THE PHARMER'S ALMANAC

·THE ULTIMATE TOILET READING FOR PHANS·

The Pharmer's Almanac Volume 4

The Unophicial Guide to Phish

Almanac Editors:
Andy Bernstein
Lockhart Steele,
Larry Chasnoff
Brian Celentano

Editorial Contributors: Jesse Appleman, Jay Archibald, Julie Beck, William Bengle, B.P., John Boeheim, Marco Burgio, James Cabot, Caroline Carillo, Tina Campbell, Jagjit Chadha, Paige Clem, David Clement, Bob Colby, Joey Conroy, Dan Corbin, Michael Davidoff, Jeremy Davis, Benjy Eisen, Dan Gibson, Chris De Gieson, Dom DeLuca, Michael & Rebecca Dougherty, Sean Ferris, Mark Fields, A.J. Fucile, Daniel Gladman, Nancy Grossman, Peter Hancock, Ric Hanna, Jason Hedrington, Christine Hollbrook, Mike Indgin, Justin Jeromon, Lane Jost, Jordan Kahn, Russell Kahn, Jon Katz, Charlie Lazarus, Adam Levine, Alyssa Litoff, Linda Mahdesian, Robert McArty, Shawn McFarland, Jon Mohr, Matt Monaco, Dan O'Brien, Monique O'Connell, Steve Paolini, Gary Perkinson, Tom Pinnick, James Pollin, David Porter, Josh Porter, Todd Prusin, Rebecca Quate, Mike Railey, Emily Rigmont, Jason Roberts, Michael Rotkowitz, Greg M. Schwartz, Kirsti Scutt, Greg Shanken, Katie Silver, Steve Silberman, Andrew Smith, Ed Smith, Ali Tariq, Mike Thomas, Steve Tremblay, Jeff Trinco, Josh Valentine, Steve Wallace, Butch Weiss, Shep Williams, Thomas Zerkowski... and hundreds more setlist and Phishtory contributors (see p. 68-70).

Consultants: Rob Dasaro, Chad Garland, Mike Graff, Greg Kelly, Jamie Janover, Matt Laurence, Brendan McKenna, Rich Seaberg, Charlene Smith, Patrick Smith

Artists: Chris Di Leo, Brian Smith, Kerri Lee Marino, Jason Estrin, E. E. Jones, Dan Gibson

Photographers: Anthony Buchla, Lucas Natali, Russell Kahn, Jay Archibald, Marco Burgio, Jason Gleason, Jessica Fausty, Christine Hollbrook, Emily Barrett, David Clement

Special Thanks: To everyone who has helped the Almanac become a reality, especially Steve Pollak, Dave Grippo, Michael Ray, Jamie Masefield, Gordon Stone, Katie McConnell, Tom Baggot, Dan Gibson, Gary Perkinson, Alyssa Litoff, Tara Chasnoff, Joanne Bernstein, Jay Archibald, Marco Burgio, Greg Schwartz, Les Kippel, Toni Brown, John Dwork, Kerri Lee Marino, Pat at Flatbush Copy, Stacey and everyone at Victor, Maria Lynch, Alison Offerman, Jessica Fausty, Adam Brinton, Bruce Burgess, Marc Allen, Leigh Gallagher, Chris Woody, Pete Shapiro, Chris Zahn, Frederick Brewery, Homegrown Music Network, Adam Levine, Larry Dobrow, Roger Ziegler and the crew at Wideband, the crew at SGB, Don Cantor from Prime Cuts, Howie Klopman, Peter Dunn from Promised Land, "Mom" Glass from Woodstock Trading, Marty Zimmerman from Grateful Threads, and all the retailers who've carried the book.
(SUPPORT YOUR LOCAL HIPPIE STORE!).

Cover Artwork by Chris Di Leo ♦ Logo Design by Brian Smith

"You've got to hear this band!"

If you're anything like most Phish fans, it was those words which introduced you to the wonderful world of Phish. It wasn't that you heard their music on the radio, or saw the band on MTV. It was probably a friend who just told you that if you hadn't heard Phish yet, you were really missing out.

"You've got to hear this band!" is what so many fans in Vermont in the 1980s told their friends after seeing Phish perform in bars in Burlington, beginning the word-of-mouth explosion which vaulted Phish to their own unique form of stardom.

It was, and continues to be, as much about the fans as about the band itself—a group process which has allowed the band and followers alike to break boundaries and discover new musical heights.

With the Pharmer's Almanac, we have sought to add to this process by creating a true collaborative project to document and detail the history of Phish.

In these pages are the words and perspectives of over 200 different fans. We estimate that Almanac contributors have attended over 5,000 combined Phish concerts and own over 20,000 hours of Phish shows on tape. The collective wisdom and experiences of these phans has created a lively and informative guide which will not only tell you everything you could possibly want to know about the band, but entertain and amuse you with wild personal tales of life as a Phish fan.

This is the fourth installment of this unofficial guide to the band, and it ranks as the largest and most comprehensive yet. Almost all of the editorial content in volume 4 either did not appear in previous volumes of the Almanac, or has been re-worked and updated.

These pages offer a ton of different features for both your reference and amusement. Volume 4's highlights include:

- **Setlists from 1983 to the present.**
- **Over 500 short show reviews to help you select concert tapes.**
- **Interviews with friends of the band.**
- **A comprehensive Phish history.**
- **An every-time-played list of original songs.**
- **Complete and off-beat 1997 show coverage.**
- **Dozens of stories written by fellow fans.**
- **Results of our most recent readers survey.**

Think of it as a Phish buffet. There are many choices, each with different flavors and each appealing to different sorts of tastes. Keep it by your bed, on the dashboard or, as we recommend, by the john.

It is, after all, the ultimate toilet reading for phans.

Now entering its third year on the bathroom floors of Phish phans, The Pharmer's Almanac extends thanks to the countless number of folks who have reached out to us with their kind words and contributions. We also wish to thank and acknowledge the many members of the online community who remain active in debating and documenting the band's history, particularly as it relates to setlists. Without them, The Pharmer's Almanac would not have been possible.

In the coming months and years, look for new and exciting projects from The Pharmer's Almanac and its many collaborators—including post-Phish show parties and music festivals, as well as other publications such as the *Tour Extra*—a free news flier we hand out at shows.

Any ideas you have on how to improve future editions of the Almanac, or how we might better serve the Phish community, are welcomed and should be directed to the Almanac editors at the address or phone number on the opposite page. Artwork, written contributions, and corrections are also encouraged. We'd love to hear from you!

Or, just sit back and enjoy.

—The Editors

The Pharmer's Almanac: The Unophicial Guide to Phish
Volume 4 — 107th Contact
Fall 1997/Winter 1998

ISBN 1-890200-03-4

The Pharmer's Almanac is never sold in venue parking lots, in accordance with guidelines set forth by Phish management. Anyone selling the Almanac on venue property is not authorized by us to do so.

A Note on Sources, Trademarks, and Copyrights

There is a great deal of concern from the band, its management company and Phish fans about trademark and copyright infringement. We are proud to say that the material in The Pharmer's Almanac is original and in no way infringes on any copyrights legally held by the band, other publications, or information services.

The setlist portion of the Almanac is based on a combination of public domain information contained in the Phish.Net archive (*www.phish.net*) and setlists and corrections supplied by Almanac contributors. The Almanac wishes to acknowledge both our direct contributors and the hundreds of fans who helped create the Phish.Net archive, without whom this publication would not be possible.

Almanac readers should be aware that other information on Phish—including setlists from mislabeled or unverified tapes not included in the this book—can be obtained free of charge to people with online access. The Pharmer's Almanac and the archive are extremely different in both editorial and informational content, and the Almanac is in no way intended to serve as a replacement or substitute for online resources.

We would also like to acknowledge dozens of publications which have printed interviews with the band and unearthed otherwise undocumented information. Their contributions are noted throughout the Almanac.

Any questions regarding sources for our information can be directed to the editors of The Pharmer's Almanac, who can easily be reached at "The Barn" in Brooklyn, NY (see contact information on the inside front cover).

It should be noted that some parties in the Phish community have claimed factual information pertaining to Phish to be their own exclusive property. It is the opinion of the Almanac that these parties have done a great disservice to the Phish community. Our goal is to compile and distribute all information pertaining to Phish, and we will not be deterred by those who seek to limit fans' access to this information by claiming, without foundation in law or common journalistic practices, ownership of that which is shared by everyone.

PHARMER'S ALMANAC CONTENTS

Photo by JASON GLEASON

A Phish Story

Band History ♦ Timeline ♦ Bios ♦ Venues ♦ Pholklore

Dublin, Ireland, June 14, 1997.
L to R, McConnell, Anastasio, Gordon.

Photo by ANTHONY BUCHLA

An Unlikely, Rags-to-Riches Journey From Dorm Room to Destiny

By Andy Bernstein and Lockhart Steele

During a 1991 interview, Phish guitarist Trey Anastasio told a reporter that the band's main goal was to make enough money to have separate rooms on the road.

Phish already had a devoted following, and was a sure draw at places like the Campus Club in Providence, RI and the Somerville Theater outside of Boston—small halls which had played host to many big-money acts on their way to the top, and a bunch more who never made it past doubling-up at Motel 6.

For a band like Phish, which was still without a major-label record contract and had labored seven years just to achieve solid regional recognition, simple comforts appeared to be a reasonable set of goals. After all, a pair of band members were essentially homeless, having given up their apartments before the '91 fall tour to save rent money.

Less than two years later, the band sold out the 17,000 capacity Great Woods Amphitheater in Mansfield, MA, and several years after that, blew the doors off its own records by attracting a city's worth of followers to the Clifford Ball in Plattsburgh, NY and The Great Went in Limestone, ME. And yet, when journalists and music pontiffs attempt to tell their oddly anachronistic story—which is void of MTV-propulsion, hit songs or genius marketing wizards—it is the roots of the band and the small bars of New England which form the crux of every narrative.

In this rags to riches story, the rags have always been more intriguing than the riches.

While the majority of fans cannot claim to have been initiated in the days of small clubs and shoestring-budget tours, it's places like the Stone Church in Newmarket, NH and, of course, Nectar's in Burlington, VT which are forever encrusted as part of the band's identity. For now at least, the colossal masses which squeeze (or break their way) into concerts remain an oddity, even to the fans who form them.

Phish, having made the transition to arena rock so seamlessly, still manages to emit the homey, detailed essence of the bar band they once were. The story of their ascension, powered by word-of-mouth hysteria and tape-trading dementia, is the same as it was when they made the then miraculous leap from part-time lounge act to small-time headliner. The band's exponential growth in popularity only serves as incentive to look back, as the music remains inextricably linked with its shadowy roots.

Phish emerged from its larvae stage in the fall of 1983, when Trey enrolled for his freshman year at the University of Vermont in Burlington.

He had been writing songs with friends from his youth since junior high school, often going off to fields near his home in New Jersey and playing guitar or writing nonsense lyrics which, speculation has it, never quite managed to impress the chicks. During his high school days at The Taft School, a boarding school in Watertown, CT, his short-lived rock band Space Antelope didn't fare much better. When he arrived on the UVM campus, he hoped to assemble a real college band.

In his first month at UVM, Trey hitched up with fellow frosh Jonathan Fishman when Trey heard drumming through his dormitory walls and investigated the source of the sublime rhythms. Listening to each other play, the two immediately knew they had found a good match. As Fishman later related to the *Boston Globe*, "As soon as I heard him [Trey] play guitar, then after I heard some of the songs he'd written, I was like, 'This is it. I'll play drums to this guy's music.' I could see immediately that he thought in a really original way and was into writing his own stuff."

Trey found rhythm guitarist Jeff Holdsworth in much the same way. Walking by Jeff's dorm room, Trey heard Jeff playing and liked what he heard. The three began jamming together in the rec room of a dormitory called Wing-Davis-Wilke. It began not really as a band rehearsal, just a sort of rolling improv. Seeking a bass player to turn their gathering into a group, Trey hung signs around campus, drawing the interest of fellow freshman Mike Gordon.

Mike, too, arrived at UVM itching to play. He had played in a cover band in high school named the Tombstone Blues Band, as well as a new wave outfit called The Edge. Mike joined the other three in the rec room and their first series of notes together attracted about 25 fellow students who heard the sounds coming through the hallways and came out and danced. When the jam wound down, Mike turned to the others and asked, "So, do I get the job?" He did.

As it turned out, Jeff knew someone who needed a band for an ROTC Halloween dance to be held in the basement of a campus dorm. The band agreed to take the gig, despite the fact they had only been playing together for a few weeks, during which time they had assembled a play list of cover tunes and made a demo tape. Lacking a name for their group, the foursome played under the temporary title "Blackwood Convention."

That the ROTC dance represented a rookie outing was clear: in lieu of microphone stands, the band relied on hockey sticks duct taped to a table to support their mics. There wasn't a stage, either, so the band set up on one side of the dark basement room, playing classic rock standards such as "Heard It Through The Grapevine" to the apparently unimpressed (and overdressed) crowd. When they stepped aside for a breather, somebody put Michael Jackson's *Thriller* on over the sound system, and taking the hint, Phish packed it in. The first gig had been a bomb.

The group retooled for several more gigs that fall, including some better-received performances in Slade Hall, an environmental cooperative house on the UVM campus.

But the new band faced a potentially devastating obstacle that winter when Trey undertook a prank of the highest order and had to pay the price. Engaged in a game of one-upsmanship with a high school friend who'd headed out west to Colorado, Trey and his friend Steve Pollak—better known by his nickname, The Dude of Life—snuck into UVM's morgue and stole a human hand and heart. They then packaged the two souvenirs and prepared to send them to their friend with a note reading, "I've got to hand it to you—you've really got heart!"

The prank would have just been a good laugh if not for one damning error and another mortal coincidence. Trey and the Dude didn't mail the package themselves—instead, they enlisted a friend, who stupidly included a return address on the package.

When their target received the little surprise, he was a good sport about it, but didn't want the decaying human organs to stink up his home. So he simply left the box out on his lawn and went out for the day. It also happened to be the day that the local firemen were walking around collecting gifts and donations from the townsfolk. One of the brave firefighters came upon the box, and thinking it was a present, opened it.

When Trey's friend returned that day, he was greeted by the flashing lights of police cars, investigating what they thought was a murder. Quick detective work traced the package and the body parts back to UVM, and to Trey and the Dude. The culprits were suspended for a semester and the band took an involuntary hiatus.

During his time away from UVM, Trey attended classes at Mercer Community College near his home in New Jersey. One day, he ran into old friends Tom Marshall and Marc Daubert, who were also at Mercer for the semester. Marshall and Daubert helped Trey set up a recording studio in his basement, where they recorded a four-track project called *Bivouac Jaun*, pieces of which would later find their way onto Phish's "white tape."

Meanwhile, Fish and Mike played together in another campus band called the Dangerous Grapes, which covered tunes by the Grateful Dead and the Allman Brothers Band, as well as some blues standards. When Trey returned to UVM in the fall of 1984, Fish and Mike faced a decision: stay with the Grapes, or re-form with Trey?

For Fish, the decision wasn't hard: he knew he wanted to play with Trey and he liked Trey's vision for the future, which included playing all original material.

The decision wasn't as easy for Mike, who later recalled to *Relix*, "When we first started jamming together in dorm rooms, I actually thought that we really didn't click together in terms of how we sounded." Fish's certainty helped solidify Mike as a member of the group, but Mike decided

Phish On Growing Up

Mike: "I was a very strange kid. I never played any sports, ever, and I spent much of my time alone. I didn't want to be a kid—I wanted to be an adult. I spent a lot of time planning projects; when I was nine I planned a full-length feature film, and I also put together these clubs that never existed...

"I was completely introverted; even when I was one or two, I'm told, I never played with toys. I preferred things in the real world, like going through the stuff in my mom's purse. I always needed to be building something, like a little-kid mad scientist. Finally, in high school, I came out of my shell, and music started to become this thing I cared about more and more."

—to Karl Coryat, Bass Player (Sept. '96)

Trey: "Growing up, I was always getting into trouble—serious trouble. I remember in the fifth grade taking a big black magic marker and writing on walls. I defaced a kids painting and tried to lie my way out of it. My parents so drilled it into me not to lie that now I don't know how to lie."

—to Lynn Minton, Parade Magazine (Feb. 6 '97)

Fish: "There were times when I caught my dad saying to my mom, 'We should never have gotten that kid a drum set.'"

—to Lynn Minton, Parade Magazine (Feb. 6 97)

Trey: "Starting in about sixth grade I had this group of friends who are very musical. We would just hang out and write songs constantly... When we would go out, it was usually five or six people, we'd go to this rhombus in Princeton. We still do—at the age of almost 30, on Tom's wedding night; it's this weird thing. We just call everybody up, people we haven't seen in years. We say, 'Rhombus, half an hour.' Everybody will show up there. It's a big black rhombus in the middle of a green field. You climb up on top of it. It's kind of a magical place for us."

—to Bob Doran, Edge City Magazine (March '93)

Mike: "We have close family ties, family values. We're not angst-ridden. We're rebellious in certain ways. We rebel against the norm. But we're not rebelling necessarily against our parents. They all have parent laminates, and they come to see us a lot. Every single parent we have a great relationship with."

—to Robin Caudell, Plattsburgh P-R (Aug 17 '96)

Page: "Both my parents are very giving people who feel it's important to give back to the community. Their lives make me feel good about what we're doing—trying to bring happiness and joy into people's lives."

—to Lynn Minton, Parade Magazine (Feb. 6 97)

Through The Ages...

1983

October 1983: After meeting Jon Fishman and Jeff Holdsworth, Trey Anastasio hangs signs around the UVM campus looking for additional people to form a band. Mike Gordon responds to the signs, and the band is born.

October 30, 1983: Phish, then called Blackwood Convention, plays its infamous first gig at an ROTC Halloween dance. The show is a bomb.

Phish On Each Other

Fish: "The first time Trey saw me, I was walking past the library. He and a friend were having a conversation about who looked like they belonged there and who didn't. I came walking by and they both fell down laughing. They pegged me from a hundred yards in a crowd of people, going, 'He doesn't look like he belongs here.'"

—to Parke Puterbaugh, Rolling Stone (Feb 20, 1997)

Trey: "For a long time, Fish had a personal rule that he'd never play the same drumbeat twice. It was a great idea, but it got to be a pain in the ass after a while."

—to Mac Randall, Musician (Dec. 1996)

Fish: "[Trey] and I lived together for about four years, and during that time there were a lot of hours that I would be practicing. My drums were in a room right off the kitchen, so, whenever Trey would be in the kitchen he'd hear some of the patterns I would be playing. He'd then go off and write a song around those beats."

—to William F. Miller, Modern Drummer (Sept. '95)

Trey: "Some songs I've written were just bad. I'd tell Page 'sing this' and he would. Most people would say 'I'm not going to sing that.'"

—to Chris Gill, Guitar Player (Vol. 28, No. 9)

Page: "It's been a many-year process to get to where I am today, which I feel like we're all equal members and we converse. There always was that feeling, but… I mean, I don't really know how to describe it except it's kind of like a marriage except you're married to three other guys and everybody's married to everybody. I can honestly say we're getting along better now than we ever have."

—to Michael Goldberg, Addicted to Noise (www.atn.com, Feb '97)

Mike: "We're pretty much lucky to have someone like Trey. I just wouldn't have the patience and the stamina to make all the decisions, to write the song lists and plan our songs, even though we don't usually stick to it. My personality is much better suited to being in the engine room, making things work from that level.

"Page and Fish—I was looking at them sitting next to each other and thinking they're sort of opposites… Page is really level-headed. He's a very reliable guy. Fish can be very disciplined. He probably practices more than any of us, but you can't count on him to be somewhere on time or that sort of thing. Fish is the most willing to do something crazy. He's the least wanting of control."

—To Robin Caudell, Plattsburgh P-R (Aug 17 '96)

Trey awaits "the note" in Divided Sky.

Photo by ANTHONY BUCHLA

They Found Goddard

WHEN WRITING ABOUT PHISH, some mainstream media publications simplify the band-member's history and say they all graduated from the University of Vermont. But that's only true for Mike Gordon, because Page, Fish and Trey all graduated from tiny Goddard College in Plainfield, Vermont.

Goddard is an alternative college based on the theories of philosopher John Dewey, and prides itself on its experimental nature. The curriculum is created anew at the start of every semester as each student works with faculty advisers to create a study plan unique to their interests. At the end of the semester, professors give their students evaluations of their work and effort in lieu of letter grades—the focus is clearly on personal development. In addition, every senior must undertake a senior project in an area of particular interest to them. For Page, this turned into a study of musical improvisation. For Trey, it was the writing and production of The Man Who Stepped Into Yesterday.

During the early 1980s, Goddard's undergraduate enrollment had dropped below 50 students, so Page received $50 each for recruiting Fish and Trey to his school. Now, though, enrollment has rebounded to over 200 undergrads. Those seeking more information can reach Goddard at (802) 454-8311.

'84

December 1, 1984: Back together again, Phish play their first show in the upstairs space at Nectar's in downtown Burlington. The Dude of Life sits in for the concert debut of Fluffhead.

Spring 1984: Trey, at home in New Jersey during his one semester suspension from UVM, records Biouvac Jaun with friends Tom Marshall and Steve Smith. During Trey's absence, Fish and Mike join another UVM band, The Dangerous Grapes.

to rejoin the band only on the condition they also could play cover songs. Trey agreed.

Around this time the band christened itself Phish. Numerous stories swirl about the genesis of the band's name, but the most believable is that they simply came up with a silly variant on Fishman's last name while hanging around the UVM student center.

The foursome played for the first time under the name Phish in the basement of a UVM dormitory called Slade Hall that fall in a gig the band still recalls fondly. In December, the band made its debut on the upstairs stage at Nectar's on Burlington's main drag, a nightspot that has offered many local area bands their first shot.

While their technical accomplishment was lacking, Trey and the band managed to do something few in the history of rock and roll have ever done. Some of the very first songs they composed were classics. Tunes such as Slave to the Traffic Light and Fluffhead—albeit without most of the complexity the four-part Fluff's Travels brings to the song—found their way into the setlist at Nectar's that night, along with a few Grateful Dead covers. Slave and Fluffhead remain two of the most climactic, adored tunes in the band's repertoire, proving that, although it would be another decade before most Phish fans would hear these songs, Phish's creative acumen was present at the band's genesis.

In early 1985, Phish signed a five-week contract to play Thursday night happy hours at Doolins, a notorious frat bar in Burlington. The Doolins shows, running from 5:00 to 6:00 p.m., didn't attract big crowds, but they did attract loyal ones. Amy Skelton, the famous "phirst phan," and Brian Long showed up each week and danced like crazy. They didn't know it—or each other—at the time, but they were grooving their way into history.

Amy would go on to serve as the band's on-tour merchandise manager. She also played host to the Amy's Farm free concert in 1991. Brian, meanwhile, moved in with the band a short time later in a red house on King Street in Burlington, across from a Hood milk factory. It was there that he helped pen some of the lyrics to Harry Hood.

In April of 1985, Brian helped Phish arrange a gig at Goddard College's annual Springfest. The organizer of the Springfest, a Goddard student originally from Basking Ridge, NJ by the name Page McConnell, liked Phish so much he volunteered to join, in the manner an overzealous little leaguer "volunteers" to bat first. Phish watched Page's band at Springfest and liked his style, and invited him to jam with them during their set.

That summer, Trey and Fish headed to Europe with several other friends during which time they played as vagabonds while Trey composed pieces including the epic You Enjoy Myself and the music to Harry Hood. Telephoning Mike in Burlington, Trey and Fish voiced their belief that Page shouldn't join Phish, but Mike spent much of the summer teaching Page early Phish compositions including Slave and Fluffhead, and by the time autumn rolled around, Page was in.

Marc Daubert, a percussionist and close friend of Trey's, also popped up in the early days, but by 1986 the lineup was solidified when Jeff supposedly "discovered Christ" and left the band. Others say Jeff simply left to pursue different interests after graduating that spring, including a trip to Alaska, but the "discovering Christ" story still circulates. (Versions of this Phishy folklore include everything from his playing in Jimmy Swaggart's church band to returning to Burlington years later in hopes of converting the rest of Phish to recognize Christ as their savior.)

The band's commitment to composing and performing original music also played a role in the original separation. Trey later told California-based *Edge City Magazine*, "Myself and Jon had gone to Europe, and we were playing street music. While we were there I wrote this thing, You Enjoy Myself. I brought it back to the band when we got back and I said, 'Let's learn this.' That was it—the tension started with Jeff. It was like beating his head against the wall. He thought it was stupid. My whole goal was, 'as different as possible.' That was the beginning of the end for him. He left the band and I started working with Ernie [Stires] and writing even more."

Page, however, loved the new direction of the band's music, and worked to convince them to play jazz standards as well. A series of trade-offs ensued when Mike, who disliked jazz, agreed to play it if the band would cover some bluegrass songs, even though both Trey and Fish professed to hate country music. In the grand art of compromise, Phish agreed to do it all; the bandmembers later would surprise themselves by each learning to enjoy parts of these varied musical styles.

In the summer of 1986, the band took the summer off while Trey spent several weeks in a secluded cabin, practicing guitar endlessly.

Phish In COLORADO

In the amphitheater at Red Rocks, August 1996.

If Phish has a home away from home, it's the great state of Colorado. No locale other than Burlington can claim such a special place in Phish history, or been witness to so many unforgettable shows.

The legacy began in 1988 when a friend booked Phish a few dates in the mining village/ski mecca of Telluride, but just days before loading up the van for the journey west, they learned the gigs had fallen through. Undeterred, they made the trek regardless, and managed to land themselves a nine-night engagement at a tiny restaurant named The Roma, playing for door earnings.

The pattern that spurred Phish's growth in the Northeast—word-of-mouth and tape trading—proved valuable in Colorado, too. "We met everybody in town and the same 20 people were coming down to see us every night. And that started off this whole Colorado thing. The next time we went back there, they each kind of brought one friend," Trey recalled to *Addicted to Noise* years later.

Their first return visit came two years later, when Phish came west for two weeks of shows. Of course the crowds were still small, but enough tape-trading students and transplanted Easterners had spread the word to make the shows a success. And one intrepid taper brought a recording and mixing rack to one show that spring (on April 22) and a string of shows during Phish's fall '90 Colorado run, starting the "Colorado Collection" of digitally-recorded concerts that rank among the best-sounding Phish tapes in existence.

From there on, Colorado Phish tours would be more spread out. But in 1993 they booked the Red Rocks Amphitheater for the first time, beginning a whole new era of legendary Phish visits that would continue through 1996, when Phish became the only band other than Huey Lewis and the News to play a four-night stand there.

They managed to grab the attention of the entire state when an incident in nearby Morrison led to a Police-Phan riot and newspaper headlines, and Red Rocks promoter Barry Fey declared that Phish had outgrown the venue.

Phish continues to play larger venues in Colorado, but in some ways, the fairy tale story which started at the Roma came to a strange end on that mysterious night.

85

Summer 1985: Trey and Fish spend part of the summer together traveling in Europe, where Trey writes a number of future Phish songs including You Enjoy Myself.

Fall 1985: Trey and Fish return from Europe to find that Mike has invited Page to join the band despite their earlier protests. Phish is now a five-piece group.

May 3, 1985: Page McConnell sits in with Phish at Goddard Springfest. By the end of the summer, he'd join the band.

November 23, 1985: Mike experiences an intensely spiritual moment playing with Phish in the Goddard cafeteria. He later recalls it as one of the most important moments in his life.

Phish On Vermont

Trey: "Vermont has everything to do with who we are. Simplicity and slowness. And cold. People here are in no rush to get anywhere. And neither is Phish."

—to Charles Hirshberg, Life (June '96)

Page: "We just really like it up here. It's out of the way and has a small town feeling to it. It definitely feels like a community. And where else would we go? I can't imagine us moving to Boston or Los Angeles. We're on the road a lot—eight or nine months last year—so why not spend the rest of our time in a beautiful place like Vermont?"

—to Steve Morse, Boston Globe (Mar. 27 '94)

Trey: "The only time we hear anything about Vermont is during the election. During the last primary, the newscasters were wondering aloud how to pronounce the capital of Vermont. It's pronounced 'mont-PEE-lee-yer.'"

—To Bill Locey, Los Angeles Times (April 16 '92)

Mike: "Had we not come from Burlington we wouldn't have made it as a band. There would have been pressure to play other kinds of music, to do certain kinds of gigs... We've found all these people in Burlington and in the outskirts of Burlington, a community of musicians."

—To Steve Rosenfeld, Vermont Times (Mar 12 '92)

Phish On Drugs

Mike: "Our fans like to alter their consciousness. Hopefully, the music, independent of the Drug, is a conscious altering thing."

—to Nate Eaton, The Best of High Times #18

Mike: "I smoke pot from time to time. Not regularly, though I really like to play music after smoking pot. I don't do it very often; I save it as a sort of ritual. It's pretty rare that I do. And I haven't tried any other drugs. That's it for me.

"Not everyone who experiments with drugs is a drug addict."

—to The Onion (www.theonion.com)

Fish: "I was never heavily into drugs. My drug is music.

"I ended up stopping quickly because I would have one experience or another where drugs would end my ability to play. Of course my first experiences inspired me to play. When you're high, your playing seems to sound better, but when you listen back to the tapes, it sucks."

—to Christopher Rossi, Relix (Oct. '96)

That fall saw Trey and Fishman transfer to Goddard College. Mike, the most serious student of the group, stayed behind at UVM, majoring in film and electrical engineering. But Trey was all too happy to get out of UVM's music department, which he thought focused too much on making students into music teachers, not musicians.

To supplement what UVM hadn't been teaching him, he had already taken music lessons from the classically trained theorist Ernie Stires, who helped teach him the art of composition. Goddard offered him college credit to continue studying with Stires, and Stires became Trey's mentor. Stires didn't have a taste for rock music. But he got Trey to focus on the art of composition, using big band music, classical music and jazz as a jumping-off points. He gave Trey compositional exercise to work on, several of which planted seeds for future Phish songs. The eager student devoured it all.

Although stationed an hour down the road in Plainfield, VT, the band became regulars at Nectar's and other small bars in Burlington, making the rounds and playing several nights a week, while also gigging at several colleges around Vermont. "A lot of who we are developed playing three sets a night at Nectar's," Trey later told *Guitar World*. "You can really do anything you wanted within reason. And we pushed reason. We tried everything including doing musical plays. There was no cover so there was always a crowd hanging at the bar drinking, whether they thought we sucked or not. Slowly but surely people actually started coming."

Eliminating the Dead covers along the way, they began filling their sets with more originals, most of which were written by Trey with lyrics often supplied by Tom Marshall. During this period, several more of the most popular Phish songs were completed, including David Bowie, Divided Sky, and Harry Hood. Gordon contributed Mike's Song to the group's repertoire, and The Dude of Life supplied Suzie Greenberg, giving Phish a solid list to choose from for any occasion.

In the fall of 1986, Phish gained a permanent soundman in Paul Languedoc, who met the band while working at Time Guitars in Burlington. Paul became the band's Mr. Everything, building custom guitars and speaker cases, carrying equipment, keeping the books, all while running the sound and monitors. He would later limit his duties to the soundboard as Phish's touring entourage swelled in size, but throughout the 1980s and into the '90s, he was the heart and soul of the Phish crew.

Mike and Page graduated in '87, Trey in '88 (Fishman wouldn't wear his graduate's cap until 1990). As they kept playing, word of their epic jams and quirky sense of on-stage fun spread around Vermont. A devoted following could be found in Burlington, at Goddard and at schools like Johnson State College in Johnson, VT, which became the first place to ban Phish from playing due to the unwelcomed convergence of VW buses that accompanied each appearance.

In March of 1988, the band clued their fans into Gamehendge, the magical musical tale of the Lizard people and their enslavement at the hands of the evil King Wilson. Songs from Gamehendge had been in the band's repertoire since 1986, but never had they performed them as a group or with a narration until the "Story Time at Nectar's" show on March 12. Few of their fans even knew there was any relationship between the songs, but during this period Trey was putting the finishing touches on the recorded version of the saga, which was called "The Man Who Stepped Into Yesterday" and served as his senior thesis at Goddard.

The early spring of 1988 also saw a student from Amherst College in Western Massachusetts take a break from a ski trip to catch a band his friends had raved about. The student was John Paluska and his impression of Phish was so strong that he immediately booked them to play three weeks later at "the Zoo," a cooperative theme house at Amherst of which he was social director.

That period saw Phish playing their first paying out-of-state shows. On March 31, they conquered New York City for the first time, playing the Greenwich Village club Kenny's Castaways with plenty of friends in attendance. Three days later, they hit Paluska's Zoo. And Amy Skelton, who had by this time moved to New Hampshire, secured them a show at the Steak House at Squam Lake, NH. It was Phish's first "spring tour." The foundation for a professional band was starting to come into place.

Paluska was so excited with the band that he called his friend Ben Hunter, a student at Boston University and a childhood chum from Maine, and convinced Ben to drive out for the Zoo show on April 2. Hunter, like Paluska, was blown away by the band's musical prowess; the two later co-founded Dionysian Productions to manage Phish. Paluska's love for Phish never faded—he still

'86

Spring 1986: After graduating from UVM, Jeff quits the band. Rumors that he "discovered Christ" will circulate for the next decade.

Fall 1986: Paul Languedoc joins on as the band's soundman and jack-of-all-trades. Phish plays their first of four Halloween concerts at Goddard College, where Trey and Fish had enrolled in September.

'87

Summer 1987: Phish starts drawing their first real crowds to its shows in Burlington and environs. Nectar's remains a favorite spot.

Fall 1987: Phish enters a Boston recording studio for the first time, recording a three-song demo tape.

Trey and Mike, mid-jam.
Photo by ANTHONY BUCHLA

manages the band (Hunter left Dionysian in the early 1990s to pursue a music journalism career).

In August, the band hit the road for two weeks worth of shows at a tiny club in Telluride, Colorado, and by the time of their return to Burlington in September, they graduated from the 200-person capacity Nectar's, which had "never a cover charge" as its motto, to The Front, which held about twice as many people.

The change was not welcomed by all. Mike still tells the story of a woman sitting at the bar at The Front wailing, "They're not our band any more!" But, as he later recounted to the *Plattsburgh Press-Republican*, "She might have been turned off, but she kept coming. She probably discovered we were pretty similar at The Front."

Times were good in Burlington, but gigs in Boston—the cultural epicenter of New England—remained elusive. Ben Hunter, still at Boston University, offered to help, landing the band a gig at a club called Molly's and plastering the area with posters. The show that November was a success (Hunter booked them again at Molly's in early December), but demo tapes the band mailed to the larger and more prestigious nightclub The Paradise were never reviewed by the club's booking agents.

So, in what the band often now points to as a major turning point, Phish rented out the club in January, 1989 to stage their own show. They expected to lose a chunk of money, but were willing to invest in making a larger Boston inroad.

To their great surprise, the show sold out. Burlington friend Tom Baggott organized a giant bus trip down to Boston, and many more loyal fans drove down from Burlington to show their support. Hunter also brought out the Boston crowd, and derisions of Paradise bouncers who asked Phish if they were "a real band" were silenced.

The winter and spring of 1989 marked one of the most important periods in the band's development. They finished up recording an album at Euphoria studios in Revere, MA, laying down six new tracks after putting four on tape the previous year. The cassette was released in May, wrapped in artwork by a former teacher of Page's at Goddard, Jim Pollock. It took its title, *Junta*, from a mispronunciation of Ben Hunter's nickname.

Meanwhile, the band's behind-the-scenes personnel also was shifting into place. Longtime "roadie extrodinaire" Del Martin called it quits that year. But a guitar student of Trey's named Chris Kuroda took a job with the band moving equipment. Then, at a March show at the Stone Church in Newmarket, NH, Kuroda stepped behind the lightboard while the band's light guy of the moment took a bathroom break. Later, Trey remarked that he liked the light work during Famous Mockingbird, and Chris told him he was responsible. One week later, Kuroda was named Phish's lighting director, a post he still holds.

Phish On the Musical Process

Fish: "I feel that the inspiration and the new directions you can achieve by opening yourself up to the other styles far outweighs anything you might lose.

"No matter how straight a thing might be, you can still find some different way to play it and still be true to the basic groove of the song."

—to William F. Miller, Modern Drummer (Sept. '95)

Trey: "The way I look at it, the music exists in the universe, and if you're lucky enough, or strong enough, to get your ego out of the way, the music comes through you. The audience that we have is open to that, and they understand that conversational transfer of energy.

—to Steve Silberman, San Diego Reader (Dec. 22, '94)

Mike: "If you were actually flying, your inner ear would be giving you information about balance, there'd be wind rushing past your face, and there'd be pressure from the altitude. All of those senses come into your brain, which perceives that you're flying. My theory is that by standing completely still, you can create not only a feeling similar to flight but the exact feeling of flight. When music is great, that's how it is for me—and the bass is the vehicle for that to happen."

—to Karl Coryat, Bass Player (Sept. '96)

Trey: "It's like you're surfing: The wave is stronger than you. If you relax and have no fear, and your with the flow of the wave, you can ride it. But if you try to fight it, you'll wipe out. The same wave can be a source of pain, or beautiful flowing grace—it's just a matter of how you respond to it."

—to Kevin Ransom, Detroit News (Oct. 26 '95)

Mike: "When I'm playing, there are times when a note can be completely thrilling in a way I couldn't even imagine when I'm not in that state, and there are other times when I play that same note and think, When am I going to get some food?

"For me, playing music isn't about creating art that will stand the test of time; it's about performing a ritual."

—to Paul Alan, Guitar World (Dec. '96)

Trey: "Music is sort of the last pure thing on earth. We've kind of always seen it as a thing where it's an escape. You can go with the music and lose yourself."

—to David Goldberg, Worcester Telegram & Gazette (Jan 1 '94)

Fish: "If you're taking a risk you've really got nothing to lose."

—to Paul Robicheau, Boston Globe (Dec 22 '96)

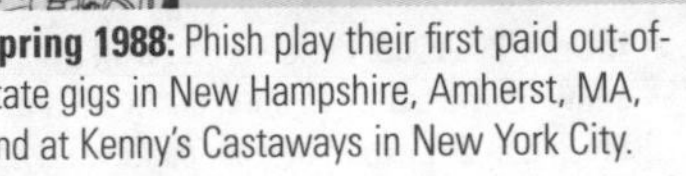
Spring 1988: Phish play their first paid out-of-state gigs in New Hampshire, Amherst, MA, and at Kenny's Castaways in New York City.

Summer 1988: Phish graduates from Nectar's in July and heads west on their first real tour, for a week's worth of shows at the tiny Roma in Telluride, Colorado.

Phish On Influences

Trey: "The thing about the influence question is understanding how many there are. All I do is listen to music. We have thousands of albums."

—to Paul Robicheau, Boston Globe (Sept. 20 '90)

Fish: "We all have a certain desire to honor the roots and traditions of music, but there's also this persistent desire to find out what else we can do rather than the common forms, the things you always hear."

—to Parke Puterbaugh, Rolling Stone (Feb. 20 '97)

Trey: "You have to at least familiarize yourself with jazz if you're going to be an American band. That's something we think about a lot. I thnk Phish is a really American kind of thing."'

—to the Times-Picayune, April '96

Trey: "There's a kind of competitive edge in the band where we hear somebody and we think 'I want to be able to do that.'"

—to Marek Kohn, The Independent (June 25 '92)

Fish: "Well of course [the Grateful Dead were an influence], along with a zillion other bands that were a huge influence. The Grateful Dead did pave the way for improvisational playing in the context of rock music and arena rock. So in that way, yeah, they really opened the doors for bands like us, and any other bands that jam. The Allmans kind of did too, but the Grateful Dead had the highest exposure. That's definitely an influence. In the structure of the shows and the whole approach, I think there are more similarities. I don't think the actual music sounds the same."

—to Paul Robicheau, Boston Globe (Dec. 22 '96)

Trey (on practicing to The Meters): "We knew it was the only way we were ever going to even resemble playing with a groove. We'd try to be as far back on the beat as they would be, knowing that we were going to speed up—there was no way to lay back as far as those guys. It was like going to school."

—to Keith Spera, Times-Picayune (April 26 '96)

Fish: "Sun Ra said he had two rules for his band: expect the unexpected and play with urgency, and I think the playing with urgency is to live as much as you can in the moment... You step foot on stage and that's who you are."

—to Paul Robicheau, Boston Globe (Dec. 22 '96)

In April, Phish competed in the "Rock Rumble" held at The Front. Competing against contemporary Burlington bands like the Hollywood Indians and Screaming Broccoli (who many Vermont music fans considered to be superior), Phish won over the diverse crowd. That performance reportedly marked the first time Fishman ever attempted a vacuum cleaner solo before an audience. The effort failed—Fish lowered himself onto the stage, stark naked, but the vacuum malfunctioned—yet the band won the Rumble and its prize, free recording time at Archer Studios.

By the summer, Phish had an entire staff in place which would remain with them through their ascent into arenas in the mid-1990s.

Santana and Phish

THERE'S ONLY ONE artist Phish has ever served as an opening act for on an extended basis—Santana, whom they supported during the summer of 1992 and again in Europe in the summer of 1996.

Carlos Santana has long been an inspiration for Phish and they frequently reference his belief that all music already exists in the universe and the musician is merely a funnel, a conduit, to bring the sound into this dimension.

Admiration turned into lifelong friendship during the summer of 1992, when Santana not only offered Phish the largest audiences they'd ever played in front of, but also invited Phish band members on stage to jam with him on an almost-nightly basis.

Carlos' guest spot with Phish, on July 25, 1992 at Stowe, has become legendary and recordings of that show are some of the heaviest circulated Phish tapes. But what many do not realize is that Phish also popped up on stage during practically every Santana performance that summer.

Trey remembers the story of how he first received an unexpected invite to join the legendary guitarist on stage:

"I didn't know it was going to happen until, like, five minutes before it happened. It was all coincidence," he told William Bengle of the University of Delaware student newspaper in 1994. "I was out in the crowd with some friends of mine who I hadn't seen since high school. We were hanging out, partying, having a great time listening to Santana and I said, 'I'll be right back. I'm going to get you some backstage passes, I'll be right back, don't leave.' I walked up to the stage and, just by coincidence, right when I walked up to the stage this road crew guy came up and said 'Carlos wants you to go on stage. Get your guitar!' I'm like 'Oh my god!' I run and get my guitar, went out on stage and did that whole thing. Then I got offstage and grabbed a couple of backstage passes and ran back out. When I got up to [my friends] I said, 'Did I miss anything?'"

It was that night, at the Garden State Art Center, that Carlos coined the phrase "The Hose" to describe the Phish concert experience.

"He had said something to me before we'd walked off stage," Trey shared with Bengle. "[Carlos] was standing in the wings and said 'I really like your band! When I listen to your band I picture the crowd as a sea of flowers, the music is the water and you guys are the hose.' That was the night he said that."

Following that summer's tour, Trey visited Carlos at his home in the San Francisco Bay Area. Early one morning, Carlos woke Trey from a sound sleep to—of all things—help take out the garbage. As Trey dragged himself to the alley, Carlos told Trey that he was about to become a big star, but he should never forget the kind of person he is, never put himself above anyone else, and always take out his own trash.

It was a lesson Trey never forgot.

'89

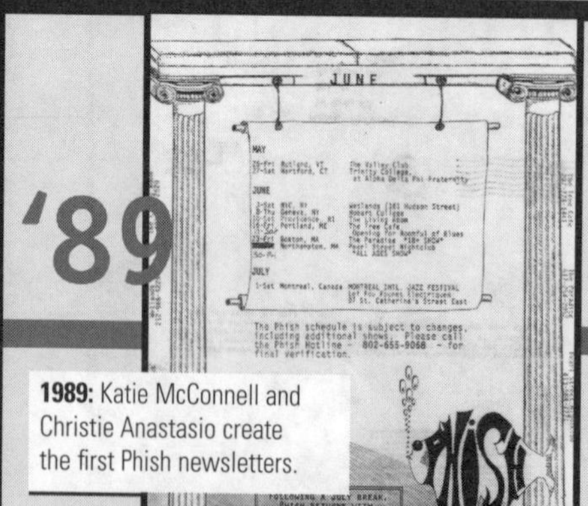

1989: Katie McConnell and Christie Anastasio create the first Phish newsletters.

January 26, 1989: Phish's first show at the Paradise in Boston is a success, as fans travel down from Vermont and New Hampshire to sell out the 650-person club.

Spring 1989: Phish wins the Rock Rumble at The Front in April, then releases *Junta* in May. The trampolines and vacuum make stage debuts.

March 30, 1989: Chris Kuroda works his first show as the band's lighting designer, and the Phish concert experience leaps forward again.

Languedoc relinquished control of Phish's books when Paluska graduated from Amherst College in May and took on the job of managing Phish full-time, creating Dionysian Productions with Hunter. The team of Paluska, Kuroda, and Languedoc, in time, would be credited with much of the band's success. While each were relative neophytes at first—only Languedoc had past experience in the role he served with Phish—they developed along with the band until they were known as masters in their field (Kuroda would later receive repeated offers to join the the Grateful Dead's lighting staff).

The band's audience steadily grew during this period, packing hundreds into a Halloween gig at Goddard, and hundreds more at their first New Year's Eve show in Boston to welcome in the new decade. The Halloween show proved to be another turning point for the band, as folks marveled at Phish's ability to draw so many fans to the Goddard campus on Halloween night. The show was videotaped and later broadcast on public access television in Burlington.

But a stronger network—word-of-mouth—propelled the band. Fans could already be found trading Phish concert tapes, and the scene at the soundboard each night was growing more chaotic as people arrived with tape decks to patch in. Everyone in Burlington, it seemed, wanted a piece of the action.

Despite the strong support at home, the band used the early part of 1990 to build audiences in more unknown regions. February saw Phish make their first run to the Southeast in a series of "gig trades" Paluska arranged with Widespread Panic, whom Phish opened for south of the Mason-Dixon Line before Widespread made it up north supporting Phish.

As sales of *Junta* helped fund the bands' exploits (and they dipped into family capital to upgrade their equipment), they also took advantage of the free studio time they'd won from the Rock Rumble to record songs which would eventually form the album *Lawn Boy*. Recorded off-and-on from May through December 1989 and originally released as a cassette tape in the spring of 1990 (which made its way to only a few hundred lucky fans) *Lawn Boy* was "officially" released that September with a new album cover on vinyl, cassette and CD on independent Absolute A-Go-Go records. *Lawn Boy* sold out its 10,000 copy run shortly after its release, but Rough Trade Records, the distributing company, went out of business, and the band never saw a cent from the deal.

Still, word about their live shows continued to spread throughout New England. The band's policy of allowing tapers to plug directly into the soundboard to make high-quality concert recordings meant thousands of crystal-clear reproductions of the Phish live experience were winding their way around college campuses and could frequently be heard in parking lots at Grateful Dead shows.

With the reputation as offering "the fabulous jam for the thinking man," Phish not only attracted a loyal team of Deadheads but also a road hungry troupe of college students who began to catch multiple shows. Hives of Phish fans seemed to be developing in places like Amherst, MA, Ithaca, NY and Boston, where even suburban high school students were catching on.

When Phish made their second and third trips to Colorado that year, a small fan base was waiting for them, familiarized through tapes which made their way across the continent. Fans who had been indoctrinated at Telluride in '88 could finally show their peers what all their talk was about.

The earnings that year were humble, but consistent, and Phish even managed to find their way on to industry top concert-earners charts, after being omitted initially when someone thought the concert gross reports on the band might be some sort of hoax.

"Phish who?" reacted music executives who, of course, had never heard of the band.

But as early as December, 1990, the record companies were on to Phish. Elektra Records A&R person Sue Drew caught Phish at several shows that month, including the band's December 28 show at the Marquee in New York City, and was stunned by the loyalty she saw from the fans.

Phish put that loyalty to the test when they left New England for their first true "tour" in February of 1991, snaking around the country over a two-month span and making it all the way to California, where they secured gigs at solid starter venues like The Catalyst in Santa Cruz and the DNA Lounge in San Francisco.

Returning from the tour, the band played their last-ever show at The Front in May. Then, still without a recording contract, though beginning to see a deal with Elektra on the horizon, they headed into Burlington's White Crow Studios at their own expense to begin recording

Phish On The Establishment

Fish: "We're already successful, and on our terms. Not everybody needs MTV. We definitely don't and I'm proud of that."

—to Peter Castro, People (June 6 '94)

Trey: "MTV is fucking up music."

—to Nate Eaton, the Best of High Times #18

Mike: "A hit single—that's the fear, because that hit single can sometimes be the curse of death."

—to Michael Mehle, Rocky Mt. News (June 9 '95)

Trey: "You have to be a very strong person not to cave in to the pressures of trying to recreate another hit. And the music that's trying to be a hit often sounds a little stale."

—to Larry Nager, Commercial Appeal (June 11 '95)

Mike: "We've spent more time avoiding growth than seeking it."

—to Entertainment Weekly

Trey: "I think the luckiest thing for us was to be ignored for 11 years. It was bliss."

—to Guitar World (August 1997)

Trey: "We never made any money off Gamehendge, and that's what kept it a cool thing. We made a vow that we will never make money off any of those songs. So we canceled the CD ROM."

—to Mac Randall, Musician (Dec. '96)

Trey: "When we first came to the awareness of the media, it would always be the Dead or Zappa they'd compare us to, all of these bands I love you know? But I got very sensitive about it.

"So if you've never seen the band, and you're reading that the 'new Grateful Dead' stuff, it doesn't really matter in my life. Because all that matters is my personal life with my family, and my musical life interacting with the people who actually come."

—to J.D. Considine, Baltimore Sun (Nov. 22 '95)

Fish: "The Grateful Dead has been part of all of our interviews for the last 12 years—why is that going to change?"

—to Paul Robicheau, Boston Globe (Dec. 22 '96)

Page: "We've been compared to more bands than any other band. It all depends what track was playing when they hear it."

—to Marek Kohn, The Independent (June 25 '92)

Fish: "There was one critic who ragged on us really creatively. I used to save her articles because her adjectives were so good."

—to Peter Castro, People (June 6 '94)

90

April 1990: Phish returns to Colorado for two weeks of shows all over the state.

June 16, 1990: Phish closes out the spring with a three-set outdoor show, then takes the summer off to rehearse.

September 21, 1990: The *Boston Globe* prints its first Phish concert review, a positive account of the previous night's show at the Somerville Theater. *Lawn Boy* released on Absolute-A-Go-Go.

Art-rocking Phish gets into the swim

By Paul Robicheau
SPECIAL TO THE GLOBE

SOMERVILLE – It's unusual for a local band to have the self-con-

Gordon and keyboardist Page McConnell. Ask them what they've been listening to lately, and you're also told Wynton Marsalis, Tom Waits, Hank Williams Sr., Fats Waller, Sun Ra, Tony Rice, Duke

PHISH
At: *The Somerville Theater, Thursday; also last night*

The Grateful Dead comparison was fueled by two sets whittled from

Phish On The Phans

Trey: "[Our fans] keep you on your toes. You have to play different songs every night, and you know they're paying attention to every single little thing you do. You don't get lazy, then."

—to J.D. Considine, Baltimore Sun (Nov. 22 '95)

Page: "A lot of Americans never get a chance to see the rest of the U.S. When kids are 18-24, following a band is a good opportunity to travel and see the rest of the country."

—to Dan Glaister, The Guardian (July 5 '96)

Mike: "We're very thankful for the people that follow us around. They listen to whatever we play—even if it's strange, even if we're taking risks."

—to Jeff Gordinier, Entertainment Weekly (Nov. 1 '96)

Trey: "There's a song we did last night, Stash, where the audience does this clapping thing. They just started doing it one night and it worked its way into the song. The audience wrote it. No matter where we go, our audience knows to do that."

—to Chris Gill, Guitar Player (Vol 28 No 9)

Mike: "[Our fans] are critical even when we're playing well. They pay attention, and they're aware of what's going on. If we have a bad gig, people backstage say, "You guys were great"—but we know that means it was a bad show. If we have a good show, the fans might say, "This was the best day of my whole life."

—to Karl Coryat, Bass Player (Sept. '96)

Trey: "God's honest truth is that they can be vicious. We have created a situation where they expect a lot from us."

—to Jeff Gordinier, Entertainment Weekly (Nov. 1 '96)

Mike: "Every time we make a new album, we get someone who calls up and says: 'How could you do it? You were the center of my universe, and I'm never going to see you again.'"

—to Scott Sutherland, New York Times (July '95)

Mike: "The worst thing for your career is to be considered Godlike by your fans. First, it's impossible to live with those expectations, and the flip side is you can't do anything wrong."

—to Dean Johnson, Boston Herald (Dec. 26 '96)

Page: "We walk even a different line, which is trying to please the hardcore fans, of which there's a certain percentage that's following us around. And then there's the people in Phoenix who get to see us when we come to Phoenix. Now who am I playing my show for? I'm playing it for both of them."

—to Michael Goldberg, Addicted to Noise (www.atn.com, Feb. '97)

the album that would become *A Picture of Nectar*. The sessions took them off the road in June, but they gave their fans a summer to remember, hitting the road for the first and only tour with The Giant Country Horns in July.

Phish had come to know Burlington musicians Dave "The Truth" Grippo, Carl "Gears" Gearhard and Russ Remington through the local music scene and a club called Sneakers in Winooski, VT. Phish began checking out the Sneakers Jazz Club there years earlier, and actually spent a year gigging with musicians at the club every Monday night under the name "The Johnny B. Fishman Jazz Ensemble."

Phish and the horns hit the road together for over a dozen legendary shows, the most popular of which came at a two-day stop at Arrowhead Ranch in upstate New York. There, they invited fans to join them several weeks later for a free show at Amy Skelton's farm in Maine, a thank-you for eight years worth of support. They also sent out personal invitations to fans on their mailing list, and thousands of folks made the trek to Auburn, ME on August 3. One fan even traveled 3,000 to catch the Amy's Farm show, which included three sets performed on the back of a platform truck. The band honored him a month later at a show in Buffalo, NY.

August also marked the formal beginnings of the Phish.Net, an Internet mailing list launched by a fan named Matt Laurence and sent to 13 people. It grew over time to become a Usenet bulletin board with over 30,000 daily readers. The growth of the Internet would contribute heavily to the band's growth in the years ahead, as setlists and concert stories were instantly devoured by online readers. More importantly, perhaps, the Internet facilitated the setting up of tape trades, allowing Phish's music to fly across the continent just days after a gig.

That fall, back on the road, Phish became the first unsigned act to sell out San Francisco's Great American Music Hall, while negotiations with Elektra kicked into full gear. Despite the fact that Gordon wore a silly wig to the final hashing out of the contract, an agreement was signed on November 22, 1991 calling for *Picture of Nectar* to be released on a major label, and *Junta* and *Lawn Boy* to also go into wide distribution sometime after *Nectar*'s release, assuming all went well.

The band had never sought a record contract—Elektra had, quite literally, come to them—so the band had some room to work during the negotiations. Phish insisted that the live tapers who'd played such an instrumental role in their growth still be allowed to tape their concerts. And they got Elektra to change contract wording that stipulated their albums had to be "commercially satisfactory" to "technically satisfactory," freeing them from a possible commitment to produce only radio-friendly songs.

With *Nectar* landing in record store racks on February 18, 1992, Phish hit the road in March with excitement at an all-time high. The tour marked their last hurrah at many of the small New England theaters they'd made home over the previous years—like the Portsmouth Music Hall in Portsmouth, NH and the Colonial Theater in Keene, NH—and the beginning of Phish's "secret language," an interactive game played with the audience using musical signals from the band.

When *Nectar* was released, it immediately became one of the top-selling albums in Boston, and sold out its initial 35,000 copy pressing in the spring of '92, but never approached gold record status. It became clear that Phish was a tough sell commercially, and not radio-friendly, although Chalk Dust Torture did get some airtime from mostly obscure stations.

But several other relatively obscure touring bands, such as Spin Doctors and Blues Traveler, were also starting to release records and get national attention at the time, and each band seemed to feed off each other's fan bases. The summer of 1992 began with a write-up for the groups in *Rolling Stone* and Phish's trip to Europe opening up for The Violent Femmes.

Then came the first HORDE Tour, the brainchild of Blues Traveler's John Popper, featuring his band along with Phish, Spin Doctors, Widespread Panic and Aquarium Rescue Unit at four northern venues. It brought Phish to huge stages such as the 12,000 seat Jones Beach Amphitheater in Long Island, NY, where they played one set as a headliner.

Four HORDE shows down south lost Phish from the package, but the band had another commitment—that of opening act for rock legend Carlos Santana. The band had previously received invitations to open for acts like the Allman Brothers and had turned them down, but the chance to spend time on the road with Santana—one of the band's heroes and major influences—proved too good to pass up. Though they generally played to small crowds, Phish was

'91

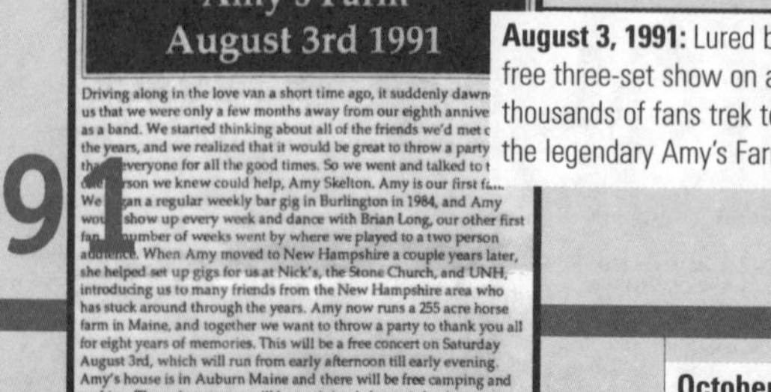
Amy's Farm
August 3rd 1991

Driving along in the love van a short time ago, it suddenly dawn[illegible] us that we were only a few months away from our eighth annive[illegible] as a band. We started thinking about all of the friends we'd met [illegible] the years, and we realized that it would be great to throw a party th[illegible] everyone for all the good times. So we went and talked to [illegible] [illegible]rson we knew could help, Amy Skelton. Amy is our first fa[illegible] We [illegible]an a regular weekly bar gig in Burlington in 1984, and Amy wou[illegible] show up every week and dance with Brian Long, our other first fan. [illegible]umber of weeks went by where we played to a two person audience. When Amy moved to New Hampshire a couple years later, she helped set up gigs for us at Nick's, the Stone Church, and UNH, introducing us to many friends from the New Hampshire area who has stuck around through the years. Amy now runs a 255 acre horse farm in Maine, and together we want to throw a party to thank you all for eight years of memories. This will be a free concert on Saturday August 3rd, which will run from early afternoon till early evening. Amy's house is in Auburn Maine and there will be free camping and parking. The only expense will be a minimal charge (a buck or two) for reseeding the fields that people will park on. There will be food and drinks available, as well as information booths, swimming and plenty of beautiful camping space. Hope to see you there.

Trey, Mike, Page, and Fish.

Rules for Amy's Farm

No campfires allowed (due to dry climate)
Bring shoes - stubbly hay field

August 3, 1991: Lured by the promise of a free three-set show on a horse ranch, thousands of fans trek to Auburn, ME for the legendary Amy's Farm show.

November 22, 1991: After months of negotiations, Phish and Elektra sign a six-album deal.

October 17-18, 1991: Phish becomes the first unsigned band to sell out San Francisco's Great American Music Hall for two consecutive nights.

Mike Gordon.
Photo by ANTHONY BUCHLA

Say 'Hey'!

WHEN NOT TOURING, Phish usually practices together five hours a day, five days a week at a studio in Paul Languedoc's home. To make the most of that time, the band has created several exercises to encourage improvisation. "We've decided that it's important to tune up our ears so that when we're on stage jamming, we don't go off in our own world," Mike told the *Sacramento Bee*. Several of their jamming exercises include:

Including Your Own Hey (also called 'Hey'). This practice routine grew out of the fact that when playing, Fish usually only followed Trey. So the band decided that they should learn to all follow each other, and this drill helped teach them how to do it. The drill progresses in the band's stage order (Page > Trey > Mike > Fish) where the first guy starts a groove, and the next guy joins in, and so on, until everyone thinks everyone else is locked in together (they say 'hey' to indicated this). Then it's up to the next guy in line to initiate a change.

Filling the Hey Hole. Each bandmember plays part of the beat not occupied by others. No one plays at the same time.

Mimicking Hey. Two people mimic and the other two specifically do not mimic the mimickers. When the mimicker matches the originator, the originator says "hey," and everyone rotates one position.

Have the drills paid off? The band sure thinks so. "We've played so much together that we've got this thing going now that we can read each other's minds," Trey told the *Commercial Appeal*. "I mean it's scary. We actually, in the practice room, sit around practicing musical communication exercises for hours and hours, so we can read each other's minds better."

Phish On The Shows

Trey: "It's the experience at the concerts. There's a real feeling between us. I don't feel like I'm performing at the audience. It's like a party. Or it's like some night in high school, where you blew off some plans and, instead, you and your friends stayed out all night. You went to the lake and watched the sun rise. It was a spontaneous bonding experience that you remember all of your life. That's how I feel at a show when everything goes right. It's much more powerful."

—to Michael Synder, S.F. Chronicle (May '94)

Trey: "If there's anything I'm thinking about before I go on stage, it's 'What are we going to do tonight that we've never done before?' And hopefully I won't know what that is until it happens."

—to Larry Nager, Commercial Appeal (June 11, '95)

Mike: "We do really weird stuff onstage sometimes, and we have a group of people listening who'd rather we did that than play the same thing each night. It's so much fun to know we can take chances and that there are people willing to come along and listen and dance.

**"These great journeys are the ideal, but there's another side. Sometimes we get off the stage and fight with each other about who wasn't concentrating.
It always comes down to hooking up."**

—to Karl Coryat, Bass Player (Sept. '96)

Trey: "We've had some really funny things happen this tour [fall '94]. Gigs where we were in smaller theaters, where one person, during a really quiet part, pulled out his car keys and started jingling them, and then everyone in the whole room pulled out their keys, and we were using the jingling as part of a jam... I love stuff like that."

—to Steve Silberman, Dupree's Diamond News (Summer '95)

Trey: "I still look down on the front row now and can probably name or recognize a third of the people there. It's weird. I feel like I'm playing in a room full of buddies."

—to Brian McCollum, Tampa Tribune (Nov 10 '95)

Trey: "[Our strangest gig ever] would have to be this gig we played at this sex commune in Vermont. It was run by this old guy named Irving who had to be about 80 years old. They were a bunch of old hippies with gardens and kids running around everywhere, and they intermingled their lovemaking...Irving showed up at the gig with a beautiful young woman on each arm... They cooked us an incredible meal, too."

—to Bill Locey, Los Angeles Times (April 16 '92)

'92

February 18, 1992: Phish's major-label debut, *A Picture of Nectar*, is released by Elektra.

March 22, 1992: Phish plays a short set on National Public Radio's MountainStage Live program, which is broadcast nationally several weeks later.

April 1992: A letters column debuts in the Phish newsletter and includes the first "What are you saying in You Enjoy Myself?" question. Mike's response: "Wasohbf woeh ejwro jeeef je ei Fndsbid."

Summer 1992: Phish plays on the first HORDE tour, then spends the summer opening for Carlos Santana on his U.S. tour.

Phish On The Future

Trey: "We won't be hitting RFK Stadium. It's too big; it's just a stupid place to have a concert. The only reason to play a room like that is because you make a whole lot of money."

—to Richard Leiby, Washington Post (Oct. 16'94)

Fish: "We've already had discussions about this—if anyone in the band goes, that it's over. The other three can continue to play together, but they've got to change the name. It's stupid [otherwise], change the name and get on with it. The only reasons to stick with the names is marketing."

—to Paul Robicheau, Boston Globe (Dec. 22 '96)

Page: "Our popularity will wane. It's on the rise now and has been. At a certain point, there will be a media backlash and then there will be sort of a social backlash and this sort of improvisational band thing, which is pretty popular right now, won't be as popular. And then if we can make it through that, eventually it will come back up again, I think if we stick around long enough."

—to Michael Goldberg, Addicted to Noise (www.atn.com, Feb '97)

Fish: "We're never going to make some ultimate song. The goals of the band aren't commercial. We are as intent as intent can be on staying together. We realize that the only thing standing between us and the record for the band with the exact same lineup staying together the longest in rock history is our getting along."

—To Peter Richmond, GQ (Jan. 97)

Mike: "I want us to be able to play in concert as sparsely as we do at soundcheck. We all want that... If we could do that, a lot of the time, then we would be a great band. But it's something to overcome..."

—To Robin Caudell, Plattsburgh P-R (Aug. 17 '96)

Trey: "Moving into the next Millennium, I'm kind of visualizing this whole new way of playing live. The Clifford Ball was the first step to that. Next summer, I'd like to do two shows like that. Because everything was different. We completely reworked the whole experience.

"There are a lot of different paths you can take. What would happen if we locked ourselves in a room for six months and just completely rewrote the entire live Phish?... Or what if you did a thing where you did a tour where the tour was four theaters across the country?... I just don't want to get trapped in every year for 20 years we do a fall tour, then we do a spring tour, then we do a summer tour and play the arenas that everybody plays."

frequently invited by Carlos to jam with him on stage during his set, and he also sat in with the boys at their hometown gig in Stowe, VT.

Yet, the national exposure did not make Phish an overnight sensation. Spin Doctors became MTV prodigies and sold millions of records, almost instantly alienating their core fans. It would take a few years, but Blues Traveler would also achieve hit-single success. Meanwhile, the musical and journalistic establishment continued to ignore Phish, and it was the continued underground communication—often via the Phish.Net—which added the most fans during this period. MTV apparently wasn't interested, and albums more or less stayed on record store shelves. But Phish tapes continued to fly around college campuses at a furious pace, beckoning even those behind on their cable bills and too broke to replace busted CD players.

New Year's Eve '92 attracted a record 6,000 fans to a sold-out Matthews Arena in Boston, and a radio audience the next day on big Boston FM station WBCN. Proving they could remain intimate with even a small town's worth of devotees, the band went without a microphone for an *a cappella* encore, showing off the product of barbershop quartet lessons they took in Burlington that year.

The winter and spring of 1993 followed with the release of *Rift* in early February and a 70-plus show tour. Some, like an April gig at the 5,000 seat-plus University of Hartford Sports Arena, were solid sellouts. Others, like the show in Bangor, ME a week later, were played before ample empty seats.

Like *Nectar*, *Rift* was a limited commercial success. But it turned a corner for the band in terms of production value and emphasis on the recorded product. For the first time, an album featured songs not previously tested on stage, and famed Muscle Shoals producer Barry Beckett produced the record in lieu of the bandmembers themselves. The title track served as the centerpiece, with each ensuing tune loosely tied into themes it laid out.

That summer, the band made one of its odder, but more magnanimous decisions. Rather than hit mid-size stages for sure sellouts on the summer tour—which would have meant less pressure and kept the veteran fans satisfied that Phish wasn't growing away from them—the band booked almost every major amphitheater on the East Coast. The brave decision meant there would be a good number of $5 tickets going around in the parking lots, but everyone who wanted to would get a chance to see the band.

Of course, the tale at that juncture could be told a different way: that Phish jumped on their first chance to hit the big leagues, ready or not. The guy who shouted "Remember Nectar's?" when Phish cut a rain-soaked gig short in Stowe probably felt that way. But that summer, the band proved they could turn their late-night, indoor shtick into an outdoor, all-ages spectacle, and still hold on to the character so precious to their long-time fans.

Following many gigs on that now-classic string of shows, Trey, Mike, Fish, and Page wandered into the parking lots. The band took the time to know many of the fans who, for the first time ever, were going cross-continent on their quest to hear the perfect show. Even as the band left the East Coast, and slipped back into smaller halls and fields, about 50 vanguards carried a flourishing "lot scene" as far south as Florida and as far west as Vancouver.

Back north for New Year's after spending the fall in Los Angeles recording their next album, Phish sold out mid-sized and large arenas for a four-show run—including the 14,500 seat Worcester Centrum in less than a day—and did more of the same the next spring. But the band continued to be an accessible presence before and after each gig.

The following spring tour coincided with the release of *Hoist*, the band's fifth album. It received mixed reviews from fans who questioned the compact format into which each song was neatly placed, and wondered if epic jams would ever be a part of new tunes the band would unleash. The Phish newsletter included letters from fans bemoaning the release of a video for the first single off *Hoist*, Down With Disease, even though none other than Mike Gordon—fulfilling a dream when a film major at UVM—directed it.

Of course, Phish had their own concerns about the video, too. They'd had plenty of conversations and arguments about making a video before, but already committed to making an album which would have several 'radio-friendly' songs, they decided to do one for a song from *Hoist* to finally "see how it feels," as Trey later put it. "What worried us about doing a video was the thought of, 'What if we suddenly have this big success?'" he told *People* magazine.

'93

February 1993: The Phish newsletter contains the first published letter from a fan urging the band to "remain as 'small' as possible."

February 3, 1993: Rift released. The album hits the Boston charts at number 7.

April 7, 1993: More than a year after its release, A Picture of Nectar wins best debut album on a major label at the Boston Music Awards.

Fall 1993: Phish spends the fall in Los Angeles recording *Hoist*, and the Phish newsletter is rechristened *Döniac Schvice*.

December 1993: A reserved-seating tapers section debuts in New Haven on December 29, then Phish closes the year on December 31 at the 14,500 seat Centrum in Worcester, MA, which includes filming for the Down With Disease video to-be.

That needn't have been a concern, as the Down With Disease video received MTV airplay only in the wee hours of the morning. And as it turned out, the band didn't like making the video—all, that is, except Mike, who enjoyed the chance to run a camera crew and mix the video in a high-tech Boston studio. The other bandmembers said they felt silly acting in the video, and none of them really appeared pleased with the results. "We did it, and I didn't like it," Trey told the *Washington Post* six months later. "It's too commercial."

But while *Hoist* missed by some accounts, the live shows of '94 did not. Songs that seemed too radio-packaged on the album, like Down With Disease, opened up in concert. Capped by an acclaimed performance halfway up a mountain at the Sugarbush ski area in July, Phish continued to prove that new, large venues gave a novel, larger-than-life feel to old and new songs alike.

A marathon Halloween show in Glens Falls, NY was remarkable not only for the much-discussed rendition of The Beatles' *White Album* and Fishman's naked run across the stage, but for the unexpectedly generous and furious third set, which stretched into the wee hours of the morning. The inaugural "musical costume," the first of three straight years in which Phish would perform an album by another artist in its entirety, also attracted an unprecedented horde of ticketless fans, who were outside waving $50 and $100 bills to no avail.

Page and Trey.

Photo by ANTHONY BUCHLA

Glens Falls also marked the first time Phish and Phish management realized the band was getting so popular, the size of the fanbase alone could be a problem. After his Halloween experience, Paluska wrote a 30-page manual for security personnel on how handle Phish fans, and band representatives began pleading with fans to not come to shows without a ticket.

Arguably the most splendid New Year's run, including the band's first show at Madison Square Garden in New York and New Year's Eve at the legendary Boston Garden, was followed by a prolonged break, during which the band's popularity only increased as the tape lists continued to fly across the Internet and cassettes buzzed through the mail.

But among the devoted, there remained a dirty, avoided topic. Just as Congress danced around the issue of Medicare cuts, Phish fans had to take the same verbal care in addressing the fact that almost all the most popular songs were at least five years old. The true crowd pleasers, to both veterans and newcomers, were mostly from the early recordings or pre-album era. Antelope, Slave, You Enjoy Myself, Harry Hood, Fluffhead, Harpua, Mike's Groove—the songs that could carry a show on their backs—were born of another time.

While the band's broad playlist could surely guarantee fresh shows into the next century, their recent offerings failed to equal the favor garnered by the Phish classics. Whether Trey could write songs on a plush touring bus as well as he could in a beat-up van was a question which had to be asked, and had seemingly been answered.

But on a warm May night in Lowell, MA, Phish took the stage for a rare benefit show and whipped out a half-dozen new songs. There may not have been a Mike's Groove among them, but tunes such as Theme From the Bottom and Free managed to combine all the elements which had vaulted the band to its current level of semi-stardom. The psychedelic abandon, the open-ended jamming, the delicate vocalization, the sound which thousands had come to know as Phish, had rarely before been realized in such a distinct manner.

The 1995 summer and fall tours saw the band fill large venues from coast to coast. The regionalism apparent two years earlier, when New England audiences numbered about 10 times the size of crowds in other time zones was lessening. The band's first show at the 20,000-seat Deer Creek Music Center in Noblesville, IN that June and their Halloween show at the 18,300-seat Rosemont Horizon near Chicago demonstrated the coming-of-age of Phish in the midwest.

Their first live album, *A Live One*, was released that June and received respectable airplay. Even *The New York Times* devoted a full page in a Sunday edition to the band, terming Phish one of the hottest acts of the summer. The secret was starting to get out. The year climaxed with two sold out gigs at Madison Square Garden. The strong finish propelled them up *Pollstar*'s ratings of the highest grossing concert acts of the year, landing them at number 15 with a gross of $15.2 million. In 1991, they'd grossed just over $200,000.

Then, when it seemed Phish couldn't climb

'94

March 15, 1993: Down With Disease released as a single to radio stations; a week later, MTV airs the video in the wee hours of the night.

March 29, 1994: *Hoist* released. It enters the *Billboard* charts at number 34.

June 6, 1994: People magazine devotes two pages to Phish. "I think Phish will have a double-platinum record in a year or two," the chairman of Elektra says.

October 31, 1994: The band performs the Beatles' *White Album* in its entirety as their first "musical costume." The show ends at 3:20 a.m.

Phish wows N.Y. crowd with Halloween marathon

By Paul Robicheau
SPECIAL TO THE GLOBE

PHISH
At: Glens Falls Civic Center, Glen Falls, N.Y., Monday night

Music Review

...NS FALLS, N.Y. – There ...rly teasers like a show-opening romp through Edgar Winter's "Frankenstein" and a snatch of Black Sabbath's ...

Album," and did a really good job at it. People may pin Phish between the Grateful Dead and Frank Zappa in style, but the band and its fans have ...

December 4, 1994: Tickets go on sale for Phish's December 30 show at Madison Square Garden and sell out in four hours; tickets for the New Year's Eve show at Boston Garden disappear within 50 minutes.

December 30, 1994: Appearing for the first time on Letterman, the band plays an awkward Chalk Dust Torture.

any higher, they once again defied gravity. After spending the winter and spring of 1996 recording the album that would become *Billy Breathes*—a studio experience the band thought to be their most pleasurable since *Junta*—Phish played one set at the New Orleans Jazz & Heritage Festival on the festival's opening day, April 26. An influx of Phish fans took New Orleans by storm.

In a city which regularly absorbs Mardi Gras and Super Bowls, the attack of the Phishheads was front-page news, and caused a panic which led JazzFest organizers to say Phish would not be welcomed back to the festival, despite a giant turnout of over 60,000 people. Though Phish's management later disputed the statement and JazzFest apologized, Phish's drawing power—and the related problems that it caused—was clearly continuing to grow.

At the opposite end of the spectrum, Phish played to only a few hundred fans at a surprise gig in Woodstock, NY in early June. Although news of the show was leaked to just a few of the band's close friends, the tiny Joyous Lake Club was packed to the hilt for a show that saw Phish play several *Billy Breathes* tracks live for the first time.

The summer of '96 saw the band spend the month of July in Europe, frequently opening for Carlos Santana and pushing a European compilation album of their recorded work titled *Stash*.

Back in the U.S. in August for two weeks worth of shows stretching from Utah to New York, Phish's popularity reached new heights. The number of fans "on tour" with the band had been growing visibly since the death of Jerry Garcia and the end of the Grateful Dead the summer before. It reached critical mass in August '96 when an incident near the Red Rocks Amphitheater in Morrison, CO led the local promoter to declare Phish had outgrown the venue.

But it was the apex of the tour in upstate New York that pushed Phish to the top of yet another plateau and earned them only accolades. The Clifford Ball, named for an obscure air mail aviator of the same name, drew almost 80,000 fans to a decomissioned Air Force Base outside of Plattsburgh, NY for two days of camping, activities galore, and six sets of Phish.

The Ball was a Phish creation in the truest sense of the word—every detail seemed to have the band's fingerprints all over it, from the Clifford Ball Town Square (complete with a 35-foot statute of the aviator himself) to the late-night Phish jazz jam performed on the back of a flatbed truck that circled through the campground. The level of organization was impeccable, drawing praise from the many fans who feared chaos. The event was later recognized as the largest concert in North America in 1996.

The television media that had been so quick to report the goings-on at Red Rocks, though, were nowhere to be found in Plattsburgh. But several magazine journalists would offer long stories on "Phish Nation" to their readers soon after.

Fall of 1996 offered another national tour, again in major-league venues from coast to coast, in support of *Billy Breathes*. Well received by fans, *Billy Breathes* also caught the attention of the national media like never before. *Entertainment Weekly* went as far as to declare Phish "the biggest band in America, no bones about it."

Articles appeared in GQ, countless local newspapers, and later *Rolling Stone*, which ran its first full Phish feature in the winter of 1997. Each article suggested that Phish was ready to break thought to the mainstream, and was in for another explosion in popularity. And though the band continued to pick up steam—receiving a reported 300,000 mail order requests for New Year's Eve tickets for the show at the FleetCenter in Boston—the crossover predicted by the media never came to pass. The album debuted on the *Billboard* charts all the way up at number seven, but dropped steadily thereafter, eventually disappearing from the top 200.

To most fans, and perhaps to the band who spoke of how hard they tried to avoid producing a hit single, it was a welcome relief.

The winter of '97 saw Phish's first ever headlining tour in Europe, a month-long affair in venues about the size of halls Phish played in the northeast in 1991. It was almost as if they were trying to do it all over again, prove they could rise to the top simply through the power of the music and word-of-mouth.

The music on the Europe tour certainly was powerful—one of the last shows of the tour, a gig in Hamburg, Germany, would later become Phish's second live album, *Slip Stitch and Pass*.

The band seemed to relish the intimate venues, and returned for another European tour in early summer. By then they had nearly 20 new songs at their disposal, including several which lent themselves to long, improvisational jams. It was just what the fans were looking for, and something the mainstream fans Phish was supposedly about to lure in wouldn't quite understand.

The month-long summer U.S. tour ended with another grand two-day finale, The Great Went in far-off Limestone, ME. A town so far North that Phish flew in through Canada and temperatures dropped into the 40s in the middle of August, Limestone grew to become the largest city in Maine for the weekend, as close to 65,000 trekked way up north. The spiritual heir of the previous summer's Clifford Ball, the Went matched the Ball in offering six sets of Phish spread over two days, camping, and a surprise pre-dawn set, this time with the band members deejaying a disco-rave affair.

In a seminal moment during the final show of the summer, the band took turns painting on stage, and then pointed to a large, towering sculpture in the midst of the crowd which fans had been building throughout the weekend. Phish proceeded to pass their creations through the crowd and had them tacked to the sculpture—a gesture of making art with the audience.

Trey then asked Chris Kuroda to shut off all the stage lights and allow the band to jam beneath the light of the moon, breaking into an emotional Harry Hood. Audience members near the stage hurled neon necklaces and lightsticks into the air by the dozen, creating a light show of their own. A misty-eyed Trey closed the set by asking fans to "get more of those, they look cool from up here."

During the encore, the art sculpture was set ablaze, and as the last notes of the summer's final song, Tweezer Reprise, soared above the assembled mass, the tower crumbled into embers, glowing brightly for the rest of the night.

The Great Went demonstrated again that, as has been noted throughout Phish's steady rise, the band has never lost its widely-recognized ability to be personal with what, to any other band, could have been a faceless mass.

Phish has proven they can maintain their identity, even if the forums in which they exercise their craft are antithetical to that persona.

Even if Phish leaves the stage for good tomorrow, the band will have left its legacy—proof that whatever the forum, inspired music can resist corporate mutation. And most of all, the thousands who came to know the band through everything but music videos and the radio will remain an undying testament to the fact that music's power can operate outside the confines of the modern business juggernaut it created.

Even in the '90s, art will find its audience.

'95

Spring 1995: Phish Tickets-by-Mail debuts for the summer tour.

May 16, 1995: Phish plays a benefit show for Voters-for-Choice in Lowell, MA, raising over $30,000 for the organization while debuting a crop of new songs.

A Benefit For Voters For Choice
EBN
JENNIFER TRYNIN
Phish
Lowell Memorial Auditorium
May 16th, 1995

June 27, 1995: *A Live One* is released. The double-live album enters the *Billboard* charts at number 18 after selling almost 50,000 copies in its first week.

July 30, 1995: *The New York Times* Sunday arts section devotes an entire page to Phish, calling them "one of the summer's most talked-about bands."

December 1995: *A Live One* sales top 270,000 copies, giving the album gold record status as a double-CD. An article in Rolling Stone refers to the poor sales of live albums throughout the music industry, and cites *ALO* as an example.

December 31, 1995: Phish plays Madison Square Garden on New Year's Eve; the concert is still ranked by fans as the band's best-ever.

Above, Trey during his senior year at the Taft School, 1982-83.

Photo by ANTHONY BUCHLA

Ernest Guiseppie "Trey" Anastasio III

Personal: Born September 30, 1964 in Fort Worth, TX; before his second birthday, his family moved to Princeton, NJ, where Trey grew up. • Mother Diane Anastasio writes and illustrates children's books (Trey has collaborated on some of them); previously, she worked as editor of *Sesame Street Magazine*. • Father Ernie Anastasio is Executive Vice President of Educational Testing Services—the SAT people—in Princeton, NJ. Trey also has one sister. • Trey married longtime girlfriend Susan Eliza Stateser on August 13, 1994 in Stowe, VT. His first daughter, Eliza Jean Anastasio, was born August 21, 1995. His second daughter, Isabella Anastasio, was born April 22, 1997.

Education: Trey attended the Taft School, a private preparatory high school, in Connecticut. • Enrolled at the University of Vermont in September, 1983, but transferred to Goddard College by fall 1986 after growing discontent with the music department at UVM. • Graduated from Goddard in spring 1988, where he wrote "The Man Who Stepped Into Yesterday" as his senior thesis.

Musical Notes: Trey began drum lessons when he was seven years old, but switched to the guitar in high school, and played in the band Space Antelope at Taft with the Dude of Life. • At UVM, he hosted an early-morning radio show on student radio called the Ambient Alarm Clock. • During his college career, he took guitar lessons from Paul Asbell, and composition lessons from neo-classical composer Ernie Stires. • Considers Sun Ra, Miles Davis and the Velvet Underground big musical influences (among many others); also credits friend Dave Grippo as an important teacher.

In the band: Trey is the closest thing Phish has to a leader, composing most of the band's music and usually selecting the setlist for shows. • Golden retriever Marley has served as "director of security" at many Phish gigs.

'96

Winter-Spring 1996: Phish records Billy Breathes in Bearsville, NY, taking a break from the studio to play the New Orleans Jazz & Heritage Festival on April 26.

August 1996: A disturbance near Red Rocks during Phish's four-night stand there draws bad press in Denver and beyond.

Rocky Mountain News
DENVER
Tuesday, August 6, 1996
Rock fans battle police
12 arrested, Morrison shut down after Phish crowd refuses to leave. 5A

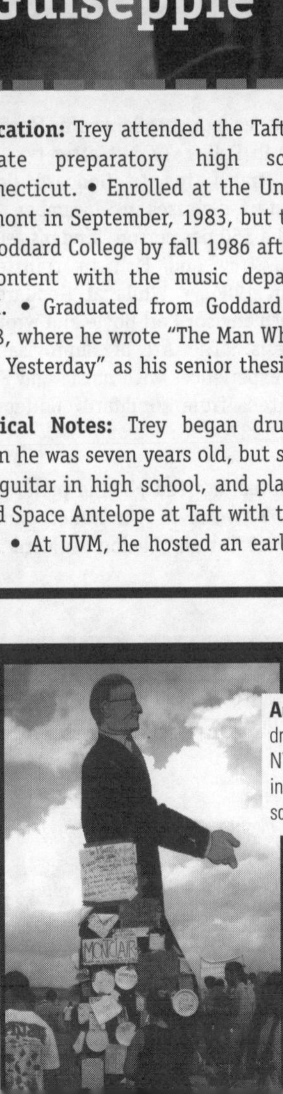

August 16-17, 1996: The Clifford Ball draws over 75,000 fans to Plattsburgh, NY, making it the largest concert event in North America in 1996, but receives scant media coverage.

October 15, 1996: *Billy Breathes* released to a four-star album review in *Rolling Stone*. Though the album debuted at No. 7 on the *Billboard* charts, it never becomes the runaway hit some expected.

December 6, 1996: Phish plays Las Vegas for the first time, a wild affair that features appearances by most of Primus and four Elvis impersonators.

Page McConnell

Photos by JAY ARCHIBALD

Personal: Born May 17, 1963 in Philadelphia, PA, Page grew up in Basking Ridge, NJ. • His father, Dr. Jack McConnell, is a big Dixieland jazz fan who helped develop Tylenol at McNeil Laboratories and later founded a health clinic on Hilton Head Island in South Carolina. His mother, Mary Ellen McConnell, is also a musician. • Has an older brother and younger sister. • Married longtime girlfriend Sofi Dillof—who has appeared onstage with Phish, most recently at Amy's Farm—in September, 1995.

Education: Attended one year of private high school at Lawrence Academy in Groton, MA, which he graduated from in 1982. • Enrolled at college at Southern Methodist University in Dallas, TX but after two years there, he transferred to Goddard College where he started classes in September, 1984. • Received a $50 per person "finder's fee" for convincing Trey and Fish to transfer to Goddard in 1986. • While at Goddard, he studied with advisor Karl Boyle and wrote his senior thesis, "The Art of Improvisation," about his experiences with music and Phish. • Graduated from Goddard College in December, 1987.

Musical Notes: Started playing piano in his childhood. • Considers Fats Waller, James P. Johnson, Art Tatum, Thelonius Monk, Lou Reed, his father, and Burlington pianist Lar Duggan as influences (among many others). • Composed the movie soundtrack for a friend's feature film, *Only in America*, which features Cars Trucks Buses, and several other original songs.

In The Band: Page holds down the calm center of the group, often functioning as a primary decision-maker with Trey. He's probably the most wary of rock-star fame of anyone in the group, and is said to be very laid-back. Helps put together show setlists with Trey, usually serving as the "proofreader" of Trey's song lists. • Nicknames include "The Chairman of the Boards" and "Leo."

'97

February-March 1997: Phish returns to Europe for three weeks of solo shows at small clubs, bars and theaters.

February 20, 1997: Ben & Jerry's releases Phish Food ice cream, and Phish pledges their portion of the proceeds to help clean up Lake Champlain.

June 13-14, 1997: Back in Europe again, Phish gives Dublin audiences two shows packed with all-new material, most of which would be heavily played throughout the summer.

August 16-17, 1997: Nearly 65,000 fans trek to far Northern Maine for The Great Went, 1997's spiritual heir to the Clifford Ball.

October 27, 1997: Live album *Slip Stitch and Patch*, recorded in Hamburg on March 1, 1997, is released.

Big photo by ANTHONY BUCHLA; inset photo by MARCO BURGIO

Michael "Cactus" Gordon

Personal: Born June 3, 1965 in Boston, MA. Grew up in nearby Sudbury, MA, where he attended the Jewish Solomon Schecter Day School. • Father founded the very successful Store 24 convenience-store chain. • Mother Marjorie (Marge) Minkin is an artist who has painted several of Phish's set backdrops, known as "Minkins." • One brother. • Engaged at presstime to Cilla Foster.

Education: Mike attended local high school near his home in Sudbury. • Enrolled at UVM in the fall of 1983. • During his time at UVM, he studied electrical engineering for two and a half years before switching his major to Film and Communications. He produced a film for his senior project called "TVF," which is apparently about the evils of television. • Graduated from UVM in the spring of 1987.

Musical Notes: Became attracted to the bass after hearing reggae group the Mustangs play poolside in the Bahamas on a family vacation in 1979, and recognizing the instrument's ability to "vibrate people." • Played in several bands in high school: the Tombstone Blues Band, which played blues and '60s rock, and The Edge, a new-wave outfit which covered bands including the Talking Heads and the Pretenders, and some originals. • Took bass classes from teacher Jim Stinnette during his time at college. • Considers bluegrass music, Phil Lesh and the Grateful Dead, Bootsy Collins, and the Mustangs as primary influences (among many others).

In The Band: The bandmember most likely to disagree with the other three, Mike is nevertheless content to not play a primary role in all decision-making. But when he disagrees, he lets them know it. • Nicknamed "Cactus." • Gets at least eight hours of sleep a night on tour. • *Mike's Corner*, a collection of his eclectic tales, was published in May '97.

Phish Phamily

BEYOND THE BAND, here are some of the Phish organization's many branches:

Paul Languedoc: Phish's sound-man and the builder of Trey's guitar and Mike's bass, as well as much of Phish's stage equipment through the mid-'90s. He joined as sound-man in 1986.

Chris Kuroda: The lighting designer and chief operator. He came on board after a short stint as a gopher in March, 1989, becoming Topher (his nickname).

John Paluska: Co-founder (along with Ben Hunter) and President of Dionysian Productions, Phish's management company which exists exclusively to serve Phish since '89. Paluska oversees all of Phish's business dealings.

Cynthia Brown: Runs the Vermont Dry Goods Department for official mail-order Phish merchandise, which employed five people full-time as of early '96.

Amy Skelton: The famous Phirst Phan. She met the band because she was a friend of Fishman's and attended their first bar shows at Doolins in Burlington back in 1985. In '92 she took control of Phish merchandise on tour, but no longer travels with the band.

Jason Colton and Shelly Culbertson: Dionysian management gurus. Shelly, a long-time phan before joining Dionysian, also serves as the band's unofficial liaison to the Phish.Net.

Kevin Shapiro: A longtime live Phish taper, Kevin now works as the band's tape vault archivist.

Brad Sands: Once known as the Big Ball guy for throwing out the balls, Brad now serves as the band's road manager.

Jonathan "Fish" Fishman

Large photo by JAY ARCHIBALD; inset photo by MARCO BURGIO

Personal: Born February 19, 1965 in Philadelphia, PA. • Grew up in Syracuse, NY. • Father Len Fishman works as an orthodontist and also as a sculptor. • Mother Mimi has become renowned as a follower of New York-area jam bands, and has appeared on stage with Phish on numerous occasions. • Has one brother and one sister; all of them (including Fish) are adopted. • Married Pam Tengiris in Las Vegas on September 28, 1997.

Education: Attended Moses Dewitt high school near his home in Syracuse. • Enrolled at UVM in September 1983, where he spent one year. • Transferred to Goddard by the fall of 1986, which after taking time off he graduated from in 1990. • Wrote his senior thesis at Goddard, "A Self-Teaching Guide to Drumming Written in Retrospect," on his experiences with music and with drumming.

Musical Notes: Started playing drums at eight years old when he played along to Led Zeppelin albums. • Took three formal drum lessons at age 13, when he learned to read music, but didn't take another lesson until several years ago when he had a session with Joe Morello. • At Goddard he was said to practice playing the drums as much as eight hours a day. • Considers King Crimson, Yes, early Genesis, Frank Zappa's band, Sun Ra, and the Velvet Underground as major influences (among many others).

In The Band: Fish is the bandmember most likely to try anything, as his vacuum-cleaner solos and occasional naked exploits have demonstrated. Content to not be a primary decision maker in the group dynamic. • Numerous nicknames include Henrietta, Zero Man, Moses Brown, Moses Dewitt and Moses Heaps, Tubbs (circa *Rift*), Greasy Fizeek (circa *Hoist*) and Norton Charleton Heston (circa fall '96). • Wears a frock on stage, a habit begun in the late 1980s, but ended the habit in 1997. During summer tour 1997, he switched to a sleek black outfit.

Fish Tools

"I play a 1967 model Electrolux."

—Fish, 4/18/92

NO ONE IN PHISH can claim the wide array of musical skills that Fishman can. During his appearances as Henrietta (and other alter-egos) over the years, Fish has mastered some of the strangest instruments:

Vacuum. His trademark piece, Fish first played the vacuum at a party in the late 1980s when Sofi Dillof (now Page's wife) asked him if he knew any instruments besides the drums. Fish replied, "Of course," and proceeded to play the house's vacuum cleaner. He subsequently translated the skill to concert.

Trombone. As the "fourth member of the Giant Country Horns," Henrietta's trombone skill has improved steadily over the years.

Madonna Washboard. So named for its conical breast features, the washboard debuted in 1992 and has been used for solos and during acoustic sets.

Cymbals. His instrument of choice for Cracklin' Rosie, the cymbals held up together spell out the word "BAH."

Plastic. For part of the '93 spring tour, Fish shook a piece of plastic to produce noise. He also "played" a cardboard picture of Otis Redding the same way on 2/5/93.

Vacuum bagpipes. This strange device surfaced for the early half of the '92 spring tour, and featured bagpipes attached to the vacuum to produce a new sucking/droning noise. The contraption gave out by 5/1/92.

"There are some things that even Fish wouldn't do on stage, and we know what they are."

—Trey, 4/21/92

Albums

Pressed Phish

The ideas, decisions and details behind Phish's albums, from the mid-1980s' White Album through 1997's Slip Stitch and Pass.

The White Album

An unofficial demo tape never officially titled, the White Album (also referred to as the "white tape") is mostly comprised of short pieces recorded separately by Trey and Mike on four-track equipment. Only a few of the songs on it feature all four of the bandmembers; friends played various instruments on some tracks. Many of the songs are abridged versions.

Recorded: Throughout the mid-1980s (1986 and 1987 in particular). Never officially released, tapes circulate among fans and for awhile in the late 1980s, the tape could be found on sale at Phish shows. Some versions of the White Album have the entire tape worth of material abridged to fit on one 45-minute side.

Track List: (A:) Alumni Blues > Steve Reich, And So To Bed, You Enjoy Myself, AC/DC Bag, Fuck Your Face, Divided Sky, Slave To The Traffic Light, Aftermath, Ingest; (B:) N2O, Fluff's Travels, Dog Log, Hamburger, Run Like An Antelope, Minkin, Letter To Jimmy Page

The Man Who Stepped Into Yesterday

Also known as Gamehendge, Trey's senior thesis at Goddard College was the recording of a musical fairy tale which he originally intended to be staged as a musical. For much of the 1990s, the band toyed with the idea of re-recording TMWSIY as an interactive CD-ROM, but decided prior to recording *Billy Breathes* that they would never record Gamehendge and hence, never profit from it.

Recorded: as Trey's senior thesis, 1987-88. Never officially released; tapes which circulate among fans have the narration on one track and the music on the other.

Track List: Wilson chant > narrative > Lizards > Tela > narrative > Wilson > narrative > AC/DC Bag > narrative> Colonel Forbin's Ascent > Famous Mockingbird > narrative > The Sloth > narrative > Possum

Junta

Phish's first studio-recorded and released album, *Junta*—named after friend Ben Hunter's nickname, which was mispronounced JOON-ta—could only be bought at Phish shows and by mail order from the band on cassette until its re-release by Elektra on CD in 1992. The album, which includes some acoustic playing, features many of the band's most popular epics.

The band now says that in some ways *Junta* is their purest album, and some longtime fans consider it Phish's best studio effort to date. In weekly record store sales, it sold better than any other Phish album prior to the release of *Billy Breathes*.

In 1992, when planning the two-disc Elektra re-release of *Junta*, Phish considered making one of the discs an interactive compact disk and including an animated Esther video (shown during setbreak at the Somerville Theater on July 19, 1991) on it. But they decided that CD-I technology had not been standardized enough to make it worthwhile. So with extra space to play with to fill the second disc, they decided to include three live tracks from the era when they recorded *Junta*. The versions of Sanity and Icculus are from the show at Nectar's on 7/24/88, not 5/3/88 as the album liner notes state. The Union Federal yields from a fabled annual jam session known as "The Oh Kee Pa Ceremony," recorded at one of the bandmember's homes in 1989.

Recorded: At Euphoria Sound Studios, Revere, MA, in two separate sessions, one during the fall of 1987 and one during the winter of 1988-89. Produced by Phish. Left on the cutting room floor: Alumni Blues, others?

Released: By Phish (cassette only) in May, 1989, with the Jim Pollock artwork that still graces it today. Re-released by Elektra on a double-CD set (featuring new Pollock longbox artwork that can no longer be found) in November, 1992.

Track List [1989]: [A:] Fee, You Enjoy Myself, Esther, Golgi Apparatus, Foam, Dinner and a Movie; [B:] Divided Sky, David Bowie, Fluffhead, Fluff's Travels (Part 1: Fluff's Travels, Part 2: The Chase, Part 3: Who Do We Do, Part 4: Clod, Part 5: Bundle of Joy, Part 6: Arrival), Contact

Track List [1992]: [Disc 1:] Fee, You Enjoy Myself, Esther, Golgi Apparatus, Foam, Dinner and a Movie, Divided Sky, David Bowie; [Disc 2:] Fluffhead, Fluff's Travels (Part 1: Fluff's Travels, Part 2: The Chase, Part 3: Who Do We Do, Part 4: Clod, Part 5: Bundle of Joy, Part 6: Arrival), Contact, Union Federal, Sanity, Icculus

Lawn Boy

Phish's second studio effort got underway soon after the release of *Junta* in May 1989. Rather than recording some of their older concert favorites like Mike's Song or Suzie Greenberg, the band decided to include mostly new material on the CD, and even arranged for a horn section on Split Open

Unreleased Studio

Like most bands, Phish has an array of studio material that's never been officially released. (Though the White Album technically falls under this category, it's covered in the main album article because it was sold at Phish shows in the late 1980s.) Here's a sampling of these unreleased gems:

Bivouac Jaun

Recorded: Spring 1984 on four-track in Trey's basement at his home in New Jersey. Features collaborations with Marc Daubert and Tom Marshall, who helped record it. Includes early versions of Slave, Antelope and I am Hydrogen. Impossible to find.

Untitled 4-Track Project

Recorded: December, 1985. Fluffhead is a live concert version featuring the Dude of Life on vocals. Copies are impossible to find.

Track List: And So To Bed, You Enjoy Myself, Green Dolphin Street, Harry Hood, Slave to the Traffic Light, Run Like an Antelope, Divided Sky, Letter to Jimmy Page, Fluffhead

1987 Promo Tape

Recorded: Exact dates unclear, the tape circulates with a "©1987 Ernest Anastasio III" tagline. Labeled simply "Phish," the tape list is grouped by "Covers" and "Originals." This tape was sent to prospective bars and clubs where the band hoped to play through 1988. All songs are in-studio versions, and the originals are the versions that eventually ended up on *Junta*.

Track List: I Know A Little, Sneakin' Sally Through the Alley, Golgi Apparatus, Fee, David Bowie, Fluffhead

Wendell Studio Sessions

Recorded: Summer 1990 at Wendell Studios in Boston, MA. The band entered the studio soon after the June 16, 1990 Townshend Family Park show, but elected not to release any of the material recorded. Tapes of the sessions circulate among phans; the first tape is more difficult to track down than the second tape.

Track List (tape one): Dog Log, Uncle Pen, Suzie Greenberg, Suzie Greenberg, Caravan, Alumni Blues, Take the A-Train, Take the A-Train, In a Mellow Tone, Possum, Mike's Song > I am Hydrogen > Weekapaug Groove

(tape two): TMWSIY > Avenu Malkenu > TMWSIY, Tweezer, Possum, Harry Hood, Rift (slow version), Runaway Jim (with alternate lyrics about Jim's death)

***Billy Breathes* Sessions**

Recorded: Spring 1996 in Bearsville, NY, for possible inclusion on *Billy Breathes*. Tapes of songs cut from the final album circulate among phans.

Track List: All of *Billy Breathes*, Glide II (instrumental), Strange Design, a Trey Song (jazzy, with lyrics), a Mike song (funky)

—thanks to Dan Gibson, Tony Hume, Michael Shtadthender, Butch Weiss

Surrender to the Air

In 1995, Trey drew together a diverse array of musicians—a "dream team" of sorts—to record an experimental jazz album. Though it was billed as a "solo project," the album that came out of several days worth of sessions didn't feature Trey prominently (though he did produce the effort). Instead, he blended his guitar into a mix that featured Marshall Allen (saxophone); Kofi Burbridge (flute); Oteil Burbridge (bass), Damon R. Choice (keyboards); Jon Fishman (drums), Bob Gullotti (drums), James Harvey (trombone), John Medeski (keyboards), Michael Ray (trumpet) and Marc Ribot.

The album, titled *Surrender to the Air*, was released by Elektra in March, 1996. In addition to the album, the Surrender to the Air crew played two live shows together on April 1 and 2, 1996. The shows were the last-ever played at The Academy in New York City, a Phish stomping ground circa '91, and included Page sitting in for the second night's second set. (Setlists from the show are easy to recall: Set I: Jam; Set II: Jam.)

Track List: Intro (Gulloti), And Furthermore, We Deflate, And Furthermore, Down (Ribot, Allen, Ray), Intro (Medeski, Ribot, Anastasio, Choice), And Furthermore, And Furthermore, Out (Allen, Choice, Ray, Fishman)

Phish Sampler CDs

Several Phish "sampler CDs" have been released over the years.

Phish: A Sampler [1993]

Released for Phish's national tour in summer 1993, the CD is, as the promotional copy on the back states, "intended to always be around, sort of like Phish... Play it in your store, play it in your room, wherever you want Phish." The CD came with an insert listing Phish's 1993 North American summer tour dates.

Track List: (from *Rift*) Fast Enough For You, The Wedge; (from *Picture of Nectar*) Chalk Dust Torture, Cavern, Stash; (from *Lawn Boy*) Bouncing Around the Room; (from *Junta*) Fee, Golgi Apparatus

Stash [1996]

Released in Europe for Phish's July '96 tour, *Stash* is another "greatest hits" compilation.

Track List: Down with Disease, If I Could, You Enjoy Myself (*Junta* version), Fast Enough For You, Scent of a Mule, Maze, Split Open and Melt, Sample in a Jar, Bouncing Around the Room, Stash (*A Live One* version), Gumbo

Free (single) [1997]

Released in Europe for Phish's '97 winter tour, the disc contains the *Billy Breathes* versions of Free and Theme, plus the previously unreleased Strange Design studio track.

and Melt. The band also opted to include the *Junta* version of Fee as the final song on the album, although they later decided to cut it from the Elektra re-release of *Lawn Boy* in 1992.

More than any other Phish album, *Lawn Boy* experienced a number of quirky problems in its post-production phase. The Absolute-A-Go-Go release switched the printed order of Reba and My Sweet One on the album case, a problem corrected for the Elektra re-release. But Elektra inadvertently slowed down the title track, Lawn Boy, on its re-release. More horribly, independent record distributor Rough Trade Records signed to distribute the album but went bankrupt by the end of 1990, taking any potential profits for Phish from the Absolute-A-Go-Go release with it and even swallowing the studio masters.

Recorded: At Archer Studios, Winooski, VT, May through December, 1989. Produced by Phish. Guest Artists: Horn section (Joseph Somerville Jr., trumpet; Dave Grippo, alto sax; Russell Remington, tenor sax; on Split Open and Melt), Christine Lynch (vocals on Split Open and Melt).

Released: On Absolute-A-Go-Go Records, in September 1990, in CD, cassette, and vinyl editions. Re-released on Elektra (CD and cassette only) on June 29, 1992.

Track List: The Squirming Coil, Reba, My Sweet One, Split Open and Melt, Oh Kee Pa Ceremony, Bathtub Gin, Run Like An Antelope, Lawn Boy, Bouncing Around The Room, [Fee]

A Picture Of Nectar

By the time Phish entered the studio to record their third album in the summer of 1991, the record companies were circling. The album which would become *A Picture Of Nectar* would give the studio execs a taste of Phish's breadth, as the album spanned a huge number of musical genres. The album also includes the only studio version of a cover song—Dizzy Gillespie's Manteca—on any Phish album. Although bandmembers say it happened as much by chance as any other reason, the album switches styles with virtually every track, a fact which later led Phish to conclude that the album lacked cohesion.

The album is named after and dedicated to Nectar Rorris (whose likeness appears in shadow on the album's citrus cover). Nectar, of course, runs the Burlington bar Nectar's.

Recorded: At White Crow Studios, Burlington, VT, in June, July and August 1991. Produced by Phish (with help from Kevin Halpin). Guest Artist: Gordon Stone (pedal steel guitar on Poor Heart). Left on the cutting room floor: Runaway Jim, Memories.

Released: On Elektra, February 18, 1992. Single released to radio: Chalk Dust Torture.

Track List: Llama, Eliza, Cavern, Poor Heart, Stash, Manteca, Guelah Papyrus, Magilla, The Landlady, Glide, Tweezer, The Mango Song, Chalk Dust Torture, Faht, Catapult, Tweezer Reprise

Rift

After the musical melange of *PON*, the band decided to make their next studio effort a more focused affair, an album which would be more cohesive than their previous studio efforts. The result was *Rift*, a concept album in which each song represents a dream by a man in the course one night of restless sleep.

In the year prior to the recording of the album, Tom Marshall had been undergoing a series of changes and challenges in his relationship, and wrote lyrics which reflected his situation (the best example being Fast Enough For You). The bandmembers found that Marshall's words also reflected some of their own struggles to carry on relationships while spending large amounts of time on the road. They selected the songs for Rift with this theme in mind; the name of the album refers to the "rift" between the fictional couple.

The contract with Elektra afforded the band the chance to work with their first producer—Muscle Shoals veteran Barry Beckett. Beckett helped the band create the arrangement on Fast Enough For You, which had never been performed live before the recording sessions, but most other songs appeared on the album in their previous concert incarnations.

The final addition to the disc was The Wedge, which Trey wrote after the recording sessions in Burlington and the band recorded at The Castle in Nashville during the mixing of the album.

Though the band initially said they were pleased with how Rift came out, they later came to see *Rift*'s concept as too much of a forced effort. "I look back at *Rift* with a lot of dismay because it was a really fertile time for us—the music was just pouring out—but we were so excited about this conceptual thing that we beat it into the ground," Trey told *Guitar World* in 1996.

Recorded: At White Crow Studios, Burlington, VT, in September and October 1992; additional recording and mixing at The Castle, Nashville TN, in October and November 1992. Produced by Barry Beckett. Guest Artist: Gordon Stone (pedal steel guitar on Fast Enough For You).

Released: On Elektra on February 2, 1993. Singles released to radio: Fast Enough For You, Maze (abridged version).

Track List: Rift, Fast Enough For You, Lengthwise > Maze, Sparkle, Horn, The Wedge, My Friend My Friend, Weigh, All Things Reconsidered, Mound, It's Ice, Lengthwise, The Horse > Silent in the Morning

Hoist

After *Rift*, Phish planned to do an album of more singable, less lyrically depressing songs. The band's idea also was to take songs they generally hadn't performed live into the studio, because they wanted the album to sound less live than *Rift* and less similar to their live concerts. Their Elektra A&R person, Nancy Jeffries, also urged them to make an album that sounded less like their live style (in hopes of netting that elusive hit single).

"We were definitely out to make this one more accessible," Page told Steve Morse of the *Boston Globe* at the time of *Hoist*'s release. "We wanted an album that didn't have as many silly lyrics or as many fantasy-oriented lyrics."

Indeed, the album followed a conscious effort by Elektra to convince Phish to put out an album with several radio-friendly songs and to make their first rock video for MTV. Paul Fox, whose producing credits included 10,000 Maniacs, Sugar Cubes, and XTC, wasn't the band's first choice as a producer, but ultimately filled that role. He used his connections to lure many guest artists into the studio.

Taking advantage of the Hollywood climate, the band did several photo sessions which resulted in the images used in the booklet accompanying the CD and promotional materials. After considering calling the album *Hung Like A Horse* (inspired by the photo which appears on the back of the case), the idea evolved into hoisting (a common way of examining horses) Amy Skelton's horse Maggie. Maggie, in hoist, appears on the album's cover.

Recorded: At American Recording Co., Woodland Hills, CA, in October and November 1993. Mixed at Can-Am Studios, Tarzana, CA, in December 1993. Produced by Paul Fox. Recorded and mixed by Ed Thacker. Guest Artists: Rickey Grundy Chorale (Julius), Tower of Power Horn Section (Julius, Wolfman's Brother), Alison Krauss (vocals on If I Could), Morgan Fichter (violin on Lifeboy), Rose Stone and Jean McClain (backing vocals on Julius and DWD), Bela Fleck (banjo on Lifeboy, Riker's Mailbox, Scent Of A Mule), The Richard Green Fourteen (strings on If I Could), and Jonathan Frakes (trombone on Riker's Mailbox). Left on the cutting room floor: Simple, Buffalo Bill (part of the song was remastered backwards, creating the Riker's Mailbox track), Frakes' trombone on Julius, long If I Could intro.

Released: On Elektra on March 29, 1994. Singles released to radio: Down With Disease, Sample in a Jar. Video: Down With Disease.

Track List: Julius, Down With Disease, If I Could, Riker's Mailbox, Axilla (Part II), Lifeboy, Sample in a Jar, Wolfman's Brother, Scent of a Mule, Dog Faced Boy, Demand

A Live One

Before *Hoist* even hit stores, Phish settled on doing a live album as their next Elektra release. Climbing concert revenues in 1994 helped sell Elektra on the idea.

To solve the dilemma of self-imposed pressure which comes from recording a select show for a live disc, Phish recorded their entire Fall Tour in 1994. On that tour, the bandmembers kept journals and wrote in them after each show, describing their feelings about that night's songs and experiences. After the tour ended, they compared notes, and shows mentioned by at least two band members went on a master list.

All told, they chose from 45 shows recorded on 32-track A-DAT machines run by Paul at the soundboard, and also had access to FM recordings from Red Rocks on June 11, Great Woods on July 8 and 9 and the Centrum on New Year's Eve 1993. The band initially considered 560 songs, roughly half of the total number they had available. They cut that group to 100, then to 30, from which they decided on the final 12. They looked mainly for great performances, and strove to get some sort of mix between songs which had previously been released and those which had not. And, before making the final cut, they also solicited the opinions of the Phish.Net community.

The Bangor Tweezer was a favorite of Page's which he worked to sell the rest of the band on, and the Great Woods Stash came to the band's attention thanks to Phish.Net suggestions (Trey later called Stash "maybe my favorite thing on the album").

The final challenge was setting an affordable price which would not only draw old fans but also attract new listeners, and they persuaded Elektra to retail the two-disc set for the low price of $19.95. The band considered naming the album *Phish*, because they felt it was the closest they had come to capturing their sound on a recording, but settled on the slightly-punny *A Live One*. The band also balked at the idea of listing the venues from which the performances were taken (reputedly because not all of them had signed off on allowing the material to appear on an album), and instead simply put "Recorded Live at Clifford Ball, 1994."

Recorded: Live in the summer and fall 1994.

Released: On Elektra as a two-disc set with booklet of band and tour photos on June 27, 1995. Singles released to radio: Bouncing, Simple

Track List: [Disc 1:] Bouncing Around the Room (12/31/94 Boston, MA), Stash (7/8/94 Mansfield, MA), Gumbo (12/2/94 Davis, CA with horns), Montana (actually a snippet from Tweezer 11/28/94 Bozeman, MT), You Enjoy Myself (12/7/94 San Diego, CA), Chalk Dust Torture (11/16/94 Ann Arbor, MI), Slave To The Traffic Light (11/26/94 Minneapolis, MN); [Disc 2:] Wilson (12/30/94 New York, NY), Tweezer (11/2/94 Bangor, ME), Simple (12/10/94 Santa Monica, CA), Harry Hood (10/23/94 Florida), The Squirming Coil (10/9/94 Pittsburgh, PA)

Billy Breathes

With about a dozen new songs already tested on stage, Phish returned to the studio in February, 1996 to create the band's sixth studio album. But their sojourn in upstate New York at Bearsville Studios wasn't just a studio session—it was a chance for Phish to get back to their roots as a band after feeling like things had gotten too big by the end of their 1995 fall tour. Trey told *Entertainment Weekly* in fall 1996, "We fulfilled this need to be completely alone, recording again and hanging out. Because things had gotten so big, we needed to get our feet back on the ground."

The recordings began with something the band called "The Blob of Music," with each member taking turns recording single notes on a variety of instruments, in hopes of creating a more textural, organic sound which got down to the roots of Phish's musical process. After almost 20 minutes worth of Blob had been recorded, the band took turns removing portions of the recording. The band also spent time recording more recognizable songs, but faced burn-out as Trey and Page spent countless hours trying to produce the album. They hoped to have the album done by early April, but they left the studio for a month to prepare for their Jazzfest appearance in late April with it unfinished.

When they headed back to the studio at Bearsville, New York, they decided they needed an outside producer. After calling former U2 producer Steve Lillywhite, he showed up two days later, and the band and Lillywhite spent six weeks re-recording and creating the album that would become *Billy Breathes*. The band later called this period one of its most pleasurable experiences as a group.

Trey told *Musician*, "This work with Steve feels like it was meant to be. I don't mean to talk in clichés, but it's been like one long party, during which some recording happened to take place. I've begun to realize that on our previous albums, we really tied the producers' hands. We were such control freaks, me particularly. Now we're loosening up."

Avoiding the endless brigade of guest and backup musicians which marked the production of *Hoist*, the band limited *Billy Breathes* to the members of Phish themselves, laying down the tracks in a studio built in a barn by a stream and going so far as even doing the album artwork themselves. The result was a highly emotive work remarkable for its consistency. Trey wrote Bliss, an acoustic instrumental, for a fan shot on his way to a show in Philadelphia the previous winter. Steep was comprised of two parts of The Blob spliced together.

On tour in Europe in July 1996, the band made the painful decision to drop Strange Design—which was supposed to close the album—from the disc. They'd tried recording it several different ways in the studio, but never quite got it right, yet they feared the song could produce the dreaded "hit single." So it was axed.

The album received four stars in *Rolling Stone*, the first time a Phish album ever to garner that treasured rating. And Free, the single, received solid radio airplay before the album was released.

Recorded: At Bearsville Studios, Bearsville, NY, February through June, 1996. Produced by Steve Lillywhite and Phish. Left on the cutting room floor: Strange Design, Glide II (instrumental), Spock's Brain, Ha Ha Ha, plus two untitled songs (one by Trey and one by Mike).

Released: On Elektra, October 15, 1996. Singles released to radio: Free, Character Zero

Track List: Free, Character Zero, Waste, Taste, Cars Trucks Buses, Talk, Theme from the Bottom, Train Song, Bliss, Billy Breathes, Swept Away, Steep, Prince Caspian

Slip Stitch and Pass

Phish made its next release another live album, the first in what the band says will be a series of "more experimental" live material to complement studio albums (the next studio album is tenatively due out in the fall of 1998). Drawing the entire album from one show—Hamburg, Germany on March 1, 1997—Phish chose material from a night that spotlighted the band's new jam style—in Trey's words, "slower, funkier, more group-oriented and less guitar-solo oriented"—that evolved on the European tour that winter.

Besides opting to include numerous cover songs for the first time (Cities, Jesus Left Chicago, Hello My Baby), the band picked one of its strangest Mike's Grooves ever—mixing intense jamming with trademark Phish musical humor.

Released: On Elektra, October 28, 1997.

Track List: Cities, Wolfman's Brother > Jesus Just Left Chicago, Weigh, Mike's Song > Lawn Boy > Weekapaug Groove, Hello My Baby, Taste

Phish On MTV

Phish has often been referred to as a band which made it big with no help from the radio industry or MTV.

Indeed, MTV virtually ignored the band (and vice-versa) through 1995. In 1996 and 1997, however, MTV hopped on the Phish bandwagon, twice airing a half-hour Clifford Ball special and dispatching MTV news crews to the band's Halloween '96 show at the Omni in Atlanta. Here's a guide to Phish spottings on MTV:

➢ A Spring, 1992 edition of Cindy Crawford's brilliantly obtuse *House Of Style* uses The Landlady as background music.

➢ Phish appears as the house band on Hangin' With MTV on July 23, 1992, almost by mistake. Surprised fans who catch the show see a snippet of Divided Sky and Fishman on vacuum. The hosts and studio audience appear befuddled, and ask Phish after their trampoline routine whether the Grateful Dead or Mary Lou Retton were a bigger influence on their band.

➢ A Summer 1994 MTV special on "Sex in the '90s" uses the Down With Disease intro as background music. It was also heard on *Road Rules* and *Real World IV*.

➢ The Down With Disease video is shown late-night on MTV for much of spring 1994; by that fall, a snippet from the video appears on *Beavis and Butt-Head*, who joke about the video's aquarium, equating it to a toilet.

➢ In their 1995 Year In Review, MTV finally caves and devotes about a minute of footage to Phish. John Popper is shown calling Phish the greatest band in the world, and a few fans from a HORDE show talk about their Phish bootleg collections. A snippet of the Down With Disease video (look quick!) also makes it in, as does a mention of the flying hot dog.

➢ Missing a story that was practically under their noses, MTV fails to send cameras or reporters to the Clifford Ball. To atone for the oversight, the station twice airs a half-hour, Dionsyian-produced video narrative on the Ball in November. Though there's precious little actual Phish performance in the show, it does include several minutes of Free from the first night of the Ball.

Videos

It's PhishTV

A guide to finding Phish on video, from Letterman to hand-held video cameras.

The members of Phish aren't exactly media darlings. If you sit on your couch with a remote control, flipping channels waiting for Phish to pop on MTV or Entertainment Tonight, you better have strong fingers. But the band does occasionally find its way to the idiot box, usually via videotape, not the airwaves.

1993 Elektra promotional video: A peek into the Phish world geared toward outsiders, mainly the music media. It includes the band explaining the concept behind *Rift*, fans explaining what it means to be a Phish fan, and some concert footage from Port Chester 11/27-28/92, including brief concert shots of Maze and YEM. This tape is frequently circulated among fans despite its short (under 15 minute) length.

Down With Disease video: The Amelia Earhardt of Phish history. Unless you stayed up late watching MTV in April of 1994, or have a rare copy on tape, you've probably never seen this little Phish venture into corp-o-rama. Directed by Mike Gordon, it features some trampoline footage and jamming from New Year's Eve 12/31/93, a shot of a real Phish tank with the bandmembers swimming and Trey's dog Marley watching them, and a cartoon moving Phish logo in front of the stage. If you really want to see it, it's occasionally shown on the big screen TV at New York's Irving Plaza between sets of shows.

Tracking: A behind-the-scenes look at the recording and mixing of *Hoist*, the fact that Phish actually markets this video via Dry Goods and charges money for it is appalling. Mike—who filmed and directed—notes on the video's box, "I sported a video camera. Sometimes I pushed the record button. Others, the stop." That isn't just Mike-speak—it's an accurate description. The 30-minute video is basically random footage; you hardly hear the band talking, then you just kind of see them singing or sitting around. It's entertainment value is virtually zero, and it's artistic merit—well, if this were figure skating, maybe a sympathetic Ukrainian judge would give a 2.4. Why this still appears in the Phish merchandise catalog is a mystery.

Late Show with David Letterman: The boys have appeared on Dave's Late Show three times, December 30, 1994 (Chalkdust Torture, played at Letterman's request); July 15, 1995 (Julius, with horns) and March 7, 1997 (Character Zero). If you can't catch them in reruns, ask around for them.

Pro-shot concert videos: Several concert videos from venues which film bands which perform there circulate among fans. The most widespread is from Waterbury, CT on April 29, 1990; it's shot from two angles and uses a straight soundboard feed for audio but strains to look professional. This video was legally taped at the venue and is still marketed, making it the only legal Phish concert video for sale—though Phish management cringes at the thought. Another video often sold illegally as "Phish: Live In A Maze" is from the Shoreline Amphitheater when Phish opened for Santanta on August 21, 1992; it's the venue videocameras that broadcast images to the lawn at Shoreline.

There's also an interesting video from the band's last Halloween show at Goddard College on October 31, 1989, clearly done with the band's cooperation, which was broadcast on public-access cable in Burlington. Look for Page's old-school haircut, Trey's devil-with-breasts costume and some funny crowd shots. (Note that the video mixes up the song order, and doesn't include all the songs played). Finally, Phish's show in Cologne, Germany on February 16, 1997 was broadcast on German TV and now circulates.

Bootleg concert videos: The band has long begged fans not to bring video cameras into shows, but in the last several years the practice has spread. The quality of the videos ranges from passable to unwatchable, mainly depending on whether the rogue cameraman used a tripod or not. There are a number of these amateur videos in circulation, the most popular of which seems to be October 31, 1994, the Halloween show in Glens Falls, which is shot from a tripod and includes most of the show, except a portion of the third set. Other amateur videos making the rounds include 12/29/93, 12/31/95 and 11/15/96, among many others.

Ball Dreams? At the Clifford Ball, it was hard not to notice the video cameras everywhere. One use for the cameras was obvious: filming the band in concert for immediate projection to the giant screens around the concert grounds. But word has it that the documentary team responsible for the critically-acclaimed *Hoop Dreams* is using that video—plus lots of other camping and phan footage gathered in the course of the weekend—in a Phish documentary, for release some time in the next few years. (Video cameras were everywhere at The Great Went, too, even at Phish's 2 a.m. disco set, but there's no word on the use for that footage.) Meanwhile, look for a copy of the video feed of the second set from the second day of the Clifford Ball (8/17/96), which circulates among phans.

Pholklore

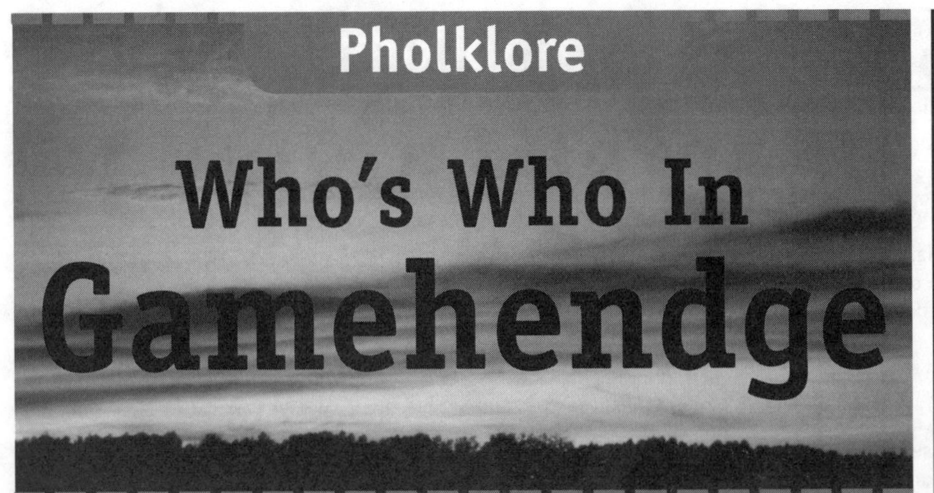

Who's Who In Gamehendge

It's not always easy to piece together who's who in Gamehendge from the songs Phish scatters throughout its shows. So herewith, The Pharmer's Almanac presents character profiles of the main characters in the Gamehendge song cycle. Those wishing to discover the full story of the mythical land of Gamehendge should consult the texts of live versions, or the ultimate Bible, The Man Who Stepped Into Yesterday recording.

The AC/DC Bag: The electronic robotic hangman of Wilson; has a black bag over its head and wheels in place of feet. Ordered by Wilson to carry out the execution of Mr. Palmer.

Colonel Forbin: A retired American Colonel who while walking his dog one morning steps through a mysterious portal and follows a long, narrow passage that leads him to Gamehendge. After meeting Rutherford the Brave upon his arrival in Gamehendge, and soon thereafter the beautiful Tela with whom he falls in love, Forbin decides to help the revolutionaries regain their freedom. He climbs the mountain in search of Icculus, seeking help in defeating Wilson.

Errand Woolfe: The leader of the revolutionaries; the song Wilson is sung from his point of view. (The character's name is a play on a childhood friend of Trey's, Aaron Woolfe).

The Famous Mockingbird: A friend of Icculus sent to retrieve the Helping Friendly Book from the tallest tower of Wilson's castle and return it to its rightful owners, the Lizards.

Icculus: The great and knowledgeable prophet of the land who, eons ago, wrote the Helping Friendly Book. According to legend, he lives atop a great mountain which is sacred ground to the Lizards; prior to Col. Forbin's climb, no one had sought out Icculus in person for thousands of years.

Kayak Guy: Yields from far north (the land where the oceans freeze), he arrives in Gamehendge on his kayak and is captured by Wilson. Punch You In The Eye is sung from his perspective and shows Wilson's xenophobic side.

Llamas: In the later years of Gamehendge—a part of the legend which has yet to be translated from oral tradition to music—the revolutionaries apparently ride llamas, the better to escape on after triggering blatoplasts (explosive devices).

The Lizards: The peaceful, loving residents of the lush, green fields of Gamehendge who after thousands of years of peace are enslaved by Wilson after he steals the Helping Friendly Book, which possesses the knowledge the Lizards need to survive. They aren't the brightest race of people, which has put them close to extinction, and they are oppressed under Wilson's dictatorship.

Multibeasts: Giant mottled, hairy, four-legged creatures used as transport by both Wilson's men and the revolutionaries.

McGrupp: Colonel Forbin's faithful and watchful dog.

Mr. Palmer: Wilson's accountant; helps fund the revolutionaries by stealing funds from Wilson and funneling them to Woolfe, et al. But Wilson discovers Palmer's deceit, and orders him assassinated by the AC/DC Bag as a warning to other revolutionaries.

The Possum: Seen by Icculus from his mountain perch, serves as a reminder of the base level of mortal existence.

Rutherford the Brave: A slightly dim-witted knight in shining armor who Colonel Forbin meets when he steps through the tunnel into Gamehendge. Rutherford, once a member of Wilson's army, works as a secret agent for the revolutionaries.

The Shepherd: Tends his flock by the shores of the Baltic Sea; McGrupp and the Watchful Hosemasters is sung from his perspective.

The Sloth: The mercenary hitman from the ghetto hired by Errand Woolfe to kill Wilson. The meanest, ugliest guy in all of Gamehendge.

Tela: The beautiful revolutionary who Colonel Forbin falls in love with, as chronicled in the song Tela which is sung from Forbin's perspective. She is a highly-placed member of the revolutionaries, but circumstantial evidence points to the fact that she might be a traitor (Trey has termed her a spy in several Gamehendge performances).

Unit Monster: Tela's sidekick; a huge, strong beast who rescues Rutherford from the river after he falls in, as chronicled in Lizards.

Wilson: Arrives in Gamehendge as a traveler from another country and becomes King of Prussia—Gamehendge's main city—and the land after stealing the Helping Friendly Book from the Lizards and enslaving them. Wilson is universally despised for his tyrannical and unjust leadership, and is apparently unable to still have fun (if he ever even was)...

Gamehendge Live

It's like a baseball pitcher's perfect game, or the landing of a meteorite—a live performance of Gamehendge. You never know when it's going to happen. Only five times in Phishtory has the blessed event occurred, each in a unique setting, sometimes appearing planned, other times spontaneous. A recap:

3/12/88 Nectar's Burlington, VT

This historical event can best be visualized through the eyes of an ancient black and white reel-to-reel projector. Those who attended were not the Gamehendge-craving folks we know today. But the audience seemed quite receptive as they interacted with yeahs and boos as Trey spoke of both the good and bad characters of his tale. As Mockingbird ends, Trey notes that Nectar's has emptied out, saying they'll continue "for those of you who are still here."

10/13/91 Surf Club, Olympia, WA

The beautiful and pristine surroundings seemed to play a huge part in Trey's decision to play Gamehendge. After opening the first set with Wilson, they went into Reba and Landlady, apparently harboring no intention of stepping into yesterday. But then something just gave. Like the original live performance, much of the crowd had yet to be exposed to such a thing. But Trey proudly acknowledged the diehards well aware of what was going on.

3/22/93 Crest Theater, Sacramento, CA

This second set begins like any other, but as we get to the middle part of It's Ice, Trey tells the audience that they are the most quiet and receptive group he's seen in years. One can never be sure, but it seems Trey made the decision to do Gamehendge right then on stage. He effectively uses the Ice imagery to take us into the land of the Lizards. Trey's narration flows more smoothly and he jokes around less. Gamehendge is now serious business.

6/26/94 Municipal Theater, Charleston, WV

It's fairly obvious that Phish planned to do Gamehendge on this particular evening prior to hitting the stage. The Kung Chant served as set opener and acted as a vehicle to bring the crowd to Gamehendge. This Gamehendge is capped off by Divided Sky, an important second cousin of the Gamehendge family. The second set was a complete rendition of *Hoist*. Gamehendge vs. *Hoist*, hmmm, tough choice.

7/8/94 Great Woods, Mansfield, MA

Perhaps the boys felt bad that each previous Gamehendge was in such an out-of-the-way place. The Great Woods Gamehendge served as a giant thank-you to the New England fans who were the first to embrace the band. Coming only weeks after the GameHoist show, some thought Gamehendge might become a semi-regular part of Phish's repertoire. Not so.

For all the rumors of "Gamehendge in London!" and "Gamehendge at Clifford Ball!" the saga as a whole remains, for now, safely stored in another time.

Phish On Halloween

Phish's Halloween antics began long before they donned their first musical costume. The tradition began back in the Sculpture Room at Goddard College in 1986, where the band put on one of the few shows from that era for which bootlegs survive.

During two of the Goddard Halloween shows, Phish switched off sets with Burlington contemporaries The Joneses.

"There was this building that wasn't in use anymore because it wasn't engineered approved. But the architectural design of it was intense," remembers Rob Dasaro, the keyboardist for the Joneses.

"There were stairways going up to these little cubicles. It was a great place. People would be drinking mushroom tea, or dosing. And we were both there, just playing for hours. It was definitely something that came close to whatever the Dead did in the Bay Area back in their day."

In 1989, Halloween marked Phish's last-ever show at Goddard College, a marathon affair in which the band wore different costumes during each set, including pajamas in set III, and pulled their first macaroni stunt, leading into Bowie as the crowd shook macaroni boxes to the rhythm. The next two years, Phish brought the party to Colorado, where they played Halloween gigs in Colorado Springs both times.

Then came a Halloween hiatus of sorts: the closest thing they came to a Halloween gig in 1992 was an October 30 shared-bill gig at the Boston Garden, and they took the entire fall off in 1993 to record *Hoist*.

But Phish turned the world upside down on October 31, 1994. The anticipation began when the fall newsletter asked fans to send in postcards voting on a "musical costume" for Phish, an album for the band to learn and play in its entirety.

The winner was officially a secret, but most fans had heard it would be The Beatles' *White Album*. And thousands drove to tiny Glens Falls, NY for the historic gig. Phish did not take the stage until just before 10 p.m. (the last of their late-late-night performances) and played into the wee hours of the morning, sandwiching an expertly-played *White Album* between two brilliant sets. During the encore, fans paraded on stage for a costume contest, won by "Mounds" candy bar Skip MacFarland.

The next year, the Rosemont Horizon near Chicago played host. Frank Zappa's *Joe's Garage* was the actual winner in the vote (due in part to light voter turnout). But the band chose the number two vote-getter, The Who's *Quadrophenia*. They capped off the show by destroying acoustic equipment on stage.

In 1996, the band decided to select an album entirely on their own, choosing a favorite of all four band members, *Remain In Light* by the Talking Heads. (Tom Marshall later joked to phan Dan Gladman that the band considered having fans vote on the album again, until the first vote arrived for Alanis). Each fan at Atlanta's Omni was handed a "Phishbill" on their way in, which included hilarious phony ads (Fishman modeled on behalf of the men's fragrance "Scent of a Fool") and an article about how much *Remain In Light* meant to the band.

Pholklore

Secret Language

"This is a very interesting sociological experiment to find out how quickly word can spread." —Trey, 3/13/92

The French phrase, "Langue D'oc" refers to an old dialect of Southern France ("Language of the 'oc'") but more importantly this dialect implies a secret language used by the troubadours, poets and knights from the era of Courtly Love (11th Century, Southern France) to woo their mistress without the husband finding out; It was a language for the poets of Arthurian Legend to enchant and enrapture, entrance and entice married ladies to the world of adulterous pleasures.

Phish's language, one of music, can also enchant and enrapture. Perhaps then it is best if we call it mere coincidence that Phish's sound engineer's last name is spelled "Languedoc." Truth be told, it doesn't really matter one way or the other—Phish's secret language has little to do with Arthurian Legends and Courts of Love and everything to do with mad science and participatory experimentation.

On March 6, 1992, at the Portsmouth Music Hall in Portsmouth, NH, the band interrupted its second set to let the audience in on a secret. Phish had been using musical signals on stage with each other for many years, but decided to cue the audience in for the first time, even making up new crowd participation signals, like "all fall down," on the spot.

Phish would give a number of tutorials through 1992, informing audiences in Providence, RI (3/13/92), Binghamton, NY (3/20/92), Atlanta, GA (3/28/92), Eugene, OR (4/22/92), Minneapolis, MN (4/29/92), and Port Chester, NY (5/14/92). More than five years later, the experiment was still continuing, though the band hasn't offered a formal lesson since its first trip to Florida on 2/22/93.

The signals sometimes feel like the most inside of inside jokes to those who don't catch a signal at a show, but this is not a joke. This is an experiment. This is an ongoing conversation between band and audience. It is a language comprised of a musical call and a verbal and/or physical response.

The conversation begins by two musical cues that the band may play in any song or jam at any given time. The first cue is always the same: a high-pitched trill, usually played on guitar by Trey, or sometimes on piano by Page or on bass by Mike. The second cue varies, depending on what the band wants to "say." There are five options:

Simpson's "D'oh." Easily the most well-known and perhaps easiest of all the language signals. When Trey plays a quick riff on the Simpson's theme song, the knowing audience yells "D'oh!"

All Fall Down. The band announces this signal by playing a series of four "falling," descending notes, each note bent down from the previous one. When the listener hears this, they are being told to fall down, along with the band. No one is to stand until the music resumes.

Turn, Turn, Turn. A take on the song by the Birds. When the band plays the melody line to the chorus, the audience is supposed to turn around and pretend that the band is playing at the back of the venue as opposed to the stage (This trick is one Phish has pretty much left in the bag since first teaching it to the audience.)

Sing a Random Note. This one is marked by the band playing a circus-like theme, after which participants are sing a random note. Most audience members generally imitate the high-pitched "lahh" favored by the band.

Ah Fuck! The only part of the language not explained to the audience at the first lesson, this was officially introduced on 5/14/92. This involves Trey making a muted brushing sound against the strings of his guitar, followed by the music stopping and the entire crowd, and band, yelling "Ah Fuck!" as Trey lifts his hand to the crowd while holding one finger back, as if the end of it was cut off.

The frequency of Secret Language signals has diminished considerably in recent years. While they surfaced regularly in 1992 and 1993, by 1994 they qualified as a special treat, and an absolute rarity thereafter.

But it would seem that in the signal's relative absence, their recognition by the audience has only grown.

In the secret laboratories of the Phish.net, fans have started creating their own signals, like the "Hood!" chant in Harry Hood, without informing the band beforehand. What started off as a "sociological experiment" has turned into an unstoppable beast: The lab animals have escaped and now may show up, unannounced, at any given moment in any Phish jam. The experiment has won. **—Benjy Eisen**

Benjy Eisen is a Roller-Coaster Engineer and one of the inventors of the "Hood!" chant.

Fun and Games

From Chess to Gliders, Phish's concerts have offered more than just music.

Phish shows have always been defined almost as much by the band's on-stage antics as by the music. Though the band has cut back on antics in recent years, putting more focus on the music, crowd-participation games and zany tricks remain part of the folklore.

Crowd-Participation Games

Besides the Secret Language, Phish has created several other games that involve the crowd, showing the band's willingness to forge new ties to their audience as venue sizes swelled in recent years.

Big Ball Jam: Officially introduced at St. Mike's College outside of Burlington, VT on November 19, 1992, the "Big Ball Jam" involves three beachballs—separately corresponding to Page, Trey and Mike—being thrown into the audience. As people bat the balls around, the band members each play when their ball is hit or held by the crowd. In this way, the crowd "jams the band."

The Big Ball Jams usually ended with Trey, Page and Brad Sands forming a giant hoop at the front of the stage while audience members tried to shoot the balls into the hoop. When the audience scored a basket, giant cheers usually erupted, a phenomenon which can be heard on many concert tapes that include a Big Ball Jam. The big balls haven't been used since the fall tour in '94, reportedly because of larger venue sizes. Or maybe the band just got bored of the game.

Chess: After years of chess tournaments in the tour bus (several Fishman-McConnell matches were detailed in the *Schvice*) the band challenged the audience to a match during the '95 fall tour. A giant chessboard hung behind the band starting at Shoreline on 9/30/95, with the band making a move at the beginning of the show and the audience responding at the start of the second set via a representative selected at the Greenpeace table during setbreak, where the audience chess move decisions were reached.

The band won the first game easily, checkmating the audience, but blew a late lead in the second game. During the show at Lake Placid, NY on 12/17/95, the band and audience traded moves throughout setbreak via walkie-talkies at the Greenpeace table and backstage, but the game was not resolved. It resumed on the New Year's Run, and the band resigned on New Year's Eve. Investigations continue into whether the band threw the second game to even the score at the end of 1995 at 1-to-1.

On-Stage Antics

Even a rookie generally walks into a show knowing about the trampolines and the vacuum cleaner, but here are some more subtle yet equally geeky tricks the band has invented over the years to get a little exercise while on stage.

Acoustic Switcheroo: Used in 1993, Trey would start The Horse or My Friend My Friend with his guitar slung over his back and an acoustic propped up on a stand. He played the first part of the song on acoustic, then Brad Sands would run out from behind the stage and grab the acoustic from him so Trey could finish the song on his electric guitar.

Creature Freak: Trey and Mike have used BBFCM as an excuse to move around the stage in dramatic and sometimes odd fashions. For parts of 1992, Trey would climb onto Page's monitors, while 1993 saw Trey and Mike lie down at the front of the stage or twist their microphone stands into strange shapes.

Going Nowhere Fast: Another 1993 creation, Trey and Mike slide from side to side on a slippery board speed-skating style during Glide or the middle segment of It's Ice.

Guelah Hop: Trey and Mike sway their legs to the music in an awkward dance during Guelah Papyrus.

Hydrogen Ride: At times in '92 and '93, Trey and Mike lay down at the front of the stage during I am Hydrogen, pedaling their feet in the air as though riding a bicycle.

Landlady Shuffle: By far the band's most ambitious foray into busting out the moves, a quick dance to the rapid beat of Landlady always gets a rise from the crowd—listen to the tapes from the Roseland Ballroom, 2/5/93, at which Trey tries to teach the dance to the New York City crowd. This one is alive and well, but Michael Jackson has nothing to fear.

Megaphone Mayhem: Employed frequently on fall tour '94 and at times in '95 and '96, Trey runs around the stage with his megaphone, pointing it at the audience and whipping the crowd into a frenzy.

Robot Waltz: During Stash, Trey and Mike walk back and forth on stage in an emotionless walk, facing each other and then turning towards the stage.

Vacuum Freeze: Used in '92 and a few times in '93, Page, Trey and Mike "freeze" in a position, often during a song, while Fish comes forward for a vacuum solo. When Fish returns to his drum set, the song resumes.

Phish on New Year's

If you haven't had the privilege of seeing Phish on New Year's Eve, then you'd better practice your mail-ordering technique and start finding transportation to the East Coast. New Year's Eve always promises to be the most impossible ticket of the year, and to this point has never ventured away from the Eastern Seaboard.

The tradition began at the World Trade Center in Boston in 1989. Phish rang in the new decade with Mike, Trey and Page all in full tuxedo garb. When they started singing I Didn't Know, Fishman emerged wearing nothing but a top hat and tails.

Phish returned to the World Trade Center in 1990, and then moved about an hour west to the New Aud in Worcester, MA in 1991. Close to 4,000 fans made their way into the sold out theater that night, marking the largest Phish show up to that point.

That record was eclipsed in 1992 when Phish filled Northeastern University's Matthews Arena to capacity, the site of their first ever New Year's prank when Brad Sands flew over the stage dressed as the Famous Mockingbird and the band used a special "secret language" created just for the show.

From there, the stunts grew even more elaborate. In 1993, Phish played in a "Phish tank" set. To mark the New Year, they lowered themselves from the ceiling in scuba gear and climbed into a giant clam at the rear of the stage before the clam counted off to midnight and fired confetti into the crowd as giant balloons dropped from above.

Then came 1994 and the most daring feat ever, as they all boarded a giant hot dog—while still playing miniature instruments—and floated through Boston Garden as fans peppered the ship with ping-pong balls tossed out by the band.

The 1995 show stands out not for its comparatively ordinary prank—in which Phish entered the Gamehendge "time lab" and Fishman emerged from a floating casket as the baby new year—but for being simply one of the most splendid musical performance ever mustered. It easily ranks as the most popular Phish show of all time in surveys conducted by The Pharmer's Almanac.

Phish returned to Boston and its new Fleet Center in 1996. Considered one of the less spectacular New Years shows, the gig's prank came in the form of tens of thousands of balloons which began falling from the ceiling at the stroke of midnight, and didn't stop for most of a marathon Down With Disease. The real zaniness came when Phish broke into Queen's Bohemian Rhapsody and a (barely audible) gospel choir joined the band on stage.

Of course, no one can predict what the future will hold for Phish and New Year's Eve, or what tricks they'll pull from their sleeves. But those looking to predict the pranks get one steady hint: the themes of the pranks are always represented on New Year's run t-shirts and mail-order tickets.

Venues

From Nectar's to Sugarbush

Surveying Several Classic, Phishy Venues

Sugarbush North, July 3, 1995
The on-mountain campground.

Over the years, Phish has taken the stage at venues ranging from the decrepit (the Campus Club in Providence, RI), to the glorious (Red Rocks in Morrison, CO and The Gorge in George, WA), to the legendary (Madison Square Garden in New York City and the Royal Albert Hall in London), and tons of places in between.

But out of the hundred of venues that Phish has played, several have developed a Phishy aura about them, becoming a part of the band's history:

Nectar's, Burlington, VT. [Number of Phish shows at venue: hundreds. Chance of Phish appearing here again: low, although a stealth show is possible. Capacity: 150-200].

The place where it all began. Owned by Nectar Rorris, who still can be seen serving fries smothered in gravy, Nectar's is a music hot spot in Burlington almost every night of the week. Its small, very shallow stage may be the origin for Phish's drums-on-the-side setup. The upstairs club, now called the Metronome, was also a favorite early stage for Phish.

Wetlands Preserve, New York City. [Number of Phish shows at venue: 8. Chance of Phish appearing here again: zip. Capacity: 600].

The club in Manhattan's TriBeCa district has helped many top acts get their starts, including Blues Traveler and, more recently, moe. With a full-time activist on its staff to promote non-profit activities, and frequent before-show environmental meetings in its cozy downstairs, Wetlands is the ultimate granola watering hole. A regular stop for Phish in 1989 and 1990, the band debuted 12 songs there during one show on September 13, 1990.

Original owner Larry Bloch put Wetlands up for sale several years ago, but held out until he could find a buyer who would promise to keep the club's environmental spirit and charity work alive. Stepping to the plate was 24-year-old Phish fan Peter Shapiro, a filmmaker whose seven-minute film "American Road," a montage of scenes from all 50 states, used You Enjoy Myself as its background music. (The film was aired on cable network MSNBC in the summer of 1997.)

The Living Room, Providence, RI. [Number of Phish shows at venue: at least 3. Chance of Phish appearing here again: zip. Capacity: approx. 450]

Tucked away in Providence's industrial district, this club was frequented by Phish and other bands on the lower rungs of their way up. The owners would often have band members over for dinner, and the crowds were always knowledgeable and appreciative, if sometimes a little put off by the decaying feel of the place. The Living Room shut down after losing its lease in 1991, but reopened at another site several years later. Gone was the factory-like feel of the spot of old. Instead, the new Living Room is in a converted family restaurant, and no longer attracts the talent the club once monopolized.

The Colonial Theater, Keene NH. [Number of Phish shows at venue: at least 6. Chance of Phish appearing here again: zip. Capacity: approx. 1,000].

The movie theater in downtown Keene—a college town about an hour north of the Massachusetts border—still occasionally plays host to a band or performer. But few have graced its tiny stage more often than Phish, which laid claim to the Colonial in the early '90s. Its cozy atmosphere, with a balcony hovering right above the stage, helped produce a perfect atmosphere for Phish as fans danced between and on top of its plush seats and wooden floors. The Colonial witnessed the debuts of Brother, It's Ice, Sparkle, and All Things Reconsidered on 9/25/91, and after retiring All Things for the fall of '91, the band brought it back at the Colonial on 3/11/92 the following year.

Warfield Theater, San Francisco, CA. [Number of Phish shows at venue: 6. Chance of Phish appearing here again: low. Capacity: 2,200].

An acoustically perfect room for a concert, and one of the last great concert theaters in the country. The band's enthusiasm for the Warfield is evident on tapes of their first show there on April 17, 1992, and Bay Area fans lament Phish's switch from this intimate hall to the huge sloping lawn of Shoreline Amphitheatre 30 minutes down the road. The main floor of the Warfield features a general admission pit in which you can literally lean on the stage; the view from the small balcony is so good that Paul and Chris set up the sound and light boards up there.

Great Woods, Mansfield, MA. [Number of Phish shows at venue: 6—includes opening for Santana once. Chance of Phish appearing here again: possible. Capacity: 19,900, expanded from 17,000 in 1994].

If there's one place and show which marks the point at which Phish "made it," Great Woods and the 7/24/93 show is it. The band sold out the venue on the night of the show, as Phish veterans mixed with thousands of first-timers and tourheads of the future. A bustling lot scene popped up around noon that day, as it became clear that Phish was going to be more than just a little New England cult band. It was apparent that Phish shows would become events that would stop towns in their tracks for years to come (such as the unbearable traffic jam at Great Woods two years later). In 1994, Phish busted out its only New England Gamehendge since Nectar's at Great Woods on 7/8/94. While Great Woods is guilty of the subpar sound and overbearing security found at many of the summer sheds, its video screens and the very fact that it's in New England somehow give it a feel some others lack.

Red Rocks, Morrison, CO. [Number of Phish shows at venue: 9. Chance of Phish appearing here again: low. Capacity: 9,450].

Probably the single prettiest place in America to see a rock concert and literally nestled of the red rocks of the Colorado countryside, this cozy amphitheatre has steep walls along the sides but opens over the stage into a magnificent vista across the surrounding counties. The venue has also hosted phenomenal Phish shows, starting with the band's debut there on 8/20/93.

The popularity of this venue caused security problems during Phish's two-night stand there in June '95, when fans ignored pleas of the band and rushed onto the rocks in an attempt to see the shows for free, and overzealous security guards responded with tear gas. A much-discussed Police-Phan incident in the nearby village of Morrison in August '96 led Red Rocks promoter Barry Fey to declare that Phish wouldn't be allowed back on the Rocks after their four-night stand concluded.

Cumberland County Civic Center, Portland, ME. [Number of Phish shows at venue: 3—includes one HORDE show. Chance of Phish appearing here again: possible. Capacity: 9,500].

In general, the hockey-style arenas which Phish hits on most cold-weather tours are monstrosities. Ugly, concrete hulks built decades ago, most feature reserved seating and stifling security personnel. In this sea of mediocrity, though, swims the CCCC, a venue which isn't aesthetically gorgeous but which hosts very mellow general admission Phish shows and draws an appreciative North-country crowd. The two Phish shows here, 12/30/93 and 12/11/95, are classics, and besides, the venue is steps away from a Hood Milk factory.

SummerStage at Sugarbush North, Fayston, VT. [Number of Phish shows at venue: 3. Chance of Phish appearing here again: unlikely. Capacity: 13,500; unofficially held well over 20,000 in July '95].

The ski slopes of Sugarbush North managed to attain legendary status with one simple show. With the stage pitched near the baselodge of the mountain, the backdrop was a 50 mile panorama over the Green Mountains which seemed to stretch all the way to Nova Scotia. Fans were treated to a legendary second set at the end of summer tour '94.

Word spread about Sugarbush the following summer, when fans who shelled out big bucks to scalpers were horrified to learn that security made no attempt to stop the thousands upon thousands of gate crashers who, as Trey described, "happened to be wandering through the woods and found [themselves] at a concert." Those high atop the mountain got another treat during the 7/3/95 show, when during a mesmerizing Makisupa distant lightning bolts seemed to fire to the beat of the music. Ask anyone there. We shit you not.

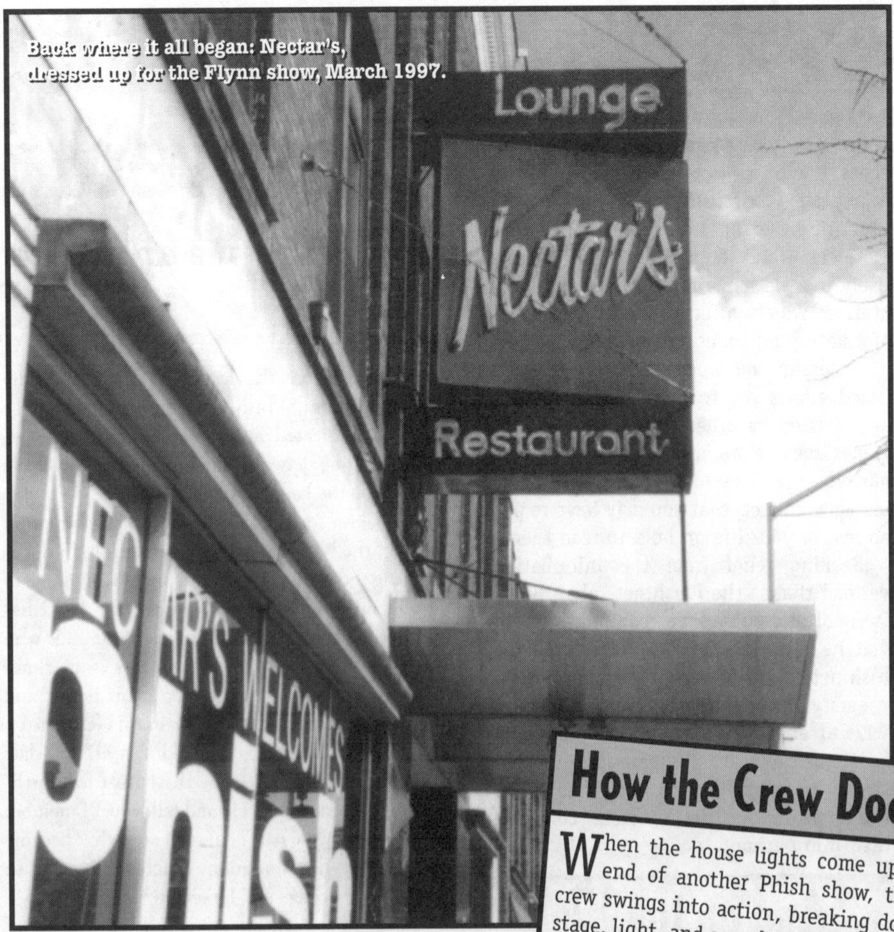

Boston Garden, Boston, MA. [Number of Phish shows at venue: 2—includes one shared bill. Capacity: 15,509. Now closed].

Decrepit and rat-infested, Phish rang in the Garden's final year with their famed flying hot dog stunt on New Year's Eve '94. Stanley Cups and NBA Championships notwithstanding, some day this too will be remembered as one of the great Boston Garden moments, at lest by the 15,000 or so lucky enough to get tickets. Rock fans lamented Boston Garden's poor acoustics and sightlines over the years, but special credit to Paul and Chris: yellow and orange lights which flooded out from the stage danced seamlessly with the Garden's colored seats, and the sound was so thunderous that the bass on Buffalo Bill sent strong vibrations through the upper balcony, leaving some wondering if the planned demolition of the building was getting a head start.

Deer Creek, Noblesville, IN. [Number of Phish shows at venue: 5. Capacity: 21,000].

Many people call Deer Creek the best shed-style amphitheatre in the country. It's a relaxed place, with crystal-clear sound, and the back of the venue opens out onto the parking lot, meaning even those who don't make it into the venue can really enjoy the music. But the really special thing about Deer Creek is the network of unofficial campgrounds that spring up in the cornfields around the venue, allowing the partying to go into the wee hours of the night.

Back where it all began: Nectar's, dressed up for the Flynn show, March 1997.

How the Crew Does It

When the house lights come up at the end of another Phish show, the road crew swings into action, breaking down the stage, light, and sound systems and packing them into the trucks which will cart them to the next venue.

While this is going on, the band hangs out backstage and then boards their tour bus, where on a typical night they might play chess or relax until checking into a hotel in the vicinity of their next show. There, they generally sleep until mid-afternoon—except Mike, who adheres to a strict sleep and exercise schedule even on rigorous tour legs.

Meanwhile, the crew has slept through the night on bunkbeds in their bus, and they arrive at the next venue by 9:00 a.m. to begin setting the show up. Riggers first locate and mark reference points for the set, lights, and speakers. The lighting crew assembles the light show and raises it into position, then the sound crew assembles the sound system and it to ascends above the stage and soundboard. Chris then updates the light positions so specific lights correspond with the placement of the band's equipment on stage and with the venue's unique layout. Following this, Paul checks the house sound, correcting any apparent problems.

By this time—usually sometime in the late afternoon if all has gone well, or the early evening if there have been snafus—the band takes the stage for their soundcheck. A couple of hours later, fans file into the venue, and then the show gets underway, while the crew prepares anew for the show's end and the beginning of their daily tour cycle.

Internet

Tangled in the Net

Back in the early 1990s, a devoted group of phans brought Phish online.

Long before the Internet became a media buzzword, Phish fans entered cyberspace and created a communication and tape-trading network which played a sizable role in spurring the band's growth.

A forum for rumors, debate and information sharing, the Net has taken an active role in documenting the band's history and influencing some of Phish's musical directions. Though the band has not heeded every request from the thousands who have posted over the years, Trey sometimes receives printouts from the Net at his home, and the band's management keeps tabs on Net chatter.

The Phish.Net was founded in 1991 by Matt Laurence, who later became the bassist for northeast touring band yeP! He and fellow yeP! member John Greene were part of a small crew that became the first Net-heads, a group which has swelled to over 40,000 posters and lurkers in recent years.

"I started noticing on Dead.Net threads of Phish-related conversation," remembers Laurence, who caught his first Phish show in 1989. "I posted a message to the Dead.Net saying 'Hey, is anyone interested in a Phish mailing list or something?' Thirteen people responded."

Laurence set up a mailing list for those 13 and the Phish.Net, in its crudest form, was born. Of course, that group quickly expanded to include many who would play a key role in Phish's future. Shelly Culbertson, now the band's assistant manager, was introduced to Phish by John Greene, and later would be among the first to inform the band of the Net's existence during the fall of 1991. She and people like Kevin Shapiro, now the band's official archivist, and Lee Silverman, who created the official Phish web site in 1996 after running the Phish.net archives off a computer at Brown University during his time there as a student, set out on a mission to document the band's history.

Another key figure was Ellis Godard, who joined the Phish.Net when it was comprised of only about 100 people. In the Spring of 1992, he formed the Phish FAQ, or Frequently Asked Questions.

"At that point it was 11 questions and answers," Godard remembers. Among them were "What's the Helping Phriendly Book?" and "What do they sing in You Enjoy Myself?"

During the Phish.Net's infancy, Godard recalls that it had a markedly different tone than today. "It was a smaller group, much more cooperative. A grovel [a plea for tapes or tickets] was not a problem. Trees were small and quick." Now, many early veterans of the Phish.Net have opted out of the loop, unwilling to deal with the torrent of postings.

But even before the Net electronic mailing list grew to the many thousands, it clearly had its impact, becoming the conduit for cross-continental tape trading which paved the path for Phish's first national tours.

"The band would play a song on one coast. By the time they got to the other coast everyone knows about it because of tape trading," Laurence said. "The net facilitated that so much."

Much of this was spurred by tape trees. A tree is a system under which one taper agrees to make copies of a tape for say, five people, and those five people agree to make copies for another five. As the tree branches out, hundreds of people gain access to tapes in a very quick fashion. Several of Phish's more recent soundboard tape releases, including 12/30/93 and 5/7/94, were offered to the Net by the band and disseminated by tape trees.

Since 1995, phan James Gray has co-ordinated the massive "Operation Everyshow" (*www.oe.org*) project that has attempted to tree every single Phish show since summer '95. Many of the highest-quality tapes in circulation are a result of OE's efforts.

The Phish.Net continues to grow, spawning various offshoots and side projects. On the 1996 summer tour, a group of Phish.Netters organized mass audience participation events, handing our flyers calling for everyone to sit down during the Divided Sky pregnant pause, and also shout "Hood" back at the band during each chant of "Harry." Thousands of fans complied during the four-day Red Rocks run.

Today, the tone and subject matter of the Phish.Net varies greatly.

"There's still plenty of the original spirit of cooperation and communal recreation. But with more people, there's plenty of flaming and antagonism and harassment," Godard said. "The other stuff has grown and that's a sociological inevitability, I suppose."

Basic tape trade requests and tape lists remain ever-present, as do simple requests for information or open-ended questions about band history. Debates on Phish fan ethics also volley back on fourth, with a staunch group of fans often seen criticizing everything from trading tapes of shows not opened to recording (such as JazzFest), to ticketless fans, to The Pharmer's Almanac.

It remains a small percentage of fans who frequently read the Net, as many remain without online access and a surprising number of fans who are hooked into the Internet still choose to get their Phish fixes elsewhere, such as in America Online's Phish Bowl (sometimes luring in Mike Gordon) or on Internet Relay Chat (IRC) on the channel *#phish*.

But even those who don't participate can clearly recognize the impact Phish.Net has made. Much of the culture and knowledge present in the Phish community originated online.

Phishing the Net

Interested in joining the cyber-Phish crowd, but don't know where to begin? To access the Phish.Net—also known by its Usenet name *rec.music.phish*—you'll need a subscription to an Internet provider that offers email and, hopefully, Usenet access. (Usenet is the name for the section of the Internet which offers bulletin boards of information on thousands of topics).

Accessing *rec.music.phish* directly via Usenet allows you to selectively read messages posted by other Phish.netters. A lot of messages. More messages about Phish than you ever imagined possible. So many messages, in fact, that you may have to put the rest of your life on hold to read them.

Seeking relief from the information overload that is the Phish.net, phan Benjy Eisen offers subjective compilations of what he considers the best stuff from the Phish.net, a job he recently assumed from Rosemary Macintosh, who stepped down in 1997 after several years of producing "Rosemary's Digest." It's perhaps the easiest way to keep up with what's going on online without suffering from complete Phish-info burnout.

...And on the Web

Andrew Gadiel's Phish Page *<<http://www.gadiel.com/phish>>* The best Phish page on the Web. From tour dates, to album info, to setlists, to whatever else, you can find it there. A great site for any and all current information about the band.

Stash Radio *<<http://www.phishradio.com>>* An online Phish radio station, 24 hours a day. All you need is a 28.8 connection and Real Audio 3.0 A live show is broadcast every Sunday night at 9pm EST.

The Helping Phriendly Program *<<http://ourworld.compuserve.com/homepages/ttphish/phishtap.htm>>* The Official homesite of a freeware program written by Tom Torrillo. The Helping Phriendly Program allows you to create and maintain a database of all the Phish tapes you have.

The Helping Phriendly Book *<<http://www.nd.edu/~pjohnso8/hpb.html>>* Created by Josh Z and Pat Johnson, this site contains a searchable, online edition of the Helping Phriendly Book with setlists from 1983 to the present.

Dan Schar's Review Page *<<http://stickman.biology.ucla.edu/~review>>* Dan has mined the Phish.net and gathered show reviews dating back to the 1980s.

Bouncin's Phish Page *<<http://www.mindspring.com/~pagey/phish>>* A good overall Phish site with lots of links, tapelist, and an online version of the Gamehendge story. A phriendly place to be.

And of course don't miss *Phish.com* and *Phish.net*, two of the best and most crucial Phish sites on the Web. **—Matt Monaco**

Musical Magic

Musicians Who Have Influenced, Collaborated With, Or Been Inspired By Phish

Good Citizen Vol. 1 performers.

Photo Courtesy of GOOD CITIZEN

New Music Thrives in Burlington, VT, the City that Spawned Phish

By Andrew Smith

The remote northeastern city of Burlington, Vermont boasts approximately 60,000 residents, five major colleges and one daily newspaper. Hometown of the nation's only independent Congressman, the outspoken Bernie Sanders, the little city on Lake Champlain is still ruled by the liberal progressive coalition and the thousands of college students who invade every September and vanish again in May.

Even though true live music clubs are few and far between, with Nectar's, Club Metronome and Club Toast providing the most consistent homes for live music, a vibrant arts community survives and flourishes. There are hundreds of bands in Burlington: the city that spawned Phish and its eclecticism offers up nightly jazz, folk, bluegrass, reggae, hardcore, alternative rock, roots rock, acid jazz—you name it, and on any given night you can probably find it in Burlington.

While Phish is the dominant musical force in the Queen City—and the only Burlington act currently on a major record label—the band has maintained its strong ties to the local music scene, often embarking on side projects with local performers, and involving many of these artists in various Phish escapades.

* * *

Jazz ensemble Bad Hat, which teams Trey Anastasio, Jon Fishman, and the Jazz Mandolin Project's Jamie Masefield and Stacey Starkweather, has been known to pop up in small clubs during breaks in the Phish schedule. Starkweather is also associated with Phish through New Orleans-based Michael Ray and the Cosmic Krewe. Ray is a trumpet player who counts past gigs with Sun Ra and Kool and the Gang to his credit, and he recently appeared on *A Live One* and *Surrender to the Air* as well. He is also featured on the Burlington compilation album *One City Under a Groove*.

Fishman sports another between-tour live outfit, Pork Tornado, which plays frequently on Monday nights at Club Toast (165 Church Street). Pork Tornado is one of several bands the drummer has been known to sit in on. Singer/songwriter/actor Martin Guigui's band Spastic got their start with Jon Fishman behind the drum kit, although he has since been replaced by Jonathan Mover of the Joe Satriani Band.

The Dude of Life's band—fronted by the famed Dude, Steve Pollak—began with the Dude playing with his friends Phish, but later evolved to include other Burlington musicians, including Dan Archer on guitar. Dan owns Archer Studio, where the Dude album *Crimes of the Mind* was recorded with Phish in 1991, and *Lawn Boy* was recorded in 1989.

Photo by MATTHEW THORSEN

Richard the Clarinet Man performs with Phish on *Burlington on Burlington.*

Other bands have benefited from the success of the piscine brethren in other ways: local group Chin Ho! penned a slightly sarcastic ditty called "(I Wish I Was A Phish) Sticker" that got a mention in *The New York Times*. Fishman and Trey allegedly both have copies of their CD *Big Crowd* in their collections.

Winning a place in Phish history, two members of local punk/alternative group The Pants performed with James Harvey, Trey and Mike under the name "New York" at Club Toast in May 1997 (Page joined for the encore). That night marked the first performance of several new Phish tunes that would surface during the '97 summer tour, including I Saw It Again and Dirt.

About a year earlier, Trey lent his studio prowess to The Pants as he produced a three-song demo for them while Phish was recording *Billy Breathes* in Bearsville, NY. The Pants returned the favor by covering "Golgi Apparatus" for the *Burlington Does Burlington* project [see sidebar at left].

Also linking up with local performers is Page McConnell, who performed on and helped produce a song for the Vermont band Uproot called "Milo." It appears on the compilation album *Digital Mystery Tour*, released on Big Noise Records [also see sidebar].

Phish often lends support by its presence at numerous other shows around Burlington as well, and bands like Strangefolk, Motel Brown and (sic) are turning heads and gaining fans the same way their friends Phish did—one at a time. These three bands lead the current "roots rock" pack in the Queen City, with hundreds more right behind them.

Strangefolk, featured previously in The Pharmer's Almanac, has toured up and down the East Coast in support of their self-released disc *Lore*, and have won legions of fans and the interest of several major labels. Motel Brown, a long-running roots reggae band, released its first CD, called *Too Much Time*, and has been gigging up and down the East Coast.

A relative newcomer to the scene, the eight-member jam band (sic), has already packed local clubs like Metronome and Toast and is probably the second-most taped live band in town (after Phish, natch). With a percussionist from local dance group Jeh Kulu (featured performers at the Clifford Ball) and members of local groups Chin Ho! DysFunkShun, Motel Brown, Cranial Perch, Bacon Sheik and Low Flying Planes, and featuring a "stick" player, (sic) shows have been littered with Phishheads grooving on their eclectic rock.

Burlington is mighty proud of its Phish, and Phish seems to be mighty proud of Burlington. Come and visit sometimes and say "hi" to Nectar while you're here.

Andrew Smith edits Good Citizen, *a publication devoted to Vermont music.*

Phish Covers Burlington Bases

As members of the local music scene who "made good," the Phish boys have not forgotten their hometown brethren. They prove their loyalty by supporting a number of projects, including a recent appearance on a compilation CD called *Burlington Does Burlington*, a disc designed to benefit Good Citizen, a Vermont-centric music publishing company.

The double CD of 38 Vermont bands covering the songs of other Vermont bands, the project was created to raise funds for the fledgling operation and foster a greater sense of community in the local music scene. The CD was released in 1996. The Phish recording of "Rocketsled's Funky Main Many Meets Big Joe on Church Street," originally by Rocketsled, is actually a collaboration of sorts with a legendary 58-year-old street musician named Richard the Clarinet Man and was partly recorded during Phish's sessions for *Billy Breathes* in the spring of 1996.

The recording is exclusive to the *Burlington Does Burlington* album and can be ordered by mail by sending $22 to Good Citizen at P.O. Box 5373, Burlington, Vermont, 05402 or via the Web: *www.bigheavyworld.com*.

Also, The Pharmer's Almanac has copies available of *Digital Mystery Tour*, featuring Page performing with Uproot for $15, postage included (Page also produced the track). Send check or money order to "The Pharmer's Almanac," 328 Flatbush Ave #122; Brooklyn NY 11238 or call us at (718) 398-4442.

Phish has been known to fly various Burlingtonians around the country for an occasional live appearances, most notably horn players Dave Grippo and Joey Somerville (see *A Live One* and *Lawn Boy*). Grippo and Somerville have also appeared with the band that leads the Burlington "acid jazz" scene, the nine-member Belizbeha. Signed to Enemy Records in Europe, Belizbeha has made the road their home for the past several years and can be found regularly haunting New York City clubs in support of their album *Charlie's Dream*.

Grippo orchestrated the horn section for Phish's appearance on The Late Show With David Letterman in summer 1995, did *Quadrophenia* in Chicago in fall 1995 and *Remain in Light* in fall 1996, and has a compact disc out with Grippo/Sklar Sextet. Joey Somerville's recent contemporary jazz album is called *Shine*. All of these artists appear on *One City Under a Groove*. Local trombonist James Harvey also appears on *A Live One* and *Surrender to the Air*; Grippo and Harvey joined Phish onstage at the band's most recent Vermont show, the March 18, 1997 gig at the Flynn Theater.

Another Burlingtonian who has appeared with Phish is the amazing pedal steel and banjo player Gordon Stone. Recording for a small Vermont label called Alcazar Records, Stone has appeared on *Picture of Nectar* and *Rift* and in 1996 his buddy Mike Gordon returned the favor by co-writing a song called "Fraction" with Stone that appears on his album *Touch and Go*.

Stone has also played with Mike Gordon on several occasions in recent years, including appearances at UVM's Slade Hall (the site of one of the first-ever Phish gigs) and in front of 6,000 people at a folk festival in Ann Arbor, MI, where they played under the name The Drop Caps. The Gordon Stone Trio frequently makes appearances on the Northeast club circuit, and performed on a small stage at the Great Went.

Dinner With The Dude

STEVE POLLAK, OTHERWISE KNOWN AS THE DUDE OF LIFE, was part of Phish history long before Phish was Phish. A high school friend of Trey's who also went to UVM for a period, the Dude can be heard on the oldest Phish bootleg in circulation—Nectar's on 12/1/84—where he sang on Skippy the Wonder Mouse and Fluffhead, two songs he helped write. The Dude also has songwriting credit on Suzie Greenberg and Sanity, and wrote the famous lyrics to Antelope, Slave to the Traffic Light and Dinner and a Movie.

◆◆◆

The Almanac editors had the pleasure of sitting down with the Dude one night, reliving his memories of high school with Trey, UVM hijinks and seeing Phish develop over the years. Not everything he told us was fit for print, but here are some highlights of our dinner with the Dude.

◆◆◆

Just in case anyone was wondering, he ordered Matzoh Ball soup.

Pharmer's Almanac: So how did you meet Trey?

Dude of Life: We actually met in high school. We went to Taft together and we had a lot of fun there [laughs]. We lived on the same floor and somehow we managed to graduate. It was like a big party. Taft was kind of like college in high school because everyone was living away from home. So we were trying to get away with as much as possible and not get caught. Usually we wound up getting caught.

And you guys were in a band back then called Space Antelope?

Yeah, I actually thought of the name. I would do special appearances with Space Antelope.

So you weren't in Space Antelope?

Well, I was the singer, but I'd only show up at certain points during the show.

Did you have the name back then?

That's when the Dude of Life was born. The name was born when a bunch of us were in somewhat of an altered state late at night in this room. I walked in wearing goggles and a tapestry and I started uttering comical phrases and suddenly I was knighted "the Dude of Life." I guess it stuck.

Were any Phish songs written that far back?

Not that early. Back then one of the songs we did was, you know, "Fire On The Mountain." We did "Fire at the Taft School." We were popular even though there were only about 200 people at the school.

Are there any tapes of Space Antelope?

I know of one, my friend has it. I'd love to hear it. It's been about 10 years.

Were you able to tell early on that Trey had it musically?

Oh, yeah. He actually didn't start playing guitar until his second or third year in high school. He was originally a drummer. Then he just got a guitar and wore it constantly. After two or three weeks, he was already playing really well. It was phenomenal to see how fast he learned it. He lived for it, he loved it.

So, after Taft, he then went to UVM.

We both went to UVM. We had some really good times back then. We actually moved off campus together. We were living on 202 1/2 Pine Street. We used to have these percussion parties with like 30 of us banging pots and pans. 30 of us stoned out of our minds.

The neighbors must of loved that.

Well the neighbors, they'd come over and join in. Those were fun days.

What was your role in each of the songs you contributed to Phish? Did you write the music or just lyrics?

I came up with the lyrics, and also the melody of the song. But then Trey would take it to another level with this incredible musicality. We wrote some great stuff together and there's some new stuff that he's helping me out on. They haven't been released yet. We have about four songs in the can and we're going to get the rest of it happening. We're just waiting for the right time.

Do you usually write with the aid of a guitar?

Well, I'm not professionally trained and I never went to music school or anything like that. I'm not a great musician at all—I get the melodies from my head and I do the best I can to get them into form. That's why I am really focusing on learning about more complex guitar and really taking it to another level. It's just a gift I have of having the song within my head.

So, first comes the melody and then comes the lyrics.

Not always. Sometimes they happen together—there are no set rules. Sometimes you can be driving at three in the morning, all burned out and be like whoa, I've got to write this song down. I take a little cassette recorder and use that to get the initial ideas and then build from there.

What's your favorite song that you've ever written, for Phish or your own band?

That's a really tough question. I have different favorite ones for different moods I'm in. But right now I'm into writing very up tunes that bring people up, just rock-n-roll in its purest form.

Suzie Greenberg—you basically wrote that whole song, right?

Yeah. She's a real person.

Did you change the name to Suzie Greenberg or is that the name of the actual person?

That is the name of the actual person. She was an ex-girlfriend of mine. Basically when I went down and had a semester at SUNY Purchase, Suzie Greenberg and I were in a film class together and I had a crush on her and we got together very quickly but we were only together for a month. We had a lot of good times in that month, but then after that, I was totally in love with her but then she broke up with me at that time and I was kind of heartbroken. It was during that time that I wrote the song.

Then five years later we got back together for a short stint but then I broke up with her the second time because I realized that she wasn't what I thought.

What did she think of the song?

I don't even know if she knows about it.

You didn't tell her?

I did tell her a long time ago but I don't think she really knows the level that it's at now. And there are other Suzie Greenbergs. When she tries to say it's about her I will get those other Suzie Greenbergs to testify that it's about them.

So the lyrics of the song were pretty dead-on?

They were written at the time when I was hurt by her, but honestly I only wish the best for Suzie Greenberg. I don't know what she's doing, man. Today I bet she's probably forgotten my name [laughs].

Do you get to play live anymore?

Sure, I played at the HORDE, with some members of Shockra. We've got some things going and I plan to be out there a lot in the near future. If I had my way I'd just be playing all the time. I'm working on a number of projects now and this is just a time for me to kick back for a while and start a few new projects.

Do you still get to see Trey a lot?

Oh yeah, he's one of my closest friends.

Space Antelope, as seen in the 1982 Taft Annual yearbook. Yes, that's Trey on electric guitar and The Dude of Life on vocals.

What's it been like seeing them go from being just your college drinking buddies to being stars?

It's just a wonderful, incredible thing to see them go from a bar band and seeing them rise up from one level to another, and see how unified the whole operation is. It's all in the name of good fun and rock-n-roll. And its done in a very true fashion—unlike some of these bands who know the right person at MTV and move right up to the top. They've done it the grassroots way—that's why they're going to be here 30 years from now, 40 years from now.

The worst fear of a Phish fan is Phish just deciding to not do Phish anymore. Is that possible?

No way, no way, they're going to be around a long, long time.

The band has always seemed like really cool people, totally down to earth, never snubbing their noses at fans.

That's really true, and I don't think that most people would handle themselves as well. Some bands have success and they just don't know what to do with it—they don't know how to handle it and that's what destroys them. Phish is anything but that.

What do you think of some of the new material coming from Phish, and Billy Breathes?

I love it. I was up there in Bearsville [NY, where Billy Breathes was recorded in the spring of 1996] hanging out with the band. Just seeing the way they work was beautiful. There was such teamwork; they were so united. Their producer Steve Lillywhite meshed beautifully with the band. He's a total genius. He sees music as a landscape and works with it in that fashion. It was quite a learning experience to see how he works. But in general, we just had a lot of fun playing ping-pong and hanging out.

So did they rent a house or something?

Trey was living in a house where Robby Robertson of The Band used to live. There were a couple of houses and a big red barn where the album was recorded.

It was just a very relaxed atmosphere. It wasn't done very commercially, it was just done in the pure Phish fashion. They did what they wanted to do, woke up when they wanted to wake up, and they had a lot of fun in the studio and it shows. It's a phenomenal album.

* * *

Looking back, what are some of your most distinct memories from the early days?

Wow, it's been a long time. I remember when Trey was getting the band together. He was putting up fliers like anyone would. And Mike became involved, and we knew Fish, he was on our floor at school.

Is it true that their first show had just one person?

Yeah. That was actually an ROTC dance kind of thing. I was at that. They also had Jeff Holdsworth as the guitarist. Trey's old girlfriend was there, and me and my buddy Rob and a cou-

The Dude of Life, fully costumed, gets down with Trey.

Photo courtesy of STEVE POLLAK

ple of other people. Then there were these military wannabes and they just didn't get it. So the show didn't last too long, but it was definitely a first gig, you know. That was the first gig. Not the Nectar's show.

How does it work when you sing with the band? Do they call you up and say come on, or…?

They usually let me know a week or so in advance. It gives me a little time to get ready.

What's your most memorable stage moment with Phish?

It's got to be the New Year's show when I came out with the lawn mower and mask [Boston 12/31/92, to perform Diamond Girl]. I'd done a number of performances with them but in much smaller venues. This one was about 8,000 people and I wasn't used to such a crowd so I was getting a little nervous and I wasn't feeling so well. But luckily, The Wife of Life showed up and calmed me down.

Was the band at your wedding?

They were my wedding band. We were one of two couples that had Phish play at their wedding.

There's one tape that's going around that's from a wedding—is that yours?

No that was not ours—ours was not bootlegged. We have pictures, though.

Did they jam? Did they go off at the wedding?

Oh it was great. I'm so close with them, it's not like I had a band playing at my wedding, it was friends playing at my wedding.

I could just see that happening right now, there would be a crowd outside the wedding with people holding their fingers up saying, "Need one invite, cash for your invite!" It must be freaky for you now to see how big they've gotten. Do you get to see them perform much these days?

Sure, I was backstage at the Clifford Ball. It was amazing to look out there and see an infinity of heads and then to say, huh, this was my wedding band.

Let The Dude Sing!

It's been a long time since The Dude of Life has shared the stage with his old friends. One has to look all the way back to Saratoga Springs in the Summer of 1994.

A lifetime's worth of Phish shows have come and gone since that night, and it's time we saw the Dude on stage with Phish again. The man behind some of the greatest Phish lyrics ever deserves to be behind the microphone.

If you've ever shouted "Set your gear shift to the high gear of your soul" while driving down the highway, then add the phrase "Let the Dude sing!" to your list of favorite phrases. Because it's up to Phish fans to let the band know they want to see the outrageous Steve Pollak on stage.

While you're at it, you may want to check out The Dude performing with his own band at clubs throughout the Northeast. Previously, the Dude toured with a backup band that included none other than Jon Fishman on drums and Dan Archer (another Phishy friend) on guitar. But now the Dude finds himself flanked by the fabulous backup band Great Red Shark, which also performs its own sets (and has been for the last 10 years).

At the new combination's debut performance at New York City's Crossroads in the Fall of 1997, The Dude and Great Red Shark packed the house for two spectacular sets, as most of the audience stayed and boogied well into the night. Performances include material from the Dude's album *Crimes of the Mind* (recorded with Phish in 1991 and released by Elektra in 1994), several new songs, and Phish tunes he helped pen like Antelope and Fluffhead.

With some help from Trey, The Dude has been recording material for an album to be released in 1998. For tour dates or booking information on The Dude of Life, call (212) 501-0584, or check out the Dude's web site at *www.dudeoflife.com*.

Horn Speak

In the summer of 1991, Phish set out on a 17-day tour with the first incarnation of The Giant Country Horns. The Horns have resurfaced several times since, most often on Spring Tour 1994 when they graced the stage at the Flynn Theater in Burlington and The Beacon Theater in New York in April, before making their way out for the encore in New Orleans the following month under the name "The Cosmic Country Horns."

In December of that year, the Horns made an appearance in California from which a performance of Gumbo was extracted for *A Live One*. That was it until a new incarnation of the Horns made it out for the *Quadrophenia* Halloween show in 1995. When another horn section formed for the 1996 *Remain in Light* Halloween show, a new tradition of sorts was cemented—horns on Halloween!

Dave Grippo, who has been with GCH since day one, and Michael Ray, who made it to a 1994 show, played on *Surrender to the Air* and shared the stage with Phish at Jazzfest in spring 1996, both took the time to give Almanac readers a behind-the-scenes look at their collaborations with Phish.

Interviews By Mike Thomas

Dave Grippo Spells Out the Truth on the GCH

There is no figure more synonymous with Phish and horns than Dave "The Truth" Grippo, the Burlington saxophonist who has served as the most consistent member of The Giant Country Horns. Grippo now spends most of his time on stage with Michael Ray and the Cosmic Krewe, but he took a few minutes out of his busy touring schedule to share some memories with the Almanac.

Pharmer's Almanac: *When did you first meet Trey?*

Dave Grippo: The first time I saw Trey play was at a jazz festival in Burlington, and he really impressed me because he could play jazz pretty well and there aren't too many jazz guitarists in Burlington. He was a young kid at the time, the new kid on the block, and I was really impressed by his band. He used to come with the whole Phish band and see the Sneakers Jazz Band at a club called Sneakers in Winooski, VT. The Sneakers Jazz Band was a seven-piece jazz group which had a three-piece horns section which later became members of the Giant Country Horns, along with some other key people. They used to come and see us play— that's where the relationship really started.

When did the whole idea to do the Giant Country Horns come about?

That was in 1990. Actually, we recorded on the *Lawn Boy* album for Split Open and Melt. Trey orchestrated some parts for alto sax and tenor sax and trumpet and he used the Sneakers band horns section. And then I guess in 1990 he started playing with the idea of having a horns section, and by 1991 it was definite that they wanted to do it. In July of 1991 it became a reality and we did a 17-day tour with Phish up and down the East Coast.

So that tour marked the first appearance of the Giant Country Horns.

Right, that was the first time Phish ever had a [formal] horns section.

So how did that work out? Because it is kind of strange to me that that the horns started with a tour, after which there was never another tour like that.

It was exciting; it was fun. I was pretty much a jazz and R&B player and hadn't had much experience with their style of music before so it was a great experience. And the tour was right before they got really big. I think after that tour they got signed to Elektra Records. So that tour was the last stage of "roughing it" as they would say, and after that came the big bus and the plane trips—all the finer points of touring.

When we toured with them, the horns section traveled in Fishman's Caravan, which was a risk to say the least [laughs]. The car overheated many a time, and I remember having to drive with the heat on in 100-degree weather just to cool the engine and keep it from overheating. That part of it wasn't so pleasurable, but the music was always great and meeting people across the country, I always enjoy that.

So are you saying that the reason there hasn't been another horns tour is because there isn't room for you guys?

It's truly their decision to do the horns when they want to do them; there was never an offer to actually do the band.

Could you possibly see another Giant Country Horns tour down the road?

A tour—sure, I'd love to do that again. Since that time we've had various configurations of the Giant Country Horns with the original being Carl Gerhard on trumpet, myself on alto sax and Russell Remington on tenor sax. And then we've had configurations with as many as six people, that was right after they came out with the *Hoist* album.

On that record they had the Tower of Power horns section record with them and when they decided to tour around, they wanted to have horns players play Julius and the Wolfman and stuff like that, that the Tower of Power had recorded. So Trey asked me if I would do that, and then who I would suggest for a horns section. And basically Carl and I were in touch with Phish, and Russell was somewhere in Texas, we had lost contact with him for a while. Joey Somerville, who's a friend of ours from Vermont, played trumpet along with Carl, and we had a baritone sax player and a trombone player, Don Glasco, and a tenor player, Chris Piederman. And we added Michael Ray and played down in New Orleans. [The group in December '94 was Peter Apfelbaum, tenor sax;

L to R, Jon Fishman, Trey Anastasio, Dave Grippo, Michael Ray.

by JEFF CLARKE/Courtesy Michael Ray & Rhythm Muse

The Cosmic Michael Ray Surrenders to the Air

Michael Ray, the clown prince of the Surrender to the Air project, boasts about the longest résumé of anyone in the music business. A 20-year veteran of The Sun Ra Arkestra and Kool and the Gang, the New Orleans-based trumpeter, keyboardist, and silly hat wearer has also appeared with Phish several times starting in May 1994 as part of the Cosmic Country Horns, as well as making a cameo at the Jazz and Heritage Festival in April 1996. Trey and Page sat in with Michael and his band, The Cosmic Krewe, at Jimmy's in New Orleans the following night. Like many of the musicians who have collaborated with Phish, Ray says the experience is something he'd certainly be willing to repeat.

Pharmer's Almanac: *How did you first get involved with Trey and Phish?*

Michael Ray: It must have been about three years ago. We were playing a gig at the Metronome [in Burlington], and Stacey Starkweather, our bass player, said he knew a guitar player we might want to use. I called Trey and he came down and played, and you know he's a real spiritual musician, and anytime we're going to play some Sun Ra material, he'll be there in a minute. Whenever we get the chance, when he gets some time off, he comes down and jams with us.

From there we went out to do *A Live One* on the West Coast, and they were down here last year for Jazzfest with about 65,000 people, and all the talk in cyberspace was about the Phishheads [laughs]. I mean, Trey's one cat that really thinks about the music and the fans.

What's it like playing a gig with the horns and Phish?

It's pretty well-organized. I come from the Sun Ra school where chaos is just another member of the band, it's riding in the van. With Phish it's a very organized unit, but what really amazes me is that a band with a huge amount of success still maintains a fan network with their newsletter. They really respect their fans and you don't see that too much, and that's one thing that I think is really remarkable. It's a rarity to do that.

How did the Surrender to the Air project come about, how did you get involved in that?

Trey said that it came to him in a dream. We all got together, and there were some very magical moments at that recording session—the stuff that they put out was just the tip of the iceberg. One thing that strikes me is when I asked Trey, "What do you want to do?" he said, "I think that some place in the cosmos there are no words, just music." And we just rolled tape. The first song was like 37 minutes, and then it was just to the next one, and two days of recording like

Michael Ray

Continued from previous page

Michael Ray.

Photo courtesy Michael Ray & Rhythm and Muse

that was just really great.

So Surrender to the Air was all improvisation?

Yeah, it was just everybody playing a part. I wish that planet Earth could do that. Every musician had a certain role, but the music was just out in the cosmos. It wasn't like Trey was Mr. Producer, even though he was, he was really just in there jamming with everybody else.

At the live Surrender shows [April 1-2, 1996 at the Academy in New York City] it seemed Trey was taking more of a back seat to other musicians, totally opposite of his role in Phish.

That was his true intention. I mean, myself being the leader of a group, it's great to be a sideman. There's so much stuff you have to consider being a leader. It's like Sun Ra said about this country, "We the people, for the people ain't say nothing about leaders." But on *Surrender to the Air* that's just the tip of the iceberg—when you've got musicians like that, it just rolls.

Could you see something like Surrender to the Air happening again?

Well, it's kind of hard because the scheduling of all the musicians is one of the hardest things. I mean the Surrender to the Air band can hold their own on any stage, but it's basically about scheduling.

If we could just get someone to schedule one big cosmic jam session—Sun Ra has done gigs with well over 100 musicians which is A Prayer for the World. We played at Carnegie Hall, and they had a choir of 30 people that would bark like dogs and then have about nine dogs that would sing, so I've seen a lot of strange shows—a 100-piece sax section in Vienna. The music's out there. No matter what language you speak you can always understand the music. How can you communicate with other worlds without the music?

How is Trey thought of in the jazz community?

Well a lot of people don't even know about him and very few people in the jazz community even know of Phish. I mean, they're a phenomenon in themselves. But he is a very well respected musician.

When was the first time you became familiar with Phish as far as hearing their music. Was that after you met Trey?

No, it was before that when my friend, videographer Eric Clapp, came down to New Orleans about five years ago with some Phish music, and he would always say, "Man, you guys should jam together," so I really have to thank him for the Phish connection.

Have you ever been to a Phish show as a fan and not playing?

I don't think I've ever been to a show unless I was playing, because if they're in town, I'm usually going to try and play with them. But I would recommend for anybody who has never seen Phish live to go and see them live—the live stuff is really worth it. For most rock acts to maintain improvisational, spontaneous secretions in their music, well that's remarkable in itself. Most of the time when you're doing a tour you have the same songs that you play night after night after night until it becomes very monotonous and robotic, but there's always a fresh edge with the Phish organization. It really builds down to their respect of the music and their respect of the fans.

What do you think of the direction they're heading in?

Well, I haven't heard too much of their new stuff—I've heard some of it down here and it's great. I mean that's new today, but right now they're probably working on some stuff for tomorrow. Like Sun Ra says, "The tomorrow never comes to a world of yesterday."

So just to be ahead and stay in touch with what's going on in music, I think they know what they're doing.

It seems that recently they've been staying away from using horns at shows.

Any time that Trey gives me a call and needs a horn, if he starts hearing horns, I'll be there and ready.

"The first song was like 37 minutes, and then it was just to the next one, and two days of recording like that was just really great."

"When we toured with Phish, the horns section traveled in Fishman's Caravan, which was a risk, to say the least."

Dave Grippo

Continued from page 36

Carl Gerhard, trumpet; Dave, alto sax; James Harvey, trombone; Michael Ray, trumpet]. That was truly the most powerful one we had.

It seems as of late that the horns have become more infrequent—Halloween appearances seem to be about it these days.

Yeah, Halloween '95 was Joey Somerville and Don Glasco, a trombone player that had played in the second configuration of the Giant Country Horns, myself and we hired a french horn player from the Vermont Symphony Orchestra, who was a teacher up at the University of Vermont. And that music designated four players.

It was great, doing *Quadrophenia* was a rush, playing music that I used to listen to when I was a kid. It was all orchestrated and it was all written down. Brian Camilio had transcribed the whole *Quadrophenia* album and put it into four parts for alto sax and baritone horn, and trumpet and french horn.

If you had to pick a moment or performance as the most enjoyable or exciting, what would it be?

Well the most exciting performance I did was doing the David Letterman show [in July '95], and I got to play with a guy from the Blues Brothers. As far as the true Giant Country Horns, when we played down in New Orleans it was a gas, because we got dressed up in costumes and we jumped on trampolines, we were just going wild—that was a lot of fun. But the shows in California were really great too, that was such a powerful group. Every time I get to play with them is better than the last, because it's so much fun, especially since they do it so infrequently.

Could you envision the next time the horns might make an appearance?

I couldn't tell you. It's the strangest thing. Trey will just call up and tell me to get together some players for a tour or he might call me up the night before and say "Hey, Dave, you want to come down to New York and do the Letterman show?" There can be no warning at all, so it can be a very spontaneous thing.

Was there ever a possibility of doing horns at the Clifford Ball?

That was never mentioned to me. I mean, I would have loved to have done it, but I wasn't gonna bug them about it either. I figure they know when they want to do it, and there's no point in pushing the issue if they don't. Funny enough, at my gig the other night, I hadn't seen those guys in almost a year and I'm playing away, and I look out the window and there's Trey, Page, and Fishman outside of the club [laughs]. And so I went outside and talked to them for quite a while.

Do they make themselves that scarce now that you haven't seen them in a year?

Well, you know, Trey and Page are married and Trey's got a kid, and they're always on the road so when they're home, they're not out and hanging about. Privacy becomes more important than anything else, and as you get older you definitely enjoy your space.

Did you ever imagine Phish turning into the phenomenon they've now become?

It is truly amazing that they have gone this far, but it's not shocking because they're the hardest working band I've ever known, I mean just in the way that they practice. I've seen them practice for six months, 10 hours a day, six days a week—that's how hard they work. And then they'll just take off for a month and go wherever they want to go and do whatever they want to do.

But they have always had that work ethic. It was never like a flash in the pan like, "Hey, I'm a star today, we've got a hit!" It never happened that way. So they have the respect of many a musician in this town here, because of that work ethic. Anyone who can play an instrument knows that these guys work hard to develop songs. You can just listen to a tape and say "Let's try and play this," and you just can't, unless you have spent all that time practicing it and memorizing it. So they have a tremendous work ethic and they're famous and huge now and rightfully so. I'm really happy to see a band like Phish making it at such a huge level because they have worked their asses off.

What's your favorite Phish stuff?

The school that I come from, tunes like Julius and the Wolfman, and even as clichéd as Suzie Greenberg sounds, that horn part and that tune—that's the balls [cracks up]. It's fat and it's in the pocket.

I think one of the things that I really love about Phish is that you can't pigeonhole them, you can't say what kind of style of music they play. One tune they're doing a really nice blues, and the next tune they're stompin' on a trashy rock sound, the next thing they're doing a salsa tune and then the next thing you know they're doing a barbershop quartet, and they kick out a bluegrass tune, and next is a free, improvisational thing. If I had to compare them to something, they remind me very much of Frank Zappa's openness. Frank Zappa didn't stop to say, "What style of music are we playing today?"

What do you see each member of Phish bringing to the table?

What I see is that Trey is a great organizer and composer, and Page also composes as well and writes some beautiful music. They all do, I mean if you go down the albums, Trey's name is after each songs and if you look for a field general, he's the one. Jon's the live wire, and he brings the unknown to the group and I think Mike Gordon is the silent type who hold things together, and is very intelligent. Of all the cats he took the longest to get to know and to this day there is still a lot I don't know about Mike, but he's certainly professional—they all are.

And they haven't lost the fun out of playing music, and I hope they never do because that's what's gotten them so far.

Think about being close with the same people for twenty years, so think how hard it must be to maintain that friendship. Think about having to go to work every day with these people, and living with these people, which is what they did for a while.

I mean, they did everything there is to do together as a band, and they still like each other after all of these years.

Better Than the Front Row

Dream of Jamming With Trey? One Dream Came True

By Jon Katz

"Nature creates ability; luck provides it with opportunity."

Jamming with Trey? Yeah, sure, buddy. Keep dreaming.

To jam with the man himself is a dream shared by guitar players out there who push and shove our way up front at every show to fix our eyes and ears on Trey, hoping to catch a few crumbs from the table of fretboard artistry. You leave the show brimming with inspiration and spend the next week in your room refining your chops, perhaps trying to reconstruct a lick. Well, all that post-show refining of the chops finally paid off for me in the summer of '93 when my dream came true.

The first week of July 1993 I returned to the National Guitar Summer Workshop in New Milford, CT for my third summer. I wasn't planning to go back but that winter, when I got word that Trey was to be one of the guest artists who would be giving a clinic, the check was in the mail.

So there I am six months later to check out Trey up close and personal. It's hot. Damn hot. It's getting close to four o'clock and Trey is doing a clinic in the auditorium in just a few minutes. Better get going. My buddy Justin comes by my room and we're off. I go to grab my keys and pause for a minute. Should I take my guitar? I mean what are the chances of me actually being called up on stage to jam with Trey? Slim to none. But wait a minute—when are they ever going to be better than that? As Wayne Gretsky put it, you miss 100 percent of the shots you never take. I strapped on the old axe and headed over.

As we approached the auditorium we heard the familiar snaps, crackles, and pops that characterized Trey's playing around that time. He was inside warming up. As we waited to enter the auditorium, we edited the gigantic list of questions we had prepared for him: "Who prepares the on tour?" "When you guys are jamming how do you know how to go back into the song?" "Did you ever leave the house?"

A NGSW intern opened the doors and we charged in. I was able to secure a seat in the second row. Trey sat at the front of the stage on top of a stage monitor with his trusty Languedoc. After the director of the program introduced Trey, as though none of us had ever heard of Phish (*with a PH*), Trey got up and began telling us about the week he spent at the NGSW as a student in 1984 and how he has applied what he learned to Phish's music (Mike also attended the workshop). After that the floor was open and we fired away. Shortly into the Q & A session Justin asked Trey what his approach to soloing over changes was. To solo over changes, there's one thing you need—*changes*. He grabbed his axe and began explaining. Midway into it, though, he got frustrated—he needed someone to back him up.

"Does anyone have a guitar?" he asked.

BOOM. I raised my hand.

"Cool!" he said. "Come on up."

Was this really happening? Was the alarm clock about to go off? Nope. This was the real deal. The hours I spent that winter working out the intricacies of Stash, YEM and the like were not about to go to waste. I walked up and introduced myself. He complemented me on my guitar and said he wanted this to be informal, so we sat down at the edge of the stage.

"So you play D minor," he said, as he strummed along, "A flat 7, E minor 7 flat 5... I dunno, uh... do you know... Stash?"

Do I know Stash? Do I know my name?

"Sure," I said, and whipped out the opening lick.

"Cool, so just jam the end part... 'Maybe so, maybe not,'" he sang to let me know where to begin. As I began playing the chords to the jam section, he explained to the crowd what we were about to do. First he was going to solo over the vamp using a strait D minor scale.

Next he would add some chromatic passing tones, and finally he would take us out into "tension land," using certain tension notes appropriate to the progression.

So there we are. Up on stage jamming Stash with Trey. As we played I thought for a moment about watching him jam Stash that past winter at the Saturday Roseland show (February 6, 1993), watching all the facial expressions: the grimaces that accompany a big bend down at the low frets, the way he moves his mouth as though he's orally articulating each note, the quizzical squints that accompany certain phrases, as though they don't make sense, and the way be bobs his head up and down when a jam gets going. Then I looked to my left. I was getting the head bobbing and a couple of squints. Cool.

While he was taking us out of tension land into "release land," I asked if I could play the main riff—"Dah-boodooboodooboodah-dah..."

"Sure," he said, between squints, as he begun one of his classic descending diminished licks. However, this time he slipped. Nothing egregious, just a slip of a sweaty finger.

"Sorry," he said, finishing off the run.

"Don't worry about it," I told him.

Everyone in the place erupted into laughter, including Trey. He patted me on the back and thanked me for helping him out.

"Anytime," I said.

Oh, and Trey, if you are reading this, thank you, and my offer still stands.

Memories of The Early Years

An Interview with Rob Dasaro

In the mid-1980s in Burlington, there were many bands that caught the attention of the locals. Among them was one called The Joneses, which attracted a similar following as Phish and often shared time with Phish both on and off the stage. Rob Dasaro, the band's keyboardist, was there when Phish came up with their name, and also on hand when the Dude of Life taught the band Suzie Greenberg.

Dasaro—who now plays with a local Colorado band called Monkey Train—shares some memories of that era with the Almanac. He admits he's not too sure which years some events occurred, but his recollections reveal some little-know facts about the band and priceless insights into how it all began.

Pharmer's Almanac: *When did you first come into contact with the members of Phish?*

Rob Dasaro: I basically met these guys through a high school buddy in the fall of 1983. I was fresh out of high school, taking a year off trying to play music, of course. I grew up outside of Burlington in a town called Jericho and went to Mt. Mansfield High School, and a few buddies of mine went to UVM.

A bunch of dudes ended up living on Patterson second floor where Jon Fishman lived. Some of those guys were jamming in a rec room called Wing-Davis-Wilke—WDW we called it. I remember sitting up in the room, one time, seeing Trey just jam. They were just perking up then—that's when they met Jeff [Holdsworth], the guitar player who's no longer with them. WDW was kind of a rec room party Friday night thing. It went for a while. Then I sort of remember them kind of turning an open jam into starting to put a band together. It started to fuse.

One thing I remember about Fish back in those days in Patterson—he would lock himself in his room and play drums all night. While everyone else was drinking and booting and doing what college kids do, he'd just be in his room drumming all night. He would have these drumming binges playing Buddy Miles, Jimmy Hendrix—just whatever he'd be playing.

Did you continue to stay in touch with them?

My friend Ken ended up living with Fish on a street near the Front. They used to do pretty funny jams there. Songs like "Hot Blooded."

I don't know how I became part of it, but I vividly remember those guys sitting in the Billings Dining Hall which, if you went upstairs, kind of had this reading place. I remember the band sitting around a table coming up with the name Phish off of Jon Fishman's name. Like right then just going, "Phish—yeah, that's it!" and going "Wow! That's cool." So they had a name for their band.

Was it just a play on Fishman's name? I've heard a lot of other explanations.

It might be deeper than that, but as far as I know everyone called Jon Fishman "Fish." That was his nickname. And they were like "Phish, what a great name for a band." But I'm sure it got deeper than that. It's kind of like the whole "Wash your feets and drive me to Firenze" line.

How long did it take before they went from just having a name to having gigs and a following?

Well, that fall I went on Dead tour and ended up out here in Colorado and spent my first year out here, went back, and ended up hooking up with the Joneses at that point. Phish had been playing the whole year at places like Finbar's. At this point Page wasn't even in the band. So this is '85. Jeff was still playing with them. It was the four of them. I think it was that spring when Page hooked up with them.

Another friend of ours from Mt. Mansfield named Josh was going to Goddard at the time, and his band was playing in this music festival at Goddard that Page organized. He was like, "We've got this band from Burlington coming down and they're called Phish." That was the time Page hooked up with them.

I came back after ski season, and The Joneses started playing. We got together for a bunch of summer gigs. Phish was playing a lot at a place called Slade Hall—the environmental students lived there. Another place they played a lot was called Hamilton Hall. There were some great jams.

I was in the Joneses and we kind of played in the same places and kind of kept running into each other. We had our thing going and had a few originals but we were definitely playing a lot of Dead. Phish was trying to get away from that. They didn't want to play the Dead.

That year [1986] they played at the Haunt on April Fool's Day. They came out and played Help on the Way into Slipknot

Slade Hall at UVM.

Wing-Davis-Wilke.

156 King Street.

and then moved into—it might have been AC/DC Bag—one of their songs. But they just ripped it, you know.

Those guys could play anything they wanted. They chose not to play the Dead but when they played it they played the hell out of it.

I started going to school at UVM. I was taking music classes and Trey was taking music classes and we used to run into each other. The classical heads hated my stuff, and I'm not sure what they though of Trey's, but I got the feeling from him that they weren't crazy about it. And that's when he's writing stuff like Fluffhead. I remember him showing me stuff and I was blown away. I mean, I was like, "Jesus, he's writing incredible stuff."

Trey is a genius. And he's a nut. He's just funny to be around. I remember one night when we were leaving Nectar's and they got everyone in the bar to go skinny dipping. And it wasn't even a jammin' night for them. It kind of quieted down by the end of the night and everyone went out and went skinny dipping. He was just like, "Let's go skinny dipping." The whole bar. It was pretty funny.

Were they getting a real fanbase then?

They definitely had a following. It seemed like at first we even had a little better following that they did—and I even got the feeling from them that they were a little resentful of that. Obviously they won out on that big time. But for a while they didn't want to play with us.

There was one summer where we played a lot, in the parks, and Phish didn't play at all. I think that was the summer of '86. I heard Trey went up to northern Vermont and rented a cabin and hung out there.

When he came back [his improvement] was really noticeable. He had all his scales, all his jazz scales. He was on it. His fingers were on the fretboard. I remember going to Nectar's and going, "Whoa, he's on it now."

The following summer I think, half of each band kind of left, so we jammed together a lot and would sometimes call ourselves "The Phonses." There was this other cool house on King Street—that's where Brian Long lived, Fishman, Trey, lived there, maybe even Mike lived there. It was a red house and it was right across from the Hood Milk plant. Hence the Harry Hood song.

That one summer, those guys started to move out, and a couple of the Joneses moved in. And they were living there and we started practicing there.

I think Mike was gone; I'm not sure if Fish was around or not. But our bass player Jim, TJ and I—the guy who hooked me up with all the Joneses guys—and Trey and Page all were jamming. And Trey said, "Oh, my buddy the Dude of Life is coming up." And that's when

"Fish would lock himself in his room and play drums all night. While everyone else was drinking and booting, he'd just be in his room drumming all night."

[The Dude] showed us Suzie Greenberg and Sanity. The next day we were playing at this Student Association Summer Festival in UVM on the steps of the theater building. We practiced that night with the intention of going out and doing this SA gig.

This is classic me right here: I friggin' went on a bike ride with a buddy, got up early, did this trail, and ended up getting to the gig 15 minutes after they were done playing. I practiced it. I got to play Suzie Greenberg the first time the Dude of Life showed any of us—Trey or anyone—Suzie Greenberg, and then I totally missed playing it live. What can you do?

The next two Halloweens we played with them and they were great jams. We would switch sets. There was this building they would play at. It wasn't in use anymore because it wasn't engineer-approved. But the architectural design of it was intense. There were stairways going up to a second floor that wasn't really a second floor. There was no second floor—it just had these little cubicles.

It was a great place. People would be drinking mushroom tea, or dosing. And we were both there, just playing for hours. It was definitely something that came close to whatever the Dead did in the Bay Area back in their day. That happened two years in a row.

Basically, that's when they started taking off, from there, '87 and '88. They really started getting tighter. Jeff had obviously left the band. He gets a lot of bad press. I read an article that says he got religious. But he just went to Alaska. He just decided that he didn't like electric music, he liked acoustic music. He was a big bluegrass influence.

Was Jeff was on the same level as a musician as the rest of the band?

At the time he was, definitely. But certainly those guys progressed.

What happened to The Joneses?

We kind of split up around '89. People were going to grad school, saying, "Where is the band going?" At that point, Phish had a light show. They were totally committed.

When you were just hanging out with them, would they talk a lot about their music?

They were the type of guys that whenever they came over, they always started jamming. You know, "So, where's the guitars?" I remember the first time I heard Tela—Trey came over and said, "Hey, check out the song I'm working on." And he started playing the chords to Tela. He just comes up with great ideas. Like when they won the Battle of the Bands at the Front. They lowered Fish down from the rafters. They rigged up a system and lowered him down with his vacuum cleaner while they're doing I Didn't Know. I think that was the first vacuum solo I saw, at the Battle of the Bands. And they won it that year.

And you're just looking at this going down and it's so bizarre, but then they jump back to their instruments and rip into Fire or something. I was like, "What the fuck's going on? He's playing a vacuum cleaner." It was all so bizarre. The thing is, you can be bizarre as long as you can get back into a jam and rip it. I don't know what they played but it was one of those in your face rock-n-roll tunes. When they used to cover a tune, they used to rip it. Some of my favorite cover tunes like Boogie on Reggae Woman, you know, Stevie Wonder. Bar bands just don't pull that out. But they were able to.

I've been talking to many early fans who say the first fans weren't Dead fans generally but more part of the general college scene. Is that right?

It was definitely alternative from that. At first, you have to remember in the early '80s the Dead were the hot thing. I went to shows with Fish. I remember seeing him sleeping in his or someone's Volkswagen bug in Portland, Maine. It's hard to say that the influence isn't there. They're not a Dead band—they're their own band. But of course we all liked the Dead too; we also liked Zappa.

I remember when Zappa came to the Memorial Auditorium. When Zappa played he had this laundry line going across the stage. He encouraged people to come up and give him undergarments, especially from the female gender. They'd go to the center of the stage and hand him a bra or panties or boxer shorts or whatever. And somebody went down and handed him a Phish shirt and he held it up to the crowd—there were a lot of Phish people there, and it raised a pretty good applause. He gave a smirk and a little puzzled expression and then put it back up on the line with the rest of the garments.

Were they there?

They were all there. When Zappa came to Burlington we were all like "Zappa's coming to Burlington!" Zappa was a big influence.

What is it like seeing Phish now?

When I saw them in Red Rocks, I saw some of the same guys that I used to hang out with in Burlington, underneath the intense light show, just playing their instruments like they always had. Only with intensity and the inspiration to go farther.

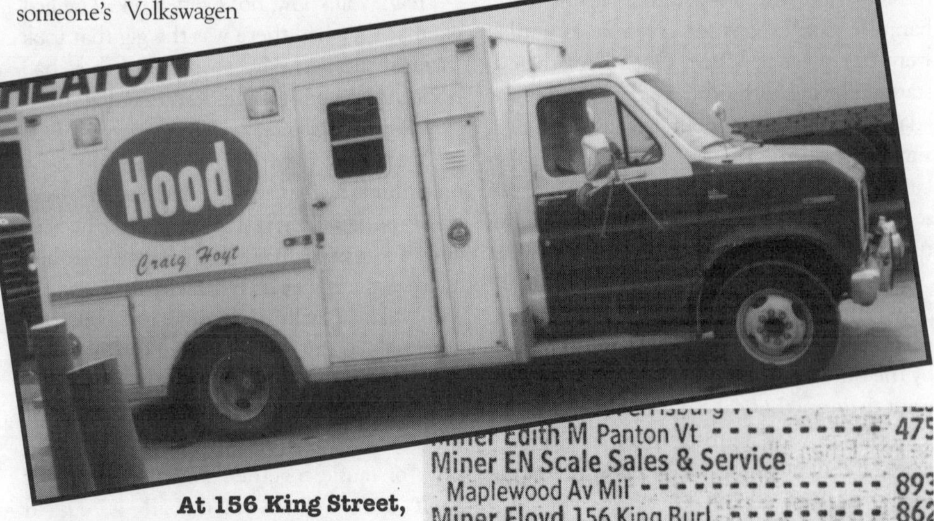

At 156 King Street, the band lived across from a Hood Milk plant (above) in the house where Floyd Miner lived before them (see 1982 Burlington phone book at right).

Miner Edith M Panton Vt - - - - - - - - - 475
Miner EN Scale Sales & Service
Maplewood Av Mil - - - - - - - - - - - 893
Miner Floyd 156 King Burl - - - - - - - - 862
Miner G E St George - - - - - - - - - - - 482
Miner H M Colchester Vt - - - - - - - - 878
Miner John Panton - - - - - - - - - - - 475
Miner John L E Charlotte Vt - - - - - - 425
Miner Keith H & Sherrie G

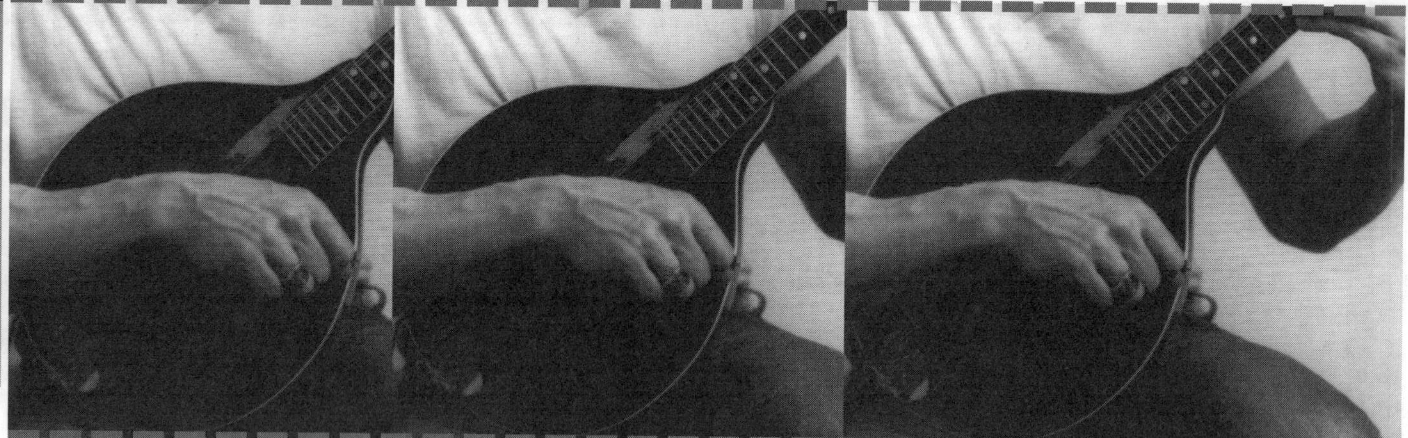

All That Jazz (Mandolin)

An Interview with JMP's Jamie Masefield

Among the many musicians whose lives have become intertwined with Phish, perhaps none has captured the allegiance of Phish fans as much as Jamie Masefield and his three-person outfit Jazz Mandolin Project.

A group whose early incarnations included Trey and Fishman under the name Bad Hat, which came together for about a dozen gigs from 1993 to 1996, JMP has built a strong individual following with Stacy Starkweather on bass and Gabe Jarret on drums. The band's superlative self-titled release on Accurate Records easily ranks as one of the most polished and captivating pieces of recorded music on the scene today. Its melodic and uplifting multi-part instrumentals can't help but draw comparisons to songs like Divided Sky and other *Junta*-era Phish epics.

Masefield was kind enough to sit down with the Almanac to discuss his own music and his collaborations with members of Phish.

Pharmer's Almanac: *Why don't you tell me a little bit about your background, and how you ended up playing the mandolin.*

Jamie Masefield: Well, I started playing music when I was 11—I started playing tenor banjo. I took lessons for seven years until I went to college at UVM. Once I got there I started playing with other students and started picking up the mandolin because it's tuned similarly—all the things I could play on the banjo I could play on the mandolin. It just seemed to be an instrument that was more in tune with the type of things I wanted to play.

The banjo has a historic sound to it. Something like a mandolin is easier to jam with other people. I started doing that, and by the time I got out of school I knew I didn't want to do anything else but be a musician, so I worked toward putting together a group where I could write tunes and play the mandolin.

What years were you at UVM?

I graduated in '88.

So, you were there around when Phish was getting started?

Yeah, as a matter of fact one of their very first gigs was in my dorm, Slade Hall.

You lived in Slade?

Yeah.

They played there pretty frequently, right?

Yeah, you know, not every week. The first gig that they had there was the gig that took them about two days to set up—they had hockey sticks out for mic stands and all that.

Did you collaborate with them early on?

Yeah, I was playing with Mike really early on. I think he was seeing someone in Slade, and I was jamming in the hallway or he was, and we started jamming together. I had another guitar player that I was playing with, and Mike actually did some gigs with us, rehearsals in my dorm room and things like that. He told me that there was this other band that he had gotten in recently and that was what he was really devoted to. We played a lot of music together, kinda bluegrassy, I don't know what you'd call it, David Grisman-y stuff.

Was it all instrumental?

Actually, at that time, this guitar player was singing and I think Mike was singing a little bit too. No drummer, just mandolin, guitar, and bass.

Was there a name for the band?

I think we played around with silly things, but it was one of those things where we only had about three or four gigs, so it didn't really take on a name.

No surviving tapes?

There actually are a couple tapes, I think. I haven't seen or listened to them in years.

Were the gigs at Slade?

We could have played at Slade, we could have played at a couple parties, I don't really remember. We didn't have equipment.

In the years that followed, Phish played in Burlington a great deal. I don't know if there's really ever been an accurate picture of what those years were like. I think that one of the visions is of a Phish utopia in the '80s in Burlington where they were playing almost every night at a bar for 50 people.

You know, that's still going on now, you've always got three or four bands that haven't broken out of their hometown and they're jumping from bar to bar. They were playing a lot in town. It just wasn't a big deal to me. For one, they never got much recognition in the

Jazz Mandolin Project:
L to R, Gabe Jarrett (drums), Jamie Masefield (mandolin), Stacy Starkweather (bass).

Photo by Lauren Stagnitti

local papers—I remember that being kind of an issue—because they were really weird, they were totally different. And now, everyone says "Oh, that's so cool, they were so weird." But at the time, it wasn't a cool weird, necessarily, it was just weird.

They had a really unique following, a small but very loyal following, and I think a lot of them came from Goddard. It was the weirdest looking crowd—I remember when there were only thirty people at a show, and they looked like they had just come out of the woodwork. It was pretty wild. I think that one of the keys for those guys was that they worked at developing it in other places and people in Burlington started hearing, "Wow, people really liked them at Goddard," I think that that was one of their initial jumping steps, and then, "Wow, they liked them at UNH," and that really helped to improve their image in Burlington.

Did you collaborate with Phish at all in those years?

In the early years it was mostly Mike that I was playing with, playing more bluegrass, sort of like Old and In the Way-type music, and then I'd say, from '90 on, or '92, Trey and I started spending more time together. He was studying with Ernie [Stires], and we started talking about music together. We were discovering jazz together; we'd pick away at the real book and find tunes and play them and show each other stuff. That was really nice.

So, that was all just basement stuff, not really performing in front of people?

Mostly basement stuff. Trey and I did a gig at the Queen City Cavern, a little Sunday brunch thing on Church Street. We just played jazz standards. That was the same weekend that Shockra came up and played a big gig and all those guys came to our brunch.

As far as I know, you've never performed with Phish in concert, is that right?

That's exactly right.

Is that on purpose?

I think it's just the way it's ended up—there's certainly no master plan in my mind.

* * *

When did Jazz Mandolin Project start?

I would say end of '92 was when something really casual started taking form. I had been working at it really really hard—one, to learn how to play jazz, and two, to just find musicians who wanted to play and wanted to rehearse. All through these years, from '88 on, I was working really hard...

You were playing in various bands in Burlington?

Yeah, exactly, I was playing in various bands and I was practicing many, many hours on my own, and trying to learn jazz, really. Then, by '92-'93, I started booking gigs in town, finding people who wanted to play with me, and then I started having a couple of tunes, original tunes, and we knew that the rest would all be jazz standards.

Phish provided a lot of inspiration to me, to see that you really can get a bunch of guys together, and work at it, and get the gig, and save up your money and buy a van, and stuff like that. That was a huge inspiration.

Stacey Starkweather also has collaborated with Trey, right?

Yeah, I think his first contact with Phish was giving Mike some lessons, and I'm not sure if I'm right or not, but I think the first time he played with Trey on a real gig was one of the first Bad Hat gigs. I could be wrong about that.

Is it right that Bad Hat was originally called Jazz Mandolin Project?

Here's how it went: Jazz Mandolin Project was lacking a drummer, and I was in between drummers...

So it was just you and Stacey?

Well, it wasn't necessarily just Stacey either. I was using many other bass players too, but sometimes Stacey was playing with me, and I needed a drummer, and I called Fish and asked him if he wanted to play, and he said "Sure," and that was at the Last Elm Cafe. Then, like, a night or two later, I went to Sneakers and Trey was playing there with those guys, and Fish had told them, and we talked it over...

Who was he playing with at Sneakers?

Oh, like Dave Grippo, Joe Somerville, and the Sneakers jazz band. He asked if he could come play too, or I might have asked him. In any case, it was decided that he would come play as well. So we played this gig at the Last Elm, and it was just great, so much fun. Basically, I had a handful of Jazz Mandolin Project gigs that I had booked that ended up becoming Bad Hat shows.

When was this?

1993, maybe? So they were booked as Jazz Mandolin Project, and it was gonna be my thing that was gonna come in, and it was so much fun, that I basically said, "Well, hey, I got this gig over in Plattsburgh, there's a gig in Portland, ME I've been trying to put together for awhile, and the guys said, "Yeah, sure, let's do it, this is fun." So that's how Bad Hat came about, basically with those guys, through Fish filling in the drums and then Trey coming, and us having so much fun that we played a handful of pre-booked gigs.

How would you describe the music of Bad Hat?

The music started out as basically being a handful of original tunes of mine and the rest were jazz standards. You know, really well-known tunes like Caravan, or Jump Monk, or Billy's Bounce, or Yardbird Suite, things like that, with our own twist on it, taking a right turn here and there, spending 20 minutes on it and then coming back, that kind of thing.

So I know you played JC's in Plattsburgh. What were some of the other places—you said Portland?

Yeah, we played at Granny Killiam's and at the Portland Performing Arts Center, we played a number of times at the Last Elm Cafe, and we played at Middlebury, and just recently, about a year and a half ago, we did a gig at UVM.

Those places were pretty packed.

Yeah, it was really exciting. They were just packed, just a lot of fun, everyone being really, really quiet—for Trey and Fish it was such a treat to play so quietly that they wanted to take it to the extreme and really take it down to a whimper.

What's the state of Bad Hat—have you guys gigged recently?

No, we haven't. We've been talking about doing things all along, and there's nothing planned specifically at this point, but I feel pretty confident that at some point we'll do something really nice.

Would there ever be a time where you do a tour that would be more accessible in terms of bigger places, announced in advance, tickets on sale over the phone, that kind of thing?

Who can say? But one of my dreams with Bad Hat would be to have a small tour in a lot of really nice old historic theaters, smaller theaters, not like little cafe places as in the past. The problem is, everyone wants to see a Bad Hat show, so it's not possible anymore to book a 200-seat capacity place and have another 700 people all pissed off outside because they can't get in. And then, I don't know if we want to get into playing these huge things, because it's really a quiet, kind of intimate experience—I don't think it would translate well in a huge situation.

When was the last time that Bad Hat played?

About a year and a half ago at UVM [January 24, 1996 in UVM's Christ Church]. It was a really great gig, a lot of fun.

* * *

At this point, Jazz Mandolin Project seems to have a pretty decent following. How did that develop? Was it a pretty gradual thing?

Yeah, I think so. A lot of touring and playing around. I think that the whole tape trading world has helped us a lot—people really have moved tapes around. And the Internet also, I guess they go hand-in-hand, tape trading and the Internet really help speed up people's interest, and we've been really busy touring a lot and playing a lot of schools. Things are going really well for us. It's really been about four years now that we've been a band.

I know it's a hard thing to do, but could you try to describe the music to somebody who's never heard it? What should they expect if they hear Jazz Mandolin Project?

One of the quotes that I've ended up using from time to time is, people come to a show, and all they knew was the name of the band, and then they tell me afterwards that it was nothing like what they expected, and I really like that. Because of the name, I think a lot of people assume that the whole band is mandolins, which to me is sort of a horror picture.

The only thing that I can think of is that it's jazz-related music, full of energy. Maybe that's the safest thing to say. It's not Charlie Parker straight-ahead stuff, it's got a lot of rock overtones, and it's got a lot of classical undertones in the way the tunes are written. We just draw upon a lot of things that intrigue us, and hope that it will intrigue the crowd.

What I really like about your music is that the mandolin sound kind of builds up a tension on its own, through melody, just sort of a swirly trippiness, and then the bass seems to release the tension—it's just such a big sound, an effect-oriented sound. Is that a way you think about the music?

I don't think it's a matter of one instrument creating a tension and another creating a sense of relief. I think the notion of tension and release is a really important notion to the music where you create that pull and then it gets relieved. I think in the band what we try to do is have it be a pretty collective thing where we're working together to build this thing up and then bring it to a climax and then bring it back down. I would think that it's kind of everybody working at it together. Maybe it's because the bass is holding the bottom end and the bass is a sound that everybody is so accustomed to.

Tension and release is obviously very important in Phish's music, and it's something Trey has talked a lot about in interviews. That is where I sense a lot of similarity between what you guys are doing. Have you influenced each other, or is it more of just a common influence in terms of jazz? Where would you say the link is?

I'm sure Trey's influenced me in some way, and maybe I've influenced him in some way. I think a big aspect of the whole thing is that basically, we're about the same age, and we're both products of the same time, and we both share a huge fascination with music in general, whether it's barbershop quartet or opera. It's an interest in music in general.

I feel like the most similar thing about the groups is a sense of optimism in the music. A love, a real love for music as a whole. And the notion of tension and release, that's the oldest, most ancient concept, that's what Western music is all about, I mean, Bach defined that centuries and centuries ago. We

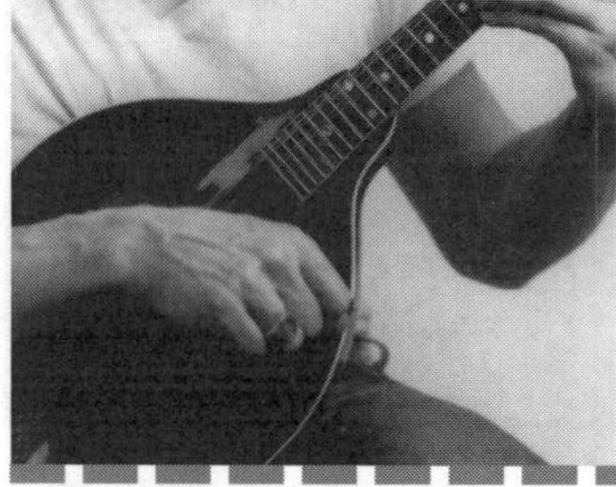

"The most similar thing about the groups [JMP and Phish] is a sense of optimism in the music. A love, a real love for music as a whole."

are just examples of how tension and release are illustrated today, in our time. It's kind of exaggerated to a huge degree, and that's kind of the way Western civilization is moving, how we have to become more and more and more exaggerated and less refined.

* * *

I know that the members of Phish appear at shows in Burlington a lot. To give somebody who doesn't live up there a picture of just how often that goes on, is it the kind of thing where on a semi-weekly basis a member of Phish takes the stage in the Burlington area, or is it more spread out?

They're on the road a lot now, so you have to consider that they're only in the Burlington area maybe a quarter of the year. I think those kinds of appearances are definitely more sporadic than they might have been three or four years ago.

Fish still bops around quite a lot. Trey's got two kids now, and it's a big effort to be a good dad, and be home, and also be this huge rock star too. So, there are a lot of pressures.

I have the impression that if there is one thing they want to support, it's the Burlington music scene, and the musicians that they've played with over the years, even though they don't do it in a very public way. I'm curious as to how that is viewed in the Burlington music scene.

Actually a couple years ago, somebody wrote an anonymous letter to the paper, just bitching them out about how they had made so much money, a "what are we going to get out of this?" type of thing. It was an amazing letter that just flipped me out. I wrote a letter back to the editor, and I was surprised because I was the only person that wrote a letter back saying, you know, what are you talking about?

What I said in my letter was, these guys have paved the road of legitimacy from Burlington to the outer world. It's so hard for a band to make it out of their hometown and become a national thing, and they put a spotlight on Burlington, and it's been great. In terms of some specific thing, there's nothing like that, and I don't really see why there should be. It's certainly helped us, when we say we're from Burlington, Vermont, people start right up and say, "Oh, yeah, that's a real happening music scene, that's where Phish came from."

But when you go out onto the stage and play, people decide if they are going to come back, and see you again, and if somebody's riding someone's wave, they don't come back again, you know? You have one chance to prove your worth. People have to paint their own picture with passion and convey to their audience and hope that it inspires them. That's what I aspire to do.

Check out the Jazz Mandolin Project Web site at www.netspace.org/jmp/music/

Doin' the Didg

From follower to friend and guest star, living a fan's and musician's dream.

By Jamie Janover *(as told to Larry Chasnoff)*

The first time I heard Phish was on a bootleg tape. I was going to Skidmore College in Sarasota Springs, NY—it was about 1987. They were doing that Jimi Hendrix tune Fire and I was like, damn, that's amazing! It's more raging than Jimi would have done it, with a different style, of course—they were stretching it a certain way.

I saw my first show in '89, at Pearl Street in Northampton. And there were probably 150 or 200 people there. I stood right in the front, checking out Fishman and thinking, "How the hell is he playing that fast and for that long?" I'm a drummer, so I was really impressed by his technique.

When I started going to shows regularly, I was always in the front row, right in front of Fishman. And Fishman knew my face after a while because I was going to so many shows. It was 1990. We were at Saratoga and there were weeks where we'd be going to class, leaving at four, driving three hours to Middlebury, or to Connecticut, to see shows. They were playing five nights, six nights a week all in the Northeast, at the most six hours from of each other. All we did was go to class, leave at four, go to the show, drive back. Go to class the next day, oh, they're playing in Burlington, go to Burlington, come back.

My face just kept appearing in the front row, and I was a drummer and I think Fishman could tell because I would stand right there and at the peak moments when he'd do something really clever or really cool, I'd say something or I'd catch his eye and he'd kind of raise his eyebrows at me or something, like, "check that out."

Trey narrates, "The villagers were playing their didgeridoos" and I walk out on stage—my friend goes, "Oh my God, it's Jamie."

I think there was a rapport there—he didn't know my name, he didn't know who I was, but he just saw me a lot.

Then I saw Fishman at the Front. He did a trombone solo where he played a note for like a minute, and in order to do that, he had to do circular breathing. So after the show he was just sitting on the stage talking to people like he usually would, and I went up to him and said, "Hey, I'm Jamie," and he was like, "Oh yeah, hey," because he recognized me.

I said, "I saw you doing circular breathing on the trombone. That's really cool, I do circular breathing too, except on the didgeridoo." And he said, "The didgeridoo, what's that?" I tried to explain it to him and he said, "Wow, that's cool, you should bring one out the next time you come to a show."

A couple months later, I went down to Poughkeepsie, NY, to The Chance. I caravaned down there with about 20 friends of mine and I carried my didgeridoo into the show. Back then there was no huge security or anything like that, so I just walked straight into the back, right up to the dressing room where I saw Trey, and he was like, "Hey, how's it going?"

I said, "I brought you guys the didgeridoo because Fishman told me to bring it—he said you might want to check it out." And they're like, "Really? What's that?" And so with everybody standing around in the dressing room, I started blowing on the didg, and Trey's mouth just dropped. He said, "Wow, man, that's the coolest sound, that sounds so cool, that's amazing!" And then he goes, "You've got to play that with us! We've got to figure out a spot where you can come in and play that on some tune, but you can't wear what you're wearing, I mean, look at you."

I had a t-shirt and shorts on like everybody else, and he's like, "You've got to come up with a costume!" We're in Poughkeepsie in the Chance—where am I going to get a costume? They looked around the room, and that night Fishman was wearing something different, that black outfit with the red cape and the zero—the Zero Man thing—so they were like, "Here, put on the Zero Man dress!" I stripped down to my underwear, put this dress on, then put my hair in a ponytail in the front of my head, instead of the back of my head.

Trey told me later that night—I don't know if it still holds true—that only Fishman, Trey and myself have worn that dress.

So Trey was like, "We've got to figure out a place for you to play this." I started naming songs and ideas of where it could be, and then he goes, "No, no, I've got it. You know that song Col. Forbin? Well, Col. Forbin goes up on the mountain. And what I'll do is say Col. Forbin went up on the mountain and he looked down into the valley and he saw all the villagers down there, playing their didgeridoos. And that's when you come out."

So here I am at The Chance in Poughkeepsie, sitting on the side of the stage. I'm with 20 people that know me from school but no one really knew that I went backstage with my didg—I didn't mention it to anybody. So people are wondering, "Where the hell is Jamie?" Three-quarters of the way through the first set, they played Col. Forbin's Ascent. Trey narrates, "Then the villagers were playing their didgeridoos" and I walk out on stage—one of my friends goes, "Oh my God, it's Jamie." I pulled out the didg and I played into Mike's vocal mic.

It wasn't very long, just a minute or so. And the didgeridoo is a really weird thing to amplify—I don't know if people could hear it very well in the audience. It wasn't like a brilliant musical expression. It was just a novelty thing.

Phish had never heard of the didgeridoo, and most of the audience probably hadn't either. But ironically, it was very shortly after that that they started springing up everywhere—you'd hear them in commercials. Now everybody knows what a didgeridoo is.

[For those that don't, it's an Australian aboriginal instrument made from tree bark which creates a deep, springy sound.]

I don't remember exactly how, but I think somebody asked or they mentioned that I could do it again at some point. It wasn't until August of '91 at Amy's Farm, the best show ever. At that show, I got to sit in again on didgeridoo, in set III, during Buried Alive.

I think I blew out Mike's monitor. On the tape it's really distorted. It's hard because his mic was cued for his vocals and here I come with this huge low-end, giant sound.

* * *

My main gig is playing hammer dulcimer. It's a string instrument from India, related to ancient Persian instruments. Its strings go across a soundboard with bridges and you hit the strings with little hammers. I play it on the street and sell my recordings.

One time, I was in Provincetown, MA at the very tip of Cape Cod playing on the street like I always do. I was just playing away, and I looked up and on the bench right next to me was Trey. And I was like, "Oh my God, there's Trey watching me play." He was like, "Hey Jamie! It's good to see you—what are you doing?" He was on vacation camping with Sue. And he was like, "Wow, that sounded really cool. I've never heard anybody play that thing, play like that, it's really cool music that you do."

We talked for a little bit, whatever, chitchatted, and he was like, "You should come bring that to a show or something, maybe play in between sets or something." And I was like, "Sure, well damn, sure."

That must have been the summer of '92. So when it came time for them to do their New Year's run, I called up the office. I talked to Shelly [Culbertson] and I said, "Shelly, will you pass along a message to Trey? Ask him if it's okay if I play in between sets at one of these shows coming up." She called me back, not very long later, and said that would be fine.

I practiced up, and then at Symphony Hall, Springfield, MA on December 30, at the end of the first set, I was on the side of the stage and Trey goes, "Now our friend Jamie Janover is going to come out and play some hammer dulcimer for you." And it was a 2,600-person show, which was one of their biggest at that point. I played for like 15 or 20 minutes, improvising. They let me put my sign and my CDs and my merchandise up with their merchandise in the hallway, in the lobby. That was the best.

Later, I became friends with Fishman more than anybody else—I've stayed at Fishman's house, the Dome, quite a few times.

Fishman is just a really great guy, he's a character, a total character. He happened to be in a band that got really good and he's really easy-going and a really good guy to hang out with. Last year when we went to the New Orleans Jazz Festival we couldn't find a place to stay, so he said, "Oh, you can come crash in my hotel room."

And I've jammed with him. There was one jam with Fish on drums, me on dulcimer, my friend Aaron on bass and another guy on guitar. Fishman would play trumpet and I'd play the kit, or different jamming, just goofing around.

Jamie Janover plays hammer dulcimer on a version of Hendrix' "Third Stone from the Sun" recorded with Stacey Starkweather and Edwin Hurwitz.

Stone Soup

The Drop Caps backstage, 1/25/97
Hill Auditorium, Ann Arbor, MI.

Discussing the many musical moods of Phish pal Gordon Stone

Few guest musicians have been showcased as prominently on Phish albums as Gordon Stone. The Burlington-based steel pedal guitarist and banjo player was the featured musician on Fast Enough For You on Rift, and also sat in on Poor Heart for Picture of Nectar.

His collaboration with Mike Gordon, however, stretches well beyond that, including a bluegrass performance under the name the Drop Caps in Ann Arbor, MI early in 1996 before a crowd of 6,000 people. Stone also released an album called Touch and Go *from Alcazar Records, and can frequently be heard performing in clubs and cafes around the country with his band The Gordon Stone Trio.*

Pharmer's Almanac: *At one time you were Mike Gordon's banjo teacher, is that right?*

Gordon Stone: That would be in the mid-'80s. He called and wanted banjo lessons. He used to come out for lessons and he would talk about this band that he was starting.

What kind of a student was he?

He was good. He's a real good banjo player now. He has sort of picked it up and put it down over the years.

For how long did you give him lessons?

I just gave him a few, two or three. And then we used to hang out—he was into bluegrass and was using the bluegrass influence in Phish when they were first starting out. I think he is the main bluegrass influence.

Was it mostly technique you were showing him, or theoretical stuff?

Just technique, how to play bluegrass banjo. Some philosophical discussions, but not much. And Phish, all of them, used to come out and hear Breakaway, which was a bluegrass band I used to play with. They used to come down to Sneakers—maybe they were influenced by listening to us, I don't know.

When was that?

Later in the eighties.

When, in your eyes, did Phish start catching on? When was the buzz really happening?

Well, I heard them—Mike would say, "Come out and hear us, come out and hear us." And I would be like, "Yeah, cool." I wasn't that excited about them at first. But when they really came together, I think, was at that band contest at the Front. When I went to hear them that time, I was like, "Whoa, this is something. This could happen."

* * *

How long has the Gordon Stone Trio been together?

Four years. There are some early tapes that are about three years old, maybe? From when we used to play at Paradise downtown here. And Mike played there twice with us, and Grippo, too.

The story behind that was, Stacey [Starkweather] suddenly couldn't play a gig and I had to find someone. I had to call around and I'm like, "Jeez, I wonder if Mike's around," so I called him. And I said, "Do you want to just come over and jam? You don't have to learn all of the material but this edge you will hear, this is not easy stuff to learn." There are stops and changes, like Phish might do live. The tempo changes, sudden hits—all that stuff. And he said, "No, give me the charts, give me the tape," because we had a lot of tapes. He learned the whole thing in two days.

We practiced once, just before we went and played, and I said, "You learned all this stuff?" And we went through the tunes and he played everything perfectly. That's what I hear they do, that Trey does the same thing. He'll go and play with Michael Ray and know the Michael Ray book better than any of the other guys in the band. They are just real dedicated and focused, real professional.

Gordon Stone photo by Laury Shea; Drop Caps photo by Randy Austin-Cardona

L to R, Jamie Masefield, Gordon Stone, and Mike Gordon.

"Mike said, 'Give me the charts, give me the tapes'... He learned the whole thing in two days."

Was Mike like that when you first came into contact with him, or was it something he developed?

He developed it from playing with Phish. He said that playing this material was not that much different because they are long tunes and they have, you would just be playing along and you would just have to be ready for the tempo change and ready for the key change. It wasn't that difficult for him.

He did some stuff with us last fall [1996], me and Doug Perkins. Doug Perkins is in the Gordon Stone Trio, he played bass and we did a Slade show and another show, too, with him. And he sang a whole bunch, like Up, Up and Away and other unusual sorts of things.

Did people know about these shows?

Oh, they were jam-packed. There were some tapers there, the tapes got out a little bit, not that much—at least not as much as the Drop Caps tape got circulated.

How did the Drop Caps come together?

Mike's idea. He did a benefit for the ARC, which is an Ann Arbor [Michigan] folk club. Two years ago in Ann Arbor, he performed by himself. I'm not sure what tune he played, but it was one of his songs—he sang and played bass. And that was it, he just went out onstage in front of 4,000 people and did a solo.

The festival featured Nancy Griffith, Leon Redbone, Dave Bromberg—really well-known folkies. The next year, they invited him back and he thought he should bring a band.

So it was a packed house, this thing.

Yeah. I really like playing in front of that many people.

Whose material were you playing?

We did some of my stuff—we didn't do anything of Mike's—and then we did some of Scott's—he's from Max Creek. And the drummer was formerly with Max Creek.

* * *

The sessions for Nectar *were your first studio sessions with Phish, right?*

Yeah, I played with them on *Picture of Nectar*—on Poor Heart, I played banjo and pedal steel.

How did that come about?

They just asked me. It was Mike's tune and Mike heard it happening and actually came over. We were going to put double banjoes on, which I would have been psyched about—they would have had both of us playing banjoes—but then they chickened out, I guess. When we got there, he said, "No, you just do it and put on the pedal steel." That was done down at White Crow Studios.

Working with Barry Beckett was pretty cool, too, during the *Rift* session. There's some textual stuff in there, I don't know if you can hear it. You have to listen pretty closely. In the end, there is some really high stuff, it almost sounds like wind chimes.

This is on Fast Enough for You?

Yeah. At the end, during the fadeout—it was an extra pedal steel track up real high. That was Barry Beckett's idea. He said, "No, twelfth fret, no fifteenth, no, go up to the twentieth-whatever," and I was just about off the neck, there was so little left of the strings. This little figure, it goes in five against the beat in a little pattern.

They were looking for something different on *Rift*, they were not looking for a country sound at all. And the pedal steel doesn't really sound country on that tune.

How would you describe Phish in the studio?

I go to the studio a lot, so for me it's just business as usual. They were really friendly and easy to work with, and pretty much left it up to me. Except when Barry was there, it was just like me and Barry working in the studio.

Do they have a pretty clear sense, when you get into the picture, of where the music is going to go, or is there a creative process going on?

They left it up to me: "Go for it." And then I went in and did my thing, which is play, and if I made a mistake, I went over it until I got a take I liked. When I got something I liked, they liked it.

* * *

We saw you perform with Phish at Stowe [7/22/93], and you performed up at the other Vermont show from that era, St. Mike's [11/19/92]. Were those the only times you performed onstage with Phish?

Yeah. It was fun. The only time I played in front of audiences that big was out at Ann Arbor at the Drop Caps show. There was a little tension at the Stowe show in terms of the rain—there was a concern about getting electrocuted. Not the band getting wet, but it being dangerous.

So they were actually thinking about not playing—there was that in-between: "Are we going on? Are we not going on?" I was just hanging in the back, waiting for these decisions to come down.

It was fun, and I could hear myself fine onstage. I was a little disappointed that it didn't come out in front very well. And the tunes that they picked for me to play were fun to play. One of them was that Hebrew prayer [Avenu Malkenu]. I also was at the Clifford Ball—we played under one of the tents. That was really fun, I really enjoyed doing that. I was thinking, "Man! This is really big!" Later, I'm standing up in the scaffolding going, "Wow, this is cool."

Yeah, it's a phenomenon. I don't know why it happens or why it continues to grow.

Check out Gordon Stone's Web site at www.nemac.com/gstone.htm

Photo by Emily Barrett, courtesy of Gordon Stone

From the Bottom

Bar Bands Take Phishy Grooves in New Directions

So you didn't get to see Phish in the pre-arena era and are still kicking yourself for all the times you said "Phish, pish," when you saw the name posted at a local bar. Or maybe you were around for those glory days, and would do anything to feel that joy again.

Well the magic of the midnight show may be gone for Phish, but not for dozens of other bands who are hitting stages today and testing the waters of 20-minute improvisations and psychedelic harmonies. In the last couple of years a disparate but recognizable group of Phish-inspired bands have surfaced on the club scene, playing to loyal pockets of tourheads and college-age crunchies while hocking self-produced, self-financed albums and building up their mailing lists and web sites.

It would be both an insult and an undue compliment to say that these bands sound like Phish—few of them do. But each taps a similar nerve as the Phish experience does, and each brings a Phish-inspired element to the stage. Loosely referred to as jam rock, this genre is emerging rapidly and may be the most remarkable phenomenon Phish has spawned.

Here's a partial summary of these road warriors. **By Andy Bernstein & Larry Chasnoff**

moe.

AFTER YEARS OF TOILING in bars and small clubs in the Northeast, moe. has suddenly burst into major theaters and 3,000 seat venues, gaining popularity by the minute. Sound familiar?

The moe.-Phish parallel is similar, in many ways, to comparisons between Phish and the Dead. They are different musically, but seem to be tapped into the fan network created by the predecessor, while subscribing to the same sort of jam ethic which drives tapers and tour heads wild. It's a ripple effect which has turned moe.—and their major label debut album *No Doy!*—into absolute sensations. Fans are already starting to rumble that moe. has gotten "too big," (again, sound familiar?), a complaint that will probably be heard more and more. Powered by guitarists Chuck Garvey and Al Schnier's scintillating trade-offs on lead, and bassist Rob Derhak's slap-happy yet precise basslines, moe. proves that trippy rock can have a razor-sharp edge.

Within that framework, moe. has found avenues for improvisation and mutation, learning to paint the edges of each song and stretch each composition out in a manner only certain types of music fans can appreciate. And moe. has stayed true to the tastes of those fans, not seeking radio play or mainstream acceptance, instead applying the Phishy-formula to an even greater degree. Yeah, they released a single, but it was a 45-minute version of the song Meat (which has only one lyric). Heck, they even allow video taping. If you haven't seen moe. yet, now is the time.

Albums: *Headseed* (1994); *Loaf* (1996); *No Doy* (1996)

Contact Info: phone: (212) 592-3542; web: *www.moe.com*; email: *moe767@aol.com*

The Ominous Seapods

THE VERITABLE GRANDFATHERS of jam rock, The Ominous Seapods have nine years and three albums under their belt, and show no signs of slowing down. The recent *Jet Smooth Ride* underscores what Seapods fans have known for close to a decade—that lead guitarist Max Verna is simply a master songwriter, and rhythm guitarist Dana Monteith is no slouch either. Songs like "Some Days," along with "Blackberry Brandy" on the previously released *Guide To Roadside Ecology*, are so memorable and enticing, that it makes one ask how a band this talented is still playing in bars after all this time.

Of course, real Seapods fans will tell you that the true gems can only be heard on those stages, as their most popular tunes have never been released on album.

Aside from strong songwriting ability, the appeal of the Seapods is their iconoclasm and utter lack of pretension. Managing to be religiously unhip without being contrived—a narrow ledge to walk—the Seapods sing about television, make fun of the Pope, and wear gas station uniforms on stage, but back their shenanigans with captivating jams and memorable guitar phrases.

Albums: *Econobrain* (1994); *Guide To Roadside Ecology* (1995); *Jet Smooth Ride* (1997)

Contact Info: phone: (518) 489-7466; web: *www.netspace.org/seapods*; email: *pod.net.request@dartmouth.edu*

Strangefolk

IF YOU BLINKED in the last year, you may have missed the fact that Strangefolk has become one of the most popular unsigned touring acts in America, and appears on the cusp of joining that elite group of jam bands who can claim to have "made it." While they may be another band which has to fight off Phish comparisons (they *are* a Burlington-based quartet), Strangefolk's unique approach to music demands a far more accurate analysis, and may even require a few listens to fully comprehend.

Combining the folky, acoustic flavor of rhythm guitarist Reid Genauer with the noodly, psychedelic precision of lead guitarist Jon Trafton, Strangefolk is irony incarnate, and creates an inherent tension and release in every tune. To some, Strangefolk represents a step away from jam rock as we know it—they've even been called

From The Bottom...

Native

mainstream or poppy by naysayers. But it comes down to what part of the music catches your ear. If you listen only to the acoustic side, you may end up thinking Eagles or worse. But try walking up to the speaker and letting the electric sounds blow you away. Quite simply, this is a very trippy band, and once you "get it," you'll never want to turn back.

Their new release, *Weightless in Water*, could prove to be a breakthrough, and their last self-release as major labels come a-knockin'.

Albums: *Strangefolk* (1994, re-released 1997); *Lore* (1996); *Weightless in Water* (1997)

Contact Info: phone: (802) 658-6453; Web: *www.strangefolk.com*; email: *yourparty@strangefolk.com*

Percy Hill

GOOD NEWS: Rumors of Percy Hill's death were greatly exaggerated, though they will be touring a bit less so band members can return to school. A victory for education is a loss for music, because Percy Hill makes every show count.

Clearly beyond their years in taste and sound, Percy Hill put out their first album just months after forming, when most of the band members were still shy of their 20th birthdays. That work, *Setting the Boat Adrift* (1993), is anything but amateur, putting forth a unique sound which mixes diverse musical influences ranging from The Allman Brothers to Steely Dan. 1995's addictive *Straight On 'Til Morning* does more of the same. In 1997, they released a two-disc live album called *Double Feature*. All of these disks are essential listening for any fan of improvisation music.

From the outset, Percy Hill brought an ironically mature, schooled combination of vocals and instrumentalization to the stage. Less guitar-driven and psychedelic than some of the bands with whom they frequently share bills, Percy Hill has still garnered a loyal, crunchy following. With an affinity toward both long improvisations and light, bouncy harmonies, Percy Hill knows how to play with and reward the audience and is fast gaining popularity.

Albums: *Setting the Boat Adrift* (1993); *Straight On 'Til Morning* (1995); *Double Feature* (1997)

Contact Info: phone: (603) 778-4242; web: *cbix.unh.edu/percy* email: *percyhill@aol.com*

The Disco Biscuits

IF BANDS LIKE moe. and the Ominous Seapods are the pioneers of the homespun jam rock scene, then the Disco Biscuits are what the scene created. Unapologetically tacking 20-minute, multi-part jams onto every song and not afraid to conquer complexity, the Disco Biscuits first generated a buzz on the Philadelphia music scene before becoming a regular headliner at the Wetlands in New York City, and also a frequent topic of discussion on the Phish.Net.

Guitarist and frontman Jon Gutwillig serves as the band's anchor, while keyboardist Aaron Magner adds the virtuoso spice that makes Biscuits jams a head-spinning, mind-altering experience.

Before anyone outside of the University of Pennsylvania had ever heard of the Disco Biscuits, Gutwillig caught the eye of Trey Anastasio during a Burlington guitar competition that Trey helped judge. With every progression in Gutwillig's one-man performance, Trey practically leapt out of his seat. And he did rise to his feet in appreciation when Gutwillig turned a tuning knob to create a desired sound, in the middle of the piece. Trey later threw his arm around the kid and pronounced that he should be known as "Jon the Jet-setter."

The quartet's first album, *Encephalous Crime*, hit the streets in 1996, marking a new level of advancement for what is, for the most part, the quintessential live band. See them now so you can say, "I saw them when."

Album: *Encephalous Crime* (1996)

Contact Info: phone: (215) 243-0410; web: *www.discobiscuits.com*; email: *saltman@discobiscuits.com*

Foxtrot Zulu

GO TO ANY FOXTROT ZULU show, and you'll probably see a good number of college-aged "mainstream" music fans, and then a bunch of Phishheads gyrating in a frenzy, literally pushing everyone else off the dance floor. The secret of Foxtrot is starting to get out.

While listening to Foxtrot Zulu and trying to identify their musical influences, one cannot avoid just giving up to bask in the pleasurable sound they've created. This band pulls off something that is seldom accomplished in today's jam rock—they've included horns which not only serve to embellish, but actually drive the groove and overall color of the music. What better to cap off a jam than a frenetic brass explosion?

The band's ability to satisfy the ears of audiences with various tastes can perhaps be attributed to the fact that Foxtrot has five songwriters each with something different to offer. What they all have in common, however, is the unmistakable ability to mesh together, producing high-energy dance rock and funk grooves with no fear of improvised exploration. Foxtrot has two high-quality albums to their credit, *Moe's Diner* and the more recent *Burn Slow*. Remarkably, they're as good in the studio as they are on stage.

Albums: *Moe's Diner* (1995); *Burn Slow* (1997)

Contact Info: phone: (401) 377-4938; web: *www.foxtrotzulu.com*; email: *zulucrew@aol.com*

String Cheese Incident

LACTOSE INTOLERANT OR NOT, String Cheese Incident will make you laugh and dance simultaneously. The Telluride, CO quintet hits you from all angles, mixing a bluegrass at the forefront with, calypso, salsa, afro-pop, funk, rock, and jazz. The collage of styles is woven by acoustic and electric mandolins which bare their distinct sound. Like Leftover Salmon, they are able to enter the depths of psychedelia while pumping out their bread and butter—high-energy bluegrass.

They've been known to appear at a bluegrass festival or two as well as draw a sell-out crowd at Boulder's Fox Theater. And word has spread quickly, making String Cheese a solid draw in almost every region of the country. But no matter where you see them, the Incident will leave you strung out and jonesing for more!

Album: *Born On the Wrong Planet* (1996)

Contact Info: Phone: (303)-417-8909; web: *www.stringcheeseincident.com*

ulu

EVERY NOW AND AGAIN you'll stumble into a gig and find an unexpected surprise. But ulu, a five-piece instrumental outfit based in New York city, is a band that will downright shock you, forcing your feet to move and your jaw to drop. The "unlabelable" groove they have mastered is as pioneering, and difficult to classify, as bands such as Medeski Martin & Wood and The Grey Boy Allstars. One can expect a distorted clavinet solo that hooks a hard harmonic left turn and settles back down to melodic pockets off the saxophone or flute. This is all happening above a relentless bass and rhythm groove skillfully providing space in the backyard of the beat. In just a few short months on the scene, ulu has generated a strong buzz and admiration among peers. This is a band that's on the way up.

Contact Info: phone: (212) 533-1075

Everything

THERE WAS ONCE this little band from Vermont that no one had ever heard of except for a few thousand diehards. Those diehards went and saw them so much that the band vaulted onto the industry charts of top concert draws. Then came the record company and the rest, as they say, was history. Washington D.C.-based Everything is holding out hope for the same story. The band has cracked the list of top 50 U.S. concert draws through its back-breaking tour schedule and enticing grooves of brass, winds, and guitar. Perhaps the only band with a guitarist, vocalist, clarinetist, and alto sax player—who's all one guy, Everything has been selling out shows along the strip of southern clubs which Phish conquered around 1991. A pair of April 1996 gigs at The Bayou in D.C. formed the band's most recent effort, a self-titled live album. It led to their signing with Blackbird-Sire records, and they will release an album called *Super Natural* in 1998.

Albums: *Labrador* (1994), *Everything* (1996)

Contact Info: phone: (540) 987-9417; web: *www.ecolon.com*; email: *everything@ecolon.com*

Freebeerandchicken

FURTHER PROOF THAT Albany, NY may be the modern hotbed for jam-oriented music, Freebeerandchicken has taken its act beyond the Capital District and become a recognized name around the country. At first listen, the band sounds like many familiar performers, throwing in a touch of bluegrass, a nice mix of acoustic and electric and solid jams. But you'll do a double take upon realizing that Freebeerandchicken's lead instrument is a saxophone, not a guitar, which opens the doors to a whole different dimension of musical adventure.

The band insists that its name is not a sleazy ploy to attract the cheap and hungry. Instead, it's an homage to the old John Lee Hooker tradition of letting people into shows for free if they brought along beer and chicken. The band cut a live album in 1995 called *Papa's Waltz*, available on cassette.

Album: *Papa's Waltz* (1995)

Contact Info: phone: (518) 438-9391; web: *members.aol.com/fb&c*; email: *FBandC@aol.com*

Schleigho

SCHLEIGHO (pronounced SHLAY-HO), has titillated audiences through thunderous jams fusing jazz, funk, and a variety of other unlikely styles which round out their heavy, yet accessible sound.

Schleigho's flawless transitions are so tight they seem virtually impossible to the naked eye (and ear). Many of their tunes aggressively and boldly take the listener down a dark and sinister path while others return to semi-reality with jazzy Latin rhythms that lighten things up—at least for a moment or two.

"The Gromlins"—from their self-titled debut album—is a classic example of what jam music is all about. Clocking in at over 26 minutes long, it begins with evil, helium-like vocals underneath a furious driving beat that swerve, sway, and meander into the bouillabaisse of sounds that you must taste to fully appreciate Schleigho. *[—By Greg Shanken]*

Albums: *Schleigho* (1995); *Farewell to the Sun (1996)*

Contact Info: phone: (508) 544-5341; web: *www.ledfeather.com/shleigho*; email: *schleigho@bigfoot.com*

Jiggle the Handle

THE 'HANDLE' ISN'T the only thing that'll 'Jiggle' while enjoying a show. Putting all the toilet humor aside, this band can move your feet along with your bowels. The Massachusetts quartet will not hold in their ability to settle into jams which build up ferociously throughout the night.

Guitarist Gary Backstrom is considered a true virtuoso, whirling through superson-

...From The Top

Of course, it's not only these more-obscure bands which tap that Phishy nerve. Others which gained fame around the same time Phish did still promise to stretch your mind while displaying their commitment to the jam ethic.

There are the well-known, MTV co-opted varieties such as **Blues Traveler** and **The Dave Matthews Band**. If you can bear the teeny-boppers and their older brothers with Hootie stubs hanging out of their pockets, these bands are still a trip—and worth making one to see.

Widespread Panic continues its ascension at a glacial pace. An original 1992 HORDE band, Widespread never received mainstream acceptance, but its national following is a loyal and growing one. It almost goes without saying that their live shows are absolutely phenomenal. **Bela Fleck and the Flecktones** can also be found playing great shows across the country, as well as on a series of outstanding studio albums and the double-CD *Live Art*.

Virtuosos **Medeski, Martin and Wood** have caught on big with the Phish audience, proving just how appreciative of good music and good musicians Phish fans can be. This jazz-fusion trio's 1996 release, *Shack-man*, continues to draw raves.

From the great state of Colorado, **Leftover Salmon** proves that more that one aquatic band can tingle the senses. The Cheech and Chong of rock and roll, these guys are the only band around that can take a mandolin, a banjo, and an irrepressible herbal theme and make an entire crowd sing "You gotta wake and bake!"

Now with Mercury Records after a failed marriage with Geffen, **God Street Wine** still manages to pack small clubs in the Northeast.

The **Aquarium Rescue Unit**, another HORDE original but now minus Col. Bruce Hampton, still hits the stage, performing tighter shows than ever. And Col. Bruce can now be found jamming with his new brainchild, the **Fiji Mariners**—perhaps the world's ugliest band, with apologies to the Stones and Zeppelin.

Meanwhile, **Michael Ray and the Cosmic Krewe** are also the rage amongst many Phishheads, including Trey and Page who appeared with them at a small club called Jimmy's during JazzFest '96. And don't forget Phish-friends **Jazz Mandolin Project** and the **Gordon Stone Trio**, both profiled elsewhere in the Almanac.

Finally, for those who can't quite break the tie, Phish cover bands are surfacing at a rapid rate. The best-known at this point, **Stash**, usually plays two sets of Phish and does a generally decent job. In the spring of 1997, Fishman joined them onstage for half a set, conferring a blessing of sorts.

From The Bottom...

ic leads while also knowing when to hold back. Jiggle the Handle has managed to gain the attention of some pretty big names in the business. They've shared the stage with icons such as Widespread Panic, Merle Saunders, The Jerry Garcia Band, and a bass player by the name of Mike Gordon. Their album *Mrs White's Party*, with an imitation hologram cover, is almost as fun to stare at as it is to hear.

Album: *Mrs White's Party* (1997)

Contact Info: phone: (508) 429-5994; web *www.moonsite.com /jiggle*

Day By The River

FRESH OFF THE 1997 HORDE tour, Athens, GA-based Day By The River has channeled band members' sophisticated musical background into soulful song writing. Their music is marked by passionate southern-style choruses which explode into musically advanced, sectional arrangements opening the doors for wistful jamming. The quintet has been improving their sound steadily since their formation in Athens in 1990. Several years spent in Miami turned out to be DBR's proving ground as they built a solid fan base there before returning home in 1995.

DBR has been extensively touring the southeast since their move, now supporting their recent release *Fly* (which was mixed by John Altschiller, the engineer of Phish's *Picture of Nectar*). Along with their repertoire of original classics, DBR has been known to bust out some influential cover tunes such as Cosmik Debris by Frank Zappa and You Enjoy Myself. You'll be soothed and pleasantly surprised if you spend A Day By The River.

Albums: *Shimmy* (1993); *Fly* (1996)

Contact Info: Phone: (706) 208-8341; *www.daybytheriver.com*; email: *info@daybytheriver.com*

Grinch

GRINCH STARTED OUT five years ago as a bunch of guys with acoustic guitars jamming together for fun at University of Delaware parties. With the addition of drums, bass, and amplification, Grinch has steamrolled the Mid-Atlantic region as an ever-present energetic groove band. Their distinctive sound contains a fusion of rock, funk, jazz, and blues which has evolved towards a psychedelic, funky platform for ambitious experimentation. Make no mistake about it, Grinch is a jam band and proud of it.

Independent label Ground Zero Records plans to release their 1997 disc nationally. But until then, enjoy their self-titled live album and catch a show. And if their drummer looks familiar, it's because he used to rattle the high-hat with moe.

Album: *Grinch* (1995)

Contact Info: phone (717) 872-8999; email: *Grinch7777@aol.com*

Hose

THE ROANOKE COLLEGE music department prides itself in having a world-renown choir and spawning an incredibly talented jam band called Hose. Greatly inspired by Phish, which might explain why they decided to name the band after the famous Carlos Santana analogy of Phish being a "hose" that waters the "sea of flowers," each of the band's four members exhibit a remarkable sense of musicianship which has crystallized from a combination of their talent as individuals, musical training at Roanoke and a love for Phish and other influential musicians. Hose has the sound of a seasoned band with the precise ability to bring out the work of each musician while emitting impressive melodies and well-conceived songs.

Hose is still making the transition from frat house gigs to flooding the local bar and club scene of Roanoke. While jamming live, the band adventurously funnels music into a fresh new direction which gives their fans reason to keep coming back for more. Still relative unknowns beyond their home base, the secret of Hose is about to get out with a big splash.

Contact Info: phone: (540)-389-3076; email: *hosers@juno.com*

Native

IT'S 3 A.M. Do you know where your flowerchild is? If it's a Wednesday night in New York City, the best place to look is McGovern's in Soho, where Native has rocked the night owls every week for the last two years with a captivating mix of ambitious musicianship and harmonies. Playing together for five years with various lineups, Native has improved steadily from both a songwriting and performance standpoint.

Their 1994 self-titled album gives a glimpse of what the band is about, but the harmonies and teamwork which mark their live shows surface best on their latest release *10 Bucks*. Lead singer Matthew Hutt, an overseas import from the British Isles, is backed by a crowded stage filled with diverse instruments and craftsmen who avoid simple clamor and find their way into cohesive jams. Native does not tour as aggressively as every band out there. But for now, their Wednesday night gigs are a regular, free treat.

Albums: *Native* (1994); *10 Bucks* (1996)

Contact Info: phone: (212) 604-0903; web: *www.nativenyc.com*; email: *native@rockweb.com*

Agents of Good Roots

WHILE FIRMLY PLANTED in the Southeast Jam Rock scene, word of Agents of Good Roots continues to germinate on a broad geographic scale. The jazz/funk based quartet refuses to lose sight of the groove even while immersed in the depths of their rich musicality. Theirs is a tightly-wound, edgy, rhythmic sound with outstanding songmanship and arrangement. Their critically acclaimed studio album, *Where Did You Get That Vibe*, was considered to be among the best homespun albums of 1996.

But there's nothing like the Agents live! *Straightaround* is a live CD which paints an even more accurate picture of the bands electrifying concert performance, and helped gain the attention of Atlantic Records, which recently signed the band to a recording contract. Also a veteran of several HORDE performances, Agents of Good Roots has established itself as a band with a present and a future.

Albums: *Where Did You Get That Vibe* (1996); *Straightaround* (1997).

Contact Info: phone: (804) 971-8117; web: *www.agentsofgoodroots.com*; email: *Agents@redlt.com*

Moon Boot Lover

SINCE ALL THE WAY back in 1992, Albany-based trio Moon Boot Lover has caused fans to gravitate to their gigs and sink into the groove. Aside from becoming a strong fixture in the upstate New York music scene (where jam rock got its start), Moon Boot Lover has caught the attention of the mainstream music world by linking up with national touring acts such as Maceo Parker.

"Immensely Boogieful" is how the *Village Voice* sums them up. Moon Boot produces a groove that slides from thunderous to delicate in one sitting. The funky rhythm is coupled with multi-dimensional keyboards and guitar that come up with improvisational inventions throughout their jams.

Albums: *Outer Space Action* (1995); *Live Down Deep* (1995)

Contact Info: phone (603) 778-4242; email: *GBEnt@aol.com* web: *www.moonbootlover.com*

On Tour

Hitting the Road with Phish to... Telluride in April '90 ♦ Midwest in summer '94 ♦ Nashville in fall '94 ♦ The Ball ♦ The Went

Gettin' down at the Clifford Ball, August 17, 1996, Plattsburgh, NY

Getting There Is Half The Fun

Phish in Telluride, CO, April 1990

By Dan Gibson

Many of us have had some problems trying to get to Phish shows, or any shows for that matter. One of my great adventures is from the early days, and looking back, it's sort of a minor miracle that I made it to Phish's stand in Telluride, Colorado in April of 1990. The fact that I got there was an interesting mix of determination and luck.

The saga began in the late 1980s. Soon after catching my first two Phish shows, in Amherst, MA, in 1988, I moved to Berkeley, California, a place Phish wouldn't play for awhile. In fact, I don't think I even met anyone who had heard of the band until I played them the few tapes I had. Home for the holidays in December of 1989 I saw an excellent Wetlands show—my first Phish concert in over a year. It motivated me to see more.

The only problem was, not only was I flying back to California, but I was going to start *walking* back to the East Coast on an environmental, educational action called The Global Walk for a Livable World. Although a fulfilling adventure, in which I would perform in a band myself, I would be somewhat out of touch with the ongoings of the rock-and-roll world for awhile.

About 120 environmental activists would walk across the U.S., covering about 20 miles on foot a day and camping out at night in tents carried by support vehicles. We planned to do a lot of educational outreaches in schools and fairs along the way.

After leaving L.A. in February of 1990, crossing the Mojave Desert, and trekking through some bizarre locations in Arizona, the Global Walk reached the hip town of Flagstaff in Northern Arizona in late March. It was here that I met my first Western Phish fans, a cool group of folks who not only took me in for a shower and a nice sleep on a couch (I had been living in a tent for two months), but turned me on to some new Phish tapes, including the legendary *White Album* of 1987.

They told me they were going to see Phish in Telluride in a few weeks. Being that we developed somewhat of a bond (I ended up hanging out with them for a few more days), and that the walk would be somewhere in New Mexico by then, I told them that I would try to meet them for the pair of shows Phish was doing in Telluride on April 10th and 11th.

On the road to Telluride, CO

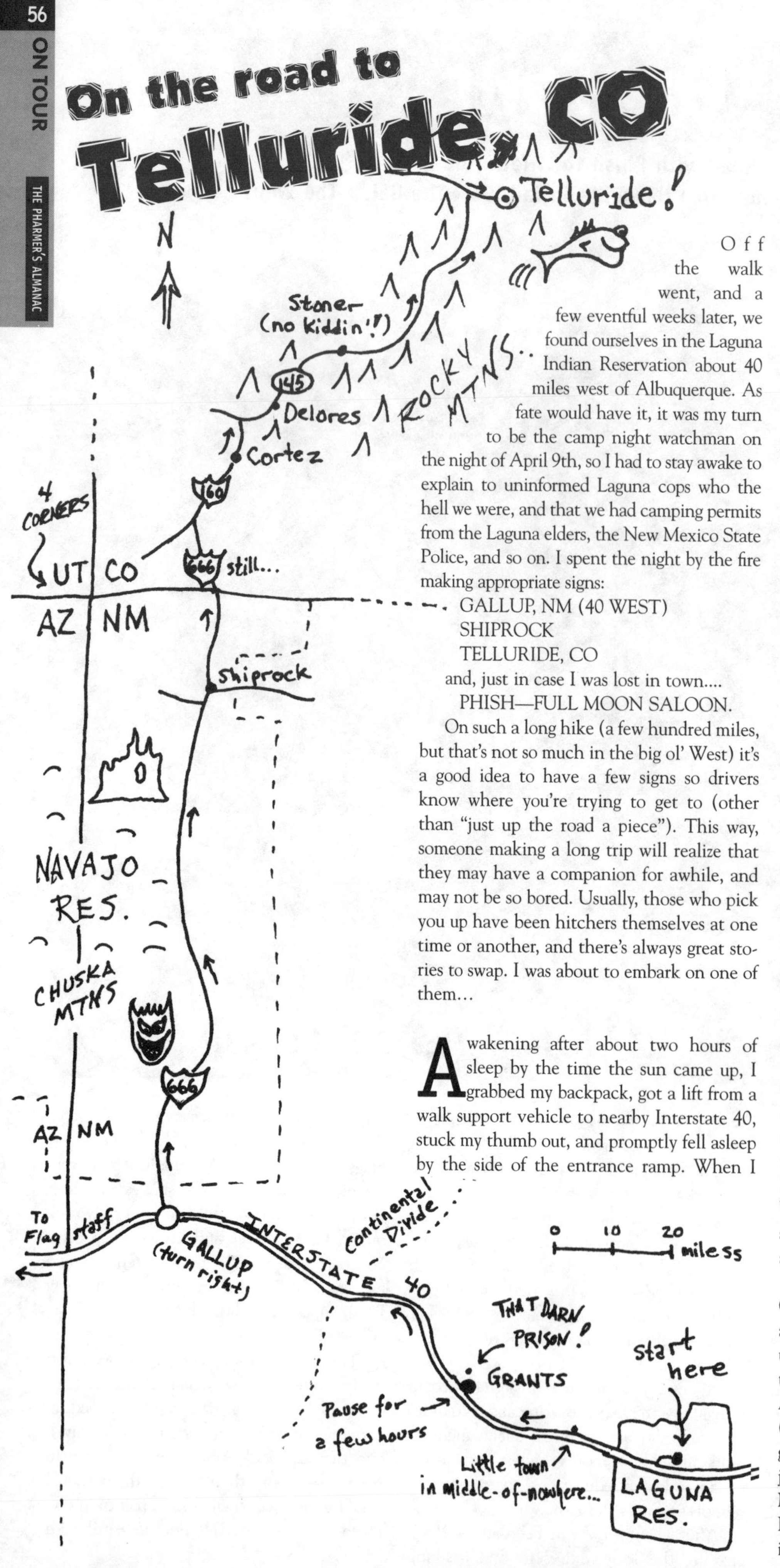

Off the walk went, and a few eventful weeks later, we found ourselves in the Laguna Indian Reservation about 40 miles west of Albuquerque. As fate would have it, it was my turn to be the camp night watchman on the night of April 9th, so I had to stay awake to explain to uninformed Laguna cops who the hell we were, and that we had camping permits from the Laguna elders, the New Mexico State Police, and so on. I spent the night by the fire making appropriate signs:

GALLUP, NM (40 WEST)
SHIPROCK
TELLURIDE, CO

and, just in case I was lost in town....

PHISH—FULL MOON SALOON.

On such a long hike (a few hundred miles, but that's not so much in the big ol' West) it's a good idea to have a few signs so drivers know where you're trying to get to (other than "just up the road a piece"). This way, someone making a long trip will realize that they may have a companion for awhile, and may not be so bored. Usually, those who pick you up have been hitchers themselves at one time or another, and there's always great stories to swap. I was about to embark on one of them…

Awakening after about two hours of sleep by the time the sun came up, I grabbed my backpack, got a lift from a walk support vehicle to nearby Interstate 40, stuck my thumb out, and promptly fell asleep by the side of the entrance ramp. When I awoke, it was probably about 10 am. Damn, I though, I've lost a few hours of valuable time.

Almost immediately, though, I was picked up by a Native American woman who didn't really speak much English… didn't speak much at all, as a matter of fact. If you're experienced with hitch-hiking, then you know it's extremely rare to be picked up by a woman who is alone, but she seemed pretty tough and seasoned in hard-knocks. She only drove me about 20 miles and left me in a tiny town in the middle of nowhere, but my journey was under way, and I was starting to feel confident I'd make it to Telluride by eight o'clock that evening.

After a half hour wait, I finally got a ride about 20 more miles to Grants, a big town for these parts, so I figured I'd get out of it soon. Even the driver said he would swing back this way in about an hour-and-a-half, and if I was still there, he'd take me to Gallup, the town where I had to turn right and head north on Route 666 (no foolin'!) to Colorado. How wrong I was. I ended up in this spot for close to three hours. The last driver never returned and this young woman with dark shades and a fast red Camaro kept cruising by me, debating whether to give me a lift somewhere or just tease the hell out of me. This was hell for the time being; the hot New Mexican sun beating down on me, sand whipping into my face, and lots of cars passing me by.

I was getting pretty frustrated, but it's not a good idea to yell at anyone who passes you, because you never know if they will stop a little farther up the road for you than expected. So there I sat at an entrance ramp to route 40 in Grants, NM, a town I had just walked through and camped in with the Global Walk only about five days before. It seemed a lot friendlier then.

At least I wrote a song about the experience—what else was there to do? I also realized, now that I had lots of time to look at my map, that I had underestimated the total mileage of the trip. I thought it was about 200, but it was closer to 400 miles—yikes! Well, I thought, I may miss most of tonight's show, but I gotta catch my Arizona friends and see tomorrow's show.

Finally, probably the only black man in Grants picked me up. He said that I was about a mile from a state prison and NO ONE picks up hitch-hikers in Grants. He was a guard there, and since I didn't look familiar.... Anyway, he was going all the way to Gallup (ya-hoo!) about an hour away, but once we got there, close to rush hour, we hit a traffic jam. What? A traffic jam in Eastern New Mexico? Would you believe that it was the Budweiser Clydesdale Horses that were causing this? Well, I didn't either, at least until I saw them for real, over in a shopping plaza parking lot.

Yeah, cool, but if I'm going to be caught in traffic, it should be over some *good* beer, you know?

Of all the places in America they could be right now, here they are in Gallup, NM, keeping a determined hitch-hiker from seeing a Phish show, which was still 200-plus miles to the North.

So this kind gentleman drops me off on 666 North, which shouldn't be problem because it goes through the Navajo Reservation, one of the best places to hitch-hike in America since it's the main mode of transportation. You don't even need to exchange words. You just hop in the back of the pick-up (and say hi to the other hitchers) and knock on the rear window when you need to get out.

That ain't what happened this time, though. After only a few minutes I got picked up by a young white guy who said he would take me all the way up 666 in his snazzy car to Shiprock, near the Colorado border! He was a cool guy and we had a great talk about the area and rock-and-roll while passing through some amazing countryside, including the Shiprock National Monument, a big hunk of old rock a few miles to our west that looks like a gigantic pirate ship (What a show this was turning out to be already.)

I almost talked him into seeing this band he'd never heard of, but he had plans. He was in a hurry and we went about 100 miles an hour, which doesn't feel that fast in a desert. I made up for some lost time, though, and before we could spin both sides of a Beartrap Road 7/88 Phish tape, we reached Shiprock, a small but pretty town with lots of trees in the Northwest corner of the state.

Out of Shiprock, I was picked up by an elderly hippy—this was my token pick-up truck experience—whose 12-year-old daughter kept rolling joints and passing them back through the window to me. They were really sweet folks and when they dropped me off just over the Colorado border, I gave them a tape of my recordings as a 'thank-you' for the ride.

Slightly dazed, I immediately got picked up by two goomers who I could hardly understand. They were friendly, of course, though conservative enough that I wasn't going to explain myself too much. They drove me through Cortez and dropped off in Dolores, CO, right on Rt. 145—which leads to Telluride! Things were actually looking good at this point. There were only about 70 more miles to go, but it was getting dark and there were hardly any cars passing me. When the road is this quiet, each passing car really stings you.

By now it was about 7:00 p.m., and if I was going to make the show, someone had better stop soon! After about 45 excruciating minutes, a car did stop. A police car. The cop told me that hitch-hiking was illegal in this town, and instructed me to check into to the motel across the street and walk out of town in the morning. He told me he would be back in 15 minutes to make sure I was off the road one way or another. He wasn't really mean—just matter-of-fact about it, but I was in a jam. If I took a motel I wouldn't see Phish that night, nor would I have money for the next night.

Before I could figure out what to do a couple of drunk golfers on there way back home to Telluride stopped and picked me up, unaware of the town's laws, I guess. I was psyched to get picked up, but not used to being around such wealthy people. They were complaining about their golf scores that day and certain investments they had made. Finally acknowledging their new passenger, the driver (at least sobering up some) said he had to stop for me because I reminded him of his daughter, "who's hitching around Thailand or some God-forsaken place right now."

Though I was getting closer to the show, this stretch seemed to take an eternity. Lots of twists and turns, but I couldn't see too much as the moon—nearly full—was still stuck behind some peaks. The driver had to drop off his friends first, and though I acted patient, I was really wasn't. I was ready to end this voyage, see my new friends from Flagstaff, and jam out to my favorite new band, hoping it would only take a few tunes to give my tired, achey body a second-wind.

When they finally dropped me off at the Full Moon Saloon (actually the Fly Me to the Moon Saloon, it turned out) I could hear the band jamming away on what seemed like the end of Cavern. Wow! I actually made it! The cover was only $5, but the door-guy told me $4 would be cool since I missed the first three songs. Ah... those were the days!

Then I got the bad news—this wasn't the first of two nights, it was the last of three! During the break, Mike Gordon told me that my new friends had already seen two shows and went back to Flagstaff. Oh well, at least I made it through a wacky adventure and made it to see most of this one.

It was the smallest place I ever saw Phish, a dimly-lit room split in two by a bar. There were probably about 45 to 50 people and only 25 of us paying attention to the band, who were as tight as I had ever seen them. They closed the first set with a blistering Mike's Groove, an absolutely stunning rendition. They also played Oh! Possum and a surprising Communication Breakdown which did get the attention of those who were just in the place to drink.

For the encore, I heard my first-ever live Contact, which had me cracking up. I also believe there was a Fluffhead and a Whipping Post in there as well, but I'm not 100 percent sure as I saw Phish a bunch more times that year. The small audience (a "crowd" in this joint) was very enthusiastic, and I quickly made some acquaintances. One guy I met had his tape stolen out of his deck, so whoever took it better circulate it around, dammit!

After the show, I talked to the band some and then tried to figure out what to do for the night. As it turned out about 15 or so fans were camping out about two blocks away in a little park. Luckily, I brought a tent and in 20-degree weather, got it set up and joined the little post show party around a campfire. It was like a little mini-Dead scene. These folks were following Phish around the state. It was then I realized that Phish was going to grow really big and that their days in small bars like this were truly numbered.

The next morning, the guy who had his tape stolen—not that he dwelled on it—drove me to Boulder where some friends drove me back to the Walk in Albuquerque a few days later. All in all, quite a successful journey.

The cover was only $5, but the door-guy told me $4 would be cool since I missed the first three songs. Ah... those were the days!

Dan Gibson now books musical acts on the East Coast.

The Clifford Ball • August 16-17, 1996 • Plattsburgh Air Force Base, Plattsburgh, NY

The Esther Doll

By Joey Conroy (with help from Caroline Carillo)

Caroline and I used to frequent the Wetlands for Dead Center every Tuesday. When we went, Caroline would wear a new dress she had sewn that week. One day this idea struck me of what I wanted to see her piece together with needle and thread. I shared this idea with her that next day, and she spent the week working on it. By the end of the week she presented me with the finished product of my idea—an Esther doll!

Now if you don't have a clue as to what this doll looks like, look at the *Junta* cover art. She's the limp white doll, with black and white stockings, and a huge smile, just hanging up there on the shelf. I was more than thrilled to have this doll. I figured that I was the only person on the face of this Earth to have an Esther doll. I had often suggested that she should sell her dresses. Now I was convinced that she should try vending Esther dolls at shows as well.

Months went by and Caroline continued her sewing. She made several beautiful dresses as well as a couple Esther dolls which she decided to vend at the Clifford Ball. She had even put together a very special Esther doll with a reversible face. One side sported the live doll's face (it had Os for eyes and a huge smile). Flip the head inside out and you had the dead doll's face (X's for eyes and a frown).

She told me that she had designed this special doll with the reversible face for Trey's daughter Eliza. Caroline even wrote an eloquent letter to Trey and his family and attached it around the doll's neck with a hemp necklace that she made. Our goal was to get this particular Esther doll on stage at the Clifford Ball.

Time came for the Northeastern shows, and Caroline had enough dresses and Esther dolls to vend up in Plattsburgh. The drive from Hershey to Plattsburgh wasn't so bad, and within the first half hour of our arrival we met Mike and Jon. They were both driving golf carts through the camping area. We talked to Fishman, and Caroline told him about the Esther dolls and how we were going to send one on stage for Trey's daughter.

Fishman's face lit up with a huge grin. He told us that all the gifts they receive are personally looked at and kept, not thrown away or stuffed in a box somewhere. She then told him that this was a special Esther doll because it had a reversible face. Fishman just laughed and said, "But of course! How else would you make it? Esther's doll needs the two faces."

At this point, Caroline and I both had hope our plan was going to work. Fishman now knew that the doll was coming and we were even more determined to get this special doll on stage.

Friday afternoon we set out to vend. All of Caroline's dresses sold amazingly fast, but for whatever reason the Esther dolls just weren't moving. Some kids (probably the ones who just bought *A Live One* before coming to Plattsburgh) thought they were voodoo dolls. There were those who thought that the dolls were a good idea but didn't have the money, and there were those who just smiled as we walked by. We did sell one to a person we had met two days before in the Hershey lot. She seemed to love the doll.

So overall the sales of the dolls didn't go so well, but we didn't care. We still had determination and a plan.

We tried to get into the concert area relatively early to ensure a place near the stage. Unfortunately, everyone else in the world all had that same idea, because by the time we got into the show there was a sea of people in front of the stage.

I though to myself, "How are we ever going to make it anywhere near the stage, much less within a good throwing distance?"

We completely missed the opener trying to find a way through the maze of people. We made it as far as the center speaker tower closest to stage when we realized that traveling any further together was going to be impossible. We gave each other a look of dismay. I handed her the doll and with a hug Caroline left to get as close to the stage as possible.

I knew that with her determination she'd eventually make it there. She later told me about her trek through the people to get to the stage. People were real cooperative knowing that she was not an irate fan just pushing to the front for her own advantage. They let her through and before she knew it she had reached the wall right in front of the stage.

She could see the security guards and the stage beyond and realized that she would need a good throwing arm to get that doll up over the speakers onto the stage. The kid in front of her seemed tall enough to help. She asked him if he had a good throwing arm and he said that he'd try to get it up there. Caroline told me that she cringed as she handed him the doll and watched him throw it.

But the doll made it up there! The doll and the small note attached to it were on stage! We had achieved our goal! Happily she rushed back to where she had left me by the center speaker tower, and was more than ecstatic when she reached me.

We walked together further back where we had enough room to dance. AC/DC Bag was still kicking strong. I happened to notice on the huge screen that the doll landed right in front of Page's piano. We were both reassured that the special Esther doll had indeed safely made it into the hands of Phish.

Then, as soon as AC/DC Bag finished, they miraculously broke into... Esther!

Tears streamed down from Caroline's eyes. This was more than we could have ever asked for, or even expected. It was more than apparent that the song was a sincere thank you. We were overwhelmed!

Time For Timer!

...And Other Experiences on Spring/Summer Tour '94
A Tour Diary by Jay Archibald

Some tours just have a way of saying, "Come with me, Jay, we made this tour just for you." Then I think, am I blessed? They must be aliens because they can read my mind!

Spring/summer '94 was that kind of tour. I lived in Minnesota in the summers, and went to school in Santa Barbara for the rest of the year. So, twice a year I made the journey from the land-o-lakes to the burnin' shore, five times all together. Only twice did I not travel with Phish. And May and June proved a perfect time for me to catch a bunch of shows.

May 17, 1994, Santa Barbara, CA

My first show of that tour came on May 17 at Santa Barbara's Arlington Theatre, an amazing part-time movie theatre with painted murals on the walls that make it look like a Spanish village. They even have false balconies with plants and stars on the ceiling.

My friend and I ended up first in line for tickets on a rainy Saturday, and while we waited the Box Office head-honcho came out and said that tickets would go on sale 15 minutes sooner where we were than at any other ticket outlet! We were able to look at the seating chart and pick out what seats we wanted because no one was ahead of us. It also turned out that they had no ticket limit, so we had everybody in the first three rows that night, thanks to Alex's Amex card.

Unfortunately, the show turned out to be one of the weaker shows I have seen to date, filled with fear about all the *Hoist* and MTV sellout talk and new songs that were still rough, but the fact remains that I still had a great time. A standard rock concert by Phish is like a standard thermonuclear bomb—it still packs one hell of a punch.

The next week of shows saw the band cruise up to the northwest, and I stayed to finish off school. But, one question remained... Two weeks from the Arlington show were three nights at the Warfield and two nights at Laguna Seca Daze with a few other bands, and for me, four weeks from then were finals.

What else is Dead Week for—a three-night stand at the Warfield or studying? (Needless to say, the Warfield run allowed me to pursue fall tour as well, seeing as how I would no longer be welcomed back to UC Santa Barbara!)

We were up close every night at the Warfield, and Phish played some solid shows. I know Trey calls this the worst tour ever, or worst at least the worst Antelope ever, but like I said, nuclear bombs.

May 27, 1994, San Francisco, CA

I remember the May 27 show *very clearly*. I was with some amazing brothers and sisters all day in line, and decided to start partying early, like noon. Market Street in San Francisco is the heart of freakdom in the world—it makes Central Station in Amsterdam look like a Disney production. The problem is is that it's not like Haight Ashbury or Venice Beach, where most of the people try to be freaks. These people are professionals, and when you're in that sketchy zone between reality and the subconscious yourself, they somehow know it and feed off it.

So, after a *long* day in line, we made it in and found ourselves up front. In a state of utter confusion, several security guards came up to me and told me to move. I was freaking out—why me? Then I saw Mimi Fishman walking up. Not bad—if I'm going to lose my place, it might as well be to the drummers' mother!

Anyway, that night I was more confused with what was happening than any other Phish show I've ever seen, especially in the second set. My Friend, Suzie > Peaches, and the first beautiful woman of the evening, Morgan Fichter on fiddle, for the acoustic bit. This section of the show is really worth finding on tape—it's a good

idea to get a great audience tapes (there are amazing ones from this night) as well as the soundboard because the latter is missing the acoustic My Mind's and Nellie Cane.

The acoustic interlude was followed by a great Mike's Song that jammed into the first Simple. Talk about confusion—I think the band was at least as confused as I was about what they were playing. (I talked to Mike in Kansas City the next month, before they tried Simple again, and he said, "Yeah, we're having problems with the chords on that one." They didn't end up getting it down until Milwaukee.)

Then, after Simple, they turned up the freakout knob and went into the fog and strobe jam and started laying back, getting quieter as the foam kept getting thicker. The crowd followed their silence as they drifted into an almost-silent jam.

The band had this evil "let's freak 'em out tonight" look on their faces as they stepped back into the fog. There was a small pause, then out came beautiful woman number two—tall, bald, and holding a box of Kraft Macaroni and Cheese in her hand! It's okay, Jay, it's okay, I reminded myself. I am still at a Phish show, even if there's a bald woman singing opera right in front of me.

Phish never has, and hopefully never will, cease to freak the living terror out of me on a surprisingly frequent basis. This was a historic show, most likely their last one ever at the Warfield, a fitting end to a great three-night stand.

May 29, 1994, Monterey, CA

I couldn't make it to the first night of Laguna Seca Daze the next day (acronym, is that the word I'm looking for?), so I missed Les Claypool and the giant YEM, but I still caught an Antelope, McGrupp, Freebird, Halley's Comet, and many many more at the Sunday LSD show.

Timer was in front of Mike, shaking his head in disbelief over the measly 13:42 Mike's Song, and fearing the worst for the Reba that might not break the eight-minute barrier.

This was the last show of the spring tour, so the band wasn't too anxious to stop playing. Wilson, Golgi, Rocky Top. One vivid memory I have of this show was during Wilson. I looked up at this huge rock band that had made it, big time. This was by far the largest Phish show I had ever seen, and during this Wilson, the lights were blazing down and they were screaming "Can you still have fun!" I was convinced at this point that despite their new-found popularity, these freaks could still rage. My fears were relieved in a major way, and with that experience, it was back to Santa Barbara after four shows in six days to take three finals in two days! I'll spare you the details of that sobering experience....

June 9, 1994, Salt Lake City, UT

Salt Lake City was the first stop on my second leg of tour, as well as the quickest stop. Before I hit the road, I invested some money in a sticker I made, but didn't end up selling one of them—I just gave or traded them away.

I met up with a soon-to-be-great friend of mine and we headed to the heart of Salt Lake City. Security was pretty intense, as you could imagine. The venue was a big courtyard between a couple of high rises, and was fenced off temporarily for concerts.

The band had taken about a week off before this show, so it took them awhile to get back in the swing of things. Halley's and Scent were sweet, but it's the Mike's Groove that I seem to remember for other reasons.

June 10 & 11, 1994, Morrison, CO

This would be the first time I made the fateful trek from Salt Lake City to Morrison, Colorado in one day, alone. I dropped off a rider in Utah, and planned to meet up with friends at Red Rocks, so solo it was.

The trip got off to a great start when I got pulled over in Laramie, Wyoming for going 82 MPH. The officer kindly asked me where I was going and coming from three times before asking if I minded him search my car—I guess he didn't like the "California, Colorado" answer. After a thoughtful pause, I politely answered, "Yes, I would mind." I was surprised to hear his reply of "Thank you very much, have a nice day, and drive safely."

I made it to Red Rocks just in time for a great show, but the next day's show proved to be one of the greatest Phish shows I have ever seen. Wilson, Chalkdust, YEM, Tela, and a Stash from who knows where. It was a magical night, with one of the best crowds I have ever been with—everybody so stoked outta their minds, it didn't even sell out, everyone got in, serious dream material.

The second set topped it all. A favorite combination of mine, 2001 into Antelope opened the freakshow. The craziest and happiest Fluffhead I've ever heard, and the finale, a Contact > Frankenstein. Now they've done it, I was sold—never going to miss another show at Red Rocks again. Certain venues bring out sacred spirits, from MSG to the Warfield, and Red Rocks does it for me more than any other I've been to.

June 13, 1994 Kansas City, MO

We spent the next day drifting to Kansas City, a day of rest and car problems. We made it with plenty of time to spare, and, since it was a GA floor, I decided to brave the 90-plus degree heat and wait in line. There, I had the *privilege* of meeting the infamous Phish fan "The Timer."

I had seen him outside the Warfield and on the rest of the tour, and couldn't forget what I saw, then or ever. From a distance (I'm not sure if this is intentional or accidental) this guy looks like a member of the Phish organization. Who else would wear a nametag to a concert while holding a clipboard with a pen in hand?

My questions were quickly answered in line. He and his travel companions were well-versed in Phishtory and Phish stat-ology.

At first, it was fun—sharing stories and favorite tapes, tour tales and the like. After a couple of minutes of talking to him, I gave him one of the stickers that I had made, as a sign of goodwill to make his day a bit brighter. He took it, looked at it briefly, then set it on the ground. I started talking to someone he was sitting with, and 30 seconds after I give him the sticker, he interrupted me and said, "Here, man, I don't want this." At least he could have given it away again, or stuck it on the underside of his muffler, but he rudely tossed it back.

So, after five or so minutes, the novelty of talking to Timer had worn off. At first, I thought this guy had a little character, maybe even a lot. Then I realized his nametag was to identify him to all the unknowledgeable fans out there who had always wanted to meet him, and who never had basked in his eternal light firsthand.

I found out that his clipboard was for making exact, on-the-spot timings of the songs Phish played. (He introduced himself as "David, the guy who timed the Bomb Factory.") Further inquiry revealed him to be a math major. Clearly, this man saw the world in binary. His only way to appreciate the show was through a sick and complex timing system. Only a long song was a good song.

With this mentality, Phish was only able to get better if they continually played longer and longer versions of their songs. By summer '98, they would be down to the opening segment of YEM for the first set, and the build up to the explosion, and maybe some lyrics if they truly were cold that night, for the second set. I guess the encore would have to be a ten-minute version of Cavern!

Anyway, as we were waiting, Mike Gordon came up to us in line. Timer took center stage and the interview began. A few questions into this historical encounter, Timer asked Mike to guestlist him for the State Theatre show in Minneapolis a few days later. Mike, with surprisingly amazing composure, agreed and then disappeared.

It turned out that Mike had come out to tell David—by this time known by the band as "Timer," too—that his timing antics were really bugging them out. (Constant reminders that your music sucks only on the basis of time would bum me out as well.)

Three days later in Minnesota, Timer found himself in the very last row of the balcony of the State Theatre, as the band dedicated the no-mic *a cappella* to him. "This is for you, Dave, we hope it's long enough," Trey said before Amazing Grace.

I put two and two together with what actually went down when I heard an interview with Trey (on the *Tank Talk Tapes*) where he told almost the same story.

Well, enough said of what went on outside the show. Me and my group were first in, we owned the rail with Time-doggity-dogger to our right. Trey was visibly disturbed by The Clipboard, looking down and glaring at times, and then doing his best to ignore it at others.

This was my first experience with "the spot," as it became known to us. This special zone was right in front of Trey, and it was the only spot where you could see Trey's feet in action. Gymnastics could have been his other calling when you see him dancing on one pedal and jumping to another right at the exact moment for that perfect sound he's looking for (Chalkdust comes to mind).

This was a solid show from start to finish. The venue was a mini-coliseum setup, but with the floor only seating about 1,000 people. Very intimate, and nowhere close to selling out. Buried Alive > Poor Heart opener was tight, as was the entire first set. I was treated to a then-rare Wolfman's Brother, my first version of that song, as well as the song it went into, Dinner and a Movie. It was a smokin' set, and one of the best shows of the tour.

The second set opened with Mike's Groove, then Esther, two rather spooky tunes in a row. The whole set had a weird feeling to it, and Trey later said it was due to the Timer factor. During Reba, The Clipboard was in full effect, and on the tapes you can hear Trey laughing at what was going down on the rail. Timer was in front of Mike, shaking his head in disbelief over the measly 13:42 Mike's Song, and fearing the worst for the Reba that might not break the eight-minute barrier.

Standing between myself and Timer was a good buddy of mine, Corey (the cookie man from the 4/9/93 Minneapolis show). He was standing next to Timer pretending he had a clipboard in his hand and looking at his watch every other second or so. Trey couldn't take it—he lost it during Reba, which was a great sight to witness.

The closest I've come to losing all control from "setlist blueballs" was during the encore. The band came out and Trey played the opening notes to Voodoo Chile, and we went nuts. He looked around the stage at the guys. Mike shrugged and mouthed "Why not?" As Page also agreed, Trey looked to Fish, and that was all she wrote. Fish shook his head no and the look on his face was enough to get Trey to play Golgi for the encore.

In a sad yet still commonplace move, I called Trey on his weak decision, yelling out "PUSSY!" as loud as I could when I saw him signal the Golgi. I guess I get a little carried away myself sometimes.

June 14, 1994 Des Moines, IA

Downtown Des Moines, the cultural hub of Iowa, is a thrilling place to hang out all day before a show! Utter boredom combined with scorching heat and locals who were driving by "to look at the freaks" made it a miserable wait. If I ever end up going to Iowa for a reserved-seating concert, I am going to do my best to get there about five minutes from showtime.

This was my second-to-last show, and I was getting sick and exhausted as I always do on tour. Home stood a mere five hours away, and we had a group of about ten of us from Minneapolis so it was an early welcome home party. The first set featured two sandwich songs, Guelah with a Sweet Adeline in between, and I Didn't Know > My Sweet One > I Didn't Know before the Split Open and Melt closer.

The second set started out with the greatest Frankenstein I have ever heard. Page let loose on the synth for the post-drums explosion, the heavy headbanging material we all love. During this set they kept toying with "On Broadway," especially during the intro to Bowie and the Possum to close the show. The whole set, from the YEM to the Bike, from the Demand to the Possum, rocked. Head to toe spaghetti bones—shaking and groovin for a good 90 minutes.

June 16, 1994 Minneapolis, MN

Well, this is it, the final stretch, a short drive to Minneapolis and that's it. My friends of course are heading on to Milwaukee the next night, but what are they gonna play there? Nothing too out of hand, right?

The State Theatre would prove to be my last show of summer '94. We had great second row seats (should have stubbed Timer down!), and we got to hear a lot of songs on the less played side of the coin. The standard first set was highlighted by Gumbo, the first one in a while, as well as my first.

The second set, however, was pure gravy throughout. Suzie, Antelope, Col. Forbin's > Kung > Mockingbird! was sickness. I don't think I've ever heard these tapes—I know they're on bootleg CD, but they haven't made it my way. I still remember the set as a non-stop rock experience.

Phish and Minneapolis have a great history together. From the unrecorded Cabooze show, to the Target Center, Phish has gone from small bar band to coliseum style venue-rock gods. At my first show in Minneapolis, also my first Phish show, 4/29/92, Trey played a Raspberry Beret jam during Weekapaug because they were playing First Ave., where Prince filmed Purple Rain.

Two years later they came back and played a surprising crowd-downer, Purple Rain. It's one thing to acknowledge Minneapolis, but as soon as you make fun of them (i.e. a guy in a dress playing vacuum), they get offended. All these Minnesotans looked like they were ready to fight.

So I departed the tour after 11 shows. I saw amazing sights, met beautiful people, saw the best venue on Earth, and got to see the best rock band in the world for two solid weeks.

The best show was by far the second night at Red Rocks, the best experience was Kansas City, and the worst drive will always belong to the journey from Salt Lake City to Morrison in one day.

Jay Archibald is the founder of The Karma Crew, a group of fans crusading for common sense and mutual respect on tour.

Halley's Coming...

By Lee LeFever

My obsession with the song Halley's Comet began when my friend Elizabeth, who I barely knew at the time, found out I was going on Phish tour in summer '97, and despite her jealousy, copied three of her favorite tapes for me and gave me her glass piece to be broken in properly.

One of the tapes was the second set of Gunnison, CO, 3/14/93, which begins with Halley's. The seed was firmly planted and though I was blown away with each and every show, my ears craved that song. My tour family scoffed at me since they had played it at the Clifford Ball (which I missed).

After a long drive to Phoenix we stopped for gas and raided the postcard aisle, not even looking at the cards we bought. The next day while flipping through the cards, Mary Miles (my car mate) freaked out when she realized we had inadvertently bought a card with Halley's Comet in the background. We decided it was a sign.

I had two choices: I could write"PLEASE" on the card and attempt to have it delivered backstage, or I could send it to a friend. I sent it to Elizabeth and felt confident that I would still get my wish.

Mary and I had not planned to go to the Great Went due to serious lack of money and tickets, but we knew deep down this was ridiculous considering we had touched each corner of the country. After a brief phone call to Mary's employer (with the inevitable news that she wasn't returning) we found ourselves in our rightful place, in our caravan headed to Limestone, ME.

We stopped at a grocery store to stock up on bread and cheese and literally dropped our baskets in surprise when we turned the corner and found ourselves on the liquor aisle. Charleston, South Carolina, where I live, is the least strict city in the Bible Belt of blue laws and there are still only certain times and places where a bottle can be purchased. We felt obligated to buy a couple of bottles. A few hours later we were in traffic for the Went and celebrating by cracking them open.

Hours later, we were still in traffic and I was crosseyed with only half a bottle of bourbon left; I remember trying to remember a time when I was happier. Eventually I had the inevitable bladder problem and stumbled off to the woods. Of course, when I emerged traffic had moved significantly and I began running to catch up with the cars. I'll admit to doing many dumb things, but I usually have brains enough to not separate from my friends and my belongings while they are still in traffic.

While I was running and stumbling to catch up to the car, a golf cart pulled up and offered me a ride to the car which I graciously accepted. I don't remember what I said, but I made the driver laugh and by the time we reached our car he decided he was taking me backstage. I happily agreed.

We pulled up to my friends and he told them to meet me at the tower at 2 a.m. We were off. I felt a tinge of panic as I saw the thousands of people pouring in, but it was too late to start thinking clearly—I was going backstage! The driver, Mike, and his friends were camped in an R.V. and had plenty of party favors which they graciously shared. I was having a great time, but as the bourbon wore off I started getting nervous about finding my friends, especially in the downpour.

Having received some mild teasing, especially about my southern accent, I scoffed when someone called, "Hey, Fishman's here." I rolled my eyes and glanced out of the R.V. In the dark I could make out a man on a golf cart with his hat pulled down low. I walked over to him, lifted his hat, and smiled when I saw that it was, in fact, Jon.

Of course we've all seen Mike cruising around or hanging out after the show, but I still get butterflies standing near the boys I consider to be among the greatest musicians ever. Imagine my stomach bugs when I introduced myself to Fishman. I managed to keep my freaking to a minimum as I sat on his cart and squeezed my tweaked-out brain for something semi-intelligent to say.

I asked him why Bob Gullotti had left the stage in the middle of a song in Austin. I told him that some people thought he was upset because he could not keep up. Fishman laughed and replied, "If anything it's the other way around—he had to take a piss!"

By then, 2 a.m. was approaching and though I was having a great time I was still worried about finding my friends. Jon said he had to go, too, so I kissed him on the cheek, thanked him for everything and watched him drive away.

Then, like an asteroid crash, I remembered my song and shouted for him to wait. He stopped and turned around and I said to him, "I know you get requests all the time, but if you remember "Oom-chic, bah-bah, chicchic…"" Jon laughed and again was off.

I missed Chelsea at the tower by five minutes and my generous new friends offered to let me sleep in their R. V. The next day we began a seemingly futile attempt to find my friends; five minutes into the search I heard Chip scream my name. I turned around and there, out of thousands of people, were Chip, Adam, and Brenden.

They jumped on the cart and guided us back to our campsite. All was well and into the show we went.

Chelsea always says that I get this maniac grin on my face with the opening song which stays in place until the encore. She claims it scares people and that's why they get out of my way. She may or may not be right, but we somehow managed to get to third row by the middle of the first set. I told Jordan that if they played my song I would lie down and roll in the mud. She went back before third set so she couldn't hold me to it.

After another never-ending break, the boys walked back on stage and although it sounds egotistical, I felt like they were looking at me. All of a sudden, Mike stepped up and started "Oom-chic…"

If anyone saw someone floating above the crowd at the beginning of third set, that was me—my body was reeling. I regained my senses and screamed "thank-you" to Jon who smiled and nodded.

Thank-you, Phish, for saying Happy Birthday to Jerry, for taking us to the Gorge, for kicking your legs at Alpine, and for finding Ken Kesey on the mountain. Thanks for the bluegrass, Mike; and thank-you especially to Jon. Thank-you, in short, for a real good time!

The Greenpeace folks man the table on the lawn at Austin, TX, July 26, 1997.

Lucky 50-Cent Piece

Thanks to a half-dollar and the Greenpeace table, a group of friends found a promised land—backstage.

By Paige Clem

That crisp autumn morning of '94, the sky was that intense color of blue that can only be seen for about two weeks a year in October. The night before had been a lot of fun, seeing Phish play the amphitheater where I'd seen countless acts perform since I was 15. The evolution of my musical experience had been marked by concerts I had attended at Oak Mountain: The early days of Buffet, Driving & Cryin', Skynard, on to my first Panic show, the HORDE, Allmans, Clapton. I've even, in an attempt for bizarre entertainment on an otherwise dull night, gone out there to see Tesla and Barry Manilow.

But now, it was Phish, and it had been exciting to see my favorite band in such a familiar setting. The show had been a great warm-up for the next few nights of being on the road. We'd catch two shows in Tennessee, and then Atlanta the next week. Then it was back to school drudgery.

But I wouldn't think about that now. The open road lay ahead of me.

The drive was beautiful as we set out on I-59 toward Chattanooga. Laura made a comment about how the trees on the humble Alabama mountains all seemed to merge together to make a huge carpet, covering the land. "Nice image," I thought to myself. The conversation on the way up was pleasant and easy. I was so relieved to finally be away from the monotony my daily life and getting to settle into what always seems to me to be my "true form"—being on the road with Phish. That peaceful easiness filled me and my two friends as "Esther," my '89 Montero, trucked along the road.

I had discovered Phish about a year and a half before. I recall my senior year of high school when a guy sitting behind me, who had a habit for pestering me randomly, recited, just loud enough for me to hear, "please her with a tweezer..." "What the hell did you just say?" I sassily called out. He mentioned something about Phish, that band I'd been hearing a few folks talk about. "Jeez, what a bunch of kinky weirdos they must be," I thought to myself.

Later that fall, in my freshman year of college, my boyfriend at the time enthusiastically played me a tape he'd just gotten from a friend. I don't recall the first song I heard. I do recall, however a strange sensation. The music made no sense to me whatsoever in melody and lyric. It seemed to be just a bunch of jumbled words and notes frantically be propelled at one another. Nothing in me went "wow, cool," yet I felt this incredible, strange pull. I didn't really care for what I was hearing, but I didn't seem able to stop listening. It was the Mango Song that finally did it for me. Page's solo pushed me over that line from which I will probably never return. Suddenly, I heard the music. It was like the Big Bang theory. Perfect law and order is created out of chaos. I was hooked. I saw my first show at the Roxy that following spring, on February 21, 1993.

A year and a half had passed and my enthusiasm only increased with every new tape, each new twisted tale or fact about this Phabulous Phoursome. I started to feel a strange connection to these people I'd never met. They seemed like close friends with whom I shared so much.

As we traveled along the road, I found that the previous night's show only affirmed those feelings. I was jealous of a few friends that had gotten the opportunity to slip backstage. I wanted that to be me. I wanted to talk to these guys and understand more. I had so many questions to ask. It pained me for a moment when I was hit with the realization of how unlikely it would be that I'd ever get to meet them with the status they were rapidly achieving. Little did I know what lay in store.

The show in Chattanooga that night was incredible. I heard my first Possum and finally understood what all the ranting was about. It was also the first time I really achieved that full cycle the music can take you through—the cycle that parallels the stages of intercourse I studied in my Human Sexuality class: build up > plateau > CLIMAX > resolution. "Wow," I thought to myself. I also got to hear my first Harpua and the last Axilla I they played until fall '96.

We spent the next two days camping on the edge of a lake in a park just outside Chattanooga, enjoying the crispness of the air and the beauty of autumn in Tennessee. Fall will probably always be my favorite time for tour.

Tuesday morning we got up and hit the road for Nashville. Once inside the arena I did my usual and immediately went for the Greenpeace table to give my $5 donation in exchange for a raffle ticket. It was a ritual I'd established ever since I'd stumbled upon the Greenpeace table at Jones Beach that summer. Now the folks at the table were starting to recognize us. I handed Henry $20 and he gave me my ticket. He didn't have change and asked if I'd break the $20 bill at the concession stand. The friendly "grandfather-type" at the stand gave me change, and to my pleasure it included a 50-cent piece. It still resides in the coin compartment of my wallet.

I gave my $5 to Henry and he gave me another ticket. "Wait, you already gave me one" I pointed out. He gave that ticket instead to my buddy, Daryll, who, along with Laura was also making a donation to increase our odds.

That night's show brought some good treats, including my first Guyute and a second set with guest Bela Fleck. On the way out we loyally stopped by the Greenpeace table, feeling great after a good show but having to face the reality that the fun was over for now and it was time to head back home to school. The (as always) surprisingly small crowd of raffle ticket holders hovered around the table. The first number was called out and, as usual, was a dud. It amazes me how many people get tickets and never show up to find out if they've won.

The second number was called out and to my dismay I heard a voice over my shoulder call out "that's me" just as I realized my ticket was only one number off! As I turned to Daryll to express my angst in being so close, I saw Henry handing him two backstage passes. Holy shit. It's us! I felt blood rush to my head. My dream was actually going to come true. I was finally going to get to talk to these people who'd added so much to my life in such a short time.

Excitement overwhelmed me and then, tragedy—there were three of us and only two passes. Shit. This is great. Mike from the table said, "You guys were bound to win some time, didn't you think this out already?" Stumped and in fear of something as awful as flipping a coin (my lucky 50 cent piece perhaps) for the extra ticket, I worried what would be decided.

Laura quickly resigned as a candidate, saying that we were much bigger fans and it was our idea to get the tickets anyway.

Feeling a bit guilty, and ready as hell to get backstage, we frantically assured her that we'd try to get another pass or something once inside. Suddenly, in the midst of struggling to come up with a place to meet back with her and with the angst of leaving her alone, an angel appeared. He may have looked like a security officer, but he had a glow in his eyes that keeps all of us convinced to this day that he was of another world. "What's the problem?" he asked with a warm smile on his face. Quicker than we could explain our dilemma, he whipped out 4 more backstage passes—two of which were all access! I reached for his arm and gave him a squeeze as I looked him deep in the eye and gave the most genuine "God bless you" I've given to anyone in my life.

Later, Daryll said the whole experience tripped him out, seeing me thank the guard and all, as if it were like witnessing some intense other-worldly moment. We got rid of the extra passes and quickly ran to the backstage area.

We found ourselves in a large, highly unglamorous room with a couple of folding tables set up with snacks on them. There were probably 20 or so folks scattered about, mostly lurking around the food. I wondered who they all were. There was no sign of the guys.

After a roadie of some sort strongly suggested that we stay in that room instead of wandering around, we tried our best to relax and wait. We pondered the letters written in black magic marker on our passes. All of ours said VD in the middle (venereal disease?), but both Daryll and Laura's passes had a GP written in the top corner. Mine said PM. Hmm? I wondered why mine was different.

The first guy to come out was Jon. He slowly wandered out and then saw someone he knew down at the end of the row of tables we were sitting on. He went over and gave her a hug and she introduced her friend. I gathered from their conversation that they were cousins or something. I felt silly for eavesdropping—I felt pretty goofy and silly all together, actually. Suddenly, I'd lost all concept of how to be cool and confident as I stood there anticipating the long-awaited moment to talk to my heroes.

Next out was Page. I'd admired him for so long. What would I say? He was stopped a few feet in front of me to sign an autograph. As he stood there talking to the guy, I noticed him glancing over his shoulder at me a few times, as if trying to make recognition. As the guy walked away, Page approached me. "Are you my guest?" he said. "How cool," I thought to myself—suddenly I was Phish's guest. I felt like royalty.

"Why, yes I am," I said coolly as I stuck out my hand. "I'm Paige too!" I said as I handed him the envelope I'd written the set list on to sign. He signed and graciously accepted my praises, though his face seemed a bit puzzled.

He then turned to my friends and greeted them. "Oh, you guys won the Greenpeace passes. Congratulations!" How did he know? Why was he addressing them and not me? He signed their passes, thanked them and walked on. It was then that Daryll made a realization, all too late. The "GP" on their passes stood for Greenpeace. The "PM" on mine stood for Page McConnell. UGGH! What did I just do?! I was acting all cool and "why yes I am your guest" when he was wondering, "Where the hell did this chick get one of my passes and why is she trying to act so cool?" How embarrassing. I meet the first of my icons and in less than one minute I have him thinking I'm an idiot.

Fortunately, my humiliation was quickly interrupted. Laura had spotted Trey. He'd slipped out a door and headed in the opposite direction towards the stage area.

We stood there, giddy as schoolgirls debating about how in the hell to approach him. Lara came up with an idea and took off in Trey's direction. Daryll and I hung back and watched. We saw her approach him and the next thing we know they're smiling and talking. Daryll and I took advantage of Laura's ice-breaking and approached them. I reached out my hand and introduced myself. "You're much better looking than the other Page," Trey commented.

We found them in a discussion about back and neck aches. In the course of our trip, Laura and I had been pondering how it is that Trey can keep that head bobbin' thing up for so long with out getting a horrible backache. He told us that sometimes it did hurt, and that in the past they've had a massage therapist travel with them on tour!

As he stood their talking, I just smiled. What a cool guy. I recall thinking that he wasn't at all the rumored snob that some of the folks who'd gone backstage at Oak Mountain had said. He stood there just as friendly and cordial as could be with his guitar strapped over one shoulder. I thought it interesting that he carried it with him. Don't they have roadies for this? It made him seem more human, like he was any other guy who loved the hell out of his guitar and wanted it to be with him.

Having just recently picked up playing the guitar myself, and having a hell of a time with building up calluses, I asked Trey to see his. I commented that they didn't seem that intense to me, thinking that they had to be peeling and mangled looking, like mine always seemed to be, to warrant anything serious. Daryll quickly corrected me and affirmed that they were indeed impressive.

As we humbly handed him our scraps to sign, we all tried to take advantage the moment to finally get the answer to some of those questions that had been in our minds for so long. "What's up with the pants, Trey?" I asked. The guy had been wearing the same pants three nights in a row. You know the ones I'm talking about, the shinny gold ones that look like pajama bottoms. He seemed genuinely concerned that I might not be fond of them. I explained to him that it wasn't the pants themselves but that, "You've been wearing them since Saturday."

"Well. actually, I just got them Saturday," Trey replied, and explained that his wife had given him two pairs, and that they were extremely comfortable and easy to move in on stage. As he signed my envelope he said he'd pull out the other pair soon. We suggested he do it in Atlanta, where we'd get to see them. My autograph from him says, "Paige, I'll wear the blue ones —Trey."

By now, Bela and Mike were nearby and we managed to somehow obtain their autographs with out breaking conversation with Trey. Daryll, who has always taken an extremely analytical approach to Phish and music in general, started in with some good questions, and Trey still seemed extremely relaxed and eager to talk to us.

Daryll expressed his curiosity about why he'd never gotten to hear a Mango Song live, commenting that it was the first Phish song he'd ever heard (I was the one that played it for him) and that it was his favorite. Trey, as if reminded of an old friend, was like, "Oh, Mango. Yeah, we haven't done that in awhile." We were quick to suggest that Atlanta be the place to pull it out (along with the blue pants).

Daryll shifted the conversation and brought up whether or not they had ever had any legal issues arise out of doing parodies of others' songs like Freebird and having them recorded by tapers. Trey said that nothing like that had arisen, but seemed more interested in talking about the "parody of Freebird" issue.

He, believe it or not, was quick to defend that it was not a parody at all. Now up to this point I was still so stunned that we were even talking to Trey that I really wasn't even listening to half of what he and Daryll were talking about. All of the sudden I found that Trey was getting really involved in this bizarre story about him and Fish in Greece back in the 1980s. I'm thinking, "Weren't we just talking about copyright laws?" and next thing I know, Trey's walking us over to the bleachers to set his guitar down so he could get more comfortable talking to us. Then, all of the sudden, as if thinking to himself "This won't do," he says, "Here, come with me."

WHAT?!! Come with you?! Now this was getting to be too much. It all seemed like some crazy dream, or like being a kid and suddenly finding out that you are actually hanging out with the one and only Papa Smurf, in the blue flesh. For so long you watched that TV screen and longed to run around the Smurf Village, and then all a sudden the Daddy of the Smurfs is inviting you into his own personal mushroom house. We followed him, grinning at each other with anticipation.

What took place over the next hour and a half will forever be one of my fondest memories. After offering us drinks, Trey invited us to sit as he picked up his Freebird story where he'd left off. The whole tale was outrageous! It was like listening to a whole new section from Gamehendge. It was the same Europe trip where he wrote You Enjoy Myself. He spoke of being on this nude beach in Greece in '85 with Fish and all these crazy things that happened to them while they were there (most of which I can't even remember because it all just seemed so outrageous). Daryll looked at me with amazement when I actually told Trey he had to be full of shit. He insisted that it was all true and that Fish would back him.

The climax of the story I do remember. Fish and Trey had been there for about a week and a half and hadn't heard any music at all. They somehow got a hold of some "highly intoxicating substances." Through the course of the very intense evening, Fish decided that it would be a good idea to swim out to this wooden raft that floats out in the ocean (Phish do like to swim, you know). Keep in mind they're both buck naked.

As they started to swim, a huge storm developed. They began to fear for their lives as the waves rose and the storm rapidly intensified. On their last breaths they make it to the raft and clung to each other for dear life. Now there's an image—20-year-old Trey and Fish, clinging to each other while freezing their naked balls off on some raft out in the middle of the ocean in Greece. See why I thought he was full of shit?

Here's the clincher. Finally they get back to shore. They'd been up all night (whether on the raft or on land I'm not clear), and it had been a crazy one. They'd had a brush with death. They sat on the beach and watched as the sun began to rise. Suddenly something formed in their ears that was strangely familiar. It was music. It'd been some time since they'd heard any. They walked over to the source and made friends with two guys sitting there with what I'm sure was a mack daddy '80s boom box.

Now there's an image—20-year-old Trey and Fish, clinging to each other while freezing their naked balls off on some raft in the middle of the ocean.

Now, unfortunately, here I have some discrepancies in memory. Through the course of the story, as Trey jumped around in his narration, he had mentioned something about hooking up with these German punks (punk in the '80s mohawk since of the word) named Jurgen and Rudy. (The names stuck in my head for some reason. I debated naming my cat after one of them just so I could tell the story when people asked why

I'd given my pet such an ugly name. The two are also acknowledged in the 'Thank You' section of *A Live One*.) They were apparently real tough guys and got in a lot of fights on the beach. Trey spoke of them very fondly as he recalled how he and Fish paled around with them through the course of their stay. Whether they were the two guys they met on the morning at hand I cannot recall.

Regardless, that morning, Trey and Fish found themselves trying to talk about music to two people with whom they didn't share the same language. When they got across that they were from the U.S., a connection was made. "Sweet Home Alabama!?" the foreigners questioned. Trey and Fish nodded yes, relieved that at last communication had been established. And there, naked on a beach in Greece, their newfound friends popped in a tape of Lynard Skynard and they watched the sun rise to the first sounds of music they'd heard since their stay had begun—Freebird. Who can deny the spirituality in that?

The rest of our conversation with Trey consisted mostly of our questions and his answers. We, of course, asked about Gamehendge, and as if he'd never had to explain it before, he leisurely told us how it was basically a familiar case of "Whoops, this project's due and I'm not done, better come up with something quick." That's why the ending is so vague. He said he's not really sure how it ends himself, and that often it's the fans that give him ideas about how it goes. "Hey Trey, does such-and-such mean such-and-such?" "Uh, yeah, that's it."

We asked how the band was "doing" in terms of sales and how it felt to be making it big. He was quick to point out that Maria Carey with X-million records sold in X-weeks was "making it big," and that they really hadn't even scraped that kind of volume. Of course, that didn't bother him much.

He was also, surprisingly, interested in us and what we thought: about the tour, that night's show, stuff in general. I recall he was excited about having played Axilla the night before. He was curious if we got the whole gist of it, so he broke into an *a cappella* rendition of the versus to both Axilla I and II. He tickled himself, laughing that trademark laugh, as he recalled the lyrics and then explained that the whole story revolved around a guy getting his testicles "dissolved."

It was about that time that some girl knocked on the door and came in and sat with us. Continuing the conversation, we questioned what the actual word "Axilla" had to do with anything and he said, point blank, that he had no idea. Go figure.

After pointing out that the axilla is that ambiguous part of the arm we all wonder about, the mystery girl told Trey that they were "about ready." WHAT? Already? Trey, still talking away, grabbed his stuff as we followed him back into that big room we'd sat waiting eagerly just two hours before.

There was a cluster of folks in the back of the room, all of whom seemed to know each other, which included the rest of the band. Not having had an opportunity to talk to Fish, and now feel quite comfortable with the whole scene, we approached the cluster of people. "Hey Jon, Jurgen and Rudy on the beach in Greece in '85," I said.

Now was my chance to catch Trey in his story-glamorizing. Jon just kinda froze and said, "Who told you about that?" in a surprised and suspicious voice. Then he immediately launches off on the exact same story that Trey had just told us, with the exact same enthusiasm and detail! It was too weird for words. As we all filed out of the gymnasium (yes, the show was in the Vandy Gym—which is what the VD stood for on the backstage passes: Vanderbilt) Jon verified Trey's whole outlandish tale, practically word-for-word.

At one point Mike, walking with some folks in front of us, stopped, turned to me and said, "muffin?" I removed the bran substance from his hand and said, "sweet cakes." With Jon still talking about Greece, we were now outside, approaching the bus. He quickly wrapped up the story and wished us a good night as he filed onto the bus with the other handful of people. We said good-bye.

Disoriented from the experience, we realized we'd exited the gym from an unfamiliar exit, so we silently walked up a slope of grass in search of the car. Esther was right there, with just a few other remaining vehicles.

After climbing inside the car we all erupted into huge screams and cheers, dissolving our cool exterior and at last being able to express our true elation. I reached in the back and grabbed a Ziplock baggy and, after dropping "Mike's muffin" into it, I placed it in the glove box as a souvenir (where it remained until Charlotte '95). I cranked up Esther and we headed for home.

A week later, Daryll and I looked out at the stage. It was our last show for the fall. We were on the first row of the mezzanine which put us very close to the front on the far left of the stage, facing Jon head-on. It seemed as thought he was looking directly at us as he methodically drummed away. Did he recognize us?

Mike stood still and tall, pants at his calves, as he studied his steady riffs. Trey strutted around the stage, head bobbing rhythmically. He sang words of "spasm waiters" and "grape apple pies." He was wearing a brand new pair of loose-fitting shiny blue pants. Page sat, graceful as ever, reciting the same sounds that had first called me to Phish two years before. Daryll and I high-fived each other in satisfaction.

Happiness filled my heart as the music filled my soul. As I listened to the music, I looked out onto the stage and saw my beloved Phish. For that one moment, I knew what it meant to feel the sunlight in my eyes.

Paige Clem is a co-founder of The Phellowship, a group of Phishheads who choose to remain substance-free because they are recovering from drug and alcohol addiction.

Emulating Fish

Recently, I was working with a construction company doing small residential jobs. Since I was the low man on the poll, I was frequently the "clean-up man" and would do various clean-up tasks at the end of the day. One day, near the end of the day, boredom started to set in as I found myself alone in this person's basement, vacuuming.

I started to think about Phish then Fishman and his vacuum, and I wondered how he got some of those noises to come out of that thing.

I then realize that I had in my hands an industrial powered shop-vac that sucks any loose object in and swallows it whole. I figured, what the hell, I might as well give it a try since I'm alone. I put this sucking machine up to my face, trying not to let it suck me in, then all of a sudden a wicked howl start roaring.

After the initial shock of "Oh my god, it's working," I realized it sounded exactly like Fish. I got so into it that I kind of zoned out for a few moments, listening to what I was doing.

When I came to, I turned around and found the homeowner's 13-year-old son staring at me in utter disbelief. The shock value of the sight of me sucking this vacuum like a hooker on 42nd Street—with the howl to go with it—was pure comedy. I wish I had a camera so I could have snapped a picture of the boy's face to remember the moment by.

—James Pollin

The Shows

Midnight, January 1, 1997,
FleetCenter, Boston, MA

Here it is... every Phish show on record. The setlist section contains several elements, each of which is explained below...

The Setlists. It's the ever-expanding compilation of Phish setlists, dating all the way back to the band's inception. In the last two years, the Almanac has undertaken a research project to document setlists previously unavailable in the public sphere, and to correct erroneous setlists. Since the publication of Volume 3 in November 1996, many Almanac readers have submitted previously-undocumented setlists and setlist corrections, while Almanac research has also uncovered new setlists, show dates and corrections. These additions have been combined with our earlier setlist archive—primarily public-domain setlist information contained in the Phish.Net archive—to create our current database. In this way, the Almanac setlist archive continues to mature. A list of new and corrected setlists appears on page 70.

Nitty-Gritty. Some setlists have descriptions written beneath them in italics. This information details guest spots, unusual performances, odd on-stage antics or other out of the ordinary occurrences. We call it the nitty-gritty, and most of these were supplied by Almanac readers during our Phishtory'97 project. It's important to note that this is an incomplete compilation, as there are many on-stage events which have never been documented. Our search continues for nitty-gritty, so please get in touch with us with any new info.

And of course, if you have setlists for any shows not included in the Almanac, or catch any errors, please contact us.

Phishtory Mini-reviews. Setlists don't tell the whole story! That's why we have also added over 500 show descriptions compiled from submissions from about 200 fans.

This project, called Phishtory'97, began in January 1997 when we printed up thousands of fliers asking fans to write short reviews of any ten Phish shows. The responses created a library of close to 3,000 reviews! We honed those down to create a collective work offering a lively and detailed account of every show of note. Contributors to this section, each of whom received a free copy of the Almanac, were also offered a free tape-trader listing. Their names and contact info can be found on pages 68-69, along with the names of Phishtory contributors who did not wish to be listed in the tape trader section.

Show stories. Nothing livens up factual history like zany personal tales from fellow Phish fans of the wild things that happened to them at shows. Included in these pages are many such stories, positioned in close proximity to the setlist for the show where the adventure occurred. These stories were selected for their ability to cast light on the scene at a show, or on the general climate of Phish shows from an era. Again, this is an ever-changing piece of the Almanac, so if you have a few nutty tales from shows past, please feel free to send them on in.

In addition, several of the show stories and mini-reviews are the result of interviews we conducted with Phish fans who attended shows in the 1980s and early '90s. Our thanks to Chad Garland, Mike Graff, Greg Kelly, Brendan McKenna, Rich Seaberg and Patrick and Charlene Smith for sharing their memories.

Historical Reviews. To add yet another dimension, we selected roughly 20 shows that we identified as the most historic nights in Phish's rich concert history and researched the stories behind those shows. These "historical reviews" appear in curved, gray-toned boxes.

Accessibility Ratings. Wondering what your chances are getting a hold of a certain show on tape? The answer can be found in the accessibility rating next to each setlist. We compared 50 fans' tapelists to get an accurate sense of which shows are in heavy circulation and which are the hardest to find. The ratings are weighted based on year. If no one had a tape from the '80s, we assume it to be a pretty rare tape, otherwise hardcore tapers would have gone after it. However, there are many tapes from the '90s which are in reasonable circulation but do not find their way to many fan's collections simply because there are so many good shows from those years to choose from. Anyone wanting to get their hands on them might have a difficult time, but would not likely run into the same barriers as they would in looking for a rare '80s show. The accessibility ratings guidelines appear on page 70.

THE PHARMER'S ALMANAC

Get A Free Pharmer's Almanac Vol. 4!

Phishtory'97

Share Your Phish Knowledge!

Tell It Like It Is!

Phishtory'97...

Phishtory'97 is the most ambitious project yet undertaken by The Pharmer's Almanac—the documentation of Phish's concert history through the memories and concert reviews of hundreds of fans.

We distributed Phishtory forms over the first three months of 1997; the results can be seen throughout the setlists section in the mini-reviews that appear under most shows and the "nitty-gritty" notes in italics under most setlists. Everyone who contributed 10 reviews was offered a free Almanac and a free tape trader listing in this volume; their names and addresses appear below and on the opposite page (the listings are offered as a courtesy, and are not verified by The Pharmer's Almanac).

Phishtory contributors who did not request a taper listing are: Eric Acquafredda, M.N.J. Adams, Josh Albini, Jonathan Ardman, Matthew Ashenfelder, Lindsey Bates, Robyn Bayetis, Waylon Baynard, Connor Bergman, David M. Brown, Emily Brown, Anthony Buchla, Angela Carrol, Bob Colby, Marcia Collins, Colm Connell, Mick Connor, Jos Conti, Mike D'Amico, James Daly, Mark Daniel, Dom DeLuca, Adam Drilhante, Ashley Davis, Amy Duncan, David Eckers, Nancy Eddies, Pat Elkins, Tim Foisser, Mark Garofalow, Daniel Grifland, Ernie Greene, Brian Gressler, Ric Hanna, Tyler Harris, Ryan Harsch, Jason Hedrington, Michelle Hirsch, Tricia Holmes, Andre Holton, Mike Hood, Tony Hume, Al Hunt, Jake Hunter, Julie Hunter, Mike Indgin, Davey Inkrea, Carri A. Johnson, Lee Johnston, Melissa Keller, Greg Kelly, James Kiddle, Langston Knipler, Richard Kot, Dan Kurtz, Shannon C. Lancaster, Russell Lane, Will Lehnert, Joseph LeRoy, Morgan Lester, Amanda Litton, Mike Livanos, Foster Lukas, Linda Mahdesian, Sarah Malo, Amy Manning, Dave Matson, Rich Mazer, Alexis Michael, Andrew Mitchell, Pete Morse, Charlie Murphy, Jefferson R. Musser, Mike Noll, Billy O'Malley, Otis, Mike Palmer, Billy Jah Patrick, Nathaniel Peirce, Brett Pessin, Bob Peterson, Bruce A. Pickell, Tom Pinnick, Brian A. Rock, Andy Ross, Hollis Rowan, Ian Rufe, Jeff Salvatore, Joesph A. Savino, Lee Schiller, Chrissy Schneider, Greg Schwartz, Dave Sharpe, Scott Sifton, Leah Shantz, J.J. Southard, Jen Spivey, Ed Smith, Pat Stanley, Teddy Stuart, Ali Tariq, Melanie and Melita Terrell, Jen Verdon, Brian Watkins, Kevin Weise, Lara Wittels, Melissa Wolcott, and Joel Zeigler.

Our thanks to the entire Phishtory'97 team!

Chuch Adams [Analog]
512 5Th Street
E. Northport, NY 11731

Chad Ashcraft [Analog]
7405 Crisp Ave
Rayrown, MO 64133

Jon Bahr [Analog]
41 Cooke Street
Providence, RI 02906
robert_bahr@brown.edu

Brent Baker [Analog]
1 Dunham Circle
Fairport, NY 14450

Alex Banks [Analog]
C/ Hontanres 7
Madrid, Spain, 28035

Libby Barrow [Analog]
1810 E. Fox Ln.
Milwaukee, WI 53217

Jonathan Bauld [Analog]
5 Ryan Circle
Simsbury, CT 06070
Jonb4131Aaol.com

R.J. Bee [Dat & Analog]
2346 Gibley Park
Toledo, OH 43617
Harpua887@aol.com

Aaron Benton [Analog]
1613 Darrel Terrace
Midlothian, VA 23113

Jeff Bernier [Analog]
A-10 Sinai
Chelmsford, MA 01824

Emily Binard [Dat & Analog]
2915 Baseline Apt.#623
Boulder, CO 808303

Chris Black [Dat & Analog]
425 Powers Court Ave
Alpharetta, GA 30201

Brian Boehm [Dat & Analog]
48 Dukes Circle
Lincolnshire, IL 60069

Peter Bukley [Analog]
408 Lareine Ave. 1ST Floor
Bradle Beach, NJ 07720

John E. Campion [Analog]
361 Greenwood Ave.
Warwick, RI 02886

Beth Castroll [Dat & Analog]
145 Osprey
Hacketstown, NJ 07840
wifeofbath@aol.com

Mike Cerniauskas [Analog]
11322 S. Homan
Chicago, IL 60655

Dan Charland [Analog]
9 Dresser Street
Providence, RI 02909
czav91b@prodigy.com

Dan Charron [Analog]
232 Marvin Rd.
Colchester, CT 06415

Chip Croteau [Analog]
433 Main Street Unit 2
Medfield, MA 02052

John Cunningham [Analog]
2589 Genesee Street
Retsof, NY 14539

Jamis Curran [Analog]
634 Cottage Grove Ave, SE
Cedor, Rapids IA 52403

Gina D'Amico [Analog]
26 Hazel Street
Harrington, Park NJ 07640

Ryan Danyew [Analog]
31 White St. PO Box 476
Clark Mills, NY 13321

Adam Davidoff [Analog]
2170 Hayes Road
Granville, OH 43023

Jason Deziel [Analog]
216 Barnes Rd.
Watertown, CT 06795

Patt Dieter [Analog]
608 Winwood Road
Balimore, MD 21212

Alb Dipasqua [Dat & Analog]
55 Church Street
Millburn, NJ 07041

Jeffrey Ellenbogen [Analog]
6612 Cliffbrook Drive
Dallas, TX 75240

Erin Ferris [Analog]
6177 Lookover Ct.
Toldeo, OH 43612

Matt Fitone [Dat & Analog]
4 Granite Rd.
Wilmington, DE 19803

John Foley [Dat & Analog]
153 Old Conn. Path
Wayland, MA 01778

Joe Galbraith [Dat & Analog]
114 Downing Ct.
MT. Laurel, NJ 08054
slipknot@bellatlantic.net

Chad Gamerke [Analog]
1556 Detroit #1
Denver, CO 80206

David George [Analog]
PO Box 7870
Radford, VA 24142
dgeorge@runet.com

Jesse Giunta [Analog]
20-D Doral Dr.
Reading, PA 19607

Jay Green [Analog]
3701 East Weyburn Rd.
Richmond, VA 23235

Aaron Grossberg [Analog]
265 Overhill Drive
Chambersburg, PA 17201

Charlie Gubman [Analog]
1046 Greenwood Ave.
Wlimette, IL 60091

Chris Haines [Analog]
31 James Street
Peabody, MA 01960

Josh Halman [Analog]
3570 Frederick Dr.
Ann Arbor, MI 48105

TapeTrader Listings

Brian Hart [Analog]
4088 Chalmette Dr.
Beaver Creek, OH 45440

Tim Herrman [Dat & Analog]
63 Phalanx Rd.
Lincroft, NJ 07738
gherrman@mail.monmouth.com

Eric Higel [Analog]
30 Michele Drive
Portland, CT 06480

Joshua Howley [Analog]
60 Pine Terrace East
Short Hills, NJ 07078
jnhhowl@eden.rutgers.edu

Mike Jett [Analog]
9619 Tamarisk Pkwy
Louisville, KY 40223
djett81588@aol.com

David Jones [Analog]
364 Red Oak Court
Auburn, AL 36830
david8503@aol.com

Andy Kahn [Analog]
5906 N. Old Orchard
Peoria, IL 61614

Robert Koeller [Analog]
450 E. Walnut Street Apt. 104
Indianapolis, IN 46202

Tony Krupka [Analog]
Rt.1 Box B-1
Koshkonong MO 65692
apk869s@smsu.nic.edu

Scott Kushner [Analog]
560 Coral Ave.
Manchester, NH 03104
gushner@aol.com

Ron Lauer [Analog]
105 Russel Street
Malden, Ma 02148

Josh Letourneau [Dat & Analog]
22 Appleton St.
Keene, NH 03431

Jeff Lozier [Dat & Analog]
17 west street
Rutland, VT 05701

Geoff Lynch [Dat & Analog]
8 Four Winds Road
Setauket, NY 11733

Aaron Mandleman [Analog]
2123 N 68TH Street
Wauwatosa, WI 53213

Greg Marceau [Analog]
109 Elm Street
Pepperell, Ma 01463

Chad Mars [Analog]
102 Rockinham Cr
Ridgeland, MS 89157

Bryan McCraner [Analog]
1266 Peavy Rd.
Howell, MI 48843

John McMeeking [Analog]
127 Great Pond Road
Simsbury, CT 06070

Scott Mele [Dat & Analog]
3080 Meadow Drive
Marietta, Ga 30062

Shawn Miller [Analog]
13654 Sycamore
Olathe, KS 66062
sdm1931@ksu.edu

Chrisopher Mills [Analog]
60 Oakwood Ave.
Farmingdale, NY 11735

Melissa Mixer [Analog]
5 Viles Court
Waltham, MA 02154

Chris Mrachek [Analog]
3413 9th Ave NW
Rochester, MN 55901

Jason Mokhtarian [Analog]
1135 King Charles Ct.
Palatine, IL 60067

Matthew Napoli [Analog]
55 Newark Street
Hoboken NJ 07030

Brendan Neagle [Analog]
Box 4446 Brown
Providence RI 02912
brendan_neagle@brown.edu

Kyle Niday [Dat & Analog]
712 52nd Street
West Des Moines, IA 50265

Trevor Norris [Analog]
8198 West 7th Ave
Pine Bluff, AR 71603
tnorris@webtv.net

Dave O'Connor [Analog]
32 Fuller Ave.
Tonawada, NY 14150

David Okimoto [Dat & Analog]
5108 W. Winona
Chicago, IL 60630

Daniel Paden [Analog]
312 Riverside Drive
Johnson City, NY 13790
padenp@maple.lemoyne.edu

Dave Parker [Analog]
510 w. scott street Apt. 4
Springfield, Mo 65802

Phil Perpich [Analog]
7753 W North Ave
River Forest, IL 60305

Michael Rambo [Analog]
305 Broad Street
Paulsboro, NJ 08066

Chris Regan [Analog]
18 Old Farm Road
Milton, MA 02186

Matt Richardson [Analog]
107 Pleasant Street
Warwick, RI 02886
fraggle99@aol.com

Rob Rimer [Dat & Analog]
48 Blueberry Lane
Hicksville, NY 11801

Adam Rizzuti [Dat & Analog]
6 Hunt Farm
Waccabus, NY 10597

Ben Ross [Analog]
5318 W. 100th Street
Overland Park, KS 66207

Craig Rothenberg [Dat & Analog]
20 Cooperhawk Drive
Manalpan, NJ 07726

Adam Satz [Analog]
215 South Mason Road
St. Louis, Mo 63141
sauktonoua@aol.com

Eric Segonia [Analog]
1125 Grandview
Boulder, CO 80303

Paul Sheets [Analog]
516 1/2 East Front Street Apt#7
Traverse City, MI 49686

Phil Shipos [Dat & Analog]
109 Althea Ave.
Morrisville, PA 19067

Sean Smith [Analog]
1205 College Ave. Apt.B
Boulder, CO 80302
Staggerlee1@juno.com

Nick Soricelli [Analog]
165 Horton Hill Rd.
Naugtuck, CT 06770

Joseph South [Analog]
597 Howards creek Road #H
Boone, NC 28607

Dave Swank [Dat & Analog]
3519 Helen Ave.
Ypsilanti, MI 48197
swankda1@pilot.masu.edu

Bob Talatzko [Dat & Analog]
2019 N86TH Street
Wauwatosa, WI 53226

William Thurston [Analog]
300 W. 14TH Street
Lawrence, KS 66044

Phil Valle [Analog]
1351 Friendensburg Road
Reading, PA,19606

Jen Verdon [Dat & Analog]
30 Romland Street
Ballston, NY 12020
jenphish@prodigy.com

Kevin M. Ward [Analog]
1480 Manchester Rd.
Erie, Pa 16505

Terry Watts [Dat & Analog]
3113 Commonwealth Ave.
Charlotte, NC 28205

Mike Wehling [Analog]
1514 Wells Ave.
Webster, MO 63119

Seth Weinglass [Analog]
296 Summit Rd.
Mountainside, NJ 07092

Justin Weiss [Analog]
2426B Blackberry Lane
Fayeteville, AR 72703

Daryl Whitcraft [Dat & Analog]
Kings Hywy and Lenola Rd.
Moorstown, NJ 08057

David White [Analog]
580 Potomac Ave.
Buffalo, NY 14222

The Almanac Setlist Team, and Setlist Notes

Setlist Team and New Setlists

Volume 4 Setlist Team (with Honors). The following people offered numerous setlist corrections and clarifications, and in some cases sent us tapes to help verify setlists. Many, many thanks to: Katie McConnell, AJ Fucile, Otis from New York, John Nalbone, Adam Rizzuti, Brian Gressler, Ryan Hersch, Dave Schall, Pat Eagle, Howie Kopman, Don and the guys at Prime Cuts in Rockville Center NY, Tim King, Michael Shtadthender, and David Stockbridge.

Volume 4 Setlist Team. These amazing folks offered setlist corrections and clarifications for Volume 4: Chuck Adams, Jeff Bergman, Chris Bertelsen, Brian Boehm, Rev. Darrin Barschdorf, Lee Boykoff, Raph Branca, Kevin Cassells, David Clement, Sam Cobb, Joey Conroy, Jamis Curran, Brian Daly, Adam Davidoff, Jeff Davis, Jason Deziel, Benjy Eisen, Steve Eisenhauer, KC Fisher, Brian Gressler, Bill Hance, Eli Hall, Andrew Hayward, Will Herrmann, Gorey Hiles, Tony Hume, Ivan James, Pete Jones, Andy Kahn, Brian Levine, Rob Livingston, Stephen Mortlock, Mike Noll, Tom Pinnick, Andrew Potter, Todd Prusin, Mike Railey, Padraic Swanton, Adam Rizzuti, Chad Redford, Peter Rocco, Greg Roth, Mike S., Lee Schaffler, Chad Shaw, Paul Sheets, Tom Smith, Paul Smiths, Padraic Swanton, Gabe Tafoya, Rob Thorne, Tinsley, Mike Waselus, Wayne, Kevin Weise, Greg Weiss, Mike Youngling, Nick Z., and others whose names we don't have. You know who you are.

They join the **Volume 3 Setlist Team** (some making a repeat appearance): Brian Carrigan, James Dunnican, Dan Freeman, AJ Fucile, Gibbee, Dan Goldstein, Eli Hall, Haney Jones, Colin Malek, Nancy, Dan O'Brien, Mark Pfister, Mike Railey, Len Stubbe Jr., Bob Talatzko, Greg Vedder, Katy Yaeland, Ross W. Yarroll, the crew at Prime Cuts, Dennis at Scarlet Begonias, and the many folks who have left information on our voicemail. Because of the incredible efforts of all these people, the Phish community is better informed. A huge thank-you to you all!

Dates of new setlists included in Volume 4: 3/11/87, 4/24/87, 11/19/87 III, 3/11/88, 3/31/88, 5/19/88, 9/8/88, 9/13/88, 11/11/88 I, 2/18/89, 3/4/89, 4/14/89, 5/21/89, 5/27/89, 8/17/89, 6/23/89 II&E, 8/23/89 II, 9/21/89, 11/3/89, 12/29/89, 2/17/90, 3/17/90 II, 3/28/90, 4/4/90, 4/8/90, 4/9/90 II, 4/12/90 I, 4/13/90, 4/20/90, 5/15/90 I, 6/1/90, 6/8/90 I, 9/15/90, 10/1/90, 10/4/90 I, 10/5/90, 12/1/90 I, 2/2/91, 2/26/91 II&E, 3/6/91, 4/6/91 I, 4/18/91 II&E, 4/26/91, 5/11/91, 5/25/91 II&E, 9/29/91, 10/27/91, 4/13/94 (radio show), and everything since 8/17/96.

New show dates, without setlists: 8/22/87, 9/3/87, 4/2/88, 3/25/89, 3/31/89, 4/1/89, 4/2/89, 4/7/89, 4/13/89, 4/19/89, 4/21-22/89, 4/27/89, 4/28/89, 4/29/89, 5/1/89, 5/3/89, 5/7/89, 5/8/89, 5/11/89, 5/12/89, 5/18/89, 5/19/89, 6/3/89, 6/7/89, 6/10/89, 6/16-17/89, 8/11/89, 8/13/89, 8/18/89, 8/23/89, 8/25/89, 9/2/89, 9/7/89, 9/8/89, 10/12/89, 10/13/89, 11/18/89, 12/3/89, 12/4/89, 12/6/89, 1/25/90, 1/26/90, 1/29/90, 2/1/90, 2/2/90, 2/3/90, 2/4/90, 2/5/90, 2/7/90, 2/16/90, 2/19/90, 4/10/90, 4/19/90, 4/21/90, 5/9/91.

Redated setlists: 1/30/88 (was 1/27/88); 8/27/88 (was Penn State '86); 5/31/90 (was 5/31/89).

Removed setlists: 3/20/88 (actually part of 5/9/89); 10/31/88 (actually part of 10/29/88); 3/17/89 (actually part of 7/23/88).

Setlists having undergone major revisions (the addition or deletion of at least one song): 12/1/84, 5/3/85, 10/30/85, 4/15/86, 10/31/86, 12/6/86, 8/21/87, 5/25/88, 7/23/88, 8/3/88, 8/6/88, 10/29/88, 11/11/88, 2/7/89, 3/3/89, 5/6/89, 4/15/89, 8/17/89, 8/19/89, 10/7/89, 10/21/89, 10/31/89, 11/2/89, 12/7/89, 12/8/89, 3/1/90, 3/7/90, 5/13/90, 6/17/90, 9/28/90, 11/4/90, 11/26/90, 2/7/91, 4/20/91, 7/25/91, 7/26/91, 10/28/91, 11/7/91, 5/3/92, 7/27/92, 11/23/92, 12/2/92, 12/11/92, 2/7/93, 2/11/93, 2/13/93, 3/5/93, 3/26/93, 3/28/93, 4/5/93, 4/14/93, 4/28/93, 4/29/93, 5/4/94, 5/7/94, 6/18/94, 10/9/94, 10/20/94, 11/18/94, and 7/21/96.

Hundreds of other setlists have undergone minor revisions, including new song orders, segues, nitty gritty additions and venue name changes for Volume 4. These are not noted separately due to space considerations.

Notes on Setlists and Nitty-Gritty

Segues. The Almanac policy on including segue notation (>) between songs in a setlist is to use an arrow any time there's no discernable pause between one song and the next. Segue corrections and additions are always welcomed.

Debuts. Concert debuts are noted in the nitty gritty starting in 1989. Of course, the "unofficial" debut dates of earlier songs can easily be figured by referencing the All The Songs section, which begins on page 223.

Last Since. Any time Phish went more than 50 shows without playing a song, the lapse—listed by total number of shows—is noted when it is finally played again.

Teases and Jams. In the nitty-gritty, we've listed some of the many times Phish has included tease or jams of other song within the song they're playing, such as "Immigrant Song jam in YEM" or "Auld Lang Syne tease in Ya Mar." Roughly speaking, we define a "tease" as a quick reference of a song, maybe a few bars played by one band member. A "jam" is a longer, more developed take which usually includes several band members. We'd love to hear from Almanac readers who have identified additional teases or jams on their Phish tapes.

Phish Jams. We've limited the use of the word "Jam" in the actual setlists for Volume 4. Because so many Phish songs include long jams, it seemed too arbitrary to assign a particular song a jam notation like Mike's > Jam > Weekapaug. "Jam" is used when Phish leaves one song completely behind, never to return, and embarks on a theme with no specific name.

Digital Delay Loop. Notation of the "digital delay loop" (known to some as "Trey's Big-Show Energy Jam") has been added to the nitty-gritty for Volume 4. Examples of this effect include the Bowie intro on 12/29/94 and the end of Mike's on 12/31/95.

Fish's Instruments. We've attempted to document every time Fish has played an instrument like the vacuum or trombone in the nitty-gritty. Separate notation is not made for versions of Cracklin' Rosie, which have all featured Fishman on cymbals. We've also added listings of the "HYHU" (Hold Your Head Up) and "Cold as Ice" intros for Fishman songs in the setlists.

Phan Picks. A special "Phan Picks" logo accompanies the setlists to denote each of the top 25 shows of all-time, as identified by Almanac readers in our Readers Survey.

Bracketed Shows. Show dates that appear in brackets, such as [3/5/97], are not considered actual "concerts," so songs played in them are not included in the All The Songs section.

Accessibility Ratings Guidelines. Next to the date of a show is a bracketed accessibility rating of how hard or easy it is to track down tapes of that show. We surveyed 50 tapes lists for our totally updated ratings:

❄ *So rare it's raw*, not appearing on any of the tape lists. Only shows from 1991 and before can get this rating.

• *Rare*. The tape appeared on only one of the tapelists (from 1991 or before) or on one or zero tapelists if it's from 1992. This rating is not given to any show from 1993 on.

•• *Medium rare*. Two to five lists claimed this one during 1992 or before. No more than three from 1993 on. A nice find.

••• *Medium*. Six to nine tapers had it on their lists. You may have to ask around to find this one, but it's definitely out there.

•••• *Well Done*. 10 to 25 tapers claimed this one. An easy find for anyone as long as you know more than a few tapers.

••••• *Singed to a crisp*. More than half the tapelists had this show. If you can't find it, you're just not looking in the right place.

The Top 25 Tapes, and Some Choice Picks

The Phan 25

The results of our Volume 3 readers survey yielded the "Phan 25," a rating of the best Phish shows of all-time. Responses were received by the Almanac between December 1, 1996 and May 1, 1997.

1) 12/31/95 New York, NY
2) 10/31/94 Glens Falls, NY
3) 02/20/93 Atlanta, GA
4) 08/16/96 Plattsburgh, NY
5) 05/07/94 Dallas, TX
6) 12/30/93 Portland, ME
7) 12/06/96 Las Vegas, NV
8) 07/16/94 Fayston, VT
9) 07/21/91 Parksville, NY (with horns)
10) 10/31/96 Atlanta, GA
11) 10/31/95 Chicago, IL
12) 08/17/96 Plattsburgh, NY
13) 12/31/96 Boston, MA
14) 03/13/92 Providence, RI
15) 12/30/95 New York, NY
16) 08/21/87 Hebron, NY
17) 12/29/95 Worcester, MA
18) 07/25/92 Stowe, VT (with Santana)
19) 03/22/93 Sacramento, CA
20) 12/01/84 Burlington, VT
21) 12/31/93 Worcester, MA
22) 08/20/93 Morrison, CO
23) 06/26/94 Charleston, WV
24) 05/25/88 Burlington, VT
25) 04/16/92 Santa Barbara, CA

The 25 Most-Circulated Tapes

During the compilation of the tape accessibility ratings for Volume 4, we tabulated the 25 most-circulated Phish tapes. The number in the right column is the percentage of tape lists that claimed that show.

1) 10/31/94	Glens Falls, NY	85%
2) 04/16/92	Santa Barbara, CA	75%
2) 10/31/95	Chicago, IL	75%
4) 12/31/93	Worcester, MA	70%
5) 07/21/91	Parksville, NY	68%
5) 12/31/95	New York, NY	68%
5) 08/16/96	Plattsburgh, NY	68%
5) 08/17/96	Plattsburgh, NY	68%
9) 07/25/92	Stowe, VT	60%
9) 02/20/93	Atlanta, GA	60%
11) 03/22/93	Sacramento, CA	58%
11) 12/30/95	New York, NY	58%
13) 08/21/87	Hebron, NY	55%
13) 08/03/91	Auburn, ME	55%
13) 03/13/92	Providence, RI	55%
13) 12/30/93	Portland, ME	55%
13) 05/07/94	Dallas, TX	55%
18) 08/20/93	Morrison, CO	53%
19) 03/12/88	Burlington, VT	50%
19) 10/20/89	Burlington, VT	50%
19) 10/31/96	Atlanta, GA	50%
22) 06/11/94	Morrison, CO	48%
22) 12/31/94	Boston, MA	48%
22) 06/06/96	Woodstock, NY	48%
25) 12/1/84, 11/4/90, 7/2/95, 12/29/95		45%

The Scoop on Soundboards

Soundman Paul Languedoc decided to end soundboard patches to most tapers after 6/16/90 because it was becoming too difficult for him to manage at shows; he was also apparently exasperated that some tapers were abusing the privilege by pulling cables out of the soundboard and plugging their decks in without asking his permission. A few long-time tapers continued to patch into the soundboard through most of 1991; the practice was all but halted by the end of that fall.

During contract negotiations with Elektra Records in 1991, the taping privilege proved to be a bit of a sticking point, but the band insisted that their contract stipulate that fans could continue to record Phish shows. By spring tour 1993, though, increasing venue sizes made it hard to manage the proliferation of tapers. The band and its management hoped to implement a designated tapers' section for summer tour 1993 but it proved too hard to organize on short notice with Ticketmaster. So mailorder ticketing for reserved seating shows debuted on the '93 New Year's Run, and has continued every tour since.

Finding soundboards from 1992 isn't tough—except for some Santana tour sets. By 1993, soundboards were released less liberally, as the band began a policy of distributing top shows to the Phish.Net on soundboard for dispersal by tape trees. Releases included 3/22/93 Sacramento, 8/20/93 Red Rocks and 12/30/93 Portland. The only show in 1994 released to the Net was the second set of Dallas, 5/7/94, which went through a cassette generation—designated as cDSBD, meaning it was originally recorded on DAT, then transferred to cassette, then back to DAT—as did the '93 boards. Apparently the distribution of the Dallas board irked one band member, and the official soundboard releases stopped. However, a number of SBDs from 1994 still made it into general circulation.

In a break with policy, Paul gave soundboard patches to the three tapers who made it to the Joyous Lake show on 6/6/96, and DSBDs were also unofficially released for 8/16/96 and 8/17/96 following the Clifford Ball. Combined with frequent radio broadcasts, including 12/31/96 and the Great Went shows, there are a handful of exceptional-quality tapes from recent years that are out there for the finding.

Kevin's Picks

Phish archivist Kevin Shapiro has a job to envy—listening to Phish tapes! The fruits of some of his efforts have been heard over Phish's radio stations at both the Clifford Ball and the Great Went, as he presented three "from the archives" shows.

Tapes of these shows—all gorgeous soundboard quality—are now in circulation among fans. Find 'em, and enjoy!

Clifford Ball Archives Show [8/15/96]: Brother (3/24/92 Richmond, VA), Catapult > Simple > Icculus (6/22/94 Columbus, OH), Setting Sail (7/15/94 Jones Beach, NY), Frankenstein (6/23/94 Pontiac, MI), Ride Captain Ride (12/12/92 Toronto, ON), Big Ball Jam, Split Open and Melt > Buffalo Bill > Makisupa (10/29/94 Spartanburg, SC), Cities (7/5/94 Ottowa, ON), PYITE (3/26/93 San Francisco, CA), Bathtub Gin > Ya Mar (8/13/93 Indianapolis, IN), Funky Bitch (2/19/93 Atlanta, GA), Curtis Loew (2/9/90 Lancaster, PA), Landlady > Destiny Unbound (11/1/91 Denver, CO), Bowie > Timber Ho > Bowie (12/30/92, Springfield, MA), Magilla (7/14/91 Townshend, VT with Horns), Tube (6/26/94 Charleston, WV), Alumni Blues > Light Up or Leave Me Alone (5/25/88 Burlington, VT). *[Thanks to Paul Sheets]*.

Great Went Archives Show 1 [8/15/97]: Bathtub Gin (8/16/96 Plattsburgh, NY), Halley's Comet > Alumni Blues (8/17/89 Burlington, VT, Halley's comet with Nancy Taube on vocals), Spock's Brain, (5/16/95 Lowell, MA), Reba (5/16/95 Lowell, MA), Fixin' to Die (11/19/94 soundcheck, Bloomington, IN), Dog Log (10/14/95 soundcheck, Austin, TX), Swing Low Sweet Chariot (8/29/87 Shelburne, VT), The Curtain With (8/29/87 Shelburne, VT), Rhombus narration > Divided Sky (11/15/91 Charlottesville, VA), Camel Walk (7/25/88 Burlington, VT), Harry Hood (4/18/92 Palo Alto, CA).

Great Went Archives Show 2 [8/16/97]: Carini (3/1/97 Hamburg, Germany), Tela (8/27/88 Penn State), Eliza (11/8/90 soundcheck, Madison, WI), Taste (11/30/96 Sacramento, CA; with Peter Apfelbaum), Hurricane (11/19/85 Burlington, VT; Bob Dylan cover, acoustic), Mike's Song > Simple > Mike's Song > I am Hydrogen > Weekapaug (6/17/94 Milwaukee, WI, the "OJ Show"), Shaggy Dog (10/31/86 Plainfield, VT), Fluffhead (10/31/86 Plainfield, VT), You Enjoy Myself (5/5/93 Albany, NY with Col. Bruce Hampton and the Aquarium Rescue Unit, and the Dude of Life).

A Taping How-To

You see them at shows, identifiable by the tall metal towers that sprout 20 feet into the air. They're the tapers, and most of them have live concert recording collections that would make your jaw drop. But let's say you're just starting to build your Phish tape collection. Here are a few things it might be helpful to know.

Taping Nuances. Tapes are either labeled SBD (for a soundboard recording; DSBD for a digital soundboard recording) or AUD (for audience recording; DAUD for a digital audience recording). Soundboard recordings come directly from the house sound, and although the sound quality is usually superior to that of audience recordings, certain instruments may sound too high or low depending on how the sound was mixed for the venue. Audience tapes are made by tapers who set up microphones at shows and capture the sound in the venue, resulting in more crowd noise and sometimes a "fuller" sound.

Many tapers record on DAT (Digital Audio Tape), but dub their DATs to analog tapes to enjoy the music in cassette decks. What makes DATs so great, besides the fact that they can record up to three hours of consecutive music on one tape with no cuts, is that they can be digitally cloned with no generational loss of tape quality. With cassette tapes, as soon as you start making copies, you face generational loss—the hiss that gets introduced as tapes are passed along. This is why analog tape collectors label the generations of their tapes; a copy of a first-generation analog tape would be 2nd gen, a copy of a 2nd gen would be 3rd gen, and so on. Generally, the lower the generation number, the better the quality.

The tape's source also affects quality, obviously. Many people swear by soundboards, but Phish hasn't officially allowed tapers to patch directly into the soundboard since the summer of 1990. A good number of soundboard tapes still make it into general circulation [see "the scoop on soundboards" on the previous page].

According to some tapers, a good audience recording can better recreate the illusion of "being there" than a soundboard can. Recordings made from in front of the soundboard ("FOB") sound best, but Phish asks tapers not to record from anywhere except the tapers' section ("TS"), so FOB tapes can be hard to come by. Most tapers will mark the type of microphones used to record shows—AKGs, B&Ks, Schoeps, and Neumanns are particularly good-sounding brands (again, generally speaking).

Starting a Collection. The best way to start a tape collection is to find a friend (or a friend of a friend) with a cache of tapes that you can raid. Once you've got a good base, you can hit the Internet and set up tape trades with others. Don't ever pay more than the price of blank tapes and postage for a tape of a show.

Another method is to ask tapers at shows to make you a copy of that night's show. If you want to go this route, there are a few points of etiquette: Put tapes—be on the safe side: use 100 minute ones—in a padded mailer, address it to yourself, and include the correct postage on the mailer. At the show, approach tapers with tact. Before the show, they'll be busy setting up and don't want to be disturbed, so it's often better to ask at setbreak or after the show. If you find a taper nice enough to take your envelope, you can reciprocate with a drink or equivalent thank-you. Then, be prepared to wait—for tapers who do a lot of trading, it can take a while to make copies.

Making Tapes. It's best if you have a three-head cassette deck to make copies—set the levels to peak at about +3, and have the levels hover between -4 to +2 otherwise. Dubbing decks are okay, but you can't set levels with them, and under no circumstances should you use high-speed dubbing to make copies (it really reduces the quality). Also, clean and demagnetize your decks religiously—cleaners and demagnetizers cost only a few bucks, and will hugely improve the quality of your recordings.

Song Title Abbreviations in the Setlists

This edition of the Almanac has contracted many song names as they appear in the setlist section for ease-of-reading. The left-hand column below is the song name as it appears in the setlist section, and the right-hand column is the real name of the song.

Abbreviation	Song
A-Train	Take the A-Train
Adeline	Sweet Adeline
All Things	All Things Reconsidered
Also Sprach	Also Sprach Zarathustra (a.k.a. 2001)
Alumni	Alumni Blues
Antelope	Run Like an Antelope
Avenu	Avenu Malkenu
BBJ	Big Ball Jam
BBFCM	Big Black Furry Creature From Mars
Bouncing	Bouncing Around the Room
Bowie	David Bowie
Brain	If I Only Had a Brain
Carini	Carini Had a Lumpy Head
Caspian	Prince Caspian
CTB	Cars Trucks Buses
Chalkdust	Chalk Dust Torture
Do It in the Road	Why Don't We Do It in the Road
FEFY	Fast Enough For You
Forbin's	Colonel Forbin's Ascent
Golgi	Golgi Apparatus
Great Gig	Great Gig in the Sky
GTBT	Good Times Bad Times
Guelah	Guelah Papyrus
Guitar Gently Weeps	While My Guitar Gently Weeps
Halley's	Halley's Comet
Hydrogen	I am Hydrogen
Jesus Left Chicago	Jesus Just Left Chicago
Jimmy Page	Letter to Jimmy Page
Makisupa	Makisupa Policeman
Mango	The Mango Song
McGrupp	McGrupp and the Watchful Hosemasters
Mike's	Mike's Song
Melt	Split Open and Melt
Mockingbird	Fly Famous Mockingbird
MSO	My Sweet One
My Friend	My Friend My Friend
My Mind's	My Mind's Got a Mind of Its Own
No Good Trying	It's No Good Trying
Oh Kee	Oh Kee Pa
Peaches	Peaches En Regalia
PYITE	Punch You in the Eye
Sample	Sample in a Jar
Silent	Silent in the Morning
Slave	Slave to the Traffic Light
Sneaking Sally	Sneaking Sally Through the Alley
Suzie	Suzie Greenberg
Theme	Theme From the Bottom
Timber Ho	Timber (Jerry)
TMWSIY	The Man Who Stepped Into Yesterday
Weekapaug	Weekapaug Groove
Wolfman's	Wolfman's Brother
YEM	You Enjoy Myself
Yerushalyaim	Yerushalayim Schel Zahav

In addition, several song titles have been changed from the last Almanac: *I'm Blue I'm Lonesome* (formerly Blue and Lonesome); *Long Journey Home* (formerly Two Dollar Bill); and *Hello My Baby* (formerly Ragtime Gal).

1983-1988 *THE EARLY YEARS*

In the formative years of the band, Phish played in and around Burlington as much as they could, often two or three times a week, and maintained a weekly stand at Nectar's before graduating to the Front in the fall of 1988. None of the shows from 1983 presently circulate, and the band went on hiatus during the spring of 1984 due to Trey's suspension from UVM. The 12/1/84 Nectar's show is the earliest Phish show fans will probably ever get to hear, though tapes apparently exist for the band's second show ever, in the Slade Hall basement.

During these early years, the band didn't have a tape deck rolling at most of their shows, so setlists and tapes this era represent only a small portion of the shows which actually occurred. There are most likely hundreds of missing setlists for every one setlist included herein. Tapes from this era largely exist because of tapers who recorded Phish shows and copied the tapes for their friends. In the days before the tapers' section became a bevy of Phish experts intent on capturing every stray note in its pure digital glory, though, tapers would commit such foul acts as not recording songs they didn't like or leaving a show partway through the band's set.

1983

[10/30/83] Show not taped
ROTC Halloween Dance, University of Vermont, Burlington, VT
Heard It Through The Grapevine, Long Cool Woman in a Black Dress

The famous "first show." The band claims its performance was so poor that when Phish took a break the event organizers put Michael Jackson on over the PA, so Phish cut their performance short. Setlist is incomplete and probably inaccurate.

1984

12/1/84 [ACCESSIBILITY: ••••]
Nectar's, Burlington, VT
Scarlet Begonias > Fire > Fire on the Mountain, Slave > Makisupa, Spanish Flea, Don't Want You No More > Cities, Skippy, Fluffhead
E: Eyes of the World

The Dude of Life on vocals for Skippy and Fluffhead. Marc Daubert plays percussion; he was a member of Phish at this point.

Phan Pick #20 ➢ This historic show is the first "official" Phish gig upstairs at Nectar's, without Page McConnell but with original band member Jeff Holdsworth on rhythm guitar. Things start off Dead, with an excellent cover of Scarlet busting into a zippy Fire and then into Fire on the Mountain (!). During an amusing Makisupa, Trey sings of how Jeff and Fishman's musical abilities are enhanced when they "go backstage and smoke a little herb." There's a garage-sounding, premature Slave as well as a cover of Herb Alpert's Spanish Flea, during which the Dude of Life introduces the band. Though their musical skills aren't as finely honed, this is interesting to hear. —RYAN HERSCH

➢ This was the first live tape I heard of Phish. Being a "big Deadhead," I thoroughly enjoyed Scarlet > Fire > Fire. It shows Phish's humor about music, which I have since found turns some people off. Still, I enjoy this. I like hearing the early roots of the band, and this tape is one of the best examples of that.—KYLE NIDAY

➢ Mike sounds phat n' phunky, but Trey doesn't sound like himself on Scarlet Begonias (more like you-know-who…). Slave is pretty rough. It's just not the same without Page. This tape is definitely worth getting, if only for nostalgia. Everything sounds ancient, but you can also hear the beginnings of something very phresh… —ANDREW MITCHELL

1980s

157 Total Show Dates
- **29** one-set shows
- **69** two-set shows
- **17** three-set shows
- **42** dates with no setlists

PHAN PICKS 1980s

SHOW	THE SKINNY
1) **08/21/87 Hebron, NY**	Phish at their early best.
2) 12/01/84 Nectar's	First Nectar's gig; w/the Dude.
3) 05/25/88 Nectar's	Great WPost, Ya Mar w/Jah Roy.
4) 05/28/89 Hebron, NY	Best musical show of the '80s?
5) 09/24/88 Amherst, MA	Full Moon at the Zoo II.
6) 03/12/88 Nectar's	First live Gamehendge.
7) 08/27/88 Penn State, PA	Awesome Tela with long jam.
8) 05/15/88 Underhill, VT	Fun on the Pharm.
9) 10/20/89 Nectar's	Horns sit in for Melt & more.
10) 12/06/86 Shelburne, VT	Lots of rarities.

MUSICAL RECAP: The 1980s saw Phish traverse the wide range of styles that would become their hallmark, from rock to jazz to reggae and bluegrass. One of the pleasures of listening to older tapes is the looser, more wide-open jam style; unlike the focused jams of the early 1990s, the 1980s saw plenty of jam-happy sets.
REPRESENTATIVE JAMS: Whipping Post, 5/25/88; David Bowie, 10/31/86; Mike's Song > I am Hydrogen > Weekapaug Groove, 5/28/89.

DARK HORSES

SHOW	THE SKINNY
1) **04/01/86 Plainfield, VT**	Help > Slip > AC/DC Bag
2) 01/30/88 Waitsfield, VT	Very well-played early show.
3) 03/04/89 New York, NY	First Phish show at Wetlands.
4) 04/20/89 Amherst, MA	Full Moon at the Zoo III
5) 10/31/89 Plainfield, VT	Last Goddard Halloween show.

Most-Played Originals:

Song	Times	%
1) You Enjoy Myself	76	48%
2) AC/DC Bag	66	42%
3) Golgi Apparatus	62	39%
4) Possum	60	36%
5) Lizards	50	32%
6) Alumni Blues	49	31%
7) Fluffhead	48	31%
8) Mike's Song	47	30%
9) Antelope	44	28%
9) Divided Sky	44	28%

Most-Played Covers:

Song	Times	%
1) GTBT	39	25%
2) Take the A Train	37	24%
3) Peaches En Regalia	34	22%
3) Walk Away	34	17%
5) Ya Mar	27	17%
6) Fire	26	16%
7) Funky Bitch	25	16%
8) La Grange	24	15%
9) Bold As Love	23	15%
10) Sneaking Sally	18	12%

First-Set Openers:

Song	Times
1) Golgi Apparatus	36
2) AC/DC Bag	8
3) I Didn't Know	6
4) Mike's Song, Oh Kee Pa, Funky Bitch	4

Second-Set Openers:

Song	Times
1) Mike's Song	6
2) David Bowie	5
3) Alumni Blues	3
3) AC/DC Bag	3
3) Oh Kee Pa	3

Nectar's: 12/1/84 Upstairs at Nectar's, Burlington, VT

There are several places to turn when talking about Phish's first show. There's the infamous ROTC Dance in October '83, and the Slade Hall gig a few days later—neither played under the "Phish" name, and neither in circulation in the taping community.

Maybe that's why so many phans turn to Phish's show at Nectar's on December 1, 1984, as Phish's "first" show. It was, apparently, the first played under the Phish name, and it marked the grand return of a band that had nearly broken up after Trey left UVM for the spring of '84 after his prank came back to haunt him. It's also the earliest-known Phish tape in general circulation, and their first show at Nectar's.

The funny thing is, the show wasn't really at Nectar's—at least, not the part of Nectar's where Phish would play so many shows in the 1985-1988 era. No, their first Nectar's gig was in the upstairs space, a smaller room than even the downstairs (which itself holds only 150 to 200 people). Nevertheless, the fact that they were given a slot at all was notable—as the band noted in the liner notes to *Picture Of Nectar*, they'd didn't have a song list long enough to fill two sets. But Nectar gave them a shot, and the boys (then comprised of Marc Daubert on percussion and Jeff Holdsworth on rhythm guitar, with Page still about six months away from his Phish debut) took it and ran with it. Almost a decade later, *PON* would be dedicated to Nectar as the band's official "thank you."

Their set showed a lot of early influences, like the Dead and Hendrix, but in a way that made their sense of humor about the music abundantly clear—who would ever conceive of a Scarlet > Fire > Fire run? And of course the show featured The Dude of Life on vocals for two tunes he penned the lyrics to, Fluffhead and Skippy (which would later be stripped of its music for use in McGrupp). The performance was raw, but the passion—even way back then—was evident. They had taken the first step.

1985

3/4/85 [ACCESSIBILITY: ••]
Hunt's, Burlington, VT
Anarchy, Camel Walk, Fire Up The Ganja, Skippy, Midnight Hour
African hunger relief benefit. Fire Up The Ganja featured members of Lamb's Bread.

5/3/85 [ACCESSIBILITY: •••]
Springfest, Goddard College, Plainfield, VT
Scarlet Begonias > Eyes of the World > Whipping Post > McGrupp > Makisupa > Antelope Jam > Other One **E:** Anarchy
Includes Page McConnell sitting in; he was not a member of Phish at this point.

➢ Page's first show. I have it on one tape that includes Scarlet Begonias into Eyes of the World, showing some major Jerry-fluence. Then comes the 25-minute Whipping Post. Oh my God—you gotta hear it to believe it! Next up is McGrupp, more spoken than played, then Makisupa and a jam that would later form into Antelope. This awesome show ends with The Other One. Man, for 1985, you gotta be kidding me! —ALEX BANKS

➢ One of the finest early Phish shows, this one circulates also as 5/19/85. Whatever the date is, it's a lot of fun to hear Page's debut with the band. He's an obvious fit, though his contributions are obviously less pronounced than in later years (hey, whattya expect from a guest?) Soon after this gig, he talked his way into history. —AL HUNT

10/17/85 [ACCESSIBILITY: ••••]
Finbar's, Burlington, VT
Star Trek Jam, Alumni > Jimmy Page > Alumni, Mike's, Dave's Energy Guide, Revolution > Anarchy, Camel Walk, Antelope, McGrupp

10/30/85 [ACCESSIBILITY: •••]
Hunt's, Burlington, VT
Harry Hood, Dog Log, Possum, Slave, Sneaking Sally, I Wish, Revival, Alumni > Jimmy Page > Alumni, Prep School Hippie, Skippy

➢ Mike is truly at his best. The bass throughout the show is direct and hard-driving. Harry Hood (the first one that exists on tape) is Mike and perfection intertwined. Prep School Hippie is always great to hear; Sneaking Sally gets weird; and the Alumni into Letter to Jimmy Page back to Alumni is an outstanding choice for breaking loose in an early show. Really, the whole show is a great part of early Phishtory. —ANDY KAHN

11/23/85 ❄
Goddard College Cafeteria, Goddard College, Plainfield, VT
Mike's > Whipping Post > Antelope > Dave's Energy Guide

1986

[1/2/86]
Penn State University, State College, PA
Tapes that circulate with this date or "Penn State '86" are apparently from 8/27/88.

4/1/86 [ACCESSIBILITY: ••]
Festival Of Fools, Goddard College, Plainfield, VT
I: Quinn the Eskimo, Have Mercy > Harry Hood, Pendulum, Bob Dylan Band Jam, Icculus, YEM
II: Help on the Way > Slipknot! > AC/DC Bag, McGrupp > Alumni > Jimmy Page > Alumni, Dear Mrs. Reagan
E: Not Fade Away
Phish shared the bill with The Joneses; each band played two sets. Members of the Joneses play on NFA.

➢ Phish sounded very young and inexperienced in 1986 compared to today, as well as different because of the two guitars (Trey and Jeff). Being a Deadhead, I like to hear the Help > Slip cover. YEM sounds great in its beginning stage but is not the powerhouse it is today. This sounds like it was a great fun festival. —ERIC HIGEL

➢ This old gem features Quinn the Eskimo with a nice guitar solo from Trey in the middle jam. Have Mercy has great piano from Page while Fishman keeps the reggae beat nicely. This flows into a very early rendition of Harry Hood, still a little rough in the transitional stages. Pendulum features a guest vocalist—I don't know who it is but he screams the lyrics "There's a war in the east! There's a war in the west! Which side are you on?" as Phish just rocks this song out. The Bob Dylan Band is Trey introducing Phish as the Bob Dylan Band while Phish plays some jazz—nothing too exciting, but kind of funny. Set II features an odd pairing of Help on the Way > Slipknot! > AC/DC Bag. This is pretty cool if you're someone who likes the Dead and Phish. This tape also features early versions of Icculus, YEM and McGrupp. Well worth hearing. —MIKE NOLL

4/15/86 [ACCESSIBILITY: ••]
University of Vermont, Burlington, VT
AC/DC Bag, Dear Mrs. Reagan, Prep School Hippie, Quinn the Eskimo, Slave, Makisupa, Have Mercy, Dog Log, Possum, YEM, Anarchy, Camel Walk, Alumni > Jimmy Page > Alumni

10/15/86 [ACCESSIBILITY: ••]
Hunt's, Burlington, VT
Wilson, Slave, Quinn The Eskimo, Mike's, Have Mercy, Harry Hood, Peaches, Golgi, Swing Low Sweet Chariot, Camel Walk, Shaggy Dog, Mustang Sally, Fluffhead, Sneaking Sally
Paul Languedoc's first show as soundman. Often misdated 4/20/87.

10/31/86 [ACCESSIBILITY: •••]
Sculpture Room, Goddard College, Plainfield, VT
I: Mustang Sally, Camel Walk, Golgi, Slave, Melt The Guns, Dave's Energy Guide, Sneaking Sally, Halley's, Creek Jam, Shaggy Dog, Fluffhead
II: AC/DC Bag, Swing Low Sweet Chariot > Peaches > Bowie, Have Mercy > Harry Hood, Sanity, Skin It Back > Icculus, Alumni > Jimmy Page > Alumni
Jah Roy on vocals for Have Mercy. First of four Phish Halloween shows at Goddard College.

➢ Phish knew how to jam right from their inception. Don't get this tape for the historical value—get it for the performance quality! The Bowie jam is something I'd be glad to hear in concert today, and Jah Roy puts in one of his many notable performances with the boys on the reggae tune Have Mercy. There's also a well-developed Hood, AC/DC Bag with a long intro jam before the current opening kicks in, and, in the comic relief department, Icculus! "This next song is the story of a great, great man," Trey says. "On Halloween, it's always important to remember this man because he was born on Halloween… in 1948… in Ancient Greece." —AMY MANNING

➢ Halloween at Goddard! This was a period of transition, with Jeff having left the band in May and Trey and Fish transferring to Goddard, but their music soars. —ERNIE GREENE

12/6/86 [ACCESSIBILITY: ••••]
The Mead Ranch, Shelburne, VT
Mike's > Little Drummer Boy > Whipping Post, She Caught The Katy, AC/DC Bag, Bowie > Clod > Bowie, YEM, Dog Log, Tush, Sneaking Sally, Prep School Hippie, Jam > Icculus, McGrupp, GTBT, Skin It Back, Cities

➢ This is a great show. For highlights, there's a long, drawn-out Whipping Post, the first Dog Log and some requests—a girl clearly asks if the band knows any Barry Manilow, to which Trey says yes, then whips into Tush by ZZ Top. But the Bowie in the set is quite lackluster, except for the neat Clod that's thrown in. —JON BAHR

➢ What went on before this show? Trey and Mike are all funked out. Mike forgets words, changes words, then just jams out. Not too many people at this show, but the crowd that's there is kind of rude. They keep talking! Is anyone paying attention? Anyway, you have to hear the old-school Phish style on tunes like She Caught the Katy, Dog Log and Tush. —JOSH LETOURNEAU

➢ Even though their music is not nearly as good as it is now, this show is great because you can tell by listening to it how much fun the band is having. Trey can be heard saying that there's a can in the bathroom for donations. Rare treats like Tush and Prep School Hippie make this tape a must-have. —MIKE JETT

1987

3/6/87 [ACCESSIBILITY: •]
Cafeteria, Goddard College, Plainfield, VT
I: Funky Bitch, GTBT, Corrina, Golgi, Quinn The Eskimo, Sneaking Sally
II: Freebird, Harry Hood, Tell Me Something Good, Possum, Free World, Wilson
Ninja Mike Billington on vocals for Freebird. "Happy Birthday" sung before Harry Hood.

➢ This is a fun-packed, funky-filled night of jams. Freebird is done with the coolest guitar trickery I've ever heard. You need to hear their performance of this song. The guy having his birthday must have laughed when Trey sang "Happy Birthday" to him because Trey makes fun of the guy's aging throughout the song. Also, when you hear this tape, you'll hear that everything is sung in a blues theme fashion. —CHAD MARS

3/11/87 [ACCESSIBILITY: •]
Goddard College, Plainfield, VT
Corrina, Golgi, Quinn the Eskimo, Sneakin' Sally, Freebird, Antelope, Flat Fee, YEM, Lushington, Possum, Sneakin' Sally reprise, Peaches, TMWSIY > Avenu > TMWSIY, Makisupa
Makisupa features a special guest on harmonica. All or part of this show may be from 5/11/87.

3/23/87 [ACCESSIBILITY: •]
Nectar's, Burlington, VT
I: Funky Bitch, Mike's, Alumni > Jimmy Page > Alumni, YEM > Sparks > Fluffhead, Peaches, Ride Captain Ride
II: Crimson Jam, Corrina, Why Don't You Love Me, Camel Walk, Golgi, Swing Low Sweet Chariot

4/24/87 [ACCESSIBILITY: •]
Billings Lounge, University of Vermont, Burlington, VT
Golgi, AC/DC Bag, Possum, Fluffhead, YEM, Dave's Energy Guide, Alumni > Jimmy Page > Alumni, Hydrogen, Bowie, Dear Mrs. Reagan, Slave

4/29/87 [ACCESSIBILITY: •••]
Nectar's, Burlington, VT
I: She Caught the Katy, Alumni > Jimmy Page > Alumni, Golgi, Swing Low Sweet Chariot, Fire > Skin It Back > Cities > Fuck Your Face
II: Lushington, Dog Log, Melt The Guns, Dave's Energy Guide, A-Train, Halley's, Quinn the Eskimo
III: Peaches > Fluffhead, GTBT, Anarchy, Makisupa, Antelope, Boogie On Reggae Woman, Timber Ho, Slave, Sparks, Jam, McGrupp, Curtis Loew, Let The Good Times Roll, Hydrogen
Setlist for third set may be incomplete.

➢ A good tape to have to chronicle how far the band has come. But even more important are the rare songs in this show full of hits. The first set contains only a few songs they still play today; most of the rest are extinct, at least for now. A ripping Lushington opens the second set, leading again into a set of almost all extinct songs. The third set is filled with tunes that seem like Phish wanted to play forever because they're classics today. If you get this show, you'll have a good idea about Phish "gems." —BRETT PESSIN

➢ This three-set show contains some real diamonds. Golgi has a funk intro that was later dropped and A-Train has a horn player (who is that?) in honor of Duke Ellington's birthday. There are also many parts of the soon-to-be-epic Fluffhead throughout this show. Lushington contains (2) The Chase. The Fluffhead played includes (1) Fluff's Travels, back into the song, and finally (6) The Arrival, the jam at the end. Finally, I Am Hydrogen eventually jams into (3) Who Do? We Do! Add another '80s tape with (4) The Clod and (5) Bundle of Joy and you have the whole shebang. —BRENDAN NEAGLE

5/11/87 [ACCESSIBILITY: ••]
Nectar's, Burlington, VT
Golgi, Corrina, Jimmy Page, YEM, Possum, Slave, Sneaking Sally, Clod, Peaches, TMWSIY > Avenu > TMWSIY, Makisupa, Ya Mar

8/9/87 [ACCESSIBILITY: •]
Nectar's, Burlington, VT
I: Fee, Harry Hood, Harpua, Suzie
II: Bowie, YEM, Ya Mar, Divided Sky, Fluffhead, McGrupp, Corrina

8/10/87 [ACCESSIBILITY: •]
Nectar's, Burlington, VT
I: Peaches, Alumni > Jimmy Page > Alumni, Golgi, Wilson, Quinn the Eskimo, Divided Sky, GTBT, Fire, AC/DC Bag, Possum, Fluffhead, Fee, Curtain
II: I Know a Little, Mustang Sally, YEM, La Grange, Icculus, Bowie, Jesus Left Chicago, Whipping Post, Anarchy, Tush, Dear Mrs. Reagan

8/21/87 [ACCESSIBILITY: •••••]
Ian McClain's Farm, Hebron, NY
I: Dog Log, Peaches, Divided Sky, Funky Bitch, Harry Hood, Clod, Curtain, Light Up Or Leave Me Alone, Shaggy Dog, Wilson, Camel Walk
II: Mike's, Harpua > Bundle of Joy > Harpua > Golgi > Sparks, Flat Fee, Fee, Skin It Back > Low Rider/La Bamba/Low Rider > Creek Jam > Sloth
III: BBFCM, McGrupp > Stir It Up > "Mousehouse Rap"/Makisupa jam, Bowie, Sanity, Swing Low Sweet Chariot
Curtain "with" (slow jam at end with music that became Rift). "HYHU" jam in Mike's. Show is often misdated 8/27/87, and the third set circulates as 1/1/87 "Private Party at Page's House."

Phan Pick #15 ➢ The two best Phish shows of the 1980s weren't really shows at all but informal affairs played before friends in Hebron, NY, right near the Vermont border. It's hard to say which show is "better," this show or their gig at Ian's place in May '89, so I won't even try. I really think you ought to hear them both, as they are as "classic" as any Phish tapes you can get your hands on. This show is a little slower and goofier than '89, as was Phish's style back then—I envision Marley and friends romping in the tall grass beneath a late-summer sun while the band weaves a complex tapestry of notes. —MELISSA WOLCOTT

➢ From the scattered barks on the tapes of this show, it sounds like there were more dogs in attendance than people. Appropriately enough, Phish starts off with Dog Log, kicking off the first of three amazing sets. Plenty of highlights here: a scorching Funky Bitch and a Harry Hood with at least five minutes of jamming before the lyrics; The Curtain, featuring the instrumental section that sounds like a slow Rift jam. Harpua is without narration, instead going into Bundle of Joy, back into a Harpua jam, then segueing smoothly into Golgi. Another highlight is a cover of Little Feat's Skin It Back, ending in squealing feedback from Trey that gives way to an amusing Low Rider. —RYAN HERSCH

➢ I have run across several versions of the famous 8/21/87 third set, and all of them have Moosehouse Rap listed before Makisupa. After Stir it Up, Trey yells, "Bass and drums! Bass and drums!" and Mike and Fish start a little reggae groove. Then, Trey spontaneously starts rapping: "You go to the house/See a little mouse/What can I do?/Go see you/Step in doggy-doo/And say pee-hew!" It goes on from there before he starts screaming, "Rasta! Jah!! Rasta is my savior! Jah is my savior!" played to a sort of Makisupa jam. Because it's an isolated incident, I think Moosehouse Rap should be given credit in the setlist for historical significance. —DAVID SCHALL

➢ This is the funniest, grooviest and coolest tape I own. Two paws up! —AMY MANNING

8/22/87 ❄
WIZN Beach Party, Burlington, VT

8/29/87 [ACCESSIBILITY: ••••]
The Mead Ranch, Shelburne, VT
I: Alumni > Jimmy Page > Alumni, Curtis Loew, Sneaking Sally, Makisupa, BBFCM, Flat Fee, Lushington, Suzie, Mustang Sally, Ya Mar, TMWSIY > Avenu > TMWSIY
II: Clod, Slave, Swing Low Sweet Chariot, Curtain, McGrupp, Possum, Harry Hood, Timber Ho, AC/DC Bag, Divided Sky, Harpua > Bundle of Joy > Harpua
"HYHU" teases in Suzie. Curtain "with."

➢ My dream show! Beautiful, perfect, 1987-era Phish that kicks off with an Alumni > J. Page > Alumni opener. The rare Lushington, complete with The Chase, is sure to make you laugh, along with Suzie G., which sounds like "Sweet Home Alabama" at first until they keep teasing HYHU to spite Fishman. Ya Mar is dedicated to Marley, Trey's dog, and Trey acknowledges this by singing, "Ya Mar, you no good dog!" The set closes with "The Man Who Stepped Into a Pile of Yesterday, and Stopped in Jerusalem on the Way"! The second set never fails to blow me away, too, beginning with Clod. Swing Low is one of my faves, followed by an unstoppable combination of: Curtain "with", McGrupp and Possum! But it doesn't stop there—Timber Ho, AC/DC Bag and Divided Sky follow! And the set closer? Harpua > Bundle of Joy > Harpua! Best show of '87? —OTIS

➢ This is without a doubt one of my favorite oldies. It opens with Alumni Blues, which appears on virtually all pre-'90s tapes. Then comes an unusually long Makisupa Policeman. The best song in the first set, though, is definitely Suzie. Whether or not this is their first time playing it, it sure sounds like it, mainly due to the fact that they seem to have real trouble getting it started. Once they do, it sounds great because it's much slower and less polished than it is now. —JONATHAN BARRO

9/3/87 ❄
Hunt's, Burlington, VT

9/12/87 [ACCESSIBILITY: •]
Nectar's, Burlington, VT
I: TMWSIY > Avenu > TMWSIY, Clod, Slave, Funky Bitch, Wilson, Dear Mrs. Reagan, Golgi, AC/DC Bag, Possum, YEM, Curtain, BBFCM
II: Suzie, Alumni > Jimmy Page, GTBT, Rocky Top, Sneaking Sally, Fee, Divided Sky, Dog Log, Curtis Loew, Antelope, Makisupa, Fire, Terrapin, La Grange, Fluffhead
Curtain "with."

9/27/87 [ACCESSIBILITY: •]
Pledge Party, Burlington, VT
I: Bowie, Funky Bitch, Golgi, Peaches, A-Train, Possum, Phase Dance, GTBT, Skin It Back
II: Wilson, I Didn't Know, Fluffhead, Fire, Fee
Date uncertain and setlist likely incomplete.

➢ Announcements made during the show include "The keg's back on tap in the basement," and "I hope all the pledges are feeling Irie," from a frat member. —AJ FUCILE

Friday, August 21, 1987 — Ian's Farm, Hebron, NY

If you've heard a tape of the classic Ian's '87 show, you know dogs bark throughout it. The Almanac tracked down one of those pooches and asked him to review the show.

What a great, tail-waggin' time I had. Lots of other canines and butts to smell. There was this one Golden Retriever with a great smelling butt, but she was all high and mighty and hanging out with these humans making weird noises on this platform. Every time I came close to them she'd growl. But the other dogs treated me better. We kept on barking at those humans, and they kept on making more noises, and so we kept on barking.

After awhile I got to like some of the noises. At first they kept on singing "dog" which is one of those noises which I know has something to do with me. They also kept saying "log." I don't know that one. So I barked. Then there were more noises without any words, then a bunch of words, then some real pretty noises, and then they started saying "Dog" again. So I kept on barking, and all the other guys joined in. The noises stopped for a while and there was a great barbecue with lots of scraps.

Then the noises started up again, and soon they were saying "dog" again, talking about someone named Harpua. I don't know him, but if I meet him, I'd like to smell his butt. **—Jim**

10/14/87 [ACCESSIBILITY: •]
Hunt's, Burlington, VT
I: Peaches, A-Train, YEM > Golgi > Slave > Chase > Fluffhead > Possum
II: Bowie, AC/DC Bag > Divided Sky > McGrupp > Clod > Makisupa

➢ This show—both sets of which fit comfortably onto a 90-minute tape—is littered with Fluffhead! The closing of Golgi slides into Slave, then the chords of The Chase emerge. It's almost unnerving to hear this part of Fluff's Travels merge into the opening "Fluffhead was a man…" refrain, but here it happens. As was standard on most early Fluffheads, the verses here are repeated at the end of the song. Clod—another future Fluff component, surfaces in the second set. Beyond Fluffhead, the second set starts immediately on my tape with Bowie—a solid portrait of the band's musicianship in late 1987. The grouping that follows would be great in concert today—AC/DC Bag into Divided Sky into McGrupp, although here the songs are shorter than their current incarnations.—LOCK STEELE

10/31/87 ❄
Sculpture Room, Goddard College, Plainfield, VT
Second annual Phish Halloween show at Goddard. Phish alternated sets with the Joneses.

11/19/87 [ACCESSIBILITY: •]
Hunt's, Burlington, VT
I: McGrupp, Sparks, Funky Bitch, YEM, Sneaking Sally, Harry Hood, Fire
II: Timber Ho, Fluffhead, I Didn't Know, Fee, Corrina, Alumni > Jimmy Page > Alumni, Suzie, Possum, Divided Sky, BBFCM
III: Dinner and a Movie, Curtis Loew, Whipping Post, Jimmy Page, A-Train, Camel Walk, La Grange, Bike, Slave

1988

1/30/88 [ACCESSIBILITY: ••]
Gallagher's, Waitsfield, VT
I: Funky Bitch, Mustang Sally, AC/DC Bag, Possum, Jesus Left Chicago, Sneaking Sally, Alumni, A-Train, GTBT
II: Wilson, Slave, Corrina, Fire, Fluffhead, Divided Sky, Curtis Loew, YEM, Sloth, Whipping Post
III: Fee, Suzie, Lizards, Golgi, Bike, BBFCM, Camel Walk, Harry Hood
Show often dated 1/27/88.

➢ Musically speaking, this is simply my favorite 1980s Phish tape (and I've heard most of them). Besides offering a good view of what Phish was up to at the time—from an opening Funky Bitch to the blues of Jesus Left Chicago and Curtis Loew to the humor of Pink Floyd's Bike—this show offers plenty of it. It's not as widely circulated as some other 1980s gigs like 10/20/89 and 8/21/87, but it's really worth seeking out. —ERNIE GREENE

2/7/88 [ACCESSIBILITY: •]
Nectar's, Burlington, VT
Fire, McGrupp, Shaggy Dog, Golgi, Alumni > Jimmy Page > Alumni, Peaches, Dear Mrs. Reagan, I Didn't Know, Bowie, AC/DC Bag, Timber Ho
Setlist incomplete.

2/8/88 [ACCESSIBILITY: •]
Nectar's, Burlington, VT
II: Fluffhead, Wilson, Peaches, Divided Sky, Lizards, Antelope, Harry Hood, Mockingbird, TMWSIY > Avenu > TMWSIY

3/11/88 [ACCESSIBILITY: •]
Johnson State College, Johnson, VT
I: The Chicken, Funky Bitch, Sneaking Sally, A-Train, YEM, Wilson, Golgi, Slave, Flat Fee, Corrina, Lizards, Bowie
II: Fluffhead, Dinner and a Movie, Harry Hood, Curtis Loew, Harpua, AC/DC Bag, Alumni > Jimmy Page > Alumni, Antelope

3/12/88 [ACCESSIBILITY: ••••]
Nectar's, Burlington, VT
Jump Monk > McGrupp > Lizards > Tela > Wilson > AC/DC Bag > Forbin's > Mockingbird > Sloth > Possum, Antelope
First live Gamehendge performance; Trey narrates between songs. Show billed as "Story Time at Nectar's."

➢ This show was the first time Phish played Gamehendge live for an audience. Even if you never get into Gamehendge, you'll appreciate this tape. It's got the usual Gamehendge setlist with the exception of the Antelope and the first song, Jump Monk, a great jazz tune they don't play often. Unlike some Gamehendge performances, Trey tells the whole story, including Col. Forbin staring in the mirror shaving. If you see this tape, grab it and listen closely. —MATT RICHARDSON

➢ I really like the way they do this Gamehendge starting with McGrupp and ending with Possum, but what I enjoy most about this version is the intimacy of it. It's so much more personal in a small place like Nectar's rather than when I saw Gamehendge at Great Woods. It's hard to get the effect of the whole story in a big place, but every show I go to, I find myself begging for it. It's too phat to describe. —NICK SORICELLI

➢ The first Gamehendge show is a necessary part of any Phish collection! —ED SMITH

[3/20/88]
Nectar's, Burlington, VT
Tapes with this date are apparently from 5/9/89.

3/21/88 [ACCESSIBILITY: ••]
Nectar's, Burlington, VT
Suzie, Golgi, McGrupp, Sneaking Sally, Divided Sky, Boogie On Reggae Woman, Timber Ho, Lizards, Fire, AC/DC Bag, Possum, Dinner and a Movie, I Didn't Know, Forbin's > Mockingbird

3/31/88 [ACCESSIBILITY: •]
Kenny's Castaways, New York City, NY
I: I Didn't Know, Golgi, Fee > AC/DC Bag > Possum, Fluffhead
II: Alumni > Jimmy Page > Alumni, Lizards, Forbin's > Mockingbird, A-Train, Fire, YEM, Wilson
AC/DC Bag sung for Roger (the "crazy little kid"), who was in attendance. First Phish New York City show.

4/2/88
Full Moon at The Zoo, Humphries House, Amherst College, Amherst, MA
First Phish "Full Moon at the Zoo" show.

5/14/88 [ACCESSIBILITY: •••]
Springfest, Goddard College, Plainfield, VT
II: Fire, I Didn't Know, Halley's, Light Up Or Leave Me Alone, YEM, Lizards, BBFCM, Jesus Left Chicago, Fluffhead, Alumni > Jimmy Page > Alumni, A-Train
Nancy Taube on vocals for I Didn't Know and Halley's. Bobby Brown on horns for Jesus Left Chicago. Karl Boyle on saxophone for A-Train. "HYHU" jam before A-Train.

5/15/88 [ACCESSIBILITY: •••]
Vermont Farm Festival, Hinesburg, VT
Alumni > Jimmy Page > Alumni, Golgi, YEM, Suzie, GTBT, Fluffhead, Shaggy Dog, Lizards, Sneaking Sally, A-Train, Curtain, Flat Fee, Whipping Post, AC/DC Bag, Possum, Icculus, McGrupp, Wilson, Peaches, I Didn't Know, Sloth, Harpua
Party at Dan Lynch's house. Song order uncertain. Curtain "with."

➢ My recollection of this show is sketchy. I do remember a tremendous Whipping Post. The rest of the show was a blur because there were several kegs sitting in the creek. I had also just gotten there after visiting Huntington Gorge and communing with the peace frog. Besides, it was senior week and I was graduating! —DAN KURTZ

➢ A unique combination of Phish performing some rare tunes. A soothing McGrupp and spacy intro to Wilson add to this tape's pleasure. Concluding with Peaches, Sloth and Harpua, I deem this tape my favorite and a necessity to all my phamily members. —MATTHEW ASHENFELDER

5/19/88
Student Union, Goddard College, Plainfield, VT
II: Fire, I Didn't Know, Halley's, Light Up or Leave Me Alone, YEM, Lizards, BBFCM, Jesus Left Chicago, Fluffhead, Alumni > Jimmy Page > Alumni, A-Train

5/23/88 [ACCESSIBILITY: ••]
Nectar's, Burlington, VT
A-Train, Golgi, YEM, Rocky Top, Light Up or Leave Me Alone, I Didn't Know, Peaches, Possum, GTBT

5/25/88 [ACCESSIBILITY: ••••]
Nectars, Burlington, VT
I: Curtain, Rocky Top, Funky Bitch, Alumni, Peaches, Golgi, Sneaking Sally, Suzie, Fire
II: Jesus Left Chicago, Fluffhead, Whipping Post
III: Sloth, I Didn't Know, Ya Mar > One Love, La Grange, Fee, I Know A Little, BBFCM, Corrina, Harpua, Antelope
Curtain "with." Jah Roy on vocals for Ya Mar and One Love. "Flintstones" jam in BBFCM.

Phan Pick #24 ➢ Another crazy night at Nectar's. Fluffhead > Whipping Post to close the second set is awesome! Trey lights the Whipping Post on fire with crazy jamming throughout—it's killer. Ya Mar is helped out by Jah Roy doing a reggae rap along with the music. Rarities I Know a Little and Corrina bring us to an early but jam-filled Antelope, and don't forget to check out the Harpua. Still, if you're a fan of wackiness, the Ya Mar at this show is worth you finding this tape to enjoy! —CHRISTOPHER MILLS

➢ The first set is led by super-energetic playing on Alumni Blues and Sneaking Sally.

Trey's guitar dominates the entire show, which is about 90 percent devoted to the group's improvisation. For example: the second set opens with a 14-minute Jesus Left Chicago and closes with a 23-minute Whipping Post during which Trey pushes the envelope of guitar ability. But the show's standout is a 20-minute Ya Mar which features Jah Roy on vocals. Phish jams into a reggae beat to which Jah Roy improvs. —AARON GROSSBERG

➢ There's a reason why the song order on most tapes of this show is a little mixed up: the original taper was smart enough to keep that incredible Whipping Post uncut! (Halley's Comet, which often appears in setlists in the third set following the Jay Roy jam, appears to be filler from a different show.) This is really just a great show, and both sets are unquestionably worth tracking down. —ERNIE GREENE

6/15/88 [ACCESSIBILITY: •••]
The Front, Burlington, VT
I: Suzie, Alumni, YEM, Wilson, Rocky Top, McGrupp, Fluffhead, Golgi, La Grange, Fee, Timber Ho, I Didn't Know
II: Lizards, AC/DC Bag, Sloth, Contact, Dinner and a Movie, A-Train, GTBT, Whipping Post, Dear Mrs. Reagan

6/18/88 [ACCESSIBILITY: •]
Nectar's, Burlington, VT
I: Curtain, Funky Bitch, Possum, Golgi, La Grange, Suzie, Big Leg Emma, YEM, GTBT, Cities

Friday, April 2, 1988 — "Full Moon at the Zoo," Humphries House, Amherst, MA

In my personal opinion, the 1980s were probably the worst decade for rock music since the genre started in the early 1950s. There were a few good things going on, of course, like the Talking Heads and the reunited King Crimson, but by the late '80s these bands were no longer touring. I dabbled in New Wave a little, but when my college friends would drag me out to a concert it was clear that most of these groups were better off in the studio, and even then, the novelty of these acts was wearing off. Musicianship didn't seem to matter as long as you had one of those poofy hairdos and some flashy (a.k.a. cheesy) outfits that MTV execs seemed to go nuts for. Even old touring warhorses like Yes and Genesis were starting to sound stale, lacking certain key members from their early days.

Fortunately there was always the good ol' Grateful Dead. In the Spring of '88 I couldn't wait for them to come to New England and shake things up a bit. I had recently met this guy Ben in a music appreciation class at Boston University and upon discovering similar tastes in rock music, it was only natural that we jaunt off to a Dead show together in Hartford. A few days before the said show (4/3/88), Ben asked if I wouldn't mind going out to his friend's dorm at Amherst College the night before the show because "he's having a cool party with some cool band playing." Sounded cool to me. Two days later we were off to Amherst playing Dead tapes and havin' a fine little road trip.

We got to the dorm, called "The Zoo," before most anyone else. There was just the band setting up and some really nice hippies who were playing hacky-sack on the other side of the room and who told me they'd come down from northern Vermont. It was just a small room with a sort of hallway leading to some stairs cutting through the middle. It was in this wooden-floored room—probably 25' X 65' at best—that I heard Phish for the first time. Before the show I met Ben's cool friend, John Paluska, who got the band down from Vermont to play their first Massachusetts show in his dorm. I also met Trey, who was noodling around with his guitar. I was intrigued, but a little skeptical and completely unprepared for the Phish onslaught. "So what kind of stuff do you guys play?" I asked, not at all thinking that I was about to be blown away.

Trey showed me a piece of paper with all the songs they play on it. Okay—first thing that jumped out at me was "Phase Dance" by Pat Metheny. Wow—this just may be really cool. "It says David Bowie. Which tune?"

"Uh... well, that's our tune. We can play it tonight if you want."

"All right, sure. You do Terrapin!?"

"That's Syd Barrett's Terrapin."

"Wow—that's cool. If you're taking more requests, then play that too!" This night was starting to look real good, especially after some pre-show festivities in someone's dorm room with all sorts of future celebrities.

Back down in the main room a bit later, the band started to tune up while a small crowd filed in. The room only needed about 50 people to feel stuffed and I'm sure there were a few more than that. Finally, at about 10 p.m. Phish started playing—with an energy that I hadn't seen live on stage (or floor, as was the case) in years. The opener—I'll never forget it—was "Golgi Apparatus." Looking back, it was a very appropriate first song to hear from those four lads. When you think about it, just about every element of Phish is in that song. Loud bursts, soft guitar lines, powerful vocals, tricky instrumental parts, thriving crescendos. All in a nice little package. You could hear their influences and yet experience something entirely new. In just a few short moments, I was an instant fan. I knew I wanted to hear everything they had to offer and see them many times, and I hadn't even heard the second song yet.

For a band that was still relatively "early" in their career, they certainly seemed like a well-oiled machine. Their playing was tight and the sound was really good, if somewhat loud for a small room. There was a mixer in the corner by the doorway and the sound-folks obviously knew what they were doing. No, there were no tapers that night, but I'm sure there must have been a board copy somewhere—though unfortunately, there's nothing in circulation.

(Funny thing: My second Phish show was in this very room, the following September. I had just returned to the U.S. and Ben told me about the show the day before it happened. The crowd was even rowdier and there was a lone microphone popping out of it. One taper, and somehow nine years later I ended up with a recording of most of the show. I guess that's all it takes sometimes.)

Ironically, I didn't even make it to the end of the show. Due to an early morning class (nine o'clock for political science) and rigorous halftime activities, by the third set I was curled up on a couch with a big smile on my face. I do remember many other phine moments, though. "Fee" was fun and the "Bowie" Trey promised me cracked me up and blew me away simultaneously. "Fluffhead" had me convinced that Prog-Rock would never die. As for covers, they did a killer "Good Times Bad Times" (from Led Zep I) and ended the second set with a scorching "Whipping Post."

I wish I remembered more, but it was all totally new to me. My mind was overloaded with incredibly cool new sounds, notes and ideas. I didn't even know the names to their originals until weeks later when John hooked us up with some studio stuff that ended up on the *Junta* album (plus some rare covers, too). But I promise you that the band was just amazing. I really enjoyed all four of the musician's contributions to the whole process. It was strange to see them whipping up such a frenzy and then, just a few moments later, to be hanging out with them, conversing. An incredible night.

My friend Ben (remember him? He took me to this party) absolutely flipped over them. He could barely contain himself. We went to Hartford the next night to see the Dead, and you know, it wasn't one of their best nights. (Giving credit where it's due, they did make up for it at the Worcester shows a week later.) We both agreed that Phish had made the weekend for us. Remember, this was the lame '80s (Duran Duran, Scandal, Van Halen)—suddenly, there was hope!

I became an early fan, but I soon graduated, toured Europe and moved out West. Ben took it one step further. He, along with John, eventually set up more New England gigs, and they soon became Phish's managers, establishing Dionysian Productions. Ben's last name was Hunter, by the way, and over time the Phish camp was calling him "Hunta" with a Bahston/New Hampsha type of accent. As Mike Gordon explained to me two springs later, somewhere along the line, someone wrote it down as JUNTA and then someone else read it and pronounced it phonetically. Apparently, this was funny as hell to everyone, and the rest is history.

Unfortunately, I lost touch with Ben (no longer with Dionysian) after a run of Colorado shows in the fall of 1990. If anyone sees him, tell him "hi" and thanks for getting me started on a wild and wacky musical adventure.

Oh, and I'm still waiting for them to play "Phase Dance"...

—Daniel Gibson

II: Alumni, BBFCM, Swing Low Sweet Chariot, Antelope, I Know A Little, Mike's, Corrina, Rocky Top, McGrupp, Jesus Left Chicago
Song order uncertain. Curtain "with."

6/20/88 [ACCESSIBILITY: ••]
Nectar's, Burlington, VT
I: Slave, Peaches, YEM, Fluffhead, AC/DC Bag, Lizards, Halley's, Wilson, Ya Mar
II: Jam, Sneaking Sally, Tela, Fee, Golgi, Satin Doll, A-Train, Curtis Loew, Bowie
Jah Roy on vocals during the Jam to start the second set.

6/21/88 [ACCESSIBILITY: •]
Nectar's, Burlington, VT
I: Fluffhead, Rocky Top, Mustang Sally, Suzie, Curtain, Lizards, Forbin's > Mockingbird, Fire
II: Harpua, I Didn't Know, AC/DC Bag, Flat Fee, Alumni, Jesus Left Chicago, GTBT, Contact, Peaches, Golgi
Curtain "with."

7/11/88 [ACCESSIBILITY: •]
Sam's Tavern, Burlington, VT
I: Satin Doll, Suzie, Curtain, Funky Bitch, Fire, Bold as Love, Forbin's > Mockingbird, Golgi, Alumni

7/12/88 [ACCESSIBILITY: ••••]
Sam's Tavern, Burlington, VT
I: A-Train > Timber Ho, Fluffhead > Jesus Left Chicago, Makisupa, Slave, AC/DC Bag, Antelope
II: Cities, Lizards, Sneaking Sally, GTBT, Peaches, YEM, I Didn't Know
Antelope sung as "Roll Like A Cantaloupe."

7/23/88 [ACCESSIBILITY: ••••]
Pete's Phabulous Phish Phest, Peter Danforth's House, Underhill, VT
I: Jam, Forbin's > Mockingbird > Mike's > Hydrogen > Weekapaug, Lizards, On Your Way Down, AC/DC Bag, Possum, Walk Away, Bold as Love, No Dogs Allowed > Divided Sky Jam > No Dogs Allowed
II: Sloth, Fire, Curtain > Wilson, Terrapin, Antelope, Satin Doll, Blue Bossa, La Grange, Alumni, Peaches
III: YEM, Contact, Harry Hood, Dinner and a Movie, Slave, Curtis Loew, GTBT
Fire featured Peter Danforth and Cameron McKinney. Slave featured a guest artist on saxophone. "Dave's Energy Guide" jam in the "with" of Curtain "with."

7/24/88 [ACCESSIBILITY: ••]
Nectar's, Burlington, VT
I: Walk Away, Golgi, Funky Bitch, Forbin's > Mockingbird, Sneaking Sally, Mike's > Hydrogen > Weekapaug, Bold as Love
II: Light Up Or Leave Me Alone, Fluffhead, La Grange, Lizards, Alumni, On Your Way Down, Cities, Bowie
III: TMWSIY > Avenu > TMWSIY, Peaches, Jesus Left Chicago, McGrupp, Antelope

7/25/88 [ACCESSIBILITY: •]
Nectar's, Burlington, VT
II: Mike's > Hydrogen > Weekapaug, Bold as Love
III: Light Up Or Leave Me Alone, Fluffhead, Skin It Back, Harpua, BBFCM, Sanity, Icculus, Camel Walk
The Sanity and Icculus from this concert appear on the Elektra re-release of Junta. Last Nectar's show.

8/3/88 [ACCESSIBILITY: •••]
The Roma, Telluride, CO
I: I Know A Little, YEM, Jesus Left Chicago
II: Peaches, Mike's > Hydrogen, Fluffhead, Harry Hood, Satin Doll, Funky Bitch, Walk Away

➢ The week of gigs in Telluride in late July-August 1988 stands as a key historical signpost in the evolution of the band. The band had been booked for a week of shows in Telluride but found out the gigs had fallen through a few days before they were to depart for Colorado. After brief hesitation, however, they decided to go anyway, and took up residence as the house band at the Italian eatery and bar The Roma on Telluride's beautiful main street. No Phish collection is complete without a Telluride tape. —PAT STANLEY

➢ Plenty of funny banter on this tape. Page, after Jesus Left Chicago, says, "We're going to take a break now and come back and play a real long set. Well, it's not gonna be that long, but it's gonna be a real short break. Well, a medium-sized break." After Fluffhead, the band sings an a cappella "Happy Birthday" to Stacy, ending it with, "It's been a long time since you were born." Before Walk Away, the band gives last call and encourages big tips for Scott, the "only one working here tonight." —BOB COLBY

➢ I sometimes hear rumors that a few Telluride fans have this entire week's worth of shows on tape. If the few sets in circulation—plus the "Jazz Odyssey" comments made during set two on 3/17/91—are any indication, this is a treasure worth uncovering! (I've also heard that soundboard masters were stolen from a house in Telluride sometime around 1990, so we may never hear these lost shows. Damn.) —ERNIE GREENE

8/6/88 [ACCESSIBILITY: ••••]
The Roma, Telluride, CO
I: La Grange, YEM > Cities > Dave's Energy Guide > Cities, A-Train, Funky Bitch, Dinner and a Movie, Fire
II: Golgi, AC/DC Bag, Satin Doll, Sanity, BBFCM, Slave
"London Bridge is Falling Down" teases in A-Train. "Jeopardy" tease before Satin Doll. Fishman on trombone for Sanity.

➢ If I could choose just one Phish tape from the 1980s for my collection, this would be it. Besides its historic value as part of Phish's week of gigs in Telluride, their first tour outside of New England, the music rocks. Cities > DEG > Cities is just phenomenal! Imagine walking down the steps into the tiny basement of the Roma and hearing a band you've never heard of playing this? No wonder the band made so many friends during their Telluride stay. —SCOTT SIFTON

➢ This show rolls along beautifully and has some really nice tunes. After an extremely slow but great YEM comes one of my favorite Cities in my collection. There are so many good songs on this tape it's unbelievable. Dave's Energy Guide is very good on this tape as well as Take the A-Train. Both sets of this show fit comfortably on one 90 minute tape, and anyone who doesn't have this tape should really try to get it. —DAVE O'CONNOR

➢ More humor on another night in Telluride. After they play AC/DC Bag with a strange intro and Page croons Satin Doll, Mike informs the miniscule crowd, "We're doing this song because Sting asked us to. I want you to know that Sting told you all to have a good time tonight." Sting's choice? Sanity. There's also the giveaway of a t-shirt from "Baked In Telluride" (a pasta and pizza joint a few blocks down from the Roma) to Tim Rogers, because as Trey says, "If anybody is baked in Telluride, it's Tim Rogers." —AMY MANNING

8/27/88 [ACCESSIBILITY: ••••]
Penn State College, State College, PA
Satin Doll, YEM, Funky Bitch, Walk Away, Fluffhead, Mike's, A-Train, Golgi, Tela
Setlist may be incomplete. Date uncertain; show often circulates as 1/2/86 or "Penn State '86."

➢ This has to be the funniest show I've ever heard. The guys obviously stopped at a bar on the way because Trey continually shouts inane ramblings and makes weird mouth noises. Another funny aspect is the lack of an audience. On one occasion I can hear *one person* clap. In response, Fish proclaims, "We're Phish…we're still Phish." Pick this one up for a great laugh and some good music. —BEN ROSS

➢ Even though the date and location are uncertain, the music quality and other virtues of this great show are known and acknowledged by those who own it. Satin Doll, a rare jazz treat, and A-Train give the set a good feel. But the true greatness lies in the Fluffhead and Tela. This Tela contains my personal favorite Phish jam and is an epic for all to enjoy. —CHIP CROTEAU

➢ After a Mike's Song that goes nowhere, A-Train and Golgi set the stage for one of the greatest treats of my tape collection. These really crisp chords emerge, coupled with a slick melody sung by Page—this is Tela in a different musical form with altered lyrics. The basic elements of the modern Tela progression are there, but this version is faster and more satisfying to the ear. Then comes a jam where Trey brilliantly flies around the neck and partially outlines the chords to the unique progression. The jam comes to a climax Harry Hood style with Page banging and sustaining the implied chords while the band vocally harmonizes "Tela, Tela." This particular Tela is something every Phish fan should hear. —LARRY CHASNOFF

9/8/88 [ACCESSIBILITY: ••]
The Front, Burlington, VT
I: Peaches, Walk Away, Slave, Wild Child, AC/DC Bag, Forbin's > Mockingbird, Bold as Love
II: Possum, YEM, Cities, GTBT, On Your Way Down, Whipping Post
Home video played for audience during YEM.

➢ This tape popped into wide circulation over the last year, perhaps a "from the vault" find. It's obvious why this one made the rounds so quickly—the soundboard sound quality is perfect, and the band smokes! The short first set (fits on one side of a 45-minute tape) features Phish covering Lou Reed's Wild Child, and doing it justice. They also sound tight on the other first-set covers: Peaches, Walk Away and Bold as Love. In the second set, Trey has the lights turned down at the start of YEM for some "home movie" screenings. (This YEM is great, by the way!) Out of that comes Cities, plus two more strong covers—On Your Way Down and the "real" (i.e., not Fishmanized) Whipping Post. —ED SMITH

9/12/88 [ACCESSIBILITY: •]
Sam's Tavern, Burlington, VT
Shaggy Dog, A-Train, Fee, Bold as Love, Timber Ho, Satin Doll, Lizards, TMWSIY > Avenu > Bundle Of Joy > Camel Walk, Harry Hood, Esther
Alternate lyrics in Esther.

9/13/88 [ACCESSIBILITY: •]
Sam's Tavern, Burlington, VT
I: Walk Away, Funky Bitch, YEM, Flat Fee > McGrupp > Wilson > Peaches, GTBT
II: Ride Captain Ride, Boogie On Reggae Woman > Cities, Antelope, Fluffhead

9/24/88 [ACCESSIBILITY: ••••]
Full Moon at The Zoo, Humphries House, Amherst College, Amherst, MA
I: Golgi, On Your Way Down, Alumni, YEM > Wilson > Peaches, La Grange, A-Train, Divided Sky, Bold as Love
II: Bowie, Lizards, Walk Away > Possum, Fee > Sparks, Whipping Post
III: GTBT, Fluffhead, Curtain, AC/DC Bag
Teases in AC/DC Bag include "London Bridge is Falling Down" and the "Flintstones" theme.

➢ This show, Phish's second gig at Humphries House "Full Moon at the Zoo" party, is a classic. The show kicks off with YEM > Wilson. The YEMs from this time period are much simpler than those of the '90s but are in my opinion much more pleasing to the ear, and the transition into Wilson is an interesting one. The other highpoint of this show is Fee > Sparks > Whipping Post. You can feel the excitement of the crowd by listening to Sparks, which is played about as well as The Who ever played it. —BEN ROSS

➢ Back when Phish still sounded amateur, but that's okay—they were still a little college band doing the New England circuit. All the soloing is simple, being that they were still at a very early stage in the great Phish experiment. Trey's guitar sounds a little bit tinny. Still, there's a great transition from YEM (no vocal jam) into Wilson and then Trey pushes into Peaches by singing the drum intro. —SCOTT KUSHNER

➢ These tapes showed me an entirely new side of Phish. It's the way the songs are played that's so intriguing. Phish seems to have brought it down a notch for this show, with slower beats, less guitar, and vocal emphasis in Golgi, Wilson, Fluffhead, Lizards and especially AC/DC Bag. Bag is played so slowly that it's transformed from an all-out jam into more of a lounge act song, allowing clear interpretation of the lyrics. Lizards has been slowed and put almost to a reggae beat. —AARON GROSSBERG

10/12/88 [ACCESSIBILITY: ••••]
Red Barn, Hampshire College, Amherst, MA
I: I Didn't Know, Golgi, Bowie, Lizards, Foam, Fee, Mike's > Hydrogen > Weekapaug, Wilson, Forbin's > Mockingbird
II: Alumni, YEM, Contact, Sloth, AC/DC Bag > Possum, GTBT **E:** Antelope
NORML benefit concert.

10/29/88 [ACCESSIBILITY: ••••]
Sculpture Room, Goddard College, Plainfield, VT
I: Suzie > Lizards, Time Loves A Hero, Golgi, Bold as Love, La Grange, Contact, Harry Hood
II: Halley's > Whipping Post, Fee, Alumni, Walk Away, Divided Sky, Curtis Loew, Mike's, A-Train, Fire
III: Fluffhead, GTBT, YEM, Possum, AC/DC Bag, Foam, Terrapin, BBFCM, Timber Ho, Slave, Donna Lee, Antelope, I Didn't Know, Wilson > Peaches, Funky Bitch
Bobby Brown on harmonica for Curtis Loew. Nancy Taube on vocals for Halley's. Third annual Phish Halloween show at Goddard College.

➢ Classic show—YEM is a killer, Possum is outstanding and they tear apart Bold as Love. The costume contest is great—"Colonel Forbin" and "Tela" both win dates with Fish. "Harry Hood" is the contest winner, though. The costume contest goes into a short but sweet Hood, ending the set on a fine note. —KEVIN WEISS

➢ After Contact, the audience cheers for the best costume. Trey comments that all of the finalists will be on the next album cover. I'm not sure what he's talking about, but it's pretty funny. —JEFFREY ELLENBOGEN

➢ Set two of this Goddard show has my very favorite Halley's Comet, which I believe features Nancy Taube, followed by a great, extended Whipping Post with Trey on vocals and guitar. Fee seems to start off with different chords. Curtis Loew is one of the best versions I've heard, and a nice A-Train follows a short Mike's Song. —PAT ELKINS

[10/31/88]
Hamilton College, Clinton, NY
Tapes from this show are actually parts of the 10/29/88 Goddard show. Phish did not play Hamilton on this date.

11/3/88 [ACCESSIBILITY: •]
Molly's, Boston, MA
I: Fire, Golgi, Fluffhead, Possum, Fee, Alumni, GTBT, Time Loves A Hero, Walk Away, Lizards, Shaggy Dog, Foam
II: Whipping Post, Contact, Bold as Love, A-Train, Antelope, Suzie, I Didn't Know, BBFCM, Harpua, Bowie
"Dave's Energy Guide" jam in Whipping Post.

➢ The band's first Boston show came three months before their more renowned debut at the Paradise. Performance-wise, little separates this show from other shows from this time period, but if you're a big fan of historical moments, you'll want to pick it up. Apparently Phish made such a big impression on the small crowd that they were immediately booked to play Molly's again in December. —TRICIA HOLMES

➢ Another good one from the bar days. You can feel the diversity in cover tunes from early on, and this show has some good ones—Fire, GTBT, Time Loves a Hero (!), Walk Away, Whipping Post and Bold as Love all sparkle with energy. Great early performance of Harpua, too. —KYLE NIDAY

11/5/88 [ACCESSIBILITY: ••]
Hamilton College, Clinton, NY
I: Slave, Time Loves A Hero, Fire, YEM, Possum, A-Train, Golgi, Walk Away, Fluffhead, Alumni, Bowie
II: Wilson, Peaches, Bold as Love, Lizards, AC/DC Bag, Fee, Mike's > Hydrogen > Weekapaug, I Didn't Know, GTBT **E:** Suzie > Sparks, Divided Sky

11/11/88 [ACCESSIBILITY: ••]
The Stone Church, Newmarket, NH
I: Divided Sky, YEM, Slave, Foam, Possum, Forbin's > Mockingbird, Bowie
II: Mike's > Hydrogen > Weekapaug, Jazz Tune, Fee, Bold as Love, Timber Ho, Lizards, Whipping Post **E:** Peaches, Funky Bitch, Donna Lee
Carl Gerhard on trumpet for the jazz tune, Timber Ho and encores.

➢ This must have been an incredible show to attend. The second set starts with a half-hour long Mike's > Weekapaug. Highlights include a great Bold as Love and Whipping

Paradise Found

1/26/89, The Paradise, Boston, MA

Phish turned many tight corners on the way to the top, but it's the January 26, 1989 show at The Paradise in Boston that the band has always pointed to as its true "turning point."

While Phish's following in Burlington, VT was well established in the late eighties, crowds and bookings outside the native state were hard to come by. Their first paying gig in Massachusetts didn't come until 1988—the first Full Moon at the Zoo show in Amherst, arranged by eventual manager John Paluska. The first Boston appearance came in the fall of '88, at a club called Molly's, after Paluska's friend Ben Hunter rented out the club and hung fliers on all the buildings in the town, successfully attracting a crowd. On November 3rd, and then again on December 2nd of that year, Phish played at the small club, filling it to the brim the second time around. The momentum was building.

But the real goal for Phish was to play the Paradise, a 650-person club where all of New England's up-and-coming bands could be found gigging regularly. The booking agents at The Paradise, however, had other things in mind. To them, Phish was just one of the hundreds of bands that sent in their demo tapes. And like most, the one marked "Phish" was never even listened to.

With the cooperation of Hunter and Paluska—who were planting the seeds that would grow into Phish's management company, Dionysian Productions—the band rented out The Paradise on its own. It was a risky, break-even-at-best sort of move, but considered necessary for Phish to make a name for itself in the hub of New England. Hunter went into action promoting the show, while Phish and friends were busy ensuring that a virtual army of faithful from Burlington made the trek.

Tom Baggot, a friend of the band's from the very first days at UVM, organized a pair of buses that transported dozens of Phish supporters down to the club, while many more caravaned in their own vehicles.

It was the true beginning of the era of Phish-heads. And the club sold out. Paradise bouncers who asked if Phish was in fact a "real band" were silenced when some fans were even turned away at the door.

The show included most of the Phish repertoire from the time, from rockers like Good Times Bad Times and Fire, to Phish trademarks like YEM, Contact and Icculus. Sadly, most tapes of this show that now circulate among fans are incomplete and poor in quality.

Nevertheless, the band had done it. From there, the bookings would follow. In 1989 other key clubs like Wetlands in New York City and the 8 X 10 Club in Baltimore would also give the band a shot. They were off and running.

Post, which is often performed by Fishman but here sung by Trey, featuring a monumental jam. And how about Peaches, Funky Bitch and Donna Lee as an encore? —JEFF SALVATORE

➢ When talking about classic Phish venues of yesterday, you can't overlook the Stone Church in Newmarket, NH. "Phirst Phan" Amy Skelton moved to New Hampshire sometime around this time and proved instrumental in getting the band gigs at Granite State venues ranging from the Squam Lake Steak House to the Stone Church. You might want to add this tape, from what I consider a particularly strong night for the boys during one of their first Stone Church appearances. —SCOTT SIFTON

12/2/88 [ACCESSIBILITY: ••]
Molly's, Boston, MA
I: Sloth, Golgi, Bold as Love, A-Train, Divided Sky, Contact, YEM
II: I Didn't Know, GTBT, Alumni > Jimmy Page, Lizards

[12/17/88]
The Stone Church, Newmarket, NH
Circulating tapes of this show are apparently from 11/11/88.

1989 *COLONIZING NEW ENGLAND*

After making their first real road trip as a band to Colorado in the summer of 1988, 1989 saw Phish spreading their roots further around the northeast. While still playing frequently in and around Burlington—where they settled in at The Front after outgrowing Nectar's—frequent tour stops included small venues like the Living Room in Providence, RI, the Wetlands Preserve in New York City, and The Paradise in Boston, MA.

By this time, Phish had achieved a level of success that allowed the band members to devote most of their time to music, as opposed to other jobs; the increased time spent practicing shows up in the music and in a series of newly-penned songs. May saw the release of their first real album, *Junta*, and July found the band playing at the prestigious Montreal Jazz Festival. After taking the rest of the month off from playing live, the band resumed touring in August and didn't stop for the rest of year. The fall finished with the band's first New Year's show in Boston, a tradition that continued in various venues around Beantown for the next five years.

Saturday, March 25, 1989 — Tree Cafe, Portland, ME

The first time I saw Phish was at the Tree Cafe in Portland, ME, I think in the spring of 1989—my memory is a bit hazy. A guy I worked with named Mike had either seen them before or had heard word-of-mouth about them, and insisted that I had to see this band. We were both pretty much confirmed Deadheads at the time, and I asked Mike if Phish was a Dead cover band, which he hedged by saying, "Sort of."

The Tree (now sadly defunct) was a pretty small place, capable of holding maybe 200 people if they ignored the fire codes. I can't remember much of what they played, other than the covers—La Grange was in there, and Peaches En Regalia, which fascinated me—you don't see a lot of bar bands covering Zappa. After the first set we went out to Mike's car which, as I recall, was parked about eight feet from the door (that should give you an idea of the size of the crowd) to augment our already-altered perceptions.

The Tree got its name (after previous owners had called it Jim's Bar & Grille, Drew's Checkerboard Lounge, et al) from its proximity to a huge, hundred-year-old oak in front of the entrance. Mike and I got out of the car, smoke billowing out the doors a la Fast Times at Ridgemont High, and ran into another Deadhead friend named Dennis, who greeted us with, "Hey, guys! Did you see the guitar player up in the tree?" We looked up and sure enough, there was Trey about ten feet over our heads, laughing his ass off.

The second set was notable for the appearance of the trampolines, which they used during Antelope (the only original song I can remember—the lyrics tend to stay with you). They encored with Rocky Top > Good Times Bad Times (how could I forget a medley that bizarre, yet strangely appropriate from this band). I was completely sold on this band, and persuaded my girlfriend (now my wife) to come see them the next time they played. I saw them at the Tree two or three more times after that, and within a couple of years they had outgrown bars.

—Bob Colby

1/26/89 [ACCESSIBILITY: •]
The Paradise, Boston, MA
I Didn't Know, Golgi, Alumni, YEM, Lizards, A-Train, Divided Sky, Fee, GTBT, Wilson, Fluffhead, Icculus, Forbin's > Mockingbird, Sloth, Possum, Contact, BBFCM, Fire
Setlist may be incomplete. Phish's first show at the Paradise.

2/5/89 [ACCESSIBILITY: •••]
The Front, Burlington, VT
I: GTBT, Walk Away, Harry Hood, BBFCM, Curtis Loew, Forbin's > Mockingbird, Whipping Post, Corrina, Bowie, La Grange, YEM
Though Phish played The Front on this date, the circulating setlist (above) is probably part of 2/6/89.

2/6/89 [ACCESSIBILITY: •••]
The Front, Burlington, VT
I: Suzie, Curtain > Wilson, Peaches > Fee > La Grange, YEM, All Blues > Sanity > A-Train, Golgi, Divided Sky, On Your Way Down, I Didn't Know
II: GTBT, Walk Away, Harry Hood, BBFCM, Curtis Loew, Icculus > Whipping Post, Corrina **E:** Bowie

➢ Besides Ian's Farm 5/28/89, this is the show to pick up if you're looking for the "new" fast version of Sanity. The fast version was only played this spring; Phish shelved the song until spring tour '92, when the original slow version made its famed comeback. As a bonus, this tape also features the only known version of Phish covering Miles Davis' All Blues. —SCOTT SIFTON

2/7/89 [ACCESSIBILITY: ••]
The Front, Burlington, VT
I: Esther, McGrupp, Foam, Sloth, Possum, Mike's > Hydrogen > Weekapaug, Golgi
II: Makisupa, Dinner and a Movie, AC/DC Bag, Lizards, Timber Ho, Contact, Alumni > Jimmy Page > Alumni, Fee, Antelope
III: Sanity, Fluffhead, Suzie, Slave, Bike, Whipping Post **E:** Fire

2/17/89 [ACCESSIBILITY: •]
The Stone Church, Newmarket, NH
AC/DC Bag, YEM, Fee, Divided Sky, Melt, Golgi, A-Train, Alumni, Antelope, Fluffhead
Setlist may be incomplete.

2/18/89 [ACCESSIBILITY: •]
The Stone Church, Newmarket, NH
Forbin's > Mockingbird, Lizards, Walk Away, Possum, GTBT, Golgi, Wilson > Peaches, YEM, La Grange, Contact, Bowie
Setlist incomplete.

2/24/89 [ACCESSIBILITY: •]
The Front, Burlington, VT
I: TMWSIY > Avenu > TMWSIY, Curtain > Foam, Forbin's > Mockingbird, Antelope, On Your Way Down
II: AC/DC Bag, YEM, Camel Walk
Setlist for second set incomplete.

3/3/89 [ACCESSIBILITY: •••]
L&L Dorm, University of Vermont, Burlington, VT
I: Wilson, McGrupp, YEM > Foam, AC/DC Bag, Curtain, Antelope, I Didn't Know, Divided Sky, Alumni, GTBT
II: Mike's > Hydrogen > Weekapaug, Fee, Possum, Walk Away, Forbin's > Mockingbird, Lizards, Melt, A-Train, Bowie
Date uncertain. Fishman on trombone for I Didn't Know.

3/4/89 [ACCESSIBILITY: •]
Wetlands, New York, NY
I: A-Train, I Didn't Know, Mike's > Hydrogen > Weekapaug, Fee, Golgi, GTBT
II: Possum, Fluffhead, Lizards, Antelope, Contact
First Phish show at the Wetlands. Fishman on trombone for I Didn't Know.

➢ Phish's first Wetlands show is a real tough tape to find—thanks to Dan Gibson for digging this one up! Even though it's the band's first time at the newly opened Wetlands, they obviously have a supportive crowd on hand—there are huge cheers when Trey introduces "Moses Brown, Moses Heaps and Moses Dewitt" for a little 'bone on I Didn't Know. After Mike's Groove, Mike tells the cheering crowd, "You're too kind." The sets are short—45 minutes each—and for historical value, check out the "upcoming band announcements" after the first set. On March 9, there's a tribute to Pig Pen, and on March 12th, "Big Fat Love, back by popular demand." —LOCK STEELE

[3/17/89]
Bear Trap Road, VT
Tapes with this date are actually part of 7/23/88.

3/25/89 ❄
Tree Cafe, Portland, ME

3/30/89 [ACCESSIBILITY: •]
The Front, Burlington, VT
I: Bold as Love, McGrupp, Divided Sky, The Price of Love, On Your Way Down, Ya Mar, Fluffhead, Antelope
II: Mango, Mike's > Hydrogen > Weekapaug, YEM > You're No Good > Undone, La Grange, Golgi
III: Peaches, Foam, AC/DC Bag, BBFCM, Satin Doll, Rocky Top
E: Makisupa

3/31/89 ❄
The Front, Burlington, VT

4/1/89 ❄
U-Joint, Northampton, MA

4/2/89 ❄
Nightshift, Naugatuck, CT

4/7/89 ❄
Stone Church, Newmarket, NH

4/13/89 ❄
Valley Club, Rutland, VT

4/14/89 [ACCESSIBILITY: •]
Base Lodge, Johnson State College, Johnson, VT
I: YEM, Bold as Love, Lizards, Sloth, Possum
II: Brain, Mike's > Hydrogen > Weekapaug, Esther

➢ Not too many folks have (or have heard) this tape; from what I've heard, there were only a few tapers there (only one or two SBDs). The band sounds excited and relaxed at the same time to be playing the Base Lodge (it's a small place). I know it's a contradiction, but the proof is in the tape. Keep your eyes peeled for this one—it's worth getting. —MIKE D'AMICO

4/15/89 [ACCESSIBILITY: •••]
Billings Hall, University of Vermont, Burlington, VT
I: Mike's > Hydrogen > Weekapaug, Esther, YEM, Wilson, Peaches, On Your Way Down, Alumni > Jimmy Page > Alumni, I Didn't Know, McGrupp, Foam, Bowie
II: Funky Bitch, Golgi, Slave, Mango, Divided Sky, Melt, Suzie, Fluffhead
E: GTBT
Soundcheck: Time Loves a Hero.

4/19/89 ❄
Johnny D's, Somerville, MA

4/20/89 [ACCESSIBILITY: ••]
Full Moon at The Zoo, Amherst College, Amherst, MA
I: AC/DC Bag, Fluffhead, You Shook Me All Night Long > Fluffhead, Fire, Esther, Suzie, Sloth, Possum, McGrupp, Foam, Bowie
II: Divided Sky, Walk Away, YEM, Melt, Lizards, Mike's > Hydrogen > Weekapaug, Love You, Harpua
Fire alarm went off during Fluffhead. After Phish returned, they started up "You Shook Me," then segued back into the unfinished Fluffhead. Phish's final "Full Moon at the Zoo" show.

4/21-22/89 ❄
The Front, Burlington, VT
Rock Rumble with five bands, including Phish. Phish won the Rumble.

4/27/89 ❄
Memorial Union Building, University of New Hampshire, Durham, NH

4/28/89 ❄
Bowdoin College, Brunswick, ME
Outdoor show.

4/29/89 ❄
The Living Room, Providence, RI
Phish shared the bill with Roomful of Blues.

4/30/89 [ACCESSIBILITY: •]
Nightstage, Cambridge, MA
I: I Didn't Know, YEM, McGrupp, Lizards, Divided Sky, Wilson, Peaches, Antelope, Terrapin, Fluffhead **E:** Possum
Setlist missing second set. Ben Hunter introduces Phish before I Didn't Know.

April 2 & May 27, 1989 — Nightshift Cafe & Trinity College

In the spring of 1989, a little tiny ad that ran in my local newspaper drew me to my first Phish show. The band played at this little tiny place called the Nightshift Cafe in Naugatuck, CT. It was a small bar—it's not even there any more—and it cost five bucks to get in. There were ten people in the audience. Two or three dedicated fans had followed Phish down there but the band really wasn't that well known in Connecticut yet.

I remember them playing Fee, YEM and BBFCFM. They also did the trampolines—I can't remember what song they did it in, though. (They didn't even tape the show—I asked Paul afterwards, and he's like, "No, we didn't tape it." I'm kind of bummed out about that.) They did two sets, and the show was great. I had a couple of tapes by then, so I knew the music but I had never seen them live before.

It was a fun night. The band came by and talked to us—they were nice guys, just regular guys, and they still are regular guys. Then I met Paul and I asked if he taped the show and he was like, "No," so he gave me his card and it had a phone number on it. I bought a red t-shirt—I still have it, my first Phish t-shirt, like a red or pink t-shirt with white letters on it. I've never even seen one like it since then. It's kind of weird.

The second show I saw is actually one of my favorites. I called up that hotline number and I heard that they were playing at Trinity College. So I called up Trinity College and nobody knew about it. And I was like, jeez, I don't know if they're really playing or not. But it said on the hotline recording that they were playing, so I went up there with my friend Jesse, real early, like one in the afternoon. I thought, maybe we'll hear something or we'll see somebody. And I was telling Jesse about the band and he was into it. So we're driving around, looking around, but we still weren't 21. I figured, what the hell. It seemed pretty hopeless until I heard this noise coming out of a building and I said, "Let's go over there and see what that is."

So we parked the car, walked in, and sure enough, there they are setting up. We walked in, didn't really say much to them—"How you doing?" that kind of thing. I remember they did a sound check with Sanity, they played that like four times, and then I remember playing pool with these guys. In the next room there was a pool table, and we were just hanging around until the evening when the show started. They were just regular guys and they weren't even famous. They were just good people—just a band.

It turned out to be a pretty good show. There was a $10 cover, which we never had to pay, and free beer. We wouldn't have gotten in anyway because you had to be 21 to get in. It was in the basement of a sorority house and they packed it in pretty well that night. There were a good 150 or 200 people there, and yes, they did tape this show.

—Rich Seaberg

Wed., June 7, 1989 — Hobart and William Smith, Geneva, NY

During our Senior Week, a couple of our friends got this band to come and play, and we didn't know anything about them. The only thing I remember about getting the band were people saying, 'Oh, well, Ross knows this band called Phish, so, you know, are you going to the Quad tonight to go listen to the Phish?" and I said, "Oh what the heck, I'll give it a try." So there were probably about maybe 75 to 100 people scattered around the Quad for that show, which probably started around 7:00 p.m. At most, there were maybe five people who didn't attend Hobart and William Smith at the show.

We were really surprised how good they were. People said things like, "Wow, this seems like a pretty good band, I wonder what they're doing bumming around on some college campus?" I don't really remember the setlist from that particular show, but it kind of set the tone for what I could expect from Phish shows after that. They pretty much always played the same songs at shows in '89 and '90—you expected to hear the same ten songs—Fee, Esther, YEM, AC/DC Bag, Lizards, Wilson, Mike's Song, Antelope, Contact and Alumni Blues. We pretty much heard that chunk of songs at every show in different kinds of orders.

—Charlene Smith

5/1/89 ❄
Pearl Street, Northampton, MA

5/3/89 ❄
Franklin & Marshall College, Lancaster, PA

5/5/89 [ACCESSIBILITY: •]
Hamilton College, Clinton, NY
I: Golgi, YEM, Ya Mar, Fluffhead, Alumni, Jazz Jam > Fee
II: Antelope, I Didn't Know, A-Train, GTBT **E:** Esther

5/6/89 [ACCESSIBILITY: •]
Collis Center, Dartmouth College, Hanover, NH
I: YEM, I Didn't Know, Mike's > Hydrogen > Weekapaug, Esther, Sloth, Possum, Bold as Love, AC/DC Bag, Forbin's > Mockingbird, Bowie
II: Donna Lee, Suzie, Contact, Fire, Harry Hood, Golgi, Slave, Divided Sky, Antelope

5/7/89 ❄
The Front, Burlington, VT

5/8/89 ❄
The Front, Burlington, VT

5/9/89 [ACCESSIBILITY: ••]
The Front, Burlington, VT
I: Wilson > Peaches, Ya Mar, Mike's > Hydrogen > Weekapaug, Sloth, Possum, Divided Sky
II: YEM, La Grange, If I Don't be There by Morning, Slave, Esther, Antelope, I Didn't Know > Nowhere Fast jam > I've Turned Bad jam > I Didn't Know, Lizards, Bold as Love, Harpua, Whipping Post
Junta release party. Sofi Dillof and Joe on vocals for Nowhere Fast and I've Turned Bad.

➢ The band took the wraps off *Junta* on this night and made it available to the public, with the cassette wrapped in artwork by Jim Pollock. The Front hosted the "Junta Release Party," though the band doesn't seem too concerned with selling albums—they're focused on the music. Check out this WILD Antelope with Trey saying, "Marco Esquandolis" in an eerie voice then asking the song's original question, "Bid you to have any spleef, man?" I Didn't Know (with a "pardon me Daubs" line) is also nuts as Sofi Dillof and Joe come on stage for a violent romp through Nowhere Fast and I've Turned Bad. ("When that angry side starts to show through, it feels so good to say 'fuck you,'" Sofi sings/yells at one point.) That leads to a drums and bass solo and then eventually back into I Didn't Know. Finally, the show is topped off by the hilarious "twice-shot ass" Harpua that includes a Poster Nutbag-like buildup for the announcement of Jimmy's name, and a rocking Whipping Post. —MELISSA WOLCOTT

➢ My favorite Front show! The second set has it all—jams, mayhem and humor. Anyone who doesn't understand Phish's dark side has got to check out the bad craziness in the middle of I Didn't Know. Yikes! —AMY MANNING

5/11/89 ❄
Pauli's Hotel, Albany, NY

5/12/89 ❄
Copperfield's, Syracuse, NY

5/13/89 [ACCESSIBILITY: ••]
The Orange Grove, Syracuse, NY
I: AC/DC Bag, Alumni > Jimmy Page > Alumni, YEM, Golgi, La Grange, Fluffhead, Possum, Foam, Walk Away, A-Train, Melt
II: Bowie, Suzie, Bold as Love, Lizards, Harry Hood, Brain, Contact
E: Fire, Whipping Post

5/14/89 ❄
University of Massachusetts, Amherst, MA
Southwest Outdoor Concert featured Canned Heat and other bands along with Phish.

5/18/89 ❄
Tree Cafe, Portland, ME

5/19/89 ❄
The Blue Pelican, Newport, RI

5/20/89 [ACCESSIBILITY: •]
Northfield Mt. Hermon School, Northfield, MA
I: AC/DC Bag, Alumni, YEM, Lizards, Wilson, Divided Sky, I Didn't Know, Possum
II: Bold as Love, Mike's > Hydrogen > Weekapaug, Foam, Contact, A-Train, Bowie, Golgi **E:** GTBT

5/21/89 [ACCESSIBILITY: •]
The Front, Burlington, VT
Harry Hood, Foam, Contact, Mike's > Hydrogen > Weekapaug, Melt, Sloth, YEM, Ya Mar, AC/DC Bag, Divided Sky
"Dazed and Confused" jam between Melt and Sloth.

5/26/89 [ACCESSIBILITY: ••]
The Valley Club, Rutland, VT
I: Bold as Love, AC/DC Bag, Mike's > Hydrogen > Weekapaug, Sanity, Halley's, Sloth, YEM
II: Bowie, Mango, Melt, Bathtub Gin, Antelope, Golgi
III: Slave, Funky Bitch, Curtis Loew, Possum, Jam
Bowie sung as "Lazy Lester." Jam at end of third set was an impromptu song the band created so they could play longer.

5/27/89 [ACCESSIBILITY: •]
Alpha Delta Phi Fraternity, Trinity College, West Hartford, CT
I: AC/DC Bag, Mike's > Hydrogen > Weekapaug, Funky Bitch, Fee, YEM, A-Train, Fluffhead, Bathtub Gin, GTBT
Setlist incomplete.

5/28/89 [ACCESSIBILITY: ••••]
Ian McClain's House, Hebron, NY
I: Divided Sky, Antelope, Forbin's > Mockingbird, Fee > Slave, Esther, Suzie, YEM
II: Fire, Mike's > Hydrogen > Weekapaug, Bathtub Gin, Sanity, Ride Captain Ride, Peaches, A-Train, Possum, Contact, "Mike and Magoo" Jam
III: Funky Bitch, La Grange, Sloth, Sneaking Sally > Vocal Jam, Ya Mar, Jesus Left Chicago, Melt, Mango, Harry Hood
Guest (Paul Ford?) on horns for A-Train. "Merry Christmas" singing after Possum. "Auld Lang Syne" jam in Contact. Ninja Mike Billington and Magoo (of Ninja Custodian) joined for the jam at the end of set II, with Fishman on trombone.

➢ A three-set show packed with highlights. I love listening to early shows, hearing them talking and having a great time up on stage. This show has special guests and funny flavors in all the songs. The third set closes perfectly with Hood, then Trey says that the cops have arrived and the show's over. If you like to hear the band talking and having a wasted good time while on stage, you have to get all three sets! —BILL PATRICK

➢ Sanity in set II is a more upbeat, fast-faced version. Then Page sings Ride Captain Ride, one of the better Page-sung tunes. In between Possum and Contact, Trey says, "It's snowing—Merry Christmas!" Some people have been misled by this since the show took place in May—really it was just ashes from the fire blowing around. Then to end Contact, they play an "Auld Lang Syne" tease. Magoo and Mike take the stage for a phunny song to close the set. —RYAN DANYEW

➢ You have to love those Ninja Custodian guys. The jam that ends set two features Magoo and Mike ("from the 'where are they now' category," Trey quips) leading the boys through a fun, funky jam. —TRICIA HOLMES

➢ Boy, Man, God, Shit, Poop—here's the best show of the 1980s, no question about it! Another party at Ian's house finds a pig over the flames and Phish kicking things off with a song Trey introduces as "Pighead" (Divided Sky). And what a set follows—Forbin/Mockingbird, Slave, Esther and a YEM in which they become fixated on the word "poop." (They actually chant "poop" in the song and the vocal jam). When it's over, Trey says, "We'd like to take a break so we can poop." The second set is even better—there's hilarious dialogue about "getting it up" (Page's department), "keeping it up" (Mike's department) and "letting it back down again" (Johnny "The Turtle" Fishman's department). Mike's Groove rocks, with Trey yelling "Here comes the beer!" in the midst of a great jam. There's also a "short visit to Weekapaug, Rhode Island," the "new" fast Sanity, a Ride Captain Ride by audience request and a hilarious Trey ribbing of Fish during A-Train. Perhaps no Phish show better combines banter and music than this one. —SCOTT SIFTON

➢ They kick some fuckin' arse! —JEN SPIVEY

6/3/89 ❄
Wetlands, New York, NY

6/8/89 ❄
The Quad, Hobart and William Smith Colleges, Geneva, NY

6/10/89 ❄
The Living Room, Providence, RI

6/16/89 ❄
Tree Cafe, Portland, ME
Phish opened for Roomful of Blues.

6/17/89 ❄
Tree Cafe, Portland, ME
Phish opened for Roomful of Blues.

6/23/89 [ACCESSIBILITY: ••]
The Paradise, Boston, MA
I: AC/DC Bag, YEM, Wilson, Peaches, Donna Lee, Fee, Mike's > Hydrogen > Weekapaug, Lizards, Antelope
II: Sloth, Fluffhead, Harry Hood, Ya Mar, Melt, Possum, Bowie
E: Contact, GTBT

6/29/89 ❄
The Front, Burlington, VT
There may not have been a show at the Front on this date.

6/30/89 [ACCESSIBILITY: •]
Pearl Street, Northampton, MA
I: Funky Bitch, YEM, McGrupp, Possum, Donna Lee, Fluffhead, Antelope
II: Walk Away, AC/DC Bag, Curtain, Slave, Bathtub Gin, Mike's > Hydrogen > Weekapaug

7/1/89 ❄
Les Fou Founes Electriques, Montreal, QC
Phish played this show as part of the Montreal International Jazz Festival.

8/11/89 ❄
Tree Cafe, Portland, ME

8/12/89 [ACCESSIBILITY: ••]
Burlington Boat House, Burlington, VT
Blue Sky > Suzie, AC/DC Bag, Ya Mar, Rocky Top, On Your Way Down, Wonderful You, Swing Tune, I Didn't Know, YEM, Possum > Icculus > Antelope
Steve and Beth's wedding party. Fishman on trombone for Icculus.

➢ For all of you who've dreamed of having Phish play at your wedding, this is a show to get. This wedding gig offers a nice setlist from top to bottom, including the only version of the Allman's Blue Sky and a couple of real dance tunes, as Trey puts it. And what wedding would be complete without the bride and groom bouncing on tramps during Suzie? —JOHN CUNNINGHAM

8/13/89 ❄
The Atlantic Connection in Oak Bluffs, Martha's Vineyard, MA

8/17/89 [ACCESSIBILITY: •]
The Front, Burlington, VT
I: Ya Mar, Suzie, McGrupp, Sloth, Rocky Top, Harry Hood, Mike's > Hydrogen > Weekapaug
II: Walk Away, AC/DC Bag, Mango, Fee, YEM > Lizards
III: Oh Kee, Bold as Love, PYITE > Possum, Halley's, Alumni, Contact, Antelope **E:** Golgi > Fire
Nancy Taube on vocals for Halley's.

➢ There were plenty of Phishtorical shows at the Front over the years, but this might be the most meaningful of all—Nancy Taube's last performance singing the words he penned to Halley's. The jam in Halley's stretches out forever, with Fish yelling things like "This song sucks!" and "I hate this song!" Because not only was this Nancy's last Halley's performance, this was Phish's last Halley's performance. They swore they'd never play it again, but four years later in Gunnison, CO, Halley's made its grand return. —ED SMITH

Saturday, October 14, 1989 — The Barn, Hobart and William Smith Colleges, Geneva, NY

The arrival of Phish at our campus on parents' weekend was our crazy secret. Only the "orphans" among us were at the show. No posters were put up and no one knew about it. Phish was brought on campus by two of my friends who also brought them to the colleges the previous spring. The day of the show we were so excited to get this band all for ourselves, we blew off classes to catch a buzz and prepare ourselves for a private party. The twilight came upon us and while we were at some off-campus house getting ready with a keg on a rather warm October night in upstate New York, Phish was having dinner at Farm House, a vegetarian co-op across the street from the Barn.

My friends and I arrived at The Barn and there was no line and, in fact, only about 50 people knew there was a concert that night. My friend who had brought the band to the colleges was collecting ticket money at the door—$2 each. Since many of us knew him personally we got in free. I was carrying a large backpack with a ten-liter bag of wine in it and once in the Barn, I looked for a place to hang the bag. I found what I was looking for—a coat hook on the wall of the dance area. I hung the bag upside down so the spigot poured strong, and went to get myself one of those VeryFine glass juice bottles out of the machine so I could drain it and use it for wine.

The Barn was a facility used for small concerts or indoor student parties. It was not used very often and only had a VeryFine juice machine and a Coke machine as amenities in the hallway, but that night we also sandwiched a keg between the juice machine and stairwell. The main hall was a large concrete slab laid in a modified barn, and it could hold 250 people. At about 10 p.m., Phish came to play. Trey and Mike were set up on a small, six-inch riser and Page and Fishman were on the concrete floor off in opposite corners flanking Trey and Mike.

They opened with a snappy version of AC/DC Bag and then proceeded to Divided Sky. People started drinking wine and frequent visits were also made to the keg using the dainty little VeryFine glass bottles or Coke cans as containers. Phish was here! Yes, our own little secret! Fishman graced us with an up-close lip-sucking on the vacuum cleaner during I Didn't Know. The show just kept rising through Golgi Apparatus, Ya Mar and Split Open and Melt. We cooled down with Fee, during which Trey skipped a line. We all knew the words and through crowd persuasion he was forced to admit his mistake by reciting the last verse—without music.

By this time the floor in front of the band was covered with broken glass, wine and beer. We all boogied in front of the six-foot high box speakers, which were soaking up their fair share of puddles of vino and beer, and often someone wiped out on the slick floor. Because there was no real stage and no definitive line between performer and audience, we all were sweating together. The stench of wine started to float in the air; was it wine-sweat or was it from the floor? Again, a rockin' rise occurred when they kicked into a supreme Alumni Blues, in which I made a fool of myself by not realizing the band had stopped. I screamed, "Because I got...!" Then the humiliation set in. The band laughed and mocked me. Fishman went so far as to ask me, "you gotta what?"

The show must have been a disappointment to the band as far as attendance was concerned. Probably only about 75 people were there at the peak, and mostly there were people who wandered in and wanted to check out what all the noise was about since The Barn bordered some dorms. However, Phish just got more hyped up. The scene was so intimate and messy it drove them to a good old jamming show. At least that's what we all felt. They then broke into what back then could have been their hallmark song, You Enjoy Myself. Inspired by the arrival of Hobart security, which Trey announced to the crowd, the band eased into a nice little version of Makisupa Policeman and it was forever made Hobart's and William Smith's own when Trey replaced "my barn" with "my house" in the lyrics. This was quickly followed by Good Times, Bad Times, which sent us all jumpin'.

Phish took a break and returned to the hallway with the keg, the coke machine and juice machine. I went over to Fishman as he was leaving and asked if he wanted some wine. He quickly replied, "yes" and we went to suckle the wine tap. After a few minutes of quenching our thirst he went to find his fellow band members. I think the short second set was the direct result of the visit by security. I also believe Phish's frustration with security inspired a particularly apropos opening of the second set—Anarchy and Highway to Hell. After Possum, I saw my buddy talking with Page and then Trey, but I couldn't figure out about what. During Harpua I found out what it was, when Trey broke into a few bars of In-A-Gadda-Da-Vida, a special treat for some of us. In addition, obviously miffed by security, even though they left as quickly as they had come, Trey told a little story during Harpua about Jimmy, who wanted to grow up to be a Hobart security officer. Man, we loved this because Trey and the rest of the band shared the same indignation we students felt for security's intrusion on our fun.

The show was over and there was just the smelly wine-slippery floor with broken glass and the sweaty people lingering and thanking the band not only with cheers but also with personal thanks. We invited them to our off-campus keg later that night, but they didn't show. Oh, well.

—Patrick Smith

8/18/89 ❄
Pearl Street, Northampton, MA

8/19/89 [ACCESSIBILITY: ••]
Collis Center, Dartmouth College, Hanover, NH
I: Oh Kee > Suzie, TMWSIY > Avenu > TMWSIY, AC/DC Bag, PYITE, Rocky Top, Bold as Love, Mango, Lizards, Mike's > Hydrogen > Weekapaug
II: Melt, A-Train, Divided Sky, Bathtub Gin, Funky Bitch, Curtis Loew, Bowie, Undone, Alumni > Jimmy Page > Alumni, YEM, Harry Hood

➢ This show circulates as 8/18/97, 8/19/88, and its correct date, 8/19/89. Any way you date it, though, it's got a good selection of Phish party tunes. —AMY MANNING

8/23/89 [ACCESSIBILITY: •]
The Living Room, Providence, RI
II: Antelope, Forbin's > Mockingbird, Ya Mar, YEM, AC/DC Bag, Foam, GTBT
Setlist missing first set.

8/25/89 ❄
The Blue Pelican, Newport, RI

8/26/89 [ACCESSIBILITY: ••]
Townshend Family Park, Townshend, VT
I: Fluffhead, Forbin's > Mockingbird, Harry Hood, Melt, Divided Sky, YEM > Possum
II: Bold as Love, Ya Mar, Slave, AC/DC Bag, Donna Lee, Funky Bitch, Foam, Bowie
III: TMWSIY > Avenu > TMWSIY, Suzie, Dinner and a Movie, Antelope
E: Contact, Lizards, La Grange
"Odd Couple" tease in Harry Hood. Show billed as "the ONLY outdoor show of the summer."

➢ As far as sets go, set I is about as perfect as I could ask for. Start out with a classic early Fluffhead then coast into a Col. Forbin > Mockingbird that easily rivals those of today, not to mention the phatty Hood that featured an "Odd Couple" theme in the intro. Set II starts out with the band asking the phans to "snap your fingers together," followed by the Andy Griffith Theme which goes into Bold as Love! Set III is equally as impressive—TMWSIY opener is beautiful, played perfectly. Every time I hear it, I am transported to another dimension. Definitely check this one out—you'll be euphoric for the whole week. —DAVID GEORGE

9/2/89 ❄
Wetlands, New York, NY

9/7/89 ❄
University of Massachusetts, Amherst, MA
Outdoor show.

9/8/89 ❄
The Front, Burlington, VT

9/9/89 [ACCESSIBILITY: ••]
Bennington College, Bennington, VT
I: Foam, Oh Kee > Suzie, Divided Sky, AC/DC Bag, McGrupp > Makisupa, Bathtub Gin, PYITE, Wilson, MSO, Bowie
II: Ya Mar, YEM, Alumni, Melt, Harry Hood, Walk Away, Possum

9/21/89 [ACCESSIBILITY: •]
Pearl Street, Northampton, MA
I: Golgi, Ya Mar, AC/DC Bag, MSO, Fee, Alumni > McGrupp, Who Do We Do, Bowie
II: Divided Sky > The Chase > Dinner and a Movie > Bundle Of Joy > Possum, Bathtub Gin, YEM, Brain, Antelope

10/1/89 [ACCESSIBILITY: ••]
The Front, Burlington, VT
I: Alumni, McGrupp > Jam, Golgi, Harry Hood > Wilson, Foam, Ya Mar, Oh Kee > Suzie, Antelope
II: AC/DC Bag > MSO, Reba, Dinner and a Movie, Fluffhead, Possum, YEM, Brain, Contact, Melt, Lizards **E:** Highway to Hell
Concert debut: Reba. Reba includes extra verse and now-defunct section following lyrics. Sunday "All Ages" show at The Front.

➢ The debut of Reba! It's a nice birth (they announce the debut, dedicated to the spirit of Nancy Taube), with the song in a bit of a different format than they play now. Other reasons to grab this tape include Ya Mar (I like the early short versions of Ya Mar like 3/1/90), Alumni and McGrupp. There's also a classic Fishman performance of If I Only Had A Brain—do you think he's telling the truth? And there's an electric My Sweet One! I miss those. —GREG MARCEAN

10/6/89 ❄
The Paradise, Boston, MA
Timber Ho, Mike's > Hydrogen > Weekapaug, Sloth, Golgi, Bold as Love, Dinner and a Movie, Alumni > Jimmy Page, Harry Hood, Possum, Highway to Hell, BBFCM **E:** GTBT
List may be incomplete.

10/7/89 [ACCESSIBILITY: ••]
Chase Hall, Bates College, Lewiston, ME
I: Golgi, Ya Mar, Mike's > Hydrogen > Weekapaug, Suzie, Fee, La Grange, Makisupa, Alumni > Jimmy Page > Alumni, GTBT
II: Dinner and a Movie, Possum, Happy Birthday Jam, Lizards, AC/DC Bag, Bowie, Contact > Highway to Hell **E:** YEM
Date of show might be 11/7/89.

10/12/89 ❄
Keene State College, Keene, NH

10/13/89 ❄
Copperfield's, Syracuse, NY

10/14/89 [ACCESSIBILITY: •••]
The Barn, Hobart and William Smith Colleges, Geneva, NY
I: AC/DC Bag, Divided Sky, I Didn't Know, Golgi, Ya Mar, Melt, Fee, Alumni > Jimmy Page > Alumni, YEM, Makisupa, GTBT
II: Anarchy In the U.K., Highway to Hell, Possum, Harpua
Setlist may be incomplete. Fishman on vacuum for I Didn't Know. "In-a-Gadda-Da-Vida" jam in Harpua.

10/20/89 [ACCESSIBILITY: ••••]
The Front, Burlington, VT
I: Harpua > Bundle of Joy > Forbin's > Mockingbird, YEM, Oh Kee, Reba, Divided Sky, Golgi, Antelope
II: No Dogs Allowed, Walk Away, Dinner and a Movie, I Didn't Know, AC/DC Bag, Donna Lee, Melt, Melt, Harry Hood, Swing Low Sweet Chariot, Hole **E:** La Grange, Slave
Reba includes extra verse and now-defunct section following lyrics. Entire second set after Dinner and a Movie featured Dave Grippo on alto saxophone and Russ Remington on tenor saxophone. Melt begun again after lighting problem. "Odd Couple" tease in Antelope and Hood. "Spiderman" tease in Antelope. "Old Macdonald" tease in Antelope.

➢ This tape offers a great glimpse of Phish early on, but late enough that they really have their act together. The Split Open restarts after a lighting problem, but it's great and features horns guests including Dave "The Truth" Grippo. Harry Hood has an "Odd Couple" jam at the beginning, which is neat. Slave to the Traffic Light is one that must be heard—it's super-fast. There's also Antelope with the "Spiderman" jam. There are many hidden treats in this show, so keep your ears open. —ADAM DAVIDOFF

➢ Amazing show! The horns sit in for most of the second set, which I find more enjoyable than many of the July '91 gigs! An absolutely rocking show. —TYLER HARRIS

10/21/89 ❄
The Front, Burlington, VT
I: Fee, Ya Mar, Hole, McGrupp > Fluffhead, Foam, AC/DC Bag, Lizards, Dog Log, Bowie
II: Mike's > Hydrogen > Weekapaug
Setlist missing rest of second set and encore.

➢ I scored this one from a buddy—wow, what an eye-opener. Great quality for an old show. There's a very stripped-down Hole, McGrupp, AC/DC Bag and of course Dog Log. Sick, I tell you! If I could be at one show that I own tapes of from '89, this would be it. Unfortunately, it's a rare tape and the setlist might be screwy. —MARK DANIEL

10/22/89 [ACCESSIBILITY: •]
The Front, Burlington, VT
I: La Grange, Forbin's > Mockingbird, YEM > Oh Kee > Suzie, Ya Mar, Foam, Rocky Top, Melt, Tela, Divided Sky, I Didn't Know, GTBT
II: Harry Hood, Reba, Golgi, Hole, McGrupp, AC/DC Bag > MSO, Fee, Possum **E:** Undone
Sunday "All Ages" show at The Front.

➢ I own close to 500 Phish tapes, including all New Year's Runs and most Halloween shows, but this is the best show I have on tape. It packs Phish's best-written songs into one show. The setlist is one beyond the dreams of fans, and the way they play the songs is flawless. The Forbin's > Mockingbird doesn't have a story and doesn't even need one. The show also contains the best Oh Kee Pa > Suzie I have ever heard, and as if that weren't enough, YEM and Divided Sky both appear in the first set. It's an excellent example of Phish's music in the late 1980s. —ADAM RIZZUTI

➢ Anyone of any age could come to this show. Ninja Mike (of Ninja Custodians) ran from the bar up onto the stage, trying to bounce on his head while Phish's trampoline act was going on. He messed up and ended up running into Trey's guitar and amp. He landed behind the backdrop. He stayed there, hiding, as Fishman made cute comments. —MELISSA MIXER

10/26/89 [ACCESSIBILITY: •••]
Wetlands, New York, NY
I: Oh Kee > Golgi, YEM, Fee > Divided Sky, I Didn't Know, Wilson, Lizards, Mike's > Hydrogen > Weekapaug
II: Dinner and a Movie > Clod > AC/DC Bag, Reba > Walk Away, Bathtub Gin > Sloth > Fluff's Travels > Possum, PYITE, Hole, "Sea Gull Poem," No Dogs Allowed, Bowie

Before PYITE, Trey clarifies that its correct title is "Punch Me In The Eye." Trey teases "Space Oddity" by Bowie while talking about the upcoming Goddard Halloween show, then the band goes into Bowie. Reba includes extra verse and now-defunct section following lyrics.

➢ The second set of this show is a great one. A Little Schoolgirl jam kicks things off, into Dinner and a Movie. Clod follows with a slower AC/DC Bag. For all Reba fans, this tape is a must-hear: there is a currently-omitted phase in this early Reba (the third ever) which no longer exists, akin to the now-omitted Tela verse (see Penn State '88). This is quite interesting and would be great to hear nowadays. Also, Trey introduces PYITE as "Punch Me in the Eye," then relatively new as well. —ADAM DAVIDOFF

➢ Great show for some "old" Phish. Nice pieces of Fluff's Travels are added in between the songs, which keep flowing from one to the next. Several classic tunes are played that you don't see on current setlists, and a rare appearance is made by Trey's mom as they explain No Dogs Allowed. This is definitely one to get a hold of to listen to the differences in Phish between '89 and '97. —TIM HERRMAN

10/28/89 ❄
The Chance, Poughkeepsie, NY

10/31/89 [ACCESSIBILITY: ••]
Sculpture Room, Goddard College, Plainfield, VT
I: Oh Kee > Suzie, AC/DC Bag, Divided Sky, Fee, Walk Away, Bathtub Gin, Possum
II: YEM, Bowie, Wilson, Reba, Forbin's > Mockingbird, Alumni, Lizards, Highway to Hell **E:** Contact > Antelope > Kung > Antelope

Final of four Phish Halloween shows at Goddard. Ninja Custodian opened. Reba includes extra verse and now-defunct section following lyrics. Band distributes macaroni and cheese boxes to the audience before David Bowie; the audience joins on percussion during Bowie. Concert debut: Kung. Portions of this show were later broadcast on public-access cable TV in Burlington.

➢ Halloween at Goddard was a huge costume party and a total blast. It was the largest Phish show I'd ever attended, but that's not saying much; there were probably two hundred people there. Everyone was dressed up, including the band. It was really dark, too—you couldn't really see anything in the crowd at this show. That was because of the not very well-lit room, which I think might have been some sort of barn. The show itself was really fun and was also a kind of a signal that Phish was getting a little bit bigger, that they could draw a few hundred people to this obscure Vermont town on Halloween night. A lot of people from Burlington, like myself, drove to Goddard for it. —CHARLENE SMITH

➢ The public-access TV video of this show is out there, and it's hilarious! You can see the costumes, the macaroni and cheese, and Page with really curly hair! It's obviously unprofessional, but man, does it make me laugh. —ED SMITH

11/2/89 [ACCESSIBILITY: ••••]
Memorial Union Building, University of New Hampshire, Durham, NH
I: Bathtub Gin, Foam, Mike's > Hydrogen > Weekapaug, Fee, Curtain, Reba, Melt, Esther, GTBT
II: Oh Kee > Golgi, YEM > Kung > Divided Sky, McGrupp > Who Do We Do > AC/DC Bag, MSO **E:** Highway to Hell

Outing Club benefit. Reba includes extra verse and now-defunct section following lyrics.

➢ A cafeteria-type room, approximate capacity 450 people. Mind-blowing first set during Reba's first tour. Reba has an extra verse, a harder-edge "bag it tag it" before the instrumental middle section. The Curtain is always a bonus, then during Divided Sky Trey speaks of the black rhombus. This was one hell of a first show for me—the band cruised around the crowd during set break. —NATHANIEL PEIRCE

➢ There are a few weird things about this show. First of all, it's one of the few early shows where good sounding digital audience tapes can be found. Also, Phish must have been playing at a school dance or something, judging from their introduction. The jammy Mike's Groove sure caught people off-guard, judging from the crowd's reaction. —BEN ROSS

➢ Quite a party at UNH this night. The start of Bathtub Gin drowned out the fire exit speech, and the show just took off from there. The YEM vocal jam was good clean fun. Our heros hammed it up and then segued straight into Kung. This was followed by a rhombus reference which gave way to Divided Sky which really moved. There have certainly been more experimental nights. This was pure fun. —SCOTT KUSHNER

11/3/89 [ACCESSIBILITY: •]
Tree Cafe, Portland, ME
I: Forbin's > Mockingbird, Bathtub Gin, MSO, Melt > Clod > Bundle of Joy, YEM, PYITE, Reba, Golgi

Reba includes extra verse and now-defunct section following lyrics.

11/4/89 ❄
College of the Atlantic, Bar Harbor, ME

Tuesday, October 31, 1989 Goddard College, Plainfield, VT

I saw my first Phish show on October 31, 1989, Halloween night, in what I believe was an art building (or something like that) at Goddard College. I kind of stumbled upon it.

I was going to school at Johnson State, which is on Route 15 in Vermont. My roommate talked me into driving to this concert and I didn't really want to go, but he told me it was kind of like a Grateful Dead cover band, so I said, "Oh, okay, what the hell."

To my surprise, Phish was much different and much to my liking. It was a really different situation—there were all kinds of people jam-packed into a tiny little place. I'd never seen anything like it before in my life, and I thought, "This is really cool."

There were about three hundred people there. That's my guess. The room felt like a garage, and the people were packed in there. What really surprised me when I got there was the partying that was going on in the parking lot for this band I had never heard of before. And everybody was dressed in costume. Trey was wearing—well, they changed in between sets—but during one set I can remember Trey wearing fake boobs with chains around them, and horns on his head. I can't remember what everybody else was wearing, but during another set, they came back and they were wearing pajamas.

I remember thinking to myself, "Wow, this is what the Grateful Dead used to be like in the good old days, and this is something that I can see, this is something of my own." And I can remember, it was Famous Mockingbird—that if I was to come away saying what tune really grabbed me, it was the Mockingbird.

At the beginning of one set, Phish just chucked all these boxes of macaroni and cheese into the crowd. Some of the students there were videotaping the show for public access TV in Burlington. So you had all kinds of people hanging from the rafters, people everywhere, and they just started chucking these macaroni and cheese boxes and everyone was getting hit by them. Then people started shaking them like they told us to, and then I think they went into a David Bowie or something like that. The shaking dissipated very soon after the David Bowie intro, but it definitely got the crowd going.

Admission to the show was free but they gladly accepted donations at the end. As I was leaving, someone shook a coffee can in my direction. I can actually remember leaving the show early because it was just so late, and driving in the rain to go home because I was the only one able to drive. We lived an hour away from Goddard, and I remember pulling into home between four and five, so the show probably didn't end until 3 a.m.

—Brendan McKenna

Friday, December 15, 1989 Ukrainian National Home, NY, NY

I sort of stumbled upon Phish by accident. I was maybe 16 or 17 hanging out with a friend on a street corner on a cold winter night in New York looking for something to do. Someone heard that Blues Traveler was playing downtown with another band who "jumped up and down on mini-tramps while they played." So we hopped in a cab and headed downtown to the Village to a Ukrainian Community Center someone rented out for the show. What a random place to see my first Phish show! What an odd place to go on a Saturday night!

I imagined that this center, with its pronounced Cyrillic signage on the building facade, was normally used for meetings, bake sales, folk-dance lessons or whatever else Ukrainians might like to do. Upstairs was a recreation room with low ceilings, funny ceiling panel-tiles, and fluorescent lighting that, suffice to say, had been turned off. I don't think there was even a stage.

That night there was no folk dancing or potluck. I caught Phish in the middle of a set and I vaguely recall jamming to YEM, although that could be a wishful memory I've planted in my head. Alas, in those days of old I had a curfew and went home before the show ended, but I'm sure the party continued into the wee hours of the morning. Those New York Ukrainian Phishheads, after all, sure know how to jam.

—Kirsti Scutt

11/9/89 [ACCESSIBILITY: •]
Mission Park Dining Hall, Williams College, Williamstown, MA
I: I Didn't Know, Golgi, Ya Mar, Curtain, MSO, Bathtub Gin, YEM, A-Train, GTBT
II: Oh Kee > AC/DC Bag, McGrupp > PYITE, Lizards, Mike's > Hydrogen > Weekapaug **E:** Highway to Hell

11/10/89 [ACCESSIBILITY: ••••]
Sigma Phi Fraternity House, Hamilton College, Clinton, NY
I: Melt, Oh Kee > Suzie, Fee, Divided Sky > AC/DC Bag, MSO, YEM, My Girl > La Grange, Harry Hood, Bathtub Gin, Mike's > Hydrogen > Weekapaug
II: McGrupp > Fluff's Travels > Sloth, Lizards, Brain, Possum, Harpua, Highway to Hell, A-Train, Antelope

11/11/89 [ACCESSIBILITY: ••]
Patrick Gymnasium, University of Vermont, Burlington, VT
Oh Kee > Golgi, Bathtub Gin, AC/DC Bag, MSO, YEM, Brain, Frankenstein
Phish played one set; Max Creek and Third World played after Phish. Concert debut: Frankenstein.

11/16/89 [ACCESSIBILITY: •]
Pearl Street, Northampton, MA
I: Mike's > Hydrogen > Weekapaug, Bathtub Gin, Foam, Oh Kee > Suzie, MSO, Reba, YEM > Frankenstein
II: Sloth, AC/DC Bag, Tela, Bowie
Show ended after Bowie when a window broke in the club. Reba includes extra verse and now-defunct section following lyrics.

11/18/89 ❄
23 East Cabaret, Ardmore, PA

➢ This was Phish's first Philadelphia-area show. To drum up fan support, the Phish newsletter advised, "These Cabaret clubs are known for their great atmosphere/good shows!" Elsewhere, the newsletter touted Phish's first show in Washington, D.C. on 12/6/89 and its show at the 8x10 Club in Baltimore the following day, saying, "What better excuse for a roadtrip than to see Phish at one of these great clubs! And make sure to spread the word to friends in these cities!" This is the famous word-of-mouth network that the band and its backers proved so good at coordinating in action. —LOCK STEELE

11/30/89 [ACCESSIBILITY: •]
The Paradise, Boston, MA
I: Bathtub Gin, Divided Sky, Ya Mar, Oh Kee > AC/DC Bag, Foam, Lizards, MSO, Antelope, Lawn Boy, Frankenstein
II: Reba, Possum, Forbin's > Mockingbird, Undone, Fee, Melt, A-Train, Suzie, Contact, Bowie
Date of show might be 12/1/89. Reba includes extra verse and now-defunct section following lyrics.

12/3/89 ❄
The Front, Burlington, VT
Sunday "All Ages" show at The Front.

12/4/89 ❄
The Front, Burlington, VT

12/6/89
The Roxy, Washington, DC

12/7/89 [ACCESSIBILITY: ••••]
8x10 Club, Baltimore, MD
I: I Didn't Know, YEM, A-Train, AC/DC Bag, Fee, Mike's > Hydrogen > Weekapaug, Alumni > Jimmy Page > Alumni, Divided Sky
II: Oh Kee > Suzie, Rocky Top, Ya Mar, Walk Away, Lizards, Antelope, Lawn Boy, Possum, Undone **E:** Golgi

12/8/89 [ACCESSIBILITY: ••••]
Green Mountain College, Poultney, VT
I: Oh Kee > Suzie, Melt, Ya Mar, Reba, McGrupp > Who Do We Do > AC/DC Bag, MSO, Bathtub Gin, Antelope
II: Harry Hood, Tela, Timber Ho, Slave, I Didn't Know, YEM, Possum, Lawn Boy, Fire
Reba includes extra verse and now-defunct section following lyrics.

➢ This tape is widely-available but tends to be somewhat overlooked. I think set II contains some of the most perfectly balanced versions of Harry, Tela and Slave I have from this era. But don't overlook the Antelope—it's not the best, but it's so, so crisp. —JUSTIN WEISS

➢ A good show from top to bottom. In the solo for Split Open, Trey sounds like a man possessed. Reba is average and so is Antelope. The boys make some funky aquatic sounds during the latter part of AC/DC Bag. Tela, Slave and I Didn't Know are must-hears on this tape. They're phantastic! The vocal jam at the end of YEM is totally insane. Grab this tape if you can find it. —TONY KRUPKA

12/9/89 [ACCESSIBILITY: •]
Castleton State College, Bomeseen, VT
I: Dinner and a Movie, La Grange, Lizards, Foam, Hole, Rocky Top, Bowie, Lawn Boy, Bathtub Gin, Golgi
II: A-Train, Fluffhead, Esther, Alumni, Fee, Mike's > Hydrogen > Weekapaug, Contact, BBFCM

12/15/89 [ACCESSIBILITY: ••]
Ukrainian National Home, New York, NY
I Didn't Know, Possum, Divided Sky, Antelope, Funky Bitch, Jesus Left Chicago, Contact, Bowie
Phish shared the bill with Blues Traveler and played one set. John Popper on harmonica for Funky Bitch and Jesus Left Chicago.

12/16/89 [ACCESSIBILITY: •]
Contois Auditorium at City Hall, Burlington, VT
Curtain > AC/DC Bag, Lawn Boy, Mike's > Hydrogen > Weekapaug, Lizards, Hole, Golgi **E:** Possum
Burlington Boathouse Benefit concert.

12/29/89 [ACCESSIBILITY: •]
23 East Cabaret, Ardmore, PA
I: Divided Sky, Ya Mar, Oh Kee > AC/DC Bag, Lizards, Lawn Boy, Mike's > Hydrogen > Weekapaug
Setlist incomplete.

12/30/89 ❄
Wetlands Preserve, New York, NY
Indecision opened.

12/31/89 ❄
Exhibition Hall, World Trade Center, Boston, MA
I: I Didn't Know, YEM, Oh Kee > AC/DC Bag, Auld Lang Syne, Antelope, Bathtub Gin, Lizards, Satin Doll, Highway to Hell
II: Mike's > Hydrogen > Weekapaug, Ya Mar, Melt, Divided Sky, Fee
E: Contact
The Ululators opened. Show billed as Phish's "1st annual New Year's Eve Extravaganza!"

➢ In a small ballroom in Beantown, the Phish New Year's Eve tradition began. The November Phish newsletter noted, "Phish is looking for a space in New England to host a New Year's Eve extravaganza! We need a room to hold 500-800 people, as well as lots of party ideas." When the venue—Boston's World Trade Center Ballroom—had been confirmed, the December newsletter said, "Creative formal dress appreciated for this grand affair!" The band provided hors d'oeuvres (fruit) and champagne to the crowd, but also (in the first of what would become an increasingly elaborate series of New Year's Eve pranks) had a few tricks up their sleeves. When Page, Trey and Mike appeared on stage in full tuxedo garb and started singing I Didn't Know, Fishman was nowhere to be seen. But when it came time for a vacuum solo in the middle of the song, Fish emerged wearing nothing but a top hat and g-string! —LOCK STEELE

1990 *MOUNTAINS TO MOUNTAINS*

1990, the first year for which setlists are generally more accurate than inaccurate—although some of the setlists from this year likely have songs or encores missing—saw Phish touring as far south as Atlanta and as far west as Wisconsin. February led the band south (for several shows with Widespread Panic), then Spring found them traveling across the midwest and back to Colorado for the first time since their August '88 Telluride sojourn. Phish took most of the summer off from gigging following a three-set show at Townshend Family Park on June 16, 1990. Starting things back up in September at the Wetlands, they unveiled a whole new slate of songs and were soon on their way west again for a run of fall shows in Colorado (including Halloween) that still rank among the most storied in Phishtory. After pressing northward to Wisconsin, the band trucked back across the country, finishing the year in the mid-Atlantic and then the Northeast with another (somewhat less successful) New Year's Eve show in Boston.

Notable debuts in the spring of 1990 include Tweezer, Cavern and Bouncing; the epic Wetlands show in September included more debuts than any show until Lowell in the spring of 1995. The year also saw frequent collaborations with Blues Traveler and especially their frontman, John Popper, with whom Trey co-wrote Don't Get Me Wrong. Excellent tapes from this year are in circulation, especially the Colorado run of 10/30-11/4 and the 4/22/90 show, for which digital soundboard/audience mixes can be found.

Though Paul stopped allowing soundboard patches for most tapers after the 6/16 Townshend show—he blamed sound difficulties at the show on the tapers patched into his soundboard—many shows from this era can be found on soundboard tapes of varying quality.

1/20/90 [ACCESSIBILITY: ••]
Webster Hall, Dartmouth College, Hanover, NH
Oh Kee > Suzie, Bouncing, Reba, Tela, La Grange, Lawn Boy, Esther, Mike's > Hydrogen > Weekapaug, Harry Hood, Carolina, Squirming Coil, Caravan
Concert debuts: Bouncing, Carolina, Caravan and Squirming Coil.

1/25/90 ❄
The Oronoko, University of Maine, Orono, ME

1/26/90 ❄
Tree Cafe, Portland, ME

1/27/90 [ACCESSIBILITY: •]
The Front, Burlington, VT
I: Carolina > Bathtub Gin, Ya Mar, Oh Kee > AC/DC Bag, MSO, Bouncing, Wilson, Reba, Funky Bitch, Mike's > Hydrogen > Weekapaug
II: Communication Breakdown, Caravan, YEM, Squirming Coil, Antelope, Terrapin, Divided Sky **E:** La Grange
Concert debut: Communication Breakdown.

1/28/90 [ACCESSIBILITY: ••]
The Front, Burlington, VT
I: Suzie, Melt, Tela, Fluffhead, La Grange, Carolina, Forbin's > Mockingbird, Communication Breakdown
II: Wilson, Antelope, Bouncing, Caravan, Squirming Coil, YEM, Bathtub Gin, Mike's > Hydrogen > Weekapaug **E:** Lawn Boy, BBFCM
Sunday "All Ages" show at The Front. Wilson played heavy-metal style.

➢ Around this time, Phish experimented with a version of Wilson that has a distinctly heavy-metal feel to it. This show offers one of the rare performances of it, as well as the great Led Zep tune Communication Breakdown, which didn't last much longer in Phish setlists than the heavy-metal Lizards. —ERNIE GREENE

1/29/90 ❄
The Haunt, Ithaca, NY

2/1/90 ❄
Georgia Theater, Athens, GA

2/2/90 ❄
Georgia Theater, Athens, GA

2/3/90 ❄
Cotton Club, Atlanta, GA

2/4/90 ❄
Greenstreets, Columbia, SC

2/5/90 ❄
Myskyne, Charleston, SC

2/7/90 ❄
Cat's Cradle, Chapel Hill, NC

2/9/90 ❄
Chameleon Club, Lancaster, PA
I: Golgi, Oh Kee > Suzie, YEM, Walk Away, Bouncing, AC/DC Bag, Squirming Coil > Mike's > Hydrogen > Weekapaug, Carolina
II: Dinner and a Movie, Ya Mar, Reba, Wilson, A-Train, Alumni, Foam, Curtis Loew, Bowie **E:** I Didn't Know

2/10/90 [ACCESSIBILITY: •]
23 East Cabaret, Ardmore, PA
I: Dinner and a Movie, Oh Kee > Suzie, YEM, Bathtub Gin, Bouncing, Possum, Carolina, Contact, Bowie
II: La Grange, Esther, AC/DC Bag, Rocky Top, Donna Lee, Fee, Mike's > Hydrogen > Weekapaug **E:** I Didn't Know, Highway to Hell

2/15/90 [ACCESSIBILITY: ••••]
The Living Room, Providence, RI
I: Carolina, Oh Kee > Suzie, Divided Sky, Dinner and a Movie, Caravan, Bathtub Gin, Mike's > Hydrogen > Weekapaug
Setlist missing second set and encore.

2/16/90 ❄
The Paradise, Boston, MA

1990

103 Total Show Dates
- **7** one-set shows
- **74** two-set shows
- **2** three-set shows
- **20** dates with no setlists

PHAN PICKS 1990

SHOW	THE SKINNY
1) 06/16/90 Townshend, VT	Three long sets in sunny VT.
2) 11/04/90 Ft. Collins, CO	The best of an amazing week.
3) 03/01/90 New Haven, CT	Widely available on bootleg CD.
4) 10/31/90 CO Springs, CO	First of two Halloweens in CO.
5) 11/02/90 Boulder, CO	The spirit of Glen Miller.
6) 11/03/90 Boulder, CO	Perhaps even better than 11/2.
7) 04/22/90 CO Springs, CO	Gorgeous Hood on perfect SBD.
8) 10/30/90 Crested Butte, CO	Another from a mystical week.
9) 04/29/90 Woodbury, CT	Find it on videotape.
10) 03/11/90 Burlington, VT	Roll like a cantaloupe!

MUSICAL RECAP: 1990 saw Phish honing their two-set live show format. Some of the long-winded craziness of the 1980s is already being toned down as more challenging compositional songs debut.
REPRESENTATIVE JAMS: Tweezer > Manteca > Tweezer, 12/28/90; Harry Hood, 11/4/90 and 4/22/90; David Bowie, 11/2/90 (w/tease medley).
ORIGINAL SONG DEBUTS: Asse Festival (9/13/90); Bouncing (1/20/90); Buried Alive (9/13/90); Cavern (3/28/90); Destiny Unbound (9/14/90); Don't Get Me Wrong (10/7/90); Eliza (11/17/90); Gumbo (9/28/90); Horn (5/24/90); Landlady (4/7/90); Magilla (9/13/90); Rift (slow version, 2/25/90); Runaway Jim (3/28/90); Squirming Coil (1/20/90); Stash (9/13/90); Tube (9/13/90); Tweezer (3/28/90).
COVER SONG DEBUTS: Caravan (1/20/90), Carolina (1/20/90); Communication Breakdown (1/27/90); Going Down Slow (9/13/90) Minute By Minute (9/13/90); It's No Good Trying (12/7/90); Paul and Silas (9/13/90); Sweet Adeline (3/28/90); Uncle Pen (3/28/90).

DARK HORSES

SHOW	THE SKINNY
1) 12/28/90 New York, NY	John Popper joins and jams.
2) 09/13/90 New York, NY	Lots of debuts, plus the Dude.
3) 04/08-09/90 Telluride, CO	Tough to find, but worth it.
4) 11/24/90 Port Chester, NY	First Phish show at the Capitol.
5) 11/08/90 Madison, WI	Another one with Popper.

Most-Played Originals:

1) Bouncing	58	56%
1) Possum	58	56%
3) You Enjoy Myself	57	55%
4) Mike's Song	54	52%
4) I am Hydrogen	54	52%
4) Weekapaug Groove	54	52%
7) Oh Kee Pa	53	51%
8) Suzie Greenberg	48	47%
9) Divided Sky	42	41%
10) Reba	36	35%

Most-Played Covers:

1) Uncle Pen	33	32%
1) Ya Mar	22	21%
3) Caravan	21	20%
3) La Grange	21	20%
3) Carolina	21	20%
6) Highway to Hell	17	17%
8) Funky Bitch	15	15%
8) Take the A-Train	15	15%
10) Donna Lee, Fire, Jesus Left Chicago	11	11%

First-Set Openers:

1) Possum	9
2) Golgi Apparatus	8
3) Suzie Greenberg	7
4) The Landlady	6
5) Buried Alive	5

Second-Set Openers:

1) Golgi Apparatus	7
2) The Landlady	6
3) Mike's Song	5
4) Buried Alive, Divided Sky, Suzie Greenberg	3

Henrietta Songs:

1) If I Only Had a Brain	8
2) Love You	8
3) Terrapin	5
4) Bike	3
4) It's No Good Trying	3
6) Minute By Minute	2

A Cappella Songs:

1) Carolina	21
2) Sweet Adeline	10
3) Memories	1

Mon., Feb. 19, 1990 Student Union, Keene State, Keene, NH

I am not your typical Phish fan. I didn't have a high school or college friend who turned me on; rather, I came across Phish by a stroke of sheer luck. Let me explain.

It was the winter of 1990, and I had just finished graduate school and was starting my first "professional" career-type job in Keene, NH, working at a municipal planning consulting firm. This was a very difficult time for me. A relationship with the love of my life ended tragically; reality and idealism were clashing at work; the money sucked; I lived in a tiny one-room closet in downtown Keene; and the scene in the area was unbelievably boring. Thinking "Welcome to the rest of my life," I was severely depressed.

At that point, our office hired an intern—Stu Schwartz, I believe (anyone know him? I need to thank this man!) from local Antioch College. We got along quite well and shared a similar taste in music. Since he lived close by, I told him to come by my place sometime and we could roll up a couple of fat boys and play some music. Well, one cold night in February he did just that. Around 8 p.m., Stu told me there was this band at Keene State that I really should check out. I hemmed and hawed and said I was pretty comfortable right where I was, but Stu insisted: "No Steve, you really need to see this band!" So he dragged me out into the cold winter night to the upstairs of the Keene State Student Union building. I walked up to the front of the stage and Phish began to play.

I absolutely flipped! This band was a blend of all my favorite bands and then some. At this time, my favorites included Zappa, Yes, King Crimson, Gentle Giant, Crack the Sky, Tull, old Genesis, and various jazz artists. They weren't aping any particular band's sound; rather, it seemed to me they were exploring uncharted territory, much like the above bands did in their primes. I remember thinking, "Oh my God... this is like seeing King Crimson before anyone knew about them!" I remember most of the songs they played: Fee, Wilson, Divided Sky, YEM, Bouncing and Lizards among them. I left that evening with much more than a shirt and a tape; I had a renewed sense that life was worth living. After two years of perpetual clouds, I felt like the sun was shining again. **—Steve Wallace**

Thursday, April 19, 1990 Boulder Theater, Boulder, CO

You gotta see these guys!"—I had heard that about Phish several times too many, but seeing how my friends in The Circle were going to be the opening band, a bunch of us decided to drive to Boulder from Colorado Springs to see our first Phish show.

The Boulder Theater was, at the time, *the* Boulder venue, with cool seating, micro-brews and southwestern murals on the walls. Getting the $6 tickets was no problem—call the venue and ask them to hold some. So, we all piled out of the car knowing that at least we were going to see The Circle in the nicest place *they'd* ever played.

My memory is fuzzy but I think Phish's opener was Good Times, Bad Times. Doing Zeppelin covers is an automatic negative-point, but as the song progressed, it was obvious that not only could Phish legitimately play this song, but they were, more than anything, players. After the cheers died down, they made their way to an original composition. This being before the LP release of *Lawn Boy*, we thought the song was called, "Bag it, tag it." Reba, as we know it today, was the first time I ever entered that special place to which only Phish can take you. As they hit the jam, we saw the trampolines for the first time. Where would we have seen the combination of aerial stunts and precision playing before this night? As "the bass player" and "the guitar player" hit their strides, we did our best to keep up.

Their talents were laid bare on Joe Walsh's Walk Away. As with Good Times, Bad Times, I had heard this song enough by the original artist, but Phish's attack on it was stellar.

As the evening progressed, it was impossible to count the number of songs they played as the jams seemed to indicate new tunes. We were sold. Phish was scheduled to do a free show in The Springs in a few days and all we could say to those who hadn't made the Boulder trip was, "You gotta see these guys!" **—Todd A. Prusin**

2/17/90 ❄
Student Union Ballroom, University of Massachusetts, Amherst, MA
Oh Kee > Suzie, Dinner and a Movie, Caravan, Bathtub Gin, Mike's > Hydrogen > Weekapaug, Melt, Bouncing, Foam, Highway to Hell
Widespread Panic and Gene Matthews opened.

2/19/90 ❄
Student Union, Keene State College, Keene, NH
Date uncertain.

2/23/90 [ACCESSIBILITY: ••••]
Haverford College, Haverford, PA
I: Alumni, YEM, Possum, Foam, Carolina, Rocky Top, Dinner and a Movie, Ya Mar, Walk Away, Bouncing, Antelope
II: Golgi, Reba, Bathtub Gin, Jesus Left Chicago, Tela, Oh Kee > Suzie, Mike's > Hydrogen > Weekapaug, Highway to Hell
E: Contact, I Didn't Know, GTBT

➢ The minute I picked up this tape I was blown away by the setlist. After listening to it, however, I'd say the setlist is probably the only thing this show has going for it. The only musical highlights for me are Walk Away and Page's playing during YEM. The disappointing playing is saved by crowd pleasers, though it sounds like there was virtually no one at this show. —CHARLIE GUBMAN

2/24/90 [ACCESSIBILITY: •]
The Bayou, Washington, DC
I: Carolina, YEM, Golgi, Divided Sky, Esther, Possum, I Didn't Know, A-Train, Antelope
II: Sloth, AC/DC Bag, Fee, Squirming Coil, La Grange, Bathtub Gin, Lawn Boy, Contact **E:** Lizards, Caravan

2/25/90 [ACCESSIBILITY: ••]
The 8x10 Club, Baltimore, MD
I: Foam, MSO, Forbin's > Mockingbird, Funky Bitch, Squirming Coil, Bouncing, Bowie, Satin Doll, Rift, Possum
II: Reba, McGrupp, Makisupa, Lizards, Fluffhead, BBFCM
Soundcheck: Jessica, Donna Lee. "Tweezer" tease in Bowie. "Jeopardy" jam before Reba. Concert debut: slow version of Rift.

➢ This tape is really nice if you're seeking some Phish rarities. Besides a really good version of Satin Doll, they play Rift for the first time. The older version of this song is light, jazzy and really interesting to hear. —JEN SPIVEY

➢ If you see this show on someone's tape list, get it! A classic show from 1990. My tape starts with the soundcheck: Jessica and Donna Lee. The opener is Foam, dedicated to Nectar's french fries! A fun, early Forbin > Mockingbird is one of the highlights from set I. The Tweezer tease (Teezer!) before Bowie is very rare, given the fact that the Tweezer debut is still a month away. For me, the slow Rift is the highlight, and being the first one ever adds to the excitement. The second set starts out with a brief Jeopardy theme jam, heading right into Reba. A great show indeed! —OTIS

3/1/90 [ACCESSIBILITY: •••]
Toad's Place, New Haven, CT
I: Golgi, Ya Mar, Divided Sky, I Didn't Know, YEM > Possum
II: Lizards, GTBT, Foam, Mike's > Hydrogen > Weekapaug
E: Carolina > Slave **E2:** Fire
Fishman on vacuum for I Didn't Know. "Bonanza" tease in Weekapaug.

➢ I remember hearing about this show on the radio, but I was only 15 years old at the time and had never heard of Phish. Oh well. I really like these old shows where things are just a little slower and more intimate. This night in New Haven served up a good setlist with YEM, Divided and Possum in set one. During Lizards, Trey invites everyone along to Gamehendge and the crowd is so quiet. Nowadays, people would go nuts for an intro like this one, but seven years ago at a club, no one seemed to care. —NICK SORICELLI

➢ Quite a good show. Absolutely awesome Divided Sky during which Trey gives a neat introduction that takes the crowd off to Gamehendge. There's also a strong YEM, a vacuum solo and a Mike's Groove. During the Weekapaug jam, Trey busts out the theme to Bonanza, which I find very amusing. —PETE MORSE

➢ I do enjoy the Mike's Groove, but I'm sorry to say the rest of this show isn't as good as it could be. A pretty average setlist that doesn't ever seem to take off. —KYLE NIDAY

3/2/90 ❄
The Chance, Poughkeepsie, NY

3/3/90 [ACCESSIBILITY: •]
Wetlands, New York, NY
I: Mike's > Hydrogen > Weekapaug, MSO, Squirming Coil, Lizards, Oh Kee > AC/DC Bag, Reba, Rocky Top, YEM, Possum
II: Dinner and a Movie, Caravan, Fluffhead, Esther, Funky Bitch, Carolina, Divided Sky **E:** Suzie
MSO and Funky Bitch featured John Popper on harmonica. Soundcheck: Tweezer.

3/7/90 [ACCESSIBILITY: •]
University Of New Hampshire, Durham, NH
I: Reba, Possum, Esther, A-Train, Lizards, Bowie
II: Oh Kee > AC/DC Bag, Squirming Coil, Bathtub Gin, Melt, Tela, Mike's > Hydrogen > Weekapaug **E:** Whipping Post

3/8/90 [ACCESSIBILITY: ••••]
Aiko's, Saratoga, NY
I: Dinner and a Movie, YEM, Possum, Ya Mar, Foam, Carolina, Oh Kee > Suzie, A-Train, Antelope
II: Divided Sky, Bathtub Gin, MSO, AC/DC Bag, Caravan, I Didn't Know, Lizards, Mike's > Hydrogen > Weekapaug, Curtis Loew, Golgi **E:** Contact, GTBT
During MSO, Mike needed to change a bass string, so Fishman launched into a drum solo for about two minutes while Trey sung, "Music to change the bass string by."

3/9/90 [ACCESSIBILITY: ••]
The Front, Burlington, VT
I: TMWSIY > Avenu > TMWSIY, Caravan, Ya Mar, Bouncing, Forbin's > Mockingbird, Sloth, Possum, Donna Lee, Antelope, Reba, Oh Kee > AC/DC Bag
II: Curtain, Dog Log, Slave, Highway to Hell, YEM, La Grange, Contact, BBFCM **E:** Whipping Post
Dave Grippo on saxophone for Caravan, Ya Mar, Donna Lee and YEM. "Frankenstein" jam in YEM. Fishman on fretless guitar for Whipping Post.

➢ With horn players (who would later help comprise the Giant Country Horns) sitting in, this is a jazzier than usual show. You Enjoy Myself is a particular highlight, with Dave Grippo wailing the riff from Frankenstein while Trey serves up a riff all his own. Is that the Andy Griffith Theme in BBFCM? —RUSSELL LANE

➢ Great early YEM on this tape, helped a whole lot by The Truth, who just rocks! After Trey drops some Hendrix licks, Grippo responds with Frankenstein and the whole band gets into it. There's also some "Sunshine of Your Love" teases in here as the band heads into a memorable vocal jam. —AMY MANNING

3/11/90 [ACCESSIBILITY: ••••]
The Front, Burlington, VT
II: Carolina, Antelope, MSO, Bouncing, Dinner and a Movie, A-Train, Sloth, Ya Mar, Melt, Harpua, Slave, AC/DC Bag, Bowie **E:** Tela
Setlist missing first set. Antelope sung as "Roll Like A Cantaloupe."

➢ The setlist is packed from beginning to end on this night in Burlington, highlighted by Antelope (Cantaloupe). Trey builds up to the climax by describing heading down the aisles in a supermarket until reaching the fruit section, then declares, "You've got to roll like a cantaloupe, out of control!" Hilarious. Harpua with a Hendrix tease after they say "Jimmy" is also cool. Otherwise, this is a fun early show to listen to, with their early talent almost ready to unfold into raging rock star-level. —BILL PATRICK

3/17/90 [ACCESSIBILITY: •]
23 East Cabaret, Ardmore, PA
II: "Killer Joe" Jam, Bold as Love, Oh Kee > AC/DC Bag > Foam, YEM
E: GTBT
Setlist missing first set.

➢ Before the second set begins, the emcee introduces the band and talks about it being set II on St. Patrick's Day. Then, before GTBT, Trey announces that this will be their final song in the Northeast before the band heads out for a midwest tour and then a southern tour. (The first tune of the set is just about a two-minute jam with Fishman mumbling the words "Killer Joe.") —CHUCK SMITH

3/28/90 [ACCESSIBILITY: ••]
Beta Intramural Hockey Team Party, Denison University, Granville, OH
I: Possum, Ya Mar, Fee, Walk Away, Tweezer, Uncle Pen, Oh Kee > Suzie, A-Train, Runaway Jim, YEM, GTBT
II: Carolina, Adeline, Whipping Post, Funky Bitch, Mike's > Hydrogen > Weekapaug, Jesus Left Chicago, Lizards, Melt, Contact, La Grange, Rift, Cavern, Highway to Hell
Slow version of Rift. Concert debuts: Tweezer, Uncle Pen, Runaway Jim, Adeline and Cavern.

➢ Credit Dean Budnick with unearthing the actual date of this show, tapes for which circulated for years as Denison '89 and Denison '90. The significance of this date comes from the fact that this show marks the debut of a whole bunch of tunes—Tweezer, Uncle Pen, Runaway Jim, Sweet Adeline and Cavern. Phish uses the informal atmosphere of an intramural team hockey party to give the new songs a go, and it's clear that they still need some work. They'd get it in Colorado, the tour's next stop. —LOCK STEELE

4/4/90 [ACCESSIBILITY: •]
Colorado University, Boulder, CO
I: Golgi, YEM, Walk Away, A-Train, Possum, Foam, Divided Sky, Carolina
II: Mike's > Hydrogen > Weekapaug, Lizards, Uncle Pen, Sloth, I Didn't Know, GTBT **E:** Contact, Highway to Hell

4/5/90 [ACCESSIBILITY: ••]
J.J. McCabe's, Boulder, CO
I: Possum, Ya Mar, Bowie, Carolina, Oh Kee > Suzie, YEM, Lizards, Fire
II: Reba, Uncle Pen, Jesus Left Chicago, AC/DC Bag, Donna Lee, Tweezer, Fee, Cavern, Mike's > Hydrogen > Weekapaug, Brain, Contact, Golgi
Page on clavinet on Suzie, Cavern, and Contact. Fishman on vacuum for Brain.

4/6/90 [ACCESSIBILITY: •]
El Dorado Cafe, Crested Butte, CO
I: Cavern, YEM, Uncle Pen, Divided Sky, Ya Mar, Dinner and a Movie, Oh Kee > Suzie, Antelope
II: Carolina, La Grange, Esther, Sloth, Harry Hood, Caravan, Reba, I Didn't Know, Alumni, GTBT, Jesus Left Chicago
E: Jesus Left Chicago, Highway to Hell

4/7/90 [ACCESSIBILITY: •]
El Dorado Cafe, Crested Butte, CO
I: Bathtub Gin, Possum, Tweezer, Mike's > Hydrogen > Weekapaug, Bowie, MSO, Suzie, AC/DC Bag, Squirming Coil, Lizards, Landlady, Walk Away
II: Golgi, Forbin's > Mockingbird, Funky Bitch, A-Train, Bold as Love, Fee, Runaway Jim, Foam, YEM, Bike, Harpua
Concert debut: Landlady.

4/8/90 [ACCESSIBILITY: •]
Fly Me to the Moon Saloon, Telluride, CO
I: Divided Sky, Funky Bitch, YEM, Brain, Oh Kee > Suzie, Uncle Pen, Possum
II: Golgi, Walk Away, Lizards, Slave, Mike's > Hydrogen > Weekapaug, Fee, MSO, Antelope **E:** Carolina, Fire

4/9/90 [ACCESSIBILITY: •]
Fly Me to the Moon Saloon, Telluride, CO
II: Funky Bitch, Esther, Uncle Pen, La Grange, Foam, Harry Hood, Jesus Left Chicago, Divided Sky, Love You, Tweezer, Whipping Post
Setlist missing first set.

4/10/90 ❄
Fly Me to the Moon Saloon, Telluride, CO
Date of the third Fly Me to the Moon show might have been 4/11/90.

4/12/90 [ACCESSIBILITY: •]
The Inferno, Steamboat Springs, CO
I: Golgi, Ya Mar, Walk Away, Uncle Pen, Possum, YEM, A-Train, Cavern, Jesus Left Chicago, Divided Sky, GTBT
Setlist missing second set.

4/13/90 [ACCESSIBILITY: •]
The Inferno, Steamboat Springs, CO
I: Funky Bitch, Dinner and a Movie, Bouncing, Fluffhead, Esther, La Grange, Oh Kee > AC/DC Bag, Reba, Fire
II: Antelope, Foam, YEM, Alumni, Curtis Loew > Sloth, Harry Hood, Caravan, Possum, Highway to Hell

4/18/90 [ACCESSIBILITY: ••]
Herman's Hideaway, Denver, CO
I: Mike's > Hydrogen > Weekapaug, Uncle Pen, Curtain, Foam, YEM, MSO, A-Train, Possum
II: La Grange, Fee, Sloth, Funky Bitch, Reba, Walk Away, Oh Kee > Bold as Love, Lawn Boy, Bowie > Jaegermeister > Bowie
"Lawn Boy" tease in Bowie intro before "sexy lights" vocals and "Jaegermeister".

➢ The "sexy lights" show is your standard spring '90 affair—the show fits on only a tape and a half—until the end of the second set. During the Bowie intro, Trey tells the small crowd, "We're trying to look for a date for our light person tonight. He wanted to make sure that we said that." Then: "We want to show you right now how sexy lights can be. Let's have a little light solo… Chris Kuroda, he's right back there, go get him." Page quips, "Those are some hot lights from a hot guy." Then, before returning to Bowie, Trey says, "This next song is dedicated to those of you who have been drinking Jaegermeister tonight." They start up this wacky ditty that goes, "Gimme some Jaegermesiter" —AMY MANNING

4/19/90 ❄
Boulder Theater, Boulder, CO
The Circle opened.

4/20/90 [ACCESSIBILITY: •]
Ramskellar, Colorado State University, Fort Collins, CO
I: A-Train, Divided Sky, Alumni, Ya Mar, Cavern, Dinner and a Movie, Bouncing, Forbin's > Mockingbird, Possum
II: Caravan, Mike's > Hydrogen > Weekapaug, La Grange, Rift, Fee, Oh Kee > AC/DC Bag, Jesus Left Chicago, YEM

4/21/90 ❄
Lincoln Center, Canyon West, Fort Collins, CO
Common Ground opened.

4/22/90 [ACCESSIBILITY: ••••]
Cutler Quad, Colorado College, Colorado Springs, CO
I: Divided Sky, Uncle Pen, Oh Kee > Suzie, Possum, I Didn't Know, Cavern, MSO, Slave, Mike's > Hydrogen > Weekapaug
II: Dinner and a Movie, Bouncing, YEM, Fluffhead, How High The Moon, Esther, BBFCM, Harry Hood, Fire
E: Lawn Boy, Golgi
Fishman on vacuum for I Didn't Know.

➢ Picking the best Harry Hood from this era isn't easy when you're comparing the 11/4/90 masterpiece and the one from this Earth Day show. Do yourself a favor and pick up this tape for Hood and for the sound quality—this is the only spring '90 show from the "Colorado Collection" of soundboard/audience mixed tapes; it's gorgeous. —ERNIE GREENE

4/25/90 [ACCESSIBILITY: ••••]
Notre Dame University, South Bend, IN
I: Brain, Divided Sky, MSO, Bowie
II: Foam, Adeline, Reba, Ya Mar, YEM, Esther, La Grange, Dinner and a Movie, Bouncing, Mike's > Hydrogen > Weekapaug **E:** Contact

4/26/90 [ACCESSIBILITY: ••]
The 'Sco, Oberlin College, Oberlin, OH
I: Possum, Foam > YEM, Uncle Pen, Dinner and a Movie > Bouncing, I Didn't Know, Antelope, Lawn Boy
II: How High The Moon, Esther, Bathtub Gin, Oh Kee > Suzie, Cavern, Adeline, Curtis Loew, Mike's > Hydrogen > Weekapaug **E:** Highway to Hell
Fishman on vacuum for I Didn't Know.

➢ Even in 1990, Trey proves his worth as a guitar great. He's all over this show, with great solo work especially in Possum, Antelope and Bathtub Gin. His best is the great Oh Kee Pa > Suzie, a high-energy jam during which the boys are obviously having fun. YEM features a perfect early vocal jam and Suzie is full of screams and laughter. Foam and Dinner also shine. A great show from the early days! —TIM FOISSER

4/28/90 [ACCESSIBILITY: •]
Strand Theater, Boston, MA
I: Adeline, Oh Kee > Suzie, Uncle Pen, Dinner and a Movie > Bouncing, Possum, YEM, Rift, Foam, Antelope
II: Cavern, Harry Hood, Caravan, I Didn't Know, Reba, MSO, Mike's > Hydrogen > Weekapaug **E:** BBFCM
Slow version of Rift.

➢ This beautiful small theater is just outside of Boston—excellent sound in this room. Phish opened with an unmiked Sweet Adeline. As the show heated up, many people jumped into the orchestra pit to dance, which left the rest of us with plenty of room. Very high energy during YEM, especially when Mike pulled out an extendo-jam solo that wouldn't quit. That was followed by a nice segue into a totally different version of Rift (also a good version). Mike led the way all night. —NATHANIEL PEIRCE

4/29/90 [ACCESSIBILITY: ••]
Woodbury Ski and Racquet Club, Woodbury, CT
Carolina, Possum, Ya Mar, YEM, Dinner and a Movie > Bouncing, Uncle Pen, Divided Sky, Fluffhead, Walk Away, Love You, Lizards, Fire

➢ My videotape of this concert shows a beautiful setting with not very many fans there. Nevertheless, Phish gave the small crowd a treat, offering up some of their best instrumental, improvisational, beautifully played tunes. YEM, Dinner and a Movie and Divided Sky take flight and soar to new heights. A great Fishman intro gives me a smile, as does Trey's super guitar work throughout the show. —ANDY KAHN

5/3/90 ❄
Somerville Theatre, Somerville, MA

5/4/90 [ACCESSIBILITY: •]
Colonial Theater, Keene, NH
I: Whipping Post, Adeline, TMWSIY > Avenu > TMWSIY, Bouncing, Possum, Reba, MSO, YEM, Lizards
II: Runaway Jim, Sloth, Uncle Pen, Tweezer, Bathtub Gin, Oh Kee > Mike's > Hydrogen > Weekapaug, Caravan, Brain, Highway to Hell, Antelope **E:** Contact

5/6/90 ❄
Toad's Place, New Haven, CT
I: Possum, Bouncing, Uncle Pen, Reba, Tweezer, Mike's > Hydrogen > Weekapaug
II: Fee, Harry Hood, Esther, Bowie, Terrapin, Jaegermeister, YEM
YEM halted before completion by club management.

5/10/90 ❄
Pearl Street, Northampton, MA
I: Suzie, Uncle Pen, Bouncing, Divided Sky, Tweezer, MSO, Bathtub Gin, Possum
II: Funky Bitch, Runaway Jim, Harry Hood, Caravan, Reba, Oh Kee > AC/DC Bag, GTBT **E:** Whipping Post

5/11/90 ❄
The Living Room, Providence, RI
I: Mike's > Hydrogen > Weekapaug > Uncle Pen, Bouncing, Possum, Reba, Highway to Hell
II: Oh Kee > AC/DC Bag, Lizards, Tweezer, Ya Mar, Love You, GTBT
E: BBFCM
Widespread Panic opened.

5/12/90 ❄
The Front, Burlington, VT

5/13/90 [ACCESSIBILITY: •]
The Front, Burlington, VT
I: Bathtub Gin, Oh Kee > AC/DC Bag, Dinner and a Movie, Bouncing, Runaway Jim, Uncle Pen, Divided Sky, Bowie
II: Mike's > Hydrogen > Weekapaug, Foam, Donna Lee, Tweezer, MSO, Reba, Funky Bitch, Adeline, La Grange, Foam, MSO, Reba
Possum tease between Adeline and La Grange. Second set setlist incomplete.

5/14/90 [ACCESSIBILITY: •]
McEwen Quad, Hamilton College, Clinton, New York
I: Fee, Reba, Alumni, Foam, Mike's > Hydrogen > Weekapaug, Uncle Pen, Bouncing, Runaway Jim, Squirming Coil, Lizards
Setlist missing second set. Second set played indoors due to inclement weather.

➢ On this date, Phish had an outdoor gig scheduled at Hamilton College. But before the second set, as the skies opened and the rain poured, Trey and Co. apologized that the show would have to be unceremoniously cancelled. Being good sports, the fellas agreed to spend the second set indoors in a dormitory lounge on our local college band's equipment. While sound quality suffered, the jams did not, and they completed the show. A bummer averted! —CHUCK SMITH

5/15/90 [ACCESSIBILITY: •]
The Front, Burlington, VT
I: Possum, Tela, Tweezer, Oh Kee > Suzie, "Happy Birthday" for Barbie, Harry Hood, Bike, Caravan, BBFCM
Setlist might be from 5/12/90; missing second set. Fishman on vacuum for Bike. "Smoke on the Water" jam in Tweezer.

➢ There's definite confusion about the date of this show, but I believe I have a set I of either the 5/12/90 or 5/15/90 shows at The Front. I can't be sure which one because it was given to me labeled as "Phish at the Front, 5/90" by a buddy of mine who had the tape given to

Friday, June 1, 1990 — The Cotton Club, Atlanta, GA

After two monstrous Colorado Phish shows the month before, I gathered a bunch of friends to go see Phish at the Cotton Club in Atlanta. This club would provide a nice small backdrop against which we could see the band. Little did I know the size of the place didn't matter—they could have been inside an enormo-dome or a closet, because nobody was there!

Phish's name had yet to arrive in Atlanta. There were about 20 people in front of the stage and we all pressed against the back wall for fear of standing alone in the middle of the dance floor.

Phish walked out on stage and greeted the Friday night concert goers with their standard smile/wave combination. The bonus here was the added audible, non-miked, "Hello" from Trey as our clapping had died down to reveal the hum of the AC units above.

My friend Julie and I braved ridicule and went up to the stage to check out their chops. She was a student at Skidmore and had seen more shows than me. She knew all the songs and even kept a setlist.

The show was great. More people showed up and the trampolines even made their way out for a visit. The lack of attendance was fine but seemed to reduce the intensity of the event a bit. We had a blast, though, and the band seemed to be glad we hollered out the songs we did. Some guy kept calling for "Suzie Greenberg," or it may have been the question, "Do you like cheeseburgers?" in an effort to provoke "Halley's Comet." He went up and placed a quarter on a monitor speaker as a bribe… I think it worked. **—Todd A. Prusin**

him by a friend of the band back in '91. Since the 5/11 show in Providence includes Possum, Tweezer and BBFCM I'm apt to believe that my tape is 5/15. During the set, between Possum and Tela, Fish tells Trey, "My kick drum is getting away," and then during Tweezer, Fish adds a line to the chorus at least three times as he sings, "My bass drum is getting away." Later in the set, he borrows duct tape to repair his drum kit. Tweezer contains a very nice, gritty "Smoke on the Water" guitar bit in the middle. I'm not sure who Barbie is, or why they decided to sing for her birthday, but Trey tells the crowd that everyone should buy Barbie a shot. Then during Bike, Fishman brings out his vacuum and proclaims, "While out west, I got a new vacuum. It's an Electrolux, like the old one, which blew a belt. This one has great sucking power." He sounds tipsy, and this song meanders until he's yelling into the microphone to the point where I have to fast-forward.—TOM SMITH

5/19/90 [ACCESSIBILITY: •]
The Upper, St. Paul's School, Concord, NH
I: Golgi, Ya Mar, Alumni, Adeline, La Grange, YEM, Lizards, Highway to Hell
II: Possum, Reba, Oh Kee > Suzie, Fee, Dinner and a Movie > Bouncing, Rift, Jesus Left Chicago, GTBT **E:** Contact
Slow version of Rift.

➢ For prep schooler Trey Anastasio, playing a gig in the Upper Dining Room at New Hampshire prep school St. Paul's must have felt like a homecoming of sorts. Despite the weird wooden acoustics of this ancient dining room, with the names of graduates from the 1800s engraved on wooden panels lining the walls, the band treated the young crowd (which included several prep schoolers who had traveled up from Exeter for the show) to quite a night. Alumni Blues is dedicated to the graduating seniors, and Rift is played in the slow spring '90 fashion. —LOCK STEELE

5/23/90 [ACCESSIBILITY: •]
The Library, Richmond, VA
I: Divided Sky, Ya Mar, YEM, Brain, Oh Kee > Suzie, Uncle Pen, Bouncing, Possum, Adeline
II: Squirming Coil, Reba, Tweezer, Lizards, La Grange, McGrupp, A-Train, Antelope, Mike's > Hydrogen > Weekapaug

5/24/90 [ACCESSIBILITY: ••]
The Brewery, Raleigh, NC
I: Sloth > Bouncing > Tweezer, Donna Lee, Reba, YEM > Oh Kee > AC/DC Bag, Golgi
II: Foam, Dinner and a Movie > Possum, I Didn't Know, MSO > Horn, Fee, Walk Away, Harry Hood, Highway to Hell > Contact **E:** GTBT
Concert debut: Horn.

5/31/90 [ACCESSIBILITY: •]
Variety Playhouse, Atlanta, GA
Possum, YEM, Dinner and a Movie, Bouncing, Caravan, Esther, Tweezer, I Didn't Know, Uncle Pen, Divided Sky, Oh Kee > Suzie **E:** GTBT
Phish opened for Aquarium Rescue Unit and played one set. Tapes of this show are sometimes misdated as 5/31/89.

6/1/90 ❄
The Cotton Club, Atlanta, GA
Bouncing, YEM, Divided Sky, Slave, Possum, Oh Kee > Suzie, Dinner and a Movie, Fee, Foam, Forbin's > Mockingbird
Setlist order uncertain and probably incomplete.

6/5/90 [ACCESSIBILITY: •••]
Cat's Cradle, Chapel Hill, NC
I: Squirming Coil, Uncle Pen, Mike's > Hydrogen > Weekapaug, Ya Mar, Oh Kee > Suzie, A-Train > Bowie, Lawn Boy, Possum
II: Adeline, Divided Sky, Caravan, Dinner and a Movie > Bouncing > MSO, Lizards, YEM > Curtis Loew, GTBT **E:** Whipping Post, Golgi
Fishman on vacuum for Whipping Post.

6/7/90 ❄
The Bayou, Washington, DC
I: Suzie, Donna Lee, Possum, Fee, Reba, YEM, Lizards, GTBT
II: MSO, Dinner and a Movie > Bouncing, Tweezer, Uncle Pen, Divided Sky, Love You, Mike's > Hydrogen > Weekapaug **E:** Lawn Boy, BBFCM
Aquarium Rescue Unit opened.

6/8/90 ❄
23 East Cabaret, Philadelphia, PA
I: Possum, MSO, Bathtub Gin, Tweezer, I Didn't Know, Mike's > Hydrogen > Weekapaug, Foam, Bouncing, YEM, Divided Sky
Setlist missing second set.

6/9/90 [ACCESSIBILITY: ••]
Wetlands, New York, NY
I: Possum, Lawn Boy, Reba, Dinner and a Movie, Bouncing, Tweezer, Uncle Pen, Mike's > Hydrogen > Weekapaug
II: GTBT, Harry Hood, TMWSIY > Avenu > TMWSIY > La Grange, Fee > Foam, Oh Kee > Suzie, Antelope, Terrapin, Harpua **E:** Landlady > Contact
"Whole Lotta Love" jam before GTBT.

➢ The second set really shines, opening with a Whole Lotta Love jam and including great tunes such as TMWSIY, La Grange and Terrapin. The reason I really enjoy this tape, though, is that it features one of my favorite Harpuas. The story wasn't any different than usual—in fact, it was a little short. But the way Trey over-over-overexaggerates on the little things (such as "Jimmy, furry little..." and the craziest, most insane introduction of Poster Nutbag I've ever heard) makes this set. —CHUCK ADAMS

6/16/90 [ACCESSIBILITY: ••]
Townshend Family Park, Townshend, VT
I: AC/DC Bag, Divided Sky > Wilson, Reba, Horn, Uncle Pen, Bouncing, Timber Ho, Lawn Boy, Possum
II: Golgi, Esther, Tweezer, MSO, Bathtub Gin, YEM, Lizards, Antelope
III: La Grange, Ya Mar, Foam, Oh Kee > Suzie, Fee, Rocky Top, Caravan, HYHU > Brain > HYHU > Mike's > Hydrogen > Weekapaug
E: Contact, BBFCM **E2:** GTBT
Soundcheck: Carolina, Funky Bitch. Fishman on vacuum for Brain. Show billed as "Phish's last show until the Fall."

➢ If you look at the setlist to this tape, it appears to be the perfect show from this era—three sets, two encores. But I have never heard Trey sound worse. This show definitely has its good moments (AC/DC, Antelope) but the band sounds tired as the show wears on. What is Trey doing in Caravan? Fishman forgets the words in Brain and Mike's Groove doesn't move mountains like it usually does. —MIKE GAROFALOW

➢ If Phish were to put together a greatest hits album, this could be it. —ADAM SATZ

➢ I know a lot of people talk about this show, but perhaps it's worth a few more words. I think the fact that this show is so much fun to listen to is derived from all its offerings. Three sets gave the guys plenty of space to play some goodies—AC/DC Bag and Bathtub Gin both rocked more than usual. The Tweezer is my earliest recording of this song and it's nice to follow its musical evolution over the years. Mike's Groove is never a letdown, and GTBT is a great encore! —DANIEL PADEN

➢ La Grange starts the third set, and Mike announces that some guy who hand-paints shirts lost one at a Max Creek show and would appreciate it if someone returned it. Trey then dedicates Ya Mar to Heather Paw because it's her birthday. Fish plays his vacuum and then does a pretty cool version of If I Only Had A Brain, telling about how his brain damage relates to the song. —JOSEPH SOUTH

[6/17/90] [ACCESSIBILITY: ••]
Wendell Studios, Boston, MA
Tape 1: Dog Log, Uncle Pen, Suzie, Suzie, Caravan, Alumni, A-Train, A-Train, In a Mellow Tone, Possum, Mike's > Hydrogen > Weekapaug
Tape 2: TMWSIY > Avenu > TMWSIY, Tweezer, Possum, Harry Hood, Rift, Runaway Jim
Unreleased studio session; date uncertain. Slow version of Rift. Alternate lyrics on Runaway Jim.

[9/90] *Lawn Boy* released on Absolute-A-Go-Go Records.

9/13/90 [ACCESSIBILITY: ••••]
Wetlands Preserve, New York, NY
I: Landlady, Divided Sky, Foam, Tube, Asse Festival, Antelope, Minute By Minute, Buried Alive, Paul and Silas, Bouncing, Possum
II: Mike's > Hydrogen > Weekapaug, Magilla, Stash, Going Down Slow, Oh Kee > AC/DC Bag > A-Train > Sparks > Reba, Self, Dahlia, Revolution's Over **E:** Lizards, La Grange
"Buried Alive" jam between AC/DC Bag and A-Train. The Dude of Life on vocals for Self, Dahlia and The Revolution's Over. Concert debuts: Tube, Asse Festival, Minute By Minute, Buried Alive, Paul and Silas, Magilla, Stash, Going Down Slow, Self, Dahlia and Revolution's Over.

➢ This show is memorable for all the debuts, ten in all. I especially enjoy Tube, which is one of (if not the) most underrated and under-played songs. It's kind of neat to hear the Asse Festival not in Guelah Papyrus. The only major downfall is Minute by Minute by the Doobie Brothers. Thank God they dropped it quickly. —RIC HANNAH

➢ A full show of new material packed with some old-time greats. Boy were they hot during this time period! Looking back, it seems as if they always played hot shows at the Wetlands Preserve. So if you need a show with a lot of song debuts, get wet at the Wetlands. (The Dude of Life was also at this show, contributing a bunch of his songs at the end of the second set.) —BILL PATRICK

9/14/90 [ACCESSIBILITY: •]
The Living Room, Providence, RI
I: Suzie, Bouncing, Landlady, Reba, Paul and Silas, Stash, Dinner and a Movie, I Didn't Know
II: Asse Festival, Squirming Coil, Buried Alive > Tweezer, Magilla, Cavern, Lizards, Destiny Unbound, Fire **E:** Going Down Slow
Concert debut: Destiny Unbound.

9/15/90 [ACCESSIBILITY: •]
Colonial Theater, Keene, NH
I: Buried Alive > Divided Sky, Paul and Silas, Landlady, Fee, Tube, Oh Kee > AC/DC Bag, Asse Festival, Bowie, Golgi, Stash, Magilla, Squirming Coil **II:** Melt, Eliza, MSO, Bathtub Gin, Foam, Minute by Minute, Harry Hood > Possum **E:** Communication Breakdown > YEM

9/16/90 [ACCESSIBILITY: ••••]
Wesleyan University, Middletown, CT
Dinner and a Movie, Bouncing, Sloth, Landlady, Reba, Ya Mar, Tube, Tweezer, Paul and Silas, Mike's > Hydrogen > Weekapaug, Magilla, Antelope **E:** Contact

9/20/90 ❄
Somerville Theatre, Somerville, MA

9/21/90 ❄
Somerville Theatre, Somerville, MA
Release party for Lawn Boy on Absolute-A-Go-Go.

9/22/90 [ACCESSIBILITY: •]
University of Massachusetts, Amherst, MA
I: Buried Alive, Horn, MSO, Divided Sky, Tela, Oh Kee > Suzie, Magilla, Wilson, Landlady, I Didn't Know, Bowie
II: Squirming Coil, Tweezer, Destiny Unbound, Fee, Uncle Pen, Bouncing, Stash, Lizards, Lawn Boy, Possum **E:** Asse Festival, Golgi

9/28/90 ❄
The Chance, Poughkeepsie, NY
I: Landlady > Bouncing, Oh Kee > Suzie, Stash, MSO, Squirming Coil > Lizards, Asse Festival, Antelope
II: AC/DC Bag > Esther > Gumbo, Dinner and a Movie, YEM > Divided Sky **E:** Paul and Silas
Concert debut: Gumbo. List may be incomplete.

[9/30/90]
The Dude Of Life's Wedding
Phish played during the wedding reception of Steve and Kathy Pollak.

10/1/90 ❄
The Haunt, Ithaca, NY
I: Possum, Squirming Coil, Lizards, Landlady, Magilla, Dinner and a Movie, Bouncing, Tweezer, Oh Kee > Suzie
II: Lawn Boy, AC/DC Bag
Setlist for second set is incomplete.

10/4/90 [ACCESSIBILITY: •]
Field House, University of New Hampshire, Durham, NH
I: Golgi, Landlady, Esther, Possum, Squirming Coil, Lizards, Destiny Unbound, Sloth, Uncle Pen, Bowie
Setlist missing second set and encore.

10/5/90 [ACCESSIBILITY: •]
Skidmore College, Saratoga Springs, NY
I: I Didn't Know, Mike's > Hydrogen > Weekapaug, MSO, Landlady, Tela, Oh Kee > Suzie, Stash, Asse Festival, Bouncing, Antelope
II: Golgi > Curtain > Ya Mar, Alumni, Uncle Pen, Melt, Fee, Possum **E:** GTBT

10/6/90 [ACCESSIBILITY: ••]
Capitol Theater, Port Chester, NY
Landlady, Squirming Coil, Dinner and a Movie, Bouncing, Foam, YEM, Oh Kee > Suzie, Esther, Possum, HYHU > Brain > HYHU, Bowie, Carolina
E: Don't Get Me Wrong
Concert debut: Don't Get Me Wrong, which featured John Popper on harmonica. Phish shared the bill with Blues Traveler and played one set.

10/7/90 ❄
Club Bene, Sayerville, NJ
I: Divided Sky, Uncle Pen, Stash, Landlady > Destiny Unbound, Forbin's > Mockingbird, Asse Festival, Squirming Coil, Mike's > Hydrogen > Weekapaug, A-Train, La Grange
II: Buried Alive, Bouncing, Tweezer, MSO, I Didn't Know, Lizards, GTBT, Golgi **E:** Contact

10/8/90 [ACCESSIBILITY: •]
The Bayou, Washington, DC
I: Don't Get Me Wrong, Landlady > Bouncing, Foam, Cavern, Reba > MSO, YEM, Oh Kee > Possum
Setlist missing second set and encore. John Popper on harmonica for Don't Get Me Wrong.

10/12/90 ❄
Cat's Cradle, Chapel Hill, NC
I: Suzie, YEM, Dinner and a Movie > Bouncing, Uncle Pen, Cavern, Esther, Tweezer, Golgi
II: Possum, Fee, Landlady, HYHU > Terrapin > HYHU, Divided Sky, Paul and Silas > Magilla, Mike's > Hydrogen > Weekapaug **E:** Carolina, GTBT

10/13/90 ❄
Greenstreets, Columbia, SC

10/30/90 [ACCESSIBILITY: ••••]
El Dorado, Crested Butte, CO
I: Landlady > Bouncing, Donna Lee, Asse Festival > Suzie, Uncle Pen, Cavern, Squirming Coil, Possum
II: Mike's > Hydrogen > Weekapaug, Magilla, Foam, Reba > Llama, Curtis Loew, Fluffhead, HYHU > Terrapin > HYHU, Buried Alive, Bowie
III: Paul and Silas, Lizards, GTBT, Contact, AC/DC Bag

➢ Phish shows in Colorado have always been super-dank, and this show is no exception. Maybe it was Colorado's wide-open spaces or a relatively new audience to play for, but this show explodes from the Landlady opener to the AC/DC Bag closer three sets later. Landlady seamlessly crosses into a stellar, laid-back Bouncing that is one of the best I have heard. If you are a Mike's > Hydrogen > Weekapaug phan like myself then you will love this great version, similar to the one on 4/16/92. I wish that I could have been at this show—thank goodness for the tapes! —DAVID GEORGE

9/13/90 The Wetlands Preserve, New York, NY

From their first show at the Wetlands in March 1989, Phish made the TriBeCa club a frequent stopping-off point on their swings south of New England.

By the time of their fall 1990 tour, which came after the band took nearly three months off from gigging and spent some time in Boston's Wendell Studios, Phish had a solid New York City fanbase, and could expect a good reception during each visit to the Big Apple.

Or so they thought. In fact, the fall 1990 Phish newsletter didn't arrive in most fan's hands until mid-September, which made Phish's last-ever show at the Wetlands a less-crowded affair than some of their earlier gigs. But perhaps the smaller audience size was a blessing in disguise, as the band used the show to introduce five new original songs, three new cover songs and three Dude of Life songs (written in conjunction with Trey and performed, of course, with the Dude himself, in his first formal appearance with Phish).

Early in the show, Trey warned the crowd that the band would be exercising a lot of new material, starting with the opening Landlady which Trey dedicated "to the spirit of Carlos." The first set also included the rollouts of Tube and the Asse Festival, as well as Fishman's take on the Doobie Brothers' Minute by Minute. Buried Alive and Paul and Silas rounded out the first-set debuts.

The second set saw more of the same, with a mid-set run three of new songs: Magilla, Stash and Going Down Slow. Then, jamming out on AC/DC Bag several songs later, the band whipped back around into a Buried Alive Reprise of sorts before taking that into Take the A-Train.

As the end of the set neared, The Dude of Life made his way onstage for the debut of three of his songs. He feigned vomiting with the dire warning, "Better get the bucket!" and assumed lead vocals for Self (his signature song, perhaps), Dahlia and The Revolution's Over. Self is notable for the guitar riff that Trey would later incorporate into Chalk Dust Torture.

The show would be Phish's last-ever at the Wetlands, as the band graduated to the larger Marquee by early 1991 and then to the Roseland Ballroom by the spring of 1992.

The Wetlands still stands today, giving jam bands on their way up a firm foothold in New York City. For Phish, the Wetlands was a friendly home-away-from home that is fondly remembered as another rung passed on their climb to the top.

➢ This is one of those real jazzy shows. Most of the first half of the first set is instrumental, partly due to the sound troubles they have. It's pretty laid back and mellow, but still very nice. After getting the gremlins worked out, they roar back strong in the second. The Mike's Groove is definitely worth checking out, as well as an incredible Reba. Go find this tape if just for this song. The rest of the set is very similar to the first. Curtis Loew, Terrapin and Buried Alive keep the jazz mood going. —BRIAN WATKINS

10/31/90 [ACCESSIBILITY: ••••]
Armstrong Hall, Colorado College, Colorado Springs, CO
I: Buried Alive > Possum, Squirming Coil, Lizards, Stash, Bouncing, YEM, Asse Festival, MSO, Cavern, Antelope
II: "Costume Contest," Landlady, Reba, Runaway Jim, Foam, Tweezer, Fee, Oh Kee > Suzie, HYHU > Love You > HYHU, Mike's > Hydrogen > Weekapaug **E:** Uncle Pen, BBFCM
Fishman on vacuum for Love You. "Heartbreaker" teases in Tweezer.

➢ Before the days of spectacular Halloween cover sets, there were just great shows. From the Buried Alive > Possum opener, you know it's going to be a smokin' show. Antelope is one of the best—very energetic. The BBFCM encore seemed appropriate, and Fish's Love You is hilarious, as usual. This is a true gem among older shows and is fairly easy to obtain. —DAVE MATSON

➢ With so much talk about the 'Ween shows from '94-'96, this one is often the forgotten gem. Very often after listening to a show people say, "Wow, Page was on tonight," or something like that, but this is one of those rare occasions that all four band members are in their zone. Just listen to the first four songs in the second set. I've never heard a show flow like this one does—a definite must for any collection. —BEN ROSS

11/2/90 [ACCESSIBILITY: ••••]
Glen Miller Ballroom, University of Colorado at Boulder, Boulder, CO
I: Golgi, Landlady > Bouncing > Divided Sky, Sloth, Mike's > Hydrogen > Weekapaug, Esther, Cavern, Asse Festival, Possum > Buried Alive > Possum
II: Suzie, Forbin's > Mockingbird, MSO, Foam, YEM, Lizards, I Didn't Know, Bowie **E:** Lawn Boy, La Grange
Fishman on trombone for I Didn't Know. "Tease medley," including teases from many other songs played at the show, in Bowie intro.

➢ The emcee tells us that Phish broke up backstage before the show started, so instead we're gonna hear a new band, "Phish 2000." But when the sweet notes of Golgi begin, you know it's just a little fun from Trey. Two nights before the epic 11/4/90 show, this concert is one of the highlights from the '90 Colorado run. The setlist really makes this show a must-have. —CHARLIE GUBMAN

➢ This is nothing more than a solid Phish concert in the classic Phish tradition. There is nothing particularly outrageous about the show, but the boys are energetic and uncompromising from the opener to the encore. There's no low point in this performance. The first set (perfect for the car) features a great Mike's Groove and Possum. —SCOTT KUSHNER

➢ There are two must-hear moments at this show (besides the outrageously wonderful Weekapaug jam); both come during the set-closers. During the Possum intro, without any warning, they're playing Buried Alive! Almost as suddenly, they're back into Possum, which rocks out. The second set closer, David Bowie, has its own craziness during the intro in the form of a "tease medley" that incorporates brief jams from many of the other songs played during the show. Like the Possum in the first set, the Bowie seems to draw on the strength of its intro to really soar. —PAT STANLEY

11/3/90 [ACCESSIBILITY: ••••]
Boulder Theater, Boulder, CO
I: Dinner and a Movie, Bouncing, Llama, Squirming Coil, Oh Kee > Suzie, Magilla, Foam, Runaway Jim, YEM, GTBT
II: Landlady, Mike's > Hydrogen > Weekapaug, Paul and Silas, Stash, Fee, Uncle Pen, Reba, Possum, HYHU > Love You > HYHU, Antelope
E: Fluffhead, Fire

➢ A classic Colorado show to acquire. The Boulder Theater is really small, with great acoustics. I have great soundboards from this show and every time I listen to it, I weep thinking about seeing these guys before 1992. Runaway, YEM, GTBT close the first set in a fierce way. In the second set, the band jumps right into an early Mike's > Hydrogen > Weekapaug. The rest of the set is what some people term SICK! Paul and Silas, Uncle Pen, Reba, Possum and Antelope. Then, hello? Take a peek at the encore: Fluffhead, Fire. It would be an understatement to say that the band didn't want to get off the stage. —BRETT PESSIN

➢ Set II features one of the best Magillas I have on tape. It's funny to hear the reaction of the crowd after each song back then—now, phans love every song, but it was different at this show. The crowd seemed so jumpy and pumped after Llama! I also like that they played all of their own music in this set, including the great Coil > Oh Kee Pa > Suzie combo. —JASON MOKHTARIAN

11/4/90 [ACCESSIBILITY: ••••]
Fort Ram Nightclub, Fort Collins, CO
I: Carolina, AC/DC Bag, Curtain, Bouncing, Tube, Harry Hood, Funky Bitch, Asse Festival, MSO, Bowie
II: Golgi, Rocky Top, Llama, Mike's > Hydrogen > Weekapaug, Manteca/Caravan/Manteca, Runaway Jim, Oh Kee > Suzie, Jesus Left Chicago, YEM **E:** Contact, Highway to Hell
Caravan jammed in the midst of Manteca.

➢ This is arguably the best Colorado show from this era. For some reason, the band keeps talking about a disco ball throughout the show. The first set is excellent—Tube is a welcome favorite, followed by a stellar Harry. It's not too often you get to hear Harry and Bowie together in a first set. The second set is good but not as exciting. —BEN ROSS

Sunday, October 7, 1990 — Club Bene, Sayerville, NJ

Nowadays I travel all over the country to see Phish, and have seen them over two hundred times. But in 1990 I had only seen three shows, and most of these in the tiny and uncomfortably packed 23 East Cabaret right near my home in Philadelphia. Thus it was a big deal when I decided that the Philadelphia show was not enough and that I wanted to travel an hour and a half to see them in New Jersey a few days later.

I had trouble convincing anyone to go, but late in the afternoon of the show day when I called my good friend Melissa and told her that this was a band she needed to see, I had a partner for my mission. As we pulled into the parking lot I began to worry. There were only a half-dozen cars in the lot and the show was due to start in an hour. Did I get the date wrong? Was this the wrong place? As we walked into the thousand-seat supper club, I really began to sweat since only five of the tables in the huge room had anyone sitting at them. However, I relaxed considerably when I noticed that at one of the tables sat the band and crew chowing down on dinner.

As we ordered drinks and I set up my taping gear, I began the lengthy task of explaining to Melissa that this was an amazing band of great renown, and not some losers playing in an empty bar in New Jersey. When the lights went down, I realized that I was about to see Phish with a grand total of 12 people in the audience, and it was to be one of my all-time favorites.

The band began by slamming into Divided Sky and spotlights came up to illuminate… a red velvet curtain? The curtain raised up eight inches and we spent the first half of the song watching the band's shoes. As the song continued, the curtain raised up to reveal partial glimpses of the band, then roll back down again. It was obvious that they were not taking the show very seriously.

A few songs into the first set, in a quiet pause between songs, I calmly and politely asked Trey (all of 10 feet away) if they could play Stash, which I had seen for the first time a few nights before. "Do you like that song?" Trey asked, looking me in the eye. "I really enjoyed it the other night," I said. "It's my favorite of the new tunes," returned Trey, "and I would love to play it for you," and he launched immediately into the opening riff. Thus began a night of requests fulfilled that felt more like an intimate gathering of friends than a rock concert.

Throughout the evening, the small audience politely made requests and the band instantly granted them. In this way, we were treated to such gems as Destiny Unbound, Good Times Bad Times, Take the A-Train, La Grange and a long and killer Colonel Forbin. At one point in the show, Trey asked, "How many people here are actually from New Jersey?… Because we are from New Jersey and this is the first time we have ever played here. So this is a real special night for us." I guess that's why for the whole show they sarcastically wove the phrase "New Jersey and you, perfect together" (the state's tourism tagline) into their lyrics.

One of the great things about this show was that since there were no loud drunks screaming at the band during and between songs, they were able to really communicate with each other on stage. Some great musical interplay such as the jam in Mike's Song was the payoff for the quiet, attentive audience.

This show is a very important one to me for many reasons. In addition to the intimacy and high level of playing, I met some people who have remained good friends throughout the years. These days, when I run into one of them at whatever enormo-dome Phish is playing, we always reminisce about the tiny show that left a huge impression. —B.P.

➢ Name the song, and this show probably has a good version of it. I love Harry Hood! This one really makes you feel good about Hood, too. Of course, any show with Mike's > Weekapaug is a good one. —LINDZ BRYAN

➢ While this is popularly viewed as a great run of shows in the tour, this show stands out for its first set. A great AC/DC Bag > Curtain warms things up. Following a mellow Bouncin', things take off like we wish they always would. Tube, Harry Hood and Funky Bitch constitute some of the most ferocious jams my ears have heard. The David Bowie to close the set is also about as good as they get. If only Phish would speed up the Tube jam more these days—it's something you must hear to believe. —ADAM DAVIDOFF

➢ The band sounds like they are really trying hard to sound good during this show. The jamming is tight and the instruments are together, but they never really find that magic. Trey finally gets his groove going on Tube but things are not as energetic as other shows from 1990. Highlights are a great up-tempo, bluesy Funky Bitch and a spooky Harry. However, as I listen to this tape, I can't help but think of Phish on this night as a good cover band. Good, but not special. —TIM FOISSER

11/8/90 [ACCESSIBILITY: ••]
Barrymore Theater, Madison, WI
I: Landlady, Possum, Lizards, Foam, Uncle Pen, Llama, Squirming Coil, Asse Festival, I Didn't Know, Mike's > Hydrogen > Weekapaug
II: Suzie, Divided Sky, Tweezer, Oh Kee > Dinner and a Movie, Bouncing, YEM, BBFCM **E:** Jesus Left Chicago, Fire
John Popper on harmonica for YEM, BBFCM, and the encores.

Friday and Saturday, November 2 & 3, 1990 — Glen Miller Ballroom and Boulder Theater, Boulder, CO

What a cool thing it is when Phish plays a show just a few blocks away from home. Home for me at this time was right in downtown Boulder and when I heard that the Vermonters were doing two nights here, at two different venues, I was ecstatic!

Although they had played Boulder the previous April—right before I saw them in Telluride—they really didn't have a big local following in the town (yet), save for some hardcores up on campus, where the first show was taking place. It was quite a struggle to get some of my "townie" friends to pay $12 to see a band they had never heard live before (I think my tape collection was up to four at this point, and mostly studio stuff) up on "The Hill" with a bunch of college kids who collectively had a reputation for not holding in their liquor as well as those of us "down the hill."

So up the hill I peddled, alone, to see what still remains one of my favorite shows. It was cold and windy out, so I felt very cozy once I made it inside the charming Ballroom. A very cool crowd, and even a few friends whose curiosity led them to the right place at the right time. The Glen Miller Ballroom, about the size of two basketball courts, was an excellent venue for Phish in 1990. Lots of dancing space on hardwood floors, a big stage that was high enough for everyone to see the band clearly, and great acoustics. This was named for one of our greatest Big Band leaders, after all....

Kicking things off with Golgi and Landlady, the band rocked out from the get-go, playing tight and feeding off the good Colorado vibes bouncing around this room. The first set was just amazing, and I witnessed my very first trampoline exhibition during a rousing Mike's Song (my 2nd coming only two hours later, in the next set). The crowd, definitely appreciating all the room to dance, was also treated to The Asse Festival by itself, and a killer Possum that segued into a twisting Buried Alive then back again to our favorite road-kill song.

During the set-break, I ran into my old college buddy Ben Hunter, who was videotaping the tour for the band (will we ever see these?). He knew the names to all the songs that I didn't and hooked me up with a ticket for the next night. Thanks again, Ben.

The next set proved transcendental for me. I heard my second Forbin's/Mockingbird, which was absolutely beautiful. They were really doing some cool things with dynamics, and Trey and Page were doing some lovely noodling, which actually spilled into the drum intro for My Sweet One. Page, whose keyboard work could be heard so distinctly (compared to his sound in a packed club), played some nice fills, continuing into a phat Foam. YEM was just fantastic.

Listening to the tape from this set, I can hear lots of whoops and hollers from the audience, and it now occurs to me that so many of these folks were probably at their very first show, being blown away by the band's skills and great, memorable melodies. The trampolines came back out and the crowd went even more ballistic. There was a funky... no, make that FUNKY! organ-based jam, and by the end of the tune the band swung into an all-out vocal assault, which evolved into an ol' Suthin' spiritual of sorts. The show ended with a tasty Lawn Boy and the rockin' La Grange, which fit in just fine in this Western town.

After the show, I asked Hunter ("Junta") if he wanted to go to a party a friend of mine told me about during the show. Ben said that would be cool, since we hadn't hung out in a while, and he didn't need to hang out with the band every night. When we got down the hill to this little soiree, there was the band, already there, Fishman controlling the stereo and playing Hendrix tapes. Small town, indeed....

The next day it was time for Phish to come down the hill to the downtown, less than a mile away, and to the newly renovated Boulder Theater, an attractive piece of real estate with two levels (18+ up top/21+ down on the floor), a bar with tables in the back, regular seating, and open space for dancing in front of the stage.

This time, I only walked three blocks to the show. I arrived a few hours early to interview the band for a CD-ROM article for a magazine that never really got going. Ben Hunter set up the interview and provided me with recording equipment (thanks again Ben, whererever you are—this was the last day I ever saw him), and the next thing I know, I'm in a room alone with Mike asking him how Phish songs are put together and about their brand new album, *Lawn Boy*.

Everything went great with Mike, but Page didn't seem into it, and Jon was mostly upset about a review from a Denver newspaper comparing them to the Dead; he said (and I agree) that although the Dead were an influence, they were just as influenced by Coltrane, Mingus, and Zappa. Trey was too busy to be interviewed, but he took the time to apologize to me later.

It seemed as if it would be hard to top the previous night's show, but that doesn't seem to be a problem for these guys. Perhaps fueled by the negative press from the Denver paper, the band cooked all night. In fact, if you have any tapes of the Colorado part of the tour, you'll hear that they were in fine form throughout, as this was their second-friendliest turf after New England.

Early in the set we were presented with one of the very first Llamas that they ever played. Wow! What a rocker! A very cool new song. Next was Squirming Coil, which always adds a little spice to a great set, although here in 1990 it's in the middle of the set and has only a very short piano solo at the end. Oh Kee Pa had everyone doing a Rocky Mountain boogie. It led right into Suzie Greenberg, which, although it had been played the night before (as had a few others), no one seemed to mind since the Theater was one massive collection of high energy. We also got another new song, Page's Magilla, performed less than 10 times by that point.

The second set was chock-full of goodies. Another Mike's Song (they loooove those trampolines), Paul and Silas, Stash (also brand new and quite the crowd-pleaser) Uncle Pen, and the rare Love You. Possum was just incredible. Phish kept teasing us with the opening riff, then drifting off into something else, back to the opening, back to drifting, and then, just when you thought they weren't going to play it after all, they launch into a full scale Possum attack! Even crazier than the night before.

The encore could not have been better. There was this very happy-go-lucky young scraggly guy wandering around all night putting out Fluffhead vibes, saying things like, "They just haaaaaaaaaaave to play it tonight!" and "Wouldn't it be just perfect if they did Fluffhead?" Well, his wish was granted because that's what they encored with, in all its glory. But wait kids—that's not all! Right when it ended they treated us to a bonus Fire that truly heated up the place before we poured back out into the cold. As the happy throngs left the theater, the first snow of the season lightly descended upon us—a wondrous sight after two great evenings of incredible music.

I can say in all honesty that Phish definitely left their mark on this Colorado town. Everyone in Boulder surely knew who they were by the end of this weekend.

—Dan Gibson

➢ Things really take off during this second set when John Popper comes to play. The YEM is one of my favorites, and John adds a lot to the vocal jam at the end. Who would have thought that BBFCM needed harmonica? Well, it sure sounds good. The Jesus Left Chicago is also awesome. —KYLE NIDAY

11/10/90 [ACCESSIBILITY: •]
Earlham College, Richmond, IN
I: Reba, Landlady > Bouncing, Runaway Jim, Cavern, MSO, Buried Alive > Lizards, Mike's > Hydrogen > Weekapaug
II: Suzie, YEM, Asse Festival, Fee, Llama, Divided Sky, HYHU > Bike > HYHU, Possum

11/16/90 [ACCESSIBILITY: •]
Campus Club, Providence, RI
I: Suzie, Buried Alive, Foam, YEM, Magilla, Llama, Divided Sky, Golgi
II: Landlady, Mike's > Hydrogen > Weekapaug, Lawn Boy, Tube, Paul and Silas, Lizards, Runaway Jim, I Didn't Know, Possum **E:** Contact, Fire

11/17/90 [ACCESSIBILITY: •]
Somerville Theater, Somerville, MA
I: Llama, Squirming Coil, Landlady, Runaway Jim, Bouncing, YEM, Cavern, Eliza, Oh Kee > Suzie, Bowie
II: Buried Alive, Fluffhead, Mike's > Hydrogen > Weekapaug, Esther, HYHU > Love You > HYHU, Possum, Lawn Boy, Rocky Top, Donna Lee, GTBT **E:** Memories, Adeline
Concert debut: Eliza. "Low Rider" jams in Suzie and Bowie intro.

11/24/90 [ACCESSIBILITY: •••]
Capitol Theater, Port Chester, NY
I: Buried Alive > Possum, Foam, Mike's > Hydrogen > Weekapaug, Squirming Coil, Lizards, Oh Kee > Suzie, Bowie
II: Llama, Bouncing, Stash, Eliza, Landlady, Runaway Jim, YEM, HYHU > Love You > HYHU, GTBT, BBFCM **E:** Lawn Boy, Divided Sky

11/26/90 ❄
The Haunt, Ithaca, NY
I: Landlady > Runaway Jim, Sloth > Reba > Buried Alive, YEM, Paul and Silas, Donna Lee, Bowie, Divided Sky, Makisupa, Llama
II: Uncle Pen, Forbin's > Mockingbird, Wilson, Mike's > Hydrogen > Weekapaug **E:** Fire, Contact, Highway to Hell

11/30/90 ❄
Colonial Theater, Keene, NH
I: Landlady, Mike's > Hydrogen > Weekapaug, Esther, Dinner and a Movie, Bouncing, Tweezer, MSO, Llama, Possum
II: Asse Festival, Squirming Coil, Runaway Jim, Stash, Lizards, Gumbo, Divided Sky, I Didn't Know, Sloth, Antelope **E:** Caravan, Oh Kee > Suzie

12/1/90 ❄
The Front, Burlington, VT
I: Cavern, Landlady, Llama, Divided Sky, Foam, Tweezer, MSO, YEM, Runaway Jim
Setlist missing second set and encore.

12/3/90 ❄
The Front, Burlington, VT
I: Bathtub Gin, Funky Bitch, Ya Mar, Reba, Divided Sky, MSO, Antelope, Lawn Boy, Frankenstein
Setlist missing second set and encore.

12/7/90 ❄
Robert Crown Center, Hampshire College, Amherst, MA
I: Golgi, Stash, Bouncing, Landlady, YEM, Asse Festival, Runaway Jim, Foam, Llama
II: Mike's > Hydrogen > Weekapaug, Donna Lee, Caravan, Tweezer, Squirming Coil, Oh Kee > Suzie, HYHU > No Good Trying > HYHU, Bowie
E: Alumni
Concert debut: No Good Trying.

12/8/90 ❄
The Chance, Poughkeepsie, NY
I: Buried Alive > Runaway Jim, Foam, AC/DC Bag, Divided Sky, Cavern, Landlady, Mike's > Hydrogen, Weekapaug
II: Llama, Asse Festival, Dinner and a Movie, Bouncing, Antelope, Tela, Golgi, HYHU > No Good Trying > HYHU, YEM, Funky Bitch
E: Contact, Highway to Hell

12/28/90 [ACCESSIBILITY: ••••]
The Marquee, New York, NY
I: Runaway Jim, Foam, Horn, Reba, Llama, Forbin's > Mockingbird, Mike's > Hydrogen > Weekapaug, Golgi
II: Landlady, Possum, Squirming Coil > Tweezer > Manteca > Tweezer, Oh Kee, MSO, Divided Sky, HYHU > No Good Trying > HYHU, Don't Get Me Wrong, Funky Bitch **E:** Bouncing, Highway to Hell
John Popper on harmonica for No Good Trying, Don't Get Me Wrong and Funky Bitch. Fishman on vacuum for No Good Trying.

➢ A basic great Phish show that benefits from the addition of John Popper from Blues Traveler on Don't Get Me Wrong and Funky Bitch. Every time I listen to this show I feel the oneness that they must have felt on stage. Everything just phlows so nicely throughout the entire show. And Popper jammed out on his harmonica. —BRYAN MCCRANER

➢ Squirming Coil > Tweezer > Manteca > Divided Sky? What more do you need in a jam? The transitions between jams is barely noticeable. I love the band's willingness to combine such different song styles into one intense jam. —RON LAUREL

➢ The second set of this show is perhaps the most popular Phish tape from 1990, helped by awesome soundboard quality, a killer setlist, great playing and an appearance from John Popper. Early in the set, the band is on fire, swinging into Manteca in the midst of Tweezer, then returning to Tweezer for the closing jam. When Fish comes forward for Syd Barrett's No Good Trying, Popper does too, and there's a real good jam in the middle of the song. After that comes a rare performance of Don't Get Me Wrong (co-written by Trey and Popper), before a funky Funky Bitch closes the set. This apparently is the show that turned Elektra on to Phish; it's easy to see why. —MELISSA WOLCOTT

12/29/90 ❄
Campus Club, Providence, RI
I: I Didn't Know, Llama, YEM, Esther, Bowie, Lawn Boy, Rocky Top, Horn > Oh Kee > Suzie
II: Buried Alive > Runaway Jim, Lizards, Cavern, Stash, Jesus Left Chicago, Dinner and a Movie > Bouncing, Destiny Unbound, Antelope
E: Donna Lee, AC/DC Bag

12/31/90 [ACCESSIBILITY: •]
Exhibition Hall, World Trade Center, Boston, MA
I: Suzie, Divided Sky, I Didn't Know, Landlady, Bouncing, MSO, Mike's > Hydrogen > Weekapaug > Auld Lang Syne, Buried Alive > Possum
II: Golgi, Stash, Squirming Coil, Runaway Jim, Magilla, YEM, Rocky Top, HYHU > Brain > HYHU, Antelope
Chucklehead opened. Venue management turned on the house lights while the band was deciding on an encore, ending the show prematurely.

1991 *SEA TO SHINING SEA*

During the year in which Phish would finally sign with a major record label, Elektra, and record the album that would become *A Picture of Nectar*, the band toured ferociously.

The '91 spring tour brought the band to California and the Pacific Northwest for the first time, as well as points as far south as Mississippi. The end of the tour found the band in their last-ever gig at The Front in Burlington, and by the time they did a short summer tour with buddies The Giant Country Horns, Phish had comfortably settled in to the small theater circuit. Places like the Capitol Theatre in Port Chester, NY, the Colonial Theatre in Keene, NH, and the Flynn Theatre in Burlington, VT would remain frequent stops over the next year.

Further south, the band became regulars at Trax in Charlottesville, VA, and Cat's Cradle in Chapel Hill, NC. The summer tour, shorter than usual to allow time for recording and mixing Nectar, saw less setlist craziness than the norm, but the presence of the horns for a sustained run of shows allowed for experimentation that had previously been impossible. The horns didn't make it to the legendary Amy's Farm show in early August, although thousands of fans who heard about the free outdoor gig on the horn tour or by a postcard-mailing from the band did.

The '91 fall tour can, by most respects, be considered the first "real" tour in the way that most people now think of a Phish tour. Kicking off the tour in Keene with a bunch of first-time-played tunes, the band wound west, pulling out an unprepared Gamehendge in Olympia, WA, and digging in for a sold out, two-night stand at The Great American Music Hall in San Francisco—impressive gigs for a band that still got by almost exclusively through word-of-mouth.

From there, the tour came back through Colorado for the now-traditional Halloween fete (this was its second year in Colorado after four years at Goddard) and then slowly back to the promised land of New England and Vermont where a record contract with Elektra awaited....

1991

127 Total Show Dates
- **5** one-set shows
- **97** two-set shows
- **2** three-set shows
- **23** dates with no setlist

PHAN PICKS 1991

SHOW	THE SKINNY
1) 07/21/91 Parksville, NY	With the horns at Arrowhead.
2) 08/03/91 Auburn, ME	Amy's Pharm, with phriends.
3) 11/30/91 Port Chester, NY	At the Capitol, a great Hood.
4) 10/19/91 Santa Cruz, CA	Very well-played show & Mimi!
5) 10/13/91 Olympia. WA	First Gamehendge since '88.
6) 04/11/91 Northfield, MN	Comic relief: the Prison Joke.
7) 07/11/91 Burlington, VT	First show of the GCH tour.
8) 07/15/91 New York, NY	Only one set, but smoking.
9) 04/16/91 Ann Arbor, MI	Band and crew football songs.
10) 03/13/91 Boulder, CO	No gimmicks, just great music.

MUSICAL RECAP: By 1991, Phish's style has become even more refined, with sets often containing as many as a dozen songs. Though the songs are generally more compact versions than would be seen in later years, the band hadn't abandoned their jamming roots. Indeed, the shift in style allowed them to hone (or attempt to hone) their technical proficiency on new songs like All Things Reconsidered, while older favorites like YEM continued to receive star treatment. Still, there are fewer "must-hear" musical moments from this year than most others, with the exception of the July tour with the Giant Country Horns that brought a new jazz sensibility to the Phish sound.

REPRESENTATIVE JAMS: Divided Sky, 7/21/91 (with horns); You Enjoy Myself, 11/16/91; Frankenstein 7/12/91 (with horns).

ORIGINAL SONG DEBUTS: All Things Reconsidered (9/25/91); Brother (9/25/91); Chalk Dust Torture (2/2/91); Glide (9/27/91); Guelah Papyrus (2/1/91); It's Ice (9/25/91); Poor Heart (4/22/91); Setting Sail (4/20/91); Sparkle (9/25/91); Tweezer Reprise (2/7/91)

COVER SONG DEBUTS: Touch Me (7/11/91); Moose the Mooche (7/12/91)

DARK HORSES

SHOW	THE SKINNY
1) 04/27/91 Port Chester, NY	Probably the best show of '91.
2) 07/24/91 Charlottesville, VA	The hidden gem of horn tour.
3) 03/16/91 Breckinridge, CO	Soft and sweet.
4) 12/05/91 Greenfield, MA	This whole week is pretty hot.
5) 05/03/91 Somerville, MA	Amazing second set.

Most-Played Originals:

Song	Times	%
1) The Landlady	82	65%
2) Cavern	74	58%
3) My Sweet One	73	58%
4) Llama	69	54%
5) Bouncing	65	51%
5) The Squirming Coil	65	51%
7) Golgi Apparatus	64	50%
8) Chalk Dust Torture	63	50%
9) Foam	61	48%
10) Runaway Jim	55	43%

Most-Played Covers:

Song	Times	%
1) Rocky Top	36	28%
2) Uncle Pen	25	20%
3) Sweet Adeline	24	19%
4) Paul and Silas	23	18%
5) Love You	21	17%
6) Take the A-Train	14	11%
7) Terrapin	13	10%
8) Memories	12	9%
9) Ya Mar	11	9%
10) Three songs with	9	7%

First-Set Openers:

Song	Times
1) Chalk Dust Torture	13
2) Golgi Apparatus	7
2) The Landlady	7
2) Llama	7
2) Runaway Jim	7

Second-Set Openers:

Song	Times
1) Llama	10
2) Chalk Dust Torture	9
3) Golgi Apparatus	7
4) The Curtain	6
5) Brother, My Sweet One	5

Henrietta Songs:

Song	Times
1) Love You	21
2) Terrapin	13
3) Touch Me	9
4) If I Only Had a Brain	4
5) Bike	2

A Cappella Songs:

Song	Times
1) Sweet Adeline	24
2) Memories	12
3) Carolina	6

2/1/91 [ACCESSIBILITY: •]
Alumnae Hall, Brown University, Providence, RI
I: MSO, Foam, Tweezer, Magilla, Guelah, Runaway Jim, Melt, Bouncing, Bowie
II: Reba, Landlady, Mango
Concert debut: Guelah. Show ended after Mango due to curfew. Last Mango, 8/19/89 Durham, NH [101 shows].

2/2/91 ❄
Bates College, Lewiston, ME
I: Oh Kee > Suzie, Guelah, Dinner and a Movie, Esther, Stash, Destiny Unbound, YEM, Chalkdust
II: Sloth, Antelope, Lawn Boy
Setlist for second set incomplete. Concert debut: Chalkdust.

2/3/91 [ACCESSIBILITY: ••]
The Front, Burlington, VT
I: Runaway Jim, Guelah > MSO > Tweezer > Esther, Destiny Unbound, Reba, Chalkdust, Foam, Golgi
II: Bowie, Squirming Coil, Landlady, Cavern, Mango, Melt, Bouncing, Oh Kee > Suzie **E:** Jesus Left Chicago, BBFCM

2/7/91 [ACCESSIBILITY: •]
Pickle Barrel Pub, Killington, VT
I: Runaway Jim, Foam, MSO, Landlady, Mango, Melt, Bouncing, Possum, Squirming Coil, Golgi
II: Chalkdust, TMWSIY > Avenu > TMWSIY, Tweezer > Tweezer Reprise, Guelah, Uncle Pen, Cavern, HYHU > Love You > HYHU, Lizards > Sloth, Destiny Unbound, YEM **E:** AC/DC Bag
Lizards aborted after Trey can't remember the lyrics. Concert debut: Tweezer Reprise.

2/8/91 [ACCESSIBILITY: ••]
Portsmouth Music Hall, Portsmouth, NH
I: AC/DC Bag, Reba, Buried Alive, Forbin's > Mockingbird, MSO, Stash, Squirming Coil, Runaway Jim, Guelah, Bowie
II: Llama, Mango, Cavern, Lawn Boy, Mike's > Hydrogen > Weekapaug, Horn, Bouncing, Lizards, Antelope **E:** Landlady, La Grange
Carl Gerhard on trumpet for Landlady and La Grange.

2/9/91 [ACCESSIBILITY: ••]
Greene Hall, Smith College, Northampton, MA
I: Mango > Sloth, TMWSIY > Avenu > TMWSIY, Runaway Jim, Foam, Guelah, MSO, Tweezer > Reba, Chalkdust
II: Golgi > Buried Alive > Fluffhead, Landlady > Bouncing, Harry Hood, Cavern, HYHU > Love You > HYHU, Squirming Coil, Llama
E: Lawn Boy, Suzie **E2:** Contact, Rocky Top
Fishman on vacuum for Love You after his vacuum fails to work.

2/14/91 [ACCESSIBILITY: •]
State Theater, Ithaca, NY
I: MSO, McGrupp, Buried Alive, Reba, Destiny Unbound, Cavern, Mango, Stash, Lawn Boy, Oh Kee > Golgi
II: Mike's > Hydrogen > Weekapaug, Foam, Squirming Coil, Runaway Jim, Esther, Alumni, Bouncing, I Didn't Know, Landlady, Possum
E: Uncle Pen, La Grange
Car giveaway during I Didn't Know.

➢ At my first Phish gig at the State Theater, the band gave away their *car*! During I Didn't Know in the second set, Fishman came out and they had a whole little ceremony about how they'd finally gotten enough money to purchase a blue minivan. They said something like, "We've finally got enough money to quit driving that junker that's parked right out front... The pink slip's in the car, yell out for the keys." And so they tossed the keys out into the crowd. This kid that we were standing with, Toast, actually caught the keys and got to drive home Phish's car that night. Toast ended up selling the car for about two thousand dollars or something, and at my next show after that, which was the next time they came further west in New York, on 4/20/91 at the University of Rochester, Fishman came out, and if you listen to tapes of the show, right at the beginning, they start talking about the car. Fishman said something like, "Maybe some of you were there." When people made it clear that they were, he said, "Yeah, well, I heard that guy sold it for like, two thousand dollars. If we knew it was worth that, we never would have given it away!" Then added, "He probably just used the money to buy dope anyway." Everybody cheered, so he yelled, "Oh yeah? Dope!" then chanted, "Dope, dope, dope" with us yelling along. —MIKE GRAFF

2/15/91 [ACCESSIBILITY: •••]
Colonial Theater, Keene, NH
I: Curtain > Wilson, Divided Sky, Melt, Fee, Buried Alive, Mango, Sloth, Dinner and a Movie, Magilla, Llama
II: Bowie, Bathtub Gin, Ya Mar, Guelah, MSO, Oh Kee > AC/DC Bag, Harry Hood, HYHU > Terrapin > HYHU, Chalkdust
E: Caravan, BBFCM **E2:** Contact, Golgi
Fishman on "industrial-strength" wet/dry vacuum for Terrapin.

2/16/91 ❄
The Marquee, New York, NY
I: Sloth, MSO, Divided Sky, Cavern, A-Train, Landlady > Bouncing, Llama, Mango, Mike's > Hydrogen > Weekapaug
II: Chalkdust, Reba, Buried Alive, Runaway Jim, Guelah, Fluffhead, Rocky Top, HYHU > Love You > HYHU, Golgi **E:** Lawn Boy, Fire **E2:** Possum
"Rocky Mountain Way" jam in Possum.

2/19/91 ❄
The Bayou, Washington, DC

2/20/91 ❄
Kahootz, Richmond, VA

2/21/91 ❄
Trax, Charlottesville, VA
I: Reba, Dinner and a Movie, Melt, Fee, Llama, Lizards, Mike's > Hydrogen > Weekapaug
II: Golgi, Cavern, Landlady, Bouncing, Stash, Guelah, Uncle Pen, Asse Festival, Bowie **E:** Suzie
The Jolly Llamas opened.

2/22/91 ❄
Cat's Cradle, Chapel Hill, NC

2/23/91 ❄
1313 Club, Charlotte, NC

2/24/91 ❄
Trax, Charlottesville, VA

2/26/91 ❄
Barrelhouse, Salem, VA
I: Foam > Squirming Coil, Llama, Guelah, MSO, Reba, Oh Kee > AC/DC Bag, Golgi, La Grange
II: Buried Alive > Runaway Jim, Dinner and a Movie, Stash, Bouncing, Landlady > Destiny Unbound, Possum, Lizards, Mike's > Hydrogen > Weekapaug **E:** HYHU > Love You > HYHU, GTBT

2/27/91 ❄
Flamingo Cafe, Knoxville, TN
I: Golgi, Divided Sky, I Didn't Know, Landlady, YEM, Fee, MSO, Melt, Bouncing, Fire
II: Suzie > Buried Alive > Cavern, Squirming Coil, Bowie, Lawn Boy > Oh Kee > Sloth, HYHU > Love You > HYHU, Possum **E:** Rocky Top

2/28/91 ❄
Sarrat Theater, Vanderbilt University, Nashville, TN
I: Landlady, Bouncing, Foam, Esther, Mike's > Hydrogen > Weekapaug, Cavern, TMWSIY > Avenu > TMWSIY, MSO, Golgi
II: Squirming Coil, Reba, Llama, Guelah, Divided Sky
Setlist for second set is likely incomplete.

3/1/91 [ACCESSIBILITY: ••••]
Georgia Theater, Athens, GA
I: Wilson, Foam, Divided Sky, Cavern, Squirming Coil, Tweezer, Dinner and a Movie, Bouncing, Buried Alive, Mike's > Hydrogen > Weekapaug
II: Golgi, Landlady, Reba, Llama, Guelah, Sloth, Possum, HYHU > Love You > HYHU, Bowie **E:** Oh Kee > Suzie

3/2/91 ❄
Cotton Club, Atlanta, GA

3/6/91 ❄
Club 616, Memphis, TN
Golgi, YEM, Landlady, Squirming Coil, Possum, Cavern, Divided Sky, HYHU > Love You > HYHU, MSO, Bouncing, Bowie **E:** Jesus Left Chicago
Setlist may be incomplete.

3/7/91 ❄
The Gim, Oxford, MS
II: Oh Kee > Landlady > Sloth, Runaway Jim, Reba, Possum, I Didn't Know, Mike's > Hydrogen > Weekapaug, Guelah, MSO, GTBT
E: Bathtub Gin
Setlist missing first set.

3/8/91 ❄
College Station Theater, Tuscaloosa, AL

3/9/91 ❄
Tipitina's, New Orleans, LA

3/13/91 [ACCESSIBILITY: ••••]
Boulder Theater, Boulder, CO
I: Fluffhead, Landlady, YEM, Cavern, Divided Sky, Esther, Llama, Squirming Coil, Bowie
II: Suzie, Melt, Bouncing, MSO, Guelah, Runaway Jim, Sloth > Reba > Tweezer, HYHU > Terrapin > HYHU, Oh Kee > Golgi **E:** A-Train, BBFCM
Fishman on vacuum for Terrapin.

3/15/91 [ACCESSIBILITY: ••••]
Gothic Theater, Denver, CO
I: Llama, Foam, MSO, Stash, Dinner and a Movie, Bouncing, Oh Kee > AC/DC Bag, Lizards, Mike's > Hydrogen > Weekapaug
II: Buried Alive > Possum, Horn, Paul and Silas, Cavern, Destiny Unbound, I Didn't Know, Harry Hood, Chalkdust
E: Squirming Coil, Runaway Jim
Fishman on trombone for I Didn't Know.

➢ I consider this one of the best shows of '91, and it's definitely one of the best tapes I own (there are plenty of phatty soundboards of this one floating around). The second set is just vintage Phish, exactly how I like it. Buried > Possum are smooth while the Paul and Silas just flat out rocks. Harry is short but oh-so-sweet, then the Runaway Jim encore is the perfect way to show Colorado exactly how much Phish loves playing there. Excellent show. —ALEX BANKS

➢ The first set Horn is so soft it makes you melt—it's by far the most peaceful Horn I've heard to date; this is when the song was still relatively new. I Didn't Know features Fishman (as Moses Brown) contributing on trombone, and a terrifying scream from the audience accompanies him. —MATTHEW ASHENFELDER

3/16/91 [ACCESSIBILITY: ••••]
The Ten Mile Room, Breckenridge, CO
I: TMWSIY > Avenu > TMWSIY, Golgi, Reba, Landlady, Bathtub Gin, Curtain, Rocky Top, Forbin's > Mockingbird, Oh Kee > Suzie, Antelope
II: Llama, Divided Sky, Guelah, MSO, Melt, Magilla > Buried Alive, Squirming Coil, Cavern, YEM **E:** Manteca > Possum

➢ Like the other shows that comprised this notable week in Phishtory, the Ten Mile Room gig is a good example of Phish's evolving style during this period. In spring 1991, the band's magic comes not in the length of the jams but rather in the tight precision with which the band executed them. Listen to how excited Trey is to play compositional tunes like TMWSIY > Avenu > TMWSIY. In some ways, I think this period serves as a bridge between the looser, jammy 1980s Phish shows and their expansive, mind-blowing jams of the mid-1990s. Even if you prefer their current style, it's worth owning a few tapes from the Colorado shows of 1990 and 1991 to better appreciate the band's evolution. —TRICIA HOLMES

➢ Oh, to see Phish in a room this small—you can hear the tiny audience cheering between the songs. With plenty of Gamehendge and Lawn Boy, it's a treat for the ears. The encore is one of the most impressive I've heard: Manteca (jazz by Duke Ellington) and Possum (classic Elvis/JGB/Mystery Train by Phish). —EMILY BINARD

3/17/91 [ACCESSIBILITY: ••••]
Wheeler Opera House, Aspen, CO
I: Carolina, Bouncing, Landlady, Mike's > Hydrogen > Weekapaug, Foam, Fluffhead, Uncle Pen, Stash, Lizards, Bowie
II: Runaway Jim, Esther, MSO, Squirming Coil, Tweezer, Fee, "Fishman Story," Slave, "Colorado Story," Chalkdust **E:** Lawn Boy, La Grange
Fishman tells a long narrative about his adventures in Telluride before Slave, and both Fishman and Trey tell stories about their adventures in Colorado after Slave. Last Slave, 4/22/90 Colorado Springs, CO [78 shows].

➢ You can tell that the band loves their western U.S. fans. They take requests throughout the show and both Trey and Fish tell the crowd some long and interesting stories. Fish tells of his adventures with a Colorado bear and her cub, and Trey picks on Fish for missing a gig because he was lost in the woods (Fish denies that any illegal substances were involved). It's hilarious. The show is also highlighted by a good early version of Chalkdust and the best Trey vocals on La Grange that I've heard. —TIM FOISSER

➢ Besides the great stories, they also explain why they get off-stage when they do, and why they don't stay on longer. This is a great tape for all who enjoy the talkative side of the band. —MATT RICHARDSON

3/19/91 ❄
Fine Arts Auditorium, Fort Lewis College, Durango, CO

➢ My first show—so many fond memories. It was in the Fine Arts Auditorium, with only about 250 people in attendance. I can say this is the smallest show I've seen. It only took this first experience for me to realize how special this group was, and I've been hooked ever since. Or maybe there was something on that animal cracker that guy gave me before the show. —JEFF SALVATORE

3/22/91 [ACCESSIBILITY: ••••]
The Inferno, Steamboat Springs, CO
I: Llama, YEM, Landlady > Destiny Unbound, Bouncing, Melt, Squirming Coil, Buried Alive > Cavern, Reba, Fire
II: Oh Kee > Suzie, Antelope, Foam, Paul and Silas, Stash, Runaway Jim, Guelah, HYHU > Terrapin > HYHU, Mike's > Hydrogen > Weekapaug
E: Magilla, Golgi
Fishman on vacuum for Terrapin.

3/23/91 [ACCESSIBILITY: •]
The Inferno, Steamboat Springs, CO
I: Sloth, Divided Sky, Fee, Llama, I Didn't Know, Curtain > Possum, Forbin's > Mockingbird, Rocky Top
II: Chalkdust, Bathtub Gin, Oh Kee > AC/DC Bag, MSO, Tweezer, Lizards, Uncle Pen, Cavern, Bowie, Contact **E:** A-Train, BBFCM

3/28/91 ❄
The Catalyst, Santa Cruz, CA
Golgi, Divided Sky, Cavern, Landlady > Bouncing, YEM, Guelah, MSO, Bowie, Squirming Coil, Oh Kee > Suzie, Magilla, Chalkdust **E:** Lawn Boy, Fire
Phish played one set.

3/29/91 ❄
DNA Lounge, San Francisco, CA

3/31/91 ❄
Berkeley Square, Berkeley, CA

4/2/91 ❄
International Beer Garden, Arcata, CA

4/3/91 ❄
Southern Oregon State College, Ashland, OR

4/4/91 [ACCESSIBILITY: •]
Woodman of the World Union Trade Hall, Eugene, OR
I: Oh Kee > Suzie, YEM, Squirming Coil, Llama, Forbin's > Mockingbird, Possum, Carolina, Golgi

Saturday, March 23, 1991 — The Inferno, Steamboat Springs, CO

Phish and Colorado go way back. When a band is based in Ski-Country East, it's only natural that many from its fan base end up going to school somewhere in Ski-Country West. In the spring of '91, Phish returned to its loyal following out there for the fourth time, only now there were many new fans who knew them not from East Coast shows but solely from their regular appearances in the Mountain State over the years. By 1990, I found myself there, in Boulder, working with my own band. When Phish came to the Boulder Theater ("Cool, I can walk to a show!") on 3/13/91, I finally managed to drag my guitarist, Bruce, to see them, hoping this would help him understand what I hoped we could achieve. We sat in the balcony watching them, mesmerized (and admiring the Minkin backdrop, of course!)—the only time, I believe, that I sat for a Phish show.

Well... Bruce was blown away, just like we all were at one time or another. He insisted that we drag our bass player, John, who mostly listened to '80s new wave, to another Colorado show. As it turned out, the only one that all three of us could logistically make was all the way on the other side of the state (okay, neither place is at the extreme side, but it's on the other side of the Continental Divide—how's that?), perhaps four hours away, in Steamboat Springs, ten days later. This was to be the second night of a two-show run there, the last show in Colorado before their first trip to California—and boy, did we pick a winner!

It may have been two days after the start of spring, but traveling through the Rocky Mountains it was still the thick of winter—we nearly flew off Rt. 40 on an ice patch. What fun. We finally made it to the town of Steamboat Springs, which isn't really a quaint ol' Western town but rather a highly developed, modern ski resort, complete with a newly built "old-looking" downtown, with bars named "Saloon." The Inferno was actually "out a ways" at the resorts. When we made it to the parking lot, there were already a few tour vehicles, some with plates from New England and southern states. After all, this was a Spring Break for many. The Inferno was actually in a complex of shops at the bottom of the slopes, but it was a rather cozy place (although no windows) and the last time I would see Phish in a room this small.

At the far end was a stage, small by today's Phish-show standards, but large enough to fit the band in its ever-popular "four across" setup—the drums far right, facing the rest of the band. My pals and I (John also brought his housemate, Jane) arrived rather early in case we needed to scramble for tickets. There certainly was no need for that. We sat down for dinner in the back half of the room, and the admission (I think it was only about eight or ten bucks) was just added to the check. About half the room was full of tables and chairs, with a bar to the side, while the other half was the dance floor in front of the stage. The place was smaller than a basketball court.

The four of us were finishing up dinner and waiting for the show to begin, but that wasn't going to happen yet. First of all, only a few fans had started to trickle in, and secondly Page walks up to our table with a plate full of chicken and asks if he can sit down and eat with us. Uh, gee, what do you think we said? We were all vegetarians, but certainly not stuck-up about it. Page remembered me from a few earlier shows out East and a rather brief interview I did with the band (but mostly Mike and Jon) at the Boulder Theater in November 1990. He probably figured we wouldn't bother him too much before the show, and he was right. It was a pleasant dinner.

Eventually, the Inferno started to fill up, though I doubt there were more than 150 folks in that room. My friends and I moved right up to the stage and there was still some room to move around. As usual, I met a few nice people in my immediate surroundings. It was all so mellow, with little hint that we would soon be whipped up into such a frenzy.

The band hit the stage and promptly ripped into Sloth—a powerful start. Suddenly the Inferno was living up to its name. Everyone, save perhaps a few uninitiated who were still at the tables, whooped it up, having a grand ol' time. Next came, for the first time (I believe) what was to be a very popular future combination—like "I Know You Rider" after "China Cat" or "Livin' Lovin' Maid" after "Heartbreaker"—yep, the lovely and wondrous Divided Sky. Surprising at the time, but it somehow seemed natural. A beautiful rendition was on display and now a phull-on-Phish-show was in effect. Other first set highlights included I Didn't Know, The Curtain and—oh, the whole set was just awesome! Look at the setlist and you'll see what I mean. The boys were playing great as the audience fed them lots of positive, wild energy.

The second set just kept getting better as it went along. Happy spring-breakers and skiers passed their drinks around, so I never had to leave the front of the stage for refreshment. Chalkdust, still quite a new song and only the second time I had heard it, was fantastic. Oh Kee Pa was a great tune for these mountains and during AC/DC Bag, I bet the dance floor never felt such happy feet. If the set had ended after the gorgeous version of Lizards, I would have been content, but this was only the middle of one lonnnnng set. After the craziness of Bowie, perhaps Phish felt that we needed a set-closing Contact to bring us back to Earth.

It was not to last, though. For the encore, we were treated to a tasty "A-Train" for last call. Then came the monster of the show, so to speak. This was perhaps the most frantic, energetic and ferocious BBFCM this here body has ever witnessed. Fishman was eerie, the band was dead on, and we were one wet drippy blob of collective sweat. After the show, every wet one of us seemed to have a big Phish-eating-grin on his or her face. This was definitely one of the "funnest" Phish shows I ever experienced.

That wasn't quite the end of the fun for the four of us from Boulder, though. We went out (into the c-c-c-cold) to an all-night diner down the road a piece with some of our new phriends and then sought out what the town was named after. Yes, in the 20-degree Colorado night, we made out way out to the hot springs, which weren't officially open yet at 5 a.m. But that didn't stop us from disrobing and sliding into the steamy sulfuric liquid. As the sun was rising, I thought that Phish should always play near a natural hot spring. Ahhhh... a great way to end an amazing evening.

—Dan Gibson

II: Curtain > Runaway Jim, Guelah, Bowie, Lawn Boy, Landlady, MSO, Divided Sky, HYHU > Love You > HYHU, BBFCM, Magilla, Highway to Hell **E:** Contact, Uncle Pen

4/5/91 [ACCESSIBILITY: ••]
Starry Night, Portland, OR
I: Landlady > Bouncing > Divided Sky, Cavern, Magilla > Reba, Chalkdust, Foam, Mike's > Hydrogen > Weekapaug
II: Rocky Top, Stash, Lizards, Sloth > Dinner and a Movie, Harry Hood, I Didn't Know, MSO, GTBT **E:** Fee, Oh Kee > Suzie

4/6/91 [ACCESSIBILITY: •]
Campus Recreation Center, Evergreen College, Olympia, WA
I: Magilla, Llama, YEM, Bathtub Gin, Icculus, Antelope, Possum, Jesus Left Chicago, Alumni
Setlist missing second set. Last Icculus, 8/12/89 Burlington, VT [181 shows].

4/11/91 [ACCESSIBILITY: ••••]
The Cave, Carleton College, Northfield, MN
I: Runaway Jim, Cavern, Paul and Silas, Tweezer, Magilla, Dinner and a Movie, Bouncing, Foam, Carolina, YEM, Squirming Coil > Chalkdust
II: MSO, Reba, Llama, TMWSIY > Avenu > TMWSIY, Lizards, Melt, Lawn Boy, Landlady > Destiny Unbound, Mike's > Hydrogen > Weekapaug
E: Fee, HYHU > "The Prison Joke" > HYHU, Possum
Between Fee and Possum, the band convinces Fishman to tell "The Prison Joke." Soundcheck: Harpua jams, local radio station promo.

➢ Ah, the (in)famous Prison Joke show. As the final notes of Fee die out, Trey encourages Henrietta to come forward, saying, "I think if you guys yell loud enough, he might be able to tell you a funny joke!" Fish responds, "I'm not telling any funny jokes. This isn't funny. There's nothing funny about this. This is serious as all hell." But Trey persists. "Maybe if you yell loud enough, Fish will tell *the Prison Joke*!" That gets a laugh out of Fishman, who goes on to explain how he bought a tape of dirty trucker's jokes for the band to listen to in their van. Then with no further prompting from Trey, he tells the Prison Joke —to a decidedly lukewarm audience response. Reflecting on the joke's failure, Fish laments, "It's all in the delivery. That's why I'm not a comedian." Like the music on this night, the whole joke sequence is a little messy. —ANDRE HOLTON

➢ At first glance, all anyone sees when they look at this setlist is the Prison Joke. Although it is hilarious (with Fishman speaking in an almost surfer-dude accent), there is plenty more to this show. Lawn Boy is extra-long and lounge-lizardy, plus there's a great Reba and of course Landlady > Destiny. Boy, how great is Destiny? —JON BAHR

4/12/91 [ACCESSIBILITY: •••]
Barrymore Theater, Madison, WI
I: Llama, Uncle Pen, Divided Sky, Guelah, Oh Kee > Suzie, Stash, Rocky Top, Golgi
II: Landlady, Runaway Jim, YEM, Fluffhead, Cavern, Tela, Buried Alive, Reba, MSO, GTBT **E:** Contact > BBFCM, Squirming Coil

➢ Some of the band's parents were apparently in the crowd this night, which seems to make the show special for the boys. There's a really nice version of Tela, the Reba jam is very intense and the YEM vocal jam is one of the best I've heard. I can definitely hear them say "Get your balls out of the butter" and "Come on, send your money." It's a totally hilarious part of a very cool show. —M.N.J. ADAMS

4/13/91 ❄
Biddy Mulligan's, Chicago, IL

4/15/91 [ACCESSIBILITY: •]
Northwestern University, Evanston, IL
I: Sloth, Ya Mar, Foam, Runaway Jim, Melt, Fee, Chalkdust, Forbin's > Mockingbird, Llama
II: Wipeout jam, Mike's > Hydrogen > Weekapaug, Horn, MSO, Landlady, Lizards, Possum, Magilla, Fire **E:** Squirming Coil, Rocky Top

4/16/91 [ACCESSIBILITY: ••••]
Rick's American Cafe, Ann Arbor, MI
I: Golgi, YEM, Paul and Silas, Cavern, Mango, Oh Kee > AC/DC Bag, Tela, Bowie
II: MSO, Reba, Chalkdust, Magilla, Buried Alive, Uncle Pen, Tweezer, Runaway Jim, Carolina, Tweezer Reprise **E:** HYHU > Brain > HYHU, GTBT
Ryth McFend opened. "Crew Football Theme Song" jam before MSO. Paul Gibbons on trombone for Magilla. Fishman on vacuum for Brain.

➢ The band sounds like they took Valium before this show, which is understandable: Rick's is known for cheap drinks and BAD cover bands. The crowd is too busy swilling Jaegermeister to dig this show until the band busts into one of the first versions of Tweezer Reprise. But it's too late, because it closed the second set. For the encore, the band responds to the lousy crowd with a vacuum solo (let 'em figure that one out!) but caves in with a Zeppelin cover. Live and learn. —PAUL SHEETS

Fri., April 26, 1991 Plymouth State College, Plymouth, NH

I was at college in the fall of 1990, and there was a little group of us who really liked Phish. We thought, "Why don't we get them to come play here? We can do it."

So (this was something you could do back then) I called John Paluska at Dionysian Productions. We spoke over and over—we practically talked every day. He told me what I had to do and he sent me some materials in the mail to present to the Student Board that decided on activities. He was the nicest guy to me—he was very decent and did everything he could. He wasn't like, "Well," you know, "we want all this money." Instead, he said, "Thanks for calling, and I'm glad you guys have an interest in them. We'll work up for your interest, and we hope you'll try to work up for ours."

It wasn't like you called and he put you on hold for an hour, either—he always had the time to talk to me, he was always concerned, and he always answered all of our concerns. He baby-stepped me right through the whole process of trying to put on a Phish show at our school. It wasn't a big deal, but there were certain steps that had to be taken, and he was always there, calling me back when problems arose—which, of course, they did.

The student committee was talking about bringing Meatloaf to play on campus, but then Meatloaf couldn't make it so they started talking about Joan Jett and the BlackHearts as the main show for the semester. I said, "Well, there's no reason why we can't do another show. Why can't we just have a small show, too?" (There usually was one big concert a semester, as it was a small college.) They seemed skeptical, so I said, "We can use the fieldhouse," but they said no, there were reasons why we couldn't use the fieldhouse—it was too big, and they worried it would cost more to set up.

So I said, "Why don't we use the little activities room?"—the band I played in had played in there, and they used it for smaller sorts of gigs. We petitioned the board and they said "Okay, we'll let you do this," and I had to call and find out how much Phish wanted for the show—originally it was $3,000 and then it was $3,500. Paluska and I agreed on $3,200.

To make it work, we had to sell 200 tickets for $20 a piece. But $20 for Phish was ridiculously high back then—they played UNH around this time for $7 a ticket. But we told everybody, "If you don't do this, if you don't fork over $20, they're not going to come here." The tickets were gone within a matter of days.

So Phish ended up coming and playing towards the end of April. It never made the newsletter for two reasons, one, it was a two hundred-ticket show—they didn't want people just showing up because it was such a tiny room. The second reason was the show was scheduled too late. They did that a lot back then—many of the shows that they played never appeared in the newsletter.

The day of the show, Fishman and Page went to a party all day on Toby Road. You see, there was this house called Toby Road which is legendary up there, a red house, the only house on the street really, and everyone used to just call it "the Toby." It was the perfect college house, full of all old hippies, and it was always the place to go to make any connections or whatever, anything—just a great place.

There were always people passing through, just staying there for a couple of days on the couch, like a little Grand Central Station. They'd have parties, and a lot of bands who played would end up there late-night or before, like this reggae band from Jamaica who played. They were there for one night and ended up staying there for two days. So Fish and Page were hanging out, enjoying the barbecue and a couple of kegs.

The show that night was just tiny. It was very loud—the room actually had good acoustics, but it was so loud that the music would hit the back wall and come right back at us as though we were attending a concert in an echo chamber.

Phish played well, though, but the show was short—they got in there and they played, nothing special. Their approach was sort of business-like: get in here, play, get out of here, move on. It seemed like it was just another stop right in the middle of their long tour. I think they left town that night.

—Chad Garland

➢ This show was at Rick's American Café, a tiny little bar in downtown Ann Arbor. Obviously it's a very intimate show. Some highlights include a solid Bowie first-set closer, Magilla with Paul Gibbons on trombone and an If I Only Had A Brain encore! At the start of set II, the band mocks some of the audience by joking about football fans in the back of the bar. —JOSH HARMAN

4/18/91 [ACCESSIBILITY: •]
Oberlin College, Oberlin, OH
II: Llama, Reba, Oh Kee Pa > Sloth, Paul and Silas, Horn, Suzie, Melt, Squirming Coil, Possum **E:** Harpua
Setlist missing first set. Last Harpua, 6/9/90 New York, NY [81 shows].

4/19/91 ❄
Nietzche's, Buffalo, NY
I: Funky Bitch, Dinner and a Movie, Bouncing, Divided Sky, Cavern, Lizards, Stash, I Didn't Know, Rocky Top, Mike's > Hydrogen > Weekapaug, Adeline
II: Harry Hood, Curtain, Golgi, Landlady > Destiny Unbound, MSO, Squirming Coil, A-Train, Antelope **E:** Paul and Silas, BBFCM

4/20/91 [ACCESSIBILITY: ••]
Cafeteria, University of Rochester, Rochester, NY
I: Runaway Jim, Reba, Llama, Fluffhead, MSO, Landlady, Esther, Chalkdust, Bouncing, YEM > Setting Sail
II: Sloth, Ya Mar, Melt, Squirming Coil, Paul and Silas, Cavern, TMWSIY > Avenu > TMWSIY, Tweezer, Oh Kee > Suzie, Adeline **E:** Horn > Alumni
Concert debut: Setting Sail.

➢ The show was in a cafeteria at the University of Rochester, so it only held two to three hundred people (including Fishman's parents). Tickets were $4 if you could find a Rochester student, and $6 to the public. (Even back then, it was a big thing to find a cheaper ticket. Now, a $6 ticket would be a dream.) They played a Bouncing in the first set, but between sets, the band threw out 300 super-bounce balls, and just filled this little tiny cafeteria with bouncy balls. It was hilarious. Everybody was bouncing these balls around, and when you've got a small little cafeteria like that and 45 minutes between sets to be throwing them around, well… I've still got my bounce ball from the show (a bunch of us held on to them). After that, it became a thing for about 30 of us from school to all throw in a buck or two whenever we went to see Phish, and we'd buy as many bouncy balls as we could. We'd all go in with our pockets full and just throw them. More than a couple of them made it onto the stage. Also, everybody says that the first Setting Sail was at Jones Beach on 7/15/94, but when I saw it at Jones Beach, I thought to myself, "I know this song." But I couldn't place where I knew it from—I thought it was a common tune, and everybody told me, "No, that was the first time." But sure enough, I went back and checked my tapes, and if you listen to the 4/20/91 YEM, they all start doing the vocal scat, and first they're doing the jumbled lyrics, so it wasn't very clear, but by the end, they're all singing the Setting Sail poem in unison. —MIKE GRAFF

➢ This show began the 4/20 tradition of opening shows on this date with Runaway Jim. The tradition continued in 1993 and 1994. —MICHELLE HIRSCH

4/21/91 [ACCESSIBILITY: ••]
SUNY Potsdam, Potsdam, NY
I: Golgi, Rocky Top, Wilson, Divided Sky, Foam, Magilla, MSO, Oh Kee, AC/DC Bag, Tela, Mike's > Hydrogen > Weekapaug, Adeline
II: Possum, Fee, Landlady, Forbin's > Mockingbird, Llama, Uncle Pen, Harry Hood, Cavern, I Didn't Know, Bowie

4/22/91 ❄
Billy's, University of Vermont, Burlington, VT
I: Curtain > Runaway Jim, Sloth, Reba, Poor Heart, Llama, Guelah, Oh Kee > Suzie
II: Chalkdust, Bathtub Gin, Uncle Pen, Landlady > Destiny Unbound, Squirming Coil, Stash, MSO, Lizards, Highway to Hell
E: Lawn Boy, Rocky Top **E2:** Tweezer, Tweezer Reprise
Concert debut: Poor Heart.

➢ Billy's is a typical Old Campus building in one of those four really nice buildings on the crest of the hill, if you know the UVM campus. It's a splendid building—lots of wooden floors and really nice interior and exterior architecture. Phish played in a room students used to study, not a concert hall at all. They moved all the desks and chairs out of the room for Phish and the band set up on a one foot riser. It was pretty crowded, maybe a few hundred people in this long, narrow room that literally was a study "hall," so the crowd (made up almost entirely of UVM students) was squashed together. It was neat to see Phish in there because what was normally this dead silent library-type building suddenly had music booming and echoing off the walls and down through the corridors. —CHARLENE SMITH

4/25/91 ❄
Field House, University of New Hampshire, Durham, NH

4/26/91 [ACCESSIBILITY: •]
Plymouth State College, Plymouth, NH
I: Chalkdust, Squirming Coil, Sloth, Possum, Fluffhead, Poor Heart, Foam > YEM > Llama
II: Uncle Pen, Melt, Bouncing, MSO, Guelah, Landlady, I Didn't Know, Harry Hood, Harpua **E:** Donna Lee > Fire
Soundcheck: Poor Heart, Paul and Silas, Funky Bitch.

4/27/91 [ACCESSIBILITY: ••••]
Capitol Theater, Port Chester, NY
I: Adeline, Asse Festival, Runaway Jim, Cavern, Landlady, MSO, Reba, Llama, Lizards, Suzie, Stash, Golgi
II: Curtain > Possum, TMWSIY > Avenu > TMWSIY, Mike's > Hydrogen > Weekapaug, Fluffhead, Tweezer, Squirming Coil, Wipeout Jam, Tweezer Reprise **E:** Bouncing, GTBT
"Sweet Emotion" teases in Tweezer. Fishman on vacuum for Wipeout Jam. Last Asse Festival (separate from Guelah), 12/8/90 Poughkeepsie, NY [55 shows].

➢ Even though the music isn't that great in the first set, all of the songs sound happy, especially Cavern, which is usually a darker song. Fish just goes crazy on the drums during the middle jam of Suzie, and when they go back into the verse he screams his head off. In the second set, the boys turn it on! They dish out everything from Curtain > Possum, Mike's Groove, the infamous Wipeout, Tweezer and Fluffhead as highlights. GTBT encore isn't too shabby either. This show is out there, so get it! —CHARLIE GUBMAN

➢ This is the way to see Phish—watching them run through a set without stopping and without turning every song into a 20 minute jam. Excellent songs during what I think was one of the best eras to see the band. The extra-funky show version of Cavern is one of the best ever. —DANIEL GILFOND

➢ Maybe the perfect sound quality of these DSBDs biases me, but I think this show is easily the best of the year (horn shows aside—those are a different beast). Besides the strong setlist and very good playing, there's also a Good Times Bad Times encore to make up for the previous time the band played in Port Chester and botched it. —ED SMITH

5/2/91 [ACCESSIBILITY: •]
The Chance, Poughkeepsie, NY
I: Rocky Top, Drum Solo > Foam, Bouncing, Landlady, Forbin's > Mockingbird, Llama, Squirming Coil, Cavern > Bowie, Adeline
II: Chalkdust, Poor Heart, Divided Sky, Fee > Melt > Tela, MSO > I Didn't Know, Buried Alive > Possum **E:** Harry Hood
Drum Solo before Foam while Mike repairs a bass string. Jamie Janover on didgeridoo during Forbin's rap. "Tease medley" in Bowie intro.

5/3/91 [ACCESSIBILITY: ••••]
Somerville Theater, Somerville, MA
I: Bouncing, Foam, Chalkdust, TMWSIY > Avenu > TMWSIY, Divided Sky, Fee, Paul and Silas, Tweezer, Lizards, Adeline
II: AC/DC Bag, Curtain > Sloth, Landlady, Runaway Jim, Tela, YEM, Harpua, Tweezer Reprise **E:** A-Train, BBFCM
Col. Bruce Hampton and the Aquarium Rescue Unit opened. "Sweet Emotion" vocals in Tweezer.

➢ The two-night stand at the Somerville Theater brought lots of good times—opening sets from the always-excellent ARU and spirited playing from Phish who obviously didn't want to be upstaged by their friends from the South. They weren't—the second set of the first night's show is Phish at their best. A strong AC/DC Bag opener leads to an inspired pairing that sends chills down my spine every time I listen to it: The Curtain's fading beats build immediately back into the opening beats of The Sloth, as though Trey always meant it to be that way. The rest of the set is packed—Tela, YEM and Harpua. This is also one of the earliest Tweezer Reps, a nice cap on a stellar set. —RICHARD KOT

➢ Trey dedicates songs to Boston Bruins' living legend Cam Neely throughout the show. The second set makes this show. During Harpua, Jimmy is watching the NHL and Cam Neely and the Bruins win the Stanley Cup. —BRIAN WATKINS

5/4/91 [ACCESSIBILITY: ••]
Somerville Theater, Somerville, MA
I: Oh Kee > Suzie, Cavern, Reba, MSO, Melt, Guelah, Fluffhead, Mike's > Hydrogen > Weekapaug
II: Dog Log, Llama, Forbin's > Mockingbird, Buried Alive, Harry Hood, Horn, Rocky Top, Possum
E: HYHU > Terrapin > HYHU, Runaway Jim, Golgi
Col. Bruce Hampton and Aquarium Rescue Unit opened. Last Dog Log, 3/11/90 Burlington, VT [129 shows].

5/9/91 ❄
Portland Performing Arts Center, Portland, ME

➢ Held in a very unique 200-person capacity theater, this show was added to the spring tour with only a few days notice. The majority of the people there didn't start dancing until the third or fourth song. Trey tells everyone how he likes to dance and Page likes to sit. They call John Paluska's younger brother Peter to the stage. To get his wallet, he requests that Phish play Moby Dick backwards (they don't do it). This is a very rare tape, with only one taper in attendance! —NATHANIEL PEIRCE

5/10/91 [ACCESSIBILITY: •••]
Student Center, Colby College, Waterville, ME
I: Bowie, Cavern, Ya Mar, Dinner and a Movie > Sloth, Landlady, Bathtub Gin, Buried Alive, Lizards, Possum, Stash
II: Harry Hood > Wilson, Poor Heart, Foam, McGrupp > Chalkdust, Love You, Mike's > Hydrogen > Weekapaug **E:** A-Train, Highway to Hell

5/11/91 [ACCESSIBILITY: •]
The Front, Burlington, VT
II: Chalkdust, YEM, Poor Heart, Reba, Oh Kee > Suzie, Tweezer Reprise
E: BBFCM
Setlist missing first set.

5/12/91 [ACCESSIBILITY: ••]
The Front, Burlington, VT
I: Chalkdust, Bouncing, Dinner and a Movie, Stash, Lizards, Landlady > Destiny Unbound, Llama, Fee, Foam, Runaway Jim
II: Bowie, Bathtub Gin, Poor Heart, Curtain > Golgi > Magilla, Mike's > Hydrogen > Weekapaug, Squirming Coil, Oh Kee > AC/DC Bag, Rocky Top
E: Antelope, Fire
David Gavidpor on horn for Magilla, AC/DC Bag and Rocky Top. Mike's featured The Dude of Life on vocals (including ad-libbed lyrics). Final Phish show at The Front.

5/16/91 [ACCESSIBILITY: •]
The Sting, New Britain, CT
I: Buried Alive, Golgi, Foam, Cavern, Divided Sky, Forbin's > Mockingbird, Chalkdust, YEM, Magilla, Llama
II: Runaway Jim, Dinner and a Movie, Bouncing, Landlady, Squirming Coil, Tweezer, MSO, Lizards, GTBT **E:** Adeline
Brian Smith on trombone for Magilla.

5/17/91 ❄
Campus Club, Providence, RI
I: Chalkdust, Drum Solo > Jam, Reba, Poor Heart, Oh Kee > Suzie, TMWSIY > Avenu > TMWSIY, Stash, I Didn't Know, Mike's > Hydrogen > Weekapaug, A-Train
II: Possum, Guelah, Rocky Top, Landlady > Fluffhead, Magilla, Cavern, HYHU > Bike > HYHU, BBFCM **E:** Lawn Boy, Golgi
Drum Solo followed a blackout in the club. Carl Gerhard on trumpet for A-Train, Magilla, Cavern, and Lawn Boy. The band delivered a birthday cake to Page during BBFCM.

5/18/91 ❄
The Marquee, New York, NY
I: Buried Alive, Golgi, Chalkdust, YEM, Paul and Silas, Foam, Divided Sky, Cavern, Possum
II: Oh Kee > Suzie, Curtain > Stash, MSO, Guelah, Bowie, HYHU > Terrapin > HYHU, Lizards **E:** Dinner and a Movie, Runaway Jim

5/25/91 [ACCESSIBILITY: •]
Salisbury School, Salisbury, CT
I: Divided Sky, Landlady, Chalkdust, Bouncing, YEM, Cavern, Squirming Coil, Llama, Oh Kee > AC/DC Bag > Fee, Foam, Reba, Dinner and a Movie > Sloth, McGrupp **II:** I Didn't Know, Golgi **E:** Possum
Fishman on vacuum for I Didn't Know. Second set cut short by school officials.

Saturday, July 14, 1991 — Family Park, Townshend, VT

My wife Charlene (who was my girlfriend back in '91) and I were driving up from Connecticut to see Phish, and all we knew was that they were playing at a place called Townshend State Park. So we got the map out, found the exit, and finally figured out where to park the car. (We had our dogs with us, too.)

When we got out of our car, we could see the band across a river—they had just started to play but we couldn't figure out how to get into this place. There were no signs. So we just waded across the river, lifted up a fishnet and just walked in. And there we were, standing with two hundred other people, jamming out with Phish.

We didn't pay a dime.

Nobody busted us. I saw that people had bracelets on, but we weren't worried about it because if somebody had come up and said, "Where's your bracelet?" I would have said, "Man, I'll be happy to give you fifteen—or whatever it was, seven bucks—but I couldn't find out how to get into this damn place. So I just walked across the river, man."

They had the Giant Country Horns there, and, if I recall correctly, it was somebody's birthday and they brought a cake out onstage with boobs on it. If my memory doesn't fail me, Trey played some of that set with an imitation breast plate on his chest. It was a great show. What made that show so special was the Giant Country Horns, and the fact that this was a joint effort.

We knew it was a joint effort when, at the beginning of the show, Trey said, "Hey, this is going to be a great show, we've got a lot of things planned, so everybody get settled in." We were all in it together, and it was a very intimate experience to have a band care so much about how much fun we were having. **—Patrick Smith**

Townshend Family Park, 7/14/91

Photos courtesy of Allison Offerman

[6/91] White Crow Studios, Burlington VT
Recording for *A Picture of Nectar*.

7/11/91 [ACCESSIBILITY: ••••]
Battery Park, Burlington, VT
I: Oh Kee > Suzie, Divided Sky, Flat Fee, MSO, Stash, Lizards, Landlady
II: Dinner and a Movie > Cavern > TMWSIY > Avenu > TMWSIY > Mike's > Hydrogen > Weekapaug, HYHU > Touch Me > HYHU, Frankenstein
E: Contact > BBFCM
With The Giant Country Horns: Dave Grippo, alto saxophone; Russ Remington, tenor saxophone, and Carl Gerhard, trumpet (the same lineup present at all shows this month). Concert debut: Touch Me.

➢ Battery Park overlooks Lake Champlain on the west side of Burlington. It's a little outdoor park, and from time to time different bands played there, all for free. Phish's show there was in the daytime, with the Giant Country Horns, who they were playing with for one of the first times. I remember the Giant Country Horns were part of it, because that was something new, so we were all like, "Wow, fancy." There were a lot more people at this show, probably because it was summer and lots of people were visiting Burlington. It also seemed like there was a greater variety of people there—it wasn't just UVM students. It was a wider age range, including some curiosity seekers—people walking down the street who thought, "Hey what's going on over here?" It was definitely a signal to us that Phish was growing in terms of their audience. I think there were 400 or 500 people at the show. —CHARLENE SMITH

➢ Vermont rules! Battery Park is beautiful. It looks out across Lake Champlain, giving a great view of the Adirondacks. The Giant Country Horns added to the musical intensity of this hot show. Touch Me was both funny and entertaining—I still get Fishman's rendition in my head whenever I hear Jim Morrison crooning this classic on the radio. —DAN KURTZ

➢ "A few hometown boys who made good," shouts an anonymous M.C. I'd say! This is a great tape. Oh Kee Pa > Suzie as an opener—they were made for each other! Flat Fee is a musical treat, horns and all. Landlady is tight, but the best is yet to come: a phat TMWSIY followed by one helluva Mike's Groove. And what better way to end a set than with Fishman doing his best Jim Morrison? —CARRIE A. JOHNSON

7/12/91 [ACCESSIBILITY: ••••]
Colonial Theater, Keene, NH
I: Dinner and a Movie > Bouncing, Buried Alive, Flat Fee, Reba, Landlady, Bathtub Gin, Donna Lee, AC/DC Bag, Rocky Top, Cavern, Bowie
II: Golgi, Squirming Coil, Moose the Mootche, Tweezer > MSO, Gumbo > Mike's > Hydrogen > Weekapaug, HYHU > Touch Me > HYHU, Oh Kee > Suzie **E:** Adeline, Frankenstein, Fee, Tweezer Reprise
With The Giant Country Horns. Concert debut: Moose The Mootche.

➢ It must have been a hot night in Keene because before the set, Trey jokes about the availability of space heaters for those who want them. The set starts off in standard fashion with Golgi and Coil before the horns come out for Moose the Mooche, a great jazz song that Trey basically controls. The opening notes of Tweezer follow the closing of Moose, and absolute chaos breaks loose after the Uncle Ebeneezer verse with Phish and the horns combining in a wild, noisy free-for-all. The encore is a generous four songs, but listen to the crowd during Adeline—I'm not sure I've heard one louder. —ED SMITH

7/13/91 [ACCESSIBILITY: ••••]
Berkshire Performing Arts Center, Lenox, MA
I: Curtain > Runaway Jim, Foam, Llama, Oh Kee > Suzie, Alumni, TMWSIY > Avenu > TMWSIY, Melt, Bouncing, Frankenstein
II: Chalkdust, Guelah, Divided Sky, Flat Fee, Paul and Silas, Lizards, Stash, HYHU > Brain > HYHU, YEM **E:** Landlady
With The Giant Country Horns.

7/14/91 [ACCESSIBILITY: ••••]
Townshend Family Park, Townshend, VT
I: Reba, Llama, Squirming Coil, Golgi, Guelah, MSO, Forbin's > Mockingbird, Sloth, I Didn't Know, Possum
II: Suzie, Caravan, Divided Sky, Gumbo, Dinner and a Movie, Bouncing, Melt, Magilla, Cavern, Antelope
III: AC/DC Bag, Landlady, Esther, Chalkdust, Bathtub Gin, Mike's > Hydrogen > Weekapaug, HYHU > Touch Me > HYHU, Harry Hood
E: Contact, BBFCM
With The Giant Country Horns. "Jeopardy" tease in Harry Hood. Trey shaves his head between sets.

➢ Phish's last show at Townshend Family Park ended a glorious tradition that began in August '89. For this grand event, Mother Nature treated us to a beautiful afternoon in the cradle of civilization and Phish provided the soundtrack. Horns and Phish—what bliss! Though Trey promised us at the end of the day that Phish would return to Townshend next year, fate had other plans in store for Vermont's Phinest. I'm glad I have my memories. —ERNIE GREENE

➢ Townshend was another great show with the GCH. It has my favorite Antelope ("Hola mijetes, como estas?" is so funny). Then, in AC/DC Bag, Trey sounds like he's laughing during the "if you've got the time, I've got the inclination" line in AC/DC Bag. Mike's Song is also really strong, and of course Touch Me is cool. After Weekapaug, Trey tells the crowd that Fish has gone to take a leak, and they stretch things out a bit while waiting for him to get back. There's also a taste of the Jeopardy theme after Hood. —CHRISSY SCHENIDER

7/15/91 [ACCESSIBILITY: ••••]
The Academy, New York, NY
Oh Kee > Suzie, Landlady, Dinner and a Movie, Stash, Bouncing, Mike's > Hydrogen > Weekapaug, Flat Fee, Lizards, Cavern, Squirming Coil, Frankenstein **E:** Caravan, Contact, Alumni
With The Giant Country Horns. The Ellen James Society and Yothu Yindi played before Phish. Phish played one set.

➢ A great show—well, how could any show with the GCH be bad? The horns add a great sound to the best Lizards I have ever heard, and they're also an excellent addition to

Arrowhead

7/20&21/91 Arrowhead Ranch, Parksville, NY

The summer of 1991 will long be remembered as the only all-out tour Phish ever did with The Giant Country Horns. And perhaps the highlight of that run was a two-night stand at Arrowhead Ranch. Without a doubt, it was the most historic.

At the time, Arrowhead served as a sort of summer getaway for the crunchy crowd—a vacation spot for those whose idea of a vacation was listening to great music and enjoying various pleasures of nature. Arrowhead owners Kenny and Michele Hoff started promoting concerts at the Ranch in the summer of 1990, hosting gigs by Hot Tuna, Max Creek and the New Riders of the Purple Sage.

The site drew the attention of legendary San Francisco promoter Bill Graham, who checked out Arrowhead and was so impressed that he told the Hoffs, "I want to create the Fillmore of the Catskills at Arrowhead." He took a stake in the venture. Graham's son, David, graduated from Columbia University in the spring of '91, and Bill put him in charge of promoting shows at Arrowhead.

The Arrowhead shows were, in part, orchestrated to capture and celebrate an emerging music scene which included bands like Blues Traveler (which had released just one album to date, a moderate success), Spin Doctors (still mostly unknown outside the club circuit), Widespread Panic (barely on the radar screen up North) and The Authority (a New York funk band which never achieved the level of success of its then-peers).

David—along with a group of his Columbia friends who were helping out—decided to host the Ranch's first small-scale festival of the summer, which was to include on-site camping and even horseback riding for those who dared, on the weekend of July 20 and 21. They faced a tough choice of which bands to book: Phish and Spin Doctors, or Bob Dylan and the Band. All of the groups were willing, but the youthful promoters picked the youthful bands, and the rest is history.

While Phish had played other outdoor gigs with nearby camping before, Arrowhead marked the first shows which seemed to tap into a crowd outside of the Vermont hardcores. About 1,000 to 1,500 fans—many of whom were seeing Phish for the first time—made it up to Arrowhead for the weekend. When, at the end of two days of great music, Trey made an announcement on stage about the upcoming Amy's Farm show to be held two weeks later, many instantly decided to make the trek to Maine. Phishheads were being born in every corner.

The Arrowhead shows themselves have stood the test of time as great performances. Though it may not be Phish's best pure-musical performance of the horn tour, it sounds unquestionably like the most fun. The weekend also featured one of the largest crowds, at the time, which Fishman had ever exposed himself to. That record has since been eclipsed, at a Halloween gig a little further north in New York State.

Despite the promoters' foresight in booking Phish and the SD's, advance ticket sales were poor for the weekend and throughout the summer. In August, the promoters canceled a Little Feat concert, and eventually, Arrowhead closed down. The memories remain.

Frankenstein. Trey forgets the lines in the middle of Cavern and asks the crowd, "Does anyone know the words to this next part, 'cause I surely don't." This is a classic one-set show that all Phish fans should have. —CHRIS BLACK

➢ Halfway through Oh Kee Pa, Trey announces: "Ladies and gentlemen, the Giant Country Horns," and we're on our way. An immediate segue into Suzie sustains the momentum. After a very technical Mike's Groove, Trey introduces the Horns. About 1:30 into Cavern, Trey stops rather suddenly and asks the audience for the lyrics. Someone reminds him and they finish the song without another glitch. As an encore, Caravan features powerful horns and Contact always enlightens with intrinsic intimacy. —ANTHONY BUCHLA

7/18/91 ❄
Casino Ballroom, Hampton Beach, NH
I: Chalkdust, Foam, Runaway Jim, Guelah, Suzie, Stash, A-Train, Cavern, Mike's > Hydrogen > Weekapaug
II: Llama, Reba, Poor Heart, Melt, Lizards, Landlady, I Didn't Know, Possum
With The Giant Country Horns.

7/19/91 [ACCESSIBILITY: •••]
Somerville Theater, Somerville, MA
I: Golgi, Landlady, Bouncing, Bowie, Fee, Cavern, Squirming Coil, YEM, Gumbo, HYHU > Touch Me
II: Suzie, Divided Sky, I Didn't Know, MSO, Magilla, Tweezer, Mango, BBFCM **E:** Lawn Boy, Runaway Jim
With The Giant Country Horns. "Jeopardy" tease in Bowie. "Frankenstein" tease in YEM. Runaway Jim sung as "Runaway Yim" for a fan whose birthday was on this day. Mimi Fishman on vacuum for I Didn't Know. Esther video produced by CoSA (including Phishhead John Greene) screened between sets.

➢ This whole tour was cool. The Somerville Theater show was the first time with Mimi Fishman. I remember seeing her in the little parking lot after the show, yelling at people for playing the Grateful Dead. She said something like, "What are you playing the Grateful Dead for? Put on Phish!" because people were playing the Grateful Dead out of the back of their cars. Then, after leaving the parking lot, I took off for home in Vermont, heading up the Mass Pike. I stopped to grab a soda at the Burger King rest stop, and the next thing I know, I'm in line in between the horns—Grippo and so on—and Trey. I told Trey "Good show," and I told the horn guys, "Good show." It came Trey's turn to order and the Burger King employee asked Trey what he wanted. In a low voice, he said, "A fish sandwich." She didn't hear him, so she said, "What?" "A fish sandwich." Again she said, "What?" Then Trey said, "A fish sandwich!" in a real loud voice, and she grabbed hold of the Burger King microphone and yelled, "Fish sandwich!" and all of us started cracking up. It was really funny because no one in there had any idea what we were all laughing at. Trey just shook his head. —BRENDAN MCKENNA

7/20/91 [ACCESSIBILITY: ••]
Arrowhead Ranch, Parksville, NY
I: Chalkdust, Foam, Squirming Coil, Llama, Oh Kee > Suzie, Landlady, Bathtub Gin, MSO, Bowie
II: Buried Alive, Reba, Caravan, Dinner and a Movie, Flat Fee, Golgi, Stash, TMWSIY > Avenu > TMWSIY, YEM, Rocky Top **E:** Possum
With The Giant Country Horns. Phish shared the bill with Spin Doctors and The Authority.

7/21/91 [ACCESSIBILITY: •••••]
Arrowhead Ranch, Parksville, NY
I: Cavern, Divided Sky, Guelah, Poor Heart, Melt, Lizards, Landlady, Bouncing, Mike's > Hydrogen > Weekapaug
II: Tweezer, I Didn't Know, Runaway Jim, Lawn Boy, Sloth, Esther, AC/DC Bag, Contact > Tweezer Reprise **E:** Gumbo, Touch Me **E2:** Fee, Suzie
With The Giant Country Horns. Phish shared the bill with the Radiators and TR3. Fishman on vacuum for I Didn't Know and trombone for the end of Gumbo. Steve "Steve-o" Nelson on washboard for encores. "Bonanza" jam in Weekapaug.

Phan Pick ➢ I know, this show has been reviewed and praised so many times, but there's a reason. Set II of this show is possibly the best set with the GCH. "Gumbo, you guys remember that one?" From the sound of it, everyone on stage sure did. This show gets my vote for best Gumbo and Lawn Boy. —JUSTIN WEISS

➢ The horns at this show were the added touch it needed. —HOLLIS ROWAN

➢ A truly classic show. The first set is highlighted by an excellent Divided Sky featuring the horns, and the closing Mike's > Hydrogen > Weekapaug which also benefitted from the new sounds created by the GCH. The second set offers an interesting Tweezer and Lawn Boy. Contact > Tweezer Reprise is very good musically and is a great jam. The encores were unusual, too—a special guest showcased his skills on washboard. —JAY GREEN

➢ You gotta love "Steve-O" from New Orleans on washboard, or "whatever the hell you call that thing," as Trey puts it. The encores of this show just rock! —RICH MAZER

➢ Everyone has their own concept of Eden. For me, it's the Divided Sky that Phish played at Arrowhead ranch. There have been versions that peaked harder, or went on longer, but none that I have heard has soared to the same spiritual heights. The horns give the song a certain mythic texture, as though all that was "yes" in the universe came together that afternoon in Parksville. Listening to it now, I feel at peace with myself and the world. —MELISSA WOLCOTT

7/23/91 [ACCESSIBILITY: ••]
The Bayou, Washington, DC
I: Chalkdust, Foam, Squirming Coil, MSO > Oh Kee > Suzie, Stash, Flat Fee, Bouncing, Mike's > Hydrogen > Weekapaug
II: Llama, Reba, Cavern, Lizards, Landlady > Tweezer, Adeline, Dinner and a Movie, Gumbo, HYHU > Touch Me **E:** Caravan, Golgi
With The Giant Country Horns.

7/24/91 [ACCESSIBILITY: •••]
Trax, Charlottesville, VA
I: Golgi, Chalkdust, Squirming Coil > Buried Alive, Melt, Bathtub Gin, Landlady, Cavern, Tela, YEM
II: Possum, Guelah, Bowie, Jesus Left Chicago, MSO, Bouncing, Funky Bitch, I Didn't Know, Frankenstein, Suzie **E:** Contact, BBFCM
With The Giant Country Horns. Fishman on vacuum for I Didn't Know. "I Love Lucy" jam in BBFCM.

7/25/91 [ACCESSIBILITY: •]
Cat's Cradle, Chapel Hill, NC
I: MSO, Sloth > Foam, Suzie, Divided Sky, Flat Fee, AC/DC Bag, Adeline, Cavern, Antelope
II: Landlady, Golgi, Squirming Coil, Llama, Poor Heart, Jesus Left Chicago, Lizards, Gumbo, HYHU > Touch Me > HYHU, Magilla, Mike's > Hydrogen > Weekapaug **E:** Melt
With The Giant Country Horns.

7/26/91 [ACCESSIBILITY: ••]
Georgia Theater, Athens, GA
I: Chalkdust, Reba, MSO, Foam, Suzie, Cavern, TMWSIY > Avenu > TMWSIY, Buried Alive > Bouncing, Landlady, Golgi
II: Stash, Dinner and a Movie > YEM, Flat Fee > Funky Bitch, Squirming Coil, Tweezer, Adeline, Lizards, Happy Birthday Jam, Tweezer Reprise
E: Lawn Boy, Frankenstein, Melt
With The Giant Country Horns. Happy Birthday Jam (with horns) played for Chris Kuroda's 26th birthday.

➢ It's really no surprise that the last few shows on the horns tour proved to be the best ones musically—after all, it took these guys a little while to find each other's grooves. But when they did, well, the results are something to see (or at least hear)! During the last two-set show of the GCH tour, the rapport between The Truth, Gears and Russell and Phish is outstanding. Listen to their interplay in the second set, especially on Stash, Tweezer and Melt. (Audience recordings of this show also reveal some poor soul screaming all night for Split Open and Melt. He finally got his wish). —ANDRE HOLTON

7/27/91 [ACCESSIBILITY: •]
Variety Playhouse, Atlanta, GA
Llama, Foam, Oh Kee > Suzie, Cavern, Poor Heart, Stash, TMWSIY > Avenu > TMWSIY, Possum, I Didn't Know, Landlady, Mike's > Hydrogen > Weekapaug **E:** Touch Me, Contact
With The Giant Country Horns. Phish shared the bill with Col. Bruce Hampton and the Aquarium Rescue Unit, and played one set.

[8/91] White Crow Studios, Burlington, VT
Recording and mixing of *A Picture of Nectar*.

8/3/91 [ACCESSIBILITY: ••••]
Larabee (Amy Skelton's) Farm, Auburn, ME
I: Wilson, Foam, Runaway Jim, Guelah, Llama, Fee, Squirming Coil, Poor Heart, Sloth, Divided Sky, Golgi
II: Curtain, Reba, Chalkdust, Bouncing, Tweezer, Esther, Cavern, I Didn't Know, YEM, Rocky Top
III: Stash, Ya Mar, Fluffhead, Lawn Boy, MSO, Lizards, Buried Alive > Possum
E: Magilla, Self, She's Bitchin' Again, Crimes of the Mind
E2: Harry Hood
Free outdoor concert. Jamie Janover on didgeridoo for Buried Alive. Self, She's Bitching Again, and Crimes of the Mind featured The Dude of Life on vocals. She's Bitching and Crimes featured Sofi Dillof on vocals. Concert debuts: She's Bitching Again, Crimes of the Mind. Fishman on vacuum for I Didn't Know. "I Love Lucy" jam in YEM and other places throughout the show.

➢ This event sounded like a blast—camping and partying and a huge offering of tunes (three sets and five encore tunes!) They really changed pace a lot and switched up all the selections to create peaks and valleys of music. I usually don't much care for Dude of Life contributions, but this show was different. Listening to this show reminds me how down to earth and cool the band is. —DAVE MATSON

➢ YEM, Ya Mar, Fluffhead, Lizards, Buried Alive > Possum *and* Harry Hood? Are they trying to give me a heart attack? This show isn't musically perfect—they never really "got it right"—but it's a great one nevertheless. I love this tape. —RON LAUER

➢ Amy had her cowboy hat on—the whole nine yards. She was very, very visible throughout the whole thing, making announcements and jumping up and down on one of the trampolines. —BRENDAN MCKENNA

Amy's Farm

8/3/91 Larabee Farm, Auburn, ME

It was only a postcard, but when it landed in the mailboxes of the thousands of people then on the Phish mailing list, its impact was most profound. A note from Trey, Mike, Page and Fish said that as the band approached its eighth anniversary, they realized "it would be great to throw a party to thank everyone for all the good times." With that, the postcard went on to invite everyone to a free Phish concert in Auburn, ME at the beginning of August.

The site? Larabee Farm, a 255-acre horse ranch owned by Amy Skelton, the acclaimed first fan who played a major role in helping Phish establish a New Hampshire fan base in the late 1980s when they were still mostly unknown outside of the Burlington, VT area. The band scouted the farm the previous fall—on horseback, no less, with Trey riding the famous Maggie, who would later be hoisted to appear on the cover of *Hoist*—and decided they'd found the perfect place to host a giant party.

Word of the event spread fast. A makeshift map on the back of the postcard served as the directions, luring people from across the country. One fan, Henry Petras, traveled coast-to-coast for the event, a fact the band acknowledged at one of their first fall shows when they presented him an award for "the longest distanced traveled to attend a Phish show." About 2,000 (the most popular estimate) fans found their way that weekend to an open field, where Phish set up a makeshift stage on the back of a truck.

There were rules, of course, but they weren't tough to abide by—no campfires were allowed because it had been a dry summer in Maine, and everyone was asked to pick up after themselves. Beyond that, as Trey said at the end of the first set, "Go wild, because nobody's going to stop you here."

It seems that everyone who attended the Amy's Farm show returned with as much excitement about the scene as about the music. While no one complained about Phish's three-set marathon, along with a six-song encore with The Dude of Life, what stood out in most people's memories was the mellow but anything goes atmosphere that pervaded the free event.

There were lots of stories that would make Pat Robertson or Jerry Fallwell cringe—nudity, mind-altering substances—but lots more that would renew any cynic's faith in society. A schoolbus unloaded a pack of campers, brought by a pretty hip camp counselor. A true communal atmosphere, where people cleaned up after themselves and took care of each other in 100-degree heat, developed. As Trey remarked at the end of three long sets of music, "Have a good time tonight—we're going to be out there partying with you." It was one long raging party, which turned strangers into friends and for some marked the start of the real Phish explosion on the East Coast.

Behind the Ryder trucks, an even more intense party raged in what was considered the "backstage area." Trey rode around on a Harley Davidson. A gaggle of the band's friends were in attendence.

For many, the highlight of the show was when Fishman appeared in the famed "Zero Man" outfit, the superhero getup that hadn't made an appearance in about a year and hasn't made it out since. There was also on-stage collaborations with The Dude of Life (on a whole bunch of songs) Sofi Dillof (then Page's girlfriend, now his wife, who claimed the role of the female singer on the Dude's classic She's Bitching Again), and Jamie Janover, who emerged to play his didgeridoo on Buried Alive.

Like so many of the stages and settings where Phish history was made, Amy's Farm is a place where the band will most likely never perform again (at least not in a concert open to the general public). And never again will an event of its intimate nature be possible. Still, the communal spirit of Amy's Farm unquestionably informed the later-year giant gatherings the Clifford Ball and the Great Went—events that have changed the very idea of what a rock concert can be.

While the Amy's Farm show is a popular and heavily-circulated set of tapes, the band had certainly achieved grander musical heights before, and have since.

But the feelings of communality the show generated may never be equaled again, and that is why the Amy's Farm show holds what is perhaps an unrivaled spot in Phish folklore.

➢ Amy's Farm is a show where every set is great. —KEVIN M. WARD

➢ This show includes a lot of incredible music. Sets I and II had standouts such as Llama, Fee, Curtain, YEM and Divided Sky, but the highlight for me is Stash. Trey holds a single note longer than I've ever heard—I thought a smoke detector in my house was going off when I first played this tape. Check it out! —MICHAEL RAMBO

[8-9/91] White Crow Studios, Burlington, VT
Recording *Crimes of the Mind* with the Dude of Life.

9/25/91 [ACCESSIBILITY: •]
Colonial Theater, Keene, NH
I: Brother, Poor Heart > Foam, Llama, Tela > MSO, It's Ice, Landlady > Caravan > Reba > Possum
II: Squirming Coil, Stash, Sparkle, Cavern, Jesus Left Chicago, Runaway Jim, YEM, Chalkdust **E:** All Things, BBFCM
Concert debuts: Brother, It's Ice, Sparkle and All Things. Carl Gerhard on trumpet for Cavern and Jesus Left Chicago.

➢ As was becoming the norm, the tour opener contained a bunch of new song debuts. The most difficult proved to be All Things Reconsidered, which the band didn't play again until Spring 1992 because they weren't yet up to its technical demands. —PAT STANLEY

➢ This show marked the start of a very strong fall tour for Phish, the first tour that saw the level of musical innovation still present today. A lot of people overlook fall '91 tapes, for no apparent reason, but you owe it to yourself to check a few out. —ED SMITH

9/26/91 [ACCESSIBILITY: •]
State Theater, Ithaca, NY
I: Llama, Bouncing, Divided Sky, Fee, It's Ice, MSO, Guelah, Lizards, Foam, Bowie
II: Golgi, Squirming Coil, Brother, Sparkle, The Landlady > Destiny Unbound > Mike's > Hydrogen > Weekapaug, Lawn Boy, Chalkdust
E: Memories, Poor Heart, Adeline
"Dr. Seuss" sung as lyrics in Bowie.

➢ There are really good tapes of this supposedly rare show circulating around Maine and New York. I'm doing my best to make sure everyone I trade with gets a copy of it.... the Landlady > Destiny > Mike's > ... is SO GOOD! —DAVID SCHALL

➢ At the State Theater show, they played the Dr. Seuss David Bowie, two days after Dr. Seuss had died. They sang, "Dr. Seuss" instead of "David Bowie." That was 9/26/91, and I think Dr. Seuss died 9/24/91 or 9/25/91. It was a great show. —MIKE GRAFF

9/27/91 ❄
The Warehouse, Rochester, NY
I: Runaway Jim, Cavern, Reba, Buried Alive, Esther, Tweezer, Paul and Silas, It's Ice, I Didn't Know
II: Possum, Tela, Sparkle, Melt, Mango, Dinner and a Movie, Oh Kee > Suzie, YEM, Tweezer Reprise **E:** Glide, Rocky Top
Concert debut: Glide. Setlist for first set may be incomplete.

➢ At the Warehouse in Rochester, during YEM, was the first time they started doing Homer Simpson's "D'oh!" During YEM, Trey started going "D'oh!" and then everybody joined in and they did an entire scat of them all going "D'oh!" "D'oh!" "D'oh!" They all really go off, all four of them trying to imitate Homer as best they could! I remember it as Phish's first "D'oh!" encounter. It was shortly after that—somewhere in the midwest, I guess—that they developed their little "D'oh!" cue. Phish's show at the Warehouse was also the last show by any band there. The Warehouse changed ownership after that show; we were hanging out with the new owner at that show, and that was what pretty much made him want to buy the place when he saw how raging it was. But that may have been the high point of that place's history—they've changed its name a couple times since. The place had a low ceiling, it was like somebody had taken an antique shop or and old junk shop and glued it to the ceiling, there were hanging bathtubs and naked mannequins in cowboy boots hanging out of them, just inches above everybody's head. Once the new owner bought the place, he cleared all that out—I bet it was a fire-hazard. But at that time of the Phish show there, the entire ceiling was covered with lamps and bikes and old machinery. —MIKE GRAFF

9/28/91 [ACCESSIBILITY: •]
The Rink, Buffalo, NY
I: Landlady > Bouncing, Chalkdust, The Squirming Coil, MSO, Stash, Foam, Brother, Golgi, Memories
II: Llama, Guelah, Sparkle, Cavern, Antelope, Lawn Boy, Lizards, Poor Heart, Mike's > Hydrogen > Weekapaug **E:** Contact, BBFCM
Before Llama, Phish presented an award to fan Henry Petras for flying 3,000 miles to catch the Amy's Farm show—the longest distance traveled to catch a Phish show. Trey solos through the crowd on rollerblades for Weekapaug. "I Love Lucy" tease in BBFCM.

➢ When the band finished the song I am Hydrogen, Trey took to his hockey roots and put on in-line skates and a wireless guitar. The song shifted into Weekapaug Groove and he skated into the crowd on his skates, jamming as he went. He took a solo and skated around the rink, inciting us all. —MELISSA MIXER

9/29/91 ❄
Agora Theater-Bar, Cleveland, OH
Cavern, Divided Sky, I Didn't Know, It's Ice, Poor Heart, Landlady > YEM, Oh Kee > Suzie
Phish played one set.

➢ This show wasn't actually at the Agora Theater—it was at the Agora theater-bar, the bar right across from the theater. The next time they played Cleveland was the first time they played the Agora Theater, on 5/7/92. It's actually the same building—the theater is on the right, and there's a little bar where bands can also play on the left. That's where Phish was this time. It was just a one-set show. —MIKE GRAFF

10/2/91 ❄
The Cubby Bear, Chicago, IL
I: Llama, Foam, Squirming Coil, Poor Heart, Cavern, Reba, Brother > Bouncing, Chalkdust, Golgi
II: Landlady, YEM, MSO, Guelah, Runaway Jim, Lawn Boy, Stash, Oh Kee > Suzie **E:** Possum, I Didn't Know, Rocky Top

10/3/91 [ACCESSIBILITY: •]
Mabel's, Champaign, IL
I: Chalkdust, Foam, Uncle Pen, It's Ice, Bouncing, Llama, Fee > Divided Sky, Cavern, Possum
II: Paul and Silas, Mike's > Hydrogen > Weekapaug, Esther, Landlady > Destiny Unbound, Buried Alive > Squirming Coil > Tweezer, Memories
E: HYHU > Terrapin > HYHU, Tweezer Reprise

10/4/91 [ACCESSIBILITY: •]
Barrymore Theater, Madison, WI
I: Memories, Chalkdust, Reba, Poor Heart, Cavern, Divided Sky, Guelah, Sparkle, Suzie, Magilla, Bowie
II: MSO, Brother, Bouncing, Foam, Runaway Jim, Lawn Boy, Stash, Squirming Coil, Mike's > Hydrogen > Weekapaug
E: Adeline, Golgi, Rocky Top, HYHU > Love You > HYHU, Llama
"Linus and Lucy" jam in Squirming Coil piano solo.

10/5/91 ❄
The Cabooze, Minneapolis, MN

10/6/91 ❄
Student Union, Macalester College, St. Paul, MN
I: Suzie, Foam, Divided Sky, Bouncing, Poor Heart, Oh Kee > AC/DC Bag, Brother, HYHU > Terrapin > HYHU, Golgi
II: MSO, Stash, Fee, Landlady > Destiny Unbound, Harry Hood, I Didn't Know, Cavern, Squirming Coil, Rocky Top
E: Adeline, Possum, Llama
Adeline performed from the balcony.

10/10/91 [ACCESSIBILITY: ••]
EMU Ballroom, University of Oregon, Eugene, OR
I: Chalkdust, Foam, Paul and Silas, Melt, Bouncing, Landlady, Runaway Jim, It's Ice, Llama, Golgi, Alumni, Lizards
II: Brother, Reba, Poor Heart, Cavern, Antelope, I Didn't Know, Sparkle, Oh Kee > Suzie, Fee > Mike's > Hydrogen > Weekapaug
E: Squirming Coil, Fire

10/11/91 ❄
Backstage, Seattle, WA
I: Landlady, MSO, Guelah, Chalkdust, YEM, Lizards, Llama, Bouncing, Runaway Jim
II: Curtain > Cavern, Foam, Bowie, Mango, Sloth, Poor Heart, Magilla, Possum **E:** Adeline, BBFCM
Setlist for first set may be incomplete.

10/12/91 ❄
Roseland Theater, Portland, OR
Artis the Spoonman opened, and played with Phish during the second set.

10/13/91 [ACCESSIBILITY: ••••]
North Shore Surf Club, Olympia, WA
I: Runaway Jim, Wilson, Reba, Landlady, Forbin's > Mockingbird > Tela > AC/DC Bag > Sloth > McGrupp, Mike's > Hydrogen > Weekapaug
II: Llama, Bathtub Gin, Squirming Coil, It's Ice, MSO, Jesus Left Chicago, Bouncing, HYHU > Love You > HYHU, Bowie
E: Eliza, Uncle Pen **E2:** Carolina
The first set features an almost complete Gamehendge saga, with narration by Trey, the second time ever performed live. Fishman on vacuum for Love You. "A-Train" jam in Bowie intro. Last complete Gamehendge, 3/12/88 Burlington, VT [316 shows].

➢ Whatever compelled Trey to tell the crowd at a tiny bar in Olympia, WA about the mystical, far-off land of Gamehendge for the first time since 1988 remains a mystery, but fast dispersal of these tapes in the early days of the Phish.Net created a far wider audience. Anyway, at least a few people in the crowd know they're witnessing history. This is the most incomplete version of the five live Gamehendge performances because Wilson had already been performed as the second song in the set before Trey decided to narrate, so Lizards (the usual starting point) had to be skipped. Still, it's obvious how excited Trey is to be telling the story—hard to believe he waited three-and-a-half years between performances! —SCOTT SIFTON

➢ This is, of course, a Gamehendge show, but it's missing one of my favorites, Lizards. I'm also bothered by the slightly illogical Gamehendge order (I would've put a few songs before Forbin's > Mockingbird), but these are Gamehendge songs after all, making the set superb. —ANDREW MITCHELL

10/15/91 ❄
International Beer Garden, Humboldt Brewery, Arcata, CA
I: Chalkdust, Foam, Squirming Coil, Melt, Sparkle, Reba, Landlady > Destiny Unbound, YEM, Rocky Top
II: Brother, Bouncing, Runaway Jim, Poor Heart, Llama, Oh Kee > Suzie, HYHU > Love You > HYHU, Funky Bitch, Golgi **E:** Memories, Harry Hood
Fishman on vacuum for Love You. Setlist for the second set is incomplete.

10/17/91 [ACCESSIBILITY: •]
Great American Music Hall, San Francisco, CA
I: Memories, Landlady > Bouncing, Divided Sky, Cavern, Poor Heart, Stash, Esther, Chalkdust, Golgi
II: Curtain, Oh Kee > Suzie, Bowie, Lawn Boy, Fluffhead, YEM, HYHU > Love You > HYHU, Possum **E:** Magilla, Rocky Top

10/18/91 [ACCESSIBILITY: ••]
Great American Music Hall, San Francisco, CA
I: Runaway Jim, Foam, Paul and Silas, Reba, Wilson > Llama, Lizards, Adeline, Antelope
II: Brother, Uncle Pen, Guelah, Dinner and a Movie, Mike's > Hydrogen > Weekapaug, I Didn't Know, Fee > Melt, MSO, Cavern
E: Sparkle, Walk Away, Squirming Coil

➢ Another Phish milestone—two sold-out shows at San Francisco's GAMH! As much as part of the folklore as the famous first Paradise gig in Boston, the band gained fame as the "first unsigned band to sell out GAMH for two nights." Get the tapes from the second night. —AMY MANNING

➢ This was the second of two nights at this classy little spot (600-person capacity). The Walk Away encore was a real treat, though they soundchecked it the night previous. —NATHANIEL PEIRCE

➢ Trey's explanations of Brother, Uncle Pen and Guelah add a little kick to the second set. He says Brother was played for Page's and Mike's brothers, who were in the audience, to "describe their personalities." He also talks about Guelah being his friend Dave's mom, and how she used to bust into his room while they wrote songs. Overall, this show gives a nice look into some early Phish tunes. Mike's > Hydrogen > Weekapaug was the set's musical highlight, followed closely by Dinner and a Movie. —NICK SORICELLI

10/19/91 [ACCESSIBILITY: ••••]
The Catalyst, Santa Cruz, CA
I: Landlady > Suzie, It's Ice, Runaway Jim, Foam, Chalkdust > Bouncing, MSO, Stash, Golgi
II: Llama, Bathtub Gin, Sparkle, Tweezer > Horn, Poor Heart, YEM, Oh Kee > HYHU > Terrapin > HYHU, Harry Hood **E:** GTBT
Terrapin featured Mimi Fishman on vacuum. MSO performed a cappella, then electric (regular).

➢ This was a very mellow show; the music was absolutely all over the place. Hold Your Head Up (which flowed into Terrapin, then back into HYHU) was played with Fishman as "Showboat Gertrude." Trey announced that Henrietta was dead ("You will never see Henrietta on the Phish stage again") and that Showboat Gertrude would take her place. The band was joined in Terrapin by Showboat Gertrude's mother, who wailed on the vacuum cleaner. —MATT FITONE

➢ The setlist doesn't do this show justice. The band cooks through the entire second set at this great little restaurant/club in downtown Santa Cruz (if you ever get a chance to see a show at the Catalyst, go!). Besides the beautiful Harry Hood that closes the set, check out the "coughing and phlegm" YEM vocal jam, which might make you lose your lunch. Terrapin, with Mimi, is also hilarious as Fish improvises some lyrics in honor of his mother's appearance. —ANDRE HOLTON

10/23/91 ❄
Chuy's, Tempe, AZ

10/24/91 [ACCESSIBILITY: ••]
Prescott College, Prescott, AZ
I: Oh Kee > Suzie, Foam, Poor Heart, Stash, Ya Mar, Divided Sky, I Didn't Know, TMWSIY > Avenu > TMWSIY, Bowie
II: Mike's > Hydrogen > Weekapaug, Lizards, Uncle Pen, Tube, Slave, Dinner and a Movie, Bouncing, HYHU > Terrapin > HYHU, Possum
E: Memories, Adeline, Rocky Top

10/26/91 ❄
Club West, Santa Fe, NM

10/27/91 [ACCESSIBILITY: •]
Elk Ballroom, Telluride, CO
I: MSO, Chalkdust, Mango, Buried Alive, Guelah, Fluffhead, Brother, Bouncing, Harry Hood, Golgi
II: Llama, Forbin's > Mockingbird, Sparkle, It's Ice, Mike's > Hydrogen > Weekapaug, Tela, Landlady > Destiny Unbound, A-Train, Antelope
E: Glide > Possum
Soundcheck: La Bamba tease, Tube, It's Ice (3x).

➢ This show was in the smallest venue I've ever seen Phish play—a room no bigger than a large living room. This was my second show and it further served to cement my appreciation of Phish. Standing only ten feet away from Trey and his newly-shaven head, with no stage, he blew me away. All the classics were here: Mango Song, Mike's, Lizards, Antelope. Another highlight was walking down the hall between sets and saying "hi" to Trey. —JEFF SALVATORE

10/28/91 [ACCESSIBILITY: ••]
Elk Ballroom, Telluride, CO
I: Curtain > Runaway Jim, Cavern, Poor Heart, Reba, I Didn't Know, Tube, Oh Kee > Foam, Fee, Bowie, Carolina
II: Divided Sky, Wilson > Dinner and a Movie > Stash, Paul and Silas, Bathtub Gin, YEM, Squirming Coil, Harpua, HYHU > Whipping Post > HYHU, Highway to Hell
E: Horn, Rocky Top
Whipping Post featured Mimi Fishman on vacuum and Fishman on slide guitar.

10/30/91 ❄
Boulder Theater, Boulder, CO

10/31/91 [ACCESSIBILITY: ••]
Armstrong Hall, Colorado Springs, CO
I: Memories, Brother, Ya Mar, Sloth, Chalkdust, Sparkle, Foam, Bathtub Gin, Paul and Silas, YEM, Runaway Jim
II: Landlady, "Wait" > Llama, Fee > "Wait", MSO > "Wait" > Bowie, Horn, Dinner and a Movie, Tube, I Didn't Know, Harry Hood
E: Glide, Rocky Top
"Wait" indicates brief musical tease then a few minutes of silence after the band says, "wait." Female show-goer dressed as Mike started the second set on stage, with Mike playing from off-stage. Costume Contest between Landlady and Llama. Fishman on vacuum for I Didn't Know.

11/1/91 [ACCESSIBILITY: ••••]
Gothic Theater, Denver, CO
I: AC/DC Bag > Sparkle, Landlady > Destiny Unbound, Squirming Coil, Melt, Fluffhead, Uncle Pen, Tube, Divided Sky, Adeline
II: Tweezer, MSO, It's Ice, Chalkdust, Eliza, Mike's > Hydrogen > Weekapaug, A-Train, Tela, Cavern, Poor Heart > Tweezer Reprise
E: HYHU > Love You > Pusher Man Jam, Stash
"Pusher Man" replaced HYHU as the outro jam on Love You. Fishman on vacuum for Love You.

➢ This show has become one of the best-circulated Phish tapes from '91, I think more for the perfect digital soundboard sound quality than for the music. There are highlights—including a powerful Landlady > Destiny, a good Divided Sky and Tube during its prime—but no must-hear jams. The Phishtoric moments come during the encore after Love You, when Phish plays "Pusher Man" as the Henrietta theme because it's a song Fish likes in place of the Hold Your Head Up jam he hates. And Stash is a request from a group of Phish.Net phans standing close to the stage—it was around this time that the band learned of the Net's existence and Trey, for one, got pretty excited about it, even if he doesn't seem to quite understand how it works. —AL HUNT

11/2/91 [ACCESSIBILITY: •]
Lory Theater, Fort Collins, CO
I: Suzie, Curtain > Llama, Reba, Paul and Silas, Foam, Bouncing, Forbin's > Mockingbird, Possum
II: Golgi, Antelope, TMWSIY > Avenu > TMWSIY, Sparkle, Guelah, Walk Away, Landlady, Runaway Jim, YEM **E:** Contact, BBFCM

11/4/91 ❄
Rhythm Room, Dallas, TX

[11/5/91]
Liberty Lunch, Austin, TX
Show canceled.

11/7/91 [ACCESSIBILITY: ••]
Tipitina's, New Orleans, LA
I: Memories, Chalkdust, Foam, Sparkle, Cavern > It's Ice, YEM, Landlady > Runaway Jim, I Didn't Know, Llama
II: Brother, Bouncing, MSO, Reba, Tube, Horn, Bowie, A-Train, HYHU > Love You > HYHU **E:** Fee, Rocky Top **E2:** Lawn Boy > Fire
Col. Bruce Hampton and the Aquarium Rescue Unit opened, and they joined Phish for Bowie, A-Train and Love You.

11/8/91 [ACCESSIBILITY: •]
The Ivory Tusk, Tuscaloosa, AL
I: Tube, Landlady > Dinner and a Movie, Stash, Poor Heart > Divided Sky, Mango, Brother > Eliza, Golgi
II: Sloth, Sparkle, Melt, Squirming Coil, I Didn't Know, Mike's > Hydrogen > Weekapaug, Jesus Left Chicago, Self, Life is a TV Show, Family Picture > Crimes of the Mind
E: Fee > Suzie
Alternate lyrics in Weekapaug: "Bucket of lard," etc. The Dude of Life on vocals for Self, Life is a TV Show, Family Picture, and Crimes of the Mind. Concert debuts: Life is a TV Show, Family Picture.

11/9/91 ❄
Variety Playhouse, Atlanta, GA
I: Curtain, Runaway Jim, Foam, Sparkle, Llama, Reba, Tube, YEM, Horn, Brother, Adeline
II: Chalkdust, Fluffhead, Poor Heart, It's Ice, Tweezer, Tela, Landlady, HYHU > Terrapin > HYHU, MSO, Tweezer Reprise
E: Glide, Possum

11/10/91 ❄
Music Farm, Charleston, SC

11/12/91 [ACCESSIBILITY: •]
Georgia Theater, Athens, GA
I: Buried Alive > Golgi, Uncle Pen, Brother, Bouncing, Tube, Sloth, Harry Hood, Fee, Foam, Llama
II: Dinner and a Movie, Stash, Squirming Coil, Paul and Silas, Mike's > Hydrogen > Weekapaug, Guelah, Chalkdust, Magilla, Cavern, HYHU > Love You > HYHU, Antelope **E:** Ya Mar, BBFCM **E2:** Melt, Memories

11/13/91 [ACCESSIBILITY: •]
Love Auditorium, Davidson College, Davidson, NC
I: Landlady > Runaway Jim, It's Ice, Sparkle, Chalkdust, Esther, Cavern, Divided Sky, I Didn't Know, HYHU > Terrapin >HYHU, YEM
II: Bowie, Forbin's > Mockingbird, Golgi, Bathtub Gin, Squirming Coil, Llama, Possum **E:** Horn, MSO, Adeline

11/14/91 [ACCESSIBILITY: ••]
Cat's Cradle, Chapel Hill, NC
I: Wilson, Uncle Pen, Llama, Reba, Foam, Tube, Sparkle, Brother, Mango, Golgi, Runaway Jim
II: Dinner and a Movie, Antelope, Fee, Paul and Silas, It's Ice, Glide, Tweezer > A-Train, HYHU > Brain > HYHU, Lizards > Tweezer Reprise
E: Bouncing, GTBT **E2:** YEM
Antelope sung as "Roll Like A Cantaloupe." "Smells Like Teen Spirit" tease in Antelope. "Frosty the Snowman" tease in A-Train.

11/15/91 [ACCESSIBILITY: ••]
Trax, Charlottesville, VA
I: Chalkdust, Sparkle, Cavern, Curtain, Melt, Squirming Coil, MSO, Divided Sky, Lawn Boy, Golgi
II: Llama, Bathtub Gin, Poor Heart > Mike's > Hydrogen > Weekapaug, Eliza > Tube, Landlady > Destiny Unbound, Harry Hood, HYHU > Love You > HYHU, Bouncing > Possum **E:** Highway to Hell, Suzie

➢ When talking about superlative Phish shows, this one must be included. The second set alone is a dandy. Llama kicks things off and flows directly into an outstanding Bathtub Gin. While Mike's is always excellent, it is the Landlady > Destiny Unbound segue that gets me going (please bring it back, guys!). Finally, the concert is topped off by an awesome Possum. —JONATHAN BAURO

11/16/91 [ACCESSIBILITY: •]
The Bayou, Washington, DC
I: Landlady, Uncle Pen, Wilson, Runaway Jim, It's Ice > Sparkle > Fluffhead, Foam, Stash, Ya Mar, Cavern
II: Tube, MSO, Bathtub Gin, Brother, YEM, Horn > Chalkdust, HYHU > Terrapin > HYHU, Llama **E:** Glide, Rocky Top
Fishman on vacuum for Terrapin.

➢ A show ahead of its time, at least as far as YEM is concerned. The boys surf the waves of beauty and wonder on this night—this is the kind of music that can change the world! I hope some of our Congressmen made it down to The Bayou, because they would have gotten to enjoy this hidden gem without the fifth-generation hiss of my analog tape. —AL HUNT

➢ For some unknown reason, Trey got fixated on the phrase "Mrs. Pizza Shit" during this show. After Gin, in an attempt to one-up Trey, Fishman rechristened Phish "Mrs. Pizza Shit," a name change that Trey reiterates during the YEM intro. The YEM vocal jam then incorporates the "Mrs. Pizza Shit" theme. Hmmm. Maybe the presence of some Phishy friends in the audience—Tom Marshall, Trey's mom and his sister—inspired the weirdness. —TRICIA HOLMES

11/19/91 ❄
The Sting, New Britain, CT
I: Uncle Pen, Foam, Runaway Jim, Fee > Sparkle, Brother, Horn, Chalkdust, HYHU > Love You > HYHU, Wilson, Divided Sky
II: Tube, MSO, Mike's > Hydrogen > Weekapaug, Mango, Sloth, Reba, Dinner and a Movie, Cavern, Bowie **E:** Glide, Rocky Top

11/20/91 [ACCESSIBILITY: •]
Campus Club, Providence, RI
I: Buried Alive > Possum, Forbin's > Mockingbird, Sparkle, Stash, Paul and Silas, Bathtub Gin, Squirming Coil, Llama, YEM
II: Golgi, It's Ice, MSO, Antelope, Tela, Landlady, HYHU > Bike > HYHU, Cavern **E:** Magilla, Brother
Fishman on fretless guitar for Bike and Cavern. Carl Gerhard on trumpet for Magilla and Brother.

11/21/91 [ACCESSIBILITY: ••]
Somerville Theater, Somerville, MA
I: Chalkdust, Bouncing, Poor Heart, Guelah, Reba, Foam, Horn, Melt, Esther, Mike's > Hydrogen > Weekapaug
II: Wilson, Harry Hood, It's Ice, Mango, Uncle Pen, Tweezer > TMWSIY > Avenu > TMWSIY, Runaway Jim **E:** Memories, Adeline, Golgi
"On Broadway" jam in Weekapaug.

11/22/91 ❄
University of Southern Maine Gymnasium, Portland, ME
I: Possum, Cavern, Sparkle, Brother, Fee, Foam, Divided Sky, Lawn Boy, Dinner and a Movie, Stash, Rocky Top
II: Tube, MSO, Landlady, Bathtub Gin, Antelope, Squirming Coil, I Didn't Know, Llama, Lizards, YEM **E:** Glide, Suzie

11/23/91 [ACCESSIBILITY: ••]
Barre Memorial Auditorium, Barre, VT
I: Llama, Reba, Foam, Runaway Jim, Guelah, Sparkle, Chalkdust, Uncle Pen, Brother, Bouncing, Golgi
II: Curtain > Mike's > Hydrogen > Weekapaug, Horn, Poor Heart, Tweezer, Eliza, Landlady, Fee, HYHU > Love You > HYHU, MSO, Tweezer Reprise **E:** Jesus Left Chicago, BBFCM
Fishman on vacuum for Love You. Dave Grippo on alto sax for Jesus Left Chicago and BBFCM.

11/24/91 ❄
Webster Hall, Dartmouth College, Hanover, NH
I: Sloth, Paul and Silas, Stash, Landlady, Fluffhead, Sparkle, It's Ice, I Didn't Know, Bowie
II: Tube, Divided Sky, Cavern, Mango, Chalkdust, A-Train, YEM, Golgi
E: Adeline, Rocky Top
Bathrobes given to members of the crew during the Bowie intro.

11/30/91 [ACCESSIBILITY: ••••]
Capitol Theater, Port Chester, NY
I: Glide, Llama, Foam, Sparkle, Divided Sky, Cavern, Squirming Coil, Brother, Paul and Silas, Guelah, YEM
II: Chalkdust, Uncle Pen, Harry Hood, It's Ice, Bouncing, MSO, Horn, I Didn't Know, Antelope, Golgi **E:** Contact, Rocky Top
Shockra opened. Fishman on trombone for I Didn't Know; he also played vacuum with Shockra.

➢ I find myself listening to this show's second set more often than many others. Originally, this was due to the fact that there is one of the hottest Harrys included. But some shows just flow so well and this is definitely one of them. Ripping open the second set with a spectacular Chalkdust, things move cooly through Uncle Pen. Then with one of the greatest intros ever (on my soundboard tape I can hear Trey call out to the rest of the guys, "Harry,") they go into it—oh, feeling good about Hood! Later comes the other major highlight of the set—a near-perfect Antelope. Like I said, it just flows oh so well. —PETER BUKLEY

➢ If you want to know why this tape is so well-circulated, I'll sum it up in two words: Harry Hood. This is one of the best versions of Harry from this era, a must-hear for all Hood aficionados. Beyond Hood, the second set is just good listening, a nice sampler of fall '91 Phish, including "new tune" It's Ice and the still-developing Chalkdust Torture. —LINDA MAHDESIAN

12/4/91 [ACCESSIBILITY: •]
Angell Ballroom, SUNY Plattsburgh, Plattsburgh, NY
I: Llama, Reba, Landlady > Runaway Jim, Cavern, Poor Heart, Brother, Squirming Coil, Dinner and a Movie, Bouncing, Bowie
II: MSO, Stash, Mango, Mike's > Hydrogen > Weekapaug, Sparkle, Lizards, Chalkdust, HYHU > Love You > HYHU, Golgi **E:** Adeline, Suzie

12/5/91 [ACCESSIBILITY: ••••]
Greenfield Armory Castle, Greenfield, MA
I: Golgi, Paul and Silas, Melt, Ya Mar, Fluffhead, Llama, Bathtub Gin, It's Ice, Bouncing, Possum
II: Tweezer, Sparkle, Tube, Foam, Mike's > Hydrogen > Weekapaug, Fee, Sloth, Squirming Coil, I Didn't Know, MSO, Tweezer Reprise
E: Glide, Cavern
Fishman on vacuum for I Didn't Know.

12/6/91 [ACCESSIBILITY: ••••]
Middlebury College, Middlebury, VT
I: Memories, Foam, Reba, Uncle Pen, Squirming Coil, Magilla, Landlady, Guelah, I Didn't Know
II: It's Ice, Eliza, Sparkle, YEM, Horn, Divided Sky, Tela, Llama, HYHU > Whipping Post > HYHU, Possum > "Wait" > Possum
E: "Wait" > Lawn Boy, Rocky Top
Guelah abandoned after something goes wrong with Trey's guitar. Fishman on fretless guitar for Whipping Post; he intentionally smashes the guitar on stage after the song. "Wait," see note with 10/31/91 setlist. Soundcheck: Memories (2x), Dog Log, Blues jam, Shaggy Dog, Makisupa.

➢ This show is a winner, but what's really worth hearing is the soundcheck, which has Trey offering some commentary on a Phish a cappella offering. After attempting Memories twice, he concludes that it's now "all the way up to the level of 'sucked.'" —AL HUNT

12/7/91 [ACCESSIBILITY: •••]
Portsmouth Music Hall, Portsmouth, NH
I: Wilson, Runaway Jim, Foam, Forbin's > Mockingbird, MSO, Stash, Curtain > Cavern > Mango, Antelope
II: Buried Alive, Reba, Chalkdust, Sparkle, Brother, Lizards, HYHU > Terrapin > HYHU, Harpua **E:** Adeline, Golgi
The band gave away their old trampolines before Adeline. "Merry Christmas" jam before and during Buried Alive. Fishman on vacuum for Terrapin.

➢ This show was actually a reasonably tough ticket, at least as those things went in 1991. Wilson—perhaps the best Phish show opener—starts things off right before a standard Runaway > Foam. Things pick up again later in the set with a great Curtain > Cavern > Mango run topped by a strong Antelope closer. As second sets go, this one lacks places for wide-open jams but the Harpua at the end makes up for it. Prior to the encore, the band announces that they will give away their old trampolines. The apparent commotion in the audience leads Fishman to urge people to calm down a bit. Eventually things get quiet enough for an unmiked Adeline. —ED SMITH

12/31/91 [ACCESSIBILITY: ••••]
The New Aud, Worcester Memorial Auditorium, Worcester, MA
I: Possum, Foam, Sparkle, Stash, Lizards, Guelah, Divided Sky, Esther > Llama, Golgi
II: Brother, Bouncing > Buried Alive > New Year's Countdown > Auld Lang Syne, Runaway Jim, Landlady, Reba, Cavern, MSO, Antelope
III: Wilson > Squirming Coil > Tweezer > McGrupp > Mike's > Hydrogen > Weekapaug **E:** Lawn Boy, Rocky Top, Tweezer Reprise
Trey used an electronic keychain to make "Fuck you," "Eat shit" and "You're an asshole" noise effects during Wilson. "Wimoweh" jam in Weekapaug.

➢ My first Phish show! I didn't intend to go, but an extra ticket was sent to me at Purdue by a buddy in Worcester. Since I had never seen Phish before, I was shocked. Opening with a fiery Possum into an extremely funky Foam set the mood for the night. The band didn't seem nervous or obligated to put on the "best" show they could do. At the New Year's countdown, I was lip-locked with a total stranger. Divided Sky, Reba, Runaway Jim and Mike's Groove all jammed. —ROB KOELLER

➢ Crazy scene outside the New Aud—this was the first time I remember seeing ticketless fans trying to break into the show any way they could. At one point, a fire exit opened and a bunch of people scampered in, only to be removed by security a moment later. All this, just to see Phish? Well, little did we know… The show was a lot of fun, everyone just having a great old time in a cool room. The show wasn't musical perfection, but that really wasn't the point. —SCOTT SIFTON

➢ Wow, a New Year's Eve show. This concert should be great, but unfortunately this show doesn't come close to Phish's normal high standards for this night. While the music is fine, it is the setlist that stands out as mediocre. Of course it's always nice to hear Brother and the third set Mike's Groove is nice, but nothing stands out that sets this night apart from any other regular Phish show. —JONATHAN BARRO

New Year's '91

12/31/91 The New Aud, Worcester, MA

Phish's growth happened so gradually, spread over so many years of touring, that it's not always easy to find the milestone shows where they took a step up to the next level of popularity. But one clear marker is the band's New Year's Eve show in Worcester, which saw almost 4,000 fans come out for year-end festivities with Phish in by far the largest venue they'd headlined at that point in their careers.

As would be the case in subsequent years, the New Year's Eve appearance allowed the band to book themselves into a larger venue than they'd play on a regular night, figuring that enough people would be drawn by the aura of a special show that demand for tickets would be greater. Of course, they were right.

The '91 New Year's gig followed a fall tour that saw the band hit the Pacific coast for second time in the year—including a two-night sellout of the Great American Music Hall in San Francisco—and the signing of a record contract with Elektra. All signs pointed to the New Year's show as the chance to put an exclamation point on what had already been an incredible year for the band.

Realizing they'd outgrown the Exhibition Hall in Boston where they spent New Year's Eve in 1989 and 1990, the band looked an hour west of Boston to Worcester. One idea they considered was booking the 14,000-seat Centrum and hanging a huge sheet to block off most of the arena, creating a smaller "theater" at one end. But then the Worcester Aud—a smaller, 3,800-person room—came through, and the die was cast. Tickets would be $16.50, and the show a general-admission affair kicking off sometime around 10 p.m. For the first time on New Year's Eve, the band decided in advance to play three sets, a tradition that echoed that of the Grateful Dead's famed New Year's affairs and one that continues to this day.

Notification of the show came, like the Amy's Farm gig the summer before, by postcard. "The New Aud [has] a nice wrap-around balcony and huge dancefloor," the postcard advised. "Plan on getting tickets early, as last year's New Year's show sold out in advance." Fans who didn't heed that advice found themselves out of luck at the door—indeed, Phish drew more than 4,000 funseekers to the cold, industrial town of Worcester to ring in 1992.

The show marked the debut of the new multi-paneled Minkin backdrops, painted by none other than Mike's mother Marjorie. They served as the band's stage backdrop for the next several years, and proved particularly inviting for Chris Kuroda, who used the unique properties of the plastic-and-paint to create stunning visual effects.

Looking back on the Worcester show five years later, Kuroda termed the New Aud show a major sign to him that the band was growing beyond the bars. Little did anyone know that, two years later, they'd be back in town on New Year's Eve, headlining the Centrum, which sold out in less than a day.

Musically, the show was solid—certainly better than the 1990 New Year's Gig, but not as vibrant as the shows that would follow on New Year's Eve in later years. There were some special moments, however, like Trey using a swearing keychain to produce a cacophony of "fuck yous" and "eat shits" during a very eerie Wilson. And there was the long jam session of the third set, which saw the band use Wilson as a springboard to a run of songs that segued from the Squirming Coil to Tweezer to the rare (even back then) McGrupp and then into a long (though mostly standard for the era) Mike's > Hydrogen > Weekapaug.

The show wasn't broadcast on the radio—that tradition wouldn't start until the next year's show at Matthews Arena in Boston—but a tape tree run on the nascent Phish.Net got the tapes out quickly.

Still, the show's lasting legacy, more than the music, was the feeling it sparked among fans that New Year's Eve had evolved from a "fun-to-attend" to a "must-attend" event. Subsequent years would see the evolution of the New Year's Eve prank and grander musical heights, but the New Aud show is remembered for laying the groundwork.

1992 Spring *CALIFORNIA DREAMIN'*

With their first album on Elektra just hitting stores, Phish opened up their 1992 spring tour with a crop of new songs, most written by the Marshall/Anastasio songwriting duo. This spring tour still ranks in some fans' minds as one of the best to date by the band—almost every night saw long shows spiced with new songs and new arrangements, and the added element of the "secret language" that debuted on March 6. The California run, beginning with the band's first show in Los Angeles on April 15, is notable for a string of outstanding performances—one of which, the April 16 gig in Santa Barbara, remains among the most well-circulated Phish tapes. Although Phish had stopped soundboard patches for tapers long before the start of this tour, the majority of shows from this tour can be found on soundboards leaked by the band and friends.

[2/18/92] *A Picture Of Nectar* released on Elektra.

3/6/92 [ACCESSIBILITY: •••]
Portsmouth Music Hall, Portsmouth, NH
I: Rift, Cavern, Sparkle, It's Ice, Oh Kee > Divided Sky, Guelah, Maze, Reba, All Things, Bowie
II: My Friend, Poor Heart, "Language Lesson", Stash, Mound, Llama, Bouncing, NICU, Possum **E:** Sleeping Monkey

Concert debuts: Rift (fast version), Maze, My Friend, Mound, NICU and Sleeping Monkey. Also the debut of the 'Language Lesson,' an explanation of the band's secret language. "Bowie" jams during Language Lesson. Last Rift (slow version), 5/19/90 Concord, NH [172 shows].

➢ A 900-seat theater, nice balcony, and the first show since New Year's. We saw many songs played for the first time: Knife (later My Friend), NICU, Sleeping Monkey, Maze, and the new Rift. Look for a video of this one floating around out there somewhere. —NATHANIEL PEIRCE

➢ The boys decided to let us in on something—The Secret Language. After an awesome My Friend (which also happens to be its debut), they laid out a nice groove and Trey started explaining the Language. If you don't know about it, don't wait any longer: get this tape and study it, because they will test you when you least expect it. —MICHAEL RAMBO

3/7/92 [ACCESSIBILITY: •••]
Portsmouth Music Hall, Portsmouth, NH
I: Brother, My Mind's, Foam, Runaway Jim, Horse > Silent, Maze, Mango, Landlady, Rift, Antelope
II: MSO, Tweezer, Squirming Coil, Weigh, Chalkdust, Horn, Mike's > Hydrogen > Weekapaug, Cold As Ice > Cracklin' Rosie > Cold As Ice, Tweezer Reprise **E:** Adeline, Golgi

Concert debuts: My Mind's, Horse, Silent, Weigh and Cracklin' Rosie (as well as the "Cold As Ice" intro and outro for Fishman, which replaced the traditional HYHU Jam for most of spring '92).

3/11/92 [ACCESSIBILITY: ••]
Colonial Theater, Keene, NH
I: Suzie, My Friend, Paul and Silas, Reba, Maze, Fee, Melt, Mound, Divided Sky, Cavern
II: Llama, NICU, Sloth, Lizards, Bathtub Gin, My Mind's, Brother, Cold As Ice > Baby Lemonade > Cold As Ice, All Things, Harry Hood, Rocky Top
E: Sanity, Memories, Carolina, Sleeping Monkey

Fishman on vacuum bagpipes for Baby Lemonade. "Smoke on the Water" jam before Llama. "Sanity" tease before All Things. Concert debut: Baby Lemonade. Last Sanity, 5/28/89 [232 shows].

➢ Proof of the band's continued growth came this night, their last gig ever at Keene's Colonial Theater. Though the show itself wasn't one of the all-time greats, it had its moments—a strong Melt jam in the first set and then a hilarious moment during the quiet segment of Divided Sky. As Trey waited to play "the note," various audience members shouted out requests. So Trey steps up to his microphone and, in classic request-style, shouted, "Possum!!" To start the second set, there's a funny "Smoke On The Water" jam while Mike makes a no smoking announcement. Later, Fishman sings Syd Barrett's Baby Lemonade for the only time and introduces us to the weird vacuum bagpipes contraption he used for much of the spring tour. There's also the return of Sanity, which the band teases the crowd with before All Things, then plays during the encore. —ANDRE HOLTON

3/12/92 [ACCESSIBILITY: ••]
Flynn Theater, Burlington, VT
I: Runaway Jim, Foam, Sparkle, Stash, I Didn't Know, Reba, Buried Alive > Rift, Magilla, Llama, YEM
II: Golgi, Tweezer, Eliza, It's Ice, Bouncing, Squirming Coil, Uncle Pen, Bowie, Cold as Ice > Cracklin' Rosie > Cold as Ice, MSO, Cavern
E: Adeline, Weigh, Tweezer Reprise

Fishman on vacuum bagpipes for I Didn't Know. Brief "tease medley" in Bowie intro.

➢ This show features what's in all likelihood the first Big Ball Jam. During a hot Tweezer, someone in the crowd lofted a giant beach ball and Trey got the idea to play a note every time someone in the audience hit the ball. Nine months later, just outside of Burlington at the Colchester show on 11/19/92, they unveiled BBJ in its "official" format. —ED SMITH

1992

121 Total Show Dates
- **40** one-set shows
- **79** two-set shows
- **1** three-set show
- **1** date with no setlist

PHAN PICKS 1992

SHOW	THE SKINNY
1) 03/13/92 Providence, RI	Big Black Furry Antelope!
2) 07/25/92 Stowe, VT	Carlos Santana sits in.
3) 04/16/92 Santa Barbara, CA	Very widely-circulated tape.
4) 03/20/92 Binghamton, NY	Terrific, jamming show.
5) 04/21/92 Redwood Ac., CA	Weirdness galore in set II.
6) 04/18/92 Palo Alto, CA	"Linus and Lucy" Hood.
7) 05/14/92 Port Chester, NY	Insane Antelope, "Aw fuck!"
8) 11/19/92 Colchester, VT	Fall tour opener just rocks.
9) 11/20/92 Albany, NY	Another all-around great show.
10) 04/17/92 S. Francisco, CA	First time at the Warfield.

MUSICAL RECAP: Leaving the more controlled days of 1991 behind, the band starts opening up its jams, taking songs like Antelope, Possum and Bowie to the edge while still retaining melodic themes. Jamming is still pretty straight-ahead, with "machine gun Trey" working the tension and release, especially on new songs like Maze.

REPRESENTATIVE JAMS: Possum, 5/17/92 and 4/5/92; Mike's Groove, 4/21/92 and 11/28/92; Antelope 3/13/92; You Enjoy Myself, 7/25/92

ORIGINAL SONG DEBUTS: Axilla (part one, 11/19/92), Big Ball Jam (11/19/92), Buffalo Bill (11/21/92); Faht (11/22/92), Fast Enough For You (11/19/92), The Horse (3/7/92), Lengthwise (11/19/92), Maze (3/6/92), Mound (3/6/92), My Friend My Friend (3/6/92), NICU (3/6/92), Rift (fast version, 3/6/92), "The Secret Language" (3/6/92), Sleeping Monkey (3/6/92), Silent in the Morning (3/7/92), Weigh (3/7/92)

COVER SONG DEBUTS: Blue Bayou (7/16/92), Cracklin' Rosie (3/7/92), Diamond Girl (12/31/92), I Walk the Line (11/19/92), My Mind's Got a Mind of Its Own (3/7/92)

DARK HORSES

SHOW	THE SKINNY
1) 05/17/92 Schenectady, NY	Incredible Possum; lots more.
2) 12/29/92 New Haven, CT	Best of '92 New Year's run?
3) 04/19/92 Santa Cruz, CA	Another gem from a magic week.
4) 05/09/92 Syracuse, NY	Harpua and a great Tweezer.
5) 08/17/92 San Juan C., CA	Somewhere Over the Rainbow.

Most-Played Originals:

1) Sparkle	64	53%
2) Llama	63	52%
3) Cavern	58	48%
4) Maze	55	45%
5) Rift	54	45%
6) Runaway Jim	54	45%
6) Stash	54	45%
8) Foam	53	44%
9) The Squirming Coil	52	43%
10) Poor Heart, YEM	47	39%

Most-Played Covers:

1) Sweet Adeline	41	34%
2) Uncle Pen	38	31%
3) Rocky Top	29	24%
4) Cracklin' Rosie	25	21%
5) Love You	20	17%
6) Memories	17	14%
7) Carolina	15	12%
8) Take the A-Train	13	11%
9) GTBT, Paul and Silas, Terrapin	12	10%

First-Set Openers:

1) The Landlady	17
2) Runaway Jim	16
2) Suzie Greenberg	13
2) Buried Alive	11
2) Chalk Dust Torture	10

Second-Set Openers:

1) Glide	8
2) Mike's Song	6
2) Suzie Greenberg	6
4) The Curtain	5
5) The Landlady	4

Top Henrietta Songs:

1) Cracklin' Rosie	25
2) Love You	20
3) Lengthwise	6
4) Faht	4
5) Bike, Brain	3

A Cappella Songs:

1) Sweet Adeline	41
2) Memories	17
3) Carolina	15

3/13/92 [ACCESSIBILITY: •••••]
Campus Club, Providence, RI
I: Curtain > Melt, Poor Heart, Guelah, Maze, Dinner and a Movie > Divided Sky, Mound, Fluffhead > Follow the Yellow Brick Road Jam > Antelope/BBFCM/Antelope
II: Wilson > Brother, Horse > Silent, Landlady, Lizards, My Mind's, Sloth, Rift, Cold as Ice > Love You > Cold As Ice, Possum > "Language Lesson" > Possum **E:** Contact, Fire

There are several teases and jams on other songs in Antelope/BBFCM/Antelope, including "Groove is in the Heart," "Lullabye of Birdland" and several vocal jams. An "Over the Rainbow" jam leads into Wilson; "Over the Rainbow" is sampled again during the Wilson intro. Fishman on vacuum bagpipes and vacuum for Love You. Mike on accordion (his first appearance on that instrument) for Contact.

Phan Pick #13 ➢ Fantastic show, totally hosed, every note is perfection and ecstacy. Great moments include two—count 'em—two, "d'oh" language signals and a full language lesson in set II; a "Somewhere Over the Rainbow" tease in both Fluffhead and Wilson; and of course the killer "Run Like A Big Black Furry Antelope From Mars" which closes set one. —JAMIS CURRAN

➢ Everyone has talked a lot about this set and its legendary Antelope, but there are a few things that don't often get mentioned. How about Mike playing the bassline for "Groove is in the Heart" (by early '90s dance band Dee-Lite)? Or the Lullabye jam? Or Trey and Page sounding like they're shattering glass at one point? All of this takes place during the Antelope mayhem. I really wish this kind of thing occurred frequently! —CHARLIE MURPHY

Man, the band loves playing in Providence, that's for sure. It seems like every show here just rocks. The second set here is pretty sweet, since Brother's in its prime. But what makes this set totally awesome is the long, hilarious signal explanation by Trey before Possum—he laughs and jokes while explaining the basic signals to the small crowd. What follows is one of the tightest and sweetest-sounding Possums of '92, which as we all know was an excellent year for Phish. —ALEX BANKS

3/14/92 [ACCESSIBILITY: ••••]
Roseland Ballroom, New York, NY
I: Runaway Jim, Cavern, Reba, Sparkle, Foam, Rift, Stash, Fee, Chalkdust, A-Train, Mike's > Hydrogen > Weekapaug
II: Golgi, Llama, Squirming Coil, Melt, Bouncing, Oh Kee > Suzie, Harry Hood, Cold As Ice > Cracklin' Rosie > Cold As Ice, Possum
E: Sleeping Monkey, GTBT

John Popper on harmonica for Sleeping Monkey and GTBT. "Funkytown" jam in Reba. "Somewhere Over the Rainbow" tease in Horn.

3/17/92 [ACCESSIBILITY: •]
Lisner Auditorium, Washington, DC
I: Buried Alive > Possum, Cavern, Sparkle, It's Ice, I Didn't Know, Divided Sky, Guelah, Rift, Bouncing, Antelope
II: Runaway Jim, Glide, Sloth, Poor Heart, Tweezer > Esther, Mike's > Hydrogen > Weekapaug, Cold As Ice > Love You > Cold As Ice, Llama
E: Memories, Adeline

Everything opened. Fishman on vacuum for I Didn't Know and vacuum bagpipes for Love You. Brief "Poor Heart" tease from Fishman before Sloth.

3/19/92 [ACCESSIBILITY: •••]
Palace Theater, New Haven, CT
I: Landlady, Rift, Melt, Sparkle, Golgi, Horse > Silent, Dinner and a Movie > Forbin's > Mockingbird, All Things, Bowie
II: Glide, Chalkdust, NICU, MSO, Stash, Oh Kee > Suzie, My Friend, Squirming Coil > Cold as Ice > Cracklin' Rosie > Cold As Ice, YEM
E: Sleeping Monkey, Rocky Top **E2:** Adeline

Soundcheck: Shaggy Dog > Jam, Lullabye of Birdland, Mound, Maze. "Michelle" tease before Glide.

3/20/92 [ACCESSIBILITY: ••••]
Broome County Forum, Binghamton, NY
I: Wilson, Reba, Brother, Glide, Rift, Fluffhead, Maze, Lizards, Mound, Antelope
II: Mike's > Hydrogen > Weekapaug, Sanity, Sloth, Mango, Cavern, Uncle Pen, Harry Hood, Cold as Ice > Terrapin > Cold as Ice, Possum > "Language Lesson" > Possum **E:** Lawn Boy, Fire

Fishman on trombone for Antelope before the "Rye, rye, rocco," lyrics, and vacuum bagpipes for Terrapin. "Roundabout" tease before Mike's. "Bowie" and "Possum" jams during Language Lesson.

➢ Phish played one of their best shows of the year on a Friday night in Binghamton. Though lacking the improvisational insanity of the previous week's Providence gig, this show shines with straight-ahead jams in the best Phish tradition. The first set highlight, besides the weirdness that erupts in Brother (Trey: "They're diving into the alligator pit!") comes in a very well-jammed Antelope that sees Fishman grabbing his trombone. Mike's Groove is the best they'd done up to this point—Weekapaug traverses hard rock, spacy vocals, melodic jams and even a few signals to reach an incredible climax. —SCOTT SIFTON

➢ I was a sophomore in high school when this "Phish group," as my friend called it, came to my hometown. Looking back, I wish I had gone. Playing in a venue of around 2,000 people, Phish treated the lucky ones to a great show. Highlights from the tapes include an early Maze, a Brother that I dearly wish I could have heard and of course Mike's Song. Trey was "en fuego" that night, making some interesting comments throughout the show, providing band-audience humor and contact that I wish was more common today. —DANIEL PADEN

➢ Besides being one of the hottest Phish sets from this era, set II is also one of the funniest. You know things are going to get interesting when Trey tells the crowd, "Help me, I'm melting and I can't solidify!" to start the set. Sanity features lots of vocal play on Mike's nicknames then gives way to a vocal jam at the end. Before Terrapin, a chant for the Prison Joke (see 4/11/91) that Trey picks up leads Fish to declare, "You're dreaming, man. You're all dreaming!" —AMY MANNING

3/21/92 [ACCESSIBILITY: ••••]
Chestnut Cabaret, Philadelphia, PA
I: Landlady, Runaway Jim, Foam, Sparkle, Melt, Horse > Silent, Dinner and a Movie, Squirming Coil, MSO, Stash, Golgi
II: Buried Alive, Oh Kee > Suzie, A-Train, My Friend, Poor Heart, All Things > Bowie, Weigh, Cold As Ice > Cracklin' Rosie > Cold As Ice, YEM
E: Bouncing, Rocky Top

Extended intro jam on MSO.

➢ Don't let anyone tell you otherwise—these really were the days! Here's Phish, playing a tiny little Cabaret, perched on a low stage so close to the crowd that you could reach out and touch them! Thinking back, this was probably the last Northeast show in a tiny venue I caught—by the fall, they hit the theater circuit pretty much exclusively. It was a great last hurrah, with the boys treating us to a jazzy A-Train and the most outrageous Bowie I'd ever seen. A great show, a great tape. —JOS CONTI

➢ Phish must've been psyched to play Philly. This was one of those fun, playful concerts. The Suzie has an organ solo in the second slot which was the habit at the time and Page tosses the horn parts in over the final refrain. Silent has the original, cheesy ending with someone singing in an unmanly range. And My Sweet One features a long, improvised hoe-down intro. —SCOTT KUSHNER

[3/22/92] [ACCESSIBILITY: •••]
Cultural Center Auditorium, Charleston, WV
Sparkle, All Things, Foam, Landlady

Mountain Stage Live performance taped for nationwide broadcast on National Public Radio. Phish played four songs. Buckwheat Zydeco headlined, and Trey came out and jammed with them during the last song of their set, "Juke-Joint Johnny."

3/24/92 [ACCESSIBILITY: •]
Flood Zone, Richmond, VA
I: Stash, Poor Heart, Foam, Eliza, Rift, Golgi, Horse > Silent, Llama, Forbin's > Mockingbird, Landlady, Bowie
II: Curtain > Mike's > Hydrogen > Weekapaug, Guelah, Mango, Brother, Uncle Pen, I Didn't Know, Oh Kee > Suzie, Harry Hood, Cavern **E:** Lawn Boy, Fire

Carl Gerhard on trumpet for Brother and Cavern.

3/25/92 [ACCESSIBILITY: ••]
Trax, Charlottesville, VA
I: Wilson > Sparkle > Melt, Rift, Fee > Maze, Glide > Runaway Jim, It's Ice > Antelope
II: Tweezer > Mound, Reba, All Things, Squirming Coil > YEM, Horn > MSO, Chalkdust, Cold As Ice > Cracklin' Rosie > Cold As Ice, Golgi
E: Sleeping Monkey > Tweezer Reprise

3/26/92 [ACCESSIBILITY: ••]
Ziggy's, Winston Salem, NC
I: Landlady, Runaway Jim, All Things, Foam, Sparkle, Stash, Fluffhead, Uncle Pen, NICU, Bowie
II: Buried Alive, Oh Kee > Suzie, Poor Heart, Brother, TMWSIY> Avenu > TMWSIY, My Friend, Lizards, Cavern, Cold as Ice > Cracklin' Rosie > Cold as Ice, Possum **E:** Sleeping Monkey, Chalkdust, Harpua

Aquarium Rescue Unit opened. Trey carries Marley out on stage during Harpua. "Fire" (Hendrix) jam in Harpua.

3/27/92 [ACCESSIBILITY: ••]
1313 Club, Charlotte, NC
I: Llama, Reba, Paul and Silas, Sloth, Divided Sky, Guelah, Maze, Glide, Bouncing, Antelope
II: Mike's > Hydrogen > Weekapaug, Horse > Silent, MSO, Rift, Bathtub Gin, Dinner and a Movie, Magilla, Harry Hood, Cold as Ice > Love You > Cold as Ice, Golgi **E:** Memories, Adeline

Extended intro jam on MSO.

3/28/92 [ACCESSIBILITY: •••]
Variety Theater, Atlanta, GA
I: Runaway Jim, Foam, Sparkle, Stash, Rift, Bouncing, Landlady, "Language Lesson," Bowie, Glide, Cavern
II: Memories, Carolina, I Didn't Know, Adeline

"Lullabye of Birdland" jam at end of Landlady. After a small flood in the theater threatened to short out the band's equipment, the abbreviated second set was performed a cappella. Fishman on trombone for I Didn't Know after his vacuum bagpipes failed because the power had been turned off. No encore.

3/30/92 [ACCESSIBILITY: ••••]
Mississippi Nights, St. Louis, MO
I: Landlady, Llama, Foam, Guelah, Sparkle, Maze, I Didn't Know, All Things, Sloth, Runaway Jim, Cavern
II: Golgi, Uncle Pen, Tweezer, Mound, YEM, BBFCM, Squirming Coil, Weigh, Chalkdust, HYHU > Cracklin' Rosie > Cold as Ice, Bouncing, Tweezer Reprise **E:** Sleeping Monkey, Oh Kee > Suzie
Fishman on vacuum for I Didn't Know. YEM vocal jam featured "Rock On" riffs, then Fishman on vacuum bagpipes leading into BBFCM. "We're Off to See the Wizard" jam in BBFCM.

3/31/92 [ACCESSIBILITY: •]
Blue Note, Columbia, MO
I: Wilson, Divided Sky, Glide, Melt, Rift, Reba, Llama, Forbin's > Mockingbird, Antelope
II: Mike's > Hydrogen > Weekapaug, Fee, Stash, Lizards, Cavern, Dinner and a Movie, My Friend, MSO, Cold as Ice > Love You > Cold as Ice, Possum
E: Adeline

➢ If you haven't listened to this show, you really must. Phish just turns it up a notch when they play in Missouri. A mini-Gamehendge in the first set should be enough to make this show great, but then comes a truly epic Mike's Groove—one of my favorite versions ever. MSO starts off in "slow motion," then goes to new levels. Love You is also great—I think Fishman should do more Syd Barrett songs. —TONY KRUPKA

4/1/92 [ACCESSIBILITY: •]
Liberty Hall, Lawrence, KS
I: Golgi, Foam, Bouncing, Brother, All Things, Sparkle, Runaway Jim, I Didn't Know, Landlady, Bowie, Carolina
II: Llama, YEM, Horse > Silent, Uncle Pen, Tweezer, Horn, Chalkdust, Cold as Ice > Cracklin' Rosie > Cold as Ice, Squirming Coil, Tweezer Reprise, Contact, Rocky Top **E:** Lawn Boy, GTBT

4/3/92 [ACCESSIBILITY: •]
Hyatt Regency Village Hall, Beaver Creek, CO
I: Landlady > Poor Heart, Stash, Rift, Guelah, Sparkle, Maze, Fluffhead, All Things, Melt, Golgi
II: Curtain > Sloth, Possum, Weigh, YEM, Mango, Llama, Harry Hood, Suzie **E:** Rocky Top

4/4/92 [ACCESSIBILITY: •]
Field House, University of Colorado, Boulder, CO
I: Runaway Jim, Foam, Reba, Uncle Pen, Chalkdust, Bouncing, It's Ice, Sparkle, Lizards, I Didn't Know, Antelope
II: Mike's > Hydrogen > Weekapaug, Glide, MSO, Tweezer, Squirming Coil, Cold as Ice > Cracklin' Rosie > Cold as Ice, My Friend, Harpua, Cavern
E: Sleeping Monkey, Tweezer Reprise
Fishman on trombone for I Didn't Know, and on vacuum bagpipes for Harpua.

4/5/92 [ACCESSIBILITY: •••]
Fox Theater, Boulder, CO
I: Llama, Guelah, Divided Sky, Wilson, Poor Heart, Stash, Rift, Horn, It's Ice, Possum, Adeline
II: Melt, All Things, YEM, Horse > Silent, Maze, Weigh, Landlady > Bowie, HYHU > Love You > Cold as Ice, A-Train > Runaway Jim
E: Lawn Boy, Rocky Top
Fishman on vacuum for Love You. "Landlady" jam in Possum intro. "Dixie" tease in A-Train.

➢ I was lucky to catch this gig. They announced they'd be doing a show at the Fox the night before at the Fieldhouse show, and we were glad to have a chance to see Phish in this cool little theater. The Fox had only been open for about a month when Phish played here, and the show blew me away. A wild, wild Possum at the end of the first set (where did that Landlady jam come from?) led us to setbreak, then a strong Melt carried us back out into the second set. YEM featured a hilarious vocal jam with the boys chanting "reggae!" then "what?" followed by evil laughter. Later in the set, Landlady > Bowie and A-Train > Runaway Jim combos rocked! —MELISSA WOLCOTT

➢ Hey kids, you like the Possum, do you? Well then, you'll love the Fox. From the time Page strikes the first note until the time Mike steps up to sing "Come from top the mountain, baby," more than *five minutes* elapse. After the first lyric segment, Trey drives the jam up to the mountain top. This version belongs in the Possum Pantheon with 5/17/92 Union College, 7/15/92 Trax and 4/30/94 Orlando. Yum. —ERNIE GREENE

4/6/92 [ACCESSIBILITY: ••••]
Western State College Gym, Gunnison, CO
I: Suzie, Foam, Sparkle, Reba, Brother, Esther, Chalkdust, Guelah, Squirming Coil, Antelope
II: Dinner and a Movie, Bathtub Gin, Paul and Silas, Mike's > Hydrogen > Weekapaug, NICU, Llama, Mound, Stash, Cold as Ice > Cracklin' Rosie > Cold as Ice, Uncle Pen, Cavern **E:** BBFCM
Cavern features "yee-haw" yells, some bluegrass-style jamming and "bluegrass" lyrics: "The foggy cavern's musty grime appeared within my palm/I saddled up horses and headed on down to the hoe-down!"

➢ This is absolutely one of my favorite shows of all time, mainly for the second set. Dinner and A Movie, Bathtub and Mike's Groove are everything you'd expect them to be, but where this tape really gets me is the NICU, the early slow version that I think is far superior to the current one. It ends with the best-timed "D'oh!" I've ever heard. The other highlight is the bluegrass version of Cavern that follows Uncle Pen. It's a completely impromptu thing, just in the spirit of the moment, and is just hilarious. It ends with "Whatever you do, take care of your boots." Then the BBCFM encore has the band shouting "Guacamole!" throughout. This show is a perfect example of Phish using their skills to mix music and humor into one. —ANDY BERNSTEIN

4/7/92 [ACCESSIBILITY: ••]
Fine Arts Auditorium, Fort Lewis College, Durango, CO
I: Buried Alive > Possum, It's Ice, Fee, Divided Sky, Horse > Silent, Melt, Bouncing, Rift, Sloth, Runaway Jim
II: Poor Heart, All Things, Tweezer, Eliza, YEM, My Friend, Lizards, Maze, Cold as Ice > Bike > Cold as Ice, My Mind's, Golgi
E: Contact, Tweezer Reprise
Fishman on vacuum for Bike.

➢ This was the second show at Fort Lewis, and once again there was a small crowd of about 300 people. There is nothing like seeing Phish in your school auditorium, and like always, the band won over the crowd, establishing many new converts with lots of new Rift material debuts. This was the last cheap Phish show for me—only $7 for three hours of bliss! —JEFF SALVATORE

4/9/92 [ACCESSIBILITY: •]
El Ray Theater, Albuquerque, NM
I: Landlady, Sparkle, Foam, Guelah, Llama, Mound, Reba, Uncle Pen, Stash, Squirming Coil, Golgi
II: Oh Kee > Suzie, Bowie, TMWSIY > Avenu > TMWSIY, MSO, Mike's > Hydrogen > Weekapaug, Horse > Silent, Chalkdust, Cold as Ice > Terrapin > Cold as Ice, Cavern **E:** Sleeping Monkey, Rocky Top

4/12/92 [ACCESSIBILITY: •]
Ballroom, University of Arizona, Tucson, AZ
I: Suzie, Poor Heart, Guelah, Divided Sky, Horse > Silent, It's Ice, Sparkle, Maze, Reba, Antelope
II: Glide, Melt, Bouncing, Rift, YEM, Lawn Boy, NICU, Cold as Ice > Cracklin' Rosie > Cold as Ice, Harry Hood, Cavern **E:** Adeline, Rocky Top

4/13/92 [ACCESSIBILITY: •••]
After The Gold Rush, Tempe, AZ
I: Golgi, Uncle Pen, Stash, Lizards, Landlady, NICU, Fee, All Things, Foam, A-Train, Bowie
II: Llama, Fluffhead, Sparkle, Mike's > Hydrogen > Weekapaug, Magilla, Ya Mar, Squirming Coil, Cold as Ice > Love You > Cold as Ice, Possum
E: Memories, Fire
Fishman on vacuum for Love You. "Smells Like Teen Spirit" tease before Llama and in Mike's intro. "We're Off to See the the Wizard" jam in Possum.

➢ This is a tape swimming in teases. Set two begins with Trey mocking Nirvana's "Smells Like Teen Spirit"—the big hit at the time—and he even reprises the tease during Mike's big, bass-heavy intro to Mike's Song. It's a really funny poke at the rock n' roll mainstream. There's also a great Bundle of Joy during Fluffhead and a "Wonderful Wizard of Oz" guitar line in Possum. You know it's a really fun show when Fish stops his vacuum solo due to "not enough suction tonight." Lots of fun! —TIM FOISSER

4/15/92 [ACCESSIBILITY: ••]
Variety Arts Theater, Los Angeles, CA
I: Oh Kee > Suzie, Foam, Guelah, Sparkle, Stash, Uncle Pen, Cavern, I Didn't Know, All Things, Runaway Jim
II: Chalkdust, YEM, Reba, Landlady, NICU, Cold as Ice > Cracklin' Rosie > Cold as Ice, MSO, Golgi **E:** Memories, Adeline, Rocky Top
Widespread Panic opened. Tapers were inadvertently shut out from this show by venue management. "Groove is in the Heart" and "Funkytown" jams in YEM. Fishman on vacuum for I Didn't Know.

4/16/92 [ACCESSIBILITY: •••••]
Anaconda Theater, University of California at Santa Barbara, Santa Barbara, CA
I: Buried Alive > Possum, It's Ice, Bouncing, Melt, Rift, Fee > Maze, Forbin's > Icculus > Mockingbird, Antelope
II: Sanity, Llama, Lizards, Mike's > Hydrogen > Weekapaug, Horn, Poor Heart, Cold as Ice > Terrapin > Cold as Ice, Carolina, Memories, Adeline, Suzie **E:** Sleeping Monkey
Widespread Panic opened. Fishman on vacuum for Terrapin. Last Icculus, 4/6/91 Olympia, WA [116 shows].

Phan Pick #25 ➢ Both sets are full of timeless treats. In set I, Split Open and Melt is mind-blowing, the transition between Fee > Maze is short but interesting and Icculus makes an appearance between Forbin and Mockingbird. The second set is also solid, from Sanity to Suzie Greenberg. There's also a smokin' Mike's Groove and an a cappella suite taboot. —CHAD ASHCRAFT

➢ For no other reason, get the Anaconda show for the Buried Alive > Possum opener. The segue is smooth as silk and contains most of the secret language signals. Then get ready for one of the most over-the-top Possums ever. Trey layers theme upon bluesy theme to create a crescendo that always does it for me. The soundboard crispness makes this tape a joy. It's a roller coaster ride! —PAUL SHEETS

➢ This is a great tape for times when people ask, "So which one of these tapes should be my first Phish tape?" It's also a great choice for those who have never heard Phish live—it hooks them every time! —JUSTIN WEISS

4/17/92 [ACCESSIBILITY: •••]
Warfield Theater, San Francisco, CA
I: Runaway Jim, Foam, Sparkle, Stash, I Didn't Know > Cavern, Reba, Maze, Bouncing, Landlady > Bowie/Catapult/Bowie
II: Brother, YEM, Fluffhead, Squirming Coil, Tweezer, Uncle Pen, Cold as Ice > Cracklin' Rosie > Cold as Ice, Tweezer Reprise **E:** Golgi

Widespread Panic opened. Fishman on vacuum for I Didn't Know. Brief "Doug" vocal jam in I Didn't Know. A bathtub was wheeled onto the stage before the start of the second set, and a parade of people walked across the stage and jumped in and out of it during Brother. Concert debut: Catapult.

➢ Setlist-wise, this show looks middle-of-the-road. But don't be fooled—this is a show you really should hear. Set one features an incredible Reba (!) and a fantastic David Bowie that includes the concert debut of Catapult woven in it. Set two is a total jam-fest: Brother, YEM and Tweezer are all strong versions, and the energy in Fluffhead is contagious. It's clear that the band enjoyed themselves, too. "We had an amazing time tonight. This is an incredible room," Trey says at the end of Golgi. The Warfield rocks. —ED SMITH

4/18/92 [ACCESSIBILITY: ••••]
Wilbur Field, Stanford University, Palo Alto, CA
I: Wilson, Divided Sky, Guelah, Poor Heart, Melt, Esther, Possum, It's Ice, Sparkle, All Things, Antelope
II: Glide, Oh Kee > Suzie, Rift, Manteca, Bathtub Gin > Manteca, Lizards, Mound, Llama, TMWSIY > Avenu > TMWSIY, Dinner and a Movie, Harry Hood, Cold as Ice > Love You > Cold as Ice, Rocky Top
E: Contact, BBFCM

Free outdoor show. "Mind Left Body" tease in Possum. "Frere Jacques" tease in Antelope intro. "Linus and Lucy" jam in Hood. Fishman on vacuum for Love You. Seven-year old Cameron McKenney played (unmiked) ukulele on BBFCM.

➢ This free afternoon show is a Phish classic. Divided Sky was beautifully hypnotic and took me to a higher ground; It's Ice was accompanied by a smooth breakdown with Trey and Page sounding off; and Antelope featured heavy jamming to end the first set. The second set has a good Oh Kee > Suzie transition, Harry Hood, and a Contact encore. —JAY GREEN

➢ This show has gained fame as one of the most perfectly played Phish concerts ever. The second set is a masterpiece of musicianship from start to finish, including an outstanding Harry Hood with a "Linus and Lucy" (a.k.a. "Peanuts") jam by Page during the quiet third segment of the song. A hot day in Palo Alto saw Trey calling for "squirt gun breaks" between songs (a roadie on the side of the stage had a SuperSoaker with him), and we're treated to a "happy Passover bass solo" from "Cactus" Gordon in Avenu. Other treats include a wonderfully playful Bathtub Gin and a double-dose of Manteca. —TRICIA HOLMES

➢ Mike Gordon fans take notice! I don't know what was going on at the soundboard, but WOW is Mike prominent in the board mix. This tape makes up for all those times you've strained to make out Mike's bass in cavernous arenas and outdoor sheds. Happily, he's on fire throughout this show, a classic Phish concert if I ever heard one. —PAT STANLEY

4/19/92 [ACCESSIBILITY: ••]
The Catalyst, Santa Cruz, CA
I: Buried Alive > NICU, Stash, Paul and Silas, My Friend, Reba, Maze, Fee > Chalkdust, I Didn't Know, Golgi
II: Curtain > Mike's > Hydrogen > Weekapaug, Horse > Silent, MSO, Tube, Mango, Llama, Lawn Boy, Cold as Ice > Brain > Cold as Ice, Runaway Jim
E: Sleeping Monkey, Cavern

Fishman on trombone for I Didn't Know and vacuum for Brain.

➢ Nearly lost among the other classic shows played this week, their return to Santa Cruz's tiny Catalyst features a great opening combo: Buried Alive > NICU. Unlike current versions of this song, NICU opens with Fish pounding out a beat (coming right out of Buried Alive) before Trey and Page drop in. By this point in the tour, NICU has already lost some of the reggae flavor apparent in March's versions but still has the "da-da-da-da" bridge to the final refrains. Hot! This show also offers a *great* Mike's Groove, Tube (as rare then as it is now) and a very jammy (not at all normal) Mango Song. —JOS CONTI

4/21/92 [ACCESSIBILITY: ••••]
Redwood Acres, Eureka, CA
I: Suzie, Uncle Pen, Melt, Rift, Guelah, Possum, It's Ice, Eliza, NICU, Bouncing, Bowie
II: Dinner and a Movie, Forbin's > Mockingbird, Tweezer, Tela, Mike's > Hydrogen > Weekapaug, Weigh, Cold as Ice > Catapult > Cold as Ice, HYHU > Lively Up Yourself > HYHU, Sanity, Maze, Memories
E: Adeline, Cavern

"Happy Birthday" jam in Weekapaug. Fishman on bass, Trey on drums and Mike on guitar and vacuum for Lively Up Yourself. "Apology" vocal jam before Sanity. Concert debut: Lively Up Yourself.

➢ What a second set! I don't know where to begin. First off, get this tape. Then check out Trey playing with echo effects during the Forbin's rap to repeat "evil King Wilson!" in a Darth Vader-like boom. Listen to Tweezer—the band finds an incredible groove and locks into it for about ten minutes of jamming that sounds so good I have to wonder if it's composed. Mike's Groove is also hot as hell, and the set continues with the famously mangled Lively Up Yourself and Sanity. This is one of the best sets of 1992. —ED SMITH

➢ This Mike's Groove is one of the early greats—no weird shit, no spacey jams, no nonsense, just a wailed-on version of this amazing suite. Mike's Song really rocks, hard as a nail, but it's in Weekapaug that the band climbs to the next plateau. Following the Weekapaug opening, several "make" chants (similar to those on 3/20/92) lead to a melodic guitar line by Trey that's just beautiful, backed ferociously by Mike. Trey's guitar sings in here, and Mike is going crazy, too! The jam gives way to a bass-dominated segment that then builds back up into the Weekapaug theme. Trey takes the jam down a bit, wishes happy birthday to two friends, does a brief "Happy Birthday" tease and then roars into a closing Weekapaug jam that is simply stupendous. —AL HUNT

➢ My vote for Phish's funniest on-stage moment comes in set II of this show. As Fishman comes to center stage for a song, someone in the crowd shouts out a request for Catapult. "That isn't my terrain," Fish says, but after a moment of contemplation he introduces Mike, who recites Catapult. That's followed by Cold as Ice, leading out of the Henrietta segment. But then Page and Trey start up the HYHU theme and Fish picks up Mike's bass. Somehow with this weird configuration the band manages to play a ridiculous version of Bob Marley's Lively Up Yourself, including Mike's debut performance on vacuum. "Thank you for tolerating that," Fish says when it's over. Suddenly everyone in the band wants to apologize, and their apologies create an odd vocal jam. —ANDRE HOLTON

4/22/92 [ACCESSIBILITY: •]
Hilton Ballroom, Eugene, OR
I: Llama, Foam, Reba, Sparkle, Guelah, Divided Sky, Mound, Stash, All Things > Suzie
II: Glide, Antelope, Horse > Silent, Rift, Wilson > "Language Lesson" > Wilson > YEM, Poor Heart > Cold as Ice > Cracklin' Rosie > Cold as Ice, Harpua, Runaway Jim **E:** A-Train, Rocky Top

Earth Day show.

➢ It's cool to hear the first West Coast "secret language" explanation before Wilson, but Harpua is definitely the great reason to hear this tape. It's Earth Day, and Trey tells a story of Johnny, little Johnny Fishman. Trey tells Paul to turn off Fish's mike so he doesn't tell what hotel room he's staying in, but Fish, in true form, sneaks it in: "623, room 623." You've got to listen to it to get the whole story. —RIC HANNAH

4/23/92 [ACCESSIBILITY: •]
Oz Nightclub, Seattle, WA
I: Cavern, Curtain > Melt, Uncle Pen, Guelah, Squirming Coil, Llama, Bouncing, It's Ice, I Didn't Know, Possum
II: Landlady, Poor Heart, Mike's > Hydrogen > Weekapaug, Lizards, NICU, Horn, Tweezer, Fee, Maze, Cold as Ice > Cracklin' Rosie > Cold as Ice, Golgi **E:** Sleeping Monkey, Tweezer Reprise

Fee lyrics: "Grab an espresso…" instead of "Grab a cup of coffee…"

4/24/92 [ACCESSIBILITY: •]
Roseland Theater, Portland, OR
I: Runaway Jim, Forbin's > Icculus > Mockingbird, Uncle Pen, Sloth, Landlady, Fluffhead, Sparkle, Stash, Squirming Coil, Golgi
II: Bowie, Cavern, Ya Mar, Foam, Mike's > Hydrogen > Weekapaug > Mango, Horn, Cold as Ice > Love You > Cold as Ice, Glide, Llama
E: Contact, BBFCM

Jim opened. Fishman on vacuum and trombone for Love You. Vocal jam in Weekapaug led to an "On Broadway" jam and segued into Mango.

4/25/92 [ACCESSIBILITY: ••]
Campus Recreation Center, Evergreen College, Olympia, WA
I: Suzie, My Friend, Paul and Silas, Reba, Brother, Tela, Chalkdust, Bouncing, Rift, Magilla, Antelope
II: Maze, Bathtub Gin, YEM, Horse > Silent, All Things, Dinner and a Movie, Harry Hood, Weigh
E: Cold as Ice > Terrapin > Cold as Ice, Poor Heart

"Sprockets" and "Chariots of Fire" themes in YEM vocal jam.

4/29/92 [ACCESSIBILITY: ••]
First Avenue, Minneapolis, MN
I: Suzie, Foam, Sparkle, It's Ice, Runaway Jim, Guelah, Rift, Bouncing, A-Train, Bowie > "Language Lesson" > Bowie
II: Landlady > Possum, Mound, Oh Kee > Llama, Lizards, Mike's > Hydrogen > Weekapaug, Cold as Ice > Love You > Cold as Ice, Golgi
E: Horn, Rocky Top

"Raspberry Beret" jam in Weekapaug. Fishman on vacuum for Love You.

➢ Welcome to Minneapolis, hometown of the Artist Who Was Still Called Prince in '92. Trey pays tribute with a very pronounced Raspberry Beret jam in Weekapaug. This show is best known for its super-stoked Possum, though, which smokes. —SCOTT SIFTON

4/30/92 [ACCESSIBILITY: ••]
Barrymore Theater, Madison, WI
I: Curtain > Melt, Fee, Maze, Reba, Uncle Pen, Stash, Rift, Esther, Antelope
II: Glide, Tweezer, Squirming Coil, My Mind's, YEM, Horse > Silent, Chalkdust, Cold as Ice > Cracklin' Rosie > Cold as Ice, Harry Hood, Tweezer Reprise **E:** Carolina, Cavern
Aquarium Rescue Unit opened.

5/1/92 [ACCESSIBILITY: ••••]
Rave at Central Park, Milwaukee, WI
I: Suzie, My Friend, Poor Heart, Landlady, NICU, Sloth, Divided Sky, Guelah, It's Ice, Horn, I Didn't Know, Possum
II: Sanity, Buried Alive > Wilson, All Things, MSO, Mike's > Hydrogen > Weekapaug, Mound, Lizards, Llama, Cold as Ice > Terrapin > Cold as Ice, Golgi **E:** Lawn Boy, GTBT **E2:** Rocky Top
Fishman on bagpipe reed (played like a kazoo) for I Didn't Know and vacuum for Terrapin.

5/2/92 [ACCESSIBILITY: ••••]
Cabaret Metro, Chicago, IL
I: Runaway Jim, Forbin's > Icculus > Mockingbird, Sparkle, Reba, Maze, Bouncing, Stash, Squirming Coil, Llama
II: Glide, Bowie, Tela, Foam, YEM, Chalkdust, Cold as Ice > Cracklin' Rosie > Cold as Ice, Cavern **E:** Sleeping Monkey, BBFCM
Aquarium Rescue Unit opened. Stash lyric: "Police pull you over, beat the shit out of you..." referencing the Rodney King verdict earlier in the week. "Wicked Witch of the West" jam before Bowie. "Band Football Theme Song" and "Crew Football Theme Song" jams in Bowie. "Funky Bitch" tease in YEM.

➢ Phish hadn't hit the big-time yet: their show at the Metro had to be over by 10 p.m. so other bands could play later in the night. Despite the early start, Phish turned in another rocking show, with lots of stage humor that isn't attempted so much these days in arenas and amphitheaters. Mike and Trey videotaped each other bouncing on trampolines during YEM, and Mike pulled out his video camera again during BBFCM when Trey stood on Page's amp to play. Antics aside, check out this Bowie. —MICK CONNOR

➢ In case you missed 4/16/91, here's another chance to get up to speed on the Band and Crew Football Theme Songs. The songs were written by Phish, one to represent their team and one for the crew's team. (Because the crew usually beats the band in their pick-up football games, they made the band theme song really strong and powerful and the crew theme song kind of wimpy.) The tunes are dusted off in the midst of the Bowie jam—that's the band theme song first, followed by the crew theme song, then back into the band theme song. —ERNIE GREENE

5/3/92 [ACCESSIBILITY: •]
Student Union Ballroom, Michigan State University, East Lansing, MI
I: Landlady, Possum, It's Ice, Uncle Pen, Fee > All Things > Melt, I Didn't Know, Rift, Horn, Runaway Jim
II: Tweezer, Horse > Silent, Fluffhead, Guelah, Mike's > Hydrogen > Weekapaug, Mango, Cold as Ice > Cracklin' Rosie > Cold as Ice, Dinner and a Movie, Bouncing, Oh Kee > Suzie
E: Memories, Adeline, Tweezer Reprise
Fishman on vacuum for I Didn't Know.

5/5/92 [ACCESSIBILITY: •]
Bogart's, Cincinnati, OH
I: Golgi, Curtain, Sparkle, Stash, Rift, Guelah, Divided Sky, I Didn't Know, It's Ice > Glide > Antelope
II: Chalkdust, Bouncing, All Things, Foam, Mike's > Hydrogen > Weekapaug, Horse > Silent, Poor Heart, Llama, Cold as Ice > Love You > Cold as Ice, Squirming Coil, Cavern
E: Contact, Rocky Top
Fishman on trombone for I Didn't Know and vacuum for Love You.

5/6/92 [ACCESSIBILITY: ••••]
St. Andrew's Hall, Detroit, MI
I: Llama, Foam, Reba, My Mind's, Maze, Tela, Brother, Forbin's > Mockingbird, Sparkle, Cavern
II: MSO, Stash, Squirming Coil, YEM, All Things, Bouncing, Uncle Pen, Chalkdust, HYHU > Terrapin > Cold as Ice, A-Train, Golgi
E: Carolina, GTBT
"Shaggy Dog" theme in YEM vocal jam. "Cold as Ice" tease before Chalkdust. Fishman on vacuum for Terrapin.

5/7/92 [ACCESSIBILITY: ••••]
Agora Theater, Cleveland, OH
I: Suzie, Poor Heart, Buried Alive, My Friend, Foam, Runaway Jim, Esther, Melt, Rift, Guelah, Possum
II: Landlady, Sparkle, Tweezer, Fluffhead, Glide, Mike's > Hydrogen > Weekapaug, Fee, Cold as Ice > Bike > Cold as Ice, Squirming Coil, Tweezer Reprise **E:** Adeline, Sleeping Monkey > Rocky Top
Fishman on vacuum for Bike. Banana tree prop lowered onto the stage during Fee.

➢ Unremarkable first set, but the second set—after a standard Landlady/Sparkle opener—is a jamfest. Experimental Tweezer > Fluff > Glide, Mike's Groove just sparkles. Cold as Ice intro to Bike as Fish announces, "Ladies and gentlemen, this is Mike Gordon tuning his bass." An epic piano solo during Coil, then my tape runs out… —BOB COLBY

5/8/92 [ACCESSIBILITY: ••]
Riviera Theater, North Tonawanda (Buffalo), NY
I: Curtain > Cavern, Reba, Uncle Pen, It's Ice > Eliza, Llama, Mound, All Things, Bouncing, Bowie, Memories
II: Wilson, MSO, Stash, Magilla > Maze, YEM, Horse > Silent, Chalkdust, Cold as Ice > Terrapin > Cold as Ice, Harry Hood, Golgi **E:** BBFCM
Fishman on vacuum for Terrapin. "Brady Bunch" and "Popeye" jams in BBFCM. House lights turned on by venue manager before BBFCM, and left on through the song.

➢ The Curtain, always a strong opener, kicks things off, then Reba keeps the upbeat tempo going into the set. Bouncing > Bowie is an infallible connection as Phish enacts the secret language by all falling down at the end of Bouncing. Set II is musically wondrous. Magilla segues into Maze, which is spacey, and YEM traverses the outer limits of improvisational music and sound. Horse > Silent is very intimate, almost like Phish is simply having a conversation with the phans instead of singing to us. Golgi and BBFCM remind us to appreciate natural humor and the art of smiling. —ANTHONY BUCHLA

5/9/92 [ACCESSIBILITY: ••••]
Syracuse Armory, Syracuse, NY
I: Runaway Jim, Foam, Sparkle, Melt, Guelah, Rift, Fee, Maze, Squirming Coil, I Didn't Know, Antelope
II: Suzie, Divided Sky, Tela, Tweezer, Harpua, Llama, Cold as Ice > Cracklin' Rosie > Cold as Ice, Golgi **E:** Poor Heart, Tweezer Reprise
Mimi Fishman and Fishman on vacuum for I Didn't Know, and Mimi on vocals for I Didn't Know. "Smells Like Teen Spirit" jam in Harpua.

5/10/92 [ACCESSIBILITY: •]
Spring Fling, University of Massachusetts, Amherst, MA
Landlady, Suzie, Sparkle, Stash, Uncle Pen, Cavern, Reba, I Didn't Know, YEM, Possum
Outdoor Spring Fling concert at which Phish played one set. The concert also featured sets by Rippopatamus and The Mighty, Mighty Bosstones, which played before Phish; and Firehose, Fishbone and the Beastie Boys, which played after Phish.

5/12/92 [ACCESSIBILITY: ••••]
St. Lawrence University, Canton, NY
I: MSO, Reba, All Things, Sloth > Possum, It's Ice, Dinner and a Movie, Bouncing, Buried Alive, Uncle Pen, Horn, Bowie
II: Landlady, Bathtub Gin, YEM, Guelah, Chalkdust, Cold as Ice > Terrapin > Cold as Ice, Poor Heart, Llama, Cavern, Runaway Jim
E: Runaway Jim
"Oye Como Va" jam in YEM.

➢ Although I only have set II, I can proudly say that this is my favorite tape—not because it's my best-sounding tape, but because of the killer playing (most obviously, Mike Gordon's bass)! The April-May '92 soundboards have Gordon particularly fat in the mix. A great Landlady melts perfectly into a great Bathtub Gin. The YEM that follows is an all-time favorite! Nice SBDs of this show are out there. —CHRIS MRACHEK

Friday, May 8, 1992 — Riviera Theater, Buffalo, NY

The Riviera Theater had just been restored—this was the first rock show they hosted there after putting a ton of money into it, and when Phish arrived, the venue staff and management thought all hell had broken loose. I asked this one old lady in the hallway what she thought of Phish's music, and her response was, and I quote, "That's what hell must sound like."

First, they didn't want to let Phish play the second set because so many people were smoking cigarettes and stuff. Page made a little announcement before Wilson, saying something like, "Please, please everybody, the fire marshall wants you to stop smoking."

Then they didn't want to let Phish do an encore. But the band was like, "We gotta do an encore." As they went to walk on the stage, the guy that owned the Riviera Theater tackled Mike to try to keep him from going on. But I guess they got on stage anyway, so the guy throws all the houselights on. Phish busted into Big Black Furry Creatures From Mars, as if these people didn't think hell had broken loose enough already. And Trey climbed on top of Page's piano, and played his whole solo behind his head, during which he played the Brady Bunch and the Popeye themes—everything behind his head. Mike, in the meantime, climbed the stacks next to Fishman and played his part from standing on top of the stacks with all the houselights on. The whole show was pretty hectic! **—Mike Graff**

5/14/92 [ACCESSIBILITY: ••••]
Capitol Theater, Port Chester, NY
I: Suzie, All Things, Sloth, Sparkle, Maze, Horn, Reba, Poor Heart, My Friend, Bouncing, Antelope > "Language Lesson" > Antelope
II: Glide, Cavern, Rift, Fluffhead, Eliza, Mike's > Hydrogen > Weekapaug, McGrupp, Stash, Cold as Ice > Cracklin' Rosie > Cold as Ice, Possum
E: Sleeping Monkey, Rocky Top
"Spiderman" jam in Antelope. "Wait" jam between Weekapaug and McGrupp.

➢ Antelope, Antelope, Antelope—can't say enough about this Antelope. Trey jams on Spiderman! A new signal ("aw fuck!") is introduced! Phish rocks out! Hear it! —ED SMITH

5/15/92 [ACCESSIBILITY: •]
Lonestar Roadhouse, New York, NY
Golgi, Foam, Cavern, Sparkle, Stash, Bouncing, Cold as Ice > Love You > Cold as Ice, Chalkdust, YEM, Adeline, Rocky Top
Private party for recording and radio industry executives. Phish played one set.

5/16/92 [ACCESSIBILITY: •••]
Orpheum Theater, Boston, MA
I: Maze, Foam, Glide, Melt, Bouncing, MSO, Horn, Golgi, Lizards, Cavern, Bowie
II: Runaway Jim, It's Ice, Paul and Silas, Tweezer, Squirming Coil, YEM, Horse > Silent, Oh Kee > AC/DC Bag, Cold as Ice > Cracklin' Rosie > Cold as Ice, Poor Heart, Tweezer Reprise **E:** Adeline, Suzie
Last AC/DC Bag, 11/1/91 Denver, CO [74 shows].

➢ My first taste of Phish madness—the crowds swarming outside the run-down but majestic Orpheum blew my mind even before the music did. Where did all these people come from? It looked like a cross between Dead tour and a prep school campus. Once we made it inside, diligent security guards kept us trapped near the back, but that didn't matter once the lights went out and the drummer emerged, wearing a dress, and tapped out a drum beat. One by one, the other band members came out and an incredible song materialized. Wow! Five years and many shows later, I still count this as one of my favorite Mazes. —TEDDY STUART

5/17/92 [ACCESSIBILITY: •••]
Achilles Rink, Union College, Schenectady, NY
I: Landlady, Llama, Forbin's > Mockingbird, MSO, Reba, I Didn't Know, Stash, Mango, Poor Heart, Chalkdust
II: Curtain > Possum, Guelah, Squirming Coil, All Things, Brother, Sanity, Cold as Ice > Love You > Cold as Ice, Sparkle, Harry Hood, Cavern
E: Lawn Boy, GTBT
Fishman on trombone for I Didn't Know and vacuum for Love You. "Rocky Mountain Way," "It's Ice" and "Divided Sky" jams in Possum. Birthday cake brought to Page during Squirming Coil. "Happy Birthday" tease in Love You.

➢ One of the most underrated shows out there, the band's Union College gig was a late but welcome addition to the tail end of the '92 spring tour. Possum is incredible! The "intro" is practically its own song, as Trey is just off somewhere else (he gets a cool groove going). Once the song kicks in, they again wander, first into Rocky Mountain Way and then into It's Ice (not a simple little jam—I keep expecting Page to sing the lyrics!) When that's calmed down a bit, Trey plays the guitar line from Divided Sky for at least a minute—then tops off an over-the-top Possum jam in incredible fashion! This is wild! Not only that, but this show has the last Sanity for awhile (and a loud one at that), plus a hilarious Fishman meditation on birthdays (it's Page's 28th) during Love You, including rare commentary from Paul at the soundboard. This set is other-worldly. —MICK CONNOR

5/18/92 [ACCESSIBILITY: ••]
Flynn Theater, Burlington, VT
I: Suzie, Maze, Bouncing, Divided Sky, Guelah, Foam, Poor Heart, Horn, Sparkle, Antelope
II: Glide, Llama, TMWSIY > Avenu > TMWSIY, Mike's > Hydrogen > Weekapaug, Fee, Rift, Cavern, Cold as Ice > Love You > HYHU, Runaway Jim **E:** Rocky Top
Fishman on vacuum for Love You.

1992 Summer/Europe

After taking a month off from touring, Phish jetted to Europe for a two-week stretch of shows at the end of June. Playing on various music festival bills and opening for an odd array of bands—primarily the Violent Femmes—the band got a taste of tour life overseas. Plans for European tours in the summers of 1993, 1994 and 1995 all failed to materialize, but summer 1996 and February 1997 took Phish back to Europe to work the connections made five years earlier.

6/19/92 [ACCESSIBILITY: ••]
Stadtpark/Freilichtbuhn, Hamburg, Germany
Landlady, Suzie, Stash, Squirming Coil, Sparkle, Cavern, YEM
Opened for the Violent Femmes. Soundcheck: MSO.

6/20/92 [ACCESSIBILITY: •]
Waldbuhn, Nordheim, Germany
Buried Alive, Bouncing, Foam, Runaway Jim, It's Ice, Horn, HYHU > Love You > HYHU, Llama
Opened for the Violent Femmes and Lou Reed. Fishman on vacuum for Love You.

6/23/92 [ACCESSIBILITY: •••]
Philipshalle, Dusseldorf, Germany
Chalkdust, Reba, Maze, Adeline, Uncle Pen, BBFCM, Brain, Golgi
Opened for the Violent Femmes. Fishman on vacuum for BBFCM.

6/24/92 [ACCESSIBILITY: •]
Resi, Nuremberg, Germany
Runaway Jim, Llama, Adeline, Uncle Pen, Guelah, I Didn't Know, Sparkle, Cavern, Rocky Top
Opened for the Violent Femmes.

6/27/92 [ACCESSIBILITY: •]
Roskilde Festival, Outside Copenhagen, Denmark
Runaway Jim, Foam, Sparkle, Reba, Maze, All Things, Chalkdust, Bouncing, Uncle Pen, Bowie **E:** I Didn't Know, GTBT
Phish played as part of the annual four-day Roskilde Festival.

[6/30/92] *Lawn Boy* re-released on Elektra.

6/30/92 [ACCESSIBILITY: •]
Elysee Montmartre, Paris, France
Golgi, Divided Sky, Guelah, Possum, Adeline, YEM
Opened for the Violent Femmes. "Frere Jacques" jam in Possum.

7/1/92 [ACCESSIBILITY: •]
Ancienne Beguique, Brussels, Belgium
Curtain > Cavern, Rift, Horn, Melt, Adeline, Rocky Top
Opened for the Violent Femmes.

7/3/92 ❄
Brixton Academy, Radio One Music Festival, London, England
Opened for the Violent Femmes and Green on Red.

1992 Summer/Santana

After returning from Europe, Phish played four concerts with Blues Traveler, Spin Doctors, Widespread Panic and Aquarium Rescue Unit on the first leg of the first HORDE (Horizons of Rock Developing Everywhere) tour, then sneaked in a couple of solo concerts before spending the rest of the summer opening for Carlos Santana—a tour that became a major turning point for the band. It was Santana who described Phish as a "hose" watering the audience, a metaphor that has come to define the peak musical experience possible at a Phish concert. Besides the hose, the summer also saw the first "vacuum freeze"—Trey, Page and Mike would freeze in position while Fishman came forward for a vacuum solo.

7/9/92 [ACCESSIBILITY: ••]
Cumberland County Civic Center, Portland, ME
Glide, Oh Kee > Suzie > Landlady, Sparkle, Stash, Squirming Coil, Runaway Jim, Guelah, Bowie, Glide Reprise **E:** Rocky Top
HORDE show with Aquarium Rescue Unit, Widespread Panic, Spin Doctors and Blues Traveler. Phish played one set, closing the show. Fishman on vacuum (vacuum freeze) during Bowie intro.

7/10/92 [ACCESSIBILITY: ••]
Empire Court, Syracuse, NY
Bouncing, Llama, Reba, Sparkle, Maze, Golgi, Lizards, Cavern, Antelope
E: MSO
HORDE show with Aquarium Rescue Unit, Widespread Panic, Spin Doctors and Blues Traveler. Phish played one set. Fishman on vacuum (vacuum freeze) near the end of Cavern.

➢ The first HORDE tour saw gem performances from Widespread, Col. Bruce & ARU, Spin Doctors, Blues Traveler and Phish. What more could you ask for? It rained all day, but I was under a tree and never noticed. Phish played a straight set with the jazz influences flying. Still, Col. Bruce and Blues Traveler blew them off the stage—well, third best isn't bad. This was a good exposure show for many "Who is this Phish band?" people. It starts getting bigger from here on. —DAVID M. BROWN

7/11/92 [ACCESSIBILITY: ••]
Garden State Arts Center, Holmdel, NJ
Landlady, Runaway Jim, Foam, Sparkle, Stash, Squirming Coil, Cavern, YEM, Suzie
HORDE show. Phish played one set. Fishman on vacuum (vacuum freeze) near the end of Cavern. Four female dancers boogied on stage with Trey and Mike during Landlady. John Popper came out to jump on trampoline during YEM, but in what turned out to be a rigged effect, the trampoline gave way under his weight.

7/12/92 [ACCESSIBILITY: ••]
Jones Beach Music Theater, Wantagh, NY
Adeline, Chalkdust, Bouncing, Divided Sky, Fluffhead, Uncle Pen, Maze, Glide, Possum
HORDE show. Phish played one set, closing the show. Fishman on vacuum (vacuum freeze) during Glide. "But Anyway" jam in Possum.

➢ Phish was the last band to take the stage during the first HORDE visit to Jones Beach. Many people had already left. I sneaked up to front row center, where there was lots of dancing room available. Phish took the stage wearing Mardi Gras masks and dancing about. The setlist was good, but the quality of the music played was great. —BRIAN A. ROCK

➢ By far the largest audience Phish had played to at that point. The crowd was genuinely enthusiastic, and even those who weren't familiar with the band did a good job pretending. I know I did. —ANDY BERNSTEIN

7/14/92 [ACCESSIBILITY: •]
The Boathouse, Norfolk, VA
I: Landlady, Rift, Guelah, Maze, Sparkle, It's Ice, Runaway Jim, Horn, Brother, I Didn't Know, Poor Heart, Cavern
II: Tweezer, Fee, All Things, Reba, Llama, Squirming Coil, Paul and Silas, YEM, A-Train, Tweezer Reprise **E:** Sleeping Monkey

7/15/92 [ACCESSIBILITY: ••••]
Trax, Charlottesville, VA
I: Glide, Oh Kee > Suzie, Foam, My Friend, Uncle Pen, Melt, Horse > Silent, Chalkdust, Lizards, Antelope
II: Sloth, Divided Sky, Esther, MSO, Stash, McGrupp, All Things, Harry Hood, Golgi **E:** Possum
Fishman on vacuum (vacuum freeze) in the middle of Possum.

7/16/92 [ACCESSIBILITY: ••]
The Flood Zone, Richmond, VA
I: Poor Heart, It's Ice, Sparkle, Wilson, Dinner and a Movie, Bouncing, Maze, Guelah, Rift, Bowie
II: Runaway Jim, Weigh, Landlady, Fluffhead, TMWSIY > Avenu Malkenu > TMWSIY, Llama, Glide, Paul and Silas, Mike's > Hydrogen > Weekapaug **E:** Blue Bayou, Squirming Coil
Concert debut: Blue Bayou.

7/17/92 ❄
Merriweather Post Pavilion, Columbia, MD
Chalkdust, Sparkle, Stash, Squirming Coil, Maze, Bouncing, Runaway Jim
Opened for Santana.

7/18/92 ❄
Mann Music Center, Philadelphia, PA
Suzie, Foam, Llama, Reba, Rift, Antelope
Opened for Santana.

7/19/92 ❄
Garden State Arts Center, Holmdel, NJ
Poor Heart, Maze, Runaway Jim, Bowie, Adeline
Opened for Santana. Trey joined Santana for one song during Santana's set.

7/21/92 [ACCESSIBILITY: •]
Great Woods, Mansfield, MA
All Things, Possum, It's Ice, Sparkle, Stash, Squirming Coil, Runaway Jim
Opened for Santana.

7/22/92 ❄
Holman Stadium, Nashua, NH
Reba, Poor Heart, Bouncing, Maze, Rift, Cavern, Bowie
Opened for Santana. Fishman on vacuum (vacuum freeze) near the end of Cavern. Trey joined Santana for a part of Santana's set.

[7/23/92] [ACCESSIBILITY: •]
Hangin' with MTV, MTV Studios, New York, NY
Phish appeared as the "house band." Snippets from Buried Alive, Divided Sky, Stash and Poor Heart, plus a Fishman vacuum solo and some trampoline action, were broadcast.

7/24/92 [ACCESSIBILITY: ••]
Jones Beach Music Theater, Wantagh, NY
MSO, Foam, Tweezer, Squirming Coil, YEM, Tweezer Reprise
Opened for Santana. Phish joined Santana for part of Santana's set.

7/25/92 [ACCESSIBILITY: •••••]
Stowe Performing Arts Center, Stowe, VT
Runaway Jim, Foam, Sparkle, Stash, Rift, YEM, Llama, Funky Bitch
Opened for Santana. YEM, Llama, and Funky Bitch featured Carlos Santana. Santana band percussionists Raul Rekow (on congas) and Karl Perazzo (on timbales) joined for YEM. Phish joined Santana for part of Santana's set.

Phan Pick #18 ➢ This was the hometown show on the Santana tour, and as a tribute, Carlos let the boys play a little longer than their normal 40-to-50-minute sets they played this summer. That was probably because Carlos joined them on stage during YEM and jammed out with Trey and the boys from YEM through Llama into Funky Bitch. The resulting music is an incredible confluence of rock's past, present and future, and is without question a seminal Phish event. No Phish tape collection is complete without a copy of this set. —SCOTT SIFTON

➢ My favorite tape in my collection! I love Santana jamming with them. This is the best Llama ever! I always listen to Trey and Carlos jam, and I don't know whose jam is better. The band seemed to be in total synch—every fan of Phish and Santana MUST own this show. Incredible! —JASON MOKHATARIAN

➢ By the way, for those of you who care about this sort of thing, the Bowie > Catapult > Bowie that follows the Funky Bitch on most copies of this tape is actually from Phish's appearance at the Warfield Theater in San Francisco on 4/17/92. Phish's set on 7/25/92 ended with Funky Bitch—and what a Bitch it was! —ERNIE GREENE

Saturday, July 25, 1992 **Stowe PAC, Stowe, VT**

Is this the ultimate Phish experience? In a word, YES. In May 1992, I called a TicketMaster-type place for tickets to Santana at the Stowe Performing Arts Center, and the dude on the phone couldn't find such a show, much less a town called Stowe. Eventually he found it listed under another town's name and I ordered the tickets.

Two months later, it was a beautiful, warm Vermont summer day, and upon arriving at the venue we saw a little shack selling cassettes and stickers for a group called Phish. Having never heard of them, I figured they must be the opening group, and after asking a few questions, I found out they were local (meaning Vermont). From there, we went to check our seats—fourth row center, NO WAY!! I guess I had ordered REAL early. The seats went right to the stage so we were only about 30 feet from the musicians.

The "local group" came on early, and the drummer started tapping. I turned to my girlfriend and said, "Oh, this must be a folk group." The song—I'm convinced the tapes have it wrong—was Glide. Next was Runaway Jim, and I was thinking, boy these guys are good, but I was still stoked for Santana. Well, Trey launched into YEM and I was hooked for life. He nailed it, standing right on the edge of the stage and making ugly faces. As you all know, Santana literally jumped out in a bright yellow t-shirt and proceeded to give us the best show of our lives.

The part you NEVER hear about came near the end of Santana's set when Santana said, "Let's bring the local boys back out." With 13 musicians on stage... well, it just can't be put into words—solos everywhere, Fishman even soloed on a small hand-held drum he beat with a weird crooked stick.

My girlfriend always says that this was the best show she's ever seen, a tall order coming from a woman who's seen Jimi Hendrix, Led Zeppelin ('73) and Janis Joplin with the Tower of Power, and who went to a picnic at Greg Allman's house after being invited by Greg himself. I'm sorry to all the folks who missed it. This was the ultimate Phish experience, Santana was Santana and Phish was the best I've ever heard them—the best. The week after the show I asked the Vermont DMV for the Phish license plate—and got it!

—David Clement

7/26/92 ❄
Big Birch Concert Pavilion, Patterson, NY
Chalkdust, It's Ice, Divided Sky, Weigh, Melt, Lizards, Llama
Opened for Santana. Trey, Page and Mike joined Santana for part of Santana's set.

7/27/92 [ACCESSIBILITY: •]
Saratoga Performing Arts Center, Saratoga Springs, NY
Golgi, All Things, Bowie, Horn, Suzie, Llama, Adeline **E:** Rocky Top
Opened for Santana. Phish joined Santana for part of Santana's set. A cappella intro to Suzie.

7/28/92 ❄
Finger Lakes Performing Arts Center, Canandaigua, NY
Chalkdust, Bouncing, Uncle Pen, Squirming Coil, Tweezer, Runaway Jim
Opened for Santana. Phish joined Santana for part of Santana's set.

7/30/92 ❄
Meadow Brook Music Festival, Rochester Hills, MI
Rift, Horn, Sparkle, It's Ice > All Things, Maze, I Didn't Know, Possum
Opened for Santana. Phish joined Santana for part of Santana's set.

7/31/92 ❄
Blossom Music Center, Cayahoga Falls, OH
Suzie, Chalkdust, Bouncing, Oh Kee > YEM, GTBT
Opened for Santana. Trey joined Santana for part of Santana's set.

8/1/92 ❄
Poplar Creek Music Center, Hoffman Estates, IL
Golgi, Foam, Poor Heart, Stash, Squirming Coil, Horn, Llama
Opened for Santana. Phish joined Santana for part of Santana's set.

8/2/92 ❄
Riverport Performing Arts Center, Marilyn Heights, MO
Chalkdust, Guelah, Rift, Oh Kee > Suzie, Bowie, Cavern, Rocky Top
Opened for Santana.

8/13/92 [ACCESSIBILITY: •]
Greek Theater, Los Angeles, CA
Chalkdust, Foam, YEM
Opened for Santana.

8/14/92 [ACCESSIBILITY: •]
Greek Theater, Los Angeles, CA
Poor Heart, Stash, Squirming Coil, Llama, Adeline
Opened for Santana.

8/15/92 [ACCESSIBILITY: •]
Greek Theater, Los Angeles, CA
Landlady, Sparkle, Guelah, Maze, Runaway Jim
Opened for Santana.

8/17/92 [ACCESSIBILITY: ••••]
The Coach House, San Juan Capistrano, CA
I: Buried Alive > Poor Heart, Landlady, Reba, Rift, Wilson, All Things, Foam, My Friend, Bouncing, Bowie
II: Suzie, It's Ice, Tweezer, Esther, Mike's > Hydrogen > Weekapaug, Horn, HYHU > Terrapin > HYHU, A-Train > Somewhere Over the Rainbow Jam, Cavern **E:** Squirming Coil
Ninja Custodian opened. "Camel Walk" jam at start of Wilson. A cappella intro to Suzie. Fishman on vacuum and Ninja Mike Billington on drums for Terrapin. "Flintstones" jams before and during A-Train. "Somewhere Over the Rainbow" jam in A-Train, followed by a separate "SOTR" jam after A-Train.

8/19/92 ❄
Pema County Fair, Tucson, AZ
Chalkdust, Landlady, Runaway Jim, Guelah, YEM, Uncle Pen, Llama
Opened for Santana. Trey, Page and Mike joined Santana for part of Santana's set.

8/20/92 ❄
Pan American Center, Las Cruces, NM
Golgi, Foam, Stash, Squirming Coil > Bowie, Adeline
Opened for Santana. Phish joined Santana for part of Santana's set.

8/23/92 ❄
Colorado State Fair, Pueblo, CO
Chalkdust, Maze, Sparkle, Cavern, Foam, Runaway Jim, Stash
Opened for Santana.

8/24/92 ❄
Gerald Ford Amphitheatre, Vail, CO
Buried Alive > Poor Heart, All Things, Tweezer, Landlady, Reba, YEM
Opened for Santana. Phish joined Santana for part of Santana's set.

8/25/92 ❄
The Downs, Santa Fe, NM
Runaway Jim, It's Ice, Sparkle, Stash, Squirming Coil, Llama, Adeline
Opened for Santana.

8/27/92 ❄
Santa Barbara County Bowl, Santa Barbara, CA
Chalkdust, Bouncing, Landlady, Horn, Sparkle, YEM, Llama
Opened for Santana.

8/28/92 ❄
Concord Pavilion, Concord, CA
Poor Heart, Foam, Stash, Adeline, Squirming Coil, Runaway Jim, Rocky Top
Opened for Santana. Phish joined Santana for part of Santana's set.

8/29/92 [ACCESSIBILITY: ••]
Shoreline Amphitheatre, Mountain View, CA
Chalkdust, Rift, Bouncing, Maze, YEM
Opened for Santana. "Oye Como Va" jam in YEM. Phish joined Santana for part of Santana's set.

8/30/92 [ACCESSIBILITY: •]
Cal Expo Amphitheatre, Sacramento, CA
Uncle Pen, Landlady, Reba, Llama, Memories, Antelope, Adeline
Music festival featuring Santana, Los Lobos and the Indigo Girls. Phish opened the festival, playing one set. Phish joined Santana for part of Santana's set.

➢ Again, Santana and Phish rock and roll together during Santana's set. Carlos and Trey have a great time going back and forth. This show ended the six-week tour with these two artists playing together almost every night. Their guitars always seem to smoke when played together. —LEAH SHANTZ

[9/7/92] White Crow Studios, Burlington, VT
Recording for *Rift* begins.

10/30/92 ❄
Boston Garden, Boston, MA
Runaway Jim, Maze, Bouncing, Rift, Cavern, Squirming Coil, Stash, Adeline, YEM
WBCN-FM new music concert featuring Spin Doctors and other groups. Phish headlined and played one set. Fishman on vacuum (vacuum freeze) near the end of Cavern.

[10/92-11/92] The Castle, Nashville TN
Additional recording and mixing for *Rift*.

1992 Fall *BIG BALL FALL*

The band put the finishing touches on the album that would become Rift in early November, then headed out for a short fall tour that culminated in the band's first "official" New Year's Run of shows. The fall tour featured debuts of several of the new Rift songs and the premiere of the Big Ball Jam, a new interactive band-audience game. Soundboard tapes from this tour are tougher to come by than those for the spring tour, though a few fall '92 boards have recently found their way into wider release.

11/19/92 [ACCESSIBILITY: ••••]
Ross Sports Center, St. Michael's College, Colchester, VT
I: Maze, Fee > Foam, Glide, Melt, Mound > Divided Sky, Esther, Axilla, Horse > Silent, Antelope
II: Mike's > Hydrogen > Weekapaug, Bouncing > It's Ice > I Walk the Line > Tweezer > BBJ, Poor Heart, FEFY, Llama, HYHU > Lengthwise > HYHU, Cavern **E:** Bold as Love
"Those Were the Days" (All in the Family theme) teases in Divided Sky, Antelope (in the intro and again before "Rye, rye, rocco…") and in Weekapaug. "Price of Love" jam in Weekapaug. "I Walk the Line" and "BBFCM" jams in Tweezer; "Burning Ring of Fire" vocal tease in Tweezer. Gordon Stone on pedal steel guitar for Poor Heart, FEFY and Llama. Fishman on vacuum for Lengthwise. Concert debuts: Axilla, I Walk the Line, BBJ, FEFY and Lengthwise. Last Mound, 5/8/92 Buffalo, NY [52 shows]. Last Bold as Love, 4/18/90 Denver, CO [285 shows].

➢ This show is kind of comparable to a show like Lowell Auditorium from May 1995. Many of the songs Phish played were first-timers, among them Lengthwise, which I would consider special nowadays, so infrequently is it played. The entire setlist rocked. Mike's > I am Hydrogen > Weekapaug was very common at the time, but Phish still managed an excellent jam. The most exciting point for me was the Bold as Love encore, a comeback appearance of a song not seen since the 1980s. —ADAM RIZZUTI

➢ This show really has a hometown feel to it. The Gordon Stone cameo adds to that, as does the debut of the Big Ball Jam. Trey explains that the big balls "let the audience jam the band," and when it's all done, Page says, "We hope you liked that as much as we did." This show also features a very rare reggae Lengthwise. When Fish finishes it, Page says, "He wrote that," and Trey adds, "We like that song so much, yes, it appears twice on the new album." —ANDY BERNSTEIN

➢ Fans of Phish chaos, like Providence's 3/13/92 Run Like a Big Black Furry Antelope, might want to check out the St. Mike's Tweezer. After a jam sequence that includes "I Walk the Line" teases, the band turns a jam that didn't seem to be going anywhere into BBFCM. But then Mike starts singing "I Walk the Line" lyrics while Trey sings "Burning Ring of Fire"! Almost immediately, the band kicks back into the Tweezer theme, which peaks right away and then dies out. Trey introduces Pete Schall, who throws out the balls for the first official (and perhaps longest) Big Ball Jam. —TEDDY STUART

11/20/92 [ACCESSIBILITY: •••]
Palace Theater, Albany, NY
I: Axilla, All Things > Suzie, Rift, Sloth, Reba, Sparkle, Stash, Lizards, Memories, I Walk the Line, Bowie
II: Chalkdust, Fluffhead, Tube, YEM, FEFY, Dinner and a Movie > Harry Hood, HYHU > Terrapin, Lengthwise
E: Self **E2:** Adeline, GTBT

"Linus and Lucy" jam in Stash. "Bowie" tease before I Walk the Line. "Jimmy Olsen's Blues" tease in Bowie (Bowie unfinished). Fishman on vacuum for Terrapin. Crowd sing-along on Lengthwise. The Dude of Life on vocals for Self. Last Tube, 4/19/92 Santa Cruz, CA [67 shows].

➢ This show was two or three years ahead of its time. On first listening to it, I thought it sounded like a '94 show. David Bowie is particularly exceptional. Granted, the I Walk the Line proceeding it was hokey, but the Bowie jam was tremendous. The boys got so wrapped up in it that they didn't even bother with the coda. It just sort of dissolved. Also, after hearing this show, I'm at a loss as to why they dropped Tube. —SCOTT KUSHNER

➢ The scene was mellow, the theater was nice and the show was phenomenal. There was ample dancing space, good sound, and the Dude of Life appeared, providing a nice twist to the show's conclusion. —BRIAN A. ROCK

➢ Everyone loves the Harry Hood from Stanford 4/18/92 with Page's jam on the Peanuts theme ("Linus and Lucy"). Less remarked upon is the Stash from this show at Albany's Palace Theater, which also features Page jamming on the Peanuts theme. And, like Stanford, this is a very well-played show—check out the outstanding jams on Stash, Bowie and Hood. —AMY MANNING

11/21/92 [ACCESSIBILITY: ••]
Sports Complex, SUNY Stony Brook, Stony Brook, NY
I: Landlady, Runaway Jim, Foam, Glide, Poor Heart, It's Ice, Bouncing, Maze, Forbin's > Mockingbird, Possum
II: Carolina, Curtain > Mike's > Hydrogen > Weekapaug, Horse > Silent, Uncle Pen, Guelah, Squirming Coil, Love You, A-Train, Llama
E: Buffalo Bill, BBFCM

Concert debut: Buffalo Bill. Fishman on vacuum for Love You and Madonna washboard for Buffalo Bill.

11/22/92 [ACCESSIBILITY: ••]
Bailey Hall, Cornell University, Ithaca, NY
I: Buried Alive > Oh Kee > Suzie, Fee > Maze, Reba, Sparkle, Horn, All Things, Bathtub Gin, Adeline, Antelope
II: Axilla, My Friend, MSO, Tweezer > BBJ > Tweezer, Tela, YEM, Faht, Golgi **E:** Bold as Love, Carolina, Tweezer Reprise

"Jimmy Olsen's Blues" jam in Suzie. "Eleanor Rigby" jam in YEM. Concert debut: Faht. Last Bathtub Gin, 5/12/92 Canton, NY [52 shows]. Last Tela, 5/9/92 Syracuse, NY [54 shows].

➢ Hot hot, tasty tasty. Was that Eleanor Rigby I heard in YEM? Trey was electric at this show. I had side seats that sucked and I was still pulled into the magic. A heavy, heady show that lead to the following night's Forum show. Without speaking, Phish told a story of passion and feeling for their music. It was Eleanor Rigby—find the tape. —DAVID M. BROWN

➢ This was the show that clinched my love for Phish. Antelope was stellar, taking me on an amazing trip (without any drugs). There were torrential downpours before the show and many people without tickets. A rumor went around that only a few tickets were left at the box office. I finagled my way inside, claiming that I had tickets at will-call and then I bought a ticket—there were plenty left! This was also the first time Faht was played, and the audience chimed in with our own jungle noises. —BRIAN A. ROCK

11/23/92 [ACCESSIBILITY: ••••]
Broome County Forum, Binghamton, NY
I: Runaway Jim, Foam, Glide, Melt, Rift, Guelah, Divided Sky, Mound, Bouncing, Memories, Bowie
II: Poor Heart, Stash, Squirming Coil, I Walk the Line, Llama, Weigh, Mike's > Hydrogen > Weekapaug > BBJ > Weekapaug, Lengthwise, Cavern **E:** Sleeping Monkey, Rocky Top

"Vibration of Life" in Bowie. Fishman on Madonna washboard for I Walk the Line. Mimi Fishman on vacuum for Lengthwise.

11/25/92 [ACCESSIBILITY: ••]
Keswick Theater, Glenside, PA
I: Buried Alive > Poor Heart, Landlady, Fee, Maze, Sparkle, It's Ice, Squirming Coil, Cavern > Adeline > Cavern, Antelope
II: Chalkdust, Foam, FEFY, YEM, Lizards, Tweezer > HYHU > Cracklin' Rosie > HYHU, MSO, Tweezer Reprise **E:** Harry Hood, Carolina

Trey twice flubs lyrics during Lizards. Last Cracklin' Rosie, 5/16/92 Boston, MA [51 shows].

11/27/92 [ACCESSIBILITY: •••]
Capitol Theater, Port Chester, NY
I: Rift, Wilson > Divided Sky, Forbin's > Mockingbird, Melt, Lawn Boy, Reba, Llama > Mound, Memories, Runaway Jim
II: Axilla, Poor Heart, Possum, Glide > It's Ice, McGrupp > I Walk the Line > Bowie, Horse > Silent, Faht, A-Train, Cavern **E:** Bold as Love

"I Walk the Line" jam in Bowie intro. "Purple Haze" jam in Cavern. Last Lawn Boy, 5/17/92 Schenectady, NY [51 shows].

11/28/92 [ACCESSIBILITY: ••••]
Capitol Theater, Port Chester, NY
I: MSO, Foam, Stash, Esther, Chalkdust, Sparkle, FEFY, All Things, Mike's > Hydrogen > Weekapaug
II: Suzie, Paul and Silas, Tweezer > BBJ, TMWSIY > Avenu > Maze > TMWSIY, Bouncing, Squirming Coil, HYHU > Love You > HYHU, Harpua, Golgi **E:** Contact > Tweezer Reprise

Bass problems in MSO led to its interruption, a long pause, and then the song's finish. "Walk this Way" jam in Mike's. "Jimmy Olsen's Blues" jam in Harpua. Trey dances on stage with his grandmother during Contact. Last Contact, 5/5/92 Cincinatti, OH [62 shows]. Last Harpua, 5/9/92 Syracuse, NY [58 shows].

➢ A nice place to see a show—the Capitol Theater has a cartoon feel to it. Many ticketless phans wandered outside, but I scored one and went inside for a show whose setlist speaks for itself. One especially funny moment came during Harpua when Trey said (mockingly), "Jimmy was listening to the number one hit," and then broke into Jimmy Olsen's Blues by the Spin Doctors. Supposedly, Phish later apologized to the SD's for making fun of them. —BRIAN A. ROCK

➢ During Mike's Song, the fog machines filled the stage with mist. From the front row, I couldn't see a thing. As the jam took "Walk This Way" around the chromatic scale, landing in many different keys, the fog cleared to show Trey standing on the very front of the stage leaning out over the audience three feet from me! Also worth noting about these shows is the continuation of a story taking place "inside Fish's head," from the Forbin's on 11/27 to the Harpua on 11/28! —BRENDAN NEAGLE

➢ This two-night stand is legendary for both the music and the vibe—these were Phish's last shows ever at the Capitol in Port Chester, the historic 1,400-seat theater they'd played regularly for two years. The whole show was great, but I wouldn't see a Mike's Groove that topped the one at Port Chester for quite a while. During the fog that filled the theater for Mike's and Hydrogen, a giant gong was brought out to the center of the stage, and Trey faked us out by pretending to hit it but never making contact. People were flipping out! We spent the whole setbreak shaking our heads in amazement. There are fun Phish shows, and there are great Phish shows. This one was both. —LOCK STEELE

11/30/92 [ACCESSIBILITY: •]
Metropol, Pittsburgh, PA
I: Llama, Foam, Bouncing, Poor Heart, Stash, Sparkle, It's Ice, I Didn't Know, Reba > Antelope
II: Buried Alive > Runaway Jim, Guelah, Maze, Glide, Uncle Pen, YEM, Squirming Coil, HYHU > Terrapin > HYHU, Cavern **E:** Fee, Fire

No whistle jam at the end of Reba, apparently for the first time ever. Fishman on Madonna washboard for I Didn't Know and vacuum for Terrapin.

12/1/92 [ACCESSIBILITY: ••]
Livingston Fieldhouse, Denison University, Granville, OH
I: Landlady > MSO, Melt, Bouncing, Rift, Cavern, Fluffhead, Maze, Adeline, Mike's > Hydrogen > Weekapaug
II: Axilla, Curtain, Chalkdust, My Friend, All Things, Uncle Pen, Llama, HYHU > Love You > HYHU, Dinner and a Movie, Bowie **E:** GTBT

"Peter and the Wolf" jams in Bowie. Fishman on vacuum for Love You.

12/2/92 [ACCESSIBILITY: ••]
Newport Music Hall, Columbus, OH
I: Suzie, Foam, Divided Sky, FEFY, Poor Heart, Stash, Lizards, Sparkle, Horn, YEM
II: Wilson > Possum, Mound, Tweezer > BBJ, Tela, Llama, Glide, HYHU > Lengthwise > HYHU, Squirming Coil, I Walk the Line, Runaway Jim
E: Golgi, Rocky Top

Fishman on vacuum for Lengthwise and Madonna washboard for I Walk the Line.

12/3/92 [ACCESSIBILITY: ••]
Bogart's, Cincinnati, OH
I: Maze, Fee > All Things, Melt, Bouncing, Uncle Pen, Chalkdust, Horse > Silent, Reba, Adeline, Antelope
II: Rift, Guelah, Fluffhead, Mike's > Hydrogen > Weekapaug, Lawn Boy, It's Ice, MSO, BBJ, HYHU > Cracklin' Rosie > HYHU, A-Train, Cavern
E: Bold as Love

12/4/92 [ACCESSIBILITY: •]
Mississippi Nights, St. Louis, MO
I: Llama, Foam, Poor Heart, Stash, Glide, Sparkle, FEFY, Maze, Forbin's > Mockingbird, Cavern

II: Suzie > Bowie, Esther, Possum, It's Ice, Squirming Coil, Carolina, Harry Hood, Faht, YEM **E:** Fee, Rocky Top

12/5/92 [ACCESSIBILITY: ••]
Vic Theater, Chicago, IL
I: Landlady, Chalkdust, Bouncing, Rift, Guelah, Melt, Lizards, Mound, Divided Sky, Adeline, Uncle Pen, Golgi
II: Poor Heart, Tweezer, Reba > I Walk the Line > Reba, Sparkle, Maze, Lawn Boy, Mike's > Hydrogen > Weekapaug, HYHU > Whipping Post > HYHU, Tweezer Reprise **E:** Memories, GTBT
Fishman on vacuum for Whipping Post.

12/6/92 [ACCESSIBILITY: ••]
Vic Theater, Chicago, IL
I: Runaway Jim, Foam, Fee, My Friend, MSO, Sloth, Squirming Coil, Llama, Fluffhead, Antelope
II: Suzie, Curtain > Stash, Paul and Silas, BBJ, Bathtub Gin, YEM, TMWSIY > Avenu > TMWSIY, HYHU > Lengthwise > HYHU, Carolina, Cavern **E:** Possum
"Vibration of Life" during jam in Possum. Fishman on vacuum for Lengthwise.

12/7/92 [ACCESSIBILITY: ••]
First Avenue, Minneapolis, MN
I: Axilla, Poor Heart, Maze, Glide, Sparkle, Foam, FEFY, Melt, Bouncing, YEM
II: Chalkdust, Reba > Llama, Horn, MSO, It's Ice, Fee, Bowie > HYHU > Love You > HYHU, Squirming Coil, Adeline **E:** Runaway Jim
"Oye Como Va" jam in YEM. "Vibration of Life" between Horn and MSO. Fishman on vacuum for Love You.

12/8/92 [ACCESSIBILITY: •]
Barrymore Theater, Madison, WI
I: Rift, Wilson, Llama, Forbin's > Mockingbird, Uncle Pen, Guelah, Divided Sky, Mound, Adeline, Stash
II: Mike's > Hydrogen > Weekapaug, Horse > Silent, It's Ice, Lizards, Antelope, Lawn Boy, Sparkle, Suzie, HYHU > Lengthwise > HYHU, MSO > BBJ, Sleeping Monkey **E:** Carolina, Fire
Fishman on vacuum for Lengthwise.

12/10/92 [ACCESSIBILITY: •]
State Theater, Kalamazoo, MI
I: Golgi, Llama, Foam, Fee, Poor Heart, Melt, I Didn't Know, All Things, Reba, Adeline, Cavern
II: Rift, Tweezer > Tela, MSO > BBJ, Maze, YEM, HYHU > Love You > HYHU, Oh Kee > Suzie **E:** Bold as Love, Carolina, Tweezer Reprise
Fishman on Madonna washboard for I Didn't Know and vacuum for Love You.

12/11/92 [ACCESSIBILITY: •••]
Michigan Theater, Ann Arbor, MI
I: Runaway Jim, It's Ice, Uncle Pen, Stash, Lizards, Chalkdust, Guelah, Sparkle, My Friend, Memories, Bowie
II: Dinner and a Movie, Mike's > Hydrogen > Weekapaug, Esther, Axilla, Bouncing, Paul and Silas > BBJ, Squirming Coil, Faht, Possum
E: Contact, GTBT
"Swing Low Sweet Chariot" jam in Bowie intro and "Moby Dick" jam in Bowie closing jam. Bowie sung as "Dana Berie" in tribute to a Greenpeace staff member.

12/12/92 [ACCESSIBILITY: •]
The Spectrum, Toronto, ON
I: Llama, Foam, Sparkle, Cavern, Reba, Landlady, Melt, Poor Heart, All Things, Bouncing, Antelope
II: Maze, Glide, Curtain > Tweezer, Rift, Guelah, YEM, HYHU > Brain > HYHU, Squirming Coil, Golgi **E:** Ride Captain Ride, Tweezer Reprise
"Davy Crockett" theme jams throughout second set; the theme is sung in the YEM vocal jam. Fishman on vacuum for Brain. Last Ride Captain Ride, 5/28/89 Hebron, NY [395 shows].

➢ One of the shows from '92 that does it for me is this one—a fairly standard setlist enhanced by wild playing. The first set is real solid from the get-go: Llama, Foam, Sparkle and Cavern sound pretty standard on paper, but I think the playing makes this set. The middle jam in Reba is sweet; Landlady and Melt make a nice pair; and Antelope is a good first-set closer. Maze starts off the second set—real nice, good and raw. Tweezer is crazy as always, then YEM stands up to the test. Then there's the break-out Ride Captain Ride encore! —PHIL VALLE

12/13/92 [ACCESSIBILITY: •]
Le Spectrum, Montreal, QC
I: Buried Alive > Wilson, Divided Sky, It's Ice, Fee, Uncle Pen, Stash, Rift, FEFY, I Didn't Know, Bowie
II: Suzie, Mound, Bouncing, Llama, Fluffhead, Chalkdust, TMWSIY > Avenu > TMWSIY, MSO > BBJ, HYHU > Cracklin' Rosie > HYHU, Harry Hood, Cavern **E:** Adeline, Rocky Top
Fishman on vacuum for I Didn't Know.

1992 New Year's Run

12/28/92 [ACCESSIBILITY: ••]
Palace Theater, New Haven, CT
I: Maze, Sparkle, Foam, Glide, It's Ice, Bouncing, Rift, Golgi, Adeline, Antelope
II: Poor Heart, Melt, Reba, Sloth, YEM, Lizards, HYHU > Bike > HYHU, Harry Hood, Cavern **E:** Memories, Fire
"Buried Alive" jam before Glide during which Trey introduces some of his relatives in the audience. Fishman on vacuum for Bike.

12/29/92 [ACCESSIBILITY: •••]
Palace Theater, New Haven, CT
I: Funky Bitch, Runaway Jim, Guelah, Llama, My Friend, Divided Sky, Wilson, Uncle Pen, Stash, Tela, Oh Kee > Suzie
II: Curtain, Tweezer, Horse > Silent, MSO > BBJ, FEFY, All Things, Mike's > Hydrogen > Weekapaug, HYHU > Terrapin > HYHU, Blue Bayou, The Squirming Coil, Tweezer Reprise **E:** Carolina, Rocky Top
"On Broadway" jam in Mike's and "Maria" jam in Weekapaug. Fishman on trombone for Terrapin, and unamplified Blue Bayou.

➢ The best show of the '92 New Year's Run, this show had a little of everything and a lot of jamming. The show rocks from the start with Funky Bitch; other great jams are heard in Mike's Song (with an "On Broadway" bit), Weekapaug (machine-gun Trey!) and of course Tweezer (probably my favorite version of the year). When Fishman comes forward for Terrapin, he tells the crowd, "I'm going to attempt a love solo on my trombone," drawing huge cheers. Trey chimes in, saying, "We will attempt now to do the slowest version of this song ever performed on the face of the Earth." They sure do! —AL HUNT

12/30/92 [ACCESSIBILITY: •••]
Symphony Hall, Springfield, MA
I: Landlady, Sparkle, Melt, Esther, Chalkdust, Fluffhead, Paul and Silas, Reba > I Walk the Line > Reba, I Didn't Know, Bowie > Timber Ho > Bowie
II: Axilla, Rift, Bathtub Gin, YEM, TMWSIY > Avenu > TMWSIY, Possum, BBJ > HYHU > Love You > HYHU, A-Train, Llama
E: Ride Captain Ride, Adeline
Fishman on trombone for I Didn't Know and vacuum for Love You. "Auld Lang Syne" tease in YEM. Last Timber Ho, 6/16/90 [275 shows].

➢ Get this show for the rarities—one of only two Ride Captain Ride performances in the 1990s and the only Timber Ho until Sugarbush '95 brought the song back into rotation. In Springfield, the band began the Bowie intro, then unexpectedly moved into the Timber Ho riff. In what turned out to be a totally unplanned move, they decided to play the whole song! This show also contains one of the funnier song dedications ever, a hilarious "cousins" send-off before TMWSIY. —ANDRE HOLTON

12/31/92 [ACCESSIBILITY: ••••]
Matthews Arena, Northeastern University, Boston, MA
I: Buried Alive > Poor Heart, Maze, Bouncing, Rift, Wilson, Divided Sky, Cavern, Foam, I Didn't Know, Antelope
II: Runaway Jim, It's Ice, Sparkle, Forbin's > Mockingbird, MSO > BBJ, Stash, Glide, GTBT
III: Mike's > New Year's Countdown > Auld Lang Syne > Weekapaug, Harpua > Kung > Harpua, Squirming Coil, Diamond Girl, Llama
E: Carolina, Fire
"Jeopardy" theme tease in Wilson. Fishman on vacuum for I Didn't Know. Brad Sands, dressed as the Mockingbird, flew over the stage during that song. Concert debut: Diamond Girl, with The Dude of Life on vocals. Last Kung, 11/2/89 Durham, NH [367 shows]. Show broadcast on WBCN-Boston on 1/1/93.

➢ Though this show sold out weeks in advance, a good deal of tickets got into the hands of scalpers, who from what I could tell managed to get little more than face value outside the arena. Inside, the crowd milled around the hockey rink and Phish opened up in strong fashion with a great Buried Alive and then an absolutely tripping Maze. The second set was more uneven—the band never really sounded 'on' until GTBT. But the energy resumed when Phish took the stage for the third set a little after 11:50 p.m. Leave it to Mike's Song to resuscitate a sagging show—the one that swung us into 1993 did the trick. The segue from Mike's into Auld Lang Syne into Weekapaug is amazing. —ALI TARIQ

➢ This show is a classic. This was my first live Phish tape, recorded off of WBCN's broadcast. Besides early show appearances of Rift and It's Ice, this show also has the best Squirming Coil I've ever heard—Page's solo is heavenly. The third set is definitely my favorite: Mike's > Auld Lang Syne > Weekapaug is awesome, as is Diamond Girl with the Dude. And there's a cool Kung and New Year's story in Harpua. —GREG MARCEAU

➢ As we entered the arena, we were given flyers with a special secret language for the night. The show was taped for broadcast on WBCN and we were to mess with the listeners' heads. Trey held up signs and we reacted by doing things like snapping our fingers, stomping our feet, yeahs, boos, random screams, crying out "Eggplant!" and doing a lip-flop. It was so much fun! —MELISSA MIXER

➢ The day after Phish's Matthews arena show, the *Boston Globe* reported on a small earthquake in Boston's North End on New Year's Eve. The article joked, "Was it an overly loud Phish concert at Matthews Arena?" Don't laugh—listen to Forbin's! —ED SMITH

1993 Spring *A 'GRAND' TOUR*

The 1993 spring tour saw one major change to the band's on-stage setup: Page's baby grand piano debuted at Portland, ME, and the band celebrated with the breakout of Loving Cup. From there, the tour wound south, then west, then to the Pacific, and finally back again—a pattern becoming familiar to Phish and the band's fans. But for the first time, the band swung through Florida, a state that would become a familiar stomping ground over the next several years. The band played outstanding shows in Colorado and Ohio and finished the tour with panache in the Northeast. A summer tour of the outdoor sheds lay ahead.

[1/28/93] Hard Rock Cafe, Boston, MA
Amazing Grace
Rift release party. Fishman donated his 1967 Electrolux vacuum to the Cafe.

[2/2/93] *Rift* released on Elektra.

2/3/93 [ACCESSIBILITY: ••]
Portland Expo, Portland, ME
I: Loving Cup, Rift, Fee, Llama, Wedge, Divided Sky, I Didn't Know, My Friend, Poor Heart, Guelah, Bowie
II: Runaway Jim, It's Ice, Tweezer, Horse > Silent, Sparkle, YEM, Lifeboy, HYHU > Terrapin > HYHU > BBJ, Possum
E: Amazing Grace, Tweezer Reprise
Fishman on trombone for I Didn't Know, a piece of cardboard for Terrapin and vacuum for BBJ. Trey on drums for BBJ. "My Girl" tease in YEM, which also featured the alternate lyrics "Water your team in a beehive, I'm a sent-you." Concert debuts: Loving Cup, Wedge, Lifeboy and Amazing Grace. Also the debut of Page's baby grand piano and Trey's use of an acoustic guitar for The Horse and the pre-lyric segment of My Friend (this continued for the rest of 1993).

➢ Newbies can debate the "YEM eternal question" because the old-school phans know. In old Phish newsletters, phans would write in asking the question "What are you saying in You Enjoy Myself?" and Mike would make up different answers. One of his responses, "Water your team in a beehive, I'm a sent you," was said very clearly during this YEM. I don't think that many people got the joke, but I thought it was pretty funny. Also, listen carefully while Fish is talking after Terrapin. The beach balls were sitting on the wings of the stage. Someone yelled out, "Give us the balls!" and Brad took the signal from Trey and right then threw them out to us! Everyone started freaking out, and Fish was running back and forth across the stage high-fiving the crowd. This is just an amazing show, one of the more underrated ever. —MIKE D'AMICO

2/4/93 [ACCESSIBILITY: •••]
Providence Performing Arts Center, Providence, RI
I: Axilla, Foam, Bouncing, Maze, FEFY, All Things, Stash, Lizards, Sample, Glide, Antelope
II: Chalkdust, Wedge, Mike's > TMWSIY > Avenu > TMWSIY > Weekapaug, Lawn Boy, Uncle Pen, BBJ, HYHU > Lengthwise > HYHU, Harry Hood, Cavern **E:** Amazing Grace, GTBT
Fishman on vacuum for Lengthwise, which was performed regular and then reggae-style. "Lengthwise" jam in Harry Hood. Concert debut: Sample.

➢ For a show that otherwise didn't let up from start to finish, this night offers one of the best-ever moments of comic relief. But in true Phish fashion, it was a moment that still made you want to boogie. Following a Big Ball Jam, Fishman appeared center stage and began crooning Lengthwise. Trey then whipped in with a reggae-ish drum beat, and Fishman gave it his best Jamaican-style bellow. As the beat sped up, it gained a sort of Elvis-ish sound. It wasn't just Lengthwise, it was "When you're gone, I sleep diagonally, in my... in my... in my bed. When you're there! When you're there! When you're there!" And the amazing thing was that it was fantastic musically—much better sounding than the similar version from 11/19/92. In fact, I once played the tape for a friend who didn't like Phish, and it was that performance that changed her mind. —ANDY BERNSTEIN

2/5/93 [ACCESSIBILITY: ••]
Roseland Ballroom, New York, NY
I: Llama, Guelah, Rift, Melt, Sparkle, PYITE, I Didn't Know, Poor Heart, Reba, Bowie
II: Curtain > Tweezer, Horse > Silent, Paul and Silas, It's Ice, YEM, HYHU > Love You > HYHU, Squirming Coil, Tweezer Reprise
E: Amazing Grace, Loving Cup
Fishman on a portrait of Otis Redding for I Didn't Know and vacuum for Love You. "Vibration of Life" before Bowie. "Funkytown" tease in Tweezer. Last PYITE, 11/9/89 Williamstown, MA [367 shows].

2/6/93 [ACCESSIBILITY: ••••]
Roseland Ballroom, New York, NY
I: Golgi, Foam, Wilson, My Friend, Maze, Horn, Divided Sky, Lawn Boy, Wedge, Bouncing, Antelope
II: Chalkdust, Mound, Stash, Adeline, All Things, Mike's > Hydrogen > Weekapaug, Lifeboy, Uncle Pen, BBJ, HYHU > Lengthwise > Buried Alive, Possum **E:** Fire
Fishman on vacuum for Lengthwise. John Popper on harmonica for Buried Alive, Possum and Fire. Noel Redding on bass for Fire, with Mike on organ.

1993

110 Total Show Dates
- **4** one-set shows
- **105** two-set shows
- **1** three-set show

PHAN PICKS 1993

SHOW	THE SKINNY
1) **02/20/93 Atlanta, GA**	Mike's > Everything > Groove
2) 12/30/93 Portland, ME	Incredible from start to finish.
3) 03/22/93 Sacramento, CA	First Gamehendge since '91.
4) 12/31/93 Worcester, MA	A Peach(es) of a show.
5) 08/20/93 Morrison, CO	Incredibly well-jammed show.
6) 08/07/93 Darien Center, NY	Wild second set.
7) 08/02/93 Tampa, FL	Breakouts in a tiny club.
8) 08/13/93 Indianapolis, IN	The famous Murat Gin.
9) 03/14/93 Gunnison, CO	First Halley's in the 1990s.
10) tie between 05/08/93 and 08/12/93	

MUSICAL RECAP: Still unwilling to fully abandon a setlist in progress, Phish nevertheless managed to stretch some songs past the 20-minute barrier in 1993. The band's improvising ability, aided by their "Hey!" exercizes, can clearly be heard in great jams like the 8/13 Bathtub Gin.
REPRESENTATIVE JAMS: Bathtub Gin, 8/13/93; Split Open and Melt, 4/21/93 and 8/20/93; Antelope 8/20/93; Mike's Groove, 5/8/93.
ORIGINAL SONG DEBUTS: Leprechaun (7/15/93), Lifeboy (2/3/93); Sample in a Jar (2/4/93); The Wedge (2/3/93);
COVER SONG DEBUTS: Also Sprach Zarathustra (7/16/93), Amazing Grace (2/3/93), Bats and Mice (8/25/93), Choo Choo Cha Boogie (3/3/93), Crossroads (5/8/93), Daniel (7/15/93), Fast Train (5/6/93), Freebird (a cappella, 7/15/93), Ginseng Sullivan (8/11/93), Great Gig in the Sky (3/14/93), It's My Life (3/3/93), Loving Cup (2/3/93), Luke-A-Roo (3/3/93), Nellie Cane (2/23/93), Pig in a Pen (2/21/93); Purple Rain (7/16/93), Tennessee Waltz (5/6/93), That's Alright Mama (5/6/93), Why You Been Gone So Long (5/6/93), Yerushalayim Schel Zahav (7/16/93)

DARK HORSES

SHOW	THE SKINNY
1) **08/06/93 Cincinatti, OH**	See the city, see the zoo.
2) 08/09/93 Toronto, ON	Very well-played show.
3) 02/19/93 Atlanta, GA	Moby Dick Bowie for Fish.
4) 08/14/93 Tinley Park, IL	Incredible Antelope.
5) 03/31/93 Portland, OR	Best of the West Coast run?

Most-Played Originals:

1) Rift	68	62%
2) Big Ball Jam	64	58%
3) Sparkle	58	53%
4) Poor Heart	57	52%
5) Stash	56	51%
6) Bouncing	55	50%
6) It's Ice	55	50%
8) Maze	54	49%
9) You Enjoy Myself	53	48%
10) Chalk Dust Torture	52	47%

Most-Played Covers:

1) Amazing Grace	54	49%
2) Uncle Pen	33	30%
3) Sweet Adeline	25	23%
4) Paul and Silas	21	19%
5) Rocky Top	20	18%
6) Also Sprach	19	17%
6) GTBT	19	17%
8) Love You	17	15%
8) Ya Mar	17	15%
10) Nellie, PRain, L'wise	15	14%

First-Set Openers:

1) Buried Alive	16
2) Chalk Dust Torture	13
2) Llama	12
2) Runaway Jim	10
2) Golgi Apparatus	7

Second-Set Openers:

1) Also Sprach Zarathustra	19
2) Runaway Jim	8
2) Wilson	6
4) Chalk Dust Torture, Llama, Rift	5

Top Henrietta Songs:

1) Love You	17
2) Purple Rain	15
2) Lengthwise	15
4) Terrapin	11
5) Great Gig in the Sky	9

A Cappella Songs:

1) Amazing Grace	54
2) Sweet Adeline	25
3) Freebird	14
4) Carolina	9
5) Memories	6

➢ I remember this night because it was so cold outside. My friend got mugged trying to sell an extra—scalpers suck, especially in NYC. Once inside, everything went real smooth. Mike sang his song in a very weird fashion, yelling and telling us how it was his song. The highlight was John Popper being wheeled out on stage for Buried Alive and Possum. It was the first appearance by him after his motorcycle wreck and he didn't disappoint, even standing up at one point. —JOSHUA HOWLEY

➢ One of the funniest Lengthwises features Fishman commenting on all the lighters being held up by people in the crowd: "When you're there/I'm burning my fingers/because I'm holding this lighter/on way too long." —MICK CONNOR

2/7/93 [ACCESSIBILITY: ••]
Lisner Auditorium, George Washington University, Washington, DC
I: Suzie, Buried Alive > Poor Heart, It's Ice, Sparkle, Forbin's > Mockingbird, Rift, I Didn't Know, Split Open And Melt, Fee, Runaway Jim
II: Llama, FEFY, My Mind's, Reba, Tweezer > BBJ, Glide, YEM, Squirming Coil, HYHU > Brain > HYHU, Tweezer Reprise
E: Amazing Grace, Contact, BBFCM
Fishman on trombone for I Didn't Know and vacuum for Brain. "Oh My Darling Clementine" sung in YEM vocal jam. Last My Mind's, 5/6/92 Detroit, MI [83 shows].

Thursday, February 4, 1993 — PPAC, Providence, RI

Over seventy shows later and counting, I'm still not sure if I've ever seen one as spectacular as my first. Certainly I haven't had a show affect me as much as the one put on by four then-strangers at the Providence Performing Arts Center in February '93.

Your first time is supposed to be messy, a little uncomfortable, and you're not supposed to know what you're doing. Perhaps the latter applies. I did ask some dude who the opening act was, but the rest of the night was a smooth deliverance into audial heaven. Phish had me, owned me, right away.

I'll admit that I sometimes get a little bored at concerts. It's rare that I walk out of a place sure that I got my thirty bucks worth, and I'm usually fairly certain that I didn't have quite as good a time as everyone else. Not so, that night. The first time you hear Bouncing Around The Room, Maze, or Lizards, it's fucking candy. Sure, I'd outgrow those tunes—and then rediscover them—but in all my virginal naivete, I could not escape the frank realization that I was experiencing the best music I'd ever heard.

Then came a second set that I'll still pit against any other ever played. The Wedge—which I wouldn't hear again until 58 shows later—then Mike's Groove, with strobe in a fully darkened concert hall. "That's the trippiest thing I ever done seen," I turned to friends as mesmerized as I. Then in Weekapaug, there was some crazy sound, some shriek that was jabbing at me from the side. It was Mike, screaming. Just screaming. And it made perfect sense, musically and environmentally. I understood. There was this band, having more fun on stage than any I'd ever seen, and even cacophonous screams were perfectly placed.

Then came a moment of history. The thrice-performed reggae Lengthwise. Imagine my reaction when I see the guitarist start banging out the drums and the little drummer boy, whom I'd barely noticed, parade about in a dress and sing some insane chant with a reggae beat.

I was owned.

Harry, then Cavern. Toto, I don't think we're in Kansas anymore.

If there's one thing that stood out as much as the captivation of the music, it was the humor and attitude that surrounded the show. Therefore, it made no sense to me, and still doesn't, when people got really pissed off when a few others wouldn't quiet down during the mic-less a cappella tune.

"Shut the fuck up!" someone screamed. And it just made no sense to me. Yeah, I wanted to hear the band too, but nothing that night was worth getting upset over. How could there be anger when it seemed so clear that the dominant emotion was amusement? Well, I guess my friend was thinking the same thing I was because when everything finally quieted down, and there was dead silence, he let out this bellowing snort that filled the entire theater. It was the hardest I ever laughed at a show, and I've seen some really funny things at Phish concerts.

Now I know that the overwhelming majority of diehards hate people who make noise during the a cappella, and a good number do get angry. Still, after seventy-plus shows, I side with the snort.

Phish means as much to me as anyone I know. But it's never been more than a laugh. It can't be. **—David Porter**

2/9/93 [ACCESSIBILITY: ••]
Auditorium Theater, Rochester, NY
I: Bowie, Bouncing, Poor Heart, My Friend, Rift, Wedge, Chalkdust, Esther > Maze, Golgi
II: PYITE > Mike's > Hydrogen > Weekapaug > Weigh, MSO, Sample, BBJ, Stash > Lizards, HYHU > Bike > HYHU, Amazing Grace
E: Cavern, Rocky Top
Fishman on vacuum for Bike.

2/10/93 [ACCESSIBILITY: ••]
Smith Opera House, Geneva, NY
I: Loving Cup, Foam, Guelah, Reba, Sloth, Divided Sky, Tela, Llama, I Didn't Know, Catapult, Antelope
II: Runaway Jim, It's Ice, Squirming Coil, Tweezer, I Walk the Line, Sparkle, YEM, Horse > Silent, HYHU > Cracklin' Rosie > HYHU, Possum
E: Adeline, Amazing Grace, Tweezer Reprise

2/11/93 [ACCESSIBILITY: ••]
Haas Center for The Arts, Bloomsburg, PA
I: Suzie, Buried Alive > Poor Heart, Stash, Fee, Rift, Fluffhead > Llama, Lawn Boy, Bowie
II: Landlady, Wilson > Uncle Pen, Mike's > Hydrogen > Weekapaug, Mound, BBJ, Bouncing, HYHU > Love You > HYHU, Lizards, Cavern
E: Bold as Love, Amazing Grace
Fishman on vacuum for Love You.

2/12/93 [ACCESSIBILITY: •••]
Mid-Hudson Civic Center, Poughkeepsie, NY
I: Golgi, Maze, Guelah, Sparkle, Melt, Esther, Wedge, Chalkdust, I Didn't Know, A-Train, Antelope
II: My Friend, All Things, Reba, Poor Heart, BBJ, FEFY, YEM, Ya Mar, HYHU > Terrapin > HYHU, Harry Hood, Harpua **E:** Amazing Grace, GTBT
Fishman on plastic for I Didn't Know and vacuum for Terrapin. "Black or White" jam in Harpua.

➢ Very, very snowy night, with not many out-of-towners there. Fish played lots of strange instruments like a placard of plexiglass and a washboard suite. The Harpua was really involved, and the Chalkdust Torture was hot. Just a big room, no chairs, with lots of freaks and Phish. That's how I like it. —EMILY BROWN

2/13/93 [ACCESSIBILITY: ••]
Bob Carpenter Center, Newark, DE
I: Bowie, Bouncing, Poor Heart, It's Ice, Glide, Rift, Stash, Lawn Boy, Maze, Golgi
II: Runaway Jim, Wilson, Uncle Pen, Tweezer, Lizards, Llama, YEM, BBJ, HYHU > Lengthwise, Squirming Coil, Cavern
E: Amazing Grace, Tweezer Reprise
Fishman on vacuum for Lengthwise. "Wimoweh" theme in YEM vocal jam.

2/15/93 [ACCESSIBILITY: ••]
Memorial Hall, University of North Carolina, Chapel Hill, NC
I: Amazing Grace, Suzie, Sparkle, Guelah, Divided Sky, Esther, Chalkdust, Mound, Stash, Guelah, I Didn't Know, Antelope
II: Rift, FEFY, Reba, Mike's > Hydrogen > Weekapaug, Wedge, Poor Heart > BBJ > HYHU > Bike > HYHU, Fee > Llama **E:** Contact > Fire
Fishman on trombone for I Didn't Know and vacuum for Bike.

2/17/93 [ACCESSIBILITY: ••]
Benton Convention Center, Winston-Salem, NC
I: Buried Alive > Possum, Weigh, All Things, Sloth, Runaway Jim, It's Ice, Bouncing, Fluffhead, Maze, Golgi
II: Axilla, Landlady, Bowie, Glide, My Friend, MSO > BBJ, Horn, YEM, HYHU > Lengthwise > HYHU, Squirming Coil **E:** Carolina, GTBT
Fishman on vacuum for Lengthwise, which was performed reggae-style.

2/18/93 [ACCESSIBILITY: ••]
Electric Ballroom, Knoxville, TN
I: Chalkdust, Guelah, Poor Heart, Tweezer > Foam, Sparkle, Cavern, Reba, Lawn Boy, Antelope
II: Rift, Stash, Lizards, PYITE, Mike's > Hydrogen > Weekapaug, Mound, Amazing Grace, Memories, Adeline, Rocky Top
Soundboard shorted out during Mound; rest of set played a cappella and, for Rocky Top, through monitors with Mike and Trey electric, Page acoustic, and Fish on trombone. No encore. "Another One Bites the Dust" jam in Weekapaug.

➢ During Mound, you could hear the sound system start to fry, so Phish decided to go a cappella, plus a Rocky Top finale played through the monitors. Wild! —JOS CONTI

2/19/93 [ACCESSIBILITY: ••••]
Roxy Theater, Atlanta, GA
I: Loving Cup, Rift, Melt, Fee > Maze, Forbin's > Mockingbird, Sparkle, My Friend, Poor Heart, Bowie
II: Runaway Jim, It's Ice, Paul and Silas, YEM, Ya Mar, BBJ, Lawn Boy, Funky Bitch, MSO, HYHU > Love You > HYHU, Llama, Amazing Grace
E: AC/DC Bag

"Moby Dick" jams during Bowie intro and outro. Bowie intro also featured Fish on vacuum and a "Happy Birthday" jam for Fish. Flavor-Flav clock presented to Fishman. Jimmy Herring on guitar for Lawn Boy, Funky Bitch, MSO, Love You and Llama. Last AC/DC Bag, 5/16/92 Boston, MA [84 shows].

➢ Fishman's birthday and the famous "Moby Dick" Bowie, which includes a Moby Dick jam in the intro and then again during the final coda. It's amazing! Jimmy Herring rocks the house in the second set. Perhaps because it falls under the shadow of the next night, this show tends to be overlooked by a lot of phans. I think it's one of the band's better shows of 1993. —TRICIA HOLMES

2/20/93 [ACCESSIBILITY: •••••]
Roxy Theater, Atlanta, GA
I: Golgi, Foam, Sloth, Possum, Weigh, All Things, Divided Sky, Horse > Silent, Fluffhead, Cavern
II: Wilson, Reba, Tweezer > Walk Away > Tweezer > Glide > Mike's > My Mind's > Mike's > Kung > Hydrogen > Weekapaug > Have Mercy > Rock and Roll All Night Jam > Weekapaug > FEFY, BBJ, HYHU > Terrapin > HYHU, Harry Hood, Tweezer Reprise **E:** Sleeping Monkey

"Iron Man" tease in Wilson. "Iron Man" and "Woody Woodpecker" teases in Reba. "Tweezer" teases in Glide and Mike's. "Tease medley" in Mike's includes teases of "Wilson," "Reba," "Tweezer," "Lizards," "Wilson" and "Stash." "Vibration of Life" before Kung, including "Nitrous" lyrics from Mike. Fishman on vacuum for Terrapin. Last Walk Away, 11/2/91 Fort Collins, CO [158 shows].

➢ I'm not sure what was going on in Gamehendge this night, but something sure was crazy. The Wilson to start set II is weird—really, the whole show has a strange feel. Inside certain songs they reference other Phish songs. At one point, Glide segues into Mike's Song. Instead of the normal Mike's, it has a Tweezer bass line. The Mike's jam includes Fluffhead, Tweezer, Lizards, Stash, My Mind, Have Mercy, and Kung, plus H2 > Weekapaug, in which Fishman introduces Gene Simmons and they play "Rock and Roll All Night" by Kiss! —JEFFREY ELLENBOGEN

➢ They weren't screwing around in the second set. After a heavy Wilson and an awe-inspiring Reba, they broke into one of THOSE Tweezers that last a whole set. Except it wasn't just Tweezer. After seguing into Walk Away and an amazing Glide, the first notes of Mike's Song were heard. This version had jams of Reba, Lizards and My Mind's until they went into a Vibration of Life/Kung/H2/Weekapaug/Have Mercy/Rock and Roll All Night/Weekapaug! As if that weren't enough, they then busted into one of the best Hoods in my collection. Amazing set! —SETH WEINGLASS

➢ I know, I know, but I had to mention this show. Not the usual praise of Mike's Groove, though, but praise for the unbelievable Tweezer. Right after the opening lyrics, Trey and Mike go on mumbling about something "coming straight from the sewer" and something about a freezer. The effect is awesome. I could listen to this Tweezer 100 times in a row and still love every minute of it! —MIKE JETT

2/21/93 [ACCESSIBILITY: ••]
Roxy Theater, Atlanta, GA
I: Suzie, Buried Alive, PYITE, Uncle Pen, Horn, Chalkdust, Esther, Dinner and a Movie, Bouncing, Antelope
II: Axilla, Curtain > Stash > Manteca > Stash > Lizards, Bathtub Gin, HYHU > Cracklin' Rosie > HYHU, Squirming Coil, BBFCM
E: Adeline, GTBT > Paul and Silas > Pig in a Pen

Encores following Adeline featured the Reverend Jeff Mosier on banjo. A cappella intro to Suzie. GTBT performed bluegrass style. Concert debut: Pig in a Pen.

2/22/93 [ACCESSIBILITY: ••]
The Moon, Tallahassee, FL
I: Rift, Guelah > "Language Lesson" > Guelah, Poor Heart, Maze, Fee, Sparkle, Foam, Cavern, I Didn't Know, Bowie
II: Runaway Jim, It's Ice, Uncle Pen, Tweezer, Glide, YEM, Oh Kee > Llama, HYHU > Love You > HYHU, Squirming Coil, Tweezer Reprise
E: Amazing Grace, Fire

Fishman on trombone for I Didn't Know and vacuum for Love You.

2/23/93 [ACCESSIBILITY: ••]
The Edge, Orlando, FL
I: Golgi, My Friend, Rift, Bouncing, Melt, Reba, Lawn Boy, Chalkdust, Wedge, Paul and Silas, Antelope
II: Axilla, MSO, Stash > Lizards, PYITE, All Things, Mike's > Hydrogen > Weekapaug > Nellie Cane > Weekapaug, HYHU > Terrapin > HYHU, Possum **E:** Adeline, Poor Heart

Fishman on vacuum for Terrapin. Concert debut: Nellie Cane.

2/25/93 [ACCESSIBILITY: ••]
Cameo Theater, Miami Beach, FL
I: Buried Alive > Poor Heart, Cavern, Maze, Forbin's > Mockingbird, Rift, Stash, Bouncing, I Didn't Know, Bowie
II: Suzie, It's Ice, Sparkle, Wilson, YEM, Uncle Pen, BBJ, FEFY, HYHU > Brain > HYHU, Golgi, BBFCM **E:** Amazing Grace, GTBT

Fishman on trombone for I Didn't Know and vacuum for Brain. Mimi Fishman on vacuum for Brain.

➢ First off, Len and Mimi Fishman were grooving right above their son for the whole show. We were also delighted to have a bit of Mimi's vacuum-playing ability displayed during If I Only Had A Brain. And how about a little Jeopardy theme song during the Bowie? The Big Ball Jam and BBFCM were highlights for me. —TONY HUME

2/26/93 [ACCESSIBILITY: ••]
Ritz Theater, Ybor City (Tampa), FL
I: Runaway Jim, Foam, Fee, Melt, Fluffhead, Llama, Horn, Divided Sky, I Didn't Know, Cavern
II: Loving Cup, Paul and Silas, Tweezer, Glide, Chalkdust, Mound, BBJ, YEM, HYHU > Lengthwise > HYHU, Squirming Coil, Tweezer Reprise
E: Bold as Love, Adeline

Fishman on vacuum for Lengthwise.

Roxy n' Roll

2/20/93 The Roxy, Atlanta, GA

When Phish visited Atlanta in the spring of 1992, their performance seemed a little soggy. That wasn't the band's fault, though—a broken water main in the venue had slowly covered the floor of the venue with water, and by the time Phish was due to come back out for their second set, the fear of electrocution loomed large. Hating to cut a gig short—what musician doesn't?—the band sang a few a cappella numbers and then did their best to apologize to the crowd. Trey in particular went out of his way to promise the crowd that the next time they played in Atlanta, they'd make sure everyone had a special time.

For some bands, such a promise might just be idle talk, a way of getting out of an awkward situation without pissing off the fans or inciting a riot. Phish, of course, wouldn't insult their fans' memories by not living up to their promise... would they?

The answer to that question came into focus on February 19, when they kicked off their first same-venue three-night stand in ages Atlanta's intimate Roxy Theater. During the narration portion of Col. Forbin's Ascent, Trey spun a tale of the concert-goers being swept away by a flood, and invoked a chant: "We will make it up to you, we will make it up to you..." True to their word, Phish hadn't forgotten.

Now, the show on the 19th was, by almost all accounts, a hell of a good time—Fishman celebrated his birthday with a David Bowie that could have just as easily been labeled on a setlist as Moby Dick > Bowie > Dick > Bowie. So as the crowds headed back to the Roxy on Saturday night, most people no longer felt that Phish owed them anything except maybe your average great Phish show. The band had other ideas.

The first set was strong, packed with crowd-favorites including Possum and Fluffhead. But there was little hint of the madness that was to follow in the second set.

Some fans in attendance that night say they sensed musical tension between Trey and Mike (leading to Fishman's comment during Terrapin, "We're a mellow band.") But if Phish's music thrives on tension and release, then perhaps a momentary spat between the bandmates was just what the doctor ordered.

When the band dropped from there into Tweezer, things start getting nutty. "How's everyone feeling out there?" Trey yells in the midst of the jam, which eventually segues into Walk Away. The departure from Tweezer is only in name, though, as Trey sticks with the Tweezer riff even in Glide and then as Mike's Song opens. Then comes the part that makes this tape so desirable—the Mike's > Everything > Groove that includes teases of numerous Phish songs, a Vibration of Life, and Kung. Then in Weekapaug, there's Have Mercy and an appearance by a phan from the audience dressed as a member of Kiss for a brief jam on Kiss' "Rock and Roll All Night." This show really has it all.

3/27/93 [ACCESSIBILITY: ••]
Florida Theater, Gainesville, FL
I: Golgi, Rift, Guelah, Maze, Bouncing Around The Room, It's Ice, Sparkle, PYITE, Lawn Boy, Antelope
II: Curtain > Stash, Poor Heart, Sample, BBJ, Ya Mar, Mike's > Hydrogen > Weekapaug, HYHU > Terrapin > HYHU, Fee, Llama
E: Sleeping Monkey, Amazing Grace, Rocky Top
Fishman on vacuum for Terrapin.

3/2/93 [ACCESSIBILITY: ••]
Tipitina's, New Orleans, LA
I: Buried Alive > Poor Heart, Stash, Reba, Sparkle, It's Ice, Fee, All Things, Chalkdust, Horse > Silent, I Didn't Know, Bowie
II: My Friend, Uncle Pen, Tweezer, Lizards, Llama, YEM, HYHU > Love You > HYHU, It's My Life, Luke-A-Roo, Choo Choo Cha Boogie, Harry Hood, Amazing Grace **E:** Golgi, Tweezer Reprise
Fishman on Madonna washboard for I Didn't Know and vacuum for Love You. Bruce "Sunpie" Barnes on washboard, harmonica and vocals for It's My Life, Luke-A-Roo and Choo Choo Cha Boogie. Concert debut: It's My Life, Luke-A-Roo and Choo Choo Cha Boogie.

3/3/93 [ACCESSIBILITY: ••]
Tipitina's, New Orleans, LA
I: Rift, Foam, Bouncing, Maze, Guelah, Paul and Silas, Sample, Runaway Jim, Lawn Boy, Cavern
II: Axilla, Curtain > Melt, Mound, Mike's > Hydrogen > Weekapaug, Glide, MSO, FEFY, HYHU > Terrapin > HYHU, Squirming Coil, Adeline **E:** Fire
Carl Gerhard on trumpet for Lawn Boy and Cavern. Fishman on vacuum for Terrapin.

3/5/93 [ACCESSIBILITY: ••]
Deep Ellum Lodge, Dallas, TX
I: Buried Alive > Poor Heart, Cavern, Foam, Sloth, Rift, Stash, Sparkle, It's Ice, I Didn't Know, Possum
II: Landlady > Chalkdust, Guelah, Uncle Pen, Mike's > Hydrogen > Weekapaug, Jesus Left Chicago, MSO > BBJ, HYHU > Love You > HYHU, Squirming Coil, Amazing Grace **E:** GTBT
Fishman on vacuum for Love You.

3/6/93 [ACCESSIBILITY: ••]
Liberty Lunch, Austin, TX
I: Llama, Horn, Curtain > Melt, Mound, PYITE, Bouncing, Maze, Golgi, Runaway Jim
II: Rift, Tweezer, Reba, Paul and Silas, BBJ, FEFY, YEM, HYHU > Cracklin' Rosie > HYHU, BBFCM **E:** Adeline, Poor Heart, Tweezer Reprise

3/8/93 [ACCESSIBILITY: •]
Sweeney Center, Santa Fe, NM
I: Golgi, Rift, Guelah, Oh Kee > Llama, Forbin's > How High the Moon > Mockingbird, Sparkle, It's Ice, Glide, Bowie
II: Poor Heart, Cavern, Uncle Pen, Stash, BBJ, My Friend > Kung > YEM, Lizards, Amazing Grace
E: HYHU > Terrapin > HYHU, Chalkdust
Last How High the Moon, 4/26/90 Oberlin, OH [329 shows].

3/9/93 [ACCESSIBILITY: ••]
Pike's Peak Center, Colorado Springs, CO
I: Runaway Jim, Foam, Bouncing, Maze, Esther, Divided Sky, Glide, PYITE, I Didn't Know, Antelope
II: Axilla, Rift, Tweezer, Reba, Lawn Boy, Mike's > Hydrogen > Weekapaug, Horse > Silent, BBJ, HYHU > Love You > HYHU, I Walk the Line, Squirming Coil, Tweezer Reprise **E:** Amazing Grace, Rocky Top
Fishman on trombone for I Didn't Know and vacuum for Love You. Before Amazing Grace, an audience member in the balcony sung an a cappella version of "The Eleven."

3/12/93 [ACCESSIBILITY: •]
Daubson Arena, Vail, CO
I: Buried Alive > Poor Heart, Cavern, Possum, Guelah, Rift, Stash, Fluffhead, Horse > Silent, Bowie
II: AC/DC Bag, My Friend, Axilla, Sparkle, YEM, Mound, BBJ, Chalkdust, HYHU > Lengthwise > HYHU, Harry Hood, Golgi
E: Adeline, Carolina, Rocky Top
Fishman on vacuum for Lengthwise.

3/13/93 [ACCESSIBILITY: ••]
Field House, University Of Colorado, Boulder, CO
I: Landlady, Funky Bitch, Bouncing, Maze, Fee, All Things, Melt, Contact, Llama, Wilson, Antelope
II: Suzie, Tweezer, Lizards, It's Ice, Glide, Uncle Pen, BBJ, Mike's > Hydrogen > Weekapaug, FEFY, HYHU > Love You > HYHU, Tweezer Reprise **E:** MSO, Amazing Grace, BBFCM
Soundcheck: Dog Log, Halley's, Blues jam, Owner of a Lonely Heart. Fishman on vacuum for Love You.

3/14/93 [ACCESSIBILITY: ••••]
Western State College Gym, Gunnison, CO
I: Loving Cup, Foam, Guelah, Sparkle, Stash, Paul and Silas, Sample, Reba, PYITE, Runaway Jim
II: Halley's > Bowie, Curtis Loew, YEM, Lifeboy, Rift, BBJ > Great Gig > HYHU, Squirming Coil **E:** Memories, Adeline, Golgi
Soundcheck: Halley's, Curtis Loew, Tales of Brave Ulysses > Sunshine of Your Love, Lifeboy. "Indian War Dance" jam before Reba whistle jam played by eight-year-old Cameron McKenney on piano. In order, jams in YEM were "Owner of a Lonely Heart," (Trey on vocals) "Low Rider," "Spooky" (Page on vocals) and "Oye Como Va." YEM vocal jam included "We are the Champions" and "Welcome to the Machine" vocal jams. Fishman on vacuum for Great Gig. Concert debut: Great Gig. Last Halley's, 8/17/89 Burlington, VT [418 shows]. Last Curtis Loew, 10/30/90 Crested Butte, CO [296 shows].

➢ After a good first set, with an always-welcome Punch and Paul & Silas, it happened. "It" being the first Halley's Comet of the '90s. A great song finally revived. Then, Bowie or Possum? Bowie or Possum? Sounds like Possum, but no, a ripping, and I mean ripping, Bowie follows. Amazingly, it's outdone by a YEM with many pleasant teases and a great vocal jam—you can actually hear them laughing and cracking up as they chant the words. —RIC HANNAH

➢ Here's my pick for the best of 1993—the revival of Halley's Comet, plus Bowie, Big Ball Jam, the tease-filled YEM—what more could you ask from a Phish show? This is truly the band at its best and most playful, as the YEM vocal jam evolves spontaneously into the chorus of "We Will Rock You" and then "Welcome to the Machine." Magnificent. —JAMIS CURRAN

➢ This is one of those shows where everyone in attendance has their own highlight. Not impressed by a first set featuring a Loving Cup opener and a killer Runaway Jim closer? Okay, how about the first Halley's in the 1990s, a song Phish swore they would never play live way back in '89? Followed by a long Bowie? And that crazy YEM? —LINDA MAHDESIAN

3/16/93 [ACCESSIBILITY: ••]
Celebrity Theater, Phoenix, AZ
I: Adeline, Buried Alive > Poor Heart, It's Ice, Fee, Maze, I Didn't Know, Divided Sky, "Harry Jones' Song," McGrupp, Cavern
II: My Friend, Curtain > Tweezer > Bathtub Gin, Esther, Chalkdust, YEM, HYHU > Bike > Lengthwise > Bike > HYHU, Lawn Boy, Llama, Amazing Grace **E:** Sparkle > Tweezer Reprise
Trey's grandfather Harry Jones came on stage and played on a song between Divided Sky and McGrupp. "Sweet Emotion" jam in Tweezer. Fishman on vacuum for Bike and Lengthwise (one verse).

3/17/93 [ACCESSIBILITY: ••]
The Palace, Hollywood, CA
I: Landlady > Runaway Jim, Foam, Bouncing, Stash, Amazing Grace, Paul and Silas, It's Ice, Oh Kee > Suzie, Antelope
II: Axilla, Glide, Reba, Jesus Left Chicago, Mound, Mike's > Hydrogen > Weekapaug, Horse > Silent, HYHU > Great Gig > HYHU, Golgi
E: Adeline, Rocky Top
"Lively Up Yourself" jam in Weekapaug. Fishman on vacuum for Great Gig.

3/18/93 [ACCESSIBILITY: ••]
The Palace, Hollywood, CA
I: Chalkdust, Guelah, Rift, Fee > Maze, Forbin's > Mockingbird, Sparkle, Horn, I Didn't Know, Bowie
II: My Friend, Poor Heart, Melt, Tela, YEM, Uncle Pen, BBJ, HYHU > Brain > HYHU, Squirming Coil, Cavern **E:** GTBT
"Little Drummer Boy" jam in My Friend. Fishman on trombone for I Didn't Know and vacuum for Brain.

3/19/93 [ACCESSIBILITY: ••]
Greek Theater, University of Redlands, Redlands, CA
I: Suzie, Llama, Foam, Bouncing, Rift, Stash, Fluffhead, Cavern, Antelope
II: Runaway Jim, It's Ice, Uncle Pen, Sample, Lizards, Mike's > Hydrogen > Weekapaug > HYHU > Love You > HYHU, Golgi
E: Amazing Grace, Chalkdust
Soundcheck: Dog Log > Heartbreaker Jam, Misty Mountain Hop, Get it On Jam, Blues Jam. Fishman on vacuum for Love You.

3/21/93 [ACCESSIBILITY: •]
Ventura Theater, Ventura, CA
I: Maze, Sparkle, Sloth, Divided Sky, Esther, All Things, Melt, Poor Heart, PYITE, Lawn Boy, Possum
II: Loving Cup, My Friend > Rift, Tweezer > Ya Mar, Llama, YEM, MSO, BBJ, HYHU > Cracklin' Rosie > HYHU, Harry Hood, Cavern
E: Sleeping Monkey, Adeline, Tweezer

3/22/93 [ACCESSIBILITY: •••••]
Crest Theater, Sacramento, CA
I: Chalkdust, Guelah, Uncle Pen, Stash, Bouncing, Rift, Weigh, Reba, Sparkle, Bowie
II: Golgi, It's Ice > Lizards > Tela > Wilson > AC/DC Bag > Forbin's > Mockingbird > Sloth > McGrupp, Mike's > Hydrogen > Weekapaug
E: Amazing Grace, Fire

Second set featured a full Gamehendge narration, beginning in the middle of It's Ice and continuing through McGrupp—third-ever live Gamehendge. Last live Gamehendge, 10/13/91 Olympia, WA [192 shows]. Last complete live Gamehendge, 3/12/88 Burlington, VT [508 shows]. "Sundown" jam in Weekapaug.

Phan Pick #19 ➢ GAMEHENDGE—what a show! The best West Coast show I've heard, and definitely one of the top three of 1993. The band is mellow, tight and tasteful and full of what they know best. This show highlights everyone doing everything right. Jon has some mighty rises, Trey takes your head off, Mike is a groovin' machine and Page is a master of the keys. You all own it, so listen to it, cherish it—it's Phish, it's Gamehendge, and it's out of this world. —DAVID M. BROWN

➢ I love this tape; it's just too perfect. Do you think maybe it was pre-planned, sort of? Maybe they had the idea in the back of their heads and were wondering when to unleash it. Anyway, this is one of the best live Gamehendges around (that's my thought). Then after all this splendor, they gave us a Mike's Groove. Wow. —RON LAUER

3/24/93 [ACCESSIBILITY: ••]
Luther Burbank Center for The Performing Arts, Santa Rosa, CA
I: Llama, Foam, Fee, Poor Heart, Maze, I Didn't Know, Sample, Amazing Grace, Cavern
II: Landlady, Melt, Sparkle, Tweezer, Mound, BBJ, FEFY, YEM, Horse > Silent, HYHU > Terrapin > HYHU, GTBT **E:** Carolina, Squirming Coil
Fishman on trombone for I Didn't Know and vacuum for Terrapin. Before Terrapin, an audience member named Sam told The Prison Joke (see 4/11/91).

3/25/93 [ACCESSIBILITY: ••]
Santa Cruz Civic Auditorium, Santa Cruz, CA
I: Chalkdust, Guelah, It's Ice, Possum, Bouncing, Stash, Glide, Rift, Horn, Magilla, Antelope
II: Axilla > Curtain > Sample, Uncle Pen, Forbin's > Icculus > Kung > Mockingbird, Wedge, Mike's > Hydrogen > Weekapaug, Golgi
E: MSO, BBJ, Adeline
"Ob-La-Di Ob-La-Da" jam in Antelope intro and in Antelope jam; "Ob-La-Di" tease in Weekapaug. Last Icculus, 5/2/92 [119 shows]. Last Magilla, 5/8/92 [114 shows].

➢ Two nights after Gamehendge, and Icculus emerges! This show (along with 3/31) are the hidden gems of the '93 spring West Coast tour. The second set of this show has the last Wedge until '95; Trey quotes the Beatles, too, especially in Antelope! —AL HUNT

3/26/93 [ACCESSIBILITY: •••]
Warfield Theater, San Francisco, CA
I: Maze, Sparkle, Foam, Fee, PYITE, All Things, Melt, Fluffhead, Divided Sky, Cavern
II: Wilson, Runaway Jim, Mound, Tweezer, Horse > Silent, YEM, BBJ, Oh Kee > Suzie, HYHU > Great Gig > HYHU, Tweezer Reprise
E: Amazing Grace, Rocky Top
Fishman on vacuum for Great Gig.

3/27/93 [ACCESSIBILITY: •••]
Warfield Theater, San Francisco, CA
I: Llama, Guelah, Rift, Stash, Reba, My Friend, Uncle Pen, Sample, I Didn't Know, Bowie
II: Buried Alive > Halley's, It's Ice, Bouncing, Chalkdust, TMWSIY > Avenu > TMWSIY, Mike's > Hydrogen > Weekapaug, HYHU > Cracklin' Rosie > HYHU, Poor Heart, Golgi **E:** Squirming Coil, Carolina
"On Broadway" jam in Weekapaug. Opening line of "Suzie" sung a cappella before Carolina.

3/28/93 [ACCESSIBILITY: ••]
East Gym, Humboldt State University, Arcata, CA
I: Landlady, Funky Bitch, Sparkle, Melt, Lizards, Sloth, Maze, Fee, It's Ice, Lawn Boy, Antelope
II: Walk Away, Runaway Jim, Mound, Bathtub Gin, YEM, Paul and Silas, BBJ, HYHU > Love You > HYHU, Possum **E:** Contact, BBFCM
"The Pez Song" sung by Trey in YEM. Fishman on vacuum for Love You.

3/30/93 [ACCESSIBILITY: ••]
Hilton Ballroom, Eugene, OR
I: Buried Alive > Poor Heart, All Things, Golgi, My Friend, Llama, Esther, Stash, Glide, Divided Sky, Cavern
II: Loving Cup, Rift, Tweezer, Lifeboy > BBJ, Weigh, Mike's > Hydrogen > Weekapaug, Horse > Silent, HYHU > Brain > HYHU, Tweezer Reprise
E: MSO, Amazing Grace
Soundcheck: She's So Cold, Funky Bitch, Theme to Sesame Street. Fishman on vacuum for Brain. "Psycho Killer" jam in Weekapaug.

3/31/93 [ACCESSIBILITY: •••]
Roseland Theater, Portland, OR
I: Runaway Jim, Foam, Sparkle, Melt, Mound, PYITE, Sample, Reba, I Didn't Know, Bowie
II: Lengthwise > Maze, Bouncing, Uncle Pen, Harry Hood, BBJ, It's Ice, YEM, Harpua, Chalkdust **E:** AC/DC Bag, Adeline
Soundcheck: Mango, Gumbo, Satisfaction. Fishman on Madonna washboard for I Didn't Know and on vacuum for YEM vocal jam. "Axel F" and "She's So Cold" jams in Harpua.

[4/1/93]
Ancient Forests Benefit, Portland, OR
Amazing Grace, I Didn't Know
Outdoor show with numerous other performers. Phish performed with no instruments.

4/1/93 [ACCESSIBILITY: ••]
Roseland Theater, Portland, OR
I: Llama, Guelah, Rift, Stash, Squirming Coil, My Friend, Paul and Silas, Fluffhead, Lawn Boy, Antelope
II: Axilla, Curtain > Possum, Fee > Ya Mar, Tweezer, Poor Heart, BBJ, HYHU > Terrapin > HYHU, Cavern **E:** Carolina, Tweezer Reprise
"Heart of Gold" tease before Llama. "Heartbreaker" tease in Antelope. April Fool's Day joke before Terrapin—a folding chair and acoustic guitar were set up and Trey announced, "Ladies and gentlemen, Neil Young!" Several audience members gave Fishman a pie in the face before Terrapin; Fishman on vacuum for Terrapin.

4/2/93 [ACCESSIBILITY: ••]
Mt. Baker Theater, Bellingham, WA
I: Buried Alive > Poor Heart, Foam, Bouncing, Divided Sky, I Didn't Know, Sparkle, Maze, Golgi
II: Runaway Jim, Sample, Uncle Pen, Llama, Horse > Silent, Mike's > Hydrogen > Weekapaug, Lizards > BBJ, HYHU > Bike > HYHU, Chalkdust
E: Amazing Grace, Rocky Top

4/3/93 [ACCESSIBILITY: ••]
86th Street Music Hall, Vancouver, BC
I: Landlady > Rift, Guelah, Sparkle, Melt, Squirming Coil, My Friend, Reba, Horn, Antelope
II: Suzie, Stash, Mound, All Things, Sloth, YEM, Jesus Left Chicago, MSO, HYHU > Love You > HYHU, Cavern **E:** GTBT
Fishman on vacuum for Love You. "My Girl" theme in YEM vocal jam.

4/5/93 [ACCESSIBILITY: ••]
Hub Ballroom, Seattle, WA
I: Llama, It's Ice, Fee, Maze, Fluffhead, Paul and Silas, Stash, Forbin's > Mockingbird, Bowie
II: Axilla, Poor Heart, Caravan, PYITE, Tweezer, Glide, YEM, HYHU > Cracklin' Rosie > HYHU, Tweezer Reprise **E:** Carolina, Fire
Last Caravan, 9/25/91 Keene, NH [216 shows].

4/9/93 [ACCESSIBILITY: ••]
State Theater, Minneapolis, MN
I: Chalkdust, Sparkle, Guelah, Stash, Horse > Silent, Maze, I Didn't Know, It's Ice, Divided Sky, Cavern
II: Buried Alive > Suzie, All Things, Llama, Mound, My Friend, YEM, MSO, HYHU > Love You > HYHU, Possum **E:** Adeline, Golgi
"Cookiehead" theme in YEM vocal jam. Fishman on vacuum for Love You.

4/10/93 [ACCESSIBILITY: •••]
Aragon Ballroom, Chicago, IL
I: Runaway Jim, Weigh, Sparkle, Melt, Squirming Coil, My Friend, Uncle Pen, Chalkdust, Lawn Boy, Bowie
II: Lengthwise > Maze, Bouncing, Rift, Glide, BBJ, Mike's > Great Gig > Weekapaug, Funky Bitch, Help Me, Hoochie Coochie Man, Cavern
E: Amazing Grace, GTBT
"Tease medley" of songs played earlier in the set during Bowie intro. "Miss You" tease in Mike's. Sugar Blue on harmonica for Funky Bitch, Help Me, Hoochie Coochie Man and Cavern. Fishman on vacuum for Great Gig. Concert debuts: Help Me, Hoochie Coochie Man.

➢ The Aragon is a terrible place to see Phish—the place isn't acoustically well-developed. But with it being so echoey, Great Gig was totally amazing. The vacuum sounded just like the big woman on Dark Side Of The Moon. I remember the smoke machine being used a few times, which completely filled the room and made it kind of mystical. —ROB KOELLER

➢ My recording of this show is not the best (tapes of most shows at the Aragon, unless they are soundboard dubs, usually suck) but the song selection and special guest Sugar Blue more than makes up for it. Several blues tunes played with Sugar Blue and an exceptional Cavern towards the end shine, thanks to the blues tinge of Sugar Blue's harmonica. Luckily I got to see this show, so the sound was as good as can be for us, although I'd love to hear a soundboard recording. —DANIEL GILFOND

4/12/93 [ACCESSIBILITY: ••]
Student Union Ballroom, Iowa City, IA
I: Golgi, Tube, Bouncing, Poor Heart, Stash, Horse > Silent, Reba, Llama, Satin Doll, Antelope
II: Dinner and a Movie, Tweezer, Fee, Paul and Silas, It's Ice, BBJ, YEM, HYHU > Terrapin > HYHU, Tweezer Reprise
E: Amazing Grace, Highway to Hell **E2:** Rocky Top
Fishman on vacuum for Terrapin. "Gumbo" (including a verse sung by Trey) and "Honky Tonk Woman" jams in YEM. "New York New York" and "Swing Low Sweet Chariot" themes in YEM vocal jam. "Ina-Gadda-Da-Vida" theme in YEM vocal jam. Last Tube, 11/20/92 Albany, NY [73 shows]. Last Highway to Hell, 11/15/91 Charlottesville, VA [184 shows]. Last Satin Doll, 2/25/90 Baltimore, MD [378 shows].

4/13/93 [ACCESSIBILITY: ••]
Memorial Hall, Kansas City, KS
I: Suzie, Foam, Sparkle, Possum, Forbin's > Mockingbird, Chalkdust, Guelah > Caravan, Cavern
II: My Friend, Rift, Sloth, Uncle Pen, FEFY, BBJ, Mike's > Hydrogen > Weekapaug, HYHU > Brain > HYHU, Squirming Coil
E: Bold as Love, Adeline
Fishman on vacuum for Brain.

4/14/93 [ACCESSIBILITY: •••]
American Theater, St. Louis, MO
I: Buried Alive > Poor Heart, Maze, Bouncing, It's Ice, Stash > Kung > Stash > Kung > Horse > Silent, Divided Sky, I Didn't Know, Golgi
II: AC/DC Bag, MSO, Tweezer, Mound, BBJ, YEM > Harpua, Runaway Jim
E: Lengthwise, Contact, Tweezer Reprise
Fishman on Madonna washboard for I Didn't Know. At the beginning of the second set, Trey's childhood friend Roger gets on stage and asks his girlfriend to marry him. She accepts, the crowd cheers, and Phish plays AC/DC Bag ("just like Roger...") in tribute. "Spooky" jam (Page on vocals) in YEM. "The End" jam in Harpua.

➢ The first set of this show features an incredible version of Stash with Kung in the middle. At the end of Stash, Trey starts up the acoustic beginning of The Horse, they whisper the lyrics to Kung again, then head into Silent. Before the second set, Trey's boyhood pal Roger asks his girlfriend Jen to marry him and the crowd screams when she says yes. Phish plays AC/DC Bag for Roger (a.k.a. "Just like Roger, he's a crazy little kid."). During the encore, they play Contact for "Roger and Jen on the road of life."—MIKE NOLL

➢ This show offers an interesting "Dreampile" Harpua narration featuring the Jetsons and a spoof on the Doors' "And he walked on down the hall!" —JUSTIN WEISS

➢ During YEM, Trey yells the lyrics "BOY! MAN! GOD! SHIT!" with much more enunciation than usual. Jeopardy theme song during the vocal craziness following YEM. Then, a chunky Harpua with Trey telling us about his dreams and the dream bubbles we all have. Our dreams become bubbles and they float together into Gamehendge. Jimmy is apparently watching the Jetsons in this particular episode. —RUSSELL LANE

4/16/93 [ACCESSIBILITY: ••]
Macauley Theater, Louisville, KY
I: Chalkdust, Guelah, Sparkle, Melt, Esther, Llama, Sample, Rift, Harry Hood, Cavern
II: Axilla, Curtain > Maze, Lizards, Mike's > Hydrogen > Weekapaug, Horse > Silent, Uncle Pen > BBJ > HYHU > Bike > HYHU, Highway to Hell
E: Gumbo, Amazing Grace
Several hundred balloons were dropped from the balcony during Lizards. Fishman on vacuum for Bike. Last Gumbo, 7/25/91 Chapel Hill, NC [230 shows].

4/17/93 [ACCESSIBILITY: ••]
Michigan Theater, Ann Arbor, MI
I: Llama, Foam, Bouncing, Stash, It's Ice, Glide, My Friend, All Things, Golgi, Antelope
II: Wilson, Reba, Landlady, Halley's > YEM, Lifeboy, Oh Kee > Suzie, HYHU > Cracklin' Rosie > HYHU > BBJ, Squirming Coil
E: Adeline, BBFCM
"Ob-La-Di Ob-La-Da" jam in My Friend. "I Wish" jam in YEM. Fishman on vacuum and Trey on drums for BBJ. Extremely long silence in BBFCM while the band waited for Trey to start the song back up.

4/18/93 [ACCESSIBILITY: •••]
Michigan Theater, Ann Arbor, MI
I: Rift, Guelah, Melt, Sparkle, Divided Sky, Fee > Maze, Horn, I Didn't Know, Cavern
II: Poor Heart, Tweezer, Horse > Silent, Possum, Mound, BBJ, Mike's > Ya Mar, Walk Away, HYHU > Love You > HYHU, Tweezer Reprise
E: Amazing Grace, Rocky Top
During I Didn't Know, Page brought audience members on stage to give their opinions of the previous night's BBFCM encore and its long pause; Brad Sands, Paul, Chris, Mike and Trey also weighed in with their opinions. "Low Rider" jam between Mike's and Ya Mar. Fishman on vacuum for Love You.

➢ During the 4/17 BBFCM encore, Trey and Mike laid down on their backs at the front of the stage during one of the song's silent moments. Apparently, Trey forgot it was his turn to start the jam back up, so the band and the crowd sat there in silence for over five minutes. Finally, Mike got up and walked over to Trey to tell him it was his turn to play. This bizarre encore got special attention during their second show at Ann Arbor the next day. Page hosted a segment in the middle of I Didn't Know where audience members came up on stage and said what they were thinking during the long BBFCM silence. —TEDDY STUART

4/20/93 [ACCESSIBILITY: ••]
Newport Music Hall, Columbus, OH
I: Runaway Jim, Weigh, Sparkle, Stash, Bouncing, It's Ice, Glide, Uncle Pen, Lawn Boy, Bowie
II: Chalkdust, Fluffhead, Sample, BBJ, TMWSIY > Avenu > TMWSIY, My Friend, Llama, YEM, HYHU > Whipping Post > HYHU, Golgi
E: Funky Bitch, Amazing Grace

4/21/93 [ACCESSIBILITY: •••]
Newport Music Hall, Columbus, OH
I: Buried Alive > Poor Heart, Foam, Guelah, Maze, Forbin's > Mockingbird, Rift, PYITE, I Didn't Know, Antelope
II: Possum, Mound, Melt, Squirming Coil, Horse > Silent, BBJ, Mike's > Great Gig > Weekapaug > Gumbo **E:** Adeline, Cavern
Fishman on trombone for I Didn't Know. A portion of Melt is featured in Demand on Hoist.

➢ We made the short trip to Newport in a highly anxious state, having missed the prior evening's show. Little did we know the historic moment that lay ahead. Buried Alive started things off rather modestly, and an excellent Poor Heart followed. Then it drifted through some average songs until Col. Forbin/Mockingbird, which for me was the highlight of the first set. The second set was kick-ass, featuring the famed Split Open and Melt, which assuredly was one to remember! —BRIAN HART

➢ You probably own part of this show without knowing it—the jam from this Split Open and Melt is part of "Demand" on Hoist. On this night, after years of playing Melt, the band finally "got it right," taking the jam places it had never traveled before. When the song ended, they stood amazed on stage, like they did after the 12/29/94 Bowie. —ERNIE GREENE

4/22/93 [ACCESSIBILITY: ••]
Agora Theater, Cleveland, OH
I: Suzie, Sparkle, It's Ice, Reba, Chalkdust, Esther, Stash, Fee, Rift, Golgi
II: Llama, Bouncing, All Things, Tweezer, Lizards, BBJ, YEM, Uncle Pen, HYHU > Love You > HYHU, Tweezer Reprise
E: AC/DC Bag, Amazing Grace
"Vibration of Life" in YEM. Fishman on vacuum for Love You.

4/23/93 [ACCESSIBILITY: ••]
Reed Athletic Center, Colgate University, Clinton, NY
I: Runaway Jim, Weigh, Sparkle, Melt, Fluffhead > My Friend, Divided Sky, Guelah, Lawn Boy, Chalkdust
II: Golgi, Maze, Curtis Loew, It's Ice, Paul and Silas, BBJ, Mike's > Hydrogen > Weekapaug, Lengthwise, Squirming Coil, Highway to Hell **E:** Fire
Soundcheck: Horn, Funky Bitch, Buffalo Bill. Lengthwise featured Mimi Fishman on vacuum. House lights turned on before encore, and left on through Fire.

4/24/93 [ACCESSIBILITY: ••]
Cheel Arena, Clarkson University, Potsdam, NY
I: Chalkdust, Guelah, Poor Heart, Stash, Horse > Silent, Rift, Caravan, Something Is Wrong with My Baby, Sparkle, Antelope
II: Llama, Foam, Bathtub Gin, Dinner and a Movie, Mound, BBJ, YEM, HYHU > Bike > HYHU, Harry Hood, Cavern
E: Amazing Grace, GTBT
Soundcheck: Something Is Wrong with My Baby. Fishman on vacuum for Bike. Concert debut: Something Is Wrong with My Baby.

4/25/93 [ACCESSIBILITY: ••]
Kuhl Gym, SUNY Geneseo, Geneseo, NY
I: Landlady, Possum, Bouncing, It's Ice, Glide, Runaway Jim, Forbin's > Mockingbird, Maze, I Didn't Know, Golgi
II: Wilson, Curtain > Tweezer, Contact, Uncle Pen > BBJ, Mike's > Hydrogen > Weekapaug, Fee, Tweezer Reprise
E: Something Is Wrong with My Baby, Carolina, Rocky Top
Fishman on Madonna washboard for I Didn't Know.

4/27/93 [ACCESSIBILITY: ••]
Concert Hall, Toronto, ON
I: Buried Alive > Poor Heart, Foam, Bouncing, Rift, Stash, Guelah, It's Ice, Sparkle, Bowie
II: Golgi, My Friend, All Things, Maze, Lizards, BBJ, YEM, Horse > Silent, HYHU > Love You > HYHU, Cavern **E:** MSO, Amazing Grace
"Sundown" jam in YEM and in the YEM vocal jam. Fishman on vacuum for Love You.

4/29/93 [ACCESSIBILITY: •••]
Le Spectrum, Montreal, QC
I: Melt, Paul and Silas, Sloth, Runaway Jim, Horn, Llama, Glide, Rift, Fee, Oh Kee > Antelope
II: Chalkdust, It's Ice, Ya Mar, Mound, BBJ, Reba, Mike's > Hydrogen > Weekapaug > Makisupa > Weekapaug, HYHU > Terrapin > HYHU, Squirming Coil **E:** My Friend, Adeline
"I've Got Spurs" jam in H2. Fishman on vacuum for Terrapin. Last Makisupa, 11/26/90 Ithaca, NY [319 shows].

4/30/93 [ACCESSIBILITY: ••••]
Sports Center, University Of Hartford, West Hartford, CT
I: Lengthwise > Maze, Bouncing, Poor Heart, Stash, Horse > Silent, Divided Sky, Cavern, Lawn Boy, All Things, Possum
II: Wilson, Sparkle, Tweezer > Walk Away, Mound, BBJ, Harry Hood, HYHU > Brain > HYHU, YEM, Golgi
E: Something Is Wrong with My Baby, Amazing Grace, Tweezer Reprise
Fishman on vacuum for Brain.

5/1/93 [ACCESSIBILITY: ••••]
Tower Theater, Upper Darby, PA
I: Runaway Jim, Foam, Guelah, Melt, Fee, Rift, Sample, It's Ice, Glide, Bowie
II: Chalkdust, Fluffhead > My Friend, Squirming Coil, BBJ > Halley's > Paul and Silas, Mike's > Great Gig > Weekapaug, Cavern
E: Carolina, Rocky Top
Fishman on vacuum for Great Gig.

➢ My first full Phish show (I had seen them open for Santana in Philly 7/15/92). Originally I only had a ticket for the next night, but I drove my friend down for the show. While hanging outside, everybody had tickets to unload for $5, but I didn't have any money. Then some guy who was drunk or just zoning on something starts yelling, "Who wants this ticket?" while holding it up in the air. I said, "Are you serious?" He said yes and gave it to me. He was in a big hurry to go in and just wanted to get rid of it. I knew this was the start of something good. I remember a good Mike's Song > Great Gig and Fluffhead. —PHIL VALLE

➢ During most of 1993, Trey used an acoustic guitar for The Horse and the intro on My Friend, which often led to cool electric-into-acoustic-into-electric segues. At this Tower show, Trey brought his acoustic guitar forward near the end of Fluffhead and played the Fluffhead outro jam acoustic into My Friend. I remember thinking, this might be as close as I'll ever come to hearing Fluffhead acoustic-style like on *Junta*. These two Tower shows were both great; the tapes are worth owning. —JOS CONTI

5/2/93 [ACCESSIBILITY: ••]
Tower Theater, Upper Darby, PA
I: Axilla, Sparkle, Divided Sky, Mound, Stash, Horse > Silent, Poor Heart, Maze, I Didn't Know, Golgi
II: Llama > PYITE, YEM > Lizards > BBJ, Uncle Pen, Bouncing > Antelope, HYHU > Cracklin' Rosie > HYHU, BBFCM
E: Sleeping Monkey, Amazing Grace
Fishman on Madonna washboard for I Didn't Know and vacuum for Love You.

5/3/93 [ACCESSIBILITY: ••]
State Theater, New Brunswick, NJ
I: Buried Alive > Rift, Weigh, Chalkdust, Esther, Melt, Forbin's > Mockingbird, Possum, Lawn Boy, Cavern
II: AC/DC Bag > Curtain > Tweezer > Manteca > Tweezer > Contact, It's Ice, McGrupp, Runaway Jim > BBJ, HYHU > Love You > HYHU, MSO, Tweezer Reprise
E: Memories, Amazing Grace, Highway to Hell
"I Feel the Earth Move" jam in Tweezer. Fishman on vacuum for Love You.

5/5/93 [ACCESSIBILITY: ••••]
Palace Theater, Albany, NY
I: Rift, Guelah, Foam, Sparkle, Stash, Bouncing, It's Ice, Glide, Maze, Golgi
II: Runaway Jim > My Friend > Manteca > My Friend, Poor Heart, Weigh, BBJ, Ya Mar, YEM
E: Amazing Grace, Cavern > A-Train > Cavern
"Two Princes" jam in Ya Mar. Col. Bruce Hampton and the Aquarium Rescue Unit joined on YEM. The jam out of YEM also featured The Dude of Life on vocals and Fish on Madonna washboard and vacuum (at various times). Original extra verse sung in Cavern.

➢ My favorite tape as of late. It has a great live feel, as both the crowd and band have such incredible energy. It feels like you're dancing three rows back from Fish. The band is in a jammy kind of mood, and it shows, as the transitions like that from Runaway into My Friend is pure Phish magic. Trey dedicates a crazy good Ya Mar to then-girlfriend Sue on her birthday. The highlight, though, is the appearance by Col. Bruce and the ARU. Ten guys onstage jamming for 30 minutes. I love this tape! —TIM FOISSER

➢ After a weak first set, the magic started with a great Runaway Jim and a MFMF that segued in and out of Manteca. After special treats Weigh and Ya Mar (with Trey teasing the Spin Doctors hit of the moment, "Two Princes") came one of the best Phish jams I've ever seen or heard—YEM with Col. Bruce and the ARU. The troops joined Phish for a long jam that (unlike some jams with special guests) never grew stale. The scene on stage was crazy—in the course of the jam, Trey grabbed a set of drumsticks and tapped on everything, the Dude of Life came out and shouted unintelligibly, Oteil gave one of his scats, singing along with the notes, Fishman donned his Madonna washboard and everyone else played their hearts out. Wow! —LOCK STEELE

5/6/93 [ACCESSIBILITY: ••]
Palace Theater, Albany, NY
I: Chalkdust, Mound, Melt, Horse > Silent, All Things, Llama, Fluffhead, Possum, Lawn Boy, Why You Been Gone So Long, Tennessee Waltz, Fast Train
II: Suzie, Tweezer, Tela, Uncle Pen, BBJ, Squirming Coil, Mike's > Ob-La-Di Ob-La-Da Jam > Bluegrass Jam > Rocky Top, HYHU > Cracklin' Rosie > HYHU, That's Alright Mama **E:** Adeline, Contact, Tweezer Reprise
Dick Solberg ("The Sun Mountain Fiddler") on fiddle for Lawn Boy and the rest of the first set, and Bluegrass Jam to the end of the second set. Jeff Walton on acoustic guitar for Why You Been Gone So Long to the end of first set, and That's Alright Mama. Concert debut: Why You Been Gone So Long, Tennessee Waltz, Fast Train, That's Alright Mama.

➢ We settled in for the second night at the beautiful Palace and Phish rocked from the get-go. After offering up Melt, Fluff and Possum (!) all in the first set, the boys were joined by their friends Dick Solberg ("the Sun Mountain Fiddler") and Jeff Walton for a rocking bluegrass affair. Solberg had no problem jumping right in, offering up a gorgeous solo in Lawn Boy. Then Trey said, "I want to get Dick to sing one for us here," and for the rest of the set, Solberg gleefully took over. He sang lead vocals on the next three songs and had us in the palm of his hand—after all, here was an older guy with bright white hair rocking out with Phish and urging them along: "Come on, Page," and "How 'bout ya, Trey?" The boys returned for the second set without Solberg and Walton but proceeded to play what was arguably the best Tweezer of the year, a 20-minute version that brought the house down. The best musical moments were still to come: in the Mike's Song jam, Trey teased Ob-La-Di-Ob-La-Da and the crowd started singing along! Then, from out of the smoke that completely engulfed the stage during Mike's, we heard Solberg's telltale fiddle. The smoke lifted, there he was! A bluegrass jam developed and for a minute it sounded like they were heading into Sparkle, but then Mike stepped up and started Rocky Top. Closing the set, a rocking That's Alright Mama provided the final exclamation point. —LOCK STEELE

5/7/93 [ACCESSIBILITY: ••]
Bangor Auditorium, Bangor, ME
I: Buried Alive > Poor Heart, Melt, Sparkle, Caravan, Lizards, Horn, Divided Sky, I Didn't Know, Antelope
II: Rift, Bouncing, Maze, Fee > BBJ, YEM > Great Gig, Harry Hood, Harpua, Highway to Hell **E:** Amazing Grace, Golgi
"Bonanza" theme in YEM vocal jam. Fishman on Madonna washboard for I Didn't Know and vacuum for Great Gig. An inflatable pig was lowered from rafters during Great Gig; Marley came onstage before the encore and sniffed it. "Crossroads" jam in Harpua.

➢ I really got the sense that the band wanted to reward everyone who drove all the way up I-95 to Bangor. (No one had even heard of Limestone yet—I thought we were about as far up North as Phish or any sane human being would ever get.) This is a great show for non-Phish snobs. There are no amazing segues, breakouts or crazy improvisations, just simply great songs and tight performances, with a healthy dose of humor. The highlights included a Great Gig in the Sky in which an inflatable pig was dropped from the rafters (with Marley brought out onstage to sniff it out), and an obviously unplanned Harpua that sampled Crossroads, a sign of things to come the next night down the road in Durham. —ANDY BERNSTEIN

5/8/93 [ACCESSIBILITY: •••]
Field House, University of New Hampshire, Durham, NH
I: Chalkdust, Guelah, Rift, Mound, Stash > Kung > Stash, Glide, My Friend, Reba, Satin Doll, Cavern
II: Bowie > Have Mercy > Bowie, Horse > Silent, It's Ice > Squirming Coil > Jam > BBJ, Mike's > Crossroads > Mike's > Hydrogen > Weekapaug > Amazing Grace > Amazing Grace Jam **E:** AC/DC Bag
"Crew appreciation" before Satin Doll. "Jessica" jam in Bowie intro. Amazing Grace Jam was electric with instruments. Concert debuts: Crossroads, Amazing Grace Jam.

➢ Our week of touring finished at the Fieldhouse, your typical college gym with bleachers against the back wall and a huge open floor. After spending the somewhat uneven first set about halfway between the soundboard and the stage, I decided to move further back for set II. The long Bowie intro mesmerized the crowd, making navigation easy, but I held my ground as Phish ripped into the song. Somewhere in the middle of the amazing jam, Trey started singing Have Mercy, but Page and Mike didn't pick up on it right away. Eventually they got the reggae groove going, sung Have Mercy, then swung back into Bowie for a climactic finale. I headed outside during Horse/Silent to cool off (there was a giant balcony off the left side of the venue) then came back in and climbed the mostly-empty bleachers in back for the jam out of Page's Coil solo and a Mike's Groove that visited Eric Clapton and Weekapaug before arriving at one of the band's most beautiful jams—an electric Amazing Grace. It still gives me goosebumps. —LOCK STEELE

➢ Anyone who doesn't have this tape in their collection is truly, truly missing out. With the possible exception of 12/29/94, this is simply the best David Bowie ever, complete with a Jessica tease, a wonderfully placed Have Mercy and an insane heavy metalish jam that manages to be melodic at the same time. Do not forget the electric Amazing Grace in which Trey thanks the crew and the fans. This show really marked the end of the last Phish tour in which Phish played modest, makeshift Northeastern venues, giving Trey's thanks and farewells a special feel in retrospect. —ANDY BERNSTEIN

5/29/93 [ACCESSIBILITY: ••]
Laguna Seca Raceway, Monterey, CA
Chalkdust, Bouncing, Rift, Stash, Squirming Coil, Sparkle, Cavern, BBJ, YEM, Runaway Jim, Amazing Grace **E:** GTBT
Laguna Seca Daze festival with Jeff Healey, Shawn Colvin, The Allman Brothers Band and Blues Traveler. Phish played one set. Vacuum freeze in Cavern.

5/30/93 [ACCESSIBILITY: ••]
Laguna Seca Raceway, Monterey, CA
Lengthwise, Maze, Guelah, Poor Heart, Foam, Ya Mar, Silent, Antelope, I Didn't Know, Melt, Contact, Llama, Golgi **E:** Possum
Laguna Seca Daze festival with The Samples, 10,000 Maniacs and Blues Traveler. Phish played one set. Fishman on Madonna washboard for I Didn't Know. First Silent without Horse.

1993 Summer *ELBOW ROOM*

When the band solicited the Phish.Net community during the spring for suggestions on where to play on summer tour, no one really expected that they'd be making the leap to the amphitheatre circuit so soon—Great Woods? Jones Beach? These were 15,000-plus capacity venues, and Phish would fill them (or at least some of them) this summer. Out of the northeast, the band often found itself playing to vast expanses of empty seats, but that didn't seem to hurt the music.

Still, the musical highlights would come during August as the band swung back to smaller venues; the month is considered by many to be one of the hottest tour months the band has ever put on. Energized by the return of La Grange and Slave (among others), Phish played their hearts out at venues as small as Club Eastbrook in Grand Rapids, MI and as big as Berkeley's Greek Theatre.

7/15/93 [ACCESSIBILITY: •••]
Cayuga County Fairgrounds, Weedsport, NY
I: Rift, Sample, Divided Sky, Mound, Stash, Foam, I Didn't Know, My Mind's, Leprechaun > Runaway Jim
II: Bowie, Horse > Silent, Sparkle, It's Ice, Lifeboy, Possum, Faht, Lizards, Walk Away, Daniel **E:** Chalkdust, Freebird
"Little Drummer Boy" jam in Stash. Fishman on Madonna washboard for I Didn't Know. Last My Mind's, 2/7/93 Washington, D.C. [69 shows]. Last Faht, 12/11/92 Ann Arbor, MI [80 shows]. Concert debuts: Leprechaun, Daniel and Freebird (the a cappella version, as are all versions hereafter).

7/16/93 [ACCESSIBILITY: ••]
Mann Music Center, Philadelphia, PA
I: Daniel, Golgi, My Friend, Ya Mar, Buried Alive, FEFY, All Things, Nellie Cane, Horn, Antelope
II: Also Sprach > Melt, Glide, Maze, Bouncing, YEM > Yerushalayim Schel Zahav > YEM, Poor Heart, Purple Rain > HYHU, Harry Hood, Cavern
E: Llama, Freebird
Fishman on vacuum for Purple Rain. Concert debuts: Also Sprach, Purple Rain and Yerushalayim Schel Zahav.

7/17/93 [ACCESSIBILITY: ••]
Filene Center at Wolf Trap, Vienna, VA
I: Landlady, Runaway Jim, Sample, My Mind's, Stash, Reba, Chalkdust, Horse > Silent, Oh Kee > Bowie
II: Also Sprach > Tweezer, Squirming Coil, It's Ice, Sparkle, BBJ, Mike's > Leprechaun > Weekapaug > HYHU > Faht, Rift, GTBT
E: Amazing Grace, Daniel, Tweezer Reprise

Sunday, July 18, 1993 — IC Light Amphitheater, Pittsburgh, PA

Pittsburgh has got to be the most underrated city in America. You think of Pittsburgh, you think of steel mills, labor strikes, and Franco Harris' breath visibly puffing out on a blustery day at Three Rivers Stadium. But the I.C. Light Amphitheater—which wasn't much of an amphitheater at all, just some makeshift bleachers between a couple sets of train tracks—managed to alter our perspective.

It was right at the confluence of the Allegeheny, Monongahela, and Ohio rivers, across from a modern, tasteful downtown that sparkled far behind the stage. In the other direction, hovering over the lot, was a cliff about 200 feet tall. That night, on a 100-yard ledge between a cliff and a river, facing a grand skyline, Phish would find ways to both accentuate and transcend the surroundings.

They didn't use a background curtain, so right behind the band there was that skyline. Something like that can add so much to a show. If your ears ever stop saying 'wow,' your eyes say it for them. The phrase multi-sensory experience, which I think has been thrown around to describe Phish a few times, was made for this show.

Trey strolled out and shielded the sun from his eyes, and peered out over and past the audience. We turned around to see what he was looking at—about 50 people who had climbed the side of the cliff and were watching the show from little rock ledges. Trey seemed pleased.

After a few songs, the band whipped into Esther. As Page played the intro, one of those freight trains started rolling by. Chugga chugga chugga chugga. Chugga chugga chugga chugga. There was a rhythm to it. A distinct rhythm. The same rhythm as Esther. Exactly. Fish couldn't have done it better himself. Page just gave this sick little amazed smile. I just turned to Larry, my tourmate, and said "The greatest band in the world." (Larry later asked Page if it was intentional, but Page said it was all just a coincidence. Great things happen to great bands).

A solid first set was followed by a spectacular second, anchored by an Antelope that still ranks as the best single-song performance I've ever seen. A sick, furious, but distinctly melodic jam that forged a new tune unto itself pounded on for about three minutes. It was so powerful that the crowd erupted right in the middle, not during any of the pauses or transitions but right in the goddamn middle. It was a jam that stretched you out so far you just couldn't contain yourself. And the band was just getting started.

It was nighttime now; the pleasant water and steel background had been replaced by the twinkle of city lights and their reflection in the river beneath. And as the jam continued, fireworks started going off at the point where the three rivers merged. The crowd was screaming again and the band didn't know why, but as the explosions continued, they turned around and saw what was happening.

It had nothing to do with the show, just something the chamber of commerce must do to keep the three tourists who visit each summer coming back. After shaking their heads a few times, the band didn't miss a beat. They started jamming to the fireworks. Big Ball jam style. With each burst, a chord. And it kept going on. Fishman tried to lead them back into Antelope a couple times but Trey was loving it, and wouldn't stop.

Every time another set went off, he'd smash the guitar in unison, followed by a thunder of applause. It never got boring. Finally, the band goes back into a tune—not Antelope, but Brother, just for a few bars. A tease. Then, after whipping the crowd up so high it almost hurt, Trey asked if we had any spike, or whatever the fuck he said that night. And there it was. The perfect climax. Unlimited tension and the ultimate relief. A time where a song was played so great, you almost want them to play a few shitty ones so you can catch your breath and get back to this planet.

Thankfully, they obliged, with Mound and Fast Enough For You, not among my favorites.

This interlude gave me the chance to listen to this dirtbag guy who pushed me out of my spot on the floor. He had just met this girl and offered to take her to the show. Apparently, they had never even heard of Phish but he had some cash and wanted to impress her. He was about 20, missing a few teeth, and she was about 30, and not looking much better. Then she started saying she had to leave, so he starts kissing her. Tounging her down, 10 feet in front of the stage, during Fast Enough For You. Really going at it. Cheap porno style.

The floor was crowded. There were some folding chairs in the mix that hadn't been tossed aside. There wasn't much room for this kind of spectacle. But not only did they find room to explore the inner reaches of each other's tonsils, but they managed to clear out a whole section of people behind them. No one wanted to look. A whole patch on the floor, a triangle stretching out around 15 feet, ended up empty because it was too nasty a sight to behold, even with Phish and the skyscrapers behind them. Finally the guy extricated himself, and she said she had to leave. He asked a few people for a pen to get her phone number but couldn't find one, and then tried to memorize it by saying it out loud, and said goodbye. A strong YEM and a few more shenanigans, including a Purple Rain in which the band rigged the vacuum cleaner to blow out, closed the show.

Hours later, we found our way to the top of the cliff, and got pulled over because I had a busted tail light. And we weren't looking pretty. A clandestine swim in a hotel pool earlier in the day notwithstanding, we stank and the car was filled with garbage. We were just begging to get searched, ticketed and booked on whatever they could come up with. I talked a good game. "We're a little messy, but try to stay on the right side of things," I said. They ran a make on my license, and kept poking around the car with a flashlight. Finally the cop saw something and got all excited. "What's that?" she asked, pointing to a box of beer which, as she was unaware, we had been storing some food in.

Larry picked it up and pulled out a thing of mustard. She smiled. "Have a nice trip." **—Andy Bernstein**

7/18/93 [ACCESSIBILITY: ••]
IC Light Amphitheatre, Pittsburgh, PA
I: Buried Alive > Rift, Foam, Guelah, Maze, Esther, Divided Sky, Uncle Pen, Cavern
II: Also Sprach > Poor Heart, Antelope, Mound, FEFY, Oh Kee > Fee, YEM, Purple Rain, Golgi
E: Rocky Top, Freebird
Soundcheck included Guyute. In order, jams in Antelope: "Whole Lotta Love," fireworks jam, and "Brother."

7/21/93 [ACCESSIBILITY: ••]
Orange County Fairgrounds, Middletown, NY
Also Sprach > Melt, Sparkle, Squirming Coil, Maze, Glide, Rift, Bouncing, Runaway Jim, BBJ, Purple Rain > HYHU, Daniel **E:** Chalkdust
HORDE Festival. Phish played one set to close the show, coming on at about 1 a.m. Fishman on vacuum in Purple Rain. "HYHU" jam in Maze.

7/22/93 [ACCESSIBILITY: ••]
Stowe Performing Arts Center, Stowe, VT
I: Llama, Foam, Horn, My Mind's, Sample, Divided Sky, Mound, Ya Mar, Poor Heart, Stash, Golgi
II: Also Sprach > Tweezer > Walk Away, Sparkle, It's Ice, Contact, Possum, Paul and Silas, TMWSIY > Avenu, Rocky Top **E:** Freebird
Gordon Stone on pedal steel guitar for Paul and Silas, Avenu and Rocky Top.

➢ This was the worst experience with Phish I have ever had. Driving up from Middletown, it was beautiful out, but as soon as we got to the lot it started pouring down rain. It also got very cold, and they almost had to cancel the show. Before Llama, Trey said something like, "Yeah, they were gonna cancel the show, but I said, 'Fuck that, stick the plug up my ass and count out Llama!" In retrospect, looking at the way they performed, they should have canceled the show. —JOSHUA HOWLEY

➢ Phish is God but they ain't Mother Nature. Hometown ambience and a Gordon Stone appearance couldn't save this show from the weather. The only thing that made this rain-soaked gig entertaining were the fans climbing high up the ski hill to get around the fence, and then bolting down past guards busily intercepting anyone they could catch. —ANDY BERNSTEIN

7/23/93 [ACCESSIBILITY: ••••]
Jones Beach Music Theater, Wantagh, NY
I: Buried Alive > Rift, Caravan, Nellie Cane, Maze, Horse > Silent, PYITE, Runaway Jim, It's Ice, Lawn Boy, Cavern
II: Also Sprach > Poor Heart, Antelope, Faht > My Friend, Uncle Pen, BBJ, YEM > BBFCM > Chalkdust, Highway to Hell
E: Amazing Grace, Daniel

7/24/93 [ACCESSIBILITY: ••••]
Great Woods, Mansfield, MA
I: Llama, Horn, Nellie Cane, Divided Sky, Guelah, Rift, Stash, Mango, Bouncing, Squirming Coil
II: Also Sprach > Melt, Fluffhead, Maze, Glide, Sparkle, Mike's > Yerushalayim Schel Zahav > Weekapaug, Purple Rain > HYHU, Daniel, GTBT **E:** Golgi, Freebird
"Also Sprach" jam in Maze. Fishman on vacuum for Purple Rain. Last Mango, 5/17/92 Schenectady, NY [150 shows].

➢ I'd like to thank my former employer, Tower Records, for scoring me fifth row center tickets for this one. The first set was solid, but the second set is where it's at. Look at the setlist... wow. Glide stepped everything up a notch with Trey and Mike donning their slippy-slidy shoes to glide back and forth on stage. After the phat Mike's, Yerushalayim was about as beautiful, calming and restful as you can get. In all of the excitement of one of my favorite Weekapaugs, I wrote down "Funky Bitch" for some reason on my setlist! Mike's bass intro matched the huge smile Trey was wearing. Then encore time, and immediately those of us who knew started a "Freebird" chant. They had done it two nights before in Stowe, VT, but we needed it here at one of their biggest sellouts to that day... and once again they did not disappoint! —TONY HUME

➢ Trey later said this show and the Murat gig on August 13 were his favorite shows of the '93 summer tour, and though the music on this night is not as incredible as the Murat's second set, it's still a great tape. Besides the Mango Song breakout in the first set, 2001 > SOAM and Mike's > Yerushalayim!! > Weekapaug are keepers. —ED SMITH

7/25/93 [ACCESSIBILITY: •••]
Waterloo Village Music Center, Stanhope, NJ
I: Wilson, Foam, Mound, Stash, Fee, Rift, Sloth, My Mind's, I Didn't Know, Bowie
II: Also Sprach > Suzie, Tweezer > Horse > Silent, Maze, Lizards, Purple Rain > HYHU, Harpua > Tweezer Reprise **E:** Cavern
"Jeopardy" jam before Foam. "Donna Lee" and "Sounds of Silence" teases in Bowie. "Taxi" theme jam in Harpua. Fishman on vacuum for Purple Rain.

7/27/93 [ACCESSIBILITY: ••]
Classic Amphitheatre, Richmond, VA
Also Sprach > Rift, Stash, Squirming Coil, Sparkle > It's Ice > Purple Rain > HYHU, YEM
HORDE festival. Phish played one set to close the show. Fishman on vacuum for Purple Rain. John Popper on harmonica and Chan Kinchla on guitar for YEM, along with other HORDE members.

➢ During the jam in YEM, Trey, Mike and several stagehands brought a large (backyard-sized) trampoline out on stage. Then John Popper—in the midst of the jam—was wheeled back offstage in his wheelchair (this was after his motorcycle accident). A few minutes later, everyone looked up to see Popper (wheelchair and all) being lowered from above the stage by a rope. The rope snapped, Popper dropped through the trampoline, and the musicians still on stage took the jam up a notch. Turned out, the "Popper" lowered from above was a dummy. —MICK CONNOR

7/28/93 [ACCESSIBILITY: ••]
Grady Cole Center, Charlotte, NC
I: All Things, Runaway Jim, Ya Mar, Sample, Foam, Nellie Cane, Melt, Horse > Silent, Poor Heart, Cavern
II: Also Sprach > Axilla, MSO, Antelope, Lizards, Mound, My Friend, Harry Hood, Great Gig > HYHU, Chalkdust
E: Father/Son Boogie, Bill Bailey
Fishman on vacuum for Great Gig. Page's father, Dr. Jack McConnell, on keyboard for Father/Son Boogie and Bill Bailey, and vocals for Bill Bailey. Concert debuts: Father/Son Boogie and Bill Bailey.

7/29/93 [ACCESSIBILITY: ••]
Tennessee Theater, Knoxville, TN
I: Funky Bitch, Divided Sky, Weigh, Rift, Landlady > Fast Enough For You, My Mind's, Forbin's > Mockingbird, Possum
II: Maze, Bouncing, It's Ice, Lifeboy, Sparkle, YEM, Purple Rain > HYHU, Daniel, GTBT **E:** Rocky Top, Freebird
Fishman on vacuum on Purple Rain.

7/30/93 [ACCESSIBILITY: ••]
The Veranda at Starwood Amphitheater, Antioch, TN
I: Contact, Llama, Uncle Pen, Stash, Esther, Chalkdust, I Didn't Know, Reba, Cavern
II: Also Sprach > Tweezer, Horse > Silent, Poor Heart, Fluffhead > My Friend, Golgi, Squirming Coil, Bowie **E:** Walk Away, Amazing Grace
Fishman on Madonna washboard for I Didn't Know.

➢ The Tweezer jam begins with Trey scratching crazy rhythms on his strings, and moves to a jam on a theme that Page creates with the low keys of his piano. The jam builds to such a full sound, it's like a '95 Free. Then Trey takes us acoustically into The Horse from the Tweezer breakdown, complete with a classical guitar solo. Later in the set, Trey segues the end of Fluffhead acoustically into My Friend My Friend. Acoustic Trey is really something. —BRENDAN NEAGLE

➢ This had to be the oddest venue Phish has ever played. Starwood is a huge amphitheater, but they played at something called "The Veranda at Starwood"—a fancy way of saying the snack bar. The thing I'll never forget from this show is seeing Trey ride around the parking lot in a golf cart, surrounded by about 25 fans. Then a security guard pulled up on a golf cart of his own and stared Trey down, asking, "Where'd you get the golf cart?" Trey replied, "I'm the guitarist." —ANDY BERNSTEIN

7/31/93 [ACCESSIBILITY: ••]
Masquerade Music Park, Atlanta, GA
I: Rift, Sample, Ya Mar, Melt, Mound, Foam, Nellie Cane, Divided Sky, Cavern
II: Wilson, Runaway Jim, It's Ice, Maze, Sparkle, Mike's > Leprechaun > Weekapaug, Purple Rain > HYHU, Daniel, Highway to Hell
E: AC/DC Bag, Freebird
"Heartbreaker" and "Black Dog" jams in Mike's. Fishman on vacuum for Purple Rain.

8/2/93 [ACCESSIBILITY: ••••]
Ritz Theater, Ybor City (Tampa), FL
I: Chalkdust, Guelah, Poor Heart, Brother, Oh Kee > Suzie, All Things, Bathtub Gin > Makisupa > My Mind's, Dog Log > La Grange
II: Also Sprach > Mike's > Sparks > Curtis Loew, Rift, Squirming Coil > Weekapaug > HYHU > Bike > HYHU, Antelope > Makisupa Jam > Antelope **E:** Sleeping Monkey, Amazing Grace
Soundcheck: Slave, Funky Bitch. "Sweet Virginia" jam in Bathtub Gin. Joe Rooney on (unintelligible) vocals during Mike's jam. Fishman on vacuum for Bike. "Saints Go Marching In" tease in Antelope intro. Last Brother, 7/14/92 Norfolk, VA [143 shows]. Last Dog Log, 5/4/91 Somerville, MA [280 shows]. Last La Grange, 3/17/91 Aspen, CO [307 shows].

➢ The venue Phish was supposed to play had gone out of business a few days before, so it was moved to a small music club in Tampa, a hot musty room that held about 500 people. Yes, this was summer of '93, and the band had sold out Great Woods about two weeks before, but it was also Florida, a state that Phish had yet to conquer. Everyone in that room walked out believers, and the band seemed to relish the atmosphere, busting out the oldies that had been created, and in some cases left behind, on stages like that one. Dog Log, Brother—songs which hadn't been played in eons and wouldn't surface again until more than two years later, as well as rarities La Grange (it hadn't been played in 307 shows) and Curtis Loew (has it been played since?)—were only part of the story.

Saturday, August 14, 1993 — The World, Tinley Park, IL

During the summer of 1993 it was possible to trade anything you owned for a Phish ticket. This period of time was known as "the Wonder Years" because if you had a half a brain and no cash you could still easily experience what I consider the most enjoyable three hours of your life, practically every night. And when Phish took a day off you were able to earn enough money from the lot scene to enjoy such places as Disney World or a water park with an all-Scandinavian female staff (Grand Rapids, check it out).

To celebrate my last show of the tour, I decided to put five doses on my tongue—what better way to end an incredible summer? I grabbed a pack full of my Phamily Phun t-shirts figuring I'd trade one for a ticket, and then move the rest inside between sets. Now, normally I'm pretty careful when selling shirts, but while I was just trying to trade one for a ticket, which is legal, I wasn't really thinking about the cops.

That was pretty dopey. The cops sure as hell didn't know or care that at that moment, as I paraded around the grounds with a backpack and a t-shirt flapping in the wind, that I was trading and not selling. Within minutes, the Tinley Park Police apprehended me for vending. One of the officers that had me in custody was a rookie cop undergoing training, and of course I was lucky enough to be the first person he ever frisked and handcuffed.

He was instructed by his superior to check my groin area for a hard object. I explained offhandedly that I wasn't that easy. The rookie cop seemed to become upset with the fact that I was cooperating with sarcasm, and the only way he was able to vent his frustration was with idiocy. That's when he proceeded to warn me not to touch his gear in the back seat of the vehicle. Now I, of course, wasn't about to touch his gear, but I was having a good time looking at it. Just as the car sped away, I was starting to get off on the five hits that I had forgotten since the start of this ordeal.

The police had a station on the premises, which moved things along relatively quickly. Even though I was in the station, I could hear the ending of Chalkdust—it even prompted me to bust a couple of moves in the fingerprint room. As the room was spinning, I smiled for my mug shot which probably outdid my yearbook picture. Divided Sky began to echo through the halls. It took me five minutes of pre-peak rhetoric to convince the authorities that I did not pose a threat to their society and that I should be permitted into the show.

I ran in at full speed and caught the end of Divided Sky. After a solid first set including a brilliantly dampened Split Open and Melt, I was mentally and physically prepared for the second set. Immediately following the 2001 Theme, which opened so many second sets in summer 1993, Antelope began its usual subtle grooves. The jam was slowly working its way up when it found its way to a repeated series of standard block rock-n-roll chords. As they brought it to a pinnacle, each member was emphasizing different rhythmic sections of the chord progression. They brilliantly combined simplicity with a very jagged finish. A few minutes later Trey composed a majestic sounding tune appropriate for a trumpeter at a Buckingham Palace royal gathering. What made it special was that each note was trilled with its half note neighbor and it was all done in a minor key that gave it a distinct Phish flavor. The Antelope lasted at least 25 minutes and included segues into and out of Walk Away, Sparks, and Have Mercy. Don't forget, I was tripping my balls off and convinced that Phish was able to manipulate the echoes generated in the spacious amphitheater. But the show fizzled out after a solid YEM.

Exiting the show, we spotted a shady-looking character who stole 100 dollars from some friends of ours who made the mistake of picking him up on the highway and giving him a ride to the show. After an hour of interrogation, this guy—who went by the name of "Free" and apparently thought everything was—admitted to the crime. He then punched me in the head. I had to spend the next eight hours of my trip with a throbbing bruise on my forehead. Believe me, I was actually able to feel the tumors forming.

Thank God for that smokin' Antelope.

—Charlie Lazarus

The Bathtub Gin is one of the best ever, and the entire second set was pretty much one long jam with Makisupa in an Antelope closer, just to make sure everyone had gotten their fill of perfection. This was a show where you could just walk up to the stage and watch from the front row, which I did during set I, but I got so hot that I had to watch set II from the bar in the back, whipping out 50¢ every few songs to buy a cup of ice water. True nourishment would come later, when Mike emerged into the tiny parking lot with a platter of food. "Eat," he said, and the band fed the tourheads. —ANDY BERNSTEIN

➢ Get this show if you don't already have it—the setlist is amazing. But the big treat of this show is what I refer to as Makisupelope. At the end of the Antelope, Mike throws the Makisupa bass line in, and the jam morphs into Makisupa. Trey sings, "Marco Policeman-Dolas," and the punchy jam moves with ease between Antelope and Makisupa before an Antelope closing. —ADAM DAVIDOFF

8/3/93 [ACCESSIBILITY: ••]
Bayfront Park Amphitheatre, Miami, FL
I: Runaway Jim, Nellie Cane, Foam, Fee > Rift, Stash, Horse > Silent, Ya Mar, Llama, Cavern
II: Lengthwise > Maze, Bouncing, It's Ice, YEM, Lizards, Sparkle, Purple Rain > HYHU, Golgi **E:** Poor Heart, Freebird
Fishman on vacuum for Purple Rain.

8/6/93 [ACCESSIBILITY: ••••]
Cincinnati Zoo Peacock Pavilion, Cincinnati, OH
I: Melt, Poor Heart, Curtain > Sample, Rift, Horn, Divided Sky, Nellie Cane, Chalkdust, Suzie
II: Buried Alive > Tweezer, Guelah, Squirming Coil, Uncle Pen, YEM > Halley's > Slave, HYHU > Cracklin' Rosie > HYHU, Tweezer Reprise
E: Amazing Grace
"Tequila" teases in Tweezer, Guelah and YEM. "Cocaine" jam in YEM, and "Cocaine" lyrics sung in YEM vocal jam. Last Slave, 10/24/91 Prescott, AZ [240 shows].

➢ This place is a nice open-air venue within the Zoo—you could leave, check out the animals, and be let back in. On stage, Mike added a small rear-view mirror to his stand so he could see the Minkin backdrop behind him. The pinnacle of the show came in the second set with YEM > Cocaine > YEM > Halley's > Slave > Cracklin' Rosie. Most were stunned upon exiting this show. —NATHANIEL PRICE

➢ Slave had been soundchecked down in Florida earlier in the week, so rumors of its imminent return at the Cincy Zoo ("See the city, see the zoo...") ran rampant. But no one could have predicted the mesmerizing way it would emerge out of the ending Halley's jam, much less the YEM > Cocaine > YEM madness that came first! —TRICIA HOLMES

➢ One of the groundbreaking '93 SOAMelts served as a very hot opener. —AL HUNT

8/7/93 [ACCESSIBILITY: ••••]
Darien Lake Performing Arts Center, Darien Center, NY
I: Llama, Bouncing, Poor Heart > Stash > Makisupa Policeman, Reba > Maze, Forbin's > Mockingbird, Cavern
II: Also Sprach > Mike's > Sparks > Kung > Mike's > TMWSIY > Avenu > Sloth, Sparkle, My Friend > McGrupp > Purple Rain > HYHU, Antelope
E: Carolina, La Grange
Fishman on vacuum for Purple Rain.

➢ The August '93 insanity continued in Darien with a segue-filled show. Stash > Makisupa and Reba > Maze in the first set are where it's at. Set II travels even farther afield with a Mike's Song complete with Kung and Sparks, a wild Avenu > Sloth pairing (no return to TMWSIY), and La Grange for an encore. —PAT STANLEY

➢ If you listen carefully to this tape during Purple Rain, you can hear a loud POP! followed by Fishman saying, "Whoa!" This is the result of someone throwing an M-80 firecracker that landed between my friend's legs. He jumped up and it exploded, raising a response from Fish. This show took place at an amusement park, which triggers an interesting dialogue in Forbin's about riding the roller coaster of the mind. This very good show should be on everyone's list of tapes. —DAVE O'CONNOR

8/8/93 [ACCESSIBILITY: ••]
Nautica Stage, Cleveland, OH
I: BBFCM, Foam, Loving Cup, Runaway Jim, Horse > Silent, PYITE, FEFY, Paul and Silas, I Didn't Know, Bowie
II: Also Sprach > Rift, Harry Hood, Wilson, It's Ice, Fluffhead, Possum, BBJ, HYHU > Love You > HYHU, Daniel, GTBT **E:** MSO, Freebird
Fishman on Madonna washboard for I Didn't Know and vacuum for Love You. "Tequila" tease in Daniel.

8/9/93 [ACCESSIBILITY: ••]
Concert Hall, Toronto, ON
I: Chalkdust, Mound, Fee > Melt, Glide, Nellie Cane > Divided Sky, Memories, Squirming Coil
II: Dinner and a Movie > Tweezer > Tela > My Friend, My Mind's, YEM > Contact, Crimes of the Mind **E:** Rocky Top
"Who Knows" jam (with lyrics) in Chalkdust. "Smoke on the Water" jam and "Speed Racer" lyrics in YEM. "Psycho Killer" and "Contact" music sung in YEM vocal jam. Dude of Life on vocal for Crimes of the Mind. Venue was changed to the Concert Hall from the Molson Place Harbourfront Pavilion a week before the show.

8/11/93 [ACCESSIBILITY: ••]
Club Eastbrook, Grand Rapids, MI
I: Buried Alive > Runaway Jim, Weigh, It's Ice, Ginseng Sullivan, My Friend, Mango, Stash, Sparkle, Cavern
II: Mike's > Great Gig > Weekapaug, Esther, All Things, Bouncing, Rift, Jesus Left Chicago, MSO, Antelope **E:** Adeline, Bold as Love

Ginseng Sullivan performed acoustic with Trey on acoustic guitar, Mike on upright bass, Fish on Madonna washboard and Page on piano. Fishman on vacuum for Great Gig. Concert debut: Ginseng Sullivan.

➢ This comes from somebody who was lucky enough to be at this show. I think the Great Gig speaks for the whole night—I actually thought the vacuum was gonna take Fishman's lips off. Weekapaug goes off—Trey was in his own zone and took it to the next level. Antelope was a great closer. In the first set, the quick drop-out transition from All Things into Bouncing is choice. The energy during Bouncing is just as strong on the tape as it was that night (minus the goosebumps). —MARK DANIEL

8/12/93 [ACCESSIBILITY: ••••]
Meadow Brook Music Theater, Rochester, MI
I: AC/DC Bag, Reba, Chalkdust, Guelah, Nellie Cane, Melt, Horse > Silent, Poor Heart, Squirming Coil
II: Also Sprach > Landlady > Tweezer > Reggae Jam > Landlady > Tweezer, Lizards, Sloth, Maze, Lawn Boy, BBJ, Golgi, Possum **E:** Fire, Freebird

"Tweezer" jam in Possum.

➢ "Get back" is a musical signal Phish sometimes uses in the midst of crazy jams to jump back into the previous song they were jamming on, like in the 3/13/92 Antelope > BBFCM > Antelope. The second set at Meadowbrook contains another prime example of this technique—Trey sends the band reeling between the slowing Tweezer jam and a faster jam, then back to the set-opening Landlady before finally returning to Tweezer. Outrageously groovy. —ANDRE HOLTON

8/13/93 [ACCESSIBILITY: ••••]
Murat Theater, Indianapolis, IN
I: Lengthwise > Llama, Makisupa > Foam, Stash, Ginseng Sullivan, Fluffhead, My Mind's, Horn, Bowie
II: Buried Alive > Rift, Bathtub Gin > Ya Mar, Mike's > Lifeboy, Oh Kee > Suzie, Amazing Grace **E:** Highway to Hell

Fishman on Madonna washboard for Ginseng Sullivan. "Ya Mar," "Mango" and "Magilla" jams in Bowie. "Weekapaug" tease in Bathtub Gin.

➢ I was in a terrible mood for this show, I mean terrible. I was quite miserable when I climbed into the ornate third balcony at the Murat Theater. But as the band had done a few nights earlier in Grand Rapids, they reminded me exactly why I was there, and floated me away from my little state of anger and disappointment. An extra-long first set was highlighted by a Makisupa, a tingly Bowie and a solid Fluffhead. Second set, during an un-fucking-real Mike's, Trey emerged from the dry ice and started chopping with his guitar like it was an axe, with only his upper body exposed through the smoke. Then they slipped into Lifeboy. Now for all you folks who bust out your lighters for Lifeboy because you think it's a touching melody, or for all you folks who can't stand Lifeboy for that very reason, try hearing the Murat version. Trippy and explosive. Yeah, Murat was so good, even Lifeboy made me cringe. —ANDY BERNSTEIN

➢ The "Murat Gin" is, of course, one of the great musical moments in Phish history. The jam segment just departs for another planet, completely leaving behind any semblance of a normal Bathtub Gin—the hose is pumping full pressure! Eventually, the jam segues into Ya Mar, and then into Mike's Song, which is just as unbelievably amazing as the Gin jam. This half-hour of Phish intensity is unmatched. (Don't miss the long, trippy Bowie that closes the first set, complete with a cool Ya Mar jam with Fishman on woodblocks that segues into the Mango Song ending, then to a jazz jam that samples Magilla.) —JOS CONTI

8/14/93 [ACCESSIBILITY: ••]
World Music Theater, Tinley Park, IL
I: Chalkdust, Guelah, Divided Sky, Horse > Silent, It's Ice, Sparkle, Melt, Esther, Poor Heart, Cavern
II: Also Sprach > Antelope > Sparks > Walk Away > Have Mercy > Antelope, Mound, Squirming Coil, Daniel, YEM, Purple Rain > HYHU, Golgi **E:** La Grange

Fishman on vacuum for Purple Rain.

➢ There's nothing as thrilling as seeing the band get "stuck in a jam," veering so far off the original tune that it seems they can't find their way back—and don't want to. This may be a bit more common today, but back in '93 it still relatively rare. So watching Phish get so far away from Antelope that they find themselves in Sparks and Walk Away—and then somehow finding their way back to Antelope—was worth the price of admission by itself. —ANDY BERNSTEIN

➢ This particular show is a favorite of mine. Though the first set is pretty much unremarkable with the exception of Divided Sky, the second set smokes. Antelope is a slice of heaven, with Sparks and Walk Away jammed in the middle. I always like Purple Rain and here Fishman doesn't disappoint. A must-have for any true Phish phan. —TONY KRUPKA

8/15/93 [ACCESSIBILITY: ••]
Macauley Theater, Louisville, KY
I: Sample, All Things, Runaway Jim, Fee, Paul and Silas, Stash, Forbin's > Mockingbird, Chalkdust
II: Rift > Tweezer, Lizards, Landlady, Bouncing, Maze, Glide, Adeline, Ginseng Sullivan, Nellie Cane, Freebird **E:** Harry Hood

Ginseng Sullivan and Nellie Cane performed acoustic with Trey on acoustic guitar, Mike on upright bass, Fishman on Madonna washboard and Page on piano.

➢ For the tape collector, the biggest problem one faces dealing with August '93 isn't deciding which tapes to seek out—it's deciding which tapes *not* to acquire! The classics (8/2, 8/13 and 8/20) are automatic. The other heavy-hitters (8/6, 8/7 and 8/14) appear on a lot of tapelists, too. From there, things get a bit trickier. 8/28 certainly has its fans, as do 8/11, 8/12, 8/16, 8/25 and 8/26—see, almost all of them. But one show I often don't see on people's tapelists is 8/15/93 Louisville, KY, and let me tell you, it's not because of the music. Though this show lacks the stellar setlists of some of those listed above, the jams in Stash and Tweezer are as hot as anything Phish played that month. —JOSH ALBINI

8/16/93 [ACCESSIBILITY: ••]
American Theater, St. Louis, MO
I: Axilla, Possum > Horn, Reba, Sparkle, Foam, I Didn't Know, Melt, Squirming Coil
II: Mike's > Faht > Weekapaug, Mound, It's Ice > My Friend, Poor Heart, BBJ, A-Train, GTBT **E:** Amazing Grace, Rocky Top

Fishman on Madonna washboard for I Didn't Know. "Black Magic Woman" jam in Weekapaug.

Rock Band

8/20/93 Red Rocks, Morrison, CO

When Phish announced their 1993 summer tour itinerary, many fans drew bright red circles around two August dates—the tour-closer at Berkeley's Greek Theater, and a night about a week before that at Red Rocks Amphitheater in Morrison, CO. Both were storied venues, home to historic shows throughout rock history. U2, it was said, made a name for itself as a band with a famous 1983 Red Rocks gig (later made available on video) in which Bono uttered the immortal line, "This is Red Rocks! This is the Edge!"

Trey had mocked that very line way back when, at a Nectar's show on 7/25/88 that ended up making it onto *Junta* as a bonus live track. Now, five years later, Phish was to play on that storied stage, nestled among the red rocks of the Colorado backcountry, with a sweeping vista that looked down over hills and the city of Denver in the distance. Of course, everyone within shouting distance of Denver wanted to be there. Happily, ticket availability wasn't a problem: 9,500 tickets were an awful lot for Phish to sell in 1993, and in fact the Red Rocks gig did not sell out. (Two years later, that situation would be drastically altered, as even four shows at the Rocks couldn't satisfy the desire for tickets).

On the day of the show, however, rain clouds blotted out the sun. Everyone who had expected to bake on a hot Colorado afternoon instead reached for their rain ponchos and prayed. The venue opened its doors, and fans rushed up front, huddling under umbrellas while rumors swirled that the show might have to be canceled.

But as the 7:30 starting time drew near, somehow the rain let up. The Phish crew scurried onto the stage, pulling back the tarps that had protected the equipment, and within minutes the crowd was on its feet, cheering the band as they came out on stage. "Cool!" Trey said, and then started up The Divided Sky. As its notes floated up the red amphitheater walls and into the sky, the unbelievable happened—a moment of true magic: the sky divided. For the first time all day, the sun peeked through the clouds. One song later, in Harpua, Trey's declaration, "Look, the storm's gone!" brought huge cheers.

Blessed by Mother Nature, the band proceeded to play what still ranks as one of their best shows ever. Incredible jams in Antelope and Split Open and Melt rank among fans' favorite versions of these songs. For many, though, the highlight came when the subtle opening of Slave to the Traffic Light (dusted off after two years of retirement two weeks earlier in Cincinnati) emerged out of 2001. Welcome to Eden.

Thursday, December 30, 1993 — CCCC, Portland, ME

There's just something special about the New Year's Run—a sense of shared camaraderie among the thousands of people who trek to all four shows, and a real feeling of communal joy when Phish makes the trip worthwhile. Of course, bonus points are added for snowstorms, ice storms and other natural disasters that have to be overcome along the way. If the idea of a winter road trip doesn't fill you with excitement, then the New Year's Run probably isn't for you.

The '93 run sure had its share of bad weather, which makes it that much more fun to remember. On our way to Bender Arena, icy road conditions made the going treacherous—we slowed to 20 MPH driving Washington D.C.'s beltway, then finally made it to the show to find a line that stretched around the building. Hundreds of people braving the cold to get up close—that's dedication.

The next night, in New Haven, we emerged hot and happy from the Coliseum to find about four inches of snow on the ground and more coming down. Anyone who could afford to spend the night in New Haven did; we were lucky to have friends nearby, so we crashed there, with visions of icy roads dancing in our heads.

We made it to Portland the next day safely, though the snow drifts were deeper in Maine than they had been in Connecticut. We emerged from our car in freezing wind to find a full-scale lot scene underway near the Civic Center, which is right in downtown Portland, across from a Hood Milk factory. People selling T-shirts in the middle of winter—we had to laugh!

Joining the lengthy line outside the Civic Center, we were comforted while we waited by a brief snippet of the Peaches En Regalia soundcheck going on inside. The venue staff was late getting the doors open, but no one really seemed angry about it even though we were jogging in place to keep our blood circulating. Everyone just took it as part of the challenge. (Trey did apologize for keeping us waiting in the cold at the beginning of Forbin's Rap, though).

When the doors finally opened and we made it in, we found the Civic Center a general-admission joy: lots of space for everyone. It's a cute little arena that feels homey, exactly the kind of place you'd expect to find in Maine. It was perfect.

And then there was the music. David Bowie, complete with a prominent Dream On tease, broke the show open from the start. The Curtain, a personal favorite, segued into the still-new Sample, and from there we got a Forbin's > Mockingbird and an outstanding Bathtub Gin. To close the set Phish pulled out the only first set a cappella Freebird they'd ever done. The energy level in the arena zoomed sky-high.

But the best was yet to come. We figured a Mike's Song might be on tap, but we didn't expect a mesmerizing version to slam out of Also Sprach Zarathustra. Mike's wound into something I labeled on my setlist as "Insane Jam!!!" (It became clear six months later that we'd heard the first Simple Jam.) That moved brilliantly into The Horse, with Trey swinging his electric guitar behind his back and strumming the opening to the Horse on his acoustic guitar. Horse/Silent calmed the place down for a minute before Trey started strumming the opening notes to PYITE. Oh, my. High above courtside, we danced our hearts out. Then, another shocker: McGrupp! I hadn't heard it live in two years, and it was a blissful delight, stretching on before a familiar Gordon bass line ambushed it… they were moving into Weekapaug. What a run of songs!

The great thing was that everyone knew it. The folks who made the trek to Portland that Holiday Tour were mostly old-school fans; it wasn't the kind of place to see your first Phish show, unlike, say, New Haven. As the band pulled out one surprise after another, the excitement kept mounting. Delirium had almost set in. Purple Rain followed Weekapaug, then for the first time in the set, there was silence from the stage.

Trey conferred with Mike as a group in front of the stage continued their "Slave! Slave! Slave!" chants. And so it was to be — as the opening notes of the first East Coast Slave to the Traffic Light in years soared out and above the crowd, I threw my head back in exultation.

It was a long, cold drive to Worcester, but no one seemed to mind.

—Lock Steele

➢ This show sticks out for one reason: the second set Mike's Song > Faht > Weekapaug Groove. Mike's is played pretty basic, nothing fancy but still great. After Mike's, Trey came forward to play the acoustic guitar commonly used at the beginning of The Horse. Then the forest animal noises of Faht came over the P.A. system. Trey threw his hands in the air like something was wrong as the forest noises continued into what becomes an amazing Weekapaug. Mike's bass holds this version down nicely, as it usually does. Another added bonus to this set was a very good rendition of Take the A-Train. —MIKE NOLL

8/17/93 [ACCESSIBILITY: ••]
Memorial Hall, Kansas City, KS
I: Wilson, Llama, Guelah, Divided Sky, Weigh, Maze, Fluffhead, FEFY, Daniel
II: Also Sprach > Bowie, Horse > Silent, Rift, Suzie, YEM, Purple Rain > HYHU, MSO, Cavern **E:** Memories, Fire
Fishman on vacuum for Purple Rain.

8/20/93 [ACCESSIBILITY: •••••]
Red Rocks Amphitheatre, Morrison, CO
I: Divided Sky, Harpua, Poor Heart, Maze, Bouncing, It's Ice > Wedge, Ginseng Sullivan, Rift, Antelope
II: Also Sprach > Slave, Melt, Squirming Coil, My Friend, Chalkdust, YEM > Purple Rain, Cavern **E:** Mango, Freebird
Ginseng Sullivan performed acoustic with Trey on acoustic guitar, Mike on bass, Fishman on Madonna washboard and Page on piano. Mimi Fishman and Fishman on vacuum for Purple Rain.

***Phan Pick* #22** ➢ This was the first Phish show at Red Rocks, and I anticipated many great things. But when I arrived, it was raining and I was seriously bummed. I went into the show wondering when it would stop, and like an act of God, it cleared five minutes before the show. What better way to start the show but with a Divided Sky, followed by a great Harpua? Red Rocks brings out the best in performers. —JEFF SALVATORE

➢ Phish's ability to somehow top everyone's already high expectations is a key to the band's magic. For their first Red Rocks show, everyone expected the world, so the band delivered a universe. The show benefits from inspired choices like the Divided Sky opener, the summer's only Wedge (the last one until 1995) and the Mango Song encore, but it's the music that really makes this show fly. Antelope and Split Open, in particular, are two of the very best performances of these songs. —MELISSA WOLCOTT

➢ I think the Split Open and Melt on this night is a true testament to the band's amazing musical skill. Page's dexterity on the piano during this song makes me long to tickle the ivories with half his talent. —AMANDA LITTON

➢ When the rain stopped, the guys played Divided Sky and the clouds literally parted and the sun came out. I laughed, cried, and danced at the same time. This is the concert where I fell in love with the making of music. —JAKE HUNTER

8/21/93 [ACCESSIBILITY: ••••]
SaltAir, Salt Lake City, UT
I: Buried Alive > Poor Heart, Foam, Guelah, Rift, Stash, Sparkle, Landlady, I Didn't Know, Runaway Jim
II: Possum, Horn, Uncle Pen, Fee, Llama, Lawn Boy, Bowie, HYHU > Brain > HYHU, Harry Hood, Daniel **E:** Amazing Grace, Nellie Cane
Bela Fleck and the Flecktones opened. Fishman on Madonna washboard for I Didn't Know. Bela Fleck on banjo, and Flecktones Victor Wooten on bass and Future Man on synth-axe drumitar joined Phish for the second set starting with Fee. Bela also sat in on Nellie Cane. Fishman on vacuum for Brain.

8/24/93 [ACCESSIBILITY: ••]
Commodore Ballroom, Vancouver, BC
I: Chalkdust, All Things, Bouncing, It's Ice, Nellie Cane, Melt, Horse > Silent, Uncle Pen, Maze, Golgi
II: Llama, Horn, Ya Mar, Mike's > Ginseng Sullivan > Weekapaug, Wilson > Rift, HYHU > Cracklin' Rosie > HYHU, Antelope
E: Halley's > Poor Heart, Adeline
Baby Gramps opened. "I Feel the Earth Move" jam in It's Ice.

8/25/93 [ACCESSIBILITY: ••]
Paramount Theater, Seattle, WA
I: AC/DC Bag, Daniel, Sample, Sparkle, Foam, Ginseng Sullivan, Nellie Cane, Amazing Grace, Stash, Glide, Cavern
II: Buried Alive, Possum, Mound, My Friend, Paul and Silas, YEM > Bats and Mice, Squirming Coil, GTBT **E:** Bold as Love, Rocky Top
Baby Gramps opened. Ginseng Sullivan and Nellie Cane performed acoustic/no amplification with Trey on acoustic guitar, Mike on upright bass, Fishman on Madonna washboard and Page on piano. Baby Gramps on YEM vocal jam and Bats and Mice. Concert debut: Bats And Mice.

➢ In the midst of an amazing Foam, Trey took the groove way down—down so far, in fact, that he wasn't actually playing at all, though he kept miming his hands as though he was (the "silent jam" reappeared during the 12/9/95 Albany YEM and the 12/30/96 FleetCenter Funky Bitch, among others). The crowd in the small theater stayed silent throughout, and Trey looked up in amazement. After finishing Foam, the band pulled out their acoustic instruments for a special "unplugged" set as a special treat for the very attentive crowd. This became commonplace in 1994, but it was special then. —LOCK STEELE

8/26/93 [ACCESSIBILITY: •••]
Arlene Schnitzer Concert Hall, Portland, OR
I: Runaway Jim, Guelah, Reba, Fee, Melt, Esther, It's Ice, Harry Hood, Golgi
II: Also Sprach > Bowie, Lifeboy, Rift, Jesus Left Chicago, Lizards, HYHU > Bats and Mice > HYHU, Chalkdust **E:** Freebird
Baby Gramps opened. Baby Gramps on Bats and Mice; Fishman on vacuum.

➢ A very well-played Jim to open up—the jam between verses was unusually extended. Also look for Split and Ice as stellar versions. The first-set Hood is unexpected and blistering. Bowie gets absolutely insane (as it always does now)—I would go as far as to say chaotic at points. The early version of Lifeboy is nice, but Jesus Left Chicago is played exquisitely with Page and Trey taking their respective solos. —BOB TALATZKO

➢ One great thing about Phish shows is the ability of music you think you know so well to surprise you. After an incredible 2001 > Bowie, during which the band showed us some new corners of this amazing song, I thought Lifeboy would give me a moment to catch my breath. But the song built and built to an incredibly moving closing jam that perfectly complemented the raging Bowie before it. —LOCK STEELE

8/28/93 [ACCESSIBILITY: ••••]
Greek Theater, University of California at Berkeley, Berkeley, CA
I: Llama, Bouncing, Foam, Ginseng Sullivan, Maze > Fluffhead, Stash, Squirming Coil, Crimes of the Mind
II: Also Sprach > Rift, Antelope, Horse > Silent, Sparkle, It's Ice > BBJ, Purple Rain > HYHU, YEM > Contact, Chalkdust
E: Daniel, Amazing Grace
J.J. Cale opened. The Dude Of Life on vocals for Crimes of the Mind. Fishman on vacuum for Purple Rain. "Brady Bunch" jams in Antelope. "Oye Como Va" in YEM. Trey acknowledges the crew in Daniel.

[10-11/93] American Recording Co., Woodland Hills, CA
Recording and mixing *Hoist*.

1993 New Year's Run

12/28/93 [ACCESSIBILITY: ••••]
Bender Arena, American University, Washington, DC
I: Peaches, Poor Heart > Melt, Esther, Oh Kee > Suzie > Ya Mar, It's Ice, Fee, Possum
II: Sample, YEM, My Friend, Lizards, Sloth, FEFY, Uncle Pen, Harry Hood, Highway to Hell **E:** Memories, Golgi
"Auld Lang Syne" tease in Ya Mar. "Kashmir" jam in Possum. Last Peaches, 6/23/89 Boston, MA [502 shows]. The show was also the debut of the aquarium stage set used for this entire New Year's Run.

12/29/93 [ACCESSIBILITY: ••••]
Veterans Memorial Coliseum, New Haven, CT
I: Runaway Jim, Peaches, Foam, Glide, Divided Sky, Wilson, Sparkle, Stash, Squirming Coil
II: Maze, Bouncing, Fluffhead, Antelope, Contact, BBFCM > Walk Away > BBJ, HYHU > Brain > HYHU, Adeline, Chalkdust **E:** Nellie Cane, Cavern
Fishman on vacuum for Brain.

➢ The entire show lacks energy. The only time the band seems to really get into the groove is during a segment of the second set that makes this tape worth listening to: Fluffhead, Antelope, Contact, BBFCM > Walk Away > Big Ball Jam. —AARON GROSSBERG

➢ The highlight of this show was the Fluffhead-Antelope combo. The Fluffhead "Arrival" section contains a jam that abandons any rhythmic structure, producing crazy ambiguity that finally resolves to the G chord. Then they do it again, even more intensely. The Antelope jam begins with a quiet guitar from Trey. At one point, the guitar gains an unbelievable sound and power to finish off the jam in uncanny fashion. —BRENDAN NEAGLE

12/30/93 [ACCESSIBILITY: •••••]
Cumberland County Civic Center, Portland, ME
I: Bowie, Weigh, Curtain > Sample, Paul and Silas, Forbin's > Mockingbird, Rift, Bathtub Gin, Freebird
II: Also Sprach > Mike's > Horse > Silent > PYITE > McGrupp > Weekapaug > Purple Rain > HYHU, Slave **E:** Rocky Top, GTBT
"Dream On" jam in Bowie. "Simple" jam in Mike's. Fishman on vacuum for Purple Rain.

Phan Pick #6 ➢ Sometimes, Phish just rewards us all. After thousands of people made it through a blizzard to get to Portland, Phish wasted no time in making the night special. Leading off with Bowie, getting to Curtain, following a Col. Forbin > Mockingbird with a great Gin and the only first set Freebird—it was just one of those nights that Phish wanted to hammer it home that everyone was in for a treat. And that was just the beginning. Set II included not only amazing songs, but splendid playing and segues as well as the first surfacing of the Simple Jam. When it seemed like there couldn't be any more, they busted out Slave, the first since Red Rocks the summer before. Just a splendid, splendid night. —ANDY BERNSTEIN

➢ This show happened to fall on my 19th birthday and is one of the most celebrated in Phishtory. There was an unbelievable amount of energy in the arena—somehow I knew this show would be special. I remember thinking after the show that I had just seen musical history. In fact, I had! —JOSHUA HOWLEY

12/31/93 [ACCESSIBILITY: •••••]
The Centrum, Worcester, MA
I: Llama, Guelah, Stash, Ginseng, Reba, Peaches, I Didn't Know, Antelope
II: Tweezer, Halley's > Poor Heart > It's Ice > Fee > Possum, Lawn Boy, YEM
III: "Into the Phishtank" > New Year's Countdown > Auld Lang Syne > Down with Disease Jam, Melt, Lizards, Sparkle, Suzie, HYHU > Cracklin' Rosie > HYHU, Harry Hood, Tweezer Reprise **E:** Golgi, Amazing Grace
Fishman on Madonna washboard for Ginseng Sullivan. "Roundabout" tease before Ginseng Sullivan. Tom Marshall on "Rye, rye, rocco, Marco Esquandolis" vocals in Antelope. "Peaches" teases in It's Ice, Possum and Suzie. "Banana Splits" theme jam in Tweezer. Bandmembers donned wetsuits during YEM vocal jam. At about 10 minutes to midnight, bandmembers (or stand-ins?) were lowered from the rafters onto the stage, where they climbed into a giant clam and disappeared. The clam counted down to midnight as the band returned for Auld Lang Syne and giant white balloons dropped from above. "Auld Lang Syne" tease in Hood. Concert debut: DWD Jam. FM broadcast on WBCN-Boston on 1/1/94.

Phan Pick #21 ➢ Here's a New Year's Eve show that exceeds Phish's standards. While the setlist may not bowl anyone over, there are some amazing moments. One must note the YEM vocal jam—just wild. Also amazing are Split Open and Harry Hood—two of my favorite versions. What I love best, though, is the Auld Lang Syne > DWD jam, which blows my mind every time I hear it. —JONATHAN BANCO

➢ Amazing show. Peaches En Regalia teases throughout the entire show, the Harry Hood rocked, and Fishman's Cracklin' Rosie was hilarious. We rung in the New Year with the band descending from the ceiling in scuba suits, then returning to play Auld Lang Syne as huge balloons fell from above. Great time!! —EMILY BROWN

➢ If you like jams, this is a show to get. Possum is insane—it just goes on and on—and YEM is great. The third set just takes the cake, though. I think that Phish should have put this Harry Hood on *A Live One* instead of the one that's on it. —DAVID ECKERS

New Year's '93

12/31/93 The Centrum, Worcester, MA

Phish fans from around the country piled into a raging lot scene across the street from the Centrum. This was not just a night of Phish—it was an enormous New Year's celebration where 15,000 partied to pay tribute to 10 years of a special band and its ultra-loyal following. For the first time in the band's history, scalpers had no problems moving tickets for $80 to $150 a pop.

For many fans, it took the first half of the first set to squeeze through the tight, unprepared door security. This dilemma was even acknowledged by Trey who asked the audience if everybody had made it in. When the crowd finally settled into Phish's groove, the atmosphere escalated into a cross between a concert and a playoff game as the crowd cheered relentlessly during recognized opening licks and piercing jams. At the end of set I, Phish lyricist Tom Marshall emerged to vocalized his lyrical contribution to Run Like an Antelope for the first time on stage.

Set II created a much darker atmosphere as fans were haunted several times by the Frank Zappa lick from Peaches en Regalia, resurrected three days earlier to pay tribute to his recent death. And when the smoke cleared during the YEM jam, all were confused to find the band members, dressed in scuba gear, leaving the stage for the second set break.

All eyes stayed focused on the stage, which had been designed just for the New Year's Run to look like the inside of a Phish tank. This was by far the most elaborate stage setting of the band's 10-year history. And to the amazement of all, Phish (or perhaps look-alikes) were lowered into the tank from the rafters of the Centrum sporting the scuba gear. But within the moments theatrical enormity, Phish brought things down to earth with light and humorous dialogue, including a mention of Fish's butt cheeks by Trey. The band members landed on stage, climbed into a giant clam shell at the back of the stage, and disappeared. The clam then rose up, counting down to New Year's, then sprayed confetti into the crowd at midnight while giant white balloons dropped from the rafters into the crowd. The band raced back on stage, in their normal clothes, and broke into Auld Lang Syne.

During Auld Lang Syne, a camera crew appeared to film concert material for Phish's first MTV video-to-be. Fans danced to an unfamiliar jam, which was later known to all as Down with Disease.

It was clear to all that the Phish Phenomenon had reached a new level. Phish fans old and new gathered to the hugest and most energetic event of its time. For most, it clinched New Year's plans for years to come.

1994

124 Total Show Dates
- **1** one-set show
- **121** two-set shows
- **2** three-set shows

PHAN PICKS 1994

SHOW	THE SKINNY
1) 10/31/94 Glens Falls, NY	*The White Album* on Halloween.
2) 05/07/94 Dallas, TX	70-minute Tweezerfest.
3) 07/16/94 Fayston, VT	Incredible second set!
4) 06/26/94 Charleston, WV	Gamehendge and *Hoist*.
5) 07/13/94 Patterson, NY	Wild and wacky second set.
6) 06/11/94 Morrison, CO	Red Rocks radio broadcast.
7) 12/31/94 Boston, MA	Flying hot dog rings in 1995.
8) 12/29/94 Providence, RI	Incredible 30+ minute Bowie.
9) 07/08/94 Mansfield, MA	Gamehendge and a great set II.
10) 12/30/94 New York, NY	Phish's first show at MSG.

MUSICAL RECAP: The Dallas Tweezerfest in May turned a new corner for Phish, and throughout the year they built on their ability to allow one massive jam to carry a set. The fall tour would see several such nights, including the Bangor Tweezer included on *A Live One*.

REPRESENTATIVE JAMS: Tweezer (et al), 5/7/94; Mike's > Simple, 11/16/ 94; Weekapaug, 12/28/94; Funky Bitch > Jam > Yerushalayim, 11/22/94.

ORIGINAL SONG DEBUTS: Axilla II (4/16/94), Demand (4/9/94), Dog Faced Boy (4/14/94), Down With Disease (4/4/94), Guyute (10/7/94), If I Could (4/4/94), Julius (4/4/94), N20 (6/25/94), Scent of a Mule (4/4/94), Simple (5/27/94), Wolfman's Brother (4/4/94)

COVER SONG DEBUTS: Bluegrass Breakdown (11/16/94), Bow Mountain Rag (10/14/94), Butter Them Biscuits (11/18/94), Dooley (11/20/94), Fixin' to Die (11/17/94), Foreplay (10/7/94), Hi-Hell Sneakers (4/23/93), I Wanna Be Like You (4/4/94), I'm Blue I'm Lonesome (11/16/94), Long Journey Home (11/16/94), Long Time (10/7/94), Old Home Place (6/26/94), Sweet Baby's Arms (11/18/94), Who By Fire (4/23/94), plus all of *The White Album* (10/31/94)

DARK HORSES

SHOW	THE SKINNY
1) 06/17/94 Milwaukee, WI	The O.J. show.
2) 11/30/94 Olympia, WA	Antelope anchors wild 2nd set.
3) 11/16/94 Ann Arbor, MI	30-minute jam out of Simple.
4) 04/29/94 Clearwater, FL	Great setlist, very well played.
5) 04/15/94 New York, NY	The horns do Broadway.

Most-Played Originals:

1) Sample in a Jar	70	56%
2) Julius	65	52%
3) Down with Disease	55	44%
4) Rift	47	38%
5) Bouncing	46	37%
5) Poor Heart	46	37%
7) Sparkle	45	36%
8) Maze	44	35%
8) Scent of a Mule	44	35%
8) Stash	44	35%

Most-Played Covers:

1) Amazing Grace	31	25%
2) Nellie Cane	26	21%
3) Ginseng Sullivan	20	16%
4) GTBT	17	14%
5) Rocky Top	16	13%
5) Uncle Pen	16	13%
7) Peaches En Regalia	15	12%
8) Old Home Place	13	10%
9) Fire	11	9%
9) Purple Rain	11	9%

First-Set Openers:

1) Runaway Jim	20
2) Llama	14
3) Chalk Dust Torture	9
3) Wilson	9
5) My Friend My Friend	7

Second-Set Openers:

1) Also Sprach Zarathustra	24
2) Suzie Greenberg	9
3) The Curtain	6
3) Maze	6
5) Wilson, Bowie, Sample	5

Top Henrietta Songs:

1) Purple Rain	11
2) I Wanna Be Like You	9
2) Cracklin' Rosie	6
4) Love You	6
5) Bike	5

A Cappella Songs:

1) Amazing Grace	31
2) Sweet Adeline	25
3) Carolina	5
4) Freebird	5
5) Memories	1

1994 Spring *TAKE ANOTHER STEP*

Spring Tour 1994 would see the band push songs from *Hoist*—it's a virtual certainty that any show from this tour contains Julius, Down With Disease or Sample, if not all three—but not much more than they had played the new songs off *Rift* a year earlier. The band's first video, directed by Mike Gordon for Down with Disease, received MTV play mostly in the wee hours of the night but never became a hit. Just a week into the tour, Trey tore ligaments in his leg at the Buffalo gig, an injury that he valiantly played through but that may have sapped some of the band's energy early in the tour. By the first week of May, though, the band would reach new heights on a quiet night in Dallas, the famous Tweezerfest, before heading once again for a rendez-vous with the Pacific.

4/4/94 [ACCESSIBILITY: ••••]
Flynn Theater, Burlington, VT
I: Divided Sky, Sample, Scent of a Mule, Maze, Fee, Reba, Horn, It's Ice, Possum
II: Down with Disease > If I Could, Buried Alive, Landlady, Julius, Magilla, Melt, Wolfman's > I Wanna Be Like You, Oh Kee > Suzie
E: Harry Hood, Cavern

Benefit show to raise money to renovate the Flynn Theatre. "My Hometown" line sung before Divided Sky. Second set, starting with Buried Alive and excluding Oh Kee, featured the six-piece Giant Country Horns: Carl Gerhard, trumpet; Dave Grippo, alto sax; Chris Peterman, tenor sax; Mike Hewitt, baritone sax; Don Glasgow, trombone; Joseph Somerville Jr., trumpet. Fishman on vacuum for I Wanna Be Like You. Dave Grippo on congas for Landlady and I Wanna Be Like You. Carl Gerhard on trumpet (solo) for Cavern. Original verse sung in Cavern. Last Magilla, 3/25/93 [73 shows]. Concert debuts: Scent of a Mule, Down with Disease, If I Could, Julius, Wolfman's, and I Wanna Be Like You.

➢ The Flynn show was a "secret" in the sense that it wasn't announced along with the other spring '94 shows—instead, tickets went on sale one morning, and anyone able to make it to the Flynn Box Office before the line grew too long found themselves in luck. The show was clearly a tough ticket, so most ticketless phans stayed away, though some were drawn by increasingly believable rumors that a horns section would show up. Inside the tiny theater, Phish payed tribute to Burlington with a "Back in my hometown" line to open the show, and then brought out the horns for most of the second set. Like most opening nights, everyone was a little rusty, but seeing the GCH back together, along with a few new friends, made for a special evening. —LOCK STEELE

➢ A perfect place to see a show. The first set is, as it appears, rather standard. But the debuts of *Hoist* songs in the second set are fantastic. At the time, I could not get over how good Disease is live (the band knew it, too). The Country Horns are fun but it limits how far the show can go as far as the song selection. Before the first encore, Trey announces an update of the Duke-Arkansas NCAA Championship Game score to a mixed crowd reaction. After Harry, he announces the final score. A funny change in one of the verses of Cavern: instead of "the foggy cavern's musty grime appeared within my palm," Trey exclaims, "the brothel wife then grabbed the knife and slashed me on the tongue." —MATTHEW NAPOLI

4/5/94 [ACCESSIBILITY: ••]
Metropolis, Montreal, QC
I: Runaway Jim, Foam, Fluffhead, Glide, Julius, Bouncing, Rift, AC/DC Bag
II: Peaches, Ya Mar, Tweezer, If I Could, YEM > I Wanna Be Like You, Chalkdust, Amazing Grace **E:** Nellie Cane, Golgi

Fishman on vacuum for I Wanna Be Like You.

4/6/94 [ACCESSIBILITY: ••]
Concert Hall, Toronto, ON
I: Llama, Guelah, Poor Heart, Stash, Lizards, Sample, Scent of a Mule, Fee > Antelope
II: Curtain > Down with Disease, Wolfman's, Sparkle, Mike's > Lifeboy > Weekapaug, Squirming Coil, Cavern
E: Ginseng Sullivan, Nellie Cane, Adeline

Ginseng Sullivan and Nellie Cane performed acoustic/no amplification, with Trey on acoustic guitar, Fishman on Madonna washboard, Mike on upright bass and Page on mouth piano. Venue changed from the Palladium in Toronto on day of show.

4/8/94 [ACCESSIBILITY: ••]
Recreation Hall, Penn State University, University Park, PA
I: Maze, Glide > Foam, I Didn't Know, PYITE, Horse > Silent > Down with Disease > If I Could, Lawn Boy, Llama
II: Melt > McGrupp, It's Ice > Sparkle, Harry Hood, Bouncing > BBJ, Bowie, Suzie **E:** Contact > BBFCM

Mimi Fishman danced on stage throughout most of the show, played cymbals for I Didn't Know, and counted out "1-2-3-4" for BBFCM. Fishman on cymbals for I Didn't Know. "Owner of a Lonely Heart" tease in Suzie.

➢ The Maze in the first set of this show ranks as one of my favorites. In usual Maze fashion the suspense builds and builds then releases. But this Maze does not want to relent. The band keeps it going until you think there is no possible way to continue—but this is no ordinary band—it's Phish, where anything is possible. I Didn't Know had Mimi Fishman on cymbals, and the Split Open and Melt that opens the second set is unrelenting, especially the jam toward the end. There is no letting up the entire show. —DAVID GEORGE

➢ An interesting show, highlighted by, of all things, It's Ice! Definitely one of the more out-there Ices, plus good jamming throughout most of the second set, makes this show a real sleeper. —ED SMITH

4/9/94 [ACCESSIBILITY: ••••]
Broome County Arena, Binghamton, NY
I: Magilla, Wilson, Rift, Bathtub Gin, Nellie Cane, Julius, Fee, All Things, Stash, Squirming Coil
II: Sample, Reba, Peaches > BBJ, Demand > Mike's > Hydrogen > Weekapaug, Tela > Slave, Cavern **E:** Amazing Grace, Highway to Hell
"Little Drummer Boy" jam in BBJ and Weekapaug. "Divided Sky" tease in Weekapaug. Concert debut: Demand.

➢ A fascinating show; the second set is essential in any collection. The first set is nice, as Magilla and Bathtub are pleasant surprises, and the smoke-filled stage during Stash was fun to see, especially considering it doesn't happen anymore. Set II offers the greatest Reba ever (everyone should hear it) and maybe the most obnoxious version of Mike's Song—it's not for the casual fan. Snippets of Divided Sky and Little Drummer Boy decorate a fabulous Weekapaug. Back then Weekapaug had more power and energy than the longer, more articulate versions of the song you hear now. A perfect spot for Tela, and, well, Slave is Slave. —MATTHEW NAPOLI

➢ I think of this as the *Deja Vu* show because it had so much in common with the Portland show from the previous New Year's run. The venue, the setlist and the quality were just so similar. The Portland show is better known, but this one really holds its own as an absolute classic. —ANDY BERNSTEIN

➢ Highway to Hell was a funny response by Phish to the "AC/DC" [Bag] chants by some fans in front of the stage. I'm sure I wasn't the only person to finally 'get it' after this show. —CHARLIE MURPHY

4/10/94 [ACCESSIBILITY: ••]
Alumni Arena, State University of New York Buffalo, Amherst, NY
I: Runaway Jim, It's Ice, Sparkle, Melt, Esther, Chalkdust, I Didn't Know, Scent of a Mule, Down with Disease
II: My Friend, Ya Mar, Antelope, Fluffhead, Ginseng Sullivan, HYHU > I Wanna Be Like You > HYHU, Harry Hood **E:** Bouncing, Golgi
Trey strained his ankle a few hours before this show, an injury that would hamper him for the next month. Fishman on vacuum for I Didn't Know and I Wanna be Like You.

➢ The show started 45 minutes late due to Trey's pre-show accident that put him on crutches, but that didn't damper the fun. Page took over immediately with brilliant performances on Ice and an amazing piano jam in Scent. Down With Disease shows that it will be a live tune to be reckoned with for years to come—great jam. The highlight, however, is the insanely funny Fish as King Louie (with an injured Trey on drums!) —TIM FOISSER

➢ Trey hobbled to center stage with a cast on his leg. Somehow, he maintained a marvelous energy and spirit throughout—he even sat in on drums as Fishman honored us with not one but two vacuum solos in I Didn't Know and I Wanna be Like You. The boys appeared to have some quality communication with each other this night, particularly noticeable during a syrupy Split Open and Melt and a show-closing, whirling Hood. Bouillabaisse indeed. —ANTHONY BUCHLA

➢ Trey played with something to prove during Harry Hood. A truly emotional version. —BOB TALATZKO

4/11/94 [ACCESSIBILITY: ••]
Snively Arena, University of New Hampshire, Durham, NH
I: Caravan, Poor Heart, Foam, FEFY, Magilla, Julius, Glide, Divided Sky, Cavern
II: Also Sprach > Maze, Forbin's > Mockingbird, Uncle Pen, Sample > BBJ, YEM, Amazing Grace, Oh Kee > Suzie **E:** Possum
YEM featured Brad Sands on trampoline, substituting for the injured Trey. During the trampoline sequence, Trey sat and read a newspaper on stage. "Sunshine of Your Love" teases in YEM.

[4/13/94] [ACCESSIBILITY: ••]
WNEW Studios, New York, NY
Sample, Down with Disease, Julius [version from *Hoist*], Rift.
Live radio broadcast in the afternoon, prior to the Beacon Theater show.

4/13/94 [ACCESSIBILITY: ••]
Beacon Theater, New York, NY
I: Buried Alive > Poor Heart, Stash, Lizards, Julius, Ginseng Sullivan, Divided Sky, Golgi
II: Faht, Curtain > Sample, Reba, BBJ, Fee, A-Train, Bowie, Purple Rain > HYHU, AC/DC Bag **E:** Adeline, GTBT
Ginseng Sullivan performed acoustic/no amplification with same setup as 4/6/94. "A-Train," "Reba" and "Sunshine of Your Love" teases in Bowie. Fishman on vacuum for Purple Rain.

➢ Phish finally hit the Beacon theater, a place Trey told us the band had always wanted to play. Though the show was sold out, tickets for the Wednesday night show were plentiful—we scored tenth-row seats for $30 each outside the venue. The second set was notable for the last A-Train the band has performed, a solid Bowie and a very good Bag, during which a very drunk fan ran across the stage, cracking up the band. —LOCK STEELE

Saturday, April 9, 1994 Broome County Arena, Binghamton, NY

"You've Never Been to a Phish Show?!" Dave yelled. "Then you don't really like them." I stood there with *Hoist* in my hand and I'd just told him that yeah, I liked Phish. But no, said Dave. Never having seen Phish live, I was not qualified to judge, he said. No, no, I argued, I had listened to *Rift* at least 30 times. I was definitely a fan. Then, fatefully, our friend Pete, a dedicated if circumspect Phishhead, announced, "They're playing Binghamton on Saturday." This was obviously celestial intervention.

Who were we to flout the will of the Almighty? Pete and I became the A-Team of Phish Tour, focused like laser beams on our goal. Binghamton was five hours away, it was a sold-out show, and we had no car or money. But details would not stop us. "Jon must come!" I proclaimed, beginning the juggernaut. Jon was a friend of ours who had heard perhaps one Phish song ever and had not expressed much enthusiasm. Pete inquired as to why Jon was an essential member of the Team. Jon had a car. He was definitely essential. Jon, however, would only go if the tickets were free. The team moved onto its next goal: obtaining tickets. At no cost.

This was a little tricky, but soon the obvious solution of impersonating journalists and scamming free tickets from the record company presented itself. I called Elektra and spoke to a very bitter woman named Sharon, who said she needed a faxed request on the publication's letterhead. And we could only have two tickets. And no photo passes. But something was better than nothing, so I wrote myself a letter of introduction, pasted a newspaper headline on top, and faxed it to Sharon. We didn't hear back for a day, and since it was now Friday, we were a little tense.

But Phish's record company is full of middle-level managers, for they not only employ Sharon to take press-pass requests, but Bill to send out the press passes. And apparently Bill and Sharon are not close. Because Friday, Bill called my roommate Alison, another Team member, and tried to verify the address for the tickets. He posed no match for Alison. "Those were four tickets, right?" she demanded. "Umm, no," said Bill. But Bill crumbled like a stale cookie. Alison convinced him to FedEx four tickets to us. He did.

On Saturday, after an extremely long drive, we arrived in Binghamton. We wandered inside and were directed to seats by Pete, then goggled at the crowd. The show started—the first set was very bouncy and happy. I was thrilled when they played Rift, because at the time I thought it was the absolute apogee of songwriting talent. I also knew all the words to Julius, because as I mentioned, I had just obtained *Hoist*. After Julius they played what I referred to as The Weasel Song, otherwise known as Fee. Then they went into Stash, which I hadn't heard before, but I got very into it.

The set closed with Squirming Coil, which featured an amazing Page solo. I was so surprised that someone was playing the piano at a rock concert, and how few opportunities to become rock stars there are for piano players, that I almost forgot to listen, which would have been a shame because this was, and still is, one of the prettiest things I have ever heard.

The second set did not feature many songs with words in them, so I was a little miffed. They started with Sample In A Jar, which was good because I knew all the words, but then they gave up on singing and just played. They played this game with beach balls bouncing around the crowd—every time one bounced back on stage, a different band member would play. Unfortunately, I was not clued into this at the time, so I was a little bored. Things picked up near the end when they played Cavern—I didn't know the words, but at least there were some.

So my first impression of Phish was that they were a band with a good piano player and not enough words in their songs. My perspective has changed since then—I now get upset if they don't jam enough, I no longer hold Rift up as the ultimate example of musical perfection, and I can pick up on a lot of the games the band plays. And I now know that Binghamton was a really great show, empirically speaking. And I was there, even if I didn't appreciate it as much as I should have, or as I would now. And in the end that's all that counts, isn't it? That I was there? **—Monique O'Connell**

4/14/94 [ACCESSIBILITY: •••]
Beacon Theater, New York, NY
I: Runaway Jim, Foam, Sparkle, Down with Disease, Glide, Rift, Demand > Melt, Squirming Coil
II: Also Sprach > Antelope, Horse > Silent, Scent of a Mule, YEM, Nellie Cane, Dog Faced Boy, Slave **E:** Rocky Top
YEM featured an audience member on trampoline, substituting for Trey. Nellie Cane and Dog Faced Boy performed acoustic/no amplification with same setup as 4/6/94. Concert debut: Dog Faced Boy.

➢ This run of shows was the best for me. I had killer seats all three nights and the shows were tremendous. This night, I remember how quiet the crowd got during Dog Faced Boy until someone yelled BABABOOHEY from Howard Stern and even Trey cracked up. I enjoyed the "If I Were a Rich Man" jam during Scent of a Mule—a real crowd-pleaser. —ROB RINER

➢ Everyone had high expectations for the Beacon run. After all, here was Phish playing a three-night stand on Broadway in a small theater they said they'd always wanted to play. Well, maybe it was the lingering results of Trey's injury earlier in the week, but the shows (with the exception of Friday night's appearance of the horns) didn't meet our expectations. Still, sometimes all it takes is one song to make the night worthwhile, and on this night, there was Slave. Ahhhhh. —LEE JOHNSTON

4/15/94 [ACCESSIBILITY: ••••]
Beacon Theater, New York, NY
I: Llama, Guelah, Paul and Silas, Harry Hood, Wilson > Chalkdust, Bouncing, It's Ice, Down with Disease
II: Maze, If I Could, Oh Kee > Suzie > Landlady, Julius, Wolfman's > Alumni > I Wanna Be Like You > HYHU, Cavern **E:** Magilla, Amazing Grace
Second set starting with Suzie, and the Magilla encore, included the six-piece Giant Country Horns with the same lineup as 4/4/94. Carl Gerhard on trumpet for Cavern. Dave Grippo on congas for Landlady and I Wanna Be Like You. Alumni was first verse only. Fishman on vacuum for I Wanna Be Like You. Last Alumni, 10/10/91 Eugene, OR [279 shows].

➢ I believe this was the best of the three at the Beacon. The Giant Country Horns added a jazz sound that enhanced the music—the combination was so tight. Fishman's Jungle Book solo was fun, Magilla is always a treat, and Alumni Blues was a surprise that is always accepted with joy. I wish Phish would play 10 shows here like the Allman Brothers do. I would attend as many as possible. —ROB RINER

➢ I got stuck with standing-room tickets—boy, was it hot and stuffy in the balcony, jammed to the rafters with phans. It shook and swayed. When the Giant Country Horns came out, the balcony rumbled. I had incredible expectations for this show. Unfortunately, I left somewhat disappointed. I suppose every night can't be magical. That's why we go to so many shows—to catch the perfect one. —DAN KURTZ

➢ As best I can remember, this show marked the first time the *entire* audience chanted the opening to "Wilson." Now it's an accepted part of the Phish experience, but back then it caught me off-guard. Even more surprising was the one verse of Alumni Blues thrown into the mix in the second set. When Trey started singing, "Woke up this morning," it seemed the whole crowd was singing along to that, too. —LOCK STEELE

4/16/94 [ACCESSIBILITY: ••••]
Mullins Center, University of Massachusetts, Amherst, MA
I: Runaway Jim, Fee, Axilla II, Rift, Stash, Fluffhead, Nellie Cane, Antelope
II: Sample, Poor Heart, Tweezer > Lizards, Julius, Bouncing, YEM, Squirming Coil, Tweezer Reprise **E:** Fire
"Vibration of Life" in YEM. "Thank You" teases in YEM. YEM also featured Brad Sands on trampoline, substituting for the injured Trey. Concert debut: Axilla II.

4/17/94 [ACCESSIBILITY: ••]
Patriot Center, George Mason University, Fairfax, VA
I: Loving Cup, Foam, I Didn't Know, Divided Sky, Mound, Down with Disease > If I Could, MSO, Cavern
II: Bowie, Wolfman's > Uncle Pen, Sloth, Reba, BBJ > Maze, Contact, Golgi
E: Cracklin' Rosie, Bold as Love
Fishman on vacuum for I Didn't Know.

4/18/94 [ACCESSIBILITY: ••]
Bob Carpenter Center, University of Delaware, Newark, DE
I: Chalkdust, Glide > Poor Heart, Julius, My Friend, Rift, Melt, Dog Faced Boy, Oh Kee > AC/DC Bag
II: Also Sprach, Sample, Sparkle > Bathtub Gin > BBJ, Ya Mar, Mike's > TMWSIY > Avenu > TMWSIY > Down with Disease > HYHU > I Wanna Be Like You > HYHU, Cavern **E:** GTBT
YEM featured Big Phil on trampoline, substituting for Trey. Fishman on vacuum for I Wanna be Like You.

4/20/94 [ACCESSIBILITY: ••••]
Virginia Horse Center, Lexington, VA
I: Runaway Jim, It's Ice, Julius, Bouncing, Axilla II, Stash, Suzie
II: Poor Heart, Antelope, Magilla, Paul and Silas, Sample, BBJ > Harry Hood, Fee, YEM > Somewhere Over the Rainbow **E:** Highway to Hell
The Dave Matthews Band opened. Dave Matthews performed trampoline routine for Trey during YEM. Somewhere Over the Rainbow featured the entire DMB.

➢ This was a nice show at a venue that no one knew anything about until we got there. Plus, it was 4/20, which made for a nice day of pre-show festivities. The Over the Rainbow jam with DMB was very sweet, as was Dave Matthews replacing the injured Trey on trampoline during YEM. —M.N.J. ADAMS

➢ So you'd think that with a date like this, this show would be good. Well, it pooh-poohed. It was hot and loud and dirty (the Horse Center had a dirt floor). The only highlight was the YEM with Dave Matthews. —TERRY WATTS

4/21/94 [ACCESSIBILITY: ••••]
Lawrence Joel Veterans Memorial Coliseum, Winston-Salem, NC
I: Chalkdust, Sparkle, Foam, Glide, Melt, Lizards, Down with Disease > If I Could, Cavern
II: Also Sprach > Maze, Fluffhead, Mike's > Hydrogen > Weekapaug, Scent of a Mule, BBJ > Possum, Amazing Grace
E: Drums > Jam > All Along the Watchtower
The Dave Matthews Band opened. "If I Were a Rich Man" tease in Scent of a Mule. YEM featured Dave Matthews on trampoline, substituting for Trey. Drum jam in encore featured DMB's Carter Beaufort and Fishman. Entire DMB joined on jam out of drums and on Watchtower, with Dave Matthews on lead vocals. Concert debut: All Along The Watchtower.

➢ For several years, phans from the South had loudly sung the praises of The Dave Matthews Band to anyone within earshot. The group had built a strong local following by gigging regularly at places like Trax in Charlottesville, and it was clear they were ready to take the next step (though few thought they'd get so big, so fast). Phish knew it, too, because they asked DMB to open for them for two nights on their spring tour, and had the band sit in with them during both shows. This night in Winston-Salem proved the more satisfying of the two, with Fishman and Carter Beaufort kicking off the encore with a long drum duo that led into a jam with all the musicians and finally into the DMB's trademark rendition of Watchtower, this time with a Phishy flavor. Jamming collaboration at its finest. —ERNIE GREENE

4/22/94 [ACCESSIBILITY: ••]
Township Auditorium, Columbia, SC
I: Llama, Horn, Uncle Pen, PYITE, Sample, All Things, Nellie Cane, Divided Sky, Horse > Silent, Bowie
II: Suzie, Julius, Reba, Tweezer, Lifeboy, Runaway Jim, HYHU > I Wanna Be Like You > HYHU, Squirming Coil **E:** Father/Son Boogie, Bill Bailey
Fishman on vacuum for I Wanna Be Like You. Jack McConnell, Page's father, on keyboards and vocals for Father/Son Boogie and Bill Bailey.

4/23/94 [ACCESSIBILITY: ••••]
Fox Theater, Atlanta, GA
I: Funky Bitch, Rift, Fee > Peaches, Poor Heart, Stash, Esther, Down with Disease, Caravan, Hi-Heel Sneakers
II: Wilson > Antelope, Mound, Sample, Sparkle, Harry Hood, Ginseng Sullivan, YEM > Who By Fire, Golgi **E:** Freebird
Merle Saunders on keyboard for Caravan and Hi-Heel Sneakers. "Rock and Roll Hoochie Koo" jam in YEM. Jam out of YEM featured Col. Bruce Hampton and all the members of Phish on keyboards. Ginseng Sullivan performed acoustic/no amplification with same setup as 4/6/94. Concert debut: Who By Fire.

➢ "Phinally the Phabulous Fox" the t-shirts said, and they were right! This gorgeous theater provided the backdrop for one of the most underrated shows of the year. Besides a Funky Bitch opener, a very strong early Down With Disease and YEM with Col. Bruce Hampton and the boys banging away on keyboards, this night also has the first guest appearance by longtime Jerry Garcia collaborator Merl Saunders. He sounds right at home with the boys. —MARCIA COLLINS

➢ Excitement ran high for this show, but it was dulled by the fact that the enormous "Freaknick" party had taken over Atlanta for the weekend, turning the town into a total madhouse and backing up traffic for miles. In the midst of it all was the Phish scene, and somehow the boys managed to pull out a great show. —RICH MAZER

➢ Besides being one of the better jammed shows of the spring '94 tour, the Fox is also the only show to feature Phish's rendering of Leonard Cohen's beautiful Who By Fire. The band apparently had a tape of Cohen songs they listened to all the time on the tour bus, and so out of the YEM vocal jam, they paid their respects. It's gorgeous. —ED SMITH

4/24/94 [ACCESSIBILITY: •••]
Grady Cole Center, Charlotte, NC
I: My Friend, Ya Mar, Axilla II, Maze, Bathtub Gin > Jump Monk > Bathtub Gin, Dog Faced Boy, Paul and Silas, It's Ice, Slave
II: Demand > Bowie, Mango, Julius, Forbin's > Mockingbird, Chalkdust, Contact, GTBT **E:** Adeline
Last Jump Monk, 3/12/88 Burlington, VT [600 shows].

4/25/94 [ACCESSIBILITY: ••]
Knoxville Civic Auditorium, Knoxville, TN
I: Landlady > Runaway Jim, Fee, Foam, Down with Disease, Ginseng Sullivan, Dog Faced Boy, Tela, Poor Heart, Melt
II: Curtain > Sample, My Mind's > Antelope > Mound, Squirming Coil > Divided Sky, Bouncing, BBJ, BBFCM **E:** Amazing Grace, Bold as Love
Ginseng Sullivan and Dog Faced Boy performed acoustic/no amplification with same setup as 4/6/94.

[4/26/94] [ACCESSIBILITY: •••]
Purple Dragon Studios, Atlanta, GA
Sample, Bouncing, Maze, Down with Disease, Fluffhead, Carefree
Live radio broadcast. Carefree is a Sun Ra song.

4/28/94 [ACCESSIBILITY: ••]
SunFest, West Palm Beach, FL
Runaway Jim, Foam, Sample, Rift, Down with Disease, Bouncing, It's Ice, Antelope, Squirming Coil, Julius, GTBT **E:** Golgi
Outdoor music festival, with Blues Traveler and others. Phish played one set.

4/29/94 [ACCESSIBILITY: •••]
Boatyard Village Pavilion, Clearwater, FL
I: Halley's, YEM > FEFY, Scent of a Mule, Sloth, Divided Sky, I Didn't Know, Dog Faced Boy, Melt > Sanity, My Mind's, Llama
II: Suzie, Maze, If I Could, Reba, Fee, Uncle Pen, Mike's > Hydrogen > Weekapaug, I Wanna Be Like You > HYHU, Cavern **E:** Fire
Fishman on washboard for I Didn't Know and vacuum for Be Like You. Last Sanity, 5/17/92 [200 shows].

➢ The Boatyard was a freaky little place—what a great breeze across the pavilion, a lot of young people walking around on a cement floor, and a small island of eight or nine tapers in the midst. The first set was hot, the sound was sweet, pure and kind. Plenty of room to dance in the rear. The second set is where it was at. Opener Suzie, and the strobes and smoke. Trey kept popping out of the fog in various places. (Word had it that right after the first set, the band jumped on a boat for their setbreak. They went for a boat ride, came back and played the second set.) —DAVE PARKER

➢ One way I judge a great show is by the amount of random screaming from the band. By that standard (and many others), this show is an absolute home-run, probably the best show of April '93—if not the entire first leg of the tour. YEM explores some interesting places, then moves (ignoring the vocal jam) seamlessly into FEFY, a beautiful combination. There's also a warped Split Open that has everyone screaming, into the first Sanity in two years. A torrid Llama closes an incredible first set. —JOSH ALBINI

4/30/94 [ACCESSIBILITY: •••]
The Edge, Orlando, FL
I: Chalkdust, Mound, Stash, Poor Heart, Sample, PYITE, Rift, Ginseng Sullivan, Adeline
II: Wilson, Bowie, Wolfman's, Peaches, Harry Hood, Axilla II, McGrupp, Possum, Purple Rain > HYHU, BBFCM
E: Sleeping Monkey, Highway to Hell
Ginseng performed acoustic/no amplification with same setup as 4/6/94. "Wimoweh" jam in Bowie intro and throughout the second set. "Tease medley" in Possum included teases of the songs played previously in the set (in order, Wilson, Bowie, Wolfman's, Peaches, Harry, Axilla II, McGrupp.) Fishman on vacuum for Purple Rain.

➢ Great set II of this show, featuring a nice combination of songs, old and new. They tease "The Lion Sleeps Tonight" throughout the set—pretty funny! Listen to the Possum on this tape for several more teases. It turns out to be one of the best versions of this song, a drawn-out version with lots of jamming. The two encores also help this show stand out from others. Phish was really on fire this night. —TIM HERRMAN

5/2/94 [ACCESSIBILITY: ••]
Five Points South Music Hall, Birmingham, AL
I: Great Gig, Melt, Bouncing, Down with Disease, It's Ice, Glide, Divided Sky, Suzie, Foam, Sample
II: Runaway Jim, Mound, Reba, Golgi, Lizards, Julius, Lawn Boy, Mike's
E: Cavern
Fishman on vacuum for Great Gig. Oteil Burbridge on guitar and Stacey Starkweather on electric bass for Mike's.

5/3/94 [ACCESSIBILITY: •••]
Starwood Amphitheater, Antioch, TN
I: Rift, Guelah, Maze, Sparkle, Stash, Squirming Coil, Scent of a Mule, Sample, Adeline
II: Bowie, If I Could, Fluffhead, Down with Disease, Harpua, Chalkdust, HYHU > I Wanna Be Like You > HYHU, Slave **E:** Nellie Cane, Fire
If I Could featured Allison Krauss on vocals. "Sunshine of Your Love" and "Sunshine of My Life" teases in Bowie and Harpua. "Black and White" jam in Bowie intro. Show moved to the main stage at Starwood (from smaller Veranda stage) because of rain.

5/4/94 [ACCESSIBILITY: ••••]
State Palace Theater, New Orleans, LA
I: Runaway Jim, Foam, Sample, It's Ice, Sparkle, Axilla II, Tweezer, Lifeboy, Rift > Tweezer Reprise
II: Antelope, Bouncing, YEM, Landlady, Buried Alive, Julius, Wolfman's, Magilla, Suzie **E:** Caravan
Second set starting with YEM and including encore featured the six-piece "Cosmic Country Horns": Carl Gerhard, trumpet; Michael Ray, trumpet; Tony Tate, tenor sax; Dave Grippo, alto sax; Jerome Theriot, baritone sax; and Rick Trolsen, trombone.

➢ The show has high energy throughout, and very enjoyable versions of Tweezer and Tweezer Reprise. But what makes the show is the Antelope, when Trey dedicates the jam to his friend's newborn baby, saying, "I hope you live your life like that last jam." It's very cool to hear. —JAMIS CURRAN

➢ The Horns played on a lot of songs they normally don't. This is the best I've ever heard such a large number of horns play at one time. They were at their best. —DAVID JONES

5/6/94 [ACCESSIBILITY: ••]
Bayou City Theater, Houston, TX
I: Down with Disease, Oh Kee > AC/DC Bag, Poor Heart, My Friend, Ya Mar, Stash, Esther, Chalkdust
II: Maze, Golgi, Uncle Pen, Sample, Reba, Axilla II, Julius, HYHU > Bike > HYHU, Bowie **E:** Ginseng Sullivan, Freebird
Fishman on vacuum for Bike. Ginseng Sullivan performed acoustic/no amplification with same setup as 4/6/94.

5/7/94 [ACCESSIBILITY: •••••]
The Bomb Factory, Dallas, TX
I: Llama, Horn > Divided Sky, Mound, FEFY, Scent of a Mule, Melt, If I Could, Suzie
II: Loving Cup, Sparkle, Tweezer > Sparks > Makisupa > Jam > Sweet Emotion Jam > Walk Away > Jam > Cannonball Jam > Purple Rain > HYHU > Jam > Tweezer Reprise **E:** Amazing Grace, Sample
Fishman on vacuum for Purple Rain.

Phan Pick #5 ➢ This show is a perfect example of how Phish can push the very boundaries of their songs. Three songs into the second set, Phish breaks into Tweezer, but this is no ordinary Tweezer. No, this is SuperTweezer! The band drifts and floats as they jam for what seems forever. They go for nearly 70 minutes as they go in and out of songs and teases and Tweezer. They even play the Breeders' Cannonball, which goes into Purple Rain with an awesome vacuum solo. The whole thing ends with a Tweezer Reprise. This show is a must-own! —CHAD ASHCRAFT

Tweezerfest

5/7/94 The Bomb Factory, Dallas, TX

It used to be the stuff of dreams. "What if," a phan would say, "Phish just jammed for an entire set? You know, what if they started a song and it just didn't end?" The dream was possible because everyone believed Phish capable of it—heck, some of their soundcheck jams stretched for 45 minutes, and Mike Gordon had said before they hoped the informal, relaxed nature of their soundchecks could some day translate to a concert.

So most everyone thought it could happen—but no one expected it, much less at a tiny venue in a state Phish had only played only a handful of times. But it was at the Bomb Factory in Dallas, TX that Phish took their next giant leap forward as a band, taking Tweezer so far afield that it—along with segues and jams into several other songs—ran nearly 70 minutes in length.

The first set of the show gave little indication of what was to follow in the second set, and the first two songs of the second set didn't hint at it either. That's because Phish themselves didn't know what was going to happen. As Trey told Michael Snyder of the *San Francisco Chronicle* a few weeks after the Bomb Factory show, "We try to let the spontaneity take over. We just played Dallas the other night, and the last 65 minutes of the show were completely improvised. It wasn't planned, but it happened, and we just took off."

Did they ever. Quickly leaving behind the Tweezer theme, Phish took their jam into bluesy jamming, a darker space Trey later said was played in tribute to the hard-rock band Gwar playing next door on the same night, pronounced "Sweet Emotion" (Aerosmith) and "Cannonball" (Breeders) sections, and full versions of longtime staples Sparks, Makisupa Policeman, Walk Away and Purple Rain, all strung together in one nonstop piece of music. The set closed with an extended Hold Your Head Up Jam that turned over into Tweezer Reprise, topping off the set.

At the time, the Bomb Factory seemed like a once-in-a-lifetime show, but by the fall tour, jams of this sort would pop up regularly. "If it wasn't for nights like that," Trey said, "I wouldn't be doing this. I'm not traveling eight months out of the year just to sit in hotel rooms."

➢ The Tweezerfest. Folks in Texas had a lot to hoot and holler about: set two had to be the coolest set of jammin' in years. Loving Cup is great and the Tweezer rips—it's got a whole bunch of songs and teases added to it. Check out Trey yelling "suck it!" while Fishman takes a vac solo on Purple Rain. —MICHAEL RAMBO

➢ When I first heard this show, I was mesmerized and considered it one of Phish's most epic, ground-breaking performances ever. I still do. My personal favorite part of Tweezerfest is the blues jam that the band howls to. All 67 minutes of this mind-blowing piece of music are held in my mind as true improvisation at its very best. —CHIP CROTEAU

➢ Truth be told, I don't really, really enjoy listening to this tape. It's interesting, sure, but it doesn't hold together as a Tweezer the way the ones from Bangor (11/2/94) or Bozeman (11/28/94) do. Still, the show bears listening for the band's willingness to throw the setlist completely out the window and devote the set to one major song. There are great digital soundboards of this set around that shouldn't be hard to find. —KATIE SILVER

➢ This show was smaller than some of the parties some of you have been to, but much bigger in a way. —DAVE PARKER

5/8/94 [ACCESSIBILITY: ••]
The Backyard Bee Cave, Austin, TX
I: Runaway Jim, Foam, Axilla II, Rift, Down with Disease, Bouncing, Stash, Squirming Coil
II: Also Sprach > Antelope > It's Ice > Fee > Julius > Cavern, YEM > Halley's > GTBT **E:** Adeline, Golgi

5/10/94 [ACCESSIBILITY: ••]
Paolo Soleri Amphitheatre, Santa Fe, NM
I: Buried Alive > Poor Heart, Sample, Divided Sky, Axilla II, It's Ice, Melt, If I Could, Cavern
II: Maze, Wilson, Julius, Reba, Scent of a Mule, Harry Hood, Ginseng Sullivan, Dog Faced Boy, Nellie Cane, Bowie **E:** Squirming Coil
Ginseng Sullivan, Dog Faced Boy and Nellie performed acoustic/no amplification with same setup as 4/6/94.

5/12/94 [ACCESSIBILITY: ••]
Buena Vista Theater, Tucson, AZ
I: Catapult > Rift, Down with Disease, Fee, Maze, Axilla II, Foam, Bathtub Gin, Lizards, Sample
II: Also Sprach > Antelope, Horse > Silent, Uncle Pen, Fluffhead, Lifeboy, Possum, HYHU > Love You > HYHU, Contact, BBFCM
E: Amazing Grace, Rocky Top
Catapult started with Mike alone onstage, singing. Fishman on vacuum for Love You. Last Catapult, 2/10/93 Geneva, NY [133 shows].

5/13/94 [ACCESSIBILITY: •••]
Hayden Square, Tempe, AZ
I: Runaway Jim, It's Ice, Julius, Mound, Stash, If I Could, My Friend, Slave, Suzie
II: Chalkdust, Bouncing, Melt, McGrupp, Peaches, Scent of a Mule, YEM, Purple Rain, GTBT **E:** Freebird
"Layla" tease in Suzie.

➢ Here's one of those shows that isn't seen on every list, but that you should seek out nonetheless. The first set is solid, with a freaky It's Ice, a rare Mound and a Suzie with a "Layla" tease, courtesy of Page. The second set starts off with an excellent Chalkdust. Split Open and Melt screams from start to finish. For you Zappa fans out there, there's a fine Peaches out of McGrupp, then a phat funky bass solo from Mike in YEM. —RYAN HIRSCH

5/14/94 [ACCESSIBILITY: ••]
Montezuma Hall, San Diego State University, San Diego, CA
I: Llama, Wilson > Down with Disease > Fee, Reba, Sample, MSO, Ginseng Sullivan, Bowie
II: Curtain > Mike's > Hydrogen > Weekapaug > TMWSIY > Avenu > TMWSIY > PYITE, FEFY, Lizards, Cavern **E:** Bold as Love
Ginseng Sullivan performed acoustic/no amplification with same setup as 4/6/94.

5/16/94 [ACCESSIBILITY: ••]
Wiltern Theater, Los Angeles, CA
I: Buried Alive > Poor Heart, Sample > Divided Sky, Axilla II, Rift, Down with Disease > Bouncing, Stash, Adeline
II: Also Sprach > Antelope, Sparkle, It's Ice, Julius > YEM, BBFCM > Amazing Grace > BBFCM **E:** Fee, Rocky Top
"BBFCM" jam in Antelope. "Louie Louie" jam in YEM.

5/17/94 [ACCESSIBILITY: ••]
Arlington Theater, Santa Barbara, CA
I: Suzie, Maze, Mound, If I Could, Scent of a Mule, Ginseng Sullivan, Dog Faced Boy, Melt, Squirming Coil
II: Runaway Jim, Glide, Tweezer > Lifeboy, Uncle Pen, BBJ, Sample, HYHU > Love You > HYHU, Slave **E:** Highway to Hell
Ginseng Sullivan and Dog Faced Boy performed acoustic/no amplification. Cake delivered to Page to celebrate his birthday during his Squirming Coil piano solo. Fishman on vacuum for Love You.

5/19/94 [ACCESSIBILITY: ••••]
Hult Center, Eugene, OR
I: Halley's > Llama, My Friend, Poor Heart > Stash, Horse > Silent, Down with Disease, Mango, Cavern
II: Sample, Sparkle, Mike's > Hydrogen > Weekapaug, Lizards, Julius, BBJ, Harry Hood, Golgi **E:** Ginseng Sullivan, Nellie Cane, Adeline, Fire
Ginseng Sullivan and Nellie Cane performed acoustic/no amplification with same setup as 4/6/94.

➢ Stellar Halley's Comet opener, right into Llama. This show took place in a pretty small room, so they used non-amplification a couple of times for some acoustic numbers. Then the second set got really out of control. Mike's Groove had a very sinister feel—it almost felt as if they were ready to jump into Simple, but that wouldn't come for a couple more weeks. —BOB TALATZKO

➢ This is simply a very well-played, well-jammed show. Stash in the first set just goes *There*—this is probably the hottest version of this song I've ever heard. There's a real feeling of intimacy at the Pacific Northwest shows from this era, and I think the music benefits from it. —MELISSA WOLCOTT

5/20/94 [ACCESSIBILITY: ••]
Campus Recreation Center, Evergreen College, Olympia, WA
I: Fee, Maze, If I Could, It's Ice, Bathtub Gin, FEFY, Scent of a Mule, Dog Faced Boy, Carolina, AC/DC Bag
II: Also Sprach > Antelope, Weigh, Axilla II, Wolfman's, Rift, YEM
E: Chalkdust
"Wimoweh" tease in Bathtub Gin. Dog Faced Boy performed acoustic/no amplification.

➢ Think the band doesn't know what's going on in the crowd? We were all surprised at the extremely short second set—it was well under an hour. Word later circulated that Trey cut the show short because he felt like the crowd wasn't really into it. Well, the crowd was into it in a way—a chant of "Fee" from the folks up front convinced the boys to open up with that song—but yeah, this was a typical newbie show with no one really digging the jams. Things got a whole lot better in Seattle and Vancouver. —TYLER HARRIS

5/21/94 [ACCESSIBILITY: ••]
Moore Theater, Seattle, WA
I: Runaway Jim, Foam, Guelah, Down with Disease, Mound, Stash, Squirming Coil, Tela, Llama
II: Dinner and A Movie > Sample, Bowie, Contact, BBJ, Julius, HYHU > Bike > HYHU, Harry Hood, Amazing Grace **E:** Bold As Love
Fishman on vacuum for Bike. Last Dinner and a Movie, 8/9/93 Toronto, ON [54 shows].

5/22/94 [ACCESSIBILITY: •••]
Vogue Theater, Vancouver, BC
I: Demand > Sloth, Divided Sky, Glide, Melt, Fluffhead, MSO, Ginseng Sullivan, Dog Faced Boy, Axilla II
II: Down with Disease, Bouncing, It's Ice, McGrupp > Tweezer > Lifeboy, Rift, Slave, Tweezer Reprise **E:** Sleeping Monkey
MSO, Ginseng Sullivan and Dog Faced Boy performed acoustic/no amplification with same setup as 4/6/94.

5/23/94 [ACCESSIBILITY: •••]
Civic Auditorium, Portland, OR
I: Chalkdust, Sample, Foam, Fee > Maze, Horse > Silent, Julius, Reba, Cavern
II: Wilson, Antelope, If I Could, Sparkle, PYITE, YEM, Possum
E: Ginseng Sullivan, Amazing Grace, Highway to Hell
Ginseng Sullivan performed acoustic/no amplification with same setup as 4/6/94.

5/25/94 [ACCESSIBILITY: ••]
Warfield Theater, San Francisco, CA
I: Curtain > Sample, Uncle Pen, Stash, Forbin's > Mockingbird, Axilla II, Scent of a Mule, MSO, Adeline, Chalkdust
II: Rift, Tweezer, Lifeboy, Maze, Contact > BBJ, Julius, HYHU > Purple Rain > HYHU, Squirming Coil **E:** Sleeping Monkey, Tweezer Reprise
MSO performed acoustic/no amplification with same setup as 4/6/94. Fishman on vacuum for Purple Rain.

5/26/94 [ACCESSIBILITY: ••]
Warfield Theater, San Francisco, CA
I: Buried Alive > Poor Heart, Cavern, Demand > Melt, Sparkle, It's Ice > Catapult, Divided Sky, Sample
II: Also Sprach > Antelope, Fluffhead, Down with Disease > Mound, Ginseng Sullivan, Dog Faced Boy, YEM, Amazing Grace **E:** GTBT
Ginseng and Dog Faced Boy performed acoustic/no amplification with same setup as 4/6/94.

➢ Like the April Beacon run, not every night at the Warfield could claim to be an above-average show. Though the setlist for this night looks solid, the band just wasn't into it at all—the high point of the show came in the first set with cool Demand > SOAM and Ice > Catapult combos. Trey was later quoted as saying that this version of Antelope was the low point of the tour for him. I didn't think it was *that* bad, but it's clear that the boys just weren't clicking. They turned that around completely the next night, though. —PAT STANLEY

5/27/94 [ACCESSIBILITY: ••••]
Warfield Theater, San Francisco, CA
I: Wilson, Runaway Jim, Foam, Bouncing, Bowie, If I Could, PYITE > Harry Hood, Golgi
II: Suzie > Peaches, My Friend, Reba, Lizards, Julius, Nellie Cane, My Mind's, Mike's > Simple > Mike's > O Mio Babbino Caro > Jam > Possum
E: Fire

Nellie Cane and My Mind's performed acoustic/no amplification with the same setup as 4/6/94, plus Morgan Fichter on fiddle. Andrea Baker of the San Francisco Opera Company on vocals for O Mio Babbino Caro. After her solo, band and crew distributed macaroni and cheese boxes to audience members, who played along on Possum and Fire. "Flintstones" tease in Possum. Concert debut: Simple.

➢ A very good show that everyone has or should have. An energetic PYITE jams straight into the Hooded one. The first set is very good (except for Bouncin'). The second set offers a psychedelic Reba (above and beyond), and the debut of Simple—it isn't one of my favorites, but this is a damn wild version. Andrea Baker comes out to sing at the end—what a voice. They also really worked up the intro into Possum. —SEAN MILLER

➢ The best cover that Phish does is Zappa's Peaches. This version is one of the best, with great keyboard work by Page. And to hear it appear out of a Suzie jam is a nice treat, a great transition. Mike's begins with great promise, and instead of forming Hydrogen and Weekapaug it jams into the concert debut of Simple. This version is raw and riotous as band members trade verses, and even Fish goes solo a few times on vocals. This crazy version goes into a stop-and-go Possum with Flintstones teases. —TIM FOISSER

➢ The opera singer, the Flintstones licks, how cool. This is another rockin' show from beginning to end. —CHAD GAMERKE

➢ As Trey took the Mike's Song jam out of the Simple debut, and pushed the groove lower and lower, I thought the band had Slave on their minds. Instead, the groove dropped out to almost nothing, and Trey and Mike crouched down with their instruments as a woman emerged from the back of the stage and walked to the front, where she sang an aria with one of the most beautiful voices I'd ever heard. The crowd fell totally silent for her performance, then exploded in cheers when she finished. She was obviously surprised by the reception, which made the moment even more special. Then the band emerged from the wings with dozens of crates of Kraft Macaroni and Cheese (decorated with Flintstones characters in support of the Flintstones movie then in theaters) and passed them out to the audience. With everyone shaking their boxes—and a few folks spraying pasta around the room, of course—Page started the Possum intro, and the place went crazy. "Shake your macaroni!" Fish bellowed. We all did! —LOCK STEELE

5/28/94 [ACCESSIBILITY: ••]
Laguna Seca Raceway, Monterey, CA
I: Rift, Sample, Foam, Bouncing, Stash, Horse > Silent, Sloth, Maze, Cavern
II: Axilla II, It's Ice, Tweezer, Lifeboy, Reba, Fee, Llama, YEM, Bass Jam
E: Poor Heart

Laguna Seca Daze festival, with a number of bands. Les Claypool on bass for YEM and Bass Jam. Fishman on vacuum in YEM. "Popeye" jam in YEM.

5/29/94 [ACCESSIBILITY: ••]
Laguna Seca Raceway, Monterey, CA
I: Divided Sky, Guelah, Halley's > Down with Disease, Sparkle, Julius, I Didn't Know, Bowie
II: Nellie Cane, Split Open and Phil, Esther, Chalkdust, McGrupp, Oh Kee > Suzie, Antelope, Freebird
E: Wilson, Golgi, Rocky Top **E2:** Harry Hood, GTBT

Laguna Seca Daze festival, with a number of bands. "Guitar Player is Taking a Leak" jam (so named by Fish) before Harry Hood.

➢ This show is Phish at their humble best, playing at an outdoor festival show in sunny California (a state Phish should play in a little more often, I think!) The first set begins with a beautiful Divided Sky. The rare Halley's Comet, showcasing the vocal talents of the band, gives way to a ripping Down With Disease. But the real high point of this show is one of my favorite Phish songs, Split Open and Melt. This one's nice and long, complete with some vocal weirdness in the end jam, false stops and plenty more sonic oddities. Phans are treated to TWO encores, the second one being Harry Hood, which just takes off and makes you feel good! —RYAN HIRSCH

1994 Summer *TUNES EXHUMED*

Starting a new practice, the band took a short break before resuming their tour in Salt Lake City. As the tour headed east, the setlists became more creative than they had been for most of the spring tour—witness the returns from hibernation of NICU and Mango, as well as continued experimentation with Simple. The use of acoustic instruments on stage, a central part of spring tour, would also continue, albeit to a slightly lesser extent in the bigger outdoor venues.

Tapes from this tour, like the spring tour, are generally high in quality, although the burgeoning size of the tapers' section in 1994 meant that some folks with $39 Walkmans were taping shows and producing tapes of predictably poor sound quality.

6/9/94 [ACCESSIBILITY: •••]
Triad Amphitheatre, Salt Lake City, UT
I: Llama, Guelah, Rift, Down with Disease, It's Ice, If I Could, Maze, Fee, Suzie
II: Melt, Glide, Julius, Halley's > Scent of a Mule, Ginseng Sullivan, Mike's > Hydrogen > Weekapaug, Golgi **E:** Highway to Hell

Ginseng Sullivan performed acoustic/no amplification with same setup as 4/6/94.

6/10/94 [ACCESSIBILITY: •••]
Red Rocks Amphitheatre, Morrison, CO
I: Runaway Jim, Foam, Sample, Nellie Cane, Demand > Bowie, Lizards, Cavern, Julius
II: Axilla II, Curtain > Tweezer > Lifeboy, Sparkle, Possum, HYHU > I Wanna Be Like You > HYHU, Harry Hood, Tweezer Reprise
E: Sleeping Monkey > Rocky Top

Fishman on vacuum for I Wanna Be Like You. "Tela" tease before Lizards.

6/11/94 [ACCESSIBILITY: •••••]
Red Rocks Amphitheatre, Morrison, CO
I: Wilson, Chalkdust, YEM > Rift, Down with Disease, It's Ice, Tela, Stash
II: Also Sprach > Antelope, Fluffhead, Scent of a Mule, Melt, Squirming Coil, Maze, Contact > Frankenstein **E:** Suzie

Live FM broadcast. Last Frankenstein, 7/26/91 Athens, GA [329 shows].

➢ This was the second of a two-show run here, on a beautiful day with the sun falling behind the towering red icons of musical energy. Being a hotter show than the first, Trey was not going to let us down. A smokin' 2001 led into Run Like an Antelope, then a fun Fluffhead got everyone bouncing. The second set ended with a Frankenstein that melted everybody, the first one in three years. —JEFF SALVATORE

➢ Anyone tuning their FM dial to this show must have been blown away during the first 45 minutes. The boys did not let up until Ice, but not before roaring out five rockers in a row, including a segue between the YEM vocal jam and Rift (perfection!) and a DWD that showed everyone that this newbie was destined for greatness. FM crispies make this one a keeper for driving without the roof. —PAUL SHEETS

➢ Although all four members of Phish always shine bright on stage, Mike Gordon played some really incredible bass throughout this show. He is master of playing that one right note instead of the ten fast notes, and this show is the perfect example of this. The highlight is in set II—the intro into the Antelope jam is just perfect. Mike weaves through Trey's licks so well! —MICHELLE HIRSCH

6/13/94 [ACCESSIBILITY: •••]
Memorial Hall, Kansas City, KS
I: Buried Alive > Poor Heart, Sample, Divided Sky, Wolfman's > Dinner and a Movie, Stash, Ginseng Sullivan, Julius
II: Mike's > Hydrogen > Weekapaug, Esther, Cavern, Reba, Jesus Left Chicago, Scent of a Mule, BBJ, HYHU > Terrapin > HYHU, Slave **E:** Golgi

Ginseng Sullivan performed acoustic/no amplification with same setup as 4/6/94. Fishman on vacuum for Terrapin.

6/14/94 [ACCESSIBILITY: ••••]
Des Moines Civic Center, Des Moines, IA
I: Llama, Guelah > Adeline > Guelah, Rift, Down with Disease, Fee, My Friend, Uncle Pen, I Didn't Know > MSO > I Didn't Know, Melt
II: Frankenstein, Demand > Bowie, If I Could, It's Ice, Sparkle, YEM, HYHU > Bike > HYHU, Possum **E:** Sample

Guelah was split between Asse Festival and The Fly. Fishman on Madonna washboard for I Didn't Know and vacuum for Bike. MSO performed acoustic/no amplification with same setup as 4/6/94. "On Broadway" jam in YEM and Possum.

6/16/94 [ACCESSIBILITY: ••••]
State Theater, Minneapolis, MN
I: Bouncing, Rift, Julius, Fee > Maze, Gumbo, Curtain > Dog Faced Boy, Stash, Squirming Coil
II: Suzie, Antelope, Forbin's > Kung > Mockingbird, BBJ, Down with Disease > Contact, BBFCM > Purple Rain > HYHU, Golgi
E: Ginseng Sullivan, Amazing Grace, GTBT

Fishman on vacuum for Purple Rain. Ginseng Sullivan performed acoustic/no amplification with same setup as 4/6/94. "Heartbreaker" tease in GTBT. Last Gumbo, 4/21/93 Columbus, OH [103 shows].

➢ Talk about filling the hey hole! After four Phishy pop tunes, this Maze is just stunning! Also in set I, a Stash of epic proportions and a Coil closer. After an energetic, exploratory Antelope in Set II, there's a trip to Gamehendge complete with Kung chant. An inspirational DWD segues nicely into Contact > BBFCM, then Fishman says (as Prince), "Hello, Minneapolis, it's good to be home!" An all-around excellent show. —BOB COLBY

➢ The Bouncing that opens up the first set is beautiful; it floats you gently through the air and sets you down when the band jumps into Rift. Gumbo is a welcome addition to this show, and they play it better than the last time they played it (at the Newport Music Hall on 4/21/93). The Forbin > Kung > Mockingbird trio in the second set is phabulous. Kung in particular stands out. A classic Phish setlist with a few twists. —DAVID GEORGE

➢ It was clear from very early on that Down With Disease was going to be a hot, jamming song, but the way Phish takes the jam far out there during set two and then slides into Contact without returning to the lyrical refrain is a sign of things to come. —ED SMITH

6/17/94 [ACCESSIBILITY: ••••]
Eagles Auditorium, Milwaukee, WI
I: Runaway Jim, Foam, Glide, Melt, If I Could, PYITE, Bathtub Gin, Scent of a Mule, Cavern
II: Also Sprach > Sample > Poor Heart, Mike's > Simple > Mike's > Hydrogen > Weekapaug, Harpua > Kung > Harpua, Sparkle > BBJ > Julius, Frankenstein **E:** Sleeping Monkey, Rocky Top

"Voodoo Chile" jam in Harpua. "Mission Impossible" jam in Mike's. "Simple" is teased/sung in "Hydrogen" and teased/sung again in "Harpua."

➢ Do you remember where you were on this night? Phish were onstage and most people in America were watching the famous white Bronco going down a California highway. The band also saw this and let everyone know it. 2001 > "What do you say OJ?" was the theme. The boys had a good time with this one, including a "Mission Impossible" jam in Mike's. This tape is a lot of fun. —MICHAEL RAMBO

➢ Second set was what made this show special—the famous OJ show. I had no idea what they were talking about, shouting "OJ!" and "Run, OJ, run!" in the middle of 2001. The theme recurred randomly throughout the set. The ballroom was roasting (really, really hot), so we were all grateful for Harpua—not just because it's always fun, but because Trey had us dreaming of cool breezes—aah. There was a girl throwing ice cubes down from the balcony that I thought was an angel. The winding down at the ending of this show was a little disappointing but Sleeping Monkey-Rocky Top always makes me laugh, at least. —LIBBY BARROW

➢ Whenever you hear about this show, it's always dubbed as the "OJ Show." That was cool, but how about listening to the music? Nice 2001 opener and the Mike's Groove is really strong, one of the best from the tour. I love Harpua where Trey tells how the old man hears the Gamehendge kids singing Simple and how it pisses him off. —NICK SORICELLI

➢ I was there, and I haven't yet read a review of this show that gives the venue justice. It was hot! And I don't just mean the music—it had to be at least 115 degrees inside. Fans were set up to cool off the band, and there were some sisters throwing ice off the balcony/bar onto the ballroom floor. Highlights included the entire second set, with the OJ chants. Many lost minds were wandering around downtown Milwaukee that night. Nothing has topped this show since. —BOB TALATZKO

6/18/94 [ACCESSIBILITY: ••••]
UIC Pavilion, University of Illinois, Chicago, IL
I: Wilson > Rift, AC/DC Bag, Maze, Mango > Down with Disease, It's Ice, Dog Faced Boy > Divided Sky, Sample
II: Peaches > Bowie > Mind Left Body Jam > Bowie, Horn, McGrupp, Tweezer > Lifeboy, YEM, Chalkdust **E:** Bouncing > Tweezer Reprise

"Mind Left Body" jam interspersed in the Bowie intro. "Three Blind Mice," "Voodoo Chile" and "Purple Haze" teases in Bowie. "Immigrant Song" tease in YEM. "Follow the Yellow Brick Road" and "Spam" themes in YEM vocal jam.

➢ The music quality of this show is awesome! They had tons of energy and it definitely came through to the crowd. First set highlights: an intense and haunting Maze and a funky Ice jam, and (of course) we all love Divided Sky. It's the second set that really blew me away, though. They busted out with Peaches (one of my favorites, even though I'm partial to Zappa's version) and then bowled me over with probably the best Bowie I've ever heard! Just look at the rest of the set, it speaks for itself (except Bouncin'). Couldn't ask for much more. This show is guaranteed to make you glow. —LIBBY BARROW

➢ One of the best-jammed shows of the year, and also one that can be found pretty easily on soundboard. The band plays a very pronounced "Mind Left Body" jam (an old favorite of the Dead's) after starting the Bowie intro, and they do it great justice. From there, they jam into an otherworldly Bowie and later toss in great versions of YEM and Tweezer. This set blows me away. —JOSH ALBINI

6/19/94 [ACCESSIBILITY: ••]
State Theater, Kalamazoo, MI
I: Suzie, Julius, Lizards, Axilla II, Curtain > FEFY, Scent of a Mule, Stash, Golgi
II: Faht, Antelope, If I Could, Reba, Makisupa, Squirming Coil, MSO, Highway to Hell **E:** Freebird

MSO performed acoustic/no amplification with same setup as 4/6/94.

6/21/94 [ACCESSIBILITY: ••]
Cincinnati Music Hall, Cincinnati, OH
I: Runaway Jim, Mound > Sample, It's Ice > Horse
II: Fire, Poor Heart, Down with Disease, My Friend, Melt, Esther, Chalkdust, BBFCM, Ginseng Sullivan, BBFCM, Dog Faced Boy, Adeline, Julius, Sparkle, Harry Hood, Suzie **E:** Amazing Grace

First set cut short during Horse after venue fire alarm went off. Ginseng Sullivan, BBFCM (after Ginseng) and Dog Faced Boy performed acoustic/no amplification with same setup as 4/6/94. "Who Knows" tease at end of My Friend.

➢This show was an interesting one to attend. Smoking was prohibited at the Music Hall, like that would stop anyone. But the alarms in the air ducts went off and Trey, in the middle of Horse, calmly came over the PA and announced that everybody had to leave the building. After what seemed like two hours (only 45 minutes), we were allowed back in. In reverence to the drill, Phish played Fire upon returning. —SEAN MILLER

➢ Hilarious. We knew something was going to come of the fire alarm. When Trey says, "No smoking," that made the set. No smoking, what else do you need? And then into Fire—hahaha. Classic. —AARON MANDELMAN

➢ Fire was the obvious choice to get the crowd back up to speed and set the tempo for the 15-song superset that followed. Several high-energy tunes gave way to a nice acoustic break because everyone had to catch their breath. Then Julius got things going again and Suzie closed the set. Harry Hood was a high point. I long for those no amplification treats that we no longer get. —JUSTIN WEISS

6/22/94 [ACCESSIBILITY: ••••]
Veterans Memorial Auditorium, Columbus, OH
I: Llama, Guelah, Rift, Gumbo, Maze, If I Could, Scent of a Mule, Stash, Golgi
II: Also Sprach > Mike's > Simple > Catapult > Mike's > Simple > Icculus, Simple > Hydrogen > Weekapaug > TMWSIY > Avenu > TMWSIY > Fluffhead, MSO > BBJ, Jesus Left Chicago, Sample **E:** Carolina, Cavern

MSO performed acoustic/no amplification. "Midnight Rider" jams in Mike's/Catapult/Mike's. Digital Delay Loop jam between TMWSIY and Fluffhead. Last Icculus, 3/25/93 Santa Cruz, CA [127 shows].

➢ If you like to hear Phish break down their jams into total looseness, then this is your kind of show. The whole second set is transitional, effortlessly moving from one jam to the next. 2001 kicks off the insanity, followed by a Mike's Groove filled to the gills with improvisation. Simple > Icculus > Simple is a great treat. After wrapping it all up with Weekapaug Groove, the band settles things down with a TMWSIY > Avenu > TMWSIY. Refusing to let things go down, Fluffhead follows, and there's also a Jesus Left Chicago, which to my ears is Page's best cover. —ADAM DAVIDOFF

The OJ Show

6/17/94 Eagles Auditorium, Milwaukee, WI

When referring to Phish shows, most people rely on the venue and year, and maybe the night of the stand, like "Red Rocks '96, third night" or "Dayton '95." Holiday shows are worthy of their own names: "Halloween '94" or "New Year's '95," and then there are the rare cases where Phish furnishes event names: "Amy's Farm" or "The Great Went."

Rarest of all, perhaps, are the shows that create a name for themselves: "The O.J. Show," so named because Phish just happened to be on tour the night O.J. Simpson took off down the highway in his white Ford Bronco.

The band members have always been astute pop culture observers—just listening to Harpua over the years gives a sense of that, as the band samples on songs as wide-ranging as "Crossroads," "Black or White" and "Smells Like Teen Spirit." Then there's Trey's penchant for reporting sports scores from the stage, whether for the NFL (8/14/93 Tinley Park), the NBA (6/22/94 Columbus) or NCAA Basketball (4/4/94 Flynn). But only once has the band directly referred to a cultural event in its show, and that event was the Simpson Bronco chase.

Coming out on stage for the second set, the band had obviously been watching the Bronco chase backstage. As Also Sprach Zarathustra starts up, Trey intones, "Run, O.J.," as Fish chants, "What do you say, O.J.?" Trey keeps repeating "O.J." as the jam progresses; at its peak, "O.J!" is yelled in sync with the music. The O.J. themes continue in Poor Heart and Mike's Song—the prelude to the funniest Phish tribute ever. Yes, Simple makes clear that "We've got O.J. in the band!", poses that timeless question, "What is a band without O.J.?", and concludes, "O.J. is grand!" before the jam dissolves back into Mike's Song.

This show would not be so widely remembered if it hadn't been musically successful. But O.J. antics aside, the second set absolutely rocks. Mike's Groove is powerful—Simple, still developing since its debut at the Warfield on May 27—is its second performance ever. Its lyrics and theme even magically surface at the beginning of I am Hydrogen. Then there's Harpua, complete with samples of Hendrix (Voodoo Child) and even Phish (Simple!).

➢ The second set is one of my favorites. 2001 > Mike's > Simple > Catapult and more Simple. The wait for Weekapaug is long, but fulfilling with Icculus and Simple (again!) to keep you guessing. The Groove is finally completed and brought down to a beautiful TMWSIY—a breath of fresh air after all the chaos of a killer Mike's. Avenu Malkenu rocks, more TMWSIY and then Fluffhead, absolute perfection! My Sweet One keeps you hanging on and Jesus Left Chicago provides a much-needed break, preparing you for a tight encore to top off a killer set. —CARRI A. JOHNSON

➢ Arguably the best set of the year, the second set in Columbus is led by Mike's Groove—one of the craziest versions ever, with themes from Catapult, Simple and Icculus magically interwoven to create a true masterpiece. After jamming out, Mike's Song drops into Simple's chords, but they don't immediately head to the lyrics—instead, there's a very cool jam for a few minutes on the Midnight Rider theme, then Catapult is sung to the tune of the jam. Catapult jumps back into Mike's Song for a minute (again, a particularly melodious Midnight Rider jam), then they start repeating "I catapult downtown" over and over. Low and behold, the Simple chords re-emerged, this time with lyrics. Out of Simple comes Icculus, including an outrageous "Read the fucking book!" sermon from Trey and "Save your life!" chants. Then they start singing Simple again! —RICH MAZER

6/23/94 [ACCESSIBILITY: ••]
Phoenix Plaza, Pontiac, MI
I: Buried Alive > Poor Heart, Melt, NICU, Foam, Bouncing, Down with Disease, Horse > Silent, PYITE, Julius
II: Frankenstein, Bowie, Mango, Axilla II, Uncle Pen, Tweezer, Lifeboy, Slave **E:** Sparkle, Tweezer Reprise
"Sunshine of Your Love" jam in Tweezer. Last NICU, 5/1/92 Milwaukee, WI [248 shows].

6/24/94 [ACCESSIBILITY: •••]
Murat Theater, Indianapolis, IN
I: Divided Sky, Wilson, It's Ice, Fee > Sloth, All Things, Paul and Silas > Horn, Reba, Adeline, Sample
II: Demand > Antelope, Halley's, Curtain > McGrupp > Simple > Sanity, Llama, Dog Faced Boy, Poor Heart, Cavern, Carolina, Down with Disease
E: Rocky Top
Dog Faced Boy, Poor Heart and Cavern performed acoustic/no amplification with same setup as 4/6/94.

6/25/94 [ACCESSIBILITY: ••]
Nautica Stage, Cleveland, OH
I: N2O, Rift, Julius, NICU, Stash, Mango, Sample, Scent of a Mule, Tela, Chalkdust
II: Suzie, Maze, Sparkle, Bathtub Gin, Axilla II, YEM, HYHU > Cracklin' Rosie > HYHU, Harry Hood, Golgi **E:** Highway to Hell
Fishman on vacuum for N2O. Concert debut: N2O.

6/26/94 [ACCESSIBILITY: ••••]
Charleston Municipal Auditorium, Charleston, WV
I: Kung > Llama > Lizards > Tela > Wilson > AC/DC Bag > Forbin's > Mockingbird > Sloth > McGrupp > Divided Sky
II: Julius, Down with Disease, If I Could, Axilla II, Lifeboy, Sample, Wolfman's, Scent of a Mule, Dog Faced Boy, Demand > Melt Jam > Yerushalayim **E:** Old Home Place, Amazing Grace, Tube, Fire
Old Home Place performed acoustic/no amplification. First set contained complete Gamehendge narration by Trey—fourth ever live Gamehendge. Second set contained the songs from Hoist, played in order and almost exactly as on the album—first live performance of the slow ending for Axilla II; Melt Jam and Yerushalayim ending for Demand. Last complete Gamehendge, 3/22/93 Sacramento, CA [133 shows]. Last Tube, 4/12/93 Iowa City, IA [119 shows]. Concert debut: Old Home Place.

Thursday, June 23, 1994 — Phoenix Plaza, Pontiac, MI

I got to the show about 2:30 or 3:00 in the afternoon, way early, and I saw this beautiful girl run into this elevator, so I went to talk to her. Next thing you know, the elevator opened up, and there we were on top of a parking garage, right where the show was going to be, four stories up. A guard recognized her, and must have just figured I was with her, so we just walked out.

Suddenly, I realized the stage was right in front of me! So I sat down, and as it turns out, this beautiful girl—I mean, a real 10—is a local stripper. The same guy running all of the concession stands at the venue—cappuccino stands and stuff—also ran a bunch of local strip clubs. Then it hits me: all these girls in here, waiting for their assignments, are strippers. And they're all just beautiful! So we're hanging out, and I'm talking to this girl next to me who had seen Phish once, but nobody else there even knew the band. All of a sudden, Phish comes out on stage. I'm thinking, "Oh my God, Phish is here, they're about to soundcheck, I know I'm not allowed to be in here, and it's only a matter of time before I get thrown out." This guy is assigning people positions, and he keeps looking at me and not really saying anything, and Phish starts playing.

I think they started doing The Wedge, and all the girls got up and started doing their dances. They're all gyrating with each other, and taking off their shirts, and they've got spandex on. I'm thinking, "I'm watching Phish play with nobody here, and a bunch of beautiful girls stripping for me. This is too good to be real!"

Meanwhile, Page kept looking at me and grinning, and I started laughing—it seemed to me that Page knew that I wasn't supposed to be in there.

Then I heard Trey start doing NICU, which they hadn't played since '92 at this point. I'm thinking, "Holy shit, NICU!" They all go into it, and they're playing through it, and they get to the verse, "I try to convey what you strive to condone," and Trey fumbles it. But he doesn't just fumble it and fix it, he looks over at Page, and he says, "What's that line?" And I'm thinking, "I try to convey what you strive to condone, I try to convey what you strive to condone!" But Page says, "I don't know." So Trey looks over at Mike and shrugs, and Trey goes back to singing the verse again, just trying to get through it, and I was like, here I've got this rare opportunity to tell Phish the line that they don't know themselves in their own song that they're playing, a song that maybe they're getting ready to bust out after two and a half years of not playing it.

But then I'd probably get thrown out. Or else I could just stay quiet.

They ended up figuring it out, and playing it four times during that soundcheck, getting it down before they broke it out during that show. By the time that happened, I was like, "Oh, NICU, this tune, this is old, this is my fifth time hearing it today." **—Mike Graff**

GameHoist: 6/26/94 Municipal Auditorium, Charleston, WV

Phish tends to diss their albums. They seem to make it through the first round of press interviews okay, but usually by the time the album has been out for a few months, the band members distance themselves from it. *Picture of Nectar* "tried to meld too many styles." *Rift* "got too caught up in its concept" and "tried too hard."

So by the middle of the summer tour in 1994, it was safe to say that Phish was probably sick of *Hoist*, too. The album had been released in March to general derision from longtime fans of the band—the tunes were too radio-friendly, and there wasn't enough jamming. Of course, critics quieted after Phish broke out the songs in concert, adding long jams to Down With Disease and the "duel" segment to Scent of a Mule.

Once the songs had established their live rhythm, Phish had a bunch of new toys to play with, and by the time the summer tour steamed through the midwest in June, the band was hitting on all cylinders. Show after show saw innovative ideas and incredible jams. As the band headed to the verdant hills of West Virginia for its first show ever in that state, many midwest tourheads had dropped off tour, and many East Coasters planned to come on board starting on June 29 in Raleigh, NC.

So the band snuck into a tiny theater in Charleston, WV, and proceeded to play a show so unusual, so totally without precedent, that it led Trey to dub this the "You Snooze, You Lose" tour, given the band's penchant of playing outstanding shows in out-of-the-way venues during the month of June (and, as it turned out, July).

Opening with Kung—the first time ever—Trey started a Gamehendge narration that ran the entire first set. The first live Gamehendge in over a year, the fourth ever, was certainly a well-earned treat. Where things got really weird, though, was in the second set. The boys offered up Julius... and DwD... and If I Could... and suddenly, people realized they were playing *Hoist*. In order. And in the style of the album—well, sort of. They played the slow Axilla II ending live for the first time (this would surface in many later performances, too), and added a Split Open and Melt jam to the end of Demand. But they also jammed out on Julius and DwD, and dueled in Scent, demonstrating what *Hoist* could have sounded like if Phish ran the record company.

Phan Pick ➢ What better place to break out a live Gamehendge, narration and all, than their first show in the state nicknamed 'Almost Heaven.' West Virginia is one of the most beautiful places east of the ol' Miss, and Gamehendge just seems appropriate here. From the opening Kung chant to capping it all off with Divided Sky, Phish just beautifully set the mood on this night. —PETER BULKLY

➢ Even with their warped minds, Phish must have had to dig pretty deep to come up with the GameHoist idea. Not content with a first-set Gamehendge (the first in well over a year, and a beautiful version at that), the band came out for the second set and played all of *Hoist*, in order, pretty much true to the album. This wacky show is a key part of any good Phish collection. —TYLER HARRIS

➢ The first-set Gamehendge is great, but a lot of people seemed turned off by the second set, in which Phish plays *Hoist* in order. If you miss the second set, though, you're missing some great music, including a *very* well-jammed DWD, Axilla II with the slow "don't shine that thing in my face, man" ending played for the first time, and Demand including the Split Open and Melt jam and the Yerushalayim ending. —MELISSA COLLINS

6/29/94 [ACCESSIBILITY: ••]
Walnut Creek Amphitheatre, Raleigh, NC
I: Curtain > Sample, Reba, Mound, Julius, Horse > Silent, Catapult > Bowie, I Didn't Know, Golgi
II: Landlady, Poor Heart, Tweezer, It's Ice, Lifeboy, Divided Sky, Suzie, Cavern **E:** Ya Mar, Tweezer Reprise
Fishman on bass drum pedal hitting his leg (amplified by Trey's megaphone and Mike's mic) for I Didn't Know.

6/30/94 [ACCESSIBILITY: ••••]
Classic Amphitheatre, Richmond, VA
I: Down with Disease, Gumbo, Rift, Guelah, Melt, Glide, Scent of a Mule, Bouncing, Frankenstein
II: Wilson, Maze, YEM > Yerushalayim > YEM, Sparkle, Axilla II, Harpua, Antelope, HYHU > Love You > HYHU, Chalkdust
E: Sleeping Monkey, Poor Heart
"Honky Tonk Woman" jam in Harpua, sung by an audience member who was brought on stage. Harpua tease in Antelope intro. Fishman on vacuum for Love You.

➢ It rained very hard before the show but that didn't dampen our fun. Harpua was a great time, with Trey calling up a guy on stage to sing karaoke for Jimmy. Everyone got a real laugh out of that. This was a solid show, nothing extraordinary, but very fun nonetheless. A good time, as always. —M.N.J. ADAMS

➢ The first set is just a warm-up with smoking versions of Rift and Scent, plus Frank for a great closer. But the real treat came in the second set. Trey fiddles with his wah-pedal all set, leading the boys through a brilliant YEM > City Of Gold > YEM. Harpua with a guest appearance from the audience for a Honky Tonk Woman tease (get the tape to find out why we needed a guest!) and a spoken Kung. And with Harpua in mind, Trey prances into Antelope. This Antelope is when it all clicked for me. —TERRY WATTS

7/1/94 [ACCESSIBILITY: ••]
Mann Music Center, Philadelphia, PA
I: Runaway Jim, Foam, Sample, NICU, Stash, Mango, It's Ice, Tela, Julius, Suzie
II: Bowie, If I Could, Fluffhead, Down with Disease, TMWSIY > Avenu > TMWSIY, Possum, HYHU > Terrapin > HYHU, Harry Hood, Cavern
E: Rocky Top
Fishman on vacuum for Terrapin.

Sunday, July 10, 1994 **SPAC, Saratoga Springs, NY**

So I lose my keys at Great Woods. Not the first time I've lost a set of keys and won't be the last. A real bitch though. I looked around my car but they were nowhere to be found. I'd been selling shirts all day and also taken a long walk through the woods. I figured I lost them then.

The next day at Saratoga I had kind of forgotten about it, intentionally. I really wasn't looking forward to making that plaintive call to my landlord, who couldn't stand me anyway. Shirt sales are going okay, and then this one dude says, "I saw you selling those shirts back in the woods yesterday."

"I lost my keys in those woods," I lament, just making small talk. It was the first time I'd mentioned it all day.

"What kind of keys?" he asks. "Was it a Volkswagon key, on a blue key chain?"

"YES!"

Turns out I didn't even lose them in the woods. He found them near his car. And he just happened to have picked them up and brought them to the next show.

One in a fuckin' million. **—Andy Bernstein**

7/2/94 [ACCESSIBILITY: ••••]
Garden State Arts Center, Holmdel, NJ
I: Golgi, Divided Sky, Guelah, FEFY, Scent of a Mule, Tweezer, Lifeboy, Sparkle, Tweezer Reprise
II: Also Sprach, Mike's > Simple > Mike's > Yerushalayim > Hydrogen > Weekapaug, McGrupp, Maze, Sample, Slave, Highway to Hell **E:** Rift
"Antelope" and "Also Sprach" teases in Weekapaug.

➢ The second set of this show left the audience delirious. I didn't know that I was that far gone. Mike's > Simple > Mike's needs absolutely no explanation, but Simple was anything but Simple, as it ascends to its complex peak and then quickly yet meticulously blends into Mike's and then Yerushalayim. Hydrogen flows through the crowd like a warm breeze and lulls everyone into a dream which is abruptly but joyfully interrupted by a welcomed Weekapaug with 2001 teases. —MATTHEW ASHENFELDER

➢ This was the first time I really saw Phish—we met a bunch of friends and headed for the amphitheater. As we awaited admittance, a thunderstorm rolled by and the sky filled with large, amazing lightning bolts that we watched from the lawn once inside. The quick storm passed, followed by a raging show complete with strobe lights in Simple, tramps in Mike's and Trey and Mike lying on their backs during Hydrogen. I was hooked! —BETH CASTROL

7/3/94 [ACCESSIBILITY: •••]
The Ballpark, Old Orchard Beach, ME
I: My Friend, Poor Heart, Down with Disease, Fee, NICU, Horn, Old Home Place, Reba, Axilla II > Bowie
II: Melt, Lizards, Bouncing, It's Ice, Horse > Silent, Julius, Squirming Coil, Antelope, Suzie **E:** Fire
Old Home Place performed acoustic, with same setup as 4/6/94. "Over the Rainbow" jam in Reba, and tease in Bowie. "3rd Stone from the Sun" jam in Melt. Fireworks jam in Antelope, leading into Suzie.

➢ Not necessarily at the level of some of Phish's other holiday performances, but this pre-Independence Day gig ranks as an all together fun show with some real highlights. A beautiful sunset descended upon this minor league baseball park as the show began, with Trey repeatedly shielding his eyes to peer out at the brilliant colors of the sunset bouncing off the clouds. By the time night fell (and they'd played their first East Coast NICU in ages), they brought the house down with a fireworks jam during Antelope, which carried into a raucous Suzie. During the appropriate Fire encore, a giant Phish logo made of sparklers was ignited to the left of the stage. —ANDY BERNSTEIN

➢ A very underrated show. Ask anyone who was actually there and they'll say it was one of their top five. The first set was basic except for a Somewhere Over the Rainbow jam during Reba and Axilla II meandering into Bowie. Everyone thought they might do some fireworks because they didn't have a show the next day, but no one knew when. The guys came out for the second set and Trey put a life-size cardboard cutout of the Simpson family on the front of the stage. At the end of the set, when Antelope emerged, so did the fireworks. —MIKE D'AMICO

7/5/94 [ACCESSIBILITY: ••]
The Congress Center, Ottawa, ON
I: Rift, Sample, Curtain > Letter to Jimmy Page > If I Could, Uncle Pen, Stash, Esther, Down with Disease, Adeline
II: Also Sprach, PYITE > Sparkle, Bathtub Gin > Lifeboy, Cities > YEM > Great Gig, Ginseng Sullivan, MSO, Amazing Grace, Golgi
E: GTBT
"Nutcracker" tease in beginning of Esther. Fishman on vacuum for Great Gig. Ginseng Sullivan and MSO performed acoustic/no amplification with same setup as 4/6/94. Last Letter to Jimmy Page, 12/7/89 Baltimore, MD [530 shows]. Last Cities, 9/8/88 Burlington, VT [627 shows].

➢ What got into Phish during their two days in Canada? The tour had already seen the breakouts of Gumbo and NICU, but apparently not content with that, the band exhumed Letter to Jimmy Page (which would appear again at Jones Beach, then move back into retirement) and Cities (which wouldn't make another appearance until 1997) for their first show in Canada's capitol. Besides the surprises, Stash rocked out, as did most of the second set. This show lacks incredible jamming, but sure pleases. —TYLER HARRIS

7/6/94 [ACCESSIBILITY: •••]
Theater St-Denis, Montreal, QC
I: Llama, Fluffhead, Julius, Bouncing, Reba, Axilla II, My Mind's, Carolina, Bowie
II: Landlady, Poor Heart, Tweezer > Lawn Boy, Chalkdust > BBFCM > Sample > BBFCM, Harry Hood, Tweezer Reprise
E: Old Home Place, Nellie Cane, Memories, Funky Bitch
"Free Ride" tease before Llama. "HYHU" and "Also Sprach" jams in Tweezer. Old Home Place and Nellie Cane performed acoustic/no amplification with same setup as 4/6/94. "Munsters" jams in Llama and Bowie.

➢ This show is rock-solid from start to end. I'd say there were about 600 phans in attendance in a theater that could hold about 1,800 people. In set I, Llama contains a five-second snippet of the Munsters theme and the jam during Julius goes some interesting places. Then, prior to the beginning of Bowie, Trey dedicates this song to the man himself before the Munster's theme rears its head again once again during the intro. And what a smoking Bowie it is. That's just set I. Set II opens with a great Landlady that finds Trey sustaining one note for a minute and 15 seconds. It moves on to one of the best Tweezers ever and a four song encore taboot! —BRIAN GRESSLER

7/8/94 [ACCESSIBILITY: ••••]
Great Woods, Mansfield, MA
I: Llama > N20 > Lizards > Tela > Wilson > AC/DC Bag > Forbin's > Mockingbird > Sloth > McGrupp > Divided Sky
II: Rift, Sample, Reba > Yerushalayim, It's Ice, Stash, YEM > Frankenstein > YEM, Julius, Golgi **E:** Nellie Cane, Cavern
First set contained a complete Gamehendge narration by Trey—fifth ever live Gamehendge. Fishman on vacuum for N20. "Manteca" tease in Reba. Stash from this show appears on A Live One.

➢ Rainy and foggy, a purple sky, and lightning? Then it happened: out came Gamehendge, and we all felt it. The craziest Phish show ever. I'll contest it with anyone! —LANGSTON KNIPER

➢ Because of this show, there are about 20,000 extra Phishheads who can claim to have seen a Gamehendge. A thrill beyond almost all thrills. One thing I really enjoyed is how they used the bass line from McGrupp during the narration between songs. On the actual Man Who Stepped into Yesterday tape, it's a portion of Esther which serves this purpose. Having the McGrupp also played in its entirety was an additional treat. —ANDY BERNSTEIN

➢ Of course the first set is Gamehendge. Wow. But the second set deserves as much recognition as the first: a powerful Rift to start, the best Stash ever in my opinion (it's on A Live One), and an awesome YEM that sucks its way beautifully into Frankenstein. A must-own show. —CHIP CROTEAU

7/9/94 [ACCESSIBILITY: ••••]
Great Woods, Mansfield, MA
I: Runaway Jim, Foam, Gumbo, Maze, Guelah, Scent of a Mule, Down with Disease, Horse > Silent, Antelope
II: Also Sprach > Melt, Fluffhead, Poor Heart, Tweezer > Lifeboy, Sparkle > BBJ, Harry Hood, Suzie **E:** Sleeping Monkey > Tweezer Reprise

7/10/94 [ACCESSIBILITY: •••]
Saratoga Performing Arts Center, Saratoga Springs, NY
I: Chalkdust, Horn, Peaches, Rift, Stash, If I Could, My Friend, Julius, Cavern
II: Sample, Bowie, Glide, Ya Mar, Mike's > Hydrogen > Weekapaug, Bouncing, Squirming Coil, Crimes of the Mind **E:** Golgi, Rocky Top
Trey yells, "Who is she?" during Ya Mar. "Low Rider" jam in Mike's. The Dude of Life on vocals for Crimes of the Mind.

7/13/94 [ACCESSIBILITY: ••••]
Big Birch Concert Pavilion, Patterson, NY
I: Buried Alive > Poor Heart, Sample, Foam, Mango, Down with Disease, Fee, It's Ice, FEFY, I Didn't Know, Melt
II: Possum, Cavern/Wilson/Cavern > NICU > Tweezer > Julius > Tweezer > BBFCM > Tweezer > Mound, Slave, Suzie **E:** MSO, Tweezer Reprise
Fishman on trombone for I Didn't Know. Aborted ending on Possum led to elongated "blues jam." Cavern started, then Wilson sung, then returned to Cavern closing chorus. "Woody Woodpecker" tease in Tweezer prior to segue into Julius; "Rock and Roll is Here to Stay" tease in Tweezer after return from Julius. BBFCM is played loosely to the tune of Scent of a Mule. "Slave" jams in Suzie.

➢ This show is the ultimate expression of Phish's transitional grooving. In the second set, there is simply nothing they can't pull off. Following Possum to open the set, the Cavern jam kicks in strong, but wait, it sounds a bit like Wilson too! Suddenly Trey busts out Wilson and afterwards they go right back into the end of Cavern. This winds right into NICU with a great swing into Tweezer. Just when you're getting lost in the Tweezer jam, Julius emerges. There is an oldies jam in the middle, then back to Tweezer, which soon finds its way to BBFCM which has a bluegrassy, Scent of a Mule tinge to it. Relentlessly, Tweezer again emerges, but morphs into Mound. Slave follows, which is excellent, then Suzie, with reoccurring Slave samples in it. —ADAM DAVIDOFF

➢ Let's talk about the second set. The madness begins at the end of Possum with an extra-long ending. Then they play the music to Cavern, but when it comes time for the first verse, Trey sings the words to Wilson! "Can you still have fun" > "Give the director a serpent deflector" ends Cavern! Tweezer features a Woody Woodpecker tease from Trey and then there's Julius, out of nowhere. Wow! Great show. —MIKE GAROFALOW

7/14/94 [ACCESSIBILITY: ••]
Finger Lakes Performing Arts Center, Canandaigua, NY
I: Runaway Jim, Bouncing > PYITE > Stash >TMWSIY > Avenu > TMWSIY, Scent of a Mule, Fluffhead, Horse > Silent, Antelope
II: Also Sprach > Sample, Maze, If I Could, Uncle Pen, YEM, Sparkle > BBJ, Harry Hood, Highway to Hell **E:** Chalkdust

7/15/94 [ACCESSIBILITY: •••]
Jones Beach Music Theater, Wantagh, NY
I: Rift, Sample, Divided Sky, Gumbo, Foam, Fee, Melt, Golgi
II: Letter to Jimmy Page > Bowie, Bouncing, Reba > It's Ice > Yerushalayim, Dog Faced Boy, Julius, HYHU > Setting Sail > HYHU, Runaway Jim
E: Sleeping Monkey, Rocky Top
First solar-powered Phish concert, administered by Greenpeace. "Jessica" jam in Bowie. "Brazil" tease in Reba. Fishman on vacuum for Setting Sail, with audience sing-along. Last Setting Sail, 4/20/91 Rochester, NY [383 shows].

Saturday, July 16, 1994 — Sugarbush North, Fayston, VT

We arrived late, and ended up in this backwoods corner of the south lot, then busted out the hits before heading to the bus. I was going to pop two, but they were folded over and I accidentally chomped three. Zack, therefore, had to do the same.

By the time we made it over to the bus it was kicking in. And by the time we got off (the bus), it was pretty damn clear that we were going to trip harder than we'd ever tripped before.

Made it into the venue after about three songs, and at this point, we were starting to enter that scared phase where communication is challenged and any sort of obstacle requires exacting care to traverse. After getting through the gates, we faced this mass of fucking people on a steep goddamn mountain. There's no way in hell we could handle the crowd, but there didn't seem to be a way around them either. That left no choice but to charge on through, heading straight for the back.

Scariest thing I've ever seen, all those faces rushing by, so fast they would have meshed together even if we hadn't been tripping bugoongas.

Bugoongas I tell you.

We made it to the way back, away from the crowds, a good 200 yards from the stage. Once you're away from people and a safe distance from the stage, everything's supposed to be okay. But it just wasn't. We were cold, and haggard. If felt like we had just gotten the shit kicked out of us. Zack said it was the climb, that we weren't used to running that high that fast. He was partially right. But most of the cause was those little pieces of paper. They were digging in hard, so hard that the amazing visual spectacle from that mountain, the stage dancing in front of a shimmering pond, flanked by a panorama which stretched 30 miles across the valley, that view was just too much. I had to remind myself that gravity only worked in one direction—that I couldn't fall *in* to the valley.

Everything was so loud. Not just the music. The breeze blowing against my arms, a sensation which in other trips I found to give a glorious sense of self-affirmation, was nails against a chalkboard. The sight of trees shaking with that same breeze: the sound of a locomotive.

Call it sensory overload.

I tried to shake everything out, to eliminate every bit of stimulus by staring into the solid blue sky which thankfully lacked even a cloud. But my mind found disturbance where there was none, as the blank sky instantly became patterned with geometric visuals, snowflakes of unwanted sensations. Then a very real horsefly buzzed through my view, and became three or four fucking horseflies, and left a wake, a wave of thick air behind it.

By the time the set break rolled around, we were still cold, still scared, and as far as we could tell, still not coming down.

It conjured memories of Arctic adventurers on National Geographic Specials sharing tales of sure doom only reversed by their experience and positive thinking. In this area, I was long on experience but short of positive thinking. As I shivered like a wet puppy whose mother had just been run over by a bus, a supple tune rang out from down the slope. I hadn't even realized that the band had taken the stage, but the staggered first notes of Antelope instantly transformed the scene.

"Phish saves the day," Zack quipped.

Now, the Antelope to start the second set at Sugarbush was not your everyday Antelope. We're talking about dueling, atonal, arrhythmic stops and starts; we're talking underwater effects; we're talking Catapult right in the fucking middle. And Trey was screaming. Fucking screaming. And I'm supposed to be coming back to reality.

As this splendid, unparalleled Antelope continued to build, sucking in the entire crowd, I felt repelled. Turning away from the stage, I began climbing away, searching for shelter from the overwhelming tidal mass which was the music.

Adding to the peril was the fact that the sound on that mountain was as crystal clear as any I'd ever experienced. It must have been the mountain air or some weird acoustic phenomenon, but

Saturday, July 16, 1994 — Sugarbush North, Fayston, VT

Continued from previous page…
a good fifth of a mile from the stage, the music was so refined, so pure, and mercilessly loud. As Trey repeatedly, unendingly begged for some spike through the climax, I continued to pace upwards, lumbering past the last approving spectators as the song's final declaration was made. With the last chords pounding away, I felt a break ensuing. An Antelope like that could only be followed by a junkie short tune which would give the band and everyone else a chance to catch their collective breath. Still climbing and looking away, I heard words so clear it was as if Trey was whispering in my ear.

"Oom Pa Pa, Oom Pa Pa, Omm Pa Paaa."

Anger, at myself, took over. I was telling myself that it was the greatest Phish show of all time, and I couldn't enjoy it because I went and took so much acid. But that feeling was soon overpowered by complete fright. The first versus of Harpua, distinctly recognized for that enticing melody I loved in every other state, retained its well-structured charm, and that, more than anything, sent me fleeing upward with greater intensity.

The sound was so good, it hurt.

I was climbing up the mountain to escape the splendor of the music.

Clearly, I had completely lost it. Zack, a true friend, took the climb with me. I looked at him and saw waves of colors unpeeling themselves from the ground

"Zack, we've never tripped this hard," I managed to say. "Oh, no," he agreed, shaking his head with assuredness.

As the band whipped in to Also Sprach inside Harpua and then explained that Poster Nutbag had been hit by a comet, the pain wouldn't let up. My best Colonel Forbin imitation continued until we were well past the spectator area, and at least 2,000 feet from the stage. Miraculously, the voice of the band only became clearer, and the bizarre, nimble pluckings of AC/DC Bag resonated with the same crushing elegance as the songs which preceded them.

Barely clinging to my wits, and still at the height of discomfort and approaching the reaches of terror, I remembered a conversation with an older friend who, long past her acid days, told me, "If you ever have a bad trip, you will never forget it and you will never trip again."

I wasn't there yet, but I could feel the precipice approaching—sense the spiraling, uncontrolled agony which awaited if I lost grasp of whatever grounding endured. Searching for any sobering, comforting thought, it became clear that I had hit the end of the road with acid. There were no regrets. I'd gotten a hell of a lot out of it, and always wondered just how far I could go; my perch upon the mountain offered a clear, concrete answer.

There was a limit, and a point at which tripping would only force me away from the things I enjoyed the most. I shared this logic with Zack. Although I don't think he really believed me, he acknowledged that it was "the end of an era." Then, still requiring comfort, I announced that it was time to tell my parents that I used LSD. This one, Zack was slower to accept: "You're joking."

But it made perfect sense. Acid was such a part of everything I was. The most productive decisions I ever made came to me while tripping. My sense of humor, in so many ways, developed around the thought patterns and experiences of taking the acid plunge. Everyone who knew me knew how I felt. Knew that half my stories began with, "So I was tripping my balls off with Zack…" And yet, to have the people who gave birth to me not know that, was nothing but a complete lie—it was like living with strangers.

And seeing as how I wasn't going to do it again, coming clean made perfect sense. This resolve somehow brought me back to this planet. Maybe not the surface but at least the breathable atmosphere. My straight-ahead climb became more of a zig-zag, and then just a broad, back-and-forth pace.

I was squeezed between competitive forces; on one side, the blanket of optimism which told me that if I was just honest, and avoided future incursions, everything would be all right. Then, from beneath, came that still menacing force which thundered its bursting magnificence with unrelenting exactitude. The Harry Hood, chimed by four minuscule figures from four football fields below, was so *big*.

A skyscraper of a Harry Hood. A colossus. Chalkdust then jabbed at me like shattered window panes with each of its advancing, layered guitar licks. My pacing continued into the encore. The Suzie proved my suspicion that Phish was, in fact, busting out one of the greatest shows of all time.

Continually I had the need to find and articulate every reason why my parents would be informed of my indiscretions, and I wondered how long after the show it would take before finally my peak was achieved and I could begin a safe rest from the goblins which clawed from the sides.

Pacing, during Suzie, speaking loudly and seriously about what I had to do to improve my life and achieve salvation, I interrupted myself. "Excuse me," I pronounced, and then momentarily turned my authoritative stomp in to a whirling, pirouetting dance to Suzie, right on the beat, until I faced my original direction and continued pontificating.

Zack cracked up. A few seconds later, I did too. It was the first time during this glorious show that my mind allowed myself unadulterated pleasure from the music. I knew I was going to be all right.

And no, I never told my parents.

—**David Porter**

7/16/94 [ACCESSIBILITY: ••••]
SummerStage, Sugarbush North, Fayston, VT
I: Golgi, Down with Disease > N2O > Stash, Lizards, Cavern, Horse > Silent, Maze, Sparkle, Sample
II: Antelope > Catapult > Antelope, Harpua > Also Sprach > Harpua > AC/DC Bag, Scent of a Mule, Harry Hood, Contact, Chalkdust **E:** Suzie
Fishman on vacuum for N2O.

Phan Pick #8 ➢ A legendary show, and I'm so glad I was there! The dentist scenario in N2O was hilarious and even had me feeling dizzy, and then they came in with the drill, metaphorically, in the second set with Antelope/Catapult/Antelope. This Catapult was particularly memorable because it was right before Trey's wedding and after he sung the lines, "There ain't gonna be no wedding," Fish came in with, "You wish!" It was also the night the Shoemaker-Levy comet slammed into Jupiter, and during Trey's narration in Harpua he reminded us of that fact. An absolute 10, wonderful, incredible, cosmic show! The only bad thing about the whole event was the bus situation. The majority of the parking area was away from the mountain, and they bused virtually the entire audience to the concert grounds with only about 10 or 20 buses. It was not unlike herding cattle into pasture—moo! —LARA WITTELS

➢ A real mental show, especially the second set. Antelope contains evil shrills and laughter throughout, not to mention Catapult and a Simpsons signal before the final jam! I think a lot of people went out of their minds. Next came Harpua, with praise for Vermont and the story of an old mountain man who wandered around during soundcheck. They see the comet crash into Jupiter, which leads to 2001, then back to the end of Harpua. —MATTHEW ASHENFELDER

➢ What would be better than hanging out on a mountain all day and seeing your favorite band that night? You know the setlist, but did you know Mike and Fish hung out in the parking lot for a good part of the day? Or that Trey was running around onstage with a megaphone like a crazy person during Antelope? —MIKE D'AMICO

1994 Fall *TRICK OR TROUT*

Continuing their heavy touring year, Phish returned to the road in early October after just a couple of months off (months which, among other things, saw Trey and Sue get married). The first show marked the debut of Guyute, a song some viewed as the next Phish epic. But the tour's biggest highlight may have been an impromptu week-long tour with bluegrass pal the Reverend Jeff Mosier across the midwest. And, of course, there were the epic Halloween and New Year's shows, too.

10/7/94 [ACCESSIBILITY: •••]
Stabler Arena, Lehigh University, Bethlehem, PA
I: My Friend, Julius, Glide, Poor Heart, Divided Sky, Guelah, Stash, Guyute, Golgi
II: Maze, Horse > Silent, Reba, Wilson, Scent of a Mule, Tweezer, Lifeboy, MSO, Tweezer Reprise **E:** Foreplay > Long Time, Cavern
Foreplay/Long Time featured Trey on acoustic guitar, Mike on banjo, Fishman on Madonna washboard and Page on stand-up bass. Concert debuts: Guyute, Foreplay, Long Time.

➢ The first show of the tour included the first Guyute ever, and also marked the debut of the spinning lights that go in circles during Tweeprise—I almost fell over when Chris turned them on. The best part of the show was the crowd, which was very aware of when to be quiet and when to participate. After this show there was one of the biggest and best drum circles I have ever seen. —JOSHUA HOWLEY

➢ The highlight of this show for me had to be the acoustic version of Boston's Long Time. We had just listened to two great sets and were hoping for a Suzie closer. Instead the boys came out with a banjo, stand up bass, guitar and Fishman on a brass-plated washboard. A hush fell over the audience. For the first few moments, no one knew what they were playing. When we realized what it was, we practically fell down laughing. —BETH CASTROL

10/8/94 [ACCESSIBILITY: ••••]
Patriot Center, George Mason University, Fairfax, VA
I: Chalkdust, Horn, Sparkle, Down with Disease, Guyute, Fee, It's Ice, Lawn Boy > Antelope
II: Also Sprach > Sample, Rift, Mike's > Simple > Mike's > Hydrogen > Weekapaug > Fluffhead, HYHU > Purple Rain > HYHU, Harry Hood > Suzie **E:** Foreplay > Long Time, Rocky Top
A dozen members of a girl's soccer team did a " We are The Muppets..." cheer between Mike's and Simple. Fishman on vacuum for Purple Rain. Foreplay/Long Time performed acoustic with setup of 10/7/94.

➢ This is my pick for the most underrated show of all time, one which I feel deserves classic status. The first set highlight was the second-ever performance of Guyute, which was so satisfying because it was still ringing in my head from the night before. It also included a wonderfully pure DwD—the jam didn't veer off very much from the dominant chords and melody, but it had so much energy, proving just how great those chords and melody are. But this show really makes its mark in Set II, an unrelenting hour and a half of music with a girls soccer team doing a cheer in Mike's and an amazing segue into Simple (where Simple works best, when you're already in psychedelic la-la land!). —ANDY BERNSTEIN

10/9/94 [ACCESSIBILITY: ••]
A.J. Palumbo Center, Pittsburgh, PA
I: Runaway Jim, Foam, FEFY, Curtain > Dog Faced Boy, Melt, Squirming Coil
II: Bowie, Bouncing, Scent of a Mule, YEM, Amazing Grace, Julius, Contact, Possum **E:** Sleeping Monkey, Poor Heart
Squirming Coil from this show appears on A Live One.

10/10/94 [ACCESSIBILITY: ••]
Palace Theater, Louisville, KY
I: Sample, Divided Sky, Horse > Silent, Sparkle, Stash, Guyute, Old Home Place, Ginseng Sullivan, Nellie Cane, Chalkdust
II: Golgi, Maze, Esther, Tweezer, Fee > Rift, Down with Disease, HYHU > Love You > HYHU, Slave **E:** Foreplay > Long Time, Tweezer Reprise
Steve Cooley on banjo for Old Home Place, Ginseng Sullivan and Nellie Cane, with Trey on acoustic guitar, Mike on banjo, Fishman on Madonna washboard and Page on mouth piano. Fishman on vacuum for Love You. Foreplay/Longtime performed acoustic with setup of 10/7/94.

10/12/94 [ACCESSIBILITY: ••]
Orpheum Theater, Memphis, TN
I: My Friend, Reba, Sloth, Poor Heart, Melt, Lizards, Guelah, Julius, Adeline
II: Peaches, Bowie, Bouncing, Scent of a Mule, YEM, Nellie Cane, Foreplay > Long Time, Harry Hood, Sample **E:** GTBT
Nellie Cane performed acoustic with Trey on acoustic guitar, Mike on banjo, Fishman on mandolin and Page on stand-up bass. Foreplay/Longtime performed acoustic with setup of 10/7/94.

10/13/94 [ACCESSIBILITY: ••]
Grove Arena, University of Mississippi, Oxford, MS
I: Llama, Gumbo, All Things, Down with Disease, I Didn't Know, Foam, FEFY, Sparkle, Stash
II: Old Home Place, Antelope, If I Could, It's Ice, Amazing Grace, Mike's > Simple > Mike's > Yerushalayim > Weekapaug, Foreplay > Long Time, Cavern **E:** Fire
Fishman on Madonna washboard for I Didn't Know. Foreplay/Longtime performed acoustic with setup of 10/7/94.

➢ The outdoor atmosphere at this show was perfect. Everyone was just chillin'; when the music started it was like an explosion of excitement with the upbeat Llama. There wasn't much deep, intense jamming in the first set, but the band still added some kicks. I must say that I Didn't Know was a five-star performance. Then came an incredible Antelope, chock full of teases, seemingly never-ending. It almost made my heart stop with the anticipation of the retreat of the magical guitar trickery. —CHAD MARS

10/14/94 [ACCESSIBILITY: •••]
McAlister Auditorium, Tulane University, New Orleans, LA
I: Buried Alive > Sample, Divided Sky, Horse > Silent, PYITE, Bathtub Gin, Adeline, Rift, Forbin's > Mockingbird, Julius
II: Curtain > Tweezer > Lifeboy, Guyute, Chalkdust, Nellie Cane, Beaumont Rag, Foreplay > Long Time, Squirming Coil, Tweezer Reprise
E: Ya Mar, Cavern
Nellie Cane and Bow Mountain Rag performed acoustic with Trey on acoustic guitar, Mike on banjo, Fishman on mandolin and Page on stand-up bass. Foreplay/Longtime performed acoustic with setup of 10/7/94. Carl Gerhard on trumpet and Michael Ray on trumpet and shaker for Ya Mar and Cavern. Concert debut: Beaumont Rag (also known incorrectly as "Bow Mountain Rag").

➢ Buried Alive is perhaps the best opener they can do, and this one is no joke. PYITE is always good, and they do a weird story in Col. Forbin's about leaving your body that was pretty cool. Second set began with The Curtain. Guyute is always a treat; this is one of the early ones. They played some little acoustic numbers, including a first-timer, before Michael Ray and Carl Gerhard played the hell out of Ya Mar and Cavern. In New Orleans, you need jazz, and the boys didn't fail to meet my expectations. —CHRISTOPHER MILLS

10/15/94 [ACCESSIBILITY: ••••]
Oak Mountain Amphitheatre, Pelham, AL
I: Wilson, Sparkle, Simple > Maze, Glide, Reba, Down with Disease, Golgi
II: Also Sprach > Runaway Jim, Halley's > Scent of a Mule, YEM > Catapult > YEM, Amazing Grace, Foreplay > Long Time, Bouncing, Suzie
E: Drums > Jam > The Maker
The Dave Matthews Band opened. Foreplay/Longtime performed acoustic with setup of 10/7/94. DMB joined Phish for the encores, which started with Fishman and Carter Beaufort drumming; Dave Matthews sung lead on The Maker. "Moby Dick" jam in Jam before The Maker. Concert debut: The Maker.

10/16/94 [ACCESSIBILITY: ••]
Chattanooga Memorial Auditorium, Chattanooga, TN
I: Rift, Horn, Foam, Fee, Melt, TMWSIY > Avenu > TMWSIY, Axilla, Possum
II: Landlady, Poor Heart, Julius, Fluffhead, BBJ, Antelope, Dog Faced Boy, Adeline, Sample **E:** Highway to Hell **E2:** Harpua
Dog Faced Boy performed acoustic with Trey on acoustic guitar, Mike on banjo, Fishman on balloon and Page on mouth piano. "Flashlight" jam in Harpua. Last Axilla (part I), 8/16/93 St. Louis, MO [93 shows].

10/18/94 [ACCESSIBILITY: •••]

Memorial Gym, Vanderbilt University, Nashville, TN

I: Simple, My Friend, I Didn't Know, Poor Heart, Stash, Tela, It's Ice, Guyute, Divided Sky, Amazing Grace
II: Bowie, Horse > Silent, Reba, Scent of a Mule, Lifeboy, Old Home Place, Beaumont Rag, Nellie Cane, Llama **E:** MSO

Fishman on vacuum for I Didn't Know. Bela Fleck on banjo for second set (starting with Scent) and encore. Old Home Place, Beaumont Rag, Nellie Cane and Llama performed acoustic with Trey on acoustic guitar, Mike on stand-up bass, Fishman on Madonna washboard and Page on mouth piano. Llama started acoustic and finished electric as the members of Phish switched back to their normal instruments in the middle of the song.

➢ During set two, Phish introduced the maestro of modern jazz/rock banjo, Bela Fleck. He hopped on stage for Scent, and after hearing the song with banjo, I felt like all the previous Scents lacked something special. The fivesome then played a series of classic bluegrass tunes that emitted a laid-back, comfortable and content feeling. The most notable, however, was Llama in a bluegrass context which led to a full-blown electric finish, during which Phish and Fleck communicated as only true musicians can. —JOHN FOLEY

➢ My God, have you heard the Llama at this show? It's amazing! Trey starts strumming the chords on his acoustic guitar, and the crowd roars in recognition when he sings the first line. After the opening acoustic segment, Bela takes a gorgeous banjo solo as the members of Phish one by one migrate back to their electric instruments. They re-enter the jam, then Trey trades licks with Bela as the song wanders for awhile, the jam growing quieter and quieter. Trey thanks the crowd before roaring the song to its finish. —ED SMITH

10/20/94 [ACCESSIBILITY: ••]

Mahaffey Theatre, St. Petersburg, FL

I: Runaway Jim, Golden Lady, Poor Heart, Guelah, Melt > Kung > Melt, Esther, Julius, Guyute, Golgi
II: Lengthwise > Maze, McGrupp, Rift, Harry Hood, Nellie Cane, Foreplay > Long Time, Chalkdust **E:** Sample

Nellie Cane and Foreplay/Longtime performed acoustic. Last Lengthwise, 8/13/93 Indianapolis, IN [98 shows]. Concert debut: Golden Lady.

➢ I thought Phish would opt for a Florida version of Harry Hood for inclusion on *A Live One*, because anyone who's heard this performance will tell you that it hasn't been matched since. And the band did go south for their pick, but they opted for the Gainsville version from a few nights later. Maybe they screwed up their notes—this Hood traverses many interesting places, rising to a glorious peak that makes you want to stand up on your heels and embrace the music. —MELISSA WOLCOTT

10/21/94 [ACCESSIBILITY: ••••]

Sunrise Musical Theatre, Sunrise, FL

I: Fee, Down with Disease > Foam, Mango, Old Home Place, Stash, Lizards, Dog Faced Boy, Antelope
II: Also Sprach > Mike's > Simple > Mike's > Hydrogen > Weekapaug, Sleeping Monkey, Curtain > FEFY, Scent of a Mule, Slave
E: Adeline, Foreplay > Long Time, Cavern

"Can't You Hear Me Knocking" jam at end of Weekapaug. Foreplay/Longtime performed acoustic with setup of 10/7/94.

10/22/94 [ACCESSIBILITY: ••]

The Edge Concert Field, Orlando, FL

I: Suzie, Divided Sky, Gumbo, Axilla II, Rift, Melt, Fluffhead, Julius
II: Peaches, Bowie, Horse > Silent, Dinner and A Movie, Tweezer > Wilson, Reba, Amazing Grace, AC/DC Bag, Highway to Hell
E: Uncle Pen, Tweezer Reprise

Fireworks from a Disney World event nearby could be seen during Fluffhead and Julius.

10/23/94 [ACCESSIBILITY: •••••]

Band Shell, University of Florida, Gainsville, FL

I: Chalkdust > My Friend, Sparkle, Simple, Poor Heart, Stash > Catapult > Stash, Tela > Maze, Sample
II: Runaway Jim, Bouncing > Halley's > YEM, Down with Disease > Purple Rain > HYHU, Harry Hood, Fee, GTBT **E:** Squirming Coil

Free outdoor concert. Soundcheck: Ginseng Sullivan, Funky Bitch, Golden Lady. "Gypsy Queen" jam in Runaway Jim. "Vibration of Life" during YEM. "Another One Bites the Dust" and "Mission Impossible" teases in YEM, and "Astronomy Domine" themes in YEM vocal jam. Fishman on vacuum for Purple Rain. Harry Hood from this show appears on A Live One.

➢ My favorite part were the trampolines during YEM. Maybe Trey's ankle was a little weak, but he literally fell jumping off. Mike starts up with Another One Bites the Dust, and Trey answers back by playing the Mission Impossible theme song. The Purple Rain actually made me cry, like no other Rain since. —TONY HUME

➢ This was a great show for several reasons. First, it was free, and the Band Shell is a great place to see a concert. Second, I got to meet Trey between sets. He was hilarious as he teased some guy who was apparently upset because his girlfriend was madly in love with Trey. Trey told the guy to bring his girlfriend over and he would act like an asshole so she wouldn't like him anymore. Finally, this was a first show for many of my friends who are now loyal phans. I love when I introduce someone to the band and they have positive reactions to it. —CHRIS HAINES

[10/25/94] ***Crimes Of The Mind*** **released on Elektra.**

10/25/94 [ACCESSIBILITY: ••]

Atlanta Civic Center, Atlanta, GA

I: Fee, Llama, Horn, Julius, Horse > Silent, Melt, Lizards, Sample
II: Mike's > Simple > Mango > Weekapaug > Yerushalayim, Glide, Axilla II > Jesus Left Chicago > BBJ, HYHU > Brain > HYHU, Possum
E: Foreplay > Long Time, Golgi

Fishman on vacuum for Brain. "Magilla" tease in Possum. Foreplay/Longtime performed acoustic with setup of 10/7/94.

10/26/94 [ACCESSIBILITY: ••]

Varsity Gym, Appalachian State University, Boone, NC

I: Simple, It's Ice, NICU, Antelope, Guyute, Dog Faced Boy, Scent of a Mule, Oh Kee > Suzie, Runaway Jim
II: Rift, Bouncing, Reba, Axilla II, YEM > Catapult, HYHU > Cracklin' Rosie > HYHU, Bowie **E:** Nellie Cane, Foreplay > Long Time, Amazing Grace

"Vibration of Life" in YEM. Nellie Cane and Foreplay/Longtime performed acoustic with setup of 10/7/94.

➢ I love to hear Trey talk to the audience. I look forward to hearing him speak, whether it be a Harpua Rap or a simple "Thanks for coming out tonight." Well, imagine my pleasure upon hearing the encore of this show. When they retake the stage, Trey comments on how much they've enjoyed their stay in the mountain-surrounded town of Boone, and even compares it to Burlington. This was ultracool for me because I lived there a while. Phish goes on to play some mountain music, followed by bluegrass Boston, then closes it up with Amazing Grace. Man, I dig Phish's diversity. —AMANDA LITTON

10/27/94 [ACCESSIBILITY: ••]

University Hall, University of Virginia, Charlottesville, VA

I: Wilson, Sparkle, Maze, Forbin's > Mockingbird, Divided Sky, Horse > Silent, Poor Heart, Cavern
II: Julius, Ya Mar, Tweezer, Contact, BBFCM, Down with Disease, Adeline
E: Slave > Icculus, Tweezer Reprise

"Vibration of Life" in Forbin's.

➢ You know it's a strange show when Phish jams out the Tweezer Reprise more than the Tweezer. No, seriously, this show does have a unique Tweezer Rep. that goes on for at least a few minutes more than normal. If you like Tweezer Reprise, you'll love this show. Otherwise, keep moving… nothing much to hear here. —LEE JOHNSTON

10/28/94 [ACCESSIBILITY: ••]

Galliard Auditorium, Charleston, SC

I: I Didn't Know, Llama, Guelah, Scent of a Mule, Stash, Glide, Axilla II, All Things, Sample, Carolina
II: Also Sprach > Bowie > Manteca > Bowie, Lizards, Rift, Lifeboy, Chalkdust, Old Home Place, Nellie Cane, Foreplay > Long Time
E: Fee, Highway to Hell

Fishman on vacuum for I Didn't Know. Old Home Place and Nellie performed acoustic with Trey on acoustic guitar, Mike on banjo, Fishman on mandolin and Page on stand-up bass. Foreplay/Longtime performed acoustic with setup of 10/7/94.

10/29/94 [ACCESSIBILITY: ••••]

Spartanburg Memorial Auditorium, Spartanburg, SC

I: My Friend, Sparkle, Simple, Runaway Jim, Foam, Lawn Boy, Melt > Buffalo Bill > Makisupa > Rift
II: Down with Disease > TMWSIY > Avenu > TMWSIY > Sparks > Uncle Pen, YEM, HYHU > Bike > HYHU, Antelope > Sleeping Monkey > Antelope
E: Harry Hood

Fishman on vacuum for Bike. Last Buffalo Bill, 11/21/92 Stony Brook, NY [224 shows].

➢ Lost in the shadow of Glens Falls is Spartanburg, a groovy gig for the thinking phan. A raging, near-chaotic Split Open and Melt jam in the first set develops a reggae beat, and before you can say "Makisupa Policeman," the boys are playing Buffalo Bill! This song, considered lost forever since its debut in November '92, has an incredible bassline that leads to another reggae jam and then, naturally, to Makisupa. Out of Makisupa, they RAGE into a jam that finally leads to… Rift. Set II is also full of interesting transitions, like TMWISY > Sparks and Antelope with Sleeping Monkey dropped in the middle. —RICH MAZER

10/31/94 [ACCESSIBILITY: •••••]

Glens Falls Civic Center, Glens Falls, NY

I: Frankenstein, Sparkle, Simple, Divided Sky, Harpua, Julius, Horse > Silent, Reba, Golgi
II: Speak To Me tease > "Ed Sullivan Introduction" > Back In The USSR, Dear Prudence, Glass Onion, Ob-La-Di Ob-La-Da, Wild Honey Pie, Continuing Story Of Bungalow Bill, Guitar Gently Weeps, Happiness is a Warm Gun, Martha My Dear, I'm So Tired, Blackbird, Piggies, Rocky Raccoon, Don't Pass Me By, Why Don't We Do It In The Road, I Will, Julia, Birthday Jam, Yer Blues, Mother Nature's Son, Everybody's Got Something To Hide Except For Me and My Monkey, Sexy Sadie, Helter Skelter, Long Long Long, Revolution 1, Honey Pie, Savoy Truffle, Cry Baby Cry, Revolution 9, Good Night

III: Bowie, Bouncing, Slave, Rift, Sleeping Monkey, Poor Heart, Antelope
E: Amazing Grace, "Costume Contest", Squirming Coil

Second set was the Beatles' White Album. All songs from the album were concert debuts. Cake presented to crew member Brad Sands during Birthday. "HYHU" tease before Why Don't We Do It. Speak To Me and Good Night were prerecorded versions played over the PA system. "Vibration of Life," "Vibration of Death" and "War Pigs" jams in Harpua. "Custard Pie" tease before Bowie. "Stash" tease in Antelope.

Phan Pick #2 ➢ Just an all-out Phishfest, with the *White Album* sandwiched between two huge sets! The best Simple you'll ever hear and one of my favorite Harpuas ever. The *White Album* was so good, coming as the effect of thinking they were about to play *Dark Side of the Moon* wore off. Page out of control on Antelope, a great Bowie, plus a bedtime serenade by Page at 3:30 a.m. What a show! —CASEY GRANT

➢ The first Halloween Phish show I saw. Musically, everyone knows the second set, but personally the first set is still one of my favorites ever. Still, the concert paled in comparison to the scene outside—I mean, the Disco Bus in the parking lot of Burger King, a guy who said he was the mayor of Glens Falls doing nitrous with us, all the costumes—what a scene! Yum! And just a heck of a concert. —BETH CASTROL

➢ Sandwiched between two great sets was The Beatles' *White Album.* "Here's another hint for you all, the walrus was Paul!"—Trey pointed and smiled as he sung this line. Weeks later, I realize he was pointing to the walrus, Paul Languedoc, at the soundboard. Trey also inserts "Guyute the pig" into this song. A great album was performed with the utmost quality. Congrats to Skippy who won the costume contest, making Ithaca College proud. I still watch this show over and over on my VCR. —RIC HANNAH

➢ Everyone knows that Phish played with people's minds by playing a "Speak to Me" tease at the beginning of the second set to trick the crowd into thinking the cover album was going to be Pink Floyd. But it's interesting that at the beginning of set III, before David Bowie, they give a tease to another great album that people thought they might play that night. The little guitar tease is the beginning of Led Zeppelin's Custard Pie, the first song off the double album *Physical Graffiti.* —BRIAN LEVINE

➢ How much stranger is seeing Fish naked? I thought this was an awesome effort. Note for note, the Green Mountain lads delivered the goods like they were from Liverpool. Was it a steady diet of stouts, porters and ESBs that had me imagining it was the Beatles? A sensational show, and a seminal event in Phishtory. —DAN KURTZ

11/2/94 [ACCESSIBILITY: ••••]
Bangor Auditorium, Bangor, ME
I: Suzie, Foam, If I Could, Maze, Guyute, Stash, Scent of a Mule, Guitar Gently Weeps
II: Halley's > Tweezer, Mango, Axilla II, Possum, Lizards, Sample
E: Old Home Place, Foreplay > Long Time, Tweezer Reprise

Old Home Place and Foreplay/Longtime performed acoustic with setup of 10/7/94. Tweezer from this show appears on A Live One.

➢ Pouring rain outside, 4,000 people inside in a really small place with wooden bleachers, even. Everyone's liquid! Trey wears the coolest shirt I've ever seen him wear. You know the setlist: TWEEZER! People were losing it. We climbed under the bleachers and ran all over the place. One of the best times of my life. —LANGSTON KNIPLER

➢ The biggest fault of *A Live One* is not including the Possum from this show along with the Tweezer. Trey jams on a very similar theme in both, making Possum almost a continuation of Tweezer. The picture in the liner notes for *A Live One* of the boys playing acoustic comes from this show because the flowers were thrown onstage by a girl in the audience. By the way, check out the first set. Each song has a great jam. —BRENDAN NEAGLE

Monday, October 31, 1994 — Civic Center, Glens Falls, NY

I was on tour during Fall '94 and had missed only a few shows when Halloween rolled around.

On our way to Glens Falls, we made a pit stop in Ithaca, NY where my friends were going to school. I really didn't have much money or time but I really waned to make a good costume. I came up with the idea to go as a "Mounds" candy bar. The only problem was how to make it, but I figured it out in a couple of hours and became convinced it would be a killer costume.

The next day showtime rolled around, and on went the most constrictive, backbreaking costume I saw that night. As I walked to the door someone handed me a little paper "treat." Subsequently, this was the last time I had a "treat." Nonetheless, there I was, a huge tripping candy bar. As I walked through the entrance somebody handed me a piece of paper saying I had qualified to be judged for the costume contest. After the first judging, about seven or eight people were eliminated, leaving myself, a Harry Hood, a Lawnboy, a Bathtub Gin, a Tela, and a Lizard. Oops, forgot about the AC/DC Bag. We were all ushered backstage—the final judging would soon take place on stage.

During the encore, they brought us onto the stage and the audience voted by applause. After an initial round I was left on stage with the Lawnboy. A couple more applause votes later I found myself with a trophy in my left hand, looking out at thousands of people cheering. This was the most intense rush I have ever felt.

A strange postscript: the very next show I was standing by the tour bus when Trey appeared. We spoke a little and I asked if there was any room on the guestlist for a wayward candybar. He said, "You got it, man." Amazing, miracled by Trey.

—Shawn "Skip" McFarland

White Album

10/31/94 Glens Falls Civic Center, Glens Falls, NY

By 1966, the Beatles had grown tired of the road. At 9:27 p.m. on August 29, 1966, the Beatles took the stage in Candlestick Park in San Francisco. At 10:00 p.m., after finishing the show with Long Tall Sally, they left the stage forever.

While the group continued to write some of the greatest songs and record some of the greatest albums ever, fans would never get a chance to see them performed live. *Sgt. Pepper's*, *Abbey Road*, *The White Album*—these brilliant musical feats would only be performed in front of mirrors, hairbrush in place of microphone, imagination creating the scene. At least until Halloween 1994.

On that night, in Glens Falls, NY, Phish opened their second set with Back in the USSR, the first song from the *White Album*, and the Beatles were magically on stage again.

People often argue over Phish shows. "It was great!" or "Just average." Opinions go on and on, and it can be fruitless to argue, as well as silly—just because you loved a show doesn't mean everyone else should. However, it's true that some shows are simply musically superior to others. That's part of why most phans don't go to just one show a year—it wouldn't be as much fun if the band were four robots and every song was always technically perfect, or every jam was played in perfect sync.

Then there are the historic moments when, regardless of the music, the show is considered a classic. When the band combines both in one night, it's perfection. Glens Falls 10/31/94 was just that.

It would have been enough simply to make a good effort at covering the *White Album*, but to nail it the way they did made it extra special. While My Guitar Gently Weeps was truly memorable, as Trey was challenged to match the great lead performed by Eric Clapton, invited into the studio for the track by close friend George Harrison. Trey proved himself up to the task, so much so that the band went on to perform the song 15 more times through the end of 1995. And of course there was Phish lunacy—Fishman pulling off his dress during Revolution 9, showing the 8,000-person crowd just what he was made of.

While Phish's musical costume—voted on by postcard by 400 fans, with about 10 percent of the votes cast for the *White Album*—was enough to make it a classic night, the first and third sets of pure Phish may have been even better. The third set in particular—highlighted by all-time great versions of Bowie, Slave and Antelope—was about as good as it gets, played to a delirous audience between 2 and 3 a.m. The encore, a perfectly-placed Squirming Coil with the traditional Page piano solo, wound down just after 3:20 a.m.

The show also proved seminal for the scene that developed outside the arena. For the first time, several thousand more fans than there were tickets arrived at the venue. The chaos that engulfed Glens Falls later led Phish manager John Paluska to write a 30-page manual for venue staffs on how to interact with Phish concert crowds. Inside, the venue security staff just gave up, and before the band took the stage, it became a general-admission affair that will never be forgotten by those lucky enough to be in attendance. The show is rightly remembered as one of Phish's most potent nights ever, and the show is the most heavily-circulated set of Phish tapes in existence.

11/3/94 [ACCESSIBILITY: ••••]
Mullins Center, University of Massachusetts, Amherst, MA
I: Fee, Divided Sky, Wilson > Peaches, Glide, Melt, Dog Faced Boy, Sparkle, Down with Disease
II: Also Sprach > Simple, Poor Heart, Julius, YEM > BBFCM, Harry Hood, Cavern **E:** MSO, Nellie Cane, Amazing Grace, Highway to Hell
"Vibration of Life" in YEM. MSO and Nellie Cane performed acoustic with Trey on acoustic guitar, Mike on banjo, Fishman on mandolin and Page on stand-up bass.

➢ This is one of my favorite tapes in my collection for three reasons: (1) Cavern's chorus is the music of Lawn Boy; (2) An insane Bowie > Yerushalayim; and (3) Fishman on mandolin! It's not as if these were the only good points of the show, either. It was just perfectly played music all night. —JOSH HALMAN

➢ Another solid show. The most memorable moment of this was the Bowie! Dang, this one got trippy, almost to the point of stopping in the middle, but they took us through a full range of emotions. Trey really got intricate in his pathways of music. This is my favorite David Bowie. There was also a great Peaches opener to set the mood and a very stellar YEM. This was a great show that gets little hype. You should check it out. —MICHELLE HIRSCH

11/4/94 [ACCESSIBILITY: ••••]
Onondaga County War Memorial, Syracuse, NY
I: Sample, It's Ice, Bouncing, Bowie, Forbin's > Mockingbird, Scent of a Mule, Suzie > Chalkdust
II: Curtain > Mike's > Simple > Mike's > Tela > Weekapaug, Ya Mar, Golgi, Slave **E:** Loving Cup, Rocky Top
"Vibration of Life" in Forbin's. "Can't You Hear Me Knocking" jam at the end of Weekapaug.

➢ A very standard setlist. However, the energy level was way greater than normal, maybe because the Vibration of Life took us to Gamehendge. It was the only time that I actually felt I was there. As my friend Gugs put it afterwards, "A stellar show." We saw Ya Mar and no vacuum. Enough said. —RIC HANNAH

➢ I was front row and had some 3-D glasses on when, at the end of Mockingbird, Trey asked for them. He wore them throughout Mule, dancing around during the duel, basically buggin' out. Everything looked so cool with those glasses on—he must have been psyched. He then passed them to Gordo for Suzie, and Mike popped and slapped throughout. Second set was old school, with no songs written in the 1990s with the exception of Simple. —JOSHUA HOWLEY

11/12/94 [ACCESSIBILITY: ••••]
Mac Center, Kent State University, Kent, OH
I: Runaway Jim, Foam, If I Could, Guyute, Maze, Stash, Esther, Chalkdust
II: Julius, Fluffhead, Down with Disease > Have Mercy > Down with Disease > Lifeboy, Rift, Old Home Place, Nellie Cane, Foreplay > Long Time, Harry Hood, Golgi **E:** Sample
Old Home Place and Nellie Cane performed acoustic with Trey on acoustic guitar, Mike on banjo, Fishman on mandolin and Page on stand-up bass. Foreplay/Longtime performed acoustic with setup of 10/7/94.

➢ The first few times I saw DwD live, I was amazed at the strength of the jam. Trey managed to play off the same basic riff for about ten minutes, just building it and building until they finished with "Na, Na, Na Na Na" refrain. But by the time I made it to Kent, the band had already discovered that DwD was a toy with more than one gadget. During the second set, they went into a rendition which began with a pretty basic jam following the lyrics, but it just kept morphing and morphing, to a point where you couldn't begin to figure out how they'd find their way back. They didn't—at least not right away. Instead they went into Have Mercy, a song which only seams to sneak into the greatest shows and the greatest jams. Then, seamlessly, they headed back into DwD and finished it off. At the time, DwD was thought of by many as the radio song, the video song, but that night it became one of my absolute favorite tunes to see live. Of course, I had no idea just what heights that song would reach. —ANDY BERNSTEIN

11/13/94 [ACCESSIBILITY: ••]
Erie Warner Theatre, Erie, PA
I: Wilson > Sparkle, Simple > Reba, Axilla II, It's Ice, Horse > Silent, Antelope
II: Suzie, Divided Sky, Lizards, Tweezer > Mango > BBFCM, Amazing Grace, Squirming Coil
E: Funky Bitch, Tweezer Reprise

➢ The venue was tiny, one of the most beautiful theaters I've ever set foot in. We drove eight hours just for this one show so we were expecting a lot. The boys did not let us down. Antelope blew my mind, not to mention the roof, right off the place—definitely the hardest I have ever seen Trey jam, and there was a small voice jam before Marco Esquandolis. Everyone should check this one out—no doubt the best one ever! Second set was great, but I could have walked out satisfied after Antelope. Amazing how far you drive and how short it takes Phish to satisfy. —JOSHUA HOWLEY

➢ I think the word for this show is phun. It was a great place for Phish to play. The energy was full. The most memorable part was Trey running around the stage with megaphone in hand during BBFCM as the strobe lights went nuts. The encore, Funky Bitch, was a request from someone in the front. —KEVIN WORD

11/14/94 [ACCESSIBILITY: ••]
Devos Hall, Grand Rapids, MI
I: My Friend, Scent of a Mule, Guelah, Melt, Bouncing, Landlady, Maze, Lawn Boy, Cavern
II: Peaches, Bowie, Yerushalayim, Slave, Poor Heart, Julius, Old Home Place, Nellie Cane, Adeline, YEM **E:** Golgi
Cavern had usual lyrics but final refrain was played to the music of Lawn Boy. Old Home Place and Nellie performed acoustic with Trey on acoustic guitar, Mike on banjo, Fishman on mandolin and Page on stand-up bass.

11/16/94 [ACCESSIBILITY: •••]
Hill Auditorium, University of Michigan, Ann Arbor, MI
I: Sample, Foam, FEFY, Reba, Axilla II, Lizards, Stash, Pig In A Pen, Tennessee Waltz, Bluegrass Breakdown, Swing Low Sweet Chariot
II: Mike's > Simple, I'm Blue I'm Lonesome, Long Journey Home, Chalkdust, Fee, Antelope **E:** Amazing Grace, Suzie
Rev. Jeff Mosier on banjo for Bluegrass Breakdown, and banjo and vocals for Pig in a Pen, Tennessee Waltz, and Swing Low Sweet Chariot. I'm Blue I'm Lonesome and Long Journey Home performed acoustic with Trey on acoustic guitar, Mike on banjo, Fishman on mandolin, and Page on stand-up bass. Last Pig In A Pen, 2/21/93 Atlanta, GA [194 shows]. Last Tennesee Waltz, 5/6/93 Albany, NY [141 shows]. Last Swing Low Sweet Chariot, 10/20/89 Burlington, VT [683 shows]. Concert debuts: Bluegrass Breakdown, I'm Blue I'm Lonesome, and Long Journey Home. Chalkdust from this show appears on A Live One.

➢ God bless the Reverend! Jeff Mosier helped make November '94 one of the hottest months of Phish ever, infusing almost every set with a bluegrass sensibility that can be heard in Phish's music to this day. This was his first night jamming on stage with the boys, and they looked damn excited to have him there. Like Dick Solberg in Albany on 5/6/93, it didn't take long for Mosier to get comfortable (perhaps because he'd played with Phish once before, on 2/21/93.) In Pig In a Pen, he introduced us to "the world's premiere bluegrass drummer… Fish!" Swing Low Sweet Chariot, with Mosier on lead vocals for the first Phish rendition since the 1980s, is another major highlight. —ERNIE GREENE

➢ Still recovering from the hot first set (Stash sizzled, Mosier cooked), I almost hit the roof as Trey started up Mike's Song to kick open the second set. Mike's > Simple was still a frequent occurrence back then, so the Simple chords came as no surprise out of the Mike's jam. It wasn't even that incredible when the band jammed out on Simple, with Trey drawing out a quietly melodious theme not unlike that of the Halloween show a few weeks earlier. But the jam kept moving—and evolving—and slowing—and then rocking, and before we knew it, we were 35 minutes into the set and still in Simple. Only after hearing the incredible Simples of Fall '96 am I willing to label the start of this set "Mike's > Simple" instead of "Mike's > Simple > Jam!" Add to this set an acoustic interlude, a killer Chalkdust (*A Live One* version), Fee > Antelope, and you'll understand why people were still cheering *outside* the venue when it was all over. —RICH MAZER

11/17/94 [ACCESSIBILITY: ••••]
Hara Arena, Dayton, OH
I: Helter Skelter, Scent of a Mule, Maze, Bouncing, Wilson, Divided Sky, Dog Faced Boy, Forbin's > Mockingbird, Down with Disease
II: Also Sprach > Bowie, Sleeping Monkey, Sparkle, YEM > HYHU > Love You > HYHU, Slave, Golgi
E: I'm Blue I'm Lonesome, Nellie Cane, Long Journey Home, Fixin' to Die
"Vibration of Life" in Forbin's. "HYHU" was sung, not played, emerging from the YEM vocal jam. Fishman on vacuum for Love You. I'm Blue I'm Lonesome, Nellie Cane and Long Journey Home performed acoustic with Trey on acoustic guitar, Mike on banjo, Fishman on mandolin and Page on stand-up bass. Rev. Jeff Mosier on spoons for Long Journey Home and on banjo (electric) and vocals for Fixin' to Die. Concert debut: Fixin' to Die.

➢ The best part is the acoustic, Dixieland-style encore. The boys sound like the mid-'60s Dead (for lack of a better comparison). Trey's got soul in his vocals and the crowd loves it! The vibes definitely come through on tape; you feel like drinkin' cheap whiskey, taking your shoes off, and stomping your feet! Long Journey and Fixin' rock. Also, the grating Fish vocals on Monkey and the venue erupting with the vocals on YEM need to be heard. —TIM FOISSER

11/18/94 [ACCESSIBILITY: •••]
MSU Auditorium, Michigan State University, East Lansing, MI
I: Rift, AC/DC Bag, Julius, Horse > Silent, It's Ice, Tela, Melt, Butter Them Biscuits, Old Home Place, Long Journey Home
II: Llama, Bathtub Gin > Lifeboy, Poor Heart, Tweezer > Contact, Possum
E: Roll In My Sweet Baby's Arms, Runaway Jim
Butter Them Biscuits, Old Home Place and Long Journey Home performed acoustic with Trey on fiddle (for Butter Them Biscuits, his debut performance on fiddle) and acoustic guitar (for Old Home Place and Long Journey Home), Mike on banjo, Fishman on mandolin and Page on stand-up bass. Rev. Jeff Mosier on banjo (acoustic) for Butter Them Biscuits, Old Home Place and Long Journey Home, and banjo (electric) for Roll In My Sweet Baby's Arms and Runaway Jim. "Bathtub Gin" teases in Possum. Concert debuts: Butter Them Biscuits, Roll In My Sweet Baby's Arms.

➢ "How about a big hand for Trey—that's the first time he's ever played the fiddle," Fish says at the end of the bluegrass instrumental Butter Them Biscuits. Three days into the Mosier Bluegrass Tour, the band sounds damn good during the three-song bluegrass series that ends the first set, even Trey on his fiddle. The Reverend also spices up the encores, including an electric Runaway Jim. Besides bluegrass, this show shines with an evil version of The Horse that cracks me up, a Bathtub Gin > Lifeboy pairing that fits wonderfully, and a great Possum with Gin jams from Trey. —TYLER HARRIS

11/19/94 [ACCESSIBILITY: •••]
University of Indiana Auditorium, Bloomington, IN
I: Golgi, Down with Disease, Guyute, Axilla II, Paul and Silas, TMWSIY > Avenu > Antelope, I'm Blue I'm Lonesome, Butter Them Biscuits, Long Journey Home
II: Suzie, Sparkle, YEM, HYHU > Cracklin' Rosie > HYHU, Harry Hood, Amazing Grace, GTBT **E:** Squirming Coil
I'm Blue I'm Lonesome, Butter Them Biscuits and Long Journey Home performed acoustic with Trey on acoustic guitar (for I'm Blue I'm Lonesome and Long Journey Home) and fiddle (for Butter Them Biscuits), Mike on banjo, Fishman on mandolin and Page on stand-up bass. Revered Jeff Mosier on banjo for Butter Them Biscuits, and banjo and vocals for I'm Blue I'm Lonesome and Long Journey Home. "Vibration of Life" in YEM. "Spooky" jam in YEM. "Can't You Hear Me Knocking" tease in YEM.

[11/19/94] [ACCESSIBILITY: ••••]
University of Indiana Auditorium Parking Lot, Bloomington, IN
Cripple Creek, Tennessee Waltz, Old Home Place, Dooley, Mountain Dew, Pig in a Pen, Roll In My Sweet Baby's Arms, Long Journey Home, Butter Them Biscuits, I'm Blue I'm Lonesome, Midnight Moonlight, Will the Circle Be Unbroken
Informal parking lot performance after the Indiana Auditorium show, with Mike (banjo and electric bass), Page (bass), Trey (fiddle and guitar), Fishman (mandolin), Rev. Jeff Mosier (banjo), Eric Merrill (fiddle and guitar), and Jeremy (banjo and jaw harp).

➢ This is a must for all phans! It's Phish and friends performing bluegrass music in a parking lot with fiddles and banjoes. Some highlights are Mountain Dew, Cripple Creek, Tennessee Waltz and Dooley. Guest appearances by Rev. Jeff Mosier and Eric Merrill. Phish sounds like a true Kentucky bluegrass band. —RYAN SATZ

➢ Great bluegrass—it makes me wonder why the band doesn't do acoustic sets. In front of a small crowd, the down-home music just rolls. Tennessee Waltz, Two Dollar Bill, Blue and Lonesome and Midnight Moonlight are my favorites of this unexpected jam. Makes me wish I was there. —KYLE NIDAY

11/20/94 [ACCESSIBILITY: ••••]
Dane County Coliseum, Madison, WI
I: Chalkdust, Fee, Scent of a Mule, Stash, If I Could, Butter Them Biscuits, Long Journey Home, Dooley, Divided Sky, Sample
II: Also Sprach > Bowie, Glide, Axilla II, Reba > Simple, Rift, HYHU > Terrapin > HYHU, Julius, Cavern **E:** Icculus **E2:** Fire
Rev. Jeff Mosier on banjo (electric) for If I Could. Butter Them Biscuits, Long Journey Home and Dooley performed acoustic with Trey on fiddle (for Butter Them Biscuits) and acoustic guitar (for Long Journey Home and Dooley), Mike on banjo, Fishman on mandolin and Page on stand-up bass. Mosier on banjo (acoustic) for Butter Them Biscuits, and on banjo (acoustic) and vocals for Long Journey Home and Dooley. Fishman on vacuum for Terrapin. Concert debut: Dooley.

11/22/94 [ACCESSIBILITY: •••]
Jesse Auditorium, University of Missouri, Columbia, MO
I: Buried Alive > Poor Heart, Horn, Foam, Guyute, I Didn't Know, Bouncing, Down with Disease, Adeline
II: Funky Bitch > Jam > Yerushalayim, Cry Baby Cry, Curtain, Blackbird, Runaway Jim > BBFCM, I'm Blue I'm Lonesome, Butter Them Biscuits, Long Journey Home, Harry Hood, Highway to Hell **E:** Lizards
End of BBFCM, I'm Blue I'm Lonesome, Butter Them Biscuits and Long Journey Home performed acoustic with Trey on acoustic guitar, Mike on banjo, Fishman on mandolin and Page on stand-up bass.

➢ Great second set! The jam in between Funky Bitch and Yerushalayim shows the band's willingness to go WAY out there. Blackbird is played perfectly, too. My highlight is when Trey asks what the band should play next. He says, "Hell, ask that guy." The guy in the crowd shouts Harry Hood. They respond with a version that is out of this world! Made that guy's night. —DAN CHARLAND

➢ This show was the closest we ever came to returning to the *White Album* because Cry Baby Cry and Blackbird both made it in. —SHAWN MILLER

➢ This show is a favorite of mine in my collection. Funky Bitch starts off a second set that's unique and different. An ode to the Beatles with Cry Baby Cry and Blackbird, and Phish does these songs justice. BBFCM is awful but the bluegrass mini-set makes up for it. Then Trey lets a fan pick the following song and they do Harry Hood. What, no Destiny Unbound or Prep School Hippie? —TONY KRUPKA

➢ This is one of those nights where trying to understand the show by looking at the setlist just won't cut it. Funky Bitch > Yerushalayim sounds like a fun little pairing, but let me warn you now, it's oh so much more than that—this very experiMENTAL jam should be heard by all phans of the Golden Hose. —RICH MAZER

11/23/94 [ACCESSIBILITY: ••]
Fox Theatre, St. Louis, MO
I: Wilson > Sparkle > Simple > It's Ice, If I Could, Oh Kee > Suzie, Divided Sky, Amazing Grace
II: Maze, Fee, Scent of a Mule, Tweezer, Lifeboy, YEM, Tweezer Reprise
E: Sample
"Vibration of Life" in YEM. "Frankenstein" jam in YEM.

➢ A must-hear second set for YEM fans. Though it's not the longest version, it's probably the spaciest. Very experimental! —SCOTT SIFTON

11/25/94 [ACCESSIBILITY: ••••]
UIC Pavilion, University of Illinois, Chicago, IL
I: Llama, Guelah, Reba, Bouncing, Melt, Esther, Julius, Golgi
II: Also Sprach > Mike's > Simple > Harpua > Weekapaug > Mango > Purple Rain > HYHU, Antelope **E:** GTBT
Fishman on vacuum for Purple Rain.

11/26/94 [ACCESSIBILITY: ••]
Orpheum Theatre, Minneapolis, MN
I: My Friend, Possum, Guyute, If I Could, Foam, Horse > Silent, Poor Heart, Cavern
II: Halley's > Bowie, Adeline, Lizards, Sample > Slave **E:** Rocky Top
Possum with alternate lyrics ("Someone hit an ostrich…"). Guyute was without second verse. Bowie jam featured, at various times, Fishman on vacuum and mandolin, Trey using a megaphone to create feedback noises and Mike on single-string bass. Slave from this show appears on A Live One.

➢ A month before the Providence Bowie we all know and love, there was the Minneapolis edition. For all of you who are sure that the 12/29 Bowie served as the groundbreaker, you should have been in the theater on this night. Almost 40 minutes of madness including Fishman on vacuum, Trey using his megaphone to create feedback effects and lots of jamming ranging from exploratory to energizing to apathetic, depending on the moment. You see, it's one of THOSE jams, and everyone in the Orpheum knew it. —LEE JOHNSTON

➢ There were waves of energy visibly emanating from the band during the opening My Friend My Friend into Possum. But set two was where it was at. Halley's Comet > David Bowie was the longest (37 minutes), spaciest, wildest version that I know of! The length says it all. A nice Lizards punctuated the middle of the set, and the "ultra-clean" Slave to the Traffic Light (A Live One version) ends this wonderfully energized show in the beautiful venue that is the Orpheum in Minneapolis! (I've never seen a soundboard of this show, and I've been looking for it since 11/27/94.) —CHRIS MRACHEK

11/28/94 [ACCESSIBILITY: ••]
Shroyer Gym, Montana State University, Bozeman, MT
I: Chalkdust, Also Sprach, Scent of a Mule, Stash, Guyute, Sparkle, Simple, Divided Sky, Adeline
II: Suzie, NICU, Tweezer, Sleeping Monkey, Julius **E:** Fee, Tweezer Reprise
Ten-year old Cameron McKenney on saxophone for Simple. Snippet from this Tweezer became Montana on A Live One.

➢ In the lexicon of Phish fans, Bozeman means one thing: Tweezer. Phish's first appearance in the Big Sky state saw them show the locals what a great night in Gamehendge is all about as they took Tweezer out for a short spin and then never returned the car. Forty-five minutes of strong improv! —PAT STANLEY

➢ If Phish is to release any show "from the vault," it should be Bozeman. In what was clearly a night of ground-breaking music, Tweezer stretched out to 45 minutes, a version which is arguably the most interesting they've ever done. A snippet from this jam comprises the "Montana" track on *A Live One*, but it's hard to enjoy the full Tweezer because no tapers that night nailed a perfect copy of it. Come on, Kevin, kick this one down! —ERNIE GREENE

11/30/94 [ACCESSIBILITY: ••••]
Campus Recreation Center, Evergreen College, Olympia, WA
I: Frankenstein, Poor Heart, My Friend, Reba, Forbin's > Mockingbird, Down with Disease, Bouncing, I'm Blue I'm Lonesome, Long Journey Home
II: Halley's > Antelope > MSO > Antelope > Fixin' to Die > Ya Mar > Mike's > Catapult > McGrupp, Cavern **E:** Horse > Silent, Amazing Grace
"Vibration of Life" in Forbin's. I'm Blue I'm Lonesome and Long Journey Home performed acoustic with Trey on acoustic guitar, Mike on banjo, Fishman on mandolin and Page on stand-up bass. Long delay at end of MSO with Trey snoring. Antelope unfinished (no lyric segment); segment before lyric segment had Trey using a megaphone to create feedback noises and Mike on one-string bass.

➢ Phish has often used Tweezer as a song around which to build a set, and on certain nights, DwD, Bowie and Mike's Groove have performed a similar feat. In Olympia, that honor fell to a well-deserving recipient: Antelope! The Antelope jam leads into MSO, complete with Trey snoring at the end, then back into an Antelope chaos jam that found Trey on megaphone. Instead of closing Antelope with the lyrics, the band headed into Fixin' to Die, the last time they've performed this song. Though Antelope "ends" at that point, the strange segues don't: Ya Mar > Mike's > Catapult > McGrupp > Cavern is a wild ride! —NANCY EDDIES

➢ This show is worthy of classic status not just because of the other-wordly second set but because it's backed up by a great, great first set. The Down With Disease jam alone is enough reason to get this tape, but add a Frankenstein opener, Reba and Forbin's > Mockingbird and you've got a great start to a great night of music. —MARCIA COLLINS

12/1/94 [ACCESSIBILITY: ••••]
Salem Armory, Salem, OR
I: Sample, Uncle Pen, FEFY, Maze, Guyute, I Didn't Know, Melt, Adeline
II: Peaches, Mound, Tweezer > BBFCM > Makisupa > NICU > Tweezer > Jesus Left Chicago > Harry Hood, Golgi
E: Sleeping Monkey > Tweezer Reprise
Fishman on vacuum for I Didn't Know. "Norwegian Wood" jam in Tweezer.

➢ Well, the boys really had it goin' on toward the end of this tour. Tweezer being absolutely incredible, Makisupa like you've never heard it before, Fishman adding some classic side comments and such a nice segue into Jesus—an impressive jam session that proves how great 1994 was in Phishland. —ALEX BANKS

➢ My favorite kind of Phish set is the kind where every song is incorporated into one massive jam. There's the more-jam-than-song variety, like the 5/7/94 Tweezerfest, and there's the more-song-than-jam sort, like this show, 12/14/95 Binghamton and the night before this show in Eugene. Salem is my favorite of this select group. The Tweezer jam is mostly Page on synth at first, then becomes a start/stop jam that spaces out before a severe Norwegian Wood jam develops that lasts several minutes and segues into BBFCM. After the usual Creature nonsense, a brief vocal jam leads into Makisupa, which itself turns into a reggae jam that Trey brings ever-so-carefully around into NICU in a perfectly-executed segue. Yes! Trey's doing his thing at the end of NICU, too, playing a pronounced closing jam that's gorgeous, then another jam that returns the band briefly to the Tweezer theme and finally to the opening notes of Jesus Left Chicago. —TYLER HARRIS

➢ This show may be on my top ten list. The first set included a trippy Maze followed by Guyute (a rare one). Once again, the second set is better. Phish started it all off with Peaches and shortly went to an award-winning Tweezer which sandwiched many versions of Phish favorites. The instrumental section after the final words in Tweezer displayed Phish communicating extremely well: so well, it reminds me of a studio version. This is one of my favorite jams. —JOHN FOLEY

12/2/94 [ACCESSIBILITY: ••]
Recreation Hall at UC Davis, Davis, CA
I: Poor Heart, Also Sprach, Sparkle, Simple > It's Ice, Lizards, Stash, Squirming Coil
II: Chalkdust, Bowie, Buried Alive, Julius, Landlady, Gumbo, Caravan, Suzie **E:** Cavern
Second set and encore, starting near the end of Bowie, featured the five-piece Giant Country Horns: Dave Grippo, alto saxophone; Carl Gerhard, trumpet; Michael Ray, trumpet; Peter Apfelbaum, baritone and tenor saxophone; and James Hardy, trombone. Gumbo from this show appears on A Live One.

12/3/94 [ACCESSIBILITY: ••••]
Event Center, San Jose State University, San Jose, CA
I: Wilson, Divided Sky, Guelah, Scent of a Mule, Antelope, Guyute, Sample
II: Frankenstein, Suzie, Buried Alive, Gumbo, Slave, Touch Me, "Horn Introductions", Julius, Cavern **E:** Golgi
The Dave Matthews Band opened. Second set (but not encore) featured the Giant Country Horns with the same lineup as 12/2/94. Jam during the horn introductions was based on "Alumni Blues." Last Touch Me, 7/27/91 Atlanta, GA [394 shows].

➢ The first set at SJSU left a little something to be desired, but the second set salvaged the show. Jamming with the Giant Country Horns, Phish produced a set that prevented anyone from catching their breath. The horns on Slave become slightly obnoxious at times, but redeem themselves in the Alumni Jam and Julius. Touch Me was also revived here for the first time since the horn tour in summer '91. —MATTHEW ASHENFELDER

➢ The horns sound a little sloppy, but add a lot to songs like Suzie, Gumbo, Landlady, Julius and Cavern. The horns are especially interesting on the Alumni Blues jam which is already cool just because, well, it's an Alumni Blues jam! Horns do not sound good on Slave, though, which is a shame because otherwise it's a really good version. —SETH WEINGLASS

12/4/94 [ACCESSIBILITY: ••]
Acker Gym, Chico State University, Chico, CA
I: Runaway Jim, Foam, If I Could, Rift, Tweezer, Fee, Mound, Adeline, Possum
II: Maze, Bouncing, Reba, Axilla II > YEM, HYHU > Purple Rain > HYHU, GTBT **E:** Sleeping Monkey > Rocky Top
Fishman on vacuum for Purple Rain.

12/6/94 [ACCESSIBILITY: ••]
Event Center, University of California at Santa Barbara, Santa Barbara, CA
I: Llama, Mound, Down with Disease, Fluffhead, Jesus Left Chicago, Sparkle, Stash, Golgi
II: Curtain > Sample, Also Sprach, Poor Heart, Mike's > Simple > Mango > Weekapaug, HYHU > Bike > HYHU, I'm Blue I'm Lonesome, Foreplay > Long Time, Antelope **E:** Back In The USSR
Fishman on vacuum for Bike. I'm Blue I'm Lonesome performed acoustic with Trey on acoustic guitar, Mike on banjo, Fishman on mandolin and Page on stand-up bass. Foreplay/Longtime performed acoustic with setup of 10/7/94.

➢ This show represents everything that was great about Phish in '94. Jams were tight, energetic, flawless and pushed to the limit without being self-indulgent. The highlight came midway through the second set, when the Burlington boys broke out the big guns. The flow of Mike's > Simple > Mango > Weekapaug worked so well, I would be surprised if it's never repeated. Weekapaug featured an extra jam that took things to yet another level. With this 44 minutes of perfection in the vault, Fishman broke out the vacuum for a rollicking version of Bike. Then the banjo and washboard came out for Blue and Lonesome, with Page nailing the high solo "suitcase" line both times. I crossed my fingers and got my wish: Foreplay > Long Time, which made my night, as I must confess this was one of my favorite albums in junior high (along with *Quadrophenia*). A tight Antelope closed things out. For the encore, we got the only Back in the USSR played after Glens Falls. The freshman in the row in front of us made the best comment of the night: "If I had stayed back in the dorm studying and missed this, I would have killed myself." —MIKE INDGIN

12/7/94 [ACCESSIBILITY: ••]
Spreckels Theatre, San Diego, CA
I: Peaches > Runaway Jim, Sloth, Ya Mar, Melt, Guyute, Lifeboy, Chalkdust
II: Rift, Frankenstein, Divided Sky, Fee > Julius, I'm Blue I'm Lonesome, Long Journey Home, Amazing Grace, YEM **E:** Cavern
"Gypsy Queen" jam in Runaway Jim. I'm Blue I'm Lonesome and Long Journey Home performed acoustic/no amplification with Trey on acoustic guitar, Mike on banjo, Fishman on mandolin and Page on upright bass. YEM from this show appears on A Live One.

12/8/94 [ACCESSIBILITY: ••••]
Spreckels Theatre, San Diego, CA
I: Makisupa > Maze, AC/DC Bag, Scent of a Mule, PYITE, Simple > Catapult > Simple, Lizards, Guitar Gently Weeps
II: Possum, My Mind's, Axilla II, Reba, Nellie Cane, Adeline, Bowie, Golgi
E: Horse > Silent, Rocky Top
Nellie Cane performed acoustic/no amplification with Trey on acoustic guitar, Mike on banjo, Fishman on mandolin and Page on upright bass.

➢ This show began the Makisupa opener tradition on nights when phans have tangled with police outside the venue (see also 6/10/95 and 8/6/96)—"Policeman came to my house" indeed! Makisupa > Maze is stunning, and from there the first set is off and running, not one down moment. Tons of energy in AC/DC Bag and PYITE, and a gorgeous Simple jam after they sneak Catapult in. Yummy. —MELISSA WOLCOTT

12/9/94 [ACCESSIBILITY: •••]
Mesa Amphitheatre, Mesa, AZ
I: Llama, Foam, Guyute, Sparkle > I Didn't Know, It's Ice > If I Could > Antelope
II: Wilson, Poor Heart > Tweezer > McGrupp, Julius > BBJ, HYHU > Cracklin' Rosie > HYHU, YEM, Suzie
E: I'm Blue I'm Lonesome, Foreplay > Long Time, Tweezer Reprise
"Slave" jam in Tweezer. I'm Blue I'm Lonesome performed acoustic with Trey on acoustic guitar, Mike on banjo, Fishman on mandolin and Page on upright bass. Foreplay/Longtime performed acoustic with setup of 10/7/94.

12/10/94 [ACCESSIBILITY: ••]
Santa Monica Civic Auditorium, Santa Monica, CA
I: Fee, Rift, Stash, Lizards, Sample, Divided Sky, Lawn Boy, Chalkdust
II: Simple, Maze, Guyute, Also Sprach, Mike's > Hydrogen > Weekapaug > HYHU > Do It in the Road > HYHU, Poor Heart, Slave, Cavern
E: "Crew Acknowledgment," GTBT
Fishman on vacuum for Do It in the Road. Jam during Crew acknowledgement was based on Chalkdust. Simple from this show appears on A Live One.

1994 New Year's Run

12/28/94 [ACCESSIBILITY: ••••]
Philadelphia Civic Center, Philadelphia, PA
I: Mound, Simple, Julius, Bathtub Gin, Bouncing, Axilla II, Reba, Dog Faced Boy, It's Ice, Antelope
II: Suzie > NICU > Mike's > Mango > Weekapaug, Contact, Llama, HYHU > Love You > HYHU, Squirming Coil **E:** Bold As Love
"Little Drummer Boy" jam in Weekapaug. Fishman on vacuum for Love You.

➢ This was a wonderful old-school Phish show, the perfect start to the '94 Holiday run. Phish treated us to a well above-average first set, complete with Gin and an unexpected Antelope closer, then took things up a notch for the second set. Suzie > NICU > Mike's > Mango proved to be an incredible series, played with just tons of energy. Then came the highlight: an incredibly well-jammed Weekapaug, complete with a long "Little Drummer Boy" jam to set the holiday mood. Strong song selection and inspired playing made this night a special one. —RICH MAZER

➢ Best Weekapaug jam ever, I must say. Like 4/9/94 Binghamton, it jams on Little Drummer Boy, but here it's even more intense. —AMY DUNCAN

➢ Whenever I take a friend to a Phish show for the first time, one of the first things they often comment on is the light show. No wonder: Chris Kuroda & Co. work magic on the raised platform in the middle of the madness. This night, I staked out space to the right of the soundboard that put me handshake distance from the lighting crew. During Antelope, I noticed that the assistant working a new spiral light didn't have a clue—30 second before Trey was to begin the "Rye, rye, rocco" line, he threw a spotlight on Trey. Chris, obvious angered, turned it back down, but the guy botched his cue again, and as the set ended, Chris threw his headset off, yelled at the guy and stormed off. But long before the start of the second set, Chris was back up there, working with the guy to make the second set go seamlessly. He did his job well—the intense Weekapaug seemed even crazier with lights going every which way. —ED SMITH

12/29/94 [ACCESSIBILITY: ••••]
Providence Civic Center, Providence, RI
I: Runaway Jim > Foam, If I Could, Melt, Horse > Silent, Uncle Pen, I Didn't Know, Possum
II: Guyute, Bowie, Halley's > Lizards, HYHU > Cracklin' Rosie > HYHU, GTBT **E:** Long Journey Home, Sleeping Monkey

"Dueling Banjos" and "LA Woman" teases in Possum. Digital Delay Loop jam in Bowie intro. "Lassie" vocal jam in Bowie. "Heartbreaker" tease in GTBT. Long Journey Home performed acoustic with Trey on acoustic guitar, Mike on banjo, Fishman on mandolin and Page on upright bass.

➢ This was the culmination of the tour in which, I believe, Phish first truly discovered that there was absolutely no limit to how far they could stretch out a jam. Most of that fall's experimentation occurred during half-hour versions of Tweezer, but in Providence, it all came together during the now-famous Bowie. After a tech'd-out beginning which sounded a lot like The Who's Eminence Front, the jam eventually found its way into a captivating and highly melodic lead by Trey, surely strong enough to be turned into its own song someday. It also had a hint of a Slave variation, before delving into a silly monologue of "Lassie, come home" chants. Not only was this the high point of Phish's 1994 super-jams, but I really think it opened the door for Phish realizing they could compose new tunes on the spot during jams, something that would eventually become commonplace in Down With Disease and frequent in Mike's Groove. —ANDY BERNSTEIN

➢ This was just your average Phish show until the second song of the second set. This was not your average Bowie. On a 90-minute tape this takes up almost all of side A and part of side B! The jam never lets down, either—it's the type of jam you can listen to all the way through, rewind, and hear again! —MATT RICHARDSON

➢ The best show of the New Year's Run in '94. The ovation after Bowie was tremendous, as the band uncharacteristically took a bow. Halley's Comet reminded the fans that they attended a special show. —MATTHEW NAPOLI

➢ A tape everyone should have in their possession. The second set provided the mother of all Bowies. It jammed for over 30 minutes and touched on every aspect and emotion that music can produce, from the flowing peacefulness of Trey's soft touch to his mad striking of chords that send chills down my spine. —MATTHEW ASHENFELDER

➢ Sweetest segue from Jim into one of the best Foams I have ever heard. —ALEX BANKS

[12/30/94] [ACCESSIBILITY: •••]
Late Show With David Letterman, Ed Sullivan Theater, New York, NY
Chalkdust

➢ Poor Phish—they looked so nervous, and boy did it show. Definitely the worst Chalkdust ever, played at the request of Sir Dave, no less. —TYLER HARRIS

12/30/94 [ACCESSIBILITY: ••••]
Madison Square Garden, New York, NY
I: Wilson > Rift, AC/DC Bag, Sparkle, Simple, Stash, Fee > Scent of a Mule, Cavern
II: Sample, Poor Heart > Tweezer, I'm Blue I'm Lonesome, YEM, Purple Rain > HYHU, Harry Hood, Tweezer Reprise **E:** Frankenstein

I'm Blue I'm Lonesome performed acoustic with Trey on acoustic guitar, Mike on banjo, Fishman on mandolin and Page on upright bass. Fishman on vacuum for Purple Rain. Wilson from this show appears on A Live One.

➢ Trey acknowledged having nerves upon taking the stage at Madison Square Garden for the first time, and it shows in the band's tame performance. Despite a heavy-duty second set that includes three of the big guns (Tweezer, YEM and Harry) all well-played and the high-octane, sold-out arena, this show was clearly the weakest of the '94 New Year's run. Still, the strength of the '94 New Year's Run is evidenced by the fact that each show has supporters who claim it was "the best of the four;" I have a few friends who swear this show changed their lives. —TYLER HARRIS

➢ Having played Letterman before the show, the guys had to be on top of the world. To start their first show at MSG, Phish chose Wilson to get the entire audience chanting. They're very tight—AC/DC is stellar, and Cavern is also so tight and hard. Set II has a Tweezer that kicks. The YEM is one of my favorites with lots of tempo and melody changes. Purple Rain with an excellent vacuum solo and the best Harry I've heard from that time. It just keeps going. —CONNOR BERGMAN

➢ This lackluster show still has some kicks, though not in the Sample second set opener or Poor Heart. Look to the second set, where Tweezer shines. Blue and Lonesome doesn't really take off, YEM as always is good to hear with the vocal breakdown jam in the middle. Also, Purple Rain kicks ass into Harry Hood > Tweezer Reprise. —AARON BENTON

12/31/94 [ACCESSIBILITY: ••••]
Boston Garden, Boston, MA
I: Golgi, NICU, Antelope, Glide, Mound, Peaches, Divided Sky, Funky Bitch
II: Old Home Place, Maze, Bouncing, Mike's > Buffalo Bill > Mike's > Yerushalayim > Weekapaug, Amazing Grace
III: "Hot Dog Vocals" > MSO, Also Sprach > James Bond Theme > New Year's Countdown > Auld Lang Syne > Tropical Hot Dog Night > Chalkdust > Horse > Silent, Suzie > Slave **E:** Simple

"Rock and Roll Part 2" played on PA while band took the stage; Trey jammed on it, then the band started Golgi. Tom Marshall on vocals for Antelope. Digital Delay Loop jam in Maze intro. "Hot Dog Vocals" had the band, offstage, talking about ordering a hot dog and french fries. MSO cut short in the middle by voice over PA system announcing the delivery of the hot dog—beginning of the New Year's celebration as the band boards giant hot dog and flies over crowd. Bond Theme/Hot Dog Night played over PA (prerecorded). Mike's grandmother walked across the stage waving a shoe during Chalkdust. Extended jam on Suzie. "Auld Lang Syne" jam at the end of Simple. Bouncing from this show appears on A Live One.

➢ This show has some sloppy playing, sure—Fishman rushes through the end of Antelope, and there's a bunch more miscues sprinkled throughout the night. But what this show lacks in technical prowess it makes up for in emotion. The second set includes the hottest version of Maze they've ever done, complete with a digital delay loop intro. In the third set, after all the midnight madness had passed, the band took Suzie around one more time. We watched in awe as Trey steered the jam into the quiet depths of the old, rotten Boston Garden and emerged with the opening chords of one of the most glorious Slave to the Traffic Lights ever. Everyone glowed. —MARCIA COLLINS

➢ My first New Year's show; it's still one of my favorite shows of all time. The energy at the start that built up into Golgi was incredible. I never knew Mike sang Phunky Bitch until he stepped up! Appropriate Old Home Place opener for the second set that also had a crazy Maze. Set III had the flying hot dog and a smoking Chalkdust to kick in the New Year that really made up for the short, cut, almost fake Chalkdust on Letterman the night before. The Simple encore was sweet with an Auld Lang Syne tease. I'm glad I saw the last Phish show ever at the old Garden. —BILL PATRICK

➢ This show has the best Silent in the Morning: if you listen to the tape, right after the "I think that this exact thing happened to me just last year" line, all you hear is the cheering and screaming of the crowd. The energy that flows out of the tape is great. It makes you want to start yelling for New Year's. Then the Simple encore serves as the perfect end to a wonderful show. The place exploded with joy. Not only did Trey laugh, he let himself go and enjoy the music. —GINA D'AMICO

➢ Everyone knows the story of this show, but I have one of my own. Before this show I was hanging out, wanting some coffee, but shit, no wallet. I really needed some java so I dug out my lucky half dollar I had carried for about five years and reluctantly used it for a cup of shitty coffee. Then I turned around and spilled it on the bro behind me. He was wearing a brand new coat and now it was soaked and stained. I felt horrible and just apologized and left. While outside in the cold Boston air the coffee-soiled stranger approached me. He handed me my lucky half dollar AND a full cup of Java. My whole attitude changed, and the show that night was the perfect way to exit a great year. I've seen the stranger many times since—it's nice to know there are brothers like him out there. —JUSTIN WEISS

New Year's '94

12/31/94 Boston Garden, Boston, MA

The Hot Dog Show, as it later became known, was Phish's first and last solo performance at the old Boston Garden. The culmination of Phish's five years of New Year's Eve shows in and around Boston, New Year's Eve '94 found Phish taking the stage like sports stars to the beat of "Rock and Roll No. 2," which Trey joined before the band dropped into Golgi. The night was off and running.

It would be a night during which Phish pulled out their most elaborate prank to date, the giant hot dog. Prior to the third set—which followed an incredible second set that featured one of the best versions of Maze ever, plus Mike's Song with the rare Buffalo Bill wedged in the middle—the band came over the PA system, and Fishman talked about his desire to order "a giant hot dog." The punchline came in the middle of My Sweet One, when a voice came over the PA system and informed the band, "Your order's ready." As the band started up Also Sprach Zarathustra, a giant hot dog, cola and fries (emblazoned with the Phish logo) dropped from the rafters. What at first seemed like a giant prop turned into something more spectacular when the band—assisted by men wearing "Rocket Scientist" jackets—boarded the hot dog and flew it down to the other end of the venue, playing instruments and throwing custom-labeled ping-pong balls into the crowd. (The band later said the hot dog was kosher, as it was blessed by a rabbi backstage).

Even funnier, perhaps, was the butcher job *Rolling Stone* editors did on Paul Robicheau's review of the show. Among the things that *did not* happen on this night: the band did not wear wetsuits, the band did not use the aquarium set (both of those were New Year's '93 props), and the band did not cover the Beatles' *White Album.*

But the band *did* finish the year with an emotional Slave and a Simple encore that returned to Auld Lang Syne, a fitting close to 1994.

1995

81 Total Show Dates
- **1** one-set show
- **78** two-set shows
- **2** three-set shows

PHAN PICKS 1995

SHOW	THE SKINNY
1) 12/31/95 New York, NY	Most popular show of all-time.
2) 10/31/95 Chicago, IL	*Quadrophenia* on Halloween.
3) 12/30/95 New York, NY	Fun show, outstanding Hood.
4) 12/29/95 Worcester, MA	"The Real Gin" in set II.
5) 12/11/95 Portland, ME	Dog Log redux, plus Warren.
6) 11/30/95 Dayton, OH	Insanely well-jammed 2nd set.
7) 06/26/95 Saratoga, NY	DWD > Free runs 30+ minutes.
8) 05/16/95 Lowell, MA	Tons of new song debuts.
9) 06/14/95 Memphis, TN	45-minute Tweezer in 2nd set.
10) 11/11/95 Atlanta, GA	Last of three nights at the Fox.

MUSICAL RECAP: 1994's logical extreme—adding epic-length jams to every show—was virtually realized in 1995. Phish's jamming continued to mature, too, reaching a peak in December that arguably marked the extreme of how far Phish could push themselves with that style.
REPRESENTATIVE JAMS: Drowned > Lizards, 12/31/95; Weekapaug > Sea and Sand, 12/31/95; Bathtub Gin > Real Me > Bathtub Gin, 12/29/95.
ORIGINAL SONG DEBUTS: Acoustic Army (6/7/95), Billy Breathes (9/27/95), Cars Trucks Buses (9/27/95), The Fog That Surrounds (9/27/95), Free (5/16/95), Glide II (5/16/95), Ha Ha Ha (5/16/95), Keyboard Kavalry (9/27/95), Prince Caspian (6/8/95), Spock's Brain (5/16/95), Taste (6/7/95), Theme from the Bottom (5/16/95),
COVER SONG DEBUTS: A Day In the Life (6/10/95), Come Together (12/8/95), Cryin' (9/29/95), Don't You Wanna Go (5/16/95), Gloria (5/16/95), I'll Come Running (5/16/95), Johnny B. Goode (6/17/95), Hello My Baby (9/27/91), Life On Mars (10/13/95), Lonesome Cowboy Bill (5/16/95), My Generation (10/31/95), Suspicious Minds (9/30/95), plus all of *Quadrophenia* (10/31/95).

DARK HORSES

SHOW	THE SKINNY
1) 12/09/95 Albany, NY	Incredible YEM w/silent jam.
2) 11/14/94 Orlando, FL	30+ Stash in second set.
3) 12/14/95 Binghamton, NY	Second set is one giant segue.
4) 12/07/95 Niagra Falls, NY	Amazing jams in Melt, Mike's.
5) 10/22/95 Champaign, IL	Gorgeous Tweezer.

Most-Played Originals:

Song	Times	%
1) Free	31	56%
2) Sample in a Jar	30	52%
3) Strange Design	28	44%
4) Acoustic Army	27	38%
5) Poor Heart	26	37%
5) Theme	26	37%
7) David Bowie	25	35%
7) Maze	25	35%
7) Antelope	25	35%
7) Stash, Sparkle	25	35%

Most-Played Covers:

Song	Times	%
1) A Day in the Life	23	25%
2) Sweet Adeline	20	21%
3) Ya Mar	18	16%
4) Also Sprach	16	14%
4) Amazing Grace	16	14%
4) Uncle Pen	16	13%
7) Hello My Baby	15	13%
8) Timber Ho	12	12%
8) Guitar Gently Weeps	12	10%
10) Fire, Frankenstein	9	9%

First-Set Openers:

Song	Times
1) My Friend My Friend	10
2) AC/DC Bag	7
3) Ya Mar	6
4) Cars Trucks Buses	5
4) Sample in a Jar	5

Second-Set Openers:

Song	Times
1) Also Sprach Zarathustra	10
2) Timber Ho	8
3) Maze	4
3) Runaway Jim	4
3) Wilson	4

Top Henrietta Songs:

Song	Times
1) Suspicious Minds	8
2) Cracklin' Rosie	3
2) Lonesome Cowboy Bill	3
4) Bike, Brain, Cryin', Love You, PRain, Terrapin	1

A Cappella Songs:

Song	Times
1) Sweet Adeline	20
2) Amazing Grace	16
3) Hello My Baby	15
4) Carolina	3

1995 Summer *STIR IT UP*

Although this tour really began in Idaho in early June, Phish snuck in a mid-May gig which gave them the opportunity to debut a slew of new tunes in front of a small crowd in Lowell, MA—tunes which would make for dramatically different setlists on this tour. Gone were the frequent Golgis, Caverns, Samples and Juliuses. Instead, the band showed a willingness to mix up their song selection more, even if some of the new setlist combinations did start to look alike a few weeks into the tour. The only problem? The tour's length. For those looking for true improvisation from Vermont's Phinest, this tour didn't offer it to the extent longer tours of the past—or future—would. But this was supposed to be a nice quick tour so Phish could enjoy some personal time off later in the summer before launching into a huge fall tour.

5/16/95 [ACCESSIBILITY: ••••]
Lowell Memorial Auditorium, Lowell, MA
Don't You Wanna Go, Ha Ha Ha > Spock's Brain, Strange Design, Reba, Theme, HYHU > Lonesome Cowboy Bill > HYHU, Free, Glide II > YEM, Adeline, Sample **E:** I'll Come Running > Gloria

Voters For Choice benefit concert. Phish headlined bill which included Jen Trynin and The Emergency Broadcast Network, and played one set. A group of fans sang "Happy Birthday" to Page before Adeline. Concert debuts: Don't You Wanna Go, Ha Ha Ha, Spock's Brain, Strange Design, Theme, Lonesome Cowboy Bill, Free, Glide II, I'll Come Running and Gloria.

➢ No one had any idea Phish planned to use the Voters For Choice benefit show as a testing ground for an entire set's worth of new material, but Gloria Steinem tipped the crowd off to that in her introduction. All of the then-new songs are now well-known, with the exception Spock's Brain (which died after summer '95) and Glide II. Too bad—I think Glide II (a.k.a. "Flip") has promise. it starts with a groove reminiscent of Hydrogen, then Trey comes in with a guitar line that's simple but sweet and seems to complement Free's melody. He slowly sings, "Gliiiiide, flip flip flip flip...," ending each verse with the refrain, "It's time." That's repeated for about five minutes, then the song suddenly ends. It's a mesmerisingly beautiful idea that's clearly a work in progress. —LEE JOHNSTON

➢ The coolest thing about this tape is the beginning where Gloria Steinem talks about the charity show and how special the atmosphere is. However, when she goes on and on for a few minutes the anxious crowd starts to let her know how they feel. The roar of the crowd is phenomenal when she mentions any name from the band and says Phish alone. —SHANNON C. LANCASTER

➢ The highlight of the show for me was Spock's Brain, a slow funk that features excellent vocal interplay between all four members. I can't understand why they dropped it after only five performances. Reba was also excellent. The jam included a light playful section, a spacey bass section, a heavy section and the climax! —BRENDAN NEAGLE

➢ What makes this tape essential in any collection is hearing Theme and Free as they were originally written. Both have become such free-form songs live and the *Billy Breathes* version of Free is so different, that only this tape offers a true representation of the well thought-out foundations for each tune. It also marks the night that Phish proved they still could write great songs. *Hoist* had made a few of us wonder. —ANDY BERNSTEIN

6/7/95 [ACCESSIBILITY: •••]
Boise State University Pavilion, Boise, ID
I: Possum, Weigh, Taste, Strange Design, Stash, If I Could, Scent of a Mule, Wedge, Funky Bitch, Slave
II: Ha Ha Ha > Maze, Spock's Brain, Theme, Lonesome Cowboy Bill, Acoustic Army, Sample, Harry Hood, Suzie **E:** Guitar Gently Weeps

Last Wedge, 8/20/93 Morrison, CO [134 shows]. Last Weigh, 5/20/94 Olympia, WA [89 shows]. Concert debuts: Taste, Acoustic Army.

➢ There couldn't have been much more anticipation for this show, the summer tour opener. In response, Phish spent well over a minute working the crowd into a frenzy, lingering on the Possum intro, getting louder, softer, louder again, softer, and then exploding into the song we know and love. When Trey chooses Weigh, at least you know he's thinking about making interesting choices. A debut therefore seems to fall into that category, as does the second performance of Strange Design. Stash was the centerpiece jam of the set. In the second, the return of the Wedge was exciting but didn't compare (in my opinion) to those 1993 versions with the extended intros. To compensate, Phish gave us Funky Bitch and Slave to close the set. The second set had much new material and was not as coherently unified but it was still far from an average Phish set. The first While My Guitar Gently Weeps encore marked the end of a particularly creative night for Trey and friends. —GREG SCHWARTZ

6/8/95 [ACCESSIBILITY: •••]
Delta Center, Salt Lake City, UT
I: Don't You Wanna Go, Ha Ha Ha, Runaway Jim, Guelah, Mound, FEFY, Reba > Caspian, Chalkdust
II: Simple, Rift, Free, Bouncing, Tweezer > Lifeboy, Poor Heart, Julius
E: GTBT

Show moved from Wolf Mountain Amphitheatre in Park City, UT because of inclement weather. Concert debut: Caspian.

➢ When we were informed that the Yanni concert was moved from Wolf Mountain to the Delta Center, we were sure they'd move the Phish show there too (disappointing—Wolf Mountain seemed like a perfect place for Phish to do their thing). The only good part, besides the music, about the Delta Center show came when I went to the box office to exchange my tickets and ended up with fifth row seats. Delta Center security was so tight that they were confiscating balloons. This led to a chant for Big Ball Jam, but I guess the band didn't want their beach balls treated as contraband so they skipped it. They did debut Price Caspian. —JUSTIN WEISS

6/9/95 [ACCESSIBILITY: ••••]
Red Rocks Amphitheatre, Morrison, CO
I: My Friend, Divided Sky, Strange Design, Oh Kee > AC/DC Bag, Theme, Taste, Sparkle, Antelope
II: Melt, Wedge, Scent of a Mule, Cavern, Bowie, Acoustic Army, Adeline, Slave **E:** Squirming Coil

➢ Holy Red Rocks! First night had such lax security and a really laid-back crowd. They treated us to an assortment of new and old. The Divided Sky seemed like a treat, then we listened objectively to new songs thereafter. Strange Design drew a lukewarm response but Theme, Taste and Acoustic Army were hits. I've never seen a crowd be so quiet as the Red Rocks crowd during Acoustic Army. Solid versions of SOAM, Bowie, Slave and a rare Wedge carried us through the second set, then Page squared things away with a beautiful Coil encore. —TREVOR NORRIS

➢ As always, Red Rocks is an experience in and of itself. It always seems like the fans are crazier and the music sounds better. Divided Sky may have been the best I'd ever heard. Overall, a nice performance. —LINDSAY BATES

➢ Tickets were harder to get this year but it seemed that everyone who went to the park got one. —JULIE HUNTER

➢ The encore, a Page solo Squirming Coil on his baby grand, sounded so sweet. The second it ended, a huge lightning bolt struck behind the stage and the wind picked up! —EMILY BROWN

6/10/95 [ACCESSIBILITY: ••••]
Red Rocks Amphitheatre, Morrison, CO
I: Makisupa > Llama, Caspian, It's Ice, Free, Rift, YEM > HYHU > Lonesome Cowboy Bill > HYHU, Suzie
II: Maze, Fee, Uncle Pen, Mike's > Hydrogen > Weekapaug, Amazing Grace, Sample **E:** Day in the Life
Fishman on vacuum for Lonesome Cowboy Bill. Concert debut: Day in the Life.

➢ Phish has this strange habit of giving me exactly what I want to hear when I want to hear it. For example, a Makisupa opener with Trey's 4:20 wake-up call. Or a YEM that ends in a vocal HYHU which introduces the last-ever (to the relief of many) Lonesome Cowboy Bill, with the only Lonesome Cowboy Bill vacuum solo. Suzie is a great closer. Similarly, Maze is always a killer opener. And Mike's > Hydrogen > Groove is the ideal centerpiece. Second set was definitely too short but the highlight of the show was the A Day in the Life encore. I instantly recognized the intro chords and immediately picked up on the band's excitement. That huge chord that marks the end of *Sgt. Pepper* (you know the one) also marked the end of the Red Rocks run, and the band left the stage triumphantly. —GREG SCHWARTZ

➢ As rain fell, the boys treated us to a massive, from-the-pages-of-history Mike's > I am Hydrogen > Weekapaug. 30 minutes of intensely inspirational jamming. —AMY DUNCAN

➢ Apparently, the boys decided on the day of the first Red Rocks show that it would be cool to learn A Day In The Life to play the next day. Word got around the scene quickly that Phish had a big musical surprise in store for us on the second night, and I could not have been more blown away when they nailed the debut performance. —TYLER HARRIS

Tuesday, May 16, 1995 — Lowell Memorial Aud, Lowell, MA

I saw a blurb for this show deep in the *Boston Globe* a few days before tickets went on sale—"Bands to play benefit concert for Pro-Choice group." So this wasn't a secret gig, per se, although you had to be relatively in-the-know to snag tickets.

I got through to Ticketmaster 20 minutes after tickets went on sale, certain that they would have sold out. But they had seats, and weeks later, I found I snagged fifth row tickets on the floor—this show took almost a day to sell out despite a venue capacity of just under 3,000. About five days before the show, the folks from Voters for Choice sent a mailer to my P.O. box thanking me for buying tickets and offering full instructions on how to claim them at the door. I don't know if they were afraid of anti-abortionist violence—the three older men holding "Abortion Kills Babies" signs outside the venue didn't seem much of a threat, at least in the physical sense—or ticket scalping, but buying tickets to this show was much easier than picking up the tickets on hold at will-call. Show ID, show Ticketmaster number, show ID again—you had to pity the Ticketless wandering in front of the venue this night.

We made it inside during Jen Trynin's set. Her band closed up shop, and a nice woman from Massachusetts Voters for Choice came out to give a lengthy intro for Gloria Steinem, at which point my friend and I turned to each other in disbelief. Steinem, the famous feminist, the former president of the National Organization for Women, was not only in the house but had the task of introducing Phish. Well, at least she tried. Most of the crowd couldn't wait for Steinem to finish. But Gloria did manage to tip the band's hand in her intro: "There'll be more new songs that you've never heard before!"

Driving to the show, I had expected one, maybe two new songs, but this night just kept coming. A gospely opener (Don't You Wanna Go), then Ha Ha Ha, into Spock's Brain, then a new (and at that point untitled) ballad sung by Page. Whew—four new ones in a row. Immediately following was one of the best Rebas ever, trailed by more rollouts: Theme From The Bottom—the best of the new batch, I thought at the time—and a cover of the Velvet Underground's Lonesome Cowboy Bill sung by Fish.

The Henrietta interlude also saw a vote for the name of the song that became Spock's Brain. Trey offered the crowd four choices: The Plane, The First Single, Israel, and Spock's Brain; as the crowd saw it, it was no contest. More new songs followed—I recall really liking Free and not comprehending what I gather is now called Glide II. A few people off to my right sang a brief Happy Birthday to Page during the a cappella part. After it was over, I couldn't say that it had felt like a Phish show. It wasn't bad, it was just something different.

But that this show happened at all deserves special note. When the Brookline Clinic shootings shocked the nation in January '95, it impacted the band—John Paluska lived next door to one of the targeted clinics and worked to arrange this gig.

A good show for a good cause. **—Chris De Gieson**

Voters For Choice
5/16/95 Lowell Memorial Auditorium, Lowell, MA

One of Phish's longest-standing band policies was not playing benefit shows for politically-charged issues. Besides a NORML benefit played for a few hundred people in the fall of 1988, Phish elected to steer clear of causes on the theory that they didn't want to infuse political messages into their music.

That all changed in January 1995, when a series of shootings at an abortion clinic in the Boston area rocked the nation. Phish's longtime manager, John Paluska, lived next door to one of the targeted clinics, and helped arrange a Voters for Choice benefit show as a way of both raising money for pro-choice causes and thanking the clinic volunteers. For one night, Phish would put aside their unofficial no-cause policy to do what felt right, and in the process, they'd raise $30,000.

The venue was a small 2,900 seat theater in the industrial Massachusetts town of Lowell, and in the crowd that night were workers and volunteers from the clinic, the guests of the bands. Also in attendance was NOW president Gloria Steinem, who served as emcee for Phish's set and later returned to the stage to hug Trey during Phish's impromptu take on "Gloria."

But Phish fans remember Lowell not so much for the cause as for the music. It was a night that saw the breakout of a next generation of Phish music, songs like Free and Theme from the Bottom that would become key components of many sets thereafter.

In the end, though, the band wondered about the costs of playing for a political cause, especially one as charged as the abortion debate. "I am supporting the right for people to make a choice, and I don't like the us-versus-them mentality," Fishman later told *Relix*. But the nature of the event meant that, for better and for worse, Phish had chosen sides. They haven't played an event like Voters For Choice since.

6/13/95 [ACCESSIBILITY: •••]
Riverport Amphitheatre, Maryland Heights, MO
I: Runaway Jim, Foam, Bouncing, Stash, Strange Design, Taste, Reba, HYHU > Terrapin > HYHU, Sparkle, Chalkdust
II: Bowie, Lizards, Axilla II, Theme, Acoustic Army, Harry Hood, Golgi
E: Adeline, Julius
Fishman on vacuum for Terrapin. "Dave's Energy Guide" tease in Chalkdust.

➢ This was definitely the worst show of the '95 summer tour. The classical Phish atmosphere was not there. Making the trip from Red Rocks was almost a waste of time. Even on tape, there is no mood. Stay away from this one. —SEAN MILLER

6/14/95 [ACCESSIBILITY: ••••]
Mud Island Amphitheatre, Memphis, TN
I: Don't You Wanna Go, Gumbo, NICU, Mound, Cavern, Possum, All Things, Amazing Grace, Horse > Silent, Spock's Brain, Melt
II: Also Sprach > Poor Heart, Tweezer, Acoustic Army, Guitar Gently Weeps **E:** Simple > Rocky Top > Tweezer Reprise

➢ It was an outdoor show on the Mississippi River—beautiful. First set was great; Don't You Wanna Go, Gumbo and NICU were great choices played well. But in the second set, the show seemed to go downhill. The Tweezer was unbearable, at least 30 minutes long. It felt never-ending—Phish is the only band that can play a song for 30 minutes without actually playing the song. But the encore made up for the Tweezer. It was three songs long: Simple, Rocky Top and Tweezer Reprise. This was a good show but definitely not one of their best. —MELANIE AND MELITA TERRELL

➢ Some Phish jams aren't for the faint of heart. The Mud Island Tweezer, another in the series of experimental Tweezers begun at Bangor on 11/2/94 and continued in Bozeman on 11/28/94—and to continue later this tour at Finger Lakes—is probably the least musically satisfying of the batch, but for those interested in hearing Phish push the boundaries of improvisational rock, potholes and all, Mud Island is worth checking out.—ED SMITH

6/15/95 [ACCESSIBILITY: •••]
Lakewood Amphitheatre, Atlanta, GA
I: My Friend, Sparkle, AC/DC Bag, Old Home Place, Taste, Wedge, Stash > I Didn't Know, Fluffhead, Antelope
II: MSO, Ha Ha Ha > Bowie, Strange Design, Theme, Scent of a Mule, Acoustic Army, Slave **E:** Bouncing, Frankenstein
Fishman on trombone, Trey on megaphone and Mike on electric drill for I Didn't Know.

➢ I thought this crowd was a real letdown. We had seats in the pavilion and our section was empty. When we moved to a different, more crowded section, everyone was sitting down. Despite the less-than-enthusiastic response, the band played well—I was pleased with the sets and psyched to have a two-song encore. I loved Fluffhead followed by Antelope and I thought Slave was unbelievable. —CHRIS HAINES

6/16/95 [ACCESSIBILITY: ••••]
Walnut Creek Amphitheatre, Raleigh, NC
I: Halley's > Down with Disease, Esther, Ya Mar, Cry Baby Cry, It's Ice, My Mind's, Dog Faced Boy, Catapult, Melt
II: Runaway Jim > Free, Carolina, YEM, Squirming Coil **E:** Bold As Love
"Melt" teases before Dog Faced Boy. YEM featured Boyd Tinsley on fiddle. "Oye Como Va" jam in YEM.

➢ This beautiful day started off with a Three Little Birds soundcheck, then the show itself offered the first-ever experimental Jim into Free. —WAYLON BAYARD

➢ Halley's > DWD opener, are you kidding? A prelude to an incredible first set. A precious Esther leads to Ya Mar. Cry Baby Cry was another treat. Fish kept teasing the SOAM opening, just trying to get this thing going. Dog Faced Boy and Catapult chilled us out before an insane SOAM finally came. The second set was one of those where you had to be there. Experimental Jim > Free was too intense. YEM with Boyd Tinsley was exciting, and Mike's bass solo at the end of YEM is sick. Nice Coil and an always-welcome Bold as Love encore. Great show at a great venue. —TREVOR NORRIS

➢ Boyd Tinsley of the Dave Matthews Band makes YEM shine at this show, but this version of Free is a definite must-listen. Wow. —DAVE SWANK

➢ They really screwed up the Cry Baby Cry; it hasn't been played since. —JOSHUA HOWLEY

6/17/95 [ACCESSIBILITY: ••••]
Nissan Pavilion at Stone Ridge, Gainsville, VA
I: Divided Sky, Suzie, Taste, Fee, Uncle Pen, Julius, Lawn Boy, Curtain > Stash
II: Wilson, Maze, Mound, Tweezer > Johnny B. Goode > Tweezer > McGrupp, Acoustic Army, Adeline, Harry Hood, Sample **E:** Three Little Birds
Dave Matthews on guitar and vocals and Leroi Moore on saxophone for Three Little Birds. Concert debuts: Johnny B. Goode, Three Little Birds.

➢ The first set opener, Divided Sky, proved to be an omen for a good show. In set one, a great version of Julius showed up, as well as an incredibly good Curtain > Stash—very trippy. The second set featured Tweezer > Johnny B. Goode > Tweezer that rocked hard. JBG was totally unexpected and rocked way harder than Chuck Berry. The encore, Three Little Birds with Dave Matthews and Leroi Moore, was a cool surprise. —JAY GREEN

➢ The band soundchecked Johnny B. Goode before the show, but no one really thought they'd play it during one of their sets. Chris Kuroda, joking around with the tapers before the first set, said, "I was wondering what they were going to break into next—Around and Around?" But then, in the midst of a very interesting Tweezer jam, out it came. The band charged through it, just ripping it up, then brought the jam back out the other side into a spacey realm similar to the portion of the Bozeman Tweezer christened "Montana" on *A Live One*. —LOCK STEELE

6/19/95 [ACCESSIBILITY: ••••]
Deer Creek Amphitheatre, Noblesville, IN
I: Theme > Poor Heart, AC/DC Bag, Tela, PYITE, Reba, Strange Design, Rift, Cavern, Antelope
II: Simple > Bowie, Mango, Loving Cup, Sparkle, YEM, Acoustic Army, Possum **E:** Day in the Life
Possum played heavy-metal style, missing final verse.

➢ This was the first time Phish ever played Deer Creek and it was a sold-out show. Deer Creek is the best place to hear any band—the sound is crystal clear and the scene is so peaceful. Loving Cup was the highlight for my show, though every song was played with exactness and clarity. Solid show from start to finish; they certainly made a mark for themselves at Deer Creek. —ROB KOELLER

➢ The first 45 minutes of this show, to my ears, is the tightest Phish has ever played. Theme From the Bottom is just so on, with Trey playing some very beautiful and soulful grooves throughout. Everything is played so well but I have to single out the PYITE and Reba. The latter in particular is flawless—guaranteed to be one of your favorite versions. There's also the worst lyric flub I've ever heard on a Phish tape. It comes during Rift and is so flubbed that Trey is obviously quite amused. —RUSSELL LANE

6/20/95 [ACCESSIBILITY: ••••]
Blossom Music Center, Cuyohoga Falls, OH
I: Llama, Spock's Brain, Ginseng Sullivan, Foam, Bathtub Gin, If I Could, Taste, I Didn't Know, Melt
II: Halley's, Chalkdust, Caspian, Uncle Pen, Mike's > Contact, Weekapaug > HYHU > Cracklin' Rosie > HYHU, Highway to Hell
E: Slave, Amazing Grace
Fishman on vacuum for I Didn't Know.

➢ The best show in the midwest in summer '95. Spock's Brain was very harmonious. Mike didn't miss a beat in Ginseng Sullivan. Damn fine rendition of I Didn't Know. Uncle Pen is always a show-stopper and this one was a beauty. The show ended with the pent-up energy enclosed in the little ditty known as Slave to the Traffic Light. —SEAN MILLER

➢ In the second set they jam a theme in between Mike's Song and Contact that will always stand out in my mind. It was like a journey into the world of the unknown, bringing me so far out of reality, carrying me around, then dropping me down into a slow-starting Contact. My friends often thank me for playing this tape during a camping trip we went on, because they hadn't realized the full power of Phish live until they heard this. —DAN CHARRON

6/22/95 [ACCESSIBILITY: •••]
Finger Lakes Performing Arts Center, Canandaigua, NY
I: Sample, Scent of a Mule, Ha Ha Ha, Divided Sky, Guelah, It's Ice, Strange Design, Maze, Cavern, Adeline
II: Theme > Tweezer > Tweezer Reprise **E:** Acoustic Army, Guitar Gently Weeps
"My Generation" jam in Tweezer.

➢ First set was great: new tunes, and I always love something a cappella. But the second set, ugh! Don't get me wrong, Tweezer is one of my faves, but halfway through I was just standing there scratching my head. The worst show I ever saw. —JOHN CUNNINGHAM

➢ Canandaigua is my favorite place to see a show. Every time Phish plays there, the weather is clear and warm and the atmosphere is groovy. First set was good, but the second set on the other hand… Tweezer > Tweezer Reprise, they played well but it was intolerable for me. Luckily, they kicked ass for While My Guitar Gently Weeps. —DAVID WHITE

➢ This second set deserves a second glance. It may not have been the best Tweezer in history, but it was the last of the great Tweezerfests of '94-'95. Theme was at that point the most intense of the new tunes, and this version is still my favorite. It never really ended, and Tweezer never really started. It never really sounded like a normal Tweezer either, though it was ferocious through and through. Trey was losing it to the point of it breaking down to just heavy noise—I had seen Trey run around screaming with the bullhorn before, but never with so much evil in him. Somewhere in the midst of this jam was a crazy My Generation jam with the strange bluegrass harmony we would hear again on Halloween. But no other recognizable themes popped up until Tweezer Reprise surfaced 45 minutes later. Out of that hell, however, came the most beautiful moment in Phish musical history. After all the screaming and aural assaults, Trey crouched down and hid under the piano, Mike crouched behind the drums, and Fish ducked to make himself disappear. They didn't stop playing, they just hid to put Page in the limelight. This is the moment that the basic melody for Keyboard Kavalry was born. Page began a simple, beautiful melody that built from nothing into sheer energy during the next few minutes. It climbed higher until the others reappeared and eventually exploded into Tweezer Reprise. The tape is worth having for these five minutes of music alone. —DAVEY INKREA

6/23/95 [ACCESSIBILITY: ••••]
Waterloo Village Music Center, Stanhope, NJ
I: Simple, Chalkdust, Caspian, Reba, Ginseng Sullivan, Free, Taste, YEM
II: Runaway Jim, Lizards, Wedge, Antelope, Harpua > Waterloo Jam > Llama, GTBT **E:** Day in the Life
Waterloo Jam, Llama and GTBT featured John Popper on harmonica. Harpua unfinished. Concert debut: Waterloo Jam.

➢ After you see a guy on a body board with a big blood spot, it's hard to have a good time. The scene was chaotic. No one had a clue, not the cops or the staff. I walked three miles and missed almost the whole first set. The encore, A Day in the Life, as well as Popper's cameo during Waterloo, were surreal. The bus ride on the way back to the auxiliary lots was also an experience, driving on two wheels going around hairpin turns. The bus driver was a heavy metal maiden from hell! —DAN KURTZ

➢ Thousands of fans got to the show late; fortunately, I wasn't one of them because this show kicked ass from the get-go. The boys were on fire throughout the first set which featured lots of classics and soon-to-be classics. The second set, however, was by far dominant. After the rocking Antelope, Harpua was an unexpected treat but what followed was even more tasty: John Popper came out to lead the boys out of Waterloo and into Llama. —ERIC ACQUAFREDDA

➢ In light of the tragedy and the mayhem at this show, it's easy to forget that it was a superb performance with everything from a YEM to close the first set, a very strong Runaway Jim, and a simply terrific Wedge, a song the band sometime struggles performing live but one that hit on all cylinders that night. —SCOTT SIFTON

6/24/95 [ACCESSIBILITY: •••]
Mann Music Center, Philadelphia, PA
I: Fee, Rift, Spock's Brain, Julius, Glide, Mound, Stash, Horse > Silent, Squirming Coil
II: Also Sprach > Halley's > Bowie, Lifeboy, Suzie, Harry Hood, Acoustic Army, Adeline, Golgi **E:** Bold As Love

➢ I thought I'd mention this show merely for the second set Bowie, but then I realized there's more to this show than one would think. It starts off with a real good Fee > Rift combo and follows with Julius which had a DWD flavor to it. The rest of the first is average… So on to set 2, with one of my all time favorite pieces: 2001 > Halley's > Bowie. The Bowie is hands-down my favorite of all time. The jam goes off into dark space, then slowly comes back and rolls like a freight train out of control. A must have! Hood is really beautiful as is the Acoustic Army where Trey thanks the crowd for being so quiet and attentive. If only all crowds would be like this. —BRIAN WATKINS

➢ When they played Spock's Brain as the third song of the night, we obviously had no idea the song was headed for the closet. Through summer '97, the band hasn't played it since. I hope Phish dusts off this forgotten gem and shines it up some time soon. Besides being a rare song with writing credited to the entire group (like Tweezer and Theme), Spock's would fit amazingly well with Phish's current funk jamming style. —SCOTT SIFTON

➢ The best Bowie I have ever seen. Even when the guys at the soundboard thought it was over (they killed the lights), Phish kept going. Also during this set, Mike and Trey chased each other around on stage. They were running around Page and behind Fishman several times. It was hilarious! —TIM HERRMANN

6/25/95 [ACCESSIBILITY: ••••]
Mann Music Center, Philadelphia, PA
I: Ya Mar > AC/DC Bag, Taste, Theme, If I Could > Sparkle, Divided Sky, I Didn't Know, Melt
II: Maze, Sample, Scent of a Mule, Mike's > Do It In The Road > HYHU > Weekapaug, Amazing Grace, Cavern **E:** Bouncing > Slave
Fishman on vacuum for I Didn't Know.

➢ The opening combo of Ya Mar > AC/DC Bag is perhaps the greatest way to open a show. My friend Jay swears he heard Page playing that classical masterpiece Rhapsody In Blue during Divided Sky. Seeing Fishman's hip thrusting motions during Why Don't We Do It In The Road has left a memorable, yet scary, impression on my mind. —RIC HANNAH

➢ In many ways, this should have been a great show: a solid first set with a strong opening duo and lots of jamming room in Theme, Divided Sky and SOAM, and a second set built around the suite of Mike's > Do it in the Road > Weekapaug, all capped off by a please-everyone Bouncin' > Slave encore. But something just didn't click on this night; though some of the jams are on, this show lacks the apparent unity of purpose that makes a show like the following night in Saratoga so special. —RICH MAZER

6/26/95 [ACCESSIBILITY: ••••]
Saratoga Performing Arts Center, Saratoga Springs, NY
I: My Friend, Don't You Wanna Go, Bathtub Gin, NICU > Sloth, My Mind's, It's Ice, Dog Faced Boy, Tela, Possum
II: Down with Disease > Free > Poor Heart > YEM, Strange Design, Antelope **E:** Sleeping Monkey > Rocky Top
"Heartbreaker" jam in Possum.

➢ This show contains, among other things, the first really huge Down with Disease, a song Phish had been avoiding most of the summer. Set I was incredible, with a Bathtub Gin in which Trey screams unintelligibly during the jam. Tela > Possum is, of course, an awesome dip into Gamehendge to close the set. The second set had a tough act to follow, so how does the band respond? Four huge jams, clearly highlighted by the new wide-open DwD which flowed surprisingly cleanly into Free. Can't complain about YEM or Antelope which more than make up for Poor Heart and Strange Design. —GREG SCHWARTZ

➢ This was one night where Phish was at their absolute best for an entire show. The crowd was so into the music: during Don't You Wanna Go, everyone was grooving in the same direction. The best Possum ever closed the first set, and the second set was unlike any other ever. The jamming was so tight, Fishman tore everything up. Poor Heart was different, and the YEM bass solo was too much. Smoke (I swear to God) started coming off Mike's bass. Sleeping Monkey was played as the encore for the only time that summer, capping off the best show that I have ever seen. —JOSHUA HOWLEY

➢ Sometimes Phish's jamming becomes so infectious that even normally tame songs fall under the sway. After the wonderful DwD (one of the most together jams the band has ever performed in that song) the jam led not to the DwD refrain but instead into a beautiful Free. The surprise came in Poor Heart—Trey became fixated on a downbeat noise and signaled Fish throughout the song to make a heavy beat effect. —TYLER HARRIS

➢ Best Possum ever. The jam had to be at least 15 to 20 minutes and in the middle of it they started to play Heartbreaker by Zeppelin. It was very vague at first but then the crowd noticed this and went insane. —DAVID ECKERS

[6/27/95] *A Live One* released on Elektra.

6/28/95 [ACCESSIBILITY: ••••]
Jones Beach Music Theater, Wantagh, NY
I: Axilla II > Foam, FEFY, Reba, PYITE, Stash, Fluffhead, Chalkdust
II: Sample, Poor Heart, Tweezer > Gumbo, Sparkle, Suzie, Harry Hood, Tweezer Reprise **E:** Adeline, Guitar Gently Weeps
"Ha Ha Ha" tease before Axilla. "Cannonball" and "Dave's Energy Guide" jams in Tweezer.

➢ What is it about Tweezer jams that provoke such strong love/hate emotions? I know people who thought this show sucked, but for me the Tweezer—complete with a full Cannonball jam and a pronounced Dave's Energy Guide—hinted at the next evolution in Phish's jamming to follow during fall tour. Instead of taking Tweezer everywhere in the course of one set, like Bozeman, Mud Island and FLPAC, they explored a more focused series of ideas. Needless to say, I thought it rocked. —PAT STANLEY

Friday, June 23, 1995 Waterloo Concert Field, Waterloo, NJ

A Phish fan named Daniel Malone died after falling from a car while on the way to this show at the Waterloo Village Concert Field.

Police told the media that he and many others chose not to wait for a bus, but if you were there, you know there were no buses available and hundreds of cars did not even make it to parking lots because highway exits were needlessly blocked off.

I have never experienced a concert-going nightmare that even compares to the hell that broke loose at Waterloo that summer. Thousands of fans jammed the highway, the off-ramps, and the "satellite" parking lots, and the system broke down.

With local police refusing to provide instructions or assistance, Malone and many of us were faced with the difficult choice of walking an unknown distance and missing at least half the show (as thousands did—I arrived at the end of the first set despite hitting the offramp to the venue a full hour before the scheduled start of the show), or jumping on the back of a car. While Daniel's decision to do just that was a tragic mistake, it was one made by many that night, and the police made no attempt to stop people or offer an alternative even after the show when they knew of the accident.

By not providing enough buses or adequate instructions, and interfering with cars' ability to get to assigned parking areas—parking spots were still open well after showtime, although some people were routed to lots more than three miles from the venue including a "Wild West Village" which, according to Waterloo officials, had never been used as a parking lot at one of their concerts before—authorities showed a complete and total contempt for Phish fans which led to disaster.

As far as I'm concerned, Waterloo, the Mt. Olive Police, and Delsener-Slater productions were directly responsible for the death of Daniel Malone. After hundreds of wonderful nights, there was one which everyone would like to forget, but no one should.

Rest in peace, Daniel. **—Andy Bernstein**

6/29/95 [ACCESSIBILITY: ••••]
Jones Beach Music Theater, Wantagh, NY
I: Runaway Jim, Taste, Horse > Silent, Divided Sky, Cavern, Rift, Simple, Melt, Carolina
II: Free > Bowie, Strange Design, YEM, Acoustic Army, Day in the Life
E: Theme
"Cannonball" jam in Runaway Jim.

➢ I have to wonder about the traffic planners who okay 19,900 person venues with a single lane of access from the highway. A huge overflow crowd for Phish on this night (and the next night, too) backed traffic up for miles. With memories of Waterloo several weeks before in our minds, a group of us decided to leave the car and walk down the shoulder of the highway. Along the way, we enjoyed a flourishing roadside lot scene; in the end, most cars made it to the lot before the band came on stage. Whew—they would have missed a very good show, capped by one of the stronger Mike's Grooves I've ever heard. —MELISSA WOLCOTT

6/30/95 [ACCESSIBILITY: ••••]
Great Woods, Mansfield, MA
I: AC/DC Bag, Scent of a Mule, Horn, Taste, Wedge, Lizards, Mound, Fee, Antelope
II: Also Sprach > Possum > Ha Ha Ha, TMWSIY > Avenu > Mike's > Contact > Weekapaug, Amazing Grace, Squirming Coil
E: HYHU > Cracklin' Rosie > HYHU, Golgi

➢ It was a hot and humid summer day. Shirts were off, liquid was pouring and the smoke was green. This is an awesome background to a killer show. (It's ten times better than the next night's; this show should have been broadcast on WBCN.) A young Taste, rare Wedge, Ha Ha Ha, and a nice Mike's > Contact > Groove arrangement. —GREG MARCEAU

➢ An interesting first set. Aside from the Wedge, the songs were standard fillers, save

Come From Top the Mountain

7/2&3/95 Sugarbush North, Fayston, VT

The legend of Sugarbush made its way around Phish circles rapidly after the band's unforgettable performance there in July 1994. A tour closer which featured an Antelope, Harpua and Harry Hood in one set, the show was even more notable for the venue—a stage perched on the side of a mountain, with a backdrop of miles of sky.

Needless to say, when Phish announced a two-day tour finale at Sugarbush for 1995, just about every fan in the Northeast marked it on their calendar. The fact that it came during the July 4 weekend, and that on-site, on-mountain camping adjacent to the concert site would be available, only further increased the anticipation.

By 11 a.m. on July 2, the day of the first show, a seemingly never-ending line of cars sloped its way up the mountain. The venue had warned that only cars with ticket-holders would be allowed in. And although the shows had only sold out days before, hordes of ticketless caravans arrived—and all somehow seemed to find their way in.

By showtime it was clear that thousands upon thousands of ticketless fans had made their way to Sugarbush, to the parking lot, and up the ski hill which formed the makeshift amphitheater. In fact, fans were pouring over the flimsy barriers which flanked the viewing area. A few guards tried to stop the first fence-hoppers, but when a sea of people oozed in from every side, venue security just gave up.

It was a free show. On a beautiful night, on a mountain, in Vermont. Nothing could have been more perfect.

A local DJ kicked off the festivities by welcoming everyone, including the gate crashers. The only request was that no one light campfires (it had been a dry summer in Vermont) and that everyone be patient with the bus system which imported and exported fans to satellite parking lots. The crowd was just a wee bit larger then they'd expected—the police estimated over 7,000 fence hoppers, plus 12,500 paid.

When Phish finally took the stage, anticipation and energy surged from the bottom of the ski hill to the very top. Thousands of bug-eyed fans squished their way up close, but an equal number fanned out up the slope, even past the downed barrier which marked the end of the viewing zone.

Rumors, accurate ones, that the best sound was actually far away from the stage in the mountain air, led many to watch from afar. The uninterrupted view of the Mad River Valley also attracted some intrepid climbers, a few of whom even made it all the way up to the top of Sugarbush North, about 4,000 feet above sea level and an equal distance from the stage.

And ah yes, there was a show. An unforgettable show. The first set featured the somewhat rare Gumbo and Curtain, and the impeccably rare Camel Walk, the first since 2/24/89—one of the longest stretches Phish had ever gone without playing a song before busting it back.

But what made the show stand out was performance more than setlists. It wasn't just that they played Camel Walk, it was that they ripped Camel Walk, played it different then ever before, with an eerie mix of restrain and abandon. That sort of tension marked the entire show. It wasn't a night of insane, down-the-neck hanging notes, it was a night of eerie precision.

The second set opened with a splendid Runaway Jim (it was this tour that the band first truly started opening up that song for extended improvisation) which segued into a slow but thundering Makisupa. Those perched high up on the ski hill were treated to a view of a far-off lighting storm which at one point actually appeared to fire to the beat of Mike's bass notes. The night went on to feature a captivating Tweezer, which morphed into Ha Ha Ha. Before it was all done there was a Slave and a Halley's Comet.

But even as the show ended, the night had just begun. On-mountain camping beckoned many, and an extended tent city stretched up a ski trail parallel to the stage area. It was Phish summer camp. The realization of a dream.

Night two was, by many opinions, not as strong as night one, but featured the breakout of Timber Ho after over 250 shows. But the weekend was about more than just music. It was about hordes of Phish fans coming together in the promised land, and realizing for the first time just how many of us there are.

for a wonderful Antelope, their best first set closer, which salvaged the set. A super second set is highlighted by a great Possum and Weekapaug. The set slows down after that point. However, being at Great Woods, arguably the best place to see Phish on the East Coast, fans knew they had the next night to look forward to. —MATTHEW NAPOLI

7/1/95 [ACCESSIBILITY: ••••]
Great Woods, Mansfield, MA
I: Ya Mar, Llama, If I Could, All Things, It's Ice, Caspian, Melt, Bouncing, Chalkdust
II: Wilson, Maze, Theme, Uncle Pen, Stash, Strange Design, Acoustic Army, Harry Hood, Suzie **E:** Funky Bitch
Live FM broadcast on WBCN in Boston. Long instrumental intro to If I Could. Fishman on vacuum and Mike on electric drill for jam in the middle of It's Ice. "Sunshine of Your Love" tease in Suzie.

➢ This show came just after the release of *A Live One* and was the first post-release show to be radio broadcast in the Boston area. In response, Phish decided not to jam, which is particularly noticeable in the second set. The show, of course, includes a handful of tunes from the album: Bouncin', Chalkdust, Wilson, Stash, Hood. Highlights are limited, including the Suzie (with Sunshine of Your Love reference) and a Funky Bitch encore dedicated to the tourheads. The mid-second set Stash was intense, but not to the level of performance a year earlier at Great Woods (which appears on the album), and was framed by songs one hopes never to see in the core of the second set: Uncle Pen, Strange Design and Acoustic Army. Basically, 7/1/95 lacked the intensity of other shows at the good Woods, probably due to the radio influence. —GREG SCHWARTZ

➢ When Phish jams, we all know we're listening to something special. But when they decide to show their softer side, be prepared to be amazed. This ballad-laden show is beautiful, particularly Strange Design. —DAVE SWANK

➢ For a somewhat maligned performance, this show does have two musical moments that stand out. After a rocking Llama, the band went into a beautiful, melodic jam that turned into If I Could. (It's been said that this is the long instrumental beginning of this song that the band axed from *Hoist* after recording it.) Then, in the second set, the band put all the pressure on Harry Hood to deliver the goods—and it did. This is one of the most profoundly moving Hoods the band has ever played. —AMY MANNING

7/2/95 [ACCESSIBILITY: •••••]
SummerStage at Sugarbush North, Fayston, VT
I: Sample, Divided Sky, Gumbo, Curtain > Julius, Camel Walk, Reba, I Didn't Know, Rift, Guitar Gently Weeps
II: Runaway Jim > Makisupa > Scent of a Mule, Tweezer > Ha Ha Ha, Sleeping Monkey, Acoustic Army, Slave **E:** Halley's, Tweezer Reprise
Last Camel Walk, 2/24/89 Burlington, VT [691 shows].

➢ What a way to end the tour, high (in more ways than one) on a mountain top. Everything about these Sugarbush shows was beautiful—the location, the music and the people. On the first night, set I proved solid with the one-time return of Camel Walk serving as the added treat. A mind-bending, 20-minute version of Runaway Jim set a trippy pace for set II. The rest of set II was smooth, jamming and flowing, leaving us asking for more in the crisp, clear Vermont night. —JASON DEZIEL

➢ The band brought back to life the funky Camel Walk, which they hadn't played since 1989. Sugarbush is just a great venue to see Phish. The mountains serve as a beautiful backdrop and the mountain on which we danced made us feel as if we were about to fall off—it's steep! Many people say that the acoustics at Sugarbush are somehow mystical in that the higher you climbed up the mountain, the better you could hear. This is just not true. I will say, though, once again, "moo." (see 7/16/94) —LARA WITTELS

➢ In the middle of the second set, people stopped watching the band and looked to the sky. Two young men climbed a ski lift tower and were swaying to the excellent music while showing off their Independence Day party favors. For a moment, it looked like the band was more interested in the young men's show than their own! —BETH CASTROL

➢ Don't overlook this show musically. The first set is nice with the first Camel Walk in over 600 shows, but the second set is incredible. The Runaway Jim goes into some kind of crazy jam which leads unexpectedly to a phat Makisupa with some Bob Marley riffs and a few pot references (4:20, dank), into Scent of a Mule and all followed by a super-funky Tweezer. One of my favorite shows. —BRYAN MCCRAMER

7/3/95 [ACCESSIBILITY: ••••]
SummerStage at Sugarbush North, Fayston, VT
I: My Friend, Poor Heart, Antelope, Loving Cup, Sparkle, It's Ice, If I Could, Maze, Strange Design, Free, Cavern
II: Timber Ho > Bowie > Johnny B. Goode > Bowie, AC/DC Bag, Lizards > BBFCM, Day in the Life, Possum, Squirming Coil
E: Simple, Amazing Grace
"Timber Ho" teases in Bowie intro. "Bathtub Gin" teases in Bowie and Possum. Lizards abandoned after Trey lyric mistake. Last Timber Ho, 12/30/92 Springfield, MA [257 shows].

➢ What can I say about the second set of the second night? It was absolutely intense; they never let up. A Day in the Life normally serves as a breather for the band; we could tell that the energy was just biding its time and waiting to resurface. And it did! Just look at the second set—look at it! —LARA WITTELS

➢ A great show turned into a hilarious one during Lizards. Trey completely blanks out on some lyrics. The music keeps playing, then an eerie silence falls on the stage. The music stops and Fish says from behind his drums, "I think you need a teleprompter there, Trey." Then they break into an unbelievable BBFCM. It was really funny. —CHRIS REGAN

➢ My sixth consecutive show of the impressive summer tour ended on the mountain. The first set was plain as day for the band was noticeably waiting for the sun to go down. The second set started with the breakout of Timber Ho, as surprising as it was rockin'. Beautiful segue into Bowie, hanging on to Timber a little. Strong jam with Johnny rocking in the middle. Trey forgot the words of Lizards as Fishman mumbled about the need for a teleprompter. This was extremely hilarious, as was Trey and Mike kicking the hacksack thrown up on stage before Amazing Grace. Ah, Phish at home! —ALEX BANKS

➢ After camping on the mountain after the first night's show, we had the entire second day to explore the mountain before the evening's show. Steep ski trails led us to gorgeous alpine fields of wildflowers and verdant pastures. Near the top, we met one group of fans who told us they'd hiked for three days over the ridges and mountains, with their final stop being the Phish shows. In my mind, this event served as the first large-scale gathering of the tribe, an annual event that would swell considerably by the time of the Clifford Ball the next summer. —MELISSA COLLINS

[7/13/95]
Late Show With David Letterman, Ed Sullivan Theater, New York, NY
Julius (with horns)

Monday, July 3, 1993 — Sugarbush North, Fayston, VT

I never talk that much about Sugarbush because *everyone* I talk to was *there*. This is one of the best concerts I've ever been to—the music was fantastic and the boys were on. However, what made this show were the thousands and thousands of Phishheads—not newbies but honest-to-God Phishheads, which definitely helped the show.

I got there real early, taking my 1963 Dodge Dart 270 with the Vermont PHISH license plates. A large crowd of people followed behind us taking pictures, and one girl said, "Oh my God, me and my friends were just talking about who in Vermont has the PHISH plates when you drove by!" Once we'd parked, we climbed up the hill to secure space close to the stage. As showtime approached, people kept squeezing in, making us all feel nervous about being crushed. As soon as the music started, though, the crowd thinned out—I could hold my arms out and twirl about without hitting anyone. I was about 30 feet from the stage all night, in ecstacy.

In the first set, this guy next to me blew up this large inflatable moose and tossed it. It bounced around the crowd for awhile with its feet sticking straight up. Finally someone whipped the moose at the stage and it sat down right by Page during Antelope. Nobody on stage noticed it until the break when Page looked to his right and saw it. He yelled to Trey and pointed, and as they left the stage Page put it under his arm and lugged it off. Very cool.

In set II, during BBFCM, it got wild. Trey threw everything off the stage—picks, water cups, whatever he could get his hands on. Then the unbelievable happened: someone threw a four-foot tall George Jetson doll on stage, Trey grabbed it and stuffed it between himself and the guitar and made it look like George was playing. Then he unstrapped and held his custom-made Paul Languedoc guitar at arm's length, straight out, and *dropped it*! Crazy!

This show also gets the best encore award, with the best version of Simple I've ever heard. They nailed it. At the end of the show, they all walked out to the edge of the stage and individually thanked the crowd for giving *them* a great tour, while still tossing things to the crowd. Trey played with a hackysack and threw it to the crowd, then they all grabbed Jon and made like they were going to throw him off the stage.

After the show, I waited for an hour to get on a bus to go back to Sugarbush South where we had parked, and finally said screw it and walked. Walking around some slow-pokes, I ran out of the way of a bus and fell on the side of the road, badly twisting my ankle. It was very dark and there was nothing around so I had to limp the six miles up to South. I was never so happy to see my car.

The next morning I couldn't even step on my ankle. I called my boss and told him I couldn't make it to work and why, and he didn't believe me. I limped around work in pain for a week.

Was the show worth it? Yes, OH GOD YES! **—David A. Clement**

1995 Fall *CHECKMATE*

For most fans, the '95 summer tour had been satisfying, but with less than a month's worth of shows, Phish did not have the opportunity to dig as far into its bag of musical tricks as they had in the past. But the vast fall tour would satiate even the most rabid of fans as the band held nothing to be sacred except the breaking of new musical ground. Songs that had been played as often as every other night only a year before seldom surfaced—Golgi, for example, was played live only three times, and Glide only twice. Other older songs received re-examination, as can be seen in the slow-shuffle version of Poor Heart that saw a November debut. And some songs seldom seen in recent years, such as Tube, returned from hibernation.

The band also experimented with setlist structure, opening the October 21 show in Lincoln, Nebraska with Tweezer Reprise, and then closing the first set with another Tweezer Reprise, despite the fact the "real" Tweezer wasn't played that night. Notably, this sort of experimentation was undertaken in front of large crowds—for the first time, the band would play arena and amphitheater-sized venues from coast to coast, starting the tour in the 14,000-seat Cal Expo Amphitheatre and finishing the year with two sold-out nights at 20,000-seat Madison Square Garden. All of this came on a stage flanked by a giant chess board, as the band challenged the audience to two games of chess in the first-ever band-versus-audience chess match.

Offstage, the Phish Tickets-By-Mail system continued to evolve, functioning with remarkable efficiency and winning praise from virtually all customers. The system proved so popular that about half of those who mailordered for New Year's Eve tickets were rejected.

9/27/95 [ACCESSIBILITY: ••••]
Cal Expo Amphitheatre, Sacramento, CA
I: Wolfman's, Rift, Free, It's Ice, I Didn't Know, Fog that Surrounds, Strange Design, Chalkdust, Squirming Coil
II: CTB, AC/DC Bag, Bowie, Billy Breathes, Keyboard Kavalry, Harry Hood, Hello My Baby, Day in the Life **E:** Possum
"Johnny B. Goode" tease in Possum. Fishman on trombone for I Didn't Know. Harry Hood unfinished. Last Wolfman's, 6/26/94 Charleston, WV [88 shows]. Concert debuts: Fog that Surrounds, CTB, Billy Breathes, Keyboard Kavalry, Hello My Baby.

9/28/95 [ACCESSIBILITY: ••]
Summer Pops, Embarcadero Center, San Diego, CA
I: CTB, Runaway Jim, Billy Breathes, Scent of a Mule, Stash, Fee, Fog that Surrounds, Acoustic Army, Slave
II: Theme, Poor Heart, Don't You Wanna Go, Tweezer, Keyboard Kavalry, Amazing Grace, Sample, Antelope **E:** Fire

➢ East Coasters, eat your heart out. Imagine an uncrowded Phish show in a wide-open outdoor venue with the sun setting over the water on one side and a sparkling skyline on the other. Highlights came in the second set, including Tweezer—not too long like the Mud Island and Finger Lakes versions—they explored it nicely before the three non-keyboardists zombie-walked their way over to Page's area where they did a four-part keyboard jam. (I think this shtick should be called "Too Much Time on the Tour Bus" because I think that's how this brainstorm came about.) Then, after Amazing Grace and Sample, IT happened. For me, the entire show can be summed up in one word: Antelope. How many climaxes can one song have? Get the tape and find out. —MIKE INDGIN

9/29/95 [ACCESSIBILITY: •••]
Greek Theater, Los Angeles, CA
I: AC/DC Bag, Sparkle, Divided Sky, Strange Design, CTB, YEM, Adeline, Suzie
II: Also Sprach > Maze, Free, Ya Mar, Melt, Billy Breathes, HYHU > Cryin' > HYHU, Day in the Life **E:** Chalkdust
Fishman on vacuum for Cryin'. Concert debut: Cryin'.

➢ Probably the funniest show I have on tape. The second set is decent but one song tops it off: Fishman took center stage and with lyrics in hand sang Cryin' by Aerosmith. This was the only time it was done and I can understand why—it's probably the worst display of vocals I've ever heard from such a talented musician. But I laugh my ass off every time I listen to it. —CHUCK ADAMS

➢ Outside, thousands of ticketless miracle seekers swam through the crowd frantically searching for that elusive extra, in sharp contrast to the scene at San Diego where the venue wasn't even sold out. Trey was ON the entire night. At one point he was flailing around so much his glasses went flying off. That kind of unbridled intensity is why I love this band. The second set began with the 2001 theme which discoed into the highlight of the show (besides Fishman's surprise): an absolutely amazing Maze. It's hard to describe what these boys are able to pull off when they're on like this, so I won't even try. After a Split Open and Melt featuring the most spaced-out jamming of the night, Fishman made his way to center stage with his vacuum in one hand and lyric sheets in the other. "I don't really know the words to this song… but that isn't the point," he said. What followed had every single person at the Greek laughing hysterically: his murderous rendition of Aerosmith's Cryin'. He botched the second half, throwing his crib notes in the air, but this just added to the hilarity of it all. In the parking lot, my friends all echoed the same sentiment: "Now I see why you like this band." —MIKE INDGIN

9/30/95 [ACCESSIBILITY: ••••]
Shoreline Amphitheatre, Mountain View, CA
I: My Friend, CTB, Chess Game Jam, Reba, Uncle Pen, Horn, Antelope, I'm Blue I'm Lonesome, Sample
II: Runaway Jim, Fog that Surrounds, If I Could, Scent of a Mule, Mike's > Keyboard Kavalry > Weekapaug, HYHU > Suspicious Minds > HYHU, Cavern **E:** Amazing Grace, GTBT
Chess Game Jam (played to tune of "White Rabbit") marked the start of the first band-versus-audience chess match. "Antelope" tease before Horn. I'm Blue I'm Lonesome performed acoustic with Trey on acoustic guitar, Mike on banjo, Fishman on mandolin and Page on upright bass, dedicated to Jerry Garcia. Concert debuts: Chess Game Jam (and the chess game), Suspicious Minds.

➢ This show features two solid sets, on Trey's birthday. It is also notable for the introduction of the band versus audience chess game. Reba is probably the fastest one I've ever heard; Antelope is smokin'; and Blue and Lonesome is touching, as Trey dedicates it to the late Jerry Garcia. The second set is highlighted by an awesome Fog and a wicked duel in Scent, yet the real centerpiece is Mike's Song and its smooth segue from a trippy, spacey jam into Keyboard Kavalry and then onto Weekapaug that put us all on a funk rollercoaster. Fishman emerges for a hilarious cover of Elvis Presley's Suspicious Minds as well. What a show! —RYAN HIRSCH

➢ Phish's first appearance at the Dead's "home," A.D. J.G., provided an interesting atmosphere. I interpreted odd feelings among the crowd and the security personnel. Phish played well, but lacked the presence of energy that a venue of this size demands of all performers. Fishman donned an Elvis cape for a hilarious rendition of Suspicious Minds that drew the loudest response of the night. —ANTHONY BUCHLA

➢ Fall Tour '95 meant chess, as the band challenged the audience to the ultimate battle of the brains. Each side made one move a night, the band at the start of the show and the audience—after setbreak consultation at the Greenpeace table—at the beginning of the second set. As a Fall '95 *Schvice* noted, "The band's convoluted strategy has kept the audience guessing. Victory is inevitable for one of the teams…" Things looked good for the audience when a northern California chess master showed up at the Greenpeace table and lent his expertise on the game's debut night at Shoreline. The audience dropped the first game, then rebounded to win the second. —MARCIA COLLINS

10/2/95 [ACCESSIBILITY: ••]
Seattle Center Arena, Seattle, WA
I: Poor Heart, Wolfman's, Rift, Chess Game Jam, Stash, Acoustic Army, Fog that Surrounds, Theme, Tela, Bowie
II: Wilson, CTB, Bathtub Gin, Llama, Simple, Keyboard Kavalry, Slave, Hello My Baby, Lizards, Antelope **E:** Day in the Life
Baby Gramps opened. "Night Moves" played as Chess Game Jam.

10/3/95 [ACCESSIBILITY: •••]
Seattle Center Arena, Seattle, WA
I: Maze, Guelah, Foam, FEFY, I'm Blue I'm Lonesome, Free, TMWSIY > Avenu > TMWSIY, Sample, YEM
II: Timber Ho, It's Ice, Sparkle, Harry Hood, Billy Breathes, Faht, Adeline, Melt, Squirming Coil **E:** Rocky Top
Baby Gramps opened. I'm Blue I'm Lonesome performed acoustic. Last Faht, 6/19/94 Kalamazoo, MI [99 shows].

10/5/95 [ACCESSIBILITY: ••]
Memorial Coliseum, Portland, OR
I: Chalkdust, Ha Ha Ha, Fog that Surrounds, Horse > Silent, CTB, Strange Design, Divided Sky, Acoustic Army, Julius, Suzie
II: Also Sprach > Runaway Jim, Forbin's > Mockingbird, Scent of a Mule, Cavern, Bowie, Lifeboy, Amazing Grace **E:** Guitar Gently Weeps

10/6/95 [ACCESSIBILITY: ••]
Orpheum Theatre, Vancouver, BC
I: Ya Mar, Stash, Billy Breathes, Reba, I'm Blue I'm Lonesome, Rift, Free, Lizards, Sample
II: Poor Heart, Maze, Theme, NICU, Tweezer, Keyboard Kavalry, Suspicious Minds, Slave **E:** Hello My Baby, Day in the Life
I'm Blue I'm Lonesome performed acoustic/no amplification.

10/7/95 [ACCESSIBILITY: ••••]
Spokane Opera House, Spokane, WA
I: Julius, Gumbo, Fog that Surrounds, Mound, Possum, Mango, Acoustic Army, Wilson, Antelope
II: Makisupa, CTB, Melt, Strange Design, It's Ice, Contact, Frankenstein, Harry Hood, Adeline **E:** Fire
Harry Hood unfinished.

➢ The Northwest shows offered the chance to see Phish in the best venues of the fall '95 tour. Each place was a small, plush, classy theater or opera house. Spokane rocked! Gumbo, Mound, Possum, Antelope all in the first set. The Acoustic Army is jammin'. Makisupa to open the second set, plus a great Frankenstein followed by a huge Harry. Fire to encore, can't ask for much more. —SEAN SMITH

➢ Every tour needs a good controversy, and during the opening leg of the fall '95 tour, everyone was talking about why Phish wasn't finishing Harry Hood. This would be the last time during the fall that they wouldn't sing the final "You can feel good about Hood" refrain, but it didn't matter—Phish devoted all their energy to the jam, unquestionably one of the best Hood jams ever. You really owe it to yourself to hear it. —SCOTT SIFTON

10/8/95 [ACCESSIBILITY: •••]
Adams Fieldhouse, University of Montana, Missoula, MT
I: AC/DC Bag, Demand > Sparkle, Wolfman's, Reba, I'm Blue I'm Lonesome, Caspian, Uncle Pen, Free
II: Keyboard Kavalry, CTB, Timber Ho, Ya Mar, Sample, YEM, Suspicious Minds, Dog Faced Boy, Bowie, Keyboard Kavalry Reprise
E: Bouncing, Rocky Top
I'm Blue I'm Lonesome performed acoustic. Last Demand, 6/26/94 Charleston, WV [97 shows].

10/11/95 [ACCESSIBILITY: ••••]
Compton Terrace Amphitheater, Tempe, AZ
I: Stash, Old Home Place, Cavern, Divided Sky, If I Could, Fog that Surrounds, Acoustic Army, Julius, Sample
II: Possum, Bathtub Gin, Mound, Mike's > McGrupp > Weekapaug, Llama, Suzie > Crossroads, Hello My Baby, Day in the Life **E:** Chalkdust
"Buried Alive" tease in Julius. "Crossroads" and "Sunshine of Your Love" teases in Suzie. Last Crossroads, 5/8/93 Durham, NH [196 shows].

10/13/95 [ACCESSIBILITY: ••••]
Will Rogers Auditorium, Fort Worth, TX
I: Ya Mar, Also Sprach > Maze, Billy Breathes, I'm Blue I'm Lonesome, Caspian, Melt, Fluffhead, Life on Mars
II: Tube, Uncle Pen, Theme, Wilson, Antelope, Keyboard Kavalry, Lizards, Guitar Gently Weeps, Adeline, Squirming Coil **E:** Bold as Love
I'm Blue I'm Lonesome performed acoustic/no amplification. Last Tube, 6/26/94 Charleston, WV [99 shows]. Concert debut: Life on Mars.

➢ This was an awesome show. Trey explained to us that this was the town in which he was born. Maybe that served as an energizer, because the show is quite pumping and fast. Wilson is particularly intense, and I was impressed with the sound of WMGGW—Trey makes his guitar cry during the solo. —JEFFREY ELLENBOGEN

➢ When a set opens with a song like Tube, you know you're in for a crazy night. (It was the first Tube we heard since June '94.) Still, the great Tube was later outdone by a Theme > Wilson > Antelope combination. Great show; the boys were on. —MARK DANIEL

10/14/95 [ACCESSIBILITY: ••••]
Austin Music Hall, Austin, TX
I: AC/DC Bag, CTB, Kung > Free, Sparkle, Stash > Catapult, Acoustic Army, It's Ice, Tela, Runaway Jim
II: Reba, Rift, YEM, Hello My Baby, Scent of a Mule, Cavern
E: Day in the Life
"Baracuda" tease before Reba. John Medeski on keyboards, Billy Martin on drums, Chris Wood on upright bass and Dominick Fallo on trumpet for YEM.

➢ Relaxing with friends before a show is fun, but when you're at home, it's great fun! I was ready for a good show after the previous night's magic, and the band didn't let me down. The first set contained a great long Stash followed by Tela a couple of songs later. The second set again felt magic with Medeski Martin and Wood and Dominick Fallo joining in on a ripping YEM, then a unique and fun Scent of a Mule. —WILLIAM THURSTON

➢ Page is joined by John Medeski on keyboard, Fish plays vacuum and trombone, Billy Martin plays drums, Chris Wood on bass, Trey on his drum kit, Mike on bass and horn, plus a little trumpet. Chaos, sweet chaos. —DAVE SWANK

➢ This night's MMW jam, unlike the one on 10/17, really works. Yum! —RICH MAZER

10/15/95 [ACCESSIBILITY: ••••]
Austin Music Hall, Austin, TX
I: Buried Alive > Poor Heart, Slave, I Didn't Know, Demand > Llama, Foam, Strange Design, I'm Blue I'm Lonesome, Bowie
II: Julius, Simple, Tweezer, Lizards, Sample, Suspicious Minds, Harry Hood, Tweezer Reprise **E:** Funky Bitch

➢ Even though neither set clicked enough to make this a great night, the boys were having fun and enjoying themselves enough to kick out several great versions of tunes. I was all smiles when the third song turned out to be Slave, and I love a first set Bowie closer. The fun they were having on this night didn't end even though the first set did. They came back out on fire for the second set. I love a Tweezer night and I especially love a Lizards and a Harry before the Reprise comes. The Lizards played on this night sounded so different than the one of two nights before, proving how special a song it is. —ERIC SEGOVIA

➢ The show was great, although more chill than the previous two. A mellow first set was followed by a surprising second set, including a groovy Suspicious Minds into a truly beautiful Harry Hood. —WILLIAM THURSTON

10/17/95 [ACCESSIBILITY: ••••]
State Palace Theatre, New Orleans, LA
I: Sample, Stash, Uncle Pen, AC/DC Bag > Maze, Glide, Sparkle, Free, Strange Design, Amazing Grace
II: Mound > Caspian, Fog that Surrounds, Suzie > Keyboard Kavalry > Jam **E:** Long Journey Home, I'm Blue I'm Lonesome
Medeski Martin & Wood opened. Nathan, a Gospel singer in the audience, sang Amazing Grace after the band performed it to close the first set. The singer later joined in on the jam at end of set two, which also featured John Medeski on keyboards, Billy Martin on drums and Chris Wood on upright bass. Fishman on vacuum and trombone during the jam. Nathan on vocals during the jam. Long Journey Home and I'm Blue I'm Lonesome performed acoustic.

➢ The second set to this show features a fabulous jam with Medeski Martin and Wood (clocking in at 25-plus minutes). Starting off slow and spacey, this jam really heats up by the end. After a slow start, things get going when each member trades licks with each other, getting faster and faster and then slowing down as Fishman brings out his vacuum, then switches to trombone. Things slowly speed up again as Fishman trades trombone licks with everybody, then as Trey switches to his percussion kit a guy named Nathan joins in on vocals, mostly using the Doo note; you'll have to hear this one because this is the best part of the jam. Everybody is into the jam playing great, as Nathan grunts and groans, "Gotta get down doo doo doo doo," then things abruptly slow down and Trey thanks the crowd on behalf of MMW. Definitely a set worth looking for if you like Surrender to the Air, but I wish it was more groovy than spacey. —MIKE NOLL

10/19/95 [ACCESSIBILITY: ••••]
Municipal Auditorium, Kansas City, MO
I: CTB, Runaway Jim, Horn, PYITE, Esther, Chalkdust, Theme, Acoustic Army, Melt, Billy Breathes, Cavern
II: Frankenstein, Poor Heart, Mike's > Hydrogen > Weekapaug > Lawn Boy, BBFCM > Kung, HYHU > Suspicious Minds > HYHU, Possum
E: Day in the Life
Recording of Trey's daughter Eliza crying was played over the PA system during Billy Breathes.

➢ This night was the beginning of the Great Midwestern Tear from KC to Cedar Rapids and Lincoln in fall '95. This show's highlights included PYITE, Billy Breathes with a Trey narration of his newborn daughter crying on a playback machine, Frankenstein and the entire second set. BBFCM was a very insane jam. —SEAN MILLER

➢ Although the setlist really isn't that bad, this show is really weak. It doesn't flow well, and never really gets going. The Mike's Groove in the second set hints at a high-energy conclusion to the show, but it's followed by four rather weak songs. Good Possum and a good encore, but it's too little, too late. —BEN ROSS

10/20/95 [ACCESSIBILITY: ••••]
Five Seasons Arena, Cedar Rapids, IA
I: My Friend, Ya Mar, Ha Ha Ha, Divided Sky, Fee, Rift, Free, Hello My Baby, Amazing Grace, Amazing Grace Jam
II: Timber Ho, Scent of a Mule, Simple, Maze, Gumbo, Guitar Gently Weeps, Long Journey Home, I'm Blue I'm Lonesome, Bouncing, Antelope
E: Sleeping Monkey, Rocky Top
Guest performer on bagpipes for Amazing Grace Jam. Long Journey Home and I'm Blue I'm Lonesome performed acoustic. Last Amazing Grace Jam, 5/8/93 Durham, NH [202 shows].

➢ Great town with good vibes and anal but harmless cops (one questioned me on my incense use), and a very small arena reminiscent of the '92-'93 tours. The show started slowly in the first set, including Trey, who with megaphone to mouth forgot the lyrics to Fee. But then things heated up: the bagpipe jam was a pleasant surprise. The second set started off with five really strong tunes that rocked! Then a sweet Antelope tease before Bouncin' got my mouth watering. It came, of course, to close the show. This was a small-time Phish party in Iowa. —ALEX BANKS

➢ The first set Amazing Grace was mind-blowing—an electric jam followed by a guest on bagpipes that just brought the house down! —JAMIS CURRAN

10/21/95 [ACCESSIBILITY: ••••]
Pershing Auditorium, Lincoln, NE
I: Tweezer Reprise, Chalkdust, Guelah, Reba, Wilson, CTB, Kung, Lizards, Strange Design, Acoustic Army, GTBT > Tweezer Reprise
II: Also Sprach > Bowie, Lifeboy, Sparkle, YEM, Purple Rain > HYHU, Harry Hood, Suzie **E:** Highway to Hell
"Black or White" tease before GTBT. "Thriller" teases before and during Harry Hood. "Beat It" teased throughout first set and in Harry Hood and Suzie. Fishman on vacuum for Purple Rain.

➢ This is probably our favorite live Phish experience. The show was full of fun stuff—they opened up and closed the first set with Tweezer Reprise. They teased Michael Jackson's "Beat It" during Harry Hood and Suzie because Halloween was coming up and everyone thought they were going to do *Thriller*, so Phish played along. During the YEM vocal jam they started snoring. It was great. The encore was Highway To Hell, and during it all the hippies started headbanging. —MELANIE AND MELITA TERRELL

➢ From the first phat bass note this show kicked ass! There were two high-school age girls with staff shirts on directly in front of Mike and Trey, and from the look on their faces they had no clue what Phish was about. When Mike dropped that first Boooooommmm, at the beginning of Tweezer Reprise, the girl in front of him (and me) just beamed a huge grin and mouthed, "Wow!" Needless to say, she had her back to the audience most of the night. Trey later treated the girls to some classic Gene Simmons-esque tongue lashing during the Highway to Hell encore. —RUSSELL LANE

➢ Tweezer Reprise for an opener? Why, that's unheard of! Well, there's a first time for everything. Reba is phenomenal—it carries the show on its back, and it's my personal favorite jam of any song in my tape collection. Purple Rain had no lyrics beside "Purple Rain"—the band just hummed the whole song. —CHAD MARS

10/22/95 [ACCESSIBILITY: ••••]
Assembly Hall, Champaign, IL
I: AC/DC Bag, My Mind's, Sloth, Runaway Jim, Weigh > NICU, FEFY, It's Ice, Poor Heart > Sample, I'm Blue I'm Lonesome, Stash
II: Golgi, Possum > Catapult > Curtain > Tweezer > Makisupa > BBFCM, Life on Mars, Uncle Pen, Slave > Cavern **E:** Adeline, Squirming Coil
Bonus lyrics in Makisupa.

➢ After a dud of a first set, as the boys always do, they saved us. The great jamming starts in Possum and, after a vocal Catapult, continues. Makisupa is a total crowd-pleaser. A jamming Uncle Pen brings back life. This is also a crazy Adeline. Pick up set II! —CHARLIE GUBMAN

➢ The Many Incredible Tweezers of Fall '95 got their start on this night with a version that might be the best of the batch and perhaps the best ever. I guess it depends how you like your Tweezers. Phish's style this fall was not to slip segues and teases into the Tweezer jams but instead to just rock out. I hear the melodious jamming in this version when I dream of what heaven might be like. —TYLER HARRIS

10/24/95 [ACCESSIBILITY: •••]
Dane County Coliseum, Madison, WI
I: My Friend, Paul and Silas, Fog that Surrounds, Fee > Llama, Horse > Silent, Demand > Maze, Wolfman's, Acoustic Army, Caspian, Melt
II: Julius, Theme, Bouncing, YEM > Sleeping Monkey, Antelope, Contact, Cavern **E:** Day in the Life
Concert debut of the reworked version of Fog That Surrounds. Last Paul and Silas, 11/19/94 Indianapolis, IN [63 shows].

➢ The beginning of this show was definitely scary. Me and my friends had secured places right down in front but with the combination of excitement, lack of air, and being smashed in the surging crowd, we all fainted! As I was getting up, I realized we weren't the only ones—people seemed to be dropping like flies. I escaped to the lobby for some air, giving up the prime floor spot and missing My Friend and most of Paul and Silas, but at least I could breathe. Then the reworked Fog That Surrounds made its debut and I knew I was still in for quite an evening. The Demand > Maze combo had me questioning my perception of time and Split Open at the end of the set reminded me of melting into the floor at the beginning. Set II was trippy! I swam with Phish underwater in Theme From the Bottom and then laughed at Lucifer in the weirdest YEM jam I've ever heard. A pre-Halloween trick (I only had to wait a few more days for the real treat!) —LIBBY BARROW

➢ A better-than-average show with great jams. One of the craziest vocal jams at the end of YEM, and the best performance of Antelope that I have witnessed. —MATT BUSSMAN

➢ The jamming in set II is absolutely out of control! This is just an absolute must-have set, a real classic of Phish's musicanship on a night where most everything soared. Things rock from the start with a Julius that's guaranteed to change the way you think of this song if you're a Julius doubter, or enlighten you further if you're a Julius believer. YEM's jam segment is also amazing, including a sung-skat segment from Trey and a series of very cohesive jams that approaches the famous 12/9/95 Albany YEM. But they save the best for last with *the most* exploratory, exuberant Antelope ever. Ever! —SCOTT SIFTON

10/25/95 [ACCESSIBILITY: ••]
St. Paul Civic Center Arena, St. Paul, MN
I: Ya Mar, Sample, Divided Sky, Wedge, Scent of a Mule, Free, Strange Design, Long Journey Home, I'm Blue I'm Lonesome, Chalkdust
II: Reba, Life on Mars, CTB, Mike's, Sparkle > Weekapaug, Suzie > Crossroads **E:** Fire
Long Journey Home and I'm Blue I'm Lonesome performed acoustic. "Breathe" jam in Mike's.

➢ Most of the show was standard fall '95 fare which, while fun, doesn't really stand out as a sweet tape. The second set does show sparks, however, with solid jamming in Reba and a spacey Mike's Groove. Life On Mars is my highlight. What a perfect cover! —JAMIS CURRAN

➢ The first set was pretty average, and I though the second set opener Reba was a disappointment, but not for long. The jam was incredibly upbeat and they soared with energy. Proceeding into Mike's Song, they broke into a Floyd tune during the jam. The controversial issue was, did they play Breathe or the beginning of Shine On You Crazy Diamond? It was odd to hear Sparkle before finishing with Weekapaug. —ERIN FERRIS

10/27/95 [ACCESSIBILITY: ••••]
Wing Stadium, Kalamazoo, MI
I: Runaway Jim, Fluffhead, Fog that Surrounds, Horn, I Didn't Know, Rift, Stash, Fee > Suspicious Minds
II: Also Sprach > Bowie, Dog Faced Boy, Poor Heart, Simple, McGrupp, Keyboard Kavalry, Bouncing, Possum **E:** Life on Mars
Fishman on vacuum for I Didn't Know.

➢ The arena was tiny to begin with so everybody knew it was gonna be an intimate jam session. Rockin' Fluffhead had everybody singing. The second set was boomin' with the greatest Poor Heart of all time—Trey just explodes with bluegrass guitar. Possum features signals including fall down, but hardly anyone knew what was going on. —ALEX BANKS

➢ This was the first chance I had to hear the boys after coming back from a stint with the Peace Corps. We entered the stadium after they had already begun the first set, and looking down the length of the rink to see them already pouring it on was as big a high as living on Kilimanjaro or on the edge of the Serengeti. —ERIC SHAW

10/28/95 [ACCESSIBILITY: •••••]
The Palace, Auburn Hills, MI
I: AC/DC Bag, Mound, Timber Ho, Uncle Pen, Sample, Lizards, Billy Breathes, Acoustic Army, Caspian, Antelope
II: Maze, Theme > Scent of a Mule, YEM, Strange Design, Frankenstein, Chalkdust **E:** Guitar Gently Weeps

➢ Hello Antelope. This was a very fun show, especially for people who came into the show thinking about how bad a venue the Palace is. Well, the show was great, with a nice Timber Ho and Lizards in set I, which concluded with an amazing Antelope! It started very delicately and exponentially acquired energy until we were running out of control (in a good way). They used their frequent tension and release method in getting everyone's soul waiting for that climax note. Oh, it felt nice when they hit it. —MICHELLE HIRSCH

➢ My brother and I took our parents to this show. What an event it was for them to experience the lot. They never imagined anything like it. Our Dad only liked it when they played cover tunes, but our Mom got connected with the energy and enjoyed all of it. She couldn't believe how friendly people were, just offering joints to her (she never has smoked). Little did they know my brother and I were huffin' some dank right next to them. What a great time! —BRYAN MCCRAMER

10/29/95 [ACCESSIBILITY: ••••]
Louisville Gardens, Louisville, KY
I: Buried Alive > Poor Heart, Julius, PYITE, CTB, Horse > Silent, Melt, NICU, Gumbo, Slave, Adeline
II: Makisupa > Bowie, Mango, It's Ice > Kung > It's Ice, Shaggy Dog, Possum, Lifeboy, Amazing Grace **E:** Funky Bitch
"Beat It" tease before Buried Alive and in Possum. Last Shaggy Dog, 11/3/88 Boston, MA [727 shows].

➢ This is a great unheard-of show. Set I proves itself with Buried Alive, PYITE, NICU, Gumbo and Slave. Then set II makes me smile with Makisupa > Bowie, Mango Song, the first Shaggy Dog in the '90s > Possum, and a favorite Funky Bitch encore. —J.J. SOUTHARD

➢ Definitely one of the best shows I've ever seen! A smoking Buried Alive > Poor Heart opener, then near the end of the first set they really cover some ground: Split Open, followed by NICU > Gumbo > Slave! Could it get any better? Obviously, I didn't realize what they had planned for the second set. It starts with a funky Makisupa, moving into a powerful Bowie. After an It's Ice with a nicely placed Kung in the middle, they brought out the first Shaggy Dog since 1988, seguing that into a phenomenal Possum, complete with "Beat It" tease. A truly unstoppable show. —OTIS

10/31/95 [ACCESSIBILITY: •••••]
Rosemont Horizon, Chicago, IL
I: Icculus, Divided Sky, Wilson, Ya Mar, Sparkle, Free, Guyute, Antelope, Harpua
II: Thriller Tease > I Am The Sea, The Real Me, Quadrophenia, Cut My Hair, The Punk Meets The Godfather, I'm One, The Dirty Jobs, Helpless Dancer, Is It In My Head, I've Had Enough, 5:15, Sea and Sand, Drowned, Bell Boy, Doctor Jimmy, The Rock, Love Reign O'er Me
III: YEM, Jesus Left Chicago, Day in the Life, Suzie **E:** My Generation
"Beat It" tease in Harpua, which also included a Mike Gordon-narrated dream sequence. Second set was The Who's Quadrophenia; all songs from the album were concert debuts. The second set featured a horn section: Dave Grippo, alto saxophone; Don Glasgo, trombone; Joe Somerville Jr., trumpet; and Alan Parshley, french horn. Bell Boy featured Phish crew member Leigh Fordham in costume and on vocals. Jesus Left Chicago featured Grippo, and Suzie featured Grippo, Glasgo and Somerville. My Generation (performed acoustic, concert debut) ended with Trey intentionally triggering a backstage explosion after the band destroyed their instruments. Last Guyute, 12/29/94 Providence, RI [50 shows]. Last Icculus, 11/20/94 Madison, WI [64 shows].

Phan Pick #11 ➢ The best show I've ever seen of any kind. The anticipation of the second set was like an hour of butterflies in my stomach. When the house lights went down and the sound of waves crashing onto the Cliffs of Dover was heard, it all became clear—*Quadrophenia*. Only Phish could pull off *Quadrophenia* better than the Who! Then, an amazing YEM, complete with trippy-huge light show and mind vocalizations that made the stage appear to melt more than normal. —DANIEL GILFOND

➢ In my opinion this is the best of Phish's three 'Ween tenures. It kicks off appropriately with a hilarious Icculus in which the book battles the Halloween spirits. Trey exclaims, "The book is getting its ass kicked!" The set ends with Guyute, a crazy Antelope and a Harpua hinting at a *Thriller* second set. *Quadrophenia* was a better choice for a cover album even than the *White Album*. Phish did much more to liven up this album. The third set is killer too. The YEM is so long, people wondered if it would be the whole set—42 minutes, to be exact. My Generation encore was weak—they didn't jam it out as much as Pete Townsend would have, although the destruction of the instruments on stage added to the ambiance. —BEN ROSS

➢ For me, this is a must-have show. Not only am I a lifetime Who fan, but *Quadrophenia* is my favorite album. Page was right on during Sea and Sand, mimicking Roger to a T. This is yet another excellent example of Phish's incredible versatility. They had everything covered—even the BBC voice-overs. I was floored! —DAN KURTZ

➢ This was hands-down the most intense Phish show I ever saw—sorry to anyone who couldn't be there to be a part of the cycle of energy. Anyhow, it is of course an amazing YEM—hard to believe they could weave through it so intensely for 40 minutes. Guyute was long-awaited but the changes were worth the wait—the tension up to Page's chords is so strong and the release from those chords makes me want to hug the person next to me. —MICHELLE HERSCH

➢ I can sum up this show in three letters: YEM. Absolutely brilliant and original, you can tell the Who influence by listening to the tape. The horns at the end of the third set are a nice treat. During Suzie, Trey sings the same verse three times. Before the final chorus, Fish says, "What the fuck?" and Trey says, "Oh, I sang that verse three times." —PETE MORSE

11/9/95 [ACCESSIBILITY: ••••]
Fox Theatre, Atlanta, GA
I: Tweezer Reprise, Divided Sky, Caspian, PYITE, Simple, Reba, Tela, Sample
II: Theme > Julius, Lizards, Bathtub Gin > TMWSIY > Avenu > TMWSIY > Life on Mars, Hello My Baby, Squirming Coil **E:** Loving Cup
"We are the Champions" tease before Theme. "Rift" jam in Bathtub Gin.

11/10/95 [ACCESSIBILITY: ••••]
Fox Theatre, Atlanta, GA
I: Bouncing, Runaway Jim, Fog that Surrounds, Old Home Place, It's Ice, Dog Faced Boy, Maze, Guyute, Cavern
II: Free, Scent of a Mule, YEM > Crossroads > YEM, Strange Design, Sparkle, AC/DC Bag, Adeline **E:** Harry Hood

➢ The Fox Theater is a great place to see a show. Inside, there are many small rooms and large velvet chairs—it resembles a castle. It is such a small venue that tickets were in high demand for this three-night stop. Outside in the streets, there seemed to be as many people searching for tickets as their were tickets. Two songs that stick out in my mind from this night are Guyute and Harry Hood. Guyute is truly one of Phish's best songs and should be included in their rotation more frequently. Harry Hood, a real crowd-pleaser, was a great treat for an encore and perfect close to the evening. —CHRIS HAINES

➢ A friend of ours from Athens sold us fourth-row seats for below face value! Too bad the setlist didn't suit my taste. Bouncin' opener? Blah! But then Page went off on Maze. Guyute was great, the first time I'd ever heard it. It gives me hope for more huge jams in the future. The second set was saved by YEM, though I wasn't crazy about the Crossroads in the middle. (Brickhouse a week later in Charleston was much better.) Hood encore was a treat as usual. —TREVOR NORRIS

11/11/95 [ACCESSIBILITY: ••••]
Fox Theatre, Atlanta, GA
I: CTB, Mike's > Day in the Life, Poor Heart, Weekapaug, Horse > Silent, Ya Mar, Stash, Amazing Grace, Fee, Chalkdust
II: Also Sprach > Bowie, Suzie, Uncle Pen, Fluffhead, Sleeping Monkey, Frankenstein > Suspicious Minds > HYHU, Antelope
E: Acoustic Army, GTBT

➢ For the last of three shows at the Fox Theater, lucky fans were treated to a tremendous show. First set Mike's Song, one of the best I've heard, caught everyone off guard. After a smoking Stash and Amazing Grace, the first set seemed to be over as band members began to exit the stage. But Page encouraged the rest to come back and they closed

Quadrophenia

10/31/95 Rosemont Horizon, Chicago, IL

With Phish's almost untarnished track record of outdoing themselves, anticipation ran high for their second annual musical costume on Halloween in 1995. Since the show was more centrally located, Phish folk flocked from around the country to squeeze in to the Rosemont Horizon, as the show became the first true national Phish event.

While Phish claimed only a small midwest following just two years before, this date would arguably become the most eagerly sought after ticket in Phish history. It sold out in a matter of hours and ticket brokers easily gouged their way to anywhere from $75 to $150 for a sacred spot inside. Of course, ticket scarcity and multitudes of counterfeits left many disappointed under the wet skies of Chicago.

As planes made their way overhead to and from O'Hare Airport, another buzz was heard in the lot prior to the show. It was that of attempting to guess what musical costume Phish would don for the second set. Many fans believed that the band would play *Thiller* by Michael Jackson, speculation fueled by "Beat It" teases from shows leading up to Rosemont. Some grew even more convinced when Trey snuck a little "Beat It" into Harpua during a startlingly good first set, one which featured the return of Guyute after nearly a year on hiatus, an Icculus show opener and one of the best early versions of Free.

During the "Beat It" jam, they actually went as far as to announce that Jimmy was listening to "the album Phish was going to play tonight." Some thought they had spilled the beans, missing the past tense of the reference. But most remained cynical. After all, why would they make it so obvious?

Other rumors persisted, such as Frank Zappa's *Joe's Garage*, The Grateful Dead's *Europe '72*, and an assortment of Zeppelin and Rolling Stones titles.

Quadrophenia was lightly rumored before the show but only one mention among many possibilities. As the rolling ocean sounds filled the dark arena at the start of the second set, most were silent with the exception of hardcore Who fans, who didn't need to think twice. And when the band exploded into the first notes of The Real Me, the portion of the audience with working knowledge of classic rock knew exactly where Phish was going.

Quadrophenia, it turns out, actually came in second in fan voting behind *Joe's Garage*, but they cashed in their executive privilege and chose The Who's rock opera about a boy named, of all things, Jimmy who has four personalities (corresponding to each member of The Who) and who embarks on a drug and fight-filled journey to Brighton in search of his true identity.

Phish played the album masterfully and one can argue they even outdid Pete Townsend and crew, who performed *Quadrophenia* months later with the help of sheet music and about a dozen backup musicians. Phish played it by heart with a relatively bare-bones setup which did include Dave Grippo and Joe Somerville of the reformed Giant Country Horns, along with Don Gasgo on trombones and Alan Parshley on French Horn. But Page masterfully handled most of *Quadrophenia*'s orchestration with his synthesizer, and Trey zealously took to Townsend's guitar parts, windmills and all.

With much of the audience lacking familiarity with *Quadrophenia*, it became a sit-down affair for many in the crowd. But the band lifted everyone to their feet with an uplifting performance of 5:15, one of many musical highlights in the set.

In subsequent interviews, Trey said he had never been a big *Quadrophenia* fan before, but learned that night what great arena rock it made. For the most part, the performance was fairly true to the album version—a simply remarkable feat—but they did mix things up a little, especially on The Dirty Jobs, during which Page plays the piano part too fast for Trey to keep up. Fishman handled vocal duties on the show's finale, the emotionally-charged Love Reign O'er Me.

Set III arguably didn't match up to the last set of the previous year's marathon but contained what was probably the longest YEM ever (including the unmistakable phrase "I want to fuck you in the ass" slipped in by one of the band members during the vocal jam) and a vicious sax solo by Dave Grippo on a great Jesus Left Chicago.

And as Phish always manages to do, they made light of the grand performance by encoring with My Generation, played bluegrass-style on old, beat-up instruments. Then, they destroyed them with a Who-esque explosion. This show was not without its critics, but by most accounts, it ranks as one of the most special nights in Phish's rich concert history.

with not only Fee but Chalkdust as well. I thought the roof would come off during Suzie and Fluffhead. This Fox show is essential in any collection. —MATTHEW NAPOLI

➢ The setlist of this show is amazing. Each song seems a perfect compliment to the one before and after it. A combination which I had never heard before, Mike's > Day in the Life, blew me away. These are two songs which have no obvious musical link but the smooth, lengthy transition is perfect. The second set features two of the rockingest covers: Frankenstein and Good Times Bad Times. —MIKE JETT

➢ An incredibly well-played show, easily one of the best of the year. The boys break out Mike's Groove in the first set for the first time since 12/1/92 Denison, a feat that wouldn't happen again until Amsterdam in summer '97. It's a Mike's with second-set intensity, really a strong version. The musical highlight of a great second set is the powerful Antelope closer. —LEE JOHNSTON

11/12/95 [ACCESSIBILITY: •••]
O'Connell Center, Gainsville, FL
I: My Friend, Llama, Bouncing, Guelah, Reba, I Didn't Know, Fog that Surrounds, If I Could, Melt, Hello My Baby
II: Curtain > Tweezer, Keyboard Kavalry, Sample, Slave, HYHU > Cracklin' Rosie > HYHU, Possum, Tweezer Reprise **E:** Fire
Fishman on vacuum for I Didn't Know.

➢ The O'Connell Center is one of the worst places you can go to see a live show. The place is like a high school gymnasium and security seems to get a kick out of shining a flashlight in your face whenever possible. The setlist wasn't anything spectacular, but one of the lighter moments of the show occurred during Fishman's rendition of Cracklin' Rosie. About halfway through the song he screwed up the lyrics, stopped and said, "Oh shit! I screwed that up. Can we do it again?" The band said no and picked up from where they left off. —CHRIS HAINES

11/14/95 [ACCESSIBILITY: ••••]
University Of Central Florida Arena, Orlando, FL
I: Chalkdust, Foam, Billy Breathes, Divided Sky, Esther, Free, Julius, I'm Blue I'm Lonesome, Cavern
II: Maze, Gumbo, Stash > Manteca > Stash > Dog Faced Boy > Stash, Strange Design, YEM **E:** Wedge, Rocky Top
Vocals only on Dog Faced Boy. 25 or 6 to 4" tease in Stash. "Immigrant Song" jam in YEM.

➢ Probably the best jam of the tour, if not the year, came during the band's Florida swing. A rare second-set Stash flows for over 30 minutes, wandering through Manteca and the Dog Faced Boy lyrics while also developing a number of very memorable, melodic themes of its own. For die-hard fans of Phish's improv, this set is just a rare, wondrous treat. —ERNIE GREENE

➢ Best version of Stash I've ever heard. It was about half an hour long and featured a Manteca jam. —TIM HERRMAN

➢ The taper section was on the side of the stage due to a smaller-than-normal floor area. First set: of course Chalkdust opens a University show; also check out the crazy Trey playing/screaming in between verses in Cavern. Second set: You see the list, you can imagine how insane Stash was. An all-a cappella Dog Faced Boy still haunts my dreams and nightmares. Be sure to listen to Trey singing the Immigrant Song intro in the middle of YEM. And don't forget the Wedge encore. —TONY HUME

➢ The first set of this show contains a beautiful Esther which flows perfectly into Free. But what a great second set. An unbelievable Stash > Manteca > Stash > Dog Faced Boy > Stash. Page does an incredible job on Strange Design. Listen closely to YEM and you will hear some Zeppelin thrown in just to make it a little sweeter. —JOHN E. CAMPION

11/15/95 [ACCESSIBILITY: ••]
Sundome, Tampa, FL
I: Poor Heart, AC/DC Bag, FEFY, Rift, Caspian, Sparkle, Melt, Adeline, Squirming Coil
II: Wilson, Theme, Scent of a Mule, Mike's > Life on Mars > Weekapaug, Fee, Guitar Gently Weeps **E:** Suzie
The band wins the first band-versus-audience chess game, taking a 1-0 lead over the audience in the match.

11/16/95 [ACCESSIBILITY: ••••]
West Palm Beach Auditorium, West Palm Beach, FL
I: CTB, Runaway Jim, Chess Game Jam, Horn, Mound, Ya Mar, Simple, Timber Ho, Guyute, Funky Bitch
II: Day in the Life, Bowie, Lifeboy, Uncle Pen, Ha Ha Ha, Harry Hood, HYHU > Brain > HYHU, Amazing Grace, Possum **E:** Brown Eyed Girl
Second band-versus-audience chess game begins during Chess Game Jam. Fishman on vacuum for Brain. Butch Trucks on drums for Possum, which also included Fishman on trombone and a "One Way Out" jam. Jimmy Buffet on vocals for Brown Eyed Girl. Concert debut: Brown Eyed Girl.

➢ The second set had some great tunes: ADITL, Uncle Pen and Ha Ha Ha. But the best part came at the end—first there was Possum with Butch Trucks, then even better was the Brown Eyed Girl encore with Jimmy Buffet. It was cool to hear a classic like that with Buffet. —CHUCK ADAMS

➢ When Possum started up, Butch Trucks from the Allman Brothers Band took over on drums and Fish played trombone, which sounded just great. I love Brown Eyed Girl, so when Jimmy Buffet is in tow I'm in a state of ecstasy. Butch and Buffet—this was a great show. —BILLY O'MALLEY

11/18/95 [ACCESSIBILITY: ••••]
North Charleston Coliseum, North Charleston, SC
I: Dinner and a Movie, Bouncing, Reba, Lawn Boy, PYITE, Slave, I'm Blue I'm Lonesome, Sample
II: AC/DC Bag, Sparkle, Free, I'm So Tired, YEM, Contact, BBFCM > Acoustic Army > BBFCM, Cavern **E:** Bill Bailey
I'm Blue I'm Lonesome performed acoustic. "Brickhouse" jam in YEM. Page's Father, Dr. Jack McConnell, on keyboard and vocals for Bill Bailey. Last Dinner and a Movie, 10/22/94 Orlando, FL [93 shows]. Last I'm So Tired, 10/31/94 Glens Falls, NY [88 shows].

➢ A sweet Dinner opener led to Fishman completely flubbing the beginning of Bouncin'. Reba, PYITE and Slave were nice first set treats. Second set had a Bag opener and the only I'm So Tired besides Halloween '94 (a cool song which was probably appropriate considering how long this tour was). YEM > Brickhouse > YEM was the bomb! The Bill Bailey encore with Dr. Jack McConnell doing the old soft-shoe was a good way to close a good show in my hometown. —TREVOR NORRIS

➢ Sometimes when you see a notation like "Brickhouse tease" on a setlist, you figure Trey maybe hit a few bars of the song somewhere in a long jam. But "Brickhouse" is ALL OVER this incredible YEM, one of the most rocking jam segments I've ever heard in this song. Trey and Mike are both on fire! —RICH MAZER

➢ Our seats were in the family section, and this was a benefit for Dr. McConnell's clinic. We met all of the friends and family of the McConnells. Then we won backstage passes from the Greenpeace brothers. So off it was to the aftershow room with a fridge full of Bass Ale. There we waited for the boys to come in. Being a guitarist, I was most excited talking to Trey. We talked about Surrender to the Air and the previous and past year's Florida shows. As it was getting near to time for us to leave, I told Trey we were driving back to Orlando because my band had to play. He told me, "It's good to see you have your priorities in order." When I told him we did some of his songs, he jokingly replied, "Oh yeah? Try Foam!" —TONY HUME

11/19/95 [ACCESSIBILITY: ••]
Charlotte Coliseum, Charlotte, NC
I: Makisupa > Maze, Poor Heart, Rift > Stash, Strange Design, It's Ice, Hello My Baby, Julius, Squirming Coil
II: Theme > Also Sprach, Curtain > Tweezer > Billy Breathes, Scent of a Mule, Harry Hood, Suzie **E:** Life on Mars, Tweezer Reprise
Slow version of Poor Heart (concert debut). "James Bond Theme" teases in Stash. "Tweezer" teases in Suzie.

11/21/95 [ACCESSIBILITY: ••••]
Lawrence Joel Coliseum, Winston Salem, NC
I: Fee, Chalkdust, Caspian, Divided Sky, Long Journey Home, I'm Blue I'm Lonesome, Guyute, My Friend, Dog Faced Boy, Runaway Jim
II: Simple, Bowie > Take Me to the River > Bowie, Glide, Ya Mar, Mike's > Keyboard Kavalry > Suspicious Minds > HYHU, Carolina, Day in the Life **E:** GTBT
I'm Blue I'm Lonesome and Long Journey Home performed acoustic. Concert debut: Take Me to the River.

➢ Perhaps my favorite of the shows I saw this fall, this show had it all—old favorites, acoustic numbers, Keyboard Kavalry, Fishman going crazy in a light-up cape singing Suspicious Minds, a cappella, Beatles, Talking Heads, Zeppelin. This show was a true carnival! Trey was killing it all night. —TERRY WATTS

➢ A unique situation at the Lawrence Joel Coliseum: no ushers for the floor seating. I didn't have floor seats but with no one checking we walked right down and sat ten rows back, center, and no one gave us any problems. Unbelievable second set. David Bowie kicked ass. The Keyboard Kavalry sounded very cool, and Fish dressed like Elvis got a laugh. An action-packed solid show. —ERIC HIGEL

➢ Absolutely the most spacey show I've ever seen. Most songs seemed to morph, like the band really had no expectations for the evening. Very groovy from start to finish though the second set takes the cake with a unique Bowie > Take Me to the River > Bowie. —WAYLON BAYARD

11/22/95 [ACCESSIBILITY: ••••]
USAir Arena, Landover, MD
I: CTB, Wilson, Antelope, Fluffhead, Uncle Pen, Cavern, Fog That Surrounds, Lizards, Sample, Adeline
II: Rift, Free > Llama, Bouncing, YEM, Strange Design
E: Poor Heart, Frankenstein
Slow version of Poor Heart. Rift abandoned after Fishman mistake.

➢ This show had the famed half-hour Free. I didn't like it. It just doesn't do anything. Its only redeeming quality is the musical debate at the end: Fish wants to segue into Bouncin'. Trey is very reluctant and ultimately chooses Llama. The transition is a tad sloppy but novel nonetheless. —SCOTT KUSHNER

➢ A memorable moment came when the second set opened with Rift: about half a minute into the song the band comes to a stop (Fish couldn't keep a beat). Trey jokingly says, "I'd like to credit that last one to our drummer, Mr. Jon Fishman." Then they burst into the most amazing Free I've ever witnessed. This Free went on for about a half hour, then they drifted beautifully into Llama in a segue highlighted by Trey's drum kit. A decent Llama followed, and a good YEM with a great vocal jam topped off the night. —JOHN FOLEY

➢ A 30-minute Free, but bigger isn't necessarily better. The improv gets a bit forced—nice try, but no cigar. Slow Poor Heart is a nice change for an encore, then Frankenstein. First set is pretty standard, with strong versions of Antelope and Sample as highlights. —BOB COLBY

➢ The Free jam is very interesting and different from the ones in 1996. You should hear it. At points, it's reminiscent of Runaway Jim. —LIBBY BARROW

11/24/95 [ACCESSIBILITY: ••]
Pittsburgh Civic Arena, Pittsburgh, PA
I: Oh Kee > AC/DC Bag, Curtain, Sparkle, Stash, Tela, I'm Blue I'm Lonesome, Maze, Suzie
II: Chalkdust, Theme, Reba, Catapult, Scent of a Mule, Bathtub Gin, Acoustic Army, HYHU > Bike > HYHU, Fee, Julius
E: Life on Mars, Rocky Top
I'm Blue I'm Lonesome performed acoustic. Fishman on vacuum for Bike. Last Oh Kee, 6/9/95 Morrison, CO [56 shows].

11/25/95 [ACCESSIBILITY: ••••]
Hampton Coliseum, Hampton, VA
I: Poor Heart, Day in the Life > Bowie, Billy Breathes, Fog that Surrounds, Bouncing, Rift, Wolfman's, Runaway Jim
II: Timber Ho > Kung > Mike's > Rotation Jam > Mike's, Long Journey Home, I'm Blue I'm Lonesome, Strange Design > Weekapaug, Harry Hood, Hello My Baby, Poor Heart **E:** Fire
Standard version of Poor Heart opened the show, then the slow version of Poor Heart closed second set. "Poor Heart" teases (slow and fast) before Fire. Long Journey Home and I'm Blue I'm Lonesome performed acoustic. Concert debut: Rotation Jam (band members rotated instruments).

➢ The first set was weak—the only songs I enjoyed were Bowie and Rift. The second set, filled with variety, made up for the first. Mike's Song showed up but segued into a weird jam. Everybody switched instruments (each taking a turn on all three other roles) allowing Fishman to make his glorious debut on electric guitar. Trey should start his own band—he sounded great on bass, drums and piano. Mike's Song came back out of this but there was no Weekapaug. It finally came after two acoustic songs and Strange Design. Poor Heart closed the set and was slowed down to counter the standard version that opened the show. —JAY GREEN

➢ After a rather textbook first set, they came back and threw us a curveball (isn't that the reason we keep coming back?), complete with a screaming Kung and a Harry Hood that was so inspired I lost total consciousness and felt like I was flying over breaking waves with the warm sun on my face—all this while completely sober. —COLM CONNELL

➢ If 5/7/94 is Tweezerfest, then I guess 11/25/95 must be PoorHeartfest. The show was bookended by Poor Hearts: set one opened with the regular, upbeat Poor Heart, and set two closed with the slow-shuffle version they started playing the week before this show. When the band came out for the encore, they teased both versions, then Trey asked the crowd, "Get it?" Ah, high-concept Phish humor—what a treat. —MARCIA COLLINS

11/28/95 [ACCESSIBILITY: ••]
Civic Coliseum, Knoxville, TN
I: Stash, Dinner and A Movie > Bouncing, Foam, I Didn't Know, Divided Sky, Guyute, Hello My Baby, Sample
II: Also Sprach > Maze, Suzie, Uncle Pen, Free, HYHU > Wind Beneath My Wings > HYHU, Antelope, Contact, BBFCM, Funky Bitch
E: Squirming Coil
"25 or 6 to 4" tease in Suzie. Fishman on vacuum for I Didn't Know. Wind Beneath My Wings was dedicated to Col. Bruce Hampton, who sat in a chair on stage reading a newspaper while Fishman sang. Concert debut: Wind Beneath My Wings.

➢ This is a perfect picture of a basically good, solid, pleasing Phish show. There weren't any standouts during set one—everything was satisfying but standard. Suzie and Uncle Pen broke up the great jams in both Maze and Free. To see Col. Bruce on stage was a thrill. —JASON DEZIEL

➢ This was my first show; I hate the fact that I am a latecomer, so to speak, but I can guarantee I heard nothing until I heard live Phish. I will never forget the image of Trey going off when they opened up with Stash and the beams of red light shined down. It was then I knew I loved this band! As far as first shows go, the music rocked, but the setlist in retrospect was weak. Regardless, it was incredible, and how could I forget Fishman serenading Col. Bruce with that all-time favorite Wind Beneath My Wings? —AMANDA LITTON

11/29/95 [ACCESSIBILITY: ••••]
Municipal Auditorium, Nashville, TN
I: AC/DC Bag, Ya Mar, Reba, If I Could, It's Ice, Theme, Acoustic Army, Fee, Melt
II: Timber Ho, Sparkle, Simple, Possum, YEM, Fog that Surrounds, Poor Heart, I'm Blue I'm Lonesome, Long Journey Home, Slave
E: Day in the Life
Bela Fleck on banjo for the second set, starting with Fog that Surrounds. "Heart and Soul" jam played to introduce Bela before Fog that Surrounds.

➢ After a fairly mediocre first set, the second set just blows my mind. A great Timber Ho kicks things off, and then comes the real fun. Halfway through the set, out comes Bela Fleck! They play some good bluegrass tunes and then the best Slave my ears have ever experienced. A banjo has never sounded so sweet as it did during this fine tune. —JOSH HARMAN

➢ Whenever Bela is involved, it's gonna be gooood, especially if it's for half a set! Check out that setlist! Also nice to hear how talented they all can be by playing acoustic guitars on Acoustic Army. —MARK SELBY

11/30/95 [ACCESSIBILITY: ••••]
Ervin J. Nutter Center, Dayton, OH
I: Sample, Curtain, Ha Ha Ha, Julius, NICU, Bathtub Gin, Rift, FEFY, Lizards, Fire
II: CTB, Tweezer > Makisupa > Antelope, Scent of a Mule, Free, Strange Design, Amazing Grace **E:** Harry Hood

➢ Many Phish shows have second sets better than the first, but seldom is the imbalance as severe as it is here. The second set is absolutely one of the must-have sets of the fall tour, featuring a wonderful Tweezer > Makisupa > Antelope trio that has to be heard to be appreciated. That's because this is no normal Tweezer—like its kindred spirit on 12/2, it explores beautiful melodious realms before seguing into Makisupa, which itself has a crazy segue into an unbelievable, unreal, thrilling Antelope (Trey starts Antelope, then returns to play around with Makisupa before churning back into Antelope.) —SCOTT SIFTON

➢ This show features one of my favorite combinations of Phish songs. It has a nicely jammed Tweezer which segues into Makisupa's reggae vibe. Then comes the part I'm fond of: Makisupa Policemantelope. There's a nice combination of the two between Makisupa and Antelope—it's a wonderful combo. —JEFFREY ELLENBOGEN

➢ My first live Phish experience, and not a bad start. The Sample opener excited me as it was something that sounded familiar. I was overwhelmed by the energy and danced like crazy until the boys slowed it down with a disappointing FEFY. Lizards kept the FEFY-heads happy but Fire brought us all back around. Second set was pretty tight; Antelope blew me away! All was well until they slowed back down, or so I thought until I listened to the lyrics to Strange Design, which inspired the first of many free hugs! Needless to say, I was hooked! —CARRI A. JOHNSON

12/1/95 [ACCESSIBILITY: ••••]
Hershey Park Arena, Hershey, PA
I: Buried Alive > Down with Disease, Theme, Poor Heart, Wolfman's, Chalkdust, Forbin's > Mockingbird, Stash, Cavern
II: Halley's > Mike's > Weekapaug, Mango, Wilson, HYHU > Suspicious Minds > HYHU, Bowie > Catapult > Bowie **E:** Suzie
"Chocolate" chants by Trey during Forbin's and Bowie.

➢ I left school early to make it to this show with my friends and it was well worth the trip. First off, the parking lot was buzzing and all of the trees inside the lot were decorated with Christmas lights, which made it extra welcoming. The Arena was a good size and security was minimal. The highlight of this show is Trey's narration after Col. Forbin in which he gives the biggest clue as to where to find the Rhombus, mentioning "King of Prussia, Pennsylvania" over and over again and telling us it would be the best clue we'd get… As well, a great chocolate story is mixed in with it. The Mike's > Weekapaug was also stellar. —DAVID GEORGE

➢ One of the best Phish shows I've been to. Hershey Park was decorated for the holidays. Christmas lights and music abound, along with the smell of "Mmmm, chocolate," as Trey, doing his Homer Simpson impression, fantasized. Buried Alive rocked the stadium as an opener. Awesome rhombus narration during Forbin's/Mockingbird (I think everybody, the following day, made way to King of Prussia, PA, in search of the elusive rhombus). Fishman's Elvis impression was mind-blowing in Suspicious Minds, especially when the lights dimmed and his Elvis cape lit the stage—beautiful! —LARA WITTELS

➢ The start of one of the sickest months of music in Phish history! What was it about December '95 that pushed them to another level? Well, in a month of incredible jams, seemingly every show has a major highlight that just HAS to be heard. Hershey's contribution? The first-ever Mike's directly into Weekapaug which is much more than the setlist indicates. Get this one and the Niagra 12/7 version (the other Mike's right into Weekapaug)—they're both awesome. —ERNIE GREENE

12/2/95 [ACCESSIBILITY: ••••]
Veterans Memorial Coliseum, New Haven, CT
I: Caspian, Runaway Jim, Mound, Guelah, Reba, MSO, Free, Fog that Surrounds, Bouncing, Possum
II: Also Sprach > Maze, Simple, Faht, Tweezer, Day in the Life, Golgi, Squirming Coil, Tweezer Reprise **E:** Bold as Love
Last MSO, 6/15/95 Atlanta, GA [58 shows].

➢ After having to travel to the past 30 or so shows, I expected a great time in my home state of Connecticut. Wrong! It was like a high school punk madhouse. The crowd seemed overtaken by troublemakers, not tourheads; some 17-year-old Pearl Jam/Nirvana wannabe pushed a girl I was with to the ground. Why? Because she asked his barely conscious friend if he was okay. Set I was basic, a few nice jams but no real standouts. The first half of set II picked up the pace, spacey but tight, and who would have expected Fishman to bust out Faht? The show lost all momentum when the set ended with selections of A Day in the Life, Golgi, and then the dreaded, slow, energy-draining piano exit Squirming Coil. Without question, this was the worst Phish show I've ever attended. —JASON DEZIEL

➢ First show! After taking Metro North two hours from New York we were greeted by nothing. New Haven was basically closed with the exception of a Burger King that should've been for lack of cleanliness. The Coliseum was a '50s-style minor league hockey arena erected between two highways. After braving three checkpoints by the police and inhaling the smoke that filled the arena, we were greeted with the magic that is Phish. After Reba, I was converted and the band, and Chris' light magic on Tweezer made me a devotee. Life would never be the same. —LEE SCHILLER

➢ A better show to hear on tape than in person, because you can fast-forward directly to Tweezer. Chris Kuroda later cited this Tweezer as a tour highlight, but it's much more than that—it's an absolute must-hear, as Phish develops several gorgeous jams in a version of the song that isn't overly long but damn sure is overly powerful! Add it to the short list of classic Phish jams, no question. —AL HUNT

12/4/95 [ACCESSIBILITY: •••]
Mullins Center, University of Massachusetts, Amherst, MA
I: Julius, Gumbo, Divided Sky, PYITE, Stash, My Mind's, Axilla II, Horse > Silent, Hello My Baby, Guitar Gently Weeps
II: Timber Ho, Sparkle, Ya Mar, Antelope, Billy Breathes, CTB, YEM, Sample, Frankenstein **E:** Bouncing, Rocky Top

12/5/95 [ACCESSIBILITY: ••••]
Mullins Center, University of Massachusetts, Amherst, MA
I: Horn, Chalkdust, Fog that Surrounds, Lizards, Free, Esther, Bowie, I'm Blue I'm Lonesome
II: Poor Heart, Bathtub Gin > Keyboard Kavalry, Scent of a Mule > Lifeboy, Harry Hood, Cavern **E:** Theme, Adeline
I'm Blue I'm Lonesome performed acoustic.

➢ At one point Trey dedicates Lizards to Dick Vitale, the sports broadcaster, whom he had just met backstage. Dick Vitale at a Phish show? What's next, Captain Lou Albano playin' the drums with Fishman? —JOSH LETOURNEAU

➢ I have friends who disagree, but I don't think Phish has ever played a great show at the Mullins Center. The place is so cavernous that the music just sort of gets lost on its way to the audience. This show might be the exception—there's a lot of meat in the first set (Free, Esther, Bowie), and an amazing Bathtub Gin in the second set that clocks in at over 25 minutes before the boys march westward for Keyboard Kavalry. The Lifeboy, Harry Hood pairing also taps an emotional reservoir, but if you're going to pick up this show, it'll be for the Gin. —PAT STANLEY

12/7/95 [ACCESSIBILITY: ••••]
Niagra Falls Convention Center, Niagra Falls, NY
I: Old Home Place, Curtain > AC/DC Bag, Demand > Rift, Slave, Guyute, Bouncing, Possum, Hello My Baby
II: Melt, Strange Design, Fog that Surrounds, Reba, Julius, Sleeping Monkey, Sparkle, Mike's > Weekapaug, Amazing Grace **E:** Uncle Pen
"In-a-Gadda-Da-Vida" jam in Melt. "Itsy Bitsy Spider" jam in Reba.

➢ One of the most underrated shows, in my opinion. An excellent Slave in the first set, then, to open off the second set is an amazing SOAMelt. They tease In-a-Gadda-Da-Vida and just jam the hell out of it. Then later in the set they pull out a phat Mike's > Weekapaug. Not as good as Hershey, but still an unbelievable version. —KEVIN WEISS

➢ In a strange attempt to alternate incredible jams with more plebian crowd-favorites, the second set of this show is truly unique. It starts with a raging Split Open and Melt that is just amazing, worthy of "best version" consideration without a doubt. As if to counter this amazing achievement with a no-improv song, the band follows with Strange Design. The opposite happens later in the set when a basic Sparkle precedes what might be the best Mike's Groove ever. The jamming that carries the band from Mike's across the great divide into Weekapaug is glorious, but then the band jams out the other side of Weekapaug, creating a Mike's > Weekapaug > Jam that is unlike any version of this song I've ever heard. —JOSH ALBINI

➢ Quite a sick tease of "Itsy Bitsy Spider" during Trey's solo in Reba. But what stole the show was Page on keys—incredible organ work during Julius. You gotta love any set that opens with good bluegrass such as My Old Home Place. I almost forgot Fishman's voice not working too well during Sleeping Money—at least he gave us a chuckle. —MARK SELBY

➢ Is this the only show where both sets end in a cappella tunes? —CHARLIE MURPHY

12/8/95 [ACCESSIBILITY: ••••]
Convocation Center, Cleveland State University, Cleveland, OH
I: Sample, Poor Heart, Simple > Runaway Jim > Fluffhead, It's Ice, Acoustic Army, Caspian, GTBT
II: Also Sprach > Tweezer > Kung > Tweezer > Love You, Squirming Coil, Tweezer Reprise, Antelope **E:** Come Together, Day in the Life
"Brady Bunch Theme" tease in Antelope. Concert debut: Come Together, in memory of John Lennon, who died 12/8/80.

➢ A few segues grab my attention. Maybe because I've only been listening for two years, but the Simple > Jim > Fluffhead is unbelievable. If I'm not mistaken you can hear the Jim teases in Simple a good minute before they kick into it. I love it. The encore of this show is amazing: back-to-back Beatles, dedicated to John Lennon on the anniversary of his death. —JEFF BERNIER

➢ This was a cold and snowy night, and also the anniversary of the day John Lennon got shot. The venue was right down the street from the Rock and Roll Hall of Fame, so I don't think anyone knew what to expect. Both sets were good, not the best, but the encores were great. Their tribute to John probably made him cry from above. —KEVIN WORD

12/9/95 [ACCESSIBILITY: ••••]
Knickerbocker Arena, Albany, NY
I: Maze, Theme, NICU, Sloth, Rift, Bouncing, Free, Billy Breathes, Dog Faced Boy, Chalkdust
II: Timber Ho, Wilson, Gumbo, YEM, Lawn Boy, Slave, Crossroads, Adeline **E:** Loving Cup
Trey triggered Beavis and Butt-head sound effects in Wilson. Silent Jam in YEM. "Shaft" line sung in YEM.

➢ The band lifted our spirits with a most memorable YEM. It was aggressive and kept the Knick grooving, including a silent jam and a stinky vocal jam. Trey sure can pull those windmills! Phish succeeded at slapping a smile on all faces that had to bear the blizzard to get to the show. Anyone else get involved in the I-90 pile-up? —MARK SELBY

➢ The band played a great silent jam that you had to see to really appreciate. About halfway through YEM, they faded the music to silence and built it back up again—but without any sound! It lasted about half a minute, and on tape all you hear is the phans' reaction. Every move was an exact replica of what it would take to play the jam with audible music! —MELISSA MIXER

➢ A simply incredible, melodic, heavily improvised YEM. Phish at their very, very, best. It's the level of performance you wait 20 to 30 shows to hear, and you damn well better appreciate it. —ANDY BERNSTEIN

➢ Phish opened up the second set with an insane Timber which displayed Phish communication at its best. Out of all my tapes, I probably listen to this one song the most. Trey tried to get the crowd psyched up for Wilson by using his Beavis and Butt-head keychain, but unfortunately the crowd just stood there and laughed. This followed with Gumbo and its saloon-style Page conclusion. Another notable was a beautiful YEM with an intense improv section. —JOHN FOLEY

12/11/95 [ACCESSIBILITY: ••••]
Cumberland County Civic Center, Portland, ME
I: My Friend, Ha Ha Ha, Stash, Caspian, Reba, Dog Log, Llama, Dog Log, Tube, McGrupp, Julius, Cavern
II: Curtain > Bowie, Mango, Fog that Surrounds, Scent of a Mule, Harry Hood, HYHU > Suspicious Minds > HYHU, Funky Bitch
E: Guitar Gently Weeps
Trey cued audience sound effects (booing) during first Dog Log. Second Dog Log performed lounge-lizard style with more cued sound effects (screaming). Warren Haynes on guitar for Funky Bitch and Guitar Gently Weeps. Last Dog Log, 8/2/93 Ybor City, FL [217 shows].

➢ North-country boys they are, Phish knew their fans deserved something special for making the trek north in the middle of December. Early in the first set, Trey revealed a secret he said he'd been keeping all tour. Noting that the band performs Dog Log during soundchecks before a lot of shows, Trey said they've been recording them for inclusion on an all-Dog Log album. And this night, Trey told us we were going to play a role in the creation of the album-to-be. The band would play Dog Log but we had to be really quiet at the beginning, mimicking the empty-room soundcheck conditions. Then, on signal, we were supposed to boo and scream at Phish as though they were the worst band in history. A minute into Dog Log, Trey lifted his arm and the Civic Center began to shake under attack from thunderous screaming and yelling. Dog Log ended there—Trey flashed one of those giddy smiles and said, "That was awesome! That's going on the album!" Then, following a great Llama, Trey decided that Dog Log was so much fun, he wanted to do another one. This time, we were told to shriek as loudly and obnoxiously as we could on his signal. Again, the effect was fantastic. As a thank you for our help, we received the tour's second Tube. —RUSSELL KAHN

➢ What a great venue—tiny for an arena. This was a goof of a show. I had a great time during Dog Log, and obviously I wasn't alone as everyone there seemed to be on that groove. My friends and I were also in town for the Gov't Mule show the following night, so Warren Haynes' presence didn't surprise us. Funky Bitch was a tasty treat. Suspicious Minds was played on the anniversary of a scheduled Elvis show in Portland that was canceled because of the King's death. The tapes don't do this gem justice. —DAN KURTZ

12/12/95 [ACCESSIBILITY: •••]
Providence Civic Center, Providence, RI
I: Ya Mar, Sample, Divided Sky, Lifeboy, PYITE, Horse > Silent, Antelope, I'm Blue I'm Lonesome, Squirming Coil
II: Free, Sparkle, Down with Disease > Lizards, Simple, Runaway Jim
E: Fire
I'm Blue I'm Lonesome performed acoustic.

➢ Bad vibes in Providence—weird after the glorious 12/29/94 show in the same room—bummed everyone out and decreased our enjoyment of what otherwise would have been a good show. A massive fight broke out on the floor during setbreak, with one guy led away in handcuffs (he tried to grab the tapers' microphone stands as the police led him past the tapers' section, which was pretty funny). A *long* Down With Disease in the second set didn't work most of the time; a tighter Runaway Jim, on the other hand, did. —TYLER HARRIS

➢ The highlight of the show was Down With Disease. Many people say '96 was the year of the DwD, but I believe DwD started to take off at this show. It clocked in at about 35 minutes. —JON BAHR

➢ This is the unknown sleeper of fall/winter '95; no one I trade with has it and no one talks about it, but it smokes! The Ya Mar opener was more funky than usual and sets a great pace. They blew up everything during set I—top-notch versions of Divided Sky and Antelope. The assholes fighting by the SBD during setbreak bummed a lot of people out, along with the large presence of drunken frat boy types. The great version of Free couldn't stand anything to the best version of Down With Disease ever—words can't describe it. There was also a terrific version of Runaway Jim to end set II (they should really use this in more places than the usual set-opening location it often gets). —JASON DEZIEL

12/14/95 [ACCESSIBILITY: ••••]
Broome County Arena, Binghamton, NY
I: Suzie, Llama, Horn, Foam, Makisupa, Melt, Tela, Fog that Surrounds, MSO, Frankenstein
II: Curtain > Tweezer > Timber Ho > Tweezer, Keyboard Kavalry, Halley's > NICU > Slave **E:** Bold as Love
Bonus lyrics in Makisupa. Silent Jam in Melt. Page solo between NICU and Slave.

➢ The most underrated tape in my collection. Second set rocks with an outstanding Tweezer > Timber > Tweezer. Page lays on the synthesizers during the jam, while Fish and Mike provide the noise. Beautiful chaos! Timber is a perfect version, as is the set-opener Curtain—the vocal harmonies are dead-on. A nice Halley's into NICU jam is all Trey. Add a brilliant Axis encore and you have yourself a great tape. —TIM FOISSER

➢ Well, I will admit to my bias to begin. This show took place in my town and to say I was excited as all hell to go is an understatement. Opening with Suzie and Llama was energizing; I also loved SOAMelt, and Makisupa had the cool Khadafi-joint narration. I got my first Frankenstein—man, what a great closer! The second set was a giant segue. Curtain was sweet, the following Tweezer was fun. Perhaps the best was Keyboard Kavalry, which was new to me, a very pretty, simple, yet powerful little tune. A final word: Halley's Comet was grrrrreat! —DANIEL PADEN

➢ The second set of this show has one of the most powerful arrangements of songs ever. Explanation won't do it justice, so I'll just spell it out for you: Curtain > Tweezer > Timber Ho > Tweezer > Keyboard Kavalry, Halley's Comet > NICU > Slave! The encore? Bold as Love! You must hear this to comprehend it! —OTIS

12/15/95 [ACCESSIBILITY: ••••]
Corestates Spectrum, Philadelphia, PA
I: Chalkdust > Harry Hood > Wilson, Maze > Ha Ha Ha > Suspicious Minds, CTB, Bouncing, Free > Possum
II: Tweezer Reprise, Runaway Jim, It's Ice > Bathtub Gin > Rotation Jam > Also Sprach > Bowie, Adeline **E:** GTBT > Tweezer Reprise
Band members rotated instruments after Fishman vacuum solo in Bathtub Gin.

➢ There are not enough good things that I can say about this show, except that it is awesome! The setlist is all that I could ever want and the band plays every song so well. Chalkdust opener is hot and segues perfectly into a Hood that would knock your fridge over. The Spectrum is where Trey saw his first concert (Jethro Tull), he tells the crowd before a smoking Ha Ha Ha that is shorter than other versions but is the tightest one I've heard. David Bowie as usual has an awesome jam included with it. I can't keep this tape out of my deck! —DAVID GEORGE

➢ They finished the Tweezer from the night before (then did it again!?). I remember Trey respectfully dedicating Good Times Bad Times to Mike Tyson, who was going to be there the next night. —COLM CONNELL

➢ Very schtick oriented-show, highlighted by the rotation jam. If you're at a show to see them jam and they end up just doing a lot of schtick, you'd better hope you're in the mood for it. I wasn't. —LISA PADDOCK

12/16/95 [ACCESSIBILITY: ••]
Olympic Center, Lake Placid, NY
I: Buried Alive > AC/DC Bag, Fog that Surrounds, Ya Mar, Sloth, Divided Sky, Dog Faced Boy, Julius, Suzie
II: Sample, Reba, Scent of a Mule, Cavern, Mike's > Simple > Weekapaug, Squirming Coil **E:** Fire

12/17/95 [ACCESSIBILITY: ••••]
Olympic Center, Lake Placid, NY
I: My Friend, Poor Heart, Day in the Life, Antelope, Mango, Tube, Stash, Lizards, Chalkdust
II: Bouncing, Maze, Free, Also Sprach > Harry Hood, Sparkle, Tweezer > Tweezer Reprise **E:** Hello My Baby, Runaway Jim
Page solo between Tweezer and Tweezer Reprise.

➢ I'd love it if every town welcomed us with the hospitality Lake Placid does. The local restaurants even incorporated Phish songs into their menus! While the setlist seems like nothing special, the music was finely crafted. I found myself constantly thinking, this is how this song is meant to be played! A perfect show to send us home with after such a phenomenal tour. —COLM CONNELL

➢ It's nice when the tour-ender falls on your birthday, especially when you know the show will be better than last night. Nothing too unusual in the first set (although Antelope through Stash was a standout portion). Chalkdust provided the tour thank-yous. The second set was interesting, not because of the song choices but the way they were ordered and combined. Bouncin' is better as an opener, because that way it doesn't destroy an amazing set. Free extends past its usual ending (to the extent that I wrote "Jam" on my setlist) before landing in 2001 land, a creative choice for mid-second set. Hood (out of 2001!) goes the same way: they play through the "You can fell good!" and eventually land in Sparkle. Tweezer develops into a Page solo, which seemed likely to end the show, but the band returned for the Reprise. Jim is a strange tour-ender, as one usually thinks of it as an opener, but on this night it seemed to fit. —GREG SCHWARTZ

New Year's '95 *TEMPORAL RIFT*

New Year's Eve '93 at The Centrum in Worcester, MA was, at the time, far and away the largest indoor venue Phish had ever played on its own. But as '95 drew to a close, the two-night stand at Worcester served as just a warm-up for Phish's most ambitious and high-profile gigs to date: a pair of shows at Madison Square Garden to close out the year.

Through the entire, no-repeats run, the band seemed to be building up to the final show, with many fans agreeing that each night was noticeably better than the one which preceded it—except perhaps for the great 12/29 show topping 12/30—and that the New Year's show took a giant step ahead of any show in memory. The midnight prank was not quite as grand as 1994's flying hot dog, with the band instead fiddling in the Gamehendge Time Laboratory at the rear of the stage and turning Fish—who had gotten a shave on stage between sets I and II—into the baby new year as he emerged from a flying crate. The first Sanity in a year and a half captured more attention.

12/28/95 [ACCESSIBILITY: ••••]
The Centrum, Worcester, MA
I: Melt, Gumbo, Curtain > Julius, Guyute, Horn, Rift, FEFY, Possum
II: Timber Ho, Theme, Wilson, Buried Alive, Tweezer, I Didn't Know, Uncle Pen, Slave **E:** Fee, Tweezer Reprise
The venue sound system cut out during Rift and the band continued to play through its monitors until the sound system came back on right before the final "and silence contagious..." line. "Johnny B. Goode" tease in Wilson. Fishman on vacuum for I Didn't Know.

➢ In my opinion (and I realize this may draw slack), this was the best show of the '95 holiday tour. Why? I think it was because it was the first holiday show and they played a lot of great tunes that you don't hear all the time. Guyute, Horn, Rift was an amazing stretch, and then the PA went out during Rift and the band kept going, realizing and smiling at what was going on as they kept playing. La Grange was great the following night, but I enjoyed this show more. —JEFF BERNIER

➢ The first of the four shows on the New Year's Run was a true indication of how great these shows would be. Although we had the worst seats possible, behind the band, it didn't stop everyone in our section from dancing and enjoying ourselves. The highlight of the night occurred during Rift. The speakers went out and there was no sound for a good part of the song. The band continued to play and the crowd kept dancing. When the sound finally kicked back on (right before the "and silence contagious in moments like these" line), the crowd let out an enormous cheer. However, there was nothing else out of the ordinary or too spectacular at this show. —CHRIS HAINES

12/29/95 [ACCESSIBILITY: ••••]
The Centrum, Worcester, MA
I: My Friend, Poor Heart, Down with Disease, Fog that Surrounds, NICU, Stash, Fluffhead, Llama, Adeline
II: Makisupa, CTB, Bathtub Gin > The Real Me > Bathtub Gin > McGrupp, BBFCM > Bass Jam > La Grange, Bouncing, Fire **E:** Golgi
Jim Stinnette (Mike's bass instructor) on bass and Mike on bass for Bass Jam. Last La Grange, 8/14/93 Tinley Park, IL [215 shows].

Sunday, December 31, 1995 — MSG, New York, NY

Phish-tacy *n. The state in which every sound made by Phish jibes perfectly with the mental state of the listener, with each note triggering endorphin secretion and unfettered bliss.*

I'd been there before, but never like at New Year's Eve. There must have been 30,000 people who showed up that night. Each waving finger outside the venue screamed of how lucky I was to have a ticket. Although I cringed at the thought of people shelling out $200 to see the show, I knew that if there was a caption under each exchange, it would read "bargain."

While the entire evening was blanketed in an aura of history, my true symbolic journey began when they kicked into Drowned, a pleasant surprise for a Who fan like myself, still recovering from the joys of Halloween. When the band morphed into a seemingly endless jam to close the tune, it went from being a pleasant little treat, to a goddamn epiphany.

Now, I've seen The Who play Drowned. They would get into it, jump around and perhaps improvise a little. But I'm sure they never dreamed of playing it as Phish did this night. I bet Pete Townsend would have liked to. He probably saw the opening. But when venturing onto a stadium stage, he knew that he must limit each song to a length palatable for the broad audience, as only radio anthems like Won't Get Fooled Again could be stretched into abandon.

As the jam unfolded, Phish revealed they had figured out that, in fact, people are tired of the palatable, tired of being addressed as a broad mass and having music funneled through the lowest common artistic denominator. Phish, and the hordes of people who converged on the Garden that night, proved that individuals want to be challenged. They want to be teased. They want to take the scenic route.

Immediate gratification is an oxymoron. MTV is irrelevant.

The secret which Phish has figured out, is that people want more. **—Andy Bernstein**

***Phan Pick* #17** ➢ A decent first set, but once again Phish unleashes during the second. Notables in the second set were an upbeat Cars Trucks Buses followed by Bathtub Gin > The Real Me > Bathtub Gin, the best sandwich sequence I have ever witnessed. Even better than any Mike's > I Am > Weekapaug I've ever heard—truly vintage Phish. They didn't stop there—McGrupp with a particularly spooky piano section was followed by a bass duet with Gordon and his instructor, Jim Stinnett. Remember, those are just the highlights of a perfect-10 show. This was the best show I've ever been to. —JOHN FOLEY

➢ Somwhere in the middle of Bathtub > Real Me > Bathtub, a.k.a. "The Real Gin," I discovered the meaning of life. Simply incredible. —MELISSA WOLCOTT

➢ While the first set seemed predictable at the time, nothing could have prepared me for the second set. Whatever was happening anywhere else in the universe did not matter. If sunlight could have made sound, it would've been Trey's guitar during the greatest Makisupa ever. From then on I didn't stop spinning. I couldn't. The set was an absolute masterpiece. Everyone was gleaming. If I could have only one live recording, this would be it. If you don't have this tape, get it! —COLM CONNELL

➢ The second set is perfect for those of you looking to turn on potential phans. It contains reggae, jazz, blues, rock, punk, a bunch of covers and the best damn segue I've ever heard (Bathtub > Real Me). It even has Bouncin', so the phan-to-be will know at least one original. For those who already know, this show will please still since it flows soooo well. What do you expect? It's the New Year's Run! —PAUL SHEETS

12/30/95 [ACCESSIBILITY: •••••]
Madison Square Garden, New York, NY
I: Caspian, Also Sprach > Suzie, Bowie, Simple, It's Ice > Kung > It's Ice, TMWSIY > Avenu > TMWSIY, Divided Sky, Sample
II: Ya Mar, Free, Harry Hood, AC/DC Bag, Lifeboy, Scent of a Mule, Cavern, Antelope **E:** Day in the Life
"Auld Lang Syne" tease in Ya Mar.

***Phan Pick* #15** ➢ There was one thing about this show that still has a big impact on me—the Hood in the second set. I think it's the best thing Phish has ever produced in concert. Yeah, their rotation jams are cool, but this song, this version is musical perfection to my ears. Whenever it is a nice day, I like to throw on my sunglasses, put on my walkman and go to class with this song ringing through my body. From the part of "Thank you Mr. Miner, thank you Mr. Hood" on, it is like jumping off a ledge and floating down slowly in a state of ecstasy. From the lows to the highs, this song is what defines Phish, and it is the most amazing thing to listen to. The crowd, obviously, felt the same way. —BRETT PESSIN

NYE '95

12/31/95 Madison Square Garden, New York, NY

The greatest show of all time. That's how readers of *The Pharmer's Almanac* rate New Year's Eve, 1995. To many, this show represents the absolute culmination of Phish's journey to greatness.

MSG. New York City. About 30,000 fans showed up and for the first time, Phish had center stage to the world—for no one can top New Year's Eve at the Garden.

But the band wasn't content just ruling three dimensions.

Trey set up their annual prank by letting fans know about Phish's "time production lab" during the Col. Forbin's narration in set one, which also found Phish lyricist Tom Marshall emerging onto the stage to sing a couple of lines from Collective Soul's 1994 hit "Shine," which allowed everyone a stroll down memory lane.

Between sets, Fishman got a shave onstage, as fans milled about in aisles so crowded it became clear that many had either sneaked in or breezed through with counterfeits—a genuine fire hazard.

But the true explosion came on stage in the second set. It opened with The Who's Drowned, which they debuted exactly two months earlier in *Quadrophenia*. But unlike Halloween, Phish took Drowned for a long spin—one of the major musical highlights of the show.

Still, it's tough to talk of highlights when practically every song in the second and third sets would stand way out at other shows. Fans tend to throw around superlatives about many songs from many nights spent with Phish, but when people discuss this show, phrases like "monumental" have completely different meanings.

The best way to put it in context is this: Ask a knowledgeable fan to rate the ten best single-song performances in Phish history. It would not be insane if that fan picked at least four from this show. Drowned, Runaway Jim, Mike's Song and Weekapaug were all miniature shows in themselves, with wonderful improvised licks and incredible melodies made up on the spot. The audience was absolutely captivated.

The middle stanza saw the breathtaking performances of Runaway Jim and Mike's, which finished with Trey alone on stage, creating a digital delay loop effect which rang out over the P.A. even when he had left the stage, reminding the crowd that, yes, there was more to come.

As the third set got underway at about five minutes to midnight, Phish unveiled the Gamehendge time laboratory, and the crowd roared in amusement when Trey, Page and Mike worked at a huge machine at the back of the stage to produce a diapered Fishman baby New Year at the stroke of midnight, hanging from the lights in what looked like a coffin. It was definitely a grand experiment, but in all its electricity, it didn't hold water to the musical brilliance of the evening.

They rang in the New Year with a Weekapaug that saw Phish jam as melodiously and powerfully as they'd ever jammed before. When the jam led to a Page piano solo, an emotional highlight of the show followed with his performance of another *Quadrophenia* remnant, Sea and Sand, the only time since Halloween '95 the song has resurfaced. An unquestionably strong YEM, and Sanity (that hadn't been heard since the spring of '94) followed, then Phish charged up the crowd for '96 by just tearing through Frankenstein and the surprise encore, Johnny B. Goode.

Everyone in the crowd had their own highlights. For some, it was enough just to be inside, on a night when the lack of security guards gave the show a general-admission feel and Phish gave everyone a night to remember.

If Phish never achieves this sort of musical height again, they should not be ashamed. For many, a show better than 12/31/95 only exists in the imagination.

➢ The setlist could not have been better for my ear. Avenu Malkenu blew my hat off. I was singing the Hebrew words and this dude next to me couldn't believe it. I told him we sang this in Temple and it blew his mind! —ROB RIMER

➢ A good upbeat setlist, but most of the songs were pretty mainstream. I would have hoped for a little more creativity during a holiday show. —KATE O'NEIL

12/31/95 [ACCESSIBILITY: •••••]
Madison Square Garden, New York, NY
I: PYITE, Sloth, Reba, Squirming Coil, Maze, Forbin's > Mockingbird, Sparkle, Chalkdust
II: Drowned > Lizards, Axilla II, Runaway Jim, Strange Design, Hello My Baby, Mike's
III: "Mad Science Experiment" > New Year's Countdown > Auld Lang Syne > Weekapaug > Sea and Sand, YEM, Sanity, Frankenstein
E: Johnny B. Goode

"Shine" jam in Forbin's, with Tom Marshall on vocals. Lyrics in Runaway Jim included "Runaway Dave" and "Runaway Daubs," referencing Trey's friends in attendance. Digital Delay Loop jam at the end of Mike's. During the mad science experiment, Page, Trey and Mike worked at a huge machine at the rear of the stage while Fishman ascended to become the New Year's baby. "Auld Lang Syne" teases in Weekapaug. Audience won the second band-versus-audience chess game as band resigned, tying the match at 1-1. The king from the chess board was thrown into crowd and caught by Rob Fasman of Springfield, NJ. Between the first and second sets, Fishman has his beard shaved off on stage. Last Sanity, 6/24/94 Indianapolis, IN [147 shows]. Last Johnny B. Goode, 7/3/95 Fayston, VT [58 shows].

Phan Pick #1 ➢ I tried to find the black cloud in the silver lining, but it wasn't happening. One of the best shows by anyone, ever. Our seats, first level about 20 feet from the stage; the fans, mellow and friendly; the music, even more astonishing; the security, what security? You could've brought in a grenade launcher. But who wanted to? Throw in an amazing interpretation of The Who's Drowned, a scintillating Mike's Song, the choreography of the Mad Scientists and Baby Fishman, and a rare Sanity, and you've got a show for the ages. The black cloud did come: our train trip back to Philly took five hours. —LEE SCHILLER

➢ The band was so on this night! The best show I've ever been to. The second set started with a kick-ass version of Drowned, which some claim contains a "Fire On the Mountain" tease. Personally, I don't hear it. The jams on all the songs were unbelievable in the second set, especially Lizards, Runaway Jim and Mike's Song. The jam in Mike's closes the set nicely with a digital delay loop effects jam by Trey. —SETH WEINGLASS

➢ All three sets of this show are incredible. A PYITE opener is a great start and I love the Reba—a great jam without whistling. Forbin/Mockingbird is cool, with Trey explaining how while not on tour, the band members make time in the Gamehendge time lab. Great Drowned > Lizards opener for set II and an excellent Runaway Jim. The Mike's into weirdness jam is nice too. Set III's Weekapaug > Sea and Sand is phat, followed by a scary YEM. Sanity is a great surprise and the encore is rippin'. Great way to ring in '96. —NICK SORICELLI

➢ It was just amazing. I was in the audience, just thinking, "This is one of the greatest moments of my life and Phish history." I heard the Who play Drowned live in 1996, but Phish just jammed it. They made everyone say, Yeah, this is music. It was a great way to ring in the New Year. —BILLY O'MALLEY

➢ Another year has gone by, and another hell of a New Year's. During Col. Forbin's, Trey got to talking about time and how the band controls time when they are off tour by making time run in Gamehendge. He then continues to say what if we were stuck in 1994, and we woke up to hearing the same song over and over. Tom Marshall then appeared on stage and sang part of Shine. —RYAN DANYEW

➢ Auld Lang Syne! I was fortunate to be in a suite for this show—drinking champagne and spraying it onto my fellow phans was a complete and joyous experience. —ROB RIMER

➢ If I have to pick one sequence of songs that showcases Phish at their very, very best, it would be the Auld Lang Syne > Weekapaug > Sea and Sand run from the third set of their MSG New Year's masterpiece. Moving from Auld Lang Syne into Weekapaug, the band's energy is incredible. They develop a jam in Weekapaug that is so powerful, so gorgeous, that I am overcome with emotion every time I hear it. Eventually, it drops into a piano solo, and Page starts singing the wonderfully moving Sea and Sand. —SCOTT SIFTON

1996 Spring *JAZZ/JOYOUS*

The winter of 1996 saw Phish disappoint its fans by calling off a tour which had been tentatively slated for the spring. Instead, they headed into the studio to record *Billy Breathes.* Phish's only scheduled performance as a band came at the New Orleans Jazz & Heritage Festival on April 26, a one-set quickie which was more remarkable for the number of Phish fans who made the pilgrimage to Louisiana than for its musical content. Later that spring, after visiting the Joyous Lake club in Woodstock, NY while recording *Billy Breathes* nearby, Phish decided to put on a secret show. Several hundred fans lucky enough to be tipped off showed up early to secure their entrance to the 200-person club, which was filled well beyond legal limit by the time the band took the stage around 11 p.m. The surprise show that many expected to someday grace the stage at Nectar's had finally happened.

1996

70 Total Show Dates
- **14** one-set shows
- **51** two-set shows
- **5** three-set shows

PHAN PICKS 1996

SHOW	THE SKINNY
1) **08/16/96 Plattsbugh, NY**	First night of the Clifford Ball.
2) 12/06/96 Las Vegas, NV	Primus and Elvii join encore.
3) 10/31/96 Atlanta, GA	*Remain in Light* on Halloween.
4) 08/17/96 Plattsburgh, NY	Ben and Jerry at the Ball.
5) 12/31/96 Boston, MA	Gospel choir for Bohemian.
6) 08/13/96 Noblesville, IN	Great from start to finish.
7) 06/06/96 Woodstock, NY	The surprise club show.
8) 04/25/96 New Orleans, LA	Jazzfest, with Michael Ray.
9) 10/23/96 Hartford, CT	Bob Gullotti joins for 2nd set.
10) 11/15/96 St. Louis, MO	The "M" set, with Popper.

MUSICAL RECAP: In a transitional stage of sorts between 1995's trademark Phish jamming and 1997's funk, the band played around with a bunch of different ideas. Some jams, like those played with Karl Perazzo on his mini-tour around Halloween, gave a hint of things to come. Others, like the Bathtub Gin from 11/7/96, showed the band's willingness to try many different themes and ideas all in the course of the same jam.

REPRESENTATIVE JAMS: Bathtub Gin, 11/7/96; Crosseyed and Painless, 11/2/96; Down with Disease, 8/16/96; Mike's Groove, 12/6/96.

ORIGINAL SONG DEBUTS: Character Zero (6/6/96), Mid-Highway Blues (11/23/96), Swept Away > Steep (10/16/96), Talk (8/5/96), Train Song (7/21/96), Waste (6/6/96)

COVER SONG DEBUTS: Bohemian Rhapsody (12/31/96), Mean Mr. Mustard (11/15/96), Sixteen Candles (12/29/96), The Star Spangled Banner (10/17/96), We're an American Band (11/16/96), and all of *Remain In Light* (10/31/96)

DARK HORSES

SHOW	THE SKINNY
1) **11/02/96 West Palm, FL**	C&P > Antelope is just nuts.
2) 11/30/96 Sacramento, CA	Horn and banjo join Phish.
3) 11/27/96 Seattle, WA	Tweezer > DWD Reprise.
4) 08/06/96 Morrison, CO	Electricity at Red Rocks.
5) 10/29/96 Tallahassee, FL	Perazzo's first night.

Most-Played Originals:

1) Taste	28	40%
2) Sample in a Jar	26	37%
3) You Enjoy Myself	23	33%
4) Chalk Dust Torture	22	31%
5) Character Zero	21	30%
5) Poor Heart	21	30%
5) Sparkle	21	30%
8) Down with Disease	20	29%
8) Runaway Jim	20	29%
8) Stash, Theme	20	29%

Most-Played Covers:

1) Ya Mar	19	27%
2) Hello My Baby	17	24%
3) Also Sprach	16	23%
4) A Day in the Life	15	21%
5) Funky Bitch	14	20%
6) Life on Mars	10	14%
7) Fire	9	13%
7) Sweet Adeline	9	13%
7) Timber Ho	9	13%
10) Star Spg. Banner	8	11%

First-Set Openers:

1) Chalk Dust Torture	8
1) Runaway Jim	8
3) Ya Mar	6
4) My Friend My Friend	5
4) Wilson	5

Second-Set Openers:

1) Also Sprach Zarathustra	7
2) AC/DC Bag	4
2) Down With Disease	4
2) Timber Ho	4
5) Bowie, Curtain, Jim	3

Top Henrietta Songs:

1) Purple Rain	3
2) Bike	2
2) Suspicious Minds	2
4) Cracklin' Rosie	1
4) Terrapin	1

A Cappella Songs:

1) Hello My Baby	17
2) Sweet Adeline	9
3) Star Spangled Banner	8
4) Amazing Grace	6
5) Carolina	1

4/26/96 [ACCESSIBILITY: ••••]
The Fairgrounds, New Orleans, LA
Ya Mar, AC/DC Bag, Sparkle, Stash, CTB, YEM > Wolfman's, Scent of a Mule, Also Sprach > Harry Hood, Sample, Day in the Life, Bowie
E: Hello My Baby, Cavern

New Orleans Jazz & Heritage Festival. Phish played one set on the main concert stage, preceding the Meters. "When the Saints Come Marching In" tease in Ya Mar. Michael Ray on trumpet for CTB. A cappella start to Wolfman's. "Caravan" tease in Bowie.

➢ All the heads at Jazzfest created a great atmosphere—everyone seemed really proud of the boys for being invited to play. But the long layoff showed as Trey was especially sloppy. Most songs were short versions that remained true to form. Michael Ray on CTB and the YEM > a cappella Wolfman's opening were highlights. Bourbon Street was a madhouse. Best time I've ever had in New Orleans. —TREVOR NORRIS

➢ This CTB is not to be missed. Michael Ray comes out and tears the whole place apart. Ya Mar is also great with a Saints Go Marching In tease. —MICHAEL ROTKOWITZ

➢ Upon listening to the Jazzfest tape, I was severely disappointed by the band's completely flat performance. Phish seemed to play the songs like it was their job, not their love. A particular lowpoint is the end of Harry Hood—what is usually a superb buildup falls flat. The only redeeming feature of this show is Michael Ray's performance on CTB. —PETE MORSE

➢ During David Bowie, Trey licks in a little "Caravan" just for the festival! Then, whoever introduces the band at the end of the encore goes through their names correctly, but when he gets to Fishman, "on drums, Fishman Jon" is what he says. —ERIC SHAW

➢ The rain at the end of Cavern was awesome! —ERIN FERRIS

6/6/96 [ACCESSIBILITY: •••••]
Joyous Lake, Woodstock, NY
I: Melt, Poor Heart, Runaway Jim, Funky Bitch, Theme From the Bottom, BBFCM, Scent of a Mule, Highway to Hell
II: AC/DC Bag, YEM, Chalkdust, Sparkle, Stash, Waste, Character Zero, Bowie, Fee > Sample **E:** Ya Mar, Fire

Unannounced show; Phish played under the name "Third Ball." Juan Hung Low opened. Soundcheck: Funky Bitch, Taste, Waste. "Wilson" tease in Runaway Jim. Trey used a beer bottle as a slide in BBFCM. "Cocaine" tease in Scent of a Mule, with Trey on keyboard for part of the jam. Waste cut short because it didn't have an ending yet. Concert debuts: Waste, Character Zero.

➢ Having attended this show, it will remain a part of my personal Phishtory forever. The sound pretty much sucked, as did all the wannabe fans. But we hung out with Page for 45 minutes during Juan Hung Low's set and no one recognized him. Just being there was the greatest highlight. —RIC HANNAH

➢ The surprise gig. Only a precious few got to enjoy this one, but boy do I wish I was one of them—just like the old days, up close and personal. And you can hear it in the music: AC/DC Bag and YEM in the second set are perfect, then comes the debut of Waste, which Fishman dubs "no ending" because Trey tells the crowd the song doesn't have an ending yet. During the Character Zero debut, Fishman again chimes in with, "This is better than Machine Gun," which was requested by an audience member. Truly another page in the Phishtory book. —PETER BUKLEY

➢ This is the best show I own. You can tell it was played in a bar from the crispness of the vocals, music and audience. —BRENT BAKER

1996 Summer/Europe

The first time Phish toured Europe, it was summer '92, and the band played several weeks of shows, most as opening act for The Violent Femmes. To say the match wasn't made in heaven would be an understatement—at the Phish/Femmes show in Paris, one Femme fan stood with his back towards Phish and his middle index finger raised in the air for Phish's entire set. The band later wondered why they'd been in such a rush to get over there.

Summer 1996 offered Phish the chance to go back to Europe, again to serve primarily as an opening act. But their tour partner this time was old friend Carlos Santana, promising a friendlier reception. Phish actually considered not including the European tour information in the newsletter or on the hotline, in the name of building new audiences. But that, it was decided, would have really sucked.

The tour didn't see as much on-stage collaboration between the two bands as there had been in '92, though Phish did sit in with Santana, and vice-versa.

For Phish, the tour served as a chance to promote a newly-released European CD, *Stash*, a greatest-hits kind of disc with tracks drawn from previous Phish albums. As a result, most of their sets opening for Santana saw certain songs appear over and over again. Phish managed to break free of that regimen by playing five solo shows, including their first gig in Amsterdam. That show, at the legendary 950-person capacity Melk Weg club, was by some accounts the toughest ticket in Phish history. The previous night's solo show at the Shepherd's Bush Empire in London, England, proved to be an easier ticket, and drew almost 1,000 local fan by some estimates. Phish had started catching on overseas.

[7/2/96]
Speedway Stadium, Lonigo, Italy

Opened for Santana. Phish's set was rained out, but Phish sat in with Santana during part of his set.

7/3/96 [ACCESSIBILITY: ••]
Stadia Brtamasco, Trento, Italy
Runaway Jim, Stash, Sparkle, Taste, Llama

Opened for Santana. Taste and Llama featured Carlos Santana and Karl Perazzo. Last Taste, 6/30/95 Mansfield, MA [64 shows].

7/5/96 [ACCESSIBILITY: ••]
Stadio Olympico, Rome, Italy
Funky Bitch, Chalkdust, AC/DC Bag, YEM, Scent of a Mule, Bowie
E: Adeline

Opened for Santana. Phish was soundchecking Funky Bitch when the venue doors opened, so they kept playing.

➢ My friends and I had been standing outside looking at the wares of the only hemp jewelry vendor when suddenly a familiar chord hit me like thunder. "Jesus, that's Funky Bitch!" I grabbed my bag and raced to the entrance. Once I got past the guards I realized there were only about 200 yards between the entrance to the stadium and the source of that sweet sound, and I fucking took off. I raced up the stairs and arrived at the floor where an enormous black stage was set up, with huge stacks of speakers on each side. And there they were—Page, Trey, Mike! There were maybe 25 fans in front of the stage with about 10,000 seats, bare, blue and without backs. The next thing I knew Chalkdust was hitting my face. I had been worried about a letdown because everyone said the Udine show was "short," but Phish never fails to amaze me. This night was just that good. —RUSSELL KAHN

7/6/96 [ACCESSIBILITY: •••]
Duomo Square, Pistoia, Italy
Also Sprach > Reba, Poor Heart, Day in the Life, Maze, Harry Hood

Opened for Santana.

7/7/96 [ACCESSIBILITY: ••]
Parco Aquatica, Milan, Italy
Sample, Divided Sky, Bouncing, Curtain > Tweezer, Adeline, Uncle Pen, Cavern, Antelope > Suzie

Opened for Santana.

7/9/96 [ACCESSIBILITY: ••]
Centre Internationale de Deauville, Deauville, France
Theme, Poor Heart, Taste, CTB, Mike's, Bouncing, Character Zero

Opened for Santana.

7/10/96 [ACCESSIBILITY: ••]
Le Zenith, Paris, France
Chalkdust, Ya Mar, Melt, Waste, Bowie, Hello My Baby, GTBT

Opened for Santana.

➢ When I sat down near the front of the stage, a young French boy with shoulder-length blond hair under a Phish cap sat down near me, smiled, and said "Bonjour." As it turned out, his name was Julian, his favorite band was Phish, and he had driven 330 kilometers (with his Dad) to see the show. I dubbed him the first French Phishhead! The kid was so pumped, getting high-fives from all around—and he was only sixteen! He had seen his first show the year before in New Jersey, and he owned one tape, which I identified as Sacramento 3/22/93. A friend of mine promised to send him more free of charge. When I imagine Julian playing Phish songs for his friends in the middle of France and another European friend dubbing the OJ show for his friends in Rome, I see the European network beginning. —RUSSELL KAHN

➢ Mike sang a verse of Ya Mar in French. His accent was so bad that several locals, when asked for a translation, said they couldn't make out a word he was saying. —SHEP WILLIAMS

7/11/96 [ACCESSIBILITY: ••••]
Shepherds Bush Empire, London, England
I: Runaway Jim, Cavern, Reba, I Didn't Know, Sparkle, Stash, Scent of a Mule, Sample
II: Harry Hood, Bouncing, Also Sprach > Maze, Lizards, HYHU > Terrapin > HYHU, YEM, Hello My Baby **E:** Day in the Life

Fishman on vacuum for I Didn't Know and Terrapin.

➢ The second set starts with a good Harry Hood. Page's piano in the beginning reggae part is very funky. The band plays nice transitions throughout the rest of Hood, going rapidly into Bouncing after the "You can feel good about Hood" refrain. A nice Also Sprach Zarathustra segues into a slowish Maze that's not as hectic as others. Fishman blows the vacuum on Terrapin, then a fairly basic YEM leads to a nice bass solo from Mike. Ragtime Gal closes out the set. The encore, A Day in the Life, gets a nice response in the home of the Beatles. —MIKE NOLL

➢The London show was a letdown. A Beatles encore was fitting in the heart of London, and the crowd exploded while I silently shook my head. You'd think after all the 45-minute sets they'd been playing, they'd be ready to go crazy. —RUSSELL KAHN

7/12/96 [ACCESSIBILITY: ••••]
Melkweg, Amsterdam, Netherlands
I: Wilson > Divided Sky, Horn, Melt, Ya Mar > Funky Bitch, Taste, Theme, Tweezer > Llama
II: It's Ice, Caspian > Mike's > Antelope, Purple Rain, Ska Groove Jam > NICU, Slave, Suzie
III: Bowie, Free, Hello My Baby **E:** Bathtub Gin, Johnny B. Goode
Antelope unfinished. "Ska Groove" Jam before NICU based on chords yelled out by audience members. Fishman on vacuum for Purple Rain.

➢ On paper, this show looks unbelievable, but actually, it's not that great. Something was definitely going on this night—the band sounds like they're practicing on their own, doing whatever they feel like. No song in the second set comes close to finishing. About a half of Slave is played and the encores are about the same length. Worth listening to as it's probably like no other show you've heard. —MATTHEW NAPOLI

➢ Although the band is not at their best musically, the smooth segues and crowd interaction make up for it. The band meanders through many of their best songs and even tries to make up a new one before going into NICU. Highlights are Ya Mar > Funky Bitch and the entire third set, as the boys rip it up. —JAMIS CURRAN

➢ The best thing about this show on tape is that you can tell this is a really small place. It sounds like the old days. —JONATHAN BANCO

7/13/96 [ACCESSIBILITY: ••]
The Dour Festival, Dour, Belgium
Sample, Runaway Jim, Cavern, Reba, Poor Heart, Melt, Fire, Funky Bitch, Chalkdust, YEM
Music festival featuring numerous bands, but not Santana. Phish played one set.

➢ This show (you can tell from the tapes) was a special one for the band. They do a little more chatting than normal on stage, emitting a friendly vibe. As far as the setlist goes, the band treated the foreigners to decent versions of Reba, SOAM and YEM (of course, these songs are always great). The ambiance of the whole European tour, which I was lucky enough to see, was similar to this show. —JOHN FOLEY

7/15/96 [ACCESSIBILITY: •••]
Lido La Marna, Sesto Calende, Italy
I: My Friend, PYITE, FEFY, Guyute, Possum, I Didn't Know, Harry Hood, Cavern
II: Down with Disease > Maze, Loving Cup, Makisupa > It's Ice > Julius, Purple Rain, Uncle Pen, Antelope **E:** Golgi
Fishman on vacuum for Purple Rain.

➢ I wasn't lucky enough to have been at the show, but a tape definitely does the job. The first set is filled with excellent songs including several surprises for the first set like Harry and Possum. But the second set proves they continued rocking with spacy jams and an always-audience pleasing Purple Rain. If that still wasn't enough, how about closing the second set with a full-jammed, energetic Antelope? —ADAM RIZZUTI

7/17/96 [ACCESSIBILITY: ••]
Theatre Antique, Vienne, France
Divided Sky, Sample, Bowie, Ya Mar, Funky Bitch
Opened for Santana.

7/18/96 [ACCESSIBILITY: ••]
Nice Jazz Festival, Nice, France
Julius, CTB, Bouncing, Stash, Hello My Baby, It's Ice, YEM
Opened for Santana.

7/19/96 [ACCESSIBILITY: ••]
Les Arenes, Arles, France
Runaway Jim, Foam, Adeline, Waste, Squirming Coil
Opened for Santana. Phish sat in with Santana for part of Santana's set.

Friday, July 12, 1996 Melk Weg, Amsterdam, Netherlands

Before the Phish show at the Melk Weg on Friday, my friend Joe and I sat outside at the Bullfrog and had a drink and a smoke with two of his friends. The girl at the table was holding the joint when the waiter came over and said, "I'm sorry, you'll have to finish that somewhere else." She apologized, took another drag and passed it to me. I hesitated and then said, "I thought he asked us not to smoke here." Everyone laughed. The waiter had been referring to her McDonald's milkshake!

Girl drinks shake and smokes joint at restaurant. Waiter asks girl to put shake away. Welcome to Amsterdam! This entire place reeks of bud. Every time you turn the corner the strong smell floats past your nose. The coffee shops are insane. I knew they would be, but I still can't get over it.

The show let in at about 10:00. The streets were filled with heads and hippies, most waving their fingers in the air. I knew that with a 950-person capacity, people were going to be shut out, so I kept checking my ticket to convince myself I was in. Phish in Amsterdam. The thought gave me chills.

My guess going into the show was that, while it would be a great deal of fun, it would not be Phish at their musical best—they'd be too fucked-up. Listen to the tape and you'll find that to be exactly true. The entire second set was chaos.

They played their first ska song... It's Ice morphed into Prince Caspian which melted into Mike's which found its way to Antelope. None of the songs was ever completed.

"Yell out a chord!" screamed Trey after "Purple Rain." He let the audience dominate the next song, "Ska Groove," whose only lyrics were, "Okay, we need some now"; and then stopped to plug in his cord, an action which Fish dubbed "the Trey-is-plugging-his-cord-in Jam." They were as random and fucked-up as I've ever seen them... The show ended at nearly 3:00 a.m, and I stumbled home at 4:00, seeing for the first time the beauty of Amsterdam. **—Russell Kahn**

Scenes from Europe Tour, July '96.

7/21/96 [ACCESSIBILITY: ••]
The Forum, Nurnburg, Germany
I: Golgi, Guelah, Rift, Tweezer, If I Could, My Mind's, Melt, Horse > Silent, Taste, Train Song, Fee > Timber Ho > Johnny B. Goode
II: Llama, Theme, Reba, Life on Mars, Free, Antelope, Simple, Caspian, Suzie **E:** Harry Hood
Concert debut: Train Song.

➢ Touring with Phish in Europe was a very intimate experience, reminiscent of the days when the band could be found hanging out around the venue before and after the show. Those of us traveling from one country to the next formed a small community, and plenty of friendships were made that continue to stand the test of time. The band payed tribute to that spirit on this night, when they dedicated the first-ever live performance of Train Song to those of us on tour. —AMY DUNCAN

7/22/96 [ACCESSIBILITY: ••]
Tanzbrunnen, Cologne, Germany
Sample, Poor Heart, Cavern, Maze, Bouncing, Stash, Day in the Life, YEM
Opened for Santana.

7/23/96 [ACCESSIBILITY: •••]
Markethalle, Hamburg, Germany
I: AC/DC Bag, Foam, Theme, Gumbo, Scent of a Mule > Down with Disease > McGrupp > Stash, Hello My Baby
II: Also Sprach > Runaway Jim, Loving Cup, Sparkle, Mike's > Hydrogen > Weekapaug, HYHU > Bike > HYHU, Slave **E:** Rocky Top
A cappella solo by Trey in Scent of a Mule. Fishman on vacuum for Bike. Last Hydrogen, 10/19/95 Kansas City, MO [61 shows].

➢ I heard the Markethalle held about 1,000 people, but in my estimate it couldn't have been more than six or seven hundred. It was a great venue with a low, close stage and a dance floor where everyone could see the band. There were elevated sides for great viewing, too. For the last solo show of the European tour, it had to be special. The first set was really, really good. I've never heard a Scent of a Mule so fierce. It was my third on the tour, and I was tired of the Fiddler on the Roof routine, but this time it really took off. Page and Trey had great communication and were the best I'd seen them in Europe. 2001 and Runaway Jim set the tone for the second set and led into Loving Cup, the song that had caused me to regret missing the Sesto Calende show—I never though they'd play it again. Phish did not disappoint. Backstage after the show, Page and I talked about the show and the tour. He said Hamburg was his favorite. —RUSSELL KAHN

➢ A promo poster in Hamburg included the words "Explosiv," "Virtuos" and "Cult" under the over-used Phish outdoors in the forest promotional photo. During the show, Trey looked at Page, Mike and Fish and shouted, "Explosiv! Virtuos! Cult!" —AMY DUNCAN

7/24/96 [ACCESSIBILITY: ••]
Music Hall, Hannover, Germany
Chalkdust, Ya Mar, Julius, YEM, Golgi
Opened for Santana.

7/25/96 [ACCESSIBILITY: ••]
Stadtpark, Hamburg, Germany
Poor Heart, PYITE, Sample, It's Ice > Antelope, Life on Mars, Harry Hood, Cavern
Opened for Santana.

1996 Summer/U.S. Tour

Returning from their month in Europe, Phish was rumored to be playing a surprise show for the Olympians in Atlanta before the start of their U.S. summer tour (no such show ever materialized). Instead, the band rested up for a week before embarking on their shortest summer tour ever—a slate of 11 gigs, starting only as far west as Utah and finishing with what promised to be an event like no other in Plattsburgh, NY.

The venues, familiar and unfamiliar, found Phish playing to crowds as small as 10,000 people at Wolf Mountain and upwards of 35,000 at Alpine Valley. Alpine Valley marked the band's biggest show ever, until the next weekend when The Clifford Ball drew 75,000 people each day to northern New York State.

At three stops on the tour—Red Rocks, Deer Creek and the Clifford Ball—Phish treated audiences to acoustic mini-sets featuring material recorded during the *Billy Breathes* sessions, plus old friend Strange Design.

Another old friend, Red Rocks, hosted Phish's first four-night run at the same venue in this decade. When a riot involving several hundred ticketless fans in the nearby town of Morrison, CO made front-page news in Denver, however, the last two nights of the Red Rocks run turned into a farewell party to one of the most beautiful places to hear live music in the country. Happily, the bad vibes disappeared by the time of the Clifford Ball, which drew thousands of people from all over the country—fitting, for the largest concert event in North America in 1996.

8/2/96 [ACCESSIBILITY: ••••]
Wolf Mountain, Park City, UT
I: Ya Mar, Down with Disease, Guelah, Poor Heart, Foam, Theme, Golgi, Tweezer, Hello My Baby, Possum
II: Runaway Jim, Simple, Taste, Free, Fluffhead, Caspian, Horse > Silent, Antelope **E:** PYITE
Page on theremin for a "Somewhere Over the Rainbow" jam before Ya Mar.

➢ Minutes prior to Phish's entrance, a double rainbow appeared on the horizon behind the stage. When they came out, Page wove a few notes of "Somewhere Over the Rainbow" on theremin. Down with Disease jammed long and solid as a prelude to its fall development. The tunes complemented each other well, and Mike's bass work was dominant from start to finish. Runaway Jim included a Dog Log tease (I think) and Antelope had a "Star Wars" tease from Trey. —ANTHONY BUCHLA

➢ Somewhere Over the Rainbow—a great opener after viewing two full rainbows over the stage. Ya Mar was very upbeat, filled with Mike's howls and yells, but the Foam was different, almost on a slower beat. This show also features the first Prince Caspian they played with the new beginning heard on *Billy Breathes*. PYITE was an odd but exhilarating encore. —ERIN FERRIS

➢ Wolf Mountain is a great place to see a show. Tucked into the base of a small ski hill, the amphitheater looks out over a ski lodge behind the stage to the valley beyond. It's an intimate venue, almost quaint in comparison to some of the fortresses Phish would play later in the tour. The ultimate Phish sunny-skies opener, Ya Mar, brought cheers from the lawn as the band got the groove going. From there, the set progressed like the first set of most tour openers: the band committed lots of little musical miscues, the song selection didn't bowl anyone over, and yet we were thrilled to be hearing Phish live again. The second set saw the American debuts of the reworked Taste and Prince Caspian, and there was Fluffhead: as its opening notes rang out, we found ourselves swamped in a wave of joyous screaming, people delighted and thrilled to be up on the mountain. —LOCK STEELE

8/4/96 [ACCESSIBILITY: ••••]
Red Rocks Amphitheatre, Morrison, CO
I: Chalkdust, Funky Bitch, Guyute, Fee, Melt, Mango, Sloth, Maze, Loving Cup
II: AC/DC Bag > Reba > Scent of a Mule, Sample, Bowie, Adeline, Slave
E: Rocky Top
Page on theremin for a "Star Trek Theme" jam before Rocky Top.

➢ Ahhh! Back at the good ole Red Rocks of Colorado. I'm so glad I made it back for Phish's last stand here, and what a fat show they pulled out to kick off the four-day stand. With a Chalkdust opener through the most intense Maze I've ever heard, I was again shocked by the musical prowess the band displayed. The first set closer, Loving Cup, really torqued on my alternate reality helmet. I'm truly sad Phish won't be back here—a beautiful venue plus a smokin' show equalled a perfect time. —WILLIAM THURSTON

➢ The first-night setlist was filled with random song choices probably meant to throw us off. Trey wore a Grinch t-shirt (from Dr. Seuss) which was funny. A good show to open up for four nights at Red Rocks, which is a beautiful place for a show. The atmosphere was great. —MELANIE AND MELITA TERRELL

➢ My first show at the Rocks. Extreme energy raged between the band and the crowd, and the setlist was stellar: Funky Bitch and Guyute in the first three songs proves that. Overall, from the time I hit the line at 4:20 to get in, to the marshmallow fights, Red Rocks will always be my favorite arena, and these shows one of the best experiences of my life. —GEOFF LYNCH

8/5/96 [ACCESSIBILITY: ••••]
Red Rocks Amphitheatre, Morrison, CO
I: Wilson, Poor Heart, Guelah, Divided Sky, Wolfman's, Foam, If I Could, Julius, Squirming Coil
II: Also Sprach, Down with Disease > It's Ice, Halley's, Waste, Talk, Train Song, Strange Design, Amazing Grace, Mike's > Hydrogen > Weekapaug
E: Cavern
Page on theremin for a "Somewhere Over the Rainbow" jam at the end of Halley's. Acoustic mini-stage featured Trey on acoustic guitar, Mike on acoustic bass, Fishman on a smaller drumset and Page on a smaller piano for Waste, Talk, Train Song and Strange Design. Concert debut: Talk, and the mini-stage.

➢ Of course every Red Rocks show is great in its own way. The setlist of this one is one of my favorites, including Halley's Comet into Somewhere Over the Rainbow, with Page on the very odd-sounding theremin, and Waste. What's unique about this show is the four acoustic songs: Waste, Talk, Train Song and Strange Design, performed on a mini stage with acoustic instruments. Page even left the baby grand and was banging keys on an upright. There's also a cool solo jam by Page and a great Mike's, which makes every show! —RYAN SATZ

➢ In the middle of Divided Sky, Trey stopped playing and everyone sat down and took a rest, an idea suggested by the "crowd participation flyers" circulated around by Phish.Net fans. —MELANIE AND MELITA TERRELL

➢ I have always wanted to hear Phish play If I Could in concert, but I never thought I would. That songs means so much to me, so when I heard them play it, I was in heaven. It was the most amazing song I have ever heard Phish play. —MELISSA KELLER

On The Rocks

8/4-7/96 Red Rocks Amphitheater, Morrison, CO

It was the best of times, it was the worst of times. When Phish announced their U.S. summer tour schedule, fans were shocked to find that the band planned only 11 North American dates. Four of those 11, however, were scheduled for Red Rocks, a venue with a very special rock history and Phish history. Since the band's inaugural show on the Rocks in August '93, the band had twice returned for two-night stands. Now, they planned to do four in a row, and fans from all over the country—somehow sensing that seeing Phish in a beautiful state park with only 9,500 other phriends might be too good to last forever—booked their plane tickets and gassed up their vans.

Those who feared Phish had already outgrown Red Rocks cited the previous year's growing pains, when police unleashed tear gas on an unruly crowd outside the venue. To counteract ticketless fans swarming the tiered parking lots of the venue and attempting to climb their way in, promoter Barry Fey closed Red Rocks Park to all non-concert goers.

Ticketless fans lined the highway to the venue, but once in the lots, it appeared the policy of keeping out the ticketless had been, for the most part, successful. A wonderfully relaxed parking lot scene developed, and most sensed that they were sharing the occasion with fans who'd gone Phishing more than a few times before. License plates from Maine, Florida and Alaska were spotted.

The first two nights came off without a hitch—Phish played well, and the scenery was as grand as everyone remembered. But while fans danced to a great Mike's Groove on night two, hundreds (some say thousands) of ticketless fans unable to gain access to the park massed two miles away in Morrison, CO, population 450. The situation clearly was already a little tense when a 21-year-old woman was hit by a pickup truck on Morrison's main drag around 8:30 p.m.

What happened next remains a source of controversy. According to the Denver media, when EMTs and police arrived at the scene to help the girl, their efforts were blocked by fans who planned to heal her holistically, or "purify the body," as one cop later told the *Rocky Mountain News*. The injured girl was eventually taken to an area hospital and treated for minor injuries, but the police seized on the incident and attempted to clear fans out of Morrison. Then things turned ugly. "Hell no, we won't go," the crowd chanted, some throwing bottles at police officers in the fight that followed.

The media went to town with the story. "Rock Fans Battle Police: 12 Arrested, Morrison Shut Down After Phish Crowd Refuses to Leave," blared the *News* in a front-page banner headline. The "disturbance," as the *News* referred to it, easily caught the attention of the Denver media who showed up at Red Rocks on Monday night to put together predictable articles on "hippies invading Red Rocks."

Of course, the 9,500 fans at the show knew nothing of the riot until they picked up newspapers the next morning. Phish took the stage on Tuesday night all smiles, despite the media blitz, and opened with Makisupa Policeman. Whether Phish meant the song as a statement about the Morrison incident was intentionally left vague, but later in the first set Trey did reference the melée. The *News* article about the Morrison incident quoted an individual identified as "21-year-old Marcus Esquandolis" shouting "You are slime!" at police officers during the standoff. During the Antelope lyric segment, Trey changed the "Marco Esquandolis" line to "21-year-old Phish fan Marcus Esquandolis," cracking up himself and the audience.

That night's show soared. As storm clouds moved in near the end of the first set, mist whipped around the venue during Lizards, engulfing the band in a fog not of their own making. This awe-inspiring sight was topped in set two when the skies opened during an electric BBFCM and Phish, charged up on their own energy and that of Mother Nature, tore into the song as rain and wind swept the amphitheater. Purple Rain and an emotional Harry Hood made the show one for the ages.

By the next day, Red Rocks promoter Barry Fey was on the front page of the *Post* stating the obvious: Phish had outgrown Red Rocks. So all the fans headed for the final night's gig knew they were probably going to witness Phish's last-ever show at Red Rocks. The atmosphere in the lot was playful but reflective, which seemed to be the band's mood, too. During Ya Mar in the first set, Trey remarked, "I want to tell you guys what an incredible time we had the last four nights. I will never forget it, and I hope you feel the same way." As the crowd cheered, he added, "This place is beautiful—I hope we can come back."

The band's final show at Red Rocks might not have achieved the heights of some of their previous engagements there, but when Trey referenced the giant iguana during a Forbin's rap in the second set, it was a nod to the band's own history—the famous Harpua of '93.

The biggest irony of the whole stand might have been that the Morrison incident may not have really happened the way most of the news media said it did. Reporter Michael Roberts of the weekly *Denver Westword* paper visited Morrison several weeks after the incident and interviewed the townsfolk. In response to the so-called "purifying the body" of the injured woman, one Red Rocks Grille staffer told Roberts, "I don't know where they got that from. I was right there, and that never happened." Another Grille staffer added, "Based on what I saw, everything in the papers was fiction."

The staffers related a very different view of the events to Roberts. After the woman was knocked down by the pickup truck, people—including an EMT and a doctor—rushed to the girl's side. A crowd gathered to watch and, when asked to take a step back, all complied, with the exception of two angry fans who jumped into the pickup truck and started jumping up and down. When police tried to haul the kids out of the truck, someone threw a bottle at the cops. "It was an isolated incident," a staffer told Roberts. But police used the incident to shut down the street, and things grew worse from there. Roberts concluded, "Reporters did their best to turn the incident into a skankier version of Riot on Sunset Strip." Phish and their fans paid the price.

➢ After an excellent second set start of 2001 > DwD > Ice > Halley's, Page moved to theremin while the rest of the band, joined by crew hands, pushed back Trey and Mike's cabinets to slide forward something that had been hidden under a tarp. When the lights came up, there stood two stools, a mini-drum kit and a standup piano. Trey relieved our curiosity: "We're taking this opportunity to play you guys some songs off the album we just recorded." After this sweet acoustic interlude—the first time they ever used the acoustic mini-stage—I was surprised and pleased when the boys cranked up Mike's Song. Like the DwD earlier in the set, the Mike's jam rose then flattened several times. The jamming, straight ahead as Mike's Songs go, was nevertheless spirited and forceful. The Weekapaug jam was similarly standard at first until Trey got a neat riff going, fast and sweet. Fish joined in, his drumming setting a relentless pace. The jam didn't wander for long before returning to the Weekapaug theme, then the band left the stage to tremendous applause. This was my favorite set of the '96 Red Rocks stand. —LOCK STEELE

8/6/96 [ACCESSIBILITY: ••••]
Red Rocks Amphitheatre, Morrison, CO
I: Makisupa, Rift, Suzie, Simple, Theme, Lizards, Dinner and a Movie, Horn, Antelope
II: Curtain > Tweezer, Caspian, Day in the Life, BBFCM, Purple Rain, Harry Hood > Tweezer Reprise **E:** Johnny B. Goode
"Simple" tease in Suzie. "21-year-old Phish fan Marcus Esquandolis" lyrics in Antelope. "Norweigan Wood" jam in Tweezer. Crowd-participation flyers got the crowd to shout "Hood!" after each "Harry" the band sang.

➢ The debate as to which Red Rocks show was the best will go on forever, but this is my choice, hands-down. A wonderful first set with some real crowd pleasers, but the real action took place in set II, when ominous thunderclouds approached the theater, and Phish seemed to feed off the energy created by the lighting behind them. Curtain was followed by an utterly blistering Tweezer, without a doubt one of the best ever, one which accomplished that level without veering away from the basics of the song all that much. They just rocked it. When the thunder turned into a downpour during BBCFM, Phish caught the cue and went into Purple Rain, with Chris shining purple lights into the sheets of water. Then came an unforgettable, emotionally charged Harry Hood. On some tapes you can here the rain hitting umbrellas, and it's not a distraction, it's perfection. —ANDY BERNSTEIN

➢ They rocked the mountain with an amazing Hood—this was the first show where all the crowd screamed "Hood" after "Harry," and Trey gave us thumbs-up for that. We all felt like there was no other place in the world we would rather be. —MICHELLE HIRSCH

➢ Makisupa opener was in context after the police fucked with everyone in Morrison. The complete focus of this show was the second set. In a couple of words, it was totally insane. During BBFCM, Trey ran around the stage (I mean, he did laps). A thunderstorm came in and the band played Purple Rain. Harry Hood with "Hood" chants proved the crowd participation flyers worked. Lightning flashes caused everyone to cheer. —MORGAN LASTER

➢ The marshmallow fight before the show was a trip. —JOE GALBRAITH

8/7/96 [ACCESSIBILITY: •••]
Red Rocks Amphitheatre, Morrison, CO
I: PYITE, Sparkle, Stash, Ya Mar, Gumbo, Taste, Lawn Boy, 99 Years, Ode to a Dream, Doin' My Time
II: Runaway Jim, Free, Forbin's > Mockingbird, Possum, Life on Mars, YEM, Hello My Baby **E:** Bouncing, Golgi
Tim O'Brien on mandolin and vocals for 99 Years and acoustic guitar and vocals for Ode to a Dream and Doin' My Time. "Gypsy Queen" jam in Runaway Jim.

➢ For the last show, anticipation ran high. According to news reports, this would be Phish's last performance here. The music was good but not anything crazy. Mandolin player Tim O'Brien served up some hot bluegrass in the first set, while the second set featured a nice Runaway Jim opener and Forbin > Mockingbird. Possum was fun to hear, but the encore was not because I hate Bouncing and Golgi. I guess they were waiting for Clifford Ball with the goods. —MORGAN LASTER

➢ Probably tired by now, the band staggered over this one. PYITE and Ya Mar get things rolling, and it was nice to hear Gumbo. First set ends with bluegrass legend Tim O'Brien on mandolin. In the second set, Runaway Jim is stellar, and Trey reminds us of the Red Rocks iguana in Col. Forbin's. After nice jamming in Possum, the rest of the set kind of drags along. —CHARLIE GUBMAN

➢ Forbin's > giant iguana > Mockingbird rekindled sentimental memories for those of us at the 1993 Red Rocks show. —JAKE HUNTER

➢ When everyone was in the parking lot before the show, a group passed out sparklers to everyone for when Phish played Sparkle. When the band pulled it out for the second song of the night, and I would say over half of those at Red Rocks lit up their sparklers. It was pretty cool. —MELISSA KELLER

8/10/96 [ACCESSIBILITY: ••••]
Alpine Valley, East Troy, WI
I: My Friend, Poor Heart, AC/DC Bag, Fee, Reba, I Didn't Know, Horse > Silent, Rift, Bathtub Gin, Cavern
II: Wilson, Down with Disease, Scent of a Mule, Free, Fluffhead, HYHU > Whipping Post > HYHU, Harry Hood, Day in the Life **E:** Contact, Fire
Fishman on vacuum for I Didn't Know. "Gypsy Queen" jam in Bathtub Gin.

➢ The sound where my seats were located (eighth row in front of Mike) was horrible—bad venue acoustics in general along with plenty of feedback. The band seemed pretty beat at Alpine, not really enthused about playing. It was the most local crowd of the summer, more of a beerfest to most; the only song most of them were interested in during set one was Silent. The only real show highlight was the revival of Whipping Post. (There was also a 14- or 15-year-old kid a few seats down from me holding a micro-cassette recorder in the air, telling people to be quiet around his tape deck.) —JASON DEZIEL

➢ The whole second set was smoking. I'll single out the comic relief portion of the show when Fishman took center stage and Trey (on drums) led the band through Hold Your Head Up. As they finished, Fishman bowed and Trey started HYHU again. Fishman looked at Trey and said, "All right, thank you," and "Thank you so much," then Trey started HYHU again. It was most humorous. When Fish finally got to sing, he chose Whipping Post, a version that rivals the shrieking rendition from 12/5/92 Chicago. —RUSSELL LANE

➢ Alpine Valley floored me by its sheer size. The sea of fans on the lawn by showtime looked incredible—35,000 phans in the middle of dairy country! The early part of the second set had hints of brilliance—the DWD jam, and a vocal jam by Trey in lieu of the guitar duel in Scent—but it wasn't until the Fishman song that things got crazy. After a long HYHU interval, Fishman started Whipping Post, the first in ages and a real treat. After the song, Trey pointed to Fish and said, "Ladies and gentlemen, the Dork!" That referenced a bootleg t-shirt Trey was wearing which had a photo of Fishman on the front and "The Dork" printed on the back. "Best t-shirt I've seen in 13 years," Trey told us, adding, "Sorry, Amy." Before the encore, the sea of lighters that floated above the lawn in tribute seemed, like the Harry Hood moments before, impossibly large. —LOCK STEELE

8/12/96 [ACCESSIBILITY: •••]
Deer Creek Amphitheatre, Noblesville, IN
I: Ya Mar, Melt, Esther, Chalkdust, Weigh, It's Ice, Dog Faced Boy, Taste, Oh Kee > Suzie
II: Timber Ho, Sparkle, Simple, Caspian > McGrupp, Antelope, Hello My Baby, Golgi, Possum **E:** Sample
"Voodoo Child" tease in Possum intro.

➢ The beautiful two-day stand started with Ya Mar into a worthy Split Open. Then Esther, which just tickled my body and soul. Weigh into It's Ice fit just right. The Suzie set closer also was great—I danced out of my shoes and found myself screaming. High points in the second set for me were McGrupp, Antelope and Possum. —BRIAN HART

➢ The opener, Ya Mar, was fun, but the rarely-played Esther and Weigh were set highlights—the selection seemed so unpredictable but so perfect. Timber Ho to kick off set II was unforgettable, but McGrupp and Antelope topped it off. Before Possum, Trey used Phish's secret on-stage language to produce a Simpson's theme into a "D'oh!" and a scene where the band drops limp over their instruments, then revives and resumes Possum's introduction. —BRIAN BOEHM

➢ We had never been to Deer Creek, so that's where we drove to instead of Noblesville. We were late but caught the second set and a good laugh. —DAVID OKIMOTO

8/13/96 [ACCESSIBILITY: ••••]
Deer Creek Amphitheatre, Nobelsville, IN
I: Divided Sky, Tube, Tela, Maze, FEFY, Old Home Place, PYITE, Llama, Glide, Slave
II: AC/DC Bag, Lizards, Mike's > Lifeboy > Weekapaug, Waste, Train Song, Strange Design, Adeline, Bowie **E:** Sleeping Monkey, Rocky Top
Short jam before AC/DC Bag. Page on theremin for a "Somewhere Over the Rainbow" jam out of Weekapaug. Acoustic mini-stage featured Trey on acoustic guitar, Mike on acoustic bass, Fishman on a smaller drumset and Page on a smaller piano for Waste, Train Song and Strange Design. Last Glide, 11/21/95 Winston-Salem, NC [51 shows].

➢ There is nothing like gettin' down in the middle of a cornfield somewhere in Indiana. I had a soul-cleansing show that I can't wait to tell my grandchildren about. Even my pet peeve, Sleeping Monkey, was enhanced by the singing of a beautiful voice coming from a nearby girl. I never even saw her face—I didn't have to. —COLM CONNELL

➢ If you were at this show, you really got your money's worth. Not only was it totally jammed out, but it was nice and long. The Slave was an absolute epic! The changes were flawless with Trey just wailing and Page answering with a delicate piano roll—back and forth until I thought Trey's guitar would just melt. —RUSSELL LANE

➢ The second set was the raw essence of the "take it to the top, drop it off and reel it back up" theory. From beginning to end, it is truly explosive, tight and absolutely unpredictable. —WAYLON BAYARD

➢ I can easily say this is in the top five Phish shows I have heard or attended. But being detoured out of the parking lot and through a drug checkpoint after the show really snapped my head back into reality after narrowly getting through. People were getting searched for no reason except for the way they looked. —JASON DEZIEL

➢ This first set is something dreams are made of. —JOSH HARMAN

8/14/96 [ACCESSIBILITY: ••••]
Hershey Park Arena, Hershey, PA
I: Wilson > Down with Disease, Fee > Poor Heart, Reba, Mango, Gumbo, Stash, Hello My Baby
II: Runaway Jim > YEM, Horse > Silent, CTB, Tweezer, Theme, HYHU > Cracklin' Rosie > HYHU, Sample > Tweezer Reprise **E:** Julius

➢ This show just screams average—pitifully low on improv, the signature of any great show. The only real jams I felt myself melting for were the opening Wilson > Down with Disease segue that whipped the crowd into a frenzy, and the jam in Tweezer. The rest of the show seemed to be just up-tempo version of album songs, rushed in one after another. —AARON GROSSBERG

➢ This is one of very few shows that I just don't care for. It's unfortunate to hear such an average show at such a great venue. —JOSH HALMAN

➢ The Wilson opener wasn't completely finished—instead, Phish went into a weird jam that had everyone confused. It's definitely worth getting a copy of this show to hear it. Reba is another highlight: Trey mimicked a little baby that was sitting on the mother's shoulders in the audience. Everyone got a good laugh out of it as the band continued a solid and tight performance of this song. —TIM HERRMAN

➢ Not the most pleasant show to attend, given the fact that horrible traffic jams snarled the roads leading to the venue. But on tape, this show is the hidden gem of the '96 summer tour. Excellent jamming in Down With Disease, Reba and especially Tweezer make this a show worth acquiring. —ERNIE GREENE

[8/15/96]
Soundcheck, Clifford Ball, Plattsburgh Air Force Base, Plattsburgh, NY
Page and Trey noodle as they enter the stage area, Long blues jam > long funk jam, HYHU > slow Tweezer Reprise > HYHU, Old Home Place, slow Little Drummer Boy (LDB) Jam, LDB jam 2 > LDB/Frankenstein jam (Mike introduced Frankenstein theme on bass) > LDB/Frankenstein Jam 2 > LDB/Frankenstein Jam 3 > Frank/Spock's Brain jam > Frankenstein/Spock's jam 2 > vocal: "Deep in the Heart of Texas!", Clifford Ball jam (as named by Trey in the jam), Clifford Ball/slow Peaches En Regalia jam > Tweezer Reprise Reprise (Page introduced Rep on piano)
Soundcheck ran from about 9:00 p.m. to about 9:55 p.m.

➢ The single most significant event for me at the Clifford Ball, musically, was the soundcheck Thursday night. Tapers were scarcely to be found, but it drew most of the campsite dwellers to the fence to hear a one-set practice session. As I recall, after they played Old Home Place, the audience cheered so loudly that the band could hear it from the half-mile (or so) away that they were. During the Little Drummer Boy jam that followed, Paul turned the PA up and Chris started doing the huge lights over the wall towards the crowd, acknowledging that they had a HUGE, FULLY-ATTENTIVE audience a HALF MILE away. My friend Michael Sauda and I began discussing and scribbling the list as soon as we realized they were soundchecking. The setlist above is what we came up with from start to finish. The titles are somewhat arbitrary—we define the jams as we hear popular Phish themes occurring and overlapping in the jam. —DAVE SCHALL

8/16/96 [ACCESSIBILITY: •••••]
The Clifford Ball, Plattsburgh Air Force Base, Plattsburgh, NY
I: Chalkdust, Bathtub Gin, Ya Mar, AC/DC Bag, Esther, Divided Sky, Halley's, Bowie
II: Melt, Sparkle, Free, Squirming Coil, Waste, Talk, Train Song, Strange Design, Hello My Baby, Mike's > Simple > Contact > Weekapaug
III: Makisupa, Also Sprach > Down with Disease > NICU, Life on Mars, Harry Hood > Fireworks Jam **E:** Amazing Grace
Acoustic mini-stage featured Trey on acoustic guitar, Mike on acoustic bass, Fishman on a smaller drumset and Page on a smaller piano for Waste, Talk, Train Song and Strange Design. Fireworks during Harry Hood and into Fireworks jam.

Phan Pick #4 ➢ The best weekend of my life, hanging out with old friends, new friends, seeing Phish outside while the sun was setting, battling to keep your spot in front of the stage was just an awesome experience. Six full sets, with festivities! It was controlled chaos. The best Phish experience to date. —ERIC HIGEL

➢ Is this Phishstock? What is going on here? Over 70,000 fans, and possibly one of the best shows ever. —DAVID ECKERS

➢ Could anyone have realized that a small, jamming band from Vermont with no media attention could attract 75,000 fans for the largest concert in North America in 1996? I don't think even the band conceived of that. They certainly didn't provide enough camping space, and water was miles away (thank god for mist tents!), but for the largest Phish concert in history the band offered fired-up versions of Disease, Hood and Weekapaug that will go down in the annals of history as some of their best. Me? My friends and I sat on top of the hill by Ball Square, taking all of this in. Information overload! —LEE SCHILLER

➢ As 70,000 people packed in, Phish kicked off the two-day festival with a kick-ass first set featuring a hot AC/DC jam, then an extended silent jam during Divided played to an incredible sunset (Fish faked the cymbal, then they finally kicked into the jam). They later played a long and amazing second set, treating us to some of their new songs acoustic, a quick a cappella and then a phatty Mike's > Simple > Contact > Weekapaug. The third set kept right up with a crazy 2001 > DwD plus a fireworks display after Hood. —RYAN DANYEW

➢ In the third set, I experienced Phishtacy—every note clicked with my psyche and the fireworks sent me into outer space. Amazing Grace brought us back to earth to get us ready for the post-show partying. Too bad it took me an hour to find my tent! —IAN RUFE

➢ Harry Hood at the Clifford Ball changed my feelings about this song. Phish played it like it was the last song they were ever going to play. Of course, the fireworks were the icing on the cake. Everyone was in awe. Even now, listening to the tape, it makes me feel like I'm hearing the song for the first time all over again. —GINA D'AMICO

➢ Until this day, I hadn't head live Phish for a long time. The entire summer I dreamed about being in Plattsburgh. As the clouds turned orange and purple, and all the people around me smiled and joked, I realized I was in heaven. When that sweet twang of Chalkdust opened this show, it gave me that feeling of freedom and happiness that I had been longing for. —JOHN MCMEECKING

[8/17/96]
Flatbed Jam, Clifford Ball, Plattsburgh Air Force Base, Plattsburgh, NY
In the pre-dawn hours following the August 16 show, Phish played a 45-minute set of mellow jazz on a flatbed truck that toured the Clifford Ball campground.

➢ It's about 3 a.m. I had just cracked the night's last brew when I noticed some lights glowing in the distance. Not too alert to what was happening, I decided to walk over and see what it was. I could not believe my eyes when I saw Phish playing softly, just barely audible. It reminded me of some dreamy Floyd, but that description does this treat no justice. One of the coolest "sets" ever. —CASEY GRANT

➢ This was very personal, very Phishlike. The music blurred as the band moved so I didn't get to listen to everything they played, but I found it very soothing. I was really excited to tell everyone in the morning what they missed while they were passed out! —JEN VERDON

8/17/96 [ACCESSIBILITY: •••••]
The Clifford Ball, Plattsburgh Air Force Base, Plattsburgh, NY
I: Old Home Place, PYITE, Reba, CTB, Lizards, Sample, Taste, Fee, Maze, Suzie
II: Curtain, Runaway Jim, It's Ice, Brother, Fluffhead, Antelope, Golgi, Slave
III: Wilson, Frankenstein, Scent of a Mule, Tweezer, Day in the Life, Possum, Tweezer Reprise **E:** Harpua
Ben Cohen and Jerry Greenfield on vocals for Brother. A female acrobat performed on ropes above the stage during Antelope, and trampolinists jumped during Tweezer. "Heartbreaker" jam in Wilson. Page/Fishman duel in Scent of a Mule instead of Page/Trey. Harpua was unfinished after a stunt plane missed its cue and the band cut the song short, leaving the stage with feedback noise ringing out.

The Clifford Ball

8/16&17/96 Plattsburgh Air Force Base, Plattsburgh, NY

Since the very beginning, Phish was never content playing traditional music venues. At the first chance they'd get, the band would invite friends and fans to outdoor gatherings which offered more than just a concert.

Perhaps the idea first blossomed with the Ian's Farm shows in the 1980s, followed by the series of Townshend Family Park shows and, of course, Amy's Farm in 1991. But in the days when Phish played from the back of a flatbed truck, they probably never imagined something of the scale of the Clifford Ball.

For one weekend in August 1996, over 70,000 Phish fans lived as family in upstate New York. A decommissioned Air Force base was transformed into a Phish theme park, a fantasy land centered by six sets of Phish and countless surprises.

Phish derived the name Clifford Ball after an Air Mail aviation pioneer of the same name. They had spotted a plaque in a Pittsburgh airport dedicated to the semi-obscure pilot, who was referred to as "a beacon of light in the world of flight." For some reason, it tickled Phish's fancy, and they tried to convince organizers of what would be the H.O.R.D.E. in 1992 to name the tour The Clifford Ball. When that failed, they wrote in the liner notes of *A Live One* that it was recorded "live at Clifford Ball."

When the real Clifford Ball kicked off after months of preparation, the first fans began arriving a full two days before the first set of music. By the time the sun came up on Friday, August 16, a tent city covered much of the base, as fans set up shop in areas called "Camping Kirk" and "Camping Picard." A licensed 24-hour radio station was "Balling all the time," playing rare Phish bootlegs and grabbing hold of band members from time to time for pointed commentary.

Planes hired by the band circled the event, dragging banners with such cryptic Phishy statements as "A Dime From Here Would Penetrate" and "Evan Dando." The aviation theme even extended to the main entrance, where all concert goers drove under a huge banner telling them to "Prepare For Flight."

Sprinkled around the campsites were several giant plywood cut-outs of Clifford Ball himself, and inside the concert ground, a 35-foot tall statue of Cliff towered over Ball Square—a land of crafts and make-believe with miniature houses. The village grounds would later play host to an actual wedding, as Michael Rehberg and Toodle Lee of Macon, GA became the first couple to ever tie the knot at a Phish show. And the event was even graced by Clifford Ball's grandson, whom the band flew up from his home in Florida for the event.

By the time the band finally took the stage at dusk on Friday night, most attendees had already shouted, "I'm having such a great time" repeatedly. For many, it was almost hard to fully digest the show with so much other excitement.

But those who kept their attention on the stage were treated to a show which easily lived up to the occasion, including one of the most melodic and heavily-improvised Bathtub Gins ever in the first set; a sublime segue between Mike's and Simple in the second that led to a "Mike's Suite" of songs—Contact and Weekapaug; and an equally brilliant Down with Disease in the third. Friday night's third set ended with fireworks going off behind the stage during Harry Hood.

Not only was Phish at their best on stage, but many fans commented on the prowess of those offstage. The sound—often impossible to perfect in large outdoor venues—was crystal clear throughout the spacious viewing area, even to fans who were stuck several football fields away from the stage. (Large video screens provided some relief, too.)

Every facet of the Ball seemed to run smoothly. Plenty of food; plenty of drink. Few lines; fewer hassles. Well past midnight on Friday night, when most exhausted fans were asleep, Phish made an appearance on the back of the same sort of flatbed truck which once served as a permanent stage in their outdoor extravaganzas. This one also had a generator, which powered Phish's instruments as they plucked their way through a mellow, rolling jam as the truck inched its way through the camping area. Hundreds of fans followed on bike or foot.

Saturday saw Phish kick off the festivities around 4 p.m., playing an afternoon set before giving the stage over to "The Clifford Ball Orchestra," a full symphony which played several of Trey's favorite classical pieces including Stravinksy's The Firebird, during which a glider flew through the air and seemed to dance to the music.

The two Phish sets that followed were a virtual buffet of fan favorites as Phish packed virtually every epic tune left in the arsenal into one evening. Fluffhead, Run Like an Antelope and Slave to the Traffic Light all surfaced in set II, along with Brother, the first since August of 1993. During that song, famous Vermont ice cream makers Ben and Jerry lent guest vocals. The shenanigans continued in the third set when trampoline artists joined the band on stage, bouncing up and down during Tweezer.

The encore offered the most confusing and debated moment of The Ball. Phish sent the crowd into a frenzy with the first notes of Harpua, soon after which a fan jumped on stage and lunged for Trey, only to be apprehended by security. The band seemed genuinely thrown off, and wound up abandoning the song half way through, leaving only ringing feedback from the amplifiers as they left the stage.

Many fans felt that the fan who jumped on stage had interrupted the band's concentration. In September, Trey addressed the confusion by going online and sharing that the band had expected to see an airplane flying overhead but couldn't (in fact, it was there, but behind the stage at an angle the band could not see, or so Trey said). That led them to cut the Harpua short.

But another theory speculates that after giving fans so much, Phish just had to leave something over for next time.

Phan Pick #12 ➢ The day began with the tiny patter of raindrops coming from a small shower from the Adirondacks to cool off me and the olfactory challenged 50,000 that shared my ground. But that didn't last as by noon the clouds disappeared, chased by the hot August sun. This set the stage for eight hours of music by Phish and their classically-minded friends. Highlight? How about everything, well, everything except for an unfinished Harpua and a foolish fan who ran onto the stage. But even before these events unfolded, I realized as I warmed my hands on a bonfire in Ball Square (to counteract the cool Adirondack winds) that nothing could mar the moment. And nothing did. —LEE SCHILLER

➢ The Clifford Ball became an instant classic, and those who were there know why. The first set of the second day was fair, basically a warm up for the night's second and third sets. The second set was perhaps the greatest single set I've seen. From a deep Runaway Jim to a surprise Brother, this set had everything. After a powerful Fluffhead and Antelope, I felt fortunate that the set would include one more—Golgi. Then the first chords of Slave started. —MATTHEW NAPOLI

➢ An endless sea of fans put the band on a pedestal from which they played intense, beautiful music. —JEFF LOZIER

➢ Day two of the gathering at the Clifford Ball. The afternoon set was typical, but the last two were extraordinary. Curtain, Runaway Jim, It's Ice got it off to an excellent start, but then they pulled Brother from its grave (last played 8/2/93) and had guest appearances by Ben & Jerry. A memorable Antelope with an acrobat swinging over the stage followed. The set ended with the best Slave I'd ever heard. Third set with a Tweezer with trampolinists. Wild! Harpua encore had Jimmy flying over the Ball (and a stunt plane)—cut short. —RYAN DANYEW

➢ Set 2 of this show is all you need to know, especially after the way-phunky jam in It's Ice. The song selection isn't what this set is about—it's about the intensity. I never felt so much intensity from the band before, though this did cause Golgi and Slave to suffer a bit from acceleration. But the intensity! Usually everyone goes nuts afterwards, but following this set, folks couldn't utter a peep. —CHARLIE MURPHY

➢ Phish sounded crystal-clear as they put their hearts out into the whole venue. They deserved this. They work harder than any band around. —LANGSTON KNIPLER

➢ A great weekend. The weather was great, the shows will live in history, and Phish put together one of the best weekends eternity will ever know. But the highlight for me was meeting Trey in Oakledge Park a couple of days later while he was Rollerblading. I told him it was the best fuckin' show I'd ever been to. He said, "Thanks. I had the best fuckin' time playing it." Let's do this every year! —BETH CASTROL

➢ When it was all over, I felt like I just got off roller skates. —JOEL ZEIGLER

1996 Fall *BILLY RAVES*

Phish hit the road in Fall '96 just as *Billy Breathes* hit stores. For the band, it was a time of renewed media interest—following the great success of the Clifford Ball, suddenly it seemed that every magazine wanted a piece of them. Articles surfaced in *Entertainment Weekly* and, by the winter of '96-'97, *GQ* and *Rolling Stone*, among others. *Rolling Stone*, in fact, awarded *Billy Breathes* a coveted four star rating, with music critic Richard Gehr (a good friend of the band) hailing the album as "a breath of fresh air." The album's single, Free, even drew significant radio play, the first Phish single to perform well on the charts.

In the concert environment, however, little changed. The band kept alternating setlists like they always had done, and in fact it was getting harder and harder to hear some songs live, what with the ever-increasing breadth of Phish's play list. Fans who just *needed* to hear a particular song had to plan on attending a long string of concerts to satiate their desire.

For those who didn't really care what the band played, so long as they played it well, the fall tour offered both satisfaction and concern. There were a bunch of real musical highlights, including the Halloween show in Atlanta which saw Phish tackle the Talking Heads with aplomb, and the band's first-ever Las Vegas gig which many immediately tagged as the best show of the year. There were super-long jams, too, like the 30-minute Bathtub Gin in Louisville and the 27-minute Crosseyed and Painless in West Palm Beach. But unlike previous tours, there didn't seem to be much played this fall that the band hadn't done before. Had Phish peaked? Fans nervously wondered. Phish's answer came the next February in Europe.

[10/15/96] *Billy Breathes* released on Elektra.

10/16/96 [ACCESSIBILITY: •••]
Olympic Center, Lake Placid, NY
I: CTB, Down with Disease, Wilson, Buried Alive, Poor Heart, Billy Breathes, Mound, Sample, It's Ice, Horse > Silent, Character Zero
II: Wolfman's, Taste, Train Song, Simple, Swept Away > Steep, Caspian, Antelope, Squirming Coil, Johnny B. Goode **E:** Waste
Concert debuts: Swept Away, Steep.

➢ This show was sour—the band just didn't seem into it at all. Songs like Ice and Antelope proved this by their lack of jamming and intensity. Lake Placid wasn't the fun spot it was the year before and I think this was because of the music. But since it was the first show of the tour, we knew that it was just going to get better from here. —GEOFF LYNCH

➢ Phish played two totally different sets. The first set was a tad flat (rusty!), and Trey seemed pissed at Fishman. Lots of subtle (and not-so-subtle) mistakes. Set II was another story as the band came out and raged. Wolfman's opener had me asking "What horns?" and Antelope had more tension and release than any version I've heard. Johnny B. Goode has been changed to Johnny B. Rockin'! —CHARLIE MURPHY

10/17/96 [ACCESSIBILITY: ••]
Bryce Jordan Center, Penn State University, State College, PA
I: Also Sprach > Funky Bitch, Sparkle > Tweezer > Theme, Talk, PYITE, Character Zero, Day in the Life, Tweezer Reprise
II: Ya Mar, Chalkdust, Bathtub Gin, Scent of a Mule, Free, Lizards, Star Spangled Banner, Bowie **E:** Golgi
Trey on acoustic guitar for Talk. Concert debut: Star Spangled Banner.

➢ The first 2001 show opener (of a two-set show) set the pace. Phish was "on" for this whole show. Tweezer flows seamlessly into Theme. Trey's vocal jam in Scent is pretty phat. I'm trying to be objective, but was this the most phar out Lizards ever? First-ever a cappella Star Spangled Banner, sung in preparation for their singing it at a L.A. Lakers game in December, followed by none other than Mr. Bowie to close set II. —CHARLIE MURPHY

➢ A spacey 2001 which Phish played completely in the dark except for red lights behind them was an unexpected first-set opener. Then, even more unexpectedly, Funky Bitch—Mike held "Every time I see her" for what felt like minutes. When Trey switched to acoustic for Talk I hoped he'd stay on it longer, but the sound of Punch You made me forget about it. "Hook it up, Trey!" —MARK GAROFALOW

➢ I talked to numerous people who were disappointed by this show. What were they listening to? Very cool Funky Bitch as Mike was really getting into it. Punch just raged! Chalkdust had a nice extended jam. Then Bathtub was taken to levels I've never seen or heard before. And the debut of the Star Spangled Banner, with one big bright spotlight shining on the U.S. flag, honestly gave me goosebumps. —RIC HANNAH

10/18/96 [ACCESSIBILITY: •••]
Pittsburgh Civic Arena, Pittsburgh, PA
I: Runaway Jim, Guelah, Old Home Place, CTB, Stash, Strange Design, Divided Sky, Billy Breathes, Taste, Sample
II: Suzie, Maze, YEM, Reba, Waste, Harry Hood **E:** Julius
"Do you Feel Like I Do?" tease in YEM.

➢ This was one of your basic Phish shows, featuring a lot of songs off *Billy Breathes*. The first set was hot—Cars Trucks Buses was key. The second set was alright but nothing to write home about. I remember it was just a rainy day. —KEVIN WORD

➢ Pittsburgh is the cleanest city I've ever seen. By the time we got to the arena it was pouring rain, but that didn't stop me from breaking out the drums and enjoying it. Someone I met complained about this show's setlist: "I've seen better." Haven't we all? I can't stand negative people at shows. Besides, I did hear a phenomenal Taste and a YEM that made me think I was gettin' down in some disco in the '70s. I didn't hear it at the show, but in the YEM jam there's a "Do You Feel Like I Do?" Frampton tease. —COLM CONNELL

10/19/96 [ACCESSIBILITY: •••]
Marine Midland Arena, Buffalo, NY
I: My Friend, Rift, Free, Esther, Llama, Gumbo, Down with Disease, Caspian, Frankenstein
II: AC/DC Bag, Sparkle, Slave, Bouncing, Melt, Fluffhead, Swept Away > Steep > Antelope, Hello My Baby **E:** Fee, Rocky Top
"Wish You Were Here" tease before AC/DC Bag.

➢ We had stopped at RIT to pick up a friend on the way to the show when we got in an accident. A girl we went to school with was driving and she handled the whole thing so well—she pushed on to the show, and we were rewarded with My Friend as an opener. My buddy loved it! I got off on the Split Open and Melt as always, and the AC/ DC Bag was rocking (the "Wish You Were Here" tease right before the Bag caught us by surprise). All in all, a great show—one that proved to us that you're lucky just to make it to any show! —DANIEL PADEN

➢ To say one word for this show, I would say "exhausted." We drove over 300 miles to Buffalo—about as long as I had ever spent in a car, and arrived to terrible weather but a fun lot scene. We were tired but so excited for the show. A packed second set was incredible, but the Fee encore just doesn't do it for me, not to mention Trey flubbed the lyrics at least twice. —JOHN MCMEECKING

➢ This was my first show since the Clifford Ball. After the band abruptly walked off stage during Harpua there, I wondered if this show's atmosphere would be any different. Definitely not. —ADAM RIZZUTI

➢ This show has no amazing parts or songs, but is still, for some odd reason, a phenomenal show. —DAVE O'CONNOR

10/21/96 [ACCESSIBILITY: ••••]
Madison Square Garden, New York, NY
I: Star Spangled Banner, Sample, CTB, Sloth, Divided Sky, Character Zero, Ginseng Sullivan, Stash, Waste, Possum
II: Wilson, Chalkdust, Wolfman's, Reba, Train Song, Maze, Life on Mars, Simple, Horse > Silent, Bowie **E:** Funky Bitch
Last Ginseng Sullivan, 6/23/95 Stanhope, NJ [103 shows].

➢ The boys opted to open with the Star Spangled Banner. The first set was all right—an electric Waste was nice but I like the acoustic version better. In the second set, a killer Simple with the nice segue into Horse led to the finale, David Bowie, a good one at that. It seemed that they held back on the jamming this night. The second set seemed like another first set, but I can't really complain with the killer Garden sound. —CHRISTOPHER MILLS

➢ Before the second set, someone threw a t-shirt up onto the stage and it landed right at Trey's feet. He picks it up, unrolls it, takes a look and nods his head like he really likes it. I found out later it was thrown by one of my friends who had 10th row seats, and it was one of the shirts we made for our trip to Hershey Park on summer tour. Besides that, this was basically a solid show. They definitely rocked the house. —PETER BUKLEY

Sat., October 26, 1996 Charlotte Coliseum, Charlotte, NC

I couldn't wait to go to this concert because I hoped to meet the band for a second time. I kind of know the band because Jon Fishman is my second cousin. Last year at the Charlotte concert I got to meet everyone, except for Mike, briefly. This year we had passes to soundcheck, dinner and the aftershow.

My dad, my brother, my friend and I arrived at Charlotte Coliseum at about 3:15 p.m. We went to will call to get our passes and they told us they didn't have them. We found a guard and he led us down to the parking lot where the buses were parked. He left us with yet another guard. This one didn't want to let us go in, but after about 15 minutes of persuading him, we got backstage. We found someone back there and asked if there were passes under our name. He called back to Jon and they gave us passes! I was so happy!! We were sitting backstage waiting for the band to start soundcheck when Trey walked out. We said hi to him and I asked him if he remembered us. I think he did! My friend and I gave him a poster that we had made and he said something like, "Cool, show that to the rest of the band and we'll hang it up in the bus or something."

Then Jon went out to test his new electric drums. We followed him out and sat in the front row while he played. Then out came Page, Mike and finally Trey. They messed around for a while and then played Dog Log, Old Home Place and Funky Bitch. Trey showed me his new Languedoc guitar. This would be only his second night playing it. While we were sitting there, Brad came out and handed us four tickets. They were about 100 times better than the seats we already had. We thanked him and later thanked Jon for the seats.

When they were finished we went backstage for dinner. The only band member that was there was Page. His parents were also there and they were as nice as he is! We ate and then got ready for the show.

The first set was fiery and had an awesome Reba in it. During intermission, I went backstage and talked to Jon and Page for a while. Mike rode his bike around backstage and strangely stared at us. My friend asked him for a pick and he threw one to him. Then came out Trey! I told him that they played a great first set. Then he said, "Aren't you Jason Roberts?" And I said, "Yeah!" He knew my name because I had recently won a Jimi Hendrix guitar competition and I got to play at Madison Square Garden in April. Jon had given him the newspaper article that I was in. We talked about the competition for a while and he wished me luck at Madison Square Garden and I thanked him and asked him for a pick. He pulled one out of his pocket and gave it to me. I ran out to see the second set.

They played a great second set with You Enjoy Myself! After they finished playing Waste, Trey stopped and said that this next song was for Fish's cousin! That's me! I couldn't believe it. He told the audience about the competition and wished me luck again. Then they started playing Run Like An Antelope! I still can't believe that they dedicated my absolute favorite song to me!! At the end of the set, I ran backstage and quickly thanked them for the wonderful night. They came back out and played an encore of Fire by Hendrix! I was so happy. One of my biggest dreams came true. **—Jason Roberts**

➢ The Yankees had a World Series game in the Bronx on this night, so it seemed appropriate to open with the Star Spangled Banner. The highlight of the first set was Stash, which took forever to come back into a recognizable form. I almost lost control before Trey brought me back—"Control for smilers can't be bought." The extra-long Simple was a much-needed addition to the second set, and the Funky Bitch encore left me heading for the exit with a big smile on my face. —MIKE GAROFALOW

➢ Though the tour was less than a week old at this point, it was already becoming clear that the boys wanted to make Simple one of their centerpiece songs for the fall. Their increased attention to Maze was also obvious, as Simple and Maze held down the middle of the second set. Simple on this night was long and cool, but not as gorgeous as some versions later in the tour would be. They were still getting warmed up. —RICH MAZER

10/22/96 [ACCESSIBILITY: ••••]
Madison Square Garden, New York, NY
I: Curtain > Runaway Jim, Bouncing, It's Ice, Talk, Melt, Sparkle > Free, YEM
II: Also Sprach > Down with Disease, Taste, Mango, Lawn Boy, Scent of a Mule, Mike's > Swept Away > Steep > Weekapaug
E: All Along the Watchtower
Trey on acoustic guitar for Talk. A dance/circus troupe (including Mimi Fishman) joined Phish onstage during Weekapaug and All Along the Watchtower. Buddy Miles on drums and vocals, and Merl Saunders on keyboard for All Along the Watchtower (Fishman played Trey's mini-drumkit.) Last Watchtower, 4/21/94 Winston-Salem, NC [226 shows].

➢ With two years of holiday tour performances at MSG under their belt, the band felt confident enough to book themselves for two nights in New York in the middle of the week, in the middle of October. Their big challenge would be recreating some of the energy and magic that flows like water around New Year's Eve. On the first night, they played a solid show, but one which seemed underwhelming given the fact that this was, after all, MSG, and Phish merchandising had printed up special "What is a band without skyscrapers?" t-shirts just for these two shows. But on the second night, from the Curtain opener to the amazing YEM set-closer (one of the year's best) in the first set, to the 2001 > DwD opener and Mike's Groove (with circus dancers!) in the second, the band proved they were capable of rockin' MSG on any occasion. Yeeha! —TYLER HARRIS

➢ The energy level in the Garden was already fever-pitched during Weekapaug, thanks to some inspired jamming and the fact that word had spread among the crowd that the Yankees, playing in the World Series against the Braves, had scored an amazing come-from-behind win in game three. But MSG got even louder when a dance/circus troupe emerged from backstage to cavort on stage during Weekapaug. With about 30 freaks gyrating among the bandmembers, climbing on top of Page's piano, spinning around Trey and just gettin' down with Phish, the arena just exploded. The band built Weekapaug up to an incredible climax, then took it around one more time, without lyrics, topping off an incredible performance with an amazing finish. —LEE JOHNSTON

➢ As the second set ended, I was screaming with so much pleasure. THIS is where I want to be, THIS is what I love. My sister, Caroline, wondered how they encore would ever top that Weekapaug. But then Trey welcomed out two new friends of his, Buddy Miles and Merl Saunders—maybe they *could* top that Weekapaug! The loveable Buddy Miles announced that he would play the drums for a Bob Dylan song, All Along the Watchtower. It was a beautiful version of the rock classic. The circus dancers reappeared and the crowd was going nuts. At the end of the song, one of the circus dancers, the Viking with the clubs, threw her clubs into the crowd. It flew by me, over my head. Then I felt something hit my ankle. THE CLUB! I stood on my chair and waved it around. Later, as I walked out onto the crowded New York street, fans hugged me and took my picture because I caught the club. As I looked around, I knew it had been, undisputedly, the greatest night of my life. —MIKE PALMER

➢ Great second set, but the encore was only enjoyable if you wanted some comic relief. "Let's hear it for Phish!" Buddy Miles screams throughout Watchtower. —RICH MAZER

10/23/96 [ACCESSIBILITY: ••••]
Hartford Civic Center, Hartford, CT
I: PYITE, Poor Heart, AC/DC Bag, Foam, Hello My Baby, Character Zero, Rift, Theme, Antelope
II: Brother, Ya Mar, Tweezer, Lizards, Llama, Suzie, Slave, Julius
E: Chalkdust
Bob Gullotti on a second drum set for the second set and encore.

➢ A fairly plain, but good, first set laid the foundation for a killer set II. Bob Gullotti (on a second drum kit) was a fantastic addition for the entire second set. Brother opened the set—only the second one since 1993! The best Ya Mar ever in my opinion (check out this drum solo!) and a great Slave are thrown in, making this show a must have. The best show I've ever attended—just an amazing vibe. —JON BAHR

➢ Bob Gullotti came out to his drum set, warmed up the skins with a few taps and I knew what we were in for. Fish kicked the opening beats for Brother and Bob jumped right in on the snare to accentuate the rhythm. The whole set, Fish and Bob played off each other. There was a drum solo during Ya Mar in which Fish and Bob just rocked out. During Tweezer, Trey got on his drum kit, and with Page on the Moog they created such a groove. The whole set amazed all. The Llama was so powerful that I almost fell down. —BRENDAN NEAGLE

10/25/96 [ACCESSIBILITY: ••••]
Hampton Coliseum, Hampton, VA
I: Ha Ha Ha, Taste, Makisupa, Maze, Billy Breathes, Mound, Guelah, I Didn't Know, Stash, Squirming Coil
II: Tube, Caspian, Timber Ho, TMWSIY > Avenu > TMWSIY, NICU, Free, Strange Design, Harry Hood, Cavern, Star Spangled Banner
E: Johnny B. Goode
Fishman on vacuum for I Didn't Know. Trey debuted a new Languedoc guitar.

➢ This show was a GREAT time—highlights include Stash, Squirming Coil, Tube and NICU. When Trey told us from the stage that Hampton was his favorite venue to play, we unanimously agreed. Many people I've talked to share the opinion that this was the best time they've ever had at a Phish show. —M.N.J. ADAMS

➢ I'm sure someone remembers the naked guy escorted out at intermission, screaming while standing up and falling down. I recall an awesome Stash in the first set; Tube and Timber Ho in the second ripped. Hampton is such a nice place to see a show. Hotels are close by and security lets you enjoy yourself. —PHIL VALLE

10/26/96 [ACCESSIBILITY: ••]
Charlotte Coliseum, Charlotte, NC
I: Julius, CTB, Wolfman's, Reba, Train Song, Character Zero, It's Ice, Theme, Sample
II: Down with Disease, YEM, Sparkle, Simple, McGrupp, Waste, Antelope
E: Fire

➢ I met Mike on his bike ride in the parking lot and talked with him for about five or 10 minutes before a crowd formed—what a nice guy and what a way to start the evening. With the exception of Julius (not a favorite of mine), set I was outstanding. The extraordinary Reba was trippy and fast-paced, whipping the crowd into a frenzy for the rest of the evening. The second set saw one jam after another with superb versions of Down with Disease and YEM. A splendid jam out of Simple really topped off the night before it even made it to McGrupp. —JASON DEZIEL

➢ Maybe the band had some pre-Halloween nerves, but they didn't take any of the shows in the week leading up to 10/31 that far out there. The setlist for this show is strong, including a second set packed with DwD, YEM, Simple and Antelope, but a truly insane jamfest this show was not. —ERNIE GREENE

10/27/96 [ACCESSIBILITY: ••]
North Charleston Coliseum, North Charleston, SC
I: Runaway Jim, PYITE, AC/DC Bag, Fee, Scent of a Mule > Catapult > Scent of a Mule, Melt, Talk, Taste, Suzie
II: Chalkdust, Bathtub Gin, Rift, Caspian, Ya Mar, Tweezer, Fluffhead, Life on Mars, Tweezer Reprise **E:** Possum, Carolina
Page on theremin for Catapult. Trey on acoustic guitar for Talk. "In-a-Gadda-Da-Vida" jam in Melt. "Norweigan Wood" jam in Taste. Last Catapult, 12/1/95 Hershey, PA [57 shows].

➢ Another wonderful switched-up, mixed-up setlist. I love when Phish plays shows like this. A bunch of Scent and Tweezer. Possum for an encore—that's splendid. Fluffhead and Catapult jam at this show—I'm lucky to own it, and to have seen it! —DARYL WHITCRAFT

➢ I love it when the band throws me for a loop in a song like Scent where I think I know what to expect. During Trey's duel segment in Scent of a Mule, Mike came out to the front of the stage with only a microphone and crooned his little ditty Catapult. When he was finished, we noticed Page had migrated to the theremin, where he teased out the Catapult tune almost perfectly. After that, they returned to their instruments and finished off Scent. Cool. —MARCIA COLLINS

10/29/96 [ACCESSIBILITY: •••]
Leon County Civic Center, Tallahassee, FL
I: Chalkdust, Guelah, CTB, Taste, Bouncing, Stash, Train Song, Billy Breathes, Poor Heart, Bowie
II: Rift, Mike's > Hydrogen > Horse > Silent, Weekapaug, Wedge, Character Zero, Suspicious Minds, Slave, Hello My Baby **E:** GTBT
Karl Perazzo on drums and percussion for the entire show. Rift intro played done by percussion instead of guitar. "Houses in Motion" jam in Mike's. Last Wedge, 11/14/95 Orlando, FL [70 shows].

➢ Front-row mailorder seats for the debut of Phish as a five-piece—this was the first of several shows with Karl Perazzo sitting in on drums and percussion. Karl even pointed at me several times with his drumsticks. Just before the second set, some guy next to me handed Page a cantaloupe that said "Welcome back to Tallahassee" and "Roll like a cantaloupe." During Mike's, the band was lagging and Trey (still in mid-jam) yells, "Come on!" and the song raised another level. Check out the Rift with a percussion intro instead of a Trey intro, and Perazzo's eggshaking beat on Hello My Baby. —TONY HUME

Remain In Light

10/31/96 The Omni, Atlanta, GA

During the days leading up to 1995's Halloween extravaganza in Chicago, Phish littered their sets with Michael Jackson musical references, screwing with phans' minds before breaking out *Quadrophenia*. In 1996, the band took the opposite tact, all but telling fans in the weeks leading up to Halloween that they'd be covering a Talking Heads album.

"It's going to be by an American band, an American album, an '80s album," Fishman told the *Atlanta Journal-Constitution* a week before the show. "There's one song that everyone has heard, but it's not as high-profile as *The White Album*. But then again, what is?"

The band had been longtime admirers of the Talking Heads, covering Cities throughout the 1980s. But no one knew for sure whether the band was really going to play "an '80s American album," or whether it was just another Phishy mind game. In any case, the decision was Phish's to make, because for the first time the band elected to choose their cover album instead of having the fans vote on it.

On the day of the show, the traditional party atmosphere surrounded the Omni. Tickets were tough—the show was, of course, an immediate sellout—but not impossible; extras changed hands in front of the venue in the $40 to $80 range. For the first time at a Phish show, MTV news cameras were on the scene, interviewing fans for *The Week in Rock*, which later included some concert footage.

Phans entering the arena received a "PHISHBILL," designed as a spoof on Playbill that listed "Phish in Talking Heads' Remain in Light," and named the band along with several guests. Inside the Phishbill was a two-page essay written by *Rolling Stone* journalist Parke Puterbaugh (who later wrote the *Rolling Stone* Phish article in winter '97) that discussed the influence *Remain in Light* had on the members of Phish. If it was all a prank, it was a pretty elaborate one.

The show started with the first Sanity since New Year's '95, a fitting opener that slammed right into Highway to Hell—another nice touch. From there, the first set soared with epics, including yet another great '96 Down with Disease and a long YEM. As the set passed the one-hour point, the band was still rocking, ripping into Col. Forbin's Ascent, where Trey spun a trippy tale of Col. Forbin climbing the mountain and the face of Icculus becoming that of Talking Heads frontman David Byrne. The "evil Halloween mockingbird" failed to return the Helping Friendly Book to the people of Gamehendge "because it's Halloween," then the band rocked out Character Zero.

As a second drum set was constructed during the setbreak, it became obvious that the Phishbill wasn't a joke. Longtime Santana band percussionist Karl Perazzo had played with Phish at their previous gig in Florida and would sit in for the musical costume. Also joining the band for set II would be GCH member Dave Grippo and trumpet player Gary Gazaway, who played on the original *Remain in Light* and wrote the horn parts to the album. The die was cast.

Instead of the drama associated with *The White Album* or *Quadrophenia*, Phish thrived on the musicality of *Remain in Light*. Whereas the band had focused in previous years on replicating the original albums, they turned *Remain in Light* into a jam showcase, taking the songs further out there than David Byrne could probably have ever imagined. Perazzo's driving percussion provided a platform for the rest of the band—as Fishman pointed out in Puterbaugh's Phishbill article, "It's almost like all the instruments are drums... Even the background vocals are like drum parts."

According to Phishbill, it was Trey who urged Phish to cover *Remain in Light*. "I practically learned how to play guitar by listening to [it]," he told Puterbaugh. Both Page and Mike covered Talking Heads songs in pre-Phishy days, too, so the album represented a homecoming of sorts for the band.

Near the end of the set, things got weird during Overload as four television sets were brought onto stage and white noise poured from the PA system. Phans watched, transfixed, as the band and friends freaked out for a few minutes—walking strangely around the stage, using jackhammers, screaming unintelligibly—then left the stage.

On a night of treats, it was the ultimate trick.

➢ Although this show did not sell out, the energy inside the Civic Center was incredible. Perazzo's playing raised the music to a whole new level, as evidenced in the amazing second set. It featured one of the best Mike's Songs I've ever heard. Fishman's performance of Suspicious Minds was his first song of the fall tour. Unfortunately, a few people ruined a perfect evening by vandalizing a police car outside the Civic Center. —CHRIS HAINES

10/31/96 [ACCESSIBILITY: ••••]
The Omni, Atlanta, GA
I: Sanity, Highway to Hell, Down with Disease > YEM > Caspian, Reba, Forbin's > Mockingbird, Character Zero, Star Spangled Banner
II: Born Under Punches (The Heat Goes On), Crosseyed and Painless, Great Curve, Once In A Lifetime, Houses In Motion, Seen And Not Seen, Listening Wind, Overload
III: Brother, Also Sprach > Maze, Simple > Swept Away > Steep, Jesus Left Chicago, Suzie **E:** Frankenstein

Second set was the Talking Heads' Remain In Light (all songs concert debut). Remain In Light featured David Grippo on saxophone, Gary Gazaway on trumpet and Karl Perazzo on drums and percussion. Armchair brought to center stage for Houses—Mike sat in the chair to sing, with Trey on bass. Industrial madness broke loose on stage at the end of the second set—four television sets were brought on stage, Fishman played vacuum and the others on stage used various tools to create weird sounds. Entire third set and encore also featured Perazzo. Jesus Left Chicago, Suzie and Frankenstein also featured Grippo and Gazaway. Last Jesus Left Chicago, 10/31/95 Chicago, IL [76 shows].

Phan Pick #10 ➢ It doesn't say enough that this show opens with Sanity. It's Halloween and I definitely had no intentions of it coming my way on this night. Every song in the first set was a highlight: DWD, Highway to Hell, YEM, Col. Forbin's. Is this some sort of sick joke? They knocked me on my ass. —BRETT PESSIN

➢ I was never a big fan of the Talking Heads so I wasn't sure if I would like set II, but it is a musical masterpiece. Phish took *Remain in Light*, tweaked it, and made it their own. Crosseyed and Painless, Houses in Motion and Overload were spectacular. A lot of good audience tapes are out there—get one and turn it up! —MICHAEL RAMBO

➢ *Remain in Light*? Talking Heads? Who would have thunk it? Most at the show agreed this was a very fresh and interesting choice for the boys. Born Under Punches was totally awesome as was Once in a Lifetime, a favorite of mine since I was younger. Lots were taken aback when the boys first started, but once the show heated up so did the crowd. Good choice, guys! —M.N.J. ADAMS

➢ All I have to say is, if Trey thinks he was shaking after this show, he should have seen us. I was a little unsure as to how I would perceive the Talking Heads set, but upon hearing set II my mind and body were sent to different realms. Crosseyed and Painless left me just that. The Great Curve and Houses in Motion traverse sequences of chords that I didn't know could be played. The conclusion of Listening Wind and Overlord was perfect for Halloween and so was Phish's performance. —MATTHEW ASHENFELDER

➢ *Remain in Light* was beautiful—David Byrne would have swooned. One of the unique things about this show was the Phishbill given out as you entered the Omni. Like the Playbills of Broadway shows, it featured ads for Gordeaux fine liquors and Scent of a Fool cologne, as well as bios on all the players and info on *Remain in Light*. —EMILY BINARD

➢ Without a doubt, the absolute highlight of the show musically is percussionist Karl Perazzo. His work in Brother and Also Sprach in particular is killer. Overall, this is musically speaking the best show I've ever heard. Jesus Left Chicago with Grippo on sax is always a plus, and the story about the evil Mockingbird is pretty cool too. —MIKE JETT

➢ Incredible, incredible show, packed to the breaking point with hot song after hot song. The first set rivaled that of 10/31/94 in its song selection (DwD, YEM, Forbin's) and song selection humor (Sanity > Hell opener). If set three of this show had been a little stronger, this might have been the greatest Phish show of all time. Still, we were more than happy to settle for Brother, plus Maze and Simple (the two unsung stars of fall tour '96) and the now-traditional Jesus Left Chicago with horns. —LEE JOHNSTON

11/2/96 [ACCESSIBILITY: ••••]
Coral Sky Amphitheater, West Palm Beach, FL
I: Ya Mar, Julius, Fee, Cavern, Taste, Stash, Free, Johnny B. Goode
II: Crosseyed and Painless, Antelope, Waste, Harry Hood, Day in the Life, Adeline **E:** Funky Bitch

Karl Perazzo on drums and percussion for the entire show. Butch Trucks on drums for Funky Bitch, with Fishman on Trey's mini-drum kit. Trey says "Norton Charleton Heston" instead of "Marco Esquandolis" in Antelope lyrics. Segments of the second set were broadcast on a syndicated nationwide FM radio program in March, 1997.

➢ A great show in a beautiful place, the only open-air venue of the tour—the skies were blue and the sun was shining. Crosseyed and Painless was the most intense Phish song I ever heard. It lasted for 27 minutes, and jammed the whole entire time. I never danced so long in my life. I was ready to take a seat when they segued right into Antelope. Let me tell you—it was the sickest Antelope I'd ever heard, too. Trey summed it up after Antelope when he walked up to his mic and simply said, "Whooaa." Thank God they played Waste next, because I had to sit down and catch my breath. I found myself up again upon hearing the opening of Hood, which proved to be one of the best of the tour. When they came out for the encore, I noticed an extra person with them. It turned out to be Butch Trucks again (he joined them at West Palm in '95). He jammed with them on a ripping version of Funky Bitch to end the show. It was the hottest second set I've heard in a while. —TOM PINNICK

➢ Ya Mar to open is a sign of good things to come, but the second set is what this show is all about. Crosseyed and Painless goes for about 25 minutes, followed by Antelope. At this point you can rewind the tape and do it all over again. A nice Hood was played, too. I highly recommend this show. —MICHAEL RAMBO

➢ In spring '97, Phish got to choose a portion of one of their fall shows for national radio broadcast. They chose part of West Palm Beach II, including the Crosseyed and Painless into Antelope, which runs about 40 minutes and is probably their best jam of the year. Mike later posted part of his journal from November 2 to *www.phish.com*. He wrote, "Playing with Karl takes away the problems of 'rushing' the rhythms… The Talking Heads song and the jam that followed were great. The whole set was great… Had a 'bit of a musical experience' in West Palm." So did everyone there! —ED SMITH

11/3/96 [ACCESSIBILITY: ••]
O'Connell Center, Gainesville, FL
I: My Friend, Runaway Jim, Billy Breathes, Sloth, NICU, Sample, Theme, Bouncing, Character Zero
II: Timber Ho, Divided Sky, Wolfman's, Sparkle, Tweezer, Life on Mars, Possum, Tweezer Reprise **E:** Fire

Karl Perazzo on drums and percussion for the entire show.

➢ This is one of the poorer Phish shows I've ever been to. We did get to hear a near-30 minute Funky Bitch soundcheck, but the crowd seemed more buzzed than into the music and believe it or not, got more excited over Sparkle than anything else. The music was actually good, but lacked the passion of most other shows. This was the last Karl Perazzo show—that man is a monster! —TONY HUME

➢ A medium-to-high-grade Phish show. There are a couple of jewels like the Tweezer jam and Possum, and the smooth My Friend opener. —DARYL WHITCRAFT

11/6/96 [ACCESSIBILITY: ••]
Knoxville Civic Coliseum, Knoxville, TN
I: Melt, CTB, FEFY, Taste, Train Song, Poor Heart, PYITE, Billy Breathes, Bowie
II: Wilson, Curtain > Mike's > Swept Away > Steep > Weekapaug, Scent of a Mule, Sample, Funky Bitch **E:** Rocky Top

➢ On the way up from Gainesville, we took the wrong highway. Needless to say, it took a while to get to Knoxville, but when we got there we went to a bar and there were Trey and Gordo. I had a nice conversation with Trey in which he kept talking about my shirt. The show was nice with a great Punch. The second set Wilson > Curtain > Mike's Groove is solid. Trey said hello to all the people he met in Knoxville—that was me!—then finished things off with an appropriate Rocky Top encore. —WILL LEHNERT

11/7/96 [ACCESSIBILITY: ••••]
Rupp Arena, Lexington, KY
I: Chalkdust, Weigh > Rift > Guelah, Stash, Waste, Guyute, Free > Tela, Character Zero
II: Suzie > Bathtub Gin, HYHU > Bike > HYHU, YEM **E:** Frankenstein

Fishman on vacuum for Bike.

➢ This was a fantastic show. Chalkdust opens, then comes the only Weigh of the tour (the show also had the only Tela of the fall, as well as the tour's first Guyute). Second set featured an amazing Bathtub Gin with the Chairman of the Boards taking control. Also, in my humble opinion, the best YEM since 6/11/94 Red Rocks. —WILL LEHNERT

➢ The second set: four songs?! The Suzie > Bathtub Gin opener has to be one of the craziest performances I have ever seen from Phish. Trey was totally going off on his guitar during Bathtub. The YEM closer topped it all off. I don't think I've ever had a more wonderful night of music than this. —DAN CHARRON

➢ The second set epitomizes what Phish was all about during the Fall '96 tour—two huge jams (Gin and YEM) that traverse a lot of places and spaces. Bathtub Gin, very arguably the best version ever, is certainly the longest—over 25 minutes. The jam segment is normal Gin-style wandering at first, but when Trey moves over to his mini-drum kit and Page steps up to his clavinet, the jam takes a U-turn. Page just dominates, absolutely rocking out while Trey, Mike and Fish provide a firm foundation for his jamming. When Trey moves back to his guitar, a wonderfully directed jam develops that rages, peaks, and heads into an entirely different jam segment, which itself transforms into a funky bass-and-drums affair that segues right into HYHU! Instead of playing six songs to showcase their different styles, Phish now does it in just one song! —JOSH ALBINI

➢ Before the second set, Trey says to the crowd, "Fish hasn't sung this tour yet, has he? He lost his privilege." (Apparently Trey forgot Suspicious Minds on 10/29). When the crowd cheers, Trey says, "You're going to have to do better than that," and the crowd goes absolutely wild. After the monstrous Suzie > Bathtub, Fishman heads for center stage with the Electrolux, declaring, "Well, by gum, you've brought me out of the penalty box. It's good to be back!" A hilarious Bike ensues. —LEE JOHNSTON

11/8/96 [ACCESSIBILITY: •••]
Assembly Hall, Champaign, IL
I: Runaway Jim > Axilla, All Things, Mound, Down with Disease, Caspian, Reba, Golgi, Antelope

II: Also Sprach > Maze, Bouncing, Simple, Loving Cup, Mike's, Star Spangled Banner, Weekapaug **E:** Theme

Last Axilla, 10/16/94 Chattanooga, TN [170 shows]. Last All Things, 7/1/95 Mansfield, MA [108 shows].

➢ Before this show, I considered Simple just another good song played between the big guns (jam songs). But once again, Phish took a step up, playing an intricate and jammed-out Simple. Clearly the best I've ever heard! Not even Trey's breaking amp (which he kicked harder than usual) stopped the intense groove. The jam included Cecilia teases, amazing Page chords and creative Mike lines. And how nice it was to follow this jam with Loving Cup—this show was a beautiful buzz! —MICHELLE HIRSCH

➢ This show was average at best. Runaway Jim was a very predictable opener, then the show became slow and methodical until Down with Disease took flight. Antelope was a nice highlight to a rather mediocre set. 2001 and the rest of the second set were subtle and a little cautious. —ANDY KAHN

➢ As Phish goes into Axilla, Trey has guitar problems and gives his amp a kick, causing a roar from the crowd. Trey does this again during Simple. Then at the beginning of Weekapaug Groove, Mike's bass makes this horrible rattling noise, ruining my enjoyment of this song. To solve a night of equipment problems and to get something out of the evening, Phish encored with a nice Theme, building up slowly then climaxing at the end. —MIKE NOLL

11/9/96 [ACCESSIBILITY: •••]
The Palace, Auburn Hills, MI
I: Buried Alive > Poor Heart, Sloth, Divided Sky, Horn, Tube, Talk, Melt, Lizards, Character Zero
II: Bowie, Day in the Life, YEM, Taste > Swept Away > Steep > Harry Hood **E:** Julius

Trey on acoustic guitar for Talk.

➢ This was a solid show. For such a large venue, Phish rocked the whole boat! And what a second set—Bowie opener was tight and great. They grasped the energy they want to obtain and held it solid throughout the song. I prefer the hard/intense Bowies, so those who agree should check this one out. The YEM was just as tight—some great bass weaving throughout. Just as I thought they would throw out a Cavern ending, they whipped out a ripping Hood with a nice transition from Steep. Thanks Page! —MICHELLE HIRSCH

➢ Phish played a great first set which yielded Sloth and a great Tube. Lizards went well, plus a good Character Zero. The second set, however, sucked. It had a decent Hood to keep it afloat, but Bowie? Day in the Life > YEM just didn't cut it, either. Julius is the worst song to end a show, but here that's what they chose. —CHRIS REGAN

11/11/96 [ACCESSIBILITY: •••••]
Van Andel Arena, Grand Rapids, MI
I: Chalkdust, Guelah, CTB, AC/DC Bag, Sparkle, Brother, Theme, Axilla, Runaway Jim
II: Timber Ho, Divided Sky, Gumbo, Curtain > Sample, Tweezer, Swept Away > Steep > Maze, Contact, Slave **E:** Waste, Cavern

➢ This was my last show of the fall tour, and I was pleased to see a good show to end (with a great view thanks to general admission). The light show pleased my senses, but my favorite part of the show had to be Page's ragtime solo at the end of Gumbo. Once finished, he cast a menacing glare on the crowd as Trey yelled in delight. —JOSH HARMAN

➢ Mother nature wasn't kind to Phish and the fans during our November trek from Michigan down across the midwest to the Pacific Northwest. Rain, sleet, ice and snow attempted to keep us away from the shows, starting in Grand Rapids, but most of us slogged through the mess and were rewarded for it. This was another solid show, nothing outrageous but nothing to gripe about either. —MELISSA WOLCOTT

➢ At first it was shocking when they broke out into Divided Sky in the second set, mostly because they played it the show before at the Palace. Thanks to G.A., I was able to ask Trey with my eyes "Why?" He looked at me with a disappointed look which reminded me of one of the most beautiful sunsets Michigan had that night. The sky was on fire with shades of red, orange and pink one can only imagine in dreams of ideal sunsets. I closed my eyes during this Divided Sky and saw those magical colors once again. —MICHELLE HIRSCH

[11/12/96]
Target Center, Minneapolis, MN
Star Spangled Banner

Phish sung a cappella before the Timberwolves-Lakers NBA game.

11/13/96 [ACCESSIBILITY: •••]
Target Center, Minneapolis, MN
I: Down with Disease, Bouncing, It's Ice, Ya Mar, Taste, Train Song, Reba, Character Zero, Adeline
II: Also Sprach > Suzie, Caspian > YEM, Theme, Golgi **E:** GTBT

Extended jam out of Suzie.

➢ It was my 21st birthday and all I wanted was to see Character Zero. They kicked down one of the fattest Zero's all tour. The Ya Mar was also huge, and Suzie Greenberg had an amazing reprise. —SEAN SMITH

Saturday, November 9, 1996 The Palace, Auburn Hills, MI

From the time my brother Mike received mail order seats for the second row, I knew the show at The Palace in Auburn Hills would be special to me. I flew to Michigan to see my brother, but it was more to see the show. I got there the night before and seeing my seat location on the seating chart, I made the decision to make a sign for a song that hopefully the band would play. I decided on Tube, a nice little rarity that rages.

We got to the Palace and met my brother's friends Jeremy, Goldie and Christina. They had come down from Buffalo and would also be sitting with my Bro's friend from school, Dave. They had awful seats so we stubbed all four of them down to our wonderful spots and the show began. I had my Buried Alive shirt on and my sign in hand as the band came out. I held my sign high. I'm sure Trey saw it as they opened with Buried Alive (coincidence, maybe) that segued into a Poor Heart. Both good show openers. Next came Sloth, which was rockin' as usual, followed by Divided Sky. After a stellar version of Divided there was a couple second pause and I held my sign high—I'm sure Mike and Trey and Fish all saw it.

But they busted into Horn, my first and a decent version of it as well. After Horn there was another pause and I held up my sign once again. Trey began strumming and I knew it from the brief little strumming it was Tube!... and a kick-ass version at that. I danced my ass off with a smile the size of Utah. After Tube, Trey went over and got his acoustic guitar, then stepped up to the mic and said hello to the crowd. He then said, "That last song was for my friend down here with a sign so he doesn't have to hold it up all night long." At that moment I almost lost my shit.

With the band's dedication to me followed by a second set featuring Bowie, YEM and Hood, it was enough to make me smile the rest of my life. **—Butch Weiss**

Wednesday, Nov. 13, 1996 Target Center, Minneapolis, MN

This was the show that made me a true believer. Until this fateful evening at Minneapolis's second largest (and worst sounding) venue, I still held on to the last of the stereotyped visions The Man had sold me about what a "Deadhead" (and subsequently, a "Phishhead") was. I caught a show here and there but I was unwilling to go that final step into drop-everything-and-hit-the-road mode, and I was still suspicious of those who did. Then Phish took the stage for the second set after an entertaining first round and spoke directly to me like missionaries on a quest to convert the last doubter.

I compiled a wish list before my partners and I left Eau Claire, WI for a Minneapolis, Ames, St. Louis jaunt. This list hung around my neck on a laminated card I named the Phish Locator. It was four songs long. Before the show I had commented to my friends Eric and Kara how it would be cool to link Theme From the Bottom and YEM somehow, since they both have a cappella vocal jams in them. Wish list song number one came with Taste in the first set.

Then Phish cranked out the second set, including wish list song number two—YEM, with intense lights and the vocal jam ending, which glided into, ohmygodcoulditbe?! Theme From The Bottom, wish list song number three. I was in tears. But as they say in the Veg-o-Matic commercials, "Wait... there's more!" Theme carried me to a new Phish height—it was Hulk Hogan, the Macho Man Savage, Rick Flair and George "The Animal" Steele (that'd be Fishman) on stage lifting me above their heads for the body slam: Golgi Apparatus, my fourth and final wish list song.

The lights went up and I had that classic glued-to-my-seat-cause-I-don't-know-what-to-do immobility. Had that just happened? I consulted the wish list. Yep, there were the four songs. I stood apart, in silence, just staring at the deconstruction of the stage and wondering if I was truly, somehow intrinsically connected with the band. Had they known and played that show for me alone? Had we connected through some mysterious ESP-like higher consciousness? It's easier to say, "No, of course not—it's coincidence," but Phish gave me that feeling of a higher power, and I knew then I could never see them enough. **—Jason Hendrington**

➢ When we arrived at the Target Center, it was freezing cold, so we boiled up some hot chocolate. There was all this talk before the show of it being a special show, that the band told the tapers to bring extra tapes because they were gonna play three sets and so on. This got me really pumped up and curious to discover what the band had in store for us. The Target Center was a nice place, just like a regular-sized arena but new. Set I proved very standard with an average DWD opener into Bouncin'. Set II opened with a funky 2001 into a incredible Suzie Greenberg. Next was Caspian which led into a phat You Enjoy Myself, including a sick vocal jam and even a very cool polka jam. I enjoyed this show, even though it ended up being nothing spectacular. —DOM DELUCA

➢ It's not often the band uses Suzie as an excuse to jam. There's the brief Suzie reprise on 12/31/94 that slides into Slave, and there's the JAM that emerges from Suzie at this show. For a solid ten minutes or so, the band leaves Suzie behind, working their way through a jam that eventually arrives at Caspian. If you're willing to call this a "Suzie Jam," then this is certainly the most jammed Suzie Greenberg ever. —ERNIE GREENE

11/14/96 [ACCESSIBILITY: •••]
Hilton Coliseum, Ames, IA
I: AC/DC Bag, Uncle Pen, Wolfman's, CTB, Free, All Things, Bathtub Gin, Talk, Julius
II: Llama, Sample, Taste, Swept Away > Steep, Scent of a Mule, Life on Mars, Demand > Antelope, Day in the Life **E:** Stash, Hello My Baby
"James Bond Theme" tease in Stash. Last Demand, 12/7/95 Niagra Falls, NY [64 shows].

➢ Very good show with good songs. AC/DC Bag gets it all started, then a short version of Free carries into a jammy Bathtub Gin and the sweet melody of Talk. The second set was good but lacked some real jams. Trey "Demand"s us to Run Like An Antelope, before telling us about A Day in the Life. ADITL popped up in such a sweet slot, after Antelope, that you're almost forced to like it even if you don't. To make up for it all, a Stash encore was well-received and helped us all leave feeling pretty happy. —CHRISTOPHER MILLS

➢ This show was relatively short, but sweet. Set-opener AC/DC Bag really jams out into a speedy Uncle Pen. Bathtub Gin seems like it's played in slow motion for a while. In the second set, Scent of a Mule into the Russian jam is awesome—they do a little vocal jamming in the middle of it. —SHANNON C. LANCASTER

➢ The band appeared to cut their performance short, probably because of the ice storm raging outside. Rumors circulated that the next day's show was going to be canceled. After it was over—including a very long and well-jammed Stash encore which shocked me because I had never heard a Stash encore before—we hopped in the car and began to drive. The weather was exceptionally bad; we saw over 10 accidents, mostly tractor-trailers that slid off the road. —DOM DELUCA

11/15/96 [ACCESSIBILITY: ••••]
Keil Center, St. Louis, MO
I: Wilson, Divided Sky, Bouncing, Character Zero, PYITE, Caspian, Ginseng Sullivan, Train Song, Chalkdust, Taste, Cavern
II: Makisupa, Maze, McGrupp, Melt, TMWSIY > Avenu > TMWSIY, My Mind's, Mike's > Sleeping Monkey > Mean Mr. Mustard > Weekapaug
E: Funky Bitch
Mean Mr. Mustard, Weekapaug and Funky Bitch featured John Popper on harmonica. Trey said the second set was "brought to you by the letter 'M' and the number '420.'" (All songs except Weekapaug included a word that started with the letter M). Concert debut: Mean Mr. Mustard.

➢ "The second set is brought to you by the letter M and the number 420." Trey's line surmises the whole second set which contains great segues, a Beatles tune and John Popper. Some people dog this set because they say it lacks extended jamming, notably on Mike's, but if your view of a great show isn't based on how few words there are, you'll love it. —PAUL SHEETS

➢ Set II is the famous "M" set—all of the songs have "M" as the main word in the title: Makisupa, Maze, McGrupp… The performance of the Beatles' Mean Mr. Mustard is fun and Trey has a good time with it. The highlight of the show is John Popper's guest appearance, which doesn't shock me because Popper seems to show up everywhere these days, with Phish, Dave Matthews and even Pearl Jam. —CRAIG ROTHENBERG

➢ The debut of Mean Mr. Mustard set the stage for the mean old man himself, John Popper (it also led to the only non-M song, Weekapaug). This was "WeekaPopper Groove" at its phinest, as it has mainly a Popper jam—so much so that some lyrics are left out. —JON BAHR

➢ The encore was a predictable Phunky Bitch, which held some confusion for the band. Trey wanted to break it down and let John go off, but the guys thought he was shutting it down and ended the song. John Popper was surprised but Fishman jumped on a phunky beat and saved it. As the guys left the stage, Trey seemed unsatisfied. I, however, was very satisfied. Do yourself a favor and get this tape. —JUSTIN WEISS

➢ The Maze was truly one of the best I've ever heard. —RUSSELL LANE

11/16/96 [ACCESSIBILITY: •••]
Civic Auditorium, Omaha, NE
I: Poor Heart, Down with Disease, Guyute, Gumbo, Rift, Free, Old Home Place, Bowie, Lawn Boy, Sparkle, Frankenstein
II: La Grange, Runaway Jim > Kung > Catapult > Axilla > Harry Hood, Suzie, Amazing Grace **E:** We're an American Band
Trey on cowbell and Mike dancing with scarf during Kung. "Vibration of Life" in Kung. "Leigh Fordham" sung in Axilla ending and in Harry Hood. "La Grange" tease in Harry Hood. "La Grange" and "Axilla" teases in Suzie. Concert debut: We're An American Band. Last Kung, 12/30/95 New York, NY [55 shows].

➢ One of the more controversial shows of the tour with the "Vibration of Life" with Trey saying, "This was written by God." For those people who have problems with this, I say, chill out. He's just having fun. Anyways, Guyute was ripping. Is it ever not? The second set offered a lot with a La Grange > Runaway. I was standing up against the front boards, and I have never seen such a huge smile on Trey's face as he had during Hood. Hood started off weird when, during the "Harry, where do you go when the lights go out?" they yelled someone else's name. I'm not sure what they were saying, but the song put a bigger smile on my face than Trey's. The American Band encore was sick—"I left my woman in Omaha"—the place erupted. Good music, good friends, good times. —BRETT PESSIN

➢ This was an excellent show in a small venue, which made it even better. It was snowing like crazy outside but it didn't stop the kids from coming out—the streets of Omaha were packed, and the setlist was fat. In the second set there was a Vibration of Life > Kung chant > Catapult during which Mike came out front and did a dance shaking his hips and waving a sash around. He actually danced on his own without Trey, who was grooving nearby on his drum kit. —MELANIE AND MELITA TERRELL

11/18/96 [ACCESSIBILITY: ••]
Mid-South Coliseum, Memphis, TN
I: CTB, Timber Ho, Poor Heart, Taste, Billy Breathes, Chalkdust, Guelah, Ginseng Sullivan, Reba, Character Zero
II: Also Sprach > Simple > Swept Away > Steep, Scent of a Mule, Tweezer, Hello My Baby, Tweezer Reprise, Llama
E: Waste, Johnny B. Goode
Gary Gazaway on trumpet for Tweezer, Hello My Baby, Tweezer Reprise, Llama and Johnny B. Goode.

➢ I am a bit partial to this show because it took place on my 21st birthday. To me the band really pushed *Billy Breathes* material on this night. Cars Trucks Buses really rocked—it's slowly becoming my favorite "new tune." Ginseng Sullivan was a rare treat and Reba was phenomenal. Also Sprach had traces of Pink Floyd in it and the 10-plus minute Scent had me dehydrated from dancing. —TONY KRUPKA

➢ A great show, thanks in large part to the trumpet stylings of Gary "El Buho" Gazaway, who played with Phish for *Remain In Light*, too (he wrote the horn parts for the album originally). This is a solid second set, both in song selection and in performance quality. Tweezer with Gary is particularly interesting, and his additions to Hello My Baby make this one a cappella song worth hearing. —ED SMITH

➢ Set II opened with a nice funked up 2001 that led into a tight Simple. I'm not a huge Simple fan, but all the Simples I saw on this tour were great—it's really developing as a jam song. Simple led into Swept Away > Steep. Out of Steep came Scent of A Mule with a nice vocal jam which they did in Mule for much of the tour. A phenomenal Tweezer followed with Gary Gazaway on trumpet—definitely my favorite version of the fall. When the boys stepped up for an a cappella Ragtime Gal, Gary took a nice solo. He stayed out there for the smokin' Reprise and then an amazing version of Llama. —DOM DELUCA

11/19/96 [ACCESSIBILITY: ••]
Municipal Auditorium, Kansas City, MO
I: Ya Mar, AC/DC Bag, Foam, Theme, Mound, Stash, Fee, Taste, Loving Cup
II: Bowie, Day in the Life, Bathtub Gin, YEM, Star Spangled Banner, Fire
E: Squirming Coil
"Vibration of Life" between Bathtub Gin and YEM. "Groove is in the Heart" jam in YEM.

➢ This setting for this show was perfect—the art-deco architecture fit nicely with Chris Kuroda's lights. AC/DC Bag was a favorite out on the dance floor. Mound made me feel like I was flying. The second set was highlighted by a You Enjoy Myself that contained a "Groove is in Your Heart" tease. I'm not real sure how long this YEM is, but let's put it this way: it's worth owning. —CHAD ASHCRAFT

➢ For the band's last show in the midwest, they treated us to a great second set reminiscent of Lexington several weeks earlier—a long (though not as long as 11/7 Lexington) Bathtub Gin and a long (even longer than 11/7) YEM, with a verse of Dee-Lite's "Groove is in the Heart" dropped right in the middle. Phish sets used to average about 10 songs each, but as their jam style continues to stretch songs waaaaay out, the number of second sets with only four to six songs continues to grow. That's a trend I can live with! —DAVE SHARPE

11/22/96 [ACCESSIBILITY: ••]
Spokane Arena, Spokane, WA
I: It's Ice, Runaway Jim, Wolfman's, Taste, Ginseng Sullivan, Sample, FEFY, Train Song, Stash, Cavern
II: Down with Disease, Caspian, Maze, Billy Breathes, Swept Away > Steep, Character Zero, Theme, Slave, Hello My Baby **E:** Julius
"Cocaine" (sung as "Spokane") jam before Julius.

➢ Treacherous road conditions and rain led to a well-put It's Ice opener (with the band completely blowing the segue back into the song after the long Page jam). Wolfman's

Brother was an interesting choice, highlighting this set of mellow jamming and new material. Down with Disease was an intense opener to a set that went downhill after the next hour and a half with lots of *Billy Breathes* material and a Julius encore. This show seemed to be a tease for the next night to come. —BRIAN BOEHM

➢ Perhaps the foul, stormy weather dampened the feeling of joy one feels seeing Phish, or maybe this was an off night. The timely It's Ice/Jim intro had me thinking 'classic show,' but on this night, naught. After a quality Taste, the first set just played itself out. The second set brought much promise with DwD and Maze being quite intense. But once again the brakes were applied and instead of grooving, I felt like snoozing (exception: Character Zero.) Even the usually lively Julius seemed a bit slow and stale. —GREG KELLY

11/23/96 [ACCESSIBILITY: •••]
Pacific Coliseum, Vancouver, BC
I: Chalkdust, Guelah, CTB, Divided Sky, PYITE, Mid-Highway Blues, Melt, Rift, Funky Bitch
II: Curtain, Mike's > Simple > Makisupa > Axilla > Weekapaug > Catapult > Waste, Amazing Grace, Harry Hood **E:** GTBT
Concert debut: Mid-Highway Blues (a.k.a. Late Night on the Highway).

➢ Classic opener Chalkdust Torture foreshadows an intense set to come. After Divided Sky and Punch was the first time they stopped this set. Midnight on the Highway, a first-ever, made the experience much more intimate before closing with the favorite Funky Bitch. Curtain > Mike's couldn't have pleased the crowd more—then came the opening notes of Makisupa. "Woke up in the morning, border guard in my bunk, turned the fucking dog on the bus, and found my dank," Trey remarked on the day's adventure. Harry Hood closes this monumental show, perfectly capping this very kind evening. —BRIAN BOEHM

➢ The setlist from this show, especially the second set, is obviously insane. The band had a lot of energy, too, with the downside being somewhat sloppy—that is, unfocused—jamming. This was a really fun show, with the boys debuting the bluegrass tune they learned while waiting at the border after their drug bust and again referencing the incident in Makisupa, but if you pick up this show expecting to be blown away by the band's musical prowess, you're barking up the wrong tape. Still, the bonus Hood after Amazing Grace sure made us happy. —MELISSA WOLCOTT

11/24/96 [ACCESSIBILITY: ••]
Memorial Coliseum, Portland, OR
I: Poor Heart, AC/DC Bag, All Things, Bouncing, Reba, Character Zero, Strange Design, Taste, I Didn't Know, Sample, Antelope
II: Also Sprach > Sparkle, Bowie, Day in the Life > YEM > Loving Cup > Suzie **E:** Ginseng Sullivan, Cavern
Fishman on vacuum for I Didn't Know. Trey says "Norton Charleton Heston" instead of "Marco Esquandolis" in Antelope lyrics.

➢ The evolution of Henrietta's nickname continues! After Zero Man, Moses Brown, Tubbs and Greasy Fizeek (among many others) came his fall '96 name, Norton Charleton Heston. In Portland, Trey introduces Norton for a vacuum solo in I Didn't Know, then substitutes "Norton Charleton Heston" for "Marco Esquandolis" in Antelope, a change made several times this month. As for the Portland show, the general feeling can be summed up by the 2001 > Sparkle combo—in other words, not one of the band's hotter nights. —DAVE SHARPE

11/27/96 [ACCESSIBILITY: ••••]
Key Arena, Seattle, WA
I: Julius > My Friend > Ya Mar, Chalkdust, Sloth, Uncle Pen, Free > Theme, Bold As Love
II: Down with Disease > Jesus Left Chicago, Scent of a Mule, Tweezer > Down with Disease, Star Spangled Banner, Fire
E: Waste, Tweezer Reprise
"Brady Bunch Theme" skatted and played by Trey in Scent of a Mule, which also included Fishman on vacuum. "Sweet Emotion" jam in Tweezer. "Can't You Hear Me Knockin'" jam at the end of the Down with Disease reprise.

➢ A sardined-packed Key Arena crowd tried to find their footing during another up-and-down first set. Even the usually forceful Sloth wilted under these cramped quarters. Axis turned my thoughts to Jimi and what could have been, much like the first set. In set II, a bombastic DwD faded into a soulful Jesus Left Chicago (sweet!). During Trey's solo/vocal part in Scent, he offered the crowd the Brady Bunch theme. Tweezer was the set's centerpiece, starting slow then growing, eventually leading to a Sweet Emotion sing-a-long which led back into the DwD jam. Fantastic! —GREG KELLY

➢ Listening to set II of this show on tape puts me in one of the best moods. Everything about it is excellent; you can't appreciate the setlist unless you hear this tape. I had never been a big Down With Disease fan but I love all 25 minutes of it. The guitar following the Mule duel in Scent is probably the coolest I have heard. But Tweezer is what really does it for me: nice jamming—a Sweet Emotion tease and chorus—and then the song somehow morphs back into DWD. This set is a DWD/Tweezerfest and it kicks ass. The feeling of hearing this tape is like the ultimate back massage. —ADAM RIZZUTI

➢ In the depths of a dense Tweezer jam, the band started singing the "Sweet Emotion" refrain. As that died out, Trey got a sweet melody going that ever so slowly drifted into the Down With Disease theme. It took about 30 seconds until it was clear he was definitely playing DwD, at which time Fishman realized it, too, and immediately accelerated his slower drum beat to the fast DwD rhythm, more or less ruining the delicacy of the segue Trey constructed. But the jam in the DwD Reprise is cool—they don't sing the refrain, instead jamming out for a few minutes before ending with the Stones jam "Can't You Hear Me Knockin.'" Great set! —TYLER HARRIS

11/29/96 [ACCESSIBILITY: ••]
Cow Palace, Daly City, CA
I: Frankenstein, NICU, CTB, Character Zero, Divided Sky, Bathtub Gin, Life on Mars, Maze, Suzie
II: Wilson > Simple > Sparks, Sparkle, Taste, Swept Away > Steep, YEM, Waste, Harry Hood **E:** Sample
Last Sparks, 10/29/94 Spartanburg, SC [173 shows].

➢ Playing at the Cow Palace on the outskirts of San Francisco, the boys didn't play a particularly bad show, but then again, they didn't play a particularly good one either. Like many of the gigs during this tour, Phish oscillated between solid jamming (including a cool Simple > Jam > Sparks and a very good Taste) and dullsville. At the Cow Palace, I found it to be more of the latter. —DAVE SHARPE

➢ I had front row seats, smack dab in between Trey and Mike. Near the end of the first set, during Maze, I was crushed into the rail. I looked back and to my surprise there was a tweaked-out hippie looking at me. He had particles of vomit dangling from his long beard and dreads. He then threw up all over the guy right next to me, as everyone pushed him around. Lots of people tried to ask him questions, but all that would come out of his mouth was a big "AAAAAAH!" All of us found him to be more entertaining than Phish. Finally the security guards let him over the rail, and walked behind him as he was jumping up and down, screaming at Trey and Page. But of course guys like that always make it back to the front. Sure enough, we looked over to our left later in the set and there he was, bothering someone else as he yelped, "AAAAAH!" So when Phish came back for the second set, we all started yelling like the guy did, pointing at Phish. Trey and Page looked at us as if we were nuts, and just laughed. The next night in Sacramento, I saw the guys I watched the show with the night before. We greeted each other, and they told me that "AAAAAAH!" was in the house. We all had a big laugh. It was a demented, memorable Phish experience! —MIKE HOOD

11/30/96 [ACCESSIBILITY: ••••]
Arco Arena, Sacramento, CA
I: Runaway Jim, PYITE, All Things, Bouncing, Stash, Fluffhead, Old Home Place, Uncle Pen, Caspian, Chalkdust
II: La Grange, It's Ice, Glide, Brother, Contact, Also Sprach > Timber Ho, Taste, Funky Bitch, Amazing Grace, Amazing Grace Jam **E:** Possum
John McEuen on banjo for Old Home Place and Uncle Pen. Peter Apfelbaum on tenor saxophone for Timber Ho, Taste and Funky Bitch. McEuen on lap slide guitar and Apfelbaum on tenor saxophone for Amazing Grace Jam and Possum. "Do That Stuff" teases in Also Sprach. Last Amazing Grace Jam, 10/20/95 Cedar Rapids, IA [103 shows].

➢ This show featured two awesome guests which definitely affected Phish's sound. In the first set, John McEuen came out for Old Home Place and Uncle Pen. Both of these songs benefitted from his banjo. Then during the second set, Peter Apfelbaum came out for Timber Ho, Taste and Funky Bitch. Taste with saxophone is so different—there's a spacey jazz feel to the jam. Later, McEuen returns with slide guitar and they jam on the Amazing Grace theme following Phish's a cappella version. —JEFFREY ELLENBOGEN

➢ My favorite non-Vegas west coast '96 show had almost all highs, with some being eight miles or so up. The opening six songs had me thinking '92-'93, not only by the titles but in style, too. Funky, intense, groovy all tweaked together, with Fluff growing to amazing status. Then John McEuen of the N.G.D.B. joined the band for two traditionals. The audience, myself included, pondered what the second set would be: no one guessed right. After opening the second set with five songs not repeated out west (in the U.S., anyway), a sax player guested on an incredible 2001 > Timber Ho. The rest of the set featured all the guests making great music and spirit. This is a must-have. —GREG KELLY

➢ Everyone I talked to loved this show, but I found it enjoyable only to the extent that the special guests infused the second set with a very different sound. (Listen to Apfelbaum's contribution to the opening of Taste for the most pleasing example of this.) The guests left Phish mostly unable to jam out, so they responded with an unusual setlist (La Grange, Glide, Brother). —DAVE SHARPE

12/1/96 [ACCESSIBILITY: •••]
Pauley Pavilion, University of California at Los Angeles, Los Angeles, CA
I: Peaches, Poor Heart, Cavern, CTB, Character Zero, Curtain > Down with Disease, Train Song, Horse > Silent, Sample, Antelope
II: Tweezer > Sparkle, Simple > Day in the Life, Reba, Swept Away > Steep > Tweezer Reprise > Johnny B. Goode, Slave **E:** Highway to Hell
Trey sings "Norton Charleton Heston" instead of "Marco Esquandolis" in Antelope. Last Peaches, 12/31/94 Boston, MA [144 shows].

➢ The revival (after almost two years) of Peaches En Regalia ("Written by a hometown boy, Frank Zappa," Trey announced) set the tone for a great evening of music in the intimate Pauley Pavilion. Both seats featured good jams that didn't stretch on for too long—DwD in the first, Tweezer and Reba in the second—and both sets appeared to close at least once before the band decided to tack on one extra song (or, in the case of the second set, two. The bonus Slave was another major highlight). —RICH MAZER

➢ It's the second set after a decent first set where we saw the first Peaches since 12/31/94. My friend Dave and I were kicking back during the setbreak when a rather large guy in the front row, wearing a Hideo Nomo jersey, went to get an ice cream sandwich. (Nomo is a pitcher for the Dodgers who is from Japan and has a wild windup.) Through Tweezer and Sparkle, this guy was jumping up and down right in front of Trey. Trey kept on looking down at him and laughing. During Simple this guy is going nuts and it looks like he's going to throw his ice cream right onto Trey. After the saxophone verse, Trey screams, "Hey Nomo!!!" It's pretty easy to hear on the tapes. No one who was at the show seems to remember it until I play the tapes for them—I don't even know if "Nomo" knew that Trey was screaming at him. He was just having such a good time (and looking funny as hell doing it.) —MARC OLSON

12/2/96 [ACCESSIBILITY: ••]
America West Arena, Phoenix, NV
I: Rocky Top > AC/DC Bag, Bouncing, YEM > I Didn't Know, Theme, Gumbo, Julius
II: Ya Mar, Divided Sky, Wolfman's, Taste, Free, Scent of a Mule > Harry Hood, Adeline **E:** Fire
Fishman on vacuum for I Didn't Know.

➢ Sunny Arizona! The weather was hot and the scene was awesome. I would never have called Rocky Top to open the show, but it was fun. A little later in the set, they pulled out YEM, the definite highlight. In set II, a nice Wolfman's flowed right into Taste, then the boys did Scent of a Mule. But before the Russian jam segment, they broke right into Harry—it really came out of nowhere. What a Harry it was, very long and the definite highlight of the show for me. It wasn't a crazy show, but I just had a wonderful time. —DOM DELUCA

[12/3/96]
Great Western Forum, Inglewood, CA
Star Spangled Banner
Phish sung a cappella before the Lakers-Supersonics NBA game.

➢ At first I didn't recognize the band (it's the first time I've ever seen Fishman in men's clothes). But once I spotted the four sharply dressed fluffheads at courtside, I grabbed my pal Frank and we ran over to meet them. We wished them all good luck and I shook Trey's hand, telling him they were going to kick ass. And kick ass they did. Clocking in at just over a minute, the boys did us proud with perfect pitch and soaring harmonies. They trotted off court to hearty applause. Then we ambushed them again, shaking their hands and engaging them in witty banter as they passed by. It wasn't much of a conversation, but at least we didn't ask them to play Destiny Unbound. —MIKE INDGIN

Friday, December 6, 1996 — Aladdin Theater, Las Vegas, NV

Wow. Las Vegas. We arrived to this show the day before and pulled right into the parking lot at the Aladdin. We were standing next to the car when this elderly couple came up to us and greeted us: "You guys must be Phish fans." We chatted with them, then they said, "You must know our daughter Amy," referring to Amy Skelton. Of course!

We walked into the Aladdin and scored a cheap room for only $25 that night. The night of the show it jumped to $80, but we got a few people in on it and figured what the heck? It was the last show of the tour—let's go out in style, plus the show was downstairs!

Still not having a ticket, I thought I would never get into the show. It was a very small theater and the last show of tour—who would want to give their ticket up? I waited in the lobby of the hotel, asking everyone who came in if they had an extra. After only an hour of doing this, I found a guy who sold me his extra for $20! I couldn't have been more thrilled—I ran upstairs and hid my golden ticket.

My friend also scored a $20 ticket from a kind guy staying across the hall from us. We put our stuff in the hotel room, settled in, then hit the streets of Las Vegas for some evening fun.

The morning of the show, I woke up excited for the last show of the tour. The will call window was right inside the Aladdin, and the heads were pouring in. The tourists had no clue what was going on. I heard Aladdin staffers whispering to people, "These guys are just like the Grateful Dead people, very nice." There was also a rodeo convention going on at the same time in the hotel so sparks flew between the cowboys and the hippies. Pretty funny stuff to watch! Vegas Ticketmaster released more tickets to the sold out show that afternoon, so most folks grabbed tickets. By 7 p.m. I saw more than 20 people selling their extras for face value (though I did see one poor guy snatch a ticket for $150.)

I headed into the show about 7:15, incredibly excited. The theatre was beautiful. I couldn't believe they were going to play there, in one of the best theatres I have seen them in. I chose my spot on Page's side right above the first section, where I had an amazing view and tons of room. The lights went down and they broke into a sweet Wilson. Peaches followed—the best version of '96, in my opinion (even though there weren't too many). The set kept rocking with an incredible 2001, the longest and funkiest version I'd ever heard; a groovy You Enjoy Myself followed by a hilarious vocal jam about donuts; and a spacey, long Down with Disease that led into Frankenstein to rock the first set out.

It was such an amazing set that I didn't know what to expect for set two. I didn't want to get my hopes up too much because I'd been to a lot of tour enders and they hadn't all been great. I was just hoping for some good songs.

After two months on the road, it had come down to only one set. The band took the stage and kicked into a smokin' Julius to start. They kept the speed up with an average, upbeat Sparkle, then dropped the bomb—an intense Mike's Song with a wicked fat jam that took off and eventually led straight into Simple. There wasn't much of a Simple tease—I could tell immediately which direction they were heading. Simple was long and great, with a cool jam afterwards, and when it ended, I thought it was time for Weekapaug.

But the boys thought differently, and before I knew it, Fish rolled out the drumbeat for Harry. I couldn't have been happier—I wanted to hear one more Harry before tour ended and I got it. Harry was beautiful—Trey's solos were amazing and Page's key work was breathtaking. After "You can feel good about Hood," they went into the jam they do after the verse and then Mike kicked into Weekapaug. Things couldn't have been going better. This Weekapaug was amazing. Almost 10 minutes into it they had a groove going where they would stop and then start back up, then stop again. Each time I thought it was over, but no, they'd kick back into it. Finally, gloriously, it finished.

After Phish took the stage for one last a cappella, Sweet Adeline, they ended the set with an amazing Good Times, Bad Times that really summed up my feelings about the tour.

Now it was time for the encore, I was just waiting for a Slave or Suzie encore, nothing special, but the lights went down and they took the stage. I noticed a few others with them, and my friend whispered to me it was Les Claypool. I had no clue what to expect. They broke into a song and I couldn't believe my ears—it was Harpua, and what a weird version it was. They totally slowed down the song. The story section arrived and Les Claypool told a little story about weed, then Trey talked about Las Vegas and camping while more special guests came out and started yodelling.

The whole place was just in shock. Everyone stared at the stage, sharing this incredible moment. The yodelling ended and Trey went back to the story, saying Jimmy was on his way to Las Vegas but was stopped at the border by four Elvises who told him couldn't come to Vegas unless he sang an Elvis song better than them.

That's when they started to play Suspicious Minds. I was freaking out. I stopped dancing for a few seconds and looked at the stage, where I saw four Elvis impersonators and Fishman, who was pretending to fight them. Then he took the mic and sang the song.

After the song, Jimmy had won and the Poster/Harpua fight materialized. I was really hoping for an ending, but I didn't know what to expect especially after this unique version and what happened when they played Harpua at the Clifford Ball. But they finished it with the wonderful ending I love, making this the best Harpua I'd ever heard and, at half an hour long, the longest encore I'd ever seen them do.

But it wasn't over. They broke into a really hot Suzie Greenberg featuring Les and most of the rest of Primus, plus everyone else (even the Elvises) just having a blast, dancing around. At the end of Suzie, an Elvis took the mic and led the band into a hilarious Suzi Q jam. Suzie/Suzi ended and they thanked us all for a great tour.

What a show! I think it may have been the best show I've ever seen, definitely top three at least. Afterwards we headed back to the hotel for the post-show festivities—it was the end of the tour and we wanted to "party down" with the family we made in the months we spent on the road. Those months of my life taught me a lot, showed me a lot and will never be forgotten. Never had such a good time—Thank You Phish!

—Dom DeLuca

12/4/96 [ACCESSIBILITY: •••]
Sports Arena, San Diego, CA
I: My Friend, Chalkdust, Horn, Uncle Pen, Timber Ho, Sample, Train Song, Guyute, Character Zero, Lizards, Bowie
II: Ha Ha Ha, Mike's > Caspian > Sparkle > PYITE, Life on Mars, Reba, Lawn Boy, Weekapaug **E:** Jesus Left Chicago

Lawn Boy dedicated to the tour's caterers, who were brought up on stage to dance during the song.

➢ Back in California once again, the weather was beautiful. We hung out on the beach all day in San Diego, enjoying the water and the weather, then headed over to the parking lot where we heard everyone grovelling for Vegas tickets. Inside, a really sweet first set included a crazy Guyute which just rocked me, a sweet Timber Ho and a ripping Bowie to end it. Set II opened with Ha Ha Ha into a Mike's Song with a phat, funky jam that led into Caspian. Later in the set, Page took the microphone for Lawn Boy and Trey invited the tour's caterers on stage and danced with two of them. A hot Weekapaug rocked this set out and closed it. Such a fun, well-played set! The encore, Jesus Left Chicago, was unusual but also fun to hear (great solos). So this was it—Las Vegas was next, the last and final stop we all so anticipated. —DOM DELUCA

➢ It was a shock when they broke out Mike's Groove during the second setin Vegas because they'd played such a strong version of it (Weekapaug especially) the show before in San Diego. The entire second set of this show is really worth hearing, for the powerful Weekapaug and gorgeous Reba. —MELISSA WOLCOTT

12/6/96 [ACCESSIBILITY: ••••]
Aladdin Theater, Las Vegas, NV
I: Wilson, Peaches, Poor Heart, Also Sprach > Llama, YEM, CTB, Down with Disease > Frankenstein
II: Julius, Sparkle, Mike's > Simple > Harry Hood > Weekapaug, Adeline, GTBT **E:** Harpua > Les Claypool Rap > Harpua > Yodeling > Harpua > Suspicious Minds > Harpua > Suzie

"Blister in the Sun" tease in Simple. Les Claypool on bass and Larry LaLonde (both of Primus) on guitar for encore. John McEuen and Anamiekl and Heather August yodeled during part of Harpua. Four Elvis impersonators joined Phish on stage during Harpua for Suspicious Minds, with Fishman taking over on lead vocals. Suzie featured everyone already on stage, plus Brian Mantia (of Primus) on drums. "Suzi Q" jam (sung by one of the Elvis impersonators) at the end of Suzie.

Phan Pick 7 ➢ I must write of this show; it was like no other. 2001 > Llama, YEM was superb, really reaching. Sweet Adeline kinda sucked because they didn't use mics—the Aladdin isn't that small, guys. Otherwise, a magical night. How about the set-long Harpua madness as an encore! I've had dreams (nightmares?) about the four Elvii singing around Fish. The band dug Vegas! —DAVE MATSON

➢ YEM featured one of Mike's finest bass jams. Mike's > Simple > Jam is one of the best ever. Harry soared high and hard into a tantalizing Weekapaug where Trey delivers a great blues solo. A truly rocking Good Times Bad Times ends it well. Did I mention the 30-minute encore with Les and Larry from Primus featuring four Elvii and yodelers during Harpua and Suzie? The best show ever! —CHIP CROTEAU

➢ This was the last show of the fall tour. The whole second set was incredible, and the encore was just all-out amazing. It started out with Harpua, then two guys from Primus came out to sing Wildwood Weed and then yodelers came out for Cowboy's Sweetheart. It then went back into Harpua then Fish and a bunch of Elvis impersonators sung Suspicious Minds (by Elvis), back into Harpua, then everything just went crazy during Suzie Greenberg. —MATT FITONE

➢ A great first set, including four instrumentals, was topped by an even greater second set. Check out the "Blister in the Sun" teases in Simple, and the encore, which needs its own tape! Basically, it's Harpua > Suzie, but there is much more: half of Primus, yodelers, and four Elvis impersonators (and Tubbs as the fifth). This is the funniest Harpua ever (always bet on 17!), then a great Suzie with something like 14 people stage! Even the Elvii took turns singing during Suzie. —JON BAHR

➢ One of the best shows of 1996. It includes the first 2001 > Llama ever and a crazy Down with Disease in the first set. The second set Mike's > Simple > Harry > Weekapaug is awesome—the best Weekapaug I've ever heard. Then a crazy jammed out Good Times Bad Times closes the set. Harpua as the encore is a slightly moderated version (they sing the chorus slower). The Elvis impersonators are great—just hilarious! —KEVIN WEISS

➢ The 30-minute encore is by far my favorite Harpua ever. In the story, Jimmy and Poster are walking through the desert when they begin to hear Suspicious Minds (this is when the Elvis impersonators came out on stage), then they ended up in a casino where Poster saw Harpua and they fought. Phish and their guests jammed into various songs such as "I Wish I was a Cowboy's Sweetheart" and "Wildwood Weed," along with yodelers. It ended with Suzie G > Suzi Q. —CHUCK ADAMS

➢ Woohoo! Elvis impersonators, Primus, 45-minute Harpua encore, a how long Mike's Groove—the list goes on! A must have show—not a poor moment for four hours! A hairy, groovin' time, fer sure! —PAUL SHEETS

➢ After a 12-hour drive from Boulder, CO, my friends and I were hurting. Driving all through the night in a snowstorm had the team morale down, but we knew what was in store: Phish's last show of the tour, and their first time in Las Vegas. After a power nap, we felt it was our duty to go check out the town before the show. As the four of us walked out of Caesar's Palace, we saw the band's bus. I knocked on the bus door but there was no one there. After a hearty meal, me and my friend Pete walked back up to the bus and gave another knock. The bus driver nodded "no," but all of a sudden, Trey came out to talk to us. "Are you psyched to play tonight Trey?" "I am so fucking psyched, man." Talking to him and Mike for awhile got us totally pumped up for the show: Trey is not only psyched to play, he is *fucking* psyched. Then my friend Pete says, "So, Mike, you gonna drop some bombs on us tonight?" Mike looked at Pete and said, "What?" Catching up with my two other friends later on, I told them what happened and their jaws hit the ground. "Yeah, we were hanging with Phish in Vegas." Not bad, considering it was my birthday. The Aladdin is a cozy venue that seats about 7,000. Wilson, Peaches really got things started off right and there were no signs of slowing down. They played the best 2001 I have ever heard with Page stealing the show early. YEM, Down with Disease > Frankenstein were all sweet and it was apparent the second set was going to rip. The Julius opener was a revival version for me, blowing the lid off the song. Mike's > Simple > Hood > Weekapaug was sick. Over an hour of music right there. Weekapaug was real good, with the band breaking in between the song and jumping right back in like it was a joke. Good Times closer summed up everything, with Page belting out his lines. I am not even going to get into the huge encore. Primus and Phish, any questions? —BRETT PESSIN

➢ Old school scene. Kids hanging out in the city of cheese. What a trip. —LANGSTON KNIPLER

Las Vegas

12/6/96 Aladdin Theater, Las Vegas, NV

The city of sin seemed like an incongruous place for a Phish concert, but the fair city of Las Vegas, NV was nevertheless tapped as the site for Phish's tour-finishing show. Though the band had played the west coast for years, they had somehow always missed Vegas. The fall Schvice made it clear that the band was excited for the gig—the band's first "casino show" since their July 18, 1991 gig with the Giant Country Horns at Hampton Beach Casino on the coast of New Hampshire.

Besides playing a town they'd never hit before, the Vegas gig also offered the only theater show of the tour—the 9,000-seat Aladdin would play host to the band. As phans started pouring into town the day before the show, a scene developed which many likened to the earlier days—the band's bus was parked out front, and a number of fans chatted it up with Trey, Page, Mike and Fish during their weekend in Vegas. Though the show was sold out, plenty of extras floated around, burning those who paid big bucks for a ticket in advance of the evening's performance.

The show—considered the best of the year by many—got off to a fast start with Wilson and Peaches En Regalia, which had been revived earlier in the week in Los Angeles for the first time since New Year's '94. Building on their early momentum, the band dove into a long Also Sprach Zarathustra (the longest-ever, at least until New Year's Eve) and an incredible You Enjoy Myself (complete with a "donut" vocal jam). And the band kept packing it in—Down With Disease, Cars Trucks Buses and a Frankenstein closer took everyone to setbreak.

When the second set opened with Julius, it seemed a fitting tribute to the nearby Caesar's Palace. But when Phish kept jamming—and jamming—on the tune, it turned into something even more powerful. After a quick Sparkle, the band erupted into Mike's Song even though they'd played it two nights earlier in San Diego. Creating a sequence that seemed the stuff of phans' dreams, the band took Mike's into a very long, gorgeous Simple and then rattled out the start of Harry Hood. When Weekapaug sandwitched this foursome, the Aladdin erupted. The rockingest GTBT ever—at least until 12/30/96—closed the set.

The encore, of course, is the stuff of which legends are made, and raises this show to the storied "all-time great" level. Les Claypool joined Phish onstage for the first time since Laguna Seca Daze 5/28/94, and this time hauled his fellow Primus bandmates along with him. That was only the start of the cavalcade of guest stars, from John McEuen and yodeling friends to four Elvis impersonators who squared off wish Fish at the front of the stage. The first Harpua since Plattsburgh was, joyously, completed, then the band took it around into Suzie Greenberg, complete with a little "Suzi Q" action from the Elvii at the end.

The tour finished, a long night of partying on the strip lay ahead.

1996 New Year's Run

After the 1995 New Year's Run, during which the band played three of their most popular concerts ever, fans embarked on the '96 run with soaring expectations. Perhaps it was inevitable that the band wouldn't rise to the incredible heights they achieved the year before, but they still gave it a hell of a shot. As had become tradition, no songs were repeated in the course of the run—something that seemed to hamper the New Year's Eve show, considering the mass of jam songs played in Philadelphia, especially during the second set on 12/29. That night's Spectrum show was named by most as the best of the lot musically, with the New Year's Eve show offering plenty of fun (a Tweezer Reprise first set closer, a massive balloon drop and an appearance by the Boston Community Choir) but not as much pure jamming as some hoped to hear. Still, it was New Year's, it was Boston, and it was a whole lot of fun.

12/28/96 [ACCESSIBILITY: ••••]
Corestates Spectrum, Philadelphia, PA
I: Runaway Jim, NICU, Wolfman's, It's Ice, Billy Breathes, Ginseng Sullivan, Melt, Mango, Frankenstein
II: Makisupa > Maze, Bouncing > TMWSIY > Avenu, Mike's > Strange Design > Weekapaug, Star Spangled Banner **E:** Johnny B. Goode
Trey spoke about his fondness for the Flyers (John Le Clair in particular) and thanked someone for throwing him a Tickle-Me-Elmo doll. (The Elmo Doll was thrown by phan Hillary Schupf.) The band also dedicated the Star Spangled Banner to Kate Smith, the singer who sang God Bless America before Flyers games.

➢ First show of the New Year's run and I just couldn't wait to get in. The Runaway Jim, NICU opener got my hopes up as we were expecting this to be an anything-goes first show of the run. Although the rest of the setlist seems pretty average, these guys were just on all night. The band came out of TMWSIY > Avenu Malkenu right into Mike's Song, which really got us going. Strange Design brought things down a little—thank God for Mike's opening notes going into Weekapaug. The closing of this show kind of killed the flow. Oh well. —PETER BUKLEY

➢ A solid first set with its fair share of treats—Jim opener, Split, Frankenstein closer. The second set was full of pleasant surprises. Maze was an early tour surprise as the band stretched it to the limits and further! But MWS > Avenu > Mike's! was an even bigger treat. —ERIC ACQUAFREDDA

➢ The first set contained an insane It's Ice bringing on a mid-set Ginseng, then closing with a kick-ass Frankenstein. A pretty decent first set beholds a killer second set! Opened with Makisupa (Trey said "stink stank stunk") into a long, drawn-out Maze. Tearing up the rest of the set was TMWSIY > a crazy Avenu which powerfully went into a fatty Mike's and then a subtle Strange Design, and, yup, Weekapaug. What a way to ring in the Holiday Tour! —ADAM BRICHANTE

12/29/96 [ACCESSIBILITY: ••••]
Corestates Spectrum, Philadelphia, PA
I: Poor Heart, Caravan, Cavern, Taste, Guelah, Train Song, Rift, Free, Squirming Coil, La Grange
II: Bowie, Day in the Life, Bathtub Gin, Lizards, YEM > Rotation Jam > Sixteen Candles > YEM, Harpua **E:** Rocky Top
Sixteen Candles performed by Mike on piano, after he repeatedly yelled "Sex!" "Champagne Supernova" jam in Harpua. Tom Marshall on lyrics for Champagne Supernova. Tom Marshall on lyrics. Last Caravan, 12/2/94 Davis, CA [160 shows]. Last Rotation Jam, 12/15/95 Philadelphia [74 shows]. Concert debut: Sixteen Candles.

➢ The second set started off with an absolutely sick Bowie. After listening to the tape, at 17+ minutes, I declared it my personal favorite Bowie since 12/29/94 Providence. In Bathtub Gin, Page absolutely destroyed his keyboard, going insane in the opening solo. After a quality Lizards, it began. The enchanting opening notes of YEM filled the Spectrum. I watched Fishman walk around the back of the stage after Trey jumped on the sticks. I expected a nice Fishman tune, but wait—rotation jam. Later, Fishman takes the bass from Page and starts slappin' away. During this, Mike is going off on the keys and Page picks up the guitar and jams. And let me tell you, Page rocks. They jammed hard, into Mike's beautiful cover of Sixteen Candles. What followed? "Oom pa pa, oom pa pa," the sounds of Harpua. —CHIP CROTEAU

➢ The second set of this show was the best of the '96 holiday run. Through trademark Phishiness (Mike's take on 16 Candles) to superb musicanship (David Bowie) to special guests (Tom Marshall doing his best Liam Gallagher) to awe-inspiring theatrics and light work (YEM), this set defined the experience that is Phish. Throw a Harpua into the broth and you've got quite a meal. —LEE SCHILLER

➢ During Harpua, Trey tells of Harpua and Poster Nutbag's trip to Hell. There they meet the Uber-Demon—Tom Marshall dressed as Liam Gallagher of Oasis. This all happens as "Champagne Supernova" plays on "Jimmy's radio." It was so funny watching all of the teeny-boppers freak out thinking it was really one of the Gallagher brothers. What a great way to build up to New Year's! —PETER BUKLEY

New Year's '96

12/31/96 FleetCenter, Boston, MA

New Year's Eve, Phish, and Boston (or at least Worcester) are linked so closely that it was only a matter of time until Phish returned to Beantown for its year-end fete. After taking off for the Big Apple for New Year's '95, Phish returned home in 1996. The final days of the year found the band at the FleetCenter for a pair of gigs *Boston Globe* writer Steve Morse termed "the toughest tickets in a long time."

Indeed, the word on the scene for New Year's at the FleetCenter was "rejected," as Phish Tickets-by-Mail was forced to turn away more fans than ever. The ticketless partied in subzero weather, hoping against hope they would make it inside for the toasty atmosphere of New Year's Phish.

Those who were lucky enough to get in witnessed history yet again. Though the new FleetCenter lacked the character of the old Boston Garden, Phish tried to make up for it with t-shirts that labeled the venue the "new Boston Garden," and of course with their music.

A generally solid first set ended on a crazy note with a Tweezer Reprise that brought closure to the previous night's Tweezer, and a solid second set included long jams in Simple and Hood. Then, between the second and third sets, the crowd watched as a remote-controlled hot air balloon motored around the venue while scoreboards counted down to midnight starting at 11:10 p.m.

Sometime within about 10 minutes of midnight, the band re-emerged and broke into Also Sprach Zarathustra. The crowd gave a huge cheer when the countdown clock hit 4:20 and an even louder roar as midnight arrived and thousands of balloons poured from the FleetCenter rafters while Phish kicked into Down with Disease. The set ended with a surprise visit by the Boston Community Choir, who backed up Phish during their first attempt at Queen's Bohemian Rhapsody. The singers stuck around for a go at Julius and Amazing Grace. Though microphone problems muted the choir in the arena, they came through loud and clear on the next day's FM-radio broadcast.

12/30/96 [ACCESSIBILITY: ••••]
FleetCenter, Boston, MA
I: Ya Mar, Sloth, Llama, Gumbo, Reba, Talk, Funky Bitch, Theme, GTBT
II: Timber Ho, Uncle Pen, AC/DC Bag, Guyute, Tweezer > Lifeboy, Scent of a Mule, Slave **E:** Possum

Trey on acoustic guitar for Talk. PA cut out during Funky Bitch, leading to a "silent jam" for about three and a half minutes before system became operational again and Funky Bitch continued. Steven Wright on bell for Scent of a Mule, which had a Page/Mike duel.

➢ Perhaps NYE fell flat because they played so hard the night before. Set one was a Page-fest: four organ solo songs to open the set, including a very grooving Ya Mar opener. We all know that the sound went out during Funky Bitch. Too bad: Trey was taking the finest, bluesiest solo he'd ever taken—nothing spacey, nothing experimental. Just raw power. Couldn't the sound have gone out during Talk when we were all sitting down? —SCOTT KUSHNER

➢ A very good show musically and a very different set list. A few phans around me commented on the set list being "songs plays less often but not often enough for NYE." One fan was very upset, saying, "They're playing all throw-backs." Personally, I found the show very enjoyable. The night was almost like waiting not to hear songs because that meant they would play them on NYE. The highlight, without a doubt, was Possum. —JEFF BERNIER

➢ My passion for Phish is outlined in the cycle of energy that flows through both the band members and all the phans at the show. How nice it is to use the Funky Bitch from set one as a clear example. Yes, the sound blew out and yes, many people were reminded of the Rift the year before at Worcester 12/28/95. But no, the energy did not stop flowing. Phish played on. We couldn't hear Trey play with his teeth, or Page play with his toes, but we still felt the energy flow—the energy that perhaps is my only healthy addiction. —MICHELLE HIRSCH

12/31/96 [ACCESSIBILITY: ••••]
FleetCenter, Boston, MA
I: Axilla, Peaches, PYITE, CTB, Stash, Horse > Silent, Divided Sky, Sample, Tweezer Reprise
II: Chalkdust, Wilson, Sparkle, Simple > Swept Away > Steep > Harry Hood > Caspian, Character Zero
III: Also Sprach > New Year's Countdown > Auld Lang Syne > Down with Disease, Suzie, Antelope, Bohemian Rhapsody, Julius **E:** Amazing Grace

Remote-controlled miniature hot air balloon floated around the venue between the second and third sets. Arena clock counted down to midnight, starting after the end of the second set at 11:10 p.m. Giant balloon drop (reportedly a world record) from arena ceiling flooded the stage and floor during Auld Lang Syne and Down with Disease. Boston Community Choir on vocals for Bohemian Rhapsody, Julius and Amazing Grace. FM broadcast on WBCN-Boston on 1/1/97. Concert debut: Bohemian Rhapsody.

Phan Pick #13 ➢ New Year's Eve!! How lucky we were to get tickets for this show. Colder on this night—the drum circle moved inside; police tried but couldn't break it up. First set was solid, second set was solid, third set was phenomenal. 2001 > ALS > DWD with the balloons set the gear shift for the high gear of my soul. I have to say I wasn't thrilled with the encore but the post-show glow lasts throughout the year. —IAN RUFE

➢ Ten minutes before midnight Phish took the stage with a slow-to-start 2001 that made me wish it was 2001 instead of 1997. Then, this is the shit: Auld Lang Syne > Down With Disease with a long end and middle jam that gave way to Suzie, new and full of life. Antelope was long and hot. Then the real magic came: the Boston Community Choir took the stage with their red robes and Phish began Bohemian Rhapsody. Next was Julius, and I've never seen a better version of this song. A sweet and mellow encore of Amazing Grace—the choir added so much. Get this tape. —AARON BENTON

➢ WOW! Amazing! This show proves Phish is only going to get better and we'd better not miss it. The first of three sets set a nice tone for a fascinating night. Horse > Silent proves to be as beautiful as ever. The new songs in set II offer a taste of an ever-expanding future. The first songs of the third set are so wide open and generally free. Queen is back with Bohemian Rhapsody and the choir only made it better. —ANDY KAHN

➢ Yeah, I know NYE shows are always favorites. This one was different, though: no theme, just music (which is okay by me!) Very solid sets I and II, great buildup to climax with 2001 > Auld Lang Syne > DWD at 12:00. Then Bohemian Rhapsody with the Boston Community Choir. Where'd they get that idea for that? Only Phish could pull something like that off. —MIKE D'AMICO

➢ This was the most disappointing Phish experience I'd ever had. My feeling has always been that the New Year's Eve show ought to be a celebration of improvisational rock (i.e., MSG '95 and Boston '94). This concert was not. Set one fell flat. Tweezer Reprise was the most energetic tune and it was half-assed. Set two was better, and the Character Zero was admittedly rocking, but it didn't make up for the show's shortcomings. I also felt very cheated that DWD was the New Year's Song instead of Brother. —SCOTT KUSHNER

➢ The band's placement of Down With Disease as the "New Year's Song," where it also appeared (as a jam, anyways) in 1993, cemented it as the song of the year. After playing it only four times in 1995, DwD was lavished with attention by the boys, raising it to the ranks of their greatest jam songs. Hurrah! —ERNIE GREENE

➢ The FleetCenter is large, sterile and boring. It was up to Phish to transform it into an intimate, friendly venue. Once again, they worked their magic and we all shared in the groove. Peace, love, and Happy New Year! —AMY MANNING

Monday, December 30, 1996 — FleetCenter, Boston, MA

During set one I was in a horrible, horrible place, physically as well as mentally. The group of boys next to the aisle where I was attempting to dance (not an inch of space for that) sang every word to Sloth in my ear and a posse of seven 16-year-old girls wearing big old vests, little backpacks and perfume crowded my moving space. I was set to move but I could barely make it up the steps it was so packed.

I started thinking some horrible thoughts. The fact that I was even thinking in the first place is pretty telling—my mind was definitely not on the show. Anyway, all of a sudden I understood what all those former Phish fans have been saying—it's just not the same—but they say it based on the sound and I think it based on the crowd. Then I realized how closely tied together these two are.

Just as the crowd affects the music, the music affects the crowd. People clap to the beat whenever there is a familiar song or rhythm, people scream during a cappella, people talk during mellow jams. In Philadelphia, Page was going off during YEM and as soon as an obvious rhythm came along, masses of people started clapping to it. It seemed like he had to change his jam. Point is, if people desire to clap, they want a "normal" beat, and a normal beat is the opposite of a crazy jam. Therefore, the masses do not want a crazy jam. And the masses have power. I believe that because they are driving me nuts.

I ended up in the hallway leading into the section to the side/rear of the stage, though even there security dudes kept coming through and telling people to leave. I perfected the ability to shut them out, to keep on twirling as they walked through all of us. Eventually they made all the twirlers go outside of the stage area by the neon nacho stands—out where it's impossible to hear the music and they pull down this big black curtain so we couldn't see in.

What do we do? I talked to lots of people who were weirded out by that stuff too—all the people exiled to the hall with me. But the band can't really say, "Please don't clap to our music."

And who am I to designate an 'us' and a 'them'? It can't be measured by the number of shows—Phish shows are the thing to do; everybody and their grandma went to Plattsburgh. Dancing is no measure—some of the most intense phans don't move a muscle during a whole show.

But that is precisely the good stuff—the membership, the community, the family. I've felt the family thing big time since Vegas and it has grown greater and greater.

The bond seems to grow out of necessity, as a means of survival. As the crowd grows bigger, the family grows tighter. I love the feeling of dancing around strangers, of stopping to catch my breath after Phish has led us on some phenomenal musical journey and smiling at the guy next to me who shares the same glow. And I have met some wonderful people and for the most part, except for the set in hell, I've found great people with whom to enjoy the show. And this fact, that there is still a family, that the smile of a stranger shared during AC/DC Bag can counter and bury all the negative feelings I experienced earlier, is what it's all about.

I know that I can get there still, that no matter what, I love these guys and will never stop going. But it has become a big challenge—of overcoming the crowd, of accepting that we are nearing the end of the decade, that Phish is huge, that MSG is a unusual venue, that tickets are not a given, that Vegas was an exception, that even Great Woods is impossible, that the whole deal is new, that this change is natural and what is inevitable is liberating.

To allow myself to grove with this, to surrender to the flow so to speak and just be comfortable with this happening as it will, of course feels better than being bitter. I still admire attempts to awaken the masses, the flyers spread out which actually have to explain that it is important to be quiet at the beginning of Foam or in Divided Sky, the built-up frustration eventually manifested by a "SHUT UP!" to the babblers and screamers during Sweet Adeline.

And I can only hope more and more people will get the bug, will feel it, and Phish won't just be a "thing" but more like a "way." All I can say right now is that I still have one more night to go and that's all that really matters.

—Julie Beck

Monday, December 31, 1996 — FleetCenter, Boston, MA

My pomposity about the previous night has lessened. New Year's Eve was totally phenomenal: great show, great crowd, great New Year's dig, thousands of balloons and a choir.

My night was just wonderful. I had a great feeling the whole show—I met a guy who is moving to New Mexico, ran into people I haven't seen since college and even high school, and found a broom.

We left our stuff under a platform, and a champagne bottle broke right there—glass everywhere. I decided to wander around the area a little bit and went over to the hallway where I had been the night before. Not surprisingly, there was this funky guy I had met last night, one of those people it was fun to just share a show experience with even though I didn't know him at all. But the amazing thing was he happened to have a broom and was sweeping the aisle. I borrowed the broom to bring to my section and swept up the glass. It felt really good to be doing that; it was totally bizarre yet natural.

The whole night was like this, even the song choices. Everything was natural in its obscurity (or obscure as its nature, I'm not sure). Axilla I and Tweezer Reprise. The simultaneous intensity and simplicity of the balloons, the professionalism yet unexpectedness of the choir and Bohemian Rhapsody.

The night was entirely magical in a very real, tangible way. I feel like I was able to break out of my rut, to dive beyond the annoyances and just fully be there and flow with everything. I had a great spot to dance in. Behind Page's side, rear stage, is definitely the place for me now. Those times that I actually opened my eyes, I found I had an amazing view. It was really cool to see the faces of the people in the front rows. The balloons were so amazing that I could barely close my eyes during Down With Disease and this experience of having my eyes open was completely new and invigorating for me.

I've met some great people these past couple of days. But the greatest individuals I encountered during these shows were a group of four guys from a high school in Boston's surrounding suburban vortex. These guys were sophomores and juniors, younger than the kids I've led on summer programs, yet I totally connected with them. They were right on, intense, funny individuals. I met them on the T into the first Boston Garden show. We talked the whole ride there, and I remember this blanket-clad guy Nick telling me about his school, show experiences, and his life's experiences.

He had some really great things to say; they all did. I ran into them again on the T on the way home after New Year's. It felt like a reunion. These guys were inspiring. Knowing that there are high school kids out there with such intense thoughts and powers of expression was redeeming after encountering the whining, drunk high school kids at the show because Phish has become the thing to do New Year's Eve. These guys were my last Phish interaction of these shows and it was with them that I said good-bye to another New Year's run. I couldn't imagine a better sense of closure.

This interaction with these guys just epitomizes my whole experience over these days. It's like this perpetual mingling of anonymity and intense belonging. Who knows if I'll ever see these kids again. I am not sure if I ever told them my name, but in our few interactions, we developed a bond, a familiarity, an appreciation of each other which I will not forget. There is just something amazing about going to shows alone, unattached to any specific individuals, any plans.

I thrived on the anonymity. I felt I was just another girl dancing, another person there for the experience that was there for all to indulge in. All the while, I know that everyone around me is equally as anonymous and this is something we all share, something that brings us together, something which allows us to belong to one another.

It is this union which I am left with, and this union which I carry with me from show to show and which carries me through the times between. And as always, as a Phish chapter closes, I am overwhelmed with mixed feelings of loss, emptiness, inspiration and rejuvenation.

And I know that no matter what, no matter how big this thing gets, no matter how overwhelmed I feel by the crowd, as long as the band still plays, the unions will inevitably exist, and I will continue to go to the shows.

—Julie Beck

1997 Winter/Europe

In February, the band headed back across the Atlantic to Europe, hoping to build on its audiences of the previous summer with three weeks of solo shows.

Musically, the tour became Phish's latest version of "let's show the doubters what we're made of." Grumblings that 1996 hadn't been the band's best year were forgotten as Phish played a string of extremely interesting, improvisational shows, utilizing a bunch of strange new tunes like Carini and Walfredo penned especially for the smaller venues of the European tour. Most notably, the tour saw the evolution of a funkier jamming style that continued to de-emphasize Trey's guitar leads that so defined Phish's style for much of the 1990s. Recognizing this musical evolution as a breakthrough for the band, Phish later mined the tour's penultimate show, in Hamburg, Germany, for the live album *Slip Stitch and Pass.*

2/13/97 [ACCESSIBILITY: •••]
Shepherds Bush Empire, London, England
I: Chalkdust, Wolfman's, Also Sprach > Stash, Walfredo, Taste, Waste, Poor Heart, Character Zero, Peaches, Love Me, Bowie
II: Julius, CTB, My Soul, PYITE > Jam > Slave, When the Circus Comes, Maze > Rocka William, Harry Hood, Frankenstein
E: Caspian, Johnny B. Goode

Maze unfinished. Concert debuts: Walfredo, Love Me (also known incorrectly as "Treat Me Like a Fool"), My Soul, When the Circus Comes and Rocka William.

➢ First show of the European tour! A very American crowd a couple thousand people strong packed into the Empire to see the boys break out a bunch of new songs, including two that feature the band members rotating instruments. For Walfredo, a little ditty about the band's experiences opening for Santana in summer '92, everyone moved one instrument to the right—Trey on piano and vocals, Mike on guitar, Fish on bass and Page on drums ("Fish played the vacuum and ruined your set" is one line I recall.) Rocka William found Trey and Fish trading places, and Mike and Page swapping, with Fish belting out the pretty dark lyrics. A fun show got the tour started right. —JAMES DALY

➢ In a radio interview broadcast in London several days before the Shepherds Bush Empire gig, Mike and Fish revealed that Trey made it all the way to Newark airport before realizing he'd forgotten his passport. I guess even rock stars aren't exempt from international laws, because he missed his flight. —SCOTT SIFTON

2/14/97 [ACCESSIBILITY: ••]
Le Botanique, Brussels, Belgium
I: Runaway Jim, NICU, YEM, Adeline, Axilla, It's Ice, Billy Breathes, Uncle Pen, Antelope
II: AC/DC Bag, Ya Mar, Down with Disease, Funky Bitch, Reba, Walfredo, Rocka William, Scent of a Mule > Day in the Life **E:** Character Zero

Scent of a Mule unfinished.

➢ Seeing Phish in Europe was amazing—the worst view in most of these clubs would be only about 20 rows back in an American venue, so it really didn't matter to us what they played. The room in Brussels was relatively clean and small, and the band responded with an incredible opening threesome: Jim, NICU, YEM! The second set drew its strength from a very good Down with Disease, plus back-to-back rotation songs Walfredo and Rocka William. Then the band came out into the bar after the show and hung out with the phans for awhile. —JAMES DALY

2/16/97 [ACCESSIBILITY: ••••]
Wartesaal, Cologne, Germany
I: Beauty of My Dreams, Melt, Bouncing, Crosseyed and Painless, Guelah, Ginseng Sullivan, Tweezer, Waste, Cavern, Chalkdust
II: Sample, CTB, Free, Sparkle, Simple > When the Circus Comes, Swept Away > Steep > Bowie, Loving Cup, Tweezer Reprise
E: Theme, Johnny B. Goode

Show was later broadcast on "Rockplast," a German television show. Concert debut: Beauty of My Dreams.

➢ This show was in the old waiting room of the Cologne train station. The band was separated from the fans by about 10 feet, a space occupied by at least six television cameras. Throughout the show, the cameras were all over the stage, getting cool angles on the band. Phish responded to this interesting scenario by playing most of the catchy songs (Bouncing, etc.). They also broke out tunes like Circus Comes to Town, which seemed to be enjoyed by the largely American audience. —JEFFREY ELLENBOGEN

➢ This show demonstrates Phish's tendency to react (in my opinion, negatively) to the concept of their show being broadcast. Numerous cameras stared at the band the whole show, contributing to the energy. The focus of the show was definitely new material: five tracks from Billy Breathes, including Theme, which is a great encore. There were also two new covers and the second post-Halloween appearance of Crosseyed and Painless. Add to the mix the favorite crowd pleasers (Bouncin', Cavern, Sparkle, Sample) and you have the makings of a pretty lame, made-for-TV show. However, even the TV audience needs a sick jam, and this show has three (Crosseyed, Tweezer and Bowie), but even those didn't get very far out there. Oh well. —GREG SCHWARTZ

2/17/97 [ACCESSIBILITY: ••••]
Paradiso, Amsterdam, Holland
I: Soul Shakedown Party > Divided Sky, Wilson, My Soul, Guyute, Timber Ho, Billy Breathes, Llama, Bathtub Gin > Golgi
II: Squirming Coil > Down with Disease > Carini > Jam > Taste > Down with Disease, Suzie, Caspian **E:** Sleeping Monkey, Rocky Top
DwD reprise out of Taste included lyrical refrain. Concert debut: Soul Shakedown Party, Carini.

➢ We arrived early to find a sparse scene of kids. We walked around back and heard what sounded like Marley playing inside. After a few moments, we realized it was Phish, soundchecking Soul Shakedown Party. Wow! Inside the renovated church was an amazing show waiting to develop. Highlights: during Wilson, the stain glass windows behind the stage lit up to the call of "Wilson... Wilson." Second set Squirming Coil segued into space, suddenly Mike stepped forward and started DwD. Mike goes sick! DwD actually becomes Lucy (or something), and there's a real segue into Taste. This was an epic jam! —JEFFREY ELLENBOGEN

➢ Obviously, the band had a tough task to follow summer '96's curfew-free Melkweg show. I heard the soundcheck, so the Soul Shakedown opener wasn't the surprise it should have been. Yet it was another excuse to partake of the diggity, in a place where you don't need excuses. Our visit to Gamehendge was cut short by fairly uncreative 12-bar blues. Thank heavens for Guyute! I've never heard Billy Breathes so jammed and in such beautiful fashion. The whole set was gorgeous, if not long enough, with Trey promising more to come. It was obvious upon returning that at least Trey had watched his set-break go up in smoke. Sometimes you can just tell that he's itching to jam. During the usual ending Coil solo by Page, Trey never really stopped playing. Instead he helped control the jam, turning it into the spacey intro that precedes Mike's huge bass intro to Down with Disease. The tempo was so fast, it was obvious that the band wanted to get right into the jam. And so they did, completely losing any semblance of the original song. After about ten minutes, a song/rap emerges (it could be described as Golden Earring meets Megadeth at a poetry workshop, but I wouldn't), and is gone like a hallucination, quickly returning to the jam. Trey pulls everyone almost seamlessly into Taste, which once again slides into jam. As Trey solos, I began to recognize a familiar melody and before I could catch my breath, they're back in DwD, more than half an hour later. Second set was also too short, but seriously sweet. —GREG SCHWARTZ

➢ The second set has an absolute must-hear, 45-minute jamfest starting and ending with Down with Disease. Starting DwD out of Coil, the band drifts into a long jam which eventually segues into the concert debut of Carini Had a Lumpy Head. The jam out of Carini is just amazing, really experimental, and finally landing in Taste. The Taste jam also takes off, with Trey bringing it back around into a full DwD reprise, with the closing lyrics. So tasty! —JOSH ALBINI

2/18/97 [ACCESSIBILITY: ••]
Bataclan, Paris, France
I: Beauty of My Dreams, Cavern, PYITE, Runaway Jim, NICU, Stash, Waste, Walfredo, Character Zero, Slave
II: Peaches, Also Sprach > My Soul, Maze, Wolfman's, Reba, Train Song, Harry Hood > Frankenstein **E:** Bold As Love

➢ It's pretty hard to be in any kind of bad mood after a Phish show, especially one like Paris, a "greatest hits" show which included a Slave dedicated to "a friend of ours [who] got hit by a car today." But after the show, my spirits were down a bit. Maybe it was because I knew the next Phish show I'd see wouldn't be for about six months. Maybe it was the remnants of rain in the air. Maybe it was the flashing neon sign right outside our hostel window. Then again, there were the three assholes I caught videotaping the show because the only security in the whole place were the coat-checkers who made everyone check in every coat and every bag before entering the show. This not only made a lot of people late getting in, but it also created an hour-or-better wait after the show to get our shit. Phish seemed a little tired, too, which, despite a pretty good show, summed up the evening—tired. —JASON HEDRINGTON

2/20/97 [ACCESSIBILITY: •••]
Teatro Smeraldo, Milan, Italy
I: Curtain > Tweezer, Soul Shakedown Party > Chalkdust, Love Me, Taste, Gumbo, When the Circus Comes > Bowie, Tweezer Reprise
II: Sample, CTB, Character Zero, Uncle Pen, Stash, Bouncing, Free, Swept Away > Steep > Day in the Life, Runaway Jim, Adeline **E:** Julius

➢ Look at the setlist for this show and tell me the sets shouldn't be reversed. Anyways, if you're getting the tapes, get the first set! It's really hot, starting with a Curtain > Tweezer opener that rocks. Follow that up with Soul Shakedown Party (glad to see they didn't limit it to just Amsterdam), strong versions of the Elvis classic Love Me, Taste and Gumbo, plus David Bowie, then Tweeprise to close? Damn fine set. —LEE JOHNSTON

2/21/97 [ACCESSIBILITY: •••]
Tenax, Florence, Italy
I: My Soul, Foam, Down with Disease, Lizards, Crosseyed and Painless, YEM
II: Ya Mar, Antelope > Wilson, Oh Kee > AC/DC Bag, Billy Breathes, Reba, Waste, Caspian **E:** Character Zero
Antelope unfinished. Wilson played heavy-metal style. Last Oh Kee, 8/12/96 Noblesville, IN [50 shows].

➢ The American scene continued in Firenze, where anticipation ran high for the first-ever solo Phish show in the city of the Uffizi. The first set was a very pleasant affair, climaxing with the song we all expected, YEM. After singing the first "Wash Uffizi, drive me to Firenze" refrain, Trey shouted, "This one's for you!" But the real highlight came in the second set, when the Antelope jam veered away from the "rye, rye rocco" closing and took on a heavy-metal feel. In the midst of a driving beat, Trey started yelling the lyrics to Wilson. He "sung" (if you could call it that) all of Wilson with this totally wild industrial beat, then finally segued into Oh Kee Pa, of all things. —JAMES DALY

2/22/97 [ACCESSIBILITY: ••]
Teatro Olympico, Rome, Italy
I: Walfredo, Also Sprach > Funky Bitch, Theme, NICU, When the Circus Comes, Talk, Melt, I Didn't Know, Character Zero
II: Chalkdust, Bathtub Gin > Sparkle, Simple > Jesus Left Chicago, Harry Hood, Free, Hello My Baby **E:** Johnny B. Goode
Fishman on vacuum for I Didn't Know. "Bowie" teases in Chalkdust. Simple featured a Page piano solo.

➢ Definitely not the pick of the Europe '97 lot, Rome was the worst of the four straight amazing Italy gigs. Can't fault the boys for that; after all, the 2/21 and 2/23 shows were practically instant classics. But the second set in Roma did have some nice touches, including Jesus Left Chicago and of course Harry Hood. —SCOTT SIFTON

2/23/97 [ACCESSIBILITY: ••••]
Fillmore, Cortemaggiore, Italy
I: Carini, Axilla, All Things, Sloth, Love Me, Rift, Fluffhead, Frankenstein, Bowie
II: Daniel, Suzie, Maze, Horse > Silent, Peaches, Mike's > Do It In the Road > HYHU, GTBT **E:** Billy Breathes, Rocky Top
To open the show, prerecorded version of Carini played over PA; Phish joined in as they took the stage. Fishman on vacuum for Do It In the Road. "Tweezer Reprise" jam in GTBT. Last Daniel, 8/28/93 Berkeley, CA [287 shows]. Last Do It In the Road, 6/25/95 Philadelphia, PA [144 shows].

➢ After Europe tour ended, everyone I talked to declared Stuttgart and Hamburg the best of the bunch, but my vote goes to Cortemaggiore. Playing the Fillmore, a cozy little hall with a garish venue logo for the backdrop behind the band, Phish just ripped it up. The first set opened with the first real Carini or Lucy or whatever it's called (the one in Amsterdam was kind of lost in the middle of a long jam), and ending with an amazing Fluffhead/Frankenstein/Bowie run. They opened the second set with the first Daniel since summer '93, went to town on Maze, then gave us the tour's first Mike's Song, which jammed way out before "the rebirth of Henrietta" (as Trey puts it) brought Fishman forward for Do It In The Road. A steaming GTBT—with a Tweezer Reprise jam!—finishes off this already-legendary set. —JAMES DALY

➢ Weird that the boys would bring back Daniel for a one-time performance, but with different lyrics and a different tempo. It's gotten a little more biblical. Besides that revival, check out the Mike's jam in this set. It never segues into Simple, but after a raging Mike's jam, they enter the outro jam and just mellow out, much like a Simple jam. There's a really gorgeous passage of quiet jamming before the music just fades to nothing for a second, then Do It In The Road cranks up. —RICH MAZER

2/25/97 [ACCESSIBILITY: ••]
Incognito, Munich, Germany
I: Runaway Jim, My Soul, One Meatball, Little Red Rooster, Got My Mojo Workin', Stash, Waste, Taste, Loving Cup
II: Beauty of My Dreams, Sample > PYITE > Free, Fee, My Friend, Down with Disease, Caspian, La Grange, Adeline **E:** Chalkdust
Sydney Ellis on vocals for One Meatball, Little Red Rooster, Got My Mojo Workin. My Friend aborted after about a minute because of Trey messup. Concert debuts: One Meatball, Little Red Rooster, Got My Mojo Workin'.

➢ Super-small venue hinted at how it must've been back at Nectar's. A special guest, Sydney Ellis, did a fabulous job on several songs in the first set. We saw another Taste, a My Friend My Friend cut short by Trey, and Mike taking over on Down With Disease. Sweet Adeline with no mics was more than awesome. —MATT BUSSMAN

2/26/97 [ACCESSIBILITY: ••••]
Longhorn, Stuttgart, Germany
I: Camel Walk, Llama, My Friend, Harry Hood, My Soul, Tube, Carini, Rocka William, Dog Log, Guitar Gently Weeps
II: Buried Alive > Poor Heart, Ha Ha Ha > Jam > YEM > Kung > Theme, Scent of a Mule > Magilla > Scent of a Mule, Slave **E:** Highway to Hell
Magilla played as Page's duel in Scent. Last Magilla, 5/4/94 New Orleans, LA [260 shows]. Last Dog Log, 12/11/95 Portland, ME [90 shows]. Last Guitar Gently Weeps, 12/11/95 Portland, ME [90 shows]. Last Camel Walk, 7/2/95 Fayston, VT [140 shows].

➢ What a cool European setting for a great selection of tunes: Camel Walk opener, Dog Log, Tube and other lesser-played gems. The second set included a reaching jazz jam. Rocka William was a switch-up of the boys (Trey on drums, Mike on keys, Page on bass and Fish on lead) which is pretty special. Overall, one of the better European shows during this tour. —DAVE MATSON

➢ One glance at the setlist makes it clear that Phish had it going on in Stuttgart! Not just Camel Walk, but Camel Walk as an opener to a set that includes rarities (Dog Log), jamming (Harry) and trademark Phish wackiness (Rocka William, Carini). The first set is so obviously phenomenal that you might be inclined to overlook the second set, but it's also a winner, built around an incredible YEM that follows a jamming (yes, really) Ha Ha Ha. Scent of a Mule has Page and Trey scatting, just wild stuff, then Slave as a finishing touch. Amazing, amazing show—if they played something like this in the states, people would lose their shit! —RICH MAZER

2/28/97 [ACCESSIBILITY: •••]
Huxley's Neue Welt, Berlin, Germany
I: Carini, Paul and Silas, My Soul, CTB, Peaches, Stash, Swept Away > Steep > Ya Mar, Character Zero
II: Taste, Drowned > Caspian > Frankenstein, Bowie, Love Me, Axilla > Waste, Julius **E:** Day in the Life

"Oh Kee" teases in Ya Mar. Page piano solo in Caspian. Last Paul and Silas, 10/24/95 Madison, WI [120 shows]. Last Drowned, 12/31/95 New York, NY [82 shows].

➢ Tucked between two of the hottest Phish shows in recent memory, Berlin is easy to overlook. Despite its paltry length (the entire show is less than two hours long), there are some sweet moments. The second set includes the first Drowned since New Year's Eve '95, and although it's not as strong a version as 12/31/95, it's good to see it back in the band's current repertoire. Caspian, which follows Drowned, includes a Page solo that eventually leads the band into a rocking Frankenstein. Trey later recalled this show as a special, softer night in front of a very attentive audience. —SCOTT SIFTON

➢ After the first-set opener, Trey remarks, "'Carini Had a Lumpy Head' is the official title of that song," ending the week-long debate about whether the tune—first played in Amsterdam—was called Lucy, Song for Carini, or something else entirely. —JAMES DALY

3/1/97 [ACCESSIBILITY: ••••]
Markthalle, Hamburg, Germany
I: Cities, Oh Kee, Down with Disease, Weigh, Beauty of My Dreams, Wolfman's > Jesus Left Chicago, Reba, Hello My Baby, Possum
II: Carini, Dinner and a Movie, Mike's > Lawn Boy > Weekapaug, Mango, Billy Breathes, Theme **E:** Taste, Adeline

"Can't You Hear Me Knocking" jams in Down with Disease and at end of Weekapaug. "The End" and "Careful With The Axe, Eugene" jams in Mike's Song. Last Cities, 7/5/94 Ottawa, ON [222 shows]. Last Dinner and a Movie, 8/6/96 Morrison, CO [59 shows]. Show was delayed broadcast on German radio. Portions of this show comprise the live Phish album Slip Stitch and Pass.

➢ It's not always safe to declare a show "classic" before the band has even left the stage, but the Hamburg show has already gained fame among fans that resembles that of 12/30/93 or 10/31/94. Though only time will tell if this show remains among the all-time favorites, it sure is a great one. Right from the opener—the first Cities in almost three years—it's clear the band is going to mix things up, then Trey tells the crowd that he's psyched to be back in the cool room that's the Markethalle. An amazing first set includes a very good Down With Disease and the first experimental Wolfman's Brother, a version that foreshadowed Phish's summer '97 versions. Though the jam never came all the way back around to the Wolfman's theme, the band followed a cool little groove into Jesus Left Chicago, then topped off the set with a great Reba and a wild "heavy-metal" Possum (hear it to understand). The second set is crazier—Mike's Song jams into "The End," and a bunch of other lyric strangeness erupts in Weekapaug. —ERNIE GREENE

3/2/97 [ACCESSIBILITY: ••]
Pumpehuset, Copenhagen, Denmark
I: Johnny B. Goode, Uncle Pen, Sample, Guyute, My Soul, Runaway Jim, Antelope > Catapult > Life on Mars, Chalkdust, Hello My Baby
II: Also Sprach > Maze, Swept Away > Steep > PYITE, Waste, Character Zero, Slave, Tweezer Reprise **E:** YEM

Antelope unfinished. "Gypsy Queen" jam in Runaway Jim.

➢ A big letdown for the European tour closer. A few nice ones in the first set, but only half of Antelope and another My Soul. 2001 > Maze was a good start for set two, but more new songs dropped the ball. Punch You is always good, but the YEM encore seemed to lack much effort and had a weak vocal jam. —MATT BUSSMAN

1997 Spring *TIME OUT*

Forsaking a U.S. spring tour for the third consecutive year, the band used the spring for practice and writing as well as several cameo appearances. The band used the release of Ben & Jerry's Phish Food ice cream as a good excuse to play their first Flynn Theater show since April '94, an affair spiced up by horn players Dave Grippo and James Harvey and the gospel stylings of Tammy Fletcher.

Besides the Flynn show, Phish made another appearance on Letterman, and individually, all of the bandmembers also remained active. Page sat in with the Allman Brothers for the second year in a row during their March stand at the Beacon Theater in New York City, while Fishman joined Phish cover band Stash for several songs during a May gig of theirs in his hometown of Syracuse. Trey and Mike, meanwhile, teamed up with several members of Burlington band The Pants and James Harvey to form "New York," which played a May gig at Club Toast in Burlington and featured the debut of several songs that would join the Phish catalog in June, including I Saw It Again and Dirt. And Mike and Fish appeared on the syndicated radio program House of Blues, treating the audience to a recorded live version of My Soul. Then, before their trip abroad in June, Phish apparently snuck in a set at Phish crew member Brad Sands' house, playing all their new material for the small crowd. What a barbecue that must have been!

[3/5/97]
Late Show With David Letterman, Ed Sullivan Theater, New York, NY
Character Zero

3/18/97 [ACCESSIBILITY: ••••]
Flynn Theater, Burlington, VT
I: Cinnamon Girl, NICU > Sample > PYITE > My Soul, Beauty of My Dreams, Harry Hood > CTB, Suzie, Character Zero
II: Taste, Drowned > Caspian, Bowie, Love Me, Reconsider Baby, Love Me Like a Man, Waste > Chalkdust, Slave
E: Hello My Baby, Funky Bitch

Benefit concert for cleanup of Lake Champlain, co-sponsored by Ben & Jerry's. Dave Grippo on alto saxophone and James Harvey on trombone for CTB, Suzie, Character Zero and Funky Bitch. Tammy Fletcher on vocals for Reconsider Baby and Love Me Like A Man. Concert debuts: Cinnamon Girl, Reconsider Baby, and Love Me Like a Man. Live FM broadcast on WIZN-Burlington.

➢ The Flynn! What can I say in such a small space to do it justice. It was everything I've ever dreamed of (literally—I had a real psychic dream about this one that came true) for a Phish show. Cinnamon Girl! The Horns on CTB, Suzie and Character Zero! Awesome Bowie! Tammy was very entertaining. You could even see little Eliza on the side of the stage. Slave, and then an awesome encore, left me just beaming. It was beautiful! People just staggered across the street to the park afterwards, stunned. I'll never forget it. By far my favorite show ever. —LIBBY BARROW

➢ Good ol' Phish—they'll never forget where they're from. Another Phish dream come true—I was one of the very lucky folks who actually got a voucher (instead of tickets, to prevent scalping). Inside the lobby of the Flynn, we were handed Phish Food in little cups. Ben and Jerry came out and introduced the band, and they weren't the first special guests—at the beginning of CTB, two mics were brought out in front of Fish, then out walked James Harvey and Dave Grippo! They raged on CTB and went off even more on Suzie. Best first set ever? Definitely in the top three I've seen. In set II, after a climactic Bowie and Treat Me Like a Fool, Trey walked to the front of the stage and introduced Tammy Fletcher (of Tammy Fletcher and the Disciples, a local blues/gospel group) for two tunes. She has such a wonderful voice—I was amazed. After Funky Bitch, again with Harvey and Grippo, I woke up... and it was the strangest thing—all my friends had the same dream. —MIKE D'AMICO

➢ I didn't get a ticket for this show because I wasn't meant to—this show was strictly for phriends of old and a few lucky Burlingtonians. Thankfully, it was radio broadcast in the area, and we decided to go to Burlington to find a spot and listen in. What a tight show! You could just tell how much fun they were having. I'm sure I wasn't the only one caught off-guard by the Cinnamon Girl opener, but Trey's guitar tone sounded great on that one. CTB, Suzie and Character Zero with Grippo and Harvey created some of the hottest musical fire I've ever heard. Just so pure. —CASEY GRANT

[5/18/97]
Corestates Spectrum, Philadelphia, PA
Star Spangled Banner

Phish performed a cappella before the Flyers-Rangers NHL playoff game.

The band gets iced for the Flyers/Rangers game.

Europe '97

On Tour with Phish in Europe, Feb.-Mar. 1997

Find yourself a city:
L to R, Brian, Andy and Larry in Stuttgart

Winter in the Olde World

Three Almanac Editors Follow Phish Abroad

By Andy Bernstein

Going to Europe was a no-brainer. In the last year, Phish had gone from being a relatively private pastime to a very public display of affliction.

The Pharmer's Almanac had somehow made it beyond "what if" status and had transformed our lives, our very identities to an extent, into a clearinghouse for Phish information and obsession. I'd stopped answering my phone with a "hello" months ago. It was always "Almanac" (or some silly variation like "Pharmer's Almond Snacks," just to keep life interesting).

And that, if anything, was a damn good excuse to pony up for a plane ticket and head overseas.

So I, along with fellow Almanac editors Larry Chasnoff and Brian Celentano—and our old friend Adam Brinton—renewed our passports, packed our bags, and jetted across the Atlantic for a week of Phish in Europe.

February 22, 1997, Rome, Italy

When we landed in Rome on the morning of the 22nd, there was nary a sign that Phish was in town.

The festivities that night—already over a week into the February tour—were set for the Teatro Olympico, a theater which dated back to the 1600s. Our cab nearly ran over a couple of motorscooters on Rome's narrow streets before dropping us off near a few hundred Phishheads sprinkled underneath the marquee.

That was it for the lot scene. It reminded me of the southern shows on the '93 tour, the last time I'd seen a turnout this small.

We quickly got a lowdown on the tour from a few friends we ran into. I asked one guy how to get to the next show, in Cortemaggiore, which we couldn't find on the map.

"Either rent a car, find someone with a car, or don't go at all," was the answer. Apparently, there was no train which stopped there, and a plan to have a bus at the nearest train station had fallen through. That was sobering, but good to know.

We then ran into Shane Johnson, the head of the Green Crew who now works for the band. He's a great guy to talk Phish with because, through all the hundreds of shows he's seen, he's never lost his enthusiasm for the band. And you know he can discern the noteworthy nights from the ordinary.

His take was that the show in Firenze had lived up to expectations, mostly on the back of the heavy-metal Wilson. He also offered an interesting observation about Italian fans—to show their appreciation during a jam, they'd clap in rhythmic unison, not really with the beat but just to show they were down with the groove. Shane demonstrated without accompanyment, and I got the idea.

Trey counts one off: February 23, 1997, Cortemaggiore, Italy

So this was fun. We were back, talking Phish, in Rome.

Then a big, blond, big bird of a bush of hair, with a sneering face underneath it, walked up, and within seconds was shouting at me. *"What are you doing here? No one wants you here! Why don't you just go home!?!"*

I don't know how he did it, but Psycho had somehow scraped up enough money to make it overseas.

You may know Psycho, as we call him. He's the guy with the curly yellow friz on his head who sells Antelope stickers in the parking lot of Phish shows. I first met him at the Chicago Halloween show, back when we had the original incarnation of the Almanac and were still selling it in the parking lots. He seemed like a nice kid at the time—well-kept and collegiate-looking—and he bought a book from us.

But three weeks later at Hampton, he was bitching us out, telling us our book was bad for this reason, that reason, and denying he'd ever picked one up in the first place.

That was the first of our many strange encounters. For a while he would at least try to issue some coherent thoughts; I believe the phrase "you're bad for the scene" was one of his favorite credos. But by the New Year's run of 1996 it had degenerated to a simple "fuck you" sent in my direction each time I crossed his path.

And unfortunately, that was pretty frequent. I mean, this guy was everywhere. As far as I know, Psycho has attended every Phish show on both sides of the Atlantic for the last several years. And it didn't stop there. He is also a regular at many of the bands we like to see at clubs—the Ominous Seapods, Jazz Mandolin Project and the like.

He even managed to be a problem at places we weren't: Larry got a call once from a friend working at a lodge in Lake Placid. "A guy came in here wearing a Phish hat and I asked him if he'd seen your book," the friend related. "Then this guy started going off that you guys were bad news or something." Larry knew just how to answer: "Did he have big, blond frizzy hair?"

* * *

Heading into the theater in Rome, the first thing that jumped out at me was the fact I could walk right up to the stage. No guards, no gates, no railings. Just a clear path to the setup in front of a mostly-empty theater.

I started talking to a girl who was doing the whole tour with her boyfriend. I asked what the scene had been like to that point. "Newbie bimbos studying abroad," she sneered.

The place was pretty full by the time the show got started, although there were rows of empty seats. We were all pretty exhausted so we didn't try to stay up front, where it became pretty crowded. But for god's sake, there wasn't a bad seat in the place.

The image is still burned in my head of the band singing Walfredo, with instrument switching. Now, if you've seen a rotation jam, you know it can be a little sloppy, a little avante-garde sounding. Well, for Walfredo, you can bet the band learned their parts. I mean, you'd never have know they weren't playing their own instruments. Trey looked totally natural on the keyboards, as he bellowed lyrics into the microphone which seemed to be telling stories from Phish's past.

It was just a great song and I certainly had no idea it would be the last time they'd play it. I'm sure it will resurface again, but as of the end of summer tour I was still waiting, and glad that its chorus still rings in my head after just one exposure.

Speaking of exposure, during the encore a girl sat up on a friend's shoulder and flashed the band. I'd heard about the topless beaches in France, but never a thing about theaters in Italy.

Upon leaving the theater, our main goal was to find out "where the heck is Cortemaggiore" and how to get there. That led us to converse with lots of interesting people, none of whom had any idea where the heck Cortemaggiore was.

We began chatting it up with a girl who, like the others, had never heard of Cortemaggiore, but had the most charming accent, and seemed to speak pretty fluent English. I asked if she'd grown up in Rome.

"No," she answered curiously, "Minnesota." So I felt pretty stupid but it was a very *strong* Minnesota accent, and not really knowing what a Minnesota accent sounds like, or a Rome accent, I think I was justifiably confused—or maybe just a dumb American who couldn't figure anything out.

Her name was Ellie, and she was studying music at a local University. We asked if she wanted to go get a beer, which she did, but she said there weren't really a lot of bars in Rome. We found that hard to believe, and all of us set out to look for one.

We walked the streets for over an hour. Not that we minded—walking through Rome at night was incredible. A dirty, crowded but beautiful city with distinctive, old-world architetcutre that made every back alley a scenic masterpiece for a bunch of Phishheads from Brooklyn.

We finally did find a bar, right next to our hotel. It proudly claimed to be an "American" bar, which disappointed us of course, but we drank like Europeans. Each of us bought a round, and I think we all coughed up for another. Ellie seemed to be enjoying herself, and we were all quite taken by her. She could belch the alphabet, which to me represents the height of evolutionary development.

We were the last ones out of that bar, and weren't done. The hotel had a roof deck and we all headed up there, staying up until the sun rose above an amazing view of ancient churches and ruins in every direction. And splendid weather. When we finally retired to our rooms, each of us commented that our first night in Europe had been absolutely perfect.

Perfect for everyone, that is, except Ellie, who immediately began throwing up in the sink.

When we parted ways the next morning, we gave her a copy of the Almanac, one of eight we'd brought with us to give away. We pointed out that it had our address and phone number in the cover, but we never heard from her again.

February 23, 1997, Cortemaggiore, Italy

We arrived at the train station about three minutes too late for the last train to Piacenza—the city closest to Cortemaggiore. But we weren't sure if that would have gotten us there anyway, so we decided to rent a car. It was colossally expensive, something like $200 American for one day, but what choice did we have?

It allowed us to make a quick stop at the Coliseum. On the way out of our tiny parking spot, I rubbed up against the car next to us and scratched up ours. Ooops.

It was a full day's drive to Cortemaggiore. We actually arrived early, though, because we drove at the same speed as the rest of the traffic—about 100 miles an hour. We'd heard about European drivers, but I couldn't believe my eyes. These little cars weren't just zipping down the highway at break-neck speeds, they were all over the road. No one stayed in lane and a couple times people nearly pushed us off the road at triple-digit velocity. Larry commented that there was a reason we didn't see any cars with dents on them—every accident in Italy was fatal.

We were really brewing with excitement as we neared Cortemaggiore. Everyone we talked to the night before guessed that because it was so hard to get to, the audience would be just a handful of people, maybe a couple hundred at most. It would be the smallest Phish show in years, and maybe never again would they play to a crowd that tiny. A circulating rumor had it that the band would play until 2 a.m.

The town turned out to be even smaller than we'd imagined. Not more than a couple of traffic lights, and every building, and resident for that matter, looked downright antique. But we followed a couple of Phishheads to the venue and found—to my continued amazement—a real live rock-n-roll club, complete with a marquee and a neon guitar.

I have no idea how it got there or who plays there, but we sure weren't the only ones to find it. There were probably about 200 people just sitting outside, including Mike Gordon, who was getting even more attention than he usually does in a U.S. parking lot.

Inside, I sensed a crowd that was proportionately a lot more Italian than the night before, and seemed to come from many walks of life. The band put on a great show that night, really high energy. Fishman wore his dress only during the second set. He hadn't worn it the night before, and as far as I know, hasn't worn it since. But he went out in style, coming to center stage for a rousing performance of Why Don't We Do It In The Road. There was a Mike's Song in the set also, and I know that a lot of people on tour were totally blown away by this show. But as far as I was concerned, it really didn't live up to the incredible atmosphere. A good, solid show no doubt, but we had psyched ourselves up for something so much more.

We hit a hotel that night in Piacenza, with Adam totally freaking that we were going to run out of gas. We said we were too tired to gas up until the next morning, and also wanted to give him a hard time.

Each of us slept like a rock that night.

February 24, 1997, Riding the Rails to Munich

I was woken up by the phone ringing. It was the front desk telling us we were way past checkout time. At that point, it occurred to me, that we were supposed to return the car in Milan by noon. It was already almost one.

We hurried out and learned that there was an Avis office in town, and headed there. By the time we arrived we were over an hour late, past the grace period. And of course there was the scratch I'd put on the car. But the Avis office was closed. They were on siesta. So we called the central office which told us to just

I asked one guy how to get to the next show, in Cortemaggiore, which we couldn't find on the map. "Find someone with a car, rent a car, or don't go," he said.

Psycho was right in front of Trey, doing some sort of karate moves or something, his bushy hair bouncing up and down.

To educate the European Phishheads, "How to Phish" fliers were distributed in Germany.

leave the car there, and leave the key and the contract in the mailbox, with the time we returned it. Of course, we wrote 12:30, within the one hour grace period. But we weren't sure if that would do the trick, so we actually took the time to set Larry's watch back to 12:30, and take a picture of him holding his watch up in front of the car, just in case we had to dispute the credit card charges.

We boarded a train to Milan, which connected to another to Munich. The train went through the Alps at night, which was disappointing because we missed all the sights, except for the gaggle of blond, female Austrian skiiers. We were very pleased to see them until they kicked us out of our seats, which they'd apparently reserved in advance.

Later in the ride we met a bunch of Phishheads, the only others on that train, and agreed to all find a youth hostel together. With their help, we located a great one right across from the Munich train station. As soon as we walked in we heard a tape blasting the Dead, and saw a good number of heads who'd come to town for the show, which wasn't until the next day.

February 25, 1997, Munich, Germany

I ate some really bad sausage that made me sick, and went off with the guys to look for a beer garden. We approached a couple of girls to ask for directions, leading off with a polite, slow, "Do you speak English?"

"Yeah," one answered, "We're from California."

We'd been in Europe for three days and I don't think we'd met one European. But it was nice to be able to converse, and they ended up drinking with us all afternoon, and we convinced them to hit the show that night.

Incognito was an aptly named venue, tucked away in a warehouse far away from downtown. This place was the smallest of the three we'd hit, although it was still a decent-sized club, much bigger than a bar.

That night we went right up to the stage, and stood between Mike and Trey—what an incredible experience. When you're that close, you just catch so many things, so many subtleties. And your attention to the music is so much greater when you can see how each note is played. It almost feels like you get into the band's mind. You're two steps behind, of course, but you feel like you're in the work room, you're seeing the process.

I remember being struck by just how much Trey is the leader of the band. Not as if that's news to anyone, and certainly not to minimize what the others do, but there are times you can just see inspiration flow out of Trey and hear the others follow. The phrase that kept hitting me was that I was watching Trey actually create the show.

I suppose it wasn't a stupendous Phish performance—in fact, Trey totally screwed up My Friend, stopping in the middle and apologizing—but I just enjoyed it so much. A female vocalist, Sydney Ellis, came out for a few blues number, including this fantastic song I'd heard once on a weird radio station called One Meatball. It's about a guy who didn't have enough cash for a two-meatball plate but tries to buy one. Ellis sang "one meatball" into Trey's microphone, while Trey and Mike sang into the other, answering "that's all" in harmony.

We also got a healthy dose of Psycho that night. We were a few people away from him, but he was right in front of Trey, doing some sort of karate moves or something throughout the show with his big bushy hair bouncing up and down.

When we got back to the hostel, we walked in on a conversation where a bunch of people were going off on someone. They were spewing about some guy who was shoving and almost hitting people so he could have room to dance. They were talking about Psycho.

Apparently he'd really pissed off an entire group of people on tour, and it had been going on since the first show in London. Psycho actually offered one guy an Antelope sticker to leave his space so he could have more room to dance. Of course, the "offer" was non-negotiable: he wouldn't take no for an answer, thrusting the guy aside and claiming the territory in front of Trey.

Man, when we heard this, we just cracked up. It was a vindication of sorts.

February 26, 1997, Stuttgart, Germany

The trip to Stuttgart was pretty short, which allowed us to wander around the area for most of the afternoon. I read a little history of the city in one of our guidebooks. It said we flattened it in the war.

The language barrier made it a little tough to find the beer garden we were seeking. I remember learning in school that English is derived more from German than Latin. Well that just can't be true. Walking around Italy, we were pretty much able to figure out what everything was—just take off a few vowels at the end to arrive at a loose English translation. In Germany I couldn't tell you what the phuck was going on. I mean, it may as well have been writings from another planet.

Finally we met some real live Germans who led us around town and to a nice bar. They were a couple of girls who, as it turned out, spent most of their time at the nearby American military base and spoke better English than we did. They had a drink with us and gave good directions to the venue, which was far away from downtown in a residential neighborhood.

We wanted to get there early because we'd heard that some people on tour had bought Fishman a birthday cake. You see, that was February 26, the date which The Pharmer's Almanac previously listed as Fish's birthday (based on an inacurrate article in *The Vermont Times*). Mimi Fishman had since informed us that we had it wrong, and we would have found someone handing him a cake to be pretty embarrassing. We wanted to get there in time to intercept that cake and offer to pay for whatever it had cost the guys who bought it.

When we got there we didn't see anyone with a cake, but went in early and spyed Trey hanging out with a bunch of fans, just milling about. We talked to him for a little while, before a more aggressive mass joined in.

The band's dressing rooms overlooked the stage up on a balcony, and they kept poking their heads out as the floor started to fill up. We grabbed a spot up front, right in the middle, and luckily Psycho decided to take a night off from being front-row center.

Waiting for the show to begin, we talked to a lot of people. There was this sweetheart of a girl named Julia who was 17-years-old and studying in Stuttgart. She proudly told us that her father named her after the Beatles song, and that the Beatles and Phish were her favorite bands. She looked a little bit like a Peanuts character, and was just bursting with enthusiasm. She just couldn't wait for the show and couldn't believe how lucky she was that Phish had come to her new town.

When you're at a place like that, you always feel like it's going to be a great show. There's a sense that it could or should be an historic night, even if they were playing places like that through the entire tour and, logically, you knew that not every night could live up to the sort of expectations the atmosphere created.

By the end of the first song, it was pretty clear that this night would. Out of nowhere, the boys led off with Camel Walk, the first since Sugarbush in '95 and only the second since the '80s. Midway through the set, they busted into Harry Hood. You know, it's a strange little thing that only Phish fans can understand, but a Harry Hood in the middle of the first set is a very special thing. Julia had found her way to the front row and was doing this little hand dance with Trey's lead. He looked over at her and smiled, and dipped the guitar in her direction. She didn't flinch at all, spiraling her hands to the music with such cohesion that it almost seemed like she was jamming Trey.

Hood was followed by My Soul, which is the song which really, in so many ways, epitomized what this tour was about musically—high energy, gospel-like arrangements as Phish seemed to be discovering blues and the soulful roots of truly American music. And then, just to remind us what a treat we were getting, they whipped out Tube. The message was clear—this was a show for the ages.

Next came Carini, an amazing song which for some reason they left overseas, and, just to make sure we were still paying attention, Dog Log. The set closed with another revival, While My Guitar Gently Weeps, and Julia led out a high-pitched scream. If Phish did nothing else on that tour but make that sweet girl that happy, the trip to Europe would have been worth it. She was bursting at the seams when the setbreak came, and seeing one person feel that much pleasure, well, you can't help but feel it rub off a bit.

Of course, the second set was just as good. The return of Ha Ha Ha, a song I absolutely love, was followed by YEM, an amazingly bluesy, funked out rendition that saw Mike Gordon really getting down before they morphed into Kung and Theme. Scent of a Mule, a song I've grown a bit tired of, became another highlight when Trey started doing a scat jam during his part of the duel with Page. He sung each note as he played it on guitar, going all over the neck as his voice meshed perfectly with the vibration of the strings.

One concept the band talks about a lot in interviews is Santana's idea that all music already exists in the universe, and that musicians are just conduits to extract it into reality.

Watching Trey sing each note on his guitar, you could almost literally see the music flowing out of him, and the look on his face was that of a man possessed. The show ended with Slave (just to *make sure* we got the idea what this show was all about) and a Highway to Hell encore.

But the show wasn't quite over.

While Larry and I were saying goodbye to some people we'd

met that night, Brian came running over to us. "You've got to see this!" he said, leading us over to a crowd of people.

We looked up and saw Fishman on the balcony *cracking up*. Then we followed his eyes down to a big head of bushy-blond hair bopping up and down. It was Psycho, in a fight! He was all red in the face, screaming at some dude, and they were shoving each other and even throwing punches. And Psycho was just flipping out, beet-red. Fishman, meanwhile, was beside himself.

Someone finally broke it up and we stuck around a little as people engaged Fish in conversation. One guy looked up and said "Happy Birthday." We all just hung our heads down and I peeped out "sorry." Not that big a deal, I guess, but from what I heard, Mimi was really miffed.

By the time we got out of there, it was past the hour that the trains were running, and there were certainly no cabs left. We were stranded. And it was pretty late so it was not like we had a whole bunch of other fans to suffer with, just one group as confused as we were. It made sense to follow their lead, which brought us to a trolley stop, as they tried to read the schedule. It was totally confusing, and at one point a trolley jetted right past us, only to stop one block up and then pull away as we were running after it.

Finally, we boarded one, but after a few stops, the driver shouted something at us in German and we all got off. As he sped away, we realized we had *no idea* what he was saying—he may have just been asking if we were from out of town. In German, everything sounds like someone's telling you to get lost.

We were stranded, and just then it started pouring. But by this point I was really enjoying hanging out with this other group. They were all from a college in Kentucky which had a satellite campus in France, and they'd taken a train to the show, planning to catch one back in the middle of the night. We were going to take the six a.m. train to Berlin, skipping a night's lodging fees and getting a whole day to explore what's left of the Wall and other sights.

Our two groups finally hunted down some cabs and divided ourselves up to all make it back to the station. Somehow, the four guys from Brooklyn ended up in something like three different cabs with girls from Kentucky.

We ended up hanging out with them two of them, Erin and Bethany, all night. They were just great, honest, down-to-earth people who knew something about the world and were having fun seeing it. Bethany flattered the shit out of us by how well she knew the Almanac. Everyone else in the station had fallen asleep or caught an earlier train to Amsterdam, where many heads were spending Phish's day off.

It ended up being the six of us, talking, running around the train station, just having fun. They were terrific people.

Sometimes, just meeting people randomly and getting to know them is the most incredible way to spend an evening, especially when you're in the middle of Europe and they happen to be attractive women. But we weren't hitting on them, barely even flirting with them. It was just a night shared with random new friends. It's not like anything spectacularly notable happened or was said—although they did assign each of us nicknames—but that night was hands-down the best night of the trip. It's funny, we had just seen one of the most incredible Phish shows of our lives, from the front row. But what happened afterwards was more special, meeting people we genuinely liked and who seemed to genuinely like us. That's something that always means something, even if you never see those people again.

February 27, 1997, Riding the Rails to Berlin

Their train left before dawn, and ours followed just as the sun was rising. We piled into a little compartment and slept almost the whole way to Berlin. When we got there, we were still exhausted, and immediately found a hostel and went to sleep, not waking up until about 9 p.m. My plan to see a European pro hockey game was thwarted; the day was pretty much shot to hell. But we did hang out in the hostel lounge for awhile, and met a whole new bunch of cool folks. I'd heard that's what it's like traveling through Europe—you just meet tons of people and they're practically all Americans. It almost made me wish Phish tour in the U.S. was done by train and backpack, because that's where the true adventure is.

February 28, 1997, Berlin, Germany

We got up pretty early to see the Wall.

Berlin is a fascinating city. The West part is busy, cosmopolitan, and extremely modern, completely rebuilt since 1945. The East side is now the world's largest construction zone, trying to get up to speed after 40 years of stagnation. Most of the Wall is gone, but you can immediately tell when you've entered the East. The buildings which aren't being torn down are falling apart on their own. Each was made from the same sallow yellow brick which really screamed with sorrow.

Those who use the phrase "capitalist" like it's a bad word should take a walk on the other side, literally. It really is an education. And you could sense that the people of this reunited city were still divided. On the West side, people walked briskly in fancy clothes. The former East Germans, meanwhile, still looked fresh from the news footage after the war.

We went to the museum by Checkpoint Charlie. It was a monument to the thousands of defectors who slipped under or over the

Trey in the light, Mike in the shadows.

Once that disaster was averted, I just spent the time looking out the window, watching Berlin fly past. This train actually went through East and West, which I'm not quite sure how they pulled off during the Cold War. It was a captivating ride, seeing the neighborhoods change, seeing the contrast between East and West again. It reminded me of New York in many ways. Each section seemed to have such different character, the people too. And the history is so rich, so recent.

It also wasn't bad getting away from my friends for the first time in a week. I'd have to say the train ride through Berlin was one of the most memorable experiences I had in Europe. Although I fear that with our Phish-focus and propensity to meet only other Americans, we may not have gotten everything we could have out of Europe, it was moments like that where the surroundings just kind of crept in, and they were priceless.

The show that night, was not. Not a terrible show, but clearly the weakest of the six we saw.

We were right up front again as Phish led off with Carini, which I was totally into at this point. But the rest of the set was Joe Average. Decent performance of basic songs. Set II led off with huge promise, Taste and then Drowned.

My all-time favorite single-song performance by Phish is the Drowned from New Year's Eve '95. What they created in Drowned that night is something that will stay with me forever, and probably had something to do with the fact that I've seen The Who perform *Quadrophenia* four times since and was never impressed. Phish just set the standard too high.

It almost made me wish Phish tour in the U.S. was done by train and backpack, because that's where the true adventure is.

Wall, and those who died trying. It was amazing to realize this wasn't 40 years ago—it didn't end until I was in college.

On the way out, we bought some sausage, which was a pretty big mistake, because it began eating through my intestine before I'd even bitten through the casing (whose ever intestine *that* was). We went to the zoo, at Larry's insistance, and by the time we were supposed to leave for the show I really needed to find a rapid exit route for the sausage and every other piece of German food I'd eaten. I told the others to go ahead and I'd catch up.

After taking my time at a private enterprise toilet station (about $1.50 for a nice, clean, private stall, *well* worth it.) I hopped on a train, heading for the show.

We each had a three-day German rail pass, which wasn't good for the subways, but if we ever had a problem we figured we'd just play dumb.

Only the real dumb part was that Brian was carrying all the passes. I realized this after a bunch of cops got on the train and started checking everyone. Now as it was, I wasn't too comfortable about riding trains in Germany. Many of my ancestors probably rode trains in Germany, once. And here were a bunch of cops in funny outfits about to bust me and do Lord-knows-what.

But for some reason, as I fiddled through my wallet for my passport and tried to think of an excuse, they just nodded and walked right by me.

Berlin was the first time they played Drowned since New Year's, and it was impossible not to hope for a divine performance. I just wasn't capable of lowering my standards for Drowned, and of course it fell short. They jammed out on it, or tried to. I could see them searching for the groove. Watching Trey's face, it was obvious to me that he knew what level they'd hit on Drowned before, and desperately wanted to get close but knew it just wasn't there. Of course, I was reading things a bit too closely, too critically, probably. And I did enjoy hearing the song again. But it wasn't, couldn't, be the same.

The rest of the set had a similar feel. After seeing four amazing shows that week, my expectations were just zooming, and an average night for Phish just wasn't doing it for me. Had I built up Phish tolerance? It happens to the best of us, especially when on tour.

The other guys were having a good time, though. That's because they were pretty drunk, spending club prices for beers, something we never do at home. But the great thing about spending a few zillion dollars on airfare, train passes and lodging is that even excessive drinking couldn't possibly make a real dent in the overall budget, so why not indulge? But my stomach still hurt so I just watched as they kept taking trips back to the long bar which faced the stage.

Photo by JAY ARCHIBALD

We didn't stay out after the show. We were still exhausted, and also had to leave the hostel by 9 a.m. the next morning or pay for the next night.

March 1, 1997, Hamburg, Germany

The 9 a.m. thing was no joke. I was the last one to get out of bed and into the shower. When I lingered past 9, some old German woman walked into the bathroom and told me to get a move on. At least that's what I think she said. It sounded like whatever the bus driver in Stuttgart was shouting. Well, I figured I'd gotten lucky with the cops but I probably wasn't going to fool a hefty old German woman, so I hurried up and got out of there.

The next stop, our last, was Hamburg, the northern port city where the Beatles did some of their first gigging 25 years ago. We got there pretty early in the day and killed the afternoon in the famed Red Light district, which turned out to be totally lame. I was expecting something really out there, but it was nothing more than a touristy Times Square. And of course each of us were competing to show who was less interested in the skin houses, so of course we didn't *do* anything, just walked around without really going in anywhere. A complete waste of time.

What a night—the band finishes the Hamburg show with an *a cappella* Adeline.

We still got to the show really early and lined up by the door with about a dozen heads. I had brought a few books with me to give copies to the band. The girl I'd met the first night, the one who described the "newbie bimbos," asked to see a copy. So I left one there with her while we went to get a beer.

When we got back the doors were open, revealing a simply awesome venue. It was tiny, but had a stepped floor where you could see the stage from any corner. I'm so used to clubs in New York where you either have to be right in front of the stage or you can't see anything.

I saw the girl who I'd lent the book to and asked what she thought. "It was alright," she said, kind of surly.

Now, that's really not what I expected.

"You sound sort of so-so on it," I said. And then she just went off. "I don't think it's fair that you unfairly stereotype Phish fans. I think your book is elitist, I don't like how it makes fun of tapers, I don't like..."

Wow. I guess she really didn't like it. And I really didn't understand. I mean, yes, there was a section in the old book that made fun of some of the stereotypes of Phish fans. But it was a joke, an obvious joke. If you can't laugh at yourself, who can you laugh at?

Now, I can't expect everyone to like or approve of every part of the book. Heck, that wouldn't be any fun. But what I just didn't understand is why that seemed to be the *only* thing she saw out of 224 pages about Phish, the band she traveled across an ocean to see. Why didn't she just turn the page?

I found myself having a similar conversation a few minutes later. I was up by the tapers section handing out fliers asking people to review shows for the next volume. Some little dude comes up to me and starts yapping in my ear.

"I'm not trying to give you a hard time," he said, "but I don't want to read about people falling in love at Phish shows. I want to read about the music!"

There was *one* story about falling in love at a Phish show and 200 pages on the music. And this dude couldn't figure out that all he had to do was *turn the page* if he didn't like something.

So I tried to take the concilliatory approach. "Well," I said, "we view it sort of as a buffet. We try to offer many different things, a lot to choose from, and make sure there's good stuff for people with different tastes, and you can just pass by the things you don't like."

But he didn't want to talk about it. He wouldn't look at me. He just kept repeating, "I'm not trying to give you a hard time."

Oh, but he was.

I've never understood why in the osten-

Trey let Fish off the hook: "I want to cook you breakfast," a voice came from the center of the stage. "I want to borrow the car."

sibly harmonious world of Phish, some people yearn for debate and controversy, and search for enemies from within and not the outside.

In the end, how absurd it all is that these four loveable dorks from Vermont inspire us all in the way they do. But they do. And that should be an excuse to create, to grow, and to bond, not to argue. Make fun of each other a little, sure, but if anyone ever looked out on stage and saw something to provoke angst or belligerence, then they sure saw something I didn't.

Of course, the other guys weren't concerned with this at all. Instead, they had just tapped into a bag of the Netherlands' kindest, freshly imported to tour. I took one toke before the show and realized just why everyone traveled to Amsterdam on the day off. It was completely unlike anthing I'd had before. One hit was enough.

It was pretty crowded on the floor by the time the show started, but we had a good spot, maybe five feet from the stage and right in the middle. As in Stuttgart, Phish made their intentions clear with a breakout for the first song, Cities. Although they'd take it to further heights during the summer, it was great version, and the excitement could literally be felt in the tiny hall, as waves of heat descended upon the audience. It must have been 100 degrees by the time Cities was over, and it got significantly hotter on the floor as the set went on. An early-show Down with Disease made it clear that Phish had lofty goals for the night. They really began hitting the zone a few songs later during Wolfman's Brother.

I had probably only seen Wolfman's about half a dozen times. I'd really enjoyed it, too, seeing it as a rocking tune which was actually much better without the horns. But Wolfman's took on a whole different life that night in Hamburg. The funky, wah-wah drenched take on the song was followed by a simply incredible jam, the kind you can really get lost in and almost forget what song started it all.

And you could see the band getting excited. They knew they were on to something and everyone in that hot little club sensed it.

By Reba, two songs later, I had inched my way closer to the stage and was looking right up at Trey.

His face exuded such intensity as the song went from section to section. Here was a song he'd played about 250 times, and yet it seemed that every single note meant so much to him. Every movement in his fingers seemed to flow from his face—buckled and bent in every direction—as his torso hovered in close to the neck of the instrument. You almost felt like you were intruding on an intimate moment between man and guitar, like should ask if they wanted to be alone together.

The set powered on and on, closing with a Possum that threatened to wipe out half the crowd with heat stroke.

The venue staff luckily opened some windows or got some fans going during set break, or they might of had a problem on their hands. We moved back a little, but were still closer to Trey than Page was to Fishman.

The Second set led off with Carini, which we'd seen nearly every night but sure as hell weren't sick of. Then Dinner and a Movie led into Mike's Song.

There are Mike's, and then there are Mike's. And there's little doubt that it's because of this Mike's that Phish later decided to make Hamburg, out of 1,000 shows to choose from, their first-ever single-show live album.

The vocal section was followed by this straight ahead, funked-out jam which really seemed to know exactly where it was headed. Kuroda immediately caught the mood with these sort of silver metallic lights. It wasn't a very long Mike's. It didn't need to be, because every progression made a point and didn't leave anything over. Page was all over his synthesizer, laying down these throaty, psychedelic grooves while Trey just went nuts.

And we're watching this splendid convergence from spitting distance.

This entire cramped little room was just on fire. Dead silence from the crowd erupted into wild applause as Trey fired the crescendo notes.

And then, in this Mike's that was so perfect everything almost seemed pre-planned, they went not into Hydrogen but into these arabic sounding notes, a familiar set of notes, something that said jungle, that said head popping from the water as the credits roll to *Apocalypse Now*. The End.

I'd always wanted Phish to play The End. I saw it as a potential Fishman tune, a joke of sorts. But here we were at the edges of sanity and, yeah, it did sort of feel like a joke as Trey sang the first lyrics, but it also felt like the most tripped out mindphuck I'd ever experienced.

A scream came, before Mike played with an effect he'd been fiddling with all tour. Trey then hit a peddle and it was all over. He began this quick rhythmic strum and Mike followed with a couple of bass notes.

The weirdest thing—it wasn't working. It just went nowhere. I was trying to follow it with my ears, waiting for it to be satisfying, believing it would be satisfying.

But after a few seconds, Trey realized he'd backed himself into a dead end, and whispered over to Page, before turning to the others to make sure they all knew what was next: Lawn Boy.

Talk about contrast. Just to remind us of that, Fishman sang "And he walked on down the hall," over the loungy lead-in notes.

Seconds later, they were back in Weekapaug, with Mike slapping away and Trey still singing "And he walked on down the hall..."

This of course leads into the Oedipal section (If you don't know it, please see the damn movie). Fish took the lead vocal: "I want to kill you." He then looked over at Trey with this nervous sort of "should I?" look. "Mother..." he sang. And then Trey let Fish off the hook. "I want to cook you breakfast," a voice came from the center of the stage. "I want to borrow the car."

It's amazing how, even in the height of inspiration, Phish always manages to be themselves, to say the things and play the notes that make them who they are.

"Tryin' to make a woman match your moves..."

The rest of Weekapaug was short, but size doesn't always matter. My favorite part came when Trey stepped off a peddle, backed up and did this happy little dance and flashed the grin of a toddler as he peered up at the lights, still jamming away.

Jesus Christ, it was downright precious. And as if I hadn't already seen enough to make my head spin, that little moment sent me on symbolic journey number 547, under the category of "Why everyone loves Phish."

It's not just the music. It's that they're so damn likeable. People forget that. You just look up at these people, so blessed, so extraordinary talented, and in the back of your mind you're thinking, "It couldn't have happened to a better bunch of guys."

* * *

At the hotel that night, we realized that we had most of an eighth left, and there was no way we were going to take it on the plane. So we rolled this big fat Cheech & Chong joint and vowed to smoke it down to nothing by the time the night was done. Only one hit of this thing just knocked you right out, and left you so high you couldn't even think about taking another puff. We put a spliff the size of Cleveland out in the ashtray and went to bed.

When we got up the next morning, none of us wanted to smoke, but we couldn't let that much, which was that good, go to waste. There was also one Almanac left after giving away the other seven we'd brought.

We took that battleship of a fatty and stuck it in the Almanac, leaving a big bulge right in the middle of the cover, and headed for the train station. As soon as we got there we passed a line of heads, trailed by this beautiful young flower whom I don't know but I've been seeing at shows for as long as I can remember.

"A gift for you," I said. "Enjoy them both."

My favorite part came when Trey did this happy little dance, and flashed the grin of a toddler as he peered up at the lights, still jamming away.

Summer '97

On Tour with Phish in Europe, June-July, 1997

Trey snaps a picture of Page during soundcheck.
July 6, 1997, Desenzano/Genova, Italy

The view from the stage.
July 6, 1997, Desenzano/Genova, Italy

Photos by MARCO BURGIO

On The Beach

On Tour in Europe, Summer '97

By Marco Burgio

Before taking one giant leap into the real world, I felt that the first part of my life would not be complete until I traveled to Europe to experience life on the road first-hand.

My graduation day was June 14, 1997. Within ten days, I was on the trail of Phish in The Old World. The following is a mini-journal of my travels, my experiences, and most of all, my thoughts during the month I traveled through half-a-dozen countries in search of the ultimate rush: Phish in Europe.

June 25, 1997, Lille, France

We arrived in Lille, France at about 5:30 p.m. and found a hotel located only three minutes away from L'Aeronef, the place Phish was playing. Upon entering the venue we were greeted by a full bar and found ourselves instantly surrounded by about 150 other American Phishheads all talking like everyone knew each other. By the time we made it into the concert area, I felt as if I knew half the crowd.

As I walked through the doors, the stage appeared in front of me and an enormous shiver ran down my spine. I knew that the venue would be intimate, but this was mind-boggling. This was hands-down the smallest crowd I'd ever seen for a Phish show.

We spent most of the first set drinking beer and dancing on Fishman's side of the stage. I felt lucky enough to be here at all, but words wouldn't do justice to what those 300 fans and myself were about to experience during the second set. It began with Down With Disease that sent the venue into a frenzy. At about this time, I was greeted with my first taste of Amsterdam hash. The joint was passed to me and I took one hit that sent me into a wonderful spin.

When they returned to Down With Disease after a nice jam and a detour through the new song Piper, everyone was excited, but it wasn't until the unfamiliar sounds of McGrupp that it became clear that this wasn't exactly going to be a standard set. This McGrupp started off sounding so strange that it took me a minute to realize what they were playing, and it continued in reggae-style, unlike any version I'd ever heard before. That found its way into Makisupa, and then into Fishman's first-ever rendition of the Simon and Garfunkle classic Cecilia. They closed it out with Antelope. What a set!

Already ecstatic over what we'd just witnessed, we took a deep breath and prepared for the encore. When they hit the opening chords to Guyute, the crowd went into complete hys-

Phish Notes from Europe

Fans gather outside Royal Albert Hall: June 16, 1997, London, England

♦ Gathered in Dublin, Ireland, for the start of the summer tour, fans debated rumors that Phish had elected to retire 25 songs from their repertoire. What made the reports especially chilling were the names of the songs supposedly put away—Mike's and You Enjoy Myself among them. Though the rumor proved to be generally unfounded, the band did make it through the entire summer without playing Suzie Greenberg, and other fan-favorites like Divided Sky and Tweezer only surfaced a handful of times.

♦ The Dublin shows saw a prodigious amount of new song debuts—14 new originals, and two new covers: Sly and the Family Stone's Stand and Jimi Hendrix's Isabella.

♦ During the David Bowie intro on the second night in Dublin, an audience clap-along led Trey to sling his guitar over his back and kick up his heels for a brief Russian folk dance before launching into the song. The night earned recognition as the strongest show of the first week of the tour.

♦ Phish's highest-profile gig of the summer Europe tour was probably their June 16 date at London's famed Royal Albert Hall. The hall was only about half-full for the show. To the surprise of many, the band opted not to play A Day in the Life, encoring instead with an also-appropriate version of Cities.

♦ Trey's "back of the worm" chants, started in Amsterdam, continued the next day in Nuremberg during a 30-minute version of Ghost (the summer's longest, topping the 27-minute take in Atlanta, GA later in the month). Trey later mentioned "the back of the worm" at the kickoff of the U.S. summer tour in Virginia Beach, too.

♦ The Mike's Song show opener on the second night in Amsterdam was the first Mike's in the first set since 11/11/95 Atlanta, GA, and the first Mike's show opener since 5/11/90 Providence, RI. The Amsterdam shows, along with 6/25/97 Lille and 7/9/97 Lyon, were generally regarded as the tour's highest musical points.

teria. From every conceivable direction, comments could be heard like, "I can't believe they're encoring with Guyute," and "Holy shit!—Guyute encore," and "This is absolutely nuts!"

After the show, we hung out in the lobby, scoping out the backstage pass situation. To my delight, the backstage passes were identical to the ones used during the spring Europe tour—one of which I was lucky enough to own. But I decided not to use it until Amsterdam. Sometimes you've got to pick your spots.

A couple minutes later, Mike Gordon strolled out and began to mingle with the crowd. I grabbed my ticket out of my pocket and got Mike to sign it. On the way out of the venue, I examined the ticket and noticed that it wasn't my Phish ticket he signed, it was my train ticket from London to Lille. Oh well.

July 1-2, 1997, Amsterdam, Holland

We arrived at the train station in Amsterdam and I was told that the best hostel in terms of price and a good time was Bob's Youth Hostel. We exited the station and walked in the rain for about an hour looking for the hostel that was supposedly a five-minute walk from the station. If you've ever been to Amsterdam, you know that the streets are incredibly unorganized. We finally found the hostel, and as we opened the door we were immediately hit in the face with a billow of pot smoke. "Ahhhh, this I can deal with," I thought to myself.

We walked into our room and to our surprise, there were 15 guys in beds, all fast asleep at 4:30 p.m. The room smelled worse than the streets of Paris and our beds were actually mattresses on the ground. Bob's Youth Hostel looked more like Bob's Halfway House. We locked our stuff up and hit the streets of Amsterdam. We checked out the city, checked out of the smelly hostel, and checked into a decent hotel.

The next day, my tour buddy Scott left and I was ready to begin the rest of my trip solo. At about 7:00 p.m., I went to the Paradiso—Phish's home for the next two nights—and hung out in the concert area with everyone else until the show started. Tonight would be the night I would use my backstage pass, I thought to myself. The Paradiso is a beautiful venue with a church-like feel to it. Behind the stage are two large stain-glass windows, and in the rear of the building is a large balcony that wraps around the sides. The only downside to the Paradiso is the terrible heat that smothers the audience.

When the band came out, I couldn't believe how crazy they looked. Mike always looks somewhat bugged out, but we are talking eyes completely shut. Trey had a huge grin on his face, and Page was just giggling, looking out at the crowd. Jon looked pretty normal behind his drums.

Highlights of the first set included an unusually placed Horn, a Reba that I thought was *definitely* going to close the first set, complete with whistling at the end. The notable part of the whistling was the fact that the crowd actually started whistling and Trey followed suit. The first set was pretty much reserved for new songs, though.

The second set, however, was something entirely different. With only five songs played, plus the encore, it was clearly a 100-percent jamming set. Bathtub Gin > Cities > Loving Cup was nuts, with serious jamming everywhere. Cities literally came out of nowhere, and because of the time, I was sure Loving Cup would close the second set. When Trey began the opening licks to Slave, the whole crowd erupted. Slave was beautiful as usual, and when the show was finally over, at least half the crowd hung around instead of leaving.

At that point, I planned to follow the other people that had backstage passes. Comparing mine to the others, I noticed the only difference was that I had AM written on my pass and everyone else had JJ written on theirs. Feeling a little nervous, I approached the security guys, and happily they let me through.

It was somewhat crowded backstage and I felt a little nervous about the whole thing, but at the same time I knew I was one of the few lucky people in this world that could say they were backstage with Phish in Amsterdam. The band didn't hang out for long—they slipped out the door within ten minutes of the backstage participants arriving. The best part of the whole experience was that I got to check out Trey's guitar up close.

I exited the Paradiso excited that I still had another night here.

* * *

I strolled into the Paradiso the next night and once again hung out, drinking a little before the show started. Everyone felt that after last night's show—which was not at all disappointing—the band would nevertheless try and top themselves tonight.

As the band stepped onto the stage, in pretty much the same state as the night before, Trey began the opening chords to Mike's Song. I thought to myself, "Thank you, now this is more like it." I love seeing Phish play this song and I had *never* seen them open a show with it. When they went into Simple, the night just kept getting better. Throughout the set, Chris Kuroda played with the lights on the stain-glass windows that they rigged up to the lightboard. Simply awesome. Strange Design and Ginseng

Photos by ANTHONY BUCHLA

Kuroda creates a mural of circles:
June 22, 1997, Loreley Festival, Koblenz, Germany

Sullivan were nicely placed, and Water In The Sky was fast becoming one of my favorites of the new tunes.

When the band stopped playing between songs, I yelled, "NO DOGS ALLOWED!" knowing full-well they would never play it. Still, I figured I had to try.

As they went into Weekapaug, I remember looking at my watch and thinking, "They will definitely play another song after this." Needless to say, they never did; the set was a short but sweet 60 minutes in length. The second set had a ridiculous three songs in it, but what was more ridiculous was that it lasted about an hour and half. One-third of the number of songs played in the first set, yet half an hour longer. Incredible.

The stretched-out set included some of the most incredible, spacey jamming I'd ever heard. Trey kept mentioning things about worms, referring to Amsterdam as "Worm Town." I wish I knew then what I know now about the meaning behind the worms. (I'll let you know a little later in my story.)

After the Free encore, I was sure the show was over. I walked to the rear of the Paradiso, near the bar, and waited there for the house lights to come on. For the next few minutes, the room stayed dark, and I became convinced they would be coming back out. As Fishman began to hit the high hat, I quickly figured it had to be David Bowie; they had already played Maze. As the energy built to the opening chords, the bartenders at the bar kept yapping loudly in Dutch. Like clockwork, someone from the audience turned around to the bartenders and yelled, "Would you shut the fuck up!" and *as soon* as that was said, Trey broke into David Bowie. If only Phish knew how in-synch the whole incident was.

Bowie smoked, as usual, and as the houselights came on, a feeling of sadness swept over me as I realized it was actually over. However, I did still have that backstage pass. So like the night before, I waited for things to settle down. This time, a member of the crew said it would be a few minutes before we could go backstage. They strung us along for about 10 minutes until they announced that the band had already left. It became clear that if I wanted to talk to the band, I'd have to use the backstage pass elsewhere on the tour. With tickets to only two more shows, I strolled back down the streets of Amsterdam to my hotel room.

July 3, 1997, Nuremberg, Germany

The next morning, I bought a train to Nuremberg and spent close to seven hours on a train filled with fellow Phishheads. We all talked about the previous few shows and traded stories of Amsterdam and our Phish experiences. The countryside in Germany was absolutely beautiful—ruins of castles strewn throughout the mountains and bright-green hills rolled endlessly past our train windows.

The train pulled into Nuremberg at around 6:15 p.m., giving me only an hour to find a hotel room and then the venue. Most people that I met on the train planned to walk directly from the station to the venue, but I took the lazy way out and got a hotel room, then a cab.

I went into the venue and purchased my ticket, and discovered that the concert area was surrounded by a 30-foot wall covered with plants. The beer sold in the venue came in *huge* one-liter cups—I had to remind myself that I was in Germany now, and this was standard size.

It felt like there were no more than 400 people at the show, almost a quarter of them German. As the band came on, Trey immediately commented on the venue, "Look at this place, it's like one giant plant." At this point it was rather pleasant outside, but I could see the clouds rolling in. As if on cue, as soon as Divided Sky began, the rain started. I was right in the front row and the only part of the venue not covered by a tent was the first three rows. But everyone in the front, including myself, decided to keep standing in the rain instead of pushing back. The showers lasted through Beauty Of My Dreams, which made for a great experience. By that time the rain passed, though, I was completely drenched, and freezing. I shivered as a pretty standard first set closed with a great Rocky Top.

As the second set opened up, we were treated to a 30-minute version of Ghost, easily the longest of the tour. As Jon began the opening drums

Photo by JASON GLEASON

Europe Summer '97
Setlists 6/13-6/27

6/13/97 S.F.X. Centre, Dublin, Ireland
I: Theme, Dogs Stole Things, Beauty of My Dreams, Billy Breathes, Limb by Limb, Wolfman's > Wading in the Velvet Sea, Taste
II: Stash, Maze, Water in the Sky, Vultures, Slave, Chalkdust > Ghost > Oblivous Fool, Character Zero **E:** Stand > Izabella
"La Bamba" and "Tequila" jams before Stash. Concert debuts: Dogs Stole Things, Limb by Limb, Wading in the Velvet Sea, Water in the Sky, Vultures, Ghost, Oblivious Fool, Stand, Izabella.

6/14/97 S.F.X. Centre, Dublin, Ireland
I: Down with Disease, NICU, Dirt, Talk, My Soul, CTB, Limb by Limb, Bye Bye Foot, Free, Caspian
II: Twist Around, Piper, I Saw It Again, Fooled by Images, Dogs Stole Things, Waste, Bowie, Cavern
E: When the Circus Comes, Rocky Top
Concert debuts: Dirt, Bye Bye Foot, Twist Around, Piper, I Saw It Again, Fooled by Images.

6/16/97 Royal Albert Hall, London, England
I: Squirming Coil > Dogs Stole Things, Taste, Water in the Sky, Sample, Beauty of My Dreams, Theme, Chalkdust, Wolfman's, Oblivious Fool
II: Limb by Limb, Ghost, I Don't Care > Reba, Wading in the Velvet Sea, Dirt, Harry Hood **E:** Cities, Poor Heart
Concert debut: I Don't Care (provisional title).

6/19/97 Arena, Vienna, Austria
I: Limb by Limb, Dogs Stole Things, Theme > PYITE, Water in the Sky, Maze, Waste, Vultures, Runaway Jim
II: Stash > Ghost > I Saw It Again, Wading in the Velvet Sea, Piper, Jesus Left Chicago, Caspian
E: Beauty of My Dreams, Character Zero, Hello My Baby

6/20/97 Archa Theatre, Prague, Czech Republic
I: Taste, Cities > Horn > Funny as it Seems > Limb by Limb > I Don't Care > Antelope
II: Bowie, Ghost, Bye Bye Foot, Ginseng Sullivan, Cavern, Twist Around, Bouncing, Julius **E:** When the Circus Comes, Rocky Top
Concert debut: Funny as it Seems.

6/21/97 Hurricane Festival, Eichenring, Scheessel, Germany
Sample, Also Sprach > Poor Heart, Taste, Dirt, Theme, Swept Away > Steep, Limb by Limb, Dogs Stole Things, Harry Hood, Chalkdust, Jam > Twist Around, Cavern **E:** My Soul
Music festival; Phish played one set.

6/22/97 WDR/Loreley Festival, Lorely, St. Goarschausem, Koblenz, Germany
Taste, Water in the Sky, Stash, Dirt, Uncle Pen, Character Zero, Theme, Hello My Baby, Ghost **E:** Limb by Limb
Music festival; Phish played one set. Delayed broadcast on German TV show "Rockplast."

6/24/97 La Laiterie, Strasbourg, France
I: Melt, Beauty of My Dreams, Dogs Stole Things, Vultures, Guelah, Runaway Jim, Talk, Free, Caspian, Rocky Top
II: Wolfman's > Reba, NICU, Twist Around, Piper, Wading in the Velvet Sea, Ghost **E:** Loving Cup
Guelah abandoned. "Gypsy Queen" jam in Runaway Jim. Live FM broadcast in Strasbourg.

6/25/97 L'Aeronef, Lille, France
I: Oblivious Fool, Dogs Stole Things, Taste, Billy Breathes, AC/DC Bag, Old Home Place, Theme, Wading in the Velvet Sea, I Saw It Again, Limb by Limb, My Soul
II: Down with Disease > Jam > Piper > Down with Disease > Time > McGrupp > Makisupa > Cecilia > HYHU > Rocka William > Antelope **E:** Guyute
"Can't You Hear Me Knocking" jam in Down with Disease. McGrupp performed reggae-style. Fishman on towel for Cecilia. Concert debuts: Time (provisional title); Cecilia.

6/27/97 Glastonbury Festival, Worthy Farm, Pilton, Somerset, England
Wilson, Chalkdust, Stash, Dogs Stole Things, Poor Heart, Taste, Bouncing, Character Zero
Music festival; Phish played one set.

Under the lights in the Paradiso: July 2, 1997, Amsterdam, Netherlands

Photo by ANTHONY BUCHLA

to Harry Hood, I was completely ecstatic—the first Hood of my tour. They closed with a nicely placed Cavern and encored with a 15-minute Character Zero.

After the show, I spoke to Mike Gordon and mentioned that I talked to his Aunt Judy a couple months back at Northeastern University. (She teaches English there.) She walked up to me in the parking lot one day because I have the PHISH license plate in Massachusetts and told me that Mike was her nephew. After we finished talking, I used my second backstage pass and this time enjoyed a five-minute conversation with Trey.

I first asked Trey for the name of the first song they played that night. People had been calling it both Words and Piper, and Trey clarified things by telling me the actual name was, in fact, Piper. I then got to the meat of our conversation, the meaning behind all the "worm" talk in Amsterdam.

The story went like this: one day in Amsterdam, Trey was using one of the toilets that openly line the streets in Amsterdam and he was completely fucked up at the time. He said while he was pissing, he actually felt like he was riding on a worm. He was completely overcome by the feeling—thus the saying, "I'm on the back of a worm!"

I left Nuremberg as fast as I came, and saw nothing of the town, something I regret now.

July 5, 1997, Como, Italy

From Nuremberg, I spent a day in Munich. Sick from being in the cold rain the night before, I spent the day in bed. The train ride from Munich to Como was a long seven hours.

I figured out the hard way that getting to Como via Milan was *much* longer than if I went through Vienna, Austria. This would explain why I saw no Phishheads on the train. During the ride, I was stuck in a cabin with a German that yelled at me for putting my feet up on the seat. He couldn't speak a word of English. Many dirty looks later, another man

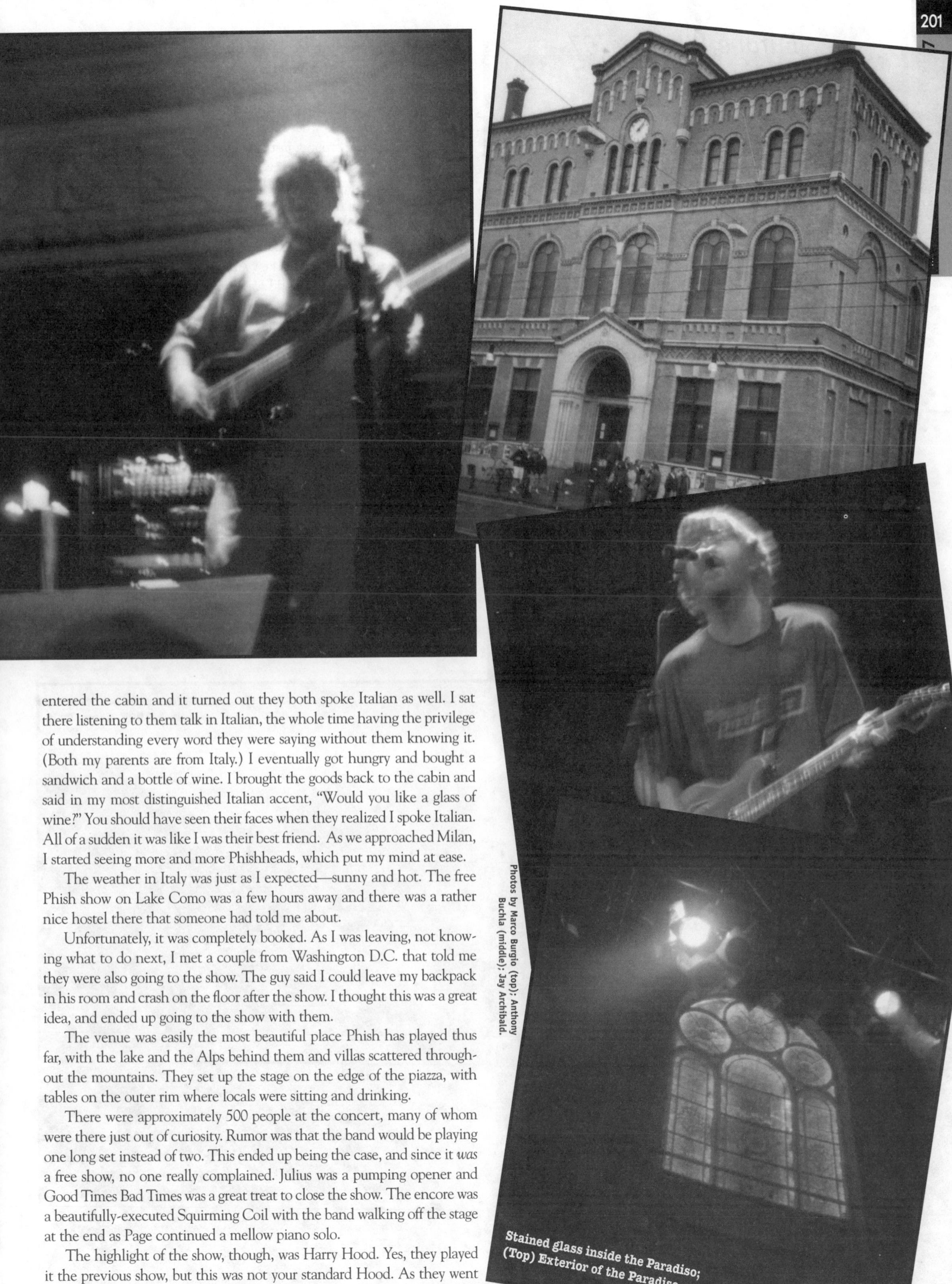

entered the cabin and it turned out they both spoke Italian as well. I sat there listening to them talk in Italian, the whole time having the privilege of understanding every word they were saying without them knowing it. (Both my parents are from Italy.) I eventually got hungry and bought a sandwich and a bottle of wine. I brought the goods back to the cabin and said in my most distinguished Italian accent, "Would you like a glass of wine?" You should have seen their faces when they realized I spoke Italian. All of a sudden it was like I was their best friend. As we approached Milan, I started seeing more and more Phishheads, which put my mind at ease.

The weather in Italy was just as I expected—sunny and hot. The free Phish show on Lake Como was a few hours away and there was a rather nice hostel there that someone had told me about.

Unfortunately, it was completely booked. As I was leaving, not knowing what to do next, I met a couple from Washington D.C. that told me they were also going to the show. The guy said I could leave my backpack in his room and crash on the floor after the show. I thought this was a great idea, and ended up going to the show with them.

The venue was easily the most beautiful place Phish has played thus far, with the lake and the Alps behind them and villas scattered throughout the mountains. They set up the stage on the edge of the piazza, with tables on the outer rim where locals were sitting and drinking.

There were approximately 500 people at the concert, many of whom were there just out of curiosity. Rumor was that the band would be playing one long set instead of two. This ended up being the case, and since it *was* a free show, no one really complained. Julius was a pumping opener and Good Times Bad Times was a great treat to close the show. The encore was a beautifully-executed Squirming Coil with the band walking off the stage at the end as Page continued a mellow piano solo.

The highlight of the show, though, was Harry Hood. Yes, they played it the previous show, but this was not your standard Hood. As they went

Photos by Marco Burgio (top); Anthony Buchla (midde); Jay Archibald.

Stained glass inside the Paradiso; (Top) Exterior of the Paradiso.

Europe Summer '97
Setlists 6/29-7/5

6/29/97 Roskilde Festival, Roskilde, Denmark
YEM, Taste, Bouncing, Beauty of My Dreams, Chalkdust, Theme, Character Zero **E:** My Soul
Music festival; Phish played one set.

7/1/97 Paradiso, Amsterdam, The Netherlands
I: Ghost, Horn, Ya Mar, Limb by Limb > Funny as it Seems, I Saw It Again, Dirt, Reba, Dogs Stole Things
II: Jam > Timber Ho, Bathtub Gin > Cities > Jam, Loving Cup, Slave
E: When the Circus Comes
"Back of the worm" vocals in Ghost, Ya Mar and Cities. Fishman on piano for jam at beginning of second set. "When the Saints Go Marching In" tease in Jam out of Cities.

7/2/97 Paradiso, Amsterdam, The Netherlands
I: Mike's > Simple > Maze, Strange Design, Ginseng Sullivan, Vultures, Water in the Sky, Weekapaug
II: Jam > Stash > Jam > Llama > "Wormtown" > Wading in the Velvet Sea **E:** Free **E2:** Bowie
"Wormtown" was Steve Miller's "Swingtown" reworked with "back of the worm" vocals and a Worm Rap by Trey.

7/3/97 Serenadenhof, Nuremberg, Germany
I: Piper, My Soul, Divided Sky, Beauty of My Dreams, Taste, Train Song, Theme, Rocky Top
II: Ghost, CTB, Billy Breathes, Sparkle, Harry Hood, Cavern
E: Character Zero

7/5/97 Piazza Risorgimento, Cernobbio (near Como), Italy
Julius, Bouncing, Uncle Pen, Sample, Theme, Caspian, Twist Around, Piper, Harry Hood > Love You > HYHU, Poor Heart, Character Zero, GTBT **E:** Squirming Coil
Free outdoor show; Phish played one set. Soundcheck: Funky Bitch, Ginseng. "Groove is in the Heart" and "Fluffhead" teases in Twist Around. Fishman on vacuum for Love You. "Walk This Way" tease in GTBT. Last Love You, 12/8/95 Cleveland, OH [111 shows].

into the song, I looked over at a couple of guys I was talking with and said, "Watch this. This is going to be a legendary Harry Hood."

As they reached the point where Trey begins the long jam right after Mr. Minor, he said, "Chris, shut the lights off so we can see the mountains." This reinforced what I had predicted. As the jam began to build, Trey slowly turned around, just staring up at the mountains. It was the most emotional Hood I have ever experienced.

After the show, we walked back to the hostel, and to my despair, there was a man at the entrance asking people to show their keys. When I couldn't supply one he told me to leave. I tried explaining that my backpack was in the room and he couldn't understand why it would be in there when I didn't have a key. After some arguing, I got him to let me in to get my backpack and I was out on the street at 1 a.m. with no place to sleep. I walked back to the train station, contemplating sleeping in the park as many were already doing, but I decided to check out a hotel across the street first. It ended up being incredibly expensive, but when I found out there was a mini-bar in the room, I took it.

July 6, 1997, Desenzano/Genova, Italy

The next morning, I strolled over to the train station and had a nice breakfast complete with a very tasty cappuccino. I met up with a group of people along the way and we all took the train to Desenzano, arriving around 11 a.m., so we had plenty of time to hang out before the show.

We ended up waiting an hour and a half for a bus that dropped us off right in front of the beach where the show would be. Not many people know about this place, but believe me when I say it is breathtaking. The town sports the biggest lake in Italy and the water was fresh and clear. As we stepped onto the rocky beach, we saw the crew setting up the stage. I never thought any venue could beat Como, but sure enough, this place was equally if not more beautiful.

Around 4 p.m. I went swimming in the lake and as I was treading

Mountains frame the soundcheck: July 5, 1997, Como, Italy

Photo by JASON GLEASON

Trey and Page jam the limbo-karaoke soundcheck: July 6, 1997, Desenzano/Genova, Italy

Mike onstage in Como, Italy, July 6, 1997

water I noticed Mike taking his clothes off. He had his fluorescent green bathing suit on and he dove into the water.

A bit later, Trey strolled down the beach and they all climbed on stage for the soundcheck. The soundcheck proved to be amazing, to say the least. I was lucky to be in the front row, pressed against the gates, where I snapped some great photos. And I wasn't the only one—the crazy soundcheck witnessed by about 90 people began with the band taking pictures of each other. I found it amusing to see the simplicity of their cameras.

After the boys were finished enjoying the moment, they picked up their instruments and began an open jam. About one minute in, Trey looked Mike's way and said, "You're the bassist, right?" Mike acknowledged the remark and kept playing. My take on it was that Trey must have felt that Mike wasn't playing hard enough, and I witnessed a quick change in sound after the comment. After jamming for a few minutes, they went into Oblivious Fool (unplayed since the remarkable show in Lille) followed by Beauty Of My Dreams.

At the conclusion of Beauty Of My Dreams, the band paused and church bells could be heard ringing from a bell tower located next to the beach. Trey found this amusing and began to play Hell's Bells. They then went into a full cover of Shook Me All Night Long.

The highlight of the soundcheck (as if everything they'd already done wasn't enough) was when Mike suggested to Trey that they get a limbo contest going. They set up Mike's microphone as the limbo pole and then asked the crowd if someone wanted to sing. An eager male obliged and jumped up on stage. Trey then summoned for a few people to come up on stage and participate in the limbo contest.

At first, I hesitated, but when I saw other people jumping the fence to the stage, I couldn't resist.

The limbo contest began with the tune Another One Bites The Dust sung by that guy from the crowd. He altered the lyrics a bit and sang, "Another one rides the bus!" which I hadn't even noticed until hearing the tapes. I stood on the stage awaiting my turn, exhilarated as I took in where I was and what I was doing. I made it through one round, but got bounced after practically falling in the second round accompanied by the boos of the crowd. I quickly stepped off the stage and left the limboing to people that had a clue.

By this point, another guy from the crowd came on stage and took over vocals. He offered to sing Stoned Me and was very impressive. After this song was over, the limbo contest was reduced to three people, all of whom were female. After a very impressive stand by all the finalists, the winner was crowned and the soundcheck came to a close.

After the soundcheck, I returned to the hotel to call my roommate back in the States to inform him of the spectacle that I both witnessed and participated in. There was no answer, so I left a detailed message on his answering machine, knowing full-well that he would never understand the experience I had just been a part of. Then I walked across the street to get some food and wine to prepare me for the show that was about two hours away.

Overall, the show wasn't that impressive. The soundcheck was easily the highlight, and the scenery was obviously another added bonus.

July 9, 1997, Lyon, France

After two perfect days in Genova, I took a train to Lyon that was *completely* filled with Phishheads. Once again, we exchanged stories as well as tapes. This guy Ashford had some really nice Widespread Panic that he let me listen to in exchange for some of my tapes.

There was a pretty solid rumor that Bela Fleck and the Flecktones

Photos by MARCO BURGIO

Europe Summer '97
Setlists 7/6-7/11

7/6/97 Spiaggia di Rivoltana, Desenzano/Genova, Italy
Soundcheck: Jam, Oblivious Fool, Beauty of My Dreams, Hell's Bells Jam, Shook Me All Night Long (Fishman on lead vocals), Oom Bop (Fishman on vocals as "James Brown performing Hansen's Oom Bop"), Karaoke Contest (all sung by audience members, except Day-O, sung by the band, with limboing by audience): Another One Bites the Dust, And It Stoned Me, Only Shallow, Day-O
I: Runaway Jim, Old Home Place, Dogs Stole Things, Stash, Horse > Silent, CTB, Scent of a Mule, Chalkdust
II: Free, YEM, Waste, Rocky Top, Funky Bitch **E:** My Soul
Soundcheck was open to the public and included audience karaoke and limbo contest.

7/9/97 Le Transbordeur, Lyon/Villeurbanne, France
I: PYITE > Caspian, Ginseng Sullivan, Melt, Dirt, Taste, Adeline, Harry Hood
II: Down with Disease > My Soul > CTB > YEM, Ghost, Poor Heart
E: Hello My Baby
Bela Fleck on banjo, Victor Wooten on bass and Future Man on synth-axe drumitar for YEM, Ghost and Poor Heart.

7/10/97 Espace Julien, Marseille, France
I: Dogs Stole Things, Limb by Limb, Ginseng Sullivan, Bathtub Gin, Llama > Wading in the Velvet Sea, Lizards, Oblivious Fool
II: Also Sprach > Julius, Magilla > Ya Mar, Ghost > Take Me to the River **E:** Funky Bitch
"Magilla" tease in Ya Mar, which also featured a number of duets between the bandmembers. Members of Son Seals' band joined for Funky Bitch: Dan Rabinovitz, trumpet; Justin Smith, rhythm guitar; Johnny B. Gayden, bass; and David Russell, drums. Last Take Me to the River, 11/21/95 Winston-Salem, NC [126 shows].

7/11/97 Doctor Music Festival, Pyrenees, Spain
Chalkdust, Bouncing, Stash, Beauty of My Dreams, Wolfman's, Johnny B. Goode, YEM **E:** Character Zero
Music festival; Phish played one set. The band following Phish at the festival was soundchecking on a nearby stage while Phish played.

would join Phish in Lyon. Someone said that on Bela Fleck's web page it said "jamming with Phish" under their tourdates for 7/9/97.

The band opened with Punch You In The Eye. During Prince Caspian I made my way to the bathroom and purchased a beer at the bar. The bar was situated in another room in the back of the venue. It had a bunch of tables where locals were eating and drinking. It was strange seeing people completely nonplused by what was going on in the adjacent room. I bought a couple of hemp necklaces from some guy selling them at the bar and rejoined the show.

They closed the first set with yet another Harry Hood, but it was once again mind-blowing.

The second set opened with a rocking Down With Disease, and everyone—including myself—was anticipating the arrival of Bela Fleck. During You Enjoy Myself, our wishes were granted as Bela Fleck and the Flecktones came out and took their positions.

The rest of the show was absolutely rocking. Highlights for me were when Flecktone bassist Victor Wooten and Mike were simultaneously playing the same bass, and when Bela and Trey faced off two feet apart from each other, exchanging licks. If you haven't heard this on tape yet, I highly recommend doing whatever it takes to get this show.

July 10, 1997, Marseille, France

The morning after the Phish/Bela Fleck show, I woke up around 9 a.m. and caught a 10:30 a.m. train bound for Marseille. Once there, I found a nice scene outside the venue where about 40 Phishheads were hanging out, eating watermelon, drinking wine, and smoking buds.

Before the show, three black guys walked up to the stage and Fishman came out. Fishman looked really happy to see them, but I had no idea who they were. As Fishman was talking to one of them, I walked up to one of the guys and said, "I don't mean to be rude, but who are you guys?" He replied, "We're the Son Seals Band out of Chicago."

About 45 minutes later, the lights went down and my last Phish show in Europe began.

On the road to the Doctor Music Festival: July 11, 1997, Pyrenees, Spain

Photo by JASON GLEASON

The highlight of the first set for me was definitely Lizards. It was the first in eight shows but I was still hoping Trey would rip up the place by cutting into Fluffhead. It never happened, but we were treated to an awesome Magilla that segued into a smoking Ya Mar. They finished up the second set with no sign of any guests on stage.

As the crowd yelled for an encore, out came Phish, and low and behold, the members of the Son Seals band. They jammed out Funky Bitch like none other and I was left walking home with a big grin on my face.

* * *

Looking back, those two weeks yielded some incredible memories that I'll never forget. As I write this I'm sitting at my desk at work. It's now September, two months since that night in Marseille, but still it feels like it was yesterday.

The last Phish show I went to in Europe had an attendance of less than 1,000 people. The last Phish show I attended in the States was The Great Went, with approximately 65,000 people. It was a contrast, to say the least.

Some people say Phish has gotten too big. My advice for them? Go see them in Europe.

Summer '97

THE X PHILES

THE TRUTH IS (WAY) OUT THERE

We are not alone:
The Great Went, Limestone, ME, August 16-17, 1997

LORING A.F.B.

CLASSIFIED

Phish played 19 shows in the United States during the summer of 1997, a tour which led off with a bunch of new tunes, and finished off in grand fashion as the band and audience created art together at the Great Went. There were many highlights in between.

Several questions surfaced throughout the tour—had the band retired certain songs? Will their new love of funk be a lasting shift? And most importantly, "Are we alone?"

The specter of UFOs and alien life forms loomed ominously over summer tour 1997, as Phish chose Loring Air Force base in far-off Limestone, ME as the site of the tour finale—the very same Loring Air Force Base which has been the site of several UFO encounters over the years. In fact, the press release sent out by Great Northeast Productions, which presented the Great Went, referred to "a well-documented incident said to have involved an alien spaceship hovering over a custer of B-52 bombers one night in 1969."

Coincidence? One phan didn't think so. That's why writer and cosmic theoretician Greg Schwartz set out to prove the existence of alien life forms on Phish tour. What he found may shock you.

Phish Notes from U.S. Summer '97

♦ The summer tour garnered rave reviews from virtually all corners of Phish phandom, with people applauding Phish's increasingly funk-oriented jam style and the transformation it brought to songs as wide-ranging as Gumbo, Also Sprach Zarathustra and You Enjoy Myself (which had its ending reworked differently during each performance, and the vocal jam all but eliminated). But the centerpiece songs of the tour were named by many as Wolfman's Brother and Cities—two songs that really allowed the band to bring on the funk. Ghost and Loving Cup also served as defining songs of the tour.

♦ With all of the new, there was of course sadness about the passing of the old. Gamehendge songs surfaced in lesser numbers than ever, and old favorites like Tweezer and Divided Sky became rarities.

♦ Continuing a fashion move started in Europe, Fishman hung up his frock for the summer tour. In its place, he sported a sleek black outfit that (as Trey remarked in Shoreline) allowed him to get the funky drumbeats right on new tunes like Limb By Limb. Traditional Fishman songs were also not to be found, though the rotation-jam Rocka William (with Fish on guitar and lead vocals) was played at Deer Creek.

♦ Throughout the summer tour, observant phans spotted Trey using a telephone mounted on top of Page's baby grand, even in the midst of jams. Theories ranged from general Phish weirdness, to Trey calling his kids, or 900 numbers.

♦ The Great Went—a name derived from a line of dialogue in the David Lynch film *Twin Peaks: Fire Walk With Me*—had trademark Phish strangeness galore with a "Port-O-Let Piazza" (a sculpture made of discarded bathroom fixtures) a maze cut in a corn field, and giant hands pointing to nowhere in the concert field. Mike Gordon told the *Boston Globe* that Lynch's movie helped inform the wacked-out spirit of the event.

♦ Vending was unofficially permitted at the Went as vendors created a giant, mile-long mall of sorts alongside the campgrounds.

♦ The Went also saw a world-record being set when over 1,000 phans posed naked for a photograph on Sunday morning (interested people actually had to be turned away!). Though the turnout was slightly tilted towards the masculine side, the split was only about 60/40, and some folks opted to spend the rest of the day naked.

♦ Unlike the Plattsburgh community, Northern Maine residents seemed united in their feelings that the Great Went was a terrific event for their region. (The Pharmer's Almanac even received several letters from Maine residents thanking Phish phans for coming.) Early indications were that the band would be invited back to Limestone for summer '98.

The intrepid research team at Deer Creek. L to R, Greg and Mike, with the "Freedom Ride" behind.

The e… Creek … Louis…

THE X PHILES

BACKGROUND

WHEREIN THE CONNECTION BETWEEN PHISH AND UFOs EMERGES, AND THE AUTHOR JOINS SUMMER TOUR

I DIDN'T GET to see any summer '96 shows because there were no West Coast shows, and I decided that I should stay in Los Angeles to continue pursuing a career in film. But here it was a year later and I wasn't much further up the ladder.

"I'm not missing summer tour again," I thought to myself, but I needed some kind of motivation beyond just having fun to justify going on tour to myself. (At age 27, it's hard to take the same carefree attitude that I had, say, five or even three years ago.)

"How could I combine my interest in film with my interest in Phish?" I wondered. A tour documentary? Sure, I could've done that, but it wouldn't have been anything particularly new. Fortunately, the fates intervened with a better idea.

Earlier in the year, I started doing some serious research into the UFO/ET phenomenon, reading all kinds of books about UFOs, ETs, and new age/metaphysical speculations about the impending evolution of humanity and planet Earth. Imagine what went through my mind while reading a book called *The UFO Coverup* that detailed a documented UFO incident at none other than the LORING AIR FORCE BASE—the site of Phish's upcoming summer festival, The Great Went!

In late October of 1975, the Loring AFB was buzzed by a UFO, which was reported to have encroached upon the base's nuclear supply depot. The Air Force went on a full alert but was never able to identify the UFO before it mysteriously vanished.

With my curiosity already piqued, I then discovered another eerie coincidence: the dates of the Went, August 16 and 17, 1997, marked the 10-year anniversary of the Mayan Harmonic Convergence! Ph.D. and Mayan expert Jose Arguelles has presented strong evidence in his writings that the Mayans were extra-terrestrials. They built the fantastic pyramids in central Mexico that are as much a mystery as the Egyptian ones, they had their own meticulously-detailed galactic calendar based on Universal constants (as opposed to our calendar which is just based on our planet and our sun and has nothing to do with the rest of the universe), and they vanished without a trace.

Arguelles deciphered the Mayan Calendar and figured out that it comes to an end on December 21, 2012. He

tended research family near Deer
L to r, Mike, Jenny, Rich,
, Charles, Brooke, Greg, Joanna.

also figured out that August 16-17, 1987 was the end of an important cycle and that those dates marked a harmonic convergence, on which cosmic light would pour into Earth, synching it up for the 25-year approach to 2012.

The combination of the Loring UFO incident and the Mayan dates seemed too unusual to dismiss. My minivan, the "Freedom Ride," already had 140,000 miles on it, but because of this new information, I felt it was absolutely meant-to-be and that the Freedom Ride would be able to make it. I knew what I had to do—I would get a camcorder and document my travels across the country.

On the road, I planned to film the parking lot scene to some extent, but my main mission was twofold: to raise awareness of the issues by distributing a newsletter summarizing my UFO research—a bright green flyer I dubbed "The 3rd Stone Chronicle"—and to interview fellow phans about their thoughts on the subject. I walked around saying, "Free info on the connection between Phish and UFOs!" I was to find that a good number of phans were already tuned into these concepts.

In the newsletter, I discussed theories on the secret government/corporate conspiracy to cover up the existence of UFOs and ETs, and the viewpoint of the ETs themselves. All my research led me to this conclusion: There is a negative faction of the ETs commonly known as the Greys, but the overwhelming majority of our visitors are benevolent, and form a sort of Federation of Planets that oversees evolution on planets in this part of the Universe. They are here to witness/help guide us toward what Pleiadian sources call the Cosmic Party, which they identify as happening on December 21, 2012.

On this date, Earth is supposed to evolve from the 3rd dimension to the 4th. What this entails is a raising of consciousness that will take humanity to a near-utopian way of life, with all of the bullshit that plagues society today left behind. This is a very rare and special cosmic event, hence all the ET interest. The Pleiadians, whom evidence says are our celestial ancestors and are the closest to us of all the ETs, also believe that a key step in the evolution of the galaxy is about to take place here on Earth on December 21, 2012. Earth is a very special place, and humanity, while obviously not without some major problems, has created one of the coolest and most unique cultures in the universe.

Lofty concepts I know, but there's a lot of evidence for this. Visionary theoretician Terence McKenna states, "The technological advances of the last 100 years make no sense unless it culminates in the utter transformation of the species." McKenna, unaware of the Mayan calendar, came up with a mathematical equation that measures novelty throughout human history. It hits what he terms "Timewave Zero" on December 21, 2012. He was stunned by the synchronicity when he found out about the Mayan calendar.

But here's what really drew me in on the Phish connection. Jose Arguelles states, "4-D reality is recreated in the 3rd dimension through the overtones of music, color, and light." Whoa! Is this not exactly what the Grateful Dead pioneered back in the '60s and what Phish carries the cosmic torch for now?

I also pointed out how I thought that Generation-X are the ones to make these changes happen. We are the flower that is blooming from the seed planted by the '60s generation. Due to our unique historical position, we can learn from their mistakes and all the other mistakes humanity has made. Come 2012, we'll be pushing 40 and we'll be the adults. We will be able to see how and why the world needs to change better than any previous generation, and I believe we will make it happen.

Trying to raise consciousness of this concept was my main goal—along with catching some great shows, of course.

THE 3RD STONE CHRONICLE - SUMMER 1997
"Beneath the tides of sleep and time, strange fish are moving" - T.Wolfe

Cosmic Speculations for Planet Earth - 1997 & Beyond : UFOs, ETs, Evolution, & Conspiracy - What You Need To Know!

By S.F. STARDOG, volunteer writer- Planetary Liberation Organization

NOTE: THIS INFORMATION IS NOT REPORTED AS FACT, BUT AS REASONABLY LIKELY SPECULATION BASED ON EXTENSIVE RESEARCH AND PONDERING OF THE PONDERINGS...

STARDATE- Summer 1997 - USA - We are not alone. This concept is supported by
overwhelming evidence including : multitudinous sightings, radar contacts, close encounters, crop
circles, animal mutilations, channeled messages, multiple-witness reports, and physical evidence such
as indented landing sites, burned vegetation, human scars and implants, as well as govt. denial of such
ludicrous proportion that it can only be meant to convince us that, yes, they have been lying to us (See
the 6/24/97 Air Force Report on Roswell). Some of the reports and evidence undoubtedly are the
product of misinterpretation and hoaxes, but the sheer volume and consistency of descriptions argues
against all of them being mistakes or fakes. Personal research concludes that there a # of varying ET
factions here on Earth, right now! IF YOU ARE CONFIDANT THAT THE GOVT. CAN REPRESENT OUR
INTERESTS AND CAN ADEQUATELY DEAL W/ A SUBJECT AS LOFTY AS ETs FROM OUTER
SPACE BETTER THAN WE CAN, YOU HAD BETTER THINK AGAIN! Our govt. has been actively aware
of space visitors for decades and by its actions has bungled its responsibility abominally. We need real
answers now. Although we have seen change on Earth accelerate dramatically over the last 50 years as
a result of technology, this is nothing compared to what will result from meeting our celestial neighbors.
Humanity is about to make its greatest leap ever. So why are the ETs here and why is the govt. hiding it?
The Energy Conspiracy - Whether you call them the Secret govt, the Illuminati, the Bilderberg
Group, the Trilateral Commission, or the Council on Foreign Relations, the name is irrelevant. The Secret
govt. is basically made up of the richest people in the world, and they have been controlling our so called
govts. for a long time. They influence who gets elected, when &where; when there is war and when
there isn't; they control planetary food shortages and inflation; and exert massive yet subtle influence in
all forms of the media. They don't always get what they want, but usually do.
*Why would the Secret govt. take interest in ETs? Just the possible impact of ET energy technology
alone is a huge source of concern to them. Through calculated and aggressive govt. & corporate
planning/conspiracy, our world has been made totally dependent on 2 major forms of energy : petroleum
& nuclear. Developing an inexpensive, abundant, & non-polluting energy source is an environmental &
social need - but it is hopeless to expect to do so on the basis of production decisions that accept as
their final test private profit rather than social value. For humanity to survive, THIS MUST CHANGE!
*Both the oil & nuclear options have brought the rise of monopolies which have functioned at the
expense of Earth's environment. It's no wonder that certain ET visitors consider Earth a wide open
insane aslyum when we consent to the adoption of such dubious energy sources which have the clear
potential of destroying the planet and its inhabitants. Any tech that might unseat these monopolies
would be viewed as dangerous to their position of power. Would the long suffering public continue to
pay ever-increasing prices for ever-decreasing reserves of gas & oil if they knew for certain that fuel-free,
non-polluting, electromagnetic and anti-gravity tech existed? Viewed from this perspective, the CAUSE
of SECRECY concerning ET CONTACT becomes CLEAR. This energy monoply has been engaged in

In late October '75, Loring AFB was buzzed by a UFO, which was reported to have encroached upon the base's nuclear supply depot.

Virginia Beach, Virginia
Monday, July 21, 1997

The pre-show parking lot scene was viciously pelted by Mother Nature. It wasn't just raining—it was bucketing. But miraculously, the sky cleared by showtime and waterlogged Phishheads scampered to the venue, where a spectacular rainbow blossomed.

Before the show, some fans claimed Phish would greet the tour with an entire set's worth of new material. They weren't that far off. The opening segment marked the first time U.S. audiences heard Ghost, Dogs Stole Things, Piper and Dirt, played in succession before the more familiar sounds of Ginseng Sullivan. The set's highlight—besides the 20-minute Ghost opener—came next in a gorgeously extended Bathtub Gin that heard Trey welcoming everyone to the tour and introducing the names of the new songs.

Set II proved to be a wild affair. Wolfman's brought out the funk, seguing into a heavily-improvised version of Magilla. A long, strong Bowie anchored the middle of the set. Then, during the Theme jam, sax player Leroi Moore of The Dave Matthews Band took the stage. After he belted out some mean solos, Trey handed him another sax, and Moore proceeded to play both at once! Not to be outdone, Trey strapped on a second and third guitar while Mike also went for extra basses. Page had each of his four limbs working different keyboards in his set up. When the craziness subsided and Moore departed, Phish closed the second set with a delicate Slave.

7/21/97 Virginia Beach Amphitheater, Virginia Beach, VA
I: Ghost, Dogs Stole Things, Piper, Dirt, Ginseng Sullivan, Bathtub Gin, Character Zero
II: Wolfman's > Magilla, Bowie, Wading in the Velvet Sea, Theme > Multi-Instrument Jam > Funky Bitch, Slave **E:** Loving Cup
"Drowned" jam in Bathtub Gin. Leroi Moore on saxophone for jam out of Theme and Funky Bitch. During the "multi-instrument jam," all five people onstage played two or three instruments (Trey on three guitars, Mike on two basses, etc.)

Raleigh, North Carolina
Tuesday, July 22, 1997

When Phish played new tune Water In the Sky in set I at Walnut Creek, it was not only a tribute to the previous 24 hours of downpours but also a foreshadowing of storms to come.

Ominous black thunderclouds built in the sky over the lawn throughout a mostly-uneven first set, finally opening during Taste. (Listen for the gigantic thunderclap on the tapes!) The rain prompted wet phans to sneak inside the crowded pavilion as security struggled to maintain order. The storm hovered directly overhead as the Taste jam matched the storm in rising intensity. Phans remaining on the lawn were treated to a spectacular lightning show as they cheered on the rain, Taste, and crackling thunder.

For set II, the rain leveled off to strong and steady pour, blowing sideways through the pavilion. But all focus was on the stage for a Down With Disease that jammed way out, then intricately segued into Mike's Song, driving the rain-drenched crowd into a frenzy. The intense jam somehow made it safely to Weekapaug through Simple and Hydrogen, comprising practically the entire set. Like the first set, the second set seemed to end prematurely, but a double encore of When the Circus Comes and—ahem—Harry Hood put an exclamation point on a wonderfully wild night.

The rain spoiled any prayer of a parking lot Shakedown, but who could be disappointed after witnessing a show for the ages?

7/22/97 Walnut Creek Amphitheater, Raleigh, NC
I: Runaway Jim > My Soul, Water in the Sky, Stash, Bouncing, Vultures, Bye Bye Foot, Taste
II: Down with Disease > Mike's > Simple > Hydrogen > Weekapaug, Hello My Baby
E: When the Circus Comes, Harry Hood
Thunder and lightning storm during Taste; rain continued for the rest of the night. "Hydrogen" teases in Weekapaug.

On the grass in Raleigh, 7.22.97

FIELDWORK

THE RESEARCHER'S TOUR BEGINS IN ARIZONA, THE SITE OF MASS-UFO SIGHTINGS IN MARCH '97

7.29.97 PHOENIX, AZ

I met up with Joanna, a girl I recruited off the Internet as an extra gas rider, and we then hooked up with some other local friends of mine for whom this would be their only Phish show of the summer.

I got some interviews in the lot, but there was not as much awareness of the UFO scenario here as I expected. I was originally going to skip this show and start at Ventura, but Arizona is well-known for UFO activity, particularly with the mass sightings that occurred in Phoenix last March 13. I thought Phish would acknowledge this with a space-themed show, including 2001, Scent of a Mule, Life on Mars, or BBFCFM, but none of that was to be. Alas, this show was to be the least satisfying of the tour. I don't know if it was the heat, but the energy just wasn't there for the most part.

One very notable exception was the first-set closer Loving Cup. I absolutely love this song, yet had never seen it live in 27 shows until Phoenix. And Trey absolutely went off on it. I would catch it three more times on tour, but this one was the best, and gave me one of my favorite Phish moments. Even though we all agreed the show was somewhat lackluster, the Loving Cup alone was a sign to me of great things to come.

7.30.97 VENTURA, CA

We hooked up with my friend Ashley, who was joining us for the rest of the West Coast run. But we got to the lot rather late, so there was no time to pass out flyers and film.

I wasn't expecting much from this show because the venue is pretty schwag—it's basically just a dirty racetrack. But this show raged! The phunky new direction of Wolfman's Brother was a pleasant surprise and sign of Phish's current musical evolution which I think is just great. The more funk the better, I always say.

There's ongoing debate on the Net about Phish having already peaked, but this tour should have convinced anyone

On the pavement in Atlanta 7.23.97

otherwise. Punch opened the second set! You know the boys mean serious business when they open with this cut—such a move always takes me back to the stupendous 12/31/95 show. I was also pleased to get my first taste of Simpsons language at a Phish show.

The Simpsons cue led into one of the top musical highlights of the year—David Bowie > Cities > David Bowie. The Bowie jam had started to ramble, but suddenly took a really funky direction. I didn't know where they were going, but I just started grooving. I looked around and saw everyone else doing the same. It was a great moment—none of us knew where we were heading, but we were all sharing in a groove.

And then they busted out Cities. What a great song! I couldn't help but feel like Trey was telling the people of L.A. to find another place to live. I already plan to since I really don't like L.A. anyway. But there is also a lot of speculation about L.A. not surviving upcoming Earth changes. So consider yourself warned, Southlanders.

7.31.97 MOUNTAIN VIEW, CA

Here we added my buddy Mike to our crew, a long-time fellow tourhead, and main co-pilot of the Freedom Ride. Again, we were running late, so there wasn't much time for flyers and filming. But I knew there'd be plenty of opportunities at the Gorge.

At this point, I must comment on the ongoing Dead/Phish debate. Many older Deadheads don't get Phish and resent the notion that another band could be in the Dead's league. I used to feel the same way, that the Dead were one of a kind. That's why Jerry's death hit me so very hard—"Oh man, this special, special thing we had is gone forever."

At that point, I'd seen Phish seven times, but still hadn't made "the connection." This came at the aforementioned cosmic barnburner, 12/31/95 at Madison Square Garden. I had a serious revelation at that show, as I became convinced beyond a shadow of a doubt that Phish were channeling the same cosmic vibes that the Dead were. Younger phans who never toured with the Dead may not want to admit this anymore than the older Deadheads, but Phish is following in the Dead's hallowed footsteps. Most everyone in their 20s who has done extensive touring with both the Dead and Phish knows this is true. The fact that Phish and the Dead are the only two bands with Ben & Jerry's ice cream flavors is a cosmic synchronici-

Atlanta, Georgia
Wednesday, July 23, 1997

As the first cars rolled onto the venue blacktop, fans discussed the relentless drive through the hurricane-driven rain and wind from Raleigh to Atlanta. Though Atlanta promised warmer, drier tidings, the show was not without threatening overcast skies (sporadic showers arrived again during the show). The first set mellowed a bit after Julius as Phish continued to showcase their new repertoire of songs. Things picked up with Split Open and Melt, and a jamming Possum set closer set the stage for the set II show-carriers.

Then there was funk! PYITE started things off cool and crisp, creating the groove momentum for a spacially-tempoed Ghost, the longest version of the U.S. tour at around 27 minutes and probably the best of the summer. YEM was also of the funky variety and featured a stylistically different ending which sounded more like a Police coda than the usual haunting vocal jam. The strange YEM ending circled back around to a familiar classic rock riff, and phans were treated to Phish's first full take on Joe Walsh's Rocky Mountain Way. A rocking Chalkdust, which heard Trey whisper the verses before chomping his guitar into the choruses, rewarded phans for their patience with Mother Nature during the Southeast run. Collective exhaustion notwithstanding, thousands headed west to continue with the tour.

7/23/97 Lakewood Amphitheater, Atlanta, GA
I: Julius, Dirt, NICU, Dogs Stole Things, Ginseng Sullivan, Water in the Sky, Limb by Limb, Melt, Billy Breathes, Possum
II: PYITE, Ghost > Sample, YEM > Rocky Mountain Way > Chalkdust
E: Frankenstein
Klezmer-type jam (similar to middle segment of Scent of a Mule) out of YEM into Rocky Mountain Way. Concert debut: Rocky Mountain Way.

Dallas, Texas
Friday, July 25, 1997

The clouds were left behind as the tour headed west to sunny Texas for a pair of well-attended gigs—by far the largest crowds ever to see Phish in the Lone Star State. Of course, Dallas is a city with quite a Phish history (site of the famous Tweezerfest of '94), but the band wouldn't top that performance this time out.

The Dallas show marked one of the rare occasions in which a first set outshined the second, as the Bathtub Gin > Makisupa > AC/DC Bag segment to close the set was a series which would have been a highlight at any show.

In set II, Bob Gullotti joined the band onstage for some double-barrel drumming action. The Surrender to the Air collaborator's appearance had been announced ahead of time, and he seemed to know Phish's music far better than during his first performance with the band, in Hartford during fall tour '96. He and Fishman shared the spotlight for a drum jam during Ya Mar, before the band joined back in for Ghost. (Some fans later complained that Gullotti's up-tempo playing didn't mesh with the rest of the band's jamming, but Phish seemed to enjoy the collaboration, and repeated it the next night in Austin.)

Although Ghost was the tour's most-played song, Dallas marked the only time the band tried to use it in the meat of the second set, without the aid of any other epic jam tune. Reviews of this setlist structure were mixed, at best.

7/25/97 Starplex Amphitheater, Dallas, TX
I: Beauty of My Dreams, Wolfman's > Maze, Water in the Sky, Bathtub Gin > Makisupa > AC/DC Bag
II: Chalkdust > Taste > Ya Mar > Drum Jam > Ghost > Character Zero **E:** Theme
Entire second set with Bob Gullotti on a second drum set. Drum Jam featured Fishman and Gullotti.

Austin, Texas
Saturday, July 26, 1997

Unlike in Dallas the night before—when Bob Gullotti took the stage only during set II—the crowd was treated to the sounds of two drummers from start to finish, and the show never let up.

From the opener—one of the best of the new songs, Limb by Limb—to a fierce YEM > Isabella to close things off, set I was a solid display of musicianship in a city that wouldn't accept anything less. (Grumblings could already be heard, however, from the folks seeing multiple shows on the tour—too many new songs too often, especially in the first sets! But Phish was going to play what they wanted to.)

Set II did not have a single dull moment, leading off with a jammed-out Timber Ho which, to some ranked as a tour highlight. A fine Bowie was followed by an unfinished Harry Hood. Although the crowd was never told to feel good about Hood, all were treated to a verse of "Blister in the Sun" by old Phish European tour buddies the Violent Femmes. That was followed shortly thereafter by a beautiful segue into Free, performed with the middle section heard only on Billy Breathes prior to the summer.

A Bouncing/Cavern encore came as a surprise in a show which seemed more geared toward veterans than beginners. Following the festivities, many phans headed back into downtown Austin to sample the city's famous nightlife.

7/26/97 South Park Meadows, Austin, TX
I: Limb by Limb, Dogs Stole Things, Poor Heart, Stash, Billy Breathes, CTB, Dirt, YEM > Isabella
II: Timber Ho > Bowie, Harry Hood > Blister in the Sun > Harry Hood > Free, Waste > Johnny B. Goode
E: Bouncing, Cavern

Bob Gullotti on a second drum set for the entire show. Blister in the Sun was one verse only; concert debut. Harry Hood unfinished.

Phoenix, Arizona
Tuesday, July 29, 1997

After the outdoor lawn of Austin, Phish returned to the shed circuit at Desert Sky in Phoenix, their first appearance at this outdoor haven. Baking under the hot Arizona sun, the band again put their focus primarily on new material, making for an interesting setlist and a show that (depending on who you talked to) was either the hidden gem of the West Coast run or the tour's most uninteresting, forgettable show.

Theme, one of the summer's most focused-on songs, opened things up in style. Other highlights in the short first set included Gumbo, featuring the summer '97 extended jam that moved this song up from a nice treat to a jaw-dropping funk tune (versions later in the tour would be even stronger than the Phoenix one), and the closing Loving Cup, already the second version of the summer just six shows into the tour. Hooray!

Set II saw long jams on two of the more infrequently played new songs—Oblivious Fool and Twist Around—with the Oblivious Fool opener being the only version Phish aired in the states. That led into the tour's first Antelope and a long, mellow Wading in the Velvet Sea. From there, the band never quite locked into the groove in Twist Around, then struggled to regain their earlier intensity, finishing with a Sample/Rocky Top/Coil run.

A welcome Possum encore bopped everyone up the highway toward Ventura, as Phish geared up for a torrid run up the West Coast that would culminate at The Gorge the next weekend.

7/29/97 Desert Sky Pavilion, Phoenix, AZ
I: Theme, Beauty of My Dreams, Gumbo, Dirt, Sparkle, Ghost, Swept Away > Steep > Loving Cup
II: Oblivious Fool, Antelope, Wading in the Velvet Sea, Twist Around, Taste, Sample, Rocky Top, Squirming Coil **E:** Possum

A mass gathering in Austin, 7.26.97

ty that illustrates this—they really are the same food, just different flavors.

This was my opinion before the Shoreline show, and the show confirmed it totally.

From the moment they hit the stage with the Ghost opener, I felt that the band was totally invoking the cosmic Bay Area/GD vibe. I can't help but feel that this song is partly about Jerry. Halfway through the set, I was able to borrow a ticket and go down to the fourth row. This is the best seat in any venue in the country! The seats slope up, so this ticket has you right on level with the stage. You can look into the musicians' eyes, and they can see yours, too. To be there again, right across from Trey, just blew me away.

The Maze they played was much to my liking, as it was more of a groove-Maze than a freak-out-Maze. Then came I Saw It Again. I couldn't help but feel like this song was symbolic of Phish being the next generation of the GD musical thing. Maybe that's just me, but it seemed even more significant in light of the fact that this was the only place they played it on the U.S. tour. And then, completely out of left field—YEM! All of us in those first few rows felt especially blessed to see a YEM like that up close.

The Runaway Jim that opened the set could well have been called Runaway Jimi—Trey was getting downright cosmic in the open-ended exploration of the tune. I thought that When the Circus Comes to Town symbolized the sadness that came with Jerry's death, as well as the passing of the "scene" from the Dead to Phish. Vultures is one of my favorite new tunes, although it wouldn't really come into its own until Deer Creek.

McGrupp proved a pleasant surprise, and I was stoked that they were invoking some Gamehendge karma, as I believe that Gamehendge is a parable for the world today—We, most of humanity, are the Lizards and the secret government/corporate fascists, that have set up the 9-to-5 economic slavery system that many of us Gen-Xers are struggling to avoid, are Wilson.

I knew that only a Mike's Groove could end this show, and so it was to be. If you look back at setlists over the years, you'll see that any show with both a YEM and a Mike's Groove is a special one, and this was to be the only such show of the tour. While it may not have been the most high-intensity version, I thought it was one of the best I'd heard.

They were locked into such a tight groove, sounding so

crisp—it was oh so sweet. When Trey started playing Happy Birthday, I knew more special vibes were heading our way. When he actually verbalized it by saying that he wanted to wish Jerry a happy birthday and vowed that "We're gonna try and keep his spirit alive in music for the next decade," all my theories were confirmed. What a special, special moment. I knew that it was no coincidence that this tour had Phish at Shoreline on the eve of Jerry's birthday and had us waking up in San Francisco on the day of his birthday, August 1.

8.1.97 SAN FRANCISCO TO STONEHENDGE

We went down to the Haight for breakfast and then hit the road. A Net phan had hipped me to the fact that there is a near-scale replica of Stonehendge right on the way to the Gorge, just over the Oregon-Washington border. This sounded incredibly cool, since there is so much speculation about the origins of Stonehendge, with ETs playing a part.

We met a phan I had met online, another Mike, at the Stonehendge monument, and I'd say it was close to 4:20 a.m. by the time we arrived. I was hoping a bunch of phans would be partying there, but there were just a few locals.

The monument was very cool. It appeared as the original Stonehendge did, with no deterioration. It had been built by a wealthy philanthropist as a monument to World War I vets. Under the beautiful starry night sky, it felt incredibly cosmic. The slab was the perfect size for four people to lay down sleeping bags and crash out there, so that's what Mike, Mike, Ashley and I did, a nice finish to a very peaceful and kind evening.

We were hoping this was a synchronicity leading to a Gamehendge show at the Gorge, since the Gorge is so "hendged" out. This, alas, was also not meant to be. The Gorge would not disappoint, however.

Unusual lifeforms encountered at Shoreline, 7.31.97

Ventura, California
Wednesday, July 30, 1997

On a night when Phish played in a giant, dusty field with not a seat to be seen, the show could be summed up in three words: Bowie > Cities > Bowie, a pairing that many later held to be the musical highlight of the West Coast run, if not the entire tour.

The stage was set for set II craziness in the first set with Phish's first-ever NICU opener. The band didn't let up for the first three songs, swinging into Wolfman's and its now-expected funk jam, then into Chalkdust. The middle of the set was anchored by a massive Stash and a rare Weigh. CTB and Character Zero brought an end to one of the more seriously-jammed first sets of the tour.

The band didn't disappoint in the second set, either. The PYITE/Free opening combo was nothing to sneer at, and it set the stage for the huge Bowie. After a long intro jam that included an increasingly-rare Simpsons "D'oh!" signal, the band took the jam segment far afield, eventually finding their way to the Cities riff for the first Cities in North America since 1994. Dizzyingly, the incredible jam out of Cities found its way back into Bowie to finish off this amazing duo.

After that kind of magic, you couldn't blame the band for falling back on more basic material for the rest of the second set, including a Bouncing/Uncle Pen/Prince Caspian run. The set's sort-of fizzle kept Ventura from being christened one of the very best all-around shows of the tour. As things ended up, it was still one of the stronger nights, at least for fans of true Phish improvisation, with Bowie > Cities > Bowie attaining "must-hear" status.

7/30/97 Ventura County Fairgrounds, Ventura, CA
I: NICU, Wolfman's > Chalkdust, Water in the Sky, Stash, Weigh, Piper, CTB, Character Zero
II: PYITE, Free, Bowie > Cities > Bowie, Bouncing, Uncle Pen, Caspian, Fire **E:** My Soul

Mountain View, California
Thursday, July 31, 1997

Prior to the summer tour, Phish's only previous appearance at Shoreline came on fall tour '95—a show that saw the debut of the band-versus-audience chess game and Trey dedicating I'm Blue I'm Lonesome to Jerry Garcia just two months after his death.

Back at the house that Bill Graham built, the ghosts palpably hung in the air once again on the eve of Garcia's birthday. The opening Ghost seemed to acknowledge those feelings, and set up a first set grounded in some of the best new material. Maze offered jamming space in the middle of the set, and the tour's only Glide brought smiles before new rocker I Saw It Again seemed to herald setbreak. But then came the opening notes of YEM. When it came to close, Phish had played for over an hour an a half.

The second set would top it. A brief "Sweet Home Alabama" tease from Trey and Mike had fans scratching their heads, but the Runaway Jim that jammed into places unknown sure didn't—the best of the tour in the minds of many. It segued into When the Circus Comes, and the intensity continued with Vultures and McGrupp before the band truly made it a night to remember by launching into Mike's Song. Though the Mike's Groove trio wasn't as long as at Raleigh, the set-closing Weekapaug included Trey jamming briefly on "Happy Birthday" and then telling the crowd that Phish planned to keep the spirit of Jerry Garcia alive through their music into the next decade. For Dead-loving phans, it was the perfect tribute; for Dead-doubters, it was maybe the only sour note on a night of pure intensity.

7/31/97 Shoreline Amphitheater, Mountain View, CA
I: Ghost, Ya Mar, Dogs Stole Things, Limb by Limb, Dirt, Maze, Glide, I Saw It Again, YEM
II: Runaway Jim > When The Circus Comes, Vultures, McGrupp, Mike's > Hydrogen > Weekapaug **E:** Cinnamon Girl

"Sweet Home Alabama" tease before Runaway Jim. "Happy Birthday" tease in Weekapaug, with Trey paying tribute to Jerry Garcia.

George, Washington
Saturday, August 2, 1997

Heralded as "The Great Went West," because of the two-night stand, on-site camping and incredible location, the Gorge led some phans to anticipate only the best. Happily, the Saturday night Gorge show lived up to those expectations for most fans (Sunday night would be a different story).

Besides another solid Ghost opener and the only Divided Sky of the U.S. Tour (a slightly sloppy version), the first set's highlight came in the incredible Wolfman's Brother jam. Yes, every version of Wolfman's in summer '97 went way out there, but the Gorge version traversed a series of wonderful funk passages before winding its way back around to the Wolfman's theme.

The incredible DWD > Tweezer > DWD madness in the second set, however, would prove to be not only the highlight of the Gorge stand but perhaps also the first half of the tour. Though the opening DWD was solid, it was in Tweezer that Trey found several melodic themes that sent jaws a' dropping. Tweezer stretched out for over 20 minutes of great improvisation before Trey found a hook and returned to the DWD theme. The DWD reprise wasn't a full-on lyrical reprise (like Amsterdam 2/17/97) or a long instrumental return (like Seattle 11/27/96). Rather, the band toyed with the theme for a few seconds, paused for a moment, then tore into Johnny B. Goode. The emotional highlight came during the encore, a beautiful Harry Hood. As the quiet jam segment started, Trey asked Chris Kuroda to turn off the lights, and everyone grooved under the stars.

8/2/97 The Gorge, George, WA
I: Theme, Ginseng Sullivan, Ghost, Dogs Stole Things, Divided Sky, Wolfman's, Water in the Sky, Melt
II: Down with Disease > Tweezer > Down with Disease > Johnny B. Goode, Sparkle, Wading in the Velvet Sea, Loving Cup, Tweezer Reprise **E:** Harry Hood
Trey asked Chris Kuroda to turn the lights off during the jam in Harry Hood.

George, Washington
Sunday, August 3, 1997

After the previous night's all-out funky jamfest, Phish took a slightly mellower approach to Sunday's Gorge show. Those who wanted more of Saturday's improv jamming left a little disappointed, but everyone who tapped in to the infectious energy enjoyed another grand night under the stars in the Columbia River basin.

The show got off on very solid footing with a Bathtub > Foam pairing. A new short, sweet instrumental surfaced next, the only time during the summer (called either Blow Wind Blow or Samson, depending on which sources you trust). Later in the set, plenty of fun was had when a very good Twist Around jam wound its way around into Jesus Left Chicago, a move reminiscent of the Wolfman's > Jesus segue from Hamburg in March.

The second set's main jamming was found in a gorgeous version of Simple, arguably the best of the tour. Later in the set, an incredible Taste earned consideration for best-of-tour honors, too. There was also plenty of energy created during Fluffhead (always a crowd favorite, especially as it grows increasingly rare), and a raging Frankenstein that rocked things out. The encore was a curveball of sorts, catering to both newbies and old phans alike.

Trey later told some fans that this show was his favorite of the first leg of the tour, expressing enthusiasm for Foam and Jesus Left Chicago in particular. But some folks could be heard complaining that the second Gorge show just didn't measure up in jam stature to most of the rest of the West Coast run.

8/3/97 The Gorge, George, WA
I: Bathtub Gin > Foam > Blow Wind Blow, Dirt, Vultures, My Mind's, Twist Around > Jesus Left Chicago, Limb by Limb, Character Zero
II: Julius, Simple, Fluffhead, Lifeboy, Taste, Hello My Baby, Frankenstein **E:** Bouncing, Slave
Concert debut: Blow Wind Blow (provisional title, might also be called Samson).

Camping at the Gorge, 8.2.97

Above photo by CHRISTIN

I noticed that the Big Dipper wa positioned directly over the bar it looked like it it was pouring cosmic ooze right onto the stage

8.2.97 GEORGE, WA [FIRST NIGHT]

When we saw the Dead in Seattle in '95, we found out the Page/Plant tour would be hitting this place called The Gorge the next night. We caught the show and were blown away by what a cool venue it was—out in the middle of nowhere; a fantastic panoramic view of a huge canyon and river behind the stage that made it look like the cover of Houses of the Holy or something; sloping ledges that composed most of the general admission section; *and* onsite camping. This place is easily on par with Red Rocks, and I knew these shows would be special.

There was a massive traffic backup when we arrived, but it was the perfect opportunity to pass out my flyers to people waiting in their cars with nothing to do. This is where the first reports of UFOs on tour started surfacing.

One guy told me he had seen a UFO during the show in Dallas. Another related a sighting the previous night as he was driving to the venue. A group from Maine told me about a sighting they had had there earlier in the summer. That was most intriguing, due to the Loring connection. I was telling everyone I came in contact with about the Loring incident, and nine out of 10 were quite intrigued.

The show was really good, with the DWD > Tweezer > DWD a major tour highlight. Many people say this show was the better of the two, but I'm a firm believer that it was the second night that was what I like to call "Da Bomb."

8.3.97 GEORGE, WA [SECOND NIGHT]

The scene seemed fairly mellow after the previous night's show, so we hadn't partied too hard. That left us really primed for this one. We staked out a place in line and scored the best

Looking down the gorge at showtime, 8.3.97

of both worlds—a spot on the floor way close up, and a great chill spot on the ledges. I watched the first set on the ledges, thinking that was the place to take it all in.

I had high hopes for this being a stupendous show, and so engaged in some "third-eye enhancement." And then Bathtub Gin opened the show! I had my true Phish "awakening" during this song at the 12/29/95 Worcester show, so it's always been very special to me. I also think the lyrics are very interesting, especially the way they correlate to the Gamehendge Time Creation Lab theme at those '95 New Year's Shows. And then I got a personal first bustout—My Mind's Got a Mind! I'd been jonesing for this song my entire Phish career. This was the show!

Later in the set, Limb by Limb made a huge impression on me. The lyrics seem to indicate a mountain climbing situation. But I got what I felt was a telepathic cosmic info download that this was a metaphor for Gen-X's uphill struggle to change the world and save the human race, that we are the ones and that we can do it. "It's up to you." This is just a terrific song.

The raging Character Zero set closer only confirmed this theme in my mind. That song is THE Gen-X anthem. I enjoyed the set very much, but by the end, I knew I had to go down front for the second set. I was still feeling blown away by the intensity of the fourth-row YEM at Shoreline, and wanted to feel that again. I thanked the concert gods that Mike, Ashley, and Joanna had staked out a blanket up front.

Before I went down, though, I noticed that the Big Dipper was positioned directly above the band—it looked like it was pouring the cosmic ooze right on to the stage! Very cool. The second set was amazing. I feel that they were at the top of their game, just playing so well. Simple was absolutely "eargasmic." It's always been one of my favorite tunes, as it sym-

St. Louis, Missouri

Wednesday, August 6, 1997

Faced with the lowest expectations of any show on the tour, Riverport was the show many of the people on tour even opted to forego (giving themselves a five-day vacation from tour between the Gorge on Sunday and the World Music Theater on Friday). But those who missed Riverport—and its many security hassles—had only themselves to blame, as Phish pulled out another solid show with several definite highlights.

Given the band's new jamming style, some phans had been waiting all tour for 2001. When it finally came in the middle of the first set, it was as drawn-out as most had hoped for, reaching levels achieved previously only on New Year's '96 (though the Great Went would later take 2001 to yet another level). When the band tacked another first set-closing YEM, fans headed into setbreak plenty content.

The second set's opening Runaway > My Soul pairing was a repeat from Raleigh, but what happened later in the set was totally fresh. Showing their desire to visit the funk on all their old friends, Phish jammed out on Antelope in a different style than most previous versions of this tune.

Things got stranger when Page stepped up to the theremin and Mike fooled around with what looked to be a mini drum-kit during a Makisupa jam that immediately preceded the Antelope lyrics. When Antelope powered to its finish, the crowd roared their approval. Phish had beaten back the bad vibes.

8/6/97 Riverport Amphitheater, Maryland Heights, MO
I: NICU, Stash, Beauty of My Dreams, Twist Around > Also Sprach > AC/DC Bag, Ya Mar, YEM
II: Runaway Jim > My Soul, Ghost, Caspian, CTB, Sample, Antelope > Makisupa Jam > Antelope **E:** Julius
Page on theremin and Mike on mini-drum kit for Makisupa Jam.

Tinley Park, Illinois
Friday, August 8, 1997

The World Music Theater is a pretty big place, but thanks to the Internet, this show was attended by plenty of people who didn't even have to navigate the industrial back-roads of Chicago in search of Phish. The nascent Internet concert broadcaster JamTV aired Phish's show live over the Internet, offering quality sound and jerky, stop-and-go video to all who tuned in.

A fairly standard, short first set got its kicks from Gumbo (and its new long jam, here a bit unfocused) and the increasingly-rare It's Ice. If that doesn't sound like a particularly jamming set, well, you're right. Phish's surest rave-up of the summer, Character Zero, energized at least part of the crowd as they headed into setbreak.

The second set offered more of the same, in a sense, as Phish served up several jamming songs—Wolfman's, Limb by Limb—but no epics. Still, the energy level ran high as the band seemed more than content just rocking out.

The show's highlight came during the encore, when blues harmonica legend Sugar Blue emerged to share the stage with Phish for the first time since 4/10/93. He led the band through Sonny Boy Williamson's Hoochie Coochie Man (previously seen at that '93 gig) and Junior Wells' Messin' With the Kid, finishing an otherwise-average show in style.

8/8/97 World Music Theatre, Tinley Park, IL
I: CTB, Gumbo > Lizards, Dirt, It's Ice, Water in the Sky, Character Zero
II: Wolfman's > Free, Limb by Limb, Loving Cup, Caspian, Chalkdust
E: Hoochie Coochie Man, Messing with the Kid

Sugar Blue on harmonica for encores. Last Hoochie Coochie Man, 4/10/93 Chicago, IL [381 shows]. Concert debut: Messing with the Kid.

East Troy, Wisconsin
Saturday, August 9, 1997

One look at the setlist makes Alpine the obvious jewel of the midwest run, and among the better shows of the tour.

Phish's new affinity for funk was apparent in new songs and old, as they stretched the intro to PYITE out to new lengths, setting the stage for a show in which the band took few shortcuts. The funk continued with Ghost—although not one of the more notable versions of the summer, some say the tune was beginning to lose steam by this point—which ran into the increasingly satisfying and respected Taste. To close the set, Phish pulled out their first version of Crossroads since fall tour 1995.

Set II was practically one long segue, with only three breaks between songs from start to finish. After kicking open with a solid Wilson > Foam pairing, a trippy-as-always Mike's Song morphed into J.J. Cale's Funny As It Seems, which went into Simple, then Swept Away, then Steep, and then a fine Scent of a Mule to finish things off. It was enough to forgive the lack of a Weekapaug, but the band had other intentions, closing the set with the remarkable Slave > Weekapaug combo.

35,000 satisfied customers left the nation's largest amphitheater, with expectations for cornfield bliss at Deer Creek running high. Traffic streamed towards Indiana, as fans had to make it to Noblesville for the next show less than 24 hours away.

8/9/97 Alpine Valley, East Troy, WI
I: Theme, PYITE, Ghost > Taste, Dogs Stole Things, Reba, Lawn Boy, Crossroads
II: Wilson > Foam, Mike's > Funny as it Seems > Simple > Swept Away > Steep > Scent of a Mule > Slave > Weekapaug
E: When the Circus Comes, Rocky Top

Last Crossroads, 12/9/95 Albany, NY [125 shows].

The looming mothership that is the World Music Theater, 8.8.97

bolizes everything the band is about to me. Trey went off on Fluffhead, which really pleased all the phans who feared it was one of the rumored "shelved" songs. Trey was on fire—the music flowed from him so vibrantly and fluidly.

But the real fireworks came during Taste. Up to this point, I had a take-it-or-leave-it attitude toward this song. But here it absolutely blew me away, probably the best version ever played. I felt like a bit of that cosmic ooze slipped into the jam at one point, and Trey just channeled it for all it was worth.

Then a rip-raging "Frankenstein" brought it all home. It's hard to put into words how much ass Phish kicks on this song. The triangular lighting rig was tripping me out too during the latter psychedelic freak-out section—I couldn't help but feel like the Mothership was landing, or that Phish was getting commands from a higher source. I was bummed that the set had to end because they were playing so well.

But the Bouncing > Slave double encore saved the day. Slave went on for so long, and Trey was right back in the intense cosmic groove from Simple, Fluffhead, and Taste. Again, "eargasmic" is the only way I can describe it.

The scene after the show was one of the all-time greats. Everyone was so happy, partying all night long. My mind was still racing a mile a minute, and I had a number of interesting conversations with a variety of cool people.

One guy, Wes, detailed a theory that Phish are Masons! NICU certainly references this, and it is intriguing, since the Masons are such a mysterious, arcane group that is speculated to be involved in all kinds of conspiracies. Another fellow explained that Mike Gordon is an extra-terrestrial. I'll add my own theory on that at the Great Went.

8.4-5.96 ON THE ROAD TO ST. LOUIS

We woke up on the 4th, bid farewell to the new Mike and Ashley, and then Mike, Joanna, and I hit the road for the long haul to Riverport. It really is too bad that there couldn't be a Colorado show in between. Surely, there must be another venue besides Red Rocks they could play?

We decided to try and make the most of this journey by seeing a few sites on the way. At Mount Rushmore, I thought George Washington looked particularly melancholic, perhaps

The A-Frame entrance to Alpine Valley beckons towards the heavens, 8.9.97

symbolic of his sure outrage at the way his beloved "sweet leaf" has been unjustly criminalized in our society. We also saw Devil's Tower in Wyoming, the site of the climactic Mothership landing in Steven Spielberg's *Close Encounters of the Third Kind*. Devil's Tower is a true vortex. This means that like other such vortex spots—Stonehendge, the Giza Pyramids, Bermuda Triangle, Sedona, AZ, Mt. Shasta in California—there are electromagnetic energies that are known to be interdimensional and intergalactic access points.

8.6.97 ST. LOUIS, MO

We finally arrived in St. Louis, where we were hooking up with a group of friends of mine from Cleveland, so our entourage grew to about 10 people for the Riverport-Deer Creek segment of the tour.

I wasn't expecting a whole lot from this show. It just seemed like one you could pinpoint as lackluster. I also don't care for the vibe here. I'd seen both Phish and the Dead here in '95, and the lot scene sucks—they have security going around all day busting people for selling jewelry, sodas, grilled cheese, or whatever. But inside, the venue is nice, much like Deer Creek, and the show was kind. This was the no-letdown tour.

The long-awaited appearance of 2001 made my day. I thought for sure we were going to get that at The Gorge, but in retrospect, this show needed it more. Getting another YEM to close the first set proved another pleasant surprise. The highlight of the second set was definitely the Antelope > Makisupa jam > Antelope. Combined with the Julius encore, it felt like the band was aware of the lot scene and making a clear statement to phans—have fun on tour, but watch it.

Once again, Phish showed how tuned in they are to what's going on around them, one of the things that continues to make them special in a way that most bands aren't. I did pass out a number of flyers before the show, but was distracted by all the security hassles that were going on, so not much awareness was raised here.

8.8.97 TINLEY PARK, IL

I'd heard nothing but bad things about this venue, concerning both the sound and the lot scene. But the lot wasn't as bad as I'd been led to believe. It wasn't raging, and cops were on the scene, but I didn't see the hassles that I'd witnessed at Riverport. I continued to receive positive reactions about my flyers, too.

This venue is not designed well, and I can understand how a lot of people had bad views and heard schwag sound, especially on the lawn. Fortunately, Mike and I "flowed" to a great spot about 10 rows back on Fish's side, and were able to hang on to it the whole show.

This was not one of the top shows of tour, but it was pretty good. When we first arrived at the venue, I thought to myself, "They'll probably bring out some old-school blues guy for the encore." And so it was, as Sugar Blue appeared. This guy is a jamming harmonica player and a clear influence on John Popper. They got down and bluesy with Hoochie Coochie Man. Then Sugar announced that the next song was a Junior Wells cut. I had seen Junior Wells play a phat show at the House of Blues in Boston in '94, so I knew we were in for a treat—Messing With the Kid! Super phunky! This second set is definitely a tape worth seeking out.

8.9.97 EAST TROY, WI

There was no time to rest in the midst of a four-night run. I looked forward to my first trip to Alpine since it has such a great tradition—many fine Dead shows and also the site of Stevie Ray Vaughn's last show. I'd also heard that it was just a major party spot. And it is.

As I was passing out flyers before the show, one girl, a cute redhead named Erin, related a very sincere tale of a close encounter of the fourth kind she had had three years ago when alien beings visited her in her bedroom. I could tell she was not making this up—it was hard for her to relate, and it was obvious that it had frightened her. But she stated that they didn't harm her, that they had actually told her the encounter was for the benefit of humanity. Very interesting. Another guy came up to me and said, "Hey, I'm going backstage to see Trey, gimme a flyer for him." All right!

It was a total mess getting into the venue and navigating down that huge hill. I had a reserve-seating ticket in the back of the reserved-seating area while Mike just a lawn ticket, but as the lights went down, there was no security at the rail and everyone just waltzed right in. It wasn't a bumrush or gatecrash—it was just unguarded, so everyone went.

We ended up around the fifteenth row. The aisles were jammed, but again, there was no security clearing things out. I felt that was meant to be because this show absolutely ruled. From start to finish, probably the most rip-rocking show of the tour, if you judge it just on pure musical intensity. The entire first set was awesome—Theme/PYITE/Ghost/Taste had this show energized from the get-go. Reba was reminiscent of the brilliant 12/31/95 version. Lawn Boy was most appropriate, since Alpine has such a huge lawn section. And then an absolutely smoking Crossroads bustout to end the set, surely a tip of the cap to Stevie Ray, I thought.

The second set raged all the way through, but it was the Scent of a > Slave to the > Groove segment that was truly mindblowing. Scent was extra-incredible because of the high strangeness that took place during the Mule Duel. I swear Trey was stalking around the stage like he was a mind-controlled android. And then he and Mike would lay on their backs and pedal their legs like on a bicycle. Then they'd get up, jam a few chords, and get back down and do it again. They must have done this five times. I know there's precedent for doing weird stuff during the Mule Duel, but I'd never seen

Noblesville, Indiana
Sunday, August 10, 1997

Traffic in the middle of Indiana? That's what phans encountered on their way from Alpine, as the interstates were mysteriously clogged from Chicago to Indianapolis, forcing many to miss out on a day of fun in the Deer Creek parking lot, considered to be one of the best places in the nation for a Phishhead to spend the afternoon (and evening).

But the band provided more than enough amusement on stage—too much if you asked some—to settle the audience in for the much anticipated two-night stand. This schtick-fest started strong in the first set, including another Bathtub opener, a nice Down With Disease, another Ginseng Sullivan (interestingly, one of the most commonly-played songs of the summer tour) and a rare Harry Hood first set closer, but became a weirdorama in set II, as a rotation jam (with Page on theremin at first) into Rocka William formed the backbone of the show.

The highlight for most phans came just before that, in a long, funked-out Cities which opened the set. Following a Bowie set II closer and Cavern encore, thousands of phans filtered out to the makeshift campsites which dotted the countryside, guaranteeing a long night of merriment, including a performance by another band on a makeshift stage in a campground.

Most felt the best of Deer Creek was yet to come.

8/10/97 Deer Creek Music Center, Noblesville, IN
I: Bathtub Gin > Sparkle, Down with Disease, Dirt, CTB, Billy Breathes, Melt, Bye Bye Foot, Ginseng Sullivan, Harry Hood
II: Cities > GTBT > Rotation Jam > HYHU > Rocka William, Bowie
E: Cavern
Page on theremin preceding Rotation Jam.

Noblesville, Indiana
Monday, August 11, 1997

When the band kicked things off with Makisupa, the sellout crowd of 20,000 knew they were probably in for a good ride. That suspicion was confirmed three songs later when the tour's first Guyute evoked a collective scream from the audience, confirming Guyute's place among the most popular and desired of Phish songs.

The first set continued to soar with a long and textured Limb by Limb, the rare Horn, and a blistering Antelope to send phans into setbreak shaking their heads. Many agreed that it was one of, if not the strongest, first set of the tour thus far.

Set II had just six songs, all played independent of each other, but the band made every one count. The Timber Ho opener, while not quite as strong as Austin's, set the table for the popular new tune Piper, and then the eerie and epic Vultures. By this point, the Deer Creek audience was as loud and enthusiastic as any Phish had played before all summer. The upbeat My Soul only brought things up a notch, followed by an oh-so-perfectly placed YEM. Turning to the surest crowd-pleaser in their repertoire, they closed the set with Character Zero, before a Squirming Coil encore offered the crowd a mellow drift back to reality.

Some thought the '97 Deer Creek stand didn't quite live up to its high expectations (following the very popular show on 8/12/96), but there was no doubt that plenty of fun was had by all both during and after the shows.

8/11/97 Deer Creek Music Center, Noblesville, IN
I: Makisupa > Maze, Water in the Sky, Guyute, Guelah, Limb by Limb, Horn, Antelope
II: Timber Ho, Piper, Vultures, My Soul, YEM, Character Zero
E: Squirming Coil

anything this bizarre. Had Trey read my newsletter? Was this some kind of tacit acknowledgement of my theories on the ET/Phish connection?

This show is an all-time keeper—one where you walk out and everyone is totally permagrin. As we were on our way to the lots, a bunch of phans were chilling on top of a hill that overlooked the gate. I yelled, "PHISH! PHIIIIIIIIIIIISH!" much like Buddy Miles had exhorted the crowd at my birthday show at MSG, and everyone cheered back loudly. The disco bus was raging, and we all partied down until they kicked us out, which wasn't until late. I was trying to interview a friend about a dream she had had the previous night. She was a newbie, and had dreamt about punching someone in the eye. And Phish had played PYITE that night! But a security guy came by and said, "All right, Spielberg, wrap it up." We all got a good laugh at that. Alpine was definitely Da Bomb.

8.10.97 NOBLESVILLE, IN [NIGHT ONE]

Again, there was no time to rest as the equally high in tradition Deer Creek awaited. I hadn't been there since the infamous 7/2/95 Dead show, and was eager to make some memories more like the GD's memorable '94 run where the place went off all three nights.

Near the venue, there's a great common grounds area where everyone mills around and hangs out; I passed out a huge amount of flyers there. They were really going like hotcakes at the Creek. One guy insisted to me that Trey is an alien. Another described a sighting he had had at The Gorge, and a third said he'd actually seen a "grey alien" on the Shakedown at the Gorge. He seemed kind of loopy, so I took that one with a grain of salt.

The 7/2/95 Dead show—when fans broke down the wall on the lawn—changed Deer Creek forever, as the workers are now totally paranoid about gate-crashing. I assured them there would be no such incident tonight. Bathtub > Sparkle > DWD started this show off in maximum style. A fine ten song first set—not as high-intensity as Alpine, but they were doing their best. The second set was super phat, highly jammed with a unique setlist. Cities to open! I just love this song, both the funk and the lyrics—"I'm checking it out... I'm the one that's got it figured out." Then Good Times Bad Times, which I'd never seen so early in a set. This was turning out to be a classic.

Then came a rare rotation jam with Fishman on slide guitar and vocal for Rocka William, singing about Malachi and "the children of the corn!" The crowd just ate this up, what with Deer Creek being surrounded by cornfields. Bowie ended the set, and then a raging Cavern encore sent everyone out whooping and hollering. How would they top this tomorrow? I wasn't sure, but we all felt they would. Security cracked down on the lot scene very quickly, which was quite disappointing. But it would change the next night.

8.11.97 NOBLESVILLE, IN [NIGHT TWO]

We knew this was going to be a special show, so we decided to have a "community shroom," brewing up tea right there in the lot, tailgating at The Freedom Ride. We felt pretty sly brewing it up practically right under the nose of the yellowjackets, not even 100 yards from the security/narc hiveshack. But hey, we "had it figured out."

The Creek is still great, but it peaked out with the '94 Dead shows. This night would harken back to those glory days, though. Makisupa opened, and it was on! Then came the freak-out Maze, which wasn't what I needed at that moment—I actually had to sit down and collect myself. Guyute had the crowd going wild, certainly the best I'd ever heard. I was thrilled to see Horn make an appearance, then came the MOST COSMIC Antelope I've ever seen. Great set.

The second set was pure kind, too. Vultures was utterly amazing—they really took it to new places, at the top of their game. This led into the smokingest My Soul I could have imagined. Trey went off on it, clearly the best version of tour. The crowd was totally primed. "The blues hath spoke," my buddy Mike declared. I feel like this song is so tuned into the zeitgeist of the '90s—another brilliant cover choice.

There was no let-up as the band headed into the only second-set YEM of the tour—what a crowd-pleaser. I had another telepathic cosmic info download here: I was picturing the song as being about a tourist-type alien that had gotten stranded in the boondocks of Italy, and just wanted to get to Florence to see the museum.

The highest of intensities was poured into the set closing Character Zero. With a Squirming Coil encore, I felt safe in declaring this show one for the ages. In fact, this four night run was right up there with the '95 New Year's run in my opinion. Who says Phish peaked in '95?

The scene raged afterwards as well. It felt like they decided that since we were good the previous night, they would let us party this night, which we did until the wee hours of the morning. After the show, I met Erin again, and we conversed about the kindness of the show. Mike, Joanna, and I went over to one of the campgrounds that had a live band playing—we just hung out and met a whole bunch of cool people all night long. Everyone was jazzed off the show and wanted to make the night last as long as possible.

8.13.97, BURGETTSTOWN, PA

This is a show that I should have enjoyed more than I did. But the combo of being slightly under-the-weather, and encountering a massive traffic jam on the way in, deterred my ability to fully appreciate it.

Arriving so late meant no time for interviews or food. But once again, there was no letdown. The second set was particularly fine—I thought Sample might end the set, but then they threw on a 2001 > Golgi > Frankenstein triad to send the set to stellar heights I hadn't expected. The momentum toward The Went just kept building.

8.14.97, DARIEN CENTER, NY

I was skeptical about this show, because I had heard many negative reports about the Hershey show that had preceded The Ball last year. But this was to be another historic moment in Phishtory.

Again, we were late arrivals, so there wasn't much time for hanging out before the show. I was missing the aspect of Dead tour where you had a day off in between each city. But you gotta play the hand you're dealt. Once inside, I encountered a phellow who informed me that Ken Kesey and the Merry Pranksters were here, and would be "coming on stage to tell stories with Phish." "No way," I exclaimed. He then showed me his Kesey autographed ticket stub. Sweet!

As the show got under way, my anticipation ran high. I was stoked for Tela in the first set, which infused a welcome Gamehendge energy into the show. The Antelope that ended the first set was a pleasant surprise, but couldn't compare to the one from Deer Creek.

The second set would turn out to be an all-time keeper. The long-awaited appearance of Col. Forbin really sent things to another level. I love Trey's stories that always accompany this song, and I fully expected this to be the moment for the Pranksters. So it was. To me, it was another unmistakable acknowledgement of the link/transference of the cosmic "scene" between the Dead and Phish, and Kesey alluded to this himself. It was a surreal scene indeed, as Kesey and the band were joined onstage by the Wizard of Oz characters and several others Kesey referred to as the "Bozos."

My buddy Mike had a view on Kesey's rap that seemed right on the money. In essence, he said that Kesey was referring to how the tour scene has always attracted two kinds of bozos—the Prankster-type bozos which are of course way cool and necessary, but also the tour rat/beggar bozos that had become such dead weight on the Dead scene in later years (no pun intended) and were now all too present on the Phish scene, too. Amen to that, Ken.

Trey was in fine form as the Pranksters left the stage, remarking, "That's what happens 30 years later when you take too much acid." Then Trey provided another classic Phish moment when he said, "We usually go into Famous Mockingbird here, but the funk's too deep." The crowd roared with approval as they continued the phunk jam and then busted out Camel Walk!

The crowd was way stoked after this one, and the mood ran high as The Great Went beckoned at last.

The tribe convenes at Deer Creek, 8.10-11.97

Burgettstown, Pennsylvania
Wednesday, August 14, 1997

With just two shows remaining before the Great Went, Phish arrived in Pittsburgh, but perhaps some of the band's focus was on Maine. For whatever reason, the Starlake show was a mix of some solid highlights and notable gaffes.

Was Mike singing off-key for at the start of Poor Heart? Sure sounded like it. But the first set—which opened strangely with the band's debut performance of Elton John's Amoreena with Page on lead vocals—did improve, highlighted by a long Gumbo and a fantastic Crosseyed and Painless, the Talking Heads song that has become a phan favorite since they fist played it on Halloween in Atlanta (this was the summer's only rendition). A fun Wilson with a severe "Little Drummer Boy" jam at the end cranked everyone up for the second set.

But the second set featured more ups and downs. When Trey goofed during the opening Runaway Jim, he announced the flub to the crowd with a "whoops." Things heated up midway through the set with a funky, long 2001, which served as the show's centerpiece jam. After an apparent Golgi set-closer, the upbeat Frankenstein emerged and closed the set with high energy. In retrospect it was less a conclusion for that night, as a preview for the historic histrionics which would follow in the next few days.

Indeed, lurking in the shadow of Deer Creek on one side and Darien and the Went on the other, Starlake is probably fated to be an underrated treat of the summer tour.

8/13/97 Starlake Amphitheater, Burgettstown, PA
I: Amoreena, Poor Heart, Water in the Sky, Gumbo, Horse > Silent, Beauty of My Dreams, Crosseyed and Painless, Wilson, Adeline
II: Runaway Jim, Ghost > Izabella, Sleeping Monkey, McGrupp, Sample, Also Sprach, Golgi, Frankenstein **E:** Theme

"Little Drummer Boy" jam at the end of Wilson. Concert debut: Amoreena

Darien Center, New York
Thursday, August 14, 1997

Sunshine, waterslides and Phish. Long haired, pierced, mentally enhanced mobs spent the day flying down water slides at the accompanying amusement park alongside perplexed upstate New Yorkers at the Darien Lake Amusement Park. And Phish, it turned out, was more than up to the task of topping off a great day.

A first set rocked with a killer opening trio of Ya Mar/Funky Bitch/Fluffhead, then a crowd-pleasing Tela (the only version of the tour) and a great Antelope closer, but the fun was just starting! A high-energy second set featured a Chalkdust opener and a great Hood, but then, during Col. Forbin's Ascent, the Bozos came.

The crowd quieted, some laughing, some staring in confusion as Ken Kesey and his Merry Pranksters took center stage in search of the missing Bozos. Instead of finding Icculus, Col. Forbin found Ken Kesey (author of One Flew Over the Cuckoos Nest and longtime Grateful Dead "collaborator") dressed as Uncle Sam, who enlisted the help of the Scarecrow, Tinman and Frankenstein (all of whom came onstage) to help him find the Bozos. Finally, the Bozos—large-headed clownlike things with white sheets—danced onto the stage. After they performed a short skit, Trey invited them to interpretively dance off the stage. He announced that they were too deep in the funk to play Mockingbird, so they instead segued into Camel Walk, capping off a historic night in Phishtory.

8/14/97 Darien Lake Performing Arts Center, Darien Center, NY
I: Ya Mar, Funky Bitch, Fluffhead, Limb by Limb, Free, CTB, Tela, Train Song, Billy Breathes, Antelope
II: Chalkdust, Love Me, Sparkle, Harry Hood > Forbin's > Pranksters Jam > Camel Walk, Taste
E: Bouncing, Rocky Top

Pranksters jam with Ken Kesey, Ken Babbs and the Merry Pranksters. "Frankenstein" jam during part of the Bozos narration.

8.16.97 THE GREAT WENT [DAY 1]

The previous night we had been listening to the last set of The Clifford Ball, with the aborted Harpua encore. I remarked to Mike, "I'll bet they finish that Harpua at The Went." He replied with great conviction, "No way they will do that."

We were among the last to arrive, I think, as we wound up getting stuck all the way at the end of the runway, what must have been some two miles from the stage. I was stoked just to finally get there, though. As I scanned the surroundings, I couldn't help but picture the scene that had occurred back in October 1975. I could sense the lingering energy of the whole incident—in my mind I could see the UFO encroaching; the blue-lights of military police flashing and sirens wailing; and the top Air Force brass freaking out about what was going on.

Here I considered the speculation that had been raised by several phans on the tour that Mike and Trey, if not the whole band, are ETs. This is not beyond the realm of conception, but is not as cut-and-dry as "they are or they aren't." My research indicated that there is a phenomenon going on on Earth, whereby a number of higher dimensional ET beings have chosen to incarnate in a 3-D body on this planet in this time, in order to help the ascension process toward the Cosmic Party in 2012. Metaphysical literature often refers to such beings as "Starseeds" or "Walk-Ins." If Trey and Mike are ETs, they are not beings that decided, "Oh, let's go to Earth and disguise ourselves as rock stars."

It would be a case wherein these ET consciousnesses were a part of them from birth and have just helped guide them on the path they need to be on. They may not even be fully aware of it, yet could sense some kind of higher purpose or inexplicable cosmic connection in their lives. Yet they are performing the valuable mission that they came here for, as their music is bringing people together and raising the vibration of Earth and humanity toward the higher, more harmonious level it needs to be at for the Cosmic Party to take place.

I think that the Grateful Dead and Jimi Hendrix initiated this process in the '60s and Phish is here to carry us through to 2012. All phans feel a sense of this energy at shows, and it is what provides that special feeling that you just can't find anywhere else. I believe that a number of phans also fit into the "Starseed/Walk-In" category, because the ascension process involves many beings, and we all have our own roles to play. I may be one myself. After graduating from film school, I felt somewhat lost as to exactly where I should be directing my energies. But since I have gotten onto the path of investigation into the UFO/ET phenomenon, I have felt a deep resonation within my soul that I am finally doing what I'm supposed to be doing—helping raise humanity's awareness of these issues, and thereby helping to catalyze the ascension/evolution process that humanity needs to go through.

So it's about four o'clock, and we figure we better get into the show. We're still a good distance from the gates when the band hits the stage at 4:20 with Makisupa! D'oh! We should have foreseen such a move. My consternation only increases when they segue into the completion of last year's Harpua, as I had predicted. We finally get in right as they went into Chalkdust. Oh well, lesson learned.

The first day's show was stellar all the way through, but I was disappointed by the overcast sky. Not a star was in sight due to the clouds, so any kind of sighting seemed pretty doubtful. The third set was a big winner though, finely jammed throughout. Halley's Comet > Cities—how phat is that? And the Funky Bitch that closed the show with accompanying spectacular fireworks display! The vibe was high as they totally jammed it out, surely one of the highlights of the summer. The Loving Cup encore was perfect—a great ending. This was truly the Loving Cup tour!

THE GREAT WENT

LORING AIR FORCE BASE, LIMESTONE, ME
AUGUST 16-17, 1997

The mile-long Shakedown was a big aspect of what made this event so unique and special. Anything and everything you could imagine for sale, all night long. Throughout the weekend, I couldn't help but have a great feeling about the sense of community. Here we were, bigger than Portland, the largest city in Maine! "And a whole lot cooler than Portland too," as Trey remarked.

It felt like a glimpse of both past and future combined—a self-reliant gypsy-type bazaar out of the past, that was also like a near-utopian glimpse of our harmonious future. The rest of the world ceased to exist. Everything we needed was right here, and nothing else mattered except "sharing in a groove." A large part of the speculation about post-Cosmic Party society is how the combination of advanced technology and higher consciousness will allow everyone's basic needs to be provided for with a minimum of effort, which will in turn free up everyone to be able to devote much more time to creative, social, and spiritual pursuits—the way I've always felt life should be.

I was pretty beat after this show, and was no longer feeling like I needed to be out and about trying to spread "the word." For one thing, I was out of flyers, having distributed all 1,000 of them from Phoenix to Darien. I also felt that we were here now, so it was time to just kick back and enjoy the vibe, and let what was going to happen go ahead and happen. We missed the band's late-night "disco/techno" performance as we were way back at our campsite, just grooving on the vibes and sharing in an extended 4:20 sesh. But that was okay. The four of us were having a blast, just cracking each other up with various musings on the the scene, the tour, and life itself.

8.17.97 THE GREAT WENT (DAY 2)

This was it. The last show.

My anticipation ran extremely high, but I must emphasize that I was not expecting the Mothership to hover over the stage and say hello or anything like that. Again, what I'd been telling people all tour was that I thought our hipper ET visitors would be looking in on the show, but that they wouldn't be real upfront about it. It would be subtle—you'd have to be looking for it.

I knew this show would be special, and was thinking about "3rd Eye Enhancement" again. I have a personal rule about such activity, which parallels Tim Leary's thoughts—mindset and location are key, and such experiences are not to be entered into whimsically. At The Great Went, I chose ecstacy, which all "X" phans know just enhances the music to almost another dimension.

I'm not afraid to admit any of this for several reasons. One, I have no intention of a political career. Two, I believe the criminalization of these substances—along with the aforementioned beloved Sweet Leaf—is an unconstitutional violation of our inherent rights as Americans. Did our founding fathers not declare that we are all entitled to the "pursuit of happiness?" If this pursuit does not include the expansion and raising of consciousness, then something is wrong with our society.

We got in early and immediately began speculating about the wooden tower being built to the right of the field. What the heck was it and what was its purpose? We were at a loss.

The first set was good, but did not have the musical fireworks I had expected. Rich, Louise, and I felt very cramped in the first set as well, so we retreated back so we could see the screens and have room to dance. I popped the X. And one of the most monumental experiences of Phish music I have ever had followed. Rich, Louise, and I all jumped for joy at the second set Down With Disease opener, as it is one of our very favorite Phish songs. To me, this song is all about the Cosmic Party—"Waiting for the time when I can finally say, that this has all been wonderful, and now I'm on my way." This clearly symbolizes that impending day when we will have the higher consciousness to use advanced medical technology to eradicate all disease, as opposed to today, where pharmaceutical companies are more interested in their financial bottom line than the social needs of society.

The song also just plain phucking jams! When they broke out the first chords of Bathtub Gin, the X kicked in at the same moment! I was in heaven as I felt the musical vibes of another favorite song flow through me. We were grooving big time. And then I started picking up on a telepathic cosmic vibe that I had first started feeling during DwD—that Trey and the boys were "playing to" the stars and those aforementioned hipper ET visitors. At this point, I started scanning the skies. It was clear, and there were many stars. And then I saw it.

I was facing away from the stage, so if you were only looking toward the stage, you would not have seen it. But it was an

around the went

In the tub on the Went fairgrounds.

odd craft that was hovering off in the distance. It had a green light on one side, a red light on the other, and a white light in the middle. This is a rare light combo that was very reminiscent of an odd craft I saw in Sedona, Arizona the night before the Summer Solstice, that I also believe was a UFO. These are the only two times I have ever seen such a craft.

So there it was, hovering in the distance and bouncing up and down in weird ways. It's conceivable that it could have been a helicopter, but it really was moving oddly. I know what I saw, and I know what I felt on a deep, soul level—that this was indeed an ET craft. I pointed it out to Rich and Louise, and they too were quite fascinated by it. Louise agreed with me that it both looked and flew in a very strange manner. I alerted the people around us that we had a UFO sighting on our hands, but I don't think they believed me. That's fine. People aren't going to learn what they don't want to know.

We turned our attentions back to the stage, periodically checking back to see it still there, and there it still was, hovering back and forth in that strange way.

Then the band broke into 2001—YAY! My three favorite Phish songs all in the same set! And what a monumental version—they were grooving out so hard, channeling the cosmic funk to the highest degree. It was pure "phishtacy"! I'll put this version right up there with any other ever played. Louise and I both thought it was better than 12/31/96. Again, I felt so deeply that they were playing to the ETs that they knew were up there; that this was why the show was held at this location; that it was a part of the grand cosmic plan.

The onstage painting took things to a new level of strangeness, as it finally started to become apparent what was going on with the tower when Trey said that the tower was now a combination of the phans' artwork (composed over the two days by phans at the free art tent) as well as the band's. The Harry Hood that ended the set was another monumental version. What an incredible set.

The lights were up and the UFO was gone. But I was incredibly stoked about the sighting and the set. This was what it was all about. Louise and I went over to the portajohn area, where there was a circle of portajohns with a big huge bathtub in the middle! I hopped up on the platform surrounding the tub and declared, "We're all in this together and we love to take a bath!" As I waited for Louise, I started spouting off about the UFOs, the 1975 incident, and the Mayan connection. I drew quite a crowd of interested onlookers. I felt so deeply that I was serving my true purpose, being all I could be, having both great fun and raising the awareness.

The third set was good, but a little anti-climactic after the cosmic spectacle that was the second set. It just didn't rock like I thought it would. Guyute was good, but didn't have the energy of the Deer Creek version. Dirt was just too mellow, belonging in the first set, in my opinion. I was so primed, I wanted high energy. Scent of a Mule was a welcome theme, though it didn't include the high-strangeness of the Alpine version. I like Caspian just fine, but didn't imagine it would close the set.

However, I did start to get that sense when I sighted the UFO again—it was beyond the stage now, flying off in the distance. How did it get over there? UFOs are known for teleporting from place to place. I pointed it out to Louise—"There goes our friend," I said. She smiled and nodded acknowledgement, surprised to see it again. As we watched it fly off, I got another telepathic cosmic info download—it had scoped out the scene, liked what it saw, and was going back to whence it came to report that things were right on track on Planet Earth.

There was one more moment of high-strangeness, when during the encore they proceeded to set fire to the entire art tower! I felt the question on everyone's mind—"What the heck is that about?" I couldn't help but feel that it somehow paralleled the Burning Man Festival that's held annually in a

Limestone, Maine—Great Went
Saturday, August 16, 1997

Most phans arrived a day in advance, or at least the night before the Went was set to kick off. In fact, those arriving in the middle of the night experienced a two-hour delay entering the compound, but those who came the morning of August 16 coasted in.

A cold and ferocious rainstorm drenched the tent city in Saturday's pre-dawn hours, leaving many shivering and exhausted as the sun rose over a sea of canvas that stretched for over two miles. Great Went radio (WENT, appropriately) declared a third campground open by mid-day, as thousands more fans streamed in and everyone trekked down the incredible vending aisle on their way to the concert grounds.

Set I began precisely at 4:20, with the apropos Makisupa Policeman, including a "goo balls" reference from Trey. Many in the crowd of 63,000 were veterans of The Clifford Ball, so they understood precisely what was going on when the band then headed into the second half of Harpua, beginning exactly where they left off during the encore at the grand Phish event in summer '96. That little musical wink from the band to the audience set the stage for two days of sharing and artistic exchange between Phish and the devotees who made it all possible. Trey followed Chalkdust with greetings and a confession that the first songs were in fact a soundcheck of sorts, as there had been no pre-show warmup this time around. The marathon set—clocking in at close to two hours—continue on with a cornucopia of crowd favorites, mostly newer songs but also YEM and Coil.

Set II led off with Wolfman's Brother, which had already been hailed the song of the tour by many. To those in attendance who had not yet been exposed to Wolfman's funky alter-ego, it was an enticing treat, especially on the Went's larger-than-life, crystal-clear sound system. It was followed by what many felt was the Went's best musical moment—a Simple jam which morphed into the familiar Odd Couple theme, into My Soul, an improvised jam, and then Slave. Capping off the set with Rocky Top and Julius, Trey announced, "in rock-n-roll tradition," that the Great Went was now the largest city in Maine. "We're bigger than Portland," he bragged. "And a whole lot cooler than Portland, too."

More memorable moments came in set III, kicking off with a slower, crisper, downright funkier take on Halley's Comet, including an unprecedented ending jam which led the band back into a lyrical reprise. It segued into the other song of 1997, Cities. Again, can you say funk? Before the night was done, the band had knocked the crowd over with a well-placed Llama and the better-every-time-they-played-it Limb by Limb. Funky Bitch, backed by fireworks, and an incredible Contact > Loving Cup encore, made Great Went night one a thrilling affair from start to finish.

But it wasn't quite done. At the end of set II, Trey told fans to be sure and check out a mysterious "disco." Savvy phans new to expect some sort of late-night appearance from the band following last year's mobile flat-bed truck jam at the Clifford Ball. This year's surprise came in the form of a stationary rave in which all band members took to keyboards and sampling devices and played weird electronic music for about 45 minutes under austere white lighting. About 500 to 1,000 phans were on hand to witness Phish making their ravemaster debuts.

8/16/97 The Great Went, Loring Air Force Base, Limestone, ME
I: Makisupa > Harpua, Chalkdust, Theme, PYITE, Ghost, Ginseng Sullivan, YEM, Train Song, Character Zero, Squirming Coil
II: Wolfman's > Simple > My Soul, Jam > Slave, Rocky Top, Julius
III: Halley's > Cities > Llama > Lawn Boy, Limb by Limb, Funky Bitch
E: Contact, Loving Cup

Harpua was second-half only, starting where the song ended at The Clifford Ball. "Odd Couple Theme" jam in jam out of Simple. Vocal reprise of Halley's chorus in jam out of Halley's. Fireworks during Funky Bitch. Last Harpua, 12/29/96 Philadelphia, PA [54 shows]. Last Halley's Comet, 8/16/96 Plattsburgh, NY [92 shows]. Last Contact, 11/30/96 Sacramento, CA [60 shows].

Limestone, Maine—Great Went
Sunday, August 17, 1997

Once again, Phish made the "night one or night two" debate—which raged at and after the Clifford Ball—an argument with no clear winner.

The second day of The Great Went kicked off with the break-out of Wedge, the first since the fall of 1996 and only the second since 1995. The band seemed to struggle with it, however, and reserved the next portion of the set for several new tunes, before going back into familiar territory with Maze and just the second Tweezer of the summer, a long but not necessarily outstanding version.

The afternoon setbreak featured The Great Went orchestra, before Phish returned for a set which would provide the most memorable, seminal moments of the Went.

It began in grand musical fashion, with a long Down With Disease morphing into a splendid Bathtub Gin, a performance that to some represented the musical highlight of the Went. But the calling-card of the weekend came during a long 2001. Throughout the set, the band had taken turns painting odd shapes on easles set up on the sides of the stage. Now it was time to act.

Trey took to the microphone and directed phans' attention to a giant sculpture to the right of the stage. To those not in the know, he explained that phans had helped build the edifice throughout the weekend. It was part of something Phish had conceived a year before, an embodiment of the band and phans creating art together. Then, the giant puzzle pieces they had painted on stage were lifted into the audience, and the crowd passed the Phish contribution toward the sculpture. As workers began tacking Phish's pieces on, the band kicked into Harry Hood.

During the jam portion of Hood, Trey asked Chris to turn off the stage lights—a tradition begun in Europe and continued at The Gorge—to allow the band to jam under only the shine of the near-full moon.

But the audience had other ideas, as Phish phandom created a light show of its own, throwing thousands of neon bracelets into the air for a display as spectacular as anything modern technology could muster. When it was all done, Trey seemed teary-eyed. "Go get more of those, they look cool," he said. The band and audience had truly created art together.

Set III began in oh-so-promising fashion, kicking off with Buffalo Bill—the first since New Year's '94—and segueing into NICU. A fire-breather spewed flames in the crowd near the stage, and the band continued with a set of relative rarities, offering up Weigh, the crowd-favorite Guyute, and the emotional new tune Dirt. But the Mike's Groove which most of the crowd was understandably expecting never came.

Instead, the weekend closed with Scent of a Mule (lacking the Duel, instead with a great jam in the middle) into a long, jammed Prince Caspian, followed by a relatively anti-climactic encore of When the Circus Comes To Town into Tweezer Reprise. The attention was directed back toward the sculpture, set ablaze by a giant match. As the crowd filed out of the concert compound, the Art Tower collapsed into embers.

The band and audiences' collaboration would be left in Limestone forever, but the memories would not.

8/17/97 The Great Went, Loring Air Force Base, Limestone, ME
I: Wedge, Beauty of My Dreams, Dogs Stole Things > Vultures, Water in the Sky, Maze, Bouncing > Tweezer > Taste, Carolina
II: Down with Disease > Bathtub Gin > Uncle Pen, Also Sprach > Art Jam > Harry Hood
III: Buffalo Bill > NICU > Weigh > Guyute > Dirt, Scent of a Mule > Caspian
E: When the Circus Comes, Tweezer Reprise

"Cities" jam in Tweezer. During the "Art Jam," the members of Phish passed paintings done onstage earlier in the set out over the heads of the crowd to the Art Tower located to the right of the stage. Trey asked Chris Kuroda to turn the lights off during the jam in Harry Hood, and the crowd created a glowstick array near the stage. The Art Tower was set aflame during Tweezer Reprise. Last Buffalo Bill, 12/31/94 Boston, MA [204 shows].

remote desert region of Nevada, where people gather for a weekend of high-strangeness and then burn down a big huge "man" that they had spent the weekend constructing.

But what was the meaning here? I read somewhere recently that an art critic or historian said, "All great art must be burned." I think that the burning of the tower, composed of artwork by both phans and the band, was both a figurative and literal melding of our energies to send out into the cosmos, and help raise the overall vibration of the planet.

The scene raged all night, of course. I spoke to one phan who told me that he had seen an apparition rise out of the crowd and into the sky during the first set. He also informed me that this past January had been the true dawn of the Aquarian Age, that we were now in it. I had read various dates for this, some saying '97, some '98. But the January '97 date makes a lot of sense—it was about this time that I started to feel myself being drawn toward this path.

It was also on their early '97 European tour that Phish's sound started evolving in this more funkified direction. My friend Mike that night described Phish as being on "the cutting edge of channeling the intergalactic cosmic funk into our lives." I couldn't have put it better. I believe that the "intergalactic cosmic funk" is the most universal language around, and therefore is a key element in bringing humanity together with our interstellar neighbors. They dig it, too—that's why they were here to check out Phish.

We partied all night and left at dawn, as the most spectacular sunrise I've ever seen lit the way. The sky was aflame with brilliant pink, orange, and purple—it was incredibly cosmic. It reminded me of the concept of Jimi Hendrix's song "First Rays of the New Rising Sun." I read an interview with Jimi in which he described the song as being about the dawning of a new age, how humanity was going to be going through some heavy changes in about 30 years. There's no doubt in my mind that Jimi was a Starseed/Walk-In. He was so far ahead of his time musically, and if you read interviews with him, he constantly alludes to the same concepts that I've been talking about regarding the Cosmic Party and the new age.

To me, Phish is THE evolution of rock and roll. I hear them as the sum total of all rock history—they have so many influences, and can bust out almost any song at anytime. Rock and Roll music is the universal language, and since Phish encompasses all rock history in creating their own original sound, that makes them THE band to lead us to the Cosmic Party.

The mythological tie to the story in the bible about Jesus telling the fishermen to go be "fishers of men" is also quite intriguing. A friend of mine who is a big phan and became a born-again Christian earlier this year pointed that out to me, and we have had an ongoing discussion of this ever since. It is very interesting, since the fish is a symbol of Christianity, and since Phish really are "fishers of men" in the way that they bring people together under one harmonious vibe. I'm not exactly sure what the religious implications here are, but it does give some credence to an idea first formed in the socio-cultural revolution of the late '60s—that rock and roll can save the world. Amen to that.

All The Songs

Every Original Song Performance ♦ Year-Play Stats ♦ Cover Tunes

The Great Went, August 17, 1997.

Original Song Performance Database

Cracking The Code...

Number of concerts played prior to the song debut (bracketed number at top of column).

Number of concerts since the song was last played (all numbers in 2nd column below the bracket).

Date of concert (first column).

Set (1 is first set, 2 is second set, 3 is third set, E is encore, E2 is separate second encore, and 1a is the first set of a single-set show.)

Song title as it appears in the setlist section.

Total number of times played (asterix indicates more info appears in the Stories sidebar).

Actual song title and authors. The [bracketed] title is the abbreviation used in the before/after columns in this section.

Songs played immediately before (left column) and immediately after (right column) on that date.

Axilla [33]*
Axilla [Axilla]
By Anastasio/Marshall

11/19/92	[480]	1	Esther	Horse
11/20/92	1	1	*OP1	All Things
11/22/92	2	2	*OP2	My Friend
11/27/92	3	2	*OP2	PoorHeart
12/01/92	3	2	*OP2	Curtain
12/07/92	6	1	*OP1	PoorHeart
12/11/92	3	2	Esther	Bouncing

All The Songs is an ultimate chronicle of every time Phish has played every original song, as documented in the Almanac's setlists section through The Great Went, 8/17/97.

There's a wealth of information if you know how to access it. This reference section is designed to allow easy determination of the number of times and dates on which Phish has played every original song. The section can also be used to help identify undated setlists, as the song performed immediately before and after the song is noted in the list.

Listed under the title, author and total number of times played is every documented show at which Phish has played the song, followed by the number of shows since they last played it, the set in which it was played, and the song played immediately before and after.

The bold-faced number following the list, e.g. [**➤ 8/17/97 633**], is the song's lapse through the second show of the Great Went, 8/17/97.

Show components listed in the setlists surrounded by quotation marks, such as "Crew Acknowledgement," are not considered songs so are omitted.

Similarly, setlists not considered to be concert performances, as noted by brackets surrounding the date in the setlist section, e.g. [7/15/95], are also omitted.

THE SONGWRITERS

Writing credit for the majority of Phish songs goes to the songwriting team of Tom Marshall and Trey Anastasio, who have collaborated since their grade-school days. Tom writes the lyrics, and Trey the music, with Tom often offering lots of poems and other writings to Trey, who then sifts through them and sets them to music. Trey has also written both the words and the music to many songs, including most of the Gamehendge saga—his senior thesis at Goddard College—and epics such as You Enjoy Myself, Reba, and David Bowie. The Dude of Life has also contributed lyrics and melodies to some of Trey's compositions, as have some other friends of the band.

Mike Gordon has written his fair share of songs, too, from Mound and Simple to Scent of a Mule and Contact. Fishman added lyrics to many earlier Phish songs but limits his songwriting skills to "deeper" songs such as Lengthwise and Ha Ha Ha nowadays (plus his new ballad, Bye Bye Foot). Page, a contributor to several songs, has written two songs performed by Phish—Magilla and Cars Trucks Buses.

Stories Behind the Songs

People can debate forever the meaning of each Phish song, because it's undoubtedly true that every song means something different to every listener. To help the quest for understanding, we present this column of notes on "the stories behind the songs," which offers lyrical analysis, stories of how the song was written, and, in some cases, notes on its in-concert history. The text continues from page to page in the left-hand column.

AC/DC Bag: A Gamehendge song, sung from Wilson's perspective. The AC/DC Bag is the electronic hangman who carries out Wilson's sentence of death on his accountant, Mr. Palmer.

Acoustic Army: This served as a defining song of summer tour 1995 when it was played at almost every show. It features the band members on acoustic guitars, performed with all four sitting on barstools at the front of the stage, but hasn't surfaced in concert since its debut year.

All Things Reconsidered: Although this song was introduced in the fall of 1991, the band only played it once on that tour because they found it so technically demanding to play. While Trey was composing the piece, he realized its similarity to the theme song for National Public Radio's popular news-information show All Things Considered, and altered his composition to make it an even-closer variation on theme on the All Things Considered theme. Phish claim they botched this song horribly when they performed it on NPR's MountainStage Live in March, 1992.

Alumni Blues: Once heavily played, this song has languished in recent years because Fishman apparently dislikes it. Prior to its one-verse-only appearance at the Beacon Theater in New York City in April 1994, it hadn't been played at all since fall '91. Trey has said that it will probably only surface if Phish tours again with a horn section.

Anarchy: More comic relief than song, this mid-1980s creation features the band chanting "Anarchy!" as they jam in punk-rock style for about 10 seconds.

AC/DC Bag [179]*

AC/DC Bag [ACDCBag]

By Anastasio

04/01/86	[4]	2	Slipknot	McGrupp
04/15/86	1	1a	*OP1	Reagan
10/31/86	2	2	*OP2	SwingLow
12/06/86	1	1a	Katy	Bowie
04/24/87	4	1a	Golgi	Possum
08/10/87	4	1	Fire	Possum
08/29/87	6	2	Timber Ho	Divided
09/12/87	2	1	Golgi	Possum
10/14/87	2	2	Bowie	Divided
01/30/88	3	1	Mustang	Possum
02/07/88	1	1a	Bowie	Timber Ho
03/11/88	2	2	Harpua	Alumni
03/12/88	1	1a	Wilson	Forbin's
03/21/88	1	1a	Fire	Possum
03/31/88	1	1	Fee	Possum
05/15/88	3	1a	WhipPost	Possum
06/15/88	3	2	Lizards	Sloth
06/20/88	2	1	Fluffhead	Lizards
06/21/88	1	2	IDK	Flat Fee
07/12/88	2	1	Slave	Antelope
07/23/88	1	1	OYWD	Possum
08/06/88	4	2	Golgi	Satin Doll
09/08/88	2	1	Wild Child	Forbin's
09/24/88	2	3	Curtain	*CL3
10/12/88	1	2	Sloth	Possum
10/29/88	1	3	Possum	Foam
11/05/88	2	2	Lizards	Fee
02/07/89	7	1	Dinner	Lizards
02/17/89	1	1a	*OP1	YEM
02/24/89	2	2	*OP2	YEM
03/03/89	1	1	Foam	Curtain
03/30/89	3	3	Foam	BBFCM
04/20/89	9	1	*OP1	Fluffhead
05/06/89	9	1	Bold	Forbin's
05/13/89	6	1	*OP1	Alumni
05/20/89	4	1	*OP1	Alumni
05/21/89	1	1	Ya Mar	Divided
05/26/89	1	1	Bold	Mike's
05/27/89	1	1	*OP1	Mike's
06/23/89	6	1	*OP1	YEM
06/30/89	2	2	WalkAway	Curtain
08/12/89	3	1a	Suzie	Ya Mar
08/17/89	1	2	WalkAway	Mango
08/19/89	2	1	TMWSIY	PYITE
08/23/89	1	2	YEM	Foam
08/26/89	1	2	Slave	Donna Lee
09/09/89	4	1	Divided	McGrupp
10/01/89	1	2	*OP2	MSO
10/07/89	2	2	Lizards	Bowie
10/14/89	3	1	*OP1	Divided
10/20/89	1	2	IDK	Donna
10/21/89	1	1	Foam	Lizards
10/22/89	1	2	McGrupp	MSO
10/26/89	1	2	Clod	Reba
10/31/89	2	1	Suzie	Divided
11/02/89	1	2	Who Do	MSO
11/09/89	3	2	Oh Kee	McGrupp
11/10/89	1	1	Divided	MSO
11/11/89	1	1a	Bathtub	MSO
11/16/89	1	2	Sloth	Tela
11/30/89	2	1	Oh Kee	Foam
12/07/89	4	1	A-Train	Fee
12/08/89	1	1	Who Do	MSO
12/16/89	3	1	Curtain	Lawn Boy
12/29/89	1	1	Oh Kee	Lizards
12/31/89	2	1	Oh Kee	Antelope
01/27/90	4	1	Oh Kee	MSO
02/09/90	8	1	Bouncing	Sqirm Coil
02/10/90	1	2	Esther	Rocky Top
02/24/90	6	2	Sloth	Fee
03/03/90	4	1	Oh Kee	Reba
03/07/90	1	2	Oh Kee	Sqirm Coil
03/08/90	1	2	MSO	Caravan
03/09/90	1	1	Oh Kee	*CL1
03/11/90	1	2	Slave	Bowie
03/17/90	1	2	Oh Kee	Foam
04/05/90	3	2	Jesus	Donna
04/07/90	2	1	Suzie	Sqirm Coil
04/13/90	5	1	Oh Kee	Reba
04/20/90	3	2	Oh Kee	Jesus
05/10/90	10	2	Oh Kee	Lizards
05/11/90	1	2	Oh Kee	Lizards
05/13/90	2	1	Oh Kee	Dinner
05/24/90	4	1	Oh Kee	Golgi
06/16/90	7	1	*OP 1	Div Sky
09/13/90	1	2	Oh Kee	Bur Alive
09/15/90	2	1	Oh Kee	Asse Fest
09/28/90	5	2	*OP 2	Esther
10/01/90	1	2	Lawn Boy	*CL2
10/30/90	8	3	Contact	*CL3
11/04/90	4	1	Carolina	Curtain
12/08/90	11	1	Foam	Divided
12/29/90	2	E	Donna	*CL E
02/07/91	5	E	*OP E	*CL E
02/08/91	1	1	*OP 1	Reba
02/15/91	3	2	Oh Kee	Harry
02/26/91	8	1	Oh Kee	Golgi
03/15/91	10	1	Oh Kee	Lizards
03/23/91	5	2	Oh Kee	MSO
04/16/91	13	1	Oh Kee	Tela
04/21/91	4	1	Oh Kee	Tela
05/03/91	5	2	*OP2	Curtain
05/12/91	3	2	Oh Kee	Antelope
05/25/91	4	1a	Oh Kee	Fee
07/12/91	2	1	Donna	Rocky Top
07/14/91	2	3	*OP3	Landlady
07/21/91	5	2	Esther	Contact
07/25/91	3	1	Flat Fee	Adeline
10/06/91	13	1	Oh Kee	Brother
10/13/91	4	1	Tela	Sloth
11/01/91	12	1	*OP1	Sparkle
05/16/92	74	2	Oh Kee	Rosie
02/19/93	84	E	*OPE	*CLE
03/12/93	14	2	*OP2	My Friend
03/22/93	8	2	Wilson	Forbin's
03/31/93	7	E	*OPE	Adeline
04/14/93	9	2	*OP2	MSO
04/22/93	6	E	*OPE	AmGrace
05/03/93	9	2	*OP2	Curtain
05/08/93	4	E	*OPE	*CLE
07/31/93	16	E	*OPE	Freebird
08/12/93	8	1	*OP1	Reba
08/25/93	9	1	*OP1	Daniel
04/05/94	8	1	Rift	*CL1
04/13/94	6	2	PurplRain	*CL2
04/18/94	5	1	Oh Kee	*CL1
05/06/94	13	1	Oh Kee	PoorHeart
05/20/94	10	1	Carolina	*CL1
06/18/94	16	1	Rift	Maze
06/26/94	7	1	Wilson	Forbin's
07/08/94	8	1	Wilson	Forbin's
07/16/94	6	2	Harpua	Scent
10/22/94	13	2	AmGrace	HwayHell
11/18/94	16	1	Rift	Julius
12/08/94	15	1	Maze	Scent
12/30/94	5	1	Rift	Sparkle
06/09/95	5	1	Oh Kee	Theme
06/15/95	4	1	Sparkle	Old Home
06/19/95	3	1	PoorHeart	Tela
06/25/95	5	1	Ya Mar	Taste
06/30/95	4	1	*OP1	Scent
07/03/95	3	2	Bowie	Lizards
09/27/95	1	1	CTB	Bowie
09/29/95	2	1	*OP1	Sparkle
10/08/95	7	1	*OP1	Demand
10/14/95	3	1	*OP1	CTB
10/17/95	2	1	Uncle Pen	Maze
10/22/95	4	1	*OP1	My Mind
10/28/95	4	1	*OP1	Mound
11/10/95	4	2	Sparkle	Adeline
11/15/95	4	1	PoorHeart	FEFY
11/18/95	2	2	*OP2	Sparkle
11/24/95	4	1	Oh Kee	Curtain
11/29/95	3	1	*OP1	Ya Mar
12/07/95	6	1	Curtain	Demand
12/16/95	7	1	BurAlive	Fog
12/30/95	4	2	Harry	Life Boy
04/26/96	2	1a	Ya Mar	Sparkle
06/06/96	1	2	*OP2	YEM
07/05/96	2	1a	Chalkdust	YEM
07/23/96	14	1	*OP1	Foam
08/04/96	4	2	*OP2	Reba
08/10/96	4	1	PoorHeart	Free
08/13/96	2	2	*OP2	Lizards
08/16/96	2	1	Ya Mar	Esther
10/19/96	5	1	*OP2	Sparkle
10/23/96	3	1	PoorHeart	Foam
10/27/96	3	1	PYITE	Fee
11/11/96	9	1	CTB	Sparkle
11/14/96	2	1	*OP1	Uncle Pen
11/19/96	4	1	Ya Mar	Foam
11/24/96	3	1	PoorHeart	All Things
12/02/96	5	1	Rocky Top	Bouncing
12/30/96	5	2	Uncle Pen	Guyute
02/14/97	3	2	*OP2	Ya Mar
02/21/97	5	2	Oh Kee	Billy
06/25/97	17	1	Billy	Old Home
07/25/97	14	1	Makisupa	*CL1
08/06/97	7	1	Also Sprac	Ya Mar
➤ 08/17/97	8			

Acoustic Army [27]*

Acoustic Army [AArmy]

By Anastasio

06/07/95	[740]	2	LCBill	Sample
06/09/95	2	2	Bowie	Adeline
06/13/95	2	2	Theme	Harry
06/14/95	1	2	Tweezer	Guitar
06/15/95	1	2	Scent	Slave
06/17/95	2	2	McGrupp	Adeline
06/19/95	1	2	YEM	Possum
06/22/95	2	E	*OPE	Guitar
06/24/95	2	2	Harry	Adeline
06/29/95	4	2	YEM	DayinLife
07/01/95	2	2	Str Design	Harry
07/02/95	1	2	Sl Monkey	Slave
09/28/95	3	1	Fog	Slave
10/02/95	3	1	Stash	Fog
10/05/95	2	1	Divided	Julius
10/07/95	2	1	Mango	Wilson
10/11/95	2	1	Fog	Julius
10/14/95	2	1	Catapult	It's Ice
10/19/95	3	1	Theme	Split&Melt
10/21/95	2	1	Str Design	GTBT
10/24/95	2	1	Wolfman's	Price
10/28/95	3	1	Billy	Caspian
11/11/95	5	E	*OPE	GTBT
11/18/95	5	2	BBFCM	BBFCM
11/24/95	4	2	Bathtub	Bike
11/29/95	3	1	Theme	Fee
12/08/95	7	1	It's Ice	Caspian
➤ 8/17/97	182			

All Things [77]*

All Things Reconsidered [All Things]

By Anastasio

09/25/91	[336]	E	*OPE	BBFCM
03/06/92	49	1	Reba	Bowie
03/11/92	2	2	BabyLem	Harry
03/19/92	5	1	Mockbird	Bowie
03/21/92	2	2	PoorHeart	Bowie
03/25/92	2	2	Reba	Sqirm Coil
03/26/92	1	1	RunJim	Foam
03/30/92	3	1	IDK	Sloth
04/01/92	2	1	Brother	Sparkle
04/03/92	1	1	Fluffhead	Split&Melt
04/05/92	2	2	Split&Melt	YEM
04/07/92	2	2	PoorHeart	Tweezer
04/13/92	3	1	Fee	Foam
04/15/92	1	1	IDK	RunJim
04/18/92	3	1	Sparkle	Antelope
04/22/92	3	1	Stash	Suzie
04/25/92	3	2	Silent	Dinner
05/01/92	3	2	Wilson	MSO
05/03/92	2	1	Fee	Split&Melt
05/05/92	1	2	Bouncing	Foam
05/06/92	1	2	YEM	Bouncing
05/08/92	2	1	Mound	Bouncing
05/12/92	3	1	Reba	Sloth
05/14/92	1	1	Suzie	Sloth
05/17/92	3	2	Sqirm Coil	Brother
06/27/92	6	1a	Maze	Chalkdust
07/14/92	8	2	Fee	Reba
07/15/92	1	2	McGrupp	Harry
07/21/92	5	1a	*OP1	Possum
07/27/92	5	1a	Golgi	Bowie
07/30/92	2	1a	It's Ice	Maze
08/17/92	7	1	Wilson	Foam
08/24/92	4	1a	PoorHeart	Tweezer
11/20/92	8	1	Axilla	Suzie
11/22/92	2	1	Horn	Gin
11/28/92	4	1	FEFY	Mike's
12/01/92	2	2	My Friend	Uncle Pen
12/03/92	2	1	Fee	Split&Melt
12/10/92	6	1	IDK	Reba
12/12/92	2	1	PoorHeart	Bouncing
12/29/92	3	2	FEFY	Mike's
02/04/93	4	1	FEFY	Stash
02/06/93	2	2	Adeline	Mike's
02/12/93	5	2	My Friend	Reba
02/17/93	3	1	Weigh	Sloth
02/20/93	3	1	Weigh	Divided
02/23/93	3	2	PYITE	Mike's
03/02/93	4	1	Fee	Chalkdust
03/13/93	7	1	Fee	Split&Melt
03/21/93	6	1	Esther	Split&Melt
03/26/93	4	1	PYITE	Split&Melt
03/30/93	3	1	PoorHeart	Golgi
04/03/93	4	2	Mound	Sloth
04/09/93	2	2	Suzie	Llama
04/17/93	6	1	My Friend	Golgi
04/22/93	4	2	Bouncing	Tweezer
04/27/93	4	2	My Friend	Maze
04/30/93	2	1	Lawn Boy	Possum
05/06/93	5	1	Silent	Llama
07/16/93	6	1	FEFY	Nellie
07/28/93	9	1	*OP1	RunJim
08/02/93	4	1	Suzie	Gin
08/11/93	6	2	Esther	Bouncing
08/15/93	4	1	Sample	RunJim
08/24/93	5	1	Chalkdust	Bouncing
04/09/94	12	1	Fee	Stash
04/22/94	11	1	Sample	Nellie
06/24/94	41	1	Sloth	Paul&Silas
10/13/94	22	1	Gumbo	DWD
10/28/94	12	1	Axilla 2	Sample
06/14/95	39	1	Possum	AmGrace
07/01/95	14	1	If I Could	It's Ice
11/08/96	108	1	Axilla	Mound

11/14/96	4	1	Free	Bathtub
11/24/96	7	1	ACDCBag	Bouncing
11/30/96	3	1	PYITE	Bouncing
02/23/97	17	1	Axilla	Sloth
➢ 8/17/97	**44**			

Alumni [64]

Alumni Blues [Alumni]

By Anastasio

10/17/85	[4]	1a	Jam	Mike's
10/30/85	1	1a	Reviv	PrepHipp
04/01/86	2	2	McGrupp	Reagan
04/15/86	1	1a	CamlWalk	*CL1
10/31/86	2	2	Icculus	*CL2
03/23/87	4	1	Mike's	YEM
04/24/87	1	1a	Dave's	I am H2
04/29/87	1	1	Katy	Golgi
08/10/87	3	1	Peaches	Golgi
08/29/87	3	1	*OP1	Curtis
09/12/87	2	2	Suzie	GTBT
11/19/87	4	2	Corrina	Suzie
01/30/88	1	1	Sally	A-Train
02/07/88	1	1a	Golgi	Peaches
03/11/88	2	2	ACDCBag	Antelope
03/31/88	3	2	*OP2	Lizards
05/14/88	2	2	Fluffhead	A-Train
05/15/88	1	1a	*OP1	Golgi
05/25/88	2	1	FunkBitch	Peaches
06/15/88	1	1	Suzie	YEM
06/18/88	1	2	*OP2	BBFCM
06/21/88	2	2	Flat Fee	Jesus
07/11/88	1	1	Golgi	*CL1
07/23/88	2	2	La Grange	Peaches
07/24/88	1	2	Lizards	OYWD
09/24/88	7	1	OYWD	YEM
10/12/88	1	2	*OP2	YEM
10/29/88	1	2	Fee	WalkAway
11/03/88	1	1	Fee	GTBT
11/05/88	1	1	Fluffhead	Bowie
12/02/88	2	2	GTBT	Lizards
01/26/89	1	1a	Golgi	YEM
02/07/89	4	2	Contact	Fee
02/17/89	1	1a	A-Train	Antelope
03/03/89	3	1	Divided	GTBT
04/15/89	10	1	OYWD	IDK
05/05/89	10	1	Fluffhead	Jam
05/13/89	7	1	ACDCBag	YEM
05/20/89	4	1	ACDCBag	YEM
08/17/89	16	3	Halley's	Contact
09/09/89	6	2	YEM	Split&Melt
10/01/89	1	1	*OP1	McGrupp
10/06/89	1	1a	Dinner	Harry
10/07/89	1	1	Makisupa	GTBT
10/14/89	3	1	Fee	YEM
10/31/89	6	2	Mockbird	Lizards
12/07/89	13	1	Weekpaug	Divided
12/09/89	2	2	Esther	Fee
02/09/90	17	2	A-Train	Foam
02/23/90	6	1	*OP1	YEM
04/06/90	14	2	IDK	GTBT
04/13/90	6	2	Foam	YEM
04/20/90	3	1	Divided	Ya Mar
05/19/90	15	1	Ya Mar	Adeline
10/05/90	20	2	Ya Mar	Uncle Pen
12/07/90	20	E	*OPE	*CLE
02/14/91	11	1	Esther	Bouncing
04/06/91	22	1	Jesus	*CL1
04/20/91	8	E	Horn	*CLE
07/13/91	19	1	Suzie	TMWSIY
07/15/91	2	E	Contact	*CLE
10/10/91	21	1	Golgi	Lizards
04/15/94	279	2	Wolfman's	BeLikeYou
➢ 8/17/97	**317**			

Anarchy [6]

Anarchy [Anarchy]

By Anastasio (?)

03/04/85	[1]	1a	*OP1	CamlWalk
05/03/85	1	E	*OPE	*CLE
10/17/85	1	1a	Revol	CamlWalk
04/15/86	4	1a	YEM	CamlWalk
04/29/87	8	3	GTBT	Makisupa
08/10/87	3	2	WhipPost	Tush
➢ 8/17/97	**923**			

Asse Festival [17]*

The Asse Festival [Asse Fest]

By Anastasio

Now played as the middle section in Guelah Papyrus.

09/13/90	[222]	1	Tube	Antelope
09/14/90	1	2	*OP2	Sqirm Coil
09/15/90	1	1	ACDCBag	Bowie
09/22/90	4	E	*OPE	Golgi
09/28/90	1	1	Lizards	Antelope
10/05/90	3	1	Stash	Bouncing
10/07/90	2	1	Mockbird	Sqirm Coil
10/30/90	4	1	Donna	Suzie
10/31/90	1	1	YEM	MSO
11/02/90	1	1	Cavern	Possum
11/04/90	2	1	FunkBitch	MSO
11/08/90	1	1	Sqirm Coil	IDK
11/10/90	1	2	YEM	Fee
11/30/90	5	2	*OP2	Sqirm Coil
12/07/90	3	1	YEM	RunJim
12/08/90	1	2	Llama	Dinner
04/27/91	55	1	Adeline	RunJim
➢ 8/17/97	**633 (as a stand-alone song)**			

Axilla [33]*

Axilla [Axilla]

By Anastasio/Marshall

11/19/92	[480]	1	Esther	Horse
11/20/92	1	1	*OP1	All Things
11/22/92	2	2	*OP2	My Friend
11/27/92	3	2	*OP2	PoorHeart
12/01/92	3	2	*OP2	Curtain
12/07/92	6	1	*OP1	PoorHeart
12/11/92	3	2	Esther	Bouncing
12/30/92	5	2	*OP2	Rift
02/04/93	3	1	*OP1	Foam
02/17/93	10	2	*OP2	Landlady
02/21/93	4	2	*OP2	Curtain
02/23/93	2	2	*OP2	MSO
03/03/93	5	2	*OP2	Curtain
03/09/93	4	2	*OP2	Rift
03/12/93	1	2	My Friend	Sparkle
03/17/93	4	2	*OP2	Glide
03/25/93	6	2	*OP2	Curtain
04/01/93	6	2	*OP2	Curtain
04/05/93	3	2	*OP2	PoorHeart
04/16/93	6	2	*OP2	Curtain
05/02/93	13	1	*OP1	Sparkle
07/28/93	18	2	Also Sprac	MSO
08/16/93	15	1	*OP1	Possum
10/16/94	93	1	TMWSIY	Possum
11/08/96	170	1	RunJim	All Things
11/11/96	2	1	Theme	RunJim
11/16/96	4	2	Catapult	Harry
11/23/96	4	2	Makisupa	Weekpaug
12/31/96	12	1	*OP1	Peaches
02/14/97	2	1	Adeline	It's Ice
02/23/97	7	1	Carini	All Things
02/28/97	3	2	Love Me	Waste
➢ 8/17/97	**41**			

Axilla II [37]*

Axilla (Part II) [Axilla 2]

By Anastasio/Marshall

04/16/94	[626]	1	Fee	Rift
04/20/94	3	1	Bouncing	Suzie
04/24/94	4	1	Ya Mar	Maze
04/30/94	4	2	Harry	McGrupp
05/04/94	3	1	Sparkle	Tweezer
05/06/94	1	2	Reba	Julius
05/08/94	2	1	Foam	Rift
05/10/94	1	1	Divided	It's Ice
05/12/94	1	1	Maze	Foam
05/16/94	3	1	Divided	Rift
05/22/94	5	1	Dog Faced	*CL1
05/25/94	2	1	Mockbird	Scent
05/28/94	3	2	*OP2	It's Ice
06/10/94	3	2	*OP2	Curtain
06/19/94	7	1	Lizards	Curtain
06/23/94	3	2	Mango	Uncle Pen
06/25/94	2	2	Gin	YEM
06/26/94	1	2	If I Could	Life Boy
06/30/94	2	2	Sparkle	Harpua
07/03/94	3	1	Reba	Bowie
07/06/94	2	1	Reba	My Mind
10/22/94	20	1	Gumbo	Rift
10/25/94	2	2	Glide	Jesus
10/26/94	1	2	Reba	YEM
10/28/94	2	1	Glide	All Things
11/02/94	3	2	Mango	Possum
11/13/94	4	1	Reba	It's Ice
11/16/94	2	1	Reba	Lizards
11/19/94	3	1	Guyute	Paul&Silas
11/20/94	1	2	Glide	Reba
12/04/94	10	2	Reba	YEM
12/08/94	3	2	My Mind	Reba
12/28/94	3	1	Bouncing	Dog Faced
06/13/95	9	2	Lizards	Theme
06/28/95	12	1	*OP1	Foam
12/04/95	49	1	My Mind	Horse
12/31/95	14	2	Lizards	RunJim
➢ 8/17/97	**123**			

Bathtub Gin [114]

Bathtub Gin [Bathtub]

By Anastasio/Goodman

05/26/89	[102]	2	Split&Melt	Antelope
05/27/89	1	1	Fluffhead	GTBT
05/28/89	1	2	Weekpaug	Sanity
06/30/89	7	2	Slave	Mike's
08/19/89	7	2	Divided	*CL2
09/09/89	6	1	Makisupa	PYITE
10/26/89	10	2	WalkAway	Sloth
10/31/89	2	1	WalkAway	Possum
11/02/89	1	1	*OP1	Foam
11/03/89	1	1	Mockbird	MSO
11/09/89	3	1	MSO	YEM
11/10/89	2	1	Harry	Mike's
11/11/89	1	1a	Golgi	ACDCBag
11/16/89	1	1	Weekpaug	Foam
11/30/89	2	1	*OP1	Divided
12/08/89	5	1	MSO	Antelope
12/09/89	1	1	Lawn Boy	Golgi
12/31/89	5	1	Antelope	Lizards
01/27/90	4	1	Carolina	Ya Mar
01/28/90	1	2	YEM	Mike's
02/10/90	8	1	YEM	Bouncing
02/15/90	1	1	Caravan	Mike's
02/17/90	2	1a	Caravan	Mike's
02/23/90	2	2	Reba	Jesus
02/24/90	1	2	La Grange	Lawn Boy
03/07/90	5	2	Sqirm Coil	Split&Melt
03/08/90	1	2	Divided	MSO
04/07/90	8	1	*OP1	Possum
04/26/90	8	2	Esther	Oh Kee
05/04/90	4	2	Tweezer	Oh Kee
05/10/90	2	1	MSO	Possum
05/13/90	3	1	*OP1	Oh Kee
06/08/90	9	1	MSO	Tweezer
06/16/90	2	2	MSO	YEM
09/15/90	3	2	MSO	Foam
12/03/90	27	1	*OP1	FunkBitch
02/15/91	13	2	Bowie	Ya Mar
03/07/91	14	E	*OPE	*CLE
03/16/91	5	1	Landlady	Curtain
03/23/91	4	2	Chalkdust	Oh Kee
04/06/91	8	1	YEM	Icculus
04/22/91	10	2	Chalkdust	Uncle Pen
05/10/91	8	1	Landlady	BurAlive
05/12/91	2	2	Bowie	PoorHeart
07/12/91	6	1	Landlady	Donna
07/14/91	2	3	Chalkdust	Mike's
07/20/91	4	1	Landlady	MSO
07/24/91	3	1	Split&Melt	Landlady
10/13/91	18	2	Llama	Sqirm Coil
10/19/91	4	2	Llama	Sparkle
10/28/91	5	2	Paul&Silas	YEM
10/31/91	2	1	Foam	Paul&Silas
11/13/91	9	2	Golgi	Sqirm Coil
11/15/91	2	2	Llama	PoorHeart
11/16/91	1	2	MSO	Brother
11/20/91	2	1	Paul&Silas	Sqirm Coil
11/22/91	2	2	Landlady	Antelope
12/05/91	5	1	Llama	It's Ice
03/11/92	6	2	Lizards	My Mind
03/27/92	11	2	Rift	Dinner
04/06/92	8	2	Dinner	Paul&Silas
04/18/92	8	2	Manteca	MtRep
04/25/92	6	2	Maze	YEM
05/12/92	12	2	Landlady	YEM
11/22/92	52	1	All Things	Adeline
12/06/92	11	2	BBJ	YEM
12/30/92	9	2	Rift	YEM
02/21/93	17	2	Lizards	Rosie
03/16/93	15	2	Tweezer	Esther
03/28/93	10	2	Mound	YEM
04/24/93	19	2	Foam	Dinner
08/02/93	28	1	All Things	Makisupa
08/13/93	8	2	Rift	Ya Mar
12/30/93	13	1	Rift	FrBir
04/09/94	6	1	Rift	Nellie
04/18/94	8	2	Sparkle	BBJ
04/24/94	5	1	Maze	Dog Faced
05/12/94	12	1	Foam	Lizards
05/20/94	6	1	It's Ice	FEFY
06/17/94	15	1	PYITE	Scent
06/25/94	7	2	Sparkle	Axilla 2
07/05/94	7	2	Sparkle	Life Boy
10/14/94	15	1	PYITE	Adeline
11/18/94	22	2	Llama	Life Boy
12/28/94	18	1	Julius	Bouncing
06/20/95	15	1	Foam	If I Could
06/26/95	5	1	Wanna Go	NICU
10/02/95	11	2	CTB	Llama
10/11/95	6	2	Possum	Mound
11/09/95	15	2	Lizards	TMWSIY
11/24/95	11	2	Scent	AArmy
11/30/95	4	1	NICU	Rift
12/05/95	4	2	PoorHeart	Keyboard
12/15/95	7	2	It's Ice	Rotation
12/29/95	4	2	CTB	McGrupp

SONGS PLAYED BY YEAR

(1997 through 8/17/97)

AC/DC Bag
1990 27
1991 18
1992 1
1993 11
1994 13
1995 21
1996 17
1997 5

Acoustic Army
1995 27
1996 0
1997 0

All Things
1991 1
1992 40
1993 24
1994 5
1995 2
1996 4
1997 1

Alumni Blues
1990 8
1991 6
1992 0
1993 1
1994 0
1995 0
1996 0
1997 0

Asse
1990 16
1991 1

Axilla I
1992 8
1993 15
1994 1
1995 0
1996 5
1997 3

Axilla II
1994 35
1995 4
1996 0
1997 0

Bathtub Gin
1990 18
1991 22
1992 9
1993 7
1994 11
1995 10
1996 10
1997 9

Big Ball Jam
1992 14
1993 64
1994 22
1995 0
1996 0
1997 0

BBFCM
1990 11
1991 20
1992 9
1993 11
1994 14
1995 6
1996 2
1997 0

Billy Breathes
1995 13
1996 8
1997 12

Bouncing
1990 58
1991 64
1992 55
1993 46
1994 40
1995 22
1996 17
1997 13

Brother
1991 26
1992 13
1993 1
1994 0
1995 0
1996 3
1997 0

Buffalo Bill
1992
1992 1
1993 0
1994 2
1995 0
1996 0
1997 1

Buried Alive
1990 16
1991 30
1992 18
1993 26
1994 13
1995 5
1996 2
1997 1

Bye Bye Foot
1997 4

Camel Walk
1990 0
1991 0
1992 0
1993 0
1994 0
1995 1
1996 0
1997 2

Carini
1997 5

Stories Behind the Songs
(Continued)

The Asse Festival: Initially performed as an individual compostion, The Asse Festival has been performed as the middle section of Guelah Papyrus since February 1991 (though it did surface once on its own after the debut of Guelah, on 4/27/91). Trey dedicated the song to his composition teacher, Ernie Stires.

Axilla/Axilla (Part II): A two-part suite about a character getting his "loins dissolved." The original Axilla featured particularly Marshallesque lyrics; the band decided not to include it on *Rift* because it didn't fit with the album's theme. But when they chose to include the song on *Hoist*, the band said they thought the lyrics would stand out for their absurdity. So, keeping the music and "Axilla!" refrain, Marshall wrote new lyrics to the song. Supposedly, Part II continues the story began in Part I, in which a witch dissolved the loins of the song's narrator. In part II, the narrator laments this unfortunate turn of events. Both Axillas are said to be set in the later years of Gamehendge, but the Gamehendge connection is unclear. Some note that Axilla means "armpit" in Italian, a fact that doesn't clarify much.

Big Ball Jam: The "music" for this song depends on how the crowd interacts with three oversized beachballs thrown into the audience that control Page, Trey, and Mike. As audience members hit the balls, the musicians play a note; should a fan hold onto a ball, the bandmember keeps jamming until the ball is released back into the air. Although other bands have thrown balls into the audience for fans to play with, Phish is apparently the first band to add this participatory element, though the band has stopped Big Balling since 1994.

Billy Breathes: Named for Eliza, Trey and Sue's first daughter, born in the summer of 1995 whom Trey bestowed the nickname "Billy" on.

Brother: A lyrically nonsensical song about somebody jumping in the tub with your brother. After not being played since August 1993, the band

07/12/96	12	E	*OPE	Johnny B.
08/10/96	16	1	Rift	Cavern
08/16/96	4	1	Chalkdust	Ya Mar
10/17/96	3	2	Chalkdust	Scent
10/27/96	8	2	Chalkdust	Rift
11/07/96	6	2	Suzie	Bike
11/14/96	5	1	All Things	Talk
11/19/96	4	2	DayinLife	YEM
11/29/96	5	1	Divided	Life Mars
12/29/96	7	2	DayinLife	Lizards
02/17/97	6	1	Llama	Golgi
02/22/97	4	2	Chalkdust	Sparkle
07/01/97	19	2	Timber Ho	Cities
07/10/97	6	1	Ginseng	Llama
07/21/97	2	1	Ginseng	CharZero
07/25/97	3	1	Water	Makisupa
08/03/93	6	1	*OP1	Foam
08/10/97	4	1	*OP1	Sparkle
08/17/97	5	2	DwD	Uncle Pen
➤ 8/17/97	0			

BBJ [99]*

Big Ball Jam [BBJ]

By Phish

11/19/92	[480]	2	Tweezer	PoorHeart
11/22/92	3	2	Tweezer	Tweezer
11/23/92	1	2	Weekpaug	Weekpaug
11/28/92	3	2	Tweezer	TMWSIY
12/02/92	3	2	Tweezer	Tela
12/03/92	1	2	BBJ	Rosie
12/06/92	3	2	Paul&Silas	Gin
12/08/92	2	2	MSO	Sl Monkey
12/10/92	1	2	MSO	Maze
12/11/92	1	2	Paul&Silas	Sqirm Coil
12/13/92	2	2	MSO	Rosie
12/29/92	2	2	MSO	FEFY
12/30/92	1	2	Possum	Love You
12/31/92	1	2	MSO	Stash
02/03/93	1	2	Terrapin	Possum
02/04/93	1	2	Uncle Pen	Lngthwise
02/06/93	2	2	Uncle Pen	Lngthwise
02/07/93	1	2	Bouncing	Glide
02/09/93	1	2	Sample	Stash
02/11/93	2	2	Mound	Bouncing
02/12/93	1	2	PoorHeart	FEFY
02/13/93	1	2	YEM	Lngthwise
02/15/93	1	2	PoorHeart	Bike
02/17/93	1	2	MSO	Horn
02/19/93	2	2	Ya Mar	Lawn Boy
02/20/93	1	2	FEFY	Terrapin
02/25/93	4	2	Uncle Pen	FEFY
02/26/93	1	2	Mound	YEM
02/27/93	1	2	Sample	Ya Mar
03/05/93	3	2	MSO	Love You
03/06/93	1	2	Paul&Silas	FEFY
03/08/93	1	2	Stash	My Friend
03/09/93	1	2	Silent	Love You
03/12/93	1	2	Mound	Chalkdust
03/13/93	1	2	Uncle Pen	Mike's
03/14/93	1	2	Rift	Great Gig
03/18/93	3	2	Uncle Pen	Brain
03/21/93	2	2	MSO	Rosie
03/24/93	2	2	Mound	FEFY
03/25/93	1	E	MSO	Adeline
03/26/93	1	2	YEM	Oh Kee
03/28/93	2	2	Paul&Silas	Love You
03/30/93	1	2	Life Boy	Weigh
03/31/93	1	2	Harry	It's Ice
04/01/93	1	2	PoorHeart	Terrapin
04/02/93	1	2	Lizards	Bike
04/10/93	4	2	Glide	Mike's
04/12/93	1	2	It's Ice	YEM
04/13/93	1	2	FEFY	Mike's
04/14/93	1	2	Mound	YEM
04/16/93	1	2	Uncle Pen	Bike
04/17/93	1	2	Suzie	Sqirm Coil
04/18/93	1	2	Mound	Mike's
04/20/93	1	2	Sample	TMWSIY
04/21/93	1	2	Silent	Mike's
04/22/93	1	2	Lizards	YEM
04/23/93	1	2	Paul&Silas	Mike's
04/24/93	1	2	Mound	YEM
04/25/93	1	2	Uncle Pen	Mike's
04/27/93	1	2	Lizards	YEM
04/29/93	1	2	Mound	Reba
04/30/93	1	2	Mound	Harry
05/01/93	1	2	Sqirm Coil	Halley's
05/02/93	1	2	Lizards	Uncle Pen
05/03/93	1	2	RunJim	Love You
05/05/93	1	2	Weigh	Ya Mar
05/06/93	1	2	Uncle Pen	Sqirm Coil
05/07/93	1	2	Fee	YEM
05/08/93	1	2	Jam	Mike's
05/29/93	1	1a	Cavern	YEM
07/17/93	4	2	Sparkle	Mike's
07/21/93	2	1a	RunJim	PurplRain
07/23/93	2	2	Uncle Pen	YEM
08/08/93	12	2	Possum	Love You
08/12/93	3	2	Lawn Boy	Golgi
08/16/93	4	2	PoorHeart	A-Train
08/28/93	7	2	It's Ice	PurplRain
12/29/93	2	2	WalkAway	Brain
04/08/94	6	2	Bouncing	Bowie
04/09/94	1	2	Peaches	Demand
04/11/94	2	2	Sample	YEM
04/13/94	1	2	Reba	Fee
04/17/94	4	2	Reba	Maze
04/18/94	1	2	Gin	Ya Mar
04/21/94	2	2	Scent	Possum
04/25/94	4	2	Bouncing	BBFCM
05/17/94	15	2	Uncle Pen	Sample
05/19/94	1	2	Julius	Harry
05/21/94	2	2	Contact	Julius
05/25/94	3	2	Contact	Julius
06/13/94	8	2	Scent	Love You
06/16/94	2	2	Mockbird	DWD
06/17/94	1	2	Sparkle	Julius
06/22/94	4	2	MSO	Jesus
07/09/94	13	2	Sparkle	Harry
07/14/94	3	2	Sparkle	Harry
10/16/94	11	2	Fluffhead	Antelope
10/25/94	6	2	Jesus	Brain
12/09/94	30	2	Julius	Rosie
➤ 8/17/97	209			

BBFCM [91]

Big Black Furry Creature From Mars [BBFCM]

By Gordon

08/21/87	[19]	3	*OP3	McGrupp
08/29/87	2	1	Makisupa	Flat Fee
09/12/87	2	1	Curtain	*CL1
11/19/87	2	2	Divided	*CL2
01/30/88	1	3	Bike	CamlWalk
05/14/88	8	2	Lizards	Jesus
05/25/88	3	3	IKALittle	Corrina
06/18/88	2	2	Alumni	SwingLow
07/25/88	7	3	Harpua	Sanity
08/06/88	2	2	Sanity	Slave
10/29/88	6	3	Terrapin	Timber Ho
11/03/88	1	2	IDK	Harpua
01/26/89	4	1a	Contact	Fire
02/05/89	2	1a	Harry	Curtis
02/06/89	1	2	Harry	Curtis
03/30/89	8	3	ACDCBag	Satin Doll
10/06/89	54	1a	HwayHell	*CL1
12/09/89	25	2	Contact	*CL2
01/28/90	10	E	Lawn Boy	*CLE
02/25/90	15	2	Fluffhead	*CL2
03/09/90	6	2	Contact	*CL2
04/22/90	17	2	Esther	Harry
04/28/90	3	E	*OPE	*CLE
05/11/90	6	E	*OPE	*CLE
05/15/90	3	1	Caravan	*CL1
06/07/90	7	E	Lawn Boy	*CLE
10/31/90	21	E	Uncle Pen	*CLE
11/08/90	4	2	YEM	*CL2
11/24/90	4	2	GTBT	*CL2
02/03/91	12	E	Jesus	*CLE
02/15/91	5	E	Caravan	*CLE
03/13/91	17	E	A-Train	*CLE
03/23/91	6	E	A-Train	*CLE
04/04/91	6	2	Love You	Magilla
04/12/91	4	E	Contact	Sqirm Coil
04/19/91	5	E	Paul&Silas	*CLE
05/03/91	8	E	A-Train	*CLE
05/11/91	4	E	*OPE	*CLE
05/17/91	3	2	Bike	*CLE
07/11/91	3	E	Contact	*CLE
07/14/91	3	E	Contact	*CLE
07/19/91	3	2	Mango	*CL2
07/24/91	4	E	Contact	*CLE
09/25/91	5	E	All Things	*CLE
09/28/91	3	E	Contact	*CLE
10/11/91	8	E	Adeline	*CLE
11/02/91	15	E	Contact	*CLE
11/12/91	6	E	Ya Mar	Split&Melt
11/23/91	9	E	Jesus	*CLE
03/13/92	12	1	Antelope	Antelope
03/30/92	11	2	YEM	Sqirm Coil
04/06/92	6	E	*OPE	*CLE
04/18/92	8	E	Contact	*CLE
04/24/92	5	E	Contact	*CLE
05/02/92	5	E	Sl Monkey	*CLE
05/08/92	5	E	*OPE	*CLE
06/23/92	11	1a	Uncle Pen	Brain
11/21/92	43	E	BuffaloBill	*CLE
02/07/93	27	E	Contact	*CLE
02/21/93	11	2	Sqirm Coil	*CL2
02/25/93	3	2	Golgi	*CL2
03/06/93	6	2	Rosie	*CL2
03/13/93	4	E	AmGrace	*CLE
03/28/93	12	E	Contact	*CLE
04/17/93	13	E	Adeline	*CLE
05/02/93	12	2	Rosie	*CL2
07/23/93	14	2	YEM	Chalkdust
08/08/93	12	1	*OP1	Foam
12/29/93	16	2	Contact	WalkAway
04/08/94	6	E	Contact	*CLE
04/25/94	15	2	BBJ	*CL2
04/30/94	3	2	PurplRain	*CL2
05/12/94	8	2	Contact	*CL2
05/16/94	3	2	YEM	*CL2
06/16/94	17	2	Contact	PurplRain
06/21/94	4	2	Chalkdust	Dog Faced
07/06/94	12	2	Chalkdust	Harry
07/13/94	4	2	Tweezer	Tweezer
10/27/94	20	2	Contact	DWD
11/03/94	5	2	YEM	Harry
11/13/94	3	2	Mango	AmGrace
11/22/94	7	2	RunJim	I'm Blue
12/01/94	6	2	Tweezer	Makisupa
07/03/95	35	2	Lizards	DayinLife
10/19/95	16	2	Lawn Boy	Kung
10/22/95	3	2	Makisupa	Life Mars
11/18/95	14	2	AArmy	Cavern
11/28/95	6	2	Contact	FunkBitch
12/29/95	17	2	McGrupp	Jam
06/06/96	4	1	Theme	Scent
08/06/96	22	2	DayinLife	PurplRain
➤ 8/17/97	99			

Billy Breathes [33]*

Billy Breathes [Billy]

By Anastasio

09/27/95	[761]	2	Bowie	Keyboard
09/28/95	1	1	RunJim	Scent
09/29/95	1	2	Split&Melt	Cryin
10/03/95	3	2	Harry	Faht
10/06/95	2	1	Stash	Reba
10/13/95	4	1	Maze	I'm Blue
10/19/95	4	1	Split&Melt	Cavern
10/28/95	7	1	Lizards	AArmy
11/14/95	7	1	Foam	Divided
11/19/95	4	2	Tweezer	Scent
11/25/95	4	1	Bowie	Fog
12/04/95	6	2	Antelope	CTB
12/09/95	4	1	Free	Dog Faced
10/16/96	42	1	PoorHeart	Mound
10/18/96	2	1	Divided	Taste
10/25/96	5	1	Maze	Mound
10/29/96	3	1	Train Song	PoorHeart
11/03/96	3	1	RunJim	Sloth
11/18/96	10	1	Taste	Chalkdust
11/22/96	2	2	Maze	SweptAwy
12/28/96	10	1	It's Ice	Ginseng
02/14/97	5	1	It's Ice	Uncle Pen
02/17/97	2	1	Timber Ho	Llama
02/21/97	3	2	ACDCBag	Reba
02/23/97	2	E	*OPE	Rocky Top
03/01/97	4	2	Mango	Theme
06/13/97	3	1	Beauty	Limb
06/25/97	8	1	Taste	ACDCBag
07/03/97	5	2	CTB	Sparkle
07/23/97	8	1	Split&Melt	Possum
07/26/97	2	1	Stash	CTB
08/10/97	9	1	CTB	Split&Melt
08/14/97	4	1	Train Song	Antelope
➤ 8/17/97	2			

Bouncing [315]

Bouncing Around the Room [Bouncing]

By Anastasio/Marshall

01/20/90	[157]	1a	Suzie	Reba
01/27/90	3	1	MSO	Wilson
01/28/90	1	2	Antelope	Caravan
02/09/90	7	1	WalkAway	ACDCBag
02/10/90	1	1	Gin	Possum
02/17/90	3	1a	Split&Melt	Foam
02/23/90	2	1	WalkAway	Antelope
02/25/90	2	1	Sqirm Coil	Bowie
03/09/90	6	1	Ya Mar	Forbin's
03/11/90	1	2	MSO	Dinner
04/13/90	11	1	Dinner	Fluffhead
04/20/90	3	1	Dinner	Forbin
04/22/90	2	2	Dinner	YEM
04/25/90	1	2	Dinner	Mike's
04/26/90	1	1	Dinner	IDK
04/28/90	1	1	Dinner	Possum
04/29/90	1	1a	Dinner	Uncle Pen
05/04/90	2	1	TMWSIY	Possum
05/06/90	1	1	Possum	Uncle Pen
05/10/90	1	1	Uncle Pen	Divided
05/11/90	1	1	Uncle Pen	Possum
05/13/90	2	1	Dinner	RunJim
05/19/90	2	2	Dinner	Rift
05/23/90	1	1	Uncle Pen	Possum
05/24/90	1	1	Sloth	Tweezer
05/31/90	1	1a	Dinner	Caravan
06/01/90	1	1a	*OP1	YEM

06/05/90	1	2	Dinner	MSO
06/07/90	1	1	Dinner	Tweezer
06/08/90	1	1	Foam	YEM
06/09/90	1	1	Dinner	Tweezer
06/16/90	1	1	Uncle Pen	Timber Ho
09/13/90	1	1	Paul&Silas	Possum
09/14/90	1	1	Suzie	Landlady
09/16/90	2	1a	Dinner	Sloth
09/22/90	3	2	Uncle Pen	Stash
09/28/90	1	1	Landlady	Oh Kee
10/01/90	1	1	Dinner	Tweezer
10/05/90	2	1	Asse Fest	Antelope
10/06/90	1	1a	Dinner	Foam
10/07/90	1	2	BurAlive	Tweezer
10/08/90	1	1	Landlady	Foam
10/12/90	1	1	Dinner	Uncle Pen
10/30/90	2	1	Landlady	Donna
10/31/90	1	1	Stash	YEM
11/02/90	1	1	Landlady	Divided
11/03/90	1	1	Dinner	Llama
11/04/90	1	1	Curtain	Tube
11/08/90	1	2	Dinner	YEM
11/10/90	1	1	Landlady	RunJim
11/17/90	2	1	RunJim	YEM
11/24/90	1	1	Llama	Stash
11/30/90	2	1	Dinner	Tweezer
12/07/90	3	1	Stash	Landlady
12/08/90	1	2	Dinner	Antelope
12/28/90	1	E	*OPE	HwayHell
12/29/90	1	2	Dinner	Destiny
12/31/90	1	1	Landlady	MSO
02/01/91	1	1	Split&Melt	Bowie
02/03/91	2	2	Split&Melt	Oh Kee
02/07/91	1	1	Split&Melt	Sqirm Coil
02/08/91	1	2	Horn	Lizards
02/09/91	1	2	Landlady	Harry
02/14/91	1	2	Alumni	IDK
02/16/91	2	1	Landlady	Llama
02/21/91	3	2	Landlady	Stash
02/26/91	4	2	Stash	Landlady
02/27/91	1	1	Split&Melt	Fire
02/28/91	1	1	Landlady	Foam
03/01/91	1	1	Dinner	BurAlive
03/06/91	2	1	MSO	Bowie
03/13/91	4	2	Split&Melt	MSO
03/15/91	1	1	Dinner	Oh Kee
03/17/91	2	1	Carolina	Landlady
03/22/91	2	1	Destiny	Split&Melt
03/28/91	2	1a	Landlady	YEM
04/05/91	6	1	Landlady	Divided
04/11/91	2	1	Dinner	Foam
04/19/91	6	1	Dinner	Divided
04/20/91	1	1	Chalkdust	YEM
04/26/91	4	2	Split&Melt	MSO
04/27/91	1	E	*OPE	GTBT
05/02/91	1	1	Foam	Landlady
05/03/91	1	1	*OP1	Foam
05/12/91	3	1	Chalkdust	Dinner
05/16/91	1	2	Dinner	Landlady
05/25/91	3	1	Chalkdust	YEM
07/12/91	2	1	Dinner	BurAlive
07/13/91	1	1	Split&Melt	Frankstein
07/14/91	1	2	Dinner	Split&Melt
07/15/91	1	1a	Stash	Mike's
07/19/91	2	1	Landlady	Bowie
07/21/91	2	1	Landlady	Mike's
07/23/91	1	1	Flat Fee	Mike's
07/24/91	1	2	MSO	FunkBitch
07/26/91	2	1	BurAlive	Landlady
08/03/91	2	2	Chalkdust	Tweezer
09/26/91	2	1	Llama	Divided
09/28/91	2	1	Landlady	Chalkdust
10/02/91	2	1	Brother	Chalkdust
10/03/91	1	1	It's Ice	Llama
10/04/91	1	2	Brother	Foam
10/06/91	2	1	Divided	PoorHeart
10/10/91	2	1	Split&Melt	Landlady
10/11/91	1	1	Llama	RunJim
10/13/91	2	2	Jesus	Love You
10/15/91	1	2	Brother	RunJim
10/17/91	1	1	Landlady	Divided
10/19/91	2	1	Chalkdust	MSO
10/24/91	2	2	Dinner	TweezRep
10/27/91	2	1	Brother	Harry
11/02/91	4	1	Foam	Forbin's
11/07/91	2	2	Brother	MSO
11/12/91	4	1	Brother	Tube
11/14/91	2	E	*OPE	GTBT
11/15/91	1	2	Love You	Possum
11/21/91	4	1	Chalkdust	PoorHeart
11/23/91	2	1	Brother	Golgi
11/30/91	2	2	It's Ice	MSO
12/04/91	1	1	Dinner	Bowie
12/05/91	1	1	It's Ice	Possum
12/31/91	3	2	Brother	BurAlive
03/06/92	1	2	Llama	NICU
03/12/92	3	2	It's Ice	Sqirm Coil
03/14/92	2	2	Split&Melt	Oh Kee
03/17/92	1	1	Rift	Antelope
03/21/92	3	E	*OPE	Rocky Top
03/27/92	4	1	Glide	Antelope
03/28/92	1	1	Rift	Landlady
03/30/92	1	2	Rosie	TweezRep
04/01/92	2	1	Foam	Brother
04/04/92	2	1	Chalkdust	It's Ice
04/07/92	3	1	Split&Melt	Rift
04/12/92	2	2	Split&Melt	Rift
04/16/92	3	1	It's Ice	Split&Melt
04/17/92	1	1	Maze	Landlady
04/21/92	3	1	NICU	Bowie
04/23/92	2	1	Llama	It's Ice
04/25/92	2	1	Chalkdust	Rift
04/29/92	1	1	Rift	A-Train
05/02/92	3	1	Maze	Stash
05/03/92	1	2	Dinner	Oh Kee
05/05/92	1	2	Chalkdust	All Things
05/06/92	1	2	All Things	Uncle Pen
05/08/92	2	1	All Things	Bowie
05/12/92	3	1	Dinner	BurAlive
05/14/92	1	1	My Friend	Antelope
05/15/92	1	1a	Stash	Love You
05/16/92	1	1	Split&Melt	MSO
05/18/92	2	1	Maze	Divided
06/20/92	2	1a	BurAlive	Foam
06/27/92	3	1a	Chalkdust	Uncle Pen
07/10/92	5	1a	*OP1	Llama
07/12/92	2	1a	Chalkdust	Divided
07/16/92	3	1	Dinner	Maze
07/17/92	1	1a	Maze	RunJim
07/22/92	4	1a	PoorHeart	Maze
07/28/92	5	1a	Chalkdust	Uncle Pen
07/31/92	2	1a	Chalkdust	Oh Kee
08/17/92	6	2	My Friend	Bowie
08/27/92	6	1a	Chalkdust	Landlady
08/29/92	2	1a	Rift	Maze
10/30/92	2	1a	Maze	Rift
11/19/92	1	2	Weekpaug	It's Ice
11/21/92	2	1	It's Ice	Maze
11/23/92	2	1	Mound	Memories
11/28/92	3	2	TMWSIY	Sqirm Coil
11/30/92	1	1	Foam	PoorHeart
12/01/92	1	1	Split&Melt	Rift
12/03/92	2	1	Split&Melt	Uncle Pen
12/05/92	2	1	Chalkdust	Rift
12/07/92	2	1	Split&Melt	YEM
12/11/92	3	2	Esther	Axilla
12/12/92	1	1	All Things	Antelope
12/13/92	1	2	Mound	Llama
12/28/92	1	1	It's Ice	Rift
12/31/92	3	1	Maze	Rift
02/04/93	2	1	Foam	Maze
02/06/93	2	1	Wedge	Antelope
02/09/93	2	1	Bowie	PoorHeart
02/11/93	2	2	BBJ	Love You
02/13/93	2	1	Bowie	PoorHeart
02/17/93	2	1	It's Ice	Fluffhead
02/21/93	4	1	Dinner	Antelope
02/23/93	2	1	Rift	Split&Melt
02/25/93	1	1	Stash	IDK
02/27/93	2	1	Maze	It's Ice
03/03/93	2	1	Foam	Maze
03/06/93	2	1	PYITE	Maze
03/09/93	2	1	Foam	Maze
03/13/93	2	1	FunkBitch	Maze
03/17/93	3	1	Foam	Stash
03/19/93	2	1	Foam	Rift
03/22/93	2	1	Stash	Rift
03/25/93	2	1	Possum	Stash
03/27/93	2	2	It's Ice	Chalkdust
03/31/93	3	2	Maze	Uncle Pen
04/02/93	2	1	Foam	Divided
04/10/93	4	2	Maze	Rift
04/12/93	1	1	Tube	PoorHeart
04/14/93	2	1	Maze	It's Ice
04/17/93	2	1	Foam	Stash
04/20/93	2	1	Stash	It's Ice
04/22/93	2	2	Llama	All Things
04/25/93	3	1	Possum	It's Ice
04/27/93	1	1	Foam	Rift
04/30/93	2	1	Maze	PoorHeart
05/02/93	2	2	Uncle Pen	Antelope
05/05/93	2	1	Stash	It's Ice
05/07/93	2	2	Rift	Maze
05/29/93	2	1a	Chalkdust	Rift
07/16/93	3	2	Maze	YEM
07/21/93	3	1a	Rift	RunJim
07/24/93	3	1	Mango	Sqirm Coil
07/29/93	4	2	Maze	It's Ice
08/03/93	4	2	Maze	It's Ice
08/07/93	2	1	Llama	PoorHeart
08/11/93	3	2	All Things	Rift
08/15/93	4	2	Landlady	Maze
08/20/93	3	1	Maze	It's Ice
08/24/93	2	1	All Things	It's Ice
08/28/93	3	1	Llama	Foam
12/29/93	2	2	Maze	Fluffhead
04/05/94	4	1	Julius	Rift
04/08/94	2	2	Harry	BBJ
04/10/94	2	E	*OPE	Golgi
04/15/94	4	1	Chalkdust	It's Ice
04/16/94	1	2	Julius	YEM
04/20/94	3	1	Julius	Axilla 2
04/25/94	5	2	Divided	BBJ
04/28/94	1	1a	DWD	It's Ice
05/02/94	3	1	Split&Melt	DWD
05/04/94	2	2	Antelope	YEM
05/08/94	3	1	DWD	Stash
05/13/94	3	2	Chalkdust	Split&Melt
05/16/94	2	1	DWD	Stash
05/22/94	5	2	DWD	It's Ice
05/27/94	4	1	Foam	Bowie
05/28/94	1	1	Foam	Stash
06/16/94	7	1	*OP1	Rift
06/18/94	2	E	*OPE	TweezRep
06/23/94	4	1	Foam	DWD
06/30/94	5	1	Scent	Frankstein
07/03/94	3	2	Lizards	It's Ice
07/06/94	2	1	Julius	YEM
07/10/94	3	2	Weekpaug	Sqirm Coil
07/14/94	2	1	RunJim	PYITE
07/15/94	1	2	Bowie	Reba
10/09/94	4	2	Bowie	Scent
10/12/94	2	2	Bowie	Scent
10/15/94	3	2	Long Time	Suzie
10/23/94	6	2	RunJim	Halley's
10/26/94	2	2	Rift	Reba
10/31/94	4	3	Bowie	Slave
11/04/94	3	1	It's Ice	Bowie
11/14/94	3	1	Split&Melt	Landlady
11/17/94	2	1	Maze	Wilson
11/22/94	4	1	IDK	DWD
11/25/94	2	1	Reba	Split&Melt
11/30/94	3	1	DWD	I'm Blue
12/04/94	4	2	Maze	Reba
12/28/94	6	1	Gin	Axilla 2
12/31/94	3	2	Maze	Mike's
06/08/95	3	2	Free	Tweezer
06/13/95	3	1	Foam	Stash
06/15/95	2	E	*OPE	Frankstein
06/25/95	8	E	*OPE	Slave
07/01/95	5	1	Split&Melt	Chalkdust
10/08/95	12	E	*OPE	Rocky Top
10/20/95	7	2	I'm Blue	Antelope
10/24/95	3	2	Theme	YEM
10/27/95	2	2	Keyboard	Possum
11/10/95	5	1	*OP1	RunJim
11/12/95	2	1	Llama	Guelah
11/18/95	4	1	Dinner	Reba
11/22/95	3	2	Llama	YEM
11/25/95	2	1	Fog	Rift
11/28/95	1	1	Dinner	Foam
12/02/95	4	1	Fog	Possum
12/04/95	1	E	*OPE	Rocky Top
12/07/95	2	1	Guyute	Possum
12/09/95	2	1	Rift	Free
12/15/95	4	1	CTB	Free
12/17/95	2	2	*OP2	Maze
12/29/95	2	2	La Grange	Fire
07/07/96	8	1a	Divided	Curtain
07/09/96	1	1a	Mike's	CharZero
07/11/96	2	1a	Harry	ASZ
07/18/96	5	1a	CTB	Stash
07/22/96	3	1a	Maze	Stash
08/07/96	8	E	*OPE	Golgi
10/19/96	10	2	Slave	Split&Melt
10/22/96	2	1	RunJim	It's Ice
10/29/96	5	1	Taste	Stash
11/03/96	3	1	Theme	CharZero
11/08/96	3	2	Maze	Simple
11/13/96	3	1	DWD	It's Ice
11/15/96	2	1	Divided	CharZero
11/24/96	6	1	All Things	Reba
11/30/96	4	1	All Things	Stash
12/02/96	2	1	ACDCBag	YEM
12/28/96	3	2	Maze	TMWSIY
02/16/97	6	1	Split&Melt	Crosseyed
02/20/97	3	2	Stash	Free
06/20/97	14	2	Twist	Julius
06/27/97	5	1a	Taste	CharZero
06/29/97	1	1a	Taste	Beauty
07/05/97	4	1a	Julius	Uncle Pen
07/11/97	4	1a	Chalkdust	Stash
07/22/97	2	1	Stash	Vultures
07/26/97	3	E	*OPE	Cavern
07/30/97	2	2	Bowie	Uncle Pen
08/03/97	3	E	*OPE	Slave
08/14/87	7	E	*OPE	Rocky Top
08/17/97	2	1	Maze	Tweezer

➢ 8/17/97 0

Brother [45]*

Brother [Brother]

By Anastasio/Marshall

09/25/91	[335]	1	*OP1	PoorHeart
09/26/91	1	2	Sqirm Coil	Sparkle
09/28/91	2	1	Foam	Golgi
10/02/91	2	1	Reba	Bouncing
10/04/91	2	2	MSO	Bouncing
10/06/91	2	1	ACDCBag	Terrapin
10/10/91	1	2	*OP2	Reba
10/12/91	2	1	Dinner	Brain
10/15/91	2	2	*OP2	Bouncing
10/18/91	2	2	*OP2	Uncle Pen
10/27/91	5	1	Fluffhead	Bouncing
10/31/91	3	1	Memories	Ya Mar
11/07/91	4	2	*OP2	Bouncing
11/08/91	1	1	Mango	Eliza
11/09/91	1	1	Horn	Adeline
11/12/91	2	1	Uncle Pen	Bouncing
11/14/91	2	1	Sparkle	Mango
11/16/91	2	2	Gin	YEM
11/19/91	1	1	Sparkle	Horn
11/20/91	1	E	Magilla	*CLE
11/22/91	2	1	Sparkle	Fee
11/23/91	1	1	Uncle Pen	Bouncing
11/30/91	2	1	Sqirm Coil	Paul&Silas
12/04/91	1	1	PoorHeart	Sqirm Coil
12/07/91	3	2	Sparkle	Lizards
12/31/91	1	2	*OP2	Bouncing
03/07/92	2	1	*OP1	My Mind
03/11/92	1	2	My Mind	BabyLem
03/13/92	1	2	Wilson	Horse
03/20/92	4	1	Reba	Glide
03/24/92	2	2	Mango	Uncle Pen
03/26/92	2	2	PoorHeart	TMWSIY
04/01/92	5	1	Bouncing	All Things
04/06/92	4	1	Reba	Esther
04/17/92	7	2	*OP2	YEM
04/25/92	7	1	Reba	Tela
05/06/92	7	1	Tela	Forbin's
05/17/92	9	2	All Things	Sanity
07/14/92	14	1	Horn	IDK
08/02/93	143	1	PoorHeart	Oh Kee
08/17/96	257	2	It's Ice	Fluffhead
10/23/96	7	2	*OP2	Ya Mar
10/31/96	5	3	*OP3	Also Sprac
11/11/96	7	1	Sparkle	Theme
11/30/96	12	2	Glide	Contact

➢ 8/17/97 61

Buffalo Bill [4]*

Buffalo Bill [BuffaloBill]

By Anastasio/Marshall

11/21/92	[482]	E	*OPE	BBFCM
10/29/94	224	1	Split&Melt	Makisupa
12/31/94	31	2	Mike's	Mike's
08/17/97	204	3	*OP3	NICU

➢ 8/17/97 0

Bundle of Joy [5]*

Bundle of Joy [BundleJoy]

By Anastasio

Now played as part of Fluff's Travels.

08/21/87	[19]	2	Harpua	Harpua
08/29/87	1	3	Harpua	Harpua
09/12/88	25	1a	Avenu	CamlWalk
10/20/89	43	1	Harpua	Forbin's
11/03/89	7	1	Clod	YEM

➢ 8/17/97 803 (as a stand-alone song)

Buried Alive [111]

Buried Alive [BurAlive]

By Anastasio

09/13/90	[222]	1	Minute	Paul&Silas
09/14/90	1	2	Sqirm Coil	Tweezer
09/15/90	1	1	*OP1	Divided
09/22/90	4	1	*OP1	Horn
10/07/90	6	2	*OP2	Bouncing
10/30/90	4	2	Terrapin	Bowie
10/31/90	1	1	*OP1	Possum
11/02/90	1	1	Possum	Possum
11/10/90	4	1	MSO	Lizards
11/16/90	1	1	Suzie	Foam
11/17/90	1	2	*OP2	Fluffhead
11/24/90	1	1	*OP1	Possum
11/26/90	1	1	Reba	YEM
12/08/90	5	1	*OP1	RunJim
12/29/90	2	2	*OP2	RunJim
12/31/90	1	1	Auld	Possum
02/08/91	5	1	Reba	Forbin's
02/09/91	1	2	Golgi	Fluffhead
02/14/91	1	1	McGrupp	Reba
02/15/91	1	1	Fee	Mango
02/16/91	1	2	Reba	RunJim
02/26/91	7	2	*OP2	RunJim
02/27/91	1	2	Suzie	Cavern
03/01/91	2	1	Bouncing	Mike's
03/15/91	7	2	*OP2	Possum
03/16/91	1	2	Magilla	Sqirm Coil
03/22/91	3	2	Sqirm Coil	Cavern
04/12/91	11	2	Tela	Reba
04/16/91	3	2	Magilla	Uncle Pen

Stories Behind the Songs
(Continued)

answered the requests of many when the song appeared at The Clifford Ball, featuring ice cream kings Ben and Jerry on lyrics. It was played twice more in the fall of 1996.

Buffalo Bill: As described by Trey in an issue of the *Döniac Schvice*, Buffalo Bill chronicles one of Fishman's backcountry adventures. After several years in hibernation, it made a return appearance at the Great Went.

Cavern: This song's lyrics came about as a result of a series of email exchanges between Tom Marshall and Scott Herman, who each added a line at a time. The original version of this song performed in 1990 included the line "a penile erector" in place of the current "a picture of nectar." The band changed it when Page said he felt silly singing the first version and they realized the change could honor Nectar Rorris, who booked Phish at his Burlington restaurant/bar Nectar's in the band's formative years. The original Cavern also had an extra verse, performed most recently on 4/4/94.

Chalk Dust Torture: Released as the only single off *Picture of Nectar* in 1992, this was the first Phish song to receive any radio airplay to speak of outside of Vermont. Two years later, appearing for the first time on Letterman in late 1994, the band performed the single worst version of this song ever at the request of Sir Dave, who had heard it on New York radio.

Colonel Forbin's Ascent: A Gamehendge song usually followed by a "Forbin's Rap," a descriptive narrative by Trey which frequently involves the audience in a trip to Gamehendge. (The song Famous Mockingbird follows the narrative.) Colonel Forbin's Ascent chronicles Col. Forbin's trek up the highest mountain in Gamehendge in search of the prophet Icculus, who lives atop it.

The Curtain: On 8/21/87, Trey explained that the fall of televangelist Jimmy Swaggart inspired the lyrics to this song (additional lyrics for The Curtain apparently exist, but are not documented on any tapes). In the late 1980s, The Curtain contained a slow

05/02/91	9	2	IDK	Possum
05/04/91	2	2	Mockbird	Harry
05/10/91	2	1	Gin	Lizards
05/16/91	3	1	*OP1	Golgi
05/18/91	2	1	*OP1	Golgi
07/12/91	3	1	Bouncing	Flat Fee
07/20/91	6	2	*OP2	Reba
07/24/91	3	1	Sqirm Coil	Split&Melt
07/26/91	2	1	TMWSIY	Bouncing
08/03/91	2	3	Lizards	Possum
09/27/91	3	1	Reba	Esther
10/03/91	4	2	Destiny	Sqirm Coil
10/27/91	15	1	Mango	Guelah
11/12/91	11	1	*OP1	Golgi
11/20/91	6	1	*OP1	Possum
12/07/91	9	2	*OP2	Reba
12/31/91	1	2	Bouncing	Auld
03/12/92	4	1	Reba	Rift
03/17/92	3	1	*OP1	Possum
03/21/92	3	2	*OP2	Oh Kee
03/26/92	3	2	*OP2	Oh Kee
04/07/92	10	1	*OP1	Possum
04/16/92	5	1	*OP1	Possum
04/19/92	3	1	*OP1	NICU
05/01/92	8	2	Sanity	Wilson
05/07/92	5	1	PoorHeart	My Friend
05/12/92	4	1	Bouncing	Uncle Pen
06/20/92	7	1a	*OP1	Bouncing
08/17/92	31	1	*OP1	PoorHeart
08/24/92	4	1a	*OP1	PoorHeart
11/22/92	10	1	*OP1	Oh Kee
11/25/92	2	1	*OP1	PoorHeart
11/30/92	3	2	*OP2	RunJim
12/13/92	12	1	*OP1	Wilson
12/31/92	4	1	*OP1	PoorHeart
02/06/93	4	2	Lngthwise	Possum
02/07/93	1	1	Suzie	PoorHeart
02/11/93	3	1	Suzie	PoorHeart
02/17/93	4	1	*OP1	Possum
02/21/93	4	1	Suzie	PYITE
02/25/93	3	1	*OP1	PoorHeart
03/02/93	3	1	*OP1	PoorHeart
03/05/93	2	1	*OP1	PoorHeart
03/12/93	4	1	*OP1	PoorHeart
03/16/93	3	1	Adeline	PoorHeart
03/27/93	9	2	*OP2	Halley's
03/30/93	2	1	*OP1	PoorHeart
04/02/93	3	1	*OP1	PoorHeart
04/09/93	3	2	*OP2	Suzie
04/14/93	4	1	*OP1	PoorHeart
04/21/93	5	1	*OP1	PoorHeart
04/27/93	5	1	*OP1	PoorHeart
05/03/93	5	1	*OP1	Rift
05/07/93	3	1	*OP1	PoorHeart
07/16/93	5	1	Ya Mar	FEFY
07/18/93	2	1	*OP1	Rift
07/23/93	3	1	*OP1	Rift
08/06/93	10	2	*OP2	Tweezer
08/11/93	14	1	*OP1	RunJim
08/13/93	2	2	*OP2	Rift
08/21/93	6	1	*OP1	PoorHeart
08/25/93	2	2	*OP2	Possum
04/04/94	7	2	If I Could	Landlady
04/13/94	7	1	*OP1	PoorHeart
05/04/94	17	2	Landlady	Julius
05/10/94	4	1	*OP1	PoorHeart
05/16/94	4	1	*OP1	PoorHeart
05/26/94	8	1	*OP1	PoorHeart
06/13/94	7	1	*OP1	PoorHeart
06/23/94	8	1	*OP1	PoorHeart
07/13/94	14	1	*OP1	PoorHeart
10/14/94	10	1	*OP1	Sample
11/22/94	25	1	*OP1	PoorHeart
12/02/94	7	2	Bowie	Julius
12/03/94	1	2	Suzie	Gumbo
10/15/95	47	1	*OP1	PoorHeart
10/29/95	10	1	*OP1	PoorHeart
12/01/95	18	1	*OP1	DWD
12/16/95	11	1	*OP1	ACDCBag
12/28/95	2	2	Wilson	Tweezer
10/16/96	36	1	Wilson	PoorHeart
11/09/96	17	1	*OP1	PoorHeart
02/26/97	32	2	*OP2	PoorHeart
➢ 8/17/97	**42**			

Bye Bye Foot [4]
Bye Bye Foot [Bye Bye]
By Fishman

06/14/97	[905]	1	Limb	Free
06/20/97	3	2	Ghost	Ginseng
07/22/97	16	1	Vultures	Taste
08/10/97	12	1	Split&Melt	Ginseng
➢ 8/17/97	**7**			

Camel Walk [15]
Camel Walk [CamlWalk]
By Holdsworth

03/04/85	[1]	1a	Anarchy	Ganja
10/17/85	2	1a	Anarchy	Antelope
04/15/86	4	1a	Anarchy	Alumni
10/15/86	1	1a	SwingLow	Shaggy
10/31/86	1	1	Sally	Golgi
03/23/87	4	1	WDYLM	Golgi
08/21/87	3	1	Wilson	*CL1
11/19/87	8	3	A-Train	La Grange
01/30/88	1	3	BBFCM	Harry
07/25/88	20	3	Icculus	*CL3
09/12/88	5	1a	BundleJoy	Harry
02/24/89	15	2	YEM	*CL2
07/02/95	691	1	Julius	Reba
02/26/97	140	1	*OP1	Llama
08/14/97	40	2	Jam	Taste
➢ 8/17/97	**2**			

Carini [5]
Carini Had a Lumpy Head [Carini]
By Phish

02/17/97	[892]	2	DWD	Jam
02/23/97	5	1	*OP1	Axilla
02/26/97	2	1	Tube	RockaW
02/28/97	1	1	*OP1	Paul&Silas
03/01/97	1	2	*OP2	Dinner
➢ 8/17/97	**40**			

CTB [54]*
Cars Trucks Buses [CTB]
By McConnell

09/27/95	[761]	2	*OP2	ACDCBag
09/28/95	1	1	*OP1	RunJim
09/29/95	1	1	Str Design	YEM
09/30/95	1	1	My Friend	Chess
10/02/95	1	2	Wilson	Bathtub
10/05/95	2	1	Silent	Str Design
10/07/95	2	1	Makisupa	Split&Melt
10/08/95	1	1	Keyboard	Timber Ho
10/14/95	3	1	ACDCBag	Kung
10/19/95	3	1	*OP1	RunJim
10/21/95	2	1	Wilson	Kung
10/25/95	3	2	Life Mars	Mike's
10/29/95	3	1	PYITE	Horse
11/11/95	4	1	*OP1	Mike's
11/16/95	4	1	*OP1	RunJim
11/22/95	4	1	*OP1	Wilson
11/30/95	5	2	*OP2	Tweezer
12/04/95	3	2	Billy	YEM
12/15/95	8	1	Suspicious	Bouncing
12/29/95	4	1	Makisupa	Bathtub
04/26/96	3	1a	Stash	YEM
07/09/96	6	1a	Taste	Mike's
07/18/96	7	1a	Julius	Bouncing
08/14/96	15	2	Silnt	Tweezer
08/17/96	2	1	Reba	Lizards
10/16/96	1	1	*OP1	DWD
10/18/96	2	1	Old Home	Stash
10/21/96	2	1	Sample	Sloth
10/26/96	4	1	Julius	Wolfman's
10/29/96	2	1	Guelah	Taste
11/06/96	4	1	Split&Melt	FEFY
11/11/96	4	1	Guelah	ACDCBag
11/14/96	2	1	Wolfman's	Free
11/18/96	3	1	*OP1	Timber Ho
11/23/96	3	1	Guelah	Divided
11/29/96	3	1	NICU	CharZero
12/01/96	2	1	Cavern	CharZero
12/06/96	3	1	YEM	DWD
12/31/96	4	1	PYITE	Stash
02/13/97	1	2	Julius	My Soul
02/16/97	2	2	Sample	Free
02/20/97	3	2	Sample	CharZero
02/28/97	6	1	My Soul	Peaches
03/18/97	3	1	Harry	Suzie
06/14/97	2	1	My Soul	Limb
07/03/97	12	2	Ghost	Billy
07/06/97	2	1	Silent	Scent
07/09/97	1	2	My Soul	YEM
07/26/97	1	7	Billy	Dirt
07/30/97	2	1	Piper	CharZero
08/06/97	4	2	Caspian	Sample
08/08/97	1	1	*OP1	Gumbo
08/10/97	2	1	Dirt	Billy
08/14/97	3	1	Free	Tela
➢ 8/17/97	**2**			

Catapult [21]
Catapult [Catapult]
By Gordon

04/17/92	[413]	1	Bowie	Bowie
04/21/92	3	2	Weigh	Lively Up
02/10/93	96	1	IDK	Antelope
05/12/94	133	1	*OP1	Rift
05/26/94	11	1	It's Ice	Divided
06/29/94	19	1	Silent	Bowie
07/16/94	13	2	Antelope	Antelope
10/15/94	8	2	YEM	YEM
10/23/94	6	1	Stash	Stash
10/26/94	2	2	YEM	Rosie
11/30/94	21	2	Mike's	McGrupp
12/08/94	7	1	Simple	Simple
06/16/95	15	1	Dog Faced	Split&Melt
10/14/95	27	1	Stash	AArmy
10/22/95	6	1	Possum	Curtain
11/24/95	18	2	Reba	Scent
12/01/95	5	2	Bowie	Bowie
10/27/96	57	1	Scent	Scent
11/16/96	13	2	Kung	Axilla
11/23/96	4	2	Weekpaug	Waste
03/02/97	26	1	Antelope	Life Mars
➢ 8/17/97	**39**			

Cavern [292]*
Cavern [Cavern]
By Anastasio/Marshall/Herman

03/28/90	[185]	2	Rift	HwayHell
04/05/90	2	2	Fee	Mike's
04/06/90	1	1	*OP1	YEM
04/12/90	5	1	A-Train	Jesus
04/20/90	4	1	Ya Mar	Dinner
04/22/90	2	1	IDK	MSO
04/26/90	2	2	Suzie	Adeline
04/28/90	1	2	*OP2	Harry
09/14/90	19	2	Magilla	Lizards
10/08/90	12	1	Foam	Reba
10/12/90	1	1	Uncle Pen	Esther
10/30/90	2	1	Uncle Pen	Sqirm Coil
10/31/90	1	1	MSO	Antelope
11/02/90	1	1	Esther	Asse Fest
11/10/90	4	1	RunJim	MSO
11/17/90	2	1	YEM	Eliza
12/01/90	4	1	*OP1	Landlady
12/08/90	3	1	Divided	Landlady
12/29/90	2	2	Lizards	Stash
02/03/91	4	2	Landlady	Mango
02/07/91	1	2	Uncle Pen	Love You
02/08/91	1	2	Mango	Lawn Boy
02/09/91	1	2	Harry	Love You
02/14/91	1	1	Destiny	Mango
02/16/91	2	1	Divided	A-Train
02/21/91	3	2	Golgi	Landlady
02/27/91	5	2	BurAlive	Sqirm Coil
02/28/91	1	1	Weekpaug	TMWSIY
03/01/91	1	1	Divided	Sqirm Coil
03/06/91	2	1	Possum	Divided
03/13/91	4	1	YEM	Divided
03/15/91	1	2	Paul&Silas	Destiny
03/16/91	1	2	Sqirm Coil	YEM
03/22/91	3	1	BurAlive	Reba
03/23/91	1	2	Uncle Pen	Bowie
03/28/91	1	1a	Divided	Landlady
04/05/91	6	1	Divided	Magilla
04/11/91	2	1	RunJim	Paul&Silas
04/12/91	1	2	Fluffhead	Tela
04/16/91	3	1	Paul&Silas	Mango
04/19/91	2	1	Divided	Lizards
04/20/91	1	2	Paul&Silas	TMWSIY
04/21/91	1	2	Harry	IDK
04/27/91	4	1	RunJim	Landlady
05/02/91	1	1	Sqirm Coil	Bowie
05/04/91	2	1	Suzie	Reba
05/10/91	1	1	Bowie	Ya Mar
05/16/91	2	1	Foam	Divided
05/17/91	1	2	Magilla	Bike
05/18/91	1	1	Divided	Possum
05/25/91	1	1a	YEM	Sqirm Coil
07/11/91	1	2	Dinner	TMWSIY
07/12/91	1	1	Rocky Top	Bowie
07/14/91	2	2	Magilla	Antelope
07/15/91	1	1a	Lizards	Sqirm Coil
07/18/91	1	1	A-Train	Mike's
07/19/91	1	1	Fee	Sqirm Coil
07/21/91	2	1	*OP1	Divided
07/23/91	1	2	Reba	Lizards
07/24/91	1	1	Landlady	Tela
07/25/91	1	1	Adeline	Antelope
07/26/91	1	1	Suzie	TMWSIY
07/27/91	1	1a	Suzie	PoorHeart
08/03/91	1	2	Esther	IDK
09/25/91	1	2	Sparkle	Jesus
09/27/91	2	1	RunJim	Reba
09/28/91	1	2	Sparkle	Antelope
09/29/91	1	1a	*OP1	Divided
10/02/91	2	1	PoorHeart	Reba
10/03/91	1	1	Divided	Possum
10/04/91	1	1	PoorHeart	Divided
10/06/91	2	2	IDK	Sqirm Coil
10/10/91	1	2	PoorHeart	Antelope
10/11/91	1	2	Curtain	Foam
10/17/91	4	1	Divided	PoorHeart
10/18/91	1	2	MSO	*CL2

10/28/91	6	1	RunJim	Reba
11/01/91	3	2	Tela	PoorHeart
11/07/91	3	1	Sparkle	It's Ice
11/12/91	4	2	Magilla	Love You
11/13/91	1	1	Esther	Divided
11/15/91	2	1	Sparkle	Curtain
11/16/91	1	1	Ya Mar	*CL1
11/19/91	1	2	Dinner	Bowie
11/20/91	1	2	Bike	*CL2
11/22/91	2	1	Possum	Sparkle
11/24/91	2	2	Divided	Mango
11/30/91	1	1	Divided	Sqirm Coil
12/04/91	1	1	RunJim	PoorHeart
12/05/91	1	E	Glide	*CLE
12/07/91	2	1	Curtain	Mango
12/31/91	1	2	Reba	MSO
03/06/92	1	1	Rift	Sparkle
03/11/92	2	1	Divided	*CL1
03/12/92	1	2	MSO	*CL2
03/14/92	2	1	RunJim	Reba
03/17/92	1	1	Possum	Sparkle
03/20/92	2	2	Mango	Uncle Pen
03/24/92	2	2	Harry	*CL2
03/26/92	2	2	Lizards	Rosie
03/28/92	2	1	Glide	*CL1
03/30/92	1	1	RunJim	*CL1
03/31/92	1	2	Lizards	Dinner
04/04/92	3	2	Harpua	*CL2
04/06/92	2	2	Uncle Pen	*CL2
04/09/92	2	2	Terrapin	*CL2
04/12/92	1	2	Harry	*CL2
04/15/92	2	1	Uncle Pen	IDK
04/17/92	2	1	IDK	Reba
04/19/92	2	1	My Friend	Maze
04/21/92	1	E	Adeline	*CLE
04/23/92	2	1	*OP1	Curtain
04/24/92	1	2	Bowie	Ya Mar
04/30/92	3	E	Carolina	*CLE
05/02/92	2	2	Rosie	*CL2
05/05/92	2	2	Sqirm Coil	*CL2
05/06/92	1	1	Sparkle	*CL1
05/08/92	2	1	Curtain	Reba
05/10/92	2	1a	Uncle Pen	Reba
05/12/92	1	2	Llama	RunJim
05/14/92	1	2	Glide	Rift
05/15/92	1	1a	Foam	Sparkle
05/16/92	1	1	Lizards	Bowie
05/17/92	1	2	Harry	*CL2
05/18/92	1	2	Rift	Love You
06/19/92	1	1a	Sparkle	YEM
06/24/92	3	1a	Sparkle	Rocky Top
07/01/92	3	1a	Curtain	Rift
07/10/92	3	1a	Lizards	Antelope
07/11/92	1	1a	Sqirm Coil	YEM
07/14/92	2	1	PoorHeart	*CL1
07/22/92	7	1a	Rift	Bowie
08/02/92	9	1a	Bowie	Rocky Top
08/17/92	4	2	A-Train	*CL2
08/23/92	3	1a	Sparkle	Foam
10/30/92	7	1a	Rift	Sqirm Coil
11/19/92	1	2	Lngthwise	*CL2
11/23/92	4	2	Lngthwise	*CL2
11/25/92	1	1	Adeline	Antelope
11/27/92	1	2	A-Train	*CL2
11/30/92	2	2	Terrapin	*CL2
12/01/92	1	1	Rift	Fluffhead
12/03/92	2	2	A-Train	*CL2
12/04/92	1	1	Mockbird	*CL1
12/06/92	2	2	Carolina	*CL2
12/10/92	3	2	Adeline	*CL1
12/12/92	2	1	Sparkle	Reba
12/13/92	1	2	Harry	*CL2
12/28/92	1	2	Harry	*CL2
12/31/92	3	1	Divided	Foam
02/04/93	2	2	Harry	*CL2
02/09/93	4	E	*OPE	Rocky Top
02/11/93	2	2	Lizards	*CL2
02/13/93	2	2	Sqirm Coil	*CL2
02/18/93	3	1	Sparkle	Reba
02/20/93	2	1	Fluffhead	*CL1
02/22/93	2	1	Foam	IDK
02/25/93	2	1	PoorHeart	Maze
02/26/93	1	1	IDK	*CL1
03/03/93	3	1	Lawn Boy	*CL1
03/05/93	1	1	PoorHeart	Foam
03/08/93	2	2	PoorHeart	Uncle Pen
03/12/93	2	1	PoorHeart	Possum
03/16/93	3	1	McGrupp	*CL1
03/18/93	2	2	Sqirm Coil	*CL2
03/19/93	1	1	Fluffhead	Antelope
03/21/93	1	2	Harry	*CL2
03/24/93	2	1	AmGrace	*CL1
03/26/93	2	1	Divided	*CL1
03/30/93	3	1	Divided	*CL1
04/01/93	2	2	Terrapin	*CL2
04/03/93	2	2	Love You	*CL2
04/09/93	2	1	Divided	*CL1
04/10/93	1	2	Hoochie	*CL2
04/13/93	2	1	Caravan	*CL1
04/16/93	2	1	Harry	*CL1
04/18/93	2	1	IDK	*CL1
04/21/93	2	E	Adeline	*CLE
04/24/93	3	2	Harry	*CL2
04/27/93	2	2	Love You	*CL2
04/30/93	2	1	Divided	Lawn Boy
05/01/93	1	2	Weekpaug	*CL2
05/03/93	2	1	Lawn Boy	*CL1
05/05/93	1	E	AmGrace	*CLE
05/08/93	3	1	Satin Doll	*CL1
05/29/93	1	1a	Sparkle	BBJ
07/16/93	3	2	Harry	*CL2
07/18/93	2	1	Uncle Pen	*CL1
07/23/93	3	1	Lawn Boy	*CL1
07/25/93	2	E	*OPE	*CLE
07/28/93	2	1	PoorHeart	*CL1
07/30/93	2	1	Reba	*CL1
07/31/93	1	1	Divided	*CL1
08/03/93	2	1	Llama	*CL1
08/07/93	2	1	Mockbird	*CL1
08/11/93	3	1	Sparkle	*CL1
08/14/93	3	1	PoorHeart	*CL1
08/17/93	3	2	MSO	*CL2
08/20/93	1	2	PurplRain	*CL2
08/25/93	3	1	Glide	*CL1
12/29/93	4	E	Nellie	*CLE
04/04/94	3	E	Harry	*CLE
04/06/94	2	2	Sqirm Coil	*CL2
04/09/94	2	2	Slave	*CL2
04/11/94	2	1	Divided	*CL1
04/15/94	3	2	BeLikeYou	*CL2
04/17/94	2	1	MSO	*CL1
04/18/94	1	2	BeLikeYou	*CL2
04/21/94	2	1	If I Could	*CL1
04/29/94	6	2	BeLikeYou	*CL2
05/02/94	2	E	*OPE	*CLE
05/08/94	5	2	Julius	YEM
05/10/94	1	1	If I Could	*CL1
05/14/94	3	2	Lizards	*CL2
05/19/94	3	1	Mango	*CL1
05/23/94	4	1	Reba	*CL1
05/26/94	2	1	PoorHeart	Demand
05/28/94	2	1	Maze	*CL1
06/10/94	3	1	Lizards	Julius
06/13/94	2	2	Esther	Reba
06/17/94	3	1	Scent	*CL1
06/22/94	4	E	Carolina	*CLE
06/24/94	2	2	PoorHeart	Carolina
06/29/94	3	2	Suzie	*CL2
07/01/94	2	2	Harry	*CL2
07/08/94	5	E	Nellie	*CLE
07/10/94	2	1	Julius	*CL1
07/13/94	1	2	Possum	NICU
07/16/94	3	1	Lizards	Horse
10/07/94	1	E	Long Time	*CLE
10/13/94	5	2	Long Time	*CL2
10/14/94	1	E	Ya Mar	*CLE
10/21/94	5	E	Long Time	*CLE
10/27/94	5	1	PoorHeart	*CL1
11/03/94	5	2	Harry	*CL2
11/14/94	4	1	Lawn Boy	*CL1
11/20/94	5	2	Julius	*CL2
11/26/94	4	1	PoorHeart	*CL1
11/30/94	2	2	McGrupp	*CL2
12/02/94	2	E	*OPE	*CLE
12/03/94	1	2	Julius	*CL2
12/07/94	3	E	*OPE	*CLE
12/10/94	3	2	Slave	*CL2
12/30/94	3	1	Scent	*CL1
06/09/95	5	2	Scent	Bowie
06/14/95	3	1	Mound	Possum
06/19/95	4	1	Rift	Antelope
06/22/95	2	1	Maze	Adeline
06/25/95	3	2	AmGrace	*CL2
06/29/95	3	1	Divided	Rift
07/03/95	4	1	Free	*CL1
09/30/95	4	2	Suspicious	*CL2
10/05/95	3	2	Scent	Bowie
10/11/95	4	1	Old Home	Divided
10/14/95	2	2	Scent	*CL2
10/19/95	3	1	Billy	*CL1
10/22/95	3	2	Slave	*CL2
10/24/95	1	2	Contact	*CL2
11/10/95	7	1	Guyute	*CL1
11/14/95	3	1	I'm Blue	*CL1
11/18/95	3	2	BBFCM	*CL2
11/22/95	3	1	Uncle Pen	Fog
12/01/95	6	1	Stash	*CL1
12/05/95	3	2	Harry	*CL2
12/11/95	4	1	Julius	*CL1
12/16/95	4	2	Scent	Mike's
12/30/95	4	2	Scent	Antelope
04/26/96	2	E	HelloBaby	*CLE
07/07/96	4	1a	Uncle Pen	Antelope
07/11/96	3	1	RunJim	Reba
07/13/96	2	1a	RunJim	Reba
07/15/96	1	1	Harry	*CL1
07/22/96	5	1a	PoorHeart	Maze
07/25/96	3	1a	Harry	*CL1
08/05/96	3	E	*OPE	*CLE
08/10/96	3	1	Bathtub	*CL1
10/25/96	13	2	Harry	SSB
11/02/96	5	1	Fee	Taste
11/11/96	6	E	Waste	*CLE
11/15/96	3	1	Taste	*CL1
11/22/96	4	1	Stash	*CL1
11/24/96	2	E	Ginseng	*CLE
12/01/96	2	1	PoorHeart	CTB
12/29/96	5	1	Caravan	Taste
02/16/97	5	1	Waste	Chalkdust
02/18/97	2	1	Beauty	PYITE
06/14/97	12	2	Bowie	*CL2
06/20/97	3	2	Ginseng	Twist
06/21/97	1	1a	Twist	*CL1
07/03/97	8	2	Harry	*CL2
07/26/97	10	E	Bouncing	*CLE
08/10/97	9	E	*OPE	*CLE
➢ 8/17/97	5			

Chalkdust [263]*

Chalk Dust Torture [Chalkdust]

By Anastasio/Marshall

02/02/91	[258]	1	YEM	*CL1
02/03/91	1	1	Reba	Foam
02/07/91	1	2	*OP2	TMWSIY
02/09/91	2	1	Reba	*CL1
02/15/91	2	2	Terrapin	*CL2
02/16/91	1	2	*OP2	Reba
03/15/91	17	2	Harry	*CL2
03/17/91	2	2	Slave	*CL1
03/23/91	3	2	*OP2	Bathtub
03/28/91	1	1a	Magilla	*CL1
04/05/91	6	1	Reba	Foam
04/11/91	2	1	Sqirm Coil	*CL1
04/15/91	3	1	Fee	Forbin's
04/16/91	1	2	Reba	Magilla
04/20/91	3	1	Esther	Bouncing
04/22/91	2	2	*OP2	Bathtub
04/26/91	1	1	*OP1	Sqirm Coil
05/02/91	2	2	*OP2	PoorHeart
05/03/91	1	1	Foam	TMWSIY
05/10/91	2	2	McGrupp	Love You
05/11/91	1	2	*OP2	YEM
05/12/91	1	1	*OP1	Bouncing
05/16/91	1	1	Mockbird	YEM
05/17/91	1	1	*OP1	Drums
05/18/91	1	1	Golgi	YEM
05/25/91	1	1	Landlady	Bouncing
07/13/91	3	2	*OP2	Guelah
07/14/91	1	3	Esther	Bathtub
07/18/91	2	1	*OP1	Foam
07/20/91	2	1	*OP1	Foam
07/23/91	2	1	*OP1	Foam
07/24/91	1	1	Golgi	Sqirm Coil
07/26/91	2	1	*OP1	Reba
08/03/91	2	2	Reba	Bouncing
09/25/91	1	2	YEM	*CL2
09/26/91	1	2	Lawn Boy	*CL2
09/28/91	2	1	Bouncing	Sqirm Coil
10/02/91	2	1	Bouncing	Golgi
10/03/91	1	1	*OP1	Foam
10/04/91	1	1	Memories	Reba
10/10/91	3	1	*OP1	Foam
10/11/91	1	1	Guelah	YEM
10/12/91	1	1	Fluffhead	A-Train
10/15/91	2	1	*OP1	Foam
10/17/91	1	1	Esther	Golgi
10/19/91	2	1	Foam	Bouncing
10/27/91	4	1	MSO	Mango
10/31/91	3	1	Sloth	Sparkle
11/01/91	1	2	It's Ice	Eliza
11/07/91	3	1	Memories	Foam
11/09/91	2	2	*OP2	Fluffhead
11/12/91	2	2	Guelah	Magilla
11/13/91	1	1	Sparkle	Esther
11/15/91	2	1	*OP1	Sparkle
11/16/91	1	2	Horn	Terrapin
11/19/91	1	1	Horn	Love You
11/21/91	2	1	*OP1	Bouncing
11/23/91	2	1	Sparkle	Uncle Pen
11/24/91	1	2	Mango	A-Train
11/30/91	1	2	*OP2	Uncle Pen
12/04/91	1	2	Lizards	Love You
12/07/91	3	2	Reba	Sparkle
03/07/92	3	2	Weigh	Horn
03/14/92	4	1	Fee	A-Train
03/19/92	2	2	Glide	NICU
03/25/92	4	2	MSO	Rosie
03/26/92	1	E	Sl Monkey	Harpua
03/30/92	3	2	Weigh	Rosie
04/01/92	2	2	Horn	Rosie
04/04/92	2	1	Uncle Pen	Bouncing
04/06/92	2	1	Esther	Guelah
04/09/92	2	2	Silent	Terrapin
04/15/92	3	2	*OP2	YEM
04/19/92	4	1	Fee	IDK
04/25/92	5	1	Tela	Bouncing
04/30/92	2	2	Silent	Rosie
05/02/92	2	2	YEM	Rosie

SONGS PLAYED BY YEAR

(1997 through 8/17/97)

CTB
1995 21
1996 19
1997 15

Catapult
1992 2
1993 1
1994 9
1995 5
1996 3
1997 1

Cavern
1990 19
1991 73
1992 58
1993 51
1994 43
1995 23
1996 17
1997 8

Chalkdust
1991 62
1992 45
1993 52
1994 38
1995 24
1996 22
1997 20

Character Zero
1996 21
1997 24

Chess Jam
1995 3
1996 0
1997 0

Col. Forbin's
1990 9
1991 16
1992 14
1993 16
1994 11
1995 3
1996 2
1997 1

Contact
1990 20
1991 15
1992 8
1993 14
1994 13
1995 6
1996 4
1997 1

Curtain
1990 4
1991 20
1992 15
1993 13
1994 17
1995 11
1996 8
1997 1

David Bowie
1990 24
1991 36
1992 37
1993 33
1994 38
1995 25
1996 19
1997 13

Demand
1994 9
1995 4
1996 1
1997 0

Destiny Unbound
1990 5
1991 18
1992 0
1993 0
1994 0
1995 0
1996 0
1997 0

Dinner
1990 35
1991 33
1992 15
1993 4
1994 3
1995 2
1996 1
1997 1

Dirt
1997 15

Divided Sky
1990 42
1991 45
1992 28
1993 31
1994 39
1995 20
1996 16
1997 3

Dog Faced Boy
1994 23
1995 9
1996 1
1997 0

Dog Log
1990 1
1991 1
1992 0
1993 1
1994 0
1995 2
1996 0
1997 1

Dogs Stole Things
1997 17

Stories Behind the Songs
(Continued)

instrumental ending Trey termed "The Curtain With." In 1992, Trey transfered that ending instrumental section into the middle section of Rift, speeding it up for the new version of the song.

Dave's Energy Guide: This song, co-written by Trey and his friend Dave Abrahams, is an instrumental that shares many musical similarities with King Crimson's "Discipline." Dave's Energy Guide has been reputedly played by Phish several times in the last couple of years. The confusion on the matter started mainly because of discussions on the Phish.Net in early 1995 about the crazy, spacey David Bowie played in Providence RI, 12/29/94. Some listeners swore they heard Dave's Energy Guide—or something that sounded a lot like it—woven therein. Other songs believed by some to contain DEG include the Tweezer at Jones Beach on 6/29/95—probably the closest they've come in this decade to pulling out a real DEG—and Trey's solo at the end of the Mike's Song at Madison Square Garden on 12/31/95. But the music produced by Trey in each of these instances are part of his (relatively new) digital feedback loop, used in numerous jams on fall tour 1994 and throughout 1995. Although these do sound like DEG at times, these performances do not match with the song as it appears on tapes from the 1980s.

David Bowie: An oldie which has in recent years expanded into a show-maker, such as the 30-minute version from 12/29/94. There's no known connection between David Bowie (the performer) and Phish.

Dear Mrs. Reagan: Like Nancy Reagan—the song's topic and target—this one is a relic of the 1980s. Performed as a sort-of Dylan parody in the mid-1980s, it contains what are clearly the most political Phish lyrics ever to reach the audience's ears.

Demand: The album version of this song is actually an amalgamy of three different songs: Demand, Split Open and Melt (the *Hoist* version includes a live recording of Split Open from 4/21/93 which kicks in after the first car sound

05/05/92	2	2	*OP2	Bouncing
05/06/92	1	2	Uncle Pen	Terrapin
05/08/92	2	2	Silent	Terrapin
05/12/92	3	2	Guelah	Terrapin
05/15/92	2	1a	Love You	YEM
05/17/92	2	1	PoorHeart	*CL1
06/23/92	4	1a	*OP1	Reba
06/27/92	2	1a	All Things	Bouncing
07/12/92	7	1a	Adeline	Bouncing
07/15/92	2	1	Silent	Lizards
07/17/92	2	1a	*OP1	Sparkle
07/26/92	7	1a	*OP1	It's Ice
07/28/92	2	1a	*OP1	Bouncing
07/31/92	2	1a	Suzie	Bouncing
08/02/92	2	1a	*OP1	Guelah
08/13/92	1	1a	*OP1	Foam
08/19/92	4	1a	*OP1	Landlady
08/23/92	2	1a	*OP1	Maze
08/27/92	3	1a	*OP1	Bouncing
08/29/92	2	1a	*OP1	Rift
11/20/92	4	2	*OP2	Fluffhead
11/25/92	4	2	*OP2	Foam
11/28/92	2	1	Esther	Sparkle
12/01/92	2	2	Curtain	My Friend
12/03/92	2	1	Uncle Pen	Horse
12/05/92	2	1	Landlady	Bouncing
12/07/92	2	2	*OP2	Reba
12/11/92	3	1	Lizards	Guelah
12/13/92	2	2	Fluffhead	TMWSIY
12/30/92	3	1	Esther	Fluffhead
02/04/93	3	2	*OP2	Wedge
02/06/93	2	2	*OP2	Mound
02/09/93	2	1	Wedge	Esther
02/12/93	3	1	Wedge	IDK
02/15/93	2	1	Esther	Mound
02/18/93	2	1	*OP1	Guelah
02/21/93	3	1	Horn	Esther
02/23/93	2	1	Lawn Boy	Wedge
02/26/93	2	2	Glide	Mound
03/02/93	2	1	All Things	Horse
03/05/93	2	2	Landlady	Guelah
03/08/93	2	E	Terrapin	*CLE
03/12/93	2	2	BBJ	Lngthwise
03/16/93	3	2	Esther	YEM
03/18/93	2	1	*OP1	Guelah
03/19/93	1	E	AmGrace	*CLE
03/22/93	2	1	*OP1	Guelah
03/25/93	2	1	*OP1	Guelah
03/27/93	2	2	Bouncing	TMWSIY
03/31/93	3	2	Harpua	*CL2
04/02/93	2	2	Bike	*CL2
04/09/93	3	1	*OP1	Sparkle
04/10/93	1	1	Uncle Pen	Lawn Boy
04/13/93	2	1	Mockbird	Guelah
04/16/93	2	1	*OP1	Guelah
04/20/93	3	2	*OP2	Fluffhead
04/22/93	2	1	Reba	Esther
04/23/93	1	1	Lawn Boy	*CL1
04/24/93	1	1	*OP1	Guelah
04/29/93	3	2	*OP2	It's Ice
05/01/93	2	2	*OP2	Fluffhead
05/03/93	2	1	Weigh	Esther
05/06/93	2	1	*OP1	Mound
05/08/93	2	1	*OP1	Guelah
05/29/93	1	1a	*OP1	Bouncing
07/15/93	2	E	*OPE	FrBir
07/17/93	2	1	Reba	Horse
07/21/93	2	E	*OPE	*CLE
07/23/93	2	2	BBFCM	HwayHell
07/28/93	4	2	Great Gig	*CL2
07/30/93	2	1	Esther	IDK
08/02/93	2	1	*OP1	Guelah
08/06/93	2	1	Nellie	Suzie
08/09/93	3	1	*OP1	Mound
08/12/93	2	1	Reba	Guelah
08/14/93	2	1	*OP1	Guelah
08/15/93	1	1	Mockbird	*CL1
08/20/93	3	2	My Friend	YEM
08/24/93	2	1	*OP1	All Things
08/26/93	2	2	Bats&Mice	*CL2
08/28/93	1	2	Contact	*CL2
12/29/93	2	2	Adeline	*CL2
04/05/94	4	2	BeLikeYou	AmGrace
04/10/94	4	1	Esther	IDK
04/15/94	4	1	Wilson	Bouncing
04/18/94	3	1	*OP1	Glide
04/21/94	2	1	*OP1	Sparkle
04/24/94	3	2	Mockbird	Contact
04/30/94	4	1	*OP1	Mound
05/03/94	2	2	Harpua	BeLikeYou
05/06/94	2	1	Esther	*CL1
05/13/94	5	2	*OP2	Bouncing
05/20/94	5	E	*OPE	*CLE
05/23/94	3	1	*OP1	Sample
05/25/94	1	1	Adeline	*CL1
05/29/94	4	2	Esther	McGrupp
06/11/94	3	1	Wilson	YEM
06/18/94	5	2	YEM	*CL2
06/21/94	2	2	Esther	BBFCM
06/25/94	4	1	Tela	*CL1
06/30/94	3	2	Love You	*CL2
07/06/94	5	2	Lawn Boy	BBFCM
07/10/94	3	1	*OP1	Horn
07/14/94	2	E	*OPE	*CLE
07/16/94	2	2	Contact	*CL2
10/08/94	2	1	*OP1	Horn
10/10/94	2	1	Nellie	*CL1
10/14/94	3	2	Guyute	Nellie
10/20/94	4	2	Long Time	*CL2
10/23/94	3	1	*OP1	My Friend
10/28/94	4	2	Life Boy	Old Home
11/04/94	5	1	Suzie	*CL1
11/12/94	1	1	Esther	*CL1
11/16/94	3	2	LongJourn	Fee
11/20/94	4	1	*OP1	Fee
11/28/94	5	1	*OP1	Also Sprac
12/02/94	3	2	*OP2	Bowie
12/07/94	4	1	Life Boy	*CL1
12/10/94	3	1	Lawn Boy	*CL1
12/31/94	4	3	Auld	Horse
06/08/95	3	1	Caspian	*CL1
06/13/95	3	1	Sparkle	*CL1
06/20/95	6	2	Halley's	Caspian
06/23/95	2	1	Simple	Caspian
06/28/95	4	1	Fluffhead	*CL1
07/01/95	3	1	Bouncing	*CL1
09/27/95	3	1	Str Design	Sqirm Coil
09/29/95	2	E	*OPE	*CLE
10/05/95	4	1	*OP1	Ha Ha Ha
10/11/95	4	E	*OPE	*CLE
10/19/95	5	1	Esther	Theme
10/21/95	2	1	TweezRep	Guelah
10/25/95	3	1	I'm Blue	*CL1
10/28/95	2	2	Frankstein	*CL2
11/11/95	5	1	Fee	*CL1
11/14/95	2	1	*OP1	Foam
11/21/95	5	1	Fee	Caspian
11/24/95	2	2	*OP2	Theme
12/01/95	5	1	Wolfman's	Forbin's
12/05/95	3	1	Horn	Fog
12/09/95	3	1	Dog Faced	*CL1
12/15/95	4	1	*OP1	Harry
12/17/95	2	1	Lizards	*CL1
12/31/95	4	1	Sparkle	*CL1
06/06/96	2	2	YEM	Sparkle
07/05/96	2	1a	FunkBitch	ACDCBag
07/10/96	4	1a	*OP1	Ya Mar
07/13/96	3	1a	FunkBitch	YEM
07/24/96	8	1a	*OP1	Ya Mar
08/04/96	3	1	*OP1	FunkBitch
08/12/96	5	1	Esther	Weigh
08/16/96	3	1	*OP1	Bathtub
10/17/96	3	2	Ya Mar	Bathtub
10/21/96	3	2	Wilson	Wolfman's
10/23/96	2	E	*OPE	*CLE
10/27/96	3	2	*OP2	Bathtub
10/29/96	1	1	*OP1	Guelah
11/07/96	5	1	*OP1	Weigh
11/11/96	3	1	*OP1	Guelah
11/15/96	2	1	Train Song	Taste
11/18/96	2	1	Billy	Guelah
11/23/96	3	1	*OP1	Guelah
11/27/96	2	1	Ya Mar	Sloth
11/30/96	2	1	Caspian	*CL1
12/04/96	3	1	My Friend	Horn
12/31/96	5	2	*OP2	Wilson
02/13/97	1	1	*OP1	Wolfman's
02/16/97	2	1	Cavern	*CL1
02/20/97	3	1	SSP	Treat
02/22/97	2	2	*OP2	Bathtub
02/25/97	2	E	*OPE	*CLE
03/02/97	4	1	Life Mars	HelloBaby
03/18/97	1	2	Waste	Slave
06/13/97	1	2	Slave	Ghost
06/16/97	2	1	Theme	Wolfman's
06/21/97	3	1a	Harry	Jam
06/27/97	4	1a	Wilson	Stash
06/29/97	1	1a	Beauty	Theme
07/06/97	5	1	Scent	*CL1
07/11/97	3	1	*OP1	Bouncing
07/23/97	3	2	RMWay	*CL2
07/25/97	1	2	*OP2	Taste
07/30/97	3	1	Wolfman's	Water
08/08/97	5	2	Caspian	*CL2
08/14/97	5	2	*OP2	Treat
08/16/97	1	1	Harpua	Theme
➢ 8/17/97	**1**			

Character Zero [45]

Character Zero [CharZero]

By Anastasio/Marshall

06/06/96	[820]	2	Waste	Bowie
07/09/96	5	1a	Bouncing	*CL1
10/16/96	25	1	Silent	*CL1
10/17/96	1	1	PYITE	DayinLife
10/21/96	3	1	Divided	Ginseng
10/23/96	2	1	HelloBaby	Rift
10/26/96	2	1	Train Song	It's Ice
10/29/96	2	2	Wedge	Suspicious
10/31/96	1	1	Mockbird	SSB
11/03/96	2	1	Bouncing	*CL1
11/07/96	2	1	Tela	*CL1
11/09/96	2	1	Lizards	*CL1
11/13/96	2	1	Reba	Adeline
11/15/96	2	1	Bouncing	PYITE
11/18/96	2	1	Reba	*CL1
11/22/96	2	2	Steep	Theme
11/24/96	2	1	Reba	Str Design
11/29/96	2	1	CTB	Divided
12/01/96	2	1	CTB	Curtain
12/04/96	2	1	Guyute	Lizards
12/31/96	5	2	Caspian	*CL2
02/13/97	1	1	PoorHeart	Peaches
02/14/97	1	E	*OPE	*CLE
02/18/97	3	1	Walfredo	Slave
02/20/97	1	2	CTB	Uncle Pen
02/21/97	1	E	*OPE	*CLE
02/22/97	1	1	IDK	*CL1
02/28/97	4	1	Ya Mar	*CL1
03/02/97	2	2	Waste	Slave
03/18/97	1	1	Suzie	*CL1
06/13/97	1	2	Oblivious	*CL2
06/19/97	3	E	Beauty	HelloBaby
06/22/97	3	1a	Uncle Pen	Theme
06/27/97	3	1a	Bouncing	*CL1
06/29/97	1	1a	Theme	*CL1
07/03/97	3	E	*OPE	*CLE
07/05/97	1	1a	PoorHeart	GTBT
07/11/97	4	E	*OPE	*CLE
07/21/97	1	1	Bathtub	*CL1
07/25/97	3	2	Ghost	*CL2
07/30/97	3	1	CTB	*CL1
08/03/97	3	1	Limb	*CL1
08/08/97	2	1	Water	*CL1
08/11/97	3	2	YEM	*CL2
08/16/97	3	1	Train Song	Sqirm Coil
➢ 8/17/97	**1**			

Chess Game Jam [3]

Chess Game Jam [Chess]

By Phish

09/30/95	[765]	1	CTB	Reba
10/02/95	1	1	Rift	Stash
11/16/95	27	1	RunJim	Horn
➢ 8/17/97	**149**			

Clod [8]*

Clod [Clod]

By Anastasio

Now played as part of Fluff's Travels.

12/06/86	[10]	1a	Bowie	Bowie
05/11/87	6	1a	Sally	Peaches
08/21/87	3	1	Harry	Curtain
08/29/87	2	2	*OP2	Slave
09/12/87	2	1	TMWSIY	Slave
10/14/87	2	2	McGrupp	Makisupa
10/26/89	109	2	Dinner	ACDCBag
11/03/89	4	1	Split&Melt	BundleJoy
➢ 8/17/97	**803 (as a stand-alone song)**			

Col. Forbin's [96]*

Colonel Forbin's Ascent [Forbin's]

By Anastasio

03/12/88	[32]	1a	ACDCBag	Mockbird
03/21/88	1	1a	IDK	Mockbird
03/31/88	1	2	Lizards	Mockbird
06/21/88	11	1	Lizards	Mockbird
07/11/88	1	1	Bold	Mockbird
07/23/88	2	1	Jam	Mockbird
07/24/88	1	1	FunkBitch	Mockbird
09/08/88	5	1	ACDCBag	Mockbird
10/12/88	3	1	Wilson	Mockbird
11/11/88	4	1	Possum	Mockbird
01/26/89	2	1a	Icculus	Mockbird
02/05/89	2	1	Curtis	Mockbird
02/18/89	4	1	*OP1	Mockbird
02/24/89	1	1	Foam	Mockbird
03/03/89	1	2	WalkAway	Mockbird
05/06/89	21	1	ACDCBag	Mockbird
05/28/89	14	1	Antelope	Mockbird
08/23/89	15	2	Antelope	Mockbird
08/26/89	1	1	Fluffhead	Mockbird
10/20/89	11	1	BundleJoy	Mockbird
10/22/89	2	1	La Grange	Mockbird
10/31/89	3	2	Reba	Mockbird
11/03/89	2	1	*OP1	Mockbird
11/30/89	7	2	Possum	Mockbird
01/28/90	22	1	Carolina	Mockbird
02/25/90	15	1	MSO	Mockbird
03/09/90	6	1	Bouncing	Mockbird
04/07/90	7	2	Golgi	Mockbird
04/20/90	8	1	Bouncing	Mockbird

10/07/90 37 1 Destiny Mockbird
11/02/90 6 2 Suzie Mockbird
11/26/90 8 2 Uncle Pen Mockbird
12/28/90 5 1 Llama Mockbird
02/08/91 7 1 BurAlive Mockbird
03/16/91 22 1 Rocky Top Mockbird
03/23/91 4 1 Possum Mockbird
04/04/91 6 1 Llama Mockbird
04/15/91 6 1 Chalkdust Mockbird
04/21/91 5 2 Landlady Mockbird
05/02/91 5 1 Landlady Mockbird
05/04/91 2 2 Llama Mockbird
05/16/91 5 1 Divided Mockbird
07/14/91 7 1 MSO Mockbird
10/13/91 25 1 Landlady Mockbird
10/27/91 8 2 Llama Mockbird
11/02/91 5 1 Bouncing Mockbird
11/13/91 7 2 Bowie Mockbird
11/20/91 5 1 Possum Mockbird
12/07/91 9 1 Foam Mockbird
03/19/92 9 1 Dinner Mockbird
03/24/92 3 1 Llama Mockbird
03/31/92 6 1 Llama Mockbird
04/16/92 11 1 Maze Icculus
04/21/92 4 2 Dinner Mockbird
04/24/92 3 1 RunJim Icculus
05/02/92 5 1 RunJim Icculus
05/06/92 3 1 Brother Mockbird
05/17/92 9 1 Llama Mockbird
11/21/92 47 1 Maze Mockbird
11/27/92 4 1 Divided Mockbird
12/04/92 6 1 Maze Mockbird
12/08/92 4 1 Llama Mockbird
12/31/92 8 2 Sparkle Mockbird
02/07/93 5 1 Sparkle Mockbird
02/19/93 9 1 Maze Mockbird
02/25/93 5 1 Maze Mockbird
03/08/93 7 1 Llama How High
03/18/93 7 1 Maze Mockbird
03/22/93 3 2 ACDCBag Mockbird
03/25/93 2 2 Uncle Pen Icculus
04/05/93 9 1 Stash Mockbird
04/13/93 4 1 Possum Mockbird
04/21/93 6 1 Maze Mockbird
04/25/93 4 1 RunJim Mockbird
05/03/93 6 1 Split&Melt Mockbird
07/29/93 18 1 My Mind Mockbird
08/07/93 6 1 Maze Mockbird
08/15/93 7 1 Stash Mockbird
12/30/93 11 1 Paul&Silas Mockbird
04/11/94 8 2 Maze Mockbird
04/24/94 11 2 Julius Mockbird
05/25/94 22 1 Stash Mockbird
06/16/94 10 2 Antelope Kung
06/26/94 9 1 ACDCBag Mockbird
07/08/94 8 1 ACDCBag Mockbird
10/14/94 13 1 Rift Mockbird
10/27/94 10 1 Maze Mockbird
11/04/94 6 1 Bowie Mockbird
11/17/94 5 1 Dog Faced Mockbird
11/30/94 9 1 Reba Mockbird
10/05/95 43 2 RunJim Mockbird
12/01/95 35 1 Chalkdust Mockbird
12/31/95 16 1 Maze Mockbird
08/07/96 25 2 Free Mockbird
10/31/96 18 1 Reba Mockbird
08/14/97 78 2 Harry Jam
➢ 8/17/97 2

Contact [107]

Contact [Contact]

By Gordon

06/15/88 [40] 2 Sloth Dinner
06/21/88 3 2 GTBT Peaches
07/23/88 3 3 YEM Harry
10/12/88 9 2 YEM Sloth
10/29/88 1 1 La Grange Harry
11/03/88 1 2 WhipPost Bold
12/02/88 3 1 Divided YEM
01/26/89 1 1a Possum BBFCM
02/07/89 4 2 Timber Ho Alumni
02/18/89 2 1a La Grange Bowie
03/04/89 3 2 Antelope *CL2
05/06/89 20 2 Suzie Fire
05/13/89 6 2 Brain *CL2
05/20/89 4 2 Foam A-Train
05/21/89 1 1 Foam Mike's
05/28/89 3 2 Possum Jam
06/23/89 5 E *OPE GTBT
08/17/89 7 3 Alumni Antelope
08/26/89 4 E *OPE Lizards
10/01/89 5 2 Brain Split&Melt
10/07/89 2 2 Bowie HwayHell
10/31/89 9 E *OPE Antelope
11/30/89 9 2 Suzie Bowie
12/09/89 6 2 Weekpaug BBFCM
12/15/89 1 1a Jesus Bowie
12/31/89 4 E *OPE *CLE
02/10/90 13 1 Carolina Bowie
02/23/90 5 E *OPE IDK
02/24/90 1 2 Lawn Boy *CL2
03/08/90 6 E *OPE GTBT
03/09/90 1 2 La Grange BBFCM
03/28/90 3 1 Split&Melt La Grange
04/04/90 1 E *OPE HwayHell
04/05/90 1 2 Brain Golgi
04/25/90 13 E *OPE *CLE
05/04/90 5 E *OPE *CLE
05/19/90 7 E *OPE *CLE
05/24/90 2 2 HwayHell *CL2
06/09/90 6 E Landlady *CLE
09/16/90 5 E *OPE *CLE
10/07/90 9 E *OPE *CLE
10/30/90 4 3 GTBT ACDCBag
11/04/90 4 E *OPE HwayHell
11/16/90 3 E *OPE Fire
11/26/90 3 E Fire HwayHell
12/08/90 5 E *OPE HwayHell
02/09/91 9 E2 *OPE2 Rocky Top
02/15/91 2 E2 *OPE2 Golgi
03/23/91 23 2 Bowie *CL2
04/04/91 6 E *OPE Uncle Pen
04/12/91 4 E *OPE BBFCM
07/11/91 23 E *OPE BBFCM
07/14/91 3 E *OPE BBFCM
07/15/91 1 E Caravan Alumni
07/21/91 4 2 ACDCBag TweezRep
07/24/91 2 E *OPE BBFCM
07/27/91 3 E Touch Me *CLE
09/28/91 5 E *OPE BBFCM
10/12/91 9 1 Rocky Top Golgi
11/02/91 14 E *OPE BBFCM
11/30/91 17 E *OPE Rocky Top
03/13/92 10 E *OPE Fire
04/01/92 13 2 TweezRep Rocky Top
04/07/92 5 E *OPE TweezRep
04/18/92 7 E *OPE BBFCM
04/24/92 5 E *OPE BBFCM
05/05/92 7 E *OPE Rocky Top
11/28/92 62 E *OPE TweezRep
12/11/92 11 E *OPE GTBT
02/07/93 11 E AmGrace BBFCM
02/15/93 6 E *OPE Fire
03/13/93 18 1 Split&Melt Llama
03/28/93 12 E *OPE BBFCM
04/14/93 11 E Lngthwise TweezRep
04/25/93 9 2 Tweezer Uncle Pen
05/03/93 6 2 Tweezer It's Ice
05/06/93 2 E Adeline TweezRep
05/30/93 4 1a Split&Melt Llama
07/22/93 6 2 It's Ice Possum
07/30/93 7 1 *OP1 Llama
08/09/93 7 2 YEM Crimes
08/28/93 13 2 YEM Chalkdust
12/29/93 2 2 Antelope BBFCM
04/08/94 6 E *OPE BBFCM
04/17/94 8 2 Maze Golgi
04/24/94 6 2 Chalkdust GTBT
05/12/94 12 2 Love You BBFCM
05/21/94 7 2 Bowie BBJ
05/25/94 3 2 Maze BBJ
06/11/94 7 2 Maze Frankstein
06/16/94 3 2 DWD BBFCM
07/16/94 23 2 Harry Chalkdust
10/09/94 3 2 Julius Possum
10/27/94 14 2 Tweezer BBFCM
11/18/94 12 2 Tweezer Possum
12/28/94 18 2 Weekpaug Llama
06/20/95 15 2 Mike's Weekpaug
06/30/95 8 2 Mike's Weekpaug
10/07/95 12 2 It's Ice Frankstein
10/24/95 11 2 Antelope Cavern
11/18/95 13 2 YEM BBFCM
11/28/95 6 2 Antelope BBFCM
08/10/96 45 E *OPE Fire
08/16/96 4 2 Simpl Weekpaug
11/11/96 20 2 Maze Slave
11/30/96 12 2 Brother Also Sprac
08/16/97 60 E *OPE Lovin Cup
➢ 8/17/97 1

Curtain [107]*

The Curtain [Curtain]

By Anastasio/Daubert

08/10/87 [18] 1 Fee *CL1
08/21/87 1 1 Clod Light Up
08/29/87 2 2 SwingLow McGrupp
09/12/87 2 1 YEM BBFCM
05/15/88 14 1a A-Train Flat Fee
05/25/88 2 1 *OP1 Rocky Top
06/18/88 2 1 *OP1 FunkBitch
06/21/88 2 1 Suzie Lizards
07/11/88 1 1 Suzie FunkBitch
07/23/88 2 2 Fire Terrapin
09/24/88 8 3 Fluffhead ACDCBag
02/06/89 10 1 Suzie Wilson
02/24/89 4 1 TMWSIY Foam
03/03/89 1 1 ACDCBag Antelope
06/30/89 42 2 ACDCBag Slave
11/02/89 26 1 Fee Reba
11/09/89 3 1 Ya Mar MSO
12/16/89 13 1a *OP1 ACDCBag
03/09/90 29 2 *OP2 Dog Log
04/18/90 13 1 Uncle Pen Foam
10/05/90 37 2 Golgi Ya Mar
11/04/90 10 1 ACDCBag Bouncing
02/15/91 22 1 *OP1 Wilson
03/16/91 19 1 Gin Rocky Top
03/23/91 4 1 IDK Possum
04/04/91 6 2 *OP2 RunJim
04/19/91 9 2 Harry Golgi
04/22/91 3 1 *OP1 RunJim
04/27/91 3 2 *OP2 Possum
05/03/91 2 2 ACDCBag Sloth
05/12/91 5 2 PoorHeart Golgi
05/18/91 3 2 Suzie Stash
07/13/91 4 1 *OP1 RunJim
08/03/91 12 2 *OP2 Reba
10/11/91 12 2 *OP2 Cavern
10/17/91 4 2 *OP2 Oh Kee
10/28/91 7 1 *OP1 RunJim
11/02/91 4 1 Suzie Llama
11/09/91 4 1 *OP1 RunJim
11/15/91 5 1 Cavern Split&Melt
11/23/91 6 2 *OP2 Mike's
12/07/91 6 1 Stash Cavern
03/13/92 6 1 *OP1 Split&Melt
03/24/92 6 2 *OP2 Mike's
04/03/92 8 2 *OP2 Sloth
04/19/92 12 2 *OP2 Mike's
04/23/92 3 1 Cavern Split&Melt
04/30/92 4 1 *OP1 Split&Melt
05/05/92 4 1 Golgi Sparkle
05/08/92 3 1 *OP1 Cavern
05/17/92 7 2 *OP2 Possum
07/01/92 8 1a *OP1 Cavern
11/21/92 39 2 Carolina Mike's
12/01/92 7 2 Axilla Chalkdust
12/06/92 5 2 Suzie Stash
12/12/92 5 2 Glide Tweezer
12/29/92 3 2 *OP2 Tweezer
02/05/93 5 2 *OP2 Tweezer
02/21/93 13 2 Axilla Stash
02/27/93 5 2 *OP2 Stash
03/03/93 2 2 Axilla Split&Melt
03/06/93 2 1 Horn Split&Melt
03/16/93 6 2 My Friend Tweezer
03/25/93 7 2 Axilla Sample
04/01/93 6 2 Axilla Possum
04/16/93 9 2 Axilla Maze
04/25/93 8 2 Wilson Tweezer
05/03/93 6 2 ACDCBag Tweezer
08/06/93 23 1 PoorHeart Sample
12/30/93 19 1 Weigh Sample
04/06/94 4 2 *OP2 DWD
04/13/94 5 2 Faht Sample
04/25/94 11 2 *OP2 Sample
05/14/94 13 2 *OP2 Mike's
05/25/94 8 1 *OP1 Sample
06/10/94 6 2 Axilla 2 Tweezer
06/16/94 4 1 Gumbo Dog Faced
06/19/94 3 1 Axila2 FEFY
06/24/94 4 2 Halley's McGrupp
06/29/94 3 1 *OP1 Sample
07/05/94 5 1 Sample LTJP
10/09/94 11 1 FEFY Dog Faced
10/14/94 4 2 *OP2 Tweezer
10/21/94 5 2 Sl Monkey FEFY
11/04/94 11 2 *OP2 Mike's
11/22/94 9 2 Cry Baby Blackbird
12/06/94 10 2 *OP2 Sample
06/17/95 18 1 Dog Faced Stash
07/02/95 12 1 Gumbo Julius
10/22/95 20 2 Catapult Tweezer
11/12/95 10 2 *OP2 Tweezer
11/19/95 5 2 Also Sprac Tweezer
11/24/95 3 1 ACDCBag Sparkle
11/30/95 4 1 Sample Ha Ha Ha
12/07/95 5 1 Old Home ACDCBag
12/11/95 3 2 *OP2 Bowie
12/14/95 2 2 *OP2 Tweezer
12/28/95 4 1 Gumbo Julius
07/07/96 9 1a Bouncing Tweezer
08/06/96 18 2 *OP2 Tweezer
08/17/96 7 2 *OP2 RunJim
10/22/96 6 1 *OP1 RunJim
11/06/96 9 2 Wilson Mike's
11/11/96 4 2 Gumbo Sample
11/23/96 8 2 *OP2 Mike's
12/01/96 5 1 CharZero DWD
02/20/97 13 1 *OP1 Tweezer
➢ 8/17/97 47

Dave's Energy Guide [6]*

Dave's Energy Guide [Dave's]

By Anastasio/Abrahams

10/17/85 [3] 1a Mike's Revol
11/23/85 2 1a Antelope *CL1
10/31/86 4 1 Melt Guns Sally
04/24/87 5 1a YEM Alumni
04/29/87 1 2 Melt Guns A-Train
08/06/88 35 1 Cities Cities
➢ 8/17/97 891

David Bowie [263]*

David Bowie [Bowie]

By Anastasio

10/31/86 [9] 2 Peaches Mercy
12/06/86 1 1a ACDCBag Fluffhead
04/24/87 4 1a I am H2 Reagan
08/09/87 3 2 *OP2 YEM
08/10/87 1 2 Icculus Jesus
08/21/87 1 3 Makisupa Jam
09/27/87 5 1 *OP1 FunkBitch
10/14/87 1 2 *OP2 ACDCBag
02/07/88 4 1a IDK ACDCBag
03/11/88 2 1 Lizards *CL1
06/20/88 9 2 Curtis *CL2
07/24/88 5 2 Cities *CL2
09/24/88 7 2 *OP2 Lizards
10/12/88 1 1 Golgi Lizards
11/03/88 2 2 Harpua *CL2
11/05/88 1 1 Alum *CL1
11/11/88 1 1 Mockbird *CL1
02/05/89 4 1 Corrina La Grange
02/06/89 1 E *OPE *CLE
02/18/89 3 1a Contact *CL1
03/03/89 2 2 A-Train *CL2
04/15/89 10 1 Foam *CL1
04/20/89 2 1 Foam *CL1
05/06/89 9 1 Mockbird *CL1
05/13/89 6 2 *OP2 Suzie
05/20/89 4 2 A-Train Golgi
05/26/89 2 2 *OP2 Mango
06/23/89 7 2 Possum *CL2
08/19/89 9 2 Curtis Undone
08/26/89 2 2 Foam *CL2
09/09/89 4 2 MSO *CL1
10/07/89 3 1 ACDCBag Contact
10/21/89 5 2 Dog Log *CL1
10/26/89 2 2 NoDog *CL2
10/31/89 2 2 YEM Wilson
11/16/89 7 2 Tela *CL2
11/30/89 2 2 Contact *CL2
12/09/89 6 1 Rocky Top Lawn Boy
12/15/89 1 1a Contact *CL1
02/09/90 16 2 Curtis *CL2
02/10/90 1 1 Contact *CL1
02/25/90 7 1 Bouncing Satin Doll
03/07/90 4 1 Lizards *CL1
03/11/90 3 2 ACDCBag *CL2
04/05/90 4 1 Ya Mar Carolina
04/07/90 2 1 Weekpaug MSO
04/18/90 6 2 Jaeg *CL2
04/25/90 5 1 MSO *CL1
05/06/90 6 2 Esther Terrapin
05/13/90 6 1 Divided *CL1
06/05/90 7 1 A-Train Lawn Boy
09/15/90 7 1 Asse Fest Golgi
09/22/90 4 1 IDK *CL1
10/04/90 3 1 Uncle Pen *CL1
10/06/90 2 1a Brain Carolina
10/30/90 5 2 BurAlive *CL2
11/02/90 2 2 IDK *CL2
11/04/90 2 1 MSO *CL1
11/17/90 4 1 Suzie *CL1
11/24/90 1 1 Suzie *CL1
11/26/90 1 1 Donna Divided
12/07/90 3 2 No Good *CL2
12/29/90 3 1 Esther Lawn Boy
02/01/91 2 1 Bouncing *CL1
02/03/91 2 2 *OP2 Sqirm Coil
02/08/91 2 1 Guelah *CL1
02/15/91 3 2 *OP2 Bathtub
02/21/91 4 2 Uncle Pen *CL2
02/27/91 5 2 Sqirm Coil Lawn Boy
03/01/91 2 2 Love You *CL2
03/06/91 2 1 Bouncing *CL1
03/13/91 4 1 Sqirm Coil *CL1
03/17/91 3 1 Lizards *CL2
03/23/91 3 2 Cavern Contact
03/28/91 1 1a MSO Sqirm Coil
04/04/91 5 2 Guelah Lawn Boy
04/16/91 7 1 Tela *CL1
04/21/91 4 2 IDK *CL2
05/02/91 5 1 Cavern Adeline
05/10/91 4 1 *OP1 Cavern
05/12/91 2 2 *OP2 Bathtub
05/18/91 3 2 Guelah Terrapin
07/12/91 3 1 Cavern *CL1
07/19/91 5 1 Bouncing Fee
07/20/91 1 1 MSO *CL2

Stories Behind the Songs
(Continued)

effects) and Yerushalayim Schel Zahav, the Hebrew prayer which appears at the very end of Hoist. In concert, the song ends where the car sound effects begin on the album.

Destiny Unbound: Last played in the fall of 1991, this song was rumored to be retired when the band feared it sounded too much like a Dead song. The band apparently promised to bring it back if the audience all yelled the song's first line in unison, but despite an incredible attempt at Red Rocks in August 1996 to coordinate this effort, the band wouldn't oblige. Trey apparently told fans in Europe during summer '96 that Destiny Unbound wouldn't be played again "for a long time."

Divided Sky: A Gamehendge song which is not part of The Man Who Stepped Into Yesterday recording but is part of an ancient Gamehendge ritual of the Lizard people in which three chosen individuals climb the rhombus in the middle of a vast field to pay homage to Icculus by way of song. Trey lifted the song's melody from an Anastasio family musical, "Gus the Christmas Dog."

Dog Log: Played sporadically in 1990 and once in 1991 (on 5/4/91), has only been played a few times since then, although the band still frequently soundchecks it — it's soundman Paul Languedoc's favorite Phish song. When the band broke it out at Portland, ME on 12/11/95, Trey joked that Phish planned to release an album of different Dog Log versions.

Dogs Stole Things: One of the many new songs debuted in summer '97, Trey told the crowd at Virginia Beach on 7/21/97 that the song is about people's pets (dogs and cats) stealing their souls while they sleep.

Down With Disease: Written by Tom Marshall during a bout with mono, Down With Disease received newfound attention from Phish in 1996. After playing it only a handful of times in 1995, the band went to town on DWD, raising it to the level of all-time jam songs in the minds of many fans. That focus continued through summer 1997, as the Disease lives on.

07/24/91	3	2	Guelah	Jesus
09/26/91	6	1	Foam	*CL1
10/04/91	6	1	Magilla	*CL1
10/11/91	4	2	Foam	Mango
10/13/91	2	2	Love You	*CL2
10/17/91	2	2	Suzie	Lawn Boy
10/24/91	4	1	TMWSIY	*CL1
10/28/91	3	1	Fee	Carolina
10/31/91	2	2	MSO	Horn
11/07/91	4	2	Horn	A-Train
11/13/91	5	2	*OP2	Forbin's
11/19/91	4	2	Cavern	*CL2
11/24/91	5	1	IDK	*CL1
12/04/91	2	1	Bouncing	*CL1
03/06/92	5	1	All Things	*CL1
03/12/92	3	2	Uncle Pen	Rosie
03/19/92	4	1	All Things	*CL1
03/21/92	2	2	All Things	Weigh
03/24/92	1	1	Landlady	*CL1
03/26/92	2	1	NICU	*CL1
03/28/92	2	1	Landlady	Glide
04/01/92	3	1	Landlady	Carolina
04/05/92	3	2	Landlady	Love You
04/09/92	3	2	Suzie	TMWSIY
04/13/92	2	1	A-Train	*CL2
04/17/92	3	1	Catapult	*CL1
04/21/92	3	1	Bouncing	*CL1
04/24/92	3	2	*OP2	Cavern
04/29/92	2	1	A-Train	*CL1
05/02/92	3	2	Glide	Tela
05/08/92	5	1	Bouncing	Memories
05/12/92	3	1	Horn	*CL1
05/16/92	3	1	Cavern	*CL1
06/27/92	7	1a	Uncle Pen	*CL1
07/09/92	4	1a	Guelah	Glide
07/16/92	6	1	Rift	*CL1
07/19/92	3	1a	RunJim	Adeline
07/22/92	2	1a	Cavern	*CL1
07/27/92	4	1a	All Things	Horn
08/02/92	5	1a	Suzie	Cavern
08/17/92	4	1	Bouncing	*CL1
08/20/92	2	1a	Sqirm Coil	Adelin
11/20/92	10	1	Walk Line	*CL1
11/23/92	3	1	Memories	*CL1
11/27/92	2	2	Walk Line	Horse
12/01/92	3	2	Dinner	*CL2
12/04/92	3	2	Suzie	Esther
12/07/92	3	2	Fee	Love You
12/11/92	3	1	Memories	*CL1
12/13/92	2	1	IDK	*CL1
12/30/92	3	1	Timber Ho	*CL1
02/03/93	2	1	Guelah	*CL1
02/05/93	2	1	Reba	*CL1
02/09/93	3	1	*OP1	Bouncing
02/11/93	2	1	Lawn Boy	*CL1
02/13/93	2	1	*OP1	Bouncing
02/17/93	2	2	Landlady	Glide
02/19/93	2	1	PoorHeart	*CL1
02/22/93	3	1	IDK	*CL1
02/25/93	2	1	IDK	*CL1
03/02/93	3	1	IDK	*CL1
03/08/93	4	1	Glide	*CL1
03/12/93	2	1	Silent	*CL1
03/14/93	2	2	Halley's	Curtis
03/18/93	3	1	IDK	*CL1
03/22/93	3	1	Sparkle	*CL1
03/27/93	4	1	IDK	*CL1
03/31/93	3	1	IDK	*CL1
04/05/93	4	1	Mockbird	*CL1
04/10/93	2	1	Lawn Boy	*CL1
04/20/93	7	1	Lawn Boy	*CL1
04/27/93	6	1	Sparkle	*CL1
05/01/93	3	1	Glide	*CL1
05/08/93	6	2	*OP2	Mercy
07/15/93	3	2	*OP2	Horse
07/17/93	2	1	Oh Kee	*CL1
07/25/93	6	1	IDK	*CL1
07/30/93	4	2	Sqirm Coil	*CL2
08/08/93	6	1	IDK	*CL1
08/13/93	4	1	Horn	*CL1
08/17/93	4	2	Also Sprac	Horse
08/21/93	2	2	Lawn Boy	Brain
08/26/93	3	2	Also Sprac	Life Boy
12/30/93	4	1	*OP1	Weigh
04/08/94	5	2	BBJ	Suzie
04/13/94	4	2	A-Train	PurplRain
04/17/94	4	2	*OP2	Wolfman's
04/22/94	4	1	Silent	*CL1
04/24/94	2	2	Demand	Mango
04/30/94	4	2	Wilson	Wolfman's
05/03/94	2	2	*OP2	If I Could
05/06/94	2	2	Bike	*CL2
05/10/94	3	2	Nellie	*CL2
05/14/94	3	1	Ginseng	*CL1
05/21/94	5	2	Sample	Contact
05/27/94	5	1	Bouncing	If I Could
05/29/94	2	1	IDK	*CL1
06/10/94	2	1	Demand	Lizards
06/14/94	3	2	Demand	If I Could
06/18/94	3	2	Peaches	Horn
06/23/94	4	2	Frankstein	Mango
06/29/94	4	1	Catapult	IDK
07/01/94	2	2	*OP2	If I Could
07/03/94	2	1	Axilla 2	*CL1
07/06/94	2	1	Carolina	*CL1
07/10/94	3	2	Sample	Glide
07/15/94	3	2	LTJP	Bouncing
10/09/94	4	2	*OP2	Bouncing
10/12/94	2	2	Peaches	Bouncing
10/18/94	5	2	*OP2	Horse
10/22/94	3	2	Peaches	Horse
10/26/94	3	2	Rosie	*CL2
10/28/94	2	2	Also Sprac	Lizards
10/31/94	2	3	*OP3	Bouncing
11/04/94	3	1	Bouncing	Forbin's
11/14/94	3	2	Peaches	YSZahov
11/17/94	2	2	Also Sprac	Manteca
11/20/94	3	2	Also Sprac	Glide
11/26/94	4	2	Halley's	Adeline
12/02/94	4	2	Chalkdust	BurAlive
12/08/94	5	2	Adeline	Golgi
12/29/94	4	2	Guyute	Halley's
06/09/95	6	2	Cavern	AArmy
06/13/95	2	2	*OP2	Lizards
06/15/95	2	2	Ha Ha Ha	Str Design
06/19/95	3	2	Simple	Mango
06/24/95	4	2	Halley's	Life Boy
06/29/95	4	2	Free	Str Design
07/03/95	4	2	Timber Ho	ACDCBag
09/27/95	1	2	ACDCBag	Billy
10/02/95	4	1	Tela	*CL1
10/05/95	2	2	Cavern	Life Boy
10/08/95	3	2	Dog Faced	KeyB
10/15/95	4	1	I'm Blue	*CL1
10/21/95	4	2	Also Sprac	Life Boy
10/27/95	4	2	Also Sprac	Dog Faced
10/29/95	2	2	Makisupa	Mango
11/11/95	4	2	Also Sprac	Suzie
11/16/95	4	2	DayinLife	Life Boy
11/21/95	3	2	Simple	Glide
11/25/95	3	1	DayinLife	Billy
12/01/95	4	2	Suspicious	*CL2
12/05/95	3	1	Esther	I'm Blue
12/11/95	4	2	Curtain	Mango
12/15/95	3	2	Also Sprac	Adeline
12/30/95	5	1	Suzie	Simple
04/26/96	2	1a	DayinLife	*CL1
06/06/96	1	2	CharZero	Fee
07/05/96	2	1a	Scent	*CL1
07/10/96	4	1a	Waste	HelloBaby
07/12/96	2	3	*OP3	Free
07/17/96	3	1a	Sample	Ya Mar
08/04/96	9	2	Sample	Adeline
08/13/96	6	2	Adeline	*CL2
08/16/96	2	1	Halley's	*CL1
10/17/96	3	2	SSB	*CL2
10/21/96	3	2	Silent	*CL2
10/29/96	6	1	PoorHeart	*CL1
11/06/96	5	1	Billy	*CL1
11/09/96	3	2	*OP2	DayinLife
11/16/96	5	1	Old Home	Lawn Boy
11/19/96	2	2	*OP2	DayinLife
11/24/96	3	2	Sparkle	DayinLife
12/04/96	6	1	Lizards	*CL1
12/29/96	3	2	*OP2	DayinLife
02/13/97	3	1	Treat	*CL1
02/16/97	2	2	Steep	Lovin Cup
02/20/97	3	1	Circus	TweezRep
02/23/97	3	1	Frankstein	*CL1
02/28/97	3	2	Frankstein	Treat
03/18/97	3	2	Caspian	Treat
06/14/97	2	2	Waste	Cavern
06/20/97	3	2	*OP2	Ghost
07/02/97	8	E2	*OPE2	*CLE2
07/21/97	7	2	Magilla	Wading
07/26/97	4	2	Timber Ho	Harry
07/30/97	2	2	Free	Bouncing
08/10/97	7	2	RockaW	*CL2
➢ 8/17/97	5			

Dear Mrs. Reagan [7]

Dear Mrs. Reagan [Reagan]

By Anastasio

04/01/86	[6]	2	Alumni	*CL2
04/15/86	1	1a	ACDCBag	PrepHipp
04/24/87	7	1a	Bowie	Slave
08/10/87	4	2	Tush	*CL2
09/12/87	5	1	Wilson	Golgi
02/07/88	6	1a	Peaches	IDK
06/15/88	12	2	WhipPost	*CL2
➢ 8/17/97	901			

Demand [14]*

Demand [Demand]

By Anastasio/Marshall

04/09/94	[619]	2	BBJ	Mike's
04/14/94	4	1	Rift	Split&Melt
04/24/94	9	2	*OP2	Bowie
05/22/94	20	1	*OP1	Sloth
05/26/94	3	1	Cavern	Split&Melt
06/10/94	5	1	Nellie	Bowie
06/14/94	3	2	Frankstein	Bowie
06/24/94	8	1	*OP2	Antelope
06/26/94	2	2	Dog Faced	SMJam
10/08/95	97	1	ACDCBag	Sparkle
10/15/95	4	1	IDK	Llama
10/24/95	6	1	Silent	Maze
12/07/95	26	1	ACDCBag	Rift
11/14/96	64	2	Life Mars	Antelope
➢ 8/17/97	71			

Destiny Unbound [23]*

Destiny Unbound [Destiny]

By Gordon

09/14/90	[223]	2	Lizards	Fire
09/22/90	5	2	Tweezer	Fee
10/04/90	3	1	Lizards	Sloth
10/07/90	3	1	Landlady	Forbin's
12/29/90	21	2	Bouncing	Antelope
02/02/91	3	1	Stash	YEM
02/03/91	1	1	Esther	Reba
02/07/91	1	2	Sloth	YEM
02/14/91	3	1	Reba	Cavern
02/26/91	9	2	Landlady	Possum
03/15/91	10	2	Cavern	IDK
03/22/91	4	1	Landlady	Bouncing
04/11/91	10	2	Landlady	Mike's
04/19/91	6	2	Landlady	MSO
04/22/91	3	2	Landlady	Sqirm Coil
05/12/91	10	1	Landlady	Llama
09/26/91	21	2	Landlady	Mike's
10/03/91	5	2	Landlady	BurAlive
10/06/91	3	2	Landlady	Harry
10/15/91	5	1	Landlady	YEM
10/27/91	7	1	Landlady	A-Train
11/01/91	4	1	Landlady	Sqirm Coil
11/15/91	10	2	Landlady	Harry
➢ 8/17/97	571			

Dinner and a Movie [108]

Dinner and a Movie [Dinner

By Anastasio/Dude of Life

11/19/87	[27]	3	*OP3	Curtis
03/11/88	4	2	Fluffhead	Harry
03/21/88	2	1a	Possum	IDK
06/15/88	7	2	Contact	A-Train
07/23/88	6	3	Harry	Slave
08/06/88	4	1	FunkBitch	Fire
02/07/89	15	1	Makisupa	ACDCBag
08/26/89	55	3	Suzie	Antelope
10/01/89	5	2	Reba	Fluffhead
10/06/89	1	1a	Bold	Alumni
10/07/89	1	2	*OP2	Possum
10/20/89	4	2	WalkAway	IDK
10/26/89	3	2	*OP2	Clod
12/09/89	17	1	*OP1	La Grange
02/09/90	17	2	*OP2	Ya Mar
02/10/90	1	1	*OP1	Oh Kee
02/15/90	1	1	Divided	Caravan
02/17/90	2	1a	Suzie	Caravan
02/23/90	2	1	Rocky Top	Ya Mar
03/03/90	5	2	*OP2	Caravan
03/08/90	2	1	*OP1	YEM
03/11/90	2	2	Bouncing	A-Train
04/06/90	5	1	Ya Mar	Oh Kee
04/13/90	6	1	FunkBitch	Bouncing
04/20/90	3	1	Cavern	Bouncing
04/22/90	2	2	*OP2	Bouncing
04/25/90	1	2	La Grange	Bouncing
04/26/90	1	1	Uncle Pen	Bouncing
04/28/90	1	1	Uncle Pen	Bouncing
04/29/90	1	1	YEM	Bouncing
05/13/90	7	1	ACDCBag	Bouncing
05/19/90	2	2	Fee	Bouncing
05/24/90	2	2	Foam	Possum
05/31/90	1	1a	YEM	Bouncing
06/01/90	1	1a	Suzie	Fee
06/05/90	1	2	Caravan	Bouncing
06/07/90	1	2	MSO	Bouncing
06/09/90	2	1	Reba	Bouncing
09/14/90	3	1	Stash	IDK
09/16/90	2	1a	*OP1	Bouncing
09/28/90	2	2	Gumbo	YEM
10/01/90	1	1	Magilla	Bouncing
10/06/90	3	1a	Sqirm Coil	Bouncing
10/12/90	3	1	YEM	Bouncing
11/03/90	5	1	*OP1	Bouncing
11/08/90	2	2	Oh Kee	Bouncing
11/30/90	6	1	Esther	Bouncing
12/08/90	3	2	Asse Fest	Bouncing
12/29/90	2	2	Jesus	Bouncing
02/02/91	3	1	Guelah	Esther

02/15/91	6	1	Sloth	Magilla
02/21/91	4	1	Reba	Split&Melt
02/26/91	4	2	RunJim	Stash
03/01/91	3	1	Tweezer	Bouncing
03/15/91	7	1	Stash	Bouncing
04/05/91	12	2	Sloth	Harry
04/11/91	2	1	Magilla	Bouncing
04/19/91	6	1	FunkBitch	Bouncing
05/10/91	11	1	Ya Mar	Sloth
05/12/91	2	1	Bouncing	Stash
05/16/91	1	2	RunJim	Bouncing
05/18/91	2	E	*OPE	RunJim
05/25/91	1	1a	Reba	Sloth
07/11/91	1	2	*OP2	Cavern
07/12/91	1	1	*OP1	Bouncing
07/14/91	2	2	Gumbo	Bouncing
07/15/91	1	1a	Landlady	Stash
07/20/91	3	2	Caravan	Flat Fee
07/23/91	2	2	Adeline	Gumbo
07/26/91	3	2	Stash	YEM
09/27/91	5	2	Mango	Oh Kee
10/12/91	10	1	A-Train	Brother
10/18/91	4	2	Guelah	Mike's
10/24/91	3	2	Slave	Bouncing
10/28/91	3	2	Wilson	Stash
10/31/91	2	2	Horn	Tube
11/08/91	5	1	Landlady	Stash
11/12/91	3	2	*OP2	Stash
11/14/91	2	2	*OP2	Antpl
11/19/91	3	2	Reba	Cavern
11/22/91	3	1	Lawn Boy	Stash
12/04/91	4	1	Sqirm Coil	Bouncing
03/13/92	9	1	Maze	Divided
03/19/92	3	1	Silent	Forbin's
03/21/92	2	1	Silent	Sqirm Coil
03/27/92	4	2	Bathtub	Magilla
03/31/92	3	2	Cavern	My Friend
04/06/92	5	2	*OP2	Bathtub
04/18/92	8	2	TMWSIY	Harry
04/21/92	2	2	*OP2	Forbin's
04/25/92	4	2	All Things	Harry
05/03/92	5	2	Rosie	Bouncing
05/12/92	7	1	It's Ice	Bouncing
07/16/92	20	1	Wilson	Bouncing
11/20/92	30	2	FEFY	Harry
12/01/92	8	2	Love You	Bowie
12/11/92	9	2	*OP2	Mike's
02/21/93	22	1	Esther	Bouncing
04/12/93	34	2	*OP2	Tweezer
04/24/93	10	2	Bathtub	Mound
08/09/93	33	2	*OP2	Tweezer
05/21/94	54	2	*OP2	Sample
06/13/94	11	1	Wolfman's	Stash
10/22/94	38	2	Silent	Tweezer
11/18/95	93	1	*OP1	Bouncing
11/28/95	6	1	Stash	Bouncing
08/06/96	43	1	Lizards	Horn
03/01/97	59	2	Carini	Mike's
➢ 8/17/97	39			

Dirt [15]

Dirt [Dirt]

By Anastasio/Marshall

06/14/97	[905]	1	NICU	Talk
06/16/97	1	2	Wading	Harry
06/21/97	3	1a	Taste	Theme
06/22/97	1	1a	Stash	Uncle Pen
07/01/97	5	1	Saw It	Reba
07/09/97	5	1	Split&Melt	Taste
07/21/97	3	1	Piper	Ginseng
07/23/97	2	1	Julius	NICU
07/26/97	2	1	CTB	YEM
07/29/97	1	1	Gumbo	Sparkle
07/31/97	2	1	Limb	Maze
08/03/97	2	1	Blow	Vultures
08/08/97	2	1	Lizards	It's Ice
08/10/97	2	1	DWD	CTB
08/17/97	5	3	Guyute	Scent
➢ 8/17/97	0			

Divided Sky [268]*

The Divided Sky [Divided]

By Anastasio

08/09/87	[17]	2	Ya Mar	Fluffhead
08/10/87	1	1	Quinn	GTBT
08/21/87	1	1	Peaches	FunkBitch
08/29/87	2	2	ACDCBag	Harpua
09/12/87	2	2	Fee	Dog Log
10/14/87	2	2	ACDCBag	McGrupp
11/19/87	2	2	Possum	BBFCM
01/30/88	1	2	Fluffhead	Curtis
02/08/88	2	2	Peaches	Lizrds
03/21/88	3	1a	Sally	Boogie On
07/23/88	13	1	No Dogs	No Dogs
09/24/88	8	1	A-Train	Bold
10/29/88	2	2	WalkAway	Curtis
11/05/88	2	2	Sparks	*CL2
11/11/88	1	1	*OP1	YEM
12/02/88	1	1	A-Train	Contact
01/26/89	1	1a	A-Train	Fee
02/06/89	3	1	Golgi	OYWD
02/17/89	2	1a	Fee	Split&Melt
03/03/89	3	1	IDK	Alumni
03/30/89	3	1	McGrupp	Price
04/15/89	7	2	Mango	Split&Melt
04/20/89	2	2	*OP2	WalkAway
04/30/89	5	1	Lizards	Wilson
05/06/89	4	2	Slave	Antelope
05/09/89	4	1	Possum	*CL1
05/20/89	7	1	Wilson	IDK
05/21/89	1	1	ACDCBag	*CL1
05/28/89	3	1	*OP1	Antelope
08/19/89	14	2	A-Train	Bathtub
08/26/89	2	1	Split&Melt	YEM
09/09/89	4	1	Suzie	ACDCBag
10/14/89	6	1	ACDCBag	IDK
10/20/89	1	1	Reba	Golgi
10/22/89	2	1	Tela	IDK
10/26/89	1	1	Fee	IDK
10/31/89	2	1	ACDCBag	Fee
11/02/89	1	2	Kung	McGrupp
11/10/89	4	1	Fee	ACDCBag
11/30/89	4	1	Bathtub	Ya Mar
12/07/89	4	1	Alumni	*CL1
12/15/89	3	1a	Possum	Antelope
12/29/89	2	1	*OP1	Ya Mar
12/31/89	2	2	Split&Melt	Fee
01/27/90	4	2	Terrapin	*Cl2
02/15/90	10	1	Suzie	Dinner
02/24/90	2	1	Golgi	Esther
03/01/90	2	1	Ya Mar	IDK
03/03/90	2	2	Carolina	*CL2
03/08/90	2	2	*OP2	Bathtub
04/06/90	5	1	Uncle Pen	Ya Mar
04/08/90	2	1	*OP1	FunkBitch
04/09/90	1	2	Jesus	Love You
04/12/90	2	1	Jesus	GTBT
04/20/90	4	1	A-Train	Alumni
04/22/90	2	1	*OP1	Uncle Pen
04/25/90	1	1	Brain	MSO
04/29/90	3	1a	Uncle Pen	Fluffhead
05/10/90	4	1	Bouncing	Tweezer
05/13/90	3	1	Uncle Pen	Bowie
05/23/90	3	1	*OP1	Ya Mar
05/31/90	2	1a	Uncle Pen	Oh Kee
06/01/90	1	1a	YEM	Slave
06/05/90	1	2	Adeline	Caravan
06/07/90	1	2	Uncle Pen	Love You
06/08/90	1	1	YEM	*CL1
06/16/90	2	1	ACDCBag	Wilson
09/13/90	1	1	Landlady	Foam
09/15/90	2	1	BurAlive	Paul&Silas
09/22/90	4	1	MSO	Tela
09/28/90	1	2	YEM	*CL2
10/07/90	5	1	*OP1	Uncle Pen
10/12/90	2	2	Terrapin	Paul&Silas
11/02/90	4	1	Bouncing	Sloth
11/08/90	3	2	Suzie	Tweezer
11/10/90	1	2	Llama	Bike
11/16/90	1	1	Llama	Golgi
11/24/90	2	E	Lawn Boy	*CLE
11/26/90	1	1	Bowie	Makisupa
11/30/90	1	2	Gumbo	IDK
12/01/90	1	1	Llama	Foam
12/03/90	1	1	Reba	MSO
12/08/90	2	1	ACDCBag	Cavern
12/28/90	1	2	MSO	No Good
12/31/90	2	1	Suzie	IDK
02/15/91	8	1	Wilson	Spilt
02/16/91	1	1	MSO	Cavern
02/27/91	8	1	Golgi	IDK
02/28/91	1	2	Guelah	*CL2
03/01/91	1	1	Foam	Cavern
03/06/91	2	1	Cavern	Love You
03/13/91	4	1	Cavern	Esther
03/16/91	2	2	Llama	Guelah
03/23/91	4	1	Sloth	Fee
03/28/91	1	1a	Golgi	Cavern
04/04/91	5	2	MSO	Love You
04/05/91	1	1	Bouncing	Cavern
04/12/91	3	1	Uncle Pen	Guelah
04/19/91	5	1	Bouncing	Cavern
04/21/91	2	1	Wilson	Foam
05/02/91	5	2	PoorHeart	Fee
05/03/91	1	1	TMWSIY	Fee
05/16/91	6	1	Cavern	Forbin's
05/18/91	2	1	Foam	Cavern
05/25/91	1	1a	*OP1	Landlady
07/11/91	1	1	Suzie	Flat Fee
07/13/91	2	2	Guelah	Flat Fee
07/14/91	1	2	Caravan	Gumbo
07/19/91	3	2	Suzie	IDK
07/21/91	2	1	Cavern	Guelah
07/25/91	3	1	Suzie	Flat Fee
08/03/91	3	1	Sloth	Golgi
09/26/91	2	1	Bouncing	Fee
09/29/91	3	1a	Cavern	IDK
10/03/91	2	1	Fee	Cavern
10/04/91	1	1	Cavern	Guelah
10/06/91	2	1	Foam	Bouncing
10/17/91	6	1	Bouncing	Cavern
10/24/91	4	1	Ya Mar	IDK
10/28/91	3	2	*OP2	Wilson
11/01/91	3	1	Tube	Adeline
11/08/91	4	1	PoorHeart	Mango
11/13/91	4	1	Cavern	IDK
11/15/91	2	1	MSO	Lawn Boy
11/19/91	2	1	Wilson	*CL1
11/22/91	3	1	Foam	Lawn Boy
11/24/91	2	2	Tube	Cavern
11/30/91	1	1	Sparkle	Cavern
12/06/91	3	2	Horn	Tela
12/31/91	2	1	Guelah	Esther
03/06/92	1	1	Oh Kee	Guelah
03/11/92	2	1	Mound	Cavern
03/13/92	2	1	Dinner	Mound
03/17/92	2	1	IDK	Guelah
03/27/92	7	1	Sloth	Guelah
03/31/92	3	1	Wilson	Glide
04/05/92	4	1	Guelah	Wilson
04/07/92	2	1	Fee	Horse
04/12/92	2	1	Guelah	Horse
04/18/92	5	1	Wilson	Guelah
04/22/92	3	1	Guelah	Mound
05/01/92	6	1	Sloth	Guelah
05/05/92	3	1	Guelah	IDN
05/09/92	4	2	Suzie	Tela
05/18/92	7	1	Bouncing	Guelah
06/30/92	6	1a	Golgi	Guelah
07/12/92	6	1a	Bouncing	Fluffhead
07/15/92	2	2	Sloth	Esther
07/26/92	9	1a	It's Ice	Weigh
11/19/92	21	1	Mound	Esther
11/23/92	4	1	Guelah	Mound
11/27/92	2	1	Wilson	Forbin's
12/02/92	4	1	Foam	FEFY
12/05/92	3	1	Mound	Adeline
12/08/92	3	1	Guelah	Mound
12/13/92	4	1	Wilson	It's Ice
12/29/92	2	1	My Friend	Wilson
12/31/92	2	1	Wilson	Cavern
02/03/93	1	1	Wedge	IDK
02/06/93	3	1	Horn	Lawn Boy
02/10/93	3	1	Sloth	Tela
02/15/93	4	1	Guelah	Esther
02/20/93	4	1	All Things	Horse
02/26/93	5	1	Horn	IDK
03/09/93	7	1	Esther	Glide
03/16/93	4	1	IDK	McGrupp
03/21/93	4	1	Sloth	Esther
03/26/93	4	1	Fluffhead	Cavern
03/30/93	3	1	Glide	Cavern
04/02/93	3	1	Bouncing	IDK
04/09/93	3	1	It's Ice	Cavern
04/14/93	4	1	Silent	IDK
04/18/93	3	1	Sparkle	Fee
04/23/93	4	1	My Friend	Guelah
04/30/93	5	1	Silent	Cavern
05/02/93	2	1	Sparkle	Mound
05/07/93	4	1	Horn	IDK
07/15/93	4	1	Sample	Mound
07/18/93	3	1	Esther	Uncle Pen
07/22/93	2	1	Sample	Mound
07/24/93	2	1	Nellie	Guelah
07/29/93	4	1	FunkBitch	Weigh
07/31/93	2	1	Nellie	Cavern
08/06/93	3	1	Horn	Nellie
08/09/93	3	1	Nellie	Memories
08/14/93	4	1	Guelah	Horse
08/17/93	3	1	Guelah	Horse
08/20/93	1	1	*OP1	Harpua
12/29/93	7	1	Glide	Wilson
04/04/94	3	1	*OP1	Sample
04/11/94	6	1	Glide	Cavern
04/13/94	1	1	Ginseng	Golgi
04/17/94	4	1	IDK	Mound
04/22/94	4	1	Nellie	Horse
04/25/94	3	2	Sqirm Coil	Bouncing
04/29/94	2	1	Sloth	IDK
05/02/94	2	1	Glide	Suzie
05/07/94	4	1	Horn	Mound
05/10/94	2	1	Sample	Axilla 2
05/16/94	4	1	Sample	Axilla 2
05/22/94	5	1	Sloth	Glide
05/26/94	3	1	Catapult	Sample
05/29/94	3	1	*OP1	Guelah
06/13/94	4	1	Sample	Wolfman's
06/18/94	4	1	Dog Faced	Sample
06/24/94	5	1	*OP2	Wilson
06/26/94	2	1	McGrupp	*CL1
06/29/94	1	2	Life Boy	Suzie
07/02/94	3	1	Golgi	Guelah
07/08/94	4	1	McGrupp	*CL1
07/15/94	5	1	Sample	Gumbo
10/07/94	2	1	PoorHeart	Guelah
10/10/94	3	1	Sample	Horse

SONGS PLAYED BY YEAR

(1997 through 8/17/97)

Don't Get Me Wrong

1990	3
1991	0
1992	0
1993	0
1994	0
1995	0
1996	0
1997	0

Down With Disease

1994	55
1995	5
1996	20
1997	12

Eliza

1990	3
1991	6
1992	6
1993	0
1994	0
1995	0
1996	0
1997	0

Esther

1990	22
1991	16
1992	12
1993	17
1994	11
1995	4
1996	3
1997	0

Faht

1992	4
1993	4
1994	2
1995	2
1996	0
1997	0

Famous Mockingbird

1990	9
1991	16
1992	14
1993	16
1994	11
1995	3
1996	2
1997	0

Fast Enough for You

1992	9
1993	17
1994	13
1995	8
1996	4
1997	0

Fee

1990	22
1991	31
1992	25
1993	33
1994	39
1995	14
1996	10
1997	1

Flat Fee

1990	0
1991	8
1992	0
1993	0
1994	0
1995	0
1996	0
1997	0

Fluffhead

1990	9
1991	19
1992	18
1993	20
1994	19
1995	8
1996	6
1997	3

Foam

1990	36
1991	61
1992	53
1993	39
1994	36
1995	8
1996	6
1997	7

Fog That Surrounds

1995	22
1996	0
1997	0

Fooled by Images

1997	1

Free

1995	31
1996	17
1997	12

Ghost

1997	20

Glide

1991	10
1992	34
1993	30
1994	20
1995	3
1996	2
1997	1

Glide II

1995	1
1996	0
1997	0

Stories Behind the Songs
(Continued)

Eliza: A Trey instrumental dedicated to his then-girlfriend, now-wife Sue, whose middle name is Eliza. Trey wrote the drum part to this song by sitting at Fish's drum set and basing the arrangement on how his drums were positioned.

Esther: In this case, the story really *is* the song. One of Trey's most unique compositions, he sounded out interesting phrases then morphed them into verses and set it to music. A computer-animated video for Esther, produced by Rhode Island video firm CoSA, was shown between sets at the Somerville Theater on July 19, 1991.

Faht: The band originally wanted to name the song "Windham Hell" for inclusion on Nectar, but the legal department of the well-known Windham Hill Records urged Phish—and Elektra—to come up with another name. Reportedly, when the band got this news, Fishman was away on vacation and in his absence the band decided to rename the song Faht. Why? The late fall 1991 Phish Update contained a Fish's Forum in which the word "raht" was misspelled "faht." The typo, at a crucial point in the essay, angered Fishman because it made the piece unintelligible. The other band members thought it would be funny to tell Fish that Elektra had misspelled "Windham Hell" as "Faht." As on *Picture of Nectar*, live versions of Faht feature sound effects (prerecorded) played through the PA system while Fishman plays the guitar line.

Famous Mockingbird: A Gamehendge song, usually preceded by a "Forbin's rap" narrative by Trey and, before that, Colonel Forbin's Ascent. Famous Mockingbird chronicles Icculus' summoning of the Mockingbird called to retrieve the Helping Friendly Book from the highest turret of Wilson's castle.

Fast Enough For You: A very literal song lyrically about love and life. Tom Marshall wrote the lyrics but Trey has said that the words had a resonance with the rest of the band, all of whom faced the challenge of staying close to loved ones while spending the majority of each year on the road. The song became the

10/14/94	3	1	Sample	Horse
10/18/94	3	1	Guyute	AmGrace
10/22/94	3	1	Suzie	Gumbo
10/27/94	4	1	Mockbird	Horse
10/31/94	3	1	Simple	Harpua
11/03/94	2	1	Fee	Wilson
11/13/94	3	2	Suzie	Lizards
11/17/94	3	1	Wilson	Dog Faced
11/20/94	3	1	Dooley	Sample
11/23/94	2	1	Suzie	AmGrace
11/28/94	3	1	Simple	Adeline
12/03/94	4	1	Wilson	Guelah
12/07/94	3	2	Frankstein	Fee
12/10/94	3	1	Sample	Lawn Boy
12/31/94	4	1	Peaches	FunkBitch
06/09/95	4	1	My Friend	Str Design
06/17/95	6	1	*OP1	Suzie
06/22/95	3	1	Ha Ha Ha	Guelah
06/25/95	3	1	Sparkle	IDK
06/29/95	3	1	Silent	Cavern
07/02/95	3	1	Sample	Gumbo
09/29/95	4	1	Sparkle	Str Design
10/05/95	4	1	Str Design	AArmy
10/11/95	4	1	Cavern	If I Could
10/20/95	6	1	Ha Ha Ha	Fee
10/25/95	4	1	Sample	Wedge
10/31/95	4	1	Icculus	Wilson
11/09/95	1	1	TweezRep	Caspian
11/14/95	4	1	Billy	Esther
11/21/95	5	1	Caspian	LongJourn
11/28/95	4	1	IDK	Guyute
12/04/95	5	1	Gumbo	PYITE
12/12/95	6	1	Sample	Life Boy
12/16/95	3	1	Sloth	Dog Faced
12/30/95	4	1	TMWSIY	Sample
07/07/96	7	1a	Sample	Bouncing
07/12/96	4	1	Wilson	Horn
07/17/96	3	1a	*OP1	Sample
08/05/96	10	1	Guelah	Wolfman's
08/13/96	5	1	*OP1	Tube
08/16/96	2	1	Esther	Halley's
10/18/96	4	1	Str Design	Billy
10/21/96	2	1	Sloth	CharZero
11/03/96	9	2	Timber Ho	Wolfman's
11/09/96	4	1	Sloth	Horn
11/11/96	1	2	Timber Ho	Gumbo
11/15/96	3	1	Wilson	Bouncing
11/23/96	5	1	CTB	PYITE
11/29/96	3	1	CharZero	Bathtub
12/02/96	3	2	Ya Mar	Wolfman's
12/31/96	6	1	Silent	Sample
02/17/97	4	1	SSP	Wilson
07/03/97	25	1	My Soul	Beauty
08/02/97	14	1	DogsStole	Wolfman's
➢ 8/17/97	**9**			

Dog Faced Boy [33]

Dog Faced Boy [Dog Faced]

By Fishman/Anastasio/Marshall/McConnell

04/14/94	[623]	2	Nellie	Slave
04/18/94	4	1	Split&Melt	Oh Kee
04/24/94	5	1	Gin	Paul&Silas
04/25/94	1	1	Ginseng	Tela
04/29/94	2	1	IDK	Split&Melt
05/10/94	8	2	Ginseng	Nellie
05/17/94	5	1	Ginseng	Split&Melt
05/20/94	2	1	Scent	Carolina
05/22/94	2	1	Ginseng	Axilla 2
05/26/94	3	2	Ginseng	YEM
06/16/94	9	1	Curtain	Stash
06/18/94	2	1	It's Ice	Divided
06/21/94	2	2	BBFCM	Adeline
06/24/94	3	2	Llama	PoorHeart
06/26/94	2	2	Scent	Demand
07/15/94	13	2	YSZahov	Julius
10/09/94	4	1	Curtain	Split&Melt
10/16/94	6	2	Antelope	Adeline
10/21/94	3	1	Lizards	Antelope
10/26/94	4	1	Guyute	Scent
11/03/94	6	1	Split&Melt	Sparkle
11/17/94	6	1	Divided	Forbin
12/28/94	19	1	Reba	It's Ice
06/16/95	12	1	My Mind	Catapult
06/26/95	8	1	It's Ice	Possum
10/08/95	16	2	Suspicious	Bowie
10/27/95	12	2	Bowie	PoorHeart
11/10/95	5	1	It's Ice	Maze
11/14/95	3	2	Stash	Stash
11/21/95	5	1	My Friend	RunJim
12/09/95	13	1	Billy	Chalkdust
12/16/95	5	1	Divided	Julius
08/12/96	40	1	It's Ice	Taste
➢ 8/17/97	**95**			

Dog Log [12]*

Dog Log [Dog Log]

By Anastasio

10/30/85	[4]	1a	Harry	Possum
04/15/86	3	1a	Mercy	Possum
12/06/86	3	1a	YEM	Tush
04/29/87	5	2	Lushngton	Melt Guns
08/21/87	4	1	*OP1	Peaches
09/12/87	4	2	Divided	Curtis
10/21/89	109	1	Lizards	Bowie
03/09/90	50	2	Curtain	Slave
05/04/91	129	2	*OP2	Llama
08/02/93	281	1	My Mind	La Grange
12/11/95	217	1	Reba	Llama
12/11/95	0	1	Llama	Tube
02/26/97	90	1	RockaW	Guitar
➢ 8/17/97	**41**			

Dogs Stole Things [18]

Dogs Stole Things [Dogs Stole]

By Anastasio/Marshall

06/13/97	[904]	1	Theme	Beauty
06/14/97	1	2	Fooled	Waste
06/16/97	1	1	Sqirm Coil	Taste
06/19/97	1	1	Limb	Theme
06/21/97	2	1a	Limb	Harry
06/24/97	2	1	Beauty	Vultures
06/25/97	1	1	Oblivious	Taste
06/27/97	1	1a	Stash	PoorHeart
07/01/97	2	1	Reba	*CL1
07/06/97	4	1	Old Home	Stash
07/10/97	2	1	*OP1	Limb
07/21/97	2	1	Ghost	Piper
07/23/97	2	1	NICU	Ginseng
07/26/97	2	1	Limb	PoorHeart
07/31/97	3	1	Ya Mar	Limb
08/02/97	1	1	Ghost	Divided
08/09/97	4	1	Taste	Reba
08/17/97	6	1	Beauty	Vultures
➢ 8/17/97	**0**			

Don't Get Me Wrong [3]

Don't Get Me Wrong [Don't Get]

By Anastasio/Popper

10/06/90	[233]	E	*OPE	*CLE
10/08/90	2	1	*OP1	Landlady
12/28/90	18	2	No Good	FunkBitch
➢ 8/17/97	**686**			

Down with Disease [92]

Down with Disease [DWD]

By Anastasio/Marshall

04/04/94	[615]	2	*OP2	If I Could
04/06/94	2	2	Curtain	Wolfman's
04/08/94	1	1	Silent	If I Could
04/10/94	2	1	Scent	*CL1
04/14/94	3	1	Sparkle	Glide
04/15/94	1	1	It's Ice	*CL1
04/17/94	2	1	Mound	If I Could
04/18/94	1	2	TMWSIY	BeLikeYou
04/21/94	2	1	Lizards	If I Could
04/23/94	2	1	Esther	Caravan
04/25/94	2	2	Foam	Ginseng
04/28/94	1	1a	Rift	Bouncing
05/02/94	3	1	Bouncing	It's Ice
05/03/94	1	2	Fluffhead	Harpua
05/06/94	2	1	*OP1	Oh Kee
05/08/94	2	1	Rift	Bouncing
05/12/94	2	2	Also Sprac	Horse
05/14/94	2	1	Wilson	Fee
05/16/94	1	1	Rift	Bouncing
05/19/94	2	1	Silent	Mango
05/21/94	2	1	Guelah	Mound
05/22/94	1	2	*OP2	Bouncing
05/26/94	3	2	Fluffhead	Mound
05/29/94	3	1	Halley's	Sparkle
06/09/94	1	1	Rift	It's Ice
06/11/94	2	1	Rift	It's Ice
06/14/94	2	1	Rift	Fee
06/16/94	1	2	BBJ	Contact
06/18/94	2	1	Mango	It's Ice
06/21/94	2	2	PoorHeart	My Friend
06/23/94	2	1	Bouncing	Horse
06/24/94	1	2	Carolina	*CL2
06/26/94	2	2	Julius	If I Could
06/30/94	2	1	*OP1	Gumbo
07/01/94	1	2	Fluffhead	TMWSIY
07/03/94	2	1	PoorHeart	Fee
07/05/94	1	1	Esther	Adeline
07/09/94	3	1	Scent	Horse
07/13/94	2	1	Mango	Fee
07/16/94	3	1	Golgi	N20

10/08/94	2	1	Sparkle	Guyute
10/10/94	2	2	Rift	Love You
10/13/94	2	1	All Things	IDK
10/15/94	2	1	Reba	Golgi
10/21/94	4	1	Fee	Foam
10/23/94	2	2	YEM	PurplRain
10/27/94	3	2	BBFCM	Adeline
10/29/94	2	2	*OP2	TMWSIY
11/03/94	3	1	Sparkle	*CL1
11/12/94	2	2	Fluffhead	Life Boy
11/17/94	4	1	Mockbird	*CL1
11/19/94	2	1	Golgi	Guyute
11/22/94	2	1	Bouncing	Adeline
11/30/94	5	1	Mockbird	Bouncing
12/06/94	5	1	Mound	Fluffhead
06/16/95	17	1	Halley's	Esther
06/26/95	8	2	*OP2	Free
12/01/95	48	1	BurAlive	Theme
12/12/95	8	2	Sparkle	Lizards
12/29/95	6	1	PoorHeart	Fog
07/15/96	14	2	*OP2	Maze
07/23/96	6	1	Scent	McGrupp
08/02/96	3	1	Ya Mar	Guelah
08/05/96	2	2	ASZ	It's Ice
08/10/96	3	2	Wilson	Scent
08/14/96	3	1	Wilson	Fee
08/16/96	1	3	ASZ	NICU
10/16/96	2	1	CTB	Wilson
10/19/96	3	1	Gumbo	Caspian
10/22/96	2	2	Also Sprac	Taste
10/26/96	3	2	*OP2	YEM
10/31/96	3	1	HwayHell	YEM
11/08/96	5	1	Mound	Caspian
11/13/96	3	1	*OP1	Bouncing
11/16/96	3	1	PoorHeart	Guyute
11/22/96	3	2	*OP2	Caspian
11/27/96	3	2	*OP2	Jesus
12/01/96	3	1	Curtain	Train Song
12/06/96	3	1	CTB	Frankstein
12/31/96	4	3	Auld	Suzie
02/14/97	2	2	Ya Mar	FunkBitch
02/17/97	2	2	Sqirm Coil	Carini
02/21/97	3	1	Foam	Lizards
02/25/97	3	2	My Friend	Caspian
03/01/97	3	1	Oh Kee	Weigh
06/14/97	4	1	*OP1	NICU
06/25/97	7	2	*OP2	Time
07/09/97	8	2	*OP2	My Soul
07/22/97	4	2	*OP2	Mike's
08/02/97	7	2	*OP2	Tweezer
08/10/97	5	1	Sparkle	Dirt
08/17/97	5	2	*OP2	Bathtub
➢ 8/17/97	**0**			

Eliza [14]*

Eliza [Eliza]

By Anastasio

09/15/90	[224]	2	Split&Melt	MSO
11/17/90	22	1	Cavern	Oh Kee
11/24/90	1	2	Stash	Landlady
10/13/91	97	E	*OPE	Uncle Pen
11/01/91	12	2	Chalkdust	Mike's
11/08/91	4	1	Brother	Golgi
11/15/91	6	2	Weekpaug	Tube
11/23/91	6	2	Tweezer	Landlady
12/06/91	5	2	It's Ice	Sparkle
03/12/92	6	2	Tweezer	It's Ice
03/24/92	7	1	Foam	Rift
04/07/92	12	2	Tweezer	YEM
04/21/92	9	1	It's Ice	NICU
05/08/92	13	1	It's Ice	Llama
05/14/92	4	2	Fluffhead	Mike's
➢ 8/17/97	**508**			

Esther [96]

Esther [Esther]

By Anastasio

09/12/88	[53]	1a	Harry	*CL1
02/07/89	12	1	*OP1	McGrupp
04/14/89	13	2	Weekpaug	*CL2
04/15/89	1	1	Weekpaug	YEM
04/20/89	2	1	Fire	Suzie
05/05/89	8	E	*OPE	*CLE
05/06/89	1	1	Weekpaug	Sloth
05/09/89	3	2	Slave	Antelope
05/28/89	11	1	Slave	Suzie
11/02/89	33	1	Split&Melt	GTBT
12/09/89	14	2	Fluffhead	Alumni
01/20/90	6	1a	Lawn Boy	Mike's
02/10/90	12	2	La Grange	ACDCBag
02/24/90	6	1	Divided	Possum
03/03/90	4	2	Fluffhead	FunkBitch
03/07/90	1	1	Possum	A-Train
04/06/90	8	2	La Grange	Sloth
04/09/90	3	2	FunkBitch	Uncle Pen
04/13/90	3	1	Fluffhead	La Grange

04/22/90	5	2	How High	BBFCM
04/25/90	1	2	YEM	La Grange
04/26/90	1	2	How High	Gin
05/06/90	5	2	Harry	Bowie
05/31/90	9	1a	Caravan	Tweezer
06/16/90	6	2	Golgi	Tweezer
09/28/90	8	2	ACDCBag	Gumbo
10/04/90	2	1	Landlady	Possum
10/06/90	2	1a	Suzie	Possum
10/12/90	3	1	Cavern	Tweezer
11/02/90	4	1	Weekpaug	Cavern
11/17/90	6	2	Weekpaug	Love You
11/30/90	3	1	Weekpaug	Dinner
12/29/90	5	1	YEM	Bowie
02/02/91	3	1	Dinner	Stash
02/03/91	1	1	Tweezer	Destiny
02/14/91	4	2	RunJim	Alumni
02/28/91	11	1	Foam	Mike's
03/13/91	7	1	Divided	Llama
03/17/91	3	2	RunJim	MSO
04/20/91	19	1	Landlady	Chalkdust
07/14/91	20	3	Landlady	Chalkdust
07/21/91	5	2	Sloth	ACDCBag
08/03/91	6	2	Tweezer	Cavern
09/27/91	3	1	BurAlive	Tweezer
10/03/91	4	2	Weekpaug	Landlady
10/17/91	9	1	Stash	Chalkdust
11/13/91	18	1	Chalkdust	Cavern
11/21/91	6	1	Split&Melt	Mike's
12/31/91	9	1	Divided	Llama
03/17/92	7	2	Tweezer	Mike's
04/06/92	15	1	Brother	Chalkdust
04/18/92	8	1	Split&Melt	Possum
04/30/92	8	1	Rift	Antelope
05/07/92	6	1	RunJim	Split&Melt
07/15/92	23	2	Divided	MSO
08/17/92	19	2	Tweezer	Mike's
11/19/92	11	1	Divided	Axilla
11/28/92	7	1	Stash	Chalkdust
12/04/92	5	2	Bowie	Possum
12/11/92	6	2	Weekpaug	Axilla
12/30/92	5	1	Split&Melt	Chalkdust
02/09/93	7	1	Chalkdust	Maze
02/12/93	3	1	Split&Melt	Wedge
02/15/93	2	1	Divided	Chalkdust
02/21/93	5	1	Chalkdust	Dinner
03/09/93	11	1	Maze	Divided
03/16/93	4	2	Gin	Chalkdust
03/21/93	4	1	Divided	All Things
03/30/93	7	1	Llama	Stash
04/16/93	11	1	Split&Melt	Llama
04/22/93	5	1	Chalkdust	Stash
05/03/93	9	1	Chalkdust	Split&Melt
07/18/93	10	1	Maze	Divided
07/30/93	9	1	Stash	Chalkdust
08/11/93	8	2	Weekpaug	All Things
08/14/93	3	1	Split&Melt	PoorHeart
08/26/93	8	1	Split&Melt	It's Ice
12/28/93	2	1	Split&Melt	Oh Kee
04/10/94	9	1	Split&Melt	Chalkdust
04/23/94	11	1	Stash	DWD
05/06/94	9	1	Stash	Chalkdust
05/29/94	18	2	Split&Melt	Chalkdust
06/13/94	4	2	Weekpaug	Cavern
06/21/94	6	2	Split&Melt	Chalkdust
07/05/94	11	1	Stash	DWD
10/10/94	12	2	Maze	Tweezer
10/20/94	7	1	Split&Melt	Julius
11/12/94	13	1	Stash	Chalkdust
11/25/94	10	1	Split&Melt	Julius
06/16/95	25	1	DWD	Ya Mar
10/19/95	30	1	PYITE	Chalkdust
11/14/95	14	1	Divided	Free
12/05/95	15	1	Free	Bowie
08/12/96	40	1	Split&Melt	Chalkdust
08/16/96	3	1	ACDCBag	Divided
10/19/96	5	1	Free	Llama
➢ 8/17/97	88			

Faht [12]*

Faht [Faht]

By Fishman

11/22/92	[483]	2	YEM	Golgi
11/27/92	3	2	Silent	A-Train
12/04/92	6	2	Harry	YEM
12/11/92	6	2	Sqirm Coil	Possum
07/15/93	80	2	Possum	Lizards
07/17/93	2	2	Weekpaug	Rift
07/23/93	4	2	Antelope	My Friend
08/16/93	19	2	Mike's	Weekpaug
04/13/94	19	2	*OP2	Curtain
06/19/94	45	2	*OP2	Antelope
10/03/95	99	2	Billy	Adeline
12/02/95	37	2	Simple	Tweezer
➢ 8/17/97	138			

Famous Mockingbird [97]*

Fly Famous Mockingbird [Mockbird]

By Anastasio

02/08/88	[30]	2	Harry	TMWSIY
03/12/88	2	1a	Forbin's	Sloth
03/21/88	1	1a	Forbin's	*CL1
03/31/88	1	2	Forbin's	A-Train
06/21/88	9	1	Forbin's	Fire
07/11/88	1	1	Forbin's	Golgi
07/23/88	2	1	Forbin's	Mike's
07/24/88	1	1	Forbin's	Sally
09/08/88	5	1	Forbin's	Bold
10/12/88	3	1	Forbin's	*CL1
11/11/88	4	1	Forbin's	Bowie
01/26/89	2	1	Forbin's	Sloth
02/05/89	2	1a	Forbin's	WhipPost
02/18/89	4	1a	Forbin's	Lizards
02/24/89	1	1	Forbin's	Antelope
03/03/89	1	2	Forbin's	Lizards
05/06/89	21	1	Forbin's	Bowie
05/28/89	14	1	Forbin's	Fee
08/23/89	15	2	Forbin's	Ya Mar
08/26/89	1	1	Forbin's	Harry
10/20/89	11	1	Forbin's	YEM
10/22/89	2	1	Forbin's	YEM
10/31/89	3	2	Forbin's	Alumni
11/03/89	2	1	Forbin's	Bathtub
11/30/89	7	2	Forbin's	Undone
01/28/90	16	1	Forbin's	Commun
02/25/90	15	1	Forbin's	FunkBitch
03/09/90	6	1	Forbin's	Sloth
04/07/90	7	2	Forbin's	FunkBitch
04/20/90	8	1	Forbin's	Possum
06/01/90	19	1a	Forbin's	*CL1
10/07/90	18	1	Forbin's	Asse Fest
11/02/90	6	2	Forbin's	MSO
11/26/90	8	2	Forbin's	Wilson
12/28/90	6	1	Forbin's	Mike's
02/08/91	7	1	Forbin's	MSO
03/16/91	22	1	Forbin's	Oh Kee
03/23/91	4	1	Forbin's	Rocky Top
04/04/91	6	1	Forbin's	Possum
04/15/91	6	1	Forbin's	Llama
04/21/91	5	1	Forbin's	LLama
05/02/91	5	1	Forbin's	Llama
05/04/91	2	2	Forbin's	BurAlive
05/16/91	5	1	Forbin's	Chalkdust
07/14/91	7	1	Forbin's	Sloth
10/13/91	25	1	Forbin's	Tela
10/27/91	8	2	Forbin's	Sparkle
11/02/91	5	1	Forbin's	Possum
11/13/91	7	2	Forbin's	Golgi
11/20/91	5	1	Forbin's	Sparkle
12/07/91	9	1	Forbin's	MSO
03/19/92	9	1	Forbin's	All Things
03/24/92	3	1	Forbin's	Landlady
03/31/92	6	1	Forbin's	Antelope
04/16/92	11	1	Icculus	Antelope
04/21/92	4	2	Forbin's	Tweezer
04/24/92	3	1	Icculus	Uncle Pen
05/02/92	5	1	Icculus	Sparkle
05/06/92	3	1	Forbin's	Sparkle
05/17/92	9	1	Forbin's	MSO
11/21/92	47	1	Forbin's	Possum
11/27/92	4	1	Forbin's	Split&Melt
12/04/92	6	1	Forbin's	Cavern
12/08/92	4	1	Forbin's	Uncle Pen
12/31/92	8	1	Forbin's	MSO
02/07/93	5	1	Forbin's	Rift
02/19/93	9	1	Forbin's	Sparkle
02/25/93	5	1	Forbin's	Rift
03/08/93	7	1	How High	Sparkle
03/18/93	7	1	Forbin's	Sparkle
03/22/93	3	2	Forbin's	Sloth
03/25/93	2	2	Kung	Wedge
04/05/93	9	1	Forbin's	Bowie
04/13/93	4	1	Forbin's	Chalkdust
04/21/93	6	1	Forbin's	Rift
04/25/93	4	1	Forbin's	Maze
05/03/93	6	1	Forbin's	Possum
07/29/93	18	1	Forbin's	Possum
08/07/93	6	1	Forbin's	Cavern
08/15/93	7	1	Forbin's	Chalkdust
12/30/93	11	1	Forbin's	Rift
04/11/94	8	2	Forbin's	Uncle Pen
04/24/94	11	2	Forbin's	Chalkdust
05/25/94	22	1	Forbin's	Axilla 2
06/16/94	10	2	Forbin's	BBJ
06/26/94	9	1	Forbin's	Sloth
07/08/94	8	1	Forbin's	Sloth
10/14/94	13	1	Forbin's	Julius
10/27/94	10	1	Forbin's	Divided
11/04/94	6	1	Forbin's	Scent
11/17/94	5	1	Forbin's	DWD
11/30/94	9	1	Forbin's	DWD
10/05/95	43	2	Forbin's	Scent
12/01/95	35	1	Forbin's	Stash
12/31/95	16	1	Forbin's	Sparkle
08/07/96	25	2	Forbin's	Possum
10/31/96	18	1	Forbin's	CharZero
➢ 8/17/97	80			

Fast Enough For You [50]*

Fast Enough For You [FEFY]

By Anastasio/Marshall

11/19/92	[480]	2	PoorHeart	Llama
11/20/92	1	2	YEM	Dinner
11/25/92	4	2	Foam	YEM
11/28/92	2	1	Sparkle	All Things
12/02/92	3	1	Divided	PoorHeart
12/04/92	2	1	Sparkle	Maze
12/07/92	3	1	Foam	Split&Melt
12/13/92	5	1	Rift	IDK
12/29/92	2	2	BBJ	All Things
02/04/93	4	1	Maze	All Things
02/07/93	3	2	Llama	My Mind
02/12/93	4	2	BBJ	YEM
02/15/93	2	2	Rift	Reba
02/20/93	4	2	Weekpaug	BBJ
02/25/93	4	2	BBJ	Brain
03/03/93	4	2	MSO	Terrapin
03/06/93	2	2	BBJ	YEM
03/13/93	4	2	Weekpaug	Love You
03/24/93	8	2	BBJ	YEM
04/13/93	14	2	Uncle Pen	BBJ
07/16/93	24	1	BurAlive	All Things
07/18/93	2	2	Mound	Oh Kee
07/29/93	8	1	Landlady	My Mind
08/08/93	7	1	PYITE	Paul&Silas
08/17/93	8	1	Fluffhead	Daniel
12/28/93	7	2	Sloth	Uncle Pen
04/11/94	10	1	Foam	Magilla
04/29/94	14	1	YEM	Scent
05/07/94	8	1	Mound	Scent
05/14/94	5	2	PYITE	Lizards
05/20/94	4	1	Gin	Scent
06/19/94	17	1	Curtain	Scent
07/02/94	10	1	Guelah	Scent
07/13/94	7	1	It's Ice	IDK
10/09/94	6	1	Foam	Curtain
10/13/94	3	1	Foam	Sparkle
10/21/94	6	2	Curtain	Scent
11/16/94	15	1	Foam	Reba
12/01/94	11	1	Uncle Pen	Maze
06/08/95	15	1	Mound	Reba
06/28/95	15	1	Foam	Reba
10/03/95	11	1	Foam	I'm Blue
10/22/95	13	1	NICU	It's Ice
11/15/95	12	1	ACDCBag	Rift
11/30/95	10	1	Rift	Lizards
12/28/95	14	1	Rift	Possum
07/15/96	15	1	PYITE	Guyute
08/13/96	16	1	Maze	Old Home
11/06/96	18	1	CTB	Train Song
11/22/96	11	1	Sample	Train Song
➢ 8/17/97	66			

Fee [216]

Fee [Fee]

By Anastasio

08/09/87	[17]	1	*OP1	Harry
08/10/87	1	1	Fluffhead	Curtain
08/21/87	1	2	Flat Fee	Skin It
09/12/87	2	2	Sally	Divided
09/27/87	1	2	Fire	*CL2
11/19/87	3	2	IDK	Corrina
01/30/88	1	3	*OP3	Suzie
03/31/88	3	1	Golgi	ACDCBag
05/25/88	2	3	La Grange	IKALittle
06/15/88	1	1	La Grange	Timber Ho
06/20/88	2	2	Tela	Golgi
09/12/88	10	1a	A-Train	Bold
09/24/88	1	2	Possum	Sparks
10/12/88	1	1	Foam	Mike's
10/29/88	1	2	WhipPost	Alumni
11/03/88	1	1	Possum	Alumni
11/05/88	1	2	ACDCBag	Mike's
11/11/88	1	2	Jazz	Bold
01/26/89	2	1a	Divided	GTBT
02/06/89	3	1	Peaches	La Grange
02/07/89	1	2	Alumni	Antelope
02/17/89	1	1a	YEM	Divided
03/04/89	1	1	Weekpaug	Golgi
05/05/89	19	1	Jam	*CL1
05/27/89	14	1	FunkBitch	YEM
05/28/89	1	1	Mockbird	Slave
06/23/89	5	1	Donna	Mike's
08/17/89	7	2	Mango	YEM
10/07/89	9	1	Suzie	La Grange
10/14/89	3	1	Split&Melt	Alumni
10/21/89	2	1	*OP1	Ya Mar
10/22/89	1	2	MSO	Possum
10/26/89	1	1	YEM	Divided
10/31/89	2	1	Divided	WalkAway
11/02/89	1	1	Weekpaug	Curtain
11/10/89	4	1	Suzie	Divided
11/30/89	4	2	Undone	Split&Melt
12/07/89	4	1	ACDCBag	Mike's
12/09/89	2	2	Alumni	Mike's
12/31/89	5	2	Divided	*CL2
02/10/90	13	2	Donna	Mike's
02/24/90	6	2	ACDCBag	Sqirm Coil
03/28/90	10	1	Ya Mar	WalkAway
04/05/90	2	2	Tweezer	Cavern
04/07/90	2	2	Bold	RunJim
04/08/90	1	2	Weekpaug	MSO
04/18/90	5	2	La Grange	Sloth
04/20/90	2	1	La Grange	Oh Kee
05/06/90	9	2	*OP2	Harry
05/19/90	6	2	Suzie	Dinner
05/24/90	2	2	Horn	WalkAway
06/01/90	2	1a	Dinner	Foam
06/07/90	2	1	Possum	Reba
06/09/90	1	2	La Grange	Foam
06/16/90	1	E	Suzie	Rocky Top
09/15/90	3	1	Landlady	Tube
09/22/90	4	2	Destiny	Uncle Pen
10/05/90	4	2	Split&Melt	Possum
10/12/90	4	2	Possum	Landlady
10/31/90	3	2	Tweezer	Oh Kee
11/03/90	2	2	Stash	Uncle Pen
11/10/90	3	2	Asse Fest	Llama
02/15/91	20	1	Spilt	BurAlive
02/21/91	4	1	Split&Melt	Llama
02/27/91	5	1	YEM	MSO
03/17/91	11	2	Tweezer	Slave
03/23/91	3	1	Divided	Llama
04/05/91	7	E	*OPE	Oh Kee
04/11/91	2	E	*OPE	Possum
04/15/91	3	1	Split&Melt	Chalkdust
04/21/91	5	2	Possum	Landlady
05/02/91	5	2	Divided	Split&Melt
05/03/91	1	1	Divided	Paul&Silas
05/12/91	5	1	Llama	Foam
05/25/91	4	1a	ACDCBag	Foam
07/12/91	1	E	Frankstein	Tweezer
07/19/91	2	1	Bowie	Cavern
07/21/91	1	E2	*OPE2	Suzie
08/03/91	2	1	Llama	Sqirm Coil
09/26/91	2	1	Divided	It's Ice
10/03/91	5	1	Llama	Divided
10/06/91	3	2	Stash	Landlady
10/10/91	1	2	Suzie	Mike's
10/18/91	6	2	IDK	Split&Melt
10/28/91	6	1	Foam	Bowie
10/31/91	2	2	Llama	MSO
11/07/91	4	E	*OPE	Rocky Top
11/08/91	1	E	*OPE	Suzie
11/12/91	3	1	Harry	Foam
11/14/91	2	2	Antelope	Paul&Silas
11/19/91	3	1	RunJim	Sparkle
11/22/91	3	1	Brother	Foam
11/23/91	1	2	Landlady	Love You
12/05/91	4	2	Weekpaug	Sloth
03/11/92	6	1	Maze	Split&Melt
03/14/92	3	1	Stash	Chalkdust
03/25/92	6	1	Rift	Maze
03/31/92	5	2	Weekpaug	Stash
04/07/92	6	1	It's Ice	Divided
04/13/92	3	1	NICU	All Things
04/16/92	3	1	Rift	Maze
04/19/92	3	1	Maze	Chalkdust
04/23/92	3	2	Tweezer	Maze
04/30/92	4	1	Split&Melt	Maze
05/03/92	3	1	Uncle Pen	All Things
05/07/92	3	2	Weekpaug	Bike
05/09/92	2	1	Rift	Maze
05/18/92	7	2	Weekpaug	Bike
07/14/92	13	2	Tweezer	All Things
11/19/92	31	1	Maze	Foam
11/22/92	3	1	Suzie	Maze
11/25/92	2	1	Landlady	Maze
11/30/92	3	E	*OPE	Fire
12/03/92	3	1	Maze	All Things
12/04/92	1	E	*OPE	Rocky Top
12/06/92	2	1	Foam	My Friend
12/07/92	1	2	It's Ice	Bowie
12/10/92	2	1	Foam	PoorHeart
12/13/92	3	1	It's Ice	Uncle Pen
02/03/93	5	1	Rift	Llama
02/07/93	4	1	Split&Melt	RunJim
02/11/93	3	1	Stash	Rift
02/15/93	3	2	Bike	Llama
02/19/93	3	1	Split&Melt	Maze
02/22/93	3	1	Maze	Sparkle
02/26/93	3	1	Foam	Split&Melt
02/27/93	1	2	Terrapin	Llama
03/02/93	1	1	It's Ice	All Things
03/13/93	7	1	Maze	All Things
03/16/93	2	1	It's Ice	Maze
03/18/93	2	1	Rift	Maze
03/24/93	4	1	Foam	PoorHeart

Stories Behind the Songs
(Continued)

thematic centerpiece of the *Rift* album concept.

Fluffhead: This song came together in its current form by the time *Junta* was recorded in 1988. The band labeled it in two parts, Fluffhead (the part for which the Dude of Life wrote the lyrics) and Fluff's Travels; some tapers label it as two songs though the two are always played together. Fluff's Travels includes four distinct parts: Fluff's Travels, The Chase, Who Do? We Do! and Clod.

The Fog That Surrounds: A reworking of Taste featuring similar music but different lyrics. For the first part of fall tour 1995, Fishman—who did not sing on the original version of Taste—sang new verses and Trey and Page joined for a chorus kept from Taste. But the version of the song played during November and December 1995 has Fishman singing some verses and Trey singing verses lifted from Taste. Unlike in Taste, the band did not return to vocals after the instrumental section of the song. Colloquial names used by fans for the reworked version of this song included 'Another Taste' and 'Taste The Fog.' But in recording sessions for Billy Breathes the band decided to rework the song yet again and call it Taste, so "The Fog That Surrounds" name appears dead.

Free: One of the debuts at the 1995 Lowell show, the band jammed on spacy versions of Free—with Trey on his mini-drum kit—in 1995 and 1996. In 1997, Trey eliminated the drum kit from his onstage toys and the jam section of the song was reworked to sound more like the version on *Billy Breathes*.

Ghost: Perhaps the most funked-out tune debuted in summer '97, the band immediately made it a showcase for their new jam style. Supposedly, Tom Marshall's lyrics refer to a childhood imaginary friend (the "ghost").

Glide II: Played in concert only once, at the 1995 Lowell show, it was soundchecked at least once on summer tour 1995 but hasn't surfaced in concert since. During the sessions for *Billy Breathes*, the band recorded an instrumental version of

03/26/93	2	1	Foam	PYITE
03/28/93	2	1	Maze	It's Ice
04/01/93	3	2	Possum	Ya Mar
04/05/93	3	1	It's Ice	Maze
04/12/93	3	2	Tweezer	Paul&Silas
04/18/93	5	1	Divided	Maze
04/22/93	3	1	Stash	Rift
04/25/93	3	2	Weekpaug	TweezRep
04/29/93	2	1	Rift	Oh Kee
05/01/93	2	1	Split&Melt	Sample
05/07/93	5	2	Maze	BBJ
07/18/93	7	2	Oh Kee	YEM
07/25/93	5	1	Stash	Rift
08/03/93	7	1	Foam	Rift
08/09/93	4	1	Mound	Split&Melt
08/15/93	5	1	RunJim	Paul&Silas
08/21/93	4	2	Uncle Pen	Llama
08/26/93	3	1	Reba	Split&Melt
12/28/93	2	1	It's Ice	Possum
12/31/93	3	2	It's Ice	Possum
04/04/94	1	1	Maze	Reba
04/06/94	2	1	Scent	Antelope
04/09/94	2	1	Julius	All Things
04/13/94	3	2	BBJ	A-Train
04/16/94	3	1	Julius	All Things
04/20/94	3	2	Harry	YEM
04/23/94	3	1	Rift	Peaches
04/25/94	2	1	RunJim	Foam
04/29/94	2	2	Reba	Uncle Pen
05/07/94	6	1	Mound	Scent
05/08/94	1	2	It's Ice	Julius
05/12/94	2	1	DWD	Maze
05/14/94	2	1	DWD	Reba
05/16/94	1	E	*OPE	Rocky Top
05/20/94	3	1	*OP1	Maze
05/23/94	3	1	Foam	Maze
05/28/94	4	2	Reba	Llama
06/09/94	2	1	Maze	Suzie
06/14/94	4	1	DWD	My Friend
06/16/94	1	1	Julius	Maze
06/24/94	7	1	It's Ice	Sloth
07/03/94	7	1	DWD	NICU
07/13/94	6	1	DWD	It's Ice
07/15/94	2	1	Foam	Split&Melt
10/08/94	3	1	Guyute	It's Ice
10/10/94	2	2	Tweezer	Rift
10/16/94	5	1	Foam	Split&Melt
10/21/94	3	1	*OP1	DWD
10/23/94	2	2	Harry	GTBT
10/25/94	1	1	*OP1	Llama
10/28/94	3	E	*OPE	HwayHell
11/03/94	4	1	*OP1	Divided
11/16/94	5	2	Chalkdust	Antpl
11/20/94	4	1	Chalkdust	Scent
11/23/94	2	2	Maze	Scent
11/28/94	3	E	*OPE	Tweezer
12/04/94	5	1	Tweezer	Mound
12/07/94	2	2	Divided	Julius
12/10/94	3	1	*OP1	Rift
12/30/94	3	1	Stash	Scent
06/10/95	6	2	Maze	Uncle Pen
06/17/95	5	1	Taste	Uncle Pen
06/24/95	5	1	*OP1	Rift
06/30/95	5	1	Mound	Antelope
09/28/95	5	1	Stash	Fog
10/20/95	15	1	Divided	Rift
10/24/95	3	1	Fog	Llama
10/27/95	2	1	Stash	Suspicious
11/11/95	6	1	AmGrace	Chalkdust
11/15/95	3	2	Weekpaug	Guitar
11/21/95	4	1	*OP1	Chalkdust
11/24/95	2	2	*OP2	Julius
11/29/95	3	1	AArmy	Split&Melt
12/28/95	15	E	*OPE	Tweezer
06/06/96	5	2	Bowie	Sample
07/21/96	14	1	Train Song	Timber Ho
08/04/96	6	1	Guyute	Split&Melt
08/10/96	4	1	ACDCBag	Reba
08/14/96	3	1	DWD	PoorHeart
08/17/96	2	1	Taste	Maze
10/19/96	4	E	*OPE	Rocky Top
10/27/96	6	1	ACDCBag	Scent
11/02/96	3	1	Julius	Cavern
11/19/96	12	1	Stash	Taste
02/25/97	24	2	Free	My Friend
➢ 8/17/97	43			

Flat Fee [12]
Flat Fee [Flat Fee]
By Anastasio

03/11/87	[12]	1a	Antelope	YEM
08/21/87	7	2	Sparks	Fee
08/29/87	2	1	BBFCM	Lushngton
03/11/88	10	1	Slave	Corrina
05/15/88	6	1a	Curtain	WhipPost
06/21/88	6	2	ACDCBag	Alumni
07/11/91	277	1	Divided	MSO
07/12/91	1	1	BurAlive	Reba
07/13/91	1	2	Divided	Paul&Silas
07/15/91	2	1a	Weekpaug	Lizards
07/20/91	3	2	Dinner	Golgi
07/23/91	2	1	Stash	Bouncing
07/25/91	2	1	Divided	ACDCBag
07/26/91	1	2	YEM	FunkBitch
➢ 8/17/97	609			

Fluffhead [150]*
Fluffhead [Fluffhead]
(includes Fluff's Travels, by Anastasio)
By Anastasio/Dude of Life

12/01/84	[0]	1a	Skip	*CL1
10/15/86	8	1a	Mustang	Sally
10/31/86	1	1	Shaggy	*CL1
03/23/87	4	1	Sparks	Peaches
04/24/87	1	1a	Possum	YEM
04/29/87	1	3	Peaches	GTBT
08/09/90	2	2	Divided	McGrupp
08/10/90	1	1	Possum	Fee
09/12/87	4	2	La Grange	*CL2
09/27/91	1	2	Fire	*CL2
10/14/87	1	1	Chase	Possum
11/19/87	2	1	Timber Ho	IDK
01/30/88	1	2	Fire	Divided
02/08/88	2	2	*OP2	Wilson
03/11/88	1	2	*OP2	Dinner
03/31/88	3	1	Possum	*CL1
05/14/88	2	2	Jesus	Alumni
05/15/88	1	1a	GTBT	Shaggy
05/25/88	2	2	Jesus	WhipPost
06/15/88	1	1	McGrupp	Golgi
06/20/88	2	1	YEM	ACDCBag
06/21/88	1	1	*OP1	Rocky Top
07/12/88	2	1	Timber Ho	Jesus
07/24/88	2	2	Light Up	La Grange
07/25/88	1	2	Light Up	*CL2
08/03/88	1	2	I am H2	Harry
08/27/88	2	1	WalkAway	Mike's
09/24/88	3	3	GTBT	Curtain
10/29/88	2	3	*OP3	GTBT
11/03/88	1	1	Golgi	Possum
11/05/88	1	1	WalkAway	Alumni
01/26/89	3	1a	Wilson	Icculus
02/07/89	4	3	Sanity	Suzie
02/17/89	1	1a	Antelope	*CL1
03/04/89	4	2	Possum	Lizards
03/30/89	2	1	Ya Mar	Antelope
04/15/89	7	2	Suzie	*CL2
04/20/89	2	1	ACDCBag	Shook
04/30/89	5	1a	Terrapin	*CL1
05/05/89	3	1	Ya Mar	Alumni
05/13/89	7	1	La Grange	Possum
05/27/89	7	1	A-Train	Bathtub
06/23/89	6	2	Sloth	Harry
06/30/89	2	1	Donna	Antelope
08/26/89	9	1	*OP1	Forbin's
10/01/89	5	2	Dinner	Possum
10/21/89	7	1	McGrupp	Foam
12/09/89	19	2	A-Train	Esther
01/28/90	10	1	Tela	La Grange
02/25/90	15	2	Lizards	BBFCM
03/03/90	3	2	Caravan	Esther
04/13/90	15	1	Bouncing	Esther
04/22/90	5	2	YEM	How High
04/29/90	4	1a	Divided	WalkAway
10/30/90	35	2	Curtis	Terrapin
11/03/90	3	E	*OPE	Fire
11/17/90	5	2	BurAlive	Mike's
02/09/91	16	2	BurAlive	Landlady
02/16/91	3	2	Guelah	Rocky Top
03/13/91	16	1	*OP1	Landlady
03/17/91	3	1	Foam	Uncle Pen
04/12/91	13	2	YEM	Cavern
04/20/91	6	1	Llama	MSO
04/26/91	4	1	Possum	PoorHeart
04/27/91	1	2	Weekpaug	Tweezer
05/04/91	3	2	Guelah	Mike's
05/17/91	6	2	Landlady	Magilla
08/03/91	17	3	Ya Mar	Lawn Boy
10/12/91	13	1	Uncle Pen	Chalkdust
10/17/91	3	2	Lawn Boy	YEM
10/27/91	6	1	Guelah	Brother
11/01/91	4	1	Split&Melt	Uncle Pen
11/09/91	5	2	Chalkdust	PoorHeart
11/16/91	6	1	Sparkle	Foam
11/24/91	6	1	Landlady	Sparkle
12/05/91	3	1	Ya Mar	Llama
03/13/92	8	1	Mound	Antelope
03/20/92	4	1	Rift	Maze
03/26/92	4	1	Stash	Uncle Pen
04/03/92	6	1	Maze	All Things
04/13/92	7	2	Llama	Sparkle
04/17/92	3	2	YEM	Sqirm Coil
04/24/92	6	1	Landlady	Sparkle
05/03/92	6	2	Silent	Guelah
05/07/92	3	2	Tweezer	Golgi
05/14/92	5	2	Rift	Eliza
07/12/92	16	1a	Divided	Uncle Pen
07/16/92	3	2	Landlady	TMWSIY
11/20/92	30	2	Chalkdust	Tube
12/01/92	8	1	Cavern	Maze
12/03/92	2	2	Guelah	Mike's
12/06/92	3	1	Llama	Antelope
12/13/92	6	2	Llama	Chalkdust
12/30/92	3	1	Chalkdust	Paul&Silas
02/11/93	9	1	Rift	Llama
02/17/93	4	1	Bouncing	Golgi
02/20/93	3	1	Silent	Cavern
02/26/93	5	1	Split&Melt	Llama
03/12/93	8	1	Stash	Horse
03/19/93	6	1	Stash	Cavern
03/26/93	5	1	Split&Melt	Divided
04/01/93	5	1	Paul&Silas	Lawn Boy
04/05/93	3	1	Maze	Paul&Silas
04/20/93	9	2	Chalkdust	Sample
04/23/93	3	1	Split&Melt	My Friend
05/01/93	6	2	Chalkdust	My Friend
05/06/93	4	1	Llama	Possum
07/24/93	12	2	Split&Melt	Maze
07/30/93	5	2	PoorHeart	My Friend
08/08/93	6	2	It's Ice	Possum
08/13/93	4	1	Ginseng	My Mind
08/17/93	4	1	Maze	FEFY
08/28/93	6	1	Maze	Stash
12/29/93	2	2	Bouncing	Antelope
04/05/94	4	1	Foam	Glide
04/10/94	4	2	Antelope	Ginseng
04/16/94	5	1	Stash	Nellie
04/21/94	4	2	Maze	Mike's
05/03/94	9	2	If I Could	DWD
05/12/94	6	2	Uncle Pen	Life Boy
05/22/94	8	1	Split&Melt	MSO
05/26/94	3	2	Antelope	DWD
06/11/94	6	2	Antelope	Scent
06/22/94	8	2	TMWSIY	MSO
07/01/94	7	2	If I Could	DWD
07/06/94	4	1	Llama	Julius
07/09/94	2	2	Split&Melt	PoorHeart
07/14/94	3	1	Scent	Horse
10/08/94	4	2	Weekpaug	PurplRain
10/16/94	7	2	Julius	BBJ
10/22/94	4	1	Split&Melt	Julius
11/12/94	11	2	Julius	DWD
12/06/94	18	1	DWD	Jesus
06/15/95	16	1	IDK	Antelope
06/28/95	10	1	Stash	Chalkdust
10/13/95	17	1	Split&Melt	Life Mars
10/27/95	10	1	RunJim	Fog
11/11/95	6	1	Uncle Pen	Sl Monkey
11/22/95	8	1	Antelope	Uncle Pen
12/08/95	11	1	RunJim	It's Ice
12/29/95	9	1	Stash	Llama
08/02/96	23	2	Free	Caspian
08/10/96	5	2	Free	WhipPost
08/17/96	5	2	Brother	Antelope
10/19/96	4	2	Split&Melt	SweptAwy
10/27/96	6	2	Tweezer	Life Mars
11/30/96	21	1	Stash	Old Home
02/23/97	17	1	Rift	Frankstein
08/03/97	35	2	Simple	Lifeboy
08/14/97	7	1	FunkBitch	Limb
➢ 8/17/97	2			

Foam [265]
Foam [Foam]
By Anastasio

10/12/88	[55]	1	Lizards	Fee
10/29/88	1	3	ACDCBag	Terrapin
11/03/88	1	1	Shaggy	*CL1
11/11/88	2	1	Slave	Possum
02/07/89	6	1	McGrupp	Sloth
02/24/89	3	1	Curtain	Forbin's
03/03/89	1	1	YEM	ACDCBag
03/30/89	3	3	Peaches	ACDCBag
04/15/89	7	1	McGrupp	Bowie
04/20/89	1	1	McGrupp	Bowie
05/13/89	15	1	Possum	WalkAway
05/20/89	4	2	Weekpaug	Contact
05/21/89	1	1	Harry	Contact
08/23/89	18	2	ACDCBag	GTBT
08/26/89	1	2	FunkBitch	Bowie
09/09/89	4	1	*OP1	Oh Kee
10/01/89	1	1	Wilson	Ya Mar
10/21/89	7	1	Fluffhead	ACDCBag
10/22/89	1	1	Ya Mar	Rocky Top
11/02/89	4	1	Gin	Mike's
11/16/89	6	1	Gin	Oh Kee
11/30/89	2	1	ACDCBag	Lizards
12/09/89	6	1	Lizards	In a Hole
02/09/90	17	2	Alumni	Curtis
02/17/90	4	1a	Bouncing	HwayHell
02/23/90	2	1	Possum	Carolina
02/25/90	2	1	*OP1	MSO

03/01/90	1	2	GTBT	Mike's
03/08/90	3	1	Ya Mar	Carolina
03/17/90	3	2	ACDCBag	YEM
04/04/90	2	1	Possum	Divided
04/07/90	3	2	RunJim	YEM
04/09/90	2	2	La Grange	Harry
04/13/90	3	2	Antelope	Alumni
04/18/90	1	1	Curtain	YEM
04/25/90	5	2	*OP2	Adeline
04/26/90	1	1	Possum	YEM
04/28/90	1	1	Rift	Antelope
05/13/90	8	2	Weekpaug	Donna
05/24/90	4	2	*OP2	Dinner
06/01/90	2	1a	Fee	Forbin's
06/08/90	3	1	Weekpaug	Bouncing
06/09/90	1	2	Fee	Oh Kee
06/16/90	1	3	Ya Mar	Oh Kee
09/13/90	1	1	Divided	Tube
09/15/90	2	2	Bathtub	Minute
10/06/90	9	1a	Bouncing	YEM
10/08/90	2	1	Bouncing	Cavern
10/30/90	3	2	Magilla	Reba
10/31/90	1	2	RunJim	Tweezer
11/02/90	1	2	MSO	YEM
11/03/90	1	1	Magilla	RunJim
11/08/90	2	1	Lizards	Uncle Pen
11/16/90	2	1	BurAlive	YEM
11/24/90	2	1	Possum	Mike's
12/01/90	3	1	Divided	Tweezer
12/07/90	2	1	RunJim	Llama
12/08/90	1	1	RunJim	ACDCBag
12/28/90	1	1	RunJim	Horn
02/01/91	3	1	MSO	Tweezer
02/03/91	2	1	Chalkdust	Golgi
02/07/91	1	1	RunJim	MSO
02/09/91	2	1	RunJim	Guelah
02/14/91	1	2	Weekpaug	Sqirm Coil
02/26/91	9	1	*OP1	Sqirm Coil
02/28/91	2	1	Bouncing	Esther
03/01/91	1	1	Wilson	Divided
03/15/91	7	1	Llama	MSO
03/17/91	2	1	Weekpaug	Fluffhead
03/22/91	2	2	Antelope	Paul&Silas
04/05/91	8	1	Chalkdust	Mike's
04/11/91	2	1	Bouncing	Carolina
04/15/91	3	1	Ya Mar	RunJim
04/21/91	5	1	Divided	Magilla
04/26/91	3	1	PoorHeart	YEM
05/02/91	4	1	Drums	Bouncing
05/03/91	1	1	Bouncing	Chalkdust
05/10/91	3	2	PoorHeart	McGrupp
05/12/91	2	1	Fee	RunJim
05/16/91	1	1	Golgi	Cavern
05/18/91	2	1	Paul&Silas	Divided
05/25/91	1	1a	Fee	Reba
07/13/91	3	1	RunJim	Llama
07/18/91	4	1	Chalkdust	RunJim
07/20/91	1	1	Chalkdust	Sqirm Coil
07/23/91	2	1	Chalkdust	Sqirm Coil
07/25/91	2	1	Sloth	Suzie
07/26/91	1	1	MSO	Suzie
07/27/91	1	1a	Llama	Oh Kee
08/03/91	1	1	Wilson	Oh Kee
09/25/91	1	1	PoorHeart	Llama
09/26/91	1	1	Lizards	Bowie
09/28/91	2	1	Stash	Brother
10/02/91	2	1	Llama	Sqirm Coil
10/03/91	1	1	Chalkdust	Uncle Pen
10/04/91	1	2	Bouncing	RunJim
10/06/91	2	1	Suzie	Divided
10/10/91	1	1	Chalkdust	Paul&Silas
10/11/91	1	2	Cavern	Bowie
10/15/91	3	1	Chalkdust	Sqirm Coil
10/18/91	2	1	RunJim	Paul&Silas
10/19/91	1	1	RunJim	Chalkdust
10/24/91	2	1	Suzie	PoorHeart
10/28/91	3	1	Oh Kee	Fee
10/31/91	2	1	Sparkle	Gin
11/02/91	2	1	Paul&Silas	Bouncing
11/07/91	2	1	Chalkdust	Sparkle
11/09/91	2	1	RunJim	Sparkle
11/12/91	2	1	Fee	Llama
11/14/91	2	1	Reba	Tube
11/16/91	2	1	Fluffhead	Stash
11/19/91	1	1	Uncle Pen	RunJim
11/21/91	2	1	Reba	Horn
11/22/91	1	1	Fee	Divided
11/23/91	1	1	Reba	RunJim
11/30/91	2	1	Llama	Sparkle
12/05/91	2	2	Tube	Mike's
12/06/91	1	1	Memories	Reba
12/07/91	1	1	RunJim	Forbin's
12/31/91	1	1	Possum	Sparkle
03/07/92	2	1	My Mind	RunJim
03/12/92	2	1	RunJim	Sparkle
03/14/92	2	1	Sparkle	Rift
03/21/92	4	1	RunJim	Sparkle
03/24/92	1	1	PoorHeart	Eliza
03/26/92	2	1	All Things	Sparkle
03/28/92	2	1	RunJim	Sparkle
03/30/92	1	1	Llama	Guelah
04/01/92	2	1	Golgi	Bouncing
04/04/92	2	1	RunJim	Reba
04/06/92	2	1	Suzie	Sparkle
04/09/92	2	1	Sparkle	Guelah
04/13/92	2	1	All Things	A-Train
04/15/92	1	1	Suzie	Guelah
04/17/92	2	1	RunJim	Sparkle
04/22/92	4	1	Llama	Reba
04/24/92	2	2	Ya Mar	Mike's
04/29/92	2	1	Suzie	Sparkle
05/02/92	3	2	Tela	YEM
05/05/92	2	2	All Things	Mike's
05/06/92	1	1	Llama	Reba
05/07/92	1	1	My Friend	RunJim
05/09/92	2	1	RunJim	Sparkle
05/15/92	4	1a	Golgi	Cavern
05/16/92	1	1	Maze	Glide
05/18/92	2	1	Guelah	PoorHeart
06/20/92	2	1a	Bouncing	RunJim
06/27/92	3	1a	RunJim	Sparkle
07/11/92	6	1a	RunJim	Sparkle
07/15/92	3	1	Suzie	My Friend
07/18/92	3	1a	Suzie	Llama
07/24/92	4	1a	MSO	Tweezer
07/25/92	1	1a	RunJim	Sparkle
08/01/92	6	1a	Golgi	PoorHeart
08/13/92	2	1a	Chalkdust	YEM
08/17/92	3	1	All Things	My Friend
08/20/92	2	1a	Golgi	Stash
08/23/92	1	1a	Cavern	RunJim
08/28/92	4	1a	PoorHeart	Stash
11/19/92	4	1	Fee	Glide
11/21/92	2	1	RunJim	Glide
11/23/92	2	1	RunJim	Glide
11/25/92	1	2	Chalkdust	FEFY
11/28/92	2	1	MSO	Stash
11/30/92	1	1	Llama	Bouncing
12/02/92	2	1	Suzie	Divided
12/04/92	2	1	Llama	PoorHeart
12/06/92	2	1	RunJim	Fee
12/07/92	1	1	Sparkle	FEFY
12/10/92	2	1	Llama	Fee
12/12/92	2	1	Llama	Sparkle
12/28/92	2	1	Sparkle	Glide
12/31/92	3	1	Cavern	IDK
02/04/93	2	1	Axilla	Bouncing
02/06/93	2	1	Golgi	Wilson
02/10/93	3	1	Lovin Cup	Guelah
02/18/93	6	1	Tweezer	Sparkle
02/20/93	2	1	Golgi	Sloth
02/22/93	2	1	Sparkle	Cavern
02/26/93	3	1	RunJim	Fee
03/03/93	3	1	Rift	Bouncing
03/05/93	1	1	Cavern	Sloth
03/09/93	3	1	RunJim	Bouncing
03/14/93	3	1	Lovin Cup	Guelah
03/17/93	2	1	RunJim	Bouncing
03/19/93	2	1	Llama	Bouncing
03/24/93	3	1	Llama	Fee
03/26/93	2	1	Sparkle	Fee
03/31/93	4	1	RunJim	Sparkle
04/02/93	2	1	PoorHeart	Bouncing
04/13/93	6	1	Suzie	Sparkle
04/17/93	3	1	Llama	Bouncing
04/21/93	3	1	PoorHeart	Guelah
04/24/93	3	2	Llama	Gin
04/27/93	2	1	PoorHeart	Bouncing
05/01/93	3	1	RunJim	Guelah
05/05/93	3	1	Guelah	Sparkle
05/30/93	5	1a	PoorHeart	Ya Mar
07/15/93	1	1	Stash	IDK
07/18/93	3	1	Rift	Guelah
07/22/93	2	1	Llama	Horn
07/25/93	3	1	Wilson	Mound
07/28/93	2	1	Sample	Nellie
07/31/93	3	1	Mound	Nellie
08/03/93	2	1	Nellie	Fee
08/08/93	3	1	BBFCM	Lovin Cup
08/13/93	4	1	Makisupa	Stash
08/16/93	3	1	Sparkle	IDK
08/21/93	3	1	PoorHeart	Guelah
08/25/93	2	1	Sparkle	Ginseng
08/28/93	2	1	Bouncing	Ginseng
12/29/93	2	1	Peaches	Glide
04/05/94	4	1	RunJim	Fluffhead
04/08/94	2	1	Glide	IDK
04/11/94	3	1	PoorHeart	FEFY
04/14/94	2	1	RunJim	Sparkle
04/17/94	3	1	Lovin Cup	IDK
04/21/94	3	1	Sparkle	Glide
04/25/94	4	1	Fee	DWD
04/28/94	1	1a	RunJim	Sample
05/02/94	3	1	Suzie	Sample
05/04/94	2	1	RunJim	Sample
05/08/94	3	1	RunJim	Axilla 2
05/12/94	2	1	Axilla 2	Gin
05/21/94	7	1	RunJim	Guelah
05/23/94	2	1	Sample	Fee
05/27/94	3	2	RunJim	Bouncing
05/28/94	1	1	Sample	Bouncing
06/10/94	3	1	RunJim	Sample
06/17/94	5	1	RunJim	Glide
06/23/94	5	1	NICU	Bouncing
07/01/94	6	1	RunJim	Foam
07/09/94	6	1	RunJim	Gumbo
07/13/94	2	1	Sample	Mango
07/15/94	2	1	Gumbo	Fee
10/09/94	4	1	RunJim	FEFY
10/13/94	3	1	IDK	FEFY
10/16/94	3	1	Horn	Fee
10/21/94	3	1	DWD	Mango
10/29/94	7	1	RunJim	Lawn Boy
11/02/94	2	1	Suzie	If I Could
11/12/94	3	1	RunJim	If I Could
11/16/94	3	1	Sample	FEFY
11/22/94	5	1	Horn	Guyute
11/26/94	3	1	If I Could	Horse
12/04/94	6	1	RunJim	If I Could
12/09/94	4	1	Llama	Guyute
12/29/94	3	1	RunJim	If I Could
06/13/95	8	1	RunJim	Bouncing
06/20/95	6	1	Ginseng	Gin
06/28/95	6	1	Axilla 2	FEFY
10/03/95	11	1	Guelah	FEFY
10/15/95	8	1	Llama	Str Design
11/14/95	16	1	Chalkdust	Billy
11/28/95	9	1	Bouncing	IDK
12/14/95	12	1	Horn	Makisupa
07/19/96	22	1a	RunJim	Adeline
07/23/96	3	1	ACDCBag	Theme
08/02/96	3	1	PoorHeart	Theme
08/05/96	2	1	Wolfman's	If I Could
10/23/96	15	1	ACDCBag	HelloBaby
11/19/96	18	1	ACDCBag	Theme
02/21/97	21	1	My Soul	DWD
08/03/97	35	1	Bathtub	Blow
08/09/97	3	2	Wilson	Mike's
➢ 8/17/97	6			

Fog That Surrounds [22]*

The Fog That Surrounds [Fog]

By Anastasio/Marshall

09/27/95	[761] 1	IDK	Str Design
09/28/95	1 1	Fee	AArmy
09/30/95	2 2	RunJim	If I Could
10/02/95	1 1	AArmy	Theme
10/05/95	2 1	Ha Ha Ha	Horse
10/07/95	2 1	Gumbo	Mound
10/11/95	2 1	If I Could	AArmy
10/17/95	4 2	Caspian	Suzie
10/24/95	5 1	Paul&Silas	Fee
10/27/95	2 1	Fluffhead	Horn
11/10/95	5 1	RunJim	Old Home
11/12/95	2 1	IDK	If I Could
11/22/95	7 1	Cavern	Lizards
11/25/95	2 1	Billy	Bouncing
11/29/95	2 2	YEM	PoorHeart
12/02/95	3 1	Free	Bouncing
12/05/95	2 1	Chalkdust	Lizards
12/07/95	1 2	Str Design	Reba
12/11/95	3 2	Mango	Scent
12/14/95	2 1	Tela	MSO
12/16/95	2 1	ACDCBag	Ya Mar
12/29/95	3 1	DWD	NICU
➢ 8/17/97	125		

Fooled by Images [1]

Fooled by Images [Fooled]

By Anastasio/Marshall

06/14/97	[905] 2	Saw It	Dogs Stole
➢ 8/17/97	36		

Free [66]*

Free [Free]

By Anastasio/Marshall

05/16/95	[738] 1a	LCBill	Flip
06/08/95	2 2	Rift	Bouncing
06/10/95	2 1	It's Ice	Rift
06/16/95	4 2	RunJim	Carolina

George Foremans

Songs that stayed on the shelf longest before making triumphant returns, with dates and the number of shows the band went without playing it:

ORIGINAL SONG NAME	WASN'T PLAYED FROM...			LAPSE
1) Camel Walk	02/24/89	to	07/02/95	691
2) Letter to Jimmy Page	12/07/89	to	07/05/94	530
3) Halley's Comet	08/17/89	to	03/14/92	418
4) Setting Sail	04/20/91	to	07/15/94	383
5) Kung	11/02/89	to	12/31/92	367
6) PYITE	11/09/89	to	02/05/93	367
7) Makisupa	11/26/90	to	04/29/93	319
8) Sanity	05/28/89	to	03/11/92	282
9) Dog Log	05/03/91	to	08/02/93	280
10) Alumni Blues	10/10/91	to	04/15/94	279
11) Magilla	05/04/94	to	02/26/97	260
12) Brother	08/02/93	to	08/17/96	257
13) NICU	05/01/92	to	06/23/94	248
14) Slave	10/24/91	to	08/06/93	240
15) Gumbo	07/25/91	to	04/16/93	230

COVER SONG NAME	WASN'T PLAYED FROM...			LAPSE
1) Shaggy Dog	11/03/88	to	10/29/95	727
2) Cities	09/08/88	to	07/05/94	627
3) Jump Monk	03/12/88	to	04/24/94	600
4) Peaches En Regalia	06/23/89	to	12/28/93	502
5) Ride Captain Ride	05/28/89	to	12/12/92	395
6) Touch Me	07/27/91	to	12/03/94	394
7) Satin Doll	02/25/90	to	04/12/93	378
8) Frankenstein	07/26/91	to	06/11/94	329
8) How High the Moon	04/26/90	to	03/08/93	329
10) La Grange	03/17/91	to	12/29/95	307
11) Curtis Loew	10/30/90	to	03/14/93	296
12) Daniel	08/28/93	to	02/23/97	287
13) Bold as Love	04/18/90	to	11/19/92	285
14) Timber Ho	06/16/90	to	12/30/92	275

Stories Behind the Songs
(Continued)

the song that did not make the final cut. Glide II is apparently the band's name for this song though some fans refer to it as "Flip" because the word "flip" is repeated over and over in the song. Part of the middle section of this song is taken almost exactly from part of Guyute.

Golgi Apparatus: Perhaps the original Phish song, the lyrics were written by Trey and Tom and their gradeschool friends, then reworked many years later for use by Phish.

Guelah Papyrus: A section of the lyrics refer nostalgically to Dave Abrahams' mother Guelah, who would intrude into Dave's bedroom and spoil the childhood fun of Trey, Tom and Dave. Guelah has never been performed without The Asse Festival included within it, but some tapers still label the song "Guelah Papyrus > Asse Festival > Guelah Papyrus."

Guyute: Debuted in October 1994, Guyute (the name of "the ugly pig" in the song) excited fans who hoped that it heralded Trey's return to writing longer-form epics. It was unplayed from 12/29/94 until Halloween '95, when contrary to rumors that it would be reworked, the song returned virtually unchanged from its fall '94 incarnation except for whistling following the opening verses.

Halley's Comet: Played in the mid- and late 1980s, the band swore they would never play this one again at their 8/17/89 Nectar's show. But low and behold, it appeared at Gunnison, CO on 3/14/93 (a seriously botched version). The song then moved back into rotation. Early versions often featured the song's lyrical author, Nancy Taube, on vocals.

Harry Hood: A very popular song among longtime fans, the source of this song's lyrics is much-debated. According to the most believable rumors, several bandmember rented an apartment on 156 King Street in Burlington around 1985 which faced a Hood Milk billboard complete with the Hood Dairy slogan "You can feel good about Hood" and the Hood cartoon mascot Harry Hood. (H.P. Hood Dairy is a large New England dairy founded in 1846 and still

06/23/95	5	1	Ginseng	Taste
06/26/95	3	2	DWD	PoorHeart
06/29/95	2	2	*OP2	Bowie
07/03/95	4	1	Str Design	Cavern
09/27/95	1	1	Rift	It's Ice
09/29/95	2	2	Maze	Ya Mar
10/03/95	3	1	I'm Blue	TMWSIY
10/06/95	2	1	Rift	Lizards
10/08/95	2	1	Uncle Pen	*CL1
10/14/95	3	1	Kung	Sparkle
10/17/95	2	1	Sparkle	Str Design
10/20/95	2	1	Rift	HelloBaby
10/25/95	4	1	Scent	Str Design
10/31/95	4	1	Sparkle	Guyute
11/10/95	2	2	*OP2	Scent
11/14/95	3	1	Esther	Julius
11/18/95	3	2	Sparkle	I'm Tired
11/22/95	3	2	Rift	Llama
11/28/95	3	2	Uncle Pen	Wind
11/30/95	2	2	Scent	Str Design
12/02/95	2	1	MSO	Fog
12/05/95	2	1	Lizards	Esther
12/09/95	3	1	Bouncing	Billy
12/12/95	2	2	*OP2	Sparkle
12/15/95	2	1	Bouncing	Possum
12/17/95	2	2	Maze	Also Sprac
12/30/95	3	2	Ya Mar	Harry
07/12/96	11	3	Bowie	HelloBaby
07/21/96	6	2	Life Mars	Antelope
08/02/96	5	2	Taste	Fluffhead
08/07/96	4	2	RunJim	Forbin's
08/10/96	1	2	Scent	Fluffhead
08/16/96	4	2	Sparkle	Sqirm Coil
10/17/96	3	2	Scent	Lizards
10/19/96	2	1	Rift	Esther
10/22/96	2	1	Sparkle	YEM
10/25/96	2	2	NICU	Str Design
11/02/96	5	1	Stash	Johnny B.
11/07/96	3	1	Guyute	Tela
11/14/96	5	1	CTB	All Things
11/16/96	2	1	Rift	Old Home
11/27/96	6	1	Uncle Pen	Theme
12/02/96	4	2	Taste	Scent
12/29/96	4	1	Rift	Sqirm Coil
02/16/97	5	2	CTB	Sparkle
02/20/97	3	2	Bouncing	SweptAwy
02/22/97	2	2	Harry	HelloBaby
02/25/97	2	2	PYITE	Fee
06/14/97	7	1	Bye Bye	Caspian
06/24/97	6	1	Talk	Caspian
07/02/97	5	E	*OPE	*CLE
07/06/97	3	2	*OP2	YEM
07/26/97	8	2	Harry	Waste
07/30/97	2	2	PYITE	Bowie
08/08/97	5	2	Wolfman's	Limb
08/14/97	5	1	Limb	CTB
➢ 8/17/97	**2**			

Fuck Your Face [1]

Fuck Your Face [Fuck]

By Gordon

04/29/87	[15]	1	Cities	*CL1
➢ 8/17/97	**926**			

Ghost [20]

Ghost [Ghost]

By Anastasio/Marshall

06/13/97	[904]	2	Chalkdust	Oblivious
06/16/97	2	2	Limb	Don't Care
06/19/97	1	2	Stash	Saw It
06/20/97	1	2	Bowie	Bye Bye
06/22/97	2	1a	HelloBaby	*CL1
06/24/97	1	2	Wading	*CL2
07/01/97	4	1	*OP1	Horn
07/03/97	2	2	*OP2	CTB
07/09/97	3	2	YEM	PoorHeart
07/10/97	1	2	Ya Mar	River
07/21/97	2	1	*OP1	Dogs Stole
07/23/97	2	2	PYITE	Sample
07/25/97	1	2	Drums	CharZero
07/29/97	2	1	Sparkle	SweptAwy
07/31/97	2	1	*OP1	Ya Mar
08/02/97	1	1	Ginseng	Dogs Stole
08/06/97	2	2	My Soul	Caspian
08/09/97	2	1	PYITE	Taste
08/13/97	3	2	RunJim	Isabella
08/16/97	2	1	PYITE	Ginseng
➢ 8/17/97	**1**			

Glide [101]

Glide [Glide]

By Phish (after Anastasio/Marshall/Abrahams)

09/27/91	[337]	E	*OPE	Rocky Top
10/27/91	19	E	*OPE	Possum
10/31/91	3	E	*OPE	Possum
11/09/91	6	E	*OPE	Possum
11/14/91	4	2	It's Ice	Tweezer
11/16/91	2	E	*OPE	Rocky Top
11/19/91	1	E	*OPE	Rocky Top
11/22/91	3	E	*OPE	Suzie
11/30/91	3	1	*OP1	Llama
12/05/91	2	E	*OPE	Cavern
03/17/92	10	2	RunJim	Sloth
03/19/92	1	2	*OP2	Chalkdust
03/20/92	1	1	Brother	Rift
03/25/92	3	1	Maze	RunJim
03/27/92	2	1	Maze	Bouncing
03/28/92	1	1	Bowie	Cavern
03/31/92	2	1	Divided	Split&Melt
04/04/92	3	2	Weekpaug	MSO
04/12/92	5	2	*OP2	Split&Melt
04/18/92	5	2	*OP2	Oh Kee
04/22/92	3	2	*OP2	Antelope
04/24/92	2	2	Love You	Llama
04/30/92	3	2	*OP2	Tweezer
05/02/92	2	2	*OP2	Bowie
05/05/92	2	1	It's Ice	Antelope
05/07/92	2	2	Fluffhead	Mike's
05/14/92	5	2	*OP2	Cavern
05/16/92	2	1	Foam	Split&Melt
05/18/92	2	2	*OP1	Llama
07/09/92	9	1a	*OP1	Oh Kee
07/12/92	3	1a	Maze	Possum
07/15/92	2	1	*OP1	Oh Kee
07/16/92	1	2	Llama	Paul&Silas'
11/19/92	29	1	Foam	Split&Melt
11/21/92	2	1	Foam	PoorHeart
11/23/92	2	1	Foam	Split&Melt
11/27/92	2	2	Possum	It's Ice
11/30/92	2	2	Maze	Uncle Pen
12/02/92	2	2	Llama	Lngthwise
12/04/92	2	1	Stash	Sparkle
12/07/92	3	1	Maze	Sparkle
12/12/92	4	2	Maze	Curtain
12/28/92	2	1	Foam	It's Ice
12/31/92	3	2	Stash	GTBT
02/04/93	2	1	Sample	Antelope
02/07/93	3	2	BBJ	YEM
02/13/93	5	1	It's Ice	Rift
02/17/93	2	2	Bowie	My Friend
02/20/93	3	2	Tweezer	Mike's
02/22/93	2	2	Tweezer	YEM
02/26/93	3	2	Tweezer	Chalkdust
03/03/93	3	2	Weekpaug	MSO
03/08/93	3	1	It's Ice	Bowie
03/09/93	1	1	Divided	PYITE
03/13/93	2	2	It's Ice	Uncle Pen
03/17/93	3	2	Axilla	Reba
03/25/93	6	1	Stash	Rift
03/30/93	4	1	Stash	Divided
04/05/93	5	2	Tweezer	YEM
04/10/93	2	2	Rift	BBJ
04/17/93	5	1	It's Ice	My Friend
04/20/93	2	1	It's Ice	Uncle Pen
04/25/93	5	1	It's Ice	RunJim
04/29/93	2	1	Llama	Rift
05/01/93	2	1	It's Ice	Bowie
05/05/93	3	1	It's Ice	Maze
05/08/93	3	1	Stash	My Friend
07/16/93	4	2	Split&Melt	Maze
07/21/93	3	1a	Maze	Rift
07/24/93	3	2	Maze	Sparkle
08/09/93	12	1	Split&Melt	Nellie
08/15/93	5	2	Maze	Adeline
08/25/93	6	1	Stash	Cavern
12/29/93	4	1	Foam	Divided
04/05/94	4	1	Fluffhead	Julius
04/08/94	2	1	Maze	Foam
04/11/94	3	1	Julius	Divided
04/14/94	2	1	DWD	Rift
04/18/94	4	1	Chalkdust	PoorHeart
04/21/94	2	1	Foam	Split&Melt
05/02/94	8	1	It's Ice	Divided
05/17/94	11	2	RunJim	Tweezer
05/22/94	4	1	Divided	Split&Melt
06/09/94	7	2	Split&Melt	Julius
06/17/94	6	1	Foam	Split&Melt
06/30/94	10	1	Split&Melt	Scent
07/10/94	8	2	Bowie	Ya Mar
10/07/94	5	1	Julius	PoorHeart
10/15/94	7	1	Maze	Reba
10/25/94	7	2	YSZahov	Axilla 2
10/28/94	3	1	Stash	Axilla 2
11/03/94	4	1	Peaches	Split&Melt
11/20/94	9	2	Bowie	Axilla 2
12/31/94	19	1	Antelope	Mound
06/24/95	15	1	Julius	Mound
10/17/95	23	1	Maze	Sparkle
11/21/95	20	1	Bowie	Ya Mar
08/13/96	51	1	Llama	Slave
11/30/96	34	2	It's Ice	Brother
07/31/97	50	1	Maze	Saw It
➢ 8/17/97	**11**			

Glide II [1]*

Glide II [Glide 2]

By Anastasio/Marshall

05/16/95	[738]	1a	Free	YEM
➢ 8/17/97	**203**			

Golgi [301]*

Golgi Apparatus [Golgi]

By Anastasio/Marshall/Woolfe/Szuter

10/15/86	[8]	1a	Peaches	SwingLow
10/31/86	1	1	CamlWalk	Slave
03/06/87	2	1	Corrina	Quinn
03/11/87	1	1a	Corrina	Quinn
03/23/87	1	2	CamlWalk	SwingLow
04/24/87	1	1	Alumni	SwingLow
04/29/87	1	1	Alumni	SwingLow
05/11/87	1	1a	*OP1	Corrina
08/10/87	2	1	Alumni	Wilson
08/21/87	1	2	Harpua	Sparks
09/12/87	2	1	Reagan	ACDCBag
09/27/87	1	1	FunkBitch	Peaches
10/14/87	1	1	YEM	Slave
01/30/88	3	3	Lizards	Bike
03/11/88	2	1	Wilson	Slave
03/21/88	2	1a	Suzie	McGrupp
03/31/88	1	1	IDK	Fee
05/15/88	3	1a	LTJP	YEM
05/23/88	1	1a	A-Train	YEM
05/25/88	1	1	Peaches	Sally
06/15/88	1	1	Fluffhead	La Grange
06/18/88	1	1	Possum	La Grange
06/20/88	1	2	Fee	Satin Doll
06/21/88	1	2	Peaches	*CL2
07/11/88	1	1	Mockbird	Alumni
07/24/88	3	1	WalkAway	FunkBitch
08/06/88	3	2	*OP2	ACDCBag
08/27/88	1	1a	A-Train	Tela
09/24/88	3	1	*OP1	OYWD
10/12/88	1	1	IDK	Bowie
10/29/88	1	1	Time Loves	Bold
11/03/88	1	1	Fire	Fluffhead
11/05/88	1	1	A-Train	WalkAway
12/02/88	2	1	Sloth	Bold
01/26/89	1	1	IDK	Alumni
02/06/89	2	1	A-Train	Divided
02/07/89	1	1	Weekpaug	*CL1
02/17/89	1	1a	Split&Melt	A-Train
02/18/89	1	1a	GTBT	Wilson
03/04/89	3	1	Fee	GTBT
03/30/89	2	2	La Grange	*CL2
04/15/89	7	2	FunkBitch	Slave
05/05/89	10	1	*OP1	YEM
05/06/89	1	2	Harry	Slave
05/13/89	6	1	YEM	La Grange
05/20/89	4	2	Bowie	*CL2
05/26/89	2	2	Antelope	*CL2
10/01/89	23	1	Jam	Harry
10/06/89	1	1a	Sloth	Bold
10/07/89	1	1	*OP1	Ya Mar
10/14/89	3	1	IDK	Ya Mar
10/20/89	1	1	Divided	Antelope
10/22/89	2	1	Reba	In a Hole
10/26/89	1	1	Oh Kee	YEM
11/02/89	3	2	Oh Kee	YEM
11/03/89	1	1	Reba	*CL1
11/09/89	2	1	IDK	Ya Mar
11/11/89	2	1a	Oh Kee	Gin
12/07/89	7	E	*OPE	*CLE
12/09/89	2	1	Gin	*CL1
12/16/89	2	1a	In a Hole	*CL1
02/09/90	15	1	*OP1	Oh Kee
02/23/90	6	2	*OP2	Reba
02/24/90	1	1	YEM	Divided
03/01/90	2	1	*OP1	Ya Mar
03/08/90	3	2	Curtis	*CL2
04/04/90	5	1	*OP1	YEM
04/05/90	1	2	Contact	*CL2
04/07/90	2	2	*OP2	Forbin's
04/08/90	1	2	*OP2	WalkAway
04/12/90	3	1	*OP1	Ya Mar
04/22/90	6	E	Lawn Boy	*CLE
05/19/90	13	1	*OP1	Ya Mar
05/24/90	2	1	ACDCBag	*CL1
06/05/90	3	E	WhipPost	*CLE
06/16/90	4	2	*OP2	Esther
09/15/90	3	1	Bowie	Stash
09/22/90	4	E	Asse Fest	*CLE
10/04/90	3	1	*OP1	Landlady
10/05/90	1	2	*OP2	Curtain
10/07/90	2	2	GTBT	*CL2
10/12/90	2	1	Tweezer	*CL1
11/02/90	4	1	*OP1	Landlady
11/04/90	2	2	*OP2	Rocky Top
11/16/90	3	1	Divided	*CL1
12/07/90	7	1	*OP1	Stash

12/08/90 1 2 Tela No Good
12/28/90 1 1 Weekpaug *CL1
12/31/90 2 2 *OP2 Stash
02/03/91 3 1 Foam *CL1
02/07/91 1 1 Sqirm Coil *CL1
02/09/91 2 2 *OP2 BurAlive
02/14/91 1 1 Oh Kee *CL1
02/15/91 1 E2 Contact *CLE2
02/16/91 1 2 Love You *CL2
02/21/91 3 2 *OP2 Cavern
02/26/91 4 1 ACDCBag La Grange
02/27/91 1 1 *OP1 Divided
02/28/91 1 1 MSO *CL1
03/01/91 1 2 *OP2 Landlady
03/06/91 2 1 *OP1 YEM
03/13/91 6 2 Oh Kee *CL2
03/16/91 2 1 TMWSIY Reba
03/22/91 3 E Magilla *CLE
03/28/91 2 1a *OP1 Divided
04/04/91 5 1 Carolina *CL1
04/12/91 4 1 Rocky Top *CL1
04/16/91 3 1 *OP1 YEM
04/19/91 2 2 Curtain Landlady
04/21/91 2 1 *OP1 Rocky Top
04/27/91 4 1 Stash *CL1
05/04/91 3 E RunJim *CLE
05/12/91 4 2 Curtain Magilla
05/16/91 1 1 BurAlive Foam
05/17/91 1 E Lawn Boy *CLE
05/18/91 1 1 BurAlive Chalkdust
07/12/91 3 2 *OP2 Sqirm Coil
07/14/91 2 1 Sqirm Coil Guelah
07/19/91 3 1 *OP1 Landlady
07/20/91 1 2 Flat Fee Stash
07/23/91 2 E Caravan *CLE
07/24/91 1 1 *OP1 Chalkdust
07/25/91 1 2 Landlady Sqirm Coil
07/26/91 1 1 Landlady *CL1
08/03/91 2 1 Divided *CL1
09/26/91 2 2 *OP2 Sqirm Coil
09/28/91 2 1 Brother Memories
10/02/91 2 1 Chalkdust *CL1
10/04/91 2 E Adeline Rocky Top
10/06/91 2 1 Terrapin *CL1
10/10/91 1 1 Llama Alumni
10/12/91 2 1 Contact *CL1
10/15/91 2 2 Ya Mar *CL2
10/17/91 1 1 Chalkdust *CL1
10/19/91 2 1 Stash *CL1
10/27/91 4 1 Harry *CL1
11/02/91 5 2 *OP2 Antelope
11/08/91 3 1 Eliza *CL1
11/12/91 3 1 BurAlive Uncle Pen
11/13/91 1 2 Mockbird Gin
11/14/91 1 1 Mango RunJim
11/15/91 1 1 Lawn Boy *CL1
11/20/91 3 2 *Op2 Uce
11/21/91 1 E Adeline *CLE
11/23/91 2 1 Bouncing *CL1
11/24/91 1 2 YEM *CL2
11/30/91 1 2 Antelope *CL2
12/04/91 1 2 Love You *CL2
12/05/91 1 1 *OP1 Paul&Silas
12/07/91 2 E Adeline *CLE
12/31/91 1 1 Llama *CL1
03/07/92 2 E Adeline *CLE
03/12/92 2 2 *OP2 Tweezer
03/14/92 2 2 *OP2 Llama
03/19/92 2 1 Sparkle Horse
03/21/92 2 1 Stash *CL1
03/24/92 1 1 Rift Horse
03/25/92 1 2 Rosie *CL2
03/27/92 2 2 Love You *CL2
03/30/92 2 2 *OP2 Uncle Pen
04/01/92 2 1 *OP1 Foam
04/03/92 1 1 Split&Melt *CL1
04/07/92 4 2 My Mind *CL2
04/09/92 1 1 Sqirm Coil *CL1
04/13/92 2 1 *OP1 Uncle Pen
04/15/92 1 2 MSO *CL2
04/17/92 2 E *OPE *CLE
04/19/92 2 1 IDK *CL1
04/23/92 3 2 Rosie *CL2
04/24/92 1 1 Sqirm Coil *CL1
04/29/92 2 2 Love You *CL2
05/01/92 2 2 Terrapin *CL2
05/05/92 3 1 *OP1 Curtain
05/06/92 1 2 A-Train *CL2
05/08/92 2 2 Harry *CL2
05/09/92 1 2 Rosie *CL2
05/15/92 4 1a *OP1 Foam
05/16/92 1 1 Horn Lizards
06/23/92 5 1a Brain *CL1
06/30/92 3 1a *OP1 Divided
07/10/92 4 1a Maze Lizards
07/15/92 4 2 Harry *CL2
07/27/92 10 1a *OP1 All Things
08/01/92 4 1a *OP1 Foam
08/20/92 7 1 *OP1 Foam
11/22/92 12 2 Faht *CL2
11/28/92 4 2 Harpua *CL2
12/02/92 3 E *OPE Rocky Top
12/05/92 3 1 Uncle Pen *CL1
12/10/92 4 1 *OP1 Llama
12/12/92 2 2 Sqirm Coil *CL2
12/28/92 2 1 Rift Adeline
02/06/93 7 1 *OP1 Foam
02/09/93 2 1 Maze *CL1
02/12/93 3 1 *OP1 Maze
02/13/93 1 1 Maze *CL1
02/17/93 2 1 Maze *CL1
02/20/93 3 1 *OP1 Foam
02/23/93 3 1 *OP1 My Friend
02/25/93 1 2 Brain BBFCM
02/27/93 2 1 *OP1 Rift
03/02/93 1 E *OPE TweezRep
03/06/93 3 1 Maze RunJim
03/08/93 1 1 *OP1 Rift
03/12/93 2 2 Harry *CL2
03/14/93 2 E Adeline *CLE
03/17/93 2 2 Great Gig *CL2
03/19/93 2 2 Love You *CL2
03/22/93 2 2 *OP2 It's Ice
03/25/93 2 2 Weekpaug *CL2
03/27/93 2 2 PoorHeart *CL2
03/30/93 2 1 All Things My Friend
04/02/93 3 1 Maze *CL1
04/09/93 3 E Adeline *CLE
04/12/93 2 1 *OP1 Tube
04/14/93 2 1 IDK *CL1
04/17/93 2 1 All Things Antelope
04/20/93 2 2 WhipPost *CL2
04/22/93 2 1 Rift *CL1
04/23/93 1 2 *OP2 Maze
04/25/93 2 1 IDK *CL1
04/27/93 1 2 *OP2 My Friend
04/30/93 2 2 YEM *CL2
05/02/93 2 1 IDK *CL1
05/05/93 2 1 Maze *CL1
05/07/93 2 E AmGrace *CLE
05/30/93 3 1a Llama *CL1
07/16/93 2 1 Daniel My Friend
07/18/93 2 2 PurplRain *CL2
07/22/93 2 1 Stash *CL1
07/24/93 2 E *OPE FrBir
07/30/93 5 2 My Friend Sqirm Coil
08/03/93 3 2 PurplRain *CL2
08/12/93 6 2 BBJ Possum
08/14/93 2 2 PurplRain *CL2
08/24/93 6 1 Maze *CL1
08/26/93 2 1 Harry *CL1
12/28/93 2 E Memories *CLE
12/31/93 3 E *OPE AmGrace
04/05/94 2 E Nellie *CLE
04/10/94 4 E Bouncing *CLE
04/13/94 2 1 Divided *CL1
04/17/94 4 2 Contact *CL2
04/23/94 5 2 Who By Fire *CL2
04/28/94 3 E *OPE *CLE
05/02/94 3 2 Reba Lizards
05/06/94 3 2 Maze Golgi
05/08/94 2 E Adeline *CLE
05/19/94 7 2 Harry *CL2
05/27/94 7 1 Harry *CL1
05/29/94 2 E Wilson Rocky Top
06/09/94 1 2 Weekpaug *CL2
06/13/94 3 E *OPE *CLE
06/16/94 2 2 PurplRain *CL2
06/19/94 3 1 Stash *CL1
06/22/94 2 1 Stash *CL1
06/25/94 3 2 Harry *CL2
06/29/94 2 1 IDK *CL1
07/02/94 3 1 *OP1 Divided
07/05/94 2 2 AmGrace *CL2
07/08/94 2 2 Julius *CL2
07/10/94 2 E *OPE Rocky Top
07/15/94 3 1 Split&Melt *CL1
07/16/94 1 1 *OP1 DWD
10/07/94 1 1 Guyute *CL1
10/10/94 3 2 *OP2 Maze
10/15/94 4 1 DWD *CL1
10/20/94 3 2 Guyute *CL1
10/25/94 4 E Long Time *CLE
10/31/94 5 1 Reba *CL1
11/04/94 3 2 Ya Mar Slave
11/12/94 1 2 Harry *CL2
11/14/94 2 E *OPE *CLE
11/17/94 2 2 Slave *CL2
11/19/94 2 1 *OP1 DWD
11/25/94 4 1 Julius *CL1
12/01/94 4 2 Harry *CL2
12/03/94 2 E *OPE *CLE
12/06/94 2 1 Stash *CL1
12/08/94 2 2 Bowie *CL2
12/31/94 6 1 *OP1 NICU
06/13/95 6 2 Harry *CL2
06/24/95 9 2 Adeline *CL2
06/30/95 5 E Rosie *CLE
10/22/95 22 2 *OP2 Possum
12/02/95 24 2 DayinLife Sqirm Coil
12/29/95 13 E *OPE *CLE
07/15/96 14 E *OPE *CLE
07/21/96 4 1 *OP1 Guelah
07/24/96 3 1a YEM *CL1
08/02/96 2 1 Theme Tweezer
08/07/96 4 E Bouncing *CLE
08/12/96 2 2 HelloBaby Possum
08/17/96 4 2 Antelope Slave
10/17/96 2 E *OPE *CLE
11/08/96 15 1 Reba Antelope
11/13/96 3 2 Theme *CL2
02/17/97 23 1 Bathtub *CL1
08/13/97 46 2 Also Sprac Frankstein
➤ 8/17/97 3

Guelah Papyrus [165]*

Guelah Papyrus [Guelah]
By Anastasio/Marshall

02/01/91 [257] 1 Magilla RunJim
02/02/91 1 1 Suzie Dinner
02/03/91 1 1 RunJim MSO
02/07/91 2 2 TweezRep Uncle Pen
02/08/91 1 1 RunJim Bowie
02/09/91 1 1 Foam MSO
02/15/91 2 2 Ya Mar MSO
02/16/91 1 2 RunJim Fluffhead
02/21/91 3 2 Stash Uncle Pen
02/26/91 4 1 Llama MSO
02/28/91 2 2 Llama Divided
03/01/91 1 2 Llama Sloth
03/07/91 3 2 Weekpaug MSO
03/13/91 3 2 MSO RunJim
03/16/91 2 2 Divided MSO
03/22/91 3 2 RunJim Terrapin
03/28/91 2 1a YEM MSO
04/04/91 5 2 RunJim Bowie
04/12/91 4 1 Divided Oh Kee
04/22/91 8 1 Llama Oh Kee
04/26/91 2 2 MSO Landlady
05/04/91 4 1 Split&Melt Fluffhead
05/17/91 6 2 Possum Rocky Top
05/18/91 1 2 MSO Bowie
07/13/91 4 2 Chalkdust Divided
07/14/91 1 1 Golgi MSO
07/18/91 3 1 RunJim Suzie
07/21/91 2 1 Divided PoorHeart
07/24/91 2 2 Possum Bowie
08/03/91 4 1 RunJim Llama
09/26/91 2 1 MSO Lizards
09/28/91 2 2 Llama Sparkle
10/02/91 2 2 MSO RunJim
10/04/91 2 1 Divided Sparkle
10/11/91 4 1 MSO Chalkdust
10/18/91 5 2 Uncle Pen Dinner
10/27/91 5 1 BurAlive Fluffhead
11/02/91 5 2 Sparkle WalkAway
11/12/91 6 2 Weekpaug Chalkdust
11/21/91 7 1 PoorHeart Reba
11/23/91 2 1 RunJim Sparkle
11/30/91 2 1 Paul&Silas YEM
12/06/91 3 1 Landlady IDK
12/31/91 2 1 Lizards Divided
03/06/92 1 1 Divided Maze
03/13/92 4 1 PoorHeart Maze
03/17/92 2 1 Divided Rift
03/24/92 4 2 Weekpaug Mango
03/27/92 3 1 Divided Maze
03/30/92 2 1 Foam Sparkle
04/03/92 3 1 Rift Sparkle
04/05/92 2 1 Llama Divided
04/06/92 1 1 Chalkdust Sqirm Coil
04/09/92 2 1 Foam Llama
04/12/92 1 1 PoorHeart Divided
04/15/92 2 1 Foam Sparkle
04/18/92 3 1 Divided PoorHeart
04/21/92 2 1 Rift Possum
04/22/92 1 1 Sparkle Divided
04/23/92 1 1 Uncle Pen Sqirm Coil
04/29/92 3 1 RunJim Rift
05/01/92 2 1 Divided It's Ice
05/03/92 2 2 Fluffhead Mike's
05/05/92 1 1 Rift Divided
05/07/92 2 1 Rift Possum
05/09/92 2 1 Split&Melt Rift
05/12/92 2 2 YEM Chalkdust
05/17/92 4 2 Possum Sqirm Coil
05/18/92 1 1 Divided Foam
06/24/92 4 1a Uncle Pen IDK
06/30/92 2 1a Divided Possum
07/09/92 3 1a RunJim Bowie
07/14/92 4 1 Rift Maze
07/16/92 2 1 Maze Rift
08/02/92 14 1a Chalkdust Rift
08/15/92 3 1a Sparkle Maze
08/19/92 2 1a RunJim YEM
11/21/92 12 2 Uncle Pen Sqirm Coil
11/23/92 2 1 Rift Divided
11/30/92 4 2 RunJim Maze

SONGS PLAYED BY YEAR
(1997 through 8/17/97)

Golgi
1990 28
1991 63
1992 41
1993 47
1994 42
1995 6
1996 10
1997 2

Guelah
1991 44
1992 42
1993 41
1994 18
1995 6
1996 11
1997 3

Gumbo
1990 2
1991 6
1992 0
1993 2
1994 9
1995 10
1996 8
1997 4

Guyute
1994 19
1995 8
1996 6
1997 5

Ha Ha Ha
1995 13
1996 2
1997 1

Halley's
1990 0
1991 0
1992 0
1993 7
1994 12
1995 6
1996 2
1997 1

Harpua
1990 3
1991 4
1992 6
1993 6
1994 7
1995 2
1996 3
1997 1

Harry Hood
1990 13
1991 22
1992 18
1993 19
1994 31
1995 22
1996 19
1997 16

Horn
1990 5
1991 17
1992 25
1993 19
1994 12
1995 9
1996 4
1997 3

Horse > Silent
1992 26
1993 39
1994 28
1995 9
1996 9
1997 3

Hydrogen
1990 53
1991 49
1992 35
1993 25
1994 14
1995 2
1996 3
1997 2

I Didn't Know
1990 24
1991 36
1992 26
1993 33
1994 15
1995 10
1996 6
1997 1

I Don't Care
1997 2

I Saw It Again
1997 5

Icculus
1990 0
1991 1
1992 3
1993 1
1994 3
1995 1
1996 0
1997 0

If I Could
1994 34
1995 9
1996 2
1997 0

It's Ice 1991
1991 21
1992 40
1993 55
1994 40
1995 18
1996 14
1997 2

Stories Behind the Songs
(Continued)

going strong). The lights going out on the billboard late at night inspired the "Harry, Harry, where do you go..." line. Mail received at the same address referred to a "Mr. Miner" who leased the apartment previously; one letter closed with the line, "Thank You, Mr. Miner." (Almanac research has documented a "Floyd Miner" at the King Street address in 1982). Several times in concert, Trey has introduced Harry Hood by telling the audience, "This is a song about milk."

Harpua: Sporadically played, much to the disappointment of fans who worship this song and consider its appearance a sign of truly great show. The misadventures of Harpua, a mangy mutt, are recounted by Trey during a hilarious "Harpua rap" in the middle of each version. The rap usually features tales of little Jimmy and his cat Poster Nutbag. The exchange between "father" and "son" in the middle of the song is a standard part of Harpua in all but the earliest versions. Also standard practice is sampling of songs by other artists in the middle of the song, which have ranged from Nirvana's Smells Like Teen Spirit (5/9/92) to Spin Doctors' Jimmy Olsen's Blues (11/28/92) to Michael Jackson's Beat It (10/31/95). Although the Harpua Rap sometimes features references to Gamehendge (like on 10/31/94), Harpua is not a Gamehendge song.

Perhaps because fans enjoy Harpua so much, the song has sparked controversies several times in the Phish phan community. A severely shortened performance of Harpua at The Clifford Ball on 8/17/96 concerned fans who wondered why the band walked off the stage with the song only half-finished. In response, Trey posted a letter on the Web several weeks later saying that a plane that was supposed to appear overhead for a special effect in the middle of the song was hidden behind the stage where the band couldn't see it, so they cut it short. Fittingly, a year later at the Great Went, Phish played the second half of Harpua, ending the version they left unfinished a year earlier.

12/03/92	3	2	Rift	Fluffhead
12/05/92	2	1	Rift	Split&Melt
12/08/92	3	1	Uncle Pen	Divided
12/11/92	2	1	Chalkdust	Sparkle
12/12/92	1	2	Rift	YEM
12/29/92	3	1	RunJim	Llama
02/03/93	3	1	PoorHeart	Bowie
02/05/93	2	1	Llama	Rift
02/10/93	4	1	Foam	Reba
02/12/93	2	1	Maze	Sparkle
02/15/93	2	1	Sparkle	Divided
02/18/93	2	1	Chalkdust	PoorHeart
02/22/93	4	1	Rift	PoorHeart
02/27/93	4	1	Rift	Maze
03/03/93	2	1	Maze	Paul&Silas
03/05/93	1	2	Chalkdust	Uncle Pen
03/08/93	2	1	Rift	Oh Kee
03/12/93	2	1	Possum	Rift
03/14/93	2	1	Foam	Sparkle
03/18/93	3	1	Chalkdust	Rift
03/22/93	3	1	Chalkdust	Uncle Pen
03/25/93	2	1	Chalkdust	It's Ice
03/27/93	2	1	Llama	Rift
04/01/93	4	1	Llama	Rift
04/03/93	2	1	Rift	Sparkle
04/09/93	2	1	Sparkle	Stash
04/13/93	3	1	Chalkdust	Caravan
04/16/93	2	1	Chalkdust	Sparkle
04/18/93	2	1	Rift	Split&Melt
04/21/93	2	1	Foam	Maze
04/23/93	2	1	Divided	Lawn Boy
04/24/93	1	1	Chalkdust	PoorHeart
04/27/93	2	1	Stash	It's Ice
05/01/93	3	1	Foam	Split&Melt
05/05/93	3	1	Rift	Foam
05/08/93	3	1	Chalkdust	Rift
05/30/93	2	1a	Maze	PoorHeart
07/18/93	4	1	Foam	Maze
07/24/93	4	1	Divided	Rift
08/02/93	7	1	Chalkdust	PoorHeart
08/06/93	2	2	Tweezer	Sqirm Coil
08/12/93	5	1	Chalkdust	Nellie
08/14/93	2	1	Chalkdust	Divided
08/17/93	3	1	Llama	Divided
08/21/93	2	1	Foam	Rift
08/26/93	3	1	RunJim	Reba
12/31/93	5	1	Llama	Stash
04/06/94	3	1	Llama	PoorHeart
04/15/94	7	1	Llama	Paul&Silas
05/03/94	14	1	Rift	Maze
05/21/94	13	1	Foam	DWD
05/29/94	7	1	Divided	Halley's
06/09/94	1	1	Llama	Rift
06/14/94	4	1	Llama	Rift
06/22/94	6	1	Llama	Rift
06/30/94	6	1	Rift	Split&Melt
07/02/94	2	1	Divided	FEFY
07/09/94	5	1	Maze	Scent
10/07/94	6	1	Divided	Stash
10/12/94	4	1	Lizards	Julius
10/20/94	6	1	PoorHeart	Split&Melt
10/28/94	7	1	Llama	Scent
11/14/94	8	1	Scent	Split&Melt
11/25/94	8	1	Llama	Reba
12/03/94	6	1	Divided	Scent
06/08/95	13	1	RunJim	Mound
06/22/95	10	1	Divided	It's Ice
10/03/95	16	1	Maze	Foam
10/21/95	12	1	Chalkdust	Reba
11/12/95	11	1	Bouncing	Reba
12/02/95	14	1	Mound	Reba
07/21/96	31	1	Golgi	Rift
08/02/96	5	1	DWD	PoorHeart
08/05/96	2	1	PoorHeart	Divided
10/18/96	11	1	RunJim	Old Home
10/25/96	5	1	Mound	IDK
10/29/96	3	1	Chalkdust	CTB
11/07/96	5	1	Rift	Stash
11/11/96	3	1	Chalkdust	CTB
11/18/96	5	1	Chalkdust	Ginseng
11/23/96	3	1	Chalkdust	CTB
12/29/96	10	1	Taste	Train Song
02/16/97	5	1	Crosseyed	Ginseng
06/24/97	20	1	Vultures	RunJim
08/11/97	26	1	Guyute	Limb
➢ 8/17/97	**5**			

Gumbo [41]

Gumbo [Gumbo]

By Anastasio/Fishman

09/28/90	[229]	2	Esther	Dinner
11/30/90	20	2	Lizards	Divided
07/12/91	72	1	MSO	Mike's
07/14/91	2	2	Divided	Dinner
07/19/91	3	1	YEM	Touch Me
07/21/91	2	E	*OPE	Touch Me
07/23/91	1	2	Dinner	Touch Me
07/25/93	2	2	Lizards	Touch Me
04/16/93	226	E	*OPE	AmGrace
04/21/93	4	2	Weekpaug	*CL2
06/16/94	103	1	Maze	Curtain
06/22/94	5	1	Rift	Maze
06/30/94	6	1	DWD	Rift
07/09/94	7	1	Foam	Maze
07/15/94	4	1	Divided	Foam
10/13/94	7	1	Divided	Axilla 2
10/22/94	7	1	Divided	Rift
12/02/94	26	2	Landlady	Caravan
12/03/94	1	2	BurAlive	Slave
06/14/95	17	1	Wanna Go	NICU
06/28/95	11	2	Tweezer	Sparkle
07/02/95	4	1	Divided	Curtain
10/07/95	10	1	Julius	Fog
10/20/95	8	2	Maze	Guitar
10/29/95	7	1	NICU	Slave
11/14/95	6	2	Maze	Stash
12/04/95	14	1	Julius	Divided
12/09/95	4	2	Wilson	YEM
12/28/95	7	1	Split&Melt	Curtain
07/23/96	21	1	Theme	Scent
08/07/96	7	1	Ya Mar	Taste
08/14/96	4	1	Mango	Stash
10/19/96	6	1	Llama	DWD
11/11/96	15	2	Divided	Curtain
11/16/96	4	1	Guyute	Rift
12/02/96	10	1	Theme	Julius
12/30/96	5	1	Llama	Reba
02/20/97	7	1	Taste	Circus
07/29/97	34	1	Beauty	Dirt
08/08/97	6	1	CTB	Lizards
08/13/97	4	1	Water	Horse
➢ 8/17/97	**3**			

Guyute [37]*

Guyute [Guyute]

By Anastasio/Marshall

10/07/94	[688]	1	Stash	Golgi
10/08/94	1	1	DWD	Fee
10/10/94	2	1	Stash	Old Home
10/14/94	3	2	Life Boy	Chalkdust
10/18/94	3	1	It's Ice	Divided
10/20/94	1	1	Julius	Golgi
10/26/94	5	1	Antelope	Dog Faced
11/02/94	5	1	Maze	Stash
11/12/94	3	1	If I Could	Maze
11/19/94	6	1	DWD	Axilla 2
11/22/94	2	1	Foam	IDK
11/26/94	3	1	Possum	If I Could
11/28/94	1	1	Stash	Sparkle
12/01/94	2	1	Maze	IDK
12/03/94	2	1	Antelope	Sample
12/07/94	3	1	Split&Melt	Life Boy
12/09/94	2	1	Foam	Sparkle
12/10/94	1	2	Maze	Also Sprac
12/29/94	2	2	*OP2	Bowie
10/31/95	50	1	Free	Antelope
11/10/95	2	1	Maze	Cavern
11/16/95	5	1	Timber Ho	FunkBitch
11/21/95	3	1	I'm Blue	My Friend
11/28/95	4	1	Divided	HelloBaby
12/07/95	7	1	Slave	Bouncing
12/28/95	9	1	Julius	Horn
07/15/96	15	1	FEFY	Possum
08/04/96	10	1	FunkBitch	Fee
11/07/96	25	1	Waste	Free
11/16/96	7	1	DWD	Gumbo
12/04/96	11	1	Train Song	CharZero
12/30/96	4	2	ACDCBag	Tweezer
02/17/97	5	1	My Soul	Timber Ho
03/02/97	10	1	Sample	My Soul
06/25/97	10	E	*OPE	*CLE
08/11/97	25	1	Water	Guelah
08/17/96	5	3	Weigh	Dirt
➢ 8/17/97	**0**			

Ha Ha Ha [16]

Ha Ha Ha [Ha Ha Ha]

By Fishman

05/16/95	[738]	1a	Wanna Go	Spock's
06/07/95	1	2	*OP2	Maze
06/08/95	1	1	Wanna Go	RunJim
06/15/95	5	2	MSO	Bowie
06/22/95	5	1	Scent	Divided
06/30/95	7	2	Possum	TMWSIY
07/02/95	2	2	Tweezer	Sl Monkey
10/05/95	8	1	Chalkdust	Fog
10/20/95	10	1	Ya Mar	Divided
11/16/95	15	2	Uncle Pen	Harry
11/30/95	9	1	Curtain	Julius
12/11/95	8	1	My Friend	Stash
12/15/95	3	1	Maze	Suspicious
10/25/96	45	1	*OP1	Taste
12/04/96	26	2	*OP2	Mike's
02/26/97	16	2	PoorHeart	YEM
➢ 8/17/97	**42**			

Halley's [34]*

Halley's Comet [Halley's]

By Phish/Nancy Taube

10/31/86	[9]	1	Sally	CrJam
04/29/87	6	2	A-Train	Quinn
05/14/88	21	2	IDK	Light Up
06/20/88	6	1	Lizards	Wilson
10/29/88	14	2	*OP2	WhipPost
05/26/89	47	1	Sanity	Sloth
08/17/89	14	3	Possum	Alumni
03/14/93	418	2	*OP2	Bowie
03/27/93	10	2	BurAlive	It's Ice
04/17/93	14	2	Landlady	YEM
05/01/93	11	2	BBJ	Paul&Silas
08/06/93	25	2	YEM	Slave
08/24/93	13	E	*OPE	PoorHeart
12/31/93	7	2	Tweezer	PoorHeart
04/29/94	21	1	*OP1	YEM
05/08/94	7	2	YEM	GTBT
05/19/94	7	1	*OP1	Llama
05/29/94	9	1	Guelah	DWD
06/09/94	1	2	Julius	Scent
06/24/94	12	2	Antelope	Curtain
10/15/94	24	2	RunJim	Scent
10/23/94	6	2	Bouncing	YEM
11/02/94	7	2	*OP2	Tweezer
11/26/94	14	2	*OP2	Bowie
11/30/94	2	2	*OP2	Antelope
12/29/94	11	2	Bowie	Lizards
06/16/95	11	1	*OP1	DWD
06/20/95	3	2	*OP2	Chalkdust
06/24/95	3	2	Also Sprac	Bowie
07/02/95	7	E	*OPE	TweezRep
12/01/95	43	2	*OP2	Mike's
12/14/95	9	2	Keyboard	NICU
08/05/96	30	2	It's Ice	Thrmn
08/16/96	7	1	Divided	Bowie
08/16/97	92	3	*OP3	Cities
➢ 8/17/97	**1**			

Harpua [47]*

Harpua [Harpua]

By Anastasio/Fishman

08/09/87	[17]	1	Harry	Suzie
08/21/87	2	2	Mike's	Golgi
08/29/87	2	2	Divided	*CL2
03/11/88	10	2	Curtis	ACDCBag
05/15/88	6	1a	Sloth	*CL1
05/25/88	2	3	Corrina	Antelope
06/21/88	4	2	*OP2	IDK
07/25/88	5	3	Skin It	BBFCM
11/03/88	9	2	BBFCM	Bowie
04/20/89	24	2	Love You	*CL2
05/09/89	12	2	Bold	WhipPost
10/14/89	37	2	Possum	*CL2
10/20/89	1	1	*OP1	BundleJoy
11/10/89	10	2	Possum	HwayHell
03/11/90	42	2	Split&Melt	Slave
04/07/90	6	2	Bike	*CL2
06/09/90	31	2	Terrapin	*CL2
04/18/91	81	E	*OPE	*CLE
04/26/91	6	2	Harry	*CL2
05/03/91	3	2	YEM	TweezRep
10/28/91	45	2	WhipPost	HwayHell
12/07/91	25	2	Terrapin	*CL2
03/26/92	14	E	Chalkdust	*CLE
04/04/92	7	2	My Friend	Cavern
04/22/92	13	2	Rosie	RunJim
05/09/92	13	2	Tweezer	Llama
11/28/92	58	2	Love You	Golgi
12/31/92	17	3	Weekpaug	Sqirm Coil
02/12/93	9	2	Harry	*CL2
03/31/93	34	2	YEM	Chalkdust
04/14/93	9	2	YEM	RunJim
05/07/93	18	2	Harry	HwayHell
07/25/93	12	2	PurplRain	TweezRep
08/20/93	19	1	Divided	PoorHeart
05/03/94	33	2	DWD	Chalkdust
06/17/94	27	2	Weekpaug	Sparkle
06/30/94	10	2	Axilla 2	Antelope
07/16/94	12	2	Antelope	ACDCBag
10/16/94	9	E2	*OPE2	*CLE2
10/31/94	11	1	Divided	Julius
11/25/94	14	2	Simple	Weekpaug
06/23/95	30	2	Antelope	WlJam
10/31/95	34	1	Antelope	*CL1
08/17/96	64	E	*OPE	*CLE
12/06/96	35	E	*OPE	Suzie
12/29/96	2	2	YEM	*CL2
08/16/97	54	1	Makisupa	Chalkdust
➢ 8/17/97	**1**			

Harry Hood [192]

Harry Hood [Harry]

By Anastasio/Phish/Brian Long

10/30/85	[4]	1a	*OP1	Dog Log
04/01/86	2	1	Mercy	Pendul
10/15/86	2	1a	Mercy	Peaches
10/31/86	1	2	Mercy	Sanity
03/06/87	2	2	FrBir	TMSG
08/09/87	6	1	Fee	Harpua
08/21/87	2	1	FunkBitch	Clod
08/29/87	2	2	Possum	Timber Ho
11/19/87	6	1	Sally	Fire
01/30/88	1	3	CamlWalk	*CL3
02/08/88	2	2	Antelope	Mockbird
03/11/88	1	2	Dinner	Curtis
07/23/88	15	3	Contact	Dinner
08/03/88	3	2	Fluffhead	Satin Doll
09/12/88	4	1a	CamlWalk	Esther
10/29/88	3	1	Contact	*CL1
02/05/89	7	1	WalkAway	BBFCM
02/06/89	1	2	WalkAway	BBFCM
05/06/89	26	2	Fire	Golgi
05/13/89	6	2	Lizards	Brain
05/21/89	5	1	*OP1	Foam
05/28/89	5	3	Mango	*CL3
06/23/89	5	2	Fluffhead	Ya Mar
08/17/89	7	1	Rocky Top	Mike's
08/19/89	2	2	YEM	*CL2
08/26/89	2	1	Mockbird	Split&Melt
09/09/89	4	2	Split&Melt	WalkAway
10/01/89	1	1	Golgi	Wilson
10/06/89	1	1a	LTJP	Possum
10/20/89	5	2	Split&Melt	SwingLow
10/22/89	2	2	*OP2	Reba
11/10/89	8	1	La Grange	Gin
12/08/89	9	2	*OP2	Tela
01/20/90	7	1a	Weekpaug	Carolina
04/06/90	31	2	Sloth	Caravan
04/09/90	3	2	Foam	Jesus
04/13/90	3	2	Sloth	Caravan
04/22/90	5	2	BBFCM	Fire
04/28/90	3	2	Cavern	Caravan
05/06/90	4	2	Fee	Esther
05/10/90	1	2	RunJim	Caravan
05/15/90	4	1	Suzie	Bike
05/24/90	3	2	WalkAway	HwayHell
06/09/90	6	2	GTBT	TMWSIY
09/15/90	4	2	Minute	Possum
11/04/90	18	1	Tube	FunkBitch
02/09/91	20	2	Bouncing	Cavern
02/15/91	2	2	ACDCBag	Terrapin
03/15/91	18	2	IDK	Chalkdust
04/05/91	12	2	Dinner	IDK
04/19/91	8	2	*OP2	Curtain
04/21/91	2	2	Uncle Pen	Cavern
04/26/91	3	2	IDK	Harpua
05/02/91	2	E	*OPE	*CLE
05/04/91	2	2	BurAlive	Horn
05/10/91	2	2	*OP2	Wilson
07/14/91	10	3	Touch Me	*CL3
08/03/91	11	E2	*OPE2	*CLE2
10/06/91	10	2	Destiny	IDK
10/12/91	3	1	Brain	TweezRep
10/15/91	2	E	Memories	*CLE
10/19/91	3	2	Terrapin	*CL2
10/27/91	4	1	Bouncing	Golgi
10/31/91	3	2	IDK	*CL2
11/12/91	8	1	Sloth	Fee
11/15/91	3	2	Destiny	Love You
11/21/91	4	2	Wilson	It's Ice
11/30/91	4	2	Uncle Pen	It's Ice
03/11/92	8	2	All Things	Rocky Top
03/14/92	3	2	Suzie	Rosie
03/20/92	3	2	Uncle Pen	Terrapin
03/24/92	2	2	Suzie	Cavern
03/27/92	3	2	Magilla	Love You
04/03/92	5	2	Llama	Suzie
04/12/92	6	2	Rosie	Cavern
04/18/92	5	2	Dinner	Love You
04/25/92	6	2	Dinner	Weigh
04/30/92	2	2	Rosie	TweezRep
05/08/92	7	2	Terrapin	Golgi
05/17/92	7	2	Sparkle	Cavern
07/15/92	15	2	All Things	Golgi
11/20/92	31	2	Dinner	Terrapin
11/25/92	4	E	*OPE	Carolina
12/04/92	7	2	Carolina	Faht
12/13/92	8	2	Rosie	Cavern
12/28/92	1	2	Bike	Cavern
02/04/93	5	2	Lngthwise	Cavern
02/12/93	7	2	Terrapin	Harpua
02/20/93	6	2	Terrapin	TweezRep
03/02/93	7	2	Choo	AmGrace
03/12/93	6	2	Lngthwise	Golgi
03/21/93	7	2	Rosie	Cavern
03/31/93	8	2	Uncle Pen	BBJ
04/16/93	10	1	Rift	Cavern
04/24/93	7	2	Bike	Cavern
04/30/93	4	2	BBJ	Brain
05/07/93	6	2	Great Gig	Harpua
07/16/93	5	2	PurplRain	Cavern
07/28/93	9	2	My Friend	Great Gig
08/08/93	8	2	Rift	Wilson
08/15/93	6	E	*OPE	*CLE
08/21/93	4	2	Brain	Daniel
08/26/93	3	1	It's Ice	Golgi
12/28/93	2	2	Uncle Pen	HwayHell
12/31/93	3	3	Rosie	TweezRep
04/04/94	1	E	*OPE	Cavern
04/08/94	3	2	Sparkle	Bouncing
04/10/94	2	2	BeLikeYou	*CL2
04/15/94	4	1	Paul&Silas	Wilson
04/20/94	4	2	BBJ	Fee
04/23/94	3	2	Ginseng	YEM
04/30/94	5	2	Peaches	Axilla 2
05/10/94	7	2	Scent	Ginseng
05/19/94	6	2	BBJ	Golgi
05/21/94	2	2	Bike	AmGrace
05/27/94	5	1	PYITE	Golgi
05/29/94	2	E2	*OPE2	GTBT
06/10/94	2	2	BeLikeYou	TweezRep
06/21/94	8	2	Sparkle	Suzie
06/25/94	4	2	Rosie	Golgi
07/01/94	4	2	Terrapin	Cavern
07/06/94	4	2	BBFCM	TweezRep
07/09/94	2	2	BBJ	Suzie
07/14/94	3	2	BBJ	HwayHell
07/16/94	2	2	Scent	Contact
10/08/94	2	2	PurplRain	Suzie
10/12/94	3	2	Long Time	Sample
10/20/94	6	2	Rift	Nellie
10/23/94	3	2	PurplRain	Fee
10/29/94	5	E	*OPE	*CLE
11/03/94	3	2	BBFCM	Cavern
11/12/94	2	2	Long Time	Golgi
11/19/94	6	2	Rosie	AmGrace
11/22/94	2	2	LongJourn	HwayHell
12/01/94	6	2	Jesus	Golgi
12/30/94	11	2	PurplRain	TweezRep
06/07/95	3	2	Sample	Suzie
06/13/95	4	2	AArmy	Golgi
06/17/95	4	2	Adeline	Sample
06/24/95	5	2	Suzie	AArmy
06/28/95	3	2	Suzie	TweezRep
07/01/95	3	2	AArmy	Suzie
09/27/95	3	2	AArmy	HelloBaby
10/03/95	5	2	Sparkle	Billy
10/07/95	3	2	Frankstein	Adeline
10/15/95	5	2	Suspicious	TweezRep
10/21/95	4	2	PurplRain	Suzie
11/10/95	9	E	*OPE	*CLE
11/16/95	5	2	Ha Ha Ha	Brain
11/19/95	2	2	Scent	Suzie
11/25/95	4	2	Weekpaug	HelloBaby
11/30/95	3	E	*OPE	*CLE
12/05/95	4	2	Life Boy	Cavern
12/11/95	4	2	Scent	Suspicious
12/15/95	3	1	Chalkdust	Wilson
12/17/95	2	2	Also Sprac	Sparkle
12/30/95	3	2	Free	ACDCBag
04/26/96	2	1a	ASZ	Sample
07/06/96	4	1a	Maze	*CL1
07/11/96	4	2	*OP2	Bouncing
07/15/96	3	1	IDK	Cavern
07/21/96	4	E	*OPE	*CLE
07/25/96	4	1a	Life Mars	Cavern
08/06/96	4	2	PurplRain	TweezRep
08/10/96	2	2	WhipPost	DayinLife
08/16/96	4	2	Life Mars	Jam
10/18/96	4	2	Waste	*CL2
10/25/96	5	2	Str Design	Cavern
11/02/96	5	2	Waste	DayinLife
11/09/96	5	2	Steep	*CL2
11/16/96	5	2	Axilla	Suzie
11/23/96	4	2	AmGrace	*CL2
11/29/96	3	2	Waste	*CL2
12/02/96	3	2	Scent	Adeline
12/06/96	2	2	Simple	Weekpaug
12/31/96	4	2	Steep	Caspian
02/13/97	1	2	RockaW	Frankstein
02/18/97	4	2	Train Song	Frankstein
02/22/97	3	2	Jesus	Free
02/26/97	3	1	My Friend	My Soul
03/18/97	4	1	Beauty	CTB
06/16/97	3	2	Dirt	*CL2
06/21/97	3	1a	Dogs Stole	Chalkdust
07/03/97	8	2	Sparkle	Cavern
07/05/97	1	1a	Piper	Love You
07/09/97	2	1	Adeline	*CL1
07/22/97	4	E	Circus	*CLE
07/26/97	3	2	Bowie	Free
08/02/97	4	E	*OPE	*CLE
08/10/97	5	1	Ginseng	*CL1
08/14/97	3	2	Sparkle	Forbin's
08/17/97	2	2	Jam	*CL2
➤ 8/17/97	0			

Horn [94]*

Horn [Horn]

By Anastasio/Marshall

05/24/90	[214]	2	MSO	Fee
06/16/90	7	1	Reba	Uncle Pen
09/22/90	7	1	BurAlive	MSO
12/28/90	26	1	Foam	Reba
12/29/90	1	1	Rocky Top	Oh Kee
02/08/91	6	2	Weekpaug	Bouncing
03/15/91	21	2	Possum	Paul&Silas
04/15/91	17	2	Weekpaug	MSO
04/18/91	2	2	Paul&Silas	Suzie
04/20/91	2	E	*OPE	Alumni
05/04/91	8	2	Harry	Rocky Top
10/19/91	41	2	Tweezer	PoorHeart
10/28/91	5	E	*OPE	Rocky Top
10/31/91	2	2	Bowie	Dinner
11/07/91	4	2	Tube	Bowie
11/09/91	2	1	YEM	Brother
11/13/91	3	E	*OPE	MSO
11/16/91	3	2	YEM	Chalkdust
11/19/91	1	1	Brother	Chalkdust
11/21/91	2	1	Foam	Split&Melt
11/23/91	2	2	Weekpaug	PoorHeart
11/30/91	2	2	MSO	IDK
12/06/91	3	2	YEM	Divided
03/07/92	4	2	Chalkdust	Mike's
03/25/92	10	2	YEM	MSO
04/01/92	6	2	Tweezer	Chalkdust
04/05/92	3	1	Rift	It's Ice
04/16/92	7	2	Weekpaug	PoorHeart
04/23/92	6	2	NICU	Tweezer
04/24/92	1	2	Mango	Love You
04/29/92	2	E	*OPE	Rocky Top
05/01/92	2	1	It's Ice	IDK
05/03/92	2	1	Rift	RunJim
05/12/92	7	1	Uncle Pen	Bowie
05/14/92	1	1	Maze	Reba
05/16/92	2	1	MSO	Golgi
05/18/92	2	1	PoorHeart	Sparkle
06/20/92	2	1a	It's Ice	Love You
07/01/92	5	1a	Rift	Split&Melt
07/14/92	6	1	RunJim	Brother
07/27/92	11	1a	Bowie	Suzie
07/30/92	2	1a	Rift	Sparkle
08/01/92	2	1a	Sqirm Coil	Llama
08/17/92	5	2	Weekpaug	Terrapin
08/27/92	6	1a	Landlady	Sparkle
11/22/92	8	1	Sparkle	All Things
12/02/92	7	1	Sparkle	YEM
12/07/92	5	2	Llama	MSO
02/06/93	13	1	Maze	Divided
02/17/93	8	2	BBJ	YEM
02/21/93	4	1	Uncle Pen	Chalkdust
02/26/93	4	1	Llama	Divided
03/06/93	5	1	Llama	Curtain
03/18/93	8	1	Sparkle	IDK
03/25/93	5	1	Rift	Magilla
04/03/93	8	1	Reba	Antelope
04/18/93	9	1	Maze	IDK
04/29/93	8	1	RunJim	Llama
05/07/93	7	1	Lizards	Divided
07/16/93	5	1	Nellie	Antelope
07/22/93	4	1	Foam	My Mind
07/24/93	2	1	Llama	Nellie
08/06/93	9	1	Rift	Divided
08/13/93	6	1	My Mind	Bowie
08/16/93	3	1	Possum	Reba
08/21/93	3	2	Possum	Uncle Pen
08/24/93	1	2	Llama	Ya Mar
04/04/94	8	1	Reba	It's Ice
04/22/94	15	1	Llama	Uncle Pen
05/07/94	11	1	Llama	Divided
06/18/94	25	2	Bowie	McGrupp
06/24/94	5	1	Paul&Silas	Reba
07/03/94	7	1	NICU	Old Home
07/10/94	5	1	Chalkdust	Peaches
10/08/94	6	1	Chalkdust	Sparkle
10/16/94	7	1	Rift	Foam
10/25/94	6	1	Llama	Julius
11/22/94	17	1	PoorHeart	Foam
06/30/95	38	1	Scent	Taste
09/30/95	7	1	Uncle Pen	Antelope
10/19/95	12	1	RunJim	PYITE
10/27/95	6	1	Fog	IDK
11/16/95	10	1	Chess	Mound
12/05/95	13	1	*OP1	Chalkdust
12/14/95	6	1	Llama	Foam
12/28/95	4	1	Guyute	Rift
07/12/96	13	1	Divided	Split&Melt
08/06/96	14	1	Dinner	Antelope
11/09/96	15	1	Divided	Tube
12/04/96	16	1	Chalkdust	Uncle Pen
06/20/97	25	1	Cities	Funny
07/01/97	7	1	Ghost	Ya Mar
08/11/97	22	1	Limb	Antelope
➤ 8/17/97	6			

Horse/Silent [114/114]*

The Horse/Silent In The Morning [Horse] [Silent]

By Anastasio/Marshall

03/07/92	[385]	1	RunJim	Maze
03/13/92	3	2	Brother	Landlady
03/19/92	3	1	Golgi	Dinner
03/21/92	2	1	Split&Melt	Dinner
03/24/92	1	1	Golgi	Llama
03/27/92	3	2	Weekpaug	MSO
04/01/92	4	2	YEM	Uncle Pen
04/05/92	3	2	YEM	Maze
04/07/92	2	1	Divided	Split&Melt
04/09/92	1	2	Weekpaug	Chalkdust
04/12/92	1	1	Divided	It's Ice
04/19/92	6	2	Weekpaug	MSO
04/22/92	2	2	Antelope	Rift
04/25/92	3	2	YEM	All Things
04/30/92	2	2	YEM	Chalkdust
05/03/92	3	2	Tweezer	Fluffhead
05/05/92	1	2	Weekpaug	PoorHeart
05/08/92	3	2	YEM	Chalkdust
05/16/92	6	2	YEM	Oh Kee
07/15/92	16	1	Split&Melt	Chalkdust
11/19/92	30	1	Axilla	Antelope
11/21/92	2	2	Weekpaug	Uncle Pen
11/27/92	4	2	Bowie	Faht
12/03/92	5	1	Chalkdust	Reba
12/08/92	5	2	Weekpaug	It's Ice
12/29/92	6	2	Tweezer	MSO
02/03/93	3	2	Tweezer	Sparkle
02/05/93	2	2	Tweezer	Paul&Silas
02/10/93	4	2	YEM	Rosie
02/20/93	8	1	Divided	Fluffhead
03/02/93	7	1	Chalkdust	IDK
03/09/93	5	2	Weekpaug	BBJ
03/12/93	1	1	Fluffhead	Bowie
03/17/93	4	2	Weekpaug	Great Gig
03/24/93	5	2	YEM	Terrapin
03/26/93	2	2	Tweezer	YEM
03/30/93	3	2	Weekpaug	Brain
04/02/93	3	2	Llama	Mike's
04/09/93	3	1	Stash	Maze
04/12/93	2	1	Stash	Reba
04/14/93	2	1	Kung	Divided
04/16/93	1	2	Weekpaug	Uncle Pen
04/18/93	2	2	Tweezer	Possum
04/21/93	2	2	Sqirm Coil	BBJ
04/24/93	3	1	Stash	Rift
04/27/93	2	2	YEM	Love You
04/30/93	2	1	Stash	Divided
05/02/93	2	1	Stash	PoorHeart
05/06/93	3	1	Split&Melt	All Things
05/08/93	2	2	Bowie	It's Ice
05/30/93*	2	1a	Ya Mar	Antelope
07/15/93	1	2	Bowie	Sparkle
07/17/93	2	1	Chalkdust	Oh Kee
07/23/93	4	1	Maze	PYITE
07/25/93	2	2	Tweezer	Maze
07/28/93	2	1	Split&Melt	PoorHeart
07/30/93	2	2	Tweezer	PoorHeart
08/03/93	3	1	Stash	Ya Mar
08/08/93	3	1	RunJim	PYITE
08/12/93	3	1	Split&Melt	PoorHeart
08/14/93	2	1	Divided	It's Ice
08/17/93	3	2	Bowie	Rift
08/24/93	3	1	Split&Melt	Uncle Pen
08/28/93	3	2	Antelope	Sparkle
12/30/93	3	2	SiJam	PYITE
04/08/94	5	1	PYITE	DWD
04/14/94	5	2	Antelope	Scent
04/22/94	7	1	Divided	Bowie
05/12/94	14	2	Antelope	Uncle Pen
05/19/94	5	1	Stash	DWD
05/23/94	4	1	Maze	Julius
05/28/94	4	1	Stash	Sloth
06/21/94*	11	1	It's Ice	*CL1
06/23/94	2	1	DWD	PYITE
06/29/94	4	1	Julius	Catapult
07/03/94	4	2	It's Ice	Julius
07/09/94	4	1	DWD	Antelope
07/14/94	3	1	Fluffhead	Antelope
07/16/94	2	1	Cavern	Maze
10/07/94	1	2	Maze	Reba
10/10/94	3	1	Divided	Sparkle
10/14/94	3	1	Divided	PYITE
10/18/94	3	2	Bowie	Reba
10/22/94	3	2	Bowie	Dinner
10/25/94	2	1	Julius	Split&Melt
10/27/94	2	1	Divided	PoorHeart
10/31/94	3	1	Julius	Reba
11/13/94	5	1	It's Ice	Antelope
11/18/94	4	1	Julius	It's Ice
11/26/94	6	1	Foam	PoorHeart
11/30/94	2	E	*OPE	AmGrace
12/08/94	7	E	*OPE	Rocky Top
12/29/94	4	1	Split&Melt	Uncle Pen

Stories Behind the Songs
(Continued)

Horn: Although Horn is not complex musically, Trey said he considered it a landmark in his songwriting career when he composed it in 1990 because of its ability to communicate emotion in a simple fashion. Tom Marshall wrote the lyrics to apparently refer to the growing bitterness the band felt in 1990 about being pursued by record companies to sign a recording contract.

The Horse: Throughout 1993, Trey played acoustic guitar on this song, then switched to electric guitar for Silent In The Morning. The song has never intentionally been played without being followed by Silent—in fact, the band never identified The Horse as a separate song until the release of *Rift,* so many tapes from 1992 label the Horse/Silent combo as just Silent In The Morning. However, when a fire alarm went off at the Cincinatti Music Hall on 6/21/94, Phish abandoned The Horse in progress, leaving it as the only Horse without Silent.

Icculus: A Gamehendge song, named for the prophet/God of the land who wrote the Helping Friendly Book. Icculus (the song) sometimes appears in concert as part of the "Forbin's Rap" between Col. Forbin's Ascent and Famous Mockingbird. If Trey gets really into it, Icculus—which urges audience members to "read the [Helping Friendly] Book!" and ends with an over-the-top, 20-second jam—can verge on epicness.

It's Ice: A close listen to the lyrics gives a sense of what this song's about: A reflected image in the Ice battling for control of the "real" person skating above.

Julius: Tom Marshall has said he wrote this song from Julius Caesar's perspective, though some Classics majors have questioned the historical veracity of the song.

Keyboard Kavalry: Played only on fall tour '95, Keyboard Kavalry (also known as Keyboard Army) features Mike, Fish and Trey robot-walking over to Page, where they each play a different keyboard instrument.

Kung: More a poem than a song, Kung appeared a few times in 1989, then was rein-

12/31/94	2	3	Chalkdust	Suzie
06/14/95	7	1	AmGrace	Spock's
06/24/95	8	1	Stash	Sqirm Coil
06/29/95	4	1	Taste	Divided
10/05/95	11	1	Fog	CTB
10/24/95	13	1	Llama	Demand
10/29/95	4	1	CTB	Split&Melt
11/11/95	4	1	Weekpaug	Ya Mar
12/04/95	16	1	Axilla 2	HelloBaby
12/12/95	6	1	PYITE	Antelope
07/21/96	24	1	Split&Melt	Taste
08/02/96	5	2	Caspian	Antelope
08/10/96	5	1	IDK	Rift
08/14/96	3	2	YEM	CTB
10/16/96	3	1	It's Ice	CharZero
10/21/96	4	2	Simple	Bowie
10/29/96	6	2	I am H2	Weekpaug
12/01/96	21	1	Train Song	Sample
12/31/96	7	1	Stash	Divided
02/23/97	9	2	Maze	Peaches
07/06/97	22	1	Stash	CTB
08/13/97	19	1	Gumbo	Beauty
➢ **8/17/97**	**3**			

Note: 5/30/93 is Silent only; 6/21/94 is Horse only.

Hydrogen [223]

I Am Hydrogen [I am H2]

By Anastasio

04/24/87	[14]	1a	Alumni	Bowie
04/29/87	1	3	LTGTR	*CL3
07/23/88	31	1	Mike's	Weekpaug
07/24/88	1	1	Mike's	Weekpaug
07/25/88	1	2	Mike's	Weekpaug
08/03/88	1	2	Mike's	Fluffhead
10/12/88	4	1	Mike's	Weekpaug
11/05/88	4	2	Mike's	Weekpaug
11/11/88	1	2	Mike's	Weekpaug
02/07/89	5	1	Mike's	Weekpaug
03/03/89	4	2	Mike's	Weekpaug
03/04/89	1	1	Mike's	Weekpaug
03/30/89	2	2	Mike's	Weekpaug
04/14/89	6	2	Mike's	Weekpaug
04/15/89	1	1	Mike's	Weekpaug
04/20/89	2	2	Mike's	Weekpaug
05/06/89	9	1	Mike's	Weekpaug
05/09/89	3	1	Mike's	Weekpaug
05/20/89	7	2	Mike's	Weekpaug
05/21/89	1	1	Mike's	Weekpaug
05/26/89	1	1	Mike's	Weekpaug
05/27/89	1	1	Mike's	Weekpaug
05/28/89	1	2	Maze	Weekpaug
06/23/89	5	1	Mike's	Weekpaug
06/30/89	2	2	Mike's	Weekpaug
08/17/89	1	1	Mike's	Weekpaug
08/19/89	2	1	Mike's	Weekpaug
10/06/89	8	1	Mike's	Weekpaug
10/07/89	1	1	Mike's	Weekpaug
10/21/89	5	2	Mike's	Weekpaug
10/26/89	2	1	Mike's	Weekpaug
11/02/89	3	1	Mike's	Weekpaug
11/09/89	3	2	Mike's	Weekpaug
11/10/89	1	1	Mike's	Weekpaug
11/16/89	2	1	Mike's	Weekpaug
12/07/89	6	1	Mike's	Weekpaug
12/09/89	2	2	Mike's	Weekpaug
12/16/89	2	1a	Mike's	Weekpaug
12/29/89	1	1	Mike's	Weekpaug
12/31/89	2	2	Mike's	Weekpaug
01/20/90	1	1a	Mike's	Weekpaug
01/27/90	3	1	Mike's	Weekpaug
01/28/90	1	2	Mike's	Weekpaug
02/09/90	7	1	Mike's	Weekpaug
02/10/90	1	1	Mike's	Weekpaug
02/15/90	1	1	Mike's	Weekpaug
02/17/90	2	1a	Mike's	Weekpaug
02/23/90	2	2	Mike's	Weekpaug
03/01/90	3	2	Mike's	Weekpaug
03/03/90	2	1	Mike's	Weekpaug
03/07/90	1	2	Mike's	Weekpaug
03/08/90	1	2	Mike's	Weekpaug
03/28/90	4	2	Mike's	Weekpaug
04/04/90	1	2	Mike's	Weekpaug
04/05/90	1	2	Mike's	Weekpaug
04/07/90	2	1	Mike's	Weekpaug
04/08/90	1	2	Mike's	Weekpaug
04/18/90	5	1	Mike's	Weekpaug
04/20/90	2	2	Mike's	Weekpaug
04/22/90	2	1	Mike's	Weekpaug
04/25/90	1	2	Mike's	Weekpaug
04/26/90	1	2	Mike's	Weekpaug
04/28/90	1	2	Mike's	Weekpaug
05/04/90	3	2	Mike's	Weekpaug
05/06/90	1	1	Mike's	Weekpaug
05/11/90	2	1	Mike's	Weekpaug
05/13/90	2	2	Mike's	Weekpaug
05/23/90	3	2	Mike's	Weekpaug
06/05/90	4	1	Mike's	Weekpaug
06/07/90	1	2	Mike's	Weekpaug
06/09/90	1	1	Mike's	Weekpaug
06/16/90	1	3	Mike's	Weekpaug
09/13/90	1	2	Mike's	Weekpaug
09/16/90	2	1a	Mike's	Weekpaug
10/05/90	7	1	Mike's	Weekpaug
10/07/90	2	1	Mike's	Weekpaug
10/12/90	2	2	Mike's	Weekpaug
10/30/90	2	2	Mike's	Weekpaug
10/31/90	1	2	Mike's	Weekpaug
11/02/90	1	1	Mike's	Weekpaug
11/03/90	1	2	Mike's	Weekpaug
11/04/90	1	2	Mike's	Weekpaug
11/08/90	1	1	Mike's	Weekpaug
11/10/90	1	1	Mike's	Weekpaug
11/16/90	1	2	Mike's	Weekpaug
11/17/90	1	2	Mike's	Weekpaug
11/24/90	1	1	Mike's	Weekpaug
11/26/90	1	2	Mike's	Weekpaug
11/30/90	1	1	Mike's	Weekpaug
12/07/90	3	2	Mike's	Weekpaug
12/08/90	1	1	Mike's	Weekpaug
12/28/90	1	1	Mike's	Weekpaug
12/31/90	2	1	Mike's	Weekpaug
02/08/91	5	2	Mike's	Weekpaug
02/14/91	2	2	Mike's	Weekpaug
02/16/91	2	1	Mike's	Weekpaug
02/21/91	3	1	Mike's	Weekpaug
02/26/91	4	2	Mike's	Weekpaug
02/28/91	2	1	Mike's	Weekpaug
03/01/91	1	1	Mike's	Weekpaug
03/07/91	3	2	Mike's	Weekpaug
03/15/91	4	1	Mike's	Weekpaug
03/17/91	2	1	Mike's	Weekpaug
03/22/91	2	2	Mike's	Weekpaug
04/05/91	8	1	Mike's	Weekpaug
04/11/91	2	2	Mike's	Weekpaug
04/15/91	3	2	Mike's	Weekpaug
04/19/91	3	1	Mike's	Weekpaug
04/21/91	2	1	Mike's	Weekpaug
04/27/91	4	2	Mike's	Weekpaug
05/04/91	3	1	Mike's	Weekpaug
05/10/91	2	2	Mike's	Weekpaug
05/12/91	2	2	Mike's	Weekpaug
05/17/91	2	1	Mike's	Weekpaug
07/11/91	3	2	Mike's	Weekpaug
07/12/91	1	2	Mike's	Weekpaug
07/14/91	2	3	Mike's	Weekpaug
07/15/91	1	1a	Mike's	Weekpaug
07/18/91	1	1	Mike's	Weekpaug
07/21/91	3	1	Mike's	Weekpaug
07/23/91	1	1	Mike's	Weekpaug
07/25/91	2	2	Mike's	Weekpaug
07/27/91	2	1a	Mike's	Weekpaug
09/26/91	3	2	Mike's	Weekpaug
09/28/91	2	2	Mike's	Weekpaug
10/03/91	3	2	Mike's	Weekpaug
10/04/91	1	2	Mike's	Weekpaug
10/10/91	3	2	Mike's	Weekpaug
10/13/91	3	1	Mike's	Weekpaug
10/18/91	3	2	Mike's	Weekpaug
10/24/91	3	2	Mike's	Weekpaug
10/27/91	2	2	Mike's	Weekpaug
11/01/91	4	2	Mike's	Weekpaug
11/08/91	4	2	Mike's	Weekpaug
11/12/91	3	2	Mike's	Weekpaug
11/15/91	3	2	Mike's	Weekpaug
11/19/91	2	2	Mike's	Weekpaug
11/21/91	2	1	Mike's	Weekpaug
11/23/91	2	2	Mike's	Weekpaug
12/04/91	3	2	Mike's	Weekpaug
12/05/91	1	2	Mike's	Weekpaug
12/31/91	3	3	Mike's	Weekpaug
03/07/92	2	2	Mike's	Weekpaug
03/14/92	4	1	Mike's	Weekpaug
03/17/92	1	2	Mike's	Weekpaug
03/20/92	2	2	Mike's	Weekpaug
03/24/92	2	2	Mike's	Weekpaug
03/27/92	3	2	Mike's	Weekpaug
03/31/92	3	2	Mike's	Weekpaug
04/04/92	3	2	Mike's	Weekpaug
04/06/92	2	2	Mike's	Weekpaug
04/09/92	2	2	Mike's	Weekpaug
04/13/92	2	2	Mike's	Weekpaug
04/16/92	2	2	Mike's	Weekpaug
04/19/92	3	2	Mike's	Weekpaug
04/21/92	1	2	Mike's	Weekpaug
04/23/92	2	2	Mike's	Weekpaug
04/24/92	1	2	Mike's	Weekpaug
04/29/92	2	2	Mike's	Weekpaug
05/01/92	2	2	Mike's	Weekpaug
05/03/92	2	2	Mike's	Weekpaug
05/05/92	1	2	Mike's	Weekpaug
05/07/92	2	2	Mike's	Weekpaug
05/14/92	5	2	Mike's	Weekpaug
05/18/92	4	2	Mike's	Weekpaug
07/16/92	15	2	Mike's	Weekpaug
08/17/92	18	2	Mike's	Weekpaug
11/19/92	11	2	Mike's	Weekpaug
11/21/92	2	2	Mike's	Weekpaug
11/23/92	2	2	Mike's	Weekpaug
11/28/92	3	1	Mike's	Weekpaug
12/01/92	2	1	Mike's	Weekpaug
12/03/92	2	2	Mike's	Weekpaug
12/05/92	2	2	Mike's	Weekpaug
12/08/92	3	2	Mike's	Weekpaug
12/11/92	2	2	Mike's	Weekpaug
12/29/92	4	2	Mike's	Weekpaug
02/06/93	6	2	Mike's	Weekpaug
02/09/93	2	2	Mike's	Weekpaug
02/11/93	2	2	Mike's	Weekpaug
02/15/93	3	2	Mike's	Weekpaug
02/18/93	2	2	Mike's	Weekpaug
02/20/93	2	2	Kung	Weekpaug
02/23/93	3	2	Mike's	Weekpaug
02/27/93	3	2	Mike's	Weekpaug
03/03/93	2	2	Mike's	Weekpaug
03/05/93	1	2	Mike's	Weekpaug
03/09/93	3	2	Mike's	Weekpaug
03/13/93	2	2	Mike's	Weekpaug
03/17/93	3	2	Mike's	Weekpaug
03/19/93	2	2	Mike's	Weekpaug
03/22/93	2	2	Mike's	Weekpaug
03/25/93	2	2	Mike's	Weekpaug
03/27/93	2	2	Mike's	Weekpaug
03/30/93	2	2	Mike's	Weekpaug
04/02/93	3	2	Mike's	Weekpaug
04/13/93	6	2	Mike's	Weekpaug
04/16/93	2	2	Mike's	Weekpaug
04/23/93	6	2	Mike's	Weekpaug
04/25/93	2	2	Mike's	Weekpaug
04/29/93	2	2	Mike's	Weekpaug
05/08/93	8	2	Mike's	Weekpaug
04/09/94	44	2	Mike's	Weekpaug
04/21/94	10	2	Mike's	Weekpaug
04/29/94	6	2	Mike's	Weekpaug
05/14/94	11	2	Mike's	Weekpaug
05/19/94	3	2	Mike's	Weekpaug
06/09/94	10	2	Mike's	Weekpaug
06/13/94	3	2	Mike's	Weekpaug
06/17/94	3	2	Mike's	Weekpaug
06/22/94	4	2	Simple	Weekpaug
07/02/94	8	2	YSZahov	Weekpaug
07/10/94	6	2	Mike's	Weekpaug
10/08/94	6	2	Mike's	Weekpaug
10/21/94	10	2	Mike's	Weekpaug
12/10/94	34	2	Mike's	Weekpaug
06/10/95	9	2	Mike's	Weekpaug
10/19/95	34	2	Mike's	Weekpaug
07/23/96	61	2	Mike's	Weekpaug
08/05/96	5	2	Mike's	Weekpaug
10/29/96	19	2	Mike's	Horse
07/22/97	64	2	Simple	Weekpaug
07/31/97	6	2	Mike's	Weekpaug
➢ **8/17/97**	**11**			

I Didn't Know [190]

I Didn't Know [IDK]

By Phish/Nancy Taube

09/27/87	[24]	2	Wilson	Fluffhead
11/19/87	3	2	Fluffhead	Fee
02/07/88	2	1a	Reagan	Bowie
03/21/88	4	1a	Dinner	Forbin's
03/31/88	1	1	*OP1	Golgi
05/14/88	2	2	Fire	Halley's
05/15/88	1	1a	Peaches	Sloth
05/23/88	1	1a	Light Up	Peaches
05/25/88	1	3	Sloth	Ya Mar
06/15/88	1	1	Timber Ho	*CL1
06/21/88	3	2	Harpua	ACDCBag
10/12/88	12	1	*OP1	Golgi
10/29/88	1	3	Antelope	Wilson
11/03/88	1	2	Suzie	BBFCM
11/05/88	1	2	Weekpaug	GTBT
12/02/88	2	2	*OP2	GTBT
01/26/89	1	1a	*OP1	Golgi
02/06/89	2	1	OYWD	*CL1
03/03/89	5	1	Antelope	Divided
03/04/89	1	1	A-Train	Mike's
04/15/89	9	1	Alumni	McGrupp
04/30/89	7	1	*OP1	YEM
05/05/89	3	2	Antelope	A-Train
05/06/89	1	1	YEM	Mike's
05/09/89	3	2	Antelope	Lizards
05/20/89	7	1	Divided	Possum
08/12/89	14	1a	Swing	YEM
10/14/89	16	1	Divided	Golgi
10/20/89	1	2	Dinner	ACDCBag
10/22/89	2	1	Divided	GTBT
10/26/89	1	1	Divided	Wilson
11/09/89	6	1	*OP1	Golgi
12/07/89	9	1	*OP1	YEM
12/08/89	1	2	Slave	YEM
12/15/89	2	1a	*OP1	Possum
12/31/89	4	1	*OP1	YEM
02/09/90	12	E	*OPE	*CLE
02/10/90	1	E	*OPE	HwayHell
02/23/90	5	E	Contact	GTBT
02/24/90	1	1	Possum	A-Train

03/01/90 2 1 Divided YEM
03/08/90 4 2 Caravan Lizards
04/04/90 5 2 Sloth GTBT
04/06/90 2 2 Reba Alumni
04/22/90 11 1 Possum Cavern
04/26/90 2 1 Bouncing Antelope
04/28/90 1 2 Caravan Reba
05/24/90 12 2 Possum MSO
05/31/90 1 1a Tweezer Uncle Pen
06/08/90 4 1 Tweezer Mike's
09/14/90 4 1 Dinner *CL1
09/22/90 5 1 Landlady Bowie
10/05/90 4 1 *OP1 Mike's
10/07/90 2 2 MSO Lizards
11/02/90 6 2 Lizards Bowie
11/08/90 3 1 Asse Fest Mike's
11/16/90 2 2 RunJim Possum
11/30/90 4 2 Divided Sloth
12/29/90 6 1 *OP1 Llama
12/31/90 1 1 Divided Landlady
02/14/91 7 2 Bouncing Landlady
02/27/91 10 1 Divided Landlady
03/07/91 5 2 Possum Mike's
03/15/91 4 2 Destiny Harry
03/23/91 5 1 Llama Curtain
04/05/91 7 2 Harry MSO
04/19/91 8 1 Stash Rocky Top
04/21/91 2 2 Cavern Bowie
04/26/91 3 2 Landlady Harry
05/02/91 2 2 MSO BurAlive
05/17/91 8 1 Stash Mike's
05/25/91 2 2 *OP2 Golgi
07/14/91 4 1 Sloth Possum
07/18/91 2 2 Landlady Possum
07/19/91 1 2 Divided MSO
07/21/91 2 2 Tweezer RunJim
07/24/91 2 2 FunkBitch Frankstein
07/27/91 3 1a Possum Landlady
08/03/91 1 2 Cavern YEM
09/27/91 3 1 It's Ice *CL1
09/29/91 2 1a Divided It's Ice
10/02/91 1 E Possum Rocky Top
10/06/91 4 2 Harry Cavern
10/10/91 1 2 Antelope Sparkle
10/18/91 6 2 Weekpaug Fee
10/24/91 3 1 Divided TMWSIY
10/28/91 3 1 Reba Tube
10/31/91 2 2 Tube Harry
11/07/91 4 1 RunJim Llama
11/08/91 1 2 Sqirm Coil Mike's
11/13/91 4 1 Divided Terrapin
11/22/91 7 2 Sqirm Coil Llama
11/24/91 2 1 It's Ice Bowie
11/30/91 1 2 Horn Antelope
12/05/91 2 2 Sqirm Coil MSO
12/06/91 1 1 Guelah *CL1
03/12/92 6 1 Stash Reba
03/17/92 3 1 It's Ice Divided
03/24/92 4 2 Uncle Pen Oh Kee
03/28/92 4 2 Carolina Adeline
03/30/92 1 1 Maze All Things
04/01/92 2 1 RunJim Landlady
04/04/92 2 1 Lizards Antelope
04/15/92 7 1 Cavern All Things
04/17/92 2 1 Stash Cavern
04/19/92 2 1 Chalkdust Golgi
04/23/92 3 1 It's Ice Possum
05/01/92 5 1 Horn Possum
05/03/92 2 1 Split&Melt Rift
05/05/92 1 1 Divided It's Ice
05/09/92 4 1 Sqirm Coil Antelope
05/10/92 1 1a Reba YEM
05/17/92 5 1 Reba Stash
06/24/92 5 1a Guelah Sparkle
06/27/92 1 E *OPE GTBT
07/14/92 8 1 Brother PoorHeart
07/30/92 13 1a Maze Possum
11/30/92 26 1 It's Ice Reba
12/10/92 9 1 Split&Melt All Things
12/13/92 3 1 FEFY Bowie
12/30/92 3 1 Reba Timber Ho
12/31/92 1 1 Foam Antelope
02/03/93 1 1 Divided My Friend
02/05/93 2 1 PYITE PoorHeart
02/07/93 2 1 Rift Split&Melt
02/10/93 2 1 Tela Catapult
02/12/93 2 1 Chalkdust A-Train
02/15/93 2 1 Guelah Antelope
02/22/93 6 1 Cavern Bowie
02/25/93 2 1 Bouncing Bowie
02/26/93 1 1 Divided Cavern
03/02/93 2 1 Silent Bowie
03/05/93 2 1 It's Ice Possum
03/09/93 3 1 PYITE Antelope
03/16/93 4 1 Maze Divided
03/18/93 2 1 Horn Bowie
03/24/93 4 1 Maze Sample
03/27/93 3 1 Sample Bowie
03/31/93 3 1 Reba Bowie
04/02/93 2 1 Divided Sparkle
04/09/93 3 1 Maze It's Ice
04/14/93 4 1 Divided Golgi
04/18/93 3 1 Horn Cavern
04/21/93 2 1 PYITE Antelope
04/25/93 4 1 Maze Golgi
05/02/93 5 1 Maze Golgi
05/07/93 4 1 Divided Antelope
05/30/93 3 1a Antelope Split&Melt
07/15/93 1 1 Foam My Mind
07/25/93 8 1 My Mind Bowie
07/30/93 4 1 Chalkdust Reba
08/08/93 6 1 Paul&Silas Bowie
08/16/93 7 1 Foam Split&Melt
08/21/93 3 1 Landlady RunJim
12/31/93 8 1 Peaches Antelope
04/08/94 4 1 Foam PYITE
04/10/94 2 1 Chalkdust Scent
04/17/94 6 1 Foam Divided
04/29/94 9 1 Divided Dog Faced
05/29/94 23 1 Julius Bowie
06/14/94 5 1 Uncle Pen MSO
06/29/94 11 1 Bowie Golgi
07/13/94 10 1 FEFY Split&Melt
10/13/94 9 1 DWD Foam
10/18/94 4 1 My Friend PoorHeart
10/28/94 8 1 *OP1 Llama
11/22/94 14 1 Guyute Bouncing
12/01/94 6 1 Guyute Split&Melt
12/09/94 7 1 Sparkle It's Ice
12/29/94 3 1 Uncle Pen Possum
06/15/95 10 1 Stash Fluffhead
06/20/95 4 1 Taste Split&Melt
06/25/95 4 1 Divided Split&Melt
07/02/95 6 1 Reba Rift
09/27/95 2 1 It's Ice Fog
10/15/95 13 1 Slave Demand
10/27/95 8 1 Horn Rift
11/12/95 7 1 Reba Fog
11/28/95 10 1 Foam Divided
12/28/95 16 2 Tweezer Uncle Pen
07/11/96 12 1 Reba Sparkle
07/15/96 3 1 Possum Harry
08/10/96 15 1 Reba Horse
10/25/96 13 1 Guelah Stash
11/24/96 20 1 Taste Sample
12/02/96 5 1 YEM Theme
02/22/97 15 1 Split&Melt CharZero
➢ 8/17/97 45

I Don't Care

I Don't Care [Don't Care]

Author Unknown

06/16/97 [906] 2 Ghost Reba
06/20/97 2 1 Limb Antelope
➢ 8/17/97 33

I Saw It Again [5]

I Saw It Again [Saw It]

By Anastasio/Marshall

06/14/97 [905] 2 Piper Fooled
06/19/97 2 2 Ghost Wading
06/25/97 5 1 Wading Limb
07/01/97 3 1 Funny Dirt
07/31/97 15 1 Glide YEM
➢ 8/17/97 11

Icculus [18]*

Icculus [Icculus]

By Anastasio/Marshall

04/01/86 [6] 1 Jam YEM
10/31/86 3 2 Skin It Alumni
12/06/86 1 1a Jam McGrupp
08/10/87 7 2 La Grange Bowie
05/15/88 19 1a Possum McGrupp
07/25/88 13 3 Sanity CamlWalk
01/26/89 13 1a Fluffhead Forbin's
02/06/89 3 2 Curtis WhipPost
08/12/89 50 1a Possum Antelope
04/06/91 181 1 Bathtub Antelope
04/16/92 116 1 Forbin's Mockbird
04/24/92 7 1 Forbin's Mockbird
05/02/92 5 1 Forbin's Mockbird
03/25/93 119 2 Forbin's Kung
06/22/94 127 2 Simple Simple
10/27/94 35 E Slave TweezRep
11/20/94 14 E *OPE Fire
10/31/95 67 1 *OP1 Divided
➢ 8/17/97 156

If I Could [45]

If I Could [If I Could]

By Anastasio

04/04/94 [615] 2 DWD BurAlive
04/05/94 1 2 Tweezer YEM
04/08/94 2 1 DWD Lawn Boy
04/15/94 6 2 Maze Oh Kee
04/17/94 2 1 DWD MSO
04/21/94 3 1 DWD Cavern
04/29/94 6 2 Maze Reba
05/03/94 3 2 Bowie Fluffhead
05/07/94 3 1 Split&Melt Suzie
05/10/94 2 1 Melt Cavern
05/13/94 2 1 Stash My Friend
05/17/94 3 1 Mound Scent
05/20/94 2 1 Maze It's Ice
05/23/94 3 2 Antelope Sparkle
05/27/94 3 1 Bowie PYITE
06/09/94 3 1 It's Ice Maze
06/14/94 4 2 Bowie It's Ice
06/17/94 2 1 Split&Melt PYITE
06/19/94 2 2 Antelope Reba
06/22/94 2 1 Maze Scent
06/26/94 4 2 DWD Axilla 2
07/01/94 3 2 Bowie Fluffhead
07/05/94 3 1 LTJP Uncle Pen
07/10/94 4 1 Stash My Friend
07/14/94 2 2 Maze Uncle Pen
10/13/94 8 2 Antelope It's Ice
11/02/94 15 1 Foam Maze
11/12/94 3 1 Foam Guyute
11/20/94 7 1 Stash Butter
11/23/94 2 1 It's Ice Oh Kee
11/26/94 2 1 Guyute Foam
12/04/94 6 1 Foam Rift
12/09/94 4 1 It's Ice Antelope
12/29/94 3 1 Foam Split&Melt
06/07/95 4 1 Stash Scent
06/20/95 10 1 Bathtub Taste
06/25/95 4 1 Theme Sparkle
07/01/95 5 1 Llama All Things
07/03/95 2 1 It's Ice Maze
09/30/95 4 2 Fog Scent
10/11/95 7 1 Divided Fog
11/12/95 18 1 Fog Split&Melt
11/29/95 11 1 Reba It's Ice
07/21/96 34 1 Tweezer My Mind
08/05/96 7 1 Foam Julius
➢ 8/17/97 100

In a Hole [6]

In a Hole [In a Hole]

By Phish

10/20/89 [131] 2 Swing *CL2
10/21/89 1 1 Ya Mar McGrupp
10/22/89 1 2 Golgi McGrupp
10/26/89 1 2 PYITE NoDog
12/09/89 17 1 Foam Rocky Top
12/16/89 2 1 Lizards Golgi
➢ 8/17/97 788

It's Ice [190]

It's Ice [It's Ice]

By Anastasio/Marshall

09/25/91 [335] 1 MSO Landlady
09/26/91 1 1 Fee MSO
09/27/91 1 1 Paul&Silas IDK
09/29/91 2 1a IDK PoorHeart
10/03/91 2 1 Uncle Pen Bouncing
10/10/91 4 1 RunJim Llama
10/13/91 3 2 Sqirm Coil MSO
10/19/91 4 1 Suzie RunJim
10/27/91 4 2 Sparkle Mike's
11/01/91 4 2 MSO Chalkdust
11/07/91 3 1 Cavern YEM
11/09/91 2 2 PoorHeart Tweezer
11/13/91 3 1 RunJim Sparkle
11/14/91 1 2 Paul&Silas Glide
11/16/91 2 1 RunJim Sparkle
11/20/91 2 2 Golgi MSO
11/21/91 1 2 Harry Mango
11/24/91 3 1 Sparkle IDK
11/30/91 1 2 Harry Bouncing
12/05/91 2 1 Gin Bouncing
12/06/91 1 2 *OP2 Eliza
03/06/92 3 1 Sparkle Oh Kee
03/12/92 3 2 Eliza Bouncing
03/17/92 3 1 Sparkle IDK
03/25/92 5 1 RunJim Antelope
04/04/92 8 1 Bouncing Sparkle
04/05/92 1 1 Horn Possum
04/07/92 2 1 Possum Fee
04/12/92 2 1 Silent Sparkle
04/16/92 3 1 Possum Bouncing
04/18/92 2 1 Possum Sparkle
04/21/92 2 1 Possum Eliza
04/23/92 2 1 Bouncing IDK
04/29/92 3 1 Sparkle RunJim
05/01/92 2 1 Guelah Horn
05/03/92 2 1 Possum Uncle Pen
05/05/92 1 1 IDK Glide
05/08/92 3 1 Uncle Pen Eliza
05/12/92 3 1 Possum Dinner
05/16/92 3 2 RunJim Paul
06/20/92 4 1a RunJim Horn
07/14/92 11 1 Sparkle RunJim
07/16/92 2 1 PoorHeart Sparkle
07/21/92 4 1a Possum Sparkle
07/26/92 4 1a Chalkdust Divided
07/30/92 3 1a Sparkle All Things
08/17/92 7 2 Suzie Tweezer
08/25/92 5 1a RunJim Sparkle
11/19/92 6 2 Bouncing Walk Line
11/21/92 2 1 PoorHeart Bouncing
11/25/92 3 1 Sparkle Sqirm Coil
11/27/92 1 2 Glide McGrupp
11/30/92 2 1 Sparkle IDK
12/03/92 3 2 Lawn Boy MSO
12/04/92 1 2 Possum Sqirm Coil
12/07/92 3 2 MSO Fee
12/08/92 1 2 Silent Lizards
12/11/92 2 1 RunJim Uncle Pen
12/13/92 2 1 Divided Fee
12/28/92 1 1 Glide Bouncing
12/31/92 3 2 RunJim Sparkle
02/03/93 1 2 RunJim Tweezer
02/05/93 2 2 Paul&Silas YEM
02/07/93 2 1 PoorHeart Sparkle
02/10/93 2 1 RunJim Sqirm Coil
02/13/93 3 1 PoorHeart Glide
02/17/93 2 1 RunJim Bouncing
02/19/93 2 2 RunJim Paul&Silas
02/22/93 3 2 RunJim Uncle Pen
02/25/93 2 2 Suzie Sparkle
02/27/93 2 1 Bouncing Sparkle
03/02/93 1 1 Sparkle Fee
03/05/93 2 1 Sparkle IDK
03/08/93 2 1 Sparkle Glide
03/13/93 3 2 Lizards Glide
03/16/93 2 1 PoorHeart Fee
03/17/93 1 1 Paul&Silas Oh Kee
03/19/93 2 2 RunJim Uncle Pen
03/22/93 2 2 Golgi Lizards
03/25/93 2 1 Guelah Possum
03/27/93 2 2 Halley's Bouncing
03/28/93 1 1 Fee Lawn Boy
03/31/93 2 2 BBJ YEM
04/05/93 4 1 Llama Fee
04/09/93 1 1 IDK Divided
04/12/93 2 2 Paul&Silas BBJ
04/14/93 2 1 Bouncing Stash
04/17/93 2 1 Stash Glide
04/20/93 2 1 Bouncing Glide
04/22/93 2 1 Sparkle Reba
04/23/93 1 2 Curtis Paul&Silas
04/25/93 2 1 Bouncing Glide
04/27/93 1 1 Guelah Sparkle
04/29/93 1 2 Chalkdust Ya Mar
05/01/93 2 1 Sample Glide
05/03/93 2 2 Contact McGrupp
05/05/93 1 1 Bouncing Glide
05/08/93 3 2 Silent Sqirm Coil
07/15/93 3 2 Sparkle Life Boy
07/17/93 2 2 Sqirm Coil Sparkle
07/22/93 3 2 Sparkle Contact
07/23/93 1 1 RunJim Lawn Boy
07/27/93 3 1a Sparkle PurplRain
07/29/93 2 2 Bouncing Life Boy
07/31/93 2 2 RunJim Maze
08/03/93 2 2 Bouncing YEM
08/08/93 3 2 Wilson Fluffhead
08/11/93 2 1 Weigh Ginseng
08/14/93 3 1 Silent Sparkle
08/16/93 2 2 Mound My Friend
08/20/93 2 1 Bouncing Wedge
08/24/93 2 1 Bouncing Nellie
08/26/93 2 1 Esther Harry
08/28/93 1 2 Sparkle BBJ
12/28/93 1 1 Ya Mar Fee
12/31/93 3 2 PoorHeart Fee
04/04/94 1 1 Horn Possum
04/08/94 3 2 McGrupp Sparkle
04/10/94 2 1 RunJim Sparkle
04/15/94 4 1 Bouncing DWD
04/20/94 4 1 RunJim Julius
04/24/94 4 1 Paul&Silas Slave
04/28/94 2 1a Bouncing Antelope
05/02/94 3 1 DWD Glide
05/04/94 2 1 Sample Sparkle
05/08/94 3 2 Antelope Fee
05/10/94 2 1 Axilla 2 Split&Melt
05/13/94 2 1 RunJim Julius
05/16/94 2 2 Sparkle Julius
05/20/94 3 1 If I Could Gin
05/22/94 2 2 Bouncing McGrupp
05/26/94 3 1 Sparkle Catapult
05/28/94 2 2 Axilla 2 Tweezer
06/09/94 2 1 DWD If I Could
06/11/94 2 1 DWD Tela
06/14/94 2 2 If I Could Sparkle

Stories Behind the Songs
(Continued)

troduced as the New Year's chant in Boston on 12/31/92. Since then, Kung has at times served as a gateway to Gamehendge—or simply as a call to stage a runaway golf cart marathon. It's often inserted in the middle of another song.

The Landlady: Originally composed as part of Punch You In The Eye, Trey extracted The Landlady and turned it into its own song during the period of Punch's retirement (in the early 1990s). It still appears in concert both on its own and as part of PYITE, though in the last couple of years, all of its appearances have come in PYITE.

Lizards: A Gamehendge song sung from the perspective of Colonel Forbin upon his arrival in Gamehendge. The Lizards are the race of native inhabitants of Gamehendge who once lived in peace in harmony (as spelled out in the Helping Friendly Book) before being enslaved by Wilson.

Llama: Set in the post-Wilson years of Gamehendge, Llama chronicles a scene from a battle. It's considered a Gamehendge tune but is not part of the original Gamehendge story.

Makisupa Policeman: This simple reggae tune has in recent years served as Trey's way of referencing pot smoking from the stage. "4:20" and "Dank" are sometimes muttered in the opening lyric segments; a strange verse about Khadafi has also surfaced (10/22/95 and 12/14/95). Most recently, Trey has offered an even wider variety of terms in the opening verse, including "schwag" at Deer Creek in summer '97 and "gooballs" at the Great Went. Some fans take this to be Trey's commentary on the drug scene at that particular show.

The Mango Song: Trey fashioned the song's refrain from a screenplay idea of his friend Aaron Woolfe that described a child of the Viet Nam War whose "hands and feet were mangled" but who grew up to be a genius. After Trey and Tom Marshall started singing a chorus slightly distorting those words, Trey wrote the verses to describe a moment in the life of waiter with a drug addiction.

McGrupp and the Watchful Hosemasters: Not part of Trey's

06/18/94	3	1	DWD	Dog Faced
06/21/94	2	1	Sample	Horse
06/24/94	3	1	Wilson	Fee
06/29/94	3	2	Tweezer	Life Boy
07/01/94	2	1	Mango	Tela
07/03/94	2	2	Bouncing	Horse
07/08/94	3	2	YSZahov	Stash
07/13/94	3	1	Fee	FEFy
07/15/94	2	2	Reba	YSZahov
10/08/94	3	1	Fee	Lawn Boy
10/13/94	4	2	If I Could	AmGrace
10/18/94	4	1	Tela	Guyute
10/26/94	6	1	Simple	NICU
11/04/94	7	1	Sample	Bouncing
11/13/94	2	1	Axilla 2	Horse
11/18/94	4	1	Silent	Tela
11/23/94	4	1	Simple	If I Could
12/02/94	6	1	Simple	Lizards
12/09/94	6	1	IDK	If I Could
12/28/94	2	1	Dog Faced	Antelope
06/10/95	8	1	Caspian	Free
06/16/95	4	1	Cry Baby	My Mind
06/22/95	4	1	Guelah	Str Design
06/26/95	4	1	My Mind	Dog Faced
07/01/95	4	1	All Things	Caspian
07/03/95	2	1	Sparkle	If I Could
09/27/95	1	1	Free	IDK
10/03/95	5	2	Timber Ho	Sparkle
10/07/95	3	2	Str Design	Contact
10/14/95	4	1	AArmy	Tela
10/22/95	6	1	FEFY	PoorHeart
10/29/95	5	2	Mango	Shagy
11/10/95	3	1	Old Home	Dog Faced
11/19/95	7	1	Str Design	HelloBaby
11/29/95	6	1	If I Could	Theme
12/08/95	7	1	Fluffhead	AArmy
12/15/95	5	2	RunJim	Gin
12/30/95	5	1	Simple	TMWSIY
07/12/96	11	2	It's Ice	Caspian
07/15/96	2	2	Makisupa	Julius
07/18/96	2	1a	HelloBaby	YEM
07/25/96	6	1a	Sample	Antelope
08/05/96	3	2	DWD	Halley's
08/12/96	4	1	Weigh	Dog Faced
08/17/96	4	2	RunJim	Brother
10/16/96	2	1	Sample	Horse
10/22/96	3	1	Bouncing	Talk
10/26/96	3	1	CharZero	Theme
11/13/96	11	1	Bouncing	Ya Mar
11/22/96	6	1	*OP1	RunJim
11/30/96	5	2	La Grange	Glide
12/28/96	5	1	Wolfman's	Billy
02/14/97	5	1	Axilla	Billy
08/08/97	44	1	Dirt	Water
➢ 8/17/97	7			

Julius [112]*

Julius [Julius]

By Anastasio/Marshall

04/04/94	[615]	2	Landlady	Magilla
04/05/94	1	1	Glide	Bouncing
04/09/94	3	1	Nellie	Fee
04/11/94	2	1	Magilla	Glide
04/13/94	1	1	Lizards	Ginseng
04/15/94	2	2	Landlady	Wolfman's
04/16/94	1	2	Lizards	Bouncing
04/18/94	2	1	PoorHeart	My Friend
04/20/94	1	1	It's Ice	Bouncing
04/22/94	2	2	Suzie	Reba
04/24/94	2	2	Mango	Forbin's
04/28/94	2	1a	Sqirm Coil	GTBT
05/02/94	3	2	Lizards	Lawn Boy
05/04/94	2	2	BurAlive	Wolfman's
05/06/94	1	2	Axilla 2	Bike
05/08/94	2	2	Fee	Cavern
05/10/94	1	2	Wilson	Reba
05/13/94	2	1	It's Ice	Mound
05/16/94	2	2	It's Ice	YEM
05/19/94	2	2	Lizards	BBJ
05/21/94	2	2	BBJ	Harry
05/23/94	2	1	Silent	Reba
05/25/94	1	2	BBJ	PurplRain
05/27/94	2	2	Lizards	Nellie
05/29/94	2	1	Sparkle	IDK
06/09/94	1	2	Glide	Halley's
06/10/94	1	1	Cavern	*CL1
06/13/94	2	1	Ginseng	*CL1
06/16/94	2	1	Rift	Fee
06/17/94	1	1	BBJ	Frankstein
06/19/94	2	1	Suzie	Lizards
06/21/94	1	2	Adeline	Sparkle
06/23/94	2	1	PYITE	*CL1
06/25/94	2	1	Rift	NICU
06/26/94	1	2	*OP2	DWD
06/29/94	1	1	Mound	Horse
07/01/94	2	1	Tela	Suzie
07/03/94	2	2	Silent	Sqirm Coil
07/06/94	2	1	Fluffhead	Bouncing
07/08/94	1	2	YEM	Golgi
07/10/94	2	1	My Friend	Cavern
07/13/94	1	2	Tweezer	Tweezer
07/15/94	2	2	Dog Faced	SettingSail
10/07/94	2	1	My Friend	Glide
10/09/94	2	2	AmGrace	Contact
10/12/94	2	1	Guelah	Adeline
10/14/94	2	1	Mockbird	*CL1
10/16/94	2	2	PoorHeart	Fluffhead
10/20/94	2	1	Esther	Guyute
10/22/94	2	1	Fluffhead	*CL1
10/25/94	2	1	Horn	Horse
10/27/94	2	2	*OP2	Ya Mar
10/31/94	3	1	Harpua	Horse
11/03/94	2	2	PoorHeart	YEM
11/12/94	2	2	*OP2	Fluffhead
11/14/94	2	2	PoorHeart	Old Home
11/18/94	3	1	ACDCBag	Horse
11/20/94	2	2	Terrapin	Cavern
11/25/94	3	1	Esther	Golgi
11/28/94	2	2	Sl Monkey	*CL2
12/02/94	3	2	BurAlive	Landlady
12/03/94	1	2	Touch Me	Cavern
12/07/94	3	2	Fee	I'm Blue
12/09/94	2	2	McGrupp	BBJ
12/28/94	2	1	Simple	Bathtub
06/08/95	6	2	PoorHeart	*CL2
06/13/95	3	E	Adln	*CLE
06/17/95	4	1	Uncle Pen	Lawn Boy
06/24/95	5	1	Spock's	Glide
07/02/95	7	1	Curtain	CamlWalk
10/05/95	8	1	AArmy	Suzie
10/07/95	2	1	*OP1	Gumbo
10/11/95	2	1	AArmy	Sample
10/15/95	3	2	*OP2	Simple
10/24/95	6	2	*OP2	Theme
10/29/95	4	1	PoorHeart	PYITE
11/09/95	2	2	Theme	Lizards
11/14/95	4	1	Free	I'm Blue
11/19/95	4	1	HelloBaby	Sqirm Coil
11/24/95	3	2	Fee	*CL2
11/30/95	4	1	Ha Ha Ha	NICU
12/04/95	3	1	*OP1	Gumbo
12/07/95	2	2	Reba	Sl Monkey
12/11/95	3	1	McGrupp	Cavern
12/16/95	4	1	Dog Faced	Suzie
12/28/95	2	1	Curtain	Guyute
07/15/96	15	2	It's Ice	PurplRain
07/18/96	2	1a	*OP1	CTB
07/24/96	5	1a	Ya Mar	YEM
08/05/96	4	1	If I Could	Sqirm Coil
08/14/96	6	E	*OPE	*CLE
10/18/96	5	E	*OPE	*CLE
10/23/96	4	2	Slave	*CL2
10/26/96	2	1	*OP1	CTB
11/02/96	4	1	Ya Mar	Fee
11/09/96	5	E	*OPE	*CLE
11/14/96	3	1	Talk	*CL1
11/22/96	5	E	*OPE	*CLE
11/27/96	3	1	*OP1	My Friend
12/02/96	4	1	Gumbo	*CL1
12/06/96	2	2	*OP2	Sparkle
12/31/96	4	3	Bohemian	*CL3
02/13/97	1	2	*OP2	CTB
02/20/97	5	E	*OPE	*CLE
02/28/97	6	2	Waste	*CL2
06/20/97	8	2	Bouncing	*CL2
07/05/97	10	1a	*OP1	Bouncing
07/10/97	3	2	Also Sprac	Magilla
07/23/97	4	1	*OP1	Dirt
08/03/97	7	2	*OP2	Simple
08/06/97	1	E	*OPE	*CLE
08/16/97	7	2	Rocky Top	*CL2
➢ 8/17/97	1			

Keyboard Kavalry [13]*

Keyboard Kavalry [Keyboard]

By Phish

09/27/95	[761]	2	Billy	Harry
09/28/95	1	2	Tweezer	AmGrace
09/30/95	2	2	Mike's	Weekpaug
10/02/95	1	2	Simple	Slave
10/06/95	3	2	Tweezer	Suspicious
10/08/95	2	2	*OP2	CTB
10/13/95	2	2	Antelope	Lizards
10/17/95	3	2	Suzie	Jam
10/27/95	7	2	McGrupp	Bouncing
11/12/95	7	2	Tweezer	Sample
11/21/95	6	2	Mike's	Suspicious
12/05/95	10	2	Bathtub	Scent
12/14/95	6	2	Tweezer	Halley's
➢ 8/17/97	130			

Kung [22]

Kung [Kung]

By Fishman

10/31/89	[136]	E	Antelope	Antelope
11/02/89	1	2	YEM	Divided
12/31/92	367	3	Harpua	Harpua
02/20/93	15	2	Mike's	I am H2
03/08/93	11	2	My Friend	YEM
03/25/93	12	2	Icculus	Mockbird
04/14/93	14	1	Stash	Horse
05/08/93	19	1	Stash	Stash
08/07/93	20	2	Sparks	Mike's
06/16/94	69	2	Forbin's	Mockbird
06/17/94	1	2	Harpua	Harpua
06/26/94	8	1	*OP1	Llama
10/20/94	25	1	Split&Melt	Split&Melt
10/14/95	75	1	CTB	Free
10/19/95	3	2	BBFCM	Suspicious
10/21/95	2	1	CTB	Lizards
10/29/95	6	2	It's Ice	It's Ice
11/25/95	14	2	Timber Ho	Mike's
12/08/95	9	2	Tweezer	Tweezer
12/30/95	10	1	It's Ice	It's Ice
11/16/96	55	2	RunJim	Catapult
02/26/97	27	2	YEM	Theme
➢ 8/17/97	42			

Landlady [165]*

The Landlady [Landlady]

By Anastasio

04/07/90	[189]	1	Lizards	WalkAway
06/09/90	31	E	*OPE	Contact
09/13/90	2	1	*OP1	Divided
09/14/90	1	2	Bouncing	Reba
09/15/90	1	1	Paul&Silas	Fee
09/16/90	1	1a	Sloth	Reba
09/22/90	3	1	Wilson	IDK
09/28/90	1	1	*OP1	Bouncing
10/01/90	1	1	Lizards	Magilla
10/04/90	1	1	Golgi	Esther
10/05/90	1	1	MSO	Tela
10/06/90	1	1a	*OP1	Sqirm Coil
10/07/90	1	1	Stash	Destiny
10/08/90	1	1	Don't Get	Bouncing
10/12/90	1	2	Fee	Terrapin
10/30/90	2	1	*OP1	Bouncing
10/31/90	1	2	*OP2	Reba
11/02/90	1	1	Golgi	Bouncing
11/03/90	1	2	*OP2	Mike's
11/08/90	2	1	*OP1	Possum
11/10/90	1	1	Reba	Bouncing
11/16/90	1	2	*OP2	Mike's
11/17/90	1	1	Sqirm Coil	RunJim
11/24/90	1	2	Eliza	RunJim
11/26/90	1	1	*OP1	RunJim
11/30/90	1	1	*OP1	Mike's
12/01/90	1	1	Cavern	Llama
12/07/90	2	1	Bouncing	YEM
12/08/90	1	1	Cavern	Mike's
12/28/90	1	2	*OP2	Possum
12/31/90	2	1	IDK	Bouncing
02/01/91	1	2	Reba	Mango
02/03/91	2	2	Sqirm Coil	Cavern
02/07/91	1	1	MSO	Mango
02/08/91	1	E	*OPE	La Grange
02/09/91	1	2	Fluffhead	Bouncing
02/14/91	1	2	IDK	Possum
02/16/91	2	1	A-Train	Bouncing
02/21/91	3	2	Cavern	Bouncing
02/26/91	4	2	Bouncing	Destiny
02/27/91	1	1	IDK	YEM
02/28/91	1	1	*OP1	Bouncing
03/01/91	1	2	Golgi	Reba
03/06/91	2	1	YEM	Sqirm Coil
03/07/91	1	2	Oh Kee	Sloth
03/13/91	3	1	Fluffhead	YEM
03/16/91	2	1	Reba	Bathtub
03/17/91	1	1	Bouncing	Mike's
03/22/91	2	1	YEM	Destiny
03/28/91	2	1a	Cavern	Bouncing
04/04/91	5	1	Lawn Boy	MSO
04/05/91	1	1	*OP1	Bouncing
04/11/91	2	2	Lawn Boy	Destiny
04/12/91	1	2	*OP2	RunJim
04/15/91	2	2	MSO	Lizards
04/19/91	3	2	Golgi	Destiny
04/20/91	1	2	MSO	Esther
04/21/91	1	2	Fee	Forbin's
04/22/91	1	2	Uncle Pen	Destiny
04/26/91	1	1	Cavern	MSO
04/27/91	1	1	Cavern	MSO
05/02/91	1	1	Bouncing	Forbin's
05/03/91	1	2	Sloth	RunJim
05/10/91	3	1	Sloth	Bathtub
05/12/91	2	1	Lizards	Destiny
05/16/91	1	2	Bouncing	Sqirm Coil
05/17/91	1	2	Rocky Top	Fluffhead
05/25/91	2	1a	Divided	Chalkdust
07/11/91	1	1	Lizards	*CL1
07/12/91	1	1	Reba	Bathtub
07/13/91	1	E	*OPE	*CLE

07/14/91 1 3 ACDCBag Esther
07/15/91 1 1a Suzie Dinner
07/18/91 1 2 Lizards IDK
07/19/91 1 1 Golgi Bouncing
07/20/91 1 1 Suzie Bathtub
07/21/91 1 1 Lizards Bouncing
07/23/91 1 2 Lizards Tweezer
07/24/91 1 1 Bathtub Cavern
07/25/91 1 2 *OP2 Golgi
07/26/91 1 1 Bouncing Golgi
07/27/91 1 1a IDK Mike's
09/25/91 2 1 It's Ice Caravan
09/26/91 1 2 Sparkle Destiny
09/28/91 2 1 *OP1 Bouncing
09/29/91 1 1a PoorHeart YEM
10/02/91 2 2 *OP2 YEM
10/03/91 1 2 Esther Destiny
10/06/91 3 2 Fee Destiny
10/10/91 1 1 Bouncing RunJim
10/11/91 1 1 *OP1 MSO
10/13/91 2 1 Reba Forbin's
10/15/91 1 1 Reba Destiny
10/17/91 1 1 Memories Bouncing
10/19/91 2 1 *OP1 Suzie
10/27/91 4 2 Tela Destiny
10/31/91 3 2 *OP2 Llama
11/01/91 1 1 Sparkle Destiny
11/02/91 1 1 WalkAway RunJim
11/07/91 2 1 YEM RunJim
11/08/91 1 1 Tube Dinner
11/09/91 1 2 Tela Terrapin
11/13/91 3 1 *OP1 RunJim
11/15/91 2 2 Tube Destiny
11/16/91 1 1 *OP1 Uncle Pen
11/20/91 2 2 Tela Bike
11/22/91 2 2 MSO Bathtub
11/23/91 1 2 Eliza Fee
11/24/91 1 1 Stash Fluffhead
12/04/91 2 1 Reba RunJim
12/06/91 2 1 Magilla Guelah
12/31/91 2 2 RunJim Reba
03/07/92 2 1 Mango Rift
03/13/92 3 2 Silent Lizards
03/19/92 3 1 *OP1 Rift
03/21/92 2 1 *OP1 RunJim
03/24/92 1 1 Mockbird Bowie
03/26/92 2 1 *OP1 RunJim
03/28/92 2 1 Bouncing Bowie
03/30/92 1 1 *OP1 Llama
04/01/92 2 1 IDK Bowie
04/03/92 1 1 *OP1 PoorHeart
04/05/92 2 2 Weigh Bowie
04/09/92 3 1 *OP1 Sparkle
04/13/92 2 1 Lizards NICU
04/15/92 1 2 Reba NICU
04/17/92 2 1 Bouncing Bowie
04/23/92 5 2 *OP2 PoorHeart
04/24/92 1 1 Sloth Fluffhead
04/29/92 2 2 *OP2 Possum
05/01/92 2 1 PoorHeart NICU
05/03/92 2 1 *OP1 Possum
05/07/92 3 2 *OP2 Sparkle
05/10/92 3 1a *OP1 Suzie
05/12/92 1 2 *OP2 Bathtub
05/17/92 4 1 *OP1 Llama
06/19/92 2 1a *OP1 Suzie
07/09/92 8 1a Suzie Sparkle
07/11/92 2 1a *OP1 RunJim
07/14/92 2 1 *OP1 Rift
07/16/92 2 2 Weigh Fluffhead
08/15/92 17 1a *OP1 Sparkle
08/17/92 1 1 PoorHeart Reba
08/19/92 1 1a Chalkdust RunJim
08/24/92 3 1a Tweezer Reba
08/27/92 2 1a Bouncing Horn
08/30/92 3 1a Uncle Pen Reba
11/21/92 4 1 *OP1 RunJim
11/25/92 3 1 PoorHeart Fee
12/01/92 4 1 *OP1 MSO
12/05/92 4 1 *OP1 Chalkdust
12/12/92 6 1 Reba Split&Melt
12/30/92 4 1 *OP1 Sparkle
02/11/93 9 2 *OP2 Wilson
02/17/93 4 2 Axilla Bowie
03/05/93 12 2 *OP2 Chalkdust
03/13/93 5 1 *OP1 FunkBitch
03/17/93 3 1 *OP1 RunJim
03/24/93 5 2 *OP1 Split&Melt
03/28/93 4 1 *OP1 FunkBitch
04/03/93 5 1 *OP1 Rift
04/17/93 8 2 Reba Halley's
04/25/93 7 1 *OP1 Possum
07/17/93 15 1 *OP1 RunJim
07/29/93 9 1 Rift FEFY
08/12/93 10 2 Also Sprac Lizards
08/15/93 3 2 Lizards Bouncing
08/21/93 4 1 Sparkle IDK
04/04/94 9 2 BurAlive Julius
04/15/94 9 2 Suzie Julius
04/25/94 9 1 *OP1 RunJim
05/04/94 6 2 YEM Julius
06/29/94 35 2 *OP2 PoorHeart
07/06/94 6 2 *OP2 PoorHeart
10/16/94 16 2 *OP2 PoorHeart
11/14/94 17 1 Bouncing Maze
12/02/94 13 2 Julius Gumbo
➢ 8/17/97 215

Lawn Boy [104]

Lawn Boy [Lawn Boy]
By Anastasio/Marshall

11/30/89 [145] 1 Antelope Frankstein
12/08/89 5 2 Possum Fire
12/09/89 1 1 Bowie Bathtub
12/16/89 2 1a ACDCBag Mike's
12/29/89 1 1 Lizards Mike's
01/20/90 3 1a La Grange Esther
01/28/90 3 E *OPE BBFCM
02/24/90 14 2 Bathtub Contact
04/18/90 20 2 Bold Jaegr
04/22/90 4 E *OPE Golgi
04/26/90 2 1 Antelope *CL1
06/05/90 14 1 Bowie Possum
06/07/90 1 E *OPE BBFCM
06/09/90 1 1 Possum Reba
06/16/90 1 1 Timber Ho Possum
09/22/90 6 1 Lizards Possum
10/01/90 2 2 *OP2 ACDCBag
11/02/90 10 E *OPE La Grange
11/16/90 5 1 Weekpaug Tube
11/17/90 1 2 Possum Rocky Top
11/24/90 1 E *OPE Divided
12/03/90 4 1 Antelope Frankstein
12/29/90 4 1 Bowie Rocky Top
02/02/91 3 2 Antelope *CL2
02/08/91 3 2 Cavern Mike's
02/09/91 1 E *OPE Suzie
02/14/91 1 1 Stash Oh Kee
02/16/91 2 E *OPE Fire
02/27/91 8 2 Bowie Oh Kee
03/17/91 11 E *OPE La Grange
03/28/91 4 E *OPE Fire
04/04/91 5 2 Bowie Landlady
04/11/91 3 2 Split&Melt Landlady
04/22/91 9 E *OPE Rocky Top
05/17/91 12 E *OPE Golgi
07/19/91 9 E *OPE RunJim
07/21/91 2 2 RunJim Sloth
07/26/91 4 E *OPE Frankstein
08/03/91 2 3 Fluffhead MSO
09/26/91 2 2 Weekpaug Chalkdust
09/28/91 2 2 Antelope Lizards
10/02/91 2 2 RunJim Stash
10/04/91 2 2 RunJim Stash
10/12/91 5 1 TweezRep Rocky Top
10/17/91 3 2 Bowie Fluffhead
11/07/91 13 E2 *OPE2 Fire
11/15/91 7 1 Divided Golgi
11/22/91 5 1 Divided Dinner
12/06/91 6 E *OPE Rocky Top
12/31/91 2 E *OPE Rocky Top
03/20/92 9 E *OPE Fire
03/24/92 2 E *OPE Fire
04/01/92 7 E *OPE GTBT
04/05/92 3 E *OPE Rocky Top
04/12/92 4 2 YEM NICU
04/19/92 6 2 Llama Brain
05/01/92 8 E *OPE GTBT
05/17/92 13 E *OPE GTBT
11/27/92 51 1 Split&Melt Reba
12/03/92 5 2 Weekpaug It's Ice
12/05/92 2 2 Maze Mike's
12/08/92 3 2 Antelope Sparkle
02/04/93 10 2 Weekpaug Uncle Pen
02/06/93 2 1 Divided Wedge
02/11/93 4 1 Llama Bowie
02/13/93 2 1 Stash Maze
02/18/93 3 1 Reba Antelope
02/19/93 1 2 BBJ FunkBitch
02/23/93 4 1 Reba Chalkdust
02/27/93 3 1 PYITE Antelope
03/03/93 2 1 RunJim Cavern
03/09/93 4 1 Reba Mike's
03/16/93 4 2 Bike Llama
03/21/93 4 1 PYITE Possum
03/28/93 6 1 It's Ice Antelope
04/01/93 3 1 Fluffhead Antelope
04/10/93 5 1 Chalkdust Bowie
04/20/93 7 1 Uncle Pen Bowie
04/23/93 3 1 Guelah Chalkdust
04/30/93 5 1 Cavern All Things
05/03/93 3 1 Possum Cavern
05/06/93 2 1 Possum WYBG
07/23/93 11 1 It's Ice Cavern
08/12/93 15 2 Maze BBJ
08/21/93 7 2 Llama Bowie
12/31/93 8 2 Possum YEM
04/08/94 4 1 If I Could Llama
05/02/94 19 2 Julius Mike's
07/06/94 43 2 Tweezer Chalkdust
10/08/94 9 1 It's Ice Antelope
10/29/94 17 1 Foam Split&Melt
11/14/94 7 1 Maze Cavern
12/10/94 20 1 Divided Chalkdust
06/17/95 14 1 Julius Curtain
10/19/95 29 2 Weekpaug BBFCM
11/18/95 17 1 Reba PYITE
12/09/95 15 2 YEM Slave
08/07/96 35 1 Taste 99 Years
10/22/96 12 2 Mango Scent
11/16/96 17 1 Bowie Sparkle
12/04/96 11 2 Reba Weekpaug
03/01/97 18 2 Mike's Weekpaug
08/09/97 34 1 Reba Crossroad
08/16/97 5 3 Llama Limb
➢ 8/17/97 1

Lengthwise [22]

Lengthwise [Lngthwise]
By Fishman

11/19/92 [480] 2 Llama Cavern
11/20/92 1 2 Terrapin *CL2
11/23/92 3 2 Weekpaug Cavern
12/02/92 6 2 Glide Sqirm Coil
12/06/92 4 2 TMWSIY Carolina
12/08/92 2 2 Suzie MSO
02/04/93 10 2 BBJ Harry
02/06/93 2 2 BBJ BurAlive
02/13/93 6 2 BBJ Sqirm Coil
02/17/93 2 2 YEM Sqirm Coil
02/26/93 8 2 YEM Sqirm Coil
03/12/93 8 2 Chalkdust Harry
03/16/93 3 2 Bike Bike
03/31/93 12 2 *OP2 Maze
04/10/93 6 2 *OP2 Maze
04/14/93 3 E *OPE Contact
04/23/93 7 2 Weekpaug Sqirm Coil
04/30/93 5 1 *OP1 Maze
05/30/93 9 1a *OP1 Maze
08/03/93 16 2 *OP2 Maze
08/13/93 7 1 *OP1 Llama
10/20/94 98 2 *OP2 Maze
➢ 8/17/97 243

Leprechaun [3]

Leprechaun
By Anastasio

07/15/93 [578] 1 My Mind RunJim
07/17/93 2 2 Mike's Weekpaug
07/31/93 11 2 Mike's Weekpaug
➢ 8/17/97 350

Letter to Jimmy Page [28]

Letter to Jimmy Page [LTJP]
By Anastasio

10/17/85 [3] 1a Alumni Alumni
10/30/85 1 1a Alumni Alumni
04/01/86 2 2 Alumni Alumni
04/15/86 1 1a Alumni Alumni
10/31/86 2 2 Alumni Alumni
03/23/87 4 1 Alumni Alumni
04/24/87 1 1 Alumni Alumni
04/29/87 1 1 Alumni Alumni
05/11/87 1 1a Corrina YEM
08/10/87 2 1 Alumni Alumni
08/29/87 3 1 Alumni Alumni
09/12/87 2 1 Alumni Alumni
11/19/87 4 2 Alumni Alumni
02/07/88 2 1a Alumni Alumni
03/11/88 2 2 Alumni Alumni
03/31/88 3 2 Alumni Alumni
05/14/88 2 2 Alumni Alumni
05/15/88 1 1a Alumni Alumni
12/02/88 23 2 Alumni Alumni
02/07/89 5 2 Alumni Alumni
04/15/89 14 2 Alumni Alumni
05/13/89 17 1 Alumni Alumni
08/19/89 22 2 Alumni Alumni
10/06/89 8 1a Alumni Alumni
10/14/89 4 1 Alumni Alumni
12/07/89 19 1 Alumni Alumni
07/05/94 530 1 Curtain If I Could
07/15/94 7 2 *OP2 Bowie
➢ 8/17/97 255

Lifeboy [45]

Lifeboy [Life Boy]
By Anastasio/Marshall

02/03/93 [505] 2 YEM Terrapin
02/06/93 3 2 Weekpaug Uncle Pen

SONGS PLAYED BY YEAR

(1997 through 8/17/97)

Julius
1994 65
1995 21
1996 16
1997 10

Keyboard Kavalry
1995 12
1996 0
1997 0

Kung
1990 0
1991 0
1992 1
1993 6
1994 4
1995 7
1996 1
1997 1

Landlady
1990 31
1991 81
1992 41
1993 15
1994 9
1995 0
1996 0
1997 0

Lawn Boy
1990 18
1991 27
1992 12
1993 24
1994 7
1995 4
1996 4
1997 3

Lengthwise
1992 6
1993 15
1994 1
1995 0
1996 0
1997 0

Leprechan
1993 3
1994 0
1995 0
1996 0
1997 0

Letter to Jimmy Page
1990 0
1991 0
1992 0
1993 0
1994 2
1995 0
1996 0
1997 0

Lifeboy
1993 9
1994 24
1995 10
1996 2
1997 1

Lizards
1990 35
1991 38
1992 24
1993 28
1994 28
1995 17
1996 9
1997 3

Limb By Limb
1997 17

Llama
1990 15
1991 67
1992 63
1993 46
1994 36
1995 13
1996 10
1997 5

Magilla
1990 11
1991 25
1992 5
1993 1
1994 6
1995 0
1996 0
1997 3

Makisupa
1990 2
1991 0
1992 0
1993 4
1994 5
1995 9
1996 7
1997 5

TMWSIY
1990 3
1991 17
1992 9
1993 5
1994 8
1995 4
1996 3
1997 0

Mango Song
1990 0
1991 20
1992 8
1993 3
1994 14
1995 6
1996 4
1997 1

Stories Behind the Songs
(Continued)

recording of The Man Who Stepped Into Yesterday, McGrupp is a Gamehendge song told from the perspective of a shepherd who has fled Prussia (the capitol city of Gamehendge) after the fall of Wilson and established a rural home on the shores of the Baltic Sea. Tom originally wrote the song as a poem and sent it to Trey, who posted it on his dorm room door. About a year later, sometime around 1986-87, the conjunction of the lyrics with the lyrics to Wilson (written by Tom and Aaron Woolfe) sparked the idea for Gamehendge as a way to tie them all together. Trey raided Skippy The Wondermouse's music and set the lyrics to McGrupp to it. Dave Abrahams, referenced in the song ("He looks too much like Dave") is a childhood friend of Trey and Tom's.

Mike's Song: A very popular song which in conjunction with Weekapaug Groove often carries a show on its back. Mike's Song almost always appears as part of "Mike's Groove"—which until 1992 was always Mike's Song > I Am Hydrogen > Weekapaug Groove. Now, it's sometimes, Mike's Song > any song > Weekapaug and was even Mike's Song > Weekapaug twice in fall '95. A tape from 1985 chronicles Trey announcing the title for Mike's Song as "Microdot"; early versions of the song were kind of bluesy before the psychedelic jam was perfected in the late 1980s. Mike's Song traditionally served, with You Enjoy Myself, as one of the band's trampoline songs, although for at least a year now the tramps have only appeared in YEM. Mike's Song is also one of the two songs during which Chris Kuroda will heavily trigger the on-stage fog machines (the other is Great Gig In The Sky).

Montana: This song title appears on *A Live One* but not on any setlists because Montana is actually a excerpt from a version of Tweezer performed in Bozeman, MT on 11/28/94.

Mound: Mike wrote many more lyrics for this song than were included in its final version; some lyrical outtakes are included in *Rift*'s liner notes. Many of Mound's lyrics also

03/14/93	26	2	YEM	Rift
03/30/93	12	2	Tweezer	BBJ
04/17/93	12	2	YEM	Oh Kee
07/15/93	20	2	It's Ice	Possum
07/29/93	11	2	It's Ice	Sparkle
08/13/93	11	2	Mike's	Oh Kee
08/26/93	9	2	Bowie	Rift
04/06/94	8	2	Mike's	Weekpaug
04/22/94	13	2	Tweezer	RunJim
05/04/94	9	1	Tweezer	Rift
05/12/94	5	2	Fluffhead	Possum
05/17/94	4	2	Tweezer	Uncle Pen
05/22/94	4	2	Tweezer	Rift
05/25/94	2	2	Tweezer	Maze
05/28/94	3	2	Tweezer	Reba
06/10/94	3	2	Tweezer	Sparkle
06/18/94	6	2	Tweezer	YEM
06/23/94	4	2	Tweezer	Slave
06/26/94	3	2	Axilla 2	Sample
06/29/94	1	2	It's Ice	Divided
07/02/94	3	1	Tweezer	Sparkle
07/05/94	2	2	Bathtub	Cities
07/09/94	3	2	Tweezer	Sparkle
10/07/94	6	2	Tweezer	MSO
10/14/94	6	2	Tweezer	Guyute
10/18/94	3	2	Scent	Old Home
10/28/94	8	2	Rift	Chalkdust
11/12/94	6	2	DwD	Rift
11/18/94	5	2	Bathtub	PoorHeart
11/23/94	4	2	Tweezer	YEM
12/07/94	10	1	Guyute	Chalkdust
06/08/95	10	2	Tweezer	PoorHeart
06/24/95	12	2	Bowie	Suzie
10/05/95	15	2	Bowie	AmGrace
10/21/95	11	2	Bowie	Sparkle
10/29/95	6	2	Possum	AmGrace
11/16/95	8	2	Bowie	Uncle Pen
12/05/95	13	2	Scent	Harry
12/12/95	5	1	Divided	PYITE
12/30/95	7	2	ACDCBag	Scent
08/13/96	29	2	Mike's	Weekpaug
12/30/96	41	2	Tweezer	Scent
08/03/97	45	2	Fluffhead	Taste
➢ 8/17/97	9			

Limb by Limb [17]

Limb by Limb [Limb]

By Anastasio/Marshall

06/13/97	[904]	1	Billy	Wolfman's
06/14/97	1	1	CTB	Bye Bye
06/16/97	1	2	*OP2	Ghost
06/19/97	1	1	*OP1	Dogs Stole
06/20/97	1	1	Funny	Don't Care
06/21/97	1	1a	Steep	Dogs Stole
06/25/97	3	1	Saw It	My Soul
07/01/97	3	1	Ya Mar	Funny
07/10/97	6	1	Dogs Stole	Ginseng
07/23/97	4	1	Water	Split&Melt
07/26/97	2	1	*OP1	Dogs Stole
07/31/97	3	1	Dogs Stole	Dirt
08/03/97	2	1	Jesus	CharZero
08/08/97	2	2	Free	Lovin Cup
08/11/97	3	1	Guelah	Horn
08/14/97	2	1	Fluffhead	Free
08/16/97	1	3	Lawn Boy	FunkBitch
➢ 8/17/97	1			

Lizards [232]*

Lizards [Lizards]

By Anastasio

01/30/88	[28]	3	Suzie	Golgi
02/08/88	2	2	Divided	Antelope
03/11/88	1	1	Corrina	Bowie
03/12/88	1	1a	McGrupp	Tela
03/21/88	1	1a	Timber Ho	Fire
03/31/88	1	2	Alumni	Forbin's
05/14/88	2	2	YEM	BBFCM
05/15/88	1	1a	Shaggy	Sally
06/15/88	3	2	*OP2	ACDCBag
06/20/88	2	1	ACDCBag	Halley's
06/21/88	1	1	Curtain	Forbin's
07/12/88	2	2	Cities	Sally
07/23/88	1	1	Weekpaug	OYWD
07/24/88	1	2	La Grange	Alumni
09/12/88	6	1a	Satin Doll	TMWSIY
09/24/88	1	2	Bowie	WalkAway
10/12/88	1	1	Bowie	Foam
10/29/88	1	1	Suzie	TimeLoves
11/03/88	1	1	WalkAway	Shaggy
11/05/88	1	2	Bold	ACDCBag
11/11/88	1	2	Timber Ho	WhipPost
12/02/88	1	2	LTJP	*CL2
01/26/89	1	1a	YEM	A-Train
02/07/89	4	1	ACDCBag	*CL1
02/18/89	2	1a	Mockbird	WalkAway
03/03/89	2	2	Mockbird	Split&Melt
03/04/89	1	2	Fluffhead	Antelope
04/14/89	8	1	Bold	Sloth
04/20/89	3	2	Split&Melt	Mike's
04/30/89	5	1	McGrupp	Divided
05/09/89	7	2	IDK	Bold
05/13/89	3	2	Bold	Harry
05/20/89	4	1	YEM	Wilson
06/23/89	9	1	Weekpaug	Antelope
08/17/89	7	2	YEM	*CL2
08/19/89	8	1	Mango	Mike's
08/26/89	2	E	Contact	La Grange
10/01/89	5	2	Split&Melt	*CL2
10/07/89	2	2	Possum	ACDCBag
10/21/89	5	1	ACDCBag	Dog Log
10/26/89	2	1	Wilson	Mike's
10/31/89	2	2	Alumni	HwayHell
11/09/89	4	2	PYITE	Mike's
11/10/89	1	2	Sloth	Brain
11/30/89	4	1	Foam	MSO
12/07/89	4	2	WalkAway	Antelope
12/09/89	2	1	La Grange	Foam
12/16/89	2	1	Weekpaug	In a Hole
12/29/89	1	1	ACDCBag	Lawn Boy
12/31/89	3	1	Bathtub	Satin Doll
02/24/90	18	E	*OPE	Cavern
02/25/90	1	2	Makisupa	Fluffhead
03/01/90	1	2	*OP2	GTBT
03/03/90	2	1	Sqirm Coil	Oh Kee
03/07/90	1	1	A-Train	Bowie
03/08/90	1	2	IDK	Mike's
03/28/90	4	2	Jesus	Split&Melt
04/04/90	1	2	Weekpaug	Uncle Pen
04/05/90	4	1	YEM	Fire
04/07/90	2	1	Sqirm Coil	Landlady
04/08/90	1	2	WalkAway	Slave
04/29/90	13	1a	Love You	Fire
05/04/90	2	1	YEM	*CL1
05/11/90	3	2	ACDCBag	Tweezer
05/19/90	4	1	YEM	HwayHell
05/23/90	1	2	Tweezer	La Grange
06/05/90	4	2	MSO	YEM
06/07/90	1	1	YEM	GTBT
06/16/90	3	2	YEM	Antelope
09/13/90	1	E	*OPE	La Grange
09/14/90	1	2	Cavern	Destiny
09/22/90	4	2	Stash	Lawn Boy
09/28/90	1	1	Sqirm Coil	Asse Fest
10/01/90	1	1	Sqirm Coil	Landlady
10/04/90	1	1	Sqirm Coil	Destiny
10/07/90	3	2	IDK	GTBT
10/30/90	4	3	Paul&Silas	GTBT
10/31/90	1	1	Sqirm Coil	Stash
11/02/90	1	2	YEM	IDK
11/08/90	3	1	Possum	Foam
11/10/90	1	1	BurAlive	Mike's
11/16/90	1	2	Paul&Silas	RunJim
11/24/90	2	1	Sqirm Coil	Oh Kee
11/30/90	2	2	Stash	Gumbo
12/29/90	6	2	RunJim	Cavern
02/07/91	5	2	Love You	Sloth
02/08/91	1	2	Bouncing	Antelope
02/21/91	7	1	Llama	Mike's
02/26/91	4	2	Possum	Mike's
03/15/91	10	1	ACDCBag	Mike's
03/17/91	2	1	Stash	Bowie
03/23/91	3	2	Tweezer	Uncle Pen
04/05/91	7	2	Stash	Sloth
04/11/91	2	2	TMWSIY	Split&Melt
04/15/91	3	2	Landlady	Possum
04/19/91	3	1	Cavern	Stash
04/22/91	3	2	MSO	HwayHell
04/27/91	3	1	Llama	Suzie
05/03/91	2	1	Tweezer	Adeline
05/10/91	3	1	BurAlive	Possum
05/12/91	2	1	Stash	Landlady
05/16/91	1	2	MSO	GTBT
05/18/91	2	2	Terrapin	*CL2
07/11/91	2	1	Stash	Landlady
07/13/91	2	2	Paul&Silas	Stash
07/15/91	2	1a	Flat Fee	Cavern
07/18/91	1	2	Split&Melt	Landlady
07/21/91	3	1	Split&Melt	Landlady
07/23/91	1	2	Cavern	Landlady
07/25/91	2	2	Jesus	Gumbo
07/26/91	1	2	Adeline	TweezRep
08/03/91	2	3	MSO	BurAlive
09/26/91	2	1	Guelah	Foam
09/28/91	2	2	Lawn Boy	PoorHeart
10/10/91	7	1	Alumni	*CL1
10/11/91	1	1	YEM	Llama
10/18/91	5	1	Llama	Adeline
10/24/91	3	2	Weekpaug	Uncle Pen
11/14/91	15	2	Brain	TweezRep
11/22/91	6	2	Llama	YEM
12/04/91	4	2	Sparkle	Chalkdust
12/07/91	3	2	Brother	Terrapin
12/31/91	1	1	Stash	Guelah
03/11/92	3	2	Sloth	Bathtub
03/13/92	2	2	Landlady	My Mind
03/20/92	4	1	Maze	Mound
03/26/92	4	2	My Friend	Cavern
03/31/92	4	2	Stash	Cavern
04/04/92	3	1	Sparkle	IDK
04/07/92	3	2	My Friend	Maze
04/13/92	3	1	Stash	Landlady
04/16/92	2	2	Llama	Mike's
04/18/92	2	2	TweezRep	Mound
04/23/92	4	1	Weekpaug	NICU
04/29/92	3	2	Llama	Mike's
05/01/92	2	2	Mound	Llama
05/16/92	12	1	Golgi	Cavern
07/10/92	12	1a	Golgi	Cavern
07/15/92	4	1	Chalkdust	Antelope
07/26/92	9	1a	Split&Melt	Llama
11/20/92	22	1	Stash	Memories
11/25/92	4	2	YEM	Tweezer
12/02/92	5	1	Stash	Sparkle
12/05/92	3	1	Split&Melt	Mound
12/08/92	3	2	It's Ice	Antelope
12/11/92	2	1	Stash	Chalkdust
12/28/92	3	2	YEM	Bike
02/04/93	5	1	Stash	Sample
02/09/93	4	2	Stash	Bike
02/13/93	4	2	Tweezer	Llama
02/18/93	3	2	Stash	PYITE
02/21/93	3	2	Stash	Bathtub
02/23/93	2	2	Stash	PYITE
03/02/93	4	2	Tweezer	Llama
03/08/93	4	2	YEM	AmGrace
03/13/93	3	2	Tweezer	It's Ice
03/19/93	5	2	Sample	Mike's
03/22/93	2	2	It's Ice	Tela
03/28/93	5	1	Split&Melt	Sloth
04/02/93	4	2	Weekpaug	BBJ
04/16/93	8	2	Maze	Mike's
04/22/93	5	2	Tweezer	BBJ
04/27/93	4	2	Maze	BBJ
05/02/93	4	2	YEM	BBJ
05/07/93	4	1	Caravan	Horn
07/15/93	4	2	Faht	WalkAway
07/25/93	8	2	Maze	PurplRain
07/28/93	2	2	Antelope	Mound
08/03/93	5	2	YEM	Sparkle
08/12/93	6	2	Landlady	Sloth
08/15/93	3	2	Tweezer	Landlady
08/26/93	7	2	Jesus	Bats&Mice
12/28/93	2	2	My Friend	Sloth
12/31/93	3	3	Split&Melt	Sparkle
04/06/94	3	1	Stash	Sample
04/13/94	5	1	Stash	Julius
04/16/94	3	2	Tweezer	Julius
04/21/94	4	1	Split&Melt	DWD
05/02/94	8	2	Golgi	Julius
05/12/94	7	1	Bathtub	Sample
05/14/94	2	2	FEFY	Cavern
05/19/94	3	2	Weekpaug	Julius
05/27/94	7	2	Reba	Julius
06/10/94	4	1	Bowie	Cavern
06/19/94	7	1	Julius	Axilla 2
06/26/94	6	1	Llama	Tela
07/03/94	5	2	Split&Melt	Bouncing
07/08/94	3	1	N20	Tela
07/16/94	6	1	Stash	Cavern
10/12/94	5	1	Split&Melt	Guelah
10/21/94	7	1	Stash	Dog Faced
10/25/94	3	1	Split&Melt	Sample
10/28/94	3	2	Bowie	Rift
11/02/94	3	2	Possum	Sample
11/13/94	4	2	Divided	Tweezer
11/16/94	2	1	Axilla 2	Stash
11/22/94	5	E	*OPE	*CLE
11/26/94	3	2	Adeline	Sample
12/02/94	4	1	It's Ice	Stash
12/08/94	5	1	Simple	Guitar
12/10/94	2	1	Stash	Sample
12/29/94	2	2	Halley's	Rosie
06/13/95	8	2	Bowie	Axilla 2
06/23/95	8	2	RunJim	Wedge
06/30/95	6	1	Wedge	Mound
07/03/95	3	2	ACDCBag	BBFCM
10/02/95	5	2	HelloBaby	Antelope
10/06/95	3	1	Free	Sample
10/13/95	4	2	Keyboard	Guitar
10/15/95	2	2	Tweezer	Sample
10/21/95	4	1	Kung	Str Design
10/28/95	5	1	Sample	Billy
11/09/95	3	2	Julius	Bathtub
11/22/95	10	1	Fog	Sample
11/30/95	5	1	FEFY	Fire
12/05/95	4	1	Fog	Free
12/12/95	5	2	DWD	Simple
12/17/95	4	1	Stash	Chalkdust
12/31/95	4	2	Drowned	Axilla 2
07/11/96	9	2	Maze	Terrapin
08/06/96	15	1	Theme	Dinner
08/13/96	4	2	ACDCBag	Mike's
08/17/96	3	1	CTB	Sample
10/17/96	2	2	Free	SSB
10/23/96	5	2	Tweezer	Llama
11/09/96	11	1	Split&Melt	CharZero

12/04/96	16	1	CharZero	Bowie
12/29/96	3	2	Bathtub	YEM
02/21/97	9	1	DWD	Crosseyed
07/10/97	26	1	Wading	Oblivious
08/08/97	13	1	Gumbo	Dirt
➤ 8/17/97	7			

Llama [246]*

Llama [Llama]

By Anastasio/Marshall

10/30/90	[238]	2	Reba	Curtis
11/03/90	3	1	Bouncing	Sqirm Coil
11/04/90	1	2	Rocky Top	Mike's
11/08/90	1	1	Uncle Pen	Sqirm Coil
11/10/90	1	2	Fee	Divided
11/16/90	1	1	Magilla	Divided
11/17/90	1	1	*OP1	Sqirm Coil
11/24/90	1	2	*OP2	Bouncing
11/26/90	1	1	Makisupa	*CL1
11/30/90	1	1	MSO	Possum
12/01/90	1	1	Landlady	Divided
12/07/90	2	1	Foam	*CL1
12/08/90	1	2	*OP2	Asse Fest
12/28/90	1	1	Reba	Forbin's
12/29/90	1	1	IDK	YEM
02/08/91	6	2	*OP2	Mango
02/09/91	1	2	Sqirm Coil	*CL2
02/15/91	2	1	Magilla	*CL1
02/16/91	1	1	Bouncing	Mango
02/21/91	3	1	Fee	Lizards
02/26/91	4	1	Sqirm Coil	Guelah
02/28/91	2	2	Reba	Guelah
03/01/91	1	2	Reba	Guelah
03/13/91	6	1	Esther	Sqirm Coil
03/15/91	1	1	*OP1	Foam
03/16/91	1	2	*OP2	Divided
03/22/91	3	1	*OP1	YEM
03/23/91	1	1	Fee	IDK
04/04/91	6	1	Sqirm Coil	Forbin's
04/06/91	2	1	Magilla	YEM
04/11/91	1	2	Reba	TMWSIY
04/12/91	1	1	*OP1	Uncle Pen
04/15/91	2	1	Mockbird	*CL1
04/18/91	2	2	*OP2	Reba
04/20/91	2	1	Reba	Fluffhead
04/21/91	1	2	Mockbird	Uncle Pen
04/22/91	1	1	PoorHeart	Guelah
04/26/91	2	1	YEM	*CL1
04/27/91	1	1	Reba	Lizards
05/02/91	1	1	Mockbird	Sqirm Coil
05/04/91	2	2	Dog Log	Forbin's
05/12/91	4	1	Destiny	Fee
05/16/91	1	1	Magilla	*CL1
05/25/91	3	1a	Sqirm Coil	Oh Kee
07/13/91	3	1	Foam	Oh Kee
07/14/91	1	1	Reba	Sqirm Coil
07/18/91	2	1	*OP2	Llama
07/20/91	2	1	Sqirm Coil	Oh Kee
07/23/91	2	2	*OP2	Reba
07/25/91	2	2	Sqirm Coil	PoorHeart
07/27/91	2	1a	*OP1	Foam
08/03/91	1	1	Guelah	Fee
09/25/91	1	1	Foam	Tela
09/26/91	1	1	*OP1	Bouncing
09/28/91	2	2	*OP2	Guelah
10/02/91	2	1	*OP1	Foam
10/03/91	1	1	Bouncing	Fee
10/04/91	1	E	Love You	*CLE
10/06/91	2	E	Possum	*CLE
10/10/91	1	1	It's Ice	Golgi
10/11/91	1	1	Lizards	Bouncing
10/13/91	2	2	*OP2	Bathtub
10/15/91	1	2	PoorHeart	Oh Kee
10/18/91	2	1	Wilson	Lizards
10/19/91	1	2	*OP2	Bathtub
10/27/91	4	2	*OP2	Forbin's
10/31/91	3	2	Landlady	Fee
11/02/91	2	1	Curtain	Reba
11/07/91	2	1	IDK	*CL1
11/09/91	2	1	Sparkle	Reba
11/12/91	2	1	Foam	*CL1
11/13/91	1	2	Sqirm Coil	Possum
11/14/91	1	1	Uncle Pen	Reba
11/15/91	1	2	*OP2	Bathtub
11/16/91	1	2	Terrapin	*CL2
11/20/91	2	1	Sqirm Coil	YEM
11/22/91	2	2	IDK	Lizards
11/23/91	1	1	*OP1	Reba
11/30/91	2	1	Glide	Foam
12/04/91	1	1	*OP1	Reba
12/05/91	1	1	Fluffhead	Bathtub
12/06/91	1	2	Tela	WhipPost
12/31/91	2	1	Esther	Golgi
03/06/92	1	2	Mound	Bouncing
03/11/92	2	2	*OP2	NICU
03/12/92	1	1	Magilla	YEM
03/14/92	2	2	Golgi	Sqirm Coil
03/17/92	1	2	Love You	*CL2
03/24/92	4	1	Silent	Forbin's
03/27/92	3	1	*OP1	Reba
03/30/92	2	1	Landlady	Foam
03/31/92	1	1	Reba	Forbin's
04/01/92	1	2	*OP2	YEM
04/03/92	1	2	Mango	Harry
04/05/92	2	1	*OP1	Guelah
04/06/92	1	2	NICU	Mound
04/09/92	2	1	Guelah	Mound
04/13/92	2	2	*OP2	Fluffhead
04/16/92	2	2	Sanity	Lizards
04/18/92	2	2	Mound	TMWSIY
04/19/92	1	2	Mango	Lawn Boy
04/22/92	2	1	*OP1	Foam
04/23/92	1	1	Sqirm Coil	Bouncing
04/24/92	1	2	Glide	*CL2
04/29/92	2	1	Oh Kee	Lizards
05/01/92	2	2	Lizards	Terrapin
05/02/92	1	1	Sqirm Coil	*CL1
05/05/92	2	2	PoorHeart	Love You
05/06/92	1	1	*OP1	Foam
05/08/92	2	1	Eliza	Mound
05/09/92	1	2	Harpua	Rosie
05/12/92	2	2	PoorHeart	Cavern
05/17/92	4	1	Landlady	Forbin's
05/18/92	1	2	Glide	TMWSIY
06/20/92	2	1a	Love You	*CL1
06/24/92	2	1a	RunJim	Adeline
07/10/92	6	1a	Bouncing	Reba
07/14/92	3	2	Reba	Sqirm Coil
07/16/92	2	2	TMWSIY	Glide
07/18/92	2	1a	Foam	Reba
07/25/92	5	1a	YEM	FunkBitch
07/26/92	1	1a	Lizards	*CL1
07/27/92	1	1a	Suzie	Adeline
08/01/92	4	1a	Horn	*CL1
08/14/92	3	1a	Sqirm Coil	Adeline
08/19/92	3	1a	Uncle Pen	*CL1
08/25/92	3	1a	Sqirm Coil	Adeline
08/27/92	2	1a	YEM	*CL1
08/30/92	3	1a	Reba	Memories
11/19/92	2	2	FEFY	Lngthwise
11/21/92	2	2	A-Train	*CL2
11/23/92	2	2	Walk Line	Weigh
11/27/92	2	1	Reba	Mound
11/30/92	2	1	*OP1	Foam
12/01/92	1	2	Uncle Pen	Love You
12/02/92	1	2	Tela	Glide
12/04/92	2	1	*OP1	Foam
12/06/92	2	1	Sqirm Coil	Fluffhead
12/07/92	1	2	Reba	Horn
12/08/92	1	1	Wilson	Forbin's
12/10/92	1	1	Golgi	Foam
12/12/92	2	1	*OP1	Foam
12/13/92	1	2	Bouncing	Fluffhead
12/29/92	2	1	Guelah	My Friend
12/30/92	1	2	A-Train	*CL2
12/31/92	1	3	DGirl	*CL3
02/03/93	1	1	Fee	Wedge
02/05/93	2	1	*OP1	Guelah
02/07/93	2	2	*OP2	FEFY
02/11/93	3	1	Fluffhead	Lawn Boy
02/13/93	2	2	Lizards	YEM
02/15/93	1	2	Fee	*CL2
02/19/93	3	2	Love You	AmGrace
02/22/93	3	2	Oh Kee	Love You
02/26/93	3	1	Fluffhead	Horn
02/27/93	1	2	Fee	*CL2
03/02/93	1	2	Lizards	YEM
03/06/93	3	1	*OP1	Horn
03/08/93	1	1	Oh Kee	Forbin's
03/13/93	3	1	Contact	Wilson
03/16/93	2	2	Lawn Boy	AmGrace
03/19/93	3	1	Suzie	Foam
03/21/93	1	2	Ya Mar	YEM
03/24/93	2	1	*OP1	Foam
03/27/93	3	1	*OP1	Guelah
03/30/93	2	1	My Friend	Esther
04/01/93	2	1	*OP1	Guelah
04/02/93	1	2	Uncle Pen	Horse
04/05/93	2	1	*OP1	It's Ice
04/09/93	1	2	All Things	Mound
04/12/93	2	1	Reba	Satin Doll
04/16/93	3	1	Esther	Sample
04/17/93	1	1	*OP1	Foam
04/20/93	2	2	My Friend	YEM
04/22/93	2	2	*OP2	Bouncing
04/24/93	2	2	*OP2	Foam
04/29/93	3	1	Horn	Glide
05/02/93	3	2	*OP2	PYITE
05/06/93	3	1	All Things	Fluffhead
05/30/93	4	1a	Contact	Golgi
07/16/93	2	E	*OPE	FrBir
07/22/93	4	1	*OP1	Foam
07/24/93	2	1	*OP1	Horn
07/30/93	5	1	Contact	Uncle Pen
08/03/93	3	1	Ya Mar	Cavern
08/07/93	2	1	*OP1	Bouncing
08/13/93	5	1	Lngthwise	Makisupa
08/17/93	4	1	Wilson	Guelah
08/21/93	2	2	Fee	Lawn Boy
08/24/93	1	2	*OP2	Horn
08/28/93	3	1	*OP1	Bouncing
12/31/93	4	1	*OP1	Guelah
04/06/94	3	1	*OP1	Guelah
04/08/94	1	1	Lawn Boy	*CL1
04/15/94	6	1	*OP1	Guelah
04/22/94	6	1	*OP1	Horn
04/29/94	5	1	My Mind	*CL1
05/07/94	6	1	*OP1	Horn
05/14/94	5	1	*OP1	Wilson
05/19/94	3	1	Halley's	My Friend
05/21/94	2	1	Tela	*CL1
05/28/94	6	2	Fee	YEM
06/09/94	2	1	*OP1	Guelah
06/14/94	4	1	*OP1	Guelah
06/22/94	6	1	*OP1	Guelah
06/24/94	2	2	Sanity	Dog Faced
06/26/94	2	1	Kung	Lizards
07/06/94	7	1	*OP1	Fluffhead
07/08/94	1	1	*OP1	N20
10/13/94	12	1	*OP1	Gumbo
10/18/94	4	2	Nellie	*CL2
10/25/94	5	1	Fee	Horn
10/28/94	3	1	IDK	Guelah
11/18/94	11	1	*OP2	Bathtub
11/25/94	5	1	*OP1	Guelah
12/06/94	8	1	*OP1	Mound
12/09/94	3	1	*OP1	Foam
12/28/94	2	2	Contact	Love You
06/10/95	8	1	Makisupa	Caspian
06/20/95	7	1	*OP1	Spock's
06/23/95	2	2	Jam	GTBT
07/01/95	7	1	Ya Mar	If I Could
10/02/95	7	2	Bathtub	Simple
10/11/95	6	2	Weekpaug	Suzie
10/15/95	3	1	Demand	Foam
10/24/95	6	1	Fee	Horse
11/12/95	9	1	My Friend	Bouncing
11/22/95	7	2	Free	Bouncing
12/11/95	13	1	Dog Log	Dog Log
12/14/95	2	1	Suzie	Horn
12/29/95	5	1	Fluffhead	Adeline
07/03/96	5	1a	Taste	*CL1
07/12/96	7	1	Tweezer	*CL1
07/21/96	6	2	*OP2	Theme
08/13/96	12	1	PYITE	Glide
10/19/96	7	1	Esther	Gumbo
10/23/96	3	2	Lizards	Suzie
11/14/96	14	2	*OP2	Sample
11/18/96	3	2	TweezRep	*CL2
12/06/96	11	1	Also Sprac	YEM
12/30/96	3	1	Sloth	Gumbo
02/17/97	5	1	Billy	Bathtub
02/26/97	7	1	CamlWalk	My Friend
07/02/97	17	2	Jam	Worms
07/10/97	5	1	Bathtub	Wading
08/16/96	19	3	Cities	Lawn Boy
➤ 8/17/97	1			

Lushington [3]

Lushington [Lushngton]

By Anastasio

03/11/87	[12]	1a	YEM	Possum
04/29/87	3	2	*OP2	Dog Log
08/29/87	6	1	Flat Fee	Suzie
➤ 8/17/97	920			

Magilla [51]

Magilla [Magilla]

By McConnell

09/13/90	[223]	2	Weekpaug	Stash
09/14/90	1	2	Tweezer	Cavern
09/15/90	1	1	Stash	Sqirm Coil
09/16/90	1	1a	Weekpaug	Antelope
09/22/90	3	1	Suzie	Wilson
10/01/90	2	1	Landlady	Dinner
10/12/90	6	2	Paul&Silas	Mike's
10/30/90	2	2	Weekpaug	Foam
11/03/90	3	1	Suzie	Foam
11/16/90	4	1	YEM	Llama
12/31/90	11	2	RunJim	YEM
02/01/91	1	1	Tweezer	Guelah
02/15/91	7	1	Dinner	Llama
03/16/91	19	2	Split&Melt	BurAlive
03/22/91	3	E	*OPE	Golgi
03/28/91	2	1a	Suzie	Chalkdust
04/04/91	5	2	BBFCM	HwayHell
04/05/91	1	1	Cavern	Reba
04/06/91	1	1	*OP1	Llama
04/11/91	1	1	Tweezer	Dinner
04/15/91	3	2	Possum	Fire
04/16/91	1	2	Chalkdust	BurAlive
04/21/91	4	1	Foam	MSO
05/12/91	11	2	Golgi	Mike's
05/16/91	1	1	YEM	Llama
05/17/91	1	2	Fluffhead	Cavern
07/14/91	6	2	Split&Melt	Cavern
07/19/91	3	2	MSO	Tweezer
07/25/91	5	2	Touch Me	Mike's
08/03/91	3	E	*OPE	Care
10/04/91	8	1	Suzie	Bowie
10/11/91	4	2	PoorHeart	Possum
10/17/91	4	E	*OPE	Rocky Top
11/12/91	17	2	Chalkdust	Cavern
11/20/91	6	E	*OPE	Brother
12/06/91	8	1	Sqirm Coil	Landlady
03/12/92	6	1	Rift	Llama
03/27/92	16	2	Dinner	Harry
04/13/92	12	2	Weekpaug	Ya Mar
04/25/92	10	1	Rift	Antelope
05/08/92	9	2	Stash	Maze
03/25/93	114	1	Horn	Antelope
04/04/94	73	2	Julius	Split&Melt
04/09/94	4	1	*OP1	Wilson
04/11/94	2	1	FEFY	Julius
04/15/94	3	E	*OPE	AmGrace
04/20/94	4	2	Antelope	Paul&Silas
05/04/94	11	2	Wolfman's	Suzie
02/26/97	260	2	Scent	Scent
07/10/97	22	2	Julius	Ya Mar
07/21/97	2	2	Wolfman's	Bowie
➤ 8/17/97	18			

Makisupa [46]*

Makisupa Policeman [Makisupa]

By Anastasio

12/01/84	[0]	1a	Slave	SpanFlea
05/03/85	1	1a	McGrupp	Antelope
04/15/86	5	1a	Slave	Mercy
03/11/87	5	1a	TMWSIY	*CL1
04/29/87	3	3	Anarchy	Antelope
05/11/87	1	1a	TMWSIY	Ya Mar
08/29/87	5	1	Sally	BBFCM
09/12/87	2	2	Antelope	Fire
10/14/87	2	2	Clod	*CL2
07/12/88	20	1	Jesus	Slave
02/07/89	20	1	Golgi	Dinner
03/30/89	7	E	*OPE	*CLE
09/09/89	52	1	McGrupp	Bathtub
10/07/89	3	1	La Grange	Alumni
10/14/89	3	1	YEM	GTBT
02/25/90	46	2	McGrupp	Lizards
11/26/90	72	1	Divided	Llama
04/29/93	319	2	Weekpaug	Weekpaug
08/02/93	25	1	Bathtub	My Mind
08/07/93	3	1	Stash	Reba
08/13/93	5	1	Llama	Foam
05/07/94	41	2	Sparks	Jam
06/19/94	26	2	Reba	Sqirm Coil
10/29/94	39	1	BuffaloBill	Rift
12/01/94	19	2	BBFCM	NICU
12/08/94	6	1	*OP1	Maze
06/10/95	11	1	*OP1	Llama
07/02/95	17	2	RunJim	Scent
10/07/95	10	2	*OP2	CTB
10/22/95	10	2	Tweezer	BBFCM
10/29/95	5	2	*OP2	Bowie
11/19/95	10	1	*OP1	Maze
11/30/95	7	2	Tweezer	Antelope
12/14/95	10	1	Foam	Split&Melt
12/29/95	5	2	*OP2	CTB
07/15/96	14	2	Lovin Cup	It's Ice
08/06/96	12	1	*OP1	Rift
08/16/96	6	3	*OP3	ASZ
10/25/96	9	1	Taste	Maze
11/15/96	14	2	*OP2	Maze
11/23/96	5	2	Simple	Axilla
12/28/96	9	2	*OP2	Maze
06/25/97	27	2	McGrupp	Cecilia
07/25/97	14	1	Bathtub	ACDCBag
08/11/97	11	1	*OP1	Maze
08/16/97	3	1	*OP1	Harpua
➤ 8/17/97	1			

TMWSIY [59]

The Man Who Stepped Into Yesterday [TMWSIY]

By Anastasio

03/11/87	[12]	1a	Peaches	Makisupa
05/11/87	4	1a	Peaches	Makisupa
08/29/87	5	1	Ya Mar	*CL1
09/12/87	2	1	*OP1	Clod
02/08/88	7	2	Mockbird	*CL2
07/24/88	17	3	*OP3	Peaches
09/12/88	6	1a	Lizards	Avenu
02/24/89	15	1	*OP1	Curtain
08/19/89	50	1	Suzie	ACDCBag
08/26/89	2	3	*OP3	Suzie
03/09/90	62	1	*OP1	Caravan
05/04/90	23	1	Adeline	Bouncing

Stories Behind the Songs
(Continued)

evolved to fit the music. During the *Rift* sessions, the band rearranged the song, making it more pleasing to play live, according to Trey.

My Friend My Friend: The song's original title, Knife, was dumped by the time of fall tour 1992. When recording the song for inclusion on *Rift* in fall '92, the band went on a Burlington radio station and announced that anyone interested in singing for the next Phish album could come down to the recording studio and join the fun. The group sing-a-long at the end of this song on the album is the result of that effort. For most of 1993, Trey performed the intro to this song (up to immediately before where the lyrics begin) on acoustic guitar, then switched to electric guitar for the rest of the song.

My Sweet One: Because Fishman wrote this song while at Mike's parents' house, the band sometimes jokes that Fish meant it as a love ballad to Mike's mom.

NICU: Originally introduced as In an Intensive Care Unit (a name which may have been a play on the lyrics in the song, "And I See You"), this song is now called NICU (pronounced N-I-C-U). NICU is apparently not meant as an acronym for anything, although fans have pointed out that the initials N.I.C.U. do substitute for "Neonatal Intensive Care Unit" in hospitals. NICU went through a number of musical revisions during spring 1992—the original version moved much slower than the current one; the band accelerated it during the spring tour in 1992, then gave up on the song altogether for a while. The version reintroduced in summer 1994 omitted a lyrical "da-da-da-da" bridge between the end of the verses and the last section of refrains. Current version features quick, ska-like guitar strumming, while original picked out the melody with a slow lead.

No Dogs Allowed: An oldie written by Trey in collaboration with his mother, who penned the lyrics.

The Oh Kee Pa Ceremony: A native American right-of-pas-

06/09/90	15	2	Harry	La Grange
02/07/91	40	2	Chalkdust	Tweezer
02/09/91	2	1	Sloth	RunJim
02/28/91	12	1	Cavern	MSO
03/16/91	9	1	*OP1	Golgi
04/11/91	13	2	Llama	Lizards
04/20/91	7	2	Cavern	Tweezer
04/27/91	5	2	Possum	Mike's
05/03/91	2	1	Chalkdust	Divided
05/17/91	7	1	Suzie	Stash
07/11/91	3	2	Cavern	Mike's
07/13/91	2	1	Alumni	Split&Melt
07/20/91	5	2	Stash	YEM
07/26/91	5	1	Cavern	BurAlive
07/27/91	1	1a	Stash	Possum
10/24/91	21	1	IDK	Bowie
11/02/91	7	2	Antelope	Sparkle
11/21/91	13	2	Tweezer	RunJim
03/26/92	22	2	Brother	My Friend
04/09/92	11	2	Bowie	MSO
04/18/92	6	2	Llama	Dinner
05/18/92	23	2	Llama	Mike's
07/16/92	15	2	Fluffhead	Llama
11/28/92	36	2	BBJ	Bouncing
12/06/92	7	2	YEM	Lngthwise
12/13/92	6	2	Chalkdust	MSO
12/30/92	3	2	YEM	Possum
02/04/93	3	2	Mike's	Weekpaug
03/27/93	38	2	Chalkdust	Mike's
04/20/93	16	2	BBJ	My Friend
07/22/93	23	2	Paul&Silas	Avenu
08/07/93	12	2	Mike's	Avenu
04/18/94	32	2	Mike's	DWD
05/14/94	19	2	Weekpaug	PYITE
06/22/94	23	2	Weekpaug	Fluffhead
07/01/94	7	2	DWD	Possum
07/14/94	9	1	Stash	Scent
10/16/94	11	1	Split&Melt	Axilla
10/29/94	10	2	DWD	Sparks
11/19/94	11	1	Paul&Silas	Avenu
06/30/95	40	2	Ha Ha Ha	Avenu
10/03/95	9	1	Free	Sample
11/09/95	20	2	Bathtub	Life Mars
12/30/95	31	1	It's Ice	Divided
10/25/96	40	2	Timber Ho	NICU
11/15/96	14	2	Split&Melt	My Mind
12/28/96	14	2	Bouncing	Mike's
➢ 8/17/97	**56**			

Mango [62]*

The Mango Song [Mango]

By Anastasio

03/30/89	[72]	2	*OP2	Mike's
04/15/89	7	2	Slave	Divided
05/26/89	23	2	Bowie	Split&Melt
05/28/89	2	3	Split&Melt	Harry
08/17/89	12	2	ACDCBag	Fee
08/19/89	2	1	Bold	Lizards
02/01/91	139	2	Landlady	*CL2
02/03/91	2	2	Cavern	Split&Melt
02/07/91	1	1	Landlady	Split&Melt
02/08/91	1	2	Llama	Cavern
02/09/91	1	1	*OP1	Sloth
02/14/91	1	1	Cavern	Stash
02/15/91	1	1	BurAlive	Sloth
02/16/91	1	1	Llama	Mike's
04/16/91	35	1	Cavern	Oh Kee
07/19/91	26	2	Tweezer	BBFCM
09/27/91	11	2	Split&Melt	Dinner
10/11/91	9	2	Bowie	Sloth
10/28/91	10	1	Chalkdust	BurAlive
11/08/91	8	1	Divided	Brother
11/14/91	5	1	Brother	Golgi
11/19/91	3	2	Weekpaug	Sloth
11/21/91	2	2	It's Ice	Uncle Pen
11/24/91	3	2	Cavern	Chalkdust
12/04/91	2	2	Stash	Mike's
12/07/91	3	1	Cavern	Antelope
03/07/92	3	1	Maze	Landlady
03/20/92	7	2	Sloth	Cavern
03/24/92	2	2	Guelah	Brother
04/03/92	8	2	YEM	Llama
04/19/92	12	2	Tube	Llama
04/24/92	4	2	Weekpaug	Horn
05/03/92	6	2	Weekpaug	Rosie
05/17/92	11	1	Stash	PoorHeart
07/24/93	150	1	Stash	Bouncing
08/11/93	13	1	My Friend	Stash
08/20/93	7	E	*OPE	FrBir
04/24/94	27	2	Bowie	Julius
05/19/94	17	1	DWD	Cavern
06/18/94	17	1	Maze	DWD
06/23/94	4	2	Bowie	Axilla 2
06/25/94	2	1	Stash	Sample
07/01/94	4	1	Stash	It's Ice
07/13/94	8	1	Foam	DWD
10/21/94	15	1	Foam	Old Home
10/25/94	3	2	Simple	Weekpaug
11/02/94	6	2	Tweezer	Axilla 2
11/13/94	4	2	Tweezer	BBFCM
11/25/94	9	2	Weekpaug	PurplRain
12/06/94	8	2	Simple	Weekpaug
12/28/94	5	2	Mike's	Weekpaug
06/19/95	14	2	Bowie	Lovin Cup
10/07/95	21	1	Possum	AArmy
10/29/95	15	2	Bowie	It's Ice
12/01/95	18	2	Weekpaug	Wilson
12/11/95	7	2	Bowie	Fog
12/17/95	5	1	Antelope	Tube
08/04/96	26	1	Split&Melt	Sloth
08/14/96	7	1	Reba	Gumbo
10/22/96	8	2	Taste	Lawn Boy
12/28/96	30	1	Split&Melt	Frankstein
03/01/97	16	2	Weekpaug	Billy
➢ 8/17/97	**40**			

Maze [206]

Maze [Maze]

By Anastasio/Marshall

03/06/92	[385]	1	Guelah	Reba
03/07/92	1	1	Silent	Mango
03/11/92	1	1	Reba	Fee
03/13/92	2	1	Guelah	Dinner
03/20/92	4	1	Fluffhead	Lizards
03/25/92	3	1	Fee	Glide
03/27/92	2	1	Guelah	Glide
03/30/92	2	1	Sparkle	IDK
04/03/92	3	1	Sparkle	Fluffhead
04/05/92	2	2	Silent	Weigh
04/07/92	2	1	Lizards	Bike
04/12/92	2	1	Sparkle	Reba
04/16/92	3	1	Fee	Forbin's
04/17/92	1	1	Reba	Bouncing
04/19/92	2	1	Reba	Fee
04/21/92	1	2	Sanity	Memories
04/23/92	2	2	Fee	Rosie
04/25/92	2	2	*OP2	Bathtub
04/30/92	2	1	Fee	Reba
05/02/92	2	1	Reba	Bouncing
05/06/92	3	1	My Mind	Tela
05/08/92	2	2	Magilla	YEM
05/09/92	1	1	Fee	Sqirm Coil
05/14/92	3	1	Sparkle	Horn
05/16/92	2	1	*OP1	Foam
05/18/92	2	1	Suzie	Bouncing
06/23/92	3	1a	Reba	Adeline
06/27/92	2	1a	Reba	All Things
07/10/92	5	1a	Sparkle	Golgi
07/12/92	2	1a	Uncle Pen	Glide
07/14/92	1	1	Guelah	Sparkle
07/16/92	2	1	Bouncing	Guelah
07/17/92	1	1a	Sqirm Coil	Bouncing
07/19/92	2	1a	PoorHeart	RunJim
07/22/92	2	1a	Bouncing	Rift
07/30/92	6	1a	All Things	IDK
08/15/92	6	1a	Guelah	RunJim
08/23/92	4	1a	Chalkdust	Sparkle
08/29/92	5	1a	Bouncing	YEM
10/30/92	2	1a	RunJim	Bouncing
11/19/92	1	1	*OP1	Fee
11/21/92	2	1	Bouncing	Forbin's
11/22/92	1	1	Fee	Reba
11/25/92	2	1	Fee	Sparkle
11/28/92	2	2	Avenu	TMWSIY
11/30/92	1	2	Guelah	Glide
12/01/92	1	1	Fluffhead	Adeline
12/03/92	2	1	*OP1	Fee
12/04/92	1	1	FEFY	Forbin's
12/05/92	1	2	Sparkle	Lawn Boy
12/07/92	2	1	PoorHeart	Glide
12/10/92	2	2	BBJ	YEM
12/12/92	2	2	*OP2	Glide
12/28/92	2	1	*OP1	Sparkle
12/31/92	3	1	PoorHeart	Bouncing
02/04/93	2	1	Bouncing	FEFY
02/06/93	2	1	My Friend	Horn
02/09/93	2	1	Esther	Golgi
02/12/93	3	1	Golgi	Guelah
02/13/93	1	1	Lawn Boy	Golgi
02/17/93	2	1	Fluffhead	Golgi
02/19/93	2	1	Fee	Forbin's
02/22/93	3	1	PoorHeart	Fee
02/25/93	2	1	Cavern	Forbin's
02/27/93	2	1	Guelah	Bouncing
03/03/93	2	1	Bouncing	Guelah
03/06/93	2	1	Bouncing	Golgi
03/09/93	2	1	Bouncing	Esther
03/13/93	2	1	Bouncing	Fee
03/16/93	2	1	Fee	IDK
03/18/93	2	1	Fee	Forbin's
03/21/93	2	1	*OP1	Sparkle
03/24/93	2	1	PoorHeart	IDK
03/26/93	2	1	*OP1	Sparkle
03/28/93	2	1	Sloth	Fee
03/31/93	2	2	Lngthwise	Bouncing
04/02/93	2	1	Sparkle	Golgi
04/05/93	2	1	Fee	Fluffhead
04/09/93	1	1	Silent	IDK
04/10/93	1	2	Lngthwise	Bouncing
04/14/93	3	1	PoorHeart	Bouncing
04/16/93	1	2	Curtain	Lizards
04/18/93	2	1	Fee	Horn
04/21/93	2	1	Guelah	Forbin's
04/23/93	2	2	Golgi	Curtis
04/25/93	2	1	Mockbird	IDK
04/27/93	1	2	All Things	Lizards
04/30/93	2	1	Lngthwise	Bouncing
05/02/93	2	1	PoorHeart	IDK
05/05/93	2	1	Glide	Golgi
05/07/93	2	2	Bouncing	Fee
05/30/93	3	1a	Lngthwise	Guelah
07/16/93	2	2	Glide	Bouncing
07/18/93	2	1	Guelah	Esther
07/21/93	1	1a	Sqirm Coil	Glide
07/23/93	2	1	Nellie	Horse
07/24/93	1	2	Fluffhead	Glide
07/25/93	1	2	Silent	Lizards
07/29/93	3	2	*OP2	Bouncing
07/31/93	2	2	It's Ice	Sparkle
08/03/93	2	2	Lngthwise	Bouncing
08/07/93	2	1	Reba	Forbin's
08/12/93	4	2	Sloth	Lawn Boy
08/15/93	3	2	Bouncing	Glide
08/17/93	2	1	Weigh	Fluffhead
08/20/93	1	1	PoorHeart	Bouncing
08/24/93	2	1	Uncle Pen	Golgi
08/28/93	3	1	Ginseng	Fluffhead
12/29/93	2	2	*OP2	Bouncing
04/04/94	3	1	Scent	Fee
04/08/94	3	1	*OP1	Glide
04/11/94	3	2	Also Sprac	Forbin's
04/15/94	3	2	*OP2	If I Could
04/17/94	2	2	BBJ	Contact
04/21/94	3	2	Also Sprac	Fluffhead
04/24/94	3	1	Axilla 2	Bathtub
04/29/94	3	2	Suzie	If I Could
05/03/94	3	1	Guelah	Sparkle
05/06/94	2	2	*OP2	Golgi
05/10/94	3	2	*OP2	Wilson
05/12/94	1	1	Fee	Axilla 2
05/17/94	4	1	Suzie	Mound
05/20/94	2	1	Fee	If I Could
05/23/94	3	1	Fee	Horse
05/25/94	1	2	Life Boy	Contact
05/28/94	3	1	Sloth	Cavern
06/09/94	2	1	If I Could	Fee
06/11/94	2	2	Sqirm Coil	Contact
06/16/94	3	1	Fee	Gumbo
06/18/94	2	1	ACDCBag	Mango
06/22/94	3	1	Gumbo	If I Could
06/25/94	3	2	Suzie	Sparkle
06/30/94	3	2	Wilson	YEM
07/02/94	2	2	McGrupp	Sample
07/09/94	5	1	Gumbo	Guelah
07/14/94	3	2	Sample	If I Could
07/16/94	2	1	Silent	Sparkle
10/07/94	1	2	*OP2	Horse
10/10/94	3	2	Golgi	Esther
10/15/94	4	1	Simple	Glide
10/20/94	3	2	Lngthwise	McGrupp
10/23/94	3	1	Tela	Sample
10/27/94	3	1	Sparkle	Forbin's
11/02/94	4	1	If I Could	Guyute
11/12/94	3	1	Guyute	Stash
11/14/94	2	1	Landlady	Lawn Boy
11/17/94	2	1	Scent	Bouncing
11/23/94	5	2	*OP2	Fee
12/01/94	5	1	FEFY	Guyute
12/04/94	3	2	*OP2	Fee
12/08/94	3	1	Makisupa	ACDCBag
12/10/94	2	2	Simple	Guyute
12/31/94	4	2	Old Home	Bouncing
06/07/95	2	2	Ha Ha Ha	Spock's
06/10/95	3	2	*OP2	Fee
06/17/95	5	2	Wilson	Mound
06/22/95	3	1	Str Design	Cavern
06/25/95	3	2	*OP2	Sample
07/01/95	5	2	Wilson	Theme
07/03/95	2	1	If I Could	Str Design
09/29/95	3	2	Also Sprac	Free
10/03/95	3	1	*OP1	Guelah
10/06/95	2	2	PoorHeart	Theme
10/13/95	4	1	Also Sprac	Billy
10/17/95	3	1	ACDCBag	Glide
10/20/95	2	2	Simple	Gumbo
10/24/95	3	1	Demand	Wolfman's
10/28/95	3	2	*OP2	Theme
11/10/95	4	1	Dog Faced	Guyute
11/14/95	3	2	*OP2	Gumbo
11/19/95	4	1	Makisupa	PoorHeart
11/24/95	3	1	I'm Blue	Suzie
11/28/95	2	2	Also Sprac	Suzie
12/02/95	4	2	Also Sprac	Simple
12/09/95	5	1	*OP1	Theme
12/15/95	4	1	Wilson	Ha Ha Ha
12/17/95	2	2	Bouncing	Free

12/31/95	4	1	Sqirm Coil	Forbin's
07/06/96	5	1a	DayinLife	Harry
07/11/96	4	2	ASZ	Lizards
07/15/96	3	2	DWD	Lovin Cup
07/22/96	5	1a	Cavern	Bouncing
08/04/96	5	1	Sloth	Lovin Cup
08/13/96	6	1	Tela	FEFY
08/17/96	3	1	Fee	Suzie
10/18/96	3	2	Suzie	YEM
10/21/96	2	2	Train Song	Life Mars
10/25/96	3	1	Makisupa	Billy
10/31/96	4	3	Also Sprac	Simple
11/08/96	5	2	Also Sprac	Bouncing
11/11/96	2	2	Steep	Contact
11/15/96	3	2	Makisupa	McGrupp
11/22/96	4	2	Caspian	Billy
11/29/96	4	1	Life Mars	Suzie
12/28/96	6	2	Makisupa	Bouncing
02/13/97	4	2	Circus	RockaW
02/18/97	4	2	My Soul	Wolfman's
02/23/97	4	2	Suzie	Horse
03/02/97	5	2	Also Sprac	SweptAwy
06/13/97	2	2	Stash	Water
06/19/97	3	1	Water	Waste
07/02/97	9	1	Simple	Str Design
07/25/97	10	1	Wolfman's	Water
07/31/97	4	1	Dirt	Glide
08/11/97	7	1	Makisupa	Water
08/17/97	4	1	Water	Bouncing
➢ **8/17/97**	**0**			

McGrupp [73]*

McGrupp and the Watchful Hosemasters [McGrupp]

By Anastasio/Marshall

05/03/85	[2]	1a	WhipPost	Makisupa
10/17/85	1	1a	Antelope	*CL1
04/01/86	3	2	ACDCBag	Alumni
12/06/86	5	1a	Icculus	GTBT
04/29/87	5	3	Jam	Curtis
08/09/87	2	2	Fluffhead	Corrina
08/21/87	2	3	BBFCM	Makisupa
08/29/87	2	2	Curtain	Possum
10/14/87	4	2	Divided	Clod
11/19/87	2	1	*OP1	Sparks
02/07/88	2	1a	Fire	Shaggy
03/12/88	2	1a	JumpMonk	Lizards
03/21/88	1	1a	Golgi	Sally
05/15/88	4	1a	Icculus	Wilson
06/15/88	3	1	Rocky Top	Fluffhead
06/18/88	1	2	Rocky Top	Jesus
07/24/88	6	3	Jesus	Antelope
02/07/89	18	1	Esther	Foam
03/03/89	4	1	Wilson	YEM
03/30/89	3	1	Bold	Divided
04/15/89	7	1	IDK	Foam
04/20/89	2	1	Possum	Foam
04/30/89	5	1	YEM	Lizards
06/30/89	25	1	YEM	Possum
08/17/89	5	1	Suzie	Sloth
09/09/89	8	1	ACDCBag	Makisupa
10/01/89	1	1	Alumni	Jam
10/21/89	7	1	In a Hole	Fluffhead
10/22/89	1	2	In a Hole	ACDCBag
11/02/89	4	2	Divided	Fluffhead
11/09/89	3	2	ACDCBag	PYITE
11/10/89	1	2	*OP2	Fluffhead
12/08/89	9	1	Reba	ACDCBag
02/25/90	22	2	Reba	Makisupa
05/23/90	37	2	La Grange	A-Train
02/14/91	50	1	MSO	BurAlive
05/10/91	50	2	Foam	Chalkdust
05/25/91	6	1	Sloth	*CL1
10/13/91	29	1	Sloth	Mike's
12/31/91	35	3	Tweezer	Mike's
05/14/92	49	2	Weekpaug	Stash
07/15/92	18	2	Stash	All Things
11/27/92	36	2	It's Ice	Walk Line
03/16/93	49	1	Divided	Cavern
03/22/93	5	2	Sloth	Mike's
05/03/93	31	2	It's Ice	RunJim
08/07/93	24	2	My Friend	PurplRain
12/30/93	18	2	PYITE	Weekpaug
04/08/94	5	2	Split&Melt	It's Ice
04/30/94	18	2	Axilla 2	Possum
05/13/94	9	2	Split&Melt	Peaches
05/22/94	7	2	It's Ice	Tweezer
05/29/94	6	2	Chalkdust	Oh Kee
06/18/94	8	2	Horn	Tweezer
06/24/94	5	2	Curtain	Simple
06/26/94	2	1	Sloth	Divided
07/02/94	4	2	Weekpaug	Maze
07/08/94	4	1	Sloth	Divided
10/20/94	17	2	Maze	Rift
11/30/94	26	2	Catapult	Cavern
12/09/94	8	2	Tweezer	Julius
06/17/95	15	2	Tweezer	AArmy
10/11/95	24	2	Mike's	Weekpaug
10/27/95	11	2	Simple	Keyboard
12/11/95	27	1	Tube	Julius
12/29/95	7	2	Bathtub	BBFCM
07/23/96	20	1	DWD	Stash
08/12/96	9	2	Caspian	Antelope
10/26/96	13	2	Simple	Waste
11/15/96	13	2	Maze	Split&Melt
06/25/97	41	2	Time	Makisupa
07/31/97	18	2	Vultures	Mike's
08/13/97	8	2	Sl Monkey	Sample
➢ **8/17/97**	**3**			

Mid-Highway Blues [1]

Mid-Highway Blues [Highway]

By Gordon

11/23/96	[877]	1	PYITE	Split&Melt
➢ **8/17/97**	**65**			

Mike's Song [291]*

Mike's Song [Mike's]

By Gordon

10/17/85	[3]	1a	Alumni	Dave's
11/23/85	2	1a	*OP1	WhipPost
10/15/86	3	1a	Quinn	Mercy
12/06/86	2	1a	*OP1	Jam
03/23/87	3	1	FunkBitch	Alumni
08/21/87	6	2	*OP2	Harpua
06/18/88	22	2	IKALittle	Corrina
07/23/88	5	1	Mockbird	I am H2
07/24/88	1	1	Sally	I am H2
07/25/88	1	2	*OP2	I am H2
08/03/88	1	2	Peaches	I am H2
08/27/88	2	1a	Fluffhead	A-Train
10/12/88	4	1	Fee	I am H2
10/29/88	1	2	Curtis	A-Train
11/05/88	2	2	Fee	I am H2
11/11/88	1	2	*OP2	I am H2
02/07/89	6	1	Possum	I am H2
03/03/89	4	2	*OP2	I am H2
03/04/89	1	1	IDK	I am H2
03/30/89	1	2	Mango	I am H2
04/14/89	6	2	Brain	I am H2
04/15/89	1	1	*OP1	I am H2
04/20/89	2	3	Lizards	I am H2
05/06/89	9	1	IDK	I am H2
05/09/89	3	1	Ya Mar	I am H2
05/20/89	7	2	Bold	I am H2
05/21/89	1	1	Contact	I am H2
05/26/89	1	1	ACDCBag	I am H2
05/27/89	1	1	ACDCBag	I am H2
05/28/89	1	2	Fire	I am H2
06/23/89	5	1	Fee	I am H2
06/30/89	2	2	Bathtub	I am H2
08/17/89	5	1	Harry	I am H2
08/19/89	2	1	Lizards	I am H2
10/06/89	8	1a	Timber Ho	I am H2
10/07/89	1	1	Ya Mar	I am H2
10/21/89	1	2	*OP2	I am H2
10/26/89	3	1	Lizards	I am H2
11/02/89	3	1	Foam	I am H2
11/09/89	3	2	Lizards	I am H2
11/10/89	1	1	Bathtub	I am H2
11/16/89	2	1	*OP1	I am H2
12/07/89	6	1	Fee	I am H2
12/09/89	2	2	Fee	I am H2
12/16/89	2	1a	Lawn Boy	I am H2
12/29/89	1	1	Lawn Boy	I am H2
12/31/89	3	2	*OP2	I am H2
01/20/90	1	1a	Esther	I am H2
01/27/90	3	1	Funky	I am H2
01/28/90	1	2	Bathtub	I am H2
02/09/90	7	1	Sqirm Coil	I am H2
02/10/90	1	2	Fee	I am H2
02/15/90	1	1	Bathtub	I am H2
02/17/90	2	1a	Bathtub	I am H2
02/23/90	2	2	Suzie	I am H2
03/01/90	3	2	Foam	I am H2
03/03/90	2	1	*OP1	I am H2
03/07/90	1	2	Tela	I am H2
03/08/90	1	2	Lizards	I am H2
03/28/90	4	2	FunkBitch	I am H2
04/04/90	1	2	*OP2	I am H2
04/05/90	1	2	Cavern	I am H2
04/07/90	2	1	Tweezer	I am H2
04/08/90	1	2	Slave	I am H2
04/18/90	5	1	*OP1	I am H2
04/20/90	2	2	Caravan	I am H2
04/22/90	2	1	Slave	I am H2
04/25/90	1	2	Bouncing	I am H2
04/26/90	1	2	Curtis	I am H2
04/28/90	1	2	MSO	I am H2
05/04/90	3	2	Oh Kee	I am H2
05/06/90	1	1	Tweezer	I am H2
05/11/90	2	1	*OP1	I am H2
05/13/90	2	2	*OP2	I am H2
05/23/90	3	2	Antelope	I am H2
06/05/90	4	1	Uncle Pen	I am H2
06/07/90	1	2	Love You	I am H2
06/08/90	1	1	IDK	I am H2
06/09/90	1	1	Uncle Pen	I am H2
06/16/90	1	3	Brain	I am H2
09/13/90	1	2	*OP2	I am H2
09/16/90	2	1a	Paul&Silas	I am H2
09/28/90	4	2	Paul&Silas	I am H2
10/05/90	7	1	IDK	I am H2
10/07/90	2	1	Sqirm Coil	I am H2
10/12/90	2	2	Magilla	I am H2
10/30/90	2	2	*OP2	I am H2
10/31/90	1	2	Love You	I am H2
11/02/90	1	1	Sloth	I am H2
11/03/90	1	2	Landlady	I am H2
11/04/90	1	2	Llama	I am H2
11/08/90	1	1	IDK	I am H2
11/10/90	1	1	Lizards	I am H2
11/16/90	1	2	Landlady	I am H2
11/17/90	1	2	Fluffhead	I am H2
11/24/90	1	1	Foam	I am H2
11/26/90	1	2	Wilson	I am H2
11/30/90	1	1	Landlady	I am H2
12/07/90	3	2	*OP2	I am H2
12/08/90	1	1	Landlady	I am H2
12/28/90	1	1	Mockbird	I am H2
12/31/90	1	2	MSO	I am H2
02/08/91	5	2	Lawn Boy	I am H2
02/14/91	2	2	*OP2	I am H2
02/16/91	2	1	Mango	I am H2
02/21/91	3	1	Lizards	I am H2
02/26/91	4	1	Lizards	I am H2
02/28/91	6	1	Esther	I am H2
03/01/91	1	1	BurAlive	I am H2
03/07/91	3	2	IDK	I am H2
03/15/91	4	1	Lizards	I am H2
03/17/91	2	1	Landlady	I am H2
03/22/91	2	2	Terrapin	I am H2
04/05/91	8	1	Foam	I am H2
04/11/91	2	2	Destiny	I am H2
04/15/91	3	2	Jam	I am H2
04/19/91	3	1	Rocky Top	I am H2
04/21/91	2	1	Tela	I am H2
04/27/91	4	2	TMWSIY	I am H2
05/04/91	3	1	Fluffhead	I am H2
05/10/91	2	2	Love You	I am H2
05/12/91	2	2	Magilla	I am H2
05/17/91	2	1	IDK	I am H2
07/11/91	3	2	TMWSIY	I am H2
07/12/91	1	2	Gumbo	I am H2
07/14/91	2	3	Bathtub	I am H2
07/15/91	1	1a	Bouncing	I am H2
07/18/91	1	1	Cavern	I am H2
07/21/91	4	1	Bouncing	I am H2
07/23/91	1	1	Bouncing	I am H2
07/25/91	2	2	Magilla	I am H2
07/27/91	2	1a	Landlady	I am H2
09/26/91	3	2	Destiny	I am H2
09/28/91	2	2	PoorHeart	I am H2
10/03/91	3	2	Paul&Silas	I am H2
10/04/91	1	2	Sqirm Coil	I am H2
10/10/91	3	2	Fee	I am H2
10/13/91	3	1	McGrupp	I am H2
10/18/91	3	2	Dinner	I am H2
10/24/91	3	2	*OP2	I am H2
10/27/91	2	2	It's Ice	I am H2
11/01/91	4	2	Eliza	I am H2
11/08/91	4	2	IDK	I am H2
11/12/91	3	2	Paul&Silas	I am H2
11/15/91	3	2	PoorHeart	I am H2
11/19/91	2	2	MSO	I am H2
11/21/91	2	1	Esther	I am H2
11/23/91	2	2	Curtain	I am H2
12/04/91	3	2	Mango	I am H2
12/05/91	1	2	Foam	I am H2
12/31/91	3	3	McGrupp	I am H2
03/07/92	2	2	Horn	I am H2
03/14/92	4	1	A-Train	I am H2
03/17/92	1	2	Esther	I am H2
03/20/92	2	2	*OP2	I am H2
03/24/92	2	2	Curtain	I am H2
03/27/92	3	2	*OP2	I am H2
03/31/92	3	2	*OP2	I am H2
04/04/92	3	2	*OP2	I am H2
04/06/92	2	2	Paul&Silas	I am H2
04/09/92	2	2	MSO	I am H2
04/13/92	2	2	Sparkle	I am H2
04/16/92	2	2	Lizards	I am H2
04/19/92	3	2	Curtain	I am H2
04/21/92	1	2	Tela	I am H2
04/23/92	2	2	PoorHeart	I am H2
04/24/92	1	2	Foam	I am H2
04/29/92	2	2	Lizards	I am H2
05/01/92	2	2	MSO	I am H2
05/03/92	2	2	Guelah	I am H2
05/05/92	1	2	Foam	I am H2
05/07/92	2	2	Glide	I am H2
05/14/92	5	2	Eliza	I am H2
05/18/92	4	2	TMWSIY	I am H2
07/16/92	15	2	Paul&Silas	I am H2
08/17/92	18	2	Esther	I am H2
11/19/92	11	2	*OP2	I am H2
11/21/92	2	2	Curtain	I am H2
11/23/92	2	2	Weigh	I am H2
11/28/92	3	1	All Things	I am H2
12/01/92	2	1	Adeline	I am H2
12/03/92	2	2	Fluffhead	I am H2
12/05/92	2	2	Lawn Boy	I am H2
12/08/92	3	2	*OP2	I am H2
12/11/92	2	2	Dinner	I am H2
12/29/92	4	2	All Things	I am H2
12/31/92	2	3	*OP3	Auld
02/04/93	2	2	Wedge	TMWSIY
02/06/93	2	2	All Things	I am H2
02/09/93	2	2	PYITE	I am H2
02/11/93	2	2	Uncle Pen	I am H2
02/15/93	3	2	Reba	I am H2
02/18/93	2	2	PYITE	I am H2
02/20/93	2	2	Glide	Kung
02/23/93	3	2	All Things	I am H2
02/27/93	3	2	Ya Mar	I am H2
03/03/93	2	2	Mound	I am H2
03/05/93	1	2	Uncle Pen	I am H2
03/09/93	3	2	Lawn Boy	I am H2
03/13/93	2	2	BBJ	I am H2
03/17/93	3	2	Mound	I am H2
03/19/93	2	2	Lizards	I am H2
03/22/93	3	2	McGrupp	I am H2
03/25/93	2	2	Wedge	I am H2
03/27/93	2	2	TMWSIY	I am H2
03/30/93	2	2	Weigh	I am H2
04/02/93	3	2	Silent	I am H2
04/10/93	4	2	BBJ	Great Gig
04/13/93	2	2	BBJ	I am H2
04/16/93	2	2	Lizards	I am H2
04/18/93	2	2	BBJ	Ya Mar
04/21/93	2	2	BBJ	Great Gig
04/23/93	2	2	BBJ	I am H2
04/25/93	2	2	BBJ	I am H2
04/29/93	2	2	Reba	I am H2
05/01/93	2	2	Paul&Silas	Great Gig
05/06/93	4	2	Sqirm Coil	ObJam
05/08/93	2	2	BBJ	I am H2
07/17/93	5	2	BBJ	Lepr
07/24/93	5	2	Sparkle	YSZahov
07/31/93	6	2	Sparkle	Lepr
08/02/93	1	2	Also Sprac	Sparks
08/07/93	3	2	Also Sprac	Sparks
08/11/93	3	2	*OP2	Great Gig
08/13/93	2	2	Ya Mar	Life Boy
08/16/93	3	2	*OP2	Faht
08/24/93	4	2	Ya Mar	Ginseng
12/30/93	6	2	Also Sprac	SiJam
04/06/94	4	2	Sparkle	Life Boy
04/09/94	2	2	Demand	I am H2
04/18/94	8	2	Ya Mar	TMWSIY
04/21/94	2	2	Fluffhead	I am H2
04/29/94	6	2	Uncle Pen	I am H2
05/02/94	2	2	Lawn Boy	*CL2
05/14/94	9	2	Curtain	I am H2
05/19/94	3	2	Sparkle	I am H2
05/27/94	7	2	My Mind	OMio
06/09/94	3	2	Ginseng	I am H2
06/13/94	3	2	*OP2	I am H2
06/17/94	3	2	PoorHeart	I am H2
06/22/94	4	2	Also Sprac	Simple
07/02/94	8	2	Also Sprac	YSZahov
07/10/94	6	2	Ya Mar	I am H2
10/08/94	6	2	Rift	I am H2
10/13/94	6	2	AmGrace	YSZahov
10/21/94	6	2	Also Sprac	I am H2
10/25/94	3	2	*OP2	Simple
11/04/94	8	2	Curtain	Tela
11/16/94	4	2	*OP2	Simple
11/25/94	7	2	Also Sprac	Simple
11/30/94	3	2	Ya Mar	Catapult
12/06/94	5	2	PoorHeart	Simple
12/10/94	4	2	Also Sprac	I am H2
12/28/94	1	2	NICU	Mango
12/31/94	3	2	Bouncing	YSZahov
06/10/95	5	2	Uncle Pen	I am H2
06/20/95	7	2	Uncle Pen	Contact
06/25/95	4	2	Scent	DoInRoad
06/30/95	4	2	Avenu	Contact
09/30/95	7	2	Scent	Keyboard
10/11/95	7	2	Mound	McGrupp
10/19/95	5	2	PoorHeart	I am H2
10/25/95	5	2	CTB	Sparkle
11/11/95	7	1	CTB	DayinLife
11/15/95	3	2	Scent	Life Mars
11/21/95	4	2	Ya Mar	Keyboard
11/25/95	3	2	Kung	LongJourn
12/01/95	4	2	Halley's	Weekpaug
12/07/95	4	2	Sparkle	Weekpaug
12/16/95	7	2	Cavern	Simple
12/31/95	5	2	HelloBaby	Jam
07/09/96	7	1a	CTB	Bouncing
07/12/96	3	2	Caspian	Antelope
07/23/96	8	2	Sparkle	I am H2

Stories Behind the Songs
(Continued)

sage takes on a slightly different meaning in the world of Phish. In the 1980s, the band would occassionally sequester themselves in a room for hours and just jam. They termed this "The Oh Kee Pa Ceremony" and affixed the title to a short instrumental piece that may have arisen from one of the sessions.

Poor Heart: Written by Mike after his four-track recording machine which he was using to complete his senior film project was ripped off, the lyrics originally referenced "my four-track" instead of "my poor heart." (The line "you won't steal my tape recorder" survived lyrical revisions in the early 1990s). There's a third verse which has never been performed in concert by Phish.

Possum: Originally written by Jeff Holdsworth about a truck driver's encounter with a Possum, Trey reworked the lyrics in the mid-1980s to turn it into a Gamehendge song. Told from the perspective of Icculus looking down from his mountain perch at a Possum on the road, its actual title is apparently Oh! Possum, but it has fallen out of use among fans.

Prep School Hippie: A favorite find on old tapes, the band retired this one long before it could offend a particular segment of their fanbase.

Prince Caspian: The song is named after the C.S. Lewis character and the lyrics reference Lewis' work. In recording sessions for *Billy Breathes*, Trey crafted a new instrumental introduction and closing jam which is became part of live performances of the song in summer 1996 and thereafter.

Punch You In The Eye: Not a part of The Man Who Stepped Into Yesterday and not included in live Gamehendge performances, PYITE is nonetheless a Gamehendge song which chronicles an outsider's visit to Gamehendge and his imprisonment by Wilson. The song underwent several major rewrites in the 1980s, and its actual title, according to Trey, is Punch Me In The Eye, but the words used in the lyrics have caught on among tapers and fans. The Landlady, which appears mixed into PYITE, was

08/05/96	4	2	AmGrace	I am H2
08/13/96	5	2	Lizards	Life Boy
08/16/96	2	2	HelloBaby	Simpl
10/22/96	7	2	Scent	SweptAwy
10/29/96	5	2	Rift	I am H2
11/06/96	4	2	Curtain	SweptAwy
11/08/96	2	2	Lovin Cup	SSB
11/15/96	5	2	My Mind	Sl Monkey
11/23/96	5	2	Curtain	Simple
12/04/96	7	2	Ha Ha Ha	Caspian
12/06/96	1	2	Sparkle	Simple
12/28/96	1	2	Avenu	Str Design
02/23/97	12	2	Peaches	DoInRoad
03/01/97	4	2	Dinner	Lawn Boy
07/02/97	15	1	*OP1	Simple
07/22/97	8	2	DWD	Simple
07/31/97	6	2	McGrupp	I am H2
08/09/97	5	2	Foam	Funny
➢ 8/17/97	**6**			

Mound [87]*

Mound [Mound]

By Gordon

03/06/92	[384]	2	Stash	Llama
03/11/92	2	1	Split&Melt	Divided
03/13/92	2	1	Divided	Fluffhead
03/20/92	4	1	Lizards	Antelope
03/25/92	3	2	Tweezer	Reba
03/30/92	4	2	Tweezer	YEM
04/06/92	6	2	Llama	Stash
04/09/92	2	1	Llama	Reba
04/18/92	6	2	Lizards	Llama
04/22/92	3	1	Divided	Stash
04/29/92	4	2	Possum	Oh Kee
05/01/92	2	2	Weekpaug	Lizards
05/08/92	6	1	Llama	All Things
11/19/92	52	1	Split&Melt	Divided
11/23/92	4	1	Divided	Bouncing
11/27/92	2	1	Llama	Memories
12/02/92	4	2	Possum	Tweezer
12/05/92	3	1	Lizards	Divided
12/08/92	3	1	Divided	Adeline
12/13/92	4	2	Suzie	Bouncing
02/06/93	8	2	Chalkdust	Stash
02/11/93	4	2	Weekpaug	BBJ
02/15/93	3	1	Chalkdust	Stash
02/18/93	2	2	Weekpaug	AmGrace
02/26/93	7	2	Chalkdust	BBJ
03/03/93	3	2	Split&Melt	Mike's
03/06/93	2	1	Split&Melt	PYITE
03/12/93	3	2	YEM	BBJ
03/17/93	4	2	Jesus	Mike's
03/24/93	5	2	Tweezer	BBJ
03/26/93	2	2	Tweezer	Horse
03/28/93	2	2	RunJim	Bathtub
03/31/93	2	1	Split&Melt	PYITE
04/03/93	3	2	Stash	All Things
04/09/93	2	2	Llama	My Friend
04/14/93	4	2	Tweezer	BBJ
04/18/93	3	2	Possum	BBJ
04/21/93	2	2	Possum	Split&Melt
04/24/93	3	2	Dinner	BBJ
04/29/93	3	2	Ya Mar	BBJ
04/30/93	1	2	Tweezer	BBJ
05/02/93	2	1	Divided	Stash
05/06/93	3	1	Chalkdust	Split&Melt
05/08/93	2	1	Rift	Stash
07/15/93	3	1	Divided	Stash
07/18/93	3	2	Antelope	FEFY
07/22/93	2	1	Divided	Ya Mar
07/25/93	3	1	Foam	Stash
07/28/93	2	2	Lizards	My Friend
07/31/93	3	1	Split&Melt	Foam
08/09/93	6	1	Chalkdust	Fee
08/14/93	4	2	Antelope	Sqirm Coil
08/16/93	2	2	Weekpaug	It's Ice
08/25/93	5	2	Possum	My Friend
04/17/94	18	1	Divided	DWD
04/23/94	5	2	Antelope	Sample
04/25/94	2	2	Antelope	Sqirm Coil
04/30/94	3	1	Chalkdust	Stash
05/02/94	1	2	RunJim	Reba
05/07/94	4	1	Divided	FEFY
05/13/94	4	1	Julius	Stash
05/17/94	3	1	Maze	If I Could
05/21/94	3	1	DWD	Stash
05/26/94	4	2	DWD	Ginseng
06/21/94	13	2	DWD	Split&Melt
06/29/94	6	1	Reba	Julius
07/13/94	10	2	Tweezer	Slave
12/01/94	41	2	Peaches	Tweezer
12/04/94	3	1	Fee	Adeline
12/06/94	1	1	Llama	DWD
12/28/94	5	1	*OP1	Simple
12/31/94	3	1	Glide	Peaches
06/08/95	3	1	Guelah	FEFY
06/14/95	4	1	NICU	Cavern
06/17/95	3	2	Maze	Tweezer
06/24/95	5	1	Glide	Stash
06/30/95	5	1	Lizards	Fee
10/07/95	12	1	Fog	Possum
10/11/95	2	2	Bathtub	Mike's
10/17/95	4	2	*OP2	Caspian
10/28/95	8	1	ACDCBag	Timber Ho
11/16/95	9	1	Horn	Ya Mar
12/02/95	11	1	RunJim	Guelah
10/16/96	47	1	Billy	Sample
10/25/96	7	1	Billy	Guelah
11/08/96	9	1	All Things	DWD
11/19/96	8	1	Theme	Stash
➢ 8/17/97	**67**			

My Friend [98]*

My Friend My Friend [My Friend]

By Anastasio/Marshall

03/06/92	[384]	2	*OP2	PoorHeart
03/11/92	2	1	Suzie	Paul&Silas
03/19/92	5	2	Suzie	Sqirm Coil
03/21/92	2	2	A-Train	PoorHeart
03/26/92	3	2	TMWSIY	Lizards
03/31/92	4	2	Dinner	MSO
04/04/92	3	2	Rosie	Harpua
04/07/92	3	2	YEM	Lizards
04/19/92	8	1	Paul&Silas	Reba
04/25/92	5	1	Suzie	Paul&Silas
05/01/92	3	1	Suzie	PoorHeart
05/07/92	5	1	BurAlive	Foam
05/14/92	5	1	PoorHeart	Bouncing
07/15/92	18	1	Foam	Uncle Pen
08/17/92	19	1	Foam	Bouncing
11/22/92	14	2	Axilla	MSO
12/01/92	6	2	Chalkdust	All Things
12/06/92	5	1	Fee	MSO
12/11/92	4	1	Sparkle	Memories
12/29/92	4	1	Llama	Divided
02/03/93	3	1	IDK	PoorHeart
02/06/93	3	1	Wilson	Maze
02/09/93	2	1	PoorHeart	Rift
02/12/93	3	2	*OP2	All Things
02/17/93	3	2	Glide	MSO
02/19/93	2	1	Sparkle	PoorHeart
02/23/93	4	1	Golgi	Rift
03/02/93	4	2	*OP2	Uncle Pen
03/08/93	4	2	BBJ	Kung
03/12/93	2	2	ACDCBag	Axilla
03/16/93	3	2	*OP2	Curtain
03/18/93	2	2	*OP2	PoorHeart
03/21/93	2	2	Lovin Cup	Rift
03/27/93	5	1	Reba	Uncle Pen
03/30/93	2	1	Golgi	Llama
04/01/93	2	1	Sqirm Coil	Paul&Silas
04/03/93	2	1	Sqirm Coil	Reba
04/09/93	2	2	Mound	YEM
04/10/93	1	1	Sqirm Coil	Uncle Pen
04/13/93	2	2	*OP2	Rift
04/17/93	3	1	Glide	All Things
04/20/93	2	2	TMWSIY	Llama
04/23/93	3	1	Fluffhead	Divided
04/27/93	3	2	Golgi	All Things
04/29/93	1	E	*OPE	*CLE
05/01/93	2	2	Fluffhead	Sqirm Coil
05/05/93	3	2	RunJim	Manteca
05/08/93	3	1	Glide	Reba
07/16/93	4	1	Golgi	Ya Mar
07/23/93	5	2	Faht	Uncle Pen
07/28/93	4	2	Mound	Harry
07/30/93	2	2	Fluffhead	Golgi
08/07/93	5	2	Sparkle	McGrupp
08/09/93	2	2	Tela	My Mind
08/11/93	1	1	Ginseng	Mango
08/16/93	5	2	It's Ice	PoorHeart
08/20/93	2	2	Sqirm Coil	Chalkdust
08/25/93	3	2	Mound	Paul&Silas
12/28/93	3	2	YEM	Lizards
04/10/94	9	2	*OP2	Ya Mar
04/18/94	7	1	Julius	Rift
04/24/94	5	1	*OP1	Ya Mar
05/06/94	8	1	PoorHeart	Ya Mar
05/13/94	5	1	If I Could	Slave
05/19/94	4	1	Llama	PoorHeart
05/27/94	7	2	Peaches	Reba
06/14/94	7	1	Fee	Uncle Pen
06/21/94	5	2	DWD	Split&Melt
07/03/94	10	1	*OP1	PoorHeart
07/10/94	5	1	If I Could	Julius
10/07/94	5	1	*OP1	Julius
10/12/94	4	1	*OP1	Reba
10/18/94	5	1	Simple	IDK
10/23/94	4	1	Chalkdust	Sparkle
10/29/94	5	1	*OP1	Sparkle
11/14/94	7	1	*OP1	Scent
11/26/94	9	1	*OP1	Possum
11/30/94	2	1	PoorHeart	Reba
06/09/95	17	1	*OP1	Divided
06/15/95	4	1	*OP1	Sparkle
06/26/95	9	1	*OP1	Wanna Go
07/03/95	6	1	*OP1	PoorHeart
09/30/95	4	1	*OP1	CTB
10/20/95	13	1	*OP1	Ya Mar
10/24/95	3	1	*OP1	Paul&Silas
11/12/95	9	1	*OP1	Llama
11/21/95	6	1	Guyute	Dog Faced
12/11/95	14	1	*OP1	Ha Ha Ha
12/17/95	5	1	*OP1	PoorHeart
12/29/95	2	1	*OP1	PoorHeart
07/15/96	14	1	*OP1	PYITE
08/10/96	14	1	*OP1	PoorHeart
10/19/96	9	1	*OP1	Rift
11/03/96	10	1	*OP1	RunJim
11/27/96	15	1	Julius	Ya Mar
12/04/96	5	1	*OP1	Chalkdust
02/25/97	15	2	Fee	DWD
02/26/97	1	1	Llama	Harry
➢ 8/17/97	**42**			

MSO [185]

My Sweet One [MSO]

By Fishman

09/09/89	[124]	1	Wilson	Bowie
10/01/89	1	2	ACDCBag	Reba
10/22/89	8	2	ACDCBag	Fee
11/02/89	4	2	ACDCBag	*CL2
11/03/89	1	1	Bathtub	Split&Melt
11/09/89	2	1	Curtain	Bathtub
11/10/89	1	1	ACDCBag	YEM
11/11/89	1	1a	ACDCBag	YEM
11/16/89	1	1	Suzie	Reba
11/30/89	2	1	Lizards	Antelope
12/08/89	5	1	ACDCBag	Bathtub
01/27/90	10	1	ACDCBag	Bouncing
02/25/90	16	1	Foam	Forbin's
03/03/90	3	1	Weekpaug	Sqirm Coil
03/08/90	2	2	Bathtub	ACDCBag
03/11/90	2	2	Antelope	Bouncing
04/07/90	6	1	Bowie	Suzie
04/08/90	1	2	Fee	Antelope
04/18/90	5	1	YEM	A-Train
04/22/90	4	1	Cavern	Slave
04/25/90	1	1	Divided	Bowie
04/28/90	2	2	Reba	Mike's
05/04/90	3	1	Reba	YEM
05/10/90	2	1	Tweezer	Bathtub
05/13/90	3	2	Tweezer	Reba
05/24/90	4	2	IDK	Horn
06/05/90	3	2	Bouncing	Lizards
06/07/90	1	2	*OP2	Dinner
06/08/90	1	1	Possum	Bathtub
06/16/90	2	2	Tweezer	Bathtub
09/15/90	3	2	Eliza	Bathtub
09/22/90	4	1	Horn	Divided
09/28/90	1	1	Stash	Sqirm Coil
10/05/90	3	1	Weekpaug	Landlady
10/07/90	2	2	Tweezer	IDK
10/08/90	1	1	Reba	YEM
10/31/90	4	1	Asse Fest	Cavern
11/02/90	1	2	Mockbird	Foam
11/04/90	2	1	Asse Fest	Bowie
11/10/90	2	1	Cavern	BurAlive
11/30/90	5	1	Tweezer	Llama
12/01/90	1	1	Tweezer	YEM
12/03/90	1	1	Divided	Antelope
12/28/90	3	2	Oh Kee	Divided
12/31/90	2	1	Bouncing	Mike's
02/01/91	1	1	*OP1	Foam
02/03/91	2	1	Guelah	Tweezer
02/07/91	1	1	Foam	Landlady
02/08/91	1	1	Mockbird	Stash
02/09/91	1	1	Guelah	Tweezer
02/14/91	1	1	*OP1	McGrupp
02/15/91	1	2	Guelah	Oh Kee
02/16/91	1	1	Sloth	Divided
02/26/91	7	1	Guelah	Reba
02/27/91	1	1	Fee	Split&Melt
02/28/91	1	1	TMWSIY	Golgi
03/06/91	3	1	Love You	Bouncing
03/07/91	1	2	Guelah	GTBT
03/13/91	3	2	Bouncing	Guelah
03/15/91	1	1	Foam	Stash
03/16/91	1	2	Guelah	Split&Melt
03/17/91	1	2	Esther	Sqirm Coil
03/23/91	3	2	ACDCBag	Tweezer
03/28/91	1	1a	Guelah	Bowie
04/04/91	5	2	Landlady	Divided
04/05/91	1	2	IDK	GTBT
04/11/91	2	2	*OP2	Reba
04/12/91	1	2	Reba	GTBT
04/15/91	2	2	Horn	Landlady
04/16/91	1	2	*OP2	Reba
04/19/91	2	2	Destiny	Sqirm Coil
04/20/91	1	1	Fluffhead	Landlady
04/21/91	1	1	Magilla	Oh Kee
04/22/91	1	2	Stash	Lizards
04/26/91	2	2	Bouncing	Guelah
04/27/91	1	1	Landlady	Reba

05/02/91	1	2	Tela	IDK
05/04/91	2	1	Reba	Split&Melt
05/16/91	5	2	Tweezer	Lizards
05/18/91	2	2	Stash	Guelah
07/11/91	2	1	Flat Fee	Stash
07/12/91	1	2	Tweezer	Gumbo
07/14/91	2	1	Guelah	Forbin's
07/19/91	3	2	IDK	Magilla
07/20/91	1	1	Bathtub	Bowie
07/23/91	2	1	Sqirm Coil	Oh Kee
07/24/91	1	2	Jesus	Bouncing
07/25/91	1	1	*OP1	Sloth
07/26/91	1	1	Reba	Foam
08/03/91	2	3	Lawn Boy	Lizards
09/25/91	1	1	Tela	It's Ice
09/26/91	1	1	It's Ice	Guelah
09/28/91	2	1	Sqirm Coil	Stash
10/02/91	2	2	YEM	Guelah
10/04/91	2	2	*OP2	Brother
10/06/91	2	2	*OP2	Stash
10/11/91	2	1	Landlady	Guelah
10/13/91	2	2	It's Ice	Jesus
10/18/91	3	2	Split&Melt	Cavern
10/19/91	1	1	Bouncing	Stash
10/27/91	4	1	*OP1	Chalkdust
10/31/91	3	2	Fee	Bowie
11/01/91	1	2	Tweezer	It's Ice
11/07/91	3	2	Bouncing	Reba
11/09/91	2	2	Terrapin	TweezRep
11/13/91	3	E	Horn	Adeline
11/15/91	2	1	Sqirm Coil	Divided
11/16/91	1	2	Tube	Bathtub
11/19/91	1	2	Tube	Mike's
11/20/91	1	2	It's Ice	Antelope
11/22/91	2	2	Tube	Landlady
11/23/91	1	2	Love You	TweezRep
11/30/91	2	2	Bouncing	Horn
12/04/91	1	2	*OP2	Stash
12/05/91	1	2	IDK	TweezRep
12/07/91	2	1	Mockbird	Stash
12/31/91	1	2	Cavern	Antelope
03/07/92	1	2	*OP2	Tweezer
03/12/92	2	2	Rosie	Cavern
03/19/92	4	2	NICU	Stash
03/21/92	2	1	Sqirm Coil	Stash
03/25/92	2	2	Horn	Chalkdust
03/27/92	2	2	Silent	Magilla
03/31/92	3	2	My Friend	Love You
04/04/92	3	2	Glide	Tweezer
04/09/92	4	2	TMWSIY	Mike's
04/15/92	3	2	Rosie	Golgi
04/19/92	4	2	Silent	Tube
05/01/92	8	2	All Things	Mike's
05/06/92	4	2	*OP2	Stash
05/08/92	2	2	Wilson	Stash
05/12/92	3	1	*OP1	Reba
05/16/92	3	1	Bouncing	Horn
05/17/92	1	1	Mockbird	Reba
07/10/92	11	E	*OPE	*CLE
07/15/92	4	2	Esther	Stash
07/24/92	7	1a	*OP1	Foam
11/22/92	26	2	My Friend	Tweezer
11/25/92	2	2	Rosie	TweezRep
11/28/92	2	1	*OP1	Foam
12/01/92	2	1	Landlady	Split&Melt
12/03/92	2	2	It's Ice	BBJ
12/06/92	3	1	My Friend	Sloth
12/07/92	1	2	Horn	It's Ice
12/08/92	1	2	Lngthwise	BBJ
12/10/92	1	2	Tela	BBJ
12/13/92	3	2	TMWSIY	BBJ
12/29/92	2	2	Silent	BBJ
12/31/92	2	2	Mockbird	BBJ
02/09/93	6	2	Weigh	Sample
02/17/93	6	2	My Friend	BBJ
02/19/93	2	2	FunkBitch	Love You
02/23/93	4	2	Axilla	Stash
03/03/93	5	2	Glide	FEFY
03/05/93	1	2	Jesus	BBJ
03/13/93	5	E	*OPE	AmGrace
03/21/93	6	2	YEM	BBJ
03/25/93	3	E	*OPE	BBJ
03/30/93	4	E	*OPE	AmGrace
04/03/93	4	2	Jesus	Love You
04/09/93	2	2	YEM	Love You
04/14/93	4	2	ACDCBag	Tweezer
05/03/93	15	2	Love You	TweezRep
07/28/93	17	2	Axilla	Antelope
08/08/93	8	E	*OPE	FrBir
08/11/93	2	2	Jesus	Antelope
08/17/93	6	2	PurplRain	Cavern
04/17/94	22	1	If I Could	Cavern
05/14/94	20	1	Sample	Ginseng
05/22/94	6	1	Fluffhead	Ginseng
05/25/94	2	1	Scent	Adeline
06/14/94	9	1	IDK	IDK
06/19/94	4	2	Sqirm Coil	HwayHell
06/22/94	2	2	Fluffhead	BBJ
07/05/94	10	2	Ginseng	AmGrace
07/13/94	5	E	*OPE	TweezRep
10/07/94	4	2	Life Boy	TweezRep
10/18/94	9	E	*OPE	*CLE
11/03/94	12	E	*OPE	Nellie
11/30/94	15	2	Antelope	Antelope
12/31/94	13	3	*OP3	Also Sprac
06/15/95	8	2	*OP2	Ha Ha Ha
12/02/95	58	1	Reba	Free
12/14/95	8	1	Fog	Frankstein
➤ 8/17/97	130			

N20 [3]

N20 [N20]

By Phish

06/25/94	[672]	1	*OP1	Rift
07/08/94	9	1	Llama	Lizards
07/16/94	6	1	DWD	Stash
➤ 8/17/97	254			

NICU [47]*

NICU [NICU]

By Anastasio/Marshall

03/06/92	[384]	2	Bouncing	Possum
03/11/92	2	2	Llama	Sloth
03/19/92	5	2	Chalkdust	MSO
03/26/92	5	1	Uncle Pen	Bowie
04/06/92	9	2	Weekpaug	Llama
04/12/92	3	2	Lawn Boy	Rosie
04/13/92	1	1	Landlady	Fee
04/15/92	1	2	Landlady	Rosie
04/19/92	4	1	BurAlive	Stash
04/21/92	1	1	Eliza	Bouncing
04/23/92	2	2	Lizards	Horn
05/01/92	5	1	Landlady	Sloth
06/23/94	248	1	Split&Melt	Foam
06/25/94	2	1	Julius	Stash
07/01/94	4	1	Sample	Stash
07/03/94	2	1	Fee	Horn
07/13/94	6	2	Cavern	Tweezer
10/26/94	19	1	It's Ice	Antelope
11/28/94	20	2	Suzie	Tweezer
12/01/94	2	2	Makisupa	Tweezer
12/28/94	9	2	Suzie	Mike's
12/31/94	3	1	Golgi	Antelope
06/14/95	7	1	Gumbo	Mound
06/26/95	10	1	Bathtub	Sloth
10/06/95	14	2	Theme	Tweezer
10/22/95	11	1	Weigh	FEFY
10/29/95	5	1	Split&Melt	Gumbo
11/30/95	17	1	Julius	Bathtub
12/09/95	7	1	Theme	Sloth
12/14/95	3	2	Halley's	Slave
12/29/95	5	1	Fog	Stash
07/12/96	12	2	PurplRain	Slave
08/16/96	20	3	DWD	Life Mars
10/25/96	9	2	TMWSIY	Free
11/03/96	6	1	Sloth	Sample
11/29/96	16	1	Frankstein	CTB
12/28/96	6	1	RunJim	Wolfman's
02/14/97	5	1	RunJim	YEM
02/18/97	3	1	RunJim	Stash
02/22/97	3	1	Theme	Circus
03/18/97	7	1	CGirl	Sample
06/14/97	2	1	DWD	Dirt
06/24/97	6	2	Reba	Twist
07/23/97	14	1	Dirt	Dogs Stole
07/30/96	4	1	*OP1	Wolfman's
08/06/97	4	1	*OP1	Stash
08/17/97	8	3	BuffaloBill	Weigh
➤ 8/17/97	1			

No Dogs Allowed [3]*

No Dogs Allowed [No Dogs]

By Anastasio

07/23/88	[46]	1	Bold	*CL1
10/20/89	85	2	*OP2	WalkAway
10/26/89	3	2	In a Hole	Bowie
➤ 8/17/97	807			

Oblivious Fool [4]

Oblivious Fool [Oblivious]

By Anastasio/Marshall

06/16/97	[906]	1	Wolfman's	*CL1
06/25/97	6	1	*OP1	Dogs Stole
07/10/97	9	1	Lizards	*CL1
07/29/97	7	2	*OP2	Antelope
➤ 8/17/97	13			

Oh Kee Pa [161]

Oh Kee Pa Ceremony [Oh Kee]

By Anastasio

08/17/89	[116]	1	Ya Mar	McGrupp
08/19/89	2	1	*OP1	Suzie
09/09/89	6	1	Foam	Suzie
10/01/89	1	1	Ya Mar	Suzie
10/20/89	6	1	YEM	Reba
10/22/89	2	1	YEM	Suzie
10/26/89	1	1	*OP1	Golgi
10/31/89	2	1	*OP1	Suzie
11/02/89	1	2	*OP2	Golgi
11/09/89	3	2	*OP2	ACDCBag
11/10/89	1	1	Split&Melt	Suzie
11/11/89	1	1a	*OP1	Golgi
11/16/89	1	1	Foam	Suzie
11/30/89	2	1	Ya Mar	ACDCBag
12/07/89	4	2	*OP2	Suzie
12/08/89	1	1	*OP1	Suzie
12/29/89	4	1	Ya Mar	ACDCBag
12/31/89	2	1	YEM	ACDCBag
01/20/90	1	1a	*OP1	Suzie
01/27/90	3	1	Ya Mar	ACDCBag
02/09/90	8	1	Golgi	Suzie
02/10/90	1	1	Dinner	Suzie
02/15/90	1	1	Carolina	Suzie
02/17/90	2	1a	*OP1	Suzie
02/23/90	2	2	Tela	Suzie
03/03/90	5	1	Lizards	ACDCBag
03/07/90	1	2	*OP2	ACDCBag
03/08/90	1	1	Carolina	Suzie
03/09/90	1	1	Reba	ACDCBag
03/17/89	2	2	Bold	ACDCBag
03/28/90	1	1	Uncle Pen	Suzie
04/05/90	2	1	Carolina	Suzie
04/06/90	1	1	Dinner	Suzie
04/08/90	2	1	Brain	Suzie
04/13/90	4	1	La Grange	ACDCBag
04/18/90	1	2	WalkAway	Bold
04/20/90	2	2	Fee	ACDCBag
04/22/90	1	1	Uncle Pen	Suzie
04/26/90	2	2	Bathtub	Suzie
04/28/90	1	1	Adeline	Suzie
05/04/90	3	2	Bathtub	Mike's
05/10/90	2	2	Reba	ACDCBag
05/11/90	1	2	*OP2	ACDCBag
05/13/90	2	1	Bathtub	ACDCBag
05/15/90	1	1	Tweezer	Suzie
05/19/90	1	2	Reba	Suzie
05/23/90	1	1	Brain	Suzie
05/24/90	1	1	YEM	ACDCBag
05/31/90	1	1a	Divided	Suzie
06/01/90	1	1a	Possum	Suzie
06/05/90	1	1	Ya Mar	Suzie
06/09/90	3	2	Foam	Suzie
06/16/90	1	3	Foam	Suzie
09/13/90	1	2	GDS	ACDCBag
09/15/90	2	1	Tube	ACDCBag
09/22/90	4	1	Tela	Suzie
09/28/90	1	1	Bouncing	Suzie
10/01/90	1	1	Tweezer	Suzie
10/05/90	2	1	Tela	Suzie
10/06/90	2	1a	YEM	Suzie
10/08/90	2	1	YEM	Possum
10/31/90	4	2	Fee	Suzie
11/03/90	2	1	Sqirm Coil	Suzie
11/04/90	1	2	RunJim	Suzie
11/08/90	1	2	Tweezer	Dinner
11/17/90	3	1	Eliza	Suzie
11/24/90	1	1	Lizards	Suzie
11/30/90	2	E	Caravan	Suzie
12/07/90	3	2	Sqirm Coil	Suzie
12/28/90	2	2	Manteca	MSO
12/29/90	1	1	Horn	Suzie
02/02/91	3	1	*OP1	Suzie
02/03/91	1	2	Bouncing	Suzie
02/14/91	4	1	Lawn Boy	Golgi
02/15/91	1	2	MSO	ACDCBag
02/26/91	8	1	Reba	ACDCBag
02/27/91	1	2	Lawn Boy	Sloth
03/01/91	2	E	*OPE	Suzie
03/07/91	3	2	*OP2	Landlady
03/13/91	3	2	Terrapin	Golgi
03/15/91	1	1	Bouncing	ACDCBag
03/16/91	1	1	Mockbird	Suzie
03/22/91	3	2	*OP2	Suzie
03/23/91	1	2	Bathtub	ACDCBag
03/28/91	1	1a	Sqirm Coil	Suzie
04/04/91	5	1	*OP1	Suzie
04/05/91	1	E	Fee	Suzie
04/12/91	3	1	Guelah	Suzie
04/16/91	3	1	Mango	ACDCBag
04/18/91	1	2	Reba	Sloth
04/20/91	2	2	Tweezer	Suzie
04/21/91	1	1	MSO	ACDCBag
04/22/91	1	1	Guelah	Suzie
05/04/91	6	1	*OP1	Suzie
05/11/91	3	2	Reba	Suzie
05/12/91	1	2	Sqirm Coil	ACDCBag
05/17/91	2	1	PoorHeart	Suzie
05/18/91	1	2	*OP2	Suzie
05/25/91	1	1a	Llama	ACDCBag
07/11/91	1	1	*OP1	ACDCBag
07/12/91	1	2	Touch Me	Suzie

SONGS PLAYED BY YEAR

(1997 through 8/17/97)

Maze

1992	55
1993	54
1994	44
1995	25
1996	17
1997	11

McGrupp

1990	2
1991	5
1992	3
1993	5
1994	13
1995	5
1996	4
1997	3

Mid-Highway Blues

1996	1
1997	0

Mike's Song

1990	54
1991	49
1992	36
1993	41
1994	27
1995	16
1996	15
1997	6

Mound

1992	20
1993	34
1994	18
1995	12
1996	4
1997	0

My Friend My Friend

1992	20
1993	39
1994	19
1995	12
1996	6
1997	2

My Sweet One

1990	34
1991	72
1992	32
1993	19
1994	14
1995	3
1996	0
1997	0

N20

1995	3
1996	0
1997	0

NICU

1992	12
1993	0
1994	10
1995	9
1996	6
1997	10

Oblivious Fool

1997	4

Oh Kee Pa

1990	53
1991	44
1992	20
1993	11
1994	8
1995	2
1996	1
1997	2

Piper

1997	9

Poor Heart

1991	33
1992	47
1993	57
1994	46
1995	26
1996	21
1997	9

Possum

1990	58
1991	49
1992	35
1993	31
1994	20
1995	21
1996	10
1997	3

Prince Caspian

1995	17
1996	17
1997	15

PYITE

1990	0
1991	0
1992	0
1993	18
1994	12
1995	9
1996	16
1997	11

Reba

1990	36
1991	52
1992	45
1993	29
1994	36
1995	23
1996	19
1997	8

Stories Behind the Songs
(Continued)

originally part of this song. As such, the correct way to label it is simply PYITE, not PYITE > Landlady > PYITE.

Reba: This song underwent slight transformation between 1989 and 1990 when Trey removed a portion that immediately followed the verses, and fashioned it into Don't Get Me Wrong (with lyrics by John Popper). A recent trend, started on 11/30/92 and employed more frequently in 1994 on, has been the omission of the whistle jam at the end during some live performances.

Rift: The original version of this song performed in 1990 had much slower music and closed with an extra couplet, printed in the liner notes of *Rift*. Trey rewrote the song because he said he thought the music didn't do justice to Tom Marshall's lyrics.

Riker's Mailbox: This "song" grew out of the Hoist recording session for Buffalo Bill and consists of a 20-second snippet of Buffalo Bill recorded backwards in some recording studio trickery. The song's only intelligible lyrics, "Olaffub!" are the word "Buffalo" repeated backwards. It's named after the unique cow mailbox of Jonathan Frakes, who played Lieutenant William Riker on Star Trek: The Next Generation and who played trombone on this song on *Hoist*.

Run Like An Antelope: A concert favorite of many. The main lyrical refrain yields from the Dude of Life, who, during his senior year at the Taft School in Watertown, CT played in the band Space Antelope with Trey. There, he coined the phrase, "Set the gearshift for the high gear of your soul, you've got to run like an antelope, out of control!" The lyrics in this song which precede this line comprise Tom Marshall's first lyrical contribution to a Phish song. Once, during a recording session in Trey's basement, Trey urged Tom to step up to the microphone and "say something." Tom looked over at friend Marc Daubert and, drawing on his knowledge of colonial Mexican history, termed him, "Marco Esquandolis." Tom sung that line with Phish on 12/31/93 and 12/31/94.

07/13/91	1	1	Llama	Suzie
07/15/91	2	1a	*OP1	Suzie
07/20/91	3	1	Llama	Suzie
07/23/91	2	1	MSO	Suzie
07/27/91	4	1a	Foam	Suzie
09/27/91	4	2	Dinner	Suzie
09/29/91	2	1a	YEM	Suzie
10/02/91	1	2	Stash	Suzie
10/06/91	4	1	PoorHeart	ACDCBag
10/10/91	1	2	Sparkle	Suzie
10/15/91	4	2	Llama	Suzie
10/17/91	1	2	Curtain	Suzie
10/19/91	2	2	YEM	Terrapin
10/24/91	2	1	*OP1	Suzie
10/28/91	3	1	Tube	Foam
03/06/92	27	1	It's Ice	Divided
03/14/92	5	2	Bouncing	Suzie
03/19/92	2	2	Stash	Suzie
03/21/92	2	2	BurAlive	Suzie
03/24/92	1	2	IDK	Suzie
03/26/92	2	2	BurAlive	Suzie
03/30/92	3	E	Sl Monkey	Suzie
04/09/92	8	2	*OP2	Suzie
04/15/92	3	1	*OP1	Suzie
04/18/92	3	2	Glide	Suzie
04/29/92	7	2	Mound	Llama
05/03/92	4	2	Bouncing	Suzie
05/16/92	10	2	Silent	ACDCBag
07/09/92	11	1a	Glide	Suzie
07/15/92	5	1	Glide	Suzie
07/31/92	13	1a	Bouncing	Suzie
08/02/92	2	1a	Rift	Suzie
11/22/92	18	1	BurAlive	Suzie
12/10/92	14	2	Love You	Suzie
12/29/92	5	1	Tela	Suzie
02/22/93	19	2	YEM	Llama
03/08/93	9	1	Guelah	Llama
03/17/93	6	1	It's Ice	Suzie
03/26/93	7	2	BBJ	Suzie
04/17/93	15	2	Life Boy	Suzie
04/29/93	9	1	Fee	Antelope
07/17/93	13	1	Silent	Bowie
07/18/93	1	2	FEFY	Fee
08/02/93	11	1	Brother	Suzie
08/13/93	8	2	Life Boy	Suzie
12/28/93	11	1	Esther	Suzie
04/04/94	4	2	BeLikeYou	Suzie
04/11/94	6	2	AmGrace	Suzie
04/15/94	3	2	If I Could	Suzie
04/18/94	3	1	Dog Faced	ACDCBag
05/06/94	13	1	DWD	ACDCBag
05/29/94	18	2	McGrupp	Suzie
10/26/94	45	1	Scent	Suzie
11/23/94	17	1	If I Could	Suzie
06/09/95	21	1	Str Design	ACDCBag
11/24/95	56	1	*OP1	ACDCBag
08/12/96	48	1	Taste	Suzie
02/21/97	50	2	Wilson	ACDCBag
03/01/97	6	1	Cities	DWD
➢ 8/17/97	40			

Piper [9]

Piper [Piper]

By Anastasio/Marshall

06/14/97	[905]	2	Twist	Saw It
06/19/97	2	2	Wading	Jesus
06/24/97	4	2	Twist	Wading
06/25/97	1	2	DWD	DWD
07/03/97	5	1	*OP1	My Soul
07/05/97	1	1a	Twist	Harry
07/21/97	5	1	Dogs Stole	Dirt
07/30/97	6	1	Weigh	CTB
08/11/97	8	2	Timber Ho	Vultures
➢ 8/17/97	5			

Poor Heart [239]*

Poor Heart [PoorHeart]

By Gordon

04/22/91	[305]	1	Reba	Llama
04/26/91	2	1	Fluffhead	Foam
05/02/91	2	2	Chalkdust	Divided
05/10/91	4	2	Wilson	Foam
05/11/91	1	2	YEM	Reba
05/12/91	1	2	Bathtub	Curtain
05/17/91	2	1	Reba	Oh Kee
07/18/91	8	2	Reba	Split&Melt
07/21/91	3	1	Guelah	Split&Melt
07/25/91	3	2	Llama	Jesus
07/27/91	2	1a	Cavern	Stash
08/03/91	1	1	Sqirm Coil	Sloth
09/25/91	1	1	Brother	Foam
09/26/91	1	E	Memories	Adeline
09/28/91	2	2	Lizards	Mike's
09/29/91	1	1a	It's Ice	Landlady
10/02/91	1	1	Sqirm Coil	Cavern
10/04/91	2	1	Reba	Cavern
10/06/91	2	1	Bouncing	Oh Kee
10/10/91	1	2	Reba	Cavern
10/11/91	1	2	Sloth	Magilla
10/15/91	3	2	RunJim	Llama
10/17/91	1	1	Cavern	Stash
10/19/91	2	2	Horn	YEM
10/24/91	2	1	Foam	Stash
10/28/91	3	1	Cavern	Reba
11/01/91	3	2	Cavern	TweezRep
11/08/91	4	1	Stash	Divided
11/09/91	1	2	Fluffhead	It's Ice
11/15/91	5	2	Bathtub	Mike's
11/21/91	4	1	Bouncing	Guelah
11/23/91	2	2	Horn	Tweezer
12/04/91	3	1	Cavern	Brother
03/06/92	5	2	My Friend	Stash
03/13/92	4	1	Split&Melt	Guelah
03/17/92	2	2	Sloth	Tweezer
03/21/92	3	2	My Friend	All Things
03/24/92	1	1	Stash	Foam
03/26/92	2	2	Suzie	Brother
04/03/92	6	1	Landlady	Stash
04/05/92	2	1	Wilson	Stash
04/07/92	2	2	*OP2	All Things
04/12/92	2	1	Suzie	Guelah
04/16/92	3	2	Horn	Terrapin
04/18/92	2	1	Guelah	Split&Melt
04/22/92	3	2	YEM	Rosie
04/23/92	1	2	Landlady	Mike's
04/25/92	2	E	Terrapin	*CLE
05/01/92	3	1	My Friend	Landlady
05/05/92	3	2	Silent	Llama
05/07/92	2	1	Suzie	BurAlive
05/09/92	2	E	*OPE	TweezRep
05/12/92	2	2	Terrapin	Llama
05/14/92	1	1	Reba	My Friend
05/16/92	2	2	Rosie	TweezRep
05/17/92	1	1	Mango	Chalkdust
05/18/92	1	1	Foam	Horn
07/14/92	13	1	IDK	Cavern
07/16/92	2	1	*OP1	It's Ice
07/19/92	3	1a	*OP1	Maze
07/22/92	2	1a	Reba	Bouncing
08/01/92	8	1a	Foam	Stash
08/14/92	3	1a	*OP1	Stash
08/17/92	2	1	BurAlive	Landlady
08/24/92	4	1a	BurAlive	All Things
08/28/92	3	1a	*OP1	Foam
11/19/92	4	2	BBJ	FEFY
11/21/92	2	1	Glide	It's Ice
11/23/92	2	2	*OP2	Stash
11/25/92	1	1	BurAlive	Landlady
11/27/92	1	2	Axilla	Possum
11/30/92	2	1	Bouncing	Stash
12/02/92	2	1	FEFY	Stash
12/04/92	2	1	Foam	Stash
12/05/92	1	2	*OP2	Tweezer
12/07/92	2	1	Axilla	Maze
12/10/92	2	1	Fee	Split&Melt
12/12/92	2	1	Split&Melt	All Things
12/28/92	2	2	*OP2	Split&Melt
12/31/92	3	1	BurAlive	Maze
02/03/93	1	1	My Friend	Guelah
02/05/93	2	1	IDK	Reba
02/07/93	2	1	BurAlive	It's Ice
02/09/93	1	1	Bouncing	My Friend
02/11/93	2	1	BurAlive	Stash
02/12/93	1	2	Reba	BBJ
02/13/93	1	1	Bouncing	It's Ice
02/15/93	1	2	Wedge	BBJ
02/18/93	2	1	Guelah	Tweezer
02/19/93	1	1	My Friend	Bowie
02/22/93	3	1	Guelah	Maze
02/23/93	1	E	Adeline	*CLE
02/25/93	1	1	BurAlive	Cavern
02/27/93	2	2	Stash	Sample
03/02/93	1	1	BurAlive	Stash
03/05/93	2	1	BurAlive	Cavern
03/06/93	1	E	Adeline	TweezRep
03/08/93	1	2	*OP2	Cavern
03/12/93	2	1	BurAlive	Cavern
03/16/93	3	1	BurAlive	It's Ice
03/18/93	2	2	My Friend	Split&Melt
03/21/93	2	1	Split&Melt	PYITE
03/24/93	2	1	Fee	Maze
03/27/93	3	2	Rosie	Golgi
03/30/93	2	1	BurAlive	All Things
04/01/93	2	2	Tweezer	BBJ
04/02/93	1	1	BurAlive	Foam
04/05/93	2	2	Axilla	Caravan
04/12/93	3	1	Bouncing	Stash
04/14/93	2	1	BurAlive	Maze
04/18/93	3	2	*OP2	Tweezer
04/21/93	2	1	BurAlive	Foam
04/24/93	3	1	Guelah	Stash
04/27/93	2	1	BurAlive	Foam
04/30/93	2	1	Bouncing	Stash
05/02/93	2	1	Silent	Maze
05/05/93	2	2	My Friend	Weigh
05/07/93	2	1	BurAlive	Split&Melt
05/30/93	3	1a	Guelah	Foam
07/16/93	2	2	YEM	PurplRain
07/18/93	2	2	Also Sprac	Antelope
07/22/93	2	1	Ya Mar	Stash
07/23/93	1	2	Also Sprac	Antelope
07/28/93	4	1	Silent	Cavern
07/30/93	2	2	Silent	Fluffhead
08/02/93	2	1	Guelah	Brother
08/03/93	1	E	*OPE	FrBir
08/06/93	1	1	Split&Melt	Curtain
08/07/93	1	1	Bouncing	Stash
08/12/93	4	1	Silent	Sqirm Coil
08/14/93	2	1	Esther	Cavern
08/16/93	2	2	My Friend	BBJ
08/20/93	2	1	Harpua	Maze
08/21/93	1	1	BurAlive	Foam
08/24/93	1	E	Halley's	Adeline
12/28/93	4	1	Peaches	Split&Melt
12/31/93	3	2	Halley's	It's Ice
04/06/94	3	1	Guelah	Stash
04/11/94	4	1	Caravan	Foam
04/13/94	1	1	BurAlive	Stash
04/16/94	3	2	Sample	Tweezer
04/18/94	2	1	Glide	Julius
04/20/94	1	2	*OP2	Antelope
04/23/94	3	1	Peaches	Stash
04/25/94	2	1	Tela	Split&Melt
04/30/94	3	1	Stash	Sample
05/06/94	4	1	ACDCBag	My Friend
05/10/94	3	1	BurAlive	Sample
05/16/94	4	1	BurAlive	Sample
05/19/94	2	1	My Friend	Stash
05/26/94	6	1	BurAlive	Cavern
05/28/94	2	E	*OPE	*CLE
06/13/94	5	1	BurAlive	Sample
06/17/94	3	2	Sample	Mike's
06/21/94	3	2	Fire	DWD
06/23/94	2	1	BurAlive	Split&Melt
06/24/94	1	2	Dog Faced	Cavern
06/29/94	3	2	Landlady	Tweezer
06/30/94	1	E	Sl Monkey	*CLE
07/03/94	3	1	My Friend	DWD
07/06/94	2	2	Landlady	Tweezer
07/09/94	2	2	Fluffhead	Tweezer
07/13/94	2	1	BurAlive	Sample
10/07/94	4	1	Glide	Divided
10/09/94	2	E	Sl Monkey	*CLE
10/12/94	2	1	Sloth	Split&Melt
10/16/94	4	2	Landlady	Julius
10/18/94	1	1	IDK	Stash
10/23/94	4	1	Simple	Stash
10/27/94	3	1	Silent	Cavern
10/31/94	3	3	Sl Monkey	Antelope
11/03/94	2	2	Simple	Julius
11/14/94	4	2	Slave	Julius
11/18/94	3	2	Life Boy	Tweezer
11/22/94	3	1	BurAlive	Horn
11/26/94	3	1	Silent	Cavern
11/30/94	2	1	Frankstein	My Friend
12/02/94	2	1	*OP1	Also Sprac
12/06/94	3	2	Also Sprac	Mike's
12/09/94	3	2	Wilson	Tweezer
12/10/94	1	2	DoInRoad	Slave
12/30/94	3	2	Sample	Tweezer
06/08/95	4	2	Life Boy	Julius
06/14/95	4	2	Also Sprac	Tweezer
06/19/95	4	1	Theme	ACDCBag
06/26/95	6	2	Free	YEM
06/28/95	1	2	Sample	Tweezer
07/03/95	5	1	My Friend	Antelope
09/28/95	2	2	Theme	Wanna Go
10/02/95	3	1	*OP1	Wolfman's
10/06/95	3	2	*OP2	Maze
10/15/95	6	1	BurAlive	Slave
10/19/95	2	2	Frankstein	Mike's
10/22/95	3	1	It's Ice	Sample
10/27/95	3	2	Dog Faced	Simple
10/29/95	2	1	BurAlive	Julius
11/11/95	4	1	DayinLife	Weekpaug
11/15/95	3	1	*OP1	ACDCBag
11/19/95	3	1	Maze	Rift
11/22/95	2	E	*OPE	Frankstein
11/25/95	2	1	*OP1	DayinLife
11/25/95	0	2	HelloBaby	*CL2
11/29/95	2	2	Fog	I'm Blue
12/01/95	2	1	Theme	Wolfman's
12/05/95	3	2	*OP2	Bathtub
12/08/95	2	1	Sample	Simple
12/17/95	7	1	My Friend	DayinLife
12/29/95	2	1	My Friend	DWD
06/06/96	4	1	Split&Melt	RunJim
07/06/96	3	1a	Reba	DayinLife
07/09/96	2	1a	Theme	Taste
07/13/96	4	1a	Reba	Split&Melt
07/22/96	6	1a	Sample	Cavern
07/25/96	3	1a	*OP1	PYITE
08/02/96	1	1	Guelah	Foam
08/05/96	2	1	Wilson	Guelah
08/10/96	3	1	My Friend	ACDCBag
08/14/96	3	1	Fee	Reba

10/16/96	3	1	BurAlive	Billy
10/23/96	6	1	PYITE	ACDCBag
10/29/96	4	1	Billy	Bowie
11/06/96	4	1	Train Song	PYITE
11/09/96	3	1	BurAlive	Sloth
11/16/96	5	1	*OP1	DWD
11/18/96	1	1	Timber Ho	Taste
11/24/96	4	1	*OP1	ACDCBag
12/01/96	4	1	Peaches	Cavern
12/06/96	3	1	Peaches	Also Sprac
12/29/96	2	1	*OP1	Caravan
02/13/97	3	1	Waste	CharZero
02/26/97	10	1	BurAlive	Ha Ha Ha
06/16/97	7	E	Cities	*CLE
06/21/97	3	1a	Also Sprac	Taste
06/27/97	4	1a	Dogs Stole	Taste
07/05/97	5	1a	Love You	CharZero
07/09/97	2	2	Ghost	*CL2
07/26/97	7	1	Dogs Stole	Stash
08/13/97	11	1	Amarina	Water
➢ 8/17/97	3			

Possum [287]*

Oh Possum [Possum]

By Holdsworth, with lyrics reworked by Anastasio

10/30/85	[4]	1a	Dog Log	Slave
04/15/86	3	1a	Dog Log	YEM
03/06/87	4	2	TellMe	FWorld
03/11/87	1	1a	Lushngton	Sally
04/24/87	2	1a	ACDCBag	Fluffhead
05/11/87	2	1a	YEM	Slave
08/10/87	2	1	ACDCBag	Fluffhead
08/29/87	3	2	McGrupp	Harry
09/12/87	2	1	ACDCBag	YEM
09/27/87	1	1	A-Train	Phase
10/14/87	1	1	Fluffhead	*CL1
11/19/87	2	2	Suzie	Divided
01/30/88	1	1	ACDCBag	Jesus
03/12/88	4	1a	Sloth	Antelope
03/21/88	1	1a	ACDCBag	Dinner
03/31/88	1	1	ACDCBag	Fluffhead
05/15/88	3	1a	ACDCBag	Icculus
05/23/88	1	1a	Peaches	GTBT
06/18/88	3	1	FunkBitch	Golgi
07/23/88	5	1	ACDCBag	WalkAway
09/08/88	6	2	*OP2	YEM
09/24/88	2	2	WalkAway	Fee
10/12/88	1	2	ACDCBag	GTBT
10/29/88	1	3	YEM	*CL3
11/03/88	1	1	Fluffhead	Fee
11/05/88	1	1	YEM	A-Train
11/11/88	1	1	Foam	Forbin's
01/26/89	2	1a	Sloth	Contact
02/07/89	4	1	Sloth	Mike's
02/18/89	2	1a	WalkAway	GTBT
03/03/89	2	2	Fee	WalkAway
03/04/89	1	2	*OP2	Fluffhead
04/14/89	8	1	Sloth	*CL1
04/20/89	3	1	Sloth	McGrupp
04/30/89	5	E	*OP1	*CL2
05/06/89	4	1	Sloth	Bold
05/09/89	3	1	Sloth	Divided
05/13/89	3	1	Fluffhead	Foam
05/20/89	4	1	IDK	*CL1
05/26/89	2	3	Curtis	Jam
05/28/89	2	2	A-Train	Contact
06/23/89	5	2	Split&Melt	Bowie
06/30/89	2	1	McGrupp	Donna
08/12/89	3	1a	YEM	Icculus
08/17/89	2	3	PYITE	Halley's
08/26/89	4	1	YEM	*CL1
09/09/89	4	2	WalkAway	*CL2
10/01/89	1	2	Fluffhead	YEM
10/06/89	1	1a	Harry	HwayHell
10/07/89	1	2	Dinner	Lizards
10/14/89	3	2	HwayHell	Harpua
10/22/89	3	2	Fee	*CL2
10/26/89	1	2	Fluffhead	PYITE
10/31/89	2	1	Bathtub	*CL1
11/10/89	5	2	Brain	Harpua
11/30/89	4	2	Reba	Forbin's
12/07/89	4	2	Lawn Boy	Undone
12/08/89	1	2	YEM	Lawn Boy
12/15/89	2	1a	IDK	Divided
12/16/89	1	E	*OPE	*CLE
02/10/90	16	1	Bouncing	Carolina
02/23/90	5	1	YEM	Foam
02/24/90	1	1	Esther	IDK
02/25/90	1	1	Rift	*CL1
03/01/90	1	1	YEM	*CL1
03/03/90	2	1	YEM	*CL1
03/07/90	1	1	Reba	Esther
03/08/90	1	1	YEM	Ya Mar
03/09/90	1	1	Sloth	Donna
03/28/90	3	1	*OP1	Ya Mar
04/04/90	1	1	A-Train	Foam
04/05/90	1	1	*OP1	Ya Mar
04/07/90	2	1	Bathtub	Tweezer
04/08/90	1	1	Uncle Pen	*CL1
04/12/90	3	1	Uncle Pen	YEM
04/13/90	1	2	Caravan	HwayHell
04/18/90	1	1	A-Train	*CL1
04/20/90	2	1	Mockbird	*CL1
04/22/90	2	1	Suzie	IDK
04/26/90	2	1	*OP1	Foam
04/28/90	1	1	Bouncing	YEM
04/29/90	1	1a	Carolina	Ya Mar
05/04/90	2	1	Bouncing	Reba
05/06/90	1	1	*OP1	Bouncing
05/10/90	1	1	Suzie	*CL1
05/11/90	1	1	Reba	Bouncing
05/13/90	2	2	Adeline	*CL2
05/15/90	3	1	*OP1	Tela
05/19/90	1	2	*OP2	Reba
05/23/90	1	1	Bouncing	Adeline
05/24/90	1	2	Dinner	IDK
05/31/90	1	1a	*OP1	YEM
06/01/90	1	1a	Slave	Oh Kee
06/05/90	1	1	Lawn Boy	*CL1
06/07/90	1	1	Donna	Fee
06/08/90	1	1	*OP1	MSO
06/09/90	1	1	*OP1	Lawn Boy
06/16/90	1	1	Lawn Boy	*CL1
09/13/90	1	1	Bouncing	*CL1
09/15/90	2	2	Lawn Boy	*CL2
09/22/90	4	2	Lawn Boy	*CL2
10/01/90	2	1	*OP1	Sqirm Coil
10/04/90	1	1	Esther	Sqirm Coil
10/05/90	1	2	Fee	*CL2
10/06/90	1	1a	Esther	Brain
10/08/90	2	1	Oh Kee	*CL1
10/12/90	1	2	*OP2	Fee
10/30/90	2	1	Sqirm Coil	*CL1
10/31/90	1	1	BurAlive	Sqirm Coil
11/02/90	1	1	BurAlive	*CL1
11/03/90	1	2	Reba	Love You
11/08/90	2	1	Landlady	Lizards
11/10/90	1	2	Bike	*CL2
11/16/90	1	2	IDK	*CL2
11/17/90	1	2	Love You	Lawn Boy
11/24/90	1	1	BurAlive	Foam
11/30/90	2	1	Llama	*CL1
12/28/90	5	2	Landlady	Sqirm Coil
12/31/90	2	1	BurAlive	*CL1
02/07/91	4	1	Bouncing	Sqirm Coil
02/14/91	3	2	Landlady	*CL2
02/16/91	2	E2	*OPE2	*CL2
02/26/91	7	2	Destiny	Lizards
02/27/91	1	2	Love You	*CL2
03/01/91	2	2	Sloth	Love You
03/06/91	2	1	Sqirm Coil	Cavern
03/07/91	1	2	Reba	IDK
03/15/91	4	2	BurAlive	Horn
03/16/91	1	E	Manteca	*CLE
03/23/91	4	1	Mockbird	Rocky Top
04/04/91	6	E	Mockbird	Carolina
04/06/91	2	1	Antelope	Jesus
04/11/91	1	E	Fee	*CLE
04/15/91	3	2	Lizards	Magilla
04/18/91	2	2	Sqirm Coil	*CL2
04/21/91	3	2	*OP2	Fee
04/26/91	3	1	Sloth	Fluffhead
04/27/91	1	2	Curtain	TMWSIY
05/02/91	1	2	BurAlive	*CL2
05/04/91	2	2	Rocky Top	*CL2
05/10/91	2	1	Lizards	Stash
05/17/91	4	2	*OP2	Guelah
05/18/91	1	1	Cavern	*CL1
05/25/91	1	E	*OPE	*CLE
07/14/91	4	1	IDK	*CL1
07/18/91	2	2	IDK	*CL2
07/20/91	2	E	*OPE	*CLE
07/24/91	3	2	*OP2	Guelah
07/27/91	3	1a	TMWSIY	IDK
08/03/91	1	3	BurAlive	*CL3
09/25/91	1	1	Reba	*CL1
09/27/91	2	2	*OP2	Tela
10/02/91	3	E	*OPE	IDK
10/03/91	1	1	Cavern	*CL1
10/06/91	3	E	Adeline	Llama
10/11/91	2	2	Magilla	*CL2
10/17/91	4	2	Love You	*CL2
10/24/91	4	2	Terrapin	*CL2
10/27/91	2	E	Glide	*CLE
11/02/91	5	1	Mockbird	*CL1
11/07/91	2	E	Glide	*CLE
11/09/91	2	E	Glide	*CLE
11/13/91	3	2	Llama	*CL2
11/15/91	2	2	Bouncing	*CL2
11/20/91	3	1	BurAlive	Forbin's
11/22/91	2	1	*OP1	Cavern
12/05/91	5	1	Bouncing	*CL1
12/06/91	1	2	WhipPost	*CL2
12/31/91	2	1	*OP1	Foam
03/06/92	1	2	NICU	*CL2
03/13/92	4	2	Love You	*CL2
03/14/92	1	2	Rosie	*CL2
03/17/92	1	1	BurAlive	Cavern
03/20/92	2	2	Terrapin	*CL2
03/26/92	4	2	Rosie	*CL2
03/31/92	4	2	Love You	*CL2
04/03/92	2	2	Sloth	Weigh
04/05/92	2	1	It's Ice	Adeline
04/07/92	2	1	BurAlive	It's Ice
04/13/92	3	2	Love You	*CL2
04/16/92	2	1	BurAlive	It's Ice
04/18/92	2	1	Esther	It's Ice
04/21/92	2	1	Guelah	It's Ice
04/23/92	2	1	IDK	*CL1
04/29/92	3	2	Landlady	Mound
05/01/92	2	1	IDK	*CL1
05/03/92	2	1	Landlady	It's Ice
05/07/92	3	1	Guelah	*CL1
05/10/92	3	1a	YEM	*CL1
05/12/92	1	1	Sloth	It's Ice
05/14/92	1	2	Rosie	*CL2
05/17/92	3	2	Curtain	Guelah
06/30/92	7	1a	Guelah	Adeline
07/12/92	6	1a	Glide	*CL1
07/15/92	2	E	*OPE	*CLE
07/21/92	5	1a	All Things	It's Ice
07/30/92	7	1a	IDK	*CL1
11/21/92	20	1	Mockbird	*CL1
11/27/92	4	2	PoorHeart	Glide
12/02/92	4	2	Wilson	Mound
12/04/92	2	2	Esther	It's Ice
12/06/92	2	E	*OPE	*CLE
12/11/92	4	2	Faht	*CL2
12/30/92	5	2	TMWSIY	BBJ
02/03/93	2	2	BBJ	*CL2
02/06/93	3	2	BurAlive	*CL2
02/10/93	3	2	Rosie	*CL2
02/17/93	5	1	BurAlive	Weigh
02/20/93	3	1	Sloth	Weigh
02/23/93	3	2	Terrapin	*CL2
03/05/93	6	1	IDK	*CL1
03/12/93	4	1	Cavern	Guelah
03/21/93	7	1	Lawn Boy	*CL1
03/25/93	3	1	It's Ice	Bouncing
03/28/93	3	2	Love You	*CL2
04/01/93	3	2	Curtain	Fee
04/09/93	4	2	Love You	*CL2
04/13/93	3	1	Sparkle	Forbin's
04/18/93	4	2	Silent	Mound
04/21/93	2	2	*OP2	Mound
04/25/93	4	2	Landlady	Bouncing
04/30/93	3	1	All Things	*CL1
05/03/93	3	1	Mockbird	Lawn Boy
05/06/93	2	1	Fluffhead	Lawn Boy
05/30/93	4	E	*OPE	*CLE
07/15/93	1	2	Life Boy	Faht
07/22/93	5	2	Contact	Paul&Silas
07/29/93	6	1	Mockbird	*CL1
08/08/93	7	2	Fluffhead	BBJ
08/12/93	3	2	Golgi	*CL2
08/16/93	4	1	Axil	Horn
08/21/93	3	2	*OP2	Horn
08/25/93	2	2	BurAlive	Mound
12/28/93	3	1	Fee	*CL1
12/31/93	3	2	Fee	Lawn Boy
04/04/94	1	1	It's Ice	*CL1
04/11/94	6	E	*OPE	*CLE
04/21/94	8	2	BBJ	AmGrace
04/30/94	7	2	McGrupp	PurplRain
05/12/94	8	2	Life Boy	Love You
05/23/94	9	2	YEM	*CL2
05/27/94	3	2	Mike's	*CL2
06/10/94	4	2	Sparkle	BeLikeYou
06/14/94	3	2	Bike	*CL2
07/01/94	13	2	TMWSIY	Terrapin
07/13/94	8	2	*OP2	Cavern
10/09/94	6	2	Contact	*CL2
10/16/94	6	1	Axil	*CL1
10/25/94	6	2	Brain	*CL2
11/02/94	6	2	Axilla 2	Lizards
11/18/94	8	2	Contact	*CL2
11/26/94	6	1	My Friend	Guyute
12/04/94	6	1	Adeline	*CL1
12/08/94	3	2	*OP2	My Mind
12/29/94	4	1	IDK	*CL1
06/07/95	4	1	*OP1	Weigh
06/14/95	5	1	Cavern	All Things
06/19/95	4	2	AArmy	*CL2
06/26/95	6	1	Tela	*CL1
06/30/95	3	2	Also Sprac	Ha Ha Ha
07/03/95	3	2	DayinLife	Sqirm Coil
09/27/95	1	E	*OPE	*CLE
10/07/95	8	1	Mound	Mango
10/11/95	2	2	*OP2	Bathtub
10/19/95	5	2	Suspicious	*CL2
10/22/95	3	2	Golgi	Catapult
10/27/95	3	2	Bouncing	*CL2
10/29/95	2	2	Shaggy	Life Boy
11/12/95	5	2	Rosie	TweezRep
11/16/95	3	2	AmGrace	*CL2
11/29/95	8	2	Simple	YEM
12/02/95	3	1	Bouncing	*CL1
12/07/95	3	1	Bouncing	HelloBaby
12/15/95	6	1	Free	*CL1
12/28/95	3	1	FEFY	*CL1
07/15/96	15	1	Guyute	IDK
08/02/96	9	1	HelloBaby	*CL1
08/07/96	4	2	Mockbird	Life Mars
08/12/96	2	1	Golgi	*CL1
08/17/96	4	3	DayinLife	TweezRep
10/21/96	5	1	Waste	*CL1
10/27/96	5	E	*OPE	Carolina
11/03/96	4	2	Life Mars	TweezRep
11/30/96	17	E	*OPE	*CLE
12/30/96	7	E	*OPE	*CLE
03/01/97	14	1	HelloBaby	*CL1
07/23/97	24	1	Billy	*CL1
07/29/97	3	E	*OPE	*CLE
➢ 8/17/97	13			

Prep School Hippie [3]*

Prep School Hippie [PrepHipp]

Author Unknown

10/30/85	[4]	1a	Alumni	Skip
04/15/86	3	1a	Reagan	Quinn
12/06/86	3	1a	Sally	Jam
➢ 8/17/97	931			

Prince Caspian [49]*

Prince Caspian [Caspian]

By Anastasio/Marshall

06/08/95	[740]	1	Reba	Chalkdust
06/10/95	2	1	Llama	It's Ice
06/20/95	7	2	Chalkdust	Uncle Pen
06/23/95	2	1	Chalkdust	Reba
07/01/95	7	1	It's Ice	Split&Melt
10/08/95	12	1	I'm Blue	Uncle Pen
10/13/95	2	1	I'm Blue	Split&Melt
10/17/95	3	2	Mound	Fog
10/24/95	5	1	AArmy	Split&Melt
10/28/95	3	1	AArmy	Antelope
11/09/95	3	1	Divided	PYITE
11/15/95	5	1	Rift	Sparkle
11/21/95	4	1	Chalkdust	Divided
12/02/95	8	1	*OP1	RunJim
12/08/95	4	1	AArmy	GTBT
12/11/95	2	1	Stash	Reba
12/30/95	8	1	*OP1	Also Sprac
07/12/96	11	2	It's Ice	Mike's
07/21/96	6	2	Simpl	Suzie
08/02/96	5	2	Fluffhead	Horse
08/06/96	3	2	Tweezer	DayinLife
08/12/96	3	2	Simpl	McGrupp
10/16/96	5	2	Steep	Antelope
10/19/96	3	1	DWD	Frankstein
10/25/96	4	2	Tube	Timber Ho
10/27/96	2	2	Rift	Ya Mar
10/31/96	2	1	YEM	Reba
11/08/96	5	1	DWD	Reba
11/13/96	3	2	Suzie	YEM
11/15/96	2	1	PYITE	Ginseng
11/22/96	4	2	DWD	Billy
11/30/96	5	1	Uncle Pen	Chalkdust
12/04/96	3	2	Mike's	Sparkle
12/31/96	5	2	Harry	CharZero
02/13/97	1	E	*OPE	Johnny B.
02/17/97	3	2	Suzie	*CL2
02/21/97	3	2	Waste	*CL2
02/25/97	3	2	DWD	La Grange
02/28/97	2	2	Drowned	Frankstein
03/18/97	3	2	Drowned	Bowie
06/14/97	2	1	Free	*CL1
06/19/97	2	2	Jesus	*CL2
06/24/97	4	1	Free	Rocky Top
07/05/97	7	1a	Theme	Twist
07/09/97	2	1	PYITE	Ginseng
07/30/97	9	2	Uncle Pen	*CL2
08/06/97	4	2	Ghost	CTB
08/08/97	1	2	Lovin Cup	Chalkdust
08/17/97	7	3	Scent	*CL3
➢ 8/17/97	0			

Punch You In The Eye [71]*

Punch You In The Eye [PYITE]

By Anastasio

08/17/89	[116]	3	Bold	Possum
08/19/89	2	1	ACDCBag	Rocky Top
09/09/89	6	1	Bathtub	Wilson
10/26/89	10	2	Possum	In a Hole
11/03/89	4	1	YEM	Reba
11/09/89	2	2	McGrupp	Lizards
02/05/93	367	1	Sparkle	IDK
02/09/93	3	2	*OP2	Mike's
02/18/93	7	2	Stash	Mike's
02/21/93	3	1	BurAlive	Uncle Pen

02/23/93	2	2	Lizards	All Things
02/27/93	3	1	Sparkle	Lawn Boy
03/06/93	4	1	Mound	Bouncing
03/09/93	2	1	Glide	IDK
03/14/93	3	1	Reba	RunJim
03/21/93	5	1	PoorHeart	Lawn Boy
03/26/93	4	1	Fee	All Things
03/31/93	4	1	Mound	Sample
04/05/93	4	2	Caravan	Tweezer
04/21/93	10	1	Rift	IDK
05/02/93	9	2	Llama	YEM
07/23/93	14	1	Silent	RunJim
08/08/93	12	1	Silent	FEFY
12/30/93	17	2	Silent	McGrupp
04/08/94	5	1	IDK	Horse
04/22/94	12	1	Uncle Pen	Sample
04/30/94	6	1	Sample	Rift
05/14/94	10	2	TMWSIY	FEFY
05/23/94	7	2	Sparkle	YEM
05/27/94	3	1	If I Could	Harry
06/17/94	9	1	If I Could	Bathtub
06/23/94	5	1	Silent	Julius
07/05/94	9	2	Also Sprac	Sparkle
07/14/94	6	1	Bouncing	Stash
10/14/94	9	1	Silent	Bathtub
12/08/94	37	1	Scent	Simple
06/19/95	17	1	Tela	Reba
06/28/95	7	1	Reba	Stash
10/19/95	21	1	Horn	Esther
10/29/95	8	1	Julius	CTB
11/09/95	2	1	Caspian	Simple
11/18/95	7	1	Lawn Boy	Slave
12/04/95	11	1	Divided	Stash
12/12/95	6	1	Life Boy	Horse
12/31/95	8	1	*OP1	Sloth
07/15/96	12	1	My Friend	FEFY
07/25/96	8	1a	PoorHeart	Sample
08/02/96	1	E	*OPE	*CLE
08/07/96	4	1	*OP1	Sparkle
08/13/96	3	1	Old Home	Llama
08/17/96	3	1	Old Home	Reba
10/17/96	2	1	Talk	CharZero
10/23/96	5	1	*OP1	PoorHeart
10/27/96	3	1	RunJim	ACDCBag
11/06/96	3	1	PoorHeart	Billy
11/15/96	7	1	CharZero	Caspian
11/23/96	5	1	Divided	Highway
11/30/96	4	1	RunJim	All Things
12/04/96	3	2	Sparkle	Life Mars
12/31/96	5	1	Peaches	CTB
02/13/97	1	2	My Soul	Slave
02/18/97	4	1	Cavern	RunJim
02/25/97	5	1	Sample	Free
03/02/97	4	2	Steep	Waste
03/18/97	1	1	Sample	My Soul
06/19/97	4	1	Theme	Water
07/09/97	13	1	*OP1	Caspian
07/23/97	5	2	*OP2	Ghost
07/30/97	4	2	*OP2	Free
08/09/97	6	1	Theme	Ghost
08/16/97	5	1	Theme	Ghost
➤ 8/17/97	**1**			

Reba [259]*

Reba [Reba]

By Anastasio

10/01/89	[125]	2	MSO	Dinner
10/20/89	6	1	Oh Kee	Divided
10/22/89	2	2	Harry	Golgi
10/26/89	1	2	ACDCBag	WalkAway
10/31/89	2	2	Wilson	Fobrn
11/02/89	1	1	Curtain	Split&Melt
11/03/89	1	1	PYITE	Golgi
11/16/89	5	1	MSO	YEM
11/30/89	2	2	*OP2	Possum
12/08/89	5	1	Ya Mar	McGrupp
01/20/90	7	1a	Bouncing	Tela
01/27/90	3	1	Wilson	FunkBitch
02/09/90	8	2	Ya Mar	Wilson
02/23/90	6	2	Golgi	Bathtub
02/25/90	2	2	Jam	McGrupp
03/03/90	3	1	ACDCBag	Rocky Top
03/07/90	1	1	*OP1	Possum
03/09/90	2	1	Antelope	Oh Kee
04/05/90	3	2	*OP2	Uncle Pen
04/06/90	1	2	Caravan	IDK
04/13/90	6	1	ACDCBag	Fire
04/18/90	1	2	FunkBitch	WalkAway
04/25/90	5	2	Adeline	Ya Mar
04/28/90	2	2	IDK	MSO
05/04/90	3	1	Possum	MSO
05/06/90	1	1	Uncle Pen	Tweezer
05/10/90	1	2	Caravan	Oh Kee
05/11/90	1	1	Possum	HwayHell
05/13/90	2	2	MSO	FunkBitch
05/19/90	2	2	Possum	Oh Kee
05/23/90	1	2	Sqirm Coil	Tweezer
05/24/90	1	1	Donna	YEM
06/07/90	4	1	Fee	YEM
06/09/90	2	1	Lawn Boy	Dinner
06/16/90	1	1	Wilson	Horn
09/13/90	1	2	Sparks	IDCA
09/14/90	1	1	Landlady	Paul&Silas
09/16/90	2	1a	Landlady	Ya Mar
10/08/90	10	1	Cavern	MSO
10/30/90	3	2	Foam	Llama
10/31/90	1	2	Landlady	RunJim
11/03/90	2	2	Uncle Pen	Possum
11/10/90	3	1	*OP1	Landlady
11/26/90	4	1	Sloth	BurAlive
12/03/90	3	1	Ya Mar	Divided
12/28/90	3	1	Horn	Llama
02/01/91	3	2	*OP2	Landlady
02/03/91	2	1	Destiny	Chalkdust
02/08/91	2	1	ACDCBag	BurAlive
02/09/91	1	1	Tweezer	Chalkdust
02/14/91	1	1	BurAlive	Destiny
02/16/91	2	2	Chalkdust	BurAlive
02/21/91	3	1	*OP1	Dinner
02/26/91	4	1	MSO	Oh Kee
02/28/91	2	2	Sqirm Coil	Llama
03/01/91	1	2	Landlady	Llama
03/07/91	3	2	RunJim	Possum
03/13/91	3	2	Sloth	Tweezer
03/16/91	2	1	Golgi	Landlady
03/22/91	3	1	Cavern	Fire
04/05/91	8	1	Magilla	Chalkdust
04/11/91	2	2	MSO	Llama
04/12/91	1	2	BurAlive	MSO
04/16/91	3	2	MSO	Chalkdust
04/18/91	1	2	Llama	Oh Kee
04/20/91	2	1	RunJim	Llama
04/22/91	1	1	Sloth	PoorHeart
04/27/91	3	1	MSO	Llama
05/04/91	3	1	Cavern	MSO
05/11/91	3	2	PoorHeart	Oh Kee
05/17/91	3	1	Jam	PoorHeart
05/25/91	2	1a	Foam	Dinner
07/12/91	2	1	Flat Fee	Landlady
07/14/91	2	1	*OP1	Llama
07/18/91	2	2	Llama	PoorHeart
07/20/91	2	2	BurAlive	Caravan
07/23/91	2	2	Llama	Cavern
07/26/91	3	1	Chalkdust	MSO
08/03/91	2	1	Curtain	Chalkdust
09/25/91	1	1	Caravan	Possum
09/27/91	2	1	Cavern	BurAlive
10/02/91	3	1	Cavern	Brother
10/04/91	2	1	Chalkdust	PoorHeart
10/10/91	3	2	Brother	PoorHeart
10/13/91	3	1	Wilson	Landlady
10/15/91	1	1	Sparkle	Landlady
10/18/91	2	1	Paul&Silas	Wilson
10/28/91	6	1	PoorHeart	IDK
11/02/91	4	1	Llama	Paul&Silas
11/07/91	2	2	MSO	Tube
11/09/91	2	1	Llama	Tube
11/14/91	4	1	Llama	Foam
11/19/91	3	2	Sloth	Dinner
11/21/91	2	1	Guelah	Foam
11/23/91	2	1	Llama	Foam
12/04/91	3	1	Llama	Landlady
12/06/91	2	1	Foam	Uncle Pen
12/07/91	1	2	BurAlive	Chalkdust
12/31/91	1	2	Landlady	Cavern
03/06/92	1	1	Maze	All Things
03/11/92	2	1	Paul&Silas	Maze
03/12/92	1	1	IDK	BurAlive
03/14/92	2	1	Cavern	Sparkle
03/20/92	3	1	Wilson	Brother
03/25/92	3	2	Mound	All Things
03/27/92	2	1	Llama	Paul&Silas
03/31/92	3	1	Rift	Llama
04/04/92	3	1	Foam	Uncle Pen
04/06/92	2	1	Sparkle	Brother
04/09/92	2	1	Mound	Uncle Pen
04/12/92	1	1	Maze	Antelope
04/15/92	2	2	YEM	Landlady
04/17/92	2	1	Cavern	Maze
04/19/92	2	1	My Friend	Maze
04/22/92	2	1	Foam	Sparkle
04/25/92	3	1	Paul&Silas	Brother
04/30/92	2	1	Maze	Uncle Pen
05/02/92	2	1	Sparkle	Maze
05/06/92	3	1	Foam	My Mind
05/08/92	2	1	Cavern	Uncle Pen
05/10/92	2	1a	Cavern	IDK
05/12/92	1	1	MSO	All Things
05/14/92	1	1	Horn	PoorHeart
05/17/92	3	1	MSO	IDK
06/23/92	4	1a	Chalkdust	Maze
06/27/92	2	1a	Sparkle	Maze
07/10/92	5	1a	Llama	Sparkle
07/14/92	3	2	All Things	Llama
07/18/92	4	1a	Llama	Rift
07/22/92	3	1a	*OP1	PoorHeart
08/17/92	13	1	Landlady	Rift
08/24/92	4	1a	Landlady	YEM
08/30/92	5	1a	Landlady	Llama
11/20/92	3	1	Sloth	Sparkle
11/22/92	2	1	Maze	Sparkle
11/27/92	3	1	Lawn Boy	Llama
11/30/92	2	1	IDK	Antelope
12/03/92	3	1	Silent	Adeline
12/05/92	2	2	Walk Line	Sparkle
12/07/92	2	2	Chalkdust	Llama
12/10/92	2	1	All Things	Adeline
12/12/92	2	1	Cavern	Landlady
12/28/92	2	2	Split&Melt	Sloth
12/30/92	2	1	Paul&Silas	IDK
02/05/93	4	1	PoorHeart	Bowie
02/07/93	2	2	My Mind	Tweezer
02/10/93	2	1	Guelah	Sloth
02/12/93	2	2	All Things	PoorHeart
02/15/93	2	2	FEFY	Mike's
02/18/93	2	1	Cavern	Lawn Boy
02/20/93	2	2	Wilson	Tweezer
02/23/93	3	1	Split&Melt	Lawn Boy
03/02/93	4	1	Stash	Sparkle
03/06/93	3	2	Tweezer	Paul&Silas
03/09/93	2	2	Tweezer	Lawn Boy
03/14/93	3	1	Sample	PYITE
03/17/93	2	2	Glide	Jesus
03/22/93	4	1	Weigh	Sparkle
03/27/93	4	1	Stash	My Friend
03/31/93	3	1	Sample	IDK
04/03/93	3	1	My Friend	Horn
04/12/93	4	1	Silent	Llama
04/17/93	4	2	Wilson	Landlady
04/22/93	4	1	It's Ice	Chalkdust
04/29/93	5	2	BBJ	Mike's
05/08/93	8	1	My Friend	Satin Doll
07/17/93	5	1	Stash	Chalkdust
07/30/93	10	1	IDK	Cavern
08/07/93	5	1	Makisupa	Maze
08/12/93	4	1	ACDCBag	Chalkdust
08/16/93	4	1	Horn	Sparkle
08/26/93	6	1	Guelah	Fee
12/31/93	5	1	Ginseng	Peaches
04/04/94	1	1	Fee	Horn
04/09/94	4	2	Sample	Peaches
04/13/94	3	2	Sample	BBJ
04/17/94	4	2	Sloth	BBJ
04/22/94	4	2	Julius	Tweezer
04/29/94	5	2	If I Could	Fee
05/02/94	2	2	Mound	Golgi
05/06/94	3	2	Sample	Axilla 2
05/10/94	3	2	Julius	Scent
05/14/94	3	1	Fee	Sample
05/23/94	7	1	Julius	Cavern
05/27/94	3	2	My Friend	Lizards
05/28/94	1	2	Life Boy	Fee
06/13/94	5	2	Cavern	Jesus
06/19/94	5	2	If I Could	Makisupa
06/24/94	4	1	Horn	Adeline
06/29/94	3	1	Sample	Mound
07/03/94	4	1	Old Home	Axilla 2
07/06/94	2	1	Bouncing	Axilla 2
07/08/94	1	2	Sample	YSZahov
07/15/94	5	2	Bouncing	It's Ice
10/07/94	2	2	Silent	Wilson
10/12/94	4	1	My Friend	Sloth
10/15/94	3	1	Glide	DWD
10/18/94	2	2	Silent	Scent
10/22/94	3	2	Wilson	AmGrace
10/26/94	3	2	Bouncing	Axilla 2
10/31/94	4	1	Silent	Golgi
11/13/94	5	1	Simple	Axilla 2
11/16/94	2	1	FEFY	Axilla 2
11/20/94	4	2	Axilla 2	Simple
11/25/94	3	1	Guelah	Bouncing
11/30/94	3	1	My Friend	Forbin's
12/04/94	4	2	Bouncing	Axilla 2
12/08/94	3	2	Axilla 2	Nellie
12/28/94	3	1	Axilla 2	Dog Faced
05/16/95	4	1a	Str Design	Theme
06/08/95	2	1	FEFY	Caspian
06/13/95	3	1	Taste	Terrapin
06/19/95	5	1	PYITE	Str Design
06/23/95	3	1	Caspian	Ginseng
06/28/95	4	1	FEFY	PYITE
07/02/95	4	1	CamlWalk	IDK
09/30/95	5	1	Chess	Uncle Pen
10/06/95	4	1	Billy	I'm Blue
10/08/95	2	1	Wolfman's	I'm Blue
10/14/95	3	2	*OP2	Rift
10/21/95	5	1	Guelah	Wilson
10/25/95	3	2	*OP2	Life Mars
11/09/95	5	1	Simple	Tela
11/12/95	3	1	Guelah	IDK
11/18/95	4	1	Bouncing	Lawn Boy
11/24/95	4	2	Theme	Catapult
11/29/95	3	1	Ya Mar	If I Could
12/02/95	3	1	Guelah	MSO
12/07/95	3	2	Fog	Julius
12/11/95	3	1	Caspian	Dog Log
12/16/95	4	2	Sample	Scent
12/31/95	5	1	Sloth	Sqirm Coil
07/06/96	5	1a	ASZ	PoorHeart
07/11/96	4	1	IDK	Cavern
07/13/96	2	1a	Cavern	PoorHeart
07/21/96	5	2	Theme	Life Mars
08/04/96	6	2	ACDCBag	Scent
08/10/96	4	1	Fee	IDK
08/14/96	3	1	PoorHeart	Mango
08/17/96	2	1	PYITE	CTB
10/18/96	3	2	YEM	Waste
10/21/96	2	2	Wolfman's	Train Song
10/26/96	4	1	Wolfman's	Train Song
10/31/96	3	1	Caspian	Forbin's
11/08/96	5	1	Caspian	Golgi
11/13/96	3	1	Train Song	CharZero
11/18/96	4	1	Ginseng	CharZero
11/24/96	4	1	Bouncing	CharZero
12/01/96	4	2	DayinLife	SweptAwy
12/04/96	2	2	Life Mars	Lawn Boy
12/30/96	4	1	Gumbo	Talk
02/14/97	3	2	FunkBitch	Walfredo
02/18/97	3	2	Wolfman's	Train Song
02/21/97	2	2	Billy	Waste
03/01/97	6	1	Jesus	HelloBaby
06/16/97	5	2	Don't Care	Wading
06/24/97	5	2	Wolfman's	NICU
07/01/97	4	1	Dirt	Dogs Stole
08/09/97	20	1	Dogs Stole	Lawn Boy
➤ 8/17/97	**6**			

Rift [206]*

Rift [Rift]

By Anastasio/Marshall

02/25/90	[176]	1	Satin Doll	Possum
03/28/90	9	2	La Grange	Cavern
04/20/90	12	2	La Grange	Fee
04/28/90	5	1	YEM	Foam
05/19/90	10	2	Bouncing	Jesus
03/06/92	172	1	*OP1	Cavern
03/07/92	1	1	Landlady	Antelope
03/12/92	2	1	BurAlive	Magilla
03/13/92	1	2	Sloth	Love You
03/14/92	1	1	Foam	Stash
03/17/92	1	1	Guelah	Bouncing
03/19/92	1	1	Landlady	Split&Melt
03/20/92	1	1	Glide	Fluffhead
03/24/92	2	1	Eliza	Golgi
03/25/92	1	1	Split&Melt	Fee
03/27/92	2	2	MSO	Bathtub
03/28/92	1	1	Stash	Bouncing
03/31/92	2	1	Split&Melt	Reba
04/03/92	2	1	Stash	Guelah
04/05/92	2	1	Stash	Horn
04/07/92	2	1	Bouncing	Sloth
04/12/92	2	2	Bouncing	YEM
04/16/92	3	1	Split&Melt	Fee
04/18/92	2	2	Suzie	Manteca
04/21/92	2	1	Split&Melt	Guelah
04/22/92	1	2	Silent	Wilson
04/25/92	3	1	Bouncing	Magilla
04/29/92	1	1	Guelah	Bouncing
04/30/92	1	1	Stash	Esther
05/03/92	3	1	IDK	Horn
05/05/92	1	1	Stash	Guelah
05/07/92	2	1	Split&Melt	Guelah
05/09/92	2	1	Guelah	Fee
05/14/92	3	2	Cavern	Fluffhead
05/18/92	4	2	Fee	Cavern
07/01/92	7	1a	Cavern	Horn
07/14/92	6	1	Landlady	Guelah
07/16/92	2	1	Guelah	Bowie
07/18/92	2	1a	Reba	Antelope
07/22/92	3	1a	Maze	Cavern
07/25/92	2	1a	Stash	YEM
07/30/92	4	1a	*OP1	Horn
08/02/92	3	1a	Guelah	Oh Kee
08/17/92	4	1	Reba	Wilson
08/29/92	8	1a	Chalkdust	Bouncing
10/30/92	2	1a	Bouncing	Cavern
11/20/92	2	1	Suzie	Sloth
11/23/92	3	1	Split&Melt	Guelah
11/27/92	2	1	*OP1	Wilson
12/01/92	3	1	Bouncing	Cavern
12/03/92	2	2	*OP2	Guelah
12/05/92	2	1	Bouncing	Guelah
12/08/92	3	1	*OP1	Wilson
12/10/92	1	2	*OP2	Tweezer
12/12/92	2	2	Tweezer	Guelah
12/13/92	1	1	Stash	FEFY
12/28/92	1	1	Bouncing	Golgi
12/30/92	2	2	Axilla	Bathtub
12/31/92	1	1	Bouncing	Wilson
02/03/93	1	1	Lovin Cup	Fee
02/05/93	2	1	Guelah	Split&Melt
02/07/93	2	1	Mockbird	IDK
02/09/93	1	1	My Friend	Wedge
02/11/93	2	1	Fee	Fluffhead
02/13/93	2	1	Glide	Stash
02/15/93	1	2	*OP2	FEFY

02/18/93	2	2	*OP2	Stash
02/19/93	1	1	Lovin Cup	Split&Melt
02/22/93	3	1	*OP1	Guelah
02/23/93	1	1	My Friend	Bouncing
02/25/93	1	1	Mockbird	Stash
02/27/93	2	1	Golgi	Guelah
03/03/93	2	1	*OP1	Foam
03/05/93	1	1	Sloth	Stash
03/06/93	1	2	*OP2	Tweezer
03/08/93	1	1	Golgi	Guelah
03/09/93	1	2	Axilla	Tweezer
03/12/93	1	1	Guelah	Stash
03/14/93	2	2	Life Boy	BBJ
03/18/93	3	1	Guelah	Fee
03/19/93	1	1	Bouncing	Stash
03/21/93	1	2	My Friend	Tweezer
03/22/93	1	1	Bouncing	Weigh
03/25/93	2	1	Glide	Horn
03/27/93	2	1	Guelah	Stash
03/30/93	2	2	Lovin Cup	Tweezer
04/01/93	2	1	Guelah	Stash
04/03/93	2	1	Landlady	Guelah
04/10/93	3	2	Bouncing	Glide
04/13/93	2	2	My Friend	Sloth
04/16/93	2	1	Sample	Harry
04/18/93	2	1	*OP1	Guelah
04/21/93	2	1	Mockbird	PYITE
04/22/93	1	1	Fee	Golgi
04/24/93	2	1	Silent	Caravan
04/27/93	2	1	Bouncing	Stash
04/29/93	1	1	Glide	Fee
05/01/93	2	1	Fee	Sample
05/03/93	2	1	BurAlive	Weigh
05/05/93	1	1	*OP1	Guelah
05/07/93	2	2	*OP2	Bouncing
05/08/93	1	1	Guelah	Mound
05/29/93	1	1a	Bouncing	Stash
07/15/93	2	1	*OP1	Sample
07/17/93	2	2	Faht	GTBT
07/18/93	1	1	BurAlive	Foam
07/21/93	1	1a	Glide	Bouncing
07/23/93	2	1	BurAlive	Caravan
07/24/93	1	1	Guelah	Stash
07/25/93	1	1	Fee	Sloth
07/27/93	1	1a	Also Sprac	Stash
07/29/93	2	1	Weigh	Landlady
07/31/93	2	1	*OP1	Sample
08/02/93	1	2	Curtis	Sqirm Coil
08/03/93	1	1	Fee	Stash
08/06/93	1	1	Sample	Horn
08/08/93	2	2	Also Sprac	Harry
08/11/93	2	1	Bouncing	Jesus
08/13/93	2	1	BurAlive	Bathtub
08/15/93	2	2	*OP2	Tweezer
08/17/93	2	2	Silent	Suzie
08/20/93	1	1	Ginseng	Antelope
08/21/93	1	1	Guelah	Stash
08/24/93	1	2	Wilson	Rosie
08/26/93	2	2	Life Boy	Jesus
08/28/93	1	2	Also Sprac	Antelope
12/30/93	3	1	Mockbird	Bathtub
04/05/94	3	1	Bouncing	ACDCBag
04/09/94	3	1	Wilson	Bathtub
04/14/94	4	1	Glide	Demand
04/16/94	2	1	Axilla 2	Stash
04/18/94	2	1	My Friend	Split&Melt
04/23/94	4	1	FunkBitch	Fee
04/28/94	3	1a	Sample	DWD
04/30/94	2	1	PYITE	Ginseng
05/03/94	2	1	*OP1	Guelah
05/04/94	1	1	Life Boy	TweezRep
05/08/94	3	1	Axilla 2	DWD
05/12/94	2	1	Catapult	DWD
05/16/94	3	1	Axilla 2	DWD
05/20/94	3	2	Wolfman's	YEM
05/22/94	2	2	Life Boy	Slave
05/25/94	2	2	*OP2	Tweezer
05/28/94	3	1	*OP1	Sample
06/09/94	2	1	Guelah	DWD
06/11/94	2	1	YEM	DWD
06/14/94	2	1	Guelah	DWD
06/16/94	1	1	Bouncing	Julius
06/18/94	2	1	Wilson	ACDCBag
06/22/94	3	1	Guelah	Gumbo
06/25/94	3	1	N20	Julius
06/30/94	3	1	Gumbo	Guelah
07/02/94	2	E	*OPE	*CLE
07/05/94	2	1	*OP1	Sample
07/08/94	2	2	*OP2	Sample
07/10/94	2	1	Peaches	Stash
07/15/94	3	1	*OP1	Sample
10/08/94	3	2	Sample	Mike's
10/10/94	2	2	Fee	DWD
10/14/94	3	1	Adeline	Forbin's
10/16/94	2	1	*OP1	Horn
10/20/94	2	2	McGrupp	Harry
10/22/94	2	1	Axilla 2	Split&Melt
10/26/94	3	2	*OP2	Bouncing
10/28/94	2	2	Lizards	Life Boy
10/29/94	1	1	Makisupa	*CL1
10/31/94	1	3	Slave	Sl Monkey
11/12/94	4	2	Life Boy	Old Home
11/18/94	5	1	*OP1	ACDCBag
11/20/94	2	2	Simple	Terrapin
12/04/94	10	1	If I Could	Tweezer
12/07/94	2	2	*OP2	Frankstein
12/10/94	3	1	Fee	Stash
12/30/94	3	1	Wilson	ACDCBag
06/08/95	4	2	Simple	Free
06/10/95	2	1	Free	YEM
06/19/95	6	1	Str Design	Cavern
06/24/95	4	1	Fee	Spock's
06/29/95	4	1	Cavern	Simple
07/02/95	3	1	IDK	Guitar
09/27/95	2	1	Wolfman's	Free
10/02/95	4	1	Wolfman's	Chess
10/06/95	3	1	I'm Blue	Free
10/14/95	5	2	Reba	YEM
10/20/95	4	1	Fee	Free
10/27/95	5	1	IDK	Stash
11/15/95	9	1	FEFY	Caspian
11/19/95	3	1	PoorHeart	Stash
11/22/95	2	2	*OP2	Free
11/25/95	2	1	Bouncing	Wolfman's
11/30/95	3	1	Bathtub	FEFY
12/07/95	5	1	Demand	Slave
12/09/95	2	1	Sloth	Bouncing
12/28/95	7	1	Horn	FEFY
07/21/96	19	1	Guelah	Tweezer
08/06/96	8	1	Makisupa	Suzie
08/10/96	2	1	Silent	Bathtub
10/19/96	9	1	My Friend	Free
10/23/96	3	1	CharZero	Theme
10/27/96	3	2	Bathtub	Caspian
10/29/96	1	2	*OP2	Mike's
11/07/96	5	1	Weigh	Guelah
11/16/96	7	1	Gumbo	Free
11/23/96	4	1	Split&Melt	FunkBitch
12/29/96	10	1	Train Song	Free
02/23/97	11	1	Treat	Fluffhead
➤ 8/17/97	44			

Rocka William [5]

Rocka William [RockaW]

By Phish

02/13/97	[889]	1	Maze	Harry
02/14/97	1	2	Wafredo	Scent
02/26/97	9	1	Carini	Dog Log
06/25/97	13	2	Cecilia	Antelope
08/10/97	24	2	Rotation	Bowie
➤ 8/17/97	7			

Rotation Jam [4]

Rotation Jam [Rotation]

By Phish

11/25/95	[798]	2	Mike's	Mike's
12/15/95	14	2	Bathtub	Also Sprac
12/29/96	74	2	YEM	Candles
08/10/97	50	2	GTBT	RockaW
➤ 8/17/97	7			

Run Like An Antelope [257]*

Run Like An Antelope [Antelope]

By Anastasio/Marshall/ Dude of Life

10/17/85	[3]	1a	CamlWalk	McGrupp
11/23/85	2	1a	WhipPost	Dave's
03/11/87	7	1a	Freebird	Flat Fee
04/29/87	3	3	Makisupa	Boogie On
09/12/87	8	2	Curtis	Makisupa
02/08/88	7	2	Lizards	Harry
03/11/88	1	2	Alumni	*CL2
03/12/88	1	1a	Possum	*CL1
05/25/88	7	3	Harpua	*CL3
06/18/88	2	2	SwingLow	IKALittle
07/12/88	4	1	ACDCBag	*CL1
07/23/88	1	2	Terrapin	Satin Doll
07/24/88	1	3	McGrupp	*CL3
10/12/88	8	E	*OPE	*CLE
10/29/88	1	3	Donna	IDK
11/03/88	1	2	A-Train	Suzie
02/07/89	8	2	Fee	*CL2
02/17/89	1	1a	Alumni	Fluffhead
02/24/89	2	1	Mockbird	OYWD
03/03/89	1	1	Curtain	IDK
03/04/89	1	2	Lizards	Contact
03/30/89	2	1	Fluffhead	*CL1
04/30/89	14	1	Peaches	Terrapin
05/05/89	3	2	*OP2	IDK
05/06/89	1	2	Divided	*CL2
05/09/89	3	2	Esther	IDK
05/26/89	9	2	Bathtub	Golgi
05/28/89	2	1	Divided	Forbin's
06/23/89	5	1	Lizards	*CL1
06/30/89	2	1	Fluffhead	*CL1
08/12/89	3	1a	Icculus	*CL1
08/17/89	2	3	Contact	*CL3
08/23/89	3	2	*OP2	Forbin's
08/26/89	1	3	Dinner	*CL3
10/01/89	5	1	Suzie	*CL1
10/20/89	6	1	Golgi	*CL1
10/31/89	5	E	Contact	*CLE
11/10/89	5	2	A-Train	*CL2
11/30/89	4	1	MSO	Lawn Boy
12/07/89	4	2	Lizards	Lawn Boy
12/08/89	1	1	Bathtub	*CL1
12/15/89	2	1a	Divided	FunkBitch
12/31/89	4	1	ACDCBag	Bathtub
01/27/90	4	2	Sqirm Coil	Terrapin
01/28/90	1	2	Wilson	Bouncing
02/23/90	13	1	Bouncing	*CL1
02/24/90	1	1	A-Train	*CL1
03/08/90	6	1	A-Train	*CL1
03/09/90	1	1	Donna	Reba
03/11/90	1	2	Carolina	MSO
04/06/90	5	1	Suzie	*CL1
04/08/90	2	2	MSO	*CL2
04/13/90	4	2	*OP2	Foam
04/26/90	7	1	IDK	Lawn Boy
04/28/90	1	1	Foam	*CL1
05/04/90	3	2	HwayHell	*CL2
05/23/90	8	2	A-Train	Mike's
06/09/90	7	2	Suzie	Terrapin
06/16/90	1	2	Lizards	*CL2
09/13/90	1	1	Asse Fest	Minute
09/16/90	3	1a	Magilla	*CL1
09/28/90	4	1	Asse Fest	*CL1
10/05/90	3	1	Bouncing	*CL1
10/31/90	7	1	Cavern	*CL1
11/03/90	2	2	Love You	*CL2
11/30/90	8	2	Sloth	*CL2
12/03/90	2	1	MSO	Lawn Boy
12/08/90	2	2	Bouncing	Tela
12/29/90	2	2	Destiny	*CL2
12/31/90	1	2	Brain	*CL2
02/02/91	2	2	Sloth	Lawn Boy
02/08/91	3	2	Lizards	*CL2
03/16/91	22	1	Suzie	*CL1
03/22/91	3	2	Suzie	Foam
04/19/91	16	2	A-Train	*CL2
05/12/91	13	E	*OPE	Fire
07/14/91	8	2	Cavern	*CL2
07/25/91	8	1	Cavern	*CL1
09/28/91	7	2	Cavern	Lawn Boy
10/10/91	7	2	Cavern	IDK
10/18/91	6	1	Adeline	*CL1
10/27/91	5	2	A-Train	*CL2
11/02/91	5	2	Golgi	TMWSIY
11/12/91	6	2	Love You	*CL2
11/14/91	2	2	Dinner	Fee
11/20/91	4	2	MSO	Tela
11/22/91	2	2	Bathtub	Sqirm Coil
11/30/91	3	2	IDK	Golgi
12/07/91	4	1	Mango	*CL1
12/31/91	1	2	MSO	*CL2
03/07/92	2	1	Rift	*CL1
03/13/92	3	1	Fluffhead	*CL1
03/17/92	2	1	Bouncing	*CL1
03/20/92	2	1	Mound	*CL1
03/25/92	3	1	It's Ice	*CL1
03/27/92	2	1	Bouncing	*CL1
03/31/92	3	1	Mockbird	*CL1
04/04/92	3	1	IDK	*CL1
04/06/92	2	1	Sqirm Coil	*CL1
04/12/92	3	1	Reba	*CL1
04/16/92	3	1	Mockbird	*CL1
04/18/92	2	1	All Things	*CL1
04/22/92	3	2	Glide	Horse
04/25/92	3	1	Magilla	*CL1
04/30/92	2	1	Esther	*CL1
05/05/92	4	1	Glide	*CL1
05/09/92	4	1	IDK	*CL1
05/14/92	3	1	Bouncing	*CL1
05/18/92	4	1	Sparkle	*CL1
07/10/92	10	1a	Cavern	*CL1
07/15/92	4	1	Lizards	*CL1
07/18/92	3	1a	Rift	*CL1
08/30/92	25	1a	Memories	Adeline
11/19/92	2	1	Silent	*CL1
11/22/92	3	1	Adeline	*CL1
11/25/92	2	1	Cavern	*CL1
11/30/92	3	1	Reba	*CL1
12/03/92	3	1	Adeline	*CL1
12/06/92	3	1	Fluffhead	*CL1
12/08/92	2	2	Lizards	Lawn Boy
12/12/92	3	1	Bouncing	*CL1
12/28/92	2	1	Adeline	*CL1
12/31/92	3	1	IDK	*CL1
02/04/93	2	1	Glide	*CL1
02/06/93	2	1	Bouncing	*CL1
02/10/93	3	1	Catapult	*CL1
02/12/93	2	1	A-Train	*CL1
02/15/93	2	1	IDK	*CL1
02/18/93	2	1	Lawn Boy	*CL1

SONGS PLAYED BY YEAR

(1997 through 8/17/97)

Rift
1990 5
1991 0
1992 54
1993 68
1994 47
1995 20
1996 11
1997 1

Rocka William
1997 5

Rotation Jam
1995 2
1996 1
1997 1

Run Like an Antelope
1990 27
1991 21
1992 33
1993 38
1994 42
1995 25
1996 19
1997 9

Runaway Jim
1990 20
1991 55
1992 54
1993 41
1994 34
1995 24
1996 20
1997 12

Sample
1993 24
1994 70
1995 30
1996 26
1997 12

Sanity
1990 0
1991 0
1992 6
1993 0
1994 2
1995 1
1996 1
1997 0

Scent of a Mule
1994 44
1995 23
1996 17
1997 5

Setting Sail
1991 1
1992 0
1993 0
1994 1
1995 0
1996 0
1997 0

Silent in the Morning [See Horse]

Simple
1994 30
1995 20
1996 16
1997 7

Slave
1990 6
1991 2
1992 0
1993 3
1994 22
1995 19
1996 12
1997 11

Sleeping Monkey
1992 18
1993 5
1994 17
1995 6
1996 2
1997 2

Sloth
1990 14
1991 30
1992 16
1993 14
1994 9
1995 5
1996 6
1997 1

Sparkle
1991 32
1992 64
1993 58
1994 45
1995 25
1996 21
1997 7

Split Open and Melt
1990 7
1991 32
1992 34
1993 42
1994 42
1995 20
1996 16
1997 7

Spock's Brain
1995 5
1996 0
1997 0

Stories Behind the Songs
(Continued)

Sanity: Played in the 1980s, the band debuted an accelerated version of the song early in 1989 before it fell out of rotation entirely in late spring/summer of that year. The "slow" (original) version of the song was revived on 3/11/92 and stayed in light rotation during spring tour 1992. The version played on 12/31/95 may have been the slowest-ever incarnation of this song.

Scent of a Mule: This song is notable in concert for the "Mule Duel" inserted in the middle of the song. From 1994 through part of 1996, Trey and Page dueled, then the music segued into a Klezmer dance before returning to the Scent lyrics. Recently, however, the band has varied the song, leading to a Fish-Page duel (8/17/96); Trey skatting his duel (most of fall tour '96); or simply a jam in place of the duel (8/17/97).

Simple: Originally titled Skyballs and Saxscrapers, the band recorded this song for inclusion on *Hoist* but decided against including it on the album. Since its debut, the song has undergone a number of subtle musical transformations as the band has worked to establish an ending for the song which satisfies them. During fall 1996, Simple often stretched out in lentgh to over 20 minutes, indicating that maybe the band had found a form they liked for it—a true jam song.

The Sloth: A Gamehendge song, The Sloth is a hitman from the ghetto who is hired by the revolutionaries to kill Wilson.

Spock's Brain: At the Lowell benefit show in 1995, the audience voted on the title for this song from among four choices given by Trey: "The Plane," "The First Single," "Israel," and "Spock's Brain." The vote was overwhelmingly in favor of Spock's Brain after Trey said the song was inspired by the Spock's Brain episode of the original Star Trek. Fans have speculated widely on why this promising song has not been played since 6/24/95. The theory that Elektra had asked Phish not to play it live so it could be released as a single off Phish's next studio album evaporated

02/21/93	3	1	Bouncing	*CL1
02/23/93	2	1	Paul&Silas	*CL1
02/27/93	3	1	Lawn Boy	*CL1
03/09/93	6	1	IDK	*CL1
03/13/93	2	1	Wilson	*CL1
03/17/93	3	1	Suzie	*CL1
03/19/93	2	1	Cavern	*CL1
03/25/93	4	1	Magilla	*CL1
03/28/93	3	1	Lawn Boy	*CL1
04/01/93	3	1	Lawn Boy	*CL1
04/03/93	2	1	Horn	*CL1
04/12/93	4	1	Satin Doll	*CL1
04/17/93	4	1	Golgi	*CL1
04/21/93	3	1	IDK	*CL1
04/24/93	3	1	Sparkle	*CL1
04/29/93	3	1	Oh Kee	*CL1
05/02/93	3	2	Bouncing	Rosie
05/07/93	4	1	IDK	*CL1
05/30/93	3	1a	Silent	IDK
07/16/93	2	1	Horn	*CL1
07/18/93	2	2	PoorHeart	Mound
07/23/93	3	2	PoorHeart	Faht
07/28/93	4	2	MSO	Lizards
08/02/93	4	2	Bike	*CL2
08/07/93	3	2	PurplRain	*CL2
08/11/93	3	2	MSO	*CL2
08/14/93	3	2	Also Sprac	Sparks
08/20/93	4	1	Rift	*CL1
08/24/93	2	2	Rosie	*CL2
08/28/93	3	2	Rift	Horse
12/29/93	2	2	Fluffhead	Contact
12/31/93	2	1	IDK	*CL1
04/06/94	3	1	Fee	*CL1
04/10/94	3	2	Ya Mar	Fluffhead
04/14/94	3	2	Also Sprac	Horse
04/16/94	2	2	Nellie	*CL1
04/20/94	3	2	PoorHeart	Magilla
04/23/94	3	2	Wilson	Mound
04/25/94	2	2	My Mind	Mound
04/28/94	1	1a	It's Ice	Sqirm Coil
05/04/94	5	2	*OP2	Bouncing
05/08/94	3	2	Also Sprac	It's Ice
05/12/94	2	2	Also Sprac	Horse
05/16/94	3	2	Also Sprac	Sparkle
05/20/94	3	2	Also Sprac	Weigh
05/23/94	3	2	Wilson	If I Could
05/26/94	2	2	Also Sprac	Fluffhead
05/29/94	3	2	Suzie	FrBir
06/11/94	3	2	Also Sprac	Fluffhead
06/16/94	3	2	Suzie	Forbin's
06/19/94	3	2	Faht	If I Could
06/24/94	4	2	Demand	Halley's
06/30/94	4	2	Harpua	Love You
07/03/94	3	2	Sqirm Coil	Suzie
07/09/94	4	1	Silent	*CL1
07/14/94	3	1	Silent	*CL1
07/16/94	2	2	*OP2	Harpua
10/08/94	2	1	Lawn Boy	*CL1
10/13/94	4	2	Old Home	If I Could
10/16/94	3	2	BBJ	Dog Faced
10/21/94	3	1	Dog Faced	*CL1
10/26/94	4	1	NICU	Guyute
10/29/94	3	2	Bike	*CL2
10/31/94	1	3	PoorHeart	*CL3
11/13/94	5	1	Silent	*CL1
11/16/94	2	2	Fee	*CL2
11/19/94	3	1	Avenu	I'm Blue
11/25/94	4	2	PurplRain	*CL2
11/30/94	3	2	MSO	Fixin' Die
12/03/94	3	1	Scent	Guyute
12/06/94	2	2	Long Time	*CL2
12/09/94	3	1	If I Could	*CL1
12/28/94	3	1	It's Ice	*CL1
12/31/94	3	1	NICU	Glide
06/09/95	4	1	Sparkle	*CL1
06/15/95	4	1	Fluffhead	*CL1
06/19/95	3	1	Cavern	*CL1
06/23/95	3	2	Wedge	Harpua
06/26/95	3	2	Str Design	*CL2
06/30/95	3	1	Fee	*CL1
07/03/95	3	1	PoorHeart	Lovin Cup
09/28/95	2	2	Sample	*CL2
09/30/95	2	1	Horn	I'm Blue
10/02/95	1	2	Lizards	*CL2
10/07/95	4	1	Wilson	*CL1
10/13/95	3	2	Wilson	Keyboard
10/20/95	5	2	Bouncing	*CL2
10/24/95	3	2	Sl Monkey	Contact
10/28/95	3	1	Caspian	*CL1
10/31/95	2	1	Guyute	Harpua
11/11/95	3	2	Suspicious	*CL2
11/22/95	8	1	Wilson	Fluffhead
11/28/95	3	2	Wind	Contact
11/30/95	2	2	Makisupa	Scent
12/04/95	3	2	Ya Mar	Billy
12/08/95	3	2	TweezRep	*CL2
12/12/95	3	1	Silent	I'm Blue
12/17/95	4	1	DayinLife	Mango
12/30/95	3	2	Cavern	*CL2
07/07/96	7	1a	Cavern	Suzie
07/12/96	4	2	Mike's	PurplRain
07/15/96	2	2	Uncle Pen	*CL2
07/21/96	4	2	Free	Simpl
07/25/96	4	1a	It's Ice	Life Mars
08/02/96	1	2	Silent	*CL2
08/06/96	3	1	Horn	*CL1
08/12/96	3	2	McGrupp	HelloBaby
08/17/96	4	2	Fluffhead	Golgi
10/16/96	1	2	Caspian	Sqirm Coil
10/19/96	3	2	Steep	HelloBaby
10/23/96	3	1	Theme	*CL1
10/26/96	2	2	Waste	*CL2
11/02/96	4	2	Crosseyed	Waste
11/08/96	4	1	Golgi	*CL1
11/14/96	4	2	Demand	DayinLife
11/24/96	7	1	Sample	*CL1
12/01/96	4	1	Sample	*CL1
12/31/96	7	3	Suzie	Bohemian
02/14/97	2	1	Uncle Pen	*CL1
02/21/97	5	2	Ya Mar	Wilson
03/02/97	7	1	RunJim	Catapult
06/20/97	6	1	I Don't Care	*CL1
06/25/97	4	2	RockaW	*CL2
07/29/97	16	2	Oblivious	Wading
08/06/97	5	2	Sample	*CL2
08/11/97	4	1	Horn	*CL1
08/14/97	2	1	Billy	*CL1
➤ 8/17/97	**2**			

Runaway Jim [259]

Runaway Jim [RunJim]

By Anastasio

03/28/90	[185]	1	A-Train	YEM
04/07/90	4	2	Fee	Foam
05/04/90	16	2	*OP2	Sloth
05/10/90	2	2	FunkBitch	Harry
05/13/90	3	1	Bouncing	Uncle Pen
10/31/90	29	2	Reba	Foam
11/03/90	2	1	Foam	YEM
11/04/90	1	2	Manteca	Oh Kee
11/10/90	2	1	Bouncing	Cavern
11/16/90	1	2	Lizards	IDK
11/17/90	1	1	Landlady	Bouncing
11/24/90	1	2	Landlady	YEM
11/26/90	1	1	Landlady	Sloth
11/30/90	1	2	Sqirm Coil	Stash
12/01/90	1	1	YEM	*CL1
12/07/90	2	1	Asse Fest	Foam
12/08/90	1	1	BurAlive	Foam
12/28/90	1	1	*OP1	Foam
12/29/90	1	2	BurAlive	Lizards
12/31/90	1	2	Sqirm Coil	Magilla
02/01/91	1	1	Guelah	Split&Melt
02/03/91	2	1	*OP1	Guelah
02/07/91	1	1	*OP1	Foam
02/08/91	1	1	Sqirm Coil	Guelah
02/09/91	1	1	TMWSIY	Foam
02/14/91	1	2	Sqirm Coil	Esther
02/16/91	2	2	BurAlive	Guelah
02/26/91	7	2	BurAlive	Dinner
03/07/91	6	2	Sloth	Reba
03/13/91	3	2	Guelah	Sloth
03/15/91	1	E	Sqirm Coil	*CLE
03/17/91	2	2	*OP2	Esther
03/22/91	2	2	Stash	Guelah
04/04/91	7	2	Curtain	Guelah
04/11/91	3	1	*OP1	Cavern
04/12/91	1	2	Landlady	YEM
04/15/91	2	1	Foam	Split&Melt
04/16/91	1	2	Tweezer	Carolina
04/20/91	3	1	*OP1	Reba
04/22/91	2	1	Curtain	Sloth
04/27/91	3	1	Asse Fest	Cavern
05/03/91	2	2	Landlady	Tela
05/04/91	1	E	Terrapin	Golgi
05/12/91	3	1	Foam	*CL1
05/16/91	1	2	*OP2	Dinner
05/18/91	2	E	Dinner	*CLE
07/13/91	4	1	Curtain	Foam
07/18/91	3	1	Foam	Guelah
07/19/91	1	E	Lawn Boy	*CLE
07/21/91	2	2	IDK	Lawn Boy
08/03/91	6	1	Foam	Guelah
09/25/91	1	2	Jesus	YEM
09/27/91	2	1	*OP1	Cavern
10/02/91	3	2	Guelah	Lawn Boy
10/04/91	2	2	Foam	Lawn Boy
10/10/91	3	1	Landlady	It's Ice
10/11/91	1	1	Bouncing	*CL1
10/13/91	2	1	*OP1	Wilson
10/15/91	1	2	Bouncing	PoorHeart
10/18/91	2	1	*OP1	Foam
10/19/91	1	1	It's Ice	Foam
10/28/91	5	1	Curtain	Cavern
10/31/91	2	1	YEM	*CL1
11/02/91	2	2	Landlady	YEM
11/07/91	2	1	Landlady	IDK
11/09/91	2	1	Curtain	Foam
11/13/91	3	1	Landlady	It's Ice
11/14/91	1	1	Golgi	*CL1
11/16/91	2	1	Wilson	It's Ice
11/19/91	1	1	Foam	Fee
11/21/91	2	2	TMWSIY	*CL2
11/23/91	2	1	Foam	Guelah
12/04/91	3	1	Landlady	Cavern
12/07/91	3	1	Wilson	Foam
12/31/91	1	2	Auld	Landlady
03/07/92	2	1	Foam	Horse
03/12/92	2	1	*OP1	Foam
03/14/92	2	1	*OP1	Cavern
03/17/92	1	2	*OP2	Glide
03/21/92	3	1	Landlady	Foam
03/25/92	2	1	Glide	It's Ice
03/26/92	1	1	Landlady	All Things
03/28/92	2	1	*OP1	Foam
03/30/92	1	1	Sloth	Cavern
04/01/92	2	1	Sparkle	IDK
04/04/92	2	1	*OP1	Foam
04/05/92	1	2	A-Train	*CL2
04/07/92	2	1	Sloth	*CL1
04/15/92	4	1	All Things	*CL1
04/17/92	2	1	*OP1	Foam
04/19/92	2	2	Brain	*CL2
04/22/92	2	2	Harpua	*CL2
04/24/92	2	1	*OP1	Forbin's
04/29/92	2	1	It's Ice	Guelah
05/02/92	3	1	*OP1	Forbin's
05/03/92	1	1	Horn	*CL1
05/07/92	3	1	Foam	Esther
05/09/92	2	1	*OP1	Foam
05/12/92	2	2	Cavern	*CL2
05/16/92	3	2	*OP2	It's Ice
05/18/92	2	2	Love You	*CL2
06/20/92	2	1a	Foam	It's Ice
06/24/92	2	1a	*OP1	Llama
06/27/92	1	1a	*OP1	Foam
07/09/92	4	1a	Sqirm Coil	Guelah
07/11/92	2	1a	Landlady	Foam
07/14/92	2	1	It's Ice	Horn
07/16/92	2	2	*OP2	Weigh
07/17/92	1	1a	Bouncing	*CL1
07/19/92	2	1a	Maze	Bowie
07/21/92	1	1a	Sqirm Coil	*CL1
07/25/92	3	1a	*OP1	Foam
07/28/92	3	1a	Tweezer	*CL1
08/15/92	7	1a	Maze	*CL1
08/19/92	2	1a	Landlady	Guelah
08/23/92	2	1a	Foam	Stash
08/25/92	2	1a	*OP1	It's Ice
08/28/92	2	1a	Sqirm Coil	Rocky Top
10/30/92	3	1a	*OP1	Maze
11/21/92	3	1	Landlady	Foam
11/23/92	2	1	*OP1	Foam
11/27/92	2	1	Memories	*CL1
11/30/92	2	2	BurAlive	Guelah
12/02/92	2	2	Walk Line	*CL2
12/06/92	4	1	*OP1	Foam
12/07/92	1	E	*OPE	*CLE
12/11/92	3	1	*OP1	It's Ice
12/29/92	4	1	FunkBitch	Guelah
12/31/92	2	2	*OP2	It's Ice
02/03/93	1	2	*OP2	It's Ice
02/07/93	4	1	Fee	*CL1
02/10/93	2	2	*OP2	It's Ice
02/13/93	2	2	*OP2	Wilson
02/17/93	3	1	Sloth	It's Ice
02/19/93	2	2	*OP2	It's Ice
02/22/93	3	2	*OP2	It's Ice
02/26/93	3	1	*OP1	Foam
03/03/93	3	1	Sample	Lawn Boy
03/06/93	2	1	Golgi	*CL1
03/09/93	2	1	*OP1	Foam
03/14/93	3	1	PYITE	*CL1
03/17/93	2	1	Landlady	Foam
03/19/93	2	2	*OP2	It's Ice
03/26/93	5	2	Wilson	Tweezer
03/28/93	2	2	WalkAway	Mound
03/31/93	2	1	*OP1	Foam
04/02/93	2	2	*OP2	Sample
04/10/93	4	1	*OP1	Weigh
04/14/93	3	2	Harpua	*CL2
04/20/93	4	1	*OP1	Weigh
04/23/93	3	1	*OP1	Weigh
04/25/93	2	1	Glide	Forbin's
04/29/93	2	1	Sloth	Horn
05/01/93	2	1	*OP1	Foam
05/03/93	2	2	McGrupp	BBJ
05/05/93	1	2	*OP2	My Friend
05/29/93	4	1a	YEM	AmGrace
07/15/93	2	2	Lepr	*CL1
07/17/93	2	1	Landlady	Sample
07/21/93	2	1a	Bouncing	BBJ
07/23/93	2	1	PYITE	It's Ice
07/28/93	4	1	All Things	Ya Mar
07/31/93	3	2	Wilson	It's Ice
08/03/93	2	1	*OP1	Nellie
08/08/93	3	1	Lovin Cup	Horse
08/11/93	2	1	BurAlive	Weigh

08/15/93	4	1	All Things	RunJim
08/21/93	4	1	IDK	*CL1
08/26/93	3	1	*OP1	Guelah
12/29/93	3	1	*OP1	Peaches
04/05/94	4	1	*OP1	Foam
04/10/94	4	1	*OP1	It's Ice
04/14/94	3	1	*OP1	Foam
04/16/94	2	1	*OP1	Fee
04/20/94	3	1	*OP1	It's Ice
04/22/94	2	2	Life Boy	BeLikeYou
04/25/94	3	1	Landlady	Fee
04/28/94	1	1a	*OP1	Foam
05/02/94	3	2	*OP2	Mound
05/04/94	2	1	*OP1	Foam
05/08/94	3	1	*OP1	Foam
05/13/94	3	1	*OP1	It's Ice
05/17/94	3	2	*OP2	Glide
05/21/94	3	1	*OP1	Foam
05/27/94	5	1	Wilson	Foam
06/10/94	4	1	*OP1	Foam
06/17/94	5	1	*OP1	Foam
06/21/94	3	1	*OP1	Foam
07/01/94	8	1	*OP1	Foam
07/09/94	6	1	*OP1	Foam
07/14/94	3	1	*OP1	Bouncing
07/15/94	1	2	SettingSail	*CL2
10/09/94	4	1	*OP1	Foam
10/15/94	5	2	Also Sprac	Halley's
10/20/94	3	1	*OP1	GoldLady
10/23/94	3	2	*OP2	Bouncing
10/26/94	2	1	Suzie	*CL1
10/29/94	3	1	Simple	Foam
11/12/94	5	1	*OP1	Foam
11/18/94	5	E	Baby Arms	*CLE
11/22/94	3	2	Blackbird	BBFCM
12/04/94	9	1	*OP1	Foam
12/07/94	2	1	Peaches	Sloth
12/29/94	5	1	*OP1	Foam
06/08/95	5	1	Ha Ha Ha	Guelah
06/13/95	3	1	*OP1	Foam
06/16/95	3	2	*OP2	Free
06/23/95	5	2	*OP2	Lizards
06/29/95	5	1	*OP1	Taste
07/02/95	3	2	*OP2	Makisupa
09/28/95	3	1	CTB	Billy
09/30/95	2	2	*OP2	Fog
10/05/95	3	2	Also Sprac	Forbin's
10/14/95	6	1	Tela	*CL1
10/19/95	3	1	CTB	Horn
10/22/95	3	1	Sloth	Weigh
10/27/95	3	1	*OP1	Fluffhead
11/10/95	5	1	Bouncing	Fog
11/16/95	5	1	CTB	Chess
11/21/95	3	1	Dog Faced	*CL1
11/25/95	3	1	Wolfman's	*CL1
12/02/95	5	1	Caspian	Mound
12/08/95	4	1	Simple	Fluffhead
12/12/95	3	2	Simple	*CL2
12/15/95	2	2	TweezRep	It's Ice
12/17/95	2	E	HelloBaby	*CLE
12/31/95	4	2	Str Design	Mike's
06/06/96	2	1	PoorHeart	FunkBitch
07/03/96	1	1a	*OP1	Stash
07/11/96	6	1	*OP1	Cavern
07/13/96	2	1a	Sample	Cavern
07/19/96	4	1a	*OP1	Foam
07/23/96	3	2	ASZ	Lovin Cup
08/02/96	3	2	*OP2	Simpl
08/07/96	4	2	*OP2	Free
08/14/96	2	2	*OP2	YEM
08/17/96	4	2	Curtain	It's Ice
10/18/96	3	1	*OP1	Guelah
10/22/96	3	1	Curtain	Bouncing
10/27/96	4	1	*OP1	PYITE
11/03/96	4	1	My Friend	Billy
11/08/96	3	1	*OP1	Axilla
11/11/96	2	1	Axilla	*CL1
11/16/96	4	2	La Grange	Kung
11/22/96	3	1	It's Ice	Wolfman's
11/30/96	5	1	*OP1	PYITE
12/28/96	5	1	*OP1	NICU
02/14/97	5	1	*OP1	NICU
02/18/97	3	1	PYITE	NICU
02/20/97	1	2	DayinLife	Adeline
02/25/97	4	1	*OP1	My Soul
03/02/97	4	1	My Soul	Antelope
06/19/97	5	1	Vultures	*CL1
06/24/97	4	1	Guelah	Talk
07/06/97	8	1	*OP1	Old Home
07/22/97	5	1	*OP1	My Soul
07/31/97	6	2	*OP2	Circus
08/06/97	3	2	*OP2	My Soul
08/13/97	5	2	*OP2	Ghost
➢ 8/17/97	**3**			

Sample In A Jar [162]

Sample In A Jar [Sample]

By Anastasio/Marshall

02/04/93	[506]	1	Lizards	Glide
02/09/93	4	2	MSO	BBJ
02/27/93	15	2	PoorHeart	BBJ
03/03/93	2	1	Paul&Silas	RunJim
03/14/93	7	1	Paul&Silas	Reba
03/19/93	4	2	Uncle Pen	Lizards
03/24/93	3	1	IDK	AmGrace
03/25/93	1	2	Curtain	Uncle Pen
03/27/93	2	1	Uncle Pen	IDK
03/31/93	3	1	PYITE	Reba
04/02/93	2	2	RunJim	Uncle Pen
04/16/93	8	1	Llama	Rift
04/20/93	3	2	Fluffhead	BBJ
05/01/93	9	1	Rift	It's Ice
07/15/93	9	1	Rift	Divided
07/17/93	2	1	RunJim	My Mind
07/22/93	3	1	My Mind	Foam
07/28/93	5	1	Ya Mar	Foam
07/31/93	3	1	Rift	Ya Mar
08/06/93	3	1	Curtain	Rift
08/15/93	8	1	*OP1	All Things
08/25/93	6	1	Divided	Sparkle
12/28/93	3	2	*OP1	YEM
12/30/93	2	1	Curtain	Paul&Silas
04/04/94	2	1	Divided	Scent
04/06/94	2	1	Lizards	Scent
04/09/94	2	2	*OP2	Reba
04/11/94	2	2	Uncle Pen	BBJ
04/13/94	1	2	Curtain	Reba
04/16/94	3	2	*OP2	PoorHeart
04/18/94	2	2	Also Sprac	Sparkle
04/20/94	1	2	Paul&Silas	BBJ
04/22/94	2	1	PYITE	All Things
04/23/94	1	2	Mound	Sparkle
04/25/94	2	2	Curtain	My Mind
04/28/94	1	1	Foam	Rift
04/30/94	2	1	PoorHeart	PYITE
05/02/94	1	1	Foam	*CL1
05/03/94	1	1	Scent	Adeline
05/04/94	1	1	Foam	It's Ice
05/06/94	1	2	Uncle Pen	Reba
05/07/94	1	E	AmGrace	*CLE
05/10/94	2	1	PoorHeart	Divided
05/12/94	1	1	Lizards	*CL1
05/14/94	2	1	Reba	MSO
05/16/94	1	1	PoorHeart	Divided
05/17/94	1	2	BBJ	Love You
05/19/94	1	2	*OP2	Sparkle
05/21/94	2	2	Dinner	Bowie
05/23/94	2	1	Chalkdust	Foam
05/25/94	1	1	Curtain	Uncle Pen
05/26/94	1	1	Divided	*CL1
05/28/94	2	1	Rift	Foam
06/10/94	3	1	Foam	Nellie
06/13/94	2	1	PoorHeart	Divided
06/14/94	1	E	*OPE	*CLE
06/17/94	2	2	Also Sprac	PoorHeart
06/18/94	1	1	Divided	*CL1
06/21/94	2	1	Mound	It's Ice
06/22/94	1	2	Jesus	*CL2
06/24/94	2	1	Adeline	*CL1
06/25/94	1	1	Mango	Scent
06/26/94	1	2	Life Boy	Wolfman's
06/29/94	1	1	Curtain	Reba
07/01/94	2	1	Foam	NICU
07/02/94	1	2	Maze	Slave
07/05/94	2	1	Rift	Curtain
07/06/94	1	2	BBFCM	BBFCM
07/08/94	1	2	Rift	Reba
07/10/94	2	2	*OP2	Bowie
07/13/94	1	1	PoorHeart	Foam
07/14/94	1	2	Also Sprac	Maze
07/15/94	1	1	Rift	Divided
07/16/94	1	1	Sparkle	*CL1
10/08/94	2	2	Also Sprac	Rift
10/10/94	2	1	*OP1	Divided
10/12/94	1	2	Harry	*CL2
10/14/94	2	1	BurAlive	Divided
10/16/94	2	2	Adeline	*CL2
10/20/94	2	E	*OPE	*CLE
10/23/94	3	1	Maze	*CL1
10/25/94	1	1	Lizards	*CL1
10/28/94	3	1	All Things	Carolina
11/02/94	3	2	Lizards	*CL2
11/04/94	2	1	*OP1	It's Ice
11/12/94	1	E	*OPE	*CLE
11/16/94	3	1	*OP1	Foam
11/20/94	4	1	Divided	*CL1
11/23/94	2	E	*OPE	*CLE
11/26/94	2	2	Lizards	Slave
12/01/94	3	1	*OP1	Uncle Pen
12/03/94	2	1	Guyute	*CL1
12/06/94	2	2	Curtain	Also Sprac
12/10/94	4	1	Lizards	Divided
12/30/94	3	2	*OP2	PoorHeart
05/16/95	2	1	Adeline	*CL1
06/07/95	1	2	AArmy	Harry
06/10/95	3	2	AmGrace	*CL2
06/17/95	5	2	Harry	*CL2
06/22/95	3	1	*OP1	Scent
06/25/95	3	2	Maze	Scent
06/28/95	2	2	*OP2	PoorHeart
07/02/95	4	1	*OP1	Divided
09/28/95	3	2	AmGrace	Antelope
09/30/95	2	1	I'm Blue	*CL1
10/03/95	2	1	TMWSIY	YEM
10/06/95	2	1	Lizards	*CL1
10/08/95	2	2	Ya Mar	YEM
10/11/95	1	1	Julius	*CL1
10/15/95	3	2	Lizards	Suspicious
10/17/95	1	1	*OP1	Stash
10/22/95	4	1	PoorHeart	I'm Blue
10/25/95	2	1	Ya Mar	Divided
10/28/95	2	1	Uncle Pen	Lizards
11/09/95	3	1	Tela	*CL1
11/12/95	3	2	Keyboard	Slave
11/18/95	4	1	I'm Blue	*CL1
11/22/95	3	1	Lizards	Adeline
11/28/95	3	1	HelloBaby	*CL1
11/30/95	2	1	*OP1	Curtain
12/04/95	3	2	YEM	Frankstein
12/08/95	3	1	*OP1	PoorHeart
12/12/95	3	1	Ya Mar	Divided
12/16/95	3	2	*OP2	Reba
12/30/95	4	1	Divided	*CL1
04/26/96	2	1a	Harry	DayinLife
06/06/96	1	2	Fee	*CL2
07/07/96	4	1a	*OP1	Divided
07/11/96	3	1	Scent	*CL1
07/13/96	2	1a	*OP1	RunJim
07/17/96	2	1a	Divided	Bowie
07/22/96	4	1a	*OP1	PoorHeart
07/25/96	3	1a	PYITE	It's Ice
08/04/96	2	2	Scent	Bowie
08/12/96	5	E	*OPE	*CLE
08/14/96	2	2	Rosie	TweezRep
08/17/96	2	1	Lizards	Taste
10/16/96	1	1	Mound	It's Ice
10/18/96	2	1	Taste	*CL1
10/21/96	2	1	SSB	CTB
10/26/96	4	1	Theme	*CL1
11/03/96	5	1	NICU	Theme
11/06/96	1	2	Scent	FunkBitch
11/11/96	4	2	Curtain	Tweezer
11/14/96	2	2	Llama	Taste
11/22/96	5	1	Ginseng	FEFY
11/24/96	2	1	IDK	Antelope
11/29/96	2	E	*OPE	*CLE
12/01/96	2	1	Silent	Antelope
12/04/96	2	1	Timber Ho	Train Song
12/31/96	5	1	Divided	TweezRep
02/16/97	3	2	*OP2	CTB
02/20/97	3	2	*OP2	CTB
02/25/97	4	2	Beauty	PYITE
03/02/97	4	1	Uncle Pen	Guyute
03/18/97	1	1	NICU	PYITE
06/16/97	3	1	Water	Beauty
06/21/97	3	1a	*OP1	Also Sprac
07/05/97	9	1a	Uncle Pen	Theme
07/23/97	7	2	Ghost	YEM
07/29/97	3	2	Taste	Rocky Top
08/06/97	5	2	CTB	Antelope
08/13/97	5	2	McGrupp	Also Sprac
➢ 8/17/97	**8 or 3**			

Sanity [18]*

Sanity [Sanity]

By Phish/Dude of Life

10/31/86	[9]	2	Harry	Skin It
08/21/87	10	3	Jam	SwingLow
07/25/88	29	3	BBFCM	Icculus
08/06/88	2	2	Satin Doll	BBFCM
02/06/89	14	1	ABlues	A-Train
02/07/89	1	3	*OP3	Fluffhead
05/26/89	37	1	Weekpaug	Halley's
05/28/89	2	2	Bathtub	Ride Capt.
03/11/92	282	E	*OPE	Memories
03/20/92	6	2	Weekpaug	Sloth
04/16/92	19	2	*OP2	Llama
04/21/92	4	2	Lively Up	Maze
05/01/92	7	2	*OP2	BurAlive
05/17/92	13	2	Brother	Love You
04/29/94	200	1	Spilt	My Mind
06/24/94	36	2	Simple	Llama
12/31/95	147	3	YEM	Frankstein
10/31/96	43	1	*OP1	HwayHell
➢ 8/17/97	**80**			

Scent Of A Mule [89]

Scent Of A Mule [Scent]

By Gordon

04/04/94	[615]	1	Sample	Maze
04/06/94	2	1	Sample	Fee
04/10/94	3	1	IDK	DWD
04/14/94	3	2	Silent	YEM
04/21/94	6	2	Weekpaug	BBJ
04/29/94	6	1	FEFY	Sloth
05/03/94	3	1	Sqirm Coil	Sample
05/07/94	3	1	FEFY	Split&Melt
05/10/94	2	2	Reba	Harry
05/13/94	2	2	Peaches	YEM
05/17/94	3	1	If I Could	Ginseng
05/20/94	2	1	FEFY	Dog Faced
05/25/94	4	1	Axilla 2	MSO
06/09/94	5	2	Halley's	Ginseng
06/11/94	2	2	Fluffhead	Split&Melt
06/13/94	1	2	Jesus	Split&Melt
06/17/94	3	2	Bathtub	Cavern
06/19/94	2	1	FEFY	Stash
06/22/94	2	1	If I Could	Stash
06/25/94	3	1	Sample	Tela
06/26/94	1	2	Wolfman's	Dog Faced
06/30/94	2	1	Glide	Bouncing
07/02/94	2	1	FEFY	Tweezer
07/09/94	5	1	Guelah	DwD
07/14/94	3	1	TMWSIY	Fluffhead
07/16/94	2	2	ACDCBag	Harry
10/07/94	1	2	Wilson	Tweezer
10/09/94	2	2	Bouncing	YEM
10/12/94	2	2	Bouncing	YEM
10/15/94	3	2	Halley's	YEM
10/18/94	2	2	Reba	Life Boy
10/21/94	2	2	FEFY	Slave
10/26/94	4	1	Dog Faced	Oh Kee
10/28/94	2	1	Guelah	Stash
11/02/94	3	1	Stash	Guitar
11/04/94	2	1	Mockbird	Suzie
11/14/94	3	1	My Friend	Guelah
11/17/94	2	1	Helter	Maze
11/20/94	3	1	Fee	Stash
11/23/94	2	2	Fee	Tweezer
11/28/94	3	1	Also Sprac	Stash
12/03/94	4	1	Guelah	Antelope
12/08/94	4	1	ACDCBag	PYITE
12/30/94	5	1	Fee	Cavern
06/07/95	3	1	If I Could	Wedge
06/09/95	2	2	Wedge	Cavern
06/15/95	4	2	Theme	AArmy
06/22/95	5	1	Sample	Ha Ha Ha
06/25/95	3	2	Sample	Mike's
06/30/95	4	1	ACDCBag	Horn
07/02/95	2	2	Makisupa	Tweezer
09/28/95	3	1	Billy	Stash
09/30/95	2	2	If I Could	Mike's
10/05/95	3	2	Mockbird	Cavern
10/14/95	6	2	HelloBaby	Cavern
10/20/95	4	2	Timber Ho	Simple
10/25/95	4	1	Wedge	Free
10/28/95	2	2	Theme	YEM
11/10/95	4	2	Free	YEM
11/15/95	4	2	Theme	Mike's
11/19/95	3	2	Billy	Harry
11/24/95	3	2	Catapult	Bathtub
11/30/95	4	2	Antelope	Free
12/05/95	4	2	Keyboard	Life Boy
12/11/95	4	2	Fog	Harry
12/16/95	4	2	Reba	Cavern
12/30/95	4	2	Life Boy	Cavern
04/26/96	2	1a	Wolfman's	Also Sprac
06/06/96	1	1	BBFCM	HwayHell
07/05/96	2	1a	YEM	Bowie
07/11/96	5	1	Stash	Sample
07/23/96	9	1	Gumbo	DWD
08/04/96	4	2	Reba	Sample
08/10/96	4	2	DWD	Free
08/17/96	5	3	Frankstein	Tweezer
10/17/96	2	2	Bathtub	Free
10/22/96	4	2	Lawn Boy	Mike's
10/27/96	4	1	Fee	Split&Melt
11/06/96	5	2	Weekpaug	Sample
11/14/96	6	2	Steep	Life Mars
11/18/96	3	2	Steep	Tweezer
11/27/96	5	2	Jesus	Tweezer
12/02/96	4	2	Free	Harry
12/30/96	5	2	Lifeboy	Slave
02/14/97	3	2	RockaW	DayinLife
02/26/97	9	2	Theme	Slave
07/06/97	20	1	CTB	Chalkdust
08/09/97	16	2	Steep	Slave
08/17/97	6	3	Dirt	Caspian
➢ 8/17/97	**0**			

Setting Sail [2]

Setting Sail [SettingSail]

By Marshall

04/20/91	[304]	1	YEM	*CL1
07/15/94	383	2	Julius	RunJim
➢ 8/17/97	**255**			

Silent In The Morning [114]

See The Horse

Simple [72]*

Simple [Simple]

By Gordon

05/27/94 [656] 2 Mike's Mike's
06/17/94 9 2 Mike's Mike's
06/22/94 4 2 Mike's I am H2
06/24/94 2 2 McGrupp Sanity
07/02/94 6 2 Mike's Mike's
10/08/94 12 2 Mike's Mike's
10/13/94 4 2 Mike's Mike's
10/15/94 2 1 Sparkle Maze
10/18/94 2 1 *OP1 My Friend
10/21/94 2 2 Mike's Mike's
10/23/94 2 1 Sparkle PoorHeart
10/25/94 1 2 Mike's Mango
10/26/94 1 1 *OP1 It's Ice
10/29/94 3 1 Sparkle RunJim
10/31/94 1 1 Sparkle Divided
11/03/94 2 2 Also Sprac PoorHeart
11/04/94 1 2 Mike's Mike's
11/13/94 2 1 Sparkle Reba
11/16/94 2 2 Mike's Jam
11/20/94 4 2 Reba Rift
11/23/94 2 1 Sparkle It's Ice
11/25/94 1 2 Mike's Harpua
11/28/94 2 1 Sparkle Divided
12/02/94 3 1 Sparkle It's Ice
12/06/94 3 2 Mike's Mango
12/08/94 2 1 Catapult Lizards
12/10/94 2 2 *OP2 Maze
12/28/94 1 1 Mound Julius
12/30/94 2 1 Sparkle Stash
12/31/94 1 E *OPE *CLE
06/08/95 3 2 *OP2 Rift
06/14/95 4 E *OPE Rocky Top
06/19/95 4 2 *OP2 Bowie
06/23/95 3 1 *OP1 Chalkdust
06/29/95 5 1 Rift Split&Melt
07/03/95 4 E *OPE AmGrace
10/02/95 5 2 Llama Keyboard
10/15/95 9 2 Julius Tweezer
10/20/95 3 2 Scent Guitar
10/27/95 5 2 PoorHeart McGrupp
11/09/95 4 1 PYITE Reba
11/16/95 6 1 Ya Mar Timber Ho
11/21/95 3 2 *OP2 Bowie
11/29/95 5 2 Sparkle Possum
12/02/95 3 2 Maze Faht
12/08/95 4 1 PoorHeart RunJim
12/12/95 3 2 Lizards RunJim
12/16/95 3 2 Mike's Weekpaug
12/30/95 4 1 Bowie It's Ice
07/21/96 17 2 Antelope Caspian
08/02/96 5 2 Taste RunJim
08/06/96 3 1 Suzie Theme
08/12/96 3 2 Sparkle Caspian
08/16/96 3 2 Mike's Contact
10/16/96 2 2 Train Song SweptAwy
10/21/96 4 2 Life Mars Horse
10/26/96 4 2 Sparkle McGrupp
10/31/96 3 3 Maze SweptAwy
11/08/96 5 2 Bouncing Lovin Cup
11/18/96 7 2 Also Sprac SweptAwy
11/23/96 3 2 Mike's Makisupa
11/29/96 3 2 Wilson Sparks
12/01/96 2 2 Sparkle DayinLife
12/06/96 3 2 Mike's Harry
12/31/96 4 2 Sparkle SweptAwy
02/16/97 3 2 Sparkle Circus
02/22/97 5 2 Sparkle Jesus
07/02/97 20 1 Mike's Maze
07/22/97 8 2 Mike's I am H2
08/03/97 8 2 Julius Fluffhead
08/09/97 3 2 Funny SweptAwy
08/16/97 5 2 Wolfman's My Soul
➢ **8/17/97 2**

Slave [107]

Slave To The Traffic Light [Slave]

By Anastasio/Dude of Life

12/01/84 [0] 1a FOTM Makisupa
10/30/85 4 1a Possum Sally
04/15/86 3 1a Quinn Makisupa
10/15/86 1 1a Wilson Makisupa
10/31/86 1 1 Golgi Melt Guns
04/24/87 5 1a Reagan *CL1
04/29/87 1 3 Timber Ho Sparks
05/11/87 1 1a Possum Sally
08/29/87 5 2 Clod SwingLow
09/12/87 2 1 Clod FunkBitch
10/14/87 2 1 Golgi Chase
01/30/88 1 2 Wilson Corrina
03/11/88 3 1 Golgi Flat Fee
06/20/88 11 1 *OP1 Peaches
07/12/88 3 1 Makisupa ACDCBag
07/23/88 1 3 Dinner Curtis
08/06/88 4 2 BBFCM *CL2
09/08/88 2 1 WalkAway WildC
10/29/88 2 3 Timber Ho Donna
11/05/88 2 1 *OP1 TimeLoves
11/11/88 1 1 YEM FOam
02/07/89 6 2 Suzie Bike
04/15/89 14 2 Golgi Mango
05/06/89 11 2 Golgi Divided
05/09/89 3 2 IIDBT Esther
05/26/89 9 3 *OP3 FunkBitch
05/28/89 2 1 Fee Esther
06/30/89 7 2 Curtain Bathtub
08/26/89 9 2 Ya Mar ACDCBag
10/20/89 11 E La Grange *CLE
12/08/89 19 2 Timber Ho IDK
03/01/90 17 E Carolina *CLE
03/09/90 5 2 Dog Log HwayHell
03/11/90 1 2 Harpua ACDCBag
04/08/90 7 2 Lizards Mike's
04/22/90 9 1 MSO Mike's
06/01/90 17 1a Divided Possum
03/17/91 68 2 Fee Chalkdust
10/24/91 70 2 Tube Dinner
08/06/93 240 2 Halley's Rosie
08/20/93 11 2 Also Sprac Split&Melt
12/30/93 8 2 PurplRain *CL2
04/09/94 6 2 Tela Cavern
04/14/94 4 2 Dog Faced *CL2
04/24/94 9 1 It's Ice *CL1
05/03/94 6 2 BeLikeYou *CL2
05/13/94 7 1 My Friend Suzie
05/17/94 3 2 Love You *CL2
05/22/94 4 2 Rift TweezRep
06/13/94 10 2 Terrapin *CL2
06/23/94 8 2 Life Boy *CL2
07/02/94 7 2 Sample HwayHell
07/13/94 7 2 Mound Suzie
10/10/94 7 2 Love You *CL2
10/21/94 8 2 Scent *CL2
10/27/94 5 E *OPE Icculus
10/31/94 3 3 Bouncing Rift
11/04/94 3 2 Golgi *CL2
11/14/94 3 2 YSZahov PoorHeart
11/17/94 2 2 Love You Golgi
11/26/94 7 2 Sample *CL2
12/03/94 5 2 Gumbo Touch Me
12/10/94 6 2 PoorHeart Cavern
12/31/94 4 3 Suzie *CL3
06/07/95 2 1 FunkBitch *CL1
06/09/95 2 2 Adeline *CL2
06/15/95 4 2 AArmy *CL2
06/20/95 4 E *OPE AmGrace
06/25/95 4 E Bouncing *CLE
07/02/95 6 2 AArmy *CL2
09/28/95 3 1 AArmy *CL1
10/02/95 3 2 Keyboard HelloBaby
10/06/95 3 2 Suspicious *CL2
10/15/95 6 1 PoorHeart IDK
10/22/95 5 2 Uncle Pen Cavern
10/29/95 5 1 Gumbo Adeline
11/12/95 5 2 Sample Rosie
11/18/95 4 1 PYITE I'm Blue
11/29/95 7 2 LongJourn *CL2
12/07/95 6 1 Rift Guyute
12/09/95 2 2 Lawn Boy Crossroad
12/14/95 3 2 NICU *CL2
12/28/95 4 2 Uncle Pen *CL2
07/12/96 13 2 NICU Suzie
07/23/96 8 2 Bike *CL2
08/04/96 4 2 Adeline *CL2
08/13/96 6 1 Glide *CL1
08/17/96 3 2 Golgi *CL2
10/19/96 4 2 Sparkle Bouncing
10/23/96 3 2 Suzie Julius
10/29/96 4 2 Suspicious HelloBaby
11/11/96 8 2 Contact *CL2
11/22/96 7 2 Theme HelloBaby
12/01/96 6 2 JGB *CL2
12/30/96 6 2 Scent *CL2
02/13/97 2 2 PYITE Circus
02/18/97 4 1 CharZero *CL1
02/26/97 6 2 Scent *CL2
03/02/97 3 2 CharZero TweezRep
03/18/97 1 2 Chalkdust *CL2
06/13/97 1 2 Vultures Chalkdust
07/01/97 11 2 Lovin Cup *CL2
07/21/97 8 2 FunkBitch *CL2
08/03/97 9 E Bouncing *CLE
08/09/97 3 2 Scent Weekpaug
08/16/97 5 2 Jam Rocky Top
➢ **8/17/97 1**

Sleeping Monkey [50]

Sleeping Monkey [Sl Monkey

By Anastasio/Marshall

03/06/92 [384] E *OPE *CLE
03/11/92 2 E Carolina *CLE
03/14/92 3 E *OPE GTBT
03/19/92 2 E *OPE Rocky Top
03/25/92 4 E *OPE TweezRep
03/26/92 1 E *OPE Chalkdust
03/30/92 3 E *OPE Oh Kee
04/04/92 4 E *OPE TweezRep
04/09/92 4 E *OPE Rocky Top
04/16/92 4 E *OPE *CLE
04/19/92 3 E *OPE Cavern
04/23/92 3 E *OPE TweezRep
05/02/92 6 E *OPE BBFCM
05/07/92 4 E Adeline Rocky Top
05/14/92 5 E *OPE Rocky Top
07/14/92 17 E *OPE *CLE
11/23/92 35 E *OPE Rocky Top
12/08/92 12 2 BBJ *CL2
02/20/93 23 E *OPE *CLE
02/27/93 6 E *OPE AmGrace
03/21/93 14 E *OPE Adeline
05/02/93 31 E *OPE AmGrace
08/02/93 22 E *OPE AmGrace
04/30/94 44 E *OPE HwayHell
05/22/94 16 E *OPE *CLE
05/25/94 2 E *OPE TweezRep
06/10/94 6 E *OPE Rocky Top
06/17/94 5 E *OPE Rocky Top
06/30/94 10 E *OPE PoorHeart
07/09/94 7 E *OPE TweezRep
07/15/94 4 E *OPE Rocky Top
10/09/94 4 E *OPE PoorHeart
10/21/94 9 2 Weekpaug Curtain
10/29/94 7 2 Antelope Antelope
10/31/94 1 3 Rift PoorHeart
11/17/94 8 2 Bowie Sparkle
11/28/94 8 2 Tweezer Julius
12/01/94 2 E *OPE TweezRep
12/04/94 3 E *OPE Rocky Top
12/29/94 7 E LongJourn *CLE
06/26/95 19 E *OPE Rocky Top
07/02/95 5 2 Ha Ha Ha AArmy
10/20/95 18 E *OPE Rocky Top
10/24/95 3 2 YEM Antelope
11/11/95 8 2 Fluffhead Frankstein
12/07/95 18 2 Julius Sparkle
08/13/96 40 E *OPE Rocky Top
11/15/96 25 2 Mike's Mustard
02/17/97 21 E *OPE Rocky Top
08/13/97 46 2 Isabella McGrupp
➢ **8/17/97 3**

The Sloth [120]*

The Sloth [Sloth]

By Anastasio

08/21/87 [19] 2 Creek *CL2
01/30/88 9 2 YEM WhipPost
03/12/88 4 1a Mockbird Possum
05/15/88 5 1a IDK Harpua
05/25/88 2 3 *OP3 IDK
06/15/88 1 2 ACDCBag Contact
07/23/88 6 2 *OP2 Fire
10/12/88 9 2 Contact ACDCBag
12/02/88 5 1 *OP1 Golgi
01/26/89 1 1a Mockbird Possum
02/07/89 4 1 Foam Possum
04/14/89 13 1 Lizards Possum
04/20/89 3 1 Suzie Possum
05/06/89 9 1 Esther Possum
05/09/89 3 1 Weekpaug Possum
05/21/89 8 1 Split&Melt YEM
05/26/89 1 1 Halley's YEM
05/28/89 2 3 La Grange Sally
06/23/89 5 2 *OP2 Fluffhead
08/17/89 7 1 McGrupp Rocky Top
10/06/89 10 1a Weekpaug Golgi
10/26/89 8 2 Bathtub Fluffhead
11/10/89 7 2 Fluffhead Lizards
11/16/89 2 2 *OP2 ACDCBag
02/24/90 32 2 *OP2 ACDCBag
03/09/90 7 1 Mockbird Possum
03/11/90 1 2 A-Train Ya Mar
04/04/90 3 2 Uncle Pen IDK
04/06/90 2 2 Esther Harry
04/13/90 6 2 Curtis Harry
04/18/90 1 2 Fee FunkBitch
05/04/90 10 2 RunJim Uncle Pen
05/24/90 9 1 *OP1 Bouncing
09/16/90 11 1a Bouncing Landlady
10/04/90 6 1 Destiny Uncle Pen
11/02/90 9 1 Divided Mike's
11/26/90 8 1 RunJim Reba
11/30/90 1 2 IDK Antelope
02/02/91 9 2 *OP2 Antelope
02/07/91 2 2 Lizards Destiny
02/09/91 2 1 Mango TMWSIY
02/15/91 2 1 Mango Dinner
02/16/91 1 1 *OP1 MSO
02/27/91 8 2 Oh Kee Love You
03/01/91 2 2 Guelah Possum
03/07/91 3 2 Landlady RunJim
03/13/91 3 2 RunJim Reba
03/23/91 6 1 *OP1 Divided
04/05/91 7 2 Lizards Dinner
04/15/91 5 1 *OP1 Ya Mar
04/18/91 2 2 Oh Kee Paul&Silas
04/20/91 2 2 *OP2 Ya Mar
04/22/91 2 1 RunJim Reba
04/26/91 2 1 Sqirm Coil Possum
05/03/91 3 2 Curtain Landlady
05/10/91 3 1 Dinner Landlady
05/25/91 6 1a Dinner McGrupp
07/14/91 4 1 Mockbird IDK
07/21/91 5 2 Lawn Boy Esther
07/25/91 3 1 MSO Foam
08/03/91 3 1 Wilson RunJim
10/11/91 12 2 Mango PoorHeart
10/13/91 2 1 ACDCBag McGrupp
10/31/91 11 1 Ya Mar Chalkdust
11/08/91 5 2 *OP2 Sparkle
11/12/91 3 1 Tube Harry
11/19/91 5 2 Mango Reba
11/24/91 5 1 *OP1 Paul&Silas
12/05/91 3 2 Fee Sqirm Coil
03/11/92 6 2 NICU Lizards
03/13/92 2 2 My Mind Rift
03/17/92 2 2 Glide PoorHeart
03/20/92 2 2 Sanity Mango
03/27/92 5 1 Paul&Silas Divided
03/30/92 2 1 All Things RunJim
04/03/92 3 2 Curtain Possum
04/07/92 4 1 Rift RunJim
04/24/92 12 1 Uncle Pen Landlady
05/01/92 4 1 NICU Divided
05/12/92 9 1 All Things Possum
05/14/92 1 1 All Things Sparkle
07/15/92 18 2 *OP2 Divided
11/20/92 31 1 Rift Reba
12/06/92 13 1 MSO Sqirm Coil
12/28/92 7 2 Reba YEM
02/10/93 10 1 Reba Divided
02/17/93 5 1 All Things RunJim
02/20/93 3 1 Foam Possum
03/05/93 9 1 Foam Rift
03/21/93 11 1 Sparkle Divided
03/22/93 1 2 Mockbird McGrupp
03/28/93 5 1 Lizards Maze
04/03/93 5 2 All Things YEM
04/13/93 5 2 Rift Uncle Pen
04/29/93 12 1 Paul&Silas RunJim
07/25/93 19 1 Rift My Mind
08/07/93 9 2 Avenu Sparkle
08/12/93 4 2 Lizards Maze
12/28/93 12 2 Lizards FEFY
04/17/94 15 2 Uncle Pen Reba
04/29/94 9 1 Scent Divided
05/22/94 17 1 Demand Divided
05/28/94 5 1 Silent Maze
06/24/94 14 1 Fee All Things
06/26/94 2 1 Mockbird McGrupp
07/08/94 8 1 Mockbird McGrupp
10/12/94 11 1 Reba PoorHeart
12/07/94 38 1 RunJim Ya Mar
06/26/95 24 1 NICU My Mind
10/22/95 25 1 My Mind RunJim
12/09/95 29 1 NICU Rift
12/16/95 5 1 Ya Mar Divided
12/31/95 5 1 PYITE Reba
08/04/96 22 1 Mango Maze
10/21/96 14 1 CTB Divided
11/03/96 9 1 Billy NICU
11/09/96 4 1 PoorHeart Divided
11/27/96 11 1 Chalkdust Uncle Pen
12/30/96 9 1 Ya Mar Llama
02/23/97 10 1 All Things Treat
➢ **8/17/97 44**

Sparkle [251]

Sparkle [Sparkle]

By Anastasio/Marshall

09/25/91 [335] 2 Stash Cavern
09/26/91 1 2 Brother Landlady
09/27/91 1 2 Tela Split&Melt
09/28/91 1 2 Guelah Cavern
10/04/91 4 1 Guelah Suzie
10/10/91 3 2 IDK Oh Kee
10/15/91 4 1 Split&Melt Reba
10/18/91 6 2 Bathtub Tweezer
10/27/91 4 2 Mockbird It's Ice
10/31/91 3 1 Chalkdust Foam
11/01/91 1 1 ACDCBag Landlady
11/02/91 1 2 TMWSIY Guelah
11/07/91 2 1 Foam Cavern
11/08/91 1 2 Sloth Split&Melt
11/09/91 1 1 Foam Llama
11/13/91 3 1 It's Ice Chalkdust
11/14/91 1 1 Tube Brother
11/15/91 1 1 Chalkdust Cavern
11/16/91 1 1 It's Ice Fluffhead

11/19/91	1	1	Fee	Brother
11/20/91	1	1	Mockbird	Stash
11/22/91	2	1	Cavern	Brother
11/23/91	1	1	Guelah	Chalkdust
11/24/91	1	1	Fluffhead	It's Ice
11/30/91	1	1	Foam	Divided
12/04/91	1	2	Weekpaug	Lizards
12/05/91	1	2	Tweezer	Tube
12/06/91	1	2	Eliza	YEM
12/07/91	1	2	Chalkdust	Brother
12/31/91	1	1	Foam	Stash
03/06/92	1	1	Cavern	It's Ice
03/12/92	3	1	Foam	Stash
03/14/92	2	1	Reba	Foam
03/17/92	1	1	Cavern	It's Ice
03/19/92	1	1	Split&Melt	Golgi
03/21/92	2	1	Foam	Split&Melt
03/25/92	2	1	Wilson	Split&Melt
03/26/92	1	1	Foam	Stash
03/28/92	2	1	Foam	Stash
03/30/92	1	1	Guelah	Maze
04/01/92	2	1	All Things	RunJim
04/03/92	1	1	Guelah	Maze
04/04/92	1	1	It's Ice	Lizards
04/06/92	2	1	Foam	Reba
04/09/92	2	1	Landlady	Foam
04/12/92	1	1	It's Ice	Maze
04/13/92	1	2	Fluffhead	Mike's
04/15/92	1	1	Guelah	Stash
04/17/92	2	1	Foam	Stash
04/18/92	1	1	It's Ice	All Things
04/22/92	3	1	Reba	Guelah
04/24/92	2	1	Fluffhead	Stash
04/29/92	2	1	Foam	It's Ice
05/02/92	3	1	Mockbird	Reba
05/05/92	2	1	Curtain	Stash
05/06/92	1	1	Mockbird	Cavern
05/07/92	1	2	Landlady	Tweezer
05/09/92	2	1	Foam	Split&Melt
05/10/92	1	1a	Suzie	Stash
05/14/92	2	1	Sloth	Maze
05/15/92	1	1a	Cavern	Stash
05/17/92	2	2	Love You	Harry
05/18/92	1	1	Horn	Antelope
06/19/92	1	1a	Sqirm Coil	Cavern
06/24/92	3	1a	IDK	Cavern
06/27/92	1	1a	Foam	Reba
07/09/92	4	1a	Landlady	Stash
07/10/92	1	1a	Reba	Maze
07/11/92	1	1a	Foam	Stash
07/14/92	2	1	Maze	It's Ice
07/16/92	2	1	It's Ice	Wilson
07/17/92	1	1a	Chalkdust	Stash
07/21/92	3	1a	It's Ice	Stash
07/25/92	3	1a	Foam	Stash
07/30/92	4	1a	Horn	It's Ice
08/15/92	6	1a	Landlady	Guelah
08/23/92	4	1a	Maze	Cavern
08/25/92	2	1a	It's Ice	Stash
08/27/92	1	1a	Horn	YEM
11/20/92	6	1	Reba	Stash
11/22/92	2	1	Reba	Horn
11/25/92	2	1	Maze	It's Ice
11/28/92	2	1	Chalkdust	FEFY
11/30/92	1	1	Stash	It's Ice
12/02/92	2	1	Lizards	Horn
12/04/92	2	1	Glide	FEFY
12/05/92	1	2	Reba	Maze
12/07/92	2	1	Glide	Foam
12/08/92	1	2	Lawn Boy	Suzie
12/11/92	2	1	Guelah	My Friend
12/12/92	1	1	Foam	Cavern
12/28/92	2	1	Maze	Foam
12/30/92	2	1	Landlady	Split&Melt
12/31/92	1	1	It's Ice	Forbin's
02/03/93	1	2	Silent	YEM
02/05/93	2	1	Split&Melt	PYITE
02/07/93	2	1	It's Ice	Forbin's
02/10/93	2	2	Walk Line	YEM
02/12/93	2	1	Guelah	Split&Melt
02/15/93	2	1	Suzie	Guelah
02/18/93	2	1	Foam	Cavern
02/19/93	1	1	Mockbird	My Friend
02/22/93	3	1	Fee	Foam
02/25/93	2	2	It's Ice	Wilson
02/27/93	2	1	It's Ice	PYITE
03/02/93	1	1	Reba	It's Ice
03/05/93	1	1	Stash	It's Ice
03/08/93	2	1	Mockbird	It's Ice
03/12/93	2	2	Axilla	YEM
03/14/93	2	1	Guelah	Stash
03/16/93	1	E	*OPE	TweezRep
03/18/93	2	1	Mockbird	Horn
03/21/93	2	1	Maze	Sloth
03/22/93	1	1	Reba	Bowie
03/24/93	1	2	Split&Melt	Tweezer
03/26/93	2	1	Maze	Foam
03/28/93	2	1	FunkBitch	Split&Melt
03/31/93	2	1	Foam	Split&Melt
04/02/93	2	1	IDK	Maze
04/03/93	1	1	Guelah	Split&Melt
04/09/93	2	1	Chalkdust	Guelah
04/10/93	1	1	Weigh	Split&Melt
04/13/93	2	1	Foam	Possum
04/16/93	2	1	Guelah	Split&Melt
04/18/93	2	1	Split&Melt	Divided
04/20/93	1	1	Weigh	Stash
04/22/93	2	1	Suzie	It's Ice
04/23/93	1	1	Weigh	Split&Melt
04/24/93	1	1	SWMB	Antelope
04/27/93	2	1	It's Ice	Bowie
04/30/93	2	2	Wilson	Tweezer
05/02/93	2	1	Axilla	Divided
05/05/93	2	1	Foam	Bouncing
05/07/93	2	1	Split&Melt	Caravan
05/29/93	2	1a	Sqirm Coil	Cavern
07/15/93	2	2	Silent	It's Ice
07/17/93	2	2	It's Ice	BBJ
07/21/93	2	1a	Split&Melt	Sqirm Coil
07/22/93	1	2	WalkAway	It's Ice
07/24/93	2	2	Glide	Mike's
07/27/93	2	1a	Sqirm Coil	It's Ice
07/29/93	2	2	Life Boy	YEM
07/31/93	2	2	Maze	Mike's
08/03/93	2	2	Lizards	PurplRain
08/07/93	2	2	Sloth	My Friend
08/11/93	3	1	Stash	Cavern
08/14/93	3	1	It's Ice	Split&Melt
08/16/93	2	1	Reba	Foam
08/21/93	3	1	Stash	Landlady
08/25/93	2	1	Sample	Foam
08/28/93	2	2	Silent	It's Ice
12/29/93	2	1	Wilson	Stash
12/31/93	2	3	Lizards	Suzie
04/06/94	3	2	Wolfman's	Mike's
04/08/94	1	2	It's Ice	Harry
04/10/94	2	1	It's Ice	Split&Melt
04/14/94	3	1	Foam	DWD
04/18/94	4	2	Sample	Bathtub
04/21/94	2	1	Chalkdust	Foam
04/23/94	2	2	Sample	Harry
05/03/94	7	1	Maze	Stash
05/04/94	1	1	It's Ice	Axilla 2
05/07/94	2	2	Lovin Cup	Tweezer
05/16/94	6	2	Antelope	It's Ice
05/19/94	2	2	Sample	Mike's
05/23/94	4	2	If I Could	PYITE
05/26/94	2	1	Split&Melt	It's Ice
05/29/94	3	1	DWD	Julius
06/10/94	2	2	Life Boy	Possum
06/14/94	3	2	It's Ice	YEM
06/17/94	2	2	Harpua	BBJ
06/21/94	3	2	Julius	Harry
06/23/94	2	E	*OPE	TweezRep
06/25/94	2	2	Maze	Bathtub
06/30/94	3	2	YEM	Axilla 2
07/02/94	2	1	Life Boy	TweezRep
07/05/94	2	2	PYITE	Bathtub
07/09/94	3	2	Life Boy	BBJ
07/14/94	3	2	YEM	BBJ
07/16/94	2	1	Maze	Sample
10/08/94	2	1	Horn	DWD
10/10/94	2	1	Silent	Stash
10/13/94	2	1	FEFY	Stash
10/15/94	2	1	Wilson	Simple
10/23/94	6	1	My Friend	Simple
10/27/94	3	1	Wilson	Maze
10/29/94	2	1	My Friend	Simple
10/31/94	1	1	Frankstein	Simple
11/03/94	2	1	Dog Faced	DWD
11/13/94	3	1	Wilson	Simple
11/17/94	3	2	Sl Monkey	YEM
11/19/94	2	2	Suzie	YEM
11/23/94	3	1	Wilson	Simple
11/28/94	3	1	Guyute	Simple
12/02/94	3	1	Also Sprac	Simple
12/06/94	3	1	Jesus	Stash
12/09/94	3	1	Guyute	IDK
12/30/94	4	1	ACDCBag	Simple
06/09/95	5	1	Taste	Antelope
06/13/95	2	1	Terrapin	Chalkdust
06/15/95	2	1	My Friend	ACDCBag
06/19/95	3	2	Lovin Cup	YEM
06/25/95	5	1	If I Could	Divided
06/28/95	2	2	Gumbo	Suzie
07/03/95	5	1	Lovin Cup	It's Ice
09/29/95	3	1	ACDCBag	Divided
10/03/95	3	2	It's Ice	HGarry
10/08/95	4	1	Demand	Wolfman's
10/14/95	3	1	Catapult	AArmy
10/17/95	2	1	Glide	Free
10/21/95	3	2	Life Boy	YEM
10/25/95	3	2	Mike's	Weekpaug
10/31/95	4	1	Ya Mar	Free
11/10/95	2	2	Str Design	ACDCBag
11/15/95	4	1	Caspian	Split&Melt
11/18/95	2	2	ACDCBag	Free
11/24/95	4	1	Curtain	Stash
11/29/95	3	2	Timber Ho	Simple
12/04/95	4	2	Timber Ho	Ya Mar
12/07/95	2	2	Sl Monkey	Mike's
12/12/95	4	2	Free	DWD
12/17/95	4	2	Harry	Tweezer
12/31/95	4	1	Mockbird	Chalkdust
04/26/96	1	1a	ACDCBag	Stash
06/06/96	1	2	Chalkdust	Stash
07/03/96	1	1a	Stash	Taste
07/11/96	6	1	IDK	Stash
07/23/96	8	2	Lovin Cup	Mike's
08/07/96	7	1	PYITE	Stash
08/12/96	2	2	Timber Ho	Simpl
08/16/96	3	2	Split&Melt	Free
10/17/96	3	1	FunkBitch	Tweezer
10/19/96	2	2	ACDCBag	Slave
10/22/96	2	1	Split&Melt	Free
10/26/96	3	2	YEM	Simple
11/03/96	5	2	Brother	Tweezer
11/11/96	5	1	ACDCBag	Brother
11/16/96	4	1	Lawn Boy	Frankstein
11/24/96	5	2	Also Sprac	Bowie
11/29/96	2	2	Sparks	Taste
12/01/96	2	2	Tweezer	Simple
12/04/96	2	2	Caspian	PYITE
12/06/96	1	2	Julius	Mike's
12/31/96	4	2	Wilson	Simple
02/16/97	3	2	Free	Simple
02/22/97	5	2	Bathtub	Simple
07/03/97	21	2	Billy	Harry
07/29/97	11	1	Dirt	Ghost
08/02/97	3	2	Johnny B.	Wading
08/10/97	5	1	Bathtub	DWD
08/14/97	3	1	Treat	Harry
➢ **8/17/97**	**2**			

Split Open and Melt [221]

Split Open and Melt [Split&Melt]

By Anastasio

02/17/89	[66]	1a	Divided	Golgi
03/03/89	3	2	Lizards	A-Train
04/15/89	10	2	Divided	Suzie
04/20/89	2	2	YEM	Lizards
05/13/89	15	1	A-Train	*CL1
05/21/89	5	1	Weekpaug	Sloth
05/26/89	1	2	Mango	Bathtub
05/28/89	2	3	Jesus	Mango
06/23/89	5	2	Ya Mar	Possum
08/19/89	9	2	*OP2	A-Train
08/26/89	2	1	Harry	Divided
09/09/89	4	2	Alumni	Harry
10/01/89	1	2	Contact	Lizards
10/14/89	5	1	Ya Mar	Fee
10/20/89	1	2	Donna	Split&Melt
10/22/89	2	1	Rocky Top	Tela
11/02/89	4	1	Reba	Esther
11/03/89	1	1	MSO	Clod
11/10/89	3	1	*OP1	Oh Kee
11/30/89	4	2	Fee	A-Train
12/08/89	5	1	Suzie	Ya Mar
12/31/89	6	2	Ya Mar	Divided
01/28/90	5	1	Suzie	Tela
02/17/90	11	1a	Weekpaug	Bouncing
03/07/90	8	2	Bathtub	Tela
03/11/90	3	2	Ya Mar	Harpua
03/28/90	2	2	Lizards	Contact
09/15/90	39	2	*OP2	Eliza
10/05/90	8	2	Uncle Pen	Fee
02/01/91	25	1	RunJim	Bouncing
02/03/91	2	2	Mango	Bouncing
02/07/91	1	1	Mango	Bouncing
02/15/91	4	1	Divided	Fee
02/21/91	4	1	Dinner	Fee
02/27/91	5	1	MSO	Bouncing
03/13/91	8	2	Suzie	Bouncing
03/16/91	2	2	MSO	Magilla
03/22/91	3	1	Bouncing	Sqirm Coil
04/11/91	10	2	Lizards	Lawn Boy
04/15/91	3	1	RunJim	Fee
04/18/91	3	2	Suzie	Sqirm Coil
04/20/91	1	2	Ya Mar	Sqirm Coil
04/26/91	4	2	Uncle Pen	Bouncing
05/02/91	2	2	Fee	Tela
05/04/91	2	1	MSO	Guelah
07/13/91	11	1	TMWSIY	Bouncing
07/14/91	1	2	Bouncing	Magilla
07/18/91	2	2	PoorHeart	Lizards
07/21/91	3	1	PoorHeart	Lizards
07/24/91	2	1	BurAlive	Bathtub
07/25/91	1	E	*OPE	*CLE
07/26/91	1	E	Frankstein	*CLE
09/27/91	5	2	Sparkle	Mango
10/10/91	8	1	Paul&Silas	Bouncing
10/15/91	4	1	Sqirm Coil	Sparkle
10/18/91	2	2	Fee	MSO
11/01/91	9	1	Sqirm Coil	Fluffhead
11/08/91	4	2	Sparkle	Sqirm Coil
11/12/91	3	E	BBFCM	Memories
11/15/91	3	1	Curtain	Sqirm Coil
11/21/91	4	1	Horn	Esther

SONGS PLAYED BY YEAR
(1997 through 8/17/97)

Squirming Coil
1990 29
1991 63
1992 52
1993 42
1994 26
1995 18
1996 7
1997 6

Stash
1990 14
1991 45
1992 54
1993 56
1994 44
1995 25
1996 20
1997 16

Strange Design
1995 28
1996 7
1997 1

Suzie
1990 48
1991 49
1992 45
1993 22
1994 42
1995 22
1996 17
1997 3

Swept Away/Steep
1996 13
1997 7

Talk
1996 8
1997 3

Taste
1995 10
1996 28
1997 24

Tela
1990 9
1991 14
1992 9
1993 5
1994 12
1995 7
1996 2
1997 1

Theme From the Bottom
1995 26
1996 20
1997 20

Time
1997 1

Train Song
1996 14
1997 4

Tube
1990 5
1991 15
1992 2
1993 1
1994 1
1995 3
1996 3
1997 1

Twist Around
1997 8

Tweezer
1990 29
1991 33
1992 30
1993 37
1994 31
1995 18
1996 16
1997 4

Tweezer Reprise
1991 18
1992 23
1993 29
1994 25
1995 16
1996 10
1997 5

Twist Around
1997 8

Vultures
1997 9

Wading in the Velvet Sea
1997 10

Walfredo
1997 4

Waste
1996 17
1997 12

Water in the Sky
1997 14

The Wedge
1993 9
1994 0
1995 7
1996 1
1997 1

Stories Behind the Songs
(Continued)

when the song wasn't even included on *Billy Breathes*.

Stash: The lyrics for this song came from a series of Tom Marshall poems which Trey excerpted specific phrases from and then wrote music around.

Steep: On Billy Breathes, Steep is two portions of the band's "Blob" stitched together. It has always been paired with Swept Away—as on the album—when performed live.

Taste: This song was temporarily superseded by The Fog That Surrounds, which used basically the same music and some of the same lyrics on fall tour 1995. But in recording sessions for *Billy Breathes,* Trey rewrote this song yet again, keeping the Fishman verse from The Fog That Surrounds but omitting a guitar solo present in original versions of Taste.

Tela: A Gamehendge song, told from the perspective of Colonel Forbin who falls in love with Tela, a revolutionary. Musically the song underwent a number of transformations before the band settled on a version they were happy with in 1991. The current version omits a long, freeform jam performed in 1988.

Union Federal: Included as a live track on *Junta,* this song was recorded during one of Phish's marathon Oh Kee Pa Ceremonies in 1989. An improvisational piece of music, it appears in no setlists.

Vibration of Life: Often included in the spacey opening segment of You Enjoy Myself, the Vibration of Life is an effect created by Trey and Mike that seeks to tap the natural vibration of the universe—seven beats per second. Trey says that creating the Vibration in concert helps recharge the crowd and the band.

The Wedge: This song was a late addition to *Rift,* and unlike all other songs on the album it was recorded at the band's mixing studio (The Castle in Nashville, TN). For the album version, all the instruments were recorded separately, and drum overdubs by Fishman were included, making the song impossible to perform live in its album form. The band experimented with different versions

12/05/91	6	1	Paul&Silas	Ya Mar
03/11/92	6	1	Fee	Mound
03/13/92	2	1	Curtain	PoorHeart
03/14/92	1	2	Sqirm Coil	Bouncing
03/19/92	2	1	Rift	Sparkle
03/21/92	2	1	Sparkle	Horse
03/25/92	2	1	Sparkle	Rift
03/31/92	5	1	Glide	Rift
04/03/92	2	1	All Things	Golgi
04/05/92	2	2	*OP2	All Things
04/07/92	2	1	Silent	Bouncing
04/12/92	2	2	Glide	Bouncing
04/16/92	3	1	Bouncing	Rift
04/18/92	2	1	PoorHeart	Esther
04/21/92	2	1	Uncle Pen	Rift
04/23/92	2	1	Curtain	Uncle Pen
04/30/92	4	1	Curtain	Fee
05/03/92	3	1	All Things	IDK
05/07/92	3	1	Esther	Rift
05/09/92	2	1	Sparkle	Guelah
05/16/92	5	1	Glide	Bouncing
07/01/92	9	1a	Horn	Adeline
07/15/92	7	1	Uncle Pen	Horse
07/26/92	9	1a	Weigh	Lizards
11/19/92	21	1	Glide	Mound
11/23/92	4	1	Glide	Rift
11/27/92	2	1	Mockbird	Lawn Boy
12/01/92	3	1	MSO	Bouncing
12/03/92	2	1	All Things	Bouncing
12/05/92	2	1	Guelah	Lizards
12/07/92	2	1	FEFY	Bouncing
12/10/92	2	1	PoorHeart	IDK
12/12/92	2	1	Landlady	PoorHeart
12/28/92	2	2	PoorHeart	Reba
12/30/92	2	1	Sparkle	Esther
02/05/93	4	1	Rift	Sparkle
02/07/93	2	1	IDK	Fee
02/12/93	4	1	Sparkle	Esther
02/19/93	5	1	Rift	Fee
02/23/93	4	1	Bouncing	Reba
02/26/93	2	1	Fee	Fluffhead
03/03/93	3	2	Curtain	Mound
03/06/93	2	1	Curtain	Mound
03/13/93	4	1	All Things	Contact
03/18/93	4	2	PoorHeart	Tela
03/21/93	2	1	All Things	PoorHeart
03/24/93	2	2	Landlady	Sparkle
03/26/93	2	1	All Things	Fluffhead
03/28/93	2	1	Sparkle	Lizards
03/31/93	2	1	Sparkle	Mound
04/03/93	3	1	Sparkle	Sqirm Coil
04/10/93	3	1	Sparkle	Sqirm Coil
04/16/93	4	1	Sparkle	Esther
04/18/93	2	1	Guelah	Sparkle
04/21/93	2	2	Mound	Sqirm Coil
04/23/93	2	1	Sparkle	Fluffhead
04/29/93	4	1	*OP1	Paul&Silas
05/01/93	2	1	Guelah	Fee
05/03/93	2	1	Esther	Forbin's
05/06/93	2	1	Mound	Horse
05/07/93	1	1	Mound	Horse
05/30/93	3	1a	IDK	Contact
07/16/93	2	2	Also Sprac	Glide
07/21/93	3	1a	Also Sprac	Sparkle
07/24/93	3	2	Also Sprac	Fluffhead
07/28/93	3	1	Nellie	Horse
07/31/93	3	1	Ya Mar	Mound
08/06/93	3	1	*OP1	PoorHeart
08/09/93	3	1	Fee	Glide
08/12/93	2	1	Nellie	Horse
08/14/93	2	1	Sparkle	Esther
08/16/93	2	1	IDK	Sqirm Coil
08/20/93	2	2	Slave	Sqirm Coil
08/24/93	2	1	Nellie	Horse
08/26/93	2	1	Fee	Esther
12/28/93	2	1	PoorHeart	Esther
12/31/93	3	3	DWD	Lizards
04/04/94	1	2	Magilla	Wolfman's
04/08/94	3	2	*OP2	McGrupp
04/10/94	2	1	Sparkle	Esther
04/14/94	3	1	Demand	Sqirm Coil
04/18/94	4	1	Rift	Dog Faced
04/21/94	2	1	Glide	Lizards
04/25/94	4	1	PoorHeart	*CL1
04/29/94	2	1	Dog Faced	Sanity
05/02/94	2	1	Great Gig	Bouncing
05/07/94	4	1	Scent	If I Could
05/10/94	2	1	It's Ice	If I Could
05/13/94	2	2	Bouncing	McGrupp
05/17/94	3	1	Dog Faced	Sqirm Coil
05/22/94	4	1	Glide	Fluffhead
05/26/94	3	1	Demand	Sparkle
05/29/94	3	2	Nellie	Esther
06/09/94	1	2	*OP2	Glide
06/11/94	2	2	Scent	Sqirm Coil
06/14/94	2	1	IDK	*CL1
06/17/94	2	1	Glide	If I Could
06/21/94	3	2	My Friend	Esther
06/23/94	2	1	PoorHeart	NICU
06/30/94	5	1	Guelah	Glide
07/03/94	3	2	*OP2	Lizards
07/09/94	4	2	Also Sprac	Fluffhead
07/13/94	2	1	IDK	*CL2
07/15/94	2	1	Fee	Golgi
10/09/94	4	1	Dog Faced	Sqirm Coil
10/12/94	2	1	PoorHeart	Lizards
10/16/94	4	1	Fee	TMWSIY
10/20/94	2	1	Kung	Esther
10/22/94	2	1	Rift	Fluffhead
10/25/94	2	1	Silent	Lizards
10/29/94	4	1	Lawn Boy	Bill
11/03/94	3	1	Glide	Dog Faced
11/14/94	4	1	Guelah	Bouncing
11/18/94	3	1	Tela	Butter
11/25/94	5	1	Bouncing	Esther
12/01/94	4	1	IDK	Adeline
12/07/94	5	1	Ya Mar	Guyute
12/29/94	5	1	If I Could	Horse
06/09/95	6	2	*OP2	Wedge
06/14/95	3	1	Spock's	*CL1
06/16/95	2	1	Catapult	*CL1
06/20/95	3	1	IDK	*CL1
06/25/95	4	1	IDK	*CL1
06/29/95	3	1	Simple	Carolina
07/01/95	2	1	Caspian	Bouncing
09/29/95	5	2	Ya Mar	Billy
10/03/95	3	2	Adeline	Sqirm Coil
10/07/95	3	1	CTB	Str Design
10/13/95	3	1	Caspian	Fluffhead
10/19/95	4	1	AArmy	Billy
10/24/95	4	1	Caspian	*CL1
10/29/95	4	1	Silent	NICU
11/12/95	5	1	If I Could	*CL1
11/15/95	2	1	Sparkle	Adeline
11/29/95	9	1	Fee	*CL1
12/07/95	6	2	*OP2	Str Design
12/14/95	5	1	Makisupa	Tela
12/28/95	4	1	*OP1	Gumbo
06/06/96	1	2	Chalkdust	Stash
07/03/96	1	1a	Stash	Taste
07/11/96	6	1	IDK	Stash
07/23/96	8	2	Lovin Cup	Mike's
08/07/96	7	1	PYITE	Stash
08/12/96	2	2	Timber Ho	Simpl
08/16/96	3	2	Split&Melt	Fee
10/19/96	5	2	Bouncing	Fluffhead
10/22/96	2	1	Talk	Sparkle
10/27/96	4	1	Scent	Talk
11/06/96	5	1	*OP1	CTB
11/09/96	3	1	Talk	Lizards
11/15/96	4	2	McGrupp	TMWSIY
11/23/96	5	1	Highway	Rift
12/28/96	9	1	Ginseng	Mango
02/16/97	6	1	Beauty	Bouncing
02/22/97	5	1	Talk	IDK
06/24/97	15	1	*OP1	Beauty
07/09/97	9	1	Ginseng	Dirt
07/23/97	5	1	Limb	Billy
08/02/97	6	1	Water	*CL1
08/10/97	5	1	Billy	Bye Bye
➢ 8/17/97	**7**			

Spock's Brain [5]*

Spock's Brain [Spock's]

By Phish

05/16/95	[738]	1a	Ha Ha Ha	Str Design
06/07/95	1	2	Maze	Theme
06/14/95	5	1	Silent	Split&Melt
06/20/95	5	1	Llama	Ginseng
06/24/95	3	1	Rift	Julius
➢ 8/17/97	**189**			

The Squirming Coil [244]

The Squirming Coil [Sqirm Coil]

By Anastasio/Marshall

01/20/90	[157]	1a	Carolina	Caravan
01/27/90	3	2	YEM	Antelope
01/28/90	1	2	Caravan	YEM
02/09/90	7	1	ACDCBag	Mike's
02/24/90	7	2	Fee	La Grange
02/25/90	1	1	FunkBitch	Bouncing
03/03/90	3	1	MSO	Lizards
03/07/90	1	2	ACDCBag	Bathtub
04/07/90	11	1	ACDCBag	Lizards
05/23/90	24	2	*OP2	Reba
06/05/90	4	1	*OP1	Uncle Pen
09/14/90	6	2	Asse Fest	BurAlive
09/15/90	1	1	Magilla	*CL1
09/22/90	4	2	*OP2	Tweezer
09/28/90	1	1	MSO	Lizards
10/01/90	1	1	Possum	Lizards
10/04/90	1	1	Possum	Lizards
10/06/90	2	1a	Landlady	Dinner
10/07/90	1	1	Asse Fest	Mike's
10/30/90	4	1	Cavern	Possum
10/31/90	1	1	Possum	Lizards
11/03/90	2	1	Llama	Oh Kee
11/08/90	2	1	Llama	Asse Fest
11/17/90	3	1	Llama	Landlady
11/24/90	1	1	Weekpaug	Lizards
11/30/90	2	2	Asse Fest	RunJim
12/07/90	3	2	Tweezer	Oh Kee
12/28/90	2	2	Possum	Tweezer
12/31/90	2	2	Stash	RunJim
02/03/91	3	2	Bowie	Landlady
02/07/91	1	1	Possum	Golgi
02/08/91	1	1	Stash	RunJim
02/09/91	1	2	Love You	Llama
02/14/91	1	2	Foam	RunJim
02/26/91	9	1	Foam	Llama
02/27/91	1	2	Cavern	Bowie
02/28/91	1	2	*OP2	Reba
03/01/91	1	1	Cavern	Tweezer
03/06/91	2	1	Landlady	Possum
03/13/91	4	1	Llama	Bowie
03/15/91	1	E	*OPE	RunJim
03/16/91	1	2	BurAlive	Cavern
03/17/91	1	2	MSO	Tweezer
03/22/91	2	1	Split&Melt	Cavern
03/28/91	2	1a	Bowie	Oh Kee
04/04/91	5	1	YEM	Llama
04/11/91	3	1	YEM	Chalkdust
04/12/91	1	E	BBFCM	*CL1
04/15/91	2	E	*OPE	Rocky Top
04/18/91	2	2	Split&Melt	Possum
04/19/91	1	2	MSO	A-Train
04/20/91	1	2	Split&Melt	Paul&Silas
04/22/91	2	2	Destiny	Stash
04/26/91	2	1	Chalkdust	Sloth
04/27/91	1	2	Tweezer	WpJam
05/02/91	1	1	Llama	Cavern
05/12/91	6	2	Weekpaug	Oh Kee
05/16/91	1	2	Landlady	Tweezer
05/25/91	3	1a	Cavern	Llama
07/12/91	2	2	Golgi	Moose
07/14/91	2	1	Llama	Golgi
07/15/91	1	1a	Cavern	Frankstein
07/19/91	2	1	Cavern	YEM
07/20/91	1	1	Foam	Llama
07/23/91	2	1	Foam	MSO
07/24/91	1	1	Chalkdust	BurAlive
07/25/91	1	2	Golgi	Llama
07/26/91	1	2	FunkBitch	Tweezer
08/03/91	2	1	Fee	PoorHeart
09/25/91	1	2	*OP2	Stash
09/26/91	1	2	Golgi	Brother
09/28/91	2	1	Chalkdust	MSO
10/02/91	2	1	Foam	PoorHeart
10/03/91	1	2	BurAlive	Tweezer
10/04/91	1	2	Stash	Mike's
10/06/91	2	2	Cavern	Rocky Top
10/10/91	1	E	*OPE	Fire
10/13/91	3	2	Bathtub	It's Ice
10/15/91	1	1	Foam	Split&Melt
10/18/91	2	E	WalkAway	*CLE
10/28/91	6	2	YEM	Harpua
11/01/91	3	1	Destiny	Split&Melt
11/08/91	4	2	Split&Melt	IDK
11/12/91	3	2	Stash	Paul&Silas
11/13/91	1	2	Bathtub	Llama
11/15/91	2	1	Split&Melt	MSO
11/20/91	3	1	Bathtub	Llama
11/22/91	2	2	Antelope	IDK
11/30/91	3	1	Cavern	Brother
12/04/91	1	1	Brother	Dinner
12/05/91	1	2	Sloth	IDK
12/06/91	1	1	Uncle Pen	Magilla
12/31/91	2	3	Wilson	Tweezer
03/07/92	2	2	Tweezer	Weigh
03/12/92	2	2	Bouncing	Uncle Pen
03/14/92	2	2	Llama	Split&Melt
03/19/92	2	2	My Friend	Rosie
03/21/92	2	1	Dinner	MSO
03/25/92	2	2	All Things	YEM
03/30/92	4	1	BBFCM	Weigh
04/01/92	2	2	Rosie	TweezRep
04/04/92	2	2	Tweezer	Rosie
04/06/92	2	1	Guelah	Antelope
04/09/92	2	1	Stash	Golgi
04/13/92	2	2	Ya Mar	Love You
04/17/92	3	2	Fluffhead	Tweezer
04/23/92	5	1	Guelah	Llama
04/24/92	1	1	Stash	Golgi
04/30/92	3	2	Tweezer	My Mind
05/02/92	2	1	Stash	Llama
05/05/92	2	2	Love You	Cavern
05/06/92	1	2	Stash	YEM
05/07/92	1	2	Bike	TweezRep
05/09/92	2	1	Maze	IDK
05/16/92	5	2	Tweezer	YEM
05/17/92	1	2	Guelah	All Things
06/19/92	2	1a	Stash	Sparkle
07/09/92	8	1a	Stash	RunJim
07/11/92	2	1a	Stash	Cavern
07/14/92	2	2	Llama	Paul&Silas
07/16/92	2	E	Bayou	*CLE

07/17/92	1	1a	Stash	Maze
07/21/92	3	1a	Stash	RunJim
07/24/92	2	1a	Tweezer	YEM
07/28/92	4	1a	Uncle Pen	Tweezer
08/01/92	3	1a	Stash	Horn
08/14/92	3	1a	Stash	Llama
08/17/92	2	E	*OPE	*CLE
08/20/92	2	1a	Stash	Bowie
08/25/92	3	1a	Stash	Llama
08/28/92	2	1a	Adeline	RunJim
10/30/92	3	1a	Cavern	Stash
11/21/92	3	2	Guelah	Love You
11/23/92	2	2	Stash	Walk Line
11/25/92	1	1	It's Ice	Cavern
11/28/92	2	2	Bouncing	Love You
11/30/92	1	2	YEM	Terrapin
12/02/92	2	2	Lngthwise	Walk Line
12/04/92	2	2	It's Ice	Carolina
12/06/92	2	1	Sloth	Llama
12/07/92	1	2	Love You	Adeline
12/11/92	3	2	BBJ	Faht
12/12/92	1	2	Brain	Golgi
12/29/92	3	2	Terrapin	TweezRep
12/31/92	2	3	Harpua	DGirl
02/05/93	3	2	Love You	TweezRep
02/07/93	2	2	YEM	Brain
02/10/93	2	2	It's Ice	Tweezer
02/13/93	3	2	Lngthwise	Cavern
02/17/93	2	2	Lngthwise	*CL2
02/21/93	4	2	Rosie	BBFCM
02/22/93	1	2	Love You	TweezRep
02/26/93	3	2	Lngthwise	TweezRep
03/03/93	3	2	Terrapin	Adeline
03/05/93	1	2	Love You	AmGrace
03/09/93	3	2	Walk Line	TweezRep
03/14/93	3	2	Great Gig	*CL2
03/18/93	3	2	Brain	Cavern
03/24/93	4	E	Carolina	*CLE
03/27/93	3	E	*OPE	Carolina
04/01/93	4	1	Stash	My Friend
04/03/93	2	1	Split&Melt	My Friend
04/10/93	3	1	Split&Melt	My Friend
04/13/93	2	2	Brain	*CL2
04/17/93	3	2	BBJ	*CL2
04/21/93	3	2	Split&Melt	Horse
04/23/93	2	2	Lngthwise	HwayHell
04/29/93	4	2	Terrapin	*CL2
05/01/93	2	2	My Friend	BBJ
05/06/93	4	2	BBJ	Mike's
05/08/93	2	2	It's Ice	Jam
05/29/93	1	1a	Stash	Sparkle
07/17/93	4	2	Tweezer	It's Ice
07/21/93	2	1a	Sparkle	Maze
07/24/93	3	1	Bouncing	*CL1
07/27/93	2	1a	Stash	Sparkle
07/30/93	3	2	Golgi	Bowie
08/02/93	2	2	Rift	Weekpaug
08/06/93	2	2	Guelah	Uncle Pen
08/09/93	3	1	Memories	*CL1
08/12/93	2	1	PoorHeart	*CL1
08/14/93	2	2	Mound	Daniel
08/16/93	2	1	Split&Melt	*CL1
08/20/93	2	2	Split&Melt	My Friend
08/25/93	3	2	Bats&Mice	GTBT
08/28/93	2	2	Stash	Crimes
12/29/93	2	1	Stash	*CL1
04/06/94	5	2	Weekpaug	Cavern
04/09/94	2	1	Stash	*CL1
04/14/94	4	1	Split&Melt	*CL1
04/16/94	2	2	YEM	TweezRep
04/22/94	5	2	BeLikeYou	*CL2
04/25/94	3	2	Mound	Divided
04/28/94	1	1a	Antelope	Julius
05/03/94	4	1	Stash	Scent
05/08/94	4	1	Stash	*CL1
05/10/94	1	E	*OPE	*CLE
05/17/94	5	1	Split&Melt	*CL1
05/21/94	3	1	Stash	Tela
05/25/94	3	2	PurplRain	*CL2
06/11/94	7	2	Split&Melt	Maze
06/16/94	3	1	Stash	*CL1
06/19/94	3	2	Makisupa	MSO
07/03/94	11	2	Julius	Antelope
07/10/94	5	2	Bouncing	Crimes
10/09/94	7	1	Split&Melt	*CL1
10/14/94	4	2	Long Time	TweezRep
10/23/94	7	E	*OPE	*CLE
10/31/94	6	E	AmGrace	*CLE
11/13/94	5	2	AmGrace	*CL2
11/19/94	5	E	*OPE	*CLE
12/02/94	9	1	Stash	*CL1
12/28/94	8	2	Love You	*CL2
06/09/95	7	E	*OPE	*CLE
06/16/95	5	2	YEM	*CL2
06/24/95	6	1	Silent	*CL1
06/30/95	5	2	AmGrace	*CL2
07/03/95	3	2	Possum	*CL2
09/27/95	1	1	Chalkdust	*CL1
10/03/95	5	2	Split&Melt	*CL2
10/13/95	6	2	Adeline	*CL2
10/22/95	7	E	Adeline	*CLE
11/09/95	7	2	HelloBaby	*CL2
11/15/95	5	1	Adeline	*CL1
11/19/95	3	1	Julius	*CL1
11/28/95	5	E	*OPE	*CLE
12/02/95	4	2	Golgi	TweezRep
12/08/95	4	2	Love You	TweezRep
12/12/95	3	1	I'm Blue	*CL1
12/16/95	3	2	Weekpaug	*CL2
12/31/95	5	1	Reba	Maze
07/19/96	15	1a	Waste	*CL1
08/05/96	8	1	Julius	*CL1
08/16/96	7	2	Free	Waste
10/16/96	2	2	Antelope	Johnny B.
10/25/96	7	1	Stash	*CL1
11/19/96	17	E	*OPE	*CLE
12/29/96	12	1	Free	La Grange
02/17/97	6	2	*OP2	DWD
06/16/97	14	1	*OP1	Dogs Stole
07/05/97	12	E	*OPE	*CLE
07/29/97	10	2	Rocky Top	*CL2
08/11/97	9	E	*OPE	*CLE
08/16/97	3	1	CharZero	*CL1
➢ 8/17/97	**1**			

Stash [274]

Stash [Stash]

By Anastasio/Marshall

09/13/90	[222]	2	Magilla	GDS
09/14/90	1	1	Paul&Silas	Dinner
09/15/90	1	1	Golgi	Magilla
09/22/90	4	2	Bouncing	Lizards
09/28/90	1	1	Suzie	MSO
10/05/90	3	1	Suzie	Asse Fest
10/07/90	2	1	Uncle Pen	Landlady
10/31/90	5	1	Lizards	Bouncing
11/03/90	2	2	Paul&Silas	Fee
11/24/90	6	2	Bouncing	Eliza
11/30/90	2	2	RunJim	Lizards
12/07/90	3	1	Golgi	Bouncing
12/29/90	3	2	Cavern	Jesus
12/31/90	1	2	Golgi	Sqirm Coil
02/02/91	2	1	Esther	Destiny
02/08/91	3	1	MSO	Sqirm Coil
02/14/91	2	1	Mango	Lawn Boy
02/21/91	5	2	Bouncing	Guelah
02/26/91	4	2	Dinner	Bouncing
03/15/91	10	1	MSO	Dinner
03/17/91	2	1	Uncle Pen	Lizards
03/22/91	2	2	Paul&Silas	RunJim
04/05/91	8	2	Rocky Top	Lizards
04/12/91	3	1	Suzie	Rocky Top
04/19/91	5	1	Lizards	IDK
04/22/91	3	2	Sqirm Coil	MSO
04/27/91	3	1	Suzie	Golgi
05/10/91	5	1	Possum	*CL1
05/12/91	2	1	Dinner	Lizards
05/17/91	2	1	TMWSIY	IDK
05/18/91	1	2	Curtain	MSO
07/11/91	2	1	MSO	Lizards
07/13/91	2	2	Lizards	Brain
07/15/91	2	1a	Dinner	Bouncing
07/18/91	1	1	Suzie	A-Train
07/20/91	2	2	Golgi	TMWSIY
07/23/91	2	1	Suzie	Flat Fee
07/25/91	2	2	Lizards	Touch Me
07/26/91	1	2	*OP2	Dinner
07/27/91	1	1a	PoorHeart	TMWSIY
08/03/91	1	3	*OP3	Ya Mar
09/25/91	1	2	Sqirm Coil	Sparkle
09/28/91	3	1	MSO	Foam
10/02/91	2	2	Lawn Boy	Oh Kee
10/04/91	2	2	Lawn Boy	Sqirm Coil
10/06/91	2	2	MSO	Fee
10/17/91	6	1	PoorHeart	Esther
10/19/91	2	1	MSO	Golgi
10/24/91	2	1	PoorHeart	Ya Mar
10/28/91	3	2	Dinner	Paul&Silas
11/01/91	3	E	Love You	*CLE
11/08/91	4	1	Dinner	PoorHeart
11/12/91	3	2	Dinner	Sqirm Coil
11/16/91	4	1	Foam	Ya Mar
11/20/91	2	1	Sparkle	Paul&Silas
11/22/91	2	1	Dinner	Rocky Top
11/24/91	2	1	Paul&Silas	Landlady
12/04/91	2	2	MSO	Mango
12/07/91	3	1	MSO	Curtain
12/31/91	1	1	Sparkle	Lizards
03/06/92	1	2	PoorHeart	Mound
03/12/92	3	1	Sparkle	IDK
03/14/92	2	1	Rift	Fee
03/19/92	2	2	MSO	Oh Kee
03/21/92	2	1	MSO	Golgi
03/24/92	1	1	*OP1	PoorHeart
03/26/92	2	1	Sparkle	Fluffhead
03/28/92	2	1	Sparkle	Rift
03/31/92	2	2	Fee	Lizards
04/03/92	2	1	PoorHeart	Rift
04/05/92	2	1	PoorHeart	Rift
04/06/92	1	2	Mound	Rosie
04/09/92	2	1	Uncle Pen	Sqirm Coil
04/13/92	2	1	Uncle Pen	Lizards
04/15/92	1	1	Sparkle	Uncle Pen
04/17/92	2	1	Sparkle	IDK
04/19/92	2	1	NICU	Paul&Silas
04/22/92	2	1	Mound	All Things
04/24/92	2	1	Sparkle	Sqirm Coil
04/30/92	3	1	Uncle Pen	Rift
05/02/92	2	1	Bouncing	Sqirm Coil
05/05/92	2	1	Sparkle	Rift
05/06/92	1	2	MSO	Sqirm Coil
05/08/92	2	2	MSO	Magilla
05/10/92	2	1a	Sparkle	Uncle Pen
05/14/92	2	2	McGrupp	Rosie
05/15/92	1	1a	Sparkle	Bouncing
05/17/92	2	1	IDK	Mango
06/19/92	2	1a	Suzie	Sqirm Coil
07/09/92	8	1a	Sparkle	Sqirm Coil
07/11/92	2	1a	Sparkle	Sqirm Coil
07/15/92	3	2	MSO	McGrupp
07/17/92	2	1a	Sparkle	Sqirm Coil
07/21/92	3	1a	Sparkle	Sqirm Coil
07/25/92	3	1a	Sparkle	Rift
08/01/92	6	1a	PoorHeart	Sqirm Coil
08/14/92	3	1a	PoorHeart	Sqirm Coil
08/20/92	4	1a	Foam	Sqirm Coil
08/23/92	1	1a	RunJim	*CL1
08/25/92	2	1a	Sparkle	Sqirm Coil
08/28/92	2	1a	Foam	Adeline
10/30/92	3	1a	Sqirm Coil	Adeline
11/20/92	2	1	Sparkle	Lizards
11/23/92	3	2	PoorHeart	Sqirm Coil
11/28/92	3	1	Foam	Esther
11/30/92	1	1	PoorHeart	Sparkle
12/02/92	2	1	PoorHeart	Lizards
12/04/92	2	1	PoorHeart	Glide
12/06/92	2	2	Curtain	Paul&Silas
12/08/92	2	1	Adeline	*CL1
12/11/92	2	1	Uncle Pen	Lizards
12/13/92	2	1	Uncle Pen	Rift
12/29/92	2	1	Uncle Pen	Tela
12/31/92	2	2	BBJ	Glide
02/04/93	2	1	All Things	Lizards
02/06/93	2	2	Mound	Adeline
02/09/93	2	2	BBJ	Lizards
02/11/93	2	1	PoorHeart	Fee
02/13/93	2	1	Rift	Lawn Boy
02/15/93	1	1	Mound	Guelah
02/18/93	2	2	Rift	Lizards
02/21/93	3	2	Curtain	Lizards
02/23/93	2	2	MSO	Lizards
02/25/93	1	2	It's Ice	Wilson
02/27/93	2	2	Curtain	PoorHeart
03/02/93	1	1	PoorHeart	Reba
03/05/93	2	1	Rift	Sparkle
03/08/93	2	2	Uncle Pen	BBJ
03/12/93	2	1	Rift	Fluffhead
03/14/93	2	1	Sparkle	Paul&Silas
03/17/93	2	1	Bouncing	AmGrace
03/19/93	2	1	Rift	Fluffhead
03/22/93	2	1	Uncle Pen	Bouncing
03/25/93	2	1	Bouncing	Glide
03/27/93	2	1	Rift	Reba
03/30/93	2	1	Esther	Glide
04/01/93	2	1	Rift	Sqirm Coil
04/03/93	2	2	Suzie	Mound
04/05/93	1	1	Paul&Silas	Forbin's
04/09/93	1	1	Guelah	Horse
04/12/93	2	1	PoorHeart	Horse
04/14/93	2	1	It's Ice	Kung
04/17/93	2	1	Bouncing	It's Ice
04/20/93	2	1	Sparkle	Bouncing
04/22/93	2	1	Esther	Fee
04/24/93	2	1	PoorHeart	Horse
04/27/93	2	1	Rift	Guelah
04/30/93	2	1	PoorHeart	Horse
05/02/93	2	1	Mound	Horse
05/05/93	2	1	Sparkle	Bouncing
05/08/93	3	1	Mound	Glide
05/29/93	1	1a	Rift	Sqirm Coil
07/15/93	2	1	Mound	Foam
07/17/93	2	1	My Mind	Reba
07/22/93	3	1	PoorHeart	Golgi
07/24/93	2	1	Rift	Mango
07/25/93	1	1	Mound	Fee
07/27/93	1	1a	Rift	Sqirm Coil
07/30/93	3	1	Uncle Pen	Esther
08/03/93	3	1	Rift	Horse
08/07/93	1	1	PoorHeart	Makisupa
08/11/93	3	1	Mango	Sparkle
08/13/93	2	1	Foam	Ginseng
08/15/93	2	1	Paul&Silas	Forbin's
08/21/93	4	1	Rift	Sparkle
08/25/93	2	1	AmGrace	Glide
08/28/93	2	1	Fluffhead	Sqirm Coil
12/29/93	2	1	Sparkle	Sqirm Coil
12/31/93	2	1	Guelah	Ginseng
04/06/94	3	1	PoorHeart	Lizards
04/09/94	2	1	All Things	Sqirm Coil
04/13/94	3	1	PoorHeart	Lizards
04/16/94	3	1	Rift	Fluffhead
04/20/94	3	1	Axilla 2	Suzie
04/23/94	3	1	PoorHeart	Esther
04/30/94	5	1	Mound	PoorHeart
05/03/94	2	1	Sparkle	Sqirm Coil
05/06/94	2	1	Ya Mar	Esther
05/08/94	2	1	Bouncing	Sqirm Coil
05/13/94	3	1	Mound	If I Could
05/16/94	2	1	Bouncing	Adeline
05/19/94	2	1	PoorHeart	Horse
05/21/94	2	1	Mound	Sqirm Coil
05/25/94	3	1	Uncle Pen	Forbin's
05/28/94	3	1	Bouncing	Horse
06/11/94	4	1	Tela	*CL1
06/13/94	1	1	Dinner	Ginseng
06/16/94	2	1	Dog Faced	Sqirm Coil
06/19/94	3	1	Scent	Golgi
06/22/94	2	1	Scent	Golgi
06/25/94	3	1	NICU	Mango
07/01/94	4	1	NICU	Mango
07/05/94	3	1	Uncle Pen	Esther
07/08/94	2	2	It's Ice	YEM
07/10/94	2	1	Rift	If I Could
07/14/94	2	1	PYITE	TMWSIY
07/16/94	2	1	N20	Lizards
10/07/94	1	1	Guelah	Guyute
10/10/94	3	1	Sparkle	Guyute
10/13/94	2	1	Sparkle	*CL1
10/18/94	4	1	PoorHeart	Tela
10/21/94	2	1	Old Home	Lizards
10/23/94	2	1	PoorHeart	Tela
10/28/94	4	1	Scent	Glide
11/02/94	3	1	Guyute	Scent
11/12/94	3	1	Maze	Esther
11/16/94	3	1	Lizards	Pig in Pen
11/20/94	4	1	Scent	If I Could
11/28/94	5	1	Scent	Guyute
12/02/94	3	1	Lizards	Sqirm Coil
12/06/94	3	1	Sparkle	Golgi
12/10/94	4	1	Rift	Lizards
12/30/94	3	1	Simple	Fee
06/07/95	3	1	Str Design	If I Could
06/13/95	4	1	Bouncing	Str Design
06/15/95	2	1	Wedge	IDK
06/17/95	2	1	Curtain	*CL1
06/24/95	5	1	Mound	Horse
06/28/95	3	1	PYITE	Fluffhead
07/01/95	3	2	Uncle Pen	Str Design
09/28/95	4	1	Scent	Fee
10/02/95	3	1	Chess	AArmy
10/06/95	3	1	Ya Mar	Billu
10/11/95	3	1	*OP1	Old Home
10/14/95	2	1	Free	Catapult
10/17/95	2	1	Sample	Uncle Pen
10/22/95	4	1	I'm Blue	*CL1
10/27/95	3	1	Rift	Fee
11/11/95	6	1	Ya Mar	AmGrace
11/14/95	2	2	Gumbo	Str Design
11/19/95	4	1	Rift	Str Design
11/24/95	3	1	Sparkle	Tela
11/28/95	2	1	*OP1	Dinner
12/01/95	3	1	Mockbird	Cavern
12/04/95	2	1	PYITE	My Mind
12/11/95	5	1	Ha Ha Ha	Caspian
12/17/95	5	1	Tube	Lizards
12/29/95	2	1	NICU	Fluffhead
04/26/96	3	1a	Sparkle	CTB
06/06/96	1	2	Sparkle	Waste
07/03/96	1	1a	RunJim	Sparkle
07/11/96	6	1	Sparkle	Scent
07/18/96	5	1a	Bouncing	HelloBaby
07/22/96	3	1a	Bouncing	DayinLife
07/23/96	1	1	McGrupp	HelloBaby
08/07/96	7	1	Sparkle	Ya Mar
08/14/96	4	1	Gumbo	HelloBaby
10/18/96	5	1	CTB	Str Design
10/21/96	2	1	Ginseng	Waste
10/25/96	3	1	IDK	Sqirm Coil
10/29/96	3	1	Bouncing	Train Song
11/02/96	2	1	Taste	Free
11/07/96	3	1	Guelah	Waste
11/14/96	5	E	*OPE	HelloBaby
11/19/96	4	1	Mound	Fee
11/22/96	1	1	Train Song	Cavern
11/30/96	5	1	Bouncing	Fluffhead
12/31/96	8	1	CTB	Horse
02/13/97	1	1	Also Sprac	Walfredo
02/18/97	4	1	NICU	Waste
02/20/97	1	2	Uncle Pen	Bouncing
02/25/97	4	1	Mojo	Waste
02/28/97	2	1	Peaches	SweptAwy
06/13/97	4	2	*OP2	Maze
06/19/97	3	2	*OP2	Ghost
06/22/97	3	1a	Water	Dirt
06/27/97	3	1a	Chalkdust	Dogs Stole
07/02/97	3	2	Jam	Llama
07/06/97	3	1	Dogs Stole	Horse
07/11/97	3	1a	Bouncing	Beauty

07/22/97	2	1	Water	Bouncing
07/26/97	3	1	PoorHeart	Billy
07/30/97	2	1	Water	Weigh
08/06/97	4	1	NICU	Beauty
➢ 8/17/97	8			

Strange Design [36]

Strange Design [Str Design]

By Anastasio/Marshall

05/16/95	[738]	1a	Spock's	Reba
06/07/95	1	1	Taste	Stash
06/09/95	2	1	Divided	Oh Kee
06/13/95	2	1	Stash	Taste
06/15/95	2	2	Bowie	Theme
06/19/95	3	1	Reba	Rift
06/22/95	2	1	It's Ice	Maze
06/26/95	4	2	YEM	Antelope
06/29/95	2	2	Bowie	YEM
07/01/95	2	2	Stash	AArmy
07/03/95	2	1	Maze	Free
09/27/95	1	1	Fog	Chalkdust
09/29/95	2	1	Divided	CTB
10/05/95	4	1	CTB	Divided
10/07/95	2	2	Split&Melt	It's Ice
10/15/95	5	1	Foam	I'm Blue
10/17/95	1	1	Free	AmGrace
10/21/95	3	1	Lizards	AArmy
10/25/95	3	1	Free	LongJourn
10/28/95	2	2	YEM	Frankstein
11/10/95	4	2	YEM	Sparkle
11/14/95	3	2	Stash	YEM
11/19/95	4	1	Stash	It's Ice
11/22/95	2	2	YEM	*CL2
11/25/95	2	2	I'm Blue	Weekpaug
11/30/95	3	2	Free	AmGrace
12/07/95	5	2	Split&Melt	Fog
12/31/95	12	2	RunJim	HelloBaby
08/05/96	23	2	Train Song	AmGrace
08/13/96	5	2	Train Song	Adeline
08/16/96	2	2	Train Song	HelloBaby
10/18/96	4	1	Stash	Divided
10/25/96	5	2	Free	Harry
11/24/96	20	1	CharZero	Taste
12/28/96	8	2	Mike's	Weekpaug
07/02/97	31	1	Maze	Ginseng
➢ 8/17/97	25			

Suzie Greenberg [285]

Suzie Greenberg [Suzie]

By Anastasio/Dude of Life

08/09/87	[17]	1	Harpua	*CL1
08/29/87	4	1	Lushngton	Mustang
09/12/87	2	2	*OP2	Alumni
11/19/87	4	2	Alumni	Possum
01/30/88	1	3	Fee	Lizards
03/21/88	5	1a	*OP1	Golgi
05/15/88	4	1a	YEM	GTBT
05/25/88	2	1	Sally	Fire
06/15/88	1	1	*OP1	Alumni
06/18/88	1	1	La Grange	Emma
06/21/88	2	1	Sally	Curtain
07/11/88	1	1	Satin Doll	Curtain
10/29/88	12	1	*OP1	Lizards
11/03/88	1	2	Antelope	IDK
11/05/88	1	E	*OPE	Sparks
02/06/89	6	1	*OP1	Curtain
02/07/89	1	3	Fluffhead	Slave
04/15/89	14	2	Split&Melt	Fluffhead
04/20/89	2	1	Esther	Sloth
05/06/89	9	2	A-Train	Contact
05/13/89	6	2	Bowie	Bold
05/28/89	8	1	Esther	YEM
08/12/89	10	1a	Blue Sky	ACDCBag
08/17/89	2	1	Ya Mar	McGrupp
08/19/89	1	1	Oh Kee	TMWSIY
08/26/89	2	3	TMWSIY	Dinner
09/09/89	4	1	Oh Kee	Divided
10/01/89	1	1	Oh Kee	Antelope
10/07/89	2	1	Weekpaug	Fee
10/22/89	6	1	Oh Kee	Ya Mar
10/31/89	3	1	Oh Kee	ACDCBag
11/10/89	5	1	Oh Kee	Fee
11/16/89	2	1	Oh Kee	MSO
11/30/89	2	2	A-Train	Contact
12/07/89	4	2	Oh Kee	Rocky Top
12/08/89	1	1	Oh Kee	Split&Melt
01/20/90	7	1a	Oh Kee	Bouncing
01/28/90	2	1	*OP1	Suzie
02/09/90	7	1	Oh Kee	YEM
02/10/90	1	1	Oh Kee	YEM
02/15/90	1	1	Oh Kee	Divided
02/17/90	2	1a	Oh Kee	Dinner
02/23/90	2	2	Oh Kee	Mike's
03/03/90	5	E	*OPE	*CLE
03/08/90	2	1	Oh Kee	A-Train
03/28/90	4	1	Oh Kee	A-Train
04/05/90	2	1	Oh Kee	YEM
04/06/90	1	1	Oh Kee	Antelope
04/07/90	1	1	MSO	ACDCBag
04/08/90	1	1	Oh Kee	Uncle Pen
04/22/90	9	1	Oh Kee	Possum
04/26/90	2	2	Oh Kee	Cavern
04/28/90	1	1	Oh Kee	Uncle Pen
05/10/90	5	1	*OP1	Uncle Pen
05/15/90	4	1	Oh Kee	Harry
05/19/90	1	2	Oh Kee	Fee
05/23/90	1	1	Oh Kee	Uncle Pen
05/31/90	2	1a	Oh Kee	*CL1
06/01/90	1	1a	Oh Kee	Dinner
06/05/90	1	1	Oh Kee	A-Train
06/07/90	1	1	*OP1	Donna
06/09/90	2	2	Oh Kee	Antelope
06/16/90	1	3	Oh Kee	Fee
09/14/90	2	1	*OP1	Bouncing
09/22/90	5	1	Oh Kee	Magilla
09/28/90	1	1	Oh Kee	Stash
10/01/90	1	1	Oh Kee	*CL1
10/05/90	2	1	Oh Kee	Stash
10/06/90	1	1a	Oh Kee	Esther
10/12/90	3	1	*OP1	YEM
10/30/90	2	1	Asse Fest	Uncle Pen
10/31/90	1	2	Oh Kee	Love You
11/02/90	1	2	*OP2	Forbin's
11/03/90	1	1	Oh Kee	Magilla
11/04/90	1	2	Oh Kee	Jesus
11/08/90	1	2	*OP2	Divided
11/10/90	1	2	*OP2	YEM
11/16/90	1	1	*OP1	BurAlive
11/17/90	1	1	Oh Kee	Bowie
11/24/90	1	1	Oh Kee	Bowie
11/30/90	2	E	Oh Kee	*CLE
12/07/90	3	2	Oh Kee	No Good
12/29/90	3	1	Oh Kee	*CL1
12/31/90	1	1	*OP1	Divided
02/02/91	2	1	Oh Kee	Guelah
02/03/91	1	2	Oh Kee	*CL2
02/09/91	3	E	Lawn Boy	*CLE
02/21/91	6	E	*OPE	*CLE
02/27/91	5	2	*OP2	BurAlive
03/01/91	2	E	Oh Kee	*CLE
03/13/91	6	2	*OP2	Split&Melt
03/16/91	2	1	Oh Kee	Antelope
03/22/91	3	2	Oh Kee	Antelope
03/28/91	2	1a	Oh Kee	Magilla
04/04/91	5	1	Oh Kee	YEM
04/05/91	1	E	Oh Kee	*CLE
04/12/91	3	1	Oh Kee	Stash
04/18/91	4	2	Horn	Split&Melt
04/20/91	2	2	Oh Kee	Adeline
04/22/91	2	1	Oh Kee	*CL1
04/27/91	3	1	Lizards	Stash
05/04/91	3	1	Oh Kee	Cavern
05/11/91	3	2	Oh Kee	TweezRep
05/17/91	3	1	Oh Kee	TMWSIY
05/18/91	1	2	Oh Kee	Curtain
07/11/91	2	1	Oh Kee	Divided
07/12/91	1	2	Oh Kee	*CL2
07/13/91	1	1	Oh Kee	Alumni
07/14/91	1	2	*OP2	Caravan
07/15/91	1	1a	Oh Kee	Landlady
07/18/91	1	1	Guelah	Stash
07/19/91	1	2	*OP2	Divided
07/20/91	1	1	Oh Kee	Landlady
07/21/91	1	E2	Fee	*CLE2
07/23/91	1	1	Oh Kee	Stash
07/24/91	1	2	Frankstein	*CL2
07/25/91	1	1	Foam	Divided
07/26/91	1	1	Foam	Cavern
07/27/91	1	1a	Oh Kee	Cavern
09/27/91	4	2	Oh Kee	YEM
09/29/91	2	1a	Oh Kee	*CL1
10/02/91	3	2	Oh Kee	*CL2
10/04/91	2	1	Sparkle	Magilla
10/06/91	2	1	*OP1	Foam
10/10/91	1	2	Oh Kee	Fee
10/15/91	4	2	Oh Kee	Love You
10/17/91	1	2	Oh Kee	Bowie
10/19/91	2	1	Landlady	It's Ice
10/24/91	2	1	Oh Kee	Foam
11/02/91	7	1	*OP1	Curtain
11/08/91	3	E	Fee	*CLE
11/15/91	6	E	HwayHell	*CLE
11/22/91	5	E	Glide	*CLE
12/04/91	4	E	Adeline	*CLE
03/11/92	7	1	*OP1	My Friend
03/14/92	3	2	Oh Kee	Harry
03/19/92	2	2	Oh Kee	My Friend
03/21/92	2	2	Oh Kee	A-Train
03/24/92	1	2	Oh Kee	Harry
03/26/92	2	2	Oh Kee	PoorHeart
03/30/92	3	E	Oh Kee	*CLE
04/03/92	3	2	Harry	*CL2
04/06/92	3	1	*OP1	Foam
04/09/92	2	2	Oh Kee	Bowie
04/12/92	1	1	*OP1	PoorHeart
04/15/92	2	1	Oh Kee	Foam
04/16/92	1	2	Adeline	*CL2
04/18/92	2	2	Oh Kee	Rift
04/21/92	2	1	*OP1	Uncle Pen
04/22/92	1	1	All Things	*CL1
04/25/92	3	1	*OP1	My Friend
04/29/92	1	1	*OP1	Foam
05/01/92	2	1	*OP1	My Friend
05/03/92	2	2	Oh Kee	*CL2
05/07/92	3	1	*OP1	PoorHeart
05/09/92	2	2	*OP2	Divided
05/10/92	1	1a	Landlady	Sparkle
05/14/92	2	1	*OP1	All Things
05/16/92	2	E	Adeline	*CLE
05/18/92	2	1	*OP1	Maze
06/19/92	1	1a	Landlady	Stash
07/09/92	8	1a	Oh Kee	Landlady
07/11/92	2	1a	YEM	*CL1
07/15/92	3	1	Oh Kee	Foam
07/18/92	3	1a	*OP1	Foam
07/27/92	7	1a	Horn	Llama
07/31/92	3	1a	*OP1	Chalkdust
08/02/92	2	1a	Oh Kee	Bowie
08/17/92	4	2	*OP2	It's Ice
11/20/92	12	1	All Things	Rift
11/22/92	2	1	Oh Kee	Fee
11/28/92	4	2	*OP2	Paul&Silas
12/02/92	3	1	*OP1	Foam
12/04/92	2	2	*OP2	Bowie
12/06/92	2	2	*OP2	Curtain
12/08/92	2	2	Sparkle	Lngthwise
12/10/92	1	2	Oh Kee	*CL2
12/13/92	3	2	*OP2	Mound
12/29/92	2	1	Oh Kee	*CL1
02/07/93	7	1	*OP1	BurAlive
02/11/93	3	1	*OP1	BurAlive
02/15/93	3	1	AmGrace	Sparkle
02/21/93	5	1	*OP1	BurAlive
02/25/93	3	2	*OP2	It's Ice
03/13/93	10	2	*OP2	Tweezer
03/17/93	3	1	Oh Kee	Antelope
03/19/93	2	1	*OP1	Llama
03/26/93	5	2	Oh Kee	Great Gig
04/03/93	7	2	*OP2	Stash
04/09/93	2	2	BurAlive	All Things
04/13/93	3	1	*OP1	Foam
04/17/93	3	2	Oh Kee	BBJ
04/22/93	4	1	*OP1	Sparkle
05/06/93	11	2	*OP2	Tweezer
07/25/93	13	2	Also Sprac	Tweezer
08/02/93	6	2	Oh Kee	All Things
08/06/93	2	1	Chalkdust	*CL1
08/13/93	6	2	Oh Kee	AmGrace
08/17/93	4	2	Rift	YEM
12/28/93	7	1	Oh Kee	Ya Mar
12/31/93	3	3	Sparkle	Rosie
04/04/94	1	2	Oh Kee	*CL2
04/08/94	3	2	Bowie	*CL2
04/11/94	3	2	Oh Kee	*CL2
04/15/94	3	2	If I Could	LLadu
04/20/94	4	1	Stash	*CL1
04/22/94	2	2	*OP2	Julius
04/29/94	5	2	*OP2	Maze
05/02/94	2	2	Divided	Foam
05/04/94	2	2	Magilla	*CL2
05/07/94	2	1	If I Could	*CL1
05/13/94	4	1	Slave	*CL1
05/17/94	3	1	*OP1	Maze
05/27/94	8	2	*OP2	Peaches
05/29/94	2	2	Oh Kee	Antelope
06/09/94	1	1	Fee	*CL1
06/11/94	2	E	*OPE	*CLE
06/16/94	3	2	*OP2	Antelope
06/19/94	3	1	*OP1	Julius
06/21/94	1	2	Harry	*CL2
06/25/94	4	2	*OP2	Maze
06/29/94	2	2	Divided	Cavern
07/01/94	2	1	Julius	*CL1
07/03/94	2	2	Antelope	*CL2
07/09/94	4	2	Harry	*CL2
07/13/94	2	2	Slave	*CL2
07/16/94	3	E	*OPE	*CLE
10/08/94	2	2	Harry	*CL2
10/15/94	6	2	Bouncing	*CL2
10/22/94	5	1	*OP1	Divided
10/26/94	3	1	Oh Kee	RunJim
11/02/94	5	1	*OP1	Foam
11/04/94	2	1	Scent	Chalkdust
11/13/94	2	2	*OP2	Divided
11/16/94	2	E	AmGrace	*CLE
11/19/94	3	2	*OP2	Sparkle
11/23/94	3	1	Oh Kee	Divided
11/28/94	3	2	*OP2	NICU
12/02/94	3	2	Caravan	*CL2
12/03/94	1	2	Frankstein	BurAlive
12/09/94	5	2	YEM	*CL2
12/28/94	2	2	*OP2	NICU
12/31/94	3	3	Silent	Slave
06/07/95	2	2	Harry	*CL2
06/10/95	3	1	LCBill	*CL1
06/17/95	5	1	Divided	Taste
06/24/95	5	1	Life Boy	Harry
06/28/95	3	1	Sparkle	Harry
07/01/95	3	1	Harry	*CL2
09/29/95	5	1	Adeline	*CL1
10/05/95	4	1	Julius	*CL1
10/11/95	4	1	Llama	Crossroad
10/17/95	4	2	Fog	Keyboard
10/21/95	3	2	Harry	*CL2
10/25/95	3	2	Weekpaug	Crossroad
10/31/95	4	3	DayinLife	*CL3
11/11/95	3	2	Bowie	Uncle Pen
11/15/95	3	E	*OPE	*CLE
11/19/95	3	2	Harry	*CL2
11/24/95	3	1	Maze	*CL1
11/28/95	2	2	Maze	Uncle Pen
12/01/95	3	E	*OPE	*CLE
12/14/95	9	1	*OP1	Llama
12/16/95	2	1	Julius	*CL1
12/30/95	4	1	Also Sprac	Bowie
07/07/96	7	1a	Antelope	*CL1
07/12/96	4	2	Slave	*CL2
07/21/96	6	2	Caspian	*CL2
08/06/96	8	1	Rift	Simpl
08/12/96	3	1	Oh Kee	*CL1
08/17/96	3	1	Maze	*CL1
10/18/96	3	2	*OP2	Maze
10/23/96	4	2	Llama	Slave
10/27/96	3	1	Taste	*CL1
10/31/96	2	3	Jesus	*CL3
11/07/96	4	2	*OP2	Bathtub
11/13/96	4	2	Also Sprac	Caspian
11/16/96	3	2	Harry	AmGrace
11/24/96	5	2	Lovin Cup	*CL2
11/29/96	2	1	Maze	*CL1
12/06/96	5	E	Harpua	*CLE
12/31/96	4	3	DWD	Antelope
02/17/97	4	2	DWD	Caspian
02/23/97	5	2	Daniel	Maze
03/18/97	6	1	CTB	CharZero
➢ 8/17/97	38			

Swept Away/Steep [20]

Swept Away [SweptAwy]/Steep [Steep]

Swept Away by Anastasio/ Marshall

Steep by Phish

10/16/96	[850]	2	Simple	Caspian
10/19/96	3	2	Fluffhead	Antelope
10/22/96	2	2	Mike's	Weekpaug
10/31/96	6	3	Simple	Jesus
11/06/96	3	2	Mike's	Weekpaug
11/09/96	3	2	Taste	Harry
11/11/96	1	2	Tweezer	Maze
11/14/96	2	2	Taste	Scent
11/18/96	3	2	Simple	Scent
11/22/96	2	2	Billy	CharZero
11/29/96	4	2	Taste	YEM
12/01/96	2	2	Reba	TweezRep
12/31/96	7	3	Simple	Harry
02/16/97	3	2	Circus	Bowie
02/20/97	3	2	Free	DayinLife
02/28/97	6	1	Stash	CharZero
03/02/97	2	1	Maze	PYITE
06/21/97	7	1a	Theme	Limb
07/29/97	19	1	Ghost	Lovin Cup
08/09/97	7	2	Simple	Scent
➢ 8/17/97	6			

Talk [11]

Talk [Talk]

By Anastasio/Marshall

08/05/96	[841]	2	Waste	Train Song
08/16/96	7	2	Waste	Train Song
10/17/96	3	1	Theme	PYITE
10/22/96	4	1	It's Ice	Split&Melt
10/27/96	4	1	Split&Melt	Taste
11/09/96	8	1	Tube	Split&Melt
11/14/96	3	1	Bathtub	Julius
12/30/96	17	1	Reba	FunkBitch
02/22/97	9	1	Circus	Split&Melt
06/14/97	9	1	Dirt	My Soul
06/24/97	6	1	RunJim	Free
➢ 8/17/97	30			

Taste [62]*

Taste [Taste]

By Phish/Marshall

06/07/95	[739]	1	Weigh	Str Design
06/09/95	2	1	Theme	Sparkle
06/13/95	2	1	Str Design	Reba
06/15/95	2	1	Old Home	Wedge
06/17/95	2	1	Suzie	Fee
06/20/95	2	1	If I Could	IDK

06/23/95 2 1 Free YEM
06/25/95 2 1 ACDCBag Theme
06/29/95 3 1 RunJim Horse
06/30/95 1 1 Horn Wedge
07/03/96 64 1a Sparkle Llama
07/09/96 4 1a PoorHeart CTB
07/12/96 3 1 FunkBitch Theme
07/21/96 6 1 Silnt Train Song
08/02/96 5 2 Simpl Free
08/07/96 4 1 Gumbo Lawn Boy
08/12/96 2 1 Dog Faced Oh Kee
08/17/96 4 1 Sample Fee
10/16/96 1 2 Wolfman's Train Song
10/18/96 2 1 Billy Sample
10/22/96 3 2 DWD Mango
10/25/96 2 1 Ha Ha Ha Makisupa
10/27/96 2 1 Talk Suzie
10/29/96 1 1 CTB Bouncing
11/02/96 2 1 Cavern Stash
11/06/96 2 1 FEFY Train Song
11/09/96 3 2 YEM SweptAwy
11/13/96 2 1 Ya Mar Train Song
11/14/96 1 2 Sample SweptAwy
11/15/96 1 1 Chalkdust Cavern
11/18/96 2 1 PoorHeart Billy
11/19/96 1 1 Fee Lovin Cup
11/22/96 1 1 Wolfman's Ginseng
11/24/96 2 1 Str Design IDK
11/29/96 2 2 Sparkle SweptAwy
11/30/96 1 2 Timber Ho FunkBitch
12/02/96 2 2 Wolfman's Free
12/29/96 4 1 Cavern Guelah
02/13/97 3 1 Walfredo Waste
02/17/97 3 2 Jam DWD
02/20/97 2 1 Treat Gumbo
02/25/97 4 1 Waste Lovin Cup
02/28/97 2 2 *OP2 Drowned
03/01/97 1 E *OPE Adeline
03/18/97 2 2 *OP2 Drowned
06/13/97 1 1 Wading *CL1
06/16/97 1 1 Dogs Stole Water
06/20/97 2 1 *OP1 Cities
06/21/97 1 1a PoorHeart Dirt
06/22/97 1 1a *OP1 Water
06/25/97 1 1 Dogs Stole Billy
06/27/97 1 1a PoorHeart Bouncing
06/29/97 1 1a YEM Bouncing
07/03/97 3 3 Beauty Train Song
07/09/97 3 1 Dirt Adeline
07/22/97 4 1 Bye Bye *CL1
07/25/97 2 2 Chalkdust Ya Mar
07/29/97 2 2 Twist Sample
08/03/97 4 2 Lifeboy HelloBaby
08/09/97 3 1 Ghost Dogs Stole
08/14/97 4 2 CamlWalk *CL2
08/17/97 2 1 Tweezer Carolina
➢ 8/17/97 0

Tela [65]*

Tela [Tela]
By Anastasio

03/12/88 [32] 1a Lizards Wilson
06/20/88 10 2 Sally Fee
08/27/88 9 1a Golgi *CL1
10/22/89 82 1 Split&Melt Divided
11/16/89 10 2 ACDCBag Bowie
12/08/89 7 2 Harry Timber Ho
01/20/90 7 1a Reba La Grange
01/28/90 4 1 Split&Melt Fluffhead
02/23/90 13 2 Jesus Oh Kee
03/07/90 6 2 Split&Melt Mike's
03/11/90 3 E *OPE *CLE
05/15/90 18 1 Possum Tweezer
09/22/90 17 1 Divided Oh Kee
10/05/90 4 1 Landlady Oh Kee
12/08/90 21 2 Antelope Golgi
04/12/91 44 2 Cavern BurAlive
04/16/91 3 1 ACDCBag Bowie
04/21/91 4 1 ACDCBag Mike's
05/02/91 5 2 Split&Melt MSO
05/03/91 1 2 RunJim YEM
07/24/91 20 1 Cavern YEM
09/25/91 5 1 Llama MSO
09/27/91 2 2 Possum Sparkle
10/13/91 11 1 Mockbird ACDCBag
10/27/91 8 2 Weekpaug Landlady
11/01/91 4 2 A-Train Cavern
11/09/91 5 2 Tweezer Landlady
11/20/91 8 2 Antelope Landlady
12/06/91 8 2 Divided Llama
04/21/92 34 2 Tweezer Mike's
04/25/92 4 1 Brother Chalkdust
05/02/92 4 2 Bowie Foam
05/06/92 3 1 Maze Brother
05/09/92 3 2 Divided Tweezer
11/22/92 54 2 Tweezer YEM
12/02/92 7 2 BBJ Llama
12/10/92 7 2 Tweezer MSO
12/29/92 5 1 Tela Oh Kee
02/10/93 9 1 Divided IDK
03/18/93 26 2 Split&Melt YEM
03/22/93 3 2 Lizards Wilson
05/06/93 33 2 Tweezer Uncle Pen
08/09/93 24 2 Tweezer My Friend
04/09/94 22 2 Weekpaug Slave
04/25/94 14 1 Dog Faced PoorHeart
05/21/94 18 1 Sqirm Coil Llama
06/11/94 10 1 It's Ice Stash
06/25/94 11 1 Scent Chalkdust
06/26/94 1 1 Lizards Wilson
07/01/94 3 1 It's Ice Julius
07/08/94 5 1 Lizards Wilson
10/18/94 16 1 Stash It's Ice
10/23/94 4 1 Stash Maze
11/04/94 9 2 Mike's Weekpaug
11/18/94 6 1 It's Ice Split&Melt
06/19/95 32 1 ACDCBag PYITE
06/26/95 6 1 Dog Faced Possum
10/02/95 11 1 Theme Bowie
10/14/95 8 1 It's Ice RunJim
11/09/95 13 1 Reba Sample
11/24/95 11 1 Stash I'm Blue
12/14/95 14 1 Split&Melt Fog
08/13/96 35 1 Tube Maze
11/07/96 19 1 Free CharZero
08/14/97 74 1 CTB Train Song
➢ 8/17/97 2

Theme From The Bottom [68]

Theme From The Bottom [Theme]
By Phish/Marshall

05/16/95 [738] 1a Reba LCBill
06/07/95 1 2 Spock's LCBill
06/09/95 2 1 ACDCBag Taste
06/13/95 2 2 Axilla 2 AArmy
06/15/95 2 2 Str Design Scent
06/19/95 3 1 *OP1 PoorHeart
06/22/95 2 2 *OP2 Tweezer
06/25/95 3 1 Taste If I Could
06/29/95 3 E *OPE *CLE
07/01/95 2 2 Maze Uncle Pen
09/28/95 4 2 *OP2 PoorHeart
10/02/95 3 1 Fog Tela
10/06/95 3 2 Maze NICU
10/13/95 4 2 Uncle Pen Wilson
10/19/95 4 1 Chalkdust AArmy
10/24/95 4 2 Julius Bouncing
10/28/95 3 2 Maze Scent
11/09/95 3 2 *OP2 Julius
11/15/95 5 2 Wilson Scent
11/19/95 3 2 *OP2 Also Sprac
11/24/95 3 2 Chalkdust Reba
11/29/95 3 1 It's Ice AArmy
12/01/95 2 1 DWD PoorHeart
12/05/95 3 E *OPE Adeline
12/09/95 3 1 Maze NICU
12/28/95 7 2 Timber Ho Wilson
06/06/96 5 1 FunkBitch BBFCM
07/09/96 5 1a *OP1 PoorHeart
07/12/96 3 1 Taste Tweezer
07/21/96 6 2 Llama Reba
07/23/96 2 1 Foam Gumbo
08/02/96 3 1 Foam Golgi
08/06/96 3 1 Simpl Lizards
08/14/96 5 2 Tweezer Rosie
10/17/96 4 1 Tweezer Talk
10/23/96 5 1 Rift Antelope
10/26/96 2 1 It's Ice Sample
11/03/96 5 1 Sample Bouncing
11/08/96 3 E *OPE *CLE
11/11/96 2 1 Brother Axilla
11/13/96 1 2 YEM Golgi
11/19/96 5 1 Foam Mound
11/22/96 1 2 CharZero Slave
11/27/96 3 1 Free Bold
12/02/96 4 1 IDK Gumbo
12/30/96 5 1 FunkBitch GTBT
02/16/97 4 E *OPE Johnny B.
02/22/97 5 1 FunkBitch NICU
02/26/97 3 2 Kung Scent
03/01/97 2 2 Billy *CL2
06/13/97 3 1 *OP1 Dogs Stole
06/16/97 2 1 Beauty Chalkdust
06/19/97 1 1 Dogs Stole PYITE
06/21/97 2 1a Dirt SweptAwy
06/22/97 1 1a CharZero HelloBaby
06/25/97 2 1 Old Home Wading
06/29/97 2 1a Chalkdust CharZero
07/03/97 3 1 Train Song Rocky Top
07/05/97 1 1a Sample Caspian
07/21/97 5 2 Wading Jam
07/25/97 3 E *OPE *CLE
07/29/97 2 1 *OP1 Beauty
08/02/97 3 1 *OP1 Ginseng
08/09/97 4 1 *OP1 PYITE
08/13/97 3 E *OPE *CLE
08/16/97 2 1 Chalkdust PYITE
➢ 8/17/97 1

Time [1]

Time [Time]
Author Unknown

06/25/97 [912] 2 DWD McGrupp
➢ 8/17/97 29

Train Song [19]

Train Song [Train Song]
By Gordon/J. Linitz

07/21/96 [834] 1 Taste Fee
08/05/96 7 2 Talk Desgn
08/13/96 5 2 Waste Desgn
08/16/96 2 2 Talk Desgn
10/16/96 2 2 Taste Simple
10/21/96 4 2 Reba Maze
10/26/96 4 1 Reba CharZero
10/29/96 2 1 Stash Billy
11/06/96 4 1 Taste PoorHeart
11/13/96 5 1 Taste Reba
11/15/96 2 1 Ginseng Chalkdust
11/22/96 4 1 FEFY Stash
12/01/96 6 1 DWD Horse
12/04/96 2 1 Sample Guyute
12/29/96 3 1 Guelah Rift
02/18/97 7 2 Reba Harry
07/03/97 24 1 Taste Theme
08/14/97 22 1 Tela Billy
08/16/97 1 1 YEM CharZero
➢ 8/17/97 1

Tube [31]

Tube [Tube]
By Anastasio/Fishman

09/13/90 [222] 1 Foam Asse Fest
09/15/90 2 1 Fee Oh Kee
09/16/90 1 1a Ya Mar Tweezer
11/04/90 17 1 Bouncing Harry
11/16/90 3 2 Lawn Boy Paul&Silas
10/24/91 109 2 Uncle Pen Slave
10/28/91 3 1 IDK Oh Kee
10/31/91 2 2 Dinner IDK
11/01/91 1 1 Uncle Pen Divided
11/07/91 3 2 Reba Horn
11/08/91 1 1 *OP1 Landlady
11/09/91 1 1 Reba YEM
11/12/91 2 1 Bouncing Sloth
11/14/91 2 1 Foam Sparkle
11/15/91 1 2 Eliza Landlady
11/16/91 1 2 *OP2 MSO
11/19/91 1 2 *OP2 MSO
11/22/91 3 2 *OP2 MSO
11/24/91 2 2 *OP2 Divided
12/05/91 3 2 Sparkle Foam
04/19/92 34 2 MSO Mango
11/20/92 67 2 Fluffhead YEM
04/12/93 73 1 Golgi Bouncing
06/26/94 119 E AmGrace Fire
10/13/95 99 2 *OP2 Uncle Pen
12/11/95 37 1 Dog Log McGrupp
12/17/95 5 1 Mango Stash
08/13/96 32 1 Divided Tela
10/25/96 11 2 *OP2 Caspian
11/09/96 10 1 Horn Talk
02/26/97 32 1 My Soul Carini
➢ 8/17/97 42

Tweezer [197]

Tweezer [Tweezer]
By Phish

03/28/90 [185] 1 WalkAway Uncle Pen
04/05/90 2 2 Donna Fee
04/07/90 2 1 Possum Mike's
04/09/90 2 2 Love You WhipPost
05/04/90 14 1 Uncle Pen Bathtub
05/06/90 1 1 Reba Mike's
05/10/90 1 1 Divided MSO
05/11/90 1 2 Lizards Ya Mar
05/13/90 2 2 Donna MSO
05/15/90 1 1 Tela Oh Kee
05/23/90 2 2 Reba Lizards
05/24/90 1 1 Bouncing Donna
05/31/90 1 1a Esther IDK
06/07/90 3 2 Bouncing Uncle Pen
06/08/90 1 1 Bathtub IDK
06/09/90 1 1 Bouncing Uncle Pen
06/16/90 1 2 Esther MSO
09/14/90 2 2 BurAlive Magilla
09/16/90 2 1a Tube Paul&Silas
09/22/90 3 2 Sqirm Coil Destiny
10/01/90 2 1 Bouncing Oh Kee
10/07/90 4 2 Bouncing MSO
10/12/90 2 1 Esther Golgi
10/31/90 3 2 Foam Fee
11/08/90 4 2 Divided Oh Kee
11/30/90 6 1 Bouncing MSO
12/01/90 1 1 Foam MSO
12/07/90 2 2 Caravan Sqirm Coil
12/28/90 2 2 Sqirm Coil Oh Kee
02/01/91 3 1 Foam Magilla
02/03/91 2 1 MSO Esther
02/07/91 1 2 Stash Guelah
02/09/91 2 1 MSO Reba
03/01/91 13 1 Sqirm Coil Dinner
03/13/91 6 2 Reba Terrapin
03/17/91 3 2 Sqirm Coil Fee
03/23/91 3 2 MSO Lizards
04/11/91 9 1 Paul&Silas Magilla
04/16/91 4 2 Uncle Pen RunJim
04/20/91 3 2 TMWSIY Oh Kee
04/22/91 2 E2 *OPE2 TweezRep
04/27/91 3 2 Fluffhead Sqirm Coil
05/03/91 2 1 Paul&Silas Lizards
05/16/91 6 2 Sqirm Coil MSO
07/12/91 5 2 Moose MSO
07/19/91 5 2 Magilla Mango
07/21/91 2 2 *OP2 IDK
07/23/91 1 2 Landlady Adeline
07/26/91 3 2 Sqirm Coil Adeline
08/03/91 2 2 Bouncing Esther
09/27/91 3 1 Esther Paul&Silas
10/03/91 4 2 Sqirm Coil Memories

In Their Sleep

Songs played so often, Phish could play them in their sleep. Here are the songs most-played by Phish in history. The most-played by year ratings show the percentage of shows featuring the song.

MOST-PLAYED, ALL-TIME	
1) YEM	**377**
2) Bouncing	**318**
3) Golgi	**301**
4) Cavern	**292**
5) Mike's	**291**
6) Possum	**287**
7) Suzie	**285**
8) Stash	**274**
9) Divided Sky	**268**
9) Weekapaug	**268**
11) Foam	**265**
12) Chalkdust	**263**
12) David Bowie	**263**
14) Reba	**259**
14) Runaway Jim	**259**

MOST-PLAYED, IN A YEAR		
1) Landlady	**1991**	**65%**
2) Rift	**1993**	**62%**
3) Big Ball Jam	**1993**	**58%**
3) Cavern	**1991**	**58%**
3) My Sweet One	**1991**	**58%**
6) Bouncing	**1990**	**56%**
6) Free	**1995**	**56%**
6) Possum	**1990**	**56%**
6) Sample	**1994**	**56%**
10) YEM	**1990**	**55%**
11) Llama	**1991**	**54%**
12) Sparkle	**1992**	**53%**
12) Sparkle	**1993**	**53%**

Stories Behind the Songs
(Continued)

of it during 1993, including a significantly revised version performed on 8/20/93. Not happy with the song (perhaps because of its often-likened similarities to a Dead song, which was apparently the reason the band did not release it as a single off *Rift*), the band put it in the closet before reviving it in a shortened version on summer tour 1995.

Weekapaug Groove: The second half of Mike's Groove (see Mike's Song); named for the town of Weekapaug, R.I., where the band played a gig at a small hotel in their early years. The lyrics of Mike's Song reportedly refer to the events of that night.

Wilson: A Gamehendge song, sung from the perspective of Errand Woolfe, the leader of the revolutionaries, who despises Wilson's imprisonment of the Lizards and his installation of himself as king of the land.

You Enjoy Myself: Perhaps the most popular Phish tune of them all, this song played a part in the departure of Jeff Holdsworth from the band in the mid-1980s.when he decided he had no interest in performing this kind of music. Lengthy and tiresome debate has ensued, both on and off the Phish.Net, over "WATSIYEM?" ("What Are They Saying In You Enjoy Myself?"). Mike has thrice published the correct version in the *Doniac Schvice*, the newsletter, but the question springs eternal.

The actual phrase, "Wash a Uffizi and drive me to Firenze," refers to a trip to Europe Trey and Fishman took in the summer of 1985 during which Trey composed this song (the famous Uffizi art gallery is in Firenze, or Florence; the song's title stems from a phrase an Italian man said to Fish and Trey when he complemented their musical acumen).

But in concert the bandmembers don't necessarily recite the "real" line; Page has said that he has no idea what they're saying most of the time. The closest approximation might be "Wash Uffizi, drive me to Firenze," dropping the "a" from the written version of the lyric.

10/12/91	6	1	*OP1	Uncle Pen
10/19/91	5	2	Sparkle	Horn
11/01/91	8	2	*OP2	MSO
11/09/91	5	2	It's Ice	Tela
11/14/91	4	2	Glide	A-Train
11/21/91	5	2	Uncle Pen	TMWSIY
11/23/91	2	2	PoorHeart	Eliza
12/05/91	4	2	*OP2	Sparkle
12/31/91	3	3	Sqirm Coil	McGrupp
03/07/92	2	2	MSO	Sqirm Coil
03/12/92	2	2	Golgi	Eliza
03/17/92	3	2	PoorHeart	Esther
03/25/92	5	2	*OP2	Mound
03/30/92	4	2	Uncle Pen	Mound
04/01/92	2	2	Uncle Pen	Horn
04/04/92	2	2	MSO	Sqirm Coil
04/07/92	3	2	All Things	Eliza
04/17/92	6	2	Sqirm Coil	Uncle Pen
04/21/92	3	2	Mockbird	Tela
04/23/92	2	2	Horn	Fee
04/30/92	4	2	Glide	Sqirm Coil
05/03/92	3	2	*OP2	Horse
05/07/92	3	2	Sparkle	Fluffhead
05/09/92	2	2	Tela	Harpua
05/16/92	5	2	Paul&Silas	Sqirm Coil
07/14/92	15	2	*OP2	Fee
07/24/92	8	1a	Foam	Sqirm Coil
07/28/92	4	1a	Sqirm Coil	RunJim
08/17/92	8	2	It's Ice	Esther
08/24/92	4	1a	All Things	Landlady
11/19/92	7	2	Walk Line	BBJ
11/22/92	3	2	MSO	Tela
11/25/92	2	2	Lizards	Rosie
11/28/92	2	2	Paul&Silas	BBJ
12/02/92	3	2	Mound	BBJ
12/05/92	3	2	PoorHeart	Reba
12/10/92	4	2	Rift	Tela
12/12/92	2	2	Curtain	Rift
12/29/92	3	2	Curtain	Horse
02/03/93	3	2	It's Ice	Horse
02/05/93	2	2	Curtain	Horse
02/07/93	2	2	Reba	BBJ
02/10/93	2	2	Sqirm Coil	Walk Line
02/13/93	3	2	Uncle Pen	Lizards
02/18/93	3	1	PoorHeart	Foam
02/20/93	2	2	Reba	Glide
02/22/93	2	2	Uncle Pen	Glide
02/26/93	3	2	Paul&Silas	Glide
03/02/93	2	2	Uncle Pen	Lizards
03/06/93	3	2	Rift	Reba
03/09/93	2	2	Rift	Reba
03/13/93	2	2	Suzie	Lizards
03/16/93	2	2	Curtain	Bathtub
03/21/93	4	2	Rift	Ya Mar
03/24/93	2	2	Sparkle	Mound
03/26/93	2	2	Curtain	Horse
03/30/93	3	2	Rift	Life Boy
04/01/93	2	2	Ya Mar	PoorHeart
04/05/93	3	2	PYITE	Glide
04/12/93	3	2	Dinner	Fee
04/14/93	2	2	MSO	Mound
04/18/93	3	2	PoorHeart	Horse
04/22/93	3	2	All Things	Lizards
04/25/93	3	2	Curtain	Contact
04/30/93	3	2	Sparkle	Mound
05/03/93	3	2	Curtain	Contact
05/06/93	2	2	Suzie	Tela
07/17/93	7	2	Also Sprac	Sqirm Coil
07/22/93	3	2	Also Sprac	WalkAway
07/25/93	3	2	Suzie	Horse
07/30/93	4	2	Also Sprac	Horse
08/06/93	4	2	Stash	Guelah
08/09/93	3	2	Dinner	Tela
08/12/93	2	2	Landlady	Jam
08/15/93	3	2	Rift	Lizards
12/31/93	12	2	*OP2	Halley's
04/05/94	2	2	Ya Mar	If I Could
04/16/94	9	2	PoorHeart	Lizards
04/22/94	5	2	Reba	Life Boy
05/04/94	9	1	Axilla 2	Life Boy
05/07/94	2	2	Sparkle	TweezRep
05/17/94	7	2	Glide	Life Boy
05/22/94	4	2	McGrupp	Life Boy
05/25/94	2	2	Rift	Life Boy
05/28/94	3	2	It's Ice	Life Boy
06/10/94	3	2	Curtain	Life Boy
06/18/94	6	2	McGrupp	Life Boy
06/23/94	4	2	Uncle Pen	Life Boy
06/29/94	4	2	PoorHeart	It's Ice
07/02/94	3	1	Scent	Life Boy
07/06/94	3	1	PoorHeart	Lawn Boy
07/09/94	2	2	PoorHeart	Life Boy
07/13/94	2	2	NICU	Mound
10/07/94	4	2	Scent	Life Boy
10/10/94	3	2	Esther	Fee
10/14/94	3	2	Curtain	Life Boy
10/22/94	6	2	Dinner	Wilson
10/27/94	4	2	Ya Mar	Contact
11/02/94	4	2	Halley's	Mango
11/13/94	4	2	Lizards	Mango
11/18/94	4	2	PoorHeart	Contact
11/23/94	4	2	Scent	Life Boy
11/28/94	3	2	NICU	Sl Monkey
12/01/94	2	2	Mound	BBFCM
12/04/94	3	1	Rift	Fee
12/09/94	4	2	PoorHeart	McGrupp
12/30/94	4	2	PoorHeart	I'm Blue
06/08/95	4	2	Bouncing	Life Boy
06/14/95	4	2	PoorHeart	AArmy
06/17/95	3	2	Mound	McGrupp
06/22/95	3	2	Theme	TweezRep
06/28/95	5	2	PoorHeart	Gumbo
07/02/95	4	2	Scent	Ha Ha Ha
09/28/95	3	2	Wanna Go	Keyboard
10/06/95	6	2	NICU	Keyboard
10/15/95	6	2	Simple	Lizards
10/22/95	5	2	Curtain	Makisupa
11/12/95	10	2	Curtain	Keyboard
11/19/95	5	2	Curtain	Billy
11/30/95	7	2	CTB	Makisupa
12/02/95	2	2	Faht	DayinLife
12/08/95	4	2	Also Sprac	Love You
12/14/95	4	2	Curtain	Keyboard
12/17/95	3	2	Sparkle	TweezRep
12/28/95	1	2	BurAlive	IDK
07/07/96	9	1a	Curtain	Adeline
07/12/96	4	1	Theme	Llama
07/21/96	6	1	Rift	If I Could
08/02/96	5	1	Golgi	HelloBaby
08/06/96	3	2	Curtain	Caspian
08/14/96	5	2	CTB	Theme
08/17/96	2	3	Scent	DayinLife
10/17/96	2	1	Sparkle	Theme
10/23/96	5	2	Ya Mar	Lizards
10/27/96	3	2	Ya Mar	Fluffhead
11/03/96	4	2	Sparkle	Life Mars
11/11/96	5	2	Sample	SweptAwy
11/18/96	5	2	Scent	HelloBaby
11/27/96	5	2	Scent	DWD
12/01/96	3	2	*OP2	Sparkle
12/30/96	6	2	Guyute	Lifeboy
02/16/97	3	1	Ginseng	Waste
02/20/97	3	1	Curtain	SSP
08/02/97	37	2	DWD	DWD
08/17/97	10	1	Bouncing	Taste
➢ 8/17/97	**0**			

Tweezer Reprise [126]

Tweezer Reprise [TweezRep]

By Phish

02/07/91	[260]	2	Tweezer	Guelah
04/16/91	40	2	Carolina	*CL2
04/22/91	5	E2	Tweezer	*CLE
04/27/91	3	2	Jam	*CL2
05/03/91	2	2	Harpua	*CL2
05/11/91	4	2	Suzie	*CL2
07/12/91	7	E	Fee	*CLE
07/21/91	7	2	Contact	*CL2
07/26/91	4	2	Lizards	*CL2
09/27/91	5	2	YEM	*CL2
10/03/91	4	E	Terrapin	*CLE
10/12/91	6	1	Harry	*CL1
11/01/91	13	2	PoorHeart	*CL2
11/09/91	5	2	MSO	*CL2
11/14/91	4	2	Lizards	*CL2
11/23/91	7	2	MSO	*CL2
12/05/91	4	2	MSO	*CL2
12/31/91	3	E	Rocky Top	*CLE
03/07/92	2	2	Rosie	*CL2
03/12/92	2	E	Weigh	*CLE
03/25/92	8	E	Sl Monkey	*CLE
03/30/92	4	2	Bouncing	*CL2
04/01/92	2	2	Sqirm Coil	Rocky Top
04/04/92	2	E	Sl Monkey	*CLE
04/07/92	3	E	Contact	*CLE
04/17/92	6	2	Rosie	*CL2
04/23/92	5	E	Sl Monkey	*CLE
04/30/92	4	2	Harry	*CL2
05/03/92	3	E	Adeline	*CLE
05/07/92	3	2	Sqirm Coil	*CL2
05/09/92	2	E	PoorHeart	*CLE
05/16/92	5	2	PoorHeart	*CL2
07/14/92	15	2	A-Train	*CL2
07/24/92	8	1a	YEM	*CL1
11/22/92	26	E	Carolina	*CLE
11/25/92	2	2	MSO	*CL2
11/28/92	2	E	Contact	*CLE
12/05/92	6	2	WhipPost	*CL2
12/10/92	4	E	Carolina	*CLE
12/12/92	2	E	Ride Capt.	*CLE
12/29/92	3	2	Sqirm Coil	*CL2
02/03/93	3	E	AmGrace	*CLE
02/05/93	2	2	Sqirm Coil	*CL2
02/07/93	2	2	Brain	*CL2
02/10/93	2	E	AmGrace	*CLE
02/13/93	3	E	AmGrace	*CLE
02/20/93	5	2	Harry	*CL2
02/22/93	2	2	Sqirm Coil	*CL2
02/26/93	3	2	Sqirm Coil	*CL2
03/02/93	2	E	Golgi	*CLE
03/06/93	3	E	PoorHeart	*CLE
03/09/93	2	2	Sqirm Coil	*CL2
03/13/93	2	2	Love You	*CL2
03/16/93	2	E	Sparkle	*CLE
03/26/93	8	2	Great Gig	*CL2
03/30/93	3	2	Brain	*CL2
04/01/93	2	E	Carolina	*CLE
04/05/93	3	2	Rosie	*CL2
04/12/93	3	2	Terrapin	*CL2
04/14/93	2	E	Contact	*CLE
04/18/93	3	2	Love You	*CL2
04/22/93	3	2	Love You	*CL2
04/25/93	3	2	Fee	*CL2
04/30/93	3	E	AmGrace	*CLE
05/03/93	3	2	MSO	*CL2
05/06/93	2	E	Contact	*CLE
07/17/93	7	E	Daniel	*CLE
07/25/93	6	2	Harpua	*CL2
08/06/93	8	2	Rosie	*CL2
12/31/93	20	3	Harry	*CL3
04/16/94	11	2	Sqirm Coil	*CL2
05/04/94	14	1	Rift	*CL1
05/07/94	2	2	HYHU	*CL2
05/22/94	11	2	Slave	*CL2
05/25/94	2	E	Sl Monkey	*CLE
06/10/94	6	2	Harry	*CL2
06/18/94	6	E	Bouncing	*CLE
06/23/94	4	E	Sparkle	*CLE
06/29/94	4	E	Ya Mar	*CLE
07/02/94	3	1	Sparkle	*CL1
07/06/94	3	2	Harry	*CL2
07/09/94	2	E	Sl Monkey	*CLE
07/13/94	2	E	MSO	*CLE
10/07/94	4	2	MSO	*CL2
10/10/94	3	E	Long Time	*CLE
10/14/94	3	2	Sqirm Coil	*CL2
10/22/94	6	E	Uncle Pen	*CLE
10/27/94	4	E	Icculus	*CLE
11/02/94	4	E	Long Time	*CLE
11/13/94	4	E	FunkBitch	*CLE
11/23/94	8	2	YEM	*CL2
11/28/94	3	E	Fee	*CLE
12/01/94	2	E	Sl Monkey	*CLE
12/09/94	7	E	Long Time	*CLE
12/30/94	4	2	Harry	*CL2
06/14/95	8	E	Rocky Top	*CLE
06/22/95	6	E	Tweezer	*CL2
06/28/95	5	2	Harry	*CL2
07/02/95	4	E	Halley's	*CLE
10/15/95	15	2	Harry	*CL2
10/21/95	4	1	*OP1	Chalkdust
10/21/95	0	1	GTBT	*CL1
11/09/95	8	1	*OP1	Divided
11/12/95	3	2	Possum	*CL2
11/19/95	5	E	Life Mars	*CLE
12/02/95	9	2	Sqirm Coil	*CL2
12/08/95	4	2	Sqirm Coil	Antelope
12/15/95	5	2	*OP2	RunJim
12/15/95	0	E	GTBT	*CLE
12/17/95	2	2	Tweezer	*CL2
12/28/95	1	E	Fee	*CLE
08/06/96	27	2	Harry	*CL2
08/14/96	5	2	Sample	*CL2
08/17/96	2	3	Possum	*CL2
10/17/96	2	1	DayinLife	*CL1
10/27/96	8	2	Life Mars	*CL2
11/03/96	4	2	Possum	*CL2
11/18/96	10	2	HelloBaby	Llama
11/27/96	5	E	Waste	*CLE
12/01/96	3	2	Steep	Johnny B.
12/31/96	7	1	Sample	*CL1
02/16/97	3	2	Lovin Cup	*CL2
02/20/97	3	1	Bowie	*CL1
03/02/97	8	2	Slave	*CL2
08/02/97	29	2	Lovin Cup	*CL2
08/17/97	10	E	Circus	*CLE
➢ 8/17/97	**0**			

Twist Around [8]

Twist Around [Twist]

By Anastasio/Marshall

06/14/97	[905]	2	*OP2	Piper
06/20/97	3	2	Cavern	Bouncing
06/21/97	1	1a	Chalkdust	Cavern
06/24/97	2	2	NICU	Piper
07/05/97	7	1a	Caspian	Piper
07/29/97	10	2	Wading	Taste
08/03/97	4	1	MyMind	Jesus
08/06/97	1	1	Beauty	Also Sprac
➢ 8/17/97	**8**			

Vultures [9]

Vultures [Vultures]

By Anastasio/Marshall

06/13/97 [904] 2 Water Slave
06/19/97 3 1 Waste RunJim
06/24/97 4 1 Dogs Stole Guelah
07/02/97 5 1 Ginseng Water
07/22/97 8 1 Bouncing Bye Bye
07/31/97 6 2 Circus McGrupp
08/03/97 2 1 Dirt MyMind
08/11/97 5 2 Piper My Soul
08/17/97 5 1 Dogs Stole Water
➢ **8/17/97 0**

Wading in the Velvet Sea [10]

Wading in the Velvet Sea [Wading]

By Anastasio/Marshall

06/13/97 [904] 1 Wolfman's Taste
06/16/97 2 2 Reba Dirt
06/19/97 1 2 Saw It Piper
06/24/97 4 2 Piper Ghost
06/25/97 1 1 Theme Saw It
07/02/97 4 2 Wormtown *CL2
07/10/97 5 1 Llama Lizards
07/21/97 2 2 Biwue Theme
07/29/97 5 1 Antelope Twist
08/02/97 3 2 Sparkle Lovin Cup
➢ **8/17/97 10**

Walfredo [4]

Walfredo [Walfredo]

By Phish

02/13/97 [889] 1 Stash Taste
02/14/97 1 2 Reba RockaW
02/18/97 3 1 Waste CharZero
02/22/97 3 1 *OP1 Also Sprac
➢ **8/17/97 45**

Waste [29]

Waste [Waste]

By Anastasio/Marshall

06/06/96 [820] 2 Stash CharZero
07/10/96 13 1a Split&Melt Bowie
07/19/96 5 1a Adeline Sqirm Coil
08/05/96 10 2 Therm Talk
08/13/96 5 2 Therm Train Song
08/16/96 2 2 Sqirm Coil Talk
10/16/96 2 E *OPE *CLE
10/18/96 2 2 Reba Harry
10/21/96 2 1 Stash Possum
10/26/96 4 2 McGrupp Antelope
11/02/96 4 2 Antelope Harry
11/07/96 3 1 Stash Guyute
11/11/96 3 E *OPE Cavern
11/18/96 5 E *OPE Johnny B.
11/23/96 3 2 Catapult AmGrace
11/27/96 2 E *OPE TweezRep
11/29/96 1 2 YEM Harry
02/13/97 10 1 Taste PoorHeart
02/16/97 2 1 Tweezer Cavern
02/18/97 2 1 Stash Walfredo
02/21/97 2 2 Reba Caspian
02/25/97 3 1 Stash Taste
02/28/97 2 2 Axilla Julius
03/02/97 2 2 PYITE CharZero
03/18/97 1 2 Love Me Chalkdust
06/14/97 2 2 Dogs Stole Bowie
06/19/97 2 1 Maze Vultures
07/06/97 12 2 YEM Rocky Top
07/26/97 8 2 Free Johnny B.
➢ **8/17/97 14**

Water in the Sky [14]

Water in the Sky [Water]

By Anastasio/Marshall

06/13/97 [904] 2 Maze Vultures
06/16/97 2 1 Taste Sample
06/19/97 1 1 PYITE Waste
06/22/97 3 1a Taste Stash
07/02/97 6 1 Vultures Weekpaug
07/22/97 8 1 My Soul Stash
07/23/97 1 1 Ginseng Limb
07/25/97 1 1 Maze Bathtub
07/30/97 3 1 Chalkdust Weigh
08/02/97 2 1 Wolfman's Split&Melt
08/08/97 3 1 It's Ice CharZero
08/11/97 3 1 Maze Guyute
08/13/97 1 1 PoorHeart Gumbo
08/17/97 3 1 Vultures Maze
➢ **8/17/97 0**

Wedge [18]*

The Wedge [Wedge]

By Anastasio/Marshall

02/03/93 [505] 1 Llama Divided
02/04/93 1 2 Chalkdust Mike's
02/06/93 2 1 Lawn Boy Bouncing
02/09/93 2 1 Rift Chalkdust
02/12/93 3 1 Esther Chalkdust
02/15/93 2 2 Weekpaug PoorHeart
02/23/93 7 1 Chalkdust Paul&Silas
03/25/93 20 2 Mockbird Mike's
08/20/93 63 1 It's Ice Ginseng
06/07/95 134 1 Scent FunkBitch
06/09/95 2 2 Split&Melt Scent
06/15/95 4 1 Taste Stash
06/23/95 6 2 Lizards Antelope
06/30/95 6 1 Taste Lizards
10/25/95 25 1 Divided Scent
11/14/95 9 E *OPE Rocky Top
10/29/96 70 2 Weekpaug CharZero
08/17/97 81 1 *OP1 Beauty
➢ **8/17/97 0**

Weekapaug [268]*

Weekapaug Groove [Weekpaug]

By Gordon

07/23/88 [46] 1 I am H2 Lizards
07/24/88 1 1 I am H2 Bold
07/25/88 1 2 I am H2 Bold
10/12/88 7 1 I am H2 Wilson
11/05/88 3 2 I am H2 IDK
11/11/88 1 2 I am H2 Jazz
02/07/89 6 1 I am H2 Golgi
03/03/89 4 2 I am H2 Fee
03/04/89 1 1 I am H2 Fee
03/30/89 2 2 I am H2 YEM
04/14/89 6 2 I am H2 Esther
04/15/89 1 1 I am H2 Esther
04/20/89 2 2 I am H2 Love You
05/06/89 9 1 I am H2 Esther
05/09/89 3 1 I am H2 Sloth
05/20/89 7 2 I am H2 Foam
05/21/89 1 1 I am H2 Split&Melt
05/26/89 1 1 I am H2 Sanity
05/27/89 1 1 I am H2 FunkBitch
05/28/89 1 2 I am H2 Bathtub
06/23/89 5 1 I am H2 Lizards
06/30/89 2 2 I am H2 *CL2
08/17/89 5 1 I am H2 *CL1
08/19/89 2 1 I am H2 *CL1
10/06/89 8 1a I am H2 Sloth
10/07/89 1 1 I am H2 Suzie
10/21/89 5 2 I am H2 *CL2
10/26/89 2 1 I am H2 *CL1
11/02/89 3 1 I am H2 Fee
11/09/89 3 2 I am H2 *CL2
11/10/89 1 1 I am H2 *CL1
11/16/89 2 1 I am H2 Bathtub
12/07/89 6 1 I am H2 Alumni
12/09/89 2 2 I am H2 Contact
12/16/89 2 1a I am H2 Lizards
12/29/89 1 1 I am H2 *CL1
12/31/89 2 2 I am H2 Ya Mar
01/20/90 1 1 I am H2 Harry
01/27/90 3 1 I am H2 *CL1
01/28/90 1 2 I am H2 *CL2
02/09/90 7 1 I am H2 Carolina
02/10/90 1 2 I am H2 *CL2
02/15/90 1 1 I am H2 *CL1
02/17/90 2 1a I am H2 Split&Melt
02/23/90 2 2 I am H2 HwayHell
03/01/90 3 2 I am H2 *CL2
03/03/90 2 1 I am H2 MSO
03/07/90 1 2 I am H2 *CL2
03/08/90 1 2 I am H2 Curtis
03/28/90 4 2 I am H2 Jesus
04/04/90 1 2 I am H2 Lizards
04/05/90 1 2 I am H2 Brain
04/07/90 2 1 I am H2 Bowie
04/08/90 1 2 I am H2 Fee
04/18/90 5 1 I am H2 Uncle Pen
04/20/90 2 2 I am H2 La Grange
04/22/90 2 1 I am H2 *CL1
04/25/90 1 2 I am H2 *CL2
04/26/90 1 2 I am H2 *CL2
04/28/90 1 2 I am H2 *CL2
05/04/90 3 2 I am H2 Caravan
05/06/90 1 1 I am H2 *CL1
05/11/90 2 1 I am H2 Uncle Pen
05/13/90 2 2 I am H2 Foam
05/23/90 3 2 I am H2 *CL2
06/05/90 4 1 I am H2 Ya Mar
06/07/90 1 2 I am H2 *CL2
06/08/90 1 1 I am H2 Foam
06/09/90 1 1 I am H2 *CL1
06/16/90 1 3 I am H2 *CL3
09/13/90 1 2 I am H2 Magilla
09/16/90 3 1a I am H2 Magilla
10/05/90 7 1 I am H2 MSO
10/07/90 2 1 I am H2 A-Train
10/12/90 2 2 I am H2 *CL2
10/30/90 2 2 I am H2 Magilla
10/31/90 1 2 I am H2 *CL2
11/02/90 1 1 I am H2 Esther
11/03/90 1 2 I am H2 Paul&Silas
11/04/90 1 2 I am H2 Manteca
11/08/90 1 1 I am H2 *CL1
11/10/90 1 1 I am H2 *CL1
11/16/90 1 2 I am H2 Lawn Boy
11/17/90 1 2 I am H2 Esther
11/24/90 1 1 I am H2 Sqirm Coil
11/26/90 1 2 I am H2 *CL2
11/30/90 1 1 I am H2 Esther
12/07/90 3 2 I am H2 Donna
12/08/90 1 1 I am H2 *CL1
12/28/90 1 1 I am H2 Golgi
12/31/90 2 1 I am H2 Auld
02/08/91 5 2 I am H2 Horn
02/14/91 2 2 I am H2 Foam
02/16/91 2 1 I am H2 *CL1
02/21/91 3 1 I am H2 *CL1
02/26/91 4 2 I am H2 *CL2
02/28/91 2 1 I am H2 Cavern
03/01/91 1 1 I am H2 *CL1
03/07/91 3 2 I am H2 Guelah
03/15/91 4 1 I am H2 *CL1
03/17/91 2 1 I am H2 Foam
03/22/91 2 2 I am H2 *CL2
04/05/91 8 1 I am H2 *CL1
04/11/91 2 2 I am H2 *CL2
04/15/91 3 2 I am H2 Horn
04/19/91 3 1 I am H2 Adeline
04/21/91 2 1 I am H2 Adeline
04/27/91 4 2 I am H2 Fluffhead
05/04/91 3 1 I am H2 *CL1
05/10/91 2 2 I am H2 *CL2
05/12/91 2 2 I am H2 Sqirm Coil
05/17/91 2 1 I am H2 A-Train
07/11/91 3 2 I am H2 Touch Me
07/12/91 1 2 I am H2 Touch Me
07/14/91 2 3 I am H2 Touch Me
07/15/91 1 1a I am H2 Flat Fee
07/18/91 1 1 I am H2 *CL1
07/21/91 3 1 I am H2 *CL1
07/23/91 1 1 I am H2 *CL1
07/25/91 2 2 I am H2 *CL2
07/27/91 2 1a I am H2 *CL1
09/26/91 3 2 I am H2 Lawn Boy
09/28/91 2 2 I am H2 *CL2
10/03/91 3 2 I am H2 Esther
10/04/91 1 2 I am H2 *CL2
10/10/91 3 2 I am H2 *CL2
10/13/91 3 1 I am H2 *CL2
10/18/91 3 2 I am H2 IDK
10/24/91 3 2 I am H2 Lizards
10/27/91 2 2 I am H2 Tela
11/01/91 4 2 I am H2 A-Train
11/08/91 4 2 I am H2 Jesus
11/12/91 3 2 I am H2 Guelah
11/15/91 3 2 I am H2 Eliza
11/19/91 2 2 I am H2 Mango
11/21/91 2 1 I am H2 *CL1
11/23/91 2 2 I am H2 Horn

Dead and Buried

ORIGINAL SONGS that haven't been played in so long they may not ever come back, with dates of the song's last live appearance:

Name	***Last***
Fuck Your Face	04/29/87
Anarchy	08/10/87
Lushington	08/29/87
Prep School Hippie	12/06/86
Dave's Energy Guide	08/06/88
Dear Mrs. Reagan	06/15/88
No Dogs Allowed	10/26/89
In a Hole	12/16/89
Don't Get Me Wrong	12/28/90
Flat Fee	07/26/91
Destiny Unbound	11/15/91
Eliza	05/14/92
Leprechaun	07/30/93

Rarities

ORIGINAL SONGS debuted before 1/1/97 that surface in concert rarely these days, with total times played since 5/16/95 and the last appearance:

Name	***Since '95***	***Last***
Glide II	1	05/16/95
Icculus	1	10/31/95
Mid-Highway Blues	1	11/23/96
Faht	2	12/02/95
Sanity	2	10/31/96
Brother	3	10/31/96
Dog Log	3	02/26/97
My Sweet One	3	12/14/95
Camel Walk	3	08/14/87
Axilla II	4	12/31/95
Rotation Jam	4	08/10/97
Spock's Brain	5	06/24/95
Harpua	6	08/16/97

SONGS PLAYED BY YEAR

(1997 through 8/17/97)

Weekapaug	
1990	54
1991	49
1992	36
1993	37
1994	22
1995	15
1996	13
1997	5

Wilson	
1990	6
1991	14
1992	17
1993	17
1994	27
1995	13
1996	12
1997	5

Weigh	
1992	11
1993	14
1994	1
1995	2
1996	2
1997	3

You Enjoy Myself	
1990	57
1991	47
1992	47
1993	53
1994	38
1995	23
1996	23
1997	14

12/04/91	3	2	I am H2	Sparkle
12/05/91	1	2	I am H2	Fee
12/31/91	3	3	I am H2	*CL3
03/07/92	2	2	I am H2	Rosie
03/14/92	4	1	I am H2	*CL1
03/17/92	1	2	I am H2	Love You
03/20/92	2	2	I am H2	Sanity
03/24/92	2	2	I am H2	Guelah
03/27/92	3	2	I am H2	Horse
03/31/92	3	2	I am H2	Fee
04/04/92	3	2	I am H2	Glide
04/06/92	2	2	I am H2	NICU
04/09/92	2	2	I am H2	Horse
04/13/92	2	2	I am H2	Magilla
04/16/92	2	2	I am H2	Horn
04/19/92	3	2	I am H2	Horse
04/21/92	1	2	I am H2	Weigh
04/23/92	2	2	I am H2	Lizards
04/24/92	1	2	I am H2	Mango
04/29/92	2	2	I am H2	Love You
05/01/92	2	2	I am H2	Mound
05/03/92	2	2	I am H2	Mango
05/05/92	1	2	I am H2	Horse
05/07/92	2	2	I am H2	Fee
05/14/92	5	2	I am H2	McGrupp
05/18/92	4	2	I am H2	Fee
07/16/92	15	2	I am H2	*CL2
08/17/92	18	2	I am H2	Horn
11/19/92	11	2	I am H2	Bouncing
11/21/92	2	2	I am H2	Horse
11/23/92	2	2	I am H2	Lngthwise
11/28/92	3	1	I am H2	*CL1
12/01/92	2	1	I am H2	*CL1
12/03/92	2	2	I am H2	Lawn Boy
12/05/92	2	2	I am H2	WhipPost
12/08/92	3	2	I am H2	Horse
12/11/92	2	2	I am H2	Esther
12/29/92	4	2	I am H2	Bayou
12/31/92	2	3	Auld	Harpua
02/04/93	2	2	TMWSIY	Lawn Boy
02/06/93	2	2	I am H2	Life Boy
02/09/93	2	2	I am H2	Weigh
02/11/93	2	2	I am H2	Mound
02/15/93	3	2	I am H2	Wedge
02/18/93	2	2	I am H2	Mound
02/20/93	2	2	I am H2	FEFY
02/23/93	3	2	I am H2	Terrapin
02/27/93	3	2	I am H2	Terrapin
03/03/93	2	2	I am H2	Glide
03/05/93	1	2	I am H2	Jesus
03/09/93	3	2	I am H2	Horse
03/13/93	2	2	I am H2	FEFY
03/17/93	3	2	I am H2	Horse
03/19/93	2	2	I am H2	Love You
03/22/93	2	2	I am H2	*CL2
03/25/93	2	2	I am H2	Golgi
03/27/93	2	2	I am H2	Rosie
03/30/93	2	2	I am H2	Horse
04/02/93	3	2	I am H2	Lizards
04/10/93	4	2	Great Gig	FunkBitch
04/13/93	2	2	I am H2	Brain
04/16/93	2	2	I am H2	Horse
04/21/93	4	2	Great Gig	Gumbo
04/23/93	2	2	I am H2	Lngthwise
04/25/93	2	2	I am H2	Fee
04/29/93	2	2	I am H2	Terrapin
05/01/93	2	2	Great Gig	Cavern
05/08/93	6	2	I am H2	AmGrace
07/17/93	5	2	Lepr	Faht
07/24/93	5	2	YSZahov	PurplRain
07/31/93	6	2	Lepr	PurplRain
08/02/93	1	2	Sqirm Coil	Bike
08/11/93	6	2	Great Gig	Esther
08/16/93	5	2	Faht	Mound
08/24/93	4	2	Ginseng	Wilson
12/30/93	6	2	McGrupp	PurplRain
04/06/94	4	2	Life Boy	Sqirm Coil
04/09/94	2	2	I am H2	Tela
04/21/94	10	2	I am H2	Scent
04/29/94	6	2	I am H2	BeLikeYou
05/14/94	11	2	I am H2	TMWSIY
05/19/94	3	2	I am H2	Lizards
06/09/94	10	2	I am H2	Golgi
06/13/94	3	2	I am H2	Esther
06/17/94	3	2	I am H2	Harpua
06/22/94	4	2	I am H2	TMWSIY
07/02/94	8	2	I am H2	McGrupp
07/10/94	6	2	I am H2	Bouncing
10/08/94	6	2	I am H2	Fluffhead
10/13/94	4	2	YSZahov	Foreplay
10/21/94	6	2	I am H2	Sl Monkey
10/25/94	3	2	Mango	YSZahov
11/04/94	8	2	Tela	Ya Mar
11/25/94	11	2	Harpua	Mango
12/06/94	8	2	Mango	Bike
12/10/94	4	2	I am H2	DoInRoad
12/28/94	1	2	Mango	Contact
12/31/94	3	2	YSZahov	AmGrace
06/10/95	5	2	I am H2	AmGrace
06/20/95	7	2	Contact	Rosie
06/25/95	4	2	DoInRoad	AmGrace
06/30/95	4	2	Contact	AmGrace
09/30/95	7	2	Keyboard	Suspicious
10/11/95	7	2	McGrupp	Llama
10/19/95	5	2	I am H2	Lawn Boy
10/25/95	5	2	Sparkle	Suzie
11/11/95	7	1	PoorHeart	Horse
11/15/95	3	2	Life Mars	Fee
11/25/95	7	2	Str Design	Harry
12/01/95	4	2	Mike's	Mango
12/07/95	4	2	Mike's	AmGrace
12/16/95	7	2	Simple	Sqirm Coil
12/31/95	5	2	Auld	Sea&Sand
07/23/96	18	2	I am H2	Bike
08/05/96	5	2	I am H2	*CL2
08/13/96	5	2	Life Boy	Therm
08/16/96	2	2	Contact	*CL2
10/22/96	7	2	Steep	*CL2
10/29/96	5	2	Silent	Wedge
11/06/96	4	2	Steep	Scent
11/08/96	2	2	SSB	*CL2
11/15/96	5	2	Mustard	*CL2
11/23/96	5	2	Axilla	Catapult
12/04/96	7	2	Lawn Boy	*CL2
12/06/96	1	2	Harry	Adeline
12/28/96	1	2	Str Design	SSB
03/01/97	16	2	Lawn Boy	Mango
07/02/97	15	1	Water	*CL1
07/22/97	8	2	I am H2	HelloBaby
07/31/97	6	2	I am H2	*CL2
08/09/97	5	2	Slave	*CL2
➢ 8/17/97	**6**			

Weigh [33]

Weigh [Weigh]

By Gordon

03/07/92	[385]	2	Sqirm Coil	Chalkdust
03/12/92	2	E	Adeline	TweezRep
03/21/92	6	2	Bowie	Rosie
03/30/92	6	2	Sqirm Coil	Chalkdust
04/03/92	3	2	Possum	YEM
04/05/92	2	2	Maze	Landlady
04/21/92	11	2	Weekpaug	Catapult
04/25/92	4	2	Harry	*CL2
07/16/92	32	2	RunJim	Landlady
07/26/92	8	1a	Divided	Split&Melt
11/23/92	25	2	Llama	Mike's
02/09/93	26	2	Weekpaug	MSO
02/17/93	6	1	Possum	All Things
02/20/93	3	1	Possum	All Things
03/22/93	21	1	Rift	Reba
03/30/93	6	2	BBJ	Mike's
04/10/93	7	1	RunJim	Sparkle
04/20/93	7	1	RunJim	Sparkle
04/23/93	3	1	RunJim	Sparkle
05/03/93	8	1	Rift	Chalkdust
05/05/93	1	2	PoorHeart	BBJ
07/29/93	17	1	Divided	Rift
08/11/93	9	1	RunJim	It's Ice
08/17/93	6	1	Divided	Maze
12/30/93	9	1	Bowie	Curtain
05/20/94	37	2	Antelope	Axilla 2
06/07/95	89	1	Possum	Taste
10/22/95	40	1	RunJim	NICU
08/13/96	66	1	Chalkdust	It's Ice
11/07/96	20	1	Chalkdust	Rift
03/01/97	36	1	DWD	Beauty
07/30/97	28	1	Stash	Piper
08/17/97	12	3	NICU	Guyute
➢ 8/17/97	**0**			

Wilson [143]*

Wilson [Wilson]

By Anastasio/Marshall/Woolfe

10/15/86	[8]	1a	*OP1	Slave
03/06/87	3	2	FWorld	*CL2
08/10/87	7	1	Golgi	Quinn
08/21/87	1	1	Shaggy	CamlWalk
09/12/87	4	1	FunkBitch	Reagan
01/30/88	4	2	*OP2	Slave
02/08/88	2	2	Fluffhead	Peaches
03/11/88	1	1	YEM	Golgi
03/12/88	1	1a	Tela	ACDCBag
03/31/88	2	2	YEM	*CL2
05/15/88	3	1a	McGrupp	Peaches
06/15/88	3	1	YEM	Rocky Top
06/20/88	2	1	Halley's	Ya Mar
07/23/88	4	2	Curtain	Terrapin
09/24/88	8	1	YEM	Peaches
10/12/88	1	1	Weekpaug	Forbin's
10/29/88	1	3	IDK	Peaches
11/05/88	2	2	*OP2	Peaches
01/26/89	3	1a	GTBT	Fluffhead
02/06/89	3	1	Curtain	Peaches
02/18/89	3	1a	Golgi	Peaches
03/03/89	2	1	*OP1	McGrupp
04/15/89	10	1	YEM	Peaches
04/30/89	7	1	Divided	Peaches
05/09/89	7	1	*OP1	Peaches
05/20/89	7	1	Lizards	Divided
06/23/89	9	1	YEM	Peaches
09/09/89	15	1	PYITE	MSO
10/01/89	1	1	Harry	Foam
10/26/89	9	1	IDK	Lizards
10/31/89	2	2	Bowie	Reba
01/27/90	24	1	Bouncing	Reba
01/28/90	1	2	*OP2	Antelope
02/09/90	7	2	Reba	A-Train
06/16/90	53	1	Divided	Reba
09/22/90	7	1	Magilla	Landlady
11/26/90	20	2	Mockbird	Mike's
02/15/91	16	1	Curtain	Divided
03/01/91	11	1	*OP1	Foam
04/21/91	29	1	Rocky Top	Divided
05/10/91	9	2	Harry	PoorHeart
08/03/91	21	1	*OP1	Foam
10/13/91	14	1	RunJim	Reba
10/18/91	3	1	Reba	Llama
10/28/91	6	2	Divided	Dinner
11/14/91	12	1	*OP1	Uncle Pen
11/16/91	2	1	Uncle Pen	RunJim
11/19/91	1	1	Love You	Divided
11/21/91	2	2	*OP2	Harry
12/07/91	8	1	*OP1	RunJim
12/31/91	1	3	*OP3	Sqirm Coil
03/13/92	5	2	*OP2	Brother
03/20/92	4	1	*OP1	Reba
03/25/92	3	1	*OP1	Sparkle
03/31/92	5	1	*OP1	Divided
04/05/92	4	1	Divided	PoorHeart
04/18/92	9	1	*OP1	Divided
04/22/92	3	2	Rift	YEM
05/01/92	6	2	BurAlive	All Things
05/08/92	6	2	*OP2	MSO
07/16/92	23	1	Sparkle	Dinner
08/17/92	18	1	Rift	All Things
11/27/92	17	1	Rift	Divided
12/02/92	4	2	*OP2	Possum
12/08/92	6	1	Rift	Llama
12/13/92	4	1	BurAlive	Divided
12/29/92	2	1	Divided	Uncle Pen
12/31/92	2	1	Rift	Divided
02/06/93	4	1	Foam	My Friend
02/11/93	4	2	Landlady	Uncle Pen
02/13/93	2	2	RunJim	Uncle Pen
02/20/93	5	2	*OP2	Reba
02/25/93	4	2	Sparkle	YEM
03/13/93	10	1	Llama	Antelope
03/22/93	7	2	Tela	ACDCBag
03/26/93	3	2	*OP2	RunJim
04/17/93	15	2	*OP2	Reba
04/25/93	7	2	*OP2	Curtain
04/30/93	3	2	*OP2	Sparkle
07/25/93	18	1	*OP1	Foam
07/31/93	5	2	*OP2	RunJim
08/08/93	5	2	Harry	It's Ice
08/17/93	8	1	*OP1	Llama
08/24/93	3	2	Weekpaug	Rift
12/29/93	5	1	Divided	Sparkle
04/09/94	7	1	Magilla	Rift
04/15/94	5	1	Harry	Chalkdust
04/23/94	7	2	*OP2	Antelope
04/30/94	5	2	*OP2	Bowie
05/10/94	7	2	Maze	Julius
05/14/94	3	1	Llama	DWD
05/23/94	7	2	*OP2	Antelope
05/27/94	3	1	*OP1	RunJim
05/29/94	2	E	*OPE	Golgi
06/11/94	3	1	*OP1	Chalkdust
06/18/94	5	1	*OP1	Rift
06/24/94	5	1	Divided	It's Ice
06/26/94	2	1	Tela	ACDCBag
06/30/94	2	2	*OP2	Maze
07/08/94	6	1	Tela	ACDCBag
07/13/94	3	2	Cavern	Cavern
10/07/94	4	2	Reba	Scent
10/15/94	7	1	*OP1	Sparkle
10/22/94	5	2	Tweezer	Reba
10/27/94	4	1	*OP1	Sparkle
11/03/94	5	1	Divided	Peaches
11/13/94	3	1	*OP1	Sparkle
11/17/94	3	1	Bouncing	Divided
11/23/94	5	1	*OP1	Sparkle
12/03/94	7	1	*OP1	Divided
12/09/94	5	2	*OP2	PoorHeart
12/30/94	4	1	*OP1	Rift
06/17/95	11	2	*OP2	Maze
07/01/95	11	2	*OP2	Maze
10/02/95	7	2	*OP2	CTB
10/07/95	4	1	AArmy	Antelope
10/13/95	3	2	Theme	Antelope
10/21/95	6	1	Reba	CTB
10/31/95	7	1	Divided	Ya Mar
11/15/95	6	2	*OP2	Theme
11/22/95	5	1	CTB	Antelope
12/01/95	6	2	Mango	Suspicious
12/09/95	6	2	Timber Ho	Gumbo
12/15/95	4	1	Harry	Maze
12/28/95	3	2	Theme	BurAlive
07/12/96	13	1	*OP1	Divided
08/05/96	13	1	*OP1	PoorHeart
08/10/96	3	2	*OP2	DWD
08/14/96	3	1	*OP1	DWD
08/17/96	2	3	*OP3	Frankstein
10/16/96	1	1	DWD	BurAlive
10/21/96	4	2	*OP2	Chalkdust
11/06/96	10	2	*OP2	Curtain
11/15/96	7	1	*OP1	Divided
11/29/96	8	2	*OP2	Simple
12/06/96	5	1	*OP1	Peaches
12/31/96	4	2	Chalkdust	Sparkle
02/17/97	4	1	Divided	My Soul
02/21/97	3	2	Antelope	Oh Kee
06/27/97	18	1a	*OP1	Chalkdust
08/09/97	22	2	*OP2	Foam
08/13/97	3	1	Crosseyed	Adeline
➢ 8/17/97	**3**			

Wolfman's Brother [38]

Wolfman's Brother [Wolfman's]

By Phish/Marshall

04/04/94	[615]	2	Split&Melt	BeLikeYou
04/06/94	2	2	DwD	Sparkle
04/15/94	7	2	Julius	Alumni
04/17/94	2	2	Bowie	Uncle Pen
04/30/94	10	2	Bowie	Peaches
05/04/94	3	2	Julius	Magilla
05/20/94	11	2	Axilla 2	Rift
06/13/94	12	1	Divided	Dinner
06/26/94	11	2	Sample	Scent
09/27/95	88	1	*OP1	Rift
10/02/95	4	1	PoorHeart	Rift
10/08/95	5	1	Sparkle	Reba
10/24/95	10	1	Maze	AArmy
11/25/95	18	1	Rift	RunJim
12/01/95	4	1	PoorHeart	Chalkdust
04/26/96	16	1a	YEM	Scent
08/05/96	22	1	Divided	Foam
10/16/96	9	2	*OP2	Taste
10/21/96	4	2	Chalkdust	Reba
10/26/96	4	1	CTB	Reba
11/03/96	5	2	Divided	Sparkle
11/14/96	7	1	Uncle Pen	CTB
11/22/96	5	1	RunJim	Taste
12/02/96	7	2	Divided	Taste
12/28/96	3	1	NICU	It's Ice
02/13/97	4	1	Chalkdust	Also Sprac
02/18/97	4	2	Maze	Reba
03/01/97	8	1	Beauty	Jesus
06/13/97	3	1	Limb	Wading
06/16/97	2	1	Chalkdust	Oblivious
06/24/97	5	2	*OP2	Reba
07/11/97	11	1a	Beauty	Johnny B.
07/21/97	1	2	*OP2	Magilla
07/25/97	3	1	Beauty	Maze
07/30/97	3	1	NICU	Chalkdust
08/02/97	2	1	Divided	Water
08/08/97	3	2	*OP2	Free
08/16/97	6	2	*OP2	Simple
➢ 8/17/97	**1**			

You Enjoy Myself [377]*

You Enjoy Myself [YEM]

By Anastasio

04/15/86	[7]	1a	Possum	Anarchy
12/06/86	3	1a	Bowie	Dog Log
03/11/87	2	1a	Flat Fee	Lushngton
03/23/87	1	1	Alumni	Sparks
04/24/87	1	1a	Fluffhead	Dave's
05/11/87	2	1a	LTJP	Possum
08/09/87	1	2	Bowie	Ya Mar
08/10/87	1	2	Sally	La Grange
09/12/87	5	1	Possum	Curtain
10/14/87	2	1	A-Train	Golgi
11/19/87	2	1	FunkBitch	Sally
01/30/88	1	2	Curtis	Sloth
03/11/88	3	1	A-Train	Wilson
03/31/88	3	2	Fire	Wilson
05/14/88	2	2	Light Up	Lizards
05/15/88	1	1a	Golgi	Suzie
05/23/88	1	1a	Golgi	Rocky Top
06/15/88	2	1	Alumni	Wilson
06/18/88	1	1	Emma	GTBT
06/20/88	1	1	Peaches	Fluffhead
07/12/88	3	1	Peaches	IDK
07/23/88	4	3	*OP3	Contact
08/03/88	3	2	IKALittle	Jesus
08/06/88	1	1	La Grange	Cities
08/27/88	1	1a	Satin Doll	FunkBitch
09/08/88	1	2	Possum	Cities
09/24/88	2	1	Alumni	Wilson
10/12/88	1	2	Alumni	Contact

10/29/88	1	3	GTBT	Possum
11/05/88	2	1	Fire	Possum
11/11/88	1	1	Divided	Slave
12/02/88	1	1	Contact	*CL1
01/26/89	1	1a	Alumni	Lizards
02/05/89	1	1a	La Grange	*CL1
02/06/89	1	1	La Grange	ABlues
02/17/89	2	1a	ACDCBag	Fee
02/18/89	1	1a	Peaches	La Grange
02/24/89	1	2	ACDCBag	CamlWalk
03/03/89	1	1	McGrupp	Foam
03/30/89	3	1	Weekpaug	You're NG
04/14/89	6	1	*OP1	Bold
04/15/89	1	1	Esther	Wilson
04/20/89	2	2	WalkAway	Split&Melt
04/30/89	5	1	IDK	McGrupp
05/05/89	3	1	Golgi	Ya Mar
05/06/89	1	1	*OP1	IDK
05/09/89	3	2	*OP2	La Grange
05/13/89	3	1	Alumni	Golgi
05/20/89	4	1	Alumni	Lizards
05/21/89	1	1	Sloth	Ya Mar
05/26/89	1	1	Sloth	*CL1
05/27/89	1	1	Fee	A-Train
05/28/89	1	1	Suzie	*CL1
06/23/89	5	1	ACDCBag	Wilson
06/30/89	2	1	FunkBitch	McGrupp
08/12/89	3	1a	IDK	Possum
08/17/89	2	2	Fee	Lizards
08/23/89	1	2	Ya Mar	ACDCBag
08/26/89	1	1	Divided	Possum
09/09/89	4	2	Ya Mar	Alumni
10/01/89	1	2	Possum	Brain
10/07/89	2	E	*OPE	*CLE
10/14/89	3	1	Alumni	Makisupa
10/20/89	1	1	Mockbird	Oh Kee
10/22/89	2	1	Mockbird	Oh Kee
10/26/89	1	1	Golgi	Fee
10/31/89	2	2	*OP2	Bowie
11/02/89	1	2	Golgi	Kung
11/03/89	1	1	BundleJoy	PYITE
11/09/89	2	1	Bathtub	A-Train
11/10/89	1	1	MSO	MyGirl
11/11/89	1	1a	MSO	Brain
11/16/89	1	1	Reba	Frankstein
12/07/89	6	1	IDK	A-Train
12/08/89	1	2	IDK	Possum
12/31/89	6	1	IDK	Oh Kee
01/27/90	4	2	Caravan	Sqirm Coil
01/28/90	1	2	Sqirm Coil	Bathtub
02/09/90	7	1	Suzie	WalkAway
02/10/90	1	1	Suzie	Bathtub
02/23/90	5	1	Alumni	Possum
02/24/90	1	1	Carolina	Golgi
03/01/90	2	1	IDK	Possum
03/03/90	2	1	Rocky Top	Possum
03/08/90	2	1	Dinner	Ya Mar
03/09/90	1	2	HwayHell	La Grange
03/17/89	2	2	Foam	*CL2
03/28/90	1	1	RunJim	GTBT
04/04/90	1	1	Golgi	WalkAway
04/05/90	1	1	Suzie	Lizards
04/06/90	1	1	Cavern	Uncle Pen
04/07/90	1	2	Foam	Bike
04/08/90	1	1	FunkBitch	Brain
04/12/90	3	1	Possum	A-Train
04/13/90	1	2	Alumni	Curtis
04/18/90	3	1	Foam	MSO
04/20/90	2	2	Jesus	*CL2
04/22/90	2	2	Bouncing	Fluffhead
04/25/90	1	2	Ya Mar	Esther
04/26/90	1	1	Foam	Uncle Pen
04/28/90	1	1	Possum	Rift
04/29/90	1	1a	Ya Mar	Dinner
05/04/90	2	1	MSO	Lizards
05/06/90	1	2	Jaeg	*CL2
05/19/90	6	1	La Grange	Lizards
05/23/90	1	1	Ya Mar	Brain
05/24/90	1	1	Reba	Oh Kee
05/31/90	1	1a	Possum	Dinner
06/01/90	1	1a	Bouncing	Divided
06/05/90	1	2	Lizards	Curtis
06/07/90	2	1	Reba	Lizards
06/08/90	1	1	Bouncing	Divided
06/16/90	2	2	Bathtub	Lizards
09/15/90	3	E	Commun	*CLE
09/28/90	5	2	Dinner	Divided
10/06/90	4	1a	Foam	Oh Kee
10/08/90	2	1	MSO	Oh Kee
10/12/90	1	1	Suzie	Dinner
10/31/90	3	1	Bouncing	Asse Fest
11/02/90	1	2	Foam	Lizards
11/03/90	1	1	RunJim	GTBT
11/04/90	1	2	Jesus	*CL2
11/08/90	1	2	Bouncing	BBFCM
11/10/90	1	2	Suzie	Asse Fest
11/16/90	1	1	Foam	Magilla
11/17/90	1	1	Bouncing	Cavern
11/24/90	1	2	RunJim	Love You
11/26/90	1	1	BurAlive	Paul&Silas
12/01/90	2	1	MSO	RunJim
12/07/90	2	1	Landlady	Asse Fest
12/08/90	1	2	No Good	FunkBitch
12/29/90	2	1	Llama	Esther
12/31/90	1	2	Magilla	Rocky Top
02/02/91	2	1	Destiny	Chalkdust
02/07/91	2	2	Destiny	*CL2
02/27/91	13	1	Landlady	Fee
03/06/91	4	1	Golgi	Landlady
03/13/91	4	1	Landlady	Cavern
03/16/91	2	2	Cavern	*CL2
03/22/91	3	1	Llama	Landlady
03/28/91	2	1a	Bouncing	Guelah
04/04/91	5	1	Suzie	Sqirm Coil
04/06/91	2	1	Llama	Bathtub
04/11/91	1	1	Carolina	Sqirm Coil
04/12/91	1	2	JIm	Fluffhead
04/16/91	3	1	Golgi	Paul&Silas
04/20/91	3	1	Bouncing	SettingSail
04/26/91	4	1	Foam	Llama
05/03/91	3	2	Tela	Harpua
05/11/91	4	2	Chalkdust	PoorHeart
05/16/91	2	1	Chalkdust	Magilla
05/18/91	2	1	Chalkdust	Paul&Silas
05/25/91	1	1a	Bouncing	Cavern
07/13/91	3	2	Brain	*CL2
07/19/91	4	1	Sqirm Coil	Gumbo
07/20/91	1	2	TMWSIY	Rocky Top
07/24/91	3	1	Tela	*CL1
07/26/91	2	2	Dinner	Flat Fee
08/03/91	2	2	IDK	Rocky Top
09/25/91	1	2	RunJim	Chalkdust
09/27/91	2	2	Suzie	TweezRep
09/29/91	2	1	Landlady	Oh Kee
10/02/91	1	2	Landlady	MSO
10/11/91	6	1	Chalkdust	Lizards
10/15/91	3	1	Destiny	Rocky Top
10/17/91	1	2	Fluffhead	Love You
10/19/91	2	2	PoorHeart	Oh Kee
10/28/91	5	2	Bathtub	Sqirm Coil
10/31/91	2	1	Paul&Silas	RunJim
11/02/91	2	2	RunJim	*CL2
11/07/91	2	1	It's Ice	Landlady
11/09/91	2	1	Tube	Horn
11/13/91	3	1	Terrapin	*CL1
11/14/91	1	E2	*OPE2	*CLE2
11/16/91	2	2	Brother	Horn
11/20/91	2	1	Llama	*CL1
11/22/91	2	2	Lizards	*CL2
11/24/91	2	2	A-Train	Golgi
11/30/91	1	1	Guelah	*CL1
12/06/91	3	2	Sparkle	Horn
03/12/92	6	1	Llama	*CL1
03/19/92	4	2	Rosie	*CL2
03/21/92	2	2	Rosie	*CL2
03/25/92	2	2	Sqirm Coil	Horn
03/30/92	4	2	Mound	BBFCM
04/01/92	2	2	Llama	Horse
04/03/92	1	2	Weigh	Mango
04/05/92	2	2	All Things	Horse
04/07/92	2	2	Eliza	My Friend
04/12/92	2	2	Rift	Lawn Boy
04/15/92	2	2	Chalkdust	Reba
04/17/92	2	2	Brother	Fluffhead
04/22/92	4	2	Wilson	PoorHeart
04/25/92	3	2	Bathtub	Horse
04/30/92	2	2	My Mind	Horse
05/02/92	2	2	Foam	Chalkdust
05/06/92	3	2	Sqirm Coil	All Things
05/08/92	2	2	Maze	Horse
05/10/92	2	1a	IDK	Possum
05/12/92	1	2	Bathtub	Guelah
05/15/92	2	1a	Chalkdust	Adeline
05/16/92	1	2	Sqirm Coil	Horse
06/19/92	3	1a	Cavern	*CL1
06/30/92	5	1a	Adeline	*CL1
07/11/92	5	1a	Cavern	Suzie
07/14/92	2	2	Paul&Silas	A-Train
07/24/92	8	1a	Sqirm Coil	TweezRep
07/25/92	1	1a	Rift	Llama
07/31/92	5	1a	Oh Kee	GTBT
08/13/92	3	1a	Foam	*CL1
08/19/92	4	1a	Guelah	Uncle Pen
08/24/92	3	1a	Reba	*CL1
08/27/92	2	1a	Sparkle	Llama
08/29/92	2	1a	Maze	*CL1
10/30/92	2	1a	Adeline	*CL1
11/20/92	2	2	Tube	FEFY
11/22/92	2	2	Tela	Faht
11/25/92	2	2	FEFY	Lizards
11/30/92	3	2	Uncle Pen	Sqirm Coil
12/02/92	2	1	Horn	*CL1
12/04/92	2	2	Faht	*CL2
12/06/92	2	2	Bathtub	TMWSIY
12/07/92	1	1	Bouncing	*CL1
12/10/92	2	2	Maze	Love You
12/12/92	2	2	Guelah	Brain
12/28/92	2	2	Sloth	Lizards
12/30/92	2	2	Bathtub	TMWSIY
02/03/93	2	2	Sparkle	Life Boy
02/05/93	2	2	It's Ice	Love You
02/07/93	2	2	Glide	BBJ
02/10/93	2	2	Sparkle	Horse
02/12/93	2	2	FEFY	Ya Mar
02/13/93	1	2	Llama	BBJ
02/17/93	2	2	Horn	Lngthwise
02/19/93	2	2	Paul&Silas	Ya Mar
02/22/93	3	2	Glide	Oh Kee
02/25/93	2	2	Wilson	Uncle Pen
02/26/93	1	2	BBJ	Lngthwise
03/02/93	2	2	Llama	Love You
03/06/93	3	2	FEFY	Rosie
03/08/93	1	2	Kung	Lizards
03/12/93	2	2	Sparkle	Mound
03/14/93	2	2	Curtis	Life Boy
03/16/93	1	2	Chalkdust	Bike
03/18/93	2	2	Tela	Uncle Pen
03/21/93	2	2	Llama	MSO
03/24/93	2	2	FEFY	Horse
03/26/93	2	2	Silent	BBJ
03/28/93	2	2	Bathtub	Paul&Silas
03/31/93	2	2	It's Ice	Harpua
04/03/93	3	2	Sloth	Jesus
04/05/93	1	2	Glide	Rosie
04/09/93	1	2	My Friend	MSO
04/12/93	2	2	BBJ	Terrapin
04/14/93	2	2	BBJ	Harpua
04/17/93	2	2	Halley's	Life Boy
04/20/93	2	2	Llama	WhipPost
04/22/93	2	2	BBJ	Uncle Pen
04/24/93	2	2	BBJ	Bike
04/27/93	2	2	BBJ	Horse
04/30/93	2	2	Brain	Golgi
05/02/93	2	2	PYITE	Lizards
05/05/93	2	2	Ya Mar	Jam
05/07/93	2	2	BBJ	Great Gig
05/29/93	2	1a	BBJ	RunJim
07/16/93	3	2	Bouncing	PoorHeart
07/18/93	2	2	Fee	PurplRain
07/23/93	3	2	BBJ	BBFCM
07/27/93	3	1a	PurplRain	*CL1
07/29/93	2	2	Sparkle	PurplRain
08/03/93	4	2	It's Ice	Lizards
08/06/93	1	2	Uncle Pen	Halley's
08/09/93	3	2	My Mind	Contact
08/14/93	4	2	Daniel	PurplRain
08/17/93	3	2	Suzie	PurplRain
08/20/93	1	2	Chalkdust	PurplRain
08/25/93	3	2	Paul&Silas	Bats&Mice
08/28/93	2	2	PurplRain	Contact
12/28/93	1	2	Sample	My Friend
12/31/93	3	2	Lawn Boy	*CL2
04/05/94	2	2	If I Could	BeLikeYou
04/11/94	5	2	BBJ	AmGrace
04/14/94	2	2	Scent	Nellie
04/16/94	2	2	Bouncing	Sqirm Coil
04/20/94	3	2	Fee	SOTR
04/23/94	3	2	Ginseng	Who Fire
04/29/94	4	1	Halley's	FEFY
05/04/94	4	2	Bouncing	Landlady
05/08/94	3	2	Cavern	Halley's
05/13/94	3	2	Scent	PurplRain
05/16/94	2	2	Julius	BBFCM
05/20/94	3	2	Rift	*CL2
05/23/94	3	2	PYITE	Possum
05/26/94	2	2	Dog Faced	AmGrace
05/28/94	2	2	Llama	Jam
06/11/94	4	1	Chalkdust	Rift
06/14/94	2	2	Sparkle	Bike
06/18/94	3	2	Life Boy	Chalkdust
06/25/94	6	2	Axilla 2	Rosie
06/30/94	3	2	Maze	Sparkle
07/05/94	4	2	Cities	Great Gig
07/08/94	2	2	Stash	Julius
07/14/94	4	2	Uncle Pen	Sparkle
10/09/94	5	2	Scent	AmGrace
10/12/94	2	2	Scent	Nellie
10/15/94	3	2	Scent	AmGrace
10/23/94	6	2	Halley's	DWD
10/26/94	2	2	Axilla 2	Catapult
10/29/94	3	2	Uncle Pen	Bike
11/03/94	3	2	Julius	BBFCM
11/14/94	4	2	Adeline	*CL2
11/17/94	2	2	Sparkle	Love You
11/19/94	2	2	Sparkle	Rosie
11/23/94	3	2	Life Boy	TweezRep
12/04/94	8	2	Axilla 2	PurplRain
12/07/94	2	2	AmGrace	*CL2
12/09/94	2	2	Rosie	Suzie
12/30/94	4	2	I'm Blue	PurplRain
05/16/95	2	1a	Glide 2	Adeline
06/10/95	4	1	Rift	LCBill
06/16/95	4	2	Carolina	Sqirm Coil
06/19/95	2	2	Sparkle	AArmy
06/23/95	3	1	Taste	*CL1
06/26/95	3	2	PoorHeart	Str Design
06/29/95	2	2	Str Design	AArmy
09/29/95	7	1	CTB	Adeline
10/03/95	3	1	Simple	*CL1
10/08/95	4	2	Sample	Suspicious
10/14/95	3	2	Rift	HelloBaby
10/21/95	5	2	Sparkle	PurplRain
10/24/95	2	2	Bouncing	Sl Monkey
10/28/95	3	2	Scent	Str Design
10/31/95	2	3	*OP3	Jesus
11/10/95	2	2	Scent	Str Design
11/14/95	3	2	Str Design	*CL2
11/18/95	3	2	I'mSoTired	Contact
11/22/95	3	2	Bouncing	Str Design
11/29/95	4	2	Possum	Fog
12/04/95	4	2	CTB	Sample
12/09/95	4	2	Gumbo	Lawn Boy
12/31/95	10	3	Sea&Sand	Sanity
04/26/96	1	1a	CTB	Wolfman's
06/06/96	1	2	ACDCBag	Chalkdust
07/05/96	2	1a	ACDCBag	Scent
07/11/96	5	2	Terrapin	HelloBaby
07/13/96	2	1a	Chalkdust	*CL1
07/18/96	3	1a	It's Ice	*CL1
07/22/96	3	1a	DayinLife	*CL1
07/24/96	2	1a	Julius	Golgi
08/07/96	6	2	Life Mars	HelloBaby
08/14/96	4	2	RunJim	Horse
10/18/96	5	2	Maze	Reba
10/22/96	3	1	Free	*CL1
10/26/96	3	2	DWD	Sparkle
10/31/96	3	1	DWD	Caspian
11/07/96	4	2	Bike	*CL2
11/09/96	2	2	DayinLife	Taste
11/13/96	2	2	Caspian	Theme
11/19/96	5	2	Bathtub	SSB
11/24/96	3	2	DayinLife	Lovin Cup
11/29/96	2	2	Steep	Waste
12/02/96	3	1	Bouncing	IDK
12/06/96	2	1	Llama	CTB
12/29/96	2	2	Lizards	Rotation
02/14/97	4	1	NICU	Adeline
02/21/97	5	1	Crosseyed	*CL1
02/26/97	4	2	Ha Ha Ha	Kung
03/02/97	3	E	*OPE	*CLE
06/29/97	12	1a	*OP1	Taste
07/06/97	5	2	Free	Waste
07/09/97	1	2	CTB	Ghost
07/11/97	2	1a	Johnny B.	*CL1
07/23/97	3	2	Sample	RMWay
07/26/97	2	1	Dirt	Isabella
07/31/97	3	1	Saw It	*CL1
08/06/97	3	1	Ya Mar	*CL1
08/11/97	4	2	My Soul	CharZero
08/16/97	3	1	Ginseng	Train Song
➢ 8/17/97	1			

Not Yet Played In Concert

Bliss, by Anastasio (on *Billy Breathes*); **Union Federal**, by Phish (on *Junta*).

Persistent Songs

ORIGINAL SONGS that have had the shortest lapses between appearances since their debuts (minimum of 50 times played; lapse is the number of shows):

1) Theme	7
2) Maze	10
2) Stash	10
4) Free	11
6) Poor Heart	13
6) YEM	13
8) Bouncing	14
9) CTB	15
9) Julius	15
9) Sample in a Jar	15
12) David Bowie	16
13) Chalkdust	17
14) Weekapaug	18

Stories Behind the Covers

Phish's huge stable of cover songs have some Phishy stories and folklore behind them, too.

Also Sprach Zarathustra: Phish learned this song for their 1993 summer tour, when the new moving Altstar moving lights allowed Chris Kuroda to create the rising lights effect that can still be seen in concert today. Though Also Sprach was originally a classical composition by Richard Strauss, Phish's version is based on Deodato's 1970s disco version of the song that can be heard on the soundtrack for the movie *Being There*.

Cities: Played very early in Phish's career, on 12/1/84, Cities lay dormant for years (save for one performance in 1994) before the band revived this Talking Heads song in 1997 and made it a focus of their new funk jamming style.

A Day in the Life: Phish's celebrated take on this Beatles' classic debuted at Red Rocks in June 1995. The band learned the song in only a day after deciding it would be cool to close the Red Rocks stand with it.

Freebird: Phish's *a cappella* take on this song became a hallmark of the summer '93 tour as the band vocalized not just the lyrics but also the instrumental segment. Old tapes document one genuine attempt by Phish to play Freebird, on 3/6/87.

Gloria: Phish's abbreviated cover of this song, on 5/16/95, was a tribute to NOW's Gloria Steinem, who served as emcee of the Voters For Choice show.

Loving Cup: When Phish debuted the song on 2/3/93, Trey said that the band had always wanted to cover it but waited until they added a baby grand piano to their touring setup. On 2/3/93—the first show with the baby grand—they opened the first set with Loving Cup. The band started playing it much more often in summer '97.

Paul and Silas: Though the band debuted this tune on 9/13/90, they didn't start singing "Paul and Silas" until the end of fall tour '91. The band learned the song from a recording, and heard the main lyrics as "Hall in Solace." After fans alerted them to their error, they corrected themselves.

Cover Songs

One-Timers

COVER SONGS THAT Phish has played only once (excepting Dude of Life songs, Fishman tunes, and Halloween albums). An asterisk after the song name indicates the song was performed with special guest(s).

Song	Date	Artist
All Blues	02/06/89	Miles Davis
Amoreena	08/13/97	Elton John/B. Taupin
Anarchy in the U.K.	10/14/89	Sex Pistols
Big Leg Emma	06/18/88	Frank Zappa
Blue Bossa	07/23/88	Kenny Dorham
Blue Sky	08/12/89	Allman Brothers
Bluegrass Breakdown*	11/16/94	Bill Monroe
Bohemian Rhapsody*	12/31/96	Queen
Boogie On Reggae Woman	03/21/88	Stevie Wonder
Brown Eyed Girl*	11/16/95	Van Morrison
Choo Choo Ch'Boogie*	03/02/93	Louis Jordan
Come Together	12/08/95	John Lennon
Diamond Girl*	12/31/92	Seals and Croft
Doin' My Time*	08/07/96	Johnny Cash
Don't Want You No More	12/01/84	Spencer Davis
Dooley*	11/20/94	The Dillards
Fire on the Mountain	12/01/84	Hart/Hunter
Gloria	05/16/95	Them
Golden Lady	10/20/94	Stevie Wonder
Got My Mojo Workin'*	02/25/97	Preston/Foster
Help Me*	04/10/93	S. Williamson/Leake
Help on the Way	04/01/86	Garcia/Hunter
Hi-Heel Sneakers*	04/23/93	Robert Higgenbotham
I'll Come Running	05/16/95	Brian Eno
It's My Life*	03/02/93	The Animals
La Bamba	08/21/87	Los Lobos
Little Red Rooster*	02/25/97	Willie Dixon
Lively Up Yourself	04/21/92	Bob Marley
Love Me Like a Man*	03/18/97	Unknown
Low Rider	08/21/87	War
Luke-A-Roo*	03/02/93	Unknown
The Maker*	10/15/94	Daniel Lanois
Mean Mr. Mustard*	11/15/96	The Beatles
Messin' With the Kid*	08/08/97	Mel London/Wells
Moose the Mootch*	07/12/91	Charlie Parker
My Generation	10/31/95	The Who
99 Years*	08/07/96	Unknown
Not Fade Away*	04/01/86	Hardin/Petty
Ode to a Dream*	08/07/96	Unknown
One Meatball*	02/25/97	Ry Cooder
Phase Dance	09/27/87	Pat Metheny
The Price of Love	03/30/89	Everly Brothers
Reconsider Baby*	03/18/97	Lowell Fulson
Revival	10/30/85	Allman Brothers
Rock and Roll All Night	02/20/93	Kiss
Rocky Mountain Way	07/23/97	Joe Walsh
Roll in my Sweet Baby's Arms*	11/18/94	Flatt/Scruggs
Slipknot!	04/01/86	Jerry Garcia
Spanish Flea	12/01/84	Herb Alpert
Stand	06/13/97	Sly & Family Stone
That's All Right (Mama)*	05/06/93	Arthur Crudup
Three Little Birds*	06/17/95	Bob Marley
We're an American Band	11/16/96	Grand Funk R'road
Why Don't You Love Me	03/23/87	R.H. Chili Peppers
Why You Been Gone So Long*	05/06/93	Traditional
Wild Child	09/08/88	Lou Reed
You're No Good	03/30/89	Carole King

Fishman Songs

Though rarer these days than the early '90s, "Fishman tunes"—during which Jon Fishman moves to center stage as Trey takes over on drums for a song—still surface. Fishman songs are often preceded and followed by a brief jam built around Argent's super-cheesy '80s hit Hold Your Head Up (HYHU), chosen because Fishman despises the song. For most of spring '92, the band segued into and out of Fishman songs with Cold As Ice by Foreigner. (#P is total number of times played by Phish.)

Song	*#P*	*Debut*	*Last*	*Original Artist*
Baby Lemonade	1	03/11/92	03/11/92	Syd Barrett
Bike	25	11/19/87	11/07/96	Syd Barrett
Cracklin' Rosie	46	03/07/92	08/14/96	Neil Diamond
Cecilia	1	06/25/97	06/25/97	Simon & Garfunkle
Cryin'	1	09/29/95	09/29/95	Aerosmith
Faht	12	11/23/92	12/02/95	Fishman
Great Gig in the Sky	11	03/14/93	07/05/94	Pink Floyd
If I Only Had a Brain	30	04/14/89	11/16/95	Wizard of Oz
I Wanna Be Like You	9	04/04/94	06/10/94	Jungle Book
It's No Good Trying	3	12/07/90	12/28/90	Syd Barrett
Lengthwise	22	11/19/92	10/20/94	Fishman
Lonesome Cowboy Bill	3	05/16/95	06/10/95	Velvet Underground
Love You	75	04/20/89	07/05/97	Syd Barrett
Minute by Minute	2	09/13/90	09/15/90	Doobie Brothers
Purple Rain	30	07/16/93	08/06/96	Prince
Suspicious Minds	10	09/30/95	12/06/96	Mark James for Elvis
Terrapin	48	09/12/87	07/11/96	Syd Barrett
Touch Me	9	07/11/91	12/02/94	The Doors
Wind Beneath My Wings	1	11/28/95	11/28/95	Bette Middler

Note: Whipping Post, though sometimes a Fishman song, appears on the opposite page.

Most Frequent Covers

PHISH'S FAVORITE COVERS, listed by order of total number of times played:

1) Uncle Pen	**176**
2) Sweet Adeline	**159**
3) Rocky Top	**147**
4) Ya Mar	**137**
5) GTBT	**136**
6) Amazing Grace	**109**
7) Fire	**94**
8) Also Sprach	**92**
9) Funky Bitch	**85**
10) Take the A-Train	**78**
11) Love You	**75**
12) Paul and Silas	**72**
13) Carolina	**61**
13) Highway to Hell	**61**
15) Peaches	**60**
16) Avenu Malkenu	**59**
17) La Grange	**57**
18) Jesus Left Chicago	**49**
19) Bold as Love	**48**
19) Terrapin	**48**
21) Cracklin' Rosie	**46**
21) Ginseng Sullivan	**46**
23) Frankenstein	**45**
24) Walk Away	**44**
25) Timber, ADITL	**42**

Cover Song Chart

THE FOLLOWING is a list of all cover songs performed by Phish at least twice, not including Fishman cover songs, Dude of Life songs, or a cappella songs [see opposite page]. Total number of times played (#P) are calculated through 8/17/97.

Song	#P	Debut	Last	Original Artist
All Along the Watchtower	2	04/21/94	10/22/96	Bob Dylan
Also Sprach Zarathustra	92	07/16/93	08/17/97	Deodato, after Strauss
Auld Lang Syne	7	12/31/89	12/31/96	Robert Burns
Avenu Malkenu	59	05/11/87	12/28/96	Traditional
Back in the USSR	2	10/31/94	12/06/94	The Beatles
Bats and Mice	2	08/25/93	08/26/93	Baby Gramps
Beaumont Rag	2	10/14/94	10/18/94	Traditional
Beauty of My Dreams	17	02/16/97	08/17/97	Del McCoury
Bill Bailey	3	07/28/93	11/18/95	Traditional
Blackbird	2	10/31/94	11/22/94	The Beatles
Blue Bayou	2	07/14/92	12/29/92	Roy Orbison
Bold as Love	48	07/11/88	02/18/97	Jimi Hendrix
Butter Them Biscuits	4	11/18/94	11/22/94	Jeff Mosier
Caravan	37	01/20/90	12/29/96	Duke Ellington
Cinnamon Girl	2	03/18/97	07/31/97	Neil Young
Cities	16	12/01/84	08/16/97	Talking Heads
Communication Breakdown	3	01/27/90	09/15/90	Led Zeppelin
Corrina Corrina	11	03/06/87	02/06/89	Bo Carter/Taj Mahal
Crosseyed and Painless	5	10/31/96	08/13/97	Talking Heads
Crossroads	6	05/08/93	08/09/97	Robert Johnston
Cry Baby Cry	3	10/31/94	06/16/95	The Beatles
Ballad of Curtis Loew	22	04/29/87	08/02/93	Lynyrd Skynyrd
Daniel (Saw the Stone)	15	07/15/93	02/23/97	Traditional
A Day in The Life	42	06/10/95	02/28/97	The Beatles
Donna Lee	20	11/11/87	07/12/91	Duke Ellington
Don't You Wanna Go	5	05/16/95	09/28/95	Missionary Sisters
Drowned	4	10/31/95	03/18/97	The Who
Eyes of the World	2	12/01/94	05/03/85	Garcia/Hunter
Fire	94	12/01/84	07/30/97	Jimi Hendrix
Fixin' To Die	2	11/17/94	11/30/94	Booker White
Foreplay	16	10/07/94	12/09/94	Boston
Frankenstein	45	11/11/89	08/16/97	Edgar Winters Group
Funky Bitch	85	03/06/87	08/16/97	Son Seals
Funny as it Seems	3	06/20/97	08/09/97	J.J. Cale
Ginseng Sullivan	46	08/11/93	08/16/97	Norman Blake
Going Down Slow	2	09/13/90	09/14/90	Allman Brothers
Good Times Bad Times	136	12/06/86	08/10/97	Led Zeppelin
Have Mercy	8	04/01/86	11/14/94	Mighty Diamonds
Helter Skelter	2	10/31/94	11/19/94	The Beatles
Highway to Hell	61	10/01/89	02/26/97	AC/DC
How High the Moon	3	04/22/90	03/08/93	Morgan Lewis
Hoochie Coochie Man	2	04/10/93	08/08/97	Willie Dixon
I'm Blue I'm Lonesome	30	11/16/94	12/12/95	James B. Smith
I'm So Tired	2	10/31/94	11/18/95	The Beatles
I Know a Little	4	08/10/87	08/03/88	Lynyrd Skynyrd
Izabella	3	06/13/97	08/13/97	Jimi Hendrix
I Walk the Line	9	11/19/92	03/09/93	Johnny Cash
Jesus Just Left Chicago	49	08/10/87	08/03/97	ZZ Top
Johnny B. Goode	19	06/17/95	08/02/97	Chuck Berry
Jump Monk	2	03/12/88	04/24/94	Charles Mingus
La Grange	57	08/10/87	02/25/97	ZZ Top
Life On Mars?	19	10/11/95	03/02/97	David Bowie
Light Up or Leave Me Alone	5	08/21/87	07/25/88	Traffic
Long Journey Home	15	11/17/94	11/29/95	Traditional
Long Time	16	10/07/94	12/09/94	Boston
Love Me	6	02/13/97	08/14/97	Leiber/Stoller for Elvis
Loving Cup	31	02/03/93	08/16/97	Rolling Stones
Manteca	9	11/04/90	11/14/95	Duke Ellington
Melt the Guns	2	10/31/86	04/29/87	XTC
Mustang Sally	6	10/15/86	06/21/88	Wilson Pickett
My Mind's Got a Mind of Its Own	26	03/07/92	08/03/97	Jimmy Dale Gilmore
My Soul	21	02/13/97	08/16/97	Clifton Chenier
Nellie Cane	41	02/23/93	12/08/94	Traditional
The Old Home Place	24	06/26/94	07/06/97	The Dillards
On Your Way Down	9	07/23/88	08/12/89	Little Feat
Paul and Silas	72	09/13/90	02/28/97	Earl Scruggs
Peaches En Regalia	60	10/15/86	02/28/97	Frank Zappa
Pig in a Pen	2	02/21/93	11/16/94	Traditional
Quinn the Eskimo	7	04/01/86	08/10/87	Bob Dylan
The Real Me	2	10/31/95	12/29/95	The Who
Ride Captain Ride	4	03/23/87	12/30/92	Blues Image
Rocky Top	147	09/12/87	08/16/97	Bordleaux/Felice
Satin Doll	12	06/20/88	05/08/93	Duke Ellington
Scarlet Begonias	2	12/01/84	05/03/85	Garcia/Hunter
Sea and Sand	2	10/31/95	12/31/95	The Who
Shaggy Dog	8	10/15/86	10/29/95	Lightning Hopkins
Soul Shakedown Party	2	02/17/97	02/20/97	Bob Marley
She Caught the Katy	2	12/06/86	04/29/87	Taj Mahal
Skin It Back	6	10/31/86	07/25/88	Little Feat
Sneaking Sally Through The Alley	19	10/30/85	05/28/89	Robert Palmer
Something's Wrong With My Baby	3	04/23/93	04/30/93	Sam and Dave
Somewhere Over the Rainbow	2	08/17/92	04/20/93	Wizard of Oz
Sparks	13	03/23/87	11/29/96	The Who
Swing Low Sweet Chariot	9	10/15/86	11/16/94	Traditional
Take the A Train	78	10/15/86	04/13/94	Duke Ellington
Take Me To The River	2	11/21/95	07/10/97	Talking Heads
Tennessee Waltz	2	05/06/93	11/16/94	Patti Page
Timber (Jerry) [Timber Ho]	42	04/29/87	08/11/97	Josh White
Time Loves a Hero	4	10/29/88	11/05/88	Little Feat
Tush	2	12/06/86	08/10/87	ZZ Top
Uncle Pen	176	03/28/90	07/15/96	Bill Monroe
Undone	5	03/30/89	12/07/89	Guess Who
Walk Away	44	07/23/88	05/07/94	James Gang
When the Circus Comes	11	02/13/97	08/17/97	Los Lobos
While My Guitar Gently Weeps	16	10/31/94	02/26/97	The Beatles
Whipping Post	31	05/03/85	08/10/96	Allman Brothers
Wipeout	2	04/15/91	04/27/91	The Ventures
Ya Mar	137	05/11/87	08/14/97	The Mustangs
Yerushalayim Schel Zahav	11	07/16/93	12/31/94	N. Scheimer-Sapir

Stories Behind the Covers
(Continued)

Peaches En Regalia: A staple of Phish's live sets in the 1980s, this song lay dormant until Phish revived it on 12/28/93 (in honor of Frank Zappa after his death earlier in the fall.) While in Los Angeles recording *Hoist* that fall, the band borrowed the original sheet music to Peaches from the Zappa estate and re-learned the song.

Somewhere Over the Rainbow: Phish's two formal takes on this Wizard of Oz classic have both been instrumental, including the version with the Dave Matthews Band on 4/20/94. During the '92 spring tour, Trey wove various Wizard of Oz themes into numerous shows, including Somewhere Over the Rainbow which makes several brief appearances on 3/13/92, among others.

Take the A Train: Like many of the jazz standards covered by Phish in their earlier days, this song lay dormant from spring '94 through summer tour '97. Word has it that the band thinks jazz songs don't translate as well to larger venues, though that didn't stop them from reviving Caravan at Philadelphia's massive Spectrum on 12/29/96.

Timber Ho: Though the actual title of this tune is "Timber (Jerry)," the Almanac elects to use the phan title for the song, Timber Ho, as a reflection of phan culture. Since its return from hibernation at Sugarbush in summer '95, it has become one of the band's favorite covers.

Whipping Post: The band has taken on Whipping Post both as a rock cover—mostly in the 1980s—and as a more humorous Fishman song in the 1990s. Fish stopped his versions when the band grew big enough that they were playing in the same venues as the Allman Brothers. After the band pulled out a surprise version of it at Alpine on 8/10/96, they considered apologizing to the Allmans for so mutilating it.

Ya Mar: A song by the reggae group the Mustangs, who Mike credits as a major influence in his decision to play the bass (he saw them while on vacation in the Caribbean in 1979). Though the song is technically a cover, Phish has made Ya Mar a trademark song, so some fans think of it as an original.

Cover Songs

Doin' It *A Cappella*

PHISH'S SMALL CROP of *a cappella* songs seems to grow at the rate of roughly one a year, with 1996's addition being the Star Spangled Banner (Phish has also performed it three times before NBA and NHL games). Below is a list of Phish's a cappella choices, including total number of times played, the debut date and most recent performance, and the original artist or composer.

Song	*#P*	*Debut*	*Last*	*Original Artist*
Amazing Grace	109	02/03/96	12/31/96	John Newton
Carolina	61	01/20/90	08/17/97	Donaldson/Kahn
Freebird	19	07/15/93	06/19/94	Lynyrd Skynard
Hello My Baby	41	09/27/95	08/03/97	Howard/Singer/Emerson
Memories	37	11/17/90	07/06/94	Traditional
Sweet Adeline	159	03/28/90	08/13/97	Richard H. Gerard
Who By Fire	1	04/23/93	04/23/93	Leonard Cohen
Star Spangled Banner	8	10/17/96	12/28/96	Francis Scott Key

After Zarathustra

SINCE ITS DEBUT in summer '93, songs that have followed Also Sprach the most number of times:

1) Antelope	**11**
2) Maze	**10**
3) David Bowie	**9**
4) Mike's Song	**8**
5) Poor Heart	**5**

The Dude of Life Onstage

WHEN PHISH TOOK the stage for the first time at Nectar's, the Dude of Life joined them to sing the lyrics to Fluffhead, which he wrote. He recorded an album, Crimes of the Mind, with Phish in 1991, and he's shown up with Phish to share his songs.

Performances by The Dude of Life in the 1990s include 9/13/90 New York City; 5/12/91 Burlington (vocals on Mike's); 8/3/91 Amy's Farm; 11/8/91 Tuscaloosa, AL; 11/20/92 Albany; 12/31/92 Boston (lead vocals on Diamond Girl); 5/6/93 (vocals in jam with ARU); 8/9/93 Toronto, ON; 8/28/93 Berkeley, CA; and 7/10/94 Saratoga, NY.

Debut dates and total number of times played for Dude of Life originals:

Crimes of the Mind	5	08/03/91
Dahlia	1	09/13/90
Family Picture	1	11/08/91
Life Is A TV Show	1	11/08/91
The Revolution's Over	1	09/13/90
Self	4	09/13/90
She's Bitching Again	1	08/03/91

Statistics

HERE ARE SOME STATISTICS on Phish song play patterns—frequent set openers and song combinations seen in concert since way back when.

Set I Openers (of a two-set show)

Runaway Jim	62
Buried Alive	44
Llama	42
Chalkdust	45
Golgi	36
The Landlady	33
Suzie Greenberg	34
Wilson	28
My Friend My Friend	22
Rift	15
The Curtain	14
Divided Sky	14
Sample in a Jar	10
Oh Kee Pa	12
Possum	12
Ya Mar	12
Maze	9
Fee	9
I Didn't Know	9

Set II Openers

Also Sprach	62
Suzie	29
The Curtain	26
Wilson	28
Runaway Jim	28
Chalkdust	27
Mike's Song	24
Golgi	23
Llama	21
The Landlady	17
Axilla I	16
AC/DC Bag	15
Buried Alive	15
Dinner and a Movie	14
Maze	14
Possum	13

Encores

Rocky Top	93
Good Times	59
Contact	47
Sleeping Monkey	39
BBFCM	39
Golgi	38
Highway	29
Suzie	29
Lawn Boy	24
Cavern	24
Possum	25
Fee	16
Poor Heart	13
Bouncing	15
Chalk Dust	13

Played on New Year's Eve

Auld Lang Syne	8
Antelope	7
Divided Sky	6
Mike's Groove	6
Sparkle	5
Stash	5

Play Patterns

Hydrogen > Weekapaug	217
Mike's > Hydrogen	209
Mike's > H2 > Week	207
Horse > Silent	112
Oh Kee Pa > Suzie	101
Forbin > Mockingbird	78
Runaway Jim, Foam	46
Dinner > Bouncing	36
Sparkle, Stash	31
Stash, Squirming Coil	30
Buried > Poor Heart	30
Stash, Lizards	26
Oh Kee Pa > AC/DC Bag	32
Poor Heart, Stash	23
Runaway Jim, It's Ice	22
Foam, Sparkle	21
Contact, BBFCM	20
It's Ice, Sparkle	20
Rift, Stash	20
Chalkdust, Bouncing	18
Divided Sky, Guelah	18
Llama, Guelah	18
Harry Hood, Cavern	20
Split Open, Bouncing	20
Landlady, Runaway Jim	18
Llama, Foam	18
Poor Heart, Tweezer	18
Rift, Guelah	17
Landlady, Bouncing	17
Fee, Maze	17
Guelah, Rift	17

Readers Survey

Results of the Almanac Volume 3 Readers Survey

The Lean on the Scene III

The Survey

Here it is—the results of our third Readers Survey. Nearly 500 Almanac readers took the time to reply to our Readers Survey in Volume 3—thanks to all the respondents! They told us about their favorite shows (the basis for the compilation of the Phan 25 noted in the setlist section; see p. 71), their favorite songs, and their funniest, strangest, and most annoying experiences at Phish shows.

The next four pages offer a glimpse into the collective mind of Phish phans. Responses were received between December 1, 1996 and July 1, 1997, with surveys tallied during summer 1997. The survey remains as unscientific as ever, but of course that isn't really the point.

Looking ahead, we invite you to join the respondent pool for our next edition. A new survey form appears on page 275.

How Old Are You?
Average: 20.22 years
Median: 20; youngest, 12; oldest, 48.

Your First Phish Show?
Median: 10/31/94
Earliest: 4/29/87

Phavorite Phish Songs *(list up to three)*

1) YEM	24%
2) Antelope	17%
3) Harry Hood	14%
4) Divided Sky	13%
5) Weekapaug	12%
6) PYITE	11%
7) Mike's Song	11%
7) Reba	11%
9) Harpua	11%
9) Guyute	11%

Which songs should Phish experiment with more? *(list up to three)*

1) Free	14%
2) Guyute	12%
3) Taste	7%
4) Character Zero	6%
5) Bouncing	5%
5) Runaway Jim	5%

Which Phish songs do you most like the lyrics to? *(list up to three)*

1) Waste	10%
2) Esther	10%
3) Lizards	8%
4) Reba	8%
5) Theme	7%
5) Sanity	7%

Which songs should Phish play more often? *(list up to three)*

1) Guyute	13%
2) Harpua	12%
3) Brother	11%
4) Dog Log	8%
4) The Wedge	8%

Which songs should Phish play less often? *(list up to three)*

1) Bouncing	30%
2) Sample in a Jar	21%
3) Sparkle	11%
4) Tweezer	11%
5) Fee	7%

How many hours of Phish do you have on tape?
Average: 50 Most: 1,100

Name three bands besides Phish that you enjoy.

1) Widespread Panic	29%
2) Allman Brothers Band	26%
3) Medeski Martin & Wood	24%
4) moe.	14%
5) Leftover Salmon	14%

What's your favorite venue to see Phish at?

1) Deer Creek, Noblesville, IN	16%
2) Red Rocks, Morrison, CO	15%
3) Madison Square Garden, New York, NY	8%
4) Plattsburgh A.F.B., Plattsburgh, NY	7%
5) Great Woods, Mansfield, MA	6%
5) Hampton Coliseum, Hampton, VA	6%

What's your least favorite venue to see Phish at?

1) Rosemont Horizon, Chicago, IL	7%
2) The Palace, Auburn Hills, MI	6%
3) Alpine Valley, East Troy, WI	5%
4) Waterloo Village, Stanhope, NJ	5%
5) Anything Inside	5%

What are the three best Phish shows you've seen?

1) 08/16/96 Clifford Ball, Plattsburgh, NY	13%
2) 12/31/95 MSG, New York, NY	10%
3) 08/17/96 Clifford Ball, Plattsburgh, NY	8%
4) 10/31/95 Rosemont, Chicago, IL	5%
4) 10/31/94 Civic Center, Glens Falls, NY	5%

How Many Phish shows have you seen?
Average: 20.11 Median: 12 Least: 1 Most: 154

Favorite Phish Musical Moment

Non-show Specific: When they are deep in a jam and Trey quotes some other song and they jam on that for a while. Awesome! • Sunshine is part of all shows. Lights. Being taken very far from the crazy world we are living in. • That moment in YEM when you feel like your whole body will explode if you have to hold out for "Boy!" one more second. • When what's left of Page's hair flops around when he's into it. • During Good Times when Page screams, "I know what it means to be alone!" • When I first walk into a show and hear everyone going wild. • No doubt it has to be the Reba jam. • Trampolines. • When, during Lizards, they stop right before the chorus, and as soon as they start playing again the whole crowd starts moving to the fast-paced jam. It's the most beautiful thing in the world. • When the four points connect to form a laser beam that is aimed between my eyes, slowly fracturing the body, allowing a glimpse of reality and realization that I am the universe. • When Trey gets stuck in a riff. • When they take me to Gamehendge. • Right when you realize it's going to be Maze, not Bowie, if you know what I'm referring to or can relate. • The beginning anticipation symbol tapping of Bowie. • The instant in Antelope where the music moves from near chaos to the quiet beat and vocals. • Every moment is magical!!!

Show-Specific: During BBFCFM at Sugarbush 7/3/95 when Trey took everything he could find on stage and threw it into the audience. • St. Louis '96 when John Popper hobbled on stage during Mean Mr. Mustard with a cane. Crowd goes nuts. Phish and Mr. Popper go Weekapaug Groovin'! I lose my voice. • New Years Eve '96 when they dropped the thousands of balloons. I felt like I was in a giant lava lamp. • A Day in the Life at Jazz Fest. I cried when they played it. I didn't know they covered it. • 6/17/95, when Dave Matthews and Phish jammed together. Wish they would do it again! • Seeing the band in London on 7/11/96. Just hanging on the floor, drinking a Guiness and hearing 2001. It was rockin'! • 10/31/96 Jesus Left Chicago • The Sweet Emotion tease at Seattle 11/27/96. I think Trey was as confused by it as the crowd was. • Brother 8/17/96. • YEM 12/31/95. • The long Runaway Jim > Free 6/16/95. • Gamehendge at Great Woods • Mike's on 2/20/93, packed full of teases. • Hood at Red rocks 8/6/96. • Harpua 12/6/96, Elvises, need I say more? • *White Album*! Amazing! • Little Drummer Boy Jam during Weekapaug, Philadelphia 12/28/94. • Dog Log twice in the first set, 12/11/95, Portland, ME. • Harpua with Tom Marshall 12/29/96. • YEM Albany 12/9/95. • Penn State '96 Sparkle. I don't know why, but I had sort of an orgasm dancing to this song. • Vocal jam 12/31/95—sick-sick-sick. • Bowie 12/29/94, where I finally "got it!" • Bohemian Rhapsody! [listed by many] • Phishin' in balloons. • Fireworks at the end of Hood, 8/16/96. • When the band kept playing HYHU at Alpine Valley to fuck with Fishman. • Watching them share the stage with Merle Saunders and Col. Bruce at the Fox Theater, 4/23/94. • 8/10/96, the band had just finished probably the best Reba I had ever heard and they paused and looked at each other in recognition of the greatness of the moment. • When Trey winked at me in Hershey after I smoked a Crypie joint. WOW!!! • The glare Page gave the crowd in Grand Rapids, MI on 11/11/96 after his solo on Gumbo. • Phish on the flatbed at The Ball. • Mike Gordon bass solo with Jim Stinnette at Worcester 12/29/95. I was blown away. • Macaroni and Cheese at the Warfield, 5/27/94 • Lightning and Purple Rain at Red Rocks, 8/6/96. • YEM 6/11/94. • Funky Bitch silent jam on 12/30/96. • Dancing with 70,000 at Clifford Ball and looking out at the sky and seeing the sunset during Divided Sky. It brought tears of joy.

If you could make one request of the band, what would it be?

Have as much fun as you used to. Have more silly things at shows. Another GCH tour. • A few more Tubes along the way. • Play an exact setlist from one of your earliest shows. • Play a concert in Toledo, OH. • More Gamehendge shows. Otherwise, keep on keepin' on! • Play Gamehendge! • Smaller venues. More tickets available by mailorder. • Play *Dark Side of the Moon*. • Play *Exile on Main Street* by the Stones. • Please play Destiny Unbound. • Have a contest for each tour so that one or two lucky ones can win tickets and transportation to the tour. • Have a festival like Clifford Ball in the desert. • Take a break if you need one—or keep on jammin' your positive vibes. • Jam out more—not so cut and dry. • Cover Floyd or Zeppelin on Halloween. • Let me work for you! • Let me do Drew's Picks. • Play myself and three of my friends at basketball. Games to 15, win by two. I get to guard Fish. • Allow cameras. • Annual show on October 5. • Stay in town for more than one day at a time! • Let me play the bell on stage. • Write more meaningful songs, not just all silly songs—some that people can get meaning out of... Well, silly songs are good too! • Play Halloween on the West Coast! • Make a movie out of Gamehendge. Have the band play some of the characters. Mike would direct, of course. • Give in and start covering the Dead again. Make an excuse like, "a tribute to Jerry and our common fans." • Don't feel the need to hold out material and energy for certain shows. • Keep having fun onstage. The more fun the band has, the more fun the phans have. • Where's the Dude of Life? I missed him in '94. • Let the Dude sing! • Be less predictable with set lists. • Cover *The Wall*. • Play at my wedding. • Be back in fifteen minutes for real! • Never play stadiums. • Come to my house and hang out for a while. • Don't ever stop! PLEASE! • Longer stands at smaller venues. • Play Radio City on Halloween. • Play a string of shows at Lambeau Field in Green Bay. • Just have fun, no matter what it is you're doing...

The Most Intense, Wacky, or Unexpected Thing at a Phish Show

On The Roads: We were told to make a u-turn on the highway by a state cop! • Getting lost for two hours in the cornfields outside of Alpine Valley, on roads that all looked the same...UGH! • As the car slowly died in Hartford, we pulled it into a parking lot near the venue. A nice tow-truck guy came over and fixed it with duct tape, for free. • Being involved in a three-car 100 MPH race down I-95 on way to the Spectrum, 12/28/96. • Following a caravan of VWs to my first Phish show at Hershey Park, loving being part of such a great family. • Driving down I-85 throwing goldfish to Phans in another car on our way to a show in Charlotte, NC. • Riding to Hampton on Fall tour '96, we spaced the gas in the middle of nowhere. A cop picked us up and he had a Phish tape in his car. It was too tripped out for me. • On the way home from The Ball we picked up a hitchhiker who lived in the same town as we did—400 miles away!!! • A cop pulled me over and asked me who the hell Phish was. I gave him a 5/16/95 tape, and avoided the ticket. • Almost hit an Elk trying to find a campground near Red Rocks. • Somehow we made it into Waterloo! What a fucking disaster that place was!!! • The blizzard after New Haven, 12/29/93, we did a 360 on the highway with trucks passing doing 70 MPH! • A really amazing chicken parm outside of Hershey. • After a show we were heading to our campground, cops were directing traffic. They stopped us and asked if we had stolen gas from a gas station. Four different cops questioned us and checked our gas gauge. After 20 minutes they apologized and let us go. What a way to kill a good buzz! • Driving home from The Ball, I realized Trey was driving in the car behind me!

In The Lots: I got lost looking for my car and I was in the drivers seat the whole time. • Buying shrooms off some guy on 12/30/94, and listening to him tell us how strong they were. After it was too late—we'd eaten too much—I realized he was not lying, and I was lost in a parking garage. • Some dude who was bragging about tripping on acid drove a brand-new Corvette into a parked car, then backed it into a barbed wire fence! • Pulled in the parking lot at Wolf Mtn. and let my friend's dogs out. They sniffed out a ground score of about 1 oz. of mushrooms, among other things. Traded for Red Rocks tickets before we found out they were fake. • Some guy on the first night of Red Rocks '96 asked me what I was listening to. I said "the radio," and he flipped out. He said I was the only person he asked who said "the radio," and that it was cool because radio is where you get the Cool '80s jams! • Seeing a Cadillac catch on fire right in front of us as we were pulling into a parking lot. I thought it was going to explode. • Someone in the parking lot offered to piss on his wife for my friend's extra. • Me and my buddy got our car towed at Jazzfest and ended up hitch hiking out to Arizona. Needless to say, we have a newfound respect for Contact. • Waiting for three hours for friends at the Waterloo box office. Missed first set and never found my friends. • Left my car door wide open at The Ball. Not one thing was missing when I got back! • Trying to find a parking space at the Palace in '95, my friend nearly hit Mike. He slammed on the brakes just in time, and apologized, but it was close. • Hailstorm in the Mullins Center parking lot with 15 people in my van. • Lost my tickets for the 12/17/95 show and the ticket lady gave us three free tix! • Smoked a bowl with a uniformed police officer at Hampton, VA, 11/25/95.

Inside The Show: The fire alarm in Cincinnati in '94. It scared me so badly I fell down the escalator. • Seeing my best friend from camp whom I hadn't seen in 12 years. She was sitting in the row in front of me. • After being on antibiotics for a day for a bad sinus infection, two hits on a j at set brake made every voice around me sound like they were processed through a delay, put trippy patterns in front of me and nearly made me pass out. That, coupled with the physical drain from dancing, made me cry when they encored with A Day in the Life, my favorite Beatles tune. • While I was walking into the FleetCenter on 12/30/96, I saw Trey run past me! • A guy (very drugged up) started whispering in my ear, "I have to take you with me, you're my angel." It took security to finally get him away. • Running into two of my best friends from Charleston at the '96 Halloween show and enjoying the next two sets with them. • My favorite song, Divided Sky, was the opener at my first show. They just know everything. • Having my privates frisked at the doors in Lake Placid by this cute chick. • Taking my mother (60) to her first show 10/19/96. She was passed a bowl, and looked at me—she didn't know what to do with it. What was I to say? • An usher at MSG on 12/31/95 confiscated a can of beer from somebody next to the tapers section, walked about 15 feet, chugged it, crushed the can and threw it on the floor. • Eating a space-cookie before the show. It hit me at the start of the second set. There were some very strange moments during that second set! • Scoring backstage passes from three drunk guys at The Ball because they felt sorry for me because someone stole my only pair of shoes. • Almost getting thrown out of venue for smoking cigars in front of luxury box seats. • When my friend Dolzi told some Jersey girls at Jones Beach to shut-up and stop talking about their hair, causing many fans to cheer. • Mail order gave me the exact same seat for all of the Deer Creek shows both in '95 and '96—seventh row, front and center! • Having Antelope dedicated to me by Trey! • Going to a show with my mother—she ditched me to get closer to the stage! • Starting to trip in Plattsburgh while not taking acid. • Two rainbows above the stage at Wolf Mountain, 8/2/96. • Trying to fit four people into a two-person tent in Plattsburgh. • Second set, Hershey Park, 8/14/96. Middle of a phat YEM groove when a tiny voice in my head told me I was thirsty. I tried to ignore it, but I couldn't, so I gave up my spot, 15 feet from where Page was blowing my mind, and headed off to the concession stand. Just as I started to leave, my foot kicked something. I looked down to find an unopened bottle of water. I chugged half, then passed it on and got to keep my killer spot for the rest of the show.

Overall: I had a really hard time getting a New Year's ticket this year and ended up paying way too much for it. When I got into the show, I got hooked up with skybox seats, and after the show I met some kids with a suite at a nearby hotel. The next morning, I found out that they were driving through my hometown on their way home. Right on! It was definitely worth it! • When I found out that my math teacher went to high school with Trey and was friends with him. • I met the guy pictured in the Pharmer's Almanac Vol. 3 from Red Rocks holding the PHISH balloon. It was in New York City on the street in front of FAO Schwartz. He made me a Mickey Mouse balloon. • Meeting Trey's father and grandfather in the parking lot of a Red Roof Inn in Albany, NY en route to the Clifford Ball. • I thought I saw a UFO but I couldn't tell for sure. • The disco party after The Ball was led by Fluffhead. • I had a beer with Gordon in a bar the night before the summer '96 opener. • Seeing the boys get inducted into the Metropolitan Music Cafe (in Royal Oak, MI) Walk of Fame. They each put their hands in wet cement and Fishman put his face in it. Funny as hell! • Mike Gordon chilling out at my tent with me and three of my friends in Plattsburgh. • Got kidnapped after my first show. I'll never go with strangers again. My mother warned me!!!

Your First Phish Experience

My friend playing Tweezer for me in the seventh grade and telling me, "They're saying step into the freezer," and laughing. • My Brother played me the song Reba. • 10th grade. I started listening to Phish to get this boy's attention. They lasted. He didn't. They were much cooler. • Sitting in a car on my first date with a boy listening to Weigh. I thought… Oh my god! What the hell is this? • I was 14 and my cousin was playing this music that I fell in love with. • Sitting in my friend Darren's room with blue twinkling X-mas lights twinkling and listening to Phish and smokin'. • My freshman roommate with all of these different colored tapes of the same band, Phish. Thanks Joe! • My cousin playing *Picture of Nectar* for me in 1994. • My friend's step-dad went to see Santana, and Phish opened for them. He came back really high on Phish. He let his son borrow *Picture of Nectar*, and he left it at my house. I listened to it a lot. • My friend Matt played me Bouncing Around the Room. From the first note, I loved it. • My cafeteria at school, probably the worst show I've see musically, but they sure did blow me away! • I worked at the Palace of Auburn Hills and before the show I met the band, having no idea how they were or what they were about. Then I went to the show… • This guy in my college dorm who kept ranting and raving about how great they were. I finally decided to go and see why he wouldn't shut up about them… • Harry Hood at a friend's house. • New Year's Eve 12/31/94 at the Boston Garden. It was a religious experience and tuned me onto the band forever. • A friend in HS placed a walkman on my ears. Cavern from *Nectar* was playing. He said, "You'll like it." I did. • Hearing their music over the PA system at the Radiators show at the Chestnut, March '92. Phish sold out their show there 3/21/92 so I didn't get to go. • I hate to admit, I fell asleep on the lawn at SPAC, my first show. It will never happen again. • Partying in Duluth, MN (winter '95) at a friends, when I heard Stash from *Nectar* and it was music to my ears. I piped up and said, "Who is this?" Someone else said Phish. • 2001 > Rift 7/27/93 Hordefest. I was a changed person. • I first heard the song Contact and thought that it was really bizarre, but great music. • Two guys singing Contact to me on a bus in Mexico. • Fall of '93 I heard the *Junta* Sanity with "this is Red Rocks, this is the Edge!" in my dorm and I wondered who it was because it sure as hell wasn't U2. • I drove 14 hours to Montana with my roommate to see the show. I didn't really even know about Phish. • The summer camp I went to, all of the other counselors listened to Phish so I was almost forced to. Thank goodness! • A friend of mine threw some Phish tapes in with a bunch of Dead bootlegs I had requested. • Listening to Weigh when I was 12 and laughing hysterically. • I was about 13 and my uncle had a Phish sticker on his van and I asked him, "Who is Pish?" • When an annoying friend convinced us to check out this band that he loved at Roseland Ballroom. • At a party at a friend's house I heard Glide and hated it, but I walked around with the song in my head until I bought the CD. • My brother would blast Reba every day when he came home from school. • Literally stumbled upon them while checking out Wesleyan on 9/16/90, my senior year of high school. • When I was 13, my dad (an ex-hippie) dragged me to a show because he didn't want to go alone. Been diggin' them ever since. • My brother getting me stoned and listening to *Junta*. • Too many drugs prevent me from remembering. • Making fun of them in my brother's car—what was I thinking?! • Dancing my ass off at the Clifford Ball. • Getting out of prison in New York on Halloween day in 1989 and seeing Phish that night in Vermont. • The OJ show. Need I say more? I was hooked. Run OJ RUN!!!

Describe the most annoying person(s) you've met at a Phish show.

In The Lots: People who sell soda for three bucks. • The person who sells your buddy three veggie burritos for five bucks and you only two for five just because your buddy has dreadlocks. • The monks that try to get you to buy books. • Guy doing the "hard sell" on religious books at the Fleet Center 12/31/96. • A girl who had never heard of Phish found an extra ticket before I did. • SCALPERS. • Nitrous vendors. • The cops who insisted that we had beepers when it turned out it was their own walkie-talkies!

Phan Types: "Hoist Rules!!!"—those people. • People who buy shirts at a show and put them on while they are still there. • Big jock-looking football player guys from Nebraska who stand with their arms folded for the entire show. • Phans that phorget that phun is the name of the game. • Assholes who think it's perfectly okay to step directly in front of me (or on me)! And stay there (and scream loudly)!

Phishier-Than-Thou: People who think that they are the only ones who deserve to see Phish because they have seen 100,000 shows. Others love them just as much as you do! • The guy who told me he was more hardcore than me because he had been on tour for the past five tours and was a taper with diggity dank bud and kind veggie burritos and wants you to feed his dog. • Anyone who says a particular show wasn't that good. • Tapers. They have bad attitudes and never have fun at the shows. • The guy who insists he knows all, but meanwhile is spouting misinformation.

Those Wacky Teenagers: Kids that sing the chorus to Sparkle and sit down the rest of the show. • All of the 12-year-old kids in Memphis 11/18/96. Too much boyfriend/girlfriend melodrama for a Phish gig. • Teenager behind me who sang every lyric to Character Zero into my left ear. Loudly. • The 12-to-14 year old teeny-bopper girls whose favorite Phish song is Bouncing. With my luck they are usually sitting next to me.

Teenager's Revenge: People who, when you walk by, say to their friends, "I hate kids." [submitted by a 13-year-old Phish fan]

Altered Experiences: The guy next to me at The Ball who was convinced that I had acid to sell to him and wouldn't stop asking me. • People looking for nugs. • The drunk guy in front of me who kept falling on me, singing at the top of his lungs, and even played a really bad air-guitar. • Some dude who was tripping at the Clifford Ball and spent an hour and a half telling us about nothing. • People who are so messed up that they distract you from the show. It's cool to have fun, but moderation is the word here.

In the Show: People who are pissed off at shows. RELAX. RELAX and SMILE!!!! • The guy at Halloween '96 with the rainbow wig who decided to wish everyone Happy Halloween the whole first set. • At the 12/28/96 show in Philly, there was a dude next to us that kept hugging my friend and I and telling us what a great show it was. • There were some people, on 10/31/94, that booed the band during the *White Album* every time they played a slow song like Dear Prudence and Julia. • The group of 20 people who tried to squeeze into the six seats next to me. • This woman sitting in front of me kept pinching her hubby's ass, then turning around and laughing.

Talkers, Singers, and Spewers: All of the people who ever sat next to me and talked for the entire show. • A guy who kept spitting in the air—I was getting hit with the spray. • People making golf plans during YEM, 8/14/96. • People who ask what song is being played during the best jam of the song. • People who pee in the sink in the bathrooms. • A lady walked up to me, and puked on my jacket.

Happy Thoughts: Everyone is really cool. • I love you all.